Canadian Journal of political science

Revue canadienne de science politique

Volume/Tome VI, 1973

nadian Journal of
olitical science
vue canadienne de
cience politique

T FAUCHER La révolution tranquillisante

HAN KNIGHT Risks of War and Deterrence Logic

BEREY Personality and Politics

W SANCTON The Latest Redistribution of the House of Commons

RESNICK The Political Theory of Extra-Parliamentarism

HULL The 1971 Survey of the Profession

RD S. SHEEHAN Federal Funds and University Research

L GRAYSON Social Position and Interest Recognition

ILLER The Canadian Constitutional Amendment Scheme

CHARLES BONENFANT Le bilinguisme et le biculturalisme

1973 mars VI no. 1

Canadian Journal of Political Science / Revue canadienne de science politique

Editorial correspondence in English should be directed to Professor David Hoffman, Division of Social Science, York University, 4700 Keele Street, Downsview 463, Ont. Subscription and business correspondence should be directed to the University of Toronto Press, Periodicals Department, Front Campus, Toronto 181, Ont.

On doit adresser toute communication en français, au sujet de la rédaction, à M. Vincent Lemieux, Département de science politique, Faculté des sciences sociales, Université Laval, Québec 10e, Qué. Les communications à caractère commercial, y compris celles concernant les abonnements, doivent être adressées à : University of Toronto Press, Periodicals Department, Front Campus, Toronto 181, Ont.

The Journal acknowledges with gratitude the generous assistance of the Canada Council. / La Revue tient à remercier le Conseil des Arts du Canada pour la généreuse subvention qu'il a bien voulu lui accorder.

Subscriptions: Membership in either the CPSA/ACSP or the SCSP includes subscription to the journal. Ordinary membership $15. Student membership $5. Joint CPSA and SCSP membership $17. Joint CPSA and Canadian Economics Association (two journals) $26.

Abonnement : la souscription à l'un des organismes ci-dessus (CPSA/ACSP ou SCSP) tient lieu d'abonnement. Montant de la souscription : tous $15, étudiants $5, conjointe aux deux organismes $17, conjointe à l'Association canadienne d'Economique (valant abonnement à *Revue canadienne d'Economique*) $26.

Postage paid in cash at third class rates — Permit no C-71, University of Toronto Press, University of Toronto, Toronto 181, Ont. / Les frais de poste sont payés au comptant selon le tarif de troisième classe — Permis no C-71, University of Toronto Press, Toronto 181, Ont.

Indexed: Index to *Canadian Legal Periodical Literature* / Indexée au *Catalogue des périodiques juridiques canadiens.*

Published by University of Toronto Press / Publiée par University of Toronto Press.

Contents

La révolution tranquillisante
ALBERT FAUCHER 3

Risks of War and Deterrence Logic
JONATHAN KNIGHT 22

Personality and Politics: A New Look at the King-Byng Dispute
J.E. ESBEREY 37

The Application of the "Senatorial Floor" Rules to the Latest Redistribution of the House of Commons: The Peculiar Case of Nova Scotia
ANDREW SANCTON 56

The Political Theory of Extra-Parliamentarism
PHILIP RESNICK 65

Notes

The 1971 Survey of the Profession
W.H.N. HULL 89

Federal Funds and University Research
BERNARD S. SHEEHAN 121

Social Position and Interest Recognition: The Voter in Broadview, *or* Are Voters Fools?
J. PAUL GRAYSON 131

A Shapley Value Analysis of the Proposed Canadian Constitutional Amendment Scheme
D.R. MILLER 140

Note bibliographique / Review Article

Les études de la Commission royale d'enquête sur le bilinguisme et le biculturalisme
JEAN-CHARLES BONENFANT 144

Recensions / Reviews 149

Avis concernant la réunion annuelle / Notice of Annual Meeting 171

La révolution tranquillisante

ALBERT FAUCHER *Université Laval*

C'est le point de vue de cette communication que rien d'intelligible ne se produit en courte période dans les changements sociaux ou mentaux, dans les mises en place de structures nouvelles, et, donc, dans ce qu'on appelle abusivement les révolutions. C'est un point de vue que les Nord-Américains ont peine à saisir parce qu'ils ont bâti un pays très vaste dans un temps très bref. Les phénomènes qu'on nomme ici révolutions sont essentiellement des accélérations turbulentes après des moments d'arrêt ou de blocage; ils appartiennent à des événements longs. Ces événements ont le caractère du chêne dont la période de croissance est longue et dont la vie se prolonge par delà plusieurs générations d'homme. Il en est ainsi d'un certain nombre d'essences dures, constituées pour durer. Le peuplier, par contre, ayant un rythme de croissance rapide, supérieur même à celui de l'homme, répond bien aux exigences des paysagistes et propriétaires impatients.

Il faudrait adopter ce point de vue dans l'analyse des phénomènes relatifs aux structures en voie de se tramer car celles-ci, par analogie, sont d'essence dure. Une fois constituées, elles résistent aux chocs d'une seule génération; elles cèdent seulement aux pressions des idées au cheminement long et tenace.[1]

Il faut être impatient pour se contenter d'une révolution qui aurait commencé en 1960 et qui se terminerait vers 1980, et naïf pour classer choses et gens selon l'avant et l'après 1960. Et pourquoi s'imaginerait-on, lorsqu'il s'agit d'expliquer nos révolutions, qu'il existe deux marches de l'humanité, celle des bons, celle des mauvais, celle des vrais, celle des faux, et qu'un bout d'histoire serait l'œuvre des bons et des vrais, qu'un autre bout serait l'œuvre des cyniques et des hypocrites, comme cela se passe dans le *Petit Manuel d'histoire du Québec*,[2] un récent succès de librairie. Disons donc que c'est aussi notre point de vue que le bien et le mal, disons *le pour* et *le contre* de quelque chose, se croisent comme les fils

[1]Cette optique des variations brusques à l'intérieur d'un événement long ouvre deux voies d'accès à l'étude du changement, objet propre de l'histoire. *La Théorie générale de l'emploi, de l'intérêt et de la monnaie*, dont il sera question ci-après repose sur une définition d'équilibre de courte période. Keynes, son auteur, n'en reconnait pas moins l'importance des facteurs qui triomphent en longue période; il termine son traité par cette paradoxale remarque : « Les hommes d'action qui se croient parfaitement affranchis des influences doctrinales sont d'ordinaire les esclaves de quelque économiste passé. Les visionnaires influents, qui entendent des voix dans le ciel, distillent des utopies nées quelques années plus tôt dans le cerveau de quelque écrivailleur de Faculté ... ce sont les idées et non les intérêts constitués qui, tôt ou tard, sont dangereuses pour le bien comme pour le mal ». J.M. Keynes, *Théorie générale*, trad. Jean de Largentage (Paris, 1949), 397.

[2]Léandre Bergeron, *Petit Manuel d'histoire du Québec* (Montréal, 1970).

Canadian Journal of Political Science/Revue canadienne de science politique, VI, no. 1 (March/mars 1973). Printed in Canada/Imprimé au Canada.

d'un même tissu, que la prudence existe parce qu'existent des imprudents, et même que les purs cohabitent avec les impurs.

Les événements longs, du fait qu'ils recouvrent parfois plusieurs générations d'homme, connaissent des phases de ralentissement, de divertissement, d'accélération. Ceux qui y participent modifient constamment leur image du monde et ils utilisent des techniques différentes; ils subissent même l'influence de l'outillage qu'ils créent ou se donnent. Tel qui travaillait dans une direction un jour, se verra remplacé par quelque autre travailleur anonyme de sa génération ou de l'autre. L'histoire ne peut pas se répéter. Elle est processus cumulatif. Et tel est le paradoxe de l'histoire que des êtres si différents par la période qui les définit existentiellement, et par l'espace qui les situe géographiquement, collaborent au processus. Nous supposons donc, en troisième hypothèse, que les hommes, et même ceux qui concourent à quelque dessein commun de longue portée, changent d'une génération à l'autre, et même à l'intérieur d'une même génération, et qu'on ne pourrait jamais les connaître une fois pour toutes. Franklin Roosevelt de 1940 n'est pas celui de 1930; il n'a pas les mêmes ennemis; on ne déduit pas la politique économique de Roosevelt du caractère politique qu'il incarnait en 1930 ; on n'explique pas non plus son évolution sans référer à l'influence de Harry Hopkins.

Enfin, dernière hypothèse, pour comprendre les transformations culturelles de notre époque, il faut élargir le champ d'observation d'une part ; et ceci nous justifie de regarder du côté des Américains. Il faut, d'autre part, découper l'événement en longueur, c'est-à-dire le présenter comme un processus de longue période. Il faut, disent les historiens de l'économique, assumer une période assez longue pour admettre un changement des paramètres ou pour mettre en question les cadres supposés invariables du champ d'analyse théorique. L'historien assume le temps concret de l'économique, il accepte le changement technologique et les variables pertinentes qui en découlent.

Voilà donc les présupposés qui vont guider quelques réflexions sur les transformations sociales et mentales du XXe siècle. Ces réflexions veulent être simplement une invitation à étudier la période 1920–40 comme phase d'un processus non achevé encore, comme prélude aux événements contemporains, comme correctif aux visions prophétiques qui refont le monde à compter de 1960.

Nous savons aujourd'hui que l'après-guerre de la première est devenu l'entre-deux guerres mondiales; nous savons aussi que cet entre-deux guerres a été aperçu par les contemporains et chroniqueurs, ou même certains historiens, en deux phases, et comme en deux épisodes distincts, pour ne pas dire dissociés, ou presque étrangers l'un à l'autre. La période des années 1920, période dite de prospérité sans précédent, véritable plateau de complaisance économique, aurait frappé à la tête : on a beaucoup dit des idées folles qui ont circulé ou de la révolte des intellectuels, des réfugiés du village de Greenwich à New York ou de la rive gauche à Paris. La période des années 1930, période de profonde dépression, aurait frappé au ventre. Comme si la période antérieure eût été exempte de souffrances, comme si la pensée eût été absente de la décennie 1930. Pourtant, la pensée progressiste, encore tout imprégnée de populisme sous le régime Théodore Roosevelt, se perpétue à travers les années de prospérité antérieures à 1929, et elle se perpétue, en se précisant davantage. Seulement, le tintamarre des an-

The tranquillizing revolution

Those phenomena that are called revolutions, *in the conventional sense of the word, are essentially moments of turbulent acceleration following periods of retardation; and such are the phenomena of the* révolution tranquille *in Québec, which are confused by some with the inclusive events of long duration. In this perspective, and as a prelude to the analysis of current conceptions of the so-called quiet revolution in Québec, the author offers a study of the economic and social history of the United States from 1920 to 1940. He sees no sharp break between the fabulous twenties and the depression decade; nor does he see a gap between the interwar period and the preceding so-called progressive period. This can be seen through the unfolding of social, political, and economic events, provided that care is taken to adopt the mental set of transcending the* conflictual *in order to assent to the* cumulative *aspects of the historical process. Seen from this angle, the issues appear more complex, and contemporaries may easily be pardoned for failing to grasp the fundamental questions or for seeing revolutions where there are none. In the freedom of dancing, smoking, and drinking with women or, again, in the freedom of teaching the theory of evolution in schools (freedoms conquered in the twenties and the early thirties), some have seen a revolution. In a like manner, the New Deal has been described as revolutionary, as has the economic theory of J.M. Keynes. But if capitalism really has undergone such trials, how then can it still carry on so vigorously? In fact, it has learned to adapt itself to the changing conditions of its survival without altering its basic character. New regimes arise and the system carries on. The New Deal created a new regime to which capitalism acclimatized itself; and in the new regime capitalism managed so well that it could take advantage of the change in mentality in order to save the system. Under the New Deal, however, capitalism reached an important stage of its politicization, as it did somewhat later, under the new fiscal policies derived from Keynes' general theory. Yet, despite all revolutionary appearances, it continued to operate on the basis of usury, and while taking hold of the new media of information it mobilized resources with a view to profit and in so doing it organized things and men with equal indifference and efficiency. The system has continued to operate on the same basis of usury and, in order to sidetrack violent protest, it has adopted the issue of social justice; it has been willing to substitute assistance for employment, destructive idleness for creative leisure. Those benefits that are labeled* social security *and are now distributed without much regard for human creativity have the properties of a tranquillizing pill. And so we are reminded of the* panem and circenses *politics of a declining Empire. Are we really prepared to swallow the tranquillizing pill?*

nées 1920 a privilégié l'homme d'affaires, c'est-à-dire, l'absence de pensée sociale et politique, et il a refoulé les éléments progressistes, il a étouffé la voix des mécontents qu'une opinion publique bien contrôlée assimilait grossièrement aux Bolsheviks. Dans les années 1930, au contraire, la conjoncture donnait raison à certains contestataires et confondait la sagesse traditionnelle de l'homme d'affaires. On aurait dit que la dépression économique rassemblait les éléments progressistes que la prospérité avait éparpillés et que, dans le courant ainsi reconstitué, on retrouvait l'essentiel du mouvement populaire pour la justice sociale. Deux décennies, un contraste.

Le contraste provient surtout d'un manque à saisir la structure et la dynamique de l'économie américaine des années 1920 d'une part, et d'une insistance indue sur le caractère subit, inattendu, catastrophique, de la crise, ou encore sur le caractère soi-disant révolutionnaire du *new deal.* Il faudrait donc revoir ces deux périodes dans le processus de la longue période et chercher comment l'une s'articule avec l'autre. On peut supposer tout de suite que, dans une perspective nouvelle, le contraste s'atténue, des accents se déplacent. Ainsi, il nous semble que la véritable catastrophe se soit produite en 1931 avec l'écroulement de l'économie dite prospère des années 1920 et de le l'euphorie économique des Améri-Or il se pourrait bien que l'effondrement de 1931 découle directement de l'économie dite prospère des années 1920 et de l'euphorie économique des Américains qui, à cette époque-là, mettaient l'astuce de Morgan de Wall Street en parallèle avec la sagesse de Jésus de Nazareth.[3]

Dans la présente étude nous allons essayer de reconstituer l'unité de la période 1920–40 en insistant sur la politique économique des divers gouvernements depuis Harding jusqu'à Truman et sur la pensée et le comportement dérogatoires ou contestataires. Il faudra, en conclusion, retenir les éléments utiles à l'examen de ce phénomène qu'on nomme drôlement « révolution tranquille ».

L'habitude qu'on a de voir les événements dans la courte période entraîne à disloquer les éléments d'un même ensemble ou à ne plus voir la trame qui les unit. On dira, par exemple, que les années 1920 sont politiquement dominées par les conservateurs et les années 1930 par les progressistes, et donc, que, dans les années 1920, l'état est absolument commis à la politique du laissez-faire, cependant que, dans la décennie suivante, il se commet résolument à la politique d'intervention.

Les prises de vue sur l'économique nous surprennent davantage. On a classé en deux périodes les événements de l'entre-deux guerres : une période de prospérité, une autre de dépression, une période constructive, une période destructive. On a cru longtemps, et certains le croient encore, que l'économie des années 1920 avait été ce que les économistes en avaient dit, commis qu'ils étaient à l'idéologie de l'homme d'affaires. L'un d'eux, Frederick Mills, pourtant féru de statistiques, écrivant en 1929, voit dans l'économie des 1920 une expérience unique et il espère faire la preuve un jour que jamais dans l'histoire économique on est venu si près de réaliser un équilibre général.[4] C'était atteindre le plateau de la complaisance. Ce plateau, les chambres de commerce et les clubs sociaux l'ont connu pour s'y être attardés trop longtemps. Plus tard, le National Bureau of Economic Research (NBER) a étendu sa recherche aux années 1930, prenant en définitive la période d'entre les deux guerres comme unité de recherche, mais sans abandonner l'idée qu'un équilibre s'était réalisé de 1922 à 1929.

Dans son ensemble, ce champ d'étude historique nous paraît étonnamment étroit; et bien curieuses nous paraissent certaines interprétations de la prospérité de la période 1922–9 qu'on donnait entre 1936 et 1940 dans l'optique de la théorie de Keynes. Ces interprétations faisaient ressortir le contraste entre les années 1920 et les années 1930 et nous présentaient la cassure de 1929 comme imputable au manque à comprendre le rôle des dépenses publiques et des budgets anticycliques avant l'avènement de Keynes. Expliquer la prospérité des années 1920, c'était montrer comment le système fonctionne à son meilleur, comment on maintient un niveau élevé d'emploi et de revenu. Nous y retrouvons les réponses clés de la catéchèse keynésienne. Allons y voir.

[3]Stuart Chase, *Prosperity, Fact or Myth* (New York, 1929).

[4]*Economic Tendencies in the United States*, Publications of the National Bureau of Economic Research, 21 (New York, 1932). Frederic C. Mills y est cité dans l'Introduction, p. vi, comme ayant écrit en 1929 : « we may hope to determine whether anything approaching true economic equilibrium was achieved within the era bounded by the two great post war recessions ».

Dans les années 1920, particulièrement de 1922 à 1929, le volume des dépenses en biens de production atteignait la somme $18.2 milliards, en moyenne annuelle, moitié pour les remplacements et renouvellements, moitié pour l'expansion et la construction nouvelle. C'était le montant requis pour relever le revenu national à $77 milliards et pour assurer le plein emploi. Au cours d'une période de grande prospérité, dit Alvin Hansen, on exploite à plein les possibilités de développement ouvertes par le progrès technique et la croissance démographique. Or, après qu'on a installé les nouvelles machines, qu'on a bien pourvu les villes de services techniques et qu'on a construit des hôtels, des logements, des écoles, en proportion des besoins de la population, il ne reste plus beaucoup à faire si ce n'est l'entretien du capital existant; et c'est ici que la prospérité s'affaisse. Voilà l'explication : n'ayant pas rempli les conditions de la prospérité, on a la dépression qu'on mérite. Et on n'a pas rempli les conditions parce que l'expansion territoriale était terminée.[5] D'autres difficultés surgissent. Pour maintenir le plein emploi, il faut continuer à dépenser, mais il arrive qu'à un moment donné les récipiendaires de revenu ne veulent plus acheter. Ils préfèrent thésauriser ou acquitter leurs dettes. De surcroît, le prix des marchandises, pourtant difficiles à vendre, s'avère inflexible, et l'attente d'une baisse de prix entraîne un fléchissement des ventes. On thésaurise de plus en plus ou on acquitte des dettes : la spirale déflationnaire est amorcée. La crise de 1929 s'y trouve ainsi élégamment présentée mais on ne dit pas pourquoi les hommes d'affaires, les banquiers, les sages de l'économie, n'ont pas tout de suite comblé la marge de revenu en effectuant les dépenses capitales nécessaires au relancement de l'économie américaine.

A la vérité, l'explication n'était qu'une grossière rationalisation *ex post.* Tous les économistes de la période, tous les contemporains, contemplateurs ou victimes de la crise, n'y ont vu qu'une récession comparable à d'autres récessions historiques. Le rapport préparé sous la direction de F.C. Mills du NBER, *Economic Tendencies*, publié en 1932 par le Committee on Recent Economic Change et subventionné par la fondation Rockefeller, Carnegie Corporation, Economic Club of Chicago, et autres associations, demeure optimiste. Frederick Mills lui-même compare 1929 à la récession de 1920–1 et espère un retour à la normale. Mais alors, la normale quelle est-elle ? Elle est toute comprise dans l'économie américaine des bonnes années. Il faut lire sur la question les propos d'un sage de l'Université Harvard, Thomas Nixon Carver. Cet économiste nous a livré son credo de la prospérité capitaliste dans ce curieux livre publié en 1925 : *The Present Economic Revolution in the United States.* L'ouvrage reflète l'indignation contre un certain évêque[6] qui voyait dans la Russie le seul pays à poursuivre un idéal. Pourtant, il existe un idéal qui inspire, anime, tous les états de l'union; on l'exprime en trois mots : prospérité, égalité, liberté. Prospérité, égale distribution de la prospérité, dans la liberté. Retenons ce passage de l'ouvrage du célèbre économiste : « A moins qu'il n'atteigne la limite de ses ressources, aucun pays ne peut manquer d'être prospère s'il poursuit sincèrement l'égalité et la liberté. Toutes ces choses nous sont données par surcroît précisément parce que nous recherchons le royaume de Dieu et sa justice, comme elles le sont et doivent, en toute nécessité logique, toujours être données par surcroît à toute nation qui poursuit sincèrement l'idéal de justice, l'essence même du royaume de Dieu ».

[5]Temporary National Economic Committee, Hearings, part 9, 3502–03.
[6]L'auteur ne révèle pas le nom de cet évêque.

Si on ne lui élève pas d'obstacles sociaux et politiques, le capitalisme « tend à éliminer ses propres inégalités et procure, non seulement grande abondance de biens pour tous, mais les distribue plus également que tout autre système ».[7]

En somme, dit Carver, les Etats-Unis ont réussi à se donner un système industriel bien équilibré. On en reconnait les bienfaits : il répand la prospérité dans toutes les catégories d'emploi, il égalise les forces entre les pouvoirs négociateurs, il diffuse le pouvoir dans toutes les classes de la société, il contribue à modifier notablement le système d'éducation. Carver, en bon partisan du vieux système, voit bien surgir du nouveau, il l'accepte même, dans la nostalgie du passé. On n'a plus les serviteurs qu'on avait, dit-il : aujourd'hui, les domestiques participent du caviar et du savon; ils sont à la fois luxe et nécessité.

Mais qu'est-ce donc que ce système d'équilibre dont parle Carver ? C'est le système américain. Voilà. On le reconnaît à ses fruits : il égalise les forces, il diffuse le pouvoir, il répand la prospérité. Malheureusement, Carver rêve; sa description ne répond pas à la réalité de l'économie américaine. Son rêve il le déduit de postulats rationalistes. Pourtant, il aurait pu en sortir en regardant la réalité et en prêtant l'oreille aux doléances de ses concitoyens. Marasme dans l'agriculture, écarts croissants entre catégories de revenu, tensions idéologiques à l'intérieur du pays et au plan international, viennent troubler l'image d'une prospérité sans ombres. Les prix agricoles baissent sous la pression de la concurrence des producteurs des pays d'Europe, cependant que le secteur industriel soumis à des contrôles monopolistiques maintient ses prix. Le syndicalisme perd du terrain. La prospérité est urbaine; elle est dominée par quelques industries clefs. Quatorze à quinze millions d'Américains s'engouffrent dans les villes dans les années 1920; les cinq villes d'un million d'habitants et plus ont absorbé plus d'un tiers de cette urbanisation; la population noire se déplace vers le nord et vers le Midwest. Les industries nouvelles battent la marche : Ford, General Motors dont le contrôle passe à Dupont et Morgan en 1921, Chrysler, organisé en 1923, qui acquiert Dodge Brothers en 1928 et Plymouth en 1929. Dans l'électricité et les accessoires électriques, Westinghouse et General Electric organisent la Radio Corporation of America et commencent en 1922 la production d'appareils récepteurs. En 1924, RCA organise la National Broadcasting Corporation et conclut des accords avec l'American Telegraph and Telephone. L'industrie du film prend un essor remarquable avec les méthodes nouvelles de distribution et l'avènement du *technicolour*. L'aviation civile et commerciale se développe, la poste aérienne s'organise en 1924 entre New York et Chicago, et, en 1926, le Congrès autorise le ministère des Postes à conclure des contrats de courrier avec des compagnies privées. Prospérité industrielle, développement urbain, oui, mais prospérité mal équilibrée et peu respectueuse des autres nations qu'elle repousse par des barrières tarifaires. Enfin, on connaît bien le reste de l'histoire. Mais, redisons-le, l'image du professeur Carver ne répond pas à la réalité. La richesse ne se diffuse pas également, non plus que le pouvoir économique. Malgré les gains apparents des classes populaires, agriculteurs et salariés, sur le plan administratif, la tendance des puissances financières à tout contrôler, même les institutions étatiques destinées à modérer le capitalisme, se perpétue. Maintenant comme auparavant sous l'ère dite progressiste, le capitalisme se politise doucement, hypocritement,

[7]Thomas Nixon Carver, *The Present Economic Revolution in the United States* (Boston, 1925), chap. 8, 208. La traduction est la mienne.

de manière que ses positions ne soient plus guère dérangées. Voilà la grande réalité d'hier, et celle d'aujourd'hui.

Au plan de l'état, tout ne se passe pas de façon conforme à l'image des hommes d'affaires, partisans du « do-nothingness ». Les pressions interventionnistes brouillent cette image.

La contestation agraire a ravivé et rassemblé les éléments d'opposition au conservatisme et à l'idéologie capitaliste, jusqu'à l'intérieur même du parti républicain. Ces éléments, associations agricoles, American Federation of Labor, ou autres, provisoirement unis, réclament la nationalisation des chemins de fer, la propriété d'état des entreprises d'utilité publique, l'abolition du recours aux injonctions dans les cas de grève. Dans les années 1920, le mouvement dirigé par le Sénateur La Follette eut toutefois la vie brève. L'American Federation of Labor a quitté les rangs, les fermiers se sont désintéressés de la cause à la suite d'une hausse de prix agricoles, le Sénateur est mort en 1925. Mais la contestation demeurait une force latente, quelques leaders s'apprêtant à la raviver en cas d'alerte.

Les politiques économiques des années 1920 portent la marque d'un freinage anti-capitaliste et, inversement, celles des années 1930 sont modérées par le poids de l'idéologie du monde des affaires. Ainsi en 1921, le *farm bloc* du parti républicain et une minorité démocrate s'accordaient pour demander le Revenue Act qui impliquait l'idée de taxe progressive. Mais l'*Ohio gang* veillait sur les intérêts des riches, Andrew W. Mellon fut nommé secrétaire du Trésor. Les riches demandaient une réduction des taxes. Mellon diminua les taxes de diverses façons, encore qu'il consentît, sous la pression des progressistes, à hausser la taxe sur la propriété foncière et à imposer une taxe sur les dons. La réduction des taxes demeurait tout de même le principal objectif des grands propriétaires, des industriels et commerçants qui contribuèrent à la caisse du parti pour l'élection de Calvin Coolidge. Et la réduction de taxes continua comme exécution de promesse électorale. Le Revenue Act de 1928 réduisait les impôts sur les corporations et les taxes de consommation. Voilà qui résume assez bien la politique fiscale d'Andrew W. Mellon, le roi de l'aluminium promu au Trésor des Etats-Unis sous le régime Harding.

Dans les années 1920, les United Farmers avaient réussi à rassembler les agriculteurs du pays dans une espèce de front commun; ils avaient plié la majorité conservatrice des Républicains à voter pour le contrôle du marché des céréales, l'aide aux coopératives agricoles, le crédit agricole. C'est encore dans les années 1920 qu'on lança la grande offensive contre le trust de l'électricité. On demandait, pour les municipalités, propriété et contrôle des compagnies, pour le fédéral la construction et l'opération de nouvelles centrales d'énergie. Pendant ce temps-là les compagnies fusionnaient si bien que, vers 1930, une douzaine de compagnies de gestion contrôlaient 85 pour cent de la capacité de production électrique des Etats-Unis. L'aversion populaire pour cette forme nouvelle de monopole reprenait et répétait d'une certaine manière la lutte organisée contre les chemins de fer à la fin du XIXe *siècle*. Les compagnies d'électricité réagissaient sournoisement et énergiquement pour protéger leur immunité de contrôle et pour empêcher l'entreprise publique de pénétrer dans le champ de la production de l'énergie. Elles formaient une association, The National Electric Light Association, dans le dessein d'organiser le *lobby* et de prendre la direction de certains journaux et d'influencer la politique éditoriale de la grande presse. Cette association constituait un comité de surveillance des idées, Textbook Committee, chargé de surveiller ce qu'on disait dans les livres d'école sur les régimes de propriété. On a payé des professeurs pour vanter les bienfaits de l'entreprise privée, on a fait la cour à des banquiers, à des leaders d'associations agricoles, et on a demandé à des politiciens de protester contre toute activité de la Federal Power Commission.

D'autre part, au cours de la même période, on faisait pression pour que le fédéral entreprenne les projets de la Tennessee Valley, de la Columbia River, et du fleuve St-Laurent conjointement avec le Canada. On avait construit le Boulder Dam sous le régime Hoover et on discutait beaucoup de Muscles Shoals (Alabama) comprenant une centrale électrique et une usine de nitrate, projet amorcé comme politique de guerre dans le dessein de libérer le pays des sources allemandes et chiliennes d'approvisionnement en nitrate. En effet, durant la guerre, le gouvernement avait construit deux usines de nitrate sur la Tennessee en Alabama et le Wilson Dam pour leur procurer de l'énergie. Or, la guerre finie, les usines étaient terminées mais la centrale d'énergie ne l'était pas, et on se demandait si on allait continuer en temps de paix une politique motivée par la guerre. En 1921, le secrétaire aux affaires de Guerre demandait au Congrès de voter les crédits nécessaires pour terminer la centrale, y mettant comme condition que l'opération et la gestion de cette entreprise seraient confiées à des intérêts privés. Henry Ford s'offrait à la louer pour cent ans, au loyer annuel de $1.5 millions et se serait engagé à produire 40,000 tonnes de nitrate annuellement. Acceptée par le Congrès, cette proposition était rejetée par le Sénat en 1924, par suite du rapport du comité Norris qui évait étudié la question depuis 1921, la conclusion du Sénateur Norris étant qu'il fallait constituer une corporation d'état pour le contrôle et l'utilisation des eaux de la vallée du Tennessee. Il avait obtenu du Congrès, en 1922, qu'on terminât le Wilson Dam et, en 1924, le comité du Sénat qu'il dirigeait recommandait que le gouvernement prît en charge l'usine de nitrate. Plus tard, en 1928, après trois ans de travail, le Sénateur faisait admettre par le Sénat que la centrale de Muscles Shoals devait être opérée par le gouvernement. Des coalitions de républicains et de démocrates faisaient pression pour obtenir du fédéral la création d'une corporation d'état qui s'occuperait du développement hydro-électrique de la vallée de la Tennessee. Des pressions s'exerçaient sur Coolidge pour l'amener à frapper de veto l'exécution de ce projet *socialiste*. Le projet a survécu au veto et, sous Hoover en 1931, le Sénateur Norris réussissait à introduire un nouveau Muscles Shoals Bill. Hoover répliqua par une défense de l'entreprise privée, sans toutefois réussir à tuer le projet.

Ainsi vont les choses sous l'administration républicaine que l'histoire conventionnelle nous présente comme absolument imperméable au courant de socialisation. A ce sujet, un économiste de l'Université de Californie, moins respectueux des bornes politiques imposées à l'histoire par les historiens, Benjamin M. Anderson, faisait cette paradoxale assertion que, si on l'envisage comme manifestation de la conscience politique, le *new deal* aurait commencé en 1924, sous le régime Coolidge.[8] Essentiellement, Anderson décrit le *new deal* par référence aux interventions de l'état sous la pression des forces contestataires, dans l'industrie, le

[8]Paul T. Homan et F. Machlup, eds., *Financing American Prosperity: A Symposium of Economists* (New York, 1945), chap. 2.

commerce, et la finance. Or, de son point de vue, l'année 1924 marque une étape importante dans l'avènement du rôle positif de l'état fédéral. C'est l'année du retour décisif du gouvernement à Wilson Dam, à Muscles Shoals, et de la mise en œuvre du Federal Reserve System, et de l'application du plan Dawes. Lorsque souffla le vent de la crise, dit encore Anderson, le *new deal* était en selle.[9] L'observation est caractéristique : elle envisage le déroulement des politiques économiques comme un processus contrarié sans doute, mais aussi entraîné par une conception nouvelle des fonctions de l'état fédéral. Dans les années 1920, les idées progressistes sont comme étouffées ou contrariées par la prosperité; dans les 1930, elles ont le vent de leur côté mais elles ne s'expriment pas à plein dans le *new deal* des premières années. Les mesures d'urgence adoptées par Roosevelt, conformément à ses promesses électorales, peuvent être interprétées comme des réflexes de *self-defence* du système. On peut en dire qu'elles vont moins loin que la pensée même de Roosevelt, comme on peut dire de certaines lois des régimes Coolidge et Hoover qu'elles ont profondément contrarié les tendances pragmatiques du parti républicain. Le processus évolutif oscille entre le pragmatisme et l'idéalisme, le pouvoir étant tempéré par la peur électorale, sans grand préjudice au système établi. Le capitalisme se politise. Telle est la constante historique. Sous l'impact de la crise économique les forces progressistes se rassemblent davantage et le gouvernement subit davantage l'influence des travailleurs industriels que des clubs sociaux, des chambres de commerce, ou des tribunes d'hommes d'affaires.

La dépression, à ses débuts, a ravivé les propos traditionnels et les déclarations de foi dans le système américain. Le président Hoover affirmait que la dépression n'était qu'une illusion et que le patriotisme exigeait qu'on n'en fît point de cas. En 1931, la situation tournant au tragique en Europe, il dénonce la crise comme étrangère au système américain et il demande à ses compatriotes de se dissocier du reste du monde : surtout il s'en prend à ceux des Américains qui voient la cause de la crise dans l'administration républicaine. En plein creux de la dépression, alors que dans les pays d'Europe la jeunesse demandait un leadership fort, ses propos ont projeté une ombre de discrédit sur le régime présidentiel. En ces circonstances, Roosevelt aurait pu annoncer un régime fort. Il s'est fait élire en 1932 sous le signe de la modération : notre première tâche, dit-il, est de trouver de l'emploi aux travailleurs; et, pour cela, point n'est besoin de changer la constitution du pays. Il propose plutôt un retour aux sources jeffersonniennes. Certains de ses propos reflètent l'influence de son cousin Théodore Roosevelt, dont un discours, prononcé en 1910, présageait une conception politique du bien-être : « I stand for a square deal ! » L'irresponsabilité de l'état en matières économiques, soutenait Théodore Roosevelt, avait engendré une caste de riches qui exercent un pouvoir sur toute la société, un pouvoir qui appartient à l'état. C'était en dire plus en 1910 que pouvait dire Franklin Roosevelt dans son discours d'inauguration en 1932; ce qui tend à montrer l'inanité des discours de l'ère dite progressiste. Franklin Roosevelt, en 1932, disait : « I pledge myself to a New Deal! » Mais les grandes mesures adoptées par son gouvernement en 1933 et 1934 visaient simplement à relancer le système par des lois d'aide à l'entreprise privée; les lois de secours, l'assistance aux nécessiteux, portent la marque de l'urgence, elles ne découlent pas d'un plan. Elles ne se déduisent pas d'une

[9]*Ibid.*, 34.

philosophie politique. Elles ont néanmoins ouvert la porte à une politique de sécurité sociale qu'il fallait bien rationaliser ensuite ou justifier au nom d'une certaine philosophie; elles ont fourni à Franklin Roosevelt l'occasion d'exposer des vues nouvelles sur les fonctions de l'état, des vues qui l'eussent stigmatisé comme Bolshevik sous les régimes antérieurs. La politique d'aide, le secours aux individus, les politiques d'emploi, les réalisaient dans les faits de l'existence. Le *new relief program*, le Works Progress Administration (WPA) de 1935, commettaient réellement l'état à des fonctions nouvelles et rompaient avec le traditionnel *do-nothingness* américain. Harry Hopkins venait de faire son entrée officielle dans la grande administration.[10] Sur le *new deal* les opinions étaient partagées. Bien sûr, il y eut l'évangéliste catholique romain, Charles Coughlin, pour dénoncer Roosevelt comme « scab president » quand celui-ci s'est mis à légiférer sur la sécurité sociale[11]; le *Chicago Tribune* y a vu la fin de l'*American way of life.* Mais la plupart des hommes d'affaires qui appréhendaient le socialisme y ont plutôt trouvé une réponse au besoin de *self-defence* qu'ils ressentaient devant le paupérisme. Ils en ont fait leur révolution, cette espèce de révolution s'effectuant dans la tranquillité de l'ordre. Ils allaient apprivoiser l'ingérence étatique.

En ces années difficiles de 1934 et 1935, des mesures d'aide qu'on avait passées timidement et par nécessité s'imposaient maintenant comme mesures normales, au nom d'une philosophie sociale. Le précédent était créé : l'état allait s'occuper systématiquement de bien-être et d'emploi. D'où les déclarations de principes sur les fonctions et responsabilités du gouvernement fédéral, sur le droit de l'individu à l'assistance et sur les initiatives de l'état au moyen de budgets déficitaires. Cette philosophie marque l'avènement d'un deuxième *new deal*, à compter de 1935. La pratique du budget déficitaire, conséquence d'une philosophie sociale, préparait la scène à l'économie politique de type keynesien. Alvin Hansen pouvait véhiculer Keynes en Amérique. La politique de guerre, le *fair deal* d'après-guerre, ont intronisé Keynes et Hansen aux Etats-Unis et au Canada.

Si le premier *new deal* repose sur une coalition des hommes d'affaires, des travailleurs, des fermiers, qu'unissait une commune croyance au système traditionnel devant les maux de la crise, le second repose sur une conception nouvelle du produit national et du rôle de l'état dans les mouvements de la conjoncture et dans la distribution du revenu. L'Emergency Relief Appropriation Act met $5 milliards à la disposition du Trésor pour financer le programme de l'année fiscale de 1935–6, programme lancé en mai 1935 avec le Works Progress Administration. A Harry Hopkins revenait la tâche d'enregistrer les chômeurs dans les régistres régionaux, d'entreprendre des travaux locaux et d'y employer 5,000,000 de chômeurs. De 1935 à 1941, le WPA dépensait $11,365 millions pour 250,000 projets dont 78 pour cent pour les travaux publics ou des travaux dits de conservation, le reste étant affecté à des travaux communautaires et à l'aide aux professions, même aux musiciens et aux artistes. Le Resettlement Administration s'occupait de déplacer 500,000 familles établies sur des terres marginales. La même année débutaient le Rural Electrification Administration et le National Youth Administration. Enfin, toute cette politique du second *new deal* implique comme philosophie sociale, que l'état a des obligations envers les citoyens, que

[10]Robert E. Sherwood, *Roosevelt and Hopkins* (New York, 1950).
[11]Charles Coughlin, *A Series of Lectures on Social Justice* (Michigan, 1935). Voir en particulier son discours du 3 mars.

l'état doit procurer de l'ouvrage là où l'entreprise privée fait défaut. Il en est résulté des mesures permanentes de sécurité. Le principe de la dépense déficitaire appliquée aux travaux publics comme source d'emploi commet l'état à la direction de la vie économique, lui confie un rôle de stabilisation, base du *fair deal* de l'administration Truman. La loi de sécurité sociale de 1935 établit un système d'assistance, de même la loi d'assurance-chômage. La loi des relations ouvrières (Wagner Act) reconnaît qu'un syndicalisme bien organisé et, surtout, reconnu officiellement, doit jouer un rôle important dans la stabilisation comme contrepoids aux penchants de la grande entreprise. La promotion du projet de la vallée du Tennessee que les présidents Coolidge et Hoover avaient repoussé nous parait aussi de cette espèce qui crée une fonction d'état dans la gestion des entreprises d'utilité publique. Les *holding companies* avaient farouchement combattu ce projet sous l'étendard de l'anti-socialisme et de l'américanisme. Expérience économique de grande portée, pourtant; première expérience d'une vaste planification sur une base interrégionale, puisque l'entreprise du TVA impliquait les états du Kentucky, du Tennessee, de l'Alabama.

Depuis la première guerre mondiale l'économie nord-américaine a traversé une phase marquante de son histoire. On y a perdu la foi dans la toute-puissance de l'entreprise libre et on a accepté que l'état assume des fonctions que le rationalisme libéral avait rejetées et que la propagande avait dénoncées comme communistes. Et pourtant, après la dernière grande guerre, on s'est bien rendu compte que rien n'avait été changé radicalement et que, les mêmes structures restant en place, les interventions compensatrices de l'état demeuraient essentielles à la survie du capitalisme. La guerre avait même renforcé les pièces les plus fortes de ces structures, elle avait fortifié les secteurs déjà privilégiés. Plus que jamais, le système se trouvait exposé aux vagues et aux turbulences qui lui sont inhérentes. D'où la nécessité de nouvelles mesures compensatrices. Il fallait s'y préparer; et à cette attitude de préparation on a donné le nom de *fair deal.* La stabilisation est son objet.

New deal et *fair deal* possèdent un fond commun d'identité : la conservation du système. Le capitalisme est sauf, on l'a coiffé d'une idéologie mitigée par l'expérience. On n'a plus foi absolue en l'entreprise libre et privée, celle que guidait la main invisible. L'expérience avait ouvert la porte aux compromis, à des interventions, à des participations. L'idéologie traditionnelle s'y trouvait modifiée d'une double façon : on admet la sécurité sociale, donc le droit de l'individu devant l'état : on admet le principe de la responsabilité par delà les mécanismes du marché, et donc le bien-fondé des initiatives et des contrôles de l'état. Mais la grande entreprise demeure maîtresse, la grande entreprise apprivoise l'état. Ne pouvant plus repousser l'ingérence étatique, elle se politise.

Les transformations récentes ont des origines lointaines. Les fonctions nouvelles qu'on assigne à l'état portent la marque historique des hommes qui ont voulu corriger les abus du système mais qui n'ont pas répudié son motif, la poursuite du gain individuel. Que s'est-il donc produit de radicalement nouveau dans ce domaine depuis 1960 ? Rien. Rien qu'une accélération de la tendance à consacrer l'inefficacité administrative et à étatiser l'usure sous le couvert d'une respectable socialisation.

Dans le domaine des idées une opposition s'est manifestée depuis la guerre civile américaine en parallèle avec l'évolution du système et de ses politiques économiques. Elle s'est affirmée en proportion des forces systémiques mais de façon sporadique et périodique, s'attaquant aux effets maléfiques du système seulement. La contestation radicale, la mise en question du système dans son ensemble, au niveau de la conscience universelle, sont des phénomènes récents.

On a donné le nom de progressisme au principe de ralliement pour les revendications populaires. Historiquement, et sur le plan politique, le ralliement prend forme de mouvement en faveur d'une intervention fédérale pour la défense des fermiers et des ouvriers contre les abus du système ou, plus particulièrement, contre les entreprises dominantes du système. L'Interstate Commerce Commission, le Federal Trade Commission, comme institutions de contrôle, proviennent de pressions populaires, celles-ci étant la réplique au *lobby* ou autres techniques de pression exercée sur le gouvernement par les intérêts constitués. Le progressisme s'exprime d'abord comme mouvement pour la défense du pauvre, puis, à la fin du siècle, il s'adresse aux institutions, aux milieux, qu'ils veulent améliorer par une législation adéquate, basée sur la recherche des travailleurs sociaux, et appliquée avec la collaboration des travailleurs sociaux. Il prépare l'avènement du *welfare state.* Le mouvement progressiste, ce rassemblement en marche guidé par l'idée de justice sociale et de la protection du faible contre le fort, s'est attaqué d'abord aux problèmes agricoles, aux problèmes ouvriers ensuite : il a arraché aux puissances dominantes les premières tranches de législation sociale.

On identifie aussi comme progressistes les adeptes de la contestation par la littérature et par la presse. Premièrement, un progressisme du type Upton Sinclair qui s'applique à voir les choses de près, de bas en haut, comptant sur la colère du peuple pour modérer le capitalisme. Le salut vient des couches populaires de la société; la contestation doit partir d'en bas : *grass roots* est son qualificatif. Deuxièmement, un progressisme de type Sinclair Lewis ou Henry Mencken, du travailleur intellectuel qui critique l'ordre établi et le dénonce comme pernicieux par les moyens du roman et du magazine, à compter de 1920.[12] Les écrivains s'attaquent à l'individualisme qu'on présentait comme source authentique d'enrichissement, et à son corollaire, la non-intervention de l'état dans les affaires économiques, ils s'appliquent à démystifier la Constitution comme document inspiré du Saint-Esprit, la Cour Suprême comme interprète du jugement de Jehovah, le héros du capitalisme – le *self-made man* qui va jusqu'à construire des chemins de fer et à les transformer en puissances financières et en instruments de contrôle politique. Dans l'ensemble, l'idée de liberté économique occupe le centre du débat; elle s'y trouve définie positivement; liberté de travailler, de sustenter à sa propre vie et à celle des dépendants, ou définie négativement, comme effort historique d'affranchissement, *freedom from ...* même des servitudes ou contraintes imposées aux hommes, au nom du progrès technique. La découverte de Thorstein Veblen favorise l'auto-critique, même dans les milieux universitaires.

Dans les années 1920, la question du pouvoir économique fait l'objet de vives discussions, et non sans raison. Les entreprises capitalistes tentent de se constituer en empires industriels ou commerciaux; commerçants et industriels organi-

[12]John Dos Passos exprime dans ses romans la désillusion des jeunes intellectuels de l'après-guerre, et leur aversion pour le capitalisme au temps de la crise.

sent ce qu'ils appellent des intégrations. La recherche du pouvoir les amène à confondre la prospérité de leurs entreprises avec le bien de la communauté et ils considèrent la docilité de l'état comme essentielle à la sécurité de leur système. Par la réclame et la propagande ils disent aux citoyens en quoi consiste leur bien; ils organisent la consommation pour la satisfaction de la production. Comme disent Adolf A. Berles Jr., et G.C. Means, le directeur d'entreprise subordonne la communauté des citoyens à l'entreprise, le communiste subordonne l'individu à l'état, le directeur d'entreprise confond la communauté des citoyens avec l'entreprise, le communiste confond la société avec l'état.[13] Dans un cas comme dans l'autre il y a asservissement, donc violence. L'entreprise contemporaine y perd ses titres de gloire. On ne défend plus l'immunité de la grande corporation au nom de la propriété privée, celle-ci étant envisagée comme extension des prérogatives de la liberté individuelle et de la conscience personnelle. Des réalités comme le Canadien Pacifique, le Standard Oil, le House of Morgan, l'International Nickel, l'Aluminium Company, ont rendu archaïque cette notion traditionnelle de propriété privée. Encore dans les années 1930 on n'avait pas pleine conscience de ces réalités brutales et on commençait à peine à démasquer l'insidieuse propagande. On avait franchi à peine le seuil de la protestation. C'était donc une lutte à poursuivre ... et une lutte sérieusement compromise par les guerres chaudes et froides qu'on a livrées ou subies depuis 1939.

Parallèlement à la protestation qui se manifeste de façon concrète à travers les magazines, les monographies, et même devant les commissions et comités du gouvernement, contre les abus du capitalisme, un autre type de protestation se manifeste, celle des écrivains qui, eux, dans leurs romans ou dans des revues de leur création, s'attaquent aux conséquences sociales du système. Leurs observations et critiques du système, *ex post*, c'est-à-dire, par le biais de ses conséquences, représentent une contribution importante au développement de la conscience collective, un prélude à la révolte de l'âge néo-électrique, une ouverture sur la prospective de l'époque contemporaine. Ces intellectuels n'ont pas tous l'intuition sociologique d'un Sinclair Lewis; la plupart font simplement la découverte du moi contre une société qu'ils trouvent chargée d'hypocrites conventions et orientée, sous l'apparence de la dignité, vers d'inavouables objets. Ils s'en prennent à leurs pères, à leur code de conduite, à l'*American way of life*. Ils ont perdu foi en leurs institutions. Certains qui avaient réclamé une extension du pouvoir étatique voient aujourd'hui le pouvoir de l'état même les empêcher de boire à leur guise. Ils sont choqués de voir que l'état use de son pouvoir pour brider les citoyens en imposant la *prohibition* à tout le pays. D'autres qui avaient eu foi en la démocratie populaire et qui avaient réclamé pour le peuple une plus grande accessibilité au gouvernement, une authentique participation du peuple au gouvernement, s'aperçoivent que, par l'intervention populaire même, la liberté subit des avatars. La majorité du peuple semble céder aux conformismes, aux peurs. Le Ku Klux Klan fait de nouveaux adeptes, le mouvement contre la théorie de l'évolution gagne la politique en certains états qui adoptent des mesures répressives contre les suspects. Des intellectuels, surpris de ce que le monde ne réponde pas à l'image qu'ils s'en étaient faite se révoltent contre l'idéalisme et se vengent

[13]*The Modern Corporation and Private Property* (New York, 1947).

de la société bourgeoise qu'ils disent hypocrite, ils se rabattent sur des propos réalistes et cyniques, ils se réfugient dans l'individualisme comme valeur première. Ils veulent faire la révolution du *moi* contre le nous contraignant et ses valeurs traditionnelles. Ils proclament la liberté sexuelle, ils cultivent l'ésotérisme : ils ont du mépris pour la masse bourgeoise et de l'aversion pour son conformisme. Ils se disent rejetés de la société et ils se réfugient, par exemple, dans le village de Greenwich à New York ou, s'ils en ont les moyens, vont rejoindre leurs congénères de la Rive Gauche à Paris. Ceux qui restent, ceux qui résistent à la société, cherchent à s'exprimer dans les media de leur création comme l'*American Mercury* lancé en 1922. Ils attaquent l'idéalisme, la démocratie, la religion organisée, les campagnes de moralité, le patriotisme, le mariage, bref, ils abattent les valeurs traditionnelles. Les canons de l'éthique traditionnelle sont soumis à l'érosion : l'autorité parentale et l'idéalisation du mari-père comme suprême autorité du foyer familial sont rejétées, la chasteté pré-maritale est ridiculisée, la fidélité conjugale dépréciée. De jeunes universitaires, instruits des théories freudiennes, cherchent dans la libération de la libido la condition de leur santé mentale. *This Side of Paradise* de F. Scott Fitzgerald fait sensation. Ce roman décrit les mœurs des jeunes à l'Université de Princeton, ce que l'auteur a vu et entendu, puisque lui-même vient d'y terminer ses études. D'autres écrivains ont complété la description de la révolution freudienne; car l'obsession sexuelle se répand chez une certaine classe populaire qui va aux vues animées et qui lit les *confession* magazines. Clara Bow la voluptueuse supplante Mary Pickford la pure. D'autres s'adonnent au *ball room dancing* où le *fast step* a remplacé les danses gracieuses. Une faction moraliste recrutée de haut constitue l'avant-garde de la réaction : on y trouve certains présidents d'université et d'honorables dames de l'église épiscopalienne, telles Madame J. Pierpont Morgan, Madame Edward Harriman, et Madame James Roosevelt.[14] Modes nouvelles et danses lascives fondent leur inquiétude. Enfin, tout part de la femme : l'émancipation de la femme entraîne le dévergondage des mœurs.

L'économiste Carver de Harvard, *laudator temporis acti*, ressent de l'anxiété devant les statistiques de l'emploi féminin dans les écoles, les professions, les services.[15] La proportion des femmes employées dans l'usine et dans le service domestique décroît. L'avènement de la femme de carrière, la promotion de la fille de bureau, sa supériorité sur la fille d'usine ou la servante domestique, modifient radicalement le statut de la femme. La révolution féminine revêt double forme : d'une part, les femmes exigent la parité, d'autre part elles adoptent certaines normes de vie jusque là réservées aux hommes. Relâchement des mœurs, bien sûr : des filles ne vivent plus avec leurs parents, elles prennent appartement. Des femmes mariées menacent d'en faire autant. On se marie plus tard, on a moins d'enfants; on envisage le divorce en cas de mésentente. Les modes changent avec les femmes; elles tendent à la parité : des femmes abandonnent leur corset, elles s'applatissent la poitrine. D'autres portent les cheveux courts; elles fument la cigarette et réclament le privilège de boire avec les hommes. Chose curieuse, a-t-on observé, plus les femmes ressemblent aux hommes plus elles

[14]Frederick L. Allen, *Only Yesterday* (New York, 1946), 110–11.
[15]Thomas N. Carver, *The Present Industrial Revolution* (Cambridge, Mass., 1925).

usent de cosmétiques. Elles abusent de *lipstick* : la face est devenue le dernier refuge de la féminité.[16]

La principale inquiétude des parents bien-pensants de cette période parait se manifester en fin de compte, non pas tellement face au communisme, comme on aurait pu s'y attendre, car celui-ci n'atteint que les jeunes gens instruits de famille à l'aise, mais face au dérèglement des mœurs envisagé comme phénomène de désagrégation ou d'érosion. Le code moral est battu en brèche, il menace de s'effriter. En tout cas, on disait que les mœurs légères d'une jeunesse en explosion, en voie de découvrir son sexe, puisque le sexe fait tant peur, mettaient en péril le code moral du pays. Ce code, selon un chroniqueur américain repose sur un certain nombre de postulats qui mettent bien en évidence les responsabilités de la femme.[17] Pour cette raison, il nous paraît opportun de les rappeler. Premièrement, les femmes sont les gardiennes de la moralité; ce qui suppose que seuls les hommes jouissent du privilège social de pécher. Deuxièmement, les femmes sont de texture fine et l'on attend d'elles qu'elles fassent preuve de finesse dans leurs sentiments et dans leurs comportements. Si les femmes ne cédaient point aux sollicitations du sexe, les hommes perdraient beaucoup d'occasion de pécher. Troisièmement, garçons et filles sont soumis à l'autorité parentale, ils acceptent gaiement le chaperonnage, en attendant d'y substituer leur propre conscience. Quatrièmement, les femmes ne boivent pas, ne fument pas – ce qui laisse supposer qu'elles boivent et fument en cachette. Surtout, elles ne vont pas montrer leur corps, elles n'utilisent pas d'artifices. Et pourtant on leur prescrit le port du corset.

Voilà le code moral. Or la moralité décline par la force d'une conspiration d'origine biblique. Les femmes attirent les regards en montrant leurs genoux; elles enlèvent leurs corsets afin de mieux danser. La bonne société frémit d'horreur en lisant la description des mœurs de leurs propres enfants au collège, mais ils ne détestent pas lire certains romanciers qui exploitent la veine freudienne. Aux lecteurs de culture moyenne (*middle brow*) on sert des magazines qui exploitent l'obsession sexuelle. *True Story* tire à 2,000,000 d'exemplaires en 1926.

De même que la protestation économique engendre une stratégie de défensive et de réadaptation chez les hommes d'affaires, ainsi les courants de la pensée *moderniste* et le débordement des mœurs rencontrent des obstacles; ils stimulent la réaction. Il en résulte une *modération* du processus évolutif. Sous le rapport des politiques économiques et sociales, nous observons un développement dans le nombre et les modes d'interventions de l'état. Sous le rapport de la pensée et des mœurs, nous assistons à une libération continue des forces individuelles, en même temps qu'à une mobilisation constante des ressources personnelles par l'état à mesure que la formation des consciences collectives réclame ou exige l'imposition de contraintes, au nom de la sécurité des citoyens.

Les forces de la réaction d'hier ont modéré en quelque sorte le processus de libération individuelle, elles ne l'ont pas arrêté; les forces de l'action progressiste ont, sous la pression conservatrice, atteint à peine le seuil de la révolution. En

[16] Arthur S. Link, *American Epoch* (New York, 1955), 321; Allen, *Only Yesterday*, 106, 126.
[17] Allen, *Only Yesterday*, chap. 5.

Amérique du Nord, dans tout révolutionnaire il y a un réactionnaire qui se cache et lui interdit d'avancer; dans tout socialiste loge le *cowboy*, ce héraut de l'individualisme. Voyons donc comment se manifestent certaines pressions réactionnaires dans le domaine des idées et des mœurs.

Des groupes de pression s'organisent en divers états du pays pour obtenir une législation sur les modes féminines ou pour interdire la vente des vêtements féminins contraires aux prescriptions de la modestie. Des familles se divisent sur la question de l'usage de la cigarette, sur la consommation du gin et sur les balades nocturnes en automobile. Durant leurs nuits d'insomnie des pères et mères de famille s'interrogent sur l'avenir éternel des enfants qui répondent trop vaguement aux questions de leurs parents. Les optimistes disent que tout cela va passer et, comme les économistes, ils attendent le retour à la normale. Ils interprètent le dérèglement des idées et le dévergondage comme une conséquence de la dégradation morale de l'Europe durant la guerre, dégradation véhiculée en Amérique par les « retours d'Europe » et diffusée par les techniques nouvelles de transport et de communication comme l'automobile, la radio, le cinéma. Pourtant, le relâchement du comportement féminin, interprété d'abord comme une menace à la suprématie et à l'indépendance des mâles finit par plaire aux hommes. On en a vu qui protestaient au commencement et qui, à la fin des années 1920, dansaient les danses modernes[18] et buvaient en compagnie de femmes dans les catacombes de la prohibition. L'Eglise s'élève contre la danse – l'étreinte syncopée de la danse qui aiguise l'instinct sexuel. Dès 1922, le révérend John William Porter, du Kentucky, publie *The Dangers of the Dance.* Autre sujet de protestation : la théorie de l'évolution provoque un mouvement de fondamentalisme biblique.

Le régime de prohibition, appliqué à l'échelle nationale de 1920 à 1933, résulte de la pression séculaire de divers groupes sociaux, *women's leagues* et autres qui s'organisent politiquement vers 1880 et engendrent, en 1895, l'Anti-saloon League of America.[19] Les maisons de débauche et de jeux se multiplient, disait-on, en proportion du nombre de *saloons.* Méthodistes et Baptistes se font ardents propagandistes du régime sec, comptant sur l'efficacité des lois comme moyens de purification des mœurs, et non sans succès, puisqu'en 1914 75 pour cent des états de l'union avaient déjà opté pour ce régime. Or voilà qu'en 1917, grâce aux circonstances de guerre, l'Anti-saloon League en fait une question de patriotisme, transposant le débat sur le plan de la politique nationale. Un amendement à la Constitution est voté afin d'appliquer la prohibition à tous les états de l'union. Aussitôt le *bootlegging* s'organise et s'articule avec le réseau des activités clandestines. En témoigne l'empire d'Alphonse Capone à Chicago. Enfin, les techniques de répression se sont avérées inefficaces : les *speakeasies* et autres nouveautés du régime sec avaient libéralement compensé la disparition des *saloons.* Avec la crise économique, les mesures de sécurité sociale ont pris le pas sur les interdictions; la prohibition fut abolie en 1933.

[18] « No longer did even an inch of space separate them; they danced as if glued together, body to body, cheek to cheek », *ibid.* 108.

[19] Sinclair Lewis voit au fond des choses : « What brought Prohibition ? ... It was the women of America ... ». Voir « Is America a Paradise for women ? » dans *The Man from Main Street,* éd. Harry E. Maule et Melville H. Cane (New York, 1953), 306.

La conjoncture économique a bouleversé l'ordre des préoccupations. Dans le creux de la crise, en 1933, on distribuait du pain et de la soupe dans les quartiers ouvriers et on parlait de révolution chez les *bourgeois*. Les radicaux intellectuels s'attendaient à une révolution de type marxiste, et non à ce phénomène banal qu'on nomme Révolution Roosevelt. Eh bien, la menace rouge s'est dissipée, le capitalisme a survécu grâce à Roosevelt, pour une bonne part. C'était frustrer l'attente de ces intellectuels, marxistes en pantoufles, qui avaient annoncé la fin du capitalisme. En 1930, la conjoncture aurait pu être favorable à la révolution, en effet, mais les radicaux intellectuels croyaient que la fin du capitalisme était imminente et que la révolution allait se faire toute seule. Or, au creux de la crise, la cause des révolutionnaires était déjà perdue. Le vent soufflait dans la voile des Démocrates. La propagande révolutionnaire, pour peu qu'on en ait fait, ne s'était pas adressée à « ceux qui n'ont rien à perdre et tout à gagner » car l'ouvrier américain a toujours eu le sentiment d'avoir quelque chose à perdre,[20] elle s'est adressée aux écrivains, aux poètes, aux intellectuels.[21] Les intellectuels n'ont pas su profiter des circonstances de la crise pour gagner des adeptes à la cause de leur radicalisme; à peine adhéraient-ils eux-mêmes à leur propre doctrine. C'est ce qui faisait dire à un observateur du temps de la crise qu'en 1932, si l'on voulait entendre parler de révolution aux Etats-Unis, il fallait aller à Park Avenue ou à Wall Street, et non aux *breadlines*.[22] Reste à voir cependant, en quel sens les riches entendent la révolution : pour eux, un simple transfert fiscal de revenu, du riche au pauvre, c'est du communisme.

Les intellectuels, par contre, se faisaient une image tout autre de la révolution, remarque l'historien Soule.[23] C'est *sentimentalement* qu'ils s'identifient à l'ouvrier

> non pas toutefois, à l'ouvrier américain tel qu'il est et tel qu'il pense en réalité dans la plupart des cas, mais tel qu'il doit être et doit penser, selon leur théorie révolutionnaire. L'ouvrier qu'ils créent n'est pas une réalité concrète mais une abstraction, un idéal platonique. Les ouvriers peuvent bien n'être pas conscients de la lutte des classes; cela ne dérange point les intellectuels. La lutte des classes existe, disent-ils, et si les ouvriers en sont inconscients, c'est que l'idéologie bourgeoise a empoisonné leurs cerveaux. S'ils étaient instruits, s'ils avaient des chefs, ils se rendraient compte de leur situation et réagiraient autrement.[24]

Conclusion

C'est dans une prise de vue à long terme des événements qu'on perçoit le changement comme processus de développement continu; dans l'optique de la courte période, c'est le processus des conflits qui frappe l'attention, et c'est à l'examen de ce processus que s'arrêtent la plupart des historiens. Parce que le métier l'oblige de coller à l'individuel et donc d'exploiter l'intelligibilité du *fait*, l'historien s'expose au danger de voir et d'interpréter l'histoire comme un déroulement con-

[20] Un point de vue que Werner Sombart s'est appliqué à élucider. Voir son essai, *Warum gibt es in den Vereinigten Staaten keine Sozialismus?* (Tübigen, 1906), le deuxième chapitre en particulier.
[21] David A. Shannon, ed., *The Great Depression* (New York, 1960), 49.
[22] George Soule, « Are we going to have a Revolution? », *Harper's Magazine* (August 1932), in *ibid.*
[23] *Ibid.*, 132.
[24] *Ibid.*, 132. La traduction est la mienne.

flictuel ou dialectique. Or il nous semble que les deux types de processus, le continuel ou l'évolutif, et le conflictuel ou le dialectique, sont contenus dans les changements de structure, mentale ou sociale. Le conflictuel s'inscrit dans l'évolutif pour le retarder ou pour l'arrêter à certains moments, pour l'accélérer ou le précipiter à d'autres, parce qu'à tout moment existent à la fois des antécédents tenaces et des projets attrayants. L'espèce humaine s'agite dans un espace où se déroulent ces deux forces de ralentissement et d'attraction. L'optique de la courte période mobilise indûment l'attention sur les forces de réaction, l'optique de la longue période nous permet de saisir le développement évolutif qui dérange les réseaux stables, c'est-à-dire, les structures.

La présente étude a voulu révéler les deux courants idéologiques de la période de l'entre-deux guerres aux Etats-Unis : un courant de libération et un courant de protection, un mouvement pour libérer la personne, un autre pour la protéger, l'un engendrant le scandale des bons, l'autre suscitant la réaction des intérêts acquis. Dans un cas, le contraire prend la forme d'une ligue de moralité, dans l'autre, le contraire revêt le manteau de la légitimité et brandit l'étendard de l'anti-communisme. Mais la marche des deux mouvements continue : libération de l'individu de ses entraves vers une société sans contrainte, protection des individus et des groupes d'individus vers une économie sans rareté; marche utopique : celle de l'homme à la recherche de sa perfection.

Au cours de la période 1920–40, période taillée, à toute fin méthodologique, dans le tissu des événements longs, se produisent des moments intéressants. Ces moments correspondent à des niveaux de conscience où toutes choses apparaissent dans des perspectives ou sous des proportions différentes. Il y a, par exemple, ces moments où l'on cesse de lutter contre la danse, et aussi ces moments où les *anti-saloon leagues* s'écroulent devant les événements majeurs de la crise économique. Ces moments-là nous intéressent, non à cause de ces phénomènes que les événements rendent futiles, mais à cause des prises de conscience qui portent à des options constructives. Avec le développement des moyens de transport et de communication se tissent des réseaux d'interdépendance de plus en plus vastes, les prises de conscience deviennent de plus en plus englobantes ou compréhensives. A ces états de conscience les institutions sont bien obligées de s'adapter, jusqu'à la limite de leur possible. Indubitablement, le *new deal* marque une étape importante dans la marche vers la libération et la protection de la personne humaine; le *new deal* entraîne des mutations de structure, mais le système demeure sauf. Aujourd'hui, une conscience mieux approfondie, plus compréhensive, perçoit ces mutations comme de banales adaptations aux pressions séculaires aussi bien qu'aux exigences de la conjoncture de crise. La conscience contemporaine, suscitée par des contacts instantanés et, grâce aux moyens récents de transport et de communication, à l'échelle mondiale, continue de se réaliser; mais c'est tout récemment qu'elle a commencé de saisir la structure des structures, c'est-à-dire, le système. A l'intérieur d'un système, le *new deal* réalise un régime qui, en s'adaptant à des mutations de structure institutionnelle et mentale, s'en empare pour sauver le système. Avec lui, le capitalisme se politise davantage; il est devenu politique, étatique.

La transformation dont on a conscience à l'heure présente se situe à l'intérieur d'un processus long : elle nous apparaît comme la fin d'un commencement. Dans notre schéma son origine remonte à l'après-guerre de la première mondiale. C'est vers cette période que l'homme, utilisant la technologie, œuvre de son propre génie, s'attaque à l'homme pour modifier son image du monde et de la vie en aménageant son cerveau. Les méthodes de violence corporelle deviennent désuètes; on s'adresse plutôt à la *chimie de l'intellect*. La corrosion se manifeste dès les années 1920, elle se propage avec le développement des techniques de diffusion de l'information, au service de la pensée pragmatique et matérialiste. On commence alors à créer des besoins pour la satisfaction des produits industriels, on va faire l'effort de transformer en centres d'achat les noyaux urbains de la civilisation industrielle. Le mouvement a été interrompu par la dépression des années 1930, apparemment; et ce fut l'occasion pour les apôtres de la justice sociale et des évangélistes de rassembler les forces progressistes, suppôts des politiques de bien-être, que l'animation économique du temps de guerre et la prospérité folle des années 1920 avaient refoulées. Après la dépression, et comme pour en disposer, la guerre, pour la deuxième fois, se présente en Amérique sous le signe de l'enrichissement et de la prospérité et elle tient en échec le progrès humain. Dans l'après-guerre et maintenant, les deux forces, celle de l'enrichissement sans fin et celle de la justice sociale, se supportent mutuellement. Au nom de la justice sociale un système croulant, féru de statistiques distribue du pain et des jeux. Le mouvement pour la justice sociale et la réforme des mentalités s'y trouve comme assoupi par toutes sortes de tranquillisants portant la commune étiquette de sécurité sociale; de sorte qu'on devrait bien parler de révolution tranquillisante. A cet âge de la drogue, la sécurité sociale est devenue l'opium des économistes. Mais les états de l'occident qui la pratiquent en la substituant à l'emploi et en continuant de servir la cause de l'enrichissement des puissants, ne font que retarder les échéances ou les agitations d'un inévitable réveil. Les *mass media* sont encore au service d'organisations ou institutions qui, selon la logique d'un système basé sur l'usure, exploitent cette tension commune aux peuples de l'occident, cette recherche persévérante « de l'économie sans rareté et de la société sans contrainte » (François Perroux). Le système, toujours basé sur l'usure, se distingue aujourd'hui par son génie d'organisation : il organise hommes et choses indifféremment; il rend les hommes interchangeables comme les pièces d'une machine fabriquées en série; puis il conditionne les hommes, au nom de l'efficacité. Et pourtant, il n'en est pas moins œuvre de l'homme. Exaspérés par la propagande insidieuse que véhiculent les formes contemporaines de communication, certains citoyens vont jusqu'à lui opposer un refus global des valeurs et des symboles de la culture qu'ils disent inhérente au système. Mais les révolutionnaires, comme les saints du XXe siècle, vont se faire de plus en plus rares s'ils continuent de jouir des aménités de l'existence, aussi inhérentes au système, et s'ils s'appliquent trop diligemment à fuir le martyre. Pour le moment, la majorité, sous l'effet des *tranquillisants*, accepte le système. Son acceptation revêt l'une quelconque des trois formes primitives d'acquiescement : celle de Barberousse qui donne dans le système pour l'exploiter à fond, celle d'Augustin qui, en philosophe, l'oppose à la Cité de Dieu; et enfin, celle de Vincent de Paul qui, sans se prononcer, s'en va servir comme aumônier des galères.

Risks of War and Deterrence Logic

JONATHAN KNIGHT *State University of New York*

Santayana once said that those who do not remember the past are condemned to relive it. Looking at the world at the edge of war in 1939, a skeptic might reply: what if the wrong lessons are remembered? What happens when men remember lessons for avoiding past calamities that cannot prevent future ones? Can the future become the past again not because we forget but because we remember too well the causes of the past and use them mistakenly as remedies for problems of today?

In the years between World War I and World War II, English and French politicians felt strongly that a major cause of the Great War was the arms race between Germany and the Allied powers and the tensions and suspicions sustained by that rivalry. To prevent war in Europe again, arms races had to be avoided at almost all costs. If nations accepted disarmament, the international community could impose its decisions peacefully. The carnage of World War I had scarred men too deeply for them to put aside this belief. The consequences of this belief, however, were disastrous, for having renounced war as evil the British and French faced men in Germany who had not.

Hitler became Chancellor of Germany on 30 January 1933 and immediately set out to rearm Germany to extend German strength throughout Europe. In a private meeting with leading German generals and admirals in early February 1933, Hitler promised a vast program of rearmament and conscription and military indoctrination of the country. What would Germany's military forces be used for? As one of those present at the meeting recalled, for the "conquest of *Lebensraum* in the East and its ruthless Germanization."[1] By the beginning of April, the German cabinet had secretly established a National Defence Council (*Reichsverteidigungsrat*) to co-ordinate military planning in the government. For Hitler, the absence of significant armed forces in France and Britain was not an inducement to negotiation but an opportunity to force the European democracies to choose between concessions and the absence of war and arming and the probability of war. Not until it was nearly too late did France and Britain begin rearming on a large scale to stop aggression.

After World War II, the lessons of the past seemed obvious. What had caused the war was appeasement and disarmament. Negotiation from strength would prevent World War III. Slowly but in ways that radically altered the defence policies of Western democracies, deterrence emerged as the central way of pre-

[1]Quoted in Gerhard L. Weinberg, *The Foreign Policy of Hitler's Germany* (Chicago and London, 1970), 27.

Canadian Journal of Political Science/Revue canadienne de science politique, VI, no. 1 (March/mars 1973). Printed in Canada/Imprimé au Canada.

Les risques de guerre et la logique de la dissuasion

La thème soutenue dans cet article est que, étant donné la façon dont les stratèges nucléaires définissent la rationalité, la logique de la dissuasion mène inévitablement à la guerre. La logique de la dissuasion dont il s'agit dans cet article est une logique causale qui s'intéresse uniquement à la prédiction et aux conséquences des décisions étatiques. La définition de la rationalité qu'elle implique insiste sur les coûts, les gains et les risques; les notions d'incertitude ainsi que d'anticipation y sont centrales. La crise des missiles cubains, en 1962, sert d'illustration à la thèse de l'article. On peut comprendre, dans un contexte de dissuasion, les mesures prises par le président Kennedy, mais il reste que la menace de représailles brandie par le président augmentait de façon sensible la possibilité d'une guerre entre les Etats-Unis et l'Union Soviétique. Kennedy courait le risque d'une guerre pour sauver la dissuasion, au nom d'une logique où l'on se devait de brandir des menaces et même d'utiliser des armes nucléaires, pour sauver cette logique même. Il n'y a pas d'apocalypse devant nous. Il se peut que la guerre nucléaire n'arrive pas d'ici cent ans. Mais on ne pourra toutefois pas l'éviter, parce que les hommes s'appuient sur une logique de la dissuasion. La sécurité est la servante de la paix, mais quand on se fait le champion d'une logique de la dissuasion on prépare peu de paix et pas de sécurité pour l'avenir.

venting general war between major powers. Arms are needed to maintain a state's credibility that it can and will use force to prevent aggression. Once an "aggressor" state believes that a "deterrer" state will carry out threats to inflict pain and suffering, regardless of the injury it will experience in return, the "aggressor" will be deterred from beginning a war. States do not make concessions to avoid war; they threaten war to make concessions. To avoid total war states accept the eventuality of war to save the peace. But with sufficient force and a readiness to use it, the "deterrer" will rarely have to do so.

Deterrence logic is, of course, quite old. It is a basic theme in the writings of Thucydides, Tacitus, Hobbes, and Churchill. What is distinctively modern about deterrence logic is that it is tied to weapons that could destroy millions of people swiftly. These weapons make it clear virtually beyond doubt, the nuclear strategists argue, that deterrence prevents war. First, nuclear powers, above all the United States and the Soviet Union, can devastate one another directly and quickly without defeating armed forces. Second, no nuclear state can prevent devastation once bombers and missiles are launched. Third, because of the sheer number of weapons and their dispersal on land and under the sea, neither the United States nor the Soviet Union can destroy completely each other's nuclear arsenals. Thus, states are deterred from firing their weapons knowing that the result would be mutual annihilation. Nuclear weapons have enormously increased the risks of war so that without the weapons there would have been a far greater chance of war between the United States and the Soviet Union.

If deterrence is the right lesson from the past for avoiding war, then we have nothing to fear and good reason for hope. Vigilance in maintaining a deterrent capability will prevent war and help lay the foundations for enduring peace between states. Yet grave doubts remain. The certainty of statesmen during the interwar years that arms races caused war was unshakeable. Only Hitler's conquest of Czechoslovakia and Poland, events unmistakeable in character, forced men to change their minds. Deterrence is similarly inviolable, similarly the bedrock assumption of state defence policies. Is deterrence also a true interpretation of the past but a tragic one for the present? Do we cling to policies that might have stopped Hitler but now lead to the very destruction the policies were designed to avoid in the first place – war between nuclear powers?

That, in fact, is the argument I want to advance. To the extent that deterrence logic becomes the fundamental way by which statesmen grasp the world, interpret their political experiences, and create state policies, so to that extent there is a great likelihood of war precisely because of the logic of deterrence thought. The thesis I will try to sustain is that given the way rationality is defined by nuclear strategists, deterrence logic inescapably leads to death. Hannah Arendt, Richard Barnet, Marc Pilisuk, Anatol Rapoport, Philip Green (the list could be extended) have commented on various facets of deterrence thought, often denouncing it severely.[2] Yet nowhere is there an effort to explain deterrence logic as causal logic with its exclusive emphasis on prediction and the consequences of state policies, or to explain why, with a concept of rationality emphasizing costs, gains, and risks, anticipation and uncertainty are at the heart of deterrence thinking. Strategists have argued that because nuclear war is possible we must think about the unthinkable in ways that will avoid war. My argument is not that we can wish away nuclear weapons by not thinking about them, but that in the particular way in which strategists think there necessarily lies greater possibility of worsening our situation.

I will accept, for the sake of argument, the assumption that without an American deterrent capability the Soviet Union might risk war, and that it is reasonable for the United States to deal with the Soviets on the basis of deterrence logic once the assumption is conceded. The assumption creates the problem of understanding what the Soviets might do in the absence of American nuclear weapons. I shall not discuss this. For it seems to me to be of considerable importance to allow the premise and consider how deterrence logic increases risks of war and does not save peace. In the second part of the essay I venture some judgements on the Cuban missile crisis, the most significant incident in the postwar years linking deterrence logic to deterrence policy.

I

Deterrence thought is a series of logically related statements that are both explanatory and normative and that can be deduced from a single proposition: states act rationally. From this single proposition flows the entire structure of deterrence thought.

How should we interpret rationality? Glenn Snyder provides a concise definition: " 'rationality' may be defined as choosing to act in the manner which gives

[2]Hannah Arendt, *On Violence* (New York, 1969), 3–8; Richard Barnet, *Roots of War* (New York, 1972), chap. 5; Marc Pilisuk, *International Conflict and Social Policy* (Englewood Cliffs, NJ, 1972), chap. 5; Anatol Rapoport, *Strategy and Conscience* (New York, 1964); Philip Green, *Deadly Logic* (New York, 1968).

best promise of maximizing one's value position, on the basis of a sober calculation of potential gains and losses, and probabilities of enemy actions."[3] Deterrence is rationality as state policy, for only by "sober calculation of potential gains and losses" can "deterrer" and "aggressor" states affect each other's capability and will to act.

> Essentially, deterrence means discouraging the enemy from taking military action by posing for him a prospect of cost and risk outweighing his prospective gain.[4]

> Deterrence may be defined as a method of forcing good (or more accurately rational) behavior through the fear of self-destruction ... [N]othing is required of the opposing side except self-interest and a certain amount of rationality.[5]

> Deterrence is concerned with influencing the choices that another party will make, and doing it by influencing his expectation of how we will behave.[6]

> A deterrence policy ... constitutes a special kind of forecast: a forecast about costs and risks that will be run by the party to be deterred, if certain actions are to be taken, and about the advantages he will gain if those actions are avoided.[7]

States are coerced through fear of pain they will suffer if they embark on war, and the calculation of cost and gain are meaningful only when "deterrer" and "aggressor" states act rationally toward each other. The threat to blow up the world, a strategy discussed by Thomas Schelling in *Arms and Influence*,[8] is rational if the Soviets are rational; that is, they act toward us in such a way that we can predict what effect our policies will have on them. When states are rational the strategist can explain, by reference to causal antecedents, why policy effects are brought about. And, because the strategist can see how policy effects come about, when similar causes are controlled similar effects are produced. Strategists are no more and no less than predicting beings, for prediction is nothing more than assessment of cause and effect relationships, while states are regarded as objects in a causal universe defined in terms of power.

The strategist makes predictions about how rational states will behave. It follows that (1) each state policy is evaluated by assessing its consequences, not by judging the rightness or wrongness of the policy itself, and (2) the future is open to prediction, for it is causally determined.

By assessment of consequence I mean questions of this sort: Will anti-ballistic missiles erode the credibility of a second-strike force? Will disarmament talks

[3]*Deterrence and Defense* (Princeton, 1961), 25. For similar understandings of rationality see Herman Kahn, *On Thermonuclear War* (Princeton, 1960) and *On Escalation* (New York, 1965); Klaus Knorr and Thornton Read, eds., *Limited Strategic War* (New York, 1962); Henry Kissinger, *Nuclear Weapons and Foreign Policy* (New York, 1957); Thomas Schelling, *The Strategy of Conflict* (Cambridge, Mass., 1960). While I recognize that strategists consider military/political issues in various ways and from different perspectives, for my purposes their similarities are more important than their differences. In particular, they share a common understanding of deterrence logic and its applicability to state policy.
[4]Snyder, *Deterrence*, 25.
[5]Chalmers W. Sherwin, "Securing Peace Through Military Technology," *Bulletin of the Atomic Scientists*, v, xii (May 1956), 160, quoted in Philip Green, *Deadly Logic*, 159.
[6]Schelling, *The Strategy of Conflict*, 13.
[7]W.W. Kaufmann, *The McNamara Strategy* (New York, 1964), 17, quoted in Green, *Deadly Logic*, 160.
[8](New Haven and London, 1967), 37–43.

undermine our bargaining relationship with China? Will limited war, conventional or nuclear, make general war more or less likely? The method is calculative: costs, gains, and risks are balanced against each other, and the right policy produces the most satisfactory result – or avoids the least satisfactory one. The strategist is more concerned with what will *happen* than with what he is *doing*.[9] He cannot stop to evaluate the intrinsic quality of a policy for he is electing choices for the future, "looking towards tomorrow from today."[10] To evaluate policy without regard to consequences assumes that policy exists apart from cause and effect relationships. Because the strategist sees states in a causal universe, every policy has consequences for prediction, and as there is no end to prediction there is no end to choosing between better and worse policies.

How does the strategist know if better or worse policies have been chosen? Lacking any way to judge the merits of policy except by considering consequences, he uses success as the test of truth. Success allows the strategist to know whether predictions have been accurate. For the strategist, nothing works like success, for success is all that works.[11] The result of this view is clear enough. No potentially useful military measure can be dismissed. The fire-bombings of Dresden and Tokyo, anti-personnel weapons used against civilian populations in airborne anti-guerilla warfare, or limited nuclear war are tolerated for they avoid greater evils. When the evil is extreme, like total nuclear war, the strategist can justify extreme action. And as the extreme evil is avoided, policies are vindicated for they have been successful. Strategists have always disagreed among themselves on defence issues. The debate on the anti-ballistic missile is a clear and recent example of this. What is crucial, however, is not disagreement among strategists, but the shared logic used to evaluate policies. Limited nuclear war may be opposed as shortsighted and imprudent not because it offends moral sensibilities, but because "sober calculation" reveals that likely costs will outweigh probable gains. If a strategist argued that it is not allowable to use nuclear

[9]The distinction is suggested by Thomas Nagel in a discussion of "War and Massacre" in *Philosophy and Public Affairs*, 1, no 2, (1972), 123–44.

[10]Richard E. Neustadt, *Presidential Power* (New York, 1960), 2. I have quoted Neustadt not because his language suits my purpose, but because he is the pre-eminent deterrence strategist for US domestic politics. At this point I can only suggest the outline of an argument supporting this position and not elaborate upon it. What must a president do to be effective? He "determinedly ... seeks power," and the more he seeks the more likely he is "to bring vigor to his clerkship" (p. 185). How shall we know if he is seeking power? By his success in "boost[ing] his chances for mastery [of Congress] in any instance, looking toward tomorrow from today" (p. 2). Why should the president look toward tomorrow? His "own choices are the only means *in his own hands* of guarding his own prospects for effective influence" (p. 57, emphasis in text). Why doesn't the president stop choosing? "[H]is choices of what he would say and do, and how and when, are his means to conserve and tap his sources of power. Alternatively, choices are the means by which he dissipates power. The outcome, case by case, will often turn on whether he perceives his risk in power terms and takes account of what he sees before he makes his choice" (p. 179). I would submit that even in this skeletal version of Neustadt's argument we have the basic ingredients of deterrence thought: rationality as causal logic, contest for success not purpose, and ceaseless seeking of power to manipulate the future.

[11]"My own bias rears itself in the view that, strategy being essentially the pursuit of success in certain types of competitive endeavor, a pragmatic approach is the only appropriate one. The basic pragmatic principle is, I suppose, that 'Truth is the idea that works.' Thus, one weighs a strategic concept or idea by investigating as thoroughly as possible the factors necessary to its successful operation." Bernard Brodie, *Survival*, V, no VII (August, 1965), 208, quoted in Green, *Deadly Logic*, 221.

weapons of whatever kind, two things would be clear. First, no argument about what would happen if the weapons were not used could show that using them would be acceptable, for use of the weapons could not be justified in terms of any consequences at all. Second, the strategist would have abandoned deterrence logic.

What does the strategist see in the future if in principle it is open to prediction? To the extent that he can make accurate predictions, the strategist foresees the possibility of death at the hands of a country with the capability of devastating the United States.

Fear of death creates a paradoxical situation for the strategist. On the one hand, fear of death provides a degree of certainty for making policy recommendations. The Soviet Union might start a general war if the United States is not prepared to use force, and therefore policies are recommended that, it is hoped, will prevent the worst possible contingency, nuclear annihilation. On the other hand, because the military capabilities of the Soviet Union are equal to those of the United States, the strategist is never certain about the results of his policy recommendations. A new weapon system, multiple re-targeted warheads for example, is favoured by American strategists for it contributes to an increase in invulnerable second-strike forces. At the same time, however, it is assumed – for it would be imprudent to do otherwise – that the Soviet Union has developed or will develop the same weapon. Worse still, the Soviet Union might find a way of countering the viability of second-strike forces. Too much is at stake to argue that this should not be a real concern, if only because of the very wide range of operational uncertainties of any weapon system, so that the strategist eventually concludes that the other side has solved the problem of finding and destroying invulnerable forces long before this has in practice been achieved. Arms competition therefore continues with greater or lesser intensity depending on the extent to which weapons systems seem suited to first-strike attacks. What appears to the American strategist as a vital contribution to assured destruction capability can appear as a threat to Soviet assured destruction, and the stability conferred by assured destruction rests on no firmer a foundation than the technological ingenuity of weapons strategists.

Given that the strategist is certain about what he ultimately fears but not certain that his predictions for avoiding catastrophe will be accurate, he is forced logically into a condition of anticipation. That is to say, he must literally foresee courses of events ("scenarios") that might bring about the worst possible contingency, so that what is unlikely yet dreaded becomes the immediate focal point for all policy proposals. A striking statement on the logical necessity of anticipation was provided by Robert McNamara as he considered why the United States expanded its nuclear forces in the early 1960s:

> In 1961 when I became Secretary of Defense, the Soviet Union had a very small operational arsenal of intercontinental missiles. However, it did possess the technological and industrial capability to enlarge that arsenal very substantially over the succeeding several years. We had no evidence that the Soviets did plan, in fact, to fully use that capability. *But ... a strategic planner must be conservative in his calculations; that is, he must prepare for the worst plausible case and not be content to hope and prepare for the most probable.*

Since we could not be certain of Soviet intentions, since we could not be sure that they would undertake such a massive build-up, we had to insure against such an eventuality by undertaking a major build-up of our own Minuteman and Polaris forces.[12]

McNamara's cautious language is important. He does not say that the Soviets might attack the United States, and much less does he raise visions of aggressive communism. He is concerned about what he does not know: whether the Soviets would develop intercontinental missiles. From this remote, conservative worry, he reaches a specific policy decision: the United States must build its own missile systems, not fearing what the Soviets nearly had done but anticipating what they might possibly do.

Clearly a nuclear preventive strike, one form of anticipation, would remove all uncertainty for the strategist about the Soviet Union.[13] Logically, death (or complete submission) eliminates the strategist's concern about what he does not know by eliminating the object of his concern. But in a world of second-strike retaliatory capabilities, a preventive strike is also self-annihilating. The only acceptable forms of anticipation are political and arms pre-emption.

Political pre-emption refers to policies that anticipate challenges to preserving options as early as possible. Why preserve options? When among equal powers there is not total certainty of successful predictions, choices are the only means completely in the hands of the strategist to conserve and advance state power. Policies of other states are important for the strategist, for out of what others think of the United States emerge opportunities for deterrence. Yet in a causal universe where there is no end to prediction it is only in making choices that the strategist minimizes chances that deterrence will fail. Without choice anticipation evaporates, for there is no way of evaluating costs and gains, and with anticipation gone there is no deterrence. Why preserve options as early as possible? Uncertain about avoiding catastrophe, the strategist cannot be certain where challenges to preserving options will stop if challenges are not met early and decisively. It is one thing to choose to act irrationally; it is quite another to be forced to choose between submission and war, for whatever the choice it will foreclose rather than keep open future state options. It even makes good sense from the logical point of view to act against hypothetical dangers, for that would narrow uncertainty about successful predictions to the vanishing point.

Arms pre-emption is weapons strategy designed to thwart the possibility of general war. If it is logical to arm to deter the Soviet Union, it would be equally illogical not to maintain a nuclear weapon capability with all that entails, as already suggested, in the way of arms competition.

In many criticisms of deterrence logic considerable emphasis is placed on the diminishing returns of additional nuclear capabilities. Defensive systems can be saturated, overwhelmed, or evaded, while additions to offensive capabilities add

[12]*The Essence of Security* (New York, Harper and Row, 1968), 57–8, emphasis added. McNamara emphasizes the capabilities of the Soviet Union, but assumptions about intentions are inescapably part of capability analysis. See Bernard Brodie, *Escalation and the Nuclear Option* (Princeton, 1966), 85–8.

[13]I raise this point not to suggest that, given the opportunity deterrence strategists would recommend a preventive strike, but rather to highlight the dilemma created for them by their own form of rationality.

nothing to military power and can be matched by the Soviet Union. With an overkill capacity of six tons of TNT per person on the planet, it is irrational to build more weapons systems, offensive or defensive.[14] For the purpose of influencing the direction of government policy, the emphasis on overkill is valuable. It calls attention to some fundamental facts about strategic weapons and defence policies: the private and public bureaucracies that help support weapons programs to support themselves; the billions of dollars spent for weapons soon obsolete; the unrivalled destructive power in the hands of the government. Yet the stress on overkill leans a long way to attempting to influence policy by presenting too optimistic a view of defence policies – optimistic in implying that if government leaders realized that defence dollars purchase shrinking amounts of security there would be a serious turn-about of weapons programs.

The United States has had nuclear overkill since at least the beginning of the Eisenhower administration, and for the past 20 years the government has enlarged and diversified its nuclear warhead arsenal. Overkill is a symptom and not a cause of this expansion. From the perspective of deterrence logic, it does not matter how many times-over each person on the planet could be killed. Overkill is the technological by-product of anticipation. The strategist's logic emphasizes taking steps to narrow uncertaintv that the Soviet Union might undermine the credibility and will of weapons' policies. The risks of nuclear war are small, but as the costs of such a war are enormous the gains of anticipation are correspondingly high even though maintaining the "integrity" of retaliatory forces means stockpiling more explosive power whether through one, two, or three independent strategic systems.[15]

Pre-emptive policies, however, only reduce uncertainty for the strategist, they cannot eliminate it. Because he cannot establish complete certainty save for risking death and because potential challenges to credibility and will cannot be totally eliminated, the strategist can never cease from his predictions, never cease from using his logic to try to avoid catastrophe. Uncertain about the results of his predictions, the strategist must devise new policies in a sisyphean quest for assurance in a world created by his own logic that is inherently uncertain.

At the centre of deterrence thought is uncertainty, the fundamental motivating force, and anticipation, the fundamental strategic principle. Together these concepts generate a self-perpetuating system of thought in which certainty is never grasped and fear of devastation is the spur to pre-emptive policies. Going one step further: once state relations are reduced to the logical categories of cause and effect, defined exclusively in terms of power, there is no way of surmounting deterrence logic except through the weapons prescribed by the logic.

Deterrence strategists obviously have a force-oriented view of international politics. After all, by definition a strategist is concerned with threat and use of force. The grave difficulty with deterrence logic is not that it is concerned with

[14]The figure of six tons is given in Seymour Melman, *Pentagon Capitalism* (New York, 1970), 165.

[15]The Nixon administration is committed to three maior systems: bombers, land-based missiles, and sea-based missiles. This is why the FY 1973 budget calls for continuation of the MIRV program, (through Poseidon missiles at sea and Minuteman III on land), strengthening ICBM silos and installing ABMs to defend land-based missiles, increased development of the B-1 bomber, undersea long-range missiles, and a new airborne warning and control system.

force. Rather, its concern is such that any use of force can be tolerated if it is rationally linked to maintaining options in an "anarchical" world where there is no certainty that force will not be used against the United States. The logic is not that states must eventually adopt policies of "unmodified counterforce attacks" or "spasm or insensate wars."[16] The logic is that it is necessary to judge *all possible options* with a view to discovering if there are "possibilities we care to risk."[17] The strategist cannot take the view that certain measures are impermissible no matter what the consequences, for he would then deny the logic which appears self-evident and compelling to him. Total nuclear war, the destruction of weapons and populations, is so abhorrent that anything short of that calamity can be rationally evaluated as successful. The end-point, then, of deterrence logic is annihilation given the reality it creates through the strength of its logic.

II

No American statesman has consistently defined political reality solely in the terms of deterrence logic set out above. No president has been rational to the point that in anticipating challenges to will and credibility he has tried to intervene against every threat, real and potential. Other values, other interests, and constraints of time, money, and manpower, have all limited the impact of deterrence logic on American foreign policy. Yet it is hardly surprising to observe that there has been impact of some sort, most clearly, perhaps, in decisions of the Kennedy administration to expand nuclear and conventional arms capabilities. My concern with impact, however, is not with determining how and why policy-makers have adopted many of the ideas of deterrence strategists. By impact I mean that policy-makers, in one degree or another, have interpreted and acted upon political events in the way that strategists would have them be rational. And that is the great concern, for the logic impels men to act in ways that significantly increase risks of war. I shall now argue that (1) steps taken by President Kennedy during the Cuban missile crisis of 1962 make good sense *in the context of deterrence logic*, and (2) the threat of nuclear retaliation laid down by the president significantly increased the possibility of war between the United States and the Soviet Union.

III

There is virtually universal agreement among the deterrence strategists and President Kennedy and his advisers that, first, the placing of medium-range and intermediate range ballistic missiles in Cuba amounted to "the supreme Soviet probe of American intentions,"[18] and that, second, action had to be taken against the missiles.

On the first point, President Kennedy's appraisal represents the common view

[16]These are "rungs" 38 and 44 on Herman Kahn's escalation ladder in *On Escalation* (Baltimore, 1968).
[17]*Ibid.*, 274.
[18]Arthur M. Schlesinger, Jr., *A Thousand Days* (Boston, 1965), 796.

of the importance of Soviet missiles in Cuba. Arthur Schlesinger recalled a conversation with the president the morning of 22 October:

He said that, first [Soviet success] might draw Russia and China closer together, or at least strengthen the Soviet position in the communist world, by showing that Moscow was capable of bold action in support of a communist revolution; second, that it would radically redefine the setting in which the Berlin problem could be reopened after the election; third, that it would deal the United States a tremendous political blow.[19]

In his televised speech that same evening the president stated that Soviet "aggressive conduct" could not be accepted if American "courage and ... commitments are ever to be trusted again by either friend or foe."[20] And nearly two months after the crisis he once again emphasized the grave political consequences of the Soviet move: "It would have politically changed the balance of power. It would have appeared to, and appearances contribute to reality."[21]

The political issues that were important for the president cannot sustain the argument that he created the crisis "because he needed a foreign policy 'victory' on the eve of congressional elections." This is Ronald Steel's position based on a distinction between military threat – an intention by the Soviet Union to use the missiles – and political threat – apparently everything worrisome to the Kennedy administration in its foreign and domestic relations short of the possibility of an attack against the United States.[22] The distinction, however, is false, for it implies drawing a sharp line between war and peace and that cannot be done. Politics was the continuation of war by other means during the crisis. If this view is accepted, difficulties are removed in interpreting evidence created either trying to pin Kennedy down and say now he felt the missiles would be used – or by the assumption that he never seriously thought they would be fired, with the consequent need to dismiss his own military directives as domestic posturings. Granting that Soviet motives were ambiguous, even granting that they were "defensive," what mattered for the president, his advisers, and deterrence strategists was the impact on the future of the Soviet move. For all these men opportunity for choice among alternative policies was essential for American efforts at maintaining stability and limiting violence in the world. With the Soviet Union successful in its fait accompli, American opportunities for choice would be drastically narrowed. Political pre-emption would turn to waiting for succeeding Soviet challenges, each one driving the United States closer to accepting coexistence on Soviet terms or launching war.

The need for action necessarily followed from this evaluation of the importance of Soviet missiles in Cuba. From the beginning of the crisis the president was convinced "that he would have to do something."[23] Except for Robert McNamara's short-lived suggestion that a missile fired from Cuba was no different than a missile fired from the Soviet Union, implying that the United States should

[19]*Ibid.*, 811.
[20]The speech is reprinted in Robert Kennedy, *Thirteen Days* (New York, 1969), 131–9.
[21]*The Washington Post* (18 December 1962), quoted in Graham Allison, *The Essence of Decision* (Boston, 1971), 51.
[22]"Endgame," *New York Review of Books*, XII (13 March 1969), 15–22, as well as his exchange with Roger Hilsman in *ibid.*, XII (8 May 1969), 36–8.
[23]Kennedy, *Thirteen Days*, 33. See also Schlesinger, *A Thousand Days*, 803, and Theodore Sorensen, *Kennedy* (New York, 1966), 761.

not act, no one in the ExCom meetings questioned the necessity for action. Indeed, it was impossible not to act for it was impossible to affirm simultaneously the gravity of the Soviet challenge and not be willing to respond to the challenge. Not to act would mean challenging the structure of deterrence thought endorsed unreservedly by the president and his advisers.

It is in this perspective that the president's choice of blockade rather than air strike appears less important than has otherwise been maintained. It has been widely argued that the crucial decision by the United States during the crisis was for blockade rather than air strike, for the United States thereby chose limited action against unlimited action. There were drawbacks to the quarantine, but it had the unparalleled advantage, so it seemed, of maintaining options. "It was a limited, low-level action" which allowed for "more controlled escalation ... gradual or rapid as the situation required."[24] *Within* the network of assumptions about the Soviet challenge and the necessity for action the blockade was, on balance, a better choice, for an air strike would have killed thousands of Russians and Soviet revenge would have poisoned Soviet-American relations for years to come. Yet the view that the choice of blockade was in some way qualitatively different from the choice of air strike may be objected to on several grounds.

First, an air strike, though perhaps imprudent, was not irrational once Soviet action was seen as a major threat to the United States. It made good sense to end the crisis quickly by an American fait accompli, something an air strike promised to do. Indeed, despite assertions during and after the crisis that the blockade maintained options, it foreclosed the option of not acting. That is, if the Soviets did not recognize the blockade and did not remove their missiles, the United States would again face the decision of escalation. It is certainly true that one could imagine "many decision points ... on the staircase of ascending steps in the use of force," but the president and his advisers did not imagine them.[25]

Their initial preference was an air strike. "The general feeling in the beginning," Robert Kennedy recalled, "was that some form of action was required ... Most felt, at that stage, that an air strike against the missile sites could be the only course."[26] By Saturday afternoon of the 20th the president had agreed to the blockade, but he still wanted explicit assurances from Air Force Tactical Bombing Command that an air strike would not destroy all the missiles. In a Sunday morning meeting with General Walter C. Sweeney, commander of Bombing Command, the president was told that "even a major surprise air attack could not be certain of destroying all the missile sites and nuclear weapons in Cuba." Robert Kennedy commented: "That ended the small, lingering doubt that might still have remained in [the President's] mind. It had worried him that a blockade would not remove the missiles – now it was clear that an attack could not accomplish that task completely, either."[27]

[24]Sorensen, *Kennedy*, 776. See also Schlesinger, *A Thousand Days*, 806; Roger Hilsman, *To Move A Nation* (New York, 1967), 205; Albert and Roberta Wohlstetter, *Controlling the Risks in Cuba* (London, 1965), 16.
[25]*Ibid.*
[26]Kennedy, *Thirteen Days*, 33. Also Sorensen, *Kennedy*, 771.
[27]Kennedy, *Thirteen Days*, 49. One effect of the meeting with Sweeney was that the president placed himself on record as having consulted fully with the Air Force. But there is nothing to indicate that this was the intent of the meeting, as implied by Allison, *Essence of Decision*, 249, and Hilsman, *To Move A Nation*, 205.

There is no way of knowing what the president would have done had he received assurance from Bombing Command of 100 per cent air strike effectiveness. Yet it is reasonably clear from the evidence, I would argue, that the president reluctantly chose the blockade *after* repeated arguments that the air strike would not be completely successful in removing the missiles. His strong inclination to use an air strike was even more apparent three days after his Monday television speech, as he and his advisers worried about continued missile construction in Cuba and Soviet refusal to recognize the blockade. The president asked for a "gradual increase in pressure," including more low-level flights over Cuba and the preparation of embargo lists.[28] Privately, however, he was deeply pessimistic about these efforts. The following morning, Friday the 26th, he "ordered the State Department to proceed with preparations for a crash program on civil government in Cuba to be established after the invasion and occupation of that country." He remarked to his advisers: "We are going to have to face the fact that, if we invade, by the time we get to these sites, after a very bloody fight, they will be pointed at us. And we must further accept the possibility that when military hostilities first begin, those missiles will be fired."[29]

In the light of what was at stake in Cuba for the president and his advisers, the initial preference for an air strike, the Sunday meeting with General Sweeney, and doubts about the effectiveness of the blockade, it seems apparent that the choice between blockade and air strike was a very narrow one, that the president probably would have gone on to invasion if the missiles had not been withdrawn, and that the president saw no "escalation steps" between blockade and higher levels of force except air strike and invasion.

But if the air strike was rational yet perhaps imprudent, what can be said of the president's threat of nuclear retaliation? Did he actually intend to launch all American nuclear weapons against the Soviet Union if a missile fired from Cuba landed in the jungles of Brazil? Were the chances of war between the United States and the Soviet Union greater because of the threat, or was the threat little more than a statement of the obvious (or perhaps not so obvious) – that the United States would defend its allies, whether in Europe or Latin America? It will be recalled that the president's statement appeared as point three in a catalogue of seven points detailing steps he had ordered in defense of American and Western Hemisphere security: "Third, It shall be the policy of this nation to regard any nuclear missile launched from Cuba against any nation in the Western Hemisphere as an attack by the Soviet Union on the United States, requiring a full retaliatory response upon the Soviet Union."[30]

There have been two reactions to this threat among presidential advisers and deterrence strategists. The first has been to ignore the threat. There is no discus-

[28]Kennedy, *Thirteen Days*, 83.

[29]*Ibid.*, 75. See also Hilsman, *To Move A Nation*, 227, and Schlesinger, *A Thousand Days*, 830. Allison argues that the missiles were withdrawn because of an "explicit threat of invasion" (*Essence of Decision*, 65). Schlesinger reports that in a conversation on Monday morning, 29 October, the president remarked that "one thing this experience shows is the value of sea power and air power; an invasion would have been a mistake – a wrong use of power. But the military are mad. They wanted to do this" (*A Thousand Days*, 831). But the president wanted to do it also, and Schlesinger himself felt that if missile construction had continued "the United States would have had no real choice but to take action against Cuba" (*Ibid.*, 830).

[30]As reprinted in Kennedy, *Thirteen Days*, 136.

sion of what President Kennedy intended by the threat or what resulted from it by Robert Kennedy, Roger Hilsman, Theodore Sorensen, or Arthur Schlesinger. There are, of course, many references in the memoirs of these men to the dangers of nuclear war and the abyss of destruction faced by the United States and the Soviet Union, but nothing which amounts to an evaluation, no matter how brief, of the importance of the threat.

The second reaction has been, in effect, to dismiss the threat as of little consequence. This is done by deterrence strategists who argue that the president did not intend to fire all American nuclear weapons, suggesting that the threat of war between the two superpowers was no greater during the crisis than at other times. Both Herman Kahn and the Wohlstetters focus on the phrase "full retaliatory response." For Kahn the phrase "does not specify the form of attack. It is still open as to whether it would be counterforce or countervalue."[31] For the Wohlstetters the policy implied by the phrase leaves open the possibility of "controlled reaction. The United States has made clear that a single nuclear missile launched against the United States need not trip an uncontrolled 'full response'."[32] Thomas Schelling is somewhat ambiguous about the matter. In an early chapter in *Arms and Influence* Schelling remarks that the threat was "not entirely incredible; and, for all I know, the President meant it."[33] Yet in a later chapter, "The Manipulation of Risk," Schelling offers an explanation of the crisis which qualifies his belief that the threat was credible or that the president meant it. And it is this explanation I shall consider briefly in arguing that the threat increased significantly the possibility of war between the United States and the Soviet Union.

Schelling's explanation begins with the assumption that neither superpower "had any desire to engage in major war" during the crisis. The crisis was "a contest in risk taking ... that would have made no sense if [it] led *predictably* and *ineluctably* to a major war." What was dangerous about the crisis was not the intention to start a war:

> If there was a danger it seems to have been that each side might have taken a series of steps, actions and reactions and countermeasures, piling up its threats and its commitments, generating a sense of showdown, demonstrating a willingness to carry the thing as far as necessary, until one side or the other began to believe that war had already started, or was so inevitable that it should be started quickly, or that so much was now at stake that general war was preferable to accommodation.[34]

Schelling appears to be doing two things in this argument. First, he does not discount the risks of war during the crisis. Yet at the same time he argues that greater risks would have developed only if a "sense of showdown" were generated by moves and countermoves by the superpowers. But as neither country wanted major war and because war did not occur (or did not nearly occur), nothing the United States did during the crisis increased the dangers of war.

The difficulty with the argument is that it is based on the misleading premise that the crisis would have been senseless had it "predictably" and "ineluctably" led to war. Certainly this was never an issue for anyone in the ExCom meetings; in fact, it is difficult to see how it could be an issue in any circumstances, imply-

[31] Kahn, *On Escalation*, 80.
[32] *Controlling the Risks in Cuba*, 18.
[33] pp.40–1.
[34] *Arms and Influence*, 95–6, emphasis added.

ing that some crises inescapably lead to war. The concern of the president and his advisers was whether war might come because of steps taken by the United States or the Soviet Union. This is exactly Schelling's concern also, but he puts the cart before the horse. The question is not whether the crisis might have led inevitably to war, but whether decisions made by the president raised or lowered the dangers of war? Schelling fastens on this as a conclusion when it should be his starting point. Considered in this way, the threat of nuclear retaliation seriously increased the possibility of war between the two superpowers. We do not know what the president meant by the phrase "full retaliatory response," but it is not necessary that we do know it. Even if the president was not certain about the meaning of the phrase, by making the threat he closed the door on not responding to a missile fired from Cuba. For given what he saw at stake in Cuba, not to react with nuclear weapons, whether few or many, would deny the very things he thought worth fighting for in Cuba – the courage and commitments of the United States.

The president and his advisers saw missiles in Cuba in the gravest way possible, as a threat to the "security" of the United States.[35] At stake was not the physical integrity of the country, but the ability to maintain freedom to use state power to preserve political options. The president was engaged in nothing less than a contest for "world leadership."[36] This was the crucial defensive reason for the threat of nuclear retaliation, for nothing short of such a threat was equal to the danger. Deterrence strategists (the Wohlstetters and Schelling, for example) cannot argue that placing of missiles in Cuba was aggression and that American reputation was worth fighting over and then conclude that the nuclear threat did not seriously raise the dangers of war. *Once the logic of deterrence thought is accepted as valid* the threat was rational precisely because it raised the risks of war. To deny that the possibility of war was grave is to deny that the president should have seen a serious challenge to the United States in Soviet action. But if that is not denied then it was rational to threaten nuclear retaliation and rational to expect that threat to increase markedly the dangers of war between the two superpowers.

What was alarming about President Kennedy's decisions was not that he was "emotional" and stressed too much the dangers of war, but that his decisions conformed only too well to the logic of deterrence thought. During those 13 days in October the president was a better deterrence strategist than the strategists themselves, as he evaluated and dealt with a foreign policy issue in the way strategists have long argued for – by "sober calculation of potential gains and losses, and probabilities of enemy actions."[37] Not what was being done but what would happen was of paramount concern to the president and his advisers. The grave threat for the president was not the possibility of missiles fired at the United States but the equally real and frightening spectre to him of narrowed political options and consequent erosion of deterrent capabilities. The president risked nuclear war to save deterrence, with the justification for this risk created and sustained by a logic that would promote threat and use of nuclear weapons to save itself. It was not unusual that the president identified America's interests

[35]Hilsman, *To Move A Nation*, 227. [36]Sorensen, *Kennedy*, 808.
[37]Snyder, *Deterrence and Defense*, 25.

in Cuba as other than sheer survival, and was prepared to take steps that might involve the country in war over interests that would not jeopardize the nation's physical survival if lost. Identification of a nation's security with survival alone is the exception rather than the rule of statecraft. The striking quality of deterrence logic is the clarity with which it requires a willingness to take risks that would lead to war for interests beyond survival.

IV

The irony and near tragedy of the missile crisis was that the logic which seemed to avoid war created the climate of statecraft for seeing missiles in Cuba as dangerous. Put differently and more generally: states arm to deal with problems created by an "anarchical" world. What problems? Problems like the threat and use of force. These are problems, however, because they are seen in the context of deterrence logic. Both the logic and states are now running in a circle: states arm to deal with force, and states use force to preserve the possibility of maintaining arms. Even worse, as deterrence logic makes greater efforts to sustain itself by the strategy of anticipation, it will logically move closer to the destruction it tries to avoid. Anything short of "complete annihilation" is successful as one can always imagine a worse circumstance – one's own death.

Statesmen do not deal with each other on the basis of deterrence logic alone; they are not yet "high causalists."[38] To the degree, however, that deterrence logic becomes more self-validating through the repeated experiences of men who take it for granted, the use of nuclear weapons will appear more suited to their political aims. The United States and the Soviet Union currently accept an array of attitudes and agreements that tend to discourage the first use of nuclear weapons. Yet this condition is precarious, characterized by uncertainties about the invulnerability of nuclear forces and the inability of any state to control the spread of nuclear weapons. Clearly the apocalypse is not before us. Nuclear war may not occur for a hundred years. It will not be avoided, though, because men rely on deterrence logic. Security is the handmaiden of peace, but to champion deterrence logic is to assure to us for the future little peace and no security.

The lesson of World War II is that disarmed states confronted by belligerent ones hasten the day when they must choose between submission and war. The lesson of deterrence logic is that armed states confronted by their own uncertainty and fear of death hasten the day when they must make the same choice. The failure of deterrence logic is not that it fails to replace a dominant concern with anticipation through pre-emption with a one-sided concern for disarmament. The failure lies in its inability to maintain a commitment to genuine security, which for nuclear powers means no serious concern that their presently invulnerable forces may be circumvented or destroyed, while calculating consequences for stopping aggression (assuming, of course, there is good reason for believing that a state is aggressive). The tension between these two commitments can be established only by moving beyond deterrence logic. I am not at all sure how this can be done, but strategists and statesmen who consider the way ahead clear are greatly to be envied.

[38] The phrase is Clifford Brown's.

Personality and Politics: A New Look at the King-Byng Dispute*

J.E. ESBEREY *University of Toronto*

Constitutional crises are a comparatively rare occurrence in Canada so it is not surprising that the electoral decision of October 1972 has rekindled interest in a well-known earlier example – the King-Byng dispute. What continues to be overlooked is the fact that the political situation in 1926 was not in itself a constitutional issue. The conventions of the constitution are flexible enough to cope with minority governments and votes of censure, as long as there is a general consensus on the precedents that are relevant and the conditions under which they should be applied. Where this consensus does not exist, a crisis may develop as a result of a clash of personalities among the major participants. Each political actor interprets the situation in terms of his own personal needs and perceptions and each response will incorporate the behaviour pattern that he has developed to cope with these needs.

If we are to fully understand the events of 1926 and their implications, it is essential that existing studies of the King-Byng dispute[1] be supplemented by other approaches that can take into account the hitherto neglected personality aspects of William Lyon Mackenzie King and the influence of specific aspects of his personality on the crisis of 1926. Concentration on Mackenzie King can be justified on the grounds that he was directly instrumental in precipitating a crisis and in the specific course and proportions of the events that followed. It is also essential that the dispute be considered in a wider time span than the period between the elections of 1925 and 1926. In political terms the dispute had its beginnings at least as early as 1919, for it embodied many aspects of party and imperial problems of the previous decade.[2] In personal terms, the dispute had its

*This article is a revised and shortened version of a paper presented to the annual meeting of the Canadian Political Science Association, Montreal, June 1972. The paper is based on a study of the relationship between Mackenzie King's personality and his politics which is being prepared as a doctoral dissertation in the Department of Political Economy, University of Toronto. The author wishes to thank the literary executors for access to the family papers in the W.L. Mackenzie King collection, Miss Tallents for access to the papers of Miss Violet Markham, and the Queen's University Archives for access to the Buchan papers. I would also like to thank Paul Fox for his advice and criticism of an earlier draft of this paper.

[1]E.A. Forsey, *The Royal Power of Dissolution in the British Commonwealth* (Toronto, 1943), W.R. Graham, *The King-Byng Affair, 1926* (Toronto, 1967), and *Arthur Meighen*, II (Toronto, 1963); H. Blair Neatby, *William Lyon Mackenzie King* II, 1924–1932 (Toronto, 1963).

[2]The years 1917–26 represented a period of flux in Canadian party development. The futures of the three leaders and the three parties were at stake. Similarly, relations with the British government were still unsettled. Canada had begun to assume a new autonomous status but a number of issues remained unsettled, including the specific role of the governor general.

Canadian Journal of Political Science/Revue canadienne de science politique, VI, no. 1 (March/mars 1973). Printed in Canada/Imprimé au Canada.

origin in the difficulties of the King family and the childhood experiences of Mackenzie King.

Any interdisciplinary approach introduces a number of special problems and seldom more so than when the approach concerns psychoanalytical psychology and politics. Because of the focus on the King-Byng dispute it is not possible to present a detailed description of Mackenzie King's personality or to discuss fully every development that contributed to the specific action being considered. A workable compromise seems to lie in isolating one pattern of behaviour observable in the dispute of 1926. This pattern can then be traced back in the solutions to the various developmental crises of the "life cycle."[3]

What are the main characteristics of this behaviour pattern?[4] It is possible to discern in the dispute a strong negative component of the crisis of basic trust, a feature both of Mackenzie King's unwillingness to trust others and of doubts of his own trustworthiness.[5] A person who is unable to rationalize these doubts of his own trustworthiness would find it difficult to function effectively in positions of responsibility, especially when these doubts are reinforced by feelings of shame and guilt. The defence mechanism by which Mackenzie King was able to make this adjustment involved both pronounced soul-searching and a pattern of unconscious confirmations. If others could be seen to trust him, then his doubts about his own trustworthiness could be disregarded as false.[6] The same people, by showing that they found Mackenzie King trustworthy, also proved themselves worthy of trust.[7] This was a standard by which an individual's worth could be reliably measured and an important aspect of his perception of Arthur Meighen and Lord Byng. Mackenzie King frequently asked for advice when what he sought was approval –a confirmation of his basic worth.

The reinforcing aspects – shame and guilt – are associated with a failure to establish autonomy within the family and to accept separation from the mother.

[3]The personality model on which the original study of Mackenzie King's personality was based is the concept of the epigenetic "Life Cycle" developed by Erik H. Erikson. Some of the terminology and concepts of this model have been included in this paper. See Erik H. Erikson, *Childhood and Society* (*Middlesex*, 1965), and *Identity, Youth and Crisis* (New York, 1968).

[4]It is not possible to document every statement about King's personality with a specific quote. Awareness of many of his attributes is based on a repetitive pattern of incidents and expressions occurring over many years rather than of any one statement. However, to provide an illustration of the type of material on which a statement is based, pertinent quotes are included in the footnotes wherever possible. It is not suggested that these individual quotes constitute evidence of the particular personality aspect by themselves.

[5]This feeling of doubt and mistrust can be seen most clearly in Mackenzie King's constant seeking for advice and the fact that he did not wait for the answers before acting or acted directly contrary to the advice when he received it. It is also visible in his reaction to new situations and to the realities of his choices.

[6]"I feel honoured beyond measure that you should have faith in me as you have." W.L.M.K. to Violet Markham, 30 June 1909, King papers, PAC. "The one thing that helps me to retain what faith I have in myself and belief in the possible fulfilment of some of the purposes of my life, as I have seen and felt it, is the belief that you have in me ... I say to myself, if you who know me so little ... continue to have the faith you have ... it is well then to go on." W.L.K.M. to V. Markham, 3 July 1912.

[7]"There are some events in life which give us a faith in a personal God who has an individual purpose in our lives and his own chosen instruments for the working out of his will ... Your letter ... has renewed this belief in God's purpose in my own life and in you as one specially chosen by Him to manifest this love to the world." W.L.M.K. to V. Markham, 12 April 1913.

Personnalité et politique : un regard neuf sur la dispute entre King et Byng

Les avantages que peut retirer la science politique des études psychanalytiques de la personnalité, appliquées au phénomène du leadership, ont été beaucoup discutés. Le modèle qui semble le plus approprié aux besoins de la discipline est le modèle épigénétique du cycle de vie dû à Erik H. Erikson. Le cadre qu'il offre permet une vérification des données utilisées qui assure à l'analyste le meilleur degré possible d'objectivité. On utilise dans cet article le modèle d'Erikson afin d'établir les principales caractéristiques de la personnalité de William Lyon Mackenzie King. Les premières crises du cycle de vie sont explorées, telles qu'elles se sont produites à l'intérieur du milieu familial, et leurs solutions sont reliées au comportement adulte de King. Cela aide à comprendre l'attitude de King envers les gouverneurs généraux du Canada. L'analyse est restreinte à la crise constitutionnelle de 1926. Elle propose que le conflit entre King et Byng en est un de personnalité, même si son importance constitutionnelle est considérable. Il est avancé également que cette crise ne fut pas un cas isolé, non plus qu'une conséquence directe de la motion de censure à la Chambre des communes. Elle faisait plutôt partie d'une série de cas, s'étendant au long de la période 1919–26, qui avaient leur origine dans des problèmes familiaux et dans la solution que King leur avait trouvée. Celui-ci a joué un rôle crucial dans l'origine de la dispute et dans les conséquences qu'elle a eues sur la politique des partis et les relations avec l'Empire.

Mrs Isabel King, the pivotal figure in the family, naturally played a key role in these developments. A daughter of the Upper Canada reformer and rebel, William Lyon Mackenzie, she had spent the early years of her life in an atmosphere of poverty, failure, disgrace, and disappointment. The inability of her husband, John King, to live up to her hopes and fulfil her ambitions had caused her to transfer her attentions and demands to her eldest son. All the intense loyalty and affection that were dominant characteristics of this unusually tight-knit family, came to be focused through her onto Mackenzie King.[8] In return she demanded nothing but the surrender of his autonomy. Self-interest and practical expediency demanded that in the King family individual needs would be subordinated to group needs. Individually they could achieve very little, but together and through the advancement of Mackenzie King they could all find fulfillment.[9]

The development of a corporate identity involves the internalization of a common set of values, and the inner unity of a person can become seriously impaired if the voices being internalized by the individual flagrantly contradict one another.[10] This appears to be the situation in Mackenzie King's case. His conscious commitment to a life of service, the dedication of self to great and noble causes, the sacrifice of pleasure to the call of duty had their origins in his upbringing and were never directly opposed by the family. But at the same time the advice and behaviour of his parents demonstrated a more pragmatic self-interest which could only be harmonized with Mackenzie King's self-image through extensive

[8]See Mrs King to W.L.M.K., 6 April 1898. For example, "I have never crossed your life and I do not intend to do so now but I think there are many things to think about." "I am very weary but that is nothing new for mother, it is only one more lesson not to put your trust in anything under the sun." "I hope you will not think me selfish when I say I had counted on you to help lift the cloud."

[9]"United we stand, divided we fall." Mrs King to W.L.M.K., 14 January 1897.

[10]E.H. Erikson, *Insight and Responsibility* (New York, 1964), 121.

rationalization. Thus selfishness could be incorporated as loyalty to one's own, snobbery became a search for worthwhile men, and patronage and influence were an opportunity for greater service. A third stream, originating with Mrs King and never consciously recognized, involved ruthlessness, abhorrence of poverty, fear of failure, and single-minded dedication to ends.

In the adult personality of Mackenzie King these contradictions could only be accommodated by suppressing or displacing all those elements which did not accord with the exaggerated virtues with which Mackenzie King endowed his family and therefore, indirectly, himself. The need to exaggerate, to maintain rigidly the corporate image, resulted from the problem of validating the self-image once the death of his parents, his sister, and his brother made Mackenzie King's identity particularly vulnerable.[11] The corporateness of the family had provided a reassuring element of security and ego support for the individual who conformed to the desired behaviour patterns.[12] The demands of the family had stopped Mackenzie King from establishing a family of his own. It was no longer possible for him to attempt to develop individual autonomy. The only solution lay in identification with a substitute family, the groups toward whom he had made a commitment – the Liberal party and the people of Canada. This solution also involved a splitting of ambivalence. The commitment was to all that was worthwhile and unselfish in his self-image and to those elements outside himself which he could associate with these virtues. All less worthy values and motives were displaced onto others – notably the Conservative party, British Tories, and those who opposed him or showed lack of trust in him. The maintenance of this distinction involved a considerable strain[13] but it provided a limited satisfaction in contrast to the precipitiousness of his reaction and the distress he felt when the illusion was challenged.

It is during the extended crisis of the adolescent period that these characteristics are clearly discernible as the problems of earlier phases are again confronted and resolved in the process of establishing a satisfactory identity and a sense of inner unity. It is also a period in which the individual seeks "men and ideas to have *faith* in, which also means men and ideals in whose service it would seem worthwhile to prove oneself trustworthy."[14] In this process of identification the earliest model will be almost completely that of his parents.[15] But Mackenzie King's image of his father was complex and ambiguous. He

[11]Even after death they could continue to exercise this role. "If reassurance was needed, he found it outside of politics, for he was sure that 'dear Mother and Father & Bell & Max the whole family in heaven are guiding and directing me." Diary, 8 November 1925, quoted in Neatby, *King*, 88.

[12]"Come home and let us talk it over dear boy and feel that wiser old heads than yours may teach you what in the future you will thank them for." John King to W.L.M.K., 9 April 1898. "We are counting the weeks until Xmas ... Oh! what talking there will be Billy. I did not believe I could have felt so lonely after my boy. Father and I have great talks about you and *such big hopes*." Mrs King to W.L.M.K., 8 November 1896.

[13]"Oh that I could get away from self, that I could cut away these chains which will make me a slave to a self-seeking existence, that I could live always and only for others." W.L.M.K. to H.A. Harper, 7 June 1896, Harper papers, PAC.

[14]Erikson, *Identity*, 129.

[15]Adults by their own example ... offer children at this age an eagerly absorbed *ethos of action* in the form of ideal types and techniques." Erikson, *Identity*, 120.

accepted John King's devoted attention and personal sacrifices as his due, for he did not develop any noticeable sense of inferiority in comparison with his father. He appreciated his father as a source of unfailing devotion and trust but not as a model, for John King wore the mantle of failure while his son was clothed in the robes of success.[16]

For a time Mackenzie King found a more acceptable model in his grandfather, William Lyon Mackenzie.[17] Here was a figure who could fulfil his needs in terms of moral qualities, strength of character, and dedication to principle, but Mackenzie was also a failure and Mackenzie King had internalized his mother's abhorrence of failure. His rejection of these models was not overt or conscious. Throughout his life Mackenzie King spoke enthusiastically of his father and grandfather, but his actions did not confirm this devotion.[18]

Intellectually Mackenzie King could find his ideal in the young English social reformer Arnold Toynbee. Fidelity is the characteristic ego strength of the adolescent period and it shows itself in the ability to give sustained loyalty to men and ideals.[19] Loyalty to the image of Toynbee was an important feature of Mackenzie King's identity solution. But Toynbee was dead and could not provide the practical aid so essential to Mackenzie King's personal security. Other men must meet this need; men of the same stamp as Toynbee; men who would not only confirm his trustworthiness but also contribute to his success.

Such men would be individuals of position and status and, at the same time, would demonstrate the characteristics he admired and sought to embody in his own life. They must be God-fearing men of social conscience and vision; men who had chosen to dedicate themselves to a worthwhile life and service to mankind. Combined with these virtues was the ability to recognize these same virtues in Mackenzie King and the willingness to promote and support his interests wherever possible.

At the summit of Mackenzie King's hierarchy of confirmations was the

[16]By 1900 Mackenzie King had begun to replace his father as provider. A series of actions pinpointed the dramatic reversal of roles. John King was forced to confess his financial muddle and to accept a lecture on financial management and an exhortion to make a greater effort to keep his affairs in order. Mrs King went to Ottawa to help Mackenzie King set up a home which became a rival to the family home in Beverly Street in terms of her time and attention. Subsequently John King was forced to go to his son for more money to pay off his debts and to pay the regular household expenses. The family begged Mackenzie King to use his influence to secure a government position for his father. The wheel seemed to have come the full circle, the father had become the dependent and the son the provider.

[17]Mackenzie King's view of Mackenzie was based on the biography written by Mackenzie's son-in-law, Charles Lindsey, which gives a very favourable opinion of Mackenzie's outlook and activities.

[18]Mackenzie King's adolescent attempt to step into Mackenzie's shoes by acting as leader in the student strike at the University of Toronto, 1895, had ended unsatisfactorily. Although a relatively minor affair, it had provoked a commission of enquiry and had certain far-reaching consequences as far as King was concerned. He had taken a leading part in proposing a boycott of lectures and in ending the boycott once an enquiry had been promised. His initial action provoked the hostility of some of the staff while the later action upset many of the students. King's subsequent response was to decry the quality of both the students and the staff of the university. The response also led to a form of avoidance behaviour in which situations resembling the student strike were to create great tension.

[19]Erikson, *Insight*, 125.

ultimate confirmation which came from being among the chosen of God.[20] Mackenzie King had sought to devote his life to God's purpose and gained immeasurable support and confirmation from the belief that God was guiding this life and making the decisions. But this confirmation, like that of his grandfather and Toynbee, was remote and impersonal and of little comfort in his loneliness and isolation. He therefore sought the halfway house of an acceptable surrogate combining in one individual all the virtues and practical attributes. But heroes are always in short supply; and this was especially so in Canada at the turn of the century. He had sought intimacy with his university teachers with some success. Biographies of great men and visits with their families provided some compensations, but not for long. Of course, only one man could ever really fit the blueprint, Mackenzie King himself, but in the meantime the search went on. In the period 1900–10 three men came closest to meeting his need – Sir William Mulock, Sir Wilfrid Laurier, and Earl Grey. In his relations with these three men Mackenzie King strengthened the ambiguous pattern of behaviour which had originated with his father and which was to come to a crisis in his clash with Lord Byng.[21]

Sir William Mulock, postmaster general (1896–1905) and later minister of labour (1900–05) in the Laurier government, had been the first person of substance to be receptive to Mackenzie King's ideas of industrial reform. He was also directly responsible for Mackenzie King's appointment to the editorship of the *Labour Gazette* and the transformation of the aspirant reformer into the deputy minister of labour. As a friend of the family, Sir William maintained a close and intimate relationship with Mackenzie King and showed a gratifying concern for his welfare. He was even prepared to allow Mackenzie King to take an increasingly dominant role in their official relationship, to advise him in many aspects. But it was difficult to maintain the illusion that Sir William shared his ideals, since the veteran politician's pragmatism and opportunism were constantly before him.

Sir Wilfrid Laurier, prime minister of Canada and leader of the Liberal party, had at times shown enthusiasm and faith in Mackenzie King's potential, but he also exasperated King by his lack of political action on the latter's behalf. Both in 1906 when Mackenzie King had thought of moving to politics and in 1911 when he needed a new constituency, Laurier proved to be unable or unwilling to meet these demands. Therefore while Sir Wilfrid remained a very important figure in the pantheon of heroes, he had not passed the practical test which involved willingness to promote Mackenzie King's cause above all else.

It is in the relationship with Albert, fourth Earl Grey, that the pattern[22] is

[20]Erikson identifies religion as the institution that works to verify basic trust (see *Identity*, 106). There is ample evidence that it occupied such a place in Mackenzie King's life.

[21]The pattern suggests strong elements of a search for father surrogates especially with governors general: men who were not necessarily great in themselves but who were clothed in greatness by virtue of their office. The pattern would thus reflect important elements of the original father-son relationship, especially the desire to challenge and defeat the father and to become the dominant element in the relationship.

[22]In a rather trivial and elementary form the pattern can be seen developing in Mackenzie King's relationship with Lord and Lady Aberdeen. A casual contact in 1894 [R. MacGregor Dawson, *William Lyon Mackenzie King: I, 1874–1923* (Toronto, 1958), 40] is followed up by a call on the Aberdeens in London (*ibid.*, 161) and a stay at the Vice Regal Lodge in

seen closest to fulfilment, for this governor general fitted Mackenzie King's model almost completely. A description of the young Gray shows all the essential attributes and could very clearly have been a self-portrait by the young Mackenzie King.[23] Such an identity of outlook and experience could hardly be coincidental. Mackenzie King was not able to admit consciously that there were other equally important factors involved. He might marvel at the coincidence that all his intimate friends, chosen for their worth and idealism, were also among the top ranks of the community, but it could be nothing more than coincidence. He was not consciously a sycophant; indeed he believed that he despised such behaviour. To him Grey was a man like Toynbee, a person he would have admired even if he had been a nobody, and he continued to admire him even though he was not. He was the governor general of Canada and to be on intimate terms with this man, while he was actually in office, and to have him take a paternal interest in him and in his career, was the realization of a deep-seated longing.

Mackenzie King found it very difficult to understand accusations made against him of opportunism, social climbing, and ambition.[24] He could not see his own political career in terms other than duty and sacrifice. He believed fervently that his own choice would have been for the quiet seclusion of the academic world. But he had torn himself away from all that he believed he longed for, because he was a "soldier of the cross," a "knight of the Holy Spirit," and could not shrink from his destiny. "Thy will be done" was his dedication and God's will as

Dublin 1912. At this stage Mackenzie King sees himself in the role of confident: "I am enjoying very much my visit here. I have had quite exceptional talks with both Lord and Lady Aberdeen who had given me many confidences and in [*sic*] the pride I feel in being a Liberal. It is a noble work – this great struggle for the rights of the people and it is a help to me to know that one fights in such noble company and that the wound inflicted are the same however exalted the station. I have been really privileged in the very intimate manner in which I have been received." W.L.M.K. to V. Markham, 19 August 1912. The relationship reached its climax in 1916 when the Aberdeens visiting the United States sought Mackenzie King's mediation in obtaining an interview with John D. Rockefeller, Jr. Lady Aberdeen to W.L.M.K., 18 January 1916. Mackenzie King was now confirmed as a man equal, if not superior, to the former governor general. It should also be noted that Lord and Lady Aberdeen resembled the parents of his self-image. They were well-born people of substance yet prepared to "labour in God's vineyards," they were friends of Gladstone and devoted to the Liberal cause in Great Britain and in Canada. [See John T. Saywell, "The Crown and the Politicians," *The Canadian Historical Review*, XXXVII, no 4 (December 1956), 315.]

[23]Grey was a man of noble character and refinement. A true Christian gentleman, a man who had chosen to dedicate his life to the service of his fellow men. As students, both had been earnest and serious with a tendency to organize their studies rigorously. They had preached duty and dedication to their sisters; they had known and admired Arnold Toynbee. (At least Grey had known Toynbee, Mackenzie King merely felt close enough to have known him.) They shared an interest in psychic phenomena, a peace-loving outlook, and a commitment to the Liberal cause. (See H. Begbie, *Albert, Fourth Earl Grey* (London, 1918), various.)

[24]If one is to understand Mackenzie King as he saw himself one must see his enthusiasm for Lord Grey and his pleasure in being on the guest list at Government House as something more than crass opportunism or calculated political expediency. It is true that Lord Grey could and did introduce him to useful people. Lord Grey had been instrumental in King's being sent on delicate missions and to international conferences. But this to Mackenzie King was no more than showing a fatherly interest and a recognition of merit. His own father, John King, had pulled such strings and exerted similar pressures to advance him along the road he had to follow. What was important was the fact that Lord Grey could make him an integral part of a warm and loving family circle where gracious living, not penny-pinching poverty, was the characteristic note.

seen in the various signs and portents was that he should shoulder the burdens of political office and carry them to the end. No matter how long the journey, no matter how weary or dispirited he might become, he could not falter. He must keep faith. To keep this trust he would sacrifice peace of mind, personal fulfilment and happiness, a home and family of his own, everything that he believed made life worthwhile. His rewards would not be of this world, but he had found that sacrifice in fact had its own rewards, even in the present, and such advancement and credit which came his way was but a token of the rewards that were to come as long as he kept to the stoney path and the "way of the cross." He longed for public recognition of these facts, for people to see his rationalized motives as the true picture. When it was not forthcoming, he devoted a great deal of his energy to the "record," so that eventually it would be known as it really was and appreciated.[25]

The roots of the misunderstanding – 1921

The departure of Lord Grey from Canada and the departure of Mackenzie King from active politics coincided in 1911. The situation was to develop one step further with the arrival of Lord Byng as governor general in 1921 and the return of the Liberal party to office. Mackenzie King, Lord Grey's former protegé, was now leader of the Liberal party and soon to be prime minister of Canada. As the representative of the Canadian people he felt himself to be second to no one. He was prepared for a new status in the old pattern of adviser-confident-friend of the governor general.

The soil in which the crisis was to grow was the set of relationships already discussed; but the impetus for the misunderstanding came from the specific acts and expectations which arose during Lord Byng's first few months in office. The conversation that laid the foundation for future misunderstandings is the one recorded in Mackenzie King's diary for 2 September 1921 in which Lord Byng is purported to have said to Mackenzie King: "Mr. King, I want to put myself in your hands. I have only one object that is to be of what service I can ... I shall be glad to have you speak very freely. As to being a constitutional gov'r, I understand that there will be little difficulty to keep on right lines."[26] That Lord Byng should express such sentiment is not out of character and quite in keeping with the general tenor of his publicly expressed views on taking up his appointment. He did not try to conceal his inexperience, his lack of interest in, or knowledge of politics. But at the same time it conveyed a false impression of his willingness to be led by the advice of others and was to produce a great deal of the subsequent misunderstanding.

[25]The references to these contentions in both the diary and the letters are too numerous for a few quotes to do them justice. The following are typical: "I can say honestly that I have given of my best every day to the work of public service, at the sacrifice of much that is personal." W.L.M.K. to V. Markham, 12 October 1922. "I am very tired ... I have felt the drain on my moral and spiritual powers, though, I thank God, I have striven, above all else, not to make sacrifices in those particulars, and such success as I have had has been due, I believe, to the fact that I have 'kept the faith' however faltering at times, the effort may have been" W.L.M.K. to V. Markham, 25 August 1930.
[26]Diary, 2 September 1921, quoted in Dawson, *King*, 374.

Lord Byng's response in the first political problem which arose during this period of office further emphasized this discrepancy. Arthur Meighen, left without a seat in the 1921 election, advised the appointment of one of the Conservative members of parliament to a position in the civil service. This device enabled him to have a by-election and be in the House of Commons for the opening of the session.[27] The governor general accepted Meighen's advice because Meighen was his constitutional adviser.[28] This at least is the version given by Mackenzie King. A version that confirmed his belief that the governor general was bound to accept the advice of the prime minister no matter how distasteful it was to him personally. Is this version fact or fantasy? Possibly it was a combination of both. Two factors seem critical: Lord Byng's gentlemanly nature and his reluctance to give offence, and Mackenzie King's tendency to see and hear what he wanted to see and hear.[29] The former produced a tendency in Lord Byng to avoid the direct request or approach, to proceed by means of hints and generalities, which allowed the listener to infer what he would. Thus it is possible that the record tends to overemphasize those things that Mackenzie King wanted to hear, but it is unlikely that it is completely fictitious. Consequently it can tell us a great deal about the kind of relationship Mackenzie King wished for and believed he had with the governor general.

The picture presented is one of complete intimacy and interdependence. Phrases such as, "I want to give you my entire confidence," "I want to know everything and to conceal nothing," "to tell you everything," "I shall keep nothing from you," which abound in the records are also characteristic of King's letters to personal friends. He constantly urged them to tell him everything, and offered to do the same himself, although he never could.[30] It gave him great reassurance to be the receiver of such confidences. On a secondary level it contained a strong element of desire to be an insider; to know things not generally known to others. At a deeper level it allowed him to identify closely with the individual, to incorporate him or her into his self-image with all the psychological benefits such a situation involved. It even allowed him to assume the role of comforter, adviser, granter of absolution, all of which confirmed his essential goodness and spiritual superiority. Thus it was for Mackenzie King to judge and forgive Lord Byng for taking a course which the former did not accept. It was for Mackenzie King to find Lord Byng acceptable and not vice versa. This attitude is expressed clearly in a letter written by Mackenzie King to Violet Markham before he became prime minister for the first time:

> I can not tell you how pleased I am with him as a man & how certain I am that his administration will prove worthy of the best that has preceded it. I took an immense liking to him from the moment we met & in each conversation I had since. I have felt

[27]Dawson, *King*, 374–6.
[28]*Ibid.*, 375.
[29]Graham, *Meighen*, 419.
[30]"I feel that I can write freely to you ... Write to me about yourself and those deep spiritual problems ... tell me of your life." W.L.M.K. to V. Markham, 5 November 1908. "I tell you this because there is nothing I would not have you know." W.L.M.K. to V. Markham, 30 June 1909. "Never feel that there is any question which you may not ask me ... I am anxious that you should know my every thought ... There is nothing I would hide from you." W.L.M.K. to V. Markham, 6 February 1911.

> a sense of oneness in aim & point of view, which is really quite remarkable. If by any chance I should come to be his adviser in the near future, I shall expect that the association will be one of the happiest and best in my life. Oddly enough when Mr. Meighen introduced me to him on his arrival in Ottawa, after mentioning that I was Leader of the Opposition Meighen went on to say that in the near future I would probably be his Prime Minister. I have spoken of this to no one ... I think the words came to Meighen's lips before he had time to really consider their significance.[31]

Mackenzie King's expectations of the relationship, as expressed in this letter, undoubtedly coloured his interpretation of Lord Byng's subsequent conversation and actions.

It is essential to decide exactly what Mackenzie King believed had happened in 1921, for it is the ground on which the latter battles were to be fought. The election of 6 December gave the Liberals 117 seats compared to 50 for the Conservatives, 64 for the Progressives, and 4 for others. Mackenzie King had, prior to the election, challenged Meighen's right to govern, on the grounds that he no longer had the confidence of the people. On 4 December, Mackenzie King had even written to Meighen advising him that if the Liberals were elected to office they would not honour anything done in the way of appointments or contracts. That Meighen would make such an appointment – A.C. Casselman to the Department of Soldier's Civil Re-establishment – after being defeated was to him an outrage. He believed that Lord Byng shared this view. When Lord Byng acted on Meighen's advice Mackenzie King was disappointed but not without comfort. A governor general who could say to Prime Minister Meighen, as Lord Byng had, "you are my constitutional advisor [*sic*] and I must act on your advice," could not in the future do anything other than take the advice of Prime Minister King. Lord Byng's actions could thus be interpreted as supporting his words and Mackenzie King could confidently look forward to a happy companionship.

The relations between Mackenzie King and Lord Byng from 1922 to 1925 seemed to have fulfilled Mackenzie King's highest expectations. His comment to Violet Markham in September 1922 is typical of his views: "You will be glad to know that I am particularly fond of Lord Byng, and that we get along splendidly together. Indeed the association is one of the pleasantest I have known and is helpful as well as happy."[32] The fact that Mackenzie King was willing to offer Lord Byng an extension of his term as governor general is further confirmation of his faith in the relationship.

The preliminary struggle – 1925

The election of 1925 produced a situation which closely resembled the events of 1921, but the roles were reversed. Mackenzie King had gone to the people and had apparently been defeated. He had also lost his own seat, as Meighen had done in 1921. Now was the time for Lord Byng to show the concern and interest that Mackenzie King expected of his close associates. More than this Mackenzie King expected Lord Byng to accept him in the dominant role. When

[31] W.L.M.K. to V. Markham, 19 September 1921.
[32] W.L.M.K. to V. Markham, 29 September 1922.

he turned to others for comfort, understanding, or reassurance about the course he had chosen he did not expect them to attempt to restrict his course or oppose his decision once it was made. Until it was made he was prepared to listen to any suggestion as long as it proposed a course which he could interpret as honourable. To him the question of who had won the election was not as simple as it might seem.

Mackenzie King felt that he was not free to follow his personal inclination for he was the instrument of God's will; his path was laid out for him. If he had been defeated and this wasn't clear, what was God's purpose? What was the message of the defeat? His diary entry for 29 October 1925 gives us the answer: "I have 'faith and courage' – will take this refining in the furnace of affliction as it is meant, and seek to rise into a nobler and higher manhood through it all."[33] If the decreased majority had been sent "to try" him, then he could not lay down the burden. Here was the core of the difficulty with Lord Byng. Both men desired to do what was best for Canada, to take the honourable, dignified course. The only problem was defining the nature of that course. Lord Byng's suggestion that King should resign immediately and that Meighen should be called on was not necessarily the right course for Mackenzie King. It might be the course of a weak, irresolute man; a man unwilling to face up to difficult responsibilities. It was also a politically dangerous course. It was obvious that the situation of 1925 made an election highly probable. Lord Byng's unwillingness to see another election could not postpone the inevitable dissolution for very long.

The decision not to resign could be rationalized on tariff grounds as well as on the grounds of political expediency, and Mackenzie King preferred to make his stand on the former. Lord Byng accepted his decision to meet parliament and the course of the relationship seemed to be smooth once more. However, while Lord Byng's response to the general issue of resignation had been acceptable in the long run, the conditions imposed on Mackenzie King were not. For, instead of allowing Mackenzie King the same freedom that Meighen had been given, Lord Byng was insisting that King do nothing of a political nature until the House met. Mackenzie King was hurt and bewildered. It was not that he intended to behave in the despicable manner that Meighen had. He would have shown his superior moral character by voluntary restraint. Lord Byng was only asking him to do what he intended to do anyway but in such a manner as to imply that there was no alternative. This was not Mackenzie King's view, since he believed that anything which was possible for Meighen in 1921 must also be possible for King in 1925, if he were unprincipled enough to want to proceed that way. There did not seem to be any significant difference in their actual positions. Certainly his party had lost seats but the Liberals had not been reduced to the smallest party in the House as the Conservatives had been in 1921, and there was every possibility that the Progressives would be persuaded to support the Liberals in a second term.

There was a great deal of personal resentment, even a feeling of betrayal in Mackenzie King's response to Lord Byng's insistence. He had always felt deeply Meighen's barbed attacks on him, and being without a seat was very unnerving for him. He could not have forgotten what capital Meighen had got out of King's

[33]Quoted in Neatby, *King*, 79.

similar predicament in 1919 when Meighen had described him as the "outside leader of the outside party in this country."[34] He might even have anticipated that Meighen would again attack him on this point, as he in fact did when asserting in January 1926 that Mackenzie King was not competent to act as an adviser to the crown because he did not have a seat.[35]

The stronger element in his growing disillusionment with Lord Byng in 1925 was the governor general's attempt to force him to resign without meeting the House. It is true that the decision not to resign was not consistent with Mackenzie King's attitude to Meighen in 1921, but it was consistent with the case he later put forward to support the claim that in fact it was not a defeat. That he was not confident of the correctness of his position can be seen in his need for reassurance. It was not enough that he should feel that his decision was right; he must have it confirmed by men of unimpeachable character. Lord Byng had refused to corroborate his decision and even if he had his credentials were no longer above suspicion. By doubting Mackenzie King's motives, by countenancing for a minute the view that King would follow anything but the path of absolute right and virtue, Lord Byng had raised doubts of his own trustworthiness.

But there must be support. If support could not come from Lord Byng it must come from someone else. Mackenzie King could not stand alone for long. His cabinet colleagues and other Canadian Liberals agreed with his decision, but it was possible that they were influenced by partisan political considerations and Mackenzie King believed that he was not. It had to be someone equal in his personal hierarchy to Lord Byng. What better person than John Buchan, not yet the governor general but one who might well be in the near future.[36] In a letter to Violet Markham Mackenzie King explained his position.

> Had Mr. Meighen not made the protection issue the main feature of the campaign and had he not won his majority by the corrupt and unfair means here described, I should possibly have not thought twice about resigning and advising His Excellency to call upon him to form a government. Indeed, my first inclination and certainly my personal desire was to resign. I had, however, carefully to consider what recognition in the circumstances would involve. I could not honestly say to His Excellency that I believed Mr. Meighen would find a majority support in the Commons as constituted, and be able to carry on ... I would have betrayed the anti-high protectionist cause had I allowed Mr. Meighen to take control of the government ... I am anxious that you should fully understand the situation. I have wished very much that both you and John Buchan could be here to talk it over with me ... I should be glad to have you let him see this letter ... just that he may be familiar with certain aspects of the present situation ... I should like Buchan to know just how I feel, and the motives which are actuating me in the course I am taking.[37]

It was following Buchan's favourable response to seeing this letter that Mackenzie King began to prepare in earnest the ground for his nomination as governor general of Canada.

[34]Graham, *Meighen*, 170.
[35]*Ibid.*, 382.
[36]This appeal to Buchan through Violet Markham is a repetition of earlier behaviour. In 1913 he had asked her to pass similar explanations of his views to reciprocity and the naval question to Lord Grey.
[37]W.L.M.K. to V. Markham, 2 December 1925.

This letter also reveals a great deal more about Mackenzie King and his personality. It may be difficult for those who have accepted the prevalent view of Mackenzie King as an unprincipled self-seeker to see his desire to resign as anything but deception, but it constitutes an important feature of the subsequent misunderstanding with Lord Byng.[38] Mackenzie King was completely convinced of his lack of personal ambition. His correspondence abounds with laments about the strain and burdens of political life, his distaste for the demands that it made on him, his longing to be free of it all. The harder he fought to retain office, the more he believed that given the personal choice he would gladly have resigned. But no matter how great the longing he must not give way or take the easy way out: it would be unworthy of all he believed in and stood for. More than that, it would be to hand over the people of Canada to the forces of "evil."[39] It would be a betrayal of the people, his party, his colleagues, his cause, and his nature. This he could not do. He must fight for the cause with all the energy of a religious zealot confronting the minions of the devil. This was his destiny; this was the will of the "unseen hand" that controlled his life; this was the basis of his quarrel with Lord Byng.

The crisis – June 1926

The King-Byng dispute is too well known to require a detailed explanation within the limits of this paper. It will suffice here to briefly summarize the points which form the basis of the discussion: (*a*) In June 1926 Prime Minister Mackenzie King, leading a miority government, was faced with possible censure in the House of Commons. (*b*) During the weekend of June 26–7, with the House adjourned, Mackenzie King abandoned his attempt to secure the acceptance of an alternative amendment and approached the governor general for a dissolution. (*c*) As he had already expressed his conviction that the leader of the opposition, Meighen, could not form a government, King believed that the governor general would have no other course but to dissolve the House and to call an election. (*d*) The governor general refused to accept the advice of his prime minister, thereby precipitating Mackenzie King's immediate resignation. (*e*) Lord Byng then asked Meighen to form a government, and he agreed to do so. (*f*) Mackenzie King concentrated his attention on defeating the Meighen government in the belief that the governor general would be forced to recall him and grant him the dissolution that would then be unavoidable. (*g*) The Meighen government, which

[38]Even before he knew the results of the election he had written, "I have no fear that we shall not be returned as an administration though should it happen that we were defeated it would not occasion me, except on the Party's account, any concern. I should welcome a breathing space; an opportunity to read, reflect, and travel a little." W.L.M.K. to V. Markham, 15 October 1925.

[39]King's suspicions of the Conservative party – his belief that they gained office only by bribery, misrepresentation of the issues, praying on the prejudices and self-interest of the people, electoral fraud, and the expenditure of large amounts of tainted money – is a constant theme in his letters. For example: "What was not seen and what contributed more than aught else to our defeat was the money which flowed into every constituency and was used without the least question in widespread corruption and bribery." W.L.M.K. to P. Larkin, 26 November 1925. "Borden will do anything rather than sacrifice power, and if a way can be found to prevent an appeal to the people he will seek it." W.L.M.K. to V. Markham, 5 March 1913.

had assumed office on 29 June was defeated 2 July on a motion which had questioned both its legality and its right to govern. (*h*) When Lord Byng accepted Meighen's advice to dissolve, Mackenzie King used this behaviour as an issue in the ensuing general election. (*i*) The Liberal success in the election of September 1926 confirmed King's belief in the correctness of his position.[40]

There are a number of pertinent questions which must be asked concerning the dispute, and a reassessment should be made of Mackenzie King's behaviour and motives. What did he see happening in 1926 and what was he trying to achieve? The King government had met the House on 8 January 1926 and on 15 January had been sustained. He was personally re-elected in Prince Albert on 15 February and by the end of May had begun to believe that his difficulties were over. He was "quite confident that his government was firmly settled in office"[41] and that in due course he would dissolve the House and have his election. Because of his commitment to a strategy of never disturbing the people unnecessarily, he was prepared to face another session or even two sessions before he asked for a dissolution.[42] His belief in his right to a dissolution predated his loss of support in the 1925 election. As early as September of that year he had said: "If we should ever be faced again with conditions such as pertained in the last four years, I could not hesitate to again call on the Governor General to dissolve Parliament and would continue until some party secures a majority to enable it to carry on the affairs of the country."[43] He had included the possibility of a dissolution in the three alternatives outlined in the statement released to the press 4 November 1925.[44] He had stated it again in the House on 15 June.[45] His behaviour does not support the view that he had promised Lord Byng not to ask for another dissolution. It does support the view that one of the dominant characteristics of his personality was perseverance and a consistent drive towards an end of his own choosing.

In the face of Lord Byng's persistent belief that Meighen must be given his chance to govern, Mackenzie King had held to his view that the dissolution was his for the asking. He might threaten awkward colleagues and the Progressives with the possibility of a Conservative government, but it did not seriously enter into his calculations. An obstinate Lord Byng, a Byng who was not prepared ultimately to accept the advice of his responsible minister was a possibility that he did not allow for. It did not fit the pattern. His whole house of cards, so carefully constructed, so apparently solid, slowly collapsed before his eyes.

As long as the probability of an election was still open he felt no need to despair. He was quite confident that there was no alternative administration in the House. He did not fear an election, although he would have preferred to have more time to reorganize the government. He was confident that the Cana-

[40]Neatby, *King*, 130–57.
[41]*Ibid.*, 129.
[42]"I am giving you my honest convictions. I was opposed to the change on the grounds of political expediency, and so stated my position strongly in the cabinet. I felt the government was taking a great risk in proposing any changes whilst the people were contented." W.L.M.K. to V. Markham, 11 October 1911.
[43]*Montreal Daily Star*, 9 September 1925, quoted in Graham, *King-Byng*, 353.
[44]Neatby, *King*, 82.
[45]*Ibid.*, 131.

dian people would recognize the true worth of his endeavours when the time came. The final stages of the report of the Special Committee on the Department of Customs and Excise changed everything. The opposition of the Conservatives was predictable and of limited concern. The probable loss of the support of the Progressives was more serious but not insurmountable; an acceptable compromise could be worked out. Mackenzie King was not personally committed to a total defence of the department. He was willing to admit a certain degree of negligence if necessary. The real danger came from within, with the possibility of a division in the Liberal caucus.

The need for unity was a driving force in Mackenzie King's life. Because of the contradictory nature of his internalized values, he had found it difficult to avoid identity confusion and to maintain a unified identity. His close identity with the Liberal party and the people of Canada formed a part of this defence against personal disintegration and meant that this intense commitment to unity was carried over into the public sphere. The reconstruction of the Liberal party on a durable basis had been a major objective of his activity as leader since 1919. This commitment was more than partisan political interest, it embodied a belief that only the Liberal party, unified under his own leadership, could truly represent the whole of the Canadian people. Any other alternative could only aggravate the divisive elements both of his own personality and of the community. The possible defection of the Progressives would mean a major setback in his efforts to bring all those committed to liberal principles under the banner of the Liberal party.

A further contributory factor in his behaviour was the belief that there was a substantial benefit in going to the country as the government. He believed that Meighen could not hope to form a stable administration and that if he tried to do so it would be because he wanted "to get control of the election machinery."[46] Lord Byng seemed to share the view that the governing party was at an advantage because the returning officers were of its way of thinking.[47] This made the granting of a dissolution to Meighen after it had been refused to Mackenzie King an even greater betrayal in King's eyes.

An additional element in the issue and an indication of how important it was to Mackenzie King to be able to stick to the literal truth relates to the censure vote. By resigning so abruptly he had technically avoided the censure of his government. The censure motion was passed once Meighen accepted office but it was now a censure of a past administration. It is doubtful if many of the electorate would draw the fine line of distinction between being censured while actually in office, and being censured after leaving office. However, the distinction was meaningful to Mackenzie King. He could say with conviction and personal satisfaction: "The government of which I had the honour to be the head never met with defeat from the day that it came into office to the day that it resigned."[48] It was a dubious satisfaction but it showed a further element of

[46]Diary, 30 October 1925, quoted in Neatby, *King*, 80.
[47]Diary, 26 July 1926, quoted in *ibid.*, 147. See also John Buchan to W.L.M.K. 26 July 1926, Buchan papers, Queen's University Archives.
[48]Graham, *Meighen*, 438.

ambiguity. Mackenzie King believed that he was guided by the spirit rather than the letter but in his actions he demonstrated a strong reliance on the letter of the text.[49]

In attempting to probe the depths of Mackenzie King's behaviour one must ask how much his action was influenced by an unconscious or even deliberate identification with William Lyon Mackenzie. King referred to the parallel during the parliamentary debate on the Robb motion but only in response to a taunt from a Conservative member. He replied: "Yes I am thinging [*sic*] of '37, and I tell my hon. friend that I was never prouder in my life than to have the privilege of standing in this parliament to-night and on behalf of British parliamentary institutions denouncing the irresponsible government of his party. Do hon. gentlemen opposite advocate that we shall go back to a condition of affairs in Canada worse than anything that existed in 1837?"[50] There are a number of possible parallels for those who wished to find them. The situation as King saw it did seem to be the same – one man, elected by no one, holding himself responsible to no one save God and his own conscience, was deciding who should be the government of Canada. Certainly Mackenzie King's rhetoric seemed to include pronounced unconscious links with his view of his grandfather as a defender of responsible government and the rights of the Canadian people against a misuse of power. If the governor general could behave in such an arbitrary fashion then Canada still needed a Mackenzie to fight its battles.

It is certain that even at a more direct level, King saw autonomy as a very delicate plant which without constant care and attention might whither and die. It is probably significant that his closest associates and friends in England were all enthusiastic imperialists.[51] Mackenzie King's official visits to England had coincided with Tory power and Tory entertainment, and men like Winston Churchill and L.S. Amery were not likely to reduce his disquiet. From all these sources as well as his own experiences at the Imperial Conference of 1923, and his problems with Ramsay MacDonald,[52] Mackenzie King could derive both conscious and unconscious impressions of danger on which to base a belief that Canadian autonomy was still in need of his vigilance, and he reacted accordingly. His speeches at this time reflected the depth of his feeling on the issue. He could sell his version to sections of the Canadian electorate because of his obvious sincerity and because it struck a similar cord of distrust in the minds of the voters.

While the governor general represented the father surrogate to him personally, the United Kingdom represented the same psychological problem on a larger scale to Canada as a whole. Canada seemed caught in the dilemma of exhibiting a strong desire to rebel against the paternal authority of the British empire and a disinclination to carry rebellion to its logical conclusion. This national am-

[49]Two examples of this are the agreement to call Parliament before holding an election in 1940 and his position on conscription in 1942–44.

[50]Canada, House of Commons, *Debates* (1926) v, 5212, quoted in Graham, *Meighen*, 437.

[51]Miss Markham and Lord Stanhope represented the moderate imperialists willing to concede full independence in theory but in a crisis inclined to put the interests of England and empire before the autonomy of the dominions. Lord Grey was an enthusiast for some form of imperial unity and had tried to win King over to his schemes. John Buchan was one of Lord Milner's circle.

[52]Neatby, *King*, 32–7.

biguity was in close accord with Mackenzie King's personal confusion. He personally had wanted to rebel, to become dominant, to be the father in practice as well as in his imagination. But the very success of his challenge produced a situation in which he was unwilling to assume the responsibilities of complete independence, and he sought the comfort and security of being the son again, of maintaining the family tie. This ambiguity was also characteristic of his attitude to the United Kingdom. He wished to go so far but no further; he wanted Canada to be autonomous but not completely independent with all the responsibilities of an independent international position. Canada within the Empire, like Mackenzie King within the family, could have the best of both worlds.

Lord Byng became the focus of all these contradictory strains. He was the obstacle in the way of the completion of Mackenzie King's plans. He had been a hero but now he had abandoned the hero's role. Yet a man who had been the recipient of Mackenzie King's respect, an intimate, a substitute father could not be bad. He must be a dupe, an honest man being manipulated by the forces of evil. These forces must be pinpointed, exposed for what they were. Obviously, they were Meighen, the Conservatives, and the jingoistic elements in the British government. They all fitted the bill perfectly, they had behaved in such ways before and must be up to their old practices.

Mackenzie King could feel sorry for Lord Byng but regrets could not deter him from the path of duty. Lord Byng, if he were half the man that Mackenzie King wanted him to be, would understand and in the end appreciate what Mackenzie King had to do. Therefore he did not expect the crisis and the unpleasantness of the subsequent election to affect his personal relations with Lord Byng. As a politician he could question Lord Byng's judgement, his understanding of the issues, his wisdom; but as a friend he could respect his sincerity and his intentions. He rejoiced at every sign that Lord Byng could do the same, for, as Neatby noted: "It would have been too disturbing for him to have to admit that anybody could doubt his rectitude."[53]

The aftermath

Just as the dispute did not begin in 1925, neither did it end in 1926. The election had given Mackenzie King the opportunity of placing the issue before the people, and he interpreted the result as sanctioning his position. However, because the crisis concerned a matter of royal prerogative, it had far-reaching implications which might not be settled at this level. The obvious solution was to place the matter before the Imperial Conference which met in October, 1926. King asked the conference for an endorsement which would confirm the correctness of his original advice to Lord Byng, even as it appeared to be concerned only with the technical status of the governor general.[54] The conference recommended "that the governor-general in a dominion should no longer act in any way as the representative or agent of the United Kingdom government and should in all essential respects hold the same position in relation to the ad-

[53]*Ibid.*, 175.
[54]N. Mansergh, *The Commonwealth Experience* (London, 1969), 230.

ministration of public affairs as the King in the United Kingdom."[55] In connection with this latter point, it should be remembered that no request for a dissolution had been denied in Britain for a hundred years.

It might be supposed that, with this double confirmation, Mackenzie King would consider the matter settled, but his subsequent behaviour shows that it had settled nothing. He continued to see threats to Canadian autonomy and Tory-Imperialist conspiracies in matters pertaining to the governor general. Consequently, it seems unlikely that the explanation of King's behaviour in terms of a desire to avoid censure and cling to office can be entirely accurate. It is possible that he continued to behave in this way because the primary issue, his personal need to seek in the governor general a counsellor and friend even as he resented having to take second place to him, remained unsettled.[56] Each new incumbent represented a challenge to his unfulfilled needs, and each new relationship contained the elements of a potential conflict. These situations could lead to a constitutional crisis because King attempted to transform formal relationships into intimate personal friendships and displaced the resulting conflicts onto public issues.

It is in the relationship with Lord Tweedsmuir that the personal aspects of the King-Byng dispute can be seen in their most developed form. Tweedsmuir was not only a personal friend of King but in a very real sense also his protegé. A protegé over whose appointment King had been prepared to precipitate another constitutional crisis in 1935. This issue cannot be considered in this paper but, along with the crisis of the royal visit in 1939, it provides further evidence to support the thesis presented in this paper. In both cases, as with the King-Byng dispute, the constitutional issues which arose were offshoots of the human dynamics of the disputes. Yet none of the incidents were concerned with trivial matters. They were all issues central to the conventions of responsible government and the functioning of the executive process. In this way they underline the fact that conventions are legally no more than patterns of acceptable behaviour moulded by men and open to disruption and transformation by the actions of men. The flexibiilty of conventions is both their strength and their weakness.

Because conventions are open to being modified by political behaviour it is not possible to limit consideration of events such as the King-Byng dispute to simple description and discussion of constitutional precedents. Even if we were only concerned to isolate what happened it would not be possible to state this with any precision without concerning ourselves with the intricacies of human behaviour and human motivation. The meaning of a particular incident can only be inferred, for motives are not open to direct observation. What is often overlooked is the fact that similar behaviour can result from different motives while similar motives can lead to different behaviour. To avoid the dangers of endowing the participants with the rationalized motives of the observer, it is necessary to ground inferences in an understanding of the total functioning organism. In this case, the personality of the "crisis maker" – William Lyon Mackenzie King.

Once it is established that it is necessary to understand the total organism, then psychoanalytical psychology is the obvious source of a framework to achieve

[55] *Ibid.*, 236.
[56] J. Adam Smith, *John Buchan* (London, 1959), 440. See also John Buchan papers, various.

this purpose. It is the discipline most concerned with the study of the functioning person as a whole. This resort to the psychoanalytical approach is also indicated by the need to establish the unconscious processes which influence apparently rational political decisions. Most of the discussion of the King-Byng dispute has carried with it this notion of an individual conscious of his motives and deliberately selecting certain courses of behaviour to reach rationally selected ends. This approach obscures the fact that an individual can be quite unaware of his most intense motivations. These elements of decision-making can only be revealed when those aspects of the developmental process which contribute to this particular behavioural response are incorporated into the inferences made. This paper is offered as a tentative step in this direction.

The Application of the "Senatorial Floor" Rules to the Latest Redistribution of the House of Commons: The Peculiar Case of Nova Scotia*

ANDREW SANCTON
University of Western Ontario

Section 51 of the British North America Act[1] lays down the rules by which Canadian House of Commons seats are allocated among the provinces.[2] Section 12 of the Electoral Boundaries Readjustment Act[3] states that it is the Representation Commissioner who has the responsibility for making the requisite calculations and publishing the results. He goes through this process every 10 years after receiving from the Dominion Statistician the figures for the total population of each province according to the latest decennial census.[4] On 13 May 1972, the Representation Commissioner published the results of his most recent calculations in the *Canada Gazette*.[5]

It is the contention of this article that in order for the Representation Commissioner to arrive at these results, in accordance with the provisions of section 51 of the BNA Act, he must defend his calculations by interpreting the Act in an unprecedented and possibly unwarranted manner. He is forced to do so because of some rather strange and unusual results which derive from the calculations concerning Nova Scotia. The article also suggests that if he is wrong in his interpretation of the Act, and he might well be, then Ontario is legally entitled to 92 rather than 91 seats and the House of Commons should consequently consist of 265 rather than 264 members.

To understand the problem that emerges in the case of Nova Scotia we must perform the calculations called for in section 51 using the 1971 census data. Rule one of section 51(1) states: "There shall be assigned to each of the Provinces a number of members computed by dividing the total population of the Provinces by two hundred and sixty-one and by dividing the population of each Province

*I am indebted to Professors W.F. Dawson and M.W. Westmacott for their helpful comments and suggestions.

1As enacted by the *British North America Act, 1952*, RSC 1952, c. 304.

2These rules have been explained and discussed in a number of works on Canadian politics, including Norman Ward, *The Canadian House of Commons: Representation*, second ed. (Toronto, 1963), 53–8; "The Redistribution of 1952," *Canadian Journal of Economics and Political Science*, XIX, no 3 (August 1953), 341–51; and "A Century of Constituencies," *Canadian Public Administration*, 10, no 1 (March 1967), 105–11; T.H. Qualter, *The Election Process in Canada* (Toronto, 1970), 111–14; W.E. Lyons, *One Man – One Vote* (Toronto, 1970), 1–11; R. MacGregor Dawson, *The Government of Canada*, fifth ed., revised by Norman Ward (Toronto, 1971), 307–11; and J.R. Mallory, *The Structure of Canadian Government* (Toronto, 1971), 185–8.

3*Statutes of Canada*, 1964–5, c. 31.

4These figures are presented in column A of Table I. They are taken from Statistics Canada, 1971 census, *Advance Bulletin*, April 1972.

5Part I, 1302. These figures are presented in column B of Table I.

Canadian Journal of Political Science/Revue canadienne de science politique, VI, no. 1 (March/mars 1973). Printed in Canada/Imprimé au Canada.

L'application des règles du « plancher sénatorial » à la redistribution actuelle des sièges à la Chambre des communes : le cas particulier de la Nouvelle-Ecosse

Cette étude se penche sur les calculs prévus par l'article 51 de l'Acte de l'Amérique du Nord Britannique pour redistribuer, d'après le recensement de 1971, les sièges des Communes entre les provinces. Dans le cas de la Nouvelle-Ecosse, ces calculs ont donné des résultats inhabituels, qui n'ont pas de précédent. On ne sait pas trop si les règles du « plancher sénatorial » doivent s'appliquer, et comment elles le doivent. On tente d'expliquer les ambiguïtés ainsi mises à jour dans l'article 51 et on propose une interprétation qui est peut-être plus plausible que d'autres. Les calculs effectués suivant cette interprétation donnent des résultats différents de ceux auxquels est arrivé le Commissaire à la représentation, en mai 1972. Même si cette différence tient à une autre façon de traiter la Nouvelle-Ecosse, c'est seulement dans le cas de l'Ontario qu'on obtient un nombre différent de sièges. D'après les calculs de l'auteur, celle-ci devrait avoir 92 sièges au lieu de 91, et la Chambre des communes devrait inclure 265 sièges au lieu de 264. Même si l'interprétation proposée dans cet article était fausse, elle ne manque pas de soulever des questions importantes sur les sens différents que peut prendre l'article 51 dans certaines circonstances inhabituelles.

by the quotient so obtained, disregarding, except as hereinafter in this section provided, the remainder, if any, after the said process of division."

By dividing 261 into 21,515,116 we obtain 82,433 as the quotient. The results of dividing the population of each province by this quotient are presented in column C of Table I. In rule one we are asked to disregard any remainders. Therefore, by this rule we have allocated 256 seats in accordance with the whole numbers listed.

Rule two of section 51(1) states: "If the total number of members assigned to all the Provinces pursuant to rule one is less than two hundred and sixty-one, additional members shall be assigned to the Provinces (one to a Province) having remainders in the computation under rule one commencing with the Province having the largest remainder and continuing with the other Provinces in the order of the magnitude of their respective remainders until the total number of members assigned is two hundred and sixty-one." Referring to the remainders in column three we note that the following five (261 − 256 = 5) provinces are entitled to one more seat: Nova Scotia, New Brunswick, Manitoba, Alberta, and British Columbia. The allocation of seats according to rules one and two is presented in column D of Table I.

Rule three of section 51(1) states: "Notwithstanding anything in this section, if upon completion of a computation under rules one and two, the number of members to be assigned to a Province is less than the number of Senators representing the said Province, rules one and two shall cease to apply in respect of the said province, and there shall be assigned to the said Province a number of members equal to the said number of Senators." To operate this rule we need to know the number of senators assigned to each province by section 22 of the BNA Act. These figures are shown in column E of Table I. From column E we note that rule three applies only to Prince Edward Island and New Brunswick,

TABLE I

RELEVANT DATA AND CALCULATIONS FOR ALLOCATING MEMBERS AMONG THE PROVINCES

	A	B	C	D	E	F	G	H	I	J	K
	Population (1971 Census)	Representation Commissioner's allocation	Application of rule one	Application of rules one and two	Senators	Calculations for remaining provinces (Part I)	Part II of F	Calculations treating NS like PEI and NB (Part I)	Part II of H	Application of rules 1-4, 1966	Final Allocation (assuming NS different from PEI & NB)
Nfld	522,104	6	6.33	6	6	6.21	6	6.19	6	7	6
PEI	111,641	4	1.35	1	4					4	4
NS	788,960	10	9.57	10	10	9.38	9			10	10
NB	634,557	10	7.70	8	10					10	10
Que	6,027,764	72	73.12	73	24	71.69	72	71.50	72	74	72
Ont	7,703,106	91	93.45	93	24	91.61	92	91.37	91	88	92
Man	988,247	12	11.99	12	6	11.75	12	11.72	12	13	12
Sask	926,242	12	11.24	11	6	11.02	11	10.99	11	13	12
Alta	1,627,874	19	19.75	20	6	19.36	19	19.31	19	19	19
BC	2,184,621	26	26.50	27	6	25.98	26	25.91	26	23	26
Prov. totals	21,515,116	262	256	261	102	243	247	233	237	261	263
Yukon	18,388	1									1
NWT	34,807	1									1
Canada totals	21,568,311	264									265

which at this stage in the calculations are definitely and finally assigned four and ten seats respectively.

Rule four of section 51(1) states: "In the event that rules one and two cease to apply in respect of a Province then, for the purposes of computing the number of members to be assigned to the Provinces in respect of which rules one and two continue to apply, the total population of the Provinces shall be reduced by the number of the population of the Province in respect of which rules one and two have ceased to apply and the number two hundred and sixty-one shall be reduced by the number of members assigned to such Province pursuant to rule three." By virtue of rule three, rules one and two have ceased to apply to Prince Edward Island and New Brunswick. We therefore reduce the total population of the provinces (21,515,116) by the combined population of these two provinces (746,198) to obtain a new total of 20,768,918. Similarly, we reduce the number of seats available by fourteen (10 + 4) to obtain a new seat total of 247 (261 − 14). The new quotient is 84,085 (20,768,918 divided by 247). Rule four then instructs us to once again follow the procedure laid down in rules one and two using the new quotient in calculating the seats to be distributed among the remaining provinces. The allocation of seats according to the calculations done so far is presented in column G of Table I. We now seem to have completed all the calculations called for under rules one to four and we find that Nova Scotia has been allocated one fewer MP than it has Senators (nine MPs, ten Senators).

There now appear to be two possible courses open to the calculator: (1) to construe rules one to four in such a way that further calculations are possible using only these rules in order to increase Nova Scotia's representation to 10; or (2) to consider calculations under rules one to four to be completed and to use other rules, if possible, to increase Nova Scotia's representation to 10.

Let us look now at the first alternative. Rule four certainly gives us no explicit instruction to perform any further calculations if any province ends up with fewer MPs than senators after applying the provisions of that rule. In fact rule four is rather misleading even in its original application for our purposes because it implies that there will never be more than one province which will have fewer members than senators after the application of rules one and two. However, since the redistribution of 1966 there have always been two provinces, Prince Edward Island and New Brunswick, protected by the "senatorial floor." The only possible interpretation of rule four is that on the last two occasions where the word "Province" occurs, "Provinces" is what is really meant. For our purposes, though, the important feature of rule four is that it, in itself, does not provide any instructions to make any further calculations.

If we look back at rule three, however, we do find possible grounds for further action. We should recall that rule three comes into effect in these circumstances: "Notwithstanding anything in this section, *if upon completion of a computation under rules one and two* [my italics] the number of members to be assigned to a Province is less than the number of Senators representing the said Province ..." At the present state of the calculations, Nova Scotia clearly has fewer members than senators. The issue, however, is whether or not this state of affairs results from "a computation under rules one and two." The case can surely be made that Nova Scotia was originally allocated 10 seats by the application of rules one and two and that it was allocated 9 seats only by the operation of a further rule. If this is the case, it is not obvious that rule three would apply.

The resolution of the problem seems to hinge on whether or not Nova Scotia was allocated 9 seats by the application of (1) rules one and two only; (2) rule four only; or (3) by some combination of rules one, two, and four. The advocate of option (1) has to argue that in fact no calculations are ever made under rule four alone; rule four simply refers us to rules one and two if certain conditions apply after the application of rule three; if this happens after rule three is applied in the first instance, there is no reason why rule four cannot apply more than once and each time refer us to rules one and two if the required circumstances exist. When faced with Nova Scotia's having one fewer member than senators, the advocate of option (1) would simply allocate 10 seats to Nova Scotia and return to rules one and two, this time excluding the three provinces of Prince Edward Island, New Brunswick, and Nova Scotia from his calculations. In this instance the quotient is 84,304 (19,979,958 divided by 237). The results of these calculations are presented in column I of Table I. To advocate option (1) is to hold that it is impossible for rules one to four to produce a situation in which a province is allocated fewer members than senators.

The advocate of option (1) must base his case on the wording of the opening lines of rule four ("in the event that rules one and two cease to apply in respect of a Province, then, for the purposes of computing the number of members to be assigned to the Provinces *in respect of which rules one and two continue to apply* ..." [my italics]). The phrase "in respect of which rules one and two continue to apply" seems to serve two grammatical purposes. First, it acts as an adjectival clause to describe the remaining provinces. Secondly, it seems to tell us to refer to rules one and two for instructions about how to perform certain further required calculations. The advocate of option (1) is not really helped by this phrase. Although it states that the provisions of rules one and two will continue to apply, it cannot and does not state that *only* they will apply in any calculation required after the application of rule three. Any such calculations must be based on the provisions of rule four, not just on those of rules one and two. Option (1) seems not to be valid on the grounds that although rules one and two are relevant to calculations made after the application of rule three, they cannot be applied without also applying the provisions of rule four.

The advocate of option (2) claims that Nova Scotia was allocated nine seats only by the application of rule four. Therefore rule three could not possibly apply in this case. Nova Scotia would be left with nine members at this stage and the calculator would then proceed to further relevant rules and sections before making a final allocation.

This argument runs into immediate difficulty because rule four is meaningless without rules one and two. If rule four simply referred us to rules one and two, the option (2) argument might be plausible. However, rule four does not do this. As shown above, it states that rules one and two do continue to apply to certain provinces although rule four is now applying to further computations as well.

It should be clear now that it is option (3) which is the most plausible. Nova

Scotia was in fact allocated 9 seats after the completion of a computation based on rules one, two, and four. Rule three only applies "upon completion of a computation under rules one and two." It might be argued, however, that a computation under rules one, two, and four could still be interpreted as being "a computation under rules one and two" on the grounds that the addition of certain other rules to the list does not change the fact that computations under rules one and two have still been completed. This argument breaks down under closer examination because rule four does not simply add a further step to the calculations already made under rules one and two. In fact, when rule four is applied, its provisions change the basic provisions of rules one and two. Therefore, when we look at the phrase "rules one, two, and four" in this context, it is not valid to claim that it can be interpreted in the same way as the phrase "rules one and two" as used in the context of rule three. This means that rule three cannot be used in this instance to boost Nova Scotia's House of Commons representation to 10 members. If this point is accepted, then the practical effects of option (3) are the same as those of option (2) outlined above and Nova Scotia is left with 9 members.

If, on the other hand, one wishes to make the implausible argument that the two phrases can be construed as meaning the same thing, then the practical effects are the same as those outlined for option (1) and Nova Scotia is allocated 10 members.

For the purposes of continuing the calculations let us assume that the argument presented above is substantially correct and that rules one to four allocate only 9 members to Nova Scotia. We can now proceed to calculations required by other rules. The provisions of rule five are not central to the arguments presented here and they therefore need only to be paraphrased. The first part of rule five states that from one redistribution to the next, no province can lose more than 15 per cent of the seats it was entitled to under rules one to four as applied in the previous redistribution. (The results of the application of rules one to four in the 1966 redistribution are presented in column J of Table I. It should be noted that Nova Scotia actually was allocated 11 members rather than 10 after all the rules were applied; 1 extra was added because of the application of this part of rule five. After the 1952 redistribution Nova Scotia had been allocated 13 seats by the application of rules one to four. The only decrease this time of more than 15 per cent is found in the case of Saskatchewan [13 − 11 = 2, 2/13 is greater than 15 per cent]. Saskatchewan is therefore allocated an additional seat.)

The second part of rule five (hitherto unused in redistributions) requires that no province be allocated fewer seats than any other province with a smaller population. This provision makes it necessary to allocate an additional seat to Nova Scotia because its population is more than that of New Brunswick and because under our present assumptions the calculations of rules one to four allocated 10 seats to New Brunswick and 9 to Nova Scotia. According to the final provision of rule five the addition of these 2 seats to Saskatchewan and Nova Scotia does not affect the calculations of rules one to four. They are simply added to the existing total.

Section 51(2) of the BNA Act allocates one seat each to the Yukon and the

Northwest Territories in addition to all the other seats allocated previously. The final allocation according to our present assumption is presented in column K of Table I.

By comparing the allocation in column K with that in column B, it can be seen that the results of the calculations just completed are not identical to those published by the Representation Commissioner. In fact, if we look at the Representation Commissioner's calculations[6] for rules one to four, we see that they are identical to those made under the interpretation of rules one to four that was rejected earlier in this paper[7] (that is, rules one to four can never produce a result in which a province has fewer members than senators).

The Representation Commissioner has not explained in his calculations why he took the course he did. In fact, he does not acknowledge that there is anything unusual about how rules one to four apply to Nova Scotia. He simply assumes from the very beginning that Nova Scotia is to be allocated 10 seats because of the operation of rule three. Nova Scotia, New Brunswick, and Prince Edward Island are treated in exactly the same way; that is, he makes no calculations for any of them. This manner of proceeding is clearly not in accordance with the rules, even though in more normal circumstances it would produce the correct results. As it appears that the Representation Commissioner has not really addressed the problem as presented in this article, there seems to be no reason why his apparent interpretation of rules one to four should be accepted.

The Representation Commissioner has implied that the provisions of section 51A of the BNA Act[8] are to be followed "at all steps in the computations of section 51A."[9] Section 51A states: "Notwithstanding anything in this Act, a province shall always be entitled to a number of members of the House of Commons not less than the number of senators representing such province." The introduction of section 51A provides an interesting new dimension to the problem. However, there are two reasons why it is essentially irrelevant to the case at hand.

First, if we in fact did apply section 51A at all stages in the computation of rules one to four, we would find that these rules would be meaningless and unworkable. The rules make sense only if one starts with the assumption that section 51A and "the senatorial floor" do not exist. One could well argue, however, that section 51A could become relevant to the computations if, after section 51 was fully applied, one province had fewer members than senators. In other words, if Nova Scotia had not received its tenth seat from the operation of the second part of rule five, we could have been justified in applying section 51A. Had we done so, this clearly could not have affected the calculations according to rules one to four. The extra tenth seat would have to have been added to the total number of House seats. The results would have been the same as those presented here in column K. This interpretation of section 51A would appear to be the only one which could give it any operational significance. If we interpret rules one to four so that Nova Scotia is given its tenth seat solely by

[6]A mimeographed copy of his calculations can be obtained from his office.
[7]See columns H and I of Table I for these calculations.
[8]As enacted by the *British North America Act, 1915*, c. 45 (UK).
[9]From a letter to the author from Mr Nelson Castonguay dated 1 November 1972.

their operation, then section 51A is clearly redundant under all conceivable circumstances. By introducing section 51A the Representation Commissioner seems to be casting doubt on, rather than defending, his own calculations.

The second reason for rejecting the Representation Commissioner's introduction of section 51A is that he has no legal authority to do so. Section 12 of the Electoral Boundaries Readjustment Act, which governs his duties in this regard, states: "... the Representation Commissioner shall calculate the number of members of the House of Commons to be assigned to each of the provinces, subject and according to section 51 of the *British North America Act, 1867* and the rules provided therein ..." It would appear from this that the Representation Commissioner is supposed to restrict himself to section 51. One can only assume that it is the Parliament of Canada which has the duty to implement section 51A if and when it is necessary, just as it was Parliament which implemented section 51 before the office of Representation Commissioner was established.

The existing section 51 was enacted by the British Parliament in 1946[10] and amended in ways not relevant to the current difficulties by the Canadian Parliament in 1952.[11] During the debates in the Canadian House of Commons on both these occasions[12] no mention was made of the possible problems caused by the kind of situation we are now in. Most of the concern in 1946 related to the fact that changes were being made in the allocation formula without the consultation or approval of the provinces. However, at one stage in the debate Louis St Laurent, the Minister of Justice and sponsor of the amending resolutions, stated: "Section 51A as I have read it and section 52 as I have read it will still continue to speak and may, if and when occasion arises to resort to them, provide authority for whatever may be found to be the right thing to do at the proper time."[13] Although Mr St Laurent probably did not have the present type of situation in mind, it is clear that he considered section 51A to be more than a redundant declaration. This is consistent with the view that, in themselves, rules one to four of section 51(1) do not provide an absolute guarantee of the "senatorial floor." The 1952 debates concern mainly rule five of section 51(1) which was introduced at that time. No reference was made to any of the matters relevant to the present case.

There have been three redistributions (1947, 1952, and 1966) based on the current formula. In no case do any of the calculations involved in these redistributions result in a situation analagous to that of Nova Scotia today. It would seem then that there is nothing that the record of the past can do to guide us in the present difficulty.

There is a pressing need for some authoritative person or institution to analyse the present ambiguities and to decide which interpretation is correct and for what reasons. Alternatively, the Canadian Parliament could clarify the situation by amending section 51 of the BNA Act while at the same time retroactively

[10]By the *British North America Act, 1946*, c. 63 (UK).
[11]The Act is cited in the first footnote. It was the first time the BNA Act was amended by the Canadian Parliament. This was made possible by *British North America (No 2) Act, 1949*, c. 36 (UK).
[12]Canada, House of Commons, *Debates* 1946, II, 1930–9, 2227–69; IV, 2404–15, 2420–41, 2460–79, 2591–2630, 2636–56, 2660–96; and *Debates* 1952, III, 3151–85.
[13]Canada, House of Commons, *Debates* 1946, IV, 2694.

applying the amended rules to the post-1971 redistribution. For the political scientist and constitutional lawyer the need is to know exactly what the "senatorial floor" rule is and how and when it is to be applied. For the citizens of Canada the immediate need is to know the number of seats to which Ontario is constitutionally entitled in the House of Commons.[14]

Even if the interpretation of section 51 advocated in this article is not accepted, the political scientist is still left with one unique and important lesson from the post-1971 calculations. The lesson is that calculations resulting from rules one to four can, in certain circumstances, be considerably more complicated than Mr St Laurent, the Representation Commissioner, or students of Canadian politics have ever suggested.

[14]The maps showing the new constituency boundaries for Ontario were published in the 27 December 1972 issue of *The Globe and Mail* by the Federal Election Boundaries Commission for Ontario. These maps, naturally enough, were drawn on the assumption that Ontario was to have 91 seats. The implication of this article is that these maps are not legally defensible because they should have been based on Ontario's having 92 seats.

The Political Theory of Extra-Parliamentarism*

PHILIP RESNICK *University of British Columbia*

Extra-parliamentarism as a political idea is not recent. Defined primarily as the rejection of the bourgeois theory of representation, extra-parliamentarism can be traced back through the development of capitalist society where it has flourished particularly during periods of economic and political crisis.

Historically, extra-parliamentarism has been associated with popular movements excluded from the formal political process and operating outside of that process. Thus, the Levellers and more especially the Diggers of the English revolution, the Sans-Culottes, and more especially, the Enragés, of the French revolution, the Soviets of 1905 and 1917, and the German and Italian factory councils of 1918–19 are historical examples of extra-parliamentary forces of a revolutionary kind.

Yet the term extra-parliamentarism can have another significance, the opposition to participation in parliamentary politics, and it is this usage that has become widely popularized in recent years. The student and youth movements of North America and Western Europe in the late 1960s insisted that parliamentarism spells co-option and that "elections equal treason." Further, they argued that politics of a radical kind could only begin when people took power into their own hands, exercising *directly* in their daily lives the control which capitalist society had alienated into institutions of class oppression. Among those institutions figured the corporation, national and multinational, the universities, agencies for the training of professional and technical cadres and workers for advanced capitalism, and at the apex, the bourgeois state, weaving its net of repression and repressive tolerance through every sinew of society.

What this paper sets out to do is first to develop a critique of the bourgeois theory of representation, and then to relate this critique to the theory of extra-parliamentarism in both its broader historical and its specifically student development. I shall argue a number of themes.

1. Representative government, as liberal theory conceives it, is, in fact, a form of counter-insurgency. It is the translation into political terms of the subordinate position that the working class occupies within the capitalist system. As such, it stands wholly opposed to the political and economic liberation of the working class through revolution, the means whereby the bourgeoisies of England, France, and the United States secured their own rise to domination.

*This paper is based on a larger study in preparation as a PHD thesis for the University of Toronto. My thanks to the Canada Council for a pre-doctoral grant that enabled me to carry out research in Europe in 1969–70.

Canadian Journal of Political Science/Revue canadienne de science politique, VI, no. 1 (March/mars 1973). Printed in Canada/Imprimé au Canada.

2. Extra-parliamentarism, historically, has implied a strong element of direct democracy, and the negation of the anti-participatory bias built into the capitalist state's political institutions. This has not necessarily implied a negation of political structures *per se*. Rather, extra-parliamentary theory has favoured popular forms of power that are the expression of the collective interest of those who work, produce, and live together.

3. In its most recent form, as in certain earlier periods, extra-parliamentarism has been critical of existing political parties of the left. In the case of social democratic parties in, for example, England, West Germany, or Canada, extra-parliamentary critics contend that these have become custodians of bourgeois interests and the bourgeois state. In the case of France or Italy, extra-parliamentary groups maintain that the communist parties have become objectively counter-revolutionary, holding back rather than fostering revolutionary consciousness, content with exercising very limited forms of parallel power within the capitalist system.

4. Extra-parliamentarism is usually characterized by a belief in militancy and direct action by the exploited and oppressed against their exploiters. In the case of the student movements, a basic argument was that the implicit violence of a global system which was mutiliating and killing people every day had to be made explicit through direct challenge if people were to become conscious of the system's repressive character and rise up against it. The alternative model to advanced capitalist society most typically put forward was one of a decentralized socialist society based on worker's control and direct democracy.

5. There is an ephemeral quality to extra-parliamentary movements, arising from the radically charged conditions under which they first develop, conditions which do not persist into a post-revolutionary or post-radical period. By definition, extra-parliamentary movements tend to be spontaneous in character, fairly resistant to strong organization; and this usually proves fatal to long-term survival. Yet extra-parliamentarism is more than a passing phase in something larger. It is as much a part of the revolutionary process as are organizations that endure. And like the revolutionary mole, it has a remarkable tendency to make its appearance when least expected.

I

Parliamentarism is the fruit of liberal theory of the seventeenth and eighteenth centuries. For Hobbes, the very basis of the commonwealth lies in a covenant among men whereby a "Man, or Assembly of Men, shall be given by the major part, the Right to Present the Person of them all, (that is to say to be their *Representative*)."[1] Sovereignty is not to be entrusted to the people themselves; rather all are to cede their power to the sovereign and be equal before his power. The representative character of Hobbes's commonwealth is an alienation of man's autonomous power in the name of a higher need – order. Yet the order of which he dreams, with the English civil war in mind, is an order which C.B. Macpherson has quite correctly analysed as possessive market society.[2]

[1]*Leviathan*, Everyman's Library (London and New York, 1959), 90.
[2]*The Political Theory of Possessive Individualism* (Oxford, 1962), 53–106.

La théorie politique de l'extraparlementarisme

Cet article se définit volontairement comme engagé, en partant à la recherche de la théorie politique de l'extraparlementarisme. Son auteur propose à la fois une critique radicale de la théorie bourgeoise de la réprésentation et une analyse de l'extraparlementarisme qui la situe dans une tradition révolutionnaire qui date au moins de la révolution française.

La première section de l'article a donc un caractère historique, et critique le rôle anti-démocratique que les institutions parlementaires ont joué dans les théories politiques de Hobbes, Locke, Montesquieu, Diderot, Madison, et John Stuart Mill. La deuxième section, par contre, analyse surtout les théories marxistes et anarchistes du 19ᵉ et de début du 20ᵉ siècle, et trouve dans les deux une conception de pouvoir ouvrier et non-parlementaire. Cependant, l'auteur fait une distinction entre la théorie anti-parlementaire des anarchistes et extra-parlementaire des marxistes.

Dans les troisiène et quatrième sections de l'article, l'auteur se penche sur les mouvements étudiants des années 1960 en France et en Allemagne de l'Ouest. Il essaie de délimiter les principes fondamentaux des mouvements étudiants et de montrer une certaine continuité entre leurs thèmes et ceux des théories antérieures.

Enfin, dans la dernière section de l'article, l'auteur résume certains points forts et faibles de l'extraparlementarisme et essaie d'analyser son importance pour l'avenir.

Hobbes's principle of representation is the principle of market sovereignty and, more fundamentally, of class sovereignty in the interests of the rising bourgeoisie.

In Locke, the bourgeois roots of parliamentarism become even more explicit. The sovereign is the "Representative of the Commonwealth," but "he has no Will, no Power, but that of the Law."[3] As for the legislative power, "the people have reserved to themselves the Choice of their *Representatives*, as the Fence to their Properties."[4] Should these representatives fail in their task, "by invading their Property,"[5] the people must be able to change this legislature. In the extreme, the body of the people have the right "to appeal to Heaven"[6] against an arbitrary legislature or executive. Yet wise rulers will ensure that such rebellion never occurs, and that the majority in a given society is placated.[7]

Locke's concept of citizenship effectively excludes the common labourers from participation in government. What it does instead is formalize the rights of the gentry and commercial classes to participation in the political system through an institution with which they can identify. It is Parliament, representing men of property and substance, "dominated by political parties one of which will be a constant ally of the commercial interest,"[8] that acquires the central function in the English state after 1688.

The English model in turn found strong support in eighteenth-century France, among the spokesmen for the rising French bourgeoisie. Montesquieu's *De l'esprit des lois* is a veritable eulogy of the English constitution, laying emphasis on the ostensible division of powers and checks and balances in the English

[3] *Two Treatises of Government*, ed. Peter Laslett, Mentor Library edition (New York, 1965), Treatise 2, no 151, 414.
[4] *Ibid.*, no 222, 461.
[5] *Ibid.*, no 226, 464.
[6] *Ibid.*, no 168, 426.
[7] *Ibid.*, 427.
[8] Harold Laski, *The Rise of European Liberalism* (London, 1962), 75.

system. His own concept of representation clearly reflects the anti-democratic role of parliamentary institutions in liberal theory. "The great advantage of representatives is that they are able to discuss public affairs. The people is quite incapable of this, which is precisely one of the great inconveniences of democracy ... There was one great vice in most ancient republics: Namely that the people had the right to make specific decisions, requiring execution, something which they are totally unfit to do. Their only role in government should be the choosing of representatives, something well within their ability."[9]

For Montesquieu, as for Locke, the franchise existed only for those who were not in an "état de bassesse." The vast majority of the nation was excluded. The nobility and the wealthy had rights to their own hereditary chamber, with appropriate veto power on the elected one. In turn, the combined legislature would both control and be limited by the executive power. Thereby, the extremes of liberty, that is, a truly popular form of government, could be avoided.

Diderot, picking up from Montesquieu, argues the case for representation in explicitly class terms: "Each class must have the right to choose its organs or *representatives*. For the latter to express the nation's will, their interests must be indivisibly tied to those of the former by the bond of possessions."[10] In Diderot's vision of society, clergy, nobility, lawyers, merchants, and landowners constitute the orders whose interests must be represented. Landless peasants, artisans, workers without property, and the destitute poor are all excluded.

Yet even had they been included, Diderot's scheme of representation would have kept them in check. For anticipating the modern concept of pluralism, Diderot defended representation by order as ensuring that no single order outweighed the others.[11] The peasants and labourers, if they had been represented, would have had to operate within a political system in which the other orders that exploited them had effective veto power over them. This is what the liberal theory of representation is in fact largely about.

No better examples of this can be offered than the writings of James Madison and John Stuart Mill. Madison makes no bones about his opposition to anything resembling direct democracy. "Such democracies have ever been the spectacles of turbulence and contention; have ever been found incompatible with personal security or the rights of property; and have in general been as short in their lives as they have been violent in their deaths."[12] The introduction of the representative principle sets off the desirable republic from the undesirable democracy. The larger the republic, the greater the variety of parties and interests in it, the lesser the chances of a coalescence of opinion "to invade the rights of other citizens."[13]

The rights that Madison, like Hamilton, was most concerned with defending

[9]*De L'esprit des lois*, ed. J.P. Mayer and A.P. Kerr, Collection Idées (Paris, 1970), Livre XI, chap. 6, 172–3. This and all subsequent translations from the French and German, except where indicated, are my own.

[10]"Représentants" in *l'Encyclopédie*, in *Œuvres Politiques* (Paris, 1963), 51.

[11]"That state is a happy one and its sovereign powerful when all the orders in the state mutually help each other. To bring about so desirable a result, the rulers of political society should seek to maintain a just equilibrium among the different classes of citizens that prevents each class from interfering with the others." *Ibid.*, 51.

[12]*The Federalist Papers*, Mentor Edition (New York, 1961), no 10, 81.

[13]*Ibid.*, 83.

were the rights of property, and the solution he hit upon was the principle of divide and rule. "The society itself will be broken into so many parts, interests, and classes of citizens, that the rights of individuals, or the minority, will be in little danger from interested combinations of the majority."[14] From this principle derive the checks and balances of the American constitution: the Senate to counteract "the propensity of all single and numerous assemblies to yield to the impulse of sudden and violent passions;"[15] the Executive, which Hamilton held essential "to the protection of property against those irregular and high-handed combinations which sometimes interrupt the ordinary sense of justice;"[16] an independent judiciary, able to check the legislature itself. The whole tenor of representation in the American system was to ensure that popular democracy did not get out of hand, and that the will of the people would be exercised within a straitjacket of countervailing rights and powers that made almost impossible any radical turn.

John Stuart Mill, in his *Representative Government*, was doing much the same for nineteenth-century England. He recognized that Parliament in his day was a class institution, framing economic policy from the point of view of the employers of labour.[17] As a liberal, he was interested in integrating the working class into the parliamentary system, yet not at the price of allowing working-class domination. "The desirable object would be that no class and no combination of classes likely to combine should be able to exercise a preponderant influence in the government."[18] Mill sought to insure that privileged minorities, particularly the employers, foremen, bankers, and those in the liberal professions, would maintain political privileges as well through, for example, multiple votes.[19] Extension of suffrage to the working class would have to involve continuous education of the working class, under the aegis of the bourgeoisie, to the art of government. "The conduct of affairs," in any case, was to remain in the hands of "skilled men, bred to it as an intellectual profession," with representatives exercising but a general control over government.[20] The destitute, the illiterate, and those who paid no taxes were to be excluded from the political process as before.

Some might wish to defend Mill by arguing that he was genuinely concerned with improving the position of the working class through political participation and public education. He may or may not have been. Objectively, however, coming when they did, his proposed reforms served quite another function. For under the guise of civilizing capitalism, Mill and his liberal successors were outlining methods of civilizing the working class to a subordinate position within the capitalist system. Representative government, with executive power in the hands of trained and qualified persons (in the bourgeois sense), and with class and sectional interests evenly balanced in the legislature, was the surest and most efficient way to secure this. The working class could participate in the political life of the nation, but the daily operation of the political system, as of the larger capitalist system, would be in the hands of those qualified to rule – the bourgeoisie.

[14] *Ibid.*, no 51, 324. [15] *Ibid.*, no 62, 379. [16] *Ibid.*, no 70, 423.
[17] *Utilitarianism, Liberty, Representative Government*, Everyman's Library (London, 1960), chap. 3, 209.
[18] *Ibid.*, 255. [19] *Ibid.*, 285. [20] *Ibid.*, 235–9.

Twentieth-century liberal theory adds little to the theory of representation. If anything, the practice of liberal democracy since Mill's time has tended to drain electoral politics of even the formal control over government which Mill had assigned it. The electorate "cannot choose the representatives it wants; it can only strike out blindly against those at whom it feels a passing indignation."[21] The tremendous ongoing power of capitalist interests over the political, economic, and ideological structures of Western societies, the bureaucratization and routinization of the political process, the taming of social democratic and other left-wing parties over time, have all contributed to the progressive eclipse of popular participation and control.

In the post-Second World War period, the exponents of liberal theory came to find the absence of such participation positively praiseworthy. "The average voter does not act, he reacts ... The majority remain passive ... not because they cannot learn about politics, but because they are not interested in it. It is nobody's fault in particular, and it is time we stopped seeking scapegoats," wrote one defender of liberal democracy.[22] "Mass Politics occur when large numbers of people engage in political activity outside of the procedures and rules instituted by a society to govern political action. Mass politics in democratic society therefore is anti-democratic ..." wrote another.[23] Polyarchy is the best we can hope for, chimed in Robert Dahl,[24] adding little to what Madison had so much more shrewdly devised.

Instead of raising fundamental questions about the function of representation in an advanced capitalist society, or the absence of day-to-day political participation by most people in such a society, Western social scientists surveyed and resurveyed voters and legislators, deducing the validity of the system from its simple existence. Political science even took the form of trying to mould human behaviour in Western and non-Western societies to conform to the norms of classical liberal theory. Politics was defined as what took place within the formal framework of elections and political parties, pressure groups and administrative decisions. Outside lay an underworld of irrationality, illegality, violence, and anomic revolt, unsafe for liberals to acknowledge except as a realm of abnormal behaviour.

II

From the seventeenth and eighteenth centuries on, however, radical theorists, including radical democrats writing in a period of bourgeois revolution, began to enunciate a critique of the bourgeois theory of representation. Jean-Jacques Rousseau's indictment of the English system of representation is still highly pertinent. "The English people think they are free; they fool themselves for they are only so during the election of Members of Parliament, as soon as these are elected, the English become slaves, become nothing. The use they make of their

[21]Harold Laski, *Democracy in Crisis* (Raleigh, NC, 1935), 75.
[22]G. Sartori, *Democratic Theory* (Detroit, 1962), 77, 88.
[23]William Kornhauser, *The Politics of Mass Society* (Glencoe, 1959), 227.
[24]*A Preface to Democratic Theory* (Chicago, 1956) and subsequent works.

freedom during the brief moments they enjoy it justifies their losing it."[25] For Rousseau, at certain moments, representative democracy represented a falling away from the ideals of classical democracy and a form of alienation of the general will. His ideal society was ostensibly one of direct democracy – elders resolving affairs of state under an oak.

In practice, however, he was prepared to settle for much less. His concept of liberty was ultimately a petty bourgeois one, individualist in the extreme: "Liberty is less a matter of exercising your own will than of not having to submit to some one else's."[26] He made his peace with the bourgeois principle of representation, and was far from consistent on direct popular rule.[27] Yet elements of extra-parliamentarism can be found in his critique of representative government, and they were to find some expression during the French revolution.

Another theorist of the eighteenth century whose ideas lend themselves to an extra-parliamentary interpretation, at least in part, is Thomas Jefferson. Unlike Madison and Hamilton, Jefferson was to go quite far in his defence of popular sovereignty against the institutionalized power of the state. "What country can preserve its liberties, if its rulers are not warned from time to time that this people preserve the spirit of resistance. Let them take arms," he wrote in 1787.[28] In a letter to Madison that same year, he set forth a rationale for extra-parliamentarism as the ultimate check on government: "A little rebellion, now and then, is a good thing, and as necessary in the political world as storms in the physical. It is a medicine necessary for the sound health of government."[29] Without disregarding Jefferson's cautious political practice, one can nonetheless see why his ideas exercised a certain amount of influence in the early days of the American new left, particularly where the concept of participatory democracy was concerned.

Nonetheless, the modern roots of extra-parliamentarism above all lie in the revolutionary and socialist tradition from the French revolution on. Since it was in the context of developing capitalist society that bourgeois spokesmen enunciated their doctrine of representative institutions, opposition to this doctrine was the expression of that class which came most directly to oppose the bourgeoisie and its conception of power: the working class and its urban precursors.

Daniel Guérin has described the role of the Sans-Culottes in the French revolution, and how the sections, communes, and popular societies of 1792–4 translated the will of the revolutionary avant-garde far more effectively than did the Constituent Assembly.[30] Indeed, the French revolution was not simply a matter of bourgeoisie versus aristocracy, or even of one faction of the bourgeoisie (Jacobins) versus another (Girondins), but also at moments a class struggle between the Sans-Culottes and the bourgeoisie. In ideological terms, this

[25] *Du contrat social*, Livre III, Chap. XV in *Œuvres complètes*, III (Paris, 1966), 430.
[26] *Huitième lettre de la montagne*, *ibid.*, 841.
[27] "If there were a people of gods, it would govern itself democratically. So perfect a government is not suitable for men." *Du contrat social*, Livre III, Chap. IV, *ibid.*, 406.
[28] *Thomas Jefferson on Democracy*, ed. S.K. Padover, Mentor edition (New York, 1939), 168.
[29] *Ibid.*, 168.
[30] *La lutte des classes sous la première république*, nouvelle édition (Paris, 1968), vol 1, chap. IV, 194–257.

struggle pitted the bourgeois concept of representative government as embodied, ultimately, in Robespierre and the Jacobins, against a popular concept of democracy based on direct Sans-Culotte rule. As Babeuf wrote shortly before the last Sans-Culotte-based insurrection of the 1790s, the Conspiracy of the Equals: "Those who govern only make revolutions to be able to continue to govern. We want to make one, at last, that will guarantee the People's well-being through true democracy."[31] Babeuf's vision of revolution was extra-parliamentary to the core in its opposition to mere institutional changes at the top, such as assemblies, that did not bring direct popular rule.

In revolutionary theory of the nineteenth and early twentieth centuries, extra-parliamentarism played a crucial role. Yet important differences which bear directly upon this discussion arose between two principal varieties of revolutionary theory in this period: anarchism and anarcho-syndicalism on the one hand, and Marxism on the other. For the anarchists, extra-parliamentarism came to mean opposition to the state itself and to *any participation* in parliamentary-type institutions. For Marx and later Marxists, opposition to parliamentary insitutions stemmed from their function as instruments of class rule in capitalist society, a function which would disappear with the coming of socialism. As long as capitalist society continued, however, socialists might continue to make *tactical* use of parliamentary institutions through electoral participation, for example, provided they did not equate parliamentarism with the whole of revolutionary class politics. The disagreement between anarchism and Marxism is thus substantial, yet I will argue that both embrace a theory of extra-parliamentarism.

Proudhon can be considered a representative spokesman for anarchism, and he was as firmly opposed to working-class participation in electoral politics as he was to the very concept of the state. "The revolutionary formula is neither *direct legislation* nor *direct government*, nor *simplified government*; it is, NO MORE GOVERNMENT," he wrote in *The General Idea of the Revolution in the XIXth Century*.[32] "One has to have lived in that isolating chamber called the National Assembly to appreciate just how much men who know almost nothing about their country almost always represent it," he wrote in his *Confessions of a Revolutionary*.[33]

In place of parliament and state, he proposed a free association of producers who would administer the mines, canals, railways, and other facilities of the society from the bottom up, participating directly in their enterprise. This system he called mutualism, or federalism.[34]

Proudhon's vision of extra-parliamentarism had a good deal of influence on the French and south European working class of the nineteenth century, and in a number of respects anticipates the modern concept of workers' control.[35] Furthermore, his indirect influence on some of the ideas of the European student

[31]*Le Tribun du Peuple* 10/18 (Paris, 1969), 317.

[32]*Idée générale de la révolution au XIX*^{e} *siècle* (Paris, 1923), Tome 2, 199.

[33]*Œuvres choisis*, ed. Jean Blancal (Paris, 1967), 192.

[34]*Ibid*., 91–146.

[35]See Daniel Guérin, "Proudhon et l'autogestion ouvrière," in *Pour un marxisme libertaire* (Paris, 1969), 99–125; Jean Bancal, "Proudhon : une sociologie de l'autogestion," *Autogestion* nos 5 and 6 (mars–juin 1968).

left, particularly with regard to decentralization of power, merits attention.[36] Yet his vision was as much a conservative as a revolutionary one rooted firmly in individual ownership of property.[37] There is no analysis in Proudhon's work of how the bourgeois political order is to suddenly disappear, and little conceptualization of a collective consciousness that transcends the individual consciousness of the diverse producers. Bakunin and later anarchists went further towards collectivism in their anti-statism, without necessarily grappling more successfully with the conditions for revolutionary transformation of society.

Blanqui was neither an anarchist nor a Marxist, but he was a practitioner of direct action which is an important component of extra-parliamentary theory. He coined the phrase, "Passions d'abord. Nous verrons là-bas,"[38] which could well have served as a motto for the student movements in their rising phase. Blanqui stood for revolutionary insurrection, without too much concern for strategy or organization.[39] This proved his undoing as far as successful insurrection was concerned, but it earns him mention as a proponent of extra-parliamentarism.

Marx's view of the state and of parliamentary institutions is of extreme importance and was firmly rooted in his analysis of all history as class history. From the *Communist Manifesto* to his last political texts, such as the *Critique of the Gotha Program*, he was concerned with a form of political power that would transcend the specific class interests of aristocracy and bourgeoisie, a form corresponding to the interests of the "immense majority" of modern society, the working class.

As early as 1841–2, he had criticized Hegel's tendency to treat the state as a finally formed entity (*fertigen* Existenz),[40] identical with the bureaucratic and class interests dominant in the Prussian regime. By 1848, he had come to see in "the modern representative State" the instrument, *par excellence*, of bourgeois political domination.[41] The communist revolution, in overthrowing bourgeois society, would also sweep away "the committee for managing common affairs of the whole bourgeoisie," the bourgeois state, through which the working class was being oppressed.

What then was Marx's view of working-class forms of power? In his *Address of the Central Committee to the Communist League* of 1850, he underlines the need for autonomous working-class organizations and centres, constituting a revolutionary power parallel to that of the bourgeoisie. "Alongside the new official governments, (the workers) must establish simultaneously their own

[36]See in particular Henri Lefebvre's references to Proudhon in *La proclamation de la commune* (Paris, 1965), 149–54, and the discussion of "The Relevance of Anarchism" by Anthony Arblaster in *The Socialist Register 1971* (London, 1971), 157–84.

[37]"Individual ownership is not an obstacle to large-scale cultivation and unity of exploitation (of land)," *Œuvres choisis*, 124, is but one such reference in Proudhon's writings.

[38]Maurice Dommanget, *Les idées politiques et sociales d'Auguste Blanqui* (Paris, 1957), 314.

[39]"[The social organism] is the work of everyone, through time, through certain changes, through progressive experience, through an unknown spontaneous current." Cited in Dommanget, *Auguste Blanqui*, 146. The key word is *spontaneous*.

[40]"Critique of Hegel's Philosophy of Right" in *Karl Marx: Die Frühschriften*, ed. S. Landshut (Stuttgart, 1968), 148.

[41]"The Communist Manifesto" in *Marx/Engels Selected Works* (London, 1968), 37.

revolutionary workers' governments, whether in the form of municipal committees and municipal councils or in the form of workers' clubs or workers' committees, so that bourgeois-democratic governments not only immediately lose the support of the workers but from the outset see themselves supervised and threatened by authorities which are backed by the whole mass of the workers."[42]

In 1864, the General Rules of the First International, which Marx inspired, declared unequivocally: "the emancipation of the working class must be the act of the workers themselves," implying the existence of specifically working-class organizations and institutions.

In 1871, Marx carried his analysis of working-class power furthest.

> The working class cannot simply lay hold of the ready-made state machinery, and wield it for its own purposes ... The Commune was to be a working, not a parliamentary, body, executive and legislative at the same time ... The communal regime once established in Paris and the secondary centres, the old centralized Government would in the provinces, too, have to give way to the self-government of the producers ... instead of deciding once in three or six years which member of the ruling class was to misrepresent the people in Parliament, universal suffrage was to serve the people, constituted in Communes, as individual suffrage serves every other employer in the search for the workmen and managers in his business.[43]

Marx's political writings thus adumbrate a theory of direct proletarian democracy and worker's self-government, radically different from the representative principle of bourgeois democracy.

Unlike the anarchists, however, Marx did not dismiss electoral participation by the working class in bourgeois democracies. Indeed, on at least one occasion, his address to the 1872 Congress of the First International, he even suggested that in such countries as England and the United States the working class might be able to achieve their aims by peaceful means.

Does this mean Marx would have subscribed to the version of the revolutionary process which Karl Kautsky, for example, painted in his *Parliamentarism and Socialism*? "The day is rapidly approaching when the all-powerful English Parliament will be an instrument of dictatorship in the hands of the Proletariat."[44] I rather doubt it. For Marx, the form of specifically working-class power was not parliamentary, but revolutionary, based on the institutions which the working class itself developed, for example, workers' committees or councils. It was this vision which allowed him, despite his fundamental antagonism to Bakunin and the anarchists, to write in 1872: "All socialists understand by anarchy the following: once the goal of the proletarian movement, the abolition of classes, is attained, the power of the State which keeps the great majority of producers under the yoke of a small minority of exploiters disappears, and governmental functions are transformed into simple administrative ones."[45] Marx's political theory was extra-parliamentary in its deepest ramifications, *because* it saw

[42]"Address of the Central Committee to the Communist League" in *Marx/Engels Selected Works*, Vol. 1 (Moscow, 1962), 112.

[43]"The Civil War in France" in *Marx/Engels Selected Works* (London, 1968), 288–92, *passim*.

[44]*Parlementarisme et socialisme* (Paris, 1900), 146.

[45]"The Alleged Splits in the International," *Archives Bakounine*, ed. A. Lehning (Leiden, 1967), vol 2, 295.

parliament as an instrument of bourgeois rule. Thus, Marx was strongly opposed to Lasalle's worship of the state "as an independent entity that possesses its own *intellectual, ethical* and *libertarian bases*," and he, not Lenin, first used the phrase "revolutionary dictatorship of the proletariat" in describing the transitional period that must follow the overthrow of capitalism.[46]

It would have been strange indeed if Marx, a strong critic of the Lasallean view of the state, should himself have developed a sudden fondness for parliamentary institutions as something to be carried over into a socialist society. Parliamentary institutions *might* have a role to play in the transition to socialism in the more developed capitalist societies, but the one example of revolutionary dictatorship of the proletariat that Marx concretely described and praised, the Paris commune, had been anti-parliamentary in inspiration.

At the very least, I would argue, Marx's view of the state (and Engels', for that matter, in *The Origins of the Family*) as a class-based institution implied a rejection by the proletariat of the political institutions which the bourgeoisie had evolved in its exercise of state power. Parliamentary assemblies were just such institutions; they might be lived with and used in the short-run by the proletariat while it gathered its strength, but they were not and could never be the expression of the proletariat's own organization and consciousness. In this rejection of the bourgeois principle of representation, therefore, Marx was not anti-parliamentary the way the anarchists were, but extra-parliamentary, looking to specifically working-class forms of organization.

Marx's principal opponent in the First International, Bakunin, was the proponent of anti-parliamentarism. Favouring a federalist form of organization that would link workers' associations, groups of communes, cantons, etc., together from the bottom up, he offered the following critique of parliamentarism: "Capitalist industry and bank speculators accommodate themselves perfectly to so-called representative democracy. For the modern structure of the state, founded on the pseudo-sovereignty of the pseudo-will of the people supposedly expressed through so-called representatives in pseudo-popular Assemblies, has two essential elements: (1) state centralization and (2) the effective subjugation of the sovereign people to an intellectual minority that governs it, ostensibly represents it, and unfailingly exploits it."[47]

These two points lead to a glorification of decentralization and of working-class spontaneity, themes that recur time and time again in the anarchist theory of extra-parliamentarism. But as I argued in the case of Proudhon, the fatal flaw in this theory is its inability to see beyond spontaneity. Hostile not only to the state, but to the very concept of authority, it raises doubts as to the viability of a would-be anarchist society in a world of antagonistic class forces and nation states.

Still the anarchist, or later anarcho-syndicalist, theory of extra-parliamentarism has had an appeal, and for understandable reasons, to militants including the student militants of the 1960s at war with their society. As the French revolutionary syndicalist, Griffuelhes, wrote in 1908: "If you think too much, you never undertake anything ... [The French worker] does not ask before acting,

[46]"Critique of the Gotha Program," in *Marx/Engels Selected Works* (London, 1968), 331.
[47]"The State and Anarchy," *Archives Bakounine*, vol 3, 211.

whether the law permits him to or not. He acts and that's that. The profound significance of direct action lies in the personal action of the workers, exercised outside of any legal consideration, and any authorization from above."[48]

What about the Marxist theory of extra-parliamentarism in the early twentieth century? For the left-wing of German social democracy before 1918, for example, Karl Liebknecht and Rosa Luxemburg, a strictly parliamentary road to power was insufficient. Luxemburg's 1906 pamphlet on *Mass Strike, Party and Unions*, stressed the importance of the direct participation of the masses in any revolutionary transformation. "Every really important class struggle entails the support and participation of the broadest masses, and any strategy of class conflict which does not entail this participation, but confines itself to the well-orchestrated march of a small disciplined section of the proletariat, is condemned beforehand to a tragic fiasco."[49] Revolutionary situations such as that in Russia in 1905, she argued, generate forms of proletarian activity, for example, the general strike, which do more to raise proletarian consciousness than ten years of public meetings and distribution of leaflets.

This did not mean that the need for a socialist party disappears, for its function in a revolutionary period was to provide resolute *political* direction that maximizes the combativeness of the mass movement. The mass movement, however, must not be subordinated in a bureaucratic or hierarchical way to the party. As Liebknecht described it: "The education of the masses and every individual to spiritual and moral independence, to the questioning of authority, to decisive initiative on one's own, to a free capacity for action, builds the only sure foundation for the development of a working class movement out of its own historical conditions, and for the avoidance of the menace of bureaucracy."[50]

In the period of the abortive German revolution, 1918–19, this view of the relations between party and masses led many revolutionaries to reject the very concept of parliamentary institutions, substituting for it the slogan, "All Power to the Workers' Councils."[51] Thus Kurt Eisner, leader of the short-lived Bavarian Soviet of 1919, could declare in November, 1918: "We do not understand by democracy citizens voting every few years and allowing themselves to be ruled by new ministers and a new Parliament. We who have founded a new kind of revolution also seek to evolve a new form of democracy. We want the co-participation of all the producers, in city and country alike."[52]

Anton Pannekoek, a Dutch communist whom Lenin denounced in *"Left-Wing" Communism*, summed up the philosophy of the workers' councils in these terms: "For the working class, parliamentary democracy is sham democracy, whereas representation through workers' councils is real democracy, the

[48]"Les caractères du syndicalisme français," *Le syndicalisme révolutionnaire*, ed. Henri Dubief (Paris, 1969), 164.

[49]*Schriften zur Theorie der Spontaneität* (Munich, 1970), 135.

[50]Karl Liebknecht, *Politische Aufzeichnangen aus seinem Nachlass 1917–18, (Posthumous Works)* (Berlin, 1921), 28.

[51]See the study by Bock, *Syndikalismus und Linkskommunismus von 1918–1923* (Meisenheim am Glan, 1969), for a fascinating account of this period. Interestingly enough, Liebknecht and Luxemburg were in the minority of the Spartacus League that voted for electoral participation in December 1918, the better to fight parliamentarism from within. Pp. 95–100.

[52]*Die Halbe Macht den Räten* (Cologne, 1969), 279.

direct control by the workers over their own affairs."[53] The analogies to the French and German student movements of the 1960s are many.

Extra-parliamentarism, however, was not strictly the reserve of left-wing militants in the German, French, or Italian working-class movements. It is important to recognize that Lenin himself, the champion of the vanguard party, was also, in part at least, a theoretician, as well as a critic, of extra-parliamentarism.

In the *April Theses*, for example, he argued for a very different form of state power from the bourgeois parliamentary republic. "A parliamentary bourgeois republic hampers and stifles the independent political life of the *masses* and their direct participation in the *democratic* organization of the life of the state from top to bottom. The contrary is the case with the Soviets of Workers' and Soldiers' Deputies."[54] The development of the Soviets as institutions of working-class parallel power in the spring and summer of 1917 opened the door to revolutionary initiatives and to "a superior type of *democratic* state ... of the type of the Paris Commune, one in which a standing army and police severed from the people are *replaced* by the directly armed people themselves."[55]

In *State and Revolution*, Lenin further attacked parliamentarism as an instrument of bourgeois class oppression,[56] while arguing for a proletarian form of political organization that "shall reduce the role of state officials to that of simply carrying out [the workers'] instructions."[57] The goal of communism, as of anarchism, was defined as the withering away of the state, *but* Lenin, like Marx, insisted on the necessity for a revolutionary dictatorship of the proletariat in the transitional period.[58]

Lenin's opposition to parliamentarism, however, was predicated on the existence of a revolutionary situation, as in Russia in 1917, with dual forms of power. Parliamentarism was not the form of power which the working class would evolve in *its* exercise of power. It might, however, have to be lived with, tactically, in non-revolutionary situations, and in capitalist societies. "It is far more difficult – and far more precious – to be a revolutionary when the conditions for direct, open, really mass, and really revolutionary struggle *do not yet exist*, to be able to champion the interests of the revolutionary in non-revolutionary bodies and quite often in downright reactionary bodies,"[59] he stated, in opposition to such anti-parliamentarians as Pannekoek.

Lenin's position on extra-parliamentarism thus contains two distinct elements. He opposed those like Pannekoek who rejected all participation in elections and parliamentary activity, arguing from the experience of the Bolsheviks who had used parliamentary institutions to carry on revolutionary propaganda prior to the October revolution. But he was quite unequivocal in declaring: "Bourgeois

[53]Serge Bricianer, *Pannekoek et les conseils ourvriers* (Paris, 1969), 275.
[54]"The Task of the Proletariat in the Present Revolution," in Lenin, *Selected Works*, 12 vols, ed. A. Fineberg (New York, no date), vol 6, 57.
[55]*Ibid.*, 56.
[56]"To decide once every few years which member of the ruling class is to repress and crush the people through parliament – this is the real essence of bourgeois parliamentarism ..." "State and Revolution," in Lenin, *Selected Works* (London, 1969), 295–6.
[57]*Ibid.*, 298.
[58]*Ibid.*, 306–9.
[59]"Left-Wing Communism – An Infantile Disorder," *ibid.*, 575–6.

parliaments must be abolished and replaced by Soviet bodies. There is no doubt about that. There is no doubt now, after the experience of Russia, Hungary, Germany and other countries, that this *absolutely must take place* during a proletarian revolution."[60] In short, Lenin was an opponent of pure anti-parliamentarism on tactical grounds, yet at the same time an opponent of the principle of parliamentarism, which he saw as a bourgeois form of power.

The official custodians of Marxism-Leninism have, since Lenin's death, been faithful on the whole to the tactical side of his position. But what of the spirit of his principled rejection of parliamentarism? Would Lenin, who as late as 1920 had recognized that "the history of revolutions ... is always richer in content ... more lively and ingenious than is imagined by even the best of parties,"[61] or who in April 1917 had fought his own party comrades to advance the position, "All Power to the Soviets," have sided with the students or with the French Communist party in May 1968? One cannot say for certain. But Lenin, the critic of anti-parliamentarism, might well have found student extra-parliamentarism more appropriate under those conditions than the cautious legalism of the French Communist party. Such may be the real legacy of Lenin where the theory of extra-parliamentarism is concerned.

III

From this discussion (which admittedly only begins to scratch the surface) of some of the roots of extra-parliamentarism, let me turn to the student movements of the 1960s, in particular to those in France and West Germany. There have by now been hundreds of studies of the causes of student revolt, so a word of reassurance to the reader is in order. I am not here interested in offering yet another explanation of the phenomenon, rather in analysing the political theory of extra-parliamentarism as developed by the student movements. Even more specifically I wish to focus on the theoretical and practical critique of parliamentarism in advanced capitalist society that these movements embodied, and assess their significance for the future.

There is a common element in the emergence of revolutionary student movements in the 1960s in countries as different as France and West Germany which needs underlining. That element lies in the failure of the major political parties of the left, the Communist party in the case of France, the Social Democratic party in the case of West Germany, to oppose in a forthright manner repressive aspects of the capitalist systems of the two countries.

In France, the Communist party took a very cautious position on Algerian independence throughout the eight years of the Algerian war, and it was the Union nationale des étudiants de France (UNEF), without Communist support, that organized the first major public rally in support of the FLN in 1961.[62] Subsequently, the French Communist party (CPF) had continuous problems with its student wing, the Union des étudiants communistes, some of whose members

[60] "Letter to Sylvia Pankhurst," 28 August 1919, in Lenin, *Collected Works* (Moscow, 1965), vol 29, 564.

[61] "Left-Wing Communism," in *Selected Works* (London, 1969), 574.

[62] See, for example, the articles by Marc Kravetz on French student syndicalism and the Algerian war in *Les temps modernes* (February 1964 and April and May 1965).

felt the CPF had "abandoned its specific function: the struggle for a socialist revolution" to play electoral games under the Fifth Republic.[63] Several of the revolutionary groups which were to figure in the May 1968 revolt, in particular the Trotskyist Jeunesse communiste révolutionnaire (JCR) and the Maoist Union des jeunesses communistes (marxiste-leniniste), were founded by ex-members of the Union des étudiants communistes. Other revolutionary students and student groups of the late 1960s, for example, the spontanist 22nd of March movement at Nanterre, never went through the school of the CPF, rejecting its Stalinism as well as its reformism, while attacking capitalist society on their own terms.[64]

In West Germany, the Social Democratic party (SPD) had stopped paying even lip-service to the Marxist credo of class consciousness and socialism at its Bad Godesberg Conference of 1959.[65] Shortly thereafter, it had expelled its left socialist youth movement, the Sozialistischer Deutscher Studentenbund, SDS, which in its early days was still committed to parliamentary democracy as the way of changing things. But the SPD itself, to cite a well-known student of German politics, "consciously strove to eliminate parliamentary opposition as a desirable pattern for the conduct of political business"[66] coming to accept the "dynamics of the market economy," and ultimately joining a government headed by Christian Democrats, the so-called Great Coalition of 1966. Moreover, as the German universities began to ban political meetings and to discipline students engaged in political activity, as internationally, the violence directed in the name of liberal democracy by West Germany's mentor and ally, the United States, against the National Liberation Front and North Vietnam increased, the SDS moved to a more radical position. It initiated mass demonstrations and direct action against such targets as the US military presence in Berlin, the Shah of Iran's visit to Germany in 1967, the Springer Press's systematic vilification of the left, and the passage of the emergency laws in the spring of 1968, coming to define itself as an Extra-Parliamentary Opposition.[67]

What themes were common to the critique of parliamentarism in advanced capitalist society which the French movement of May–June 1968 and the German student movement of 1967–8 advanced?

Firstly, parliament was seen as an instrument of class rule, whereby the working class was made to accept the legality of its own oppression. "It is because the [May] movement has developed outside of Parliament that it has forced the bosses to back down. Parliament is an arm of the bourgeoisie which uses it as it chooses. It is not an arm of the workers. The arm of the workers is the mass

[63]*L'année politique 1967* (Paris, 1968), 4. See also *L'année politique 1963* (Paris, 1964), for an account of the purging of so-called pro-Italian elements from the leadership of the Union des étudiants communistes.

[64]For a good discussion of the development of the principal revolutionary groups up to and including May 1968 see Richard Gombin, *Le projet révolutionnaire* (Paris, 1969).

[65]The 1959 Program of the SPD talks of freedom and justice, without mentioning either capitalism or classes. See *Die deutschen Parteiprogramme*, ed. Otto Bezold (Munich, 1967).

[66]Otto Kirchheimer, "Germany," *Political Opposition in Western Democracies*, ed. Robert Dahl (New Haven, 1966), 243, 245.

[67]See for example Meino Buning, "The West Berlin Student Movement," *International Socialist Journal*, 23 (October 1967); F.C. Hunnius, "The New Left in Germany," *Our Generation*, 6, nos 1–2 (July, 1968).

struggle and the general strike ... The bourgeoisie does not surrender its power at the ballot box. You have to wrest it away in the factories and in the street."[68]

Secondly, Parliament was the symbol of a dying civilization, incapable of solving fundamental social problems.

[The electoral game] touches only a miniscule part of the possibilities which the modern epoch opens for human society. The fundamental problems of our society are not posed by the parliamentary system for the simple reason that that system cannot resolve them ... To put into question the existing model of consumption and civilization is to put into question the capitalist system which creates it. This demands other weapons than the ballot, other arenas of battle than the parliamentary ... To build a new model of consumption means giving those who cannot speak the right to speak. That is already the Revolution.[69]

Thirdly, capitalist democracy was seen as a system which frequently violates its own self-proclaimed principles of democracy, for example, de Gaulle's coming to power in 1958 through the French army revolt. Another excellent example of this were the emergency laws passed by the West German Parliament in 1968, allowing the government to suspend the civil liberty provisions of the constitution under conditions of emergency which it itself would define. "When State and Bundestag violate democracy, the people have the right and the duty to take to the streets and fight for democracy,"[70] was the reply of the German Extra-Parliamentary opposition.

Finally, there was a critique of the alienation of political power from the people that the representative principle entails. Some of the wall posters and slogans of May 1968 express this perfectly:

Liberty is not something we have. It is something we have been prevented from acquiring through laws, regulations, etc. (Nanterre)

If you start thinking for others, others will start thinking for you. (Nanterre)

No to parliamentary solutions. (24 May demonstration)

When the National Assembly becomes a bourgeois theatre, all the bourgeois theatres must become national assemblies. (Odeon Theatre)

Power lies in the streets. (Beaux Arts)[71]

The practice of the student movements was no less extra-parliamentary than their theory. Great emphasis was placed on concrete struggles within the universities, the work place, and so on, "that help people to shake themselves free of the institutions in which they are oppressed."[72] The student movement evolved a new style of action, "installing itself in full illegality on the public place, visible

[68]"Elections – A Poisoned Gift," a tract published by the Coordinated Action Committees, 31 May 1968, reproduced in *Journal de la commune étudiante*, ed. Alain Schnapp and Pierre Vidal-Naquet (Paris, 1969), 501–2.
[69]*Action*, a newspaper published by the Union nationale des étudiants de France, the Comités d'action Lycéens and the Syndicat national de l'enseignement supérieur during the May–June revolt, no 13 (19 June 1968).
[70]Hans-Jurgen Krahl, "Römerbergrede," *Universität und Widerstand*, ed. D. Claussen and Regine Dermitzel (Frankfurt am Main, 1968), 37.
[71]*Les murs ont la parole – mai 1968* (Paris, 1968); *Partisans* (Paris), no 42.
[72]Erhard Lucas, "Thesen zum Parlamentarismus," *Sozialistische Korrespondenz*, no 9 (Frankfurt, 19 July 1969).

to everyone, rendering the institutions incapable of functioning and the authorities powerless, counting on mass support to counteract any repression against it."[73] In turn, the militancy of the French student movement in early May in fighting the CRS (riot police) and occupying the universities, served as a catalyst for the wave of strikes and occupations that swept the country from 15 May on. Like the students, many workers, especially younger ones, decided that "the 'normal' strike had lost its 'power of dissuasion,' " and that "power can only be conquered through action."[74]

Inevitably, the development of the student movements led to a good deal of antagonism with the established parties of the left and with the leadership of much of the trade union movement. The French Communist party had denounced the student movements as "leftists" and "adventurists" in the first week of the May revolt, leading such students as Daniel Cohn-Bendit to dismiss the CP leadership as "Communist hacks." Throughout the strike movement in the second half of May, the leaders of the Communist-led Confédération générale du travail did all they could to prevent contacts between students and workers, denouncing the Union nationale des étudiants de France for provocation, all the while pursuing a strategy of negotiation with the government and the Conseil national du patronat français to end the strike.[75] For the student movement and its supporters, the Communist party was guilty of sabotaging the May movement and the possibility of revolution in France.[76] Even Raymond Aron, no friend of the students, could write: "The Communist party is experiencing the same contradiction as European social democracy experienced between the end of the nineteenth century and 1940. You cannot keep on talking indefinitely about revolution, condemning the Gaullist regime and personal power with all severity, while leaving most observers with the impression that you want everything but revolution."[77] Whether the Communist party is or is not the party of order, it most certainly is no longer the party of revolution.[78]

In West Germany, where the student movements did not spark a mass working-class revolt the hatred by the extra-parliamentary left for the Social Democrats was perhaps less intense than that of the French student left for the Communist party. Yet the analysis of the failure of the SPD is not that different. "No one should be surprised that the SPD and the DGB [German Trade Union Federation] have refused to take part in the fight against the emergency laws.

[73]Claude Lefort, "Le désordre nouveau," *Mai 1968: La brèche*, ed. E. Morin, C. Lefort, J-M Coudray (Paris, 1968), 45.
[74]Centre national d'information pour la productivité des entreprises, *Les événements de mai-juin vus à travers cent entreprises* (Paris, 1969), 22, 28. Interviews with factory heads, unionists, etc.
[75]See, for example, Patrick Seale and Maureen McConville, *French Revolution: 1968* (Hammondsworth, 1968) for a good short account of the principal events.
[76]Andre Barjonet, *La révolution trahie de 1968* (Paris, 1968) writes one of the strongest indictments. Daniel Singer, *Prelude to Revolution: France in May 1968* (New York, 1970) is equally critical of the CPF.
[77]*La Révolution Introuvable* (Paris, 1968), 101.
[78]In an opinion poll taken by the Institut française de l'opinion publique in 1967, 63 per cent of Communist party supporters defined the party as "the party of the working class," 26 per cent as "the most important force of the left," and only 1 per cent as "the party that wants revolution." Fondation nationale des sciences politiques, *Le communisme en France*, Cahier 175, 289, *et seq.*

The elected organizations of the working class cannot defend the workers within the parliamentary system. They only administer and rule, eliminating the control of the voters after their election, and evolving a bureaucratic apparatus that is independent and can prevent the workers from exercising power." And later: "This process will go on as long as the workers do not recognize that no one can help them, if they do not help themselves."[79]

For the extra-parliamentary left the road to revolution and socialism did not lie through the Social Democratic or Communist parties, any more than through the parliamentary process. To hazard a partial definition of its strategy: "Not through a majority to revolutionary tactics, but through revolutionary tactics to a majority."[80]

IV

This question of strategy leads naturally to asking just what the student movements stood for in contradistinction to the bourgeois parliamentary system. To declare that "the people in a democracy is the real sovereign, not the Parliament"[81] is well and good. It does not, however, tell us how the popular will is to manifest itself, or what structures are to eventually replace the class-based structures of advanced capitalism.

There was far greater disagreement within the extra-parliamentary left on strategy than on the critique of capitalism. The gulf between the Situationists in France, for example, for whom "it is work itself which must be called into question,"[82] and the Maoists, for whom the role of the students was "to support the bastions of proletarian resistance, such as Renault, Citroën, and Peugot,"[83] was clearly large. Similarly there were important differences between the anti-authoritarian theory of the German SDS in the period 1967–8 and the more Leninist definitions of class and organization that came to prevail by 1969 within the same organization.

We must, therefore, try to isolate those themes which were in some sense characteristic of the French and West German student movements as a whole, at the height of their activity. Let me suggest the following strands in student extra-parliamentary theory, of which (1) and (2) alone need concern us here.

1. A commitment to direct action and confrontation politics, aimed at exposing the repressive and manipulative character of the system, and at producing revolutionary solidarity among those taking part in such actions.
2. Self-organization as a revolutionary principle, with students, workers, and citizens democratically running their organizations from below. A belief in direct democracy, a hostile attitude towards bureaucratic processes, and a vision of a more decentralized society.

[79]Leaflet no 3, Der Basisgruppe des SDS *Heidelberg* (5 June 1968).
[80]Singer, *Prelude to Revolution*, 303.
[81]*Diskus*, a Frankfurt student newspaper, special issue on the emergency laws (May, 1968).
[82]Situationist International, *Of Student Poverty Considered it its Economic, Political, Psychological, Sexual and, Particularly, Intellectual Aspects, and a Modest Proposal for its Remedy* (England, no date), 19.
[83]"La cause du peuple," no 16 (13 June 1968), in Schnapp and Vidal-Naquet, "Commune étudiante, 361.

3. A view of the class basis of revolution which strongly privileged the working class of traditional Marxist theory, while embracing new elements, students, technical workers, and professionals as part of the revolutionary subject.
4. A strong internationalism, in which the student movements identified with student struggles in other countries (Berkeley-Berlin-Nanterre), and with national liberation and anti-imperialist struggles in the third world, especially in Vietnam.
5. Attacks on bourgeois alienation, morality, and culture in the name of a revolutionary culture and consciousness.

The emphasis on direct action recurs in various documents of the student movement. One early, fairly moderate formulation reads: "Direct action begins in small things, through involvement in the daily struggle for existence that most people lead. Its necessity arises out of specific, concrete situations which people come to see as unbearable ... Direct action must be defensive, concrete. Through the struggle for existence, people can link up with the political struggle."[84]

As the student movements developed, direct action came to mean something more militant:

> Demonstrations and protests are the first steps in changing people's consciousness. We must make more and more people politically conscious, bringing them over to the anti-authoritarian camp through direct action.[85]

> When things have reached the stage where the act of caricaturing violence through eggs and tomatoes unleashes an ostensibly tolerant police apparatus to disregard democratic and civil rights and "get straight down to business," that is, violently repressing people, our so-called provocation has done more for political enlightenment than most platform discussions.[86]

In the week-long confrontations between students and police in the Latin Quarter in early May 1968, direct action served to create a strong sense of solidarity among those taking part: "All experienced solidarity. For the first time young workers, students, apprentices, and teen-agers were united in action. No one could tell what was going to happen, but that wasn't important ... In a society which atomizes individuals ... a profound feeling of collective force developed the night [of the barricades]."[87]

Still another justification of direct action by a young student stated simply: "Faced with a Government, which while not absolutely authoritarian is nonetheless anti-democratic, we can only succeed through rioting."[88] Carried one step further, direct action was the very precondition for sweeping away the framework of repressive laws and class relations of capitalism: "You do not ask for your rights, you have to take them." "It is forbidden to occupy factories and universities ... The workers have gone on strike and prolonged and intensified it quite illegally." "Confrontation sweeps away all laws."[89]

[84]Michael Vester, "Die Strategie der direkten Aktion," *Neue Kritik* (Frankfurt, June, 1965), no 30, 13.
[85]Rudi Dutschke, in an interview in *Der Spiegel* (10 July 1967), 29–33.
[86]Wolfgang Lefevre and Walter Weller, "Towards a History of the Berlin Student Movement," in *Wider die Untertanenfabrik*, ed. Stephen Liebfied (Cologne, 1967), 212.
[87]Daniel Cohn-Bendit, *Le Gauchisme* (Paris, 1968), 66.
[88]*Un mois de mai orageux*, an interview with 113 Paris students, Privat (Paris, 1968), 50–5.
[89]*Action*, no VII, 11 June, and no X, 14 June 1968.

Once the student revolts had reached their peak, however, a more critical note began to be sounded. "Mass demonstrations are necessary, but not sufficient," a leaflet published by UNEF on 30 May 1968 stated, stressing the need for students and workers to actually make the universities and factories function.[90] An SDS publication of April 1969 condemned action "freakism" (*Aktionismus*) and an exaggerated anti-authoritarianism, underlining the fact that every university strike or action will not bring the system down, and emphasizing the importance of student self-organization.[91] If militant confrontation therefore had its place as an offensive as well as defensive strategy in student extra-parliamentary theory, it was not the sum total of that theory.

In our discussion above, we stressed the theme of direct working-class power in both the Marxist and anarchist critiques of parliamentarism. This theme and that of direct democracy were central to the French and West German student movements, and played a significant role in the May 1968 revolt in France. The forum of radical student activity was the general assembly or mass rally, not some parliamentary body. Moreover, the structures of both the German SDS and the French May movement were extremely decentralized with most activity being initiated quite indepedently by militants and local associations, and in a spontaneous fashion.

In the anti-authoritarian phase of the SDS for example, much emphasis was placed on the anti-bureaucratic character of the movement: "The greatest effectiveness of the extra-parliamentary movement lies in its accepting only structures and organizational forms arising out of its concrete struggles ... Students must evolve counter-structures to those in existing society."[92] The movement's structures were explicitly identified with direct democracy by people like Rudi Dutschke: "When we say extra-parliamentary opposition, we have in mind a system of direct democracy, that is to say council democracy, which allows people to directly elect and impeach their representatives ... Our new form of state organization will do away with the inner laws of interest group democracy; the compromise character of politics will disappear."[93] West German extra-parliamentary theory tended to oppose the freely given participation and consent of the population, particularly the working class, in institutions such as workers' councils, to the imposed, arbitrary and manipulative character of political authority under capitalism.

Interestingly enough, the goal of student and working-class self-organization did not prevent most SDS groups from participating in student elections and parliaments parallel to their other activities. In the closing days of the SDS (1969–early 1970), in addition, there was growing consciousness of the danger that small base groups, in the absence of a strong cadre organization, would become isolated, and perhaps even co-opted by technocratic university reforms.[94] Still,

[90] Leaflet signed Union nationale des étudiants de France, in Schnapp and Vidal-Naquet, *Commune étudiante*, 310.

[91] *Sozialistische Korrespondenz*, info 2 (26 April 1969).

[92] *Ibid.*, info 9 (July, 1969), reproducing the discussion of parliamentarism that took place at the SDS federal convention in March 1968.

[93] *Der Spiegel* interview, 10 July 1967; "Demokratie, Universitat und Gessellschaft," *Demonstrationen: Ein Berliner Modell*, ed. B. Larsson (Berlin), 156.

[94] *Neue Kritik*, nos 51–2 (February 1969), 5. A Heidelberg SDS publication (16 April 1970), *Rote Zelle Soziologie*, argued the need to go beyond anti-authoritarianism in the student movement and raise class issues.

the principles of direct democracy at the base and of revolutionary self-organization typified the SDS through much of its existence.

In France, the concept of direct democracy goes back to the Paris commune and the French revolution. The very name some of the student militants adopted, les Enragés, evoked the Sans-Culottes of 1794, while certain organizational forms of the May movement recalled the revolutionary *sections* of an earlier day. One of the most important of these forms were the *comités d'action*, which made their appearance during the first days of May. "Political groups that are too divided, too large, will not suffice. Yet we must organize for combat in the streets and for propaganda activity among the workers, for organization of the amphitheatres no less than of demonstrations. The only adequate form of organization is the creation, *at the base, in unity, for action, of action committees*."[95] Action committees were units of agitation and contestation in the student milieu and outside, formed on an *ad hoc* basis and opposed to any hierarchical authority.[96] At the height of the university occupations, they were eclipsed by the general assemblies, which were institutions of mass democracy and permanent discussion. But the cumbersomeness of assembly proceedings made the action committees the fighting edge of the student movement.

The wave of strikes that swept French factories and enterprises from 14 May on was an expression of working-class self-organization. The initiative for strike action usually came from the base, and the militancy of the strikers, for example, those at Sud Aviation in Nantes or at Renault's plant in Cléon who sequestered their directors, owed little to trade union leaders. Indeed, as a number of accounts testify, the trade union delegate in France owed greater responsibility to his central than to the rank and file, with spontaneity the trait most discouraged in militants.[97] It was only poetic justice that May 1968 saw members of the Confédération générale des cadres, a moderate organization, "occupying their union headquarters like one occupies a factory, and treating their leaders like vulgar bosses."[98]

The May–June strikes brought spontaneity to the fore, with strike committees, base committees, and general assemblies the real decision-making bodies in various sectors.[99] One proof of this was the rejection by a mass meeting of the base at Renault of the so-called Grenelle Accords worked out by the unions, business, and government. Another was the reluctance with which many workers finally returned to their jobs under pressure from both government and union hierarchies in June. "We left discontented, we return discontented,"[100] was a typical comment.

[95]Leaflet signed "Les comités d'action" (8 May 1968) in Schnapp and Vidal Naquet, *Commune étudiante*, 212.
[96]"Organization is created in and by the movement itself ... The movement has no need for leaders or professional guides; it can lead itself ..." reads one definition, *Mouvement* (4 June 1968), *ibid.*, 496.
[97]See for example Daniel Mothé, *Militant chez Renault* (Paris, 1965), 102, 125; and Ernest Monpied, *Militant de base* (Clermont Ferrand, 1969), 115.
[98]A. Lefranc, *Le mouvement syndical – de la liberation aux événements de mai-juin 1968* (Paris, 1969), 251.
[99]See the article by Claude Durand, "Ouvriers et techniciens en mai 1968," in *Grèves Revendicatives ou Grèves Politiques?* (Paris, 1971), 44–53 for a discussion of the technical sectors in particular.
[100]Cited in Centre nationale d'information pour la productivité des entreprises, *Evénements de mai-juin.*

In at least one case, the strike went a step beyond occupation. At Nantes, the strike committee was in control of the city for a number of days, regulating the distribution of goods and gasoline, and well-nigh functioning as a parallel power.[101] What did not occur, however, were instances of workers actually running the factories they had occupied.

If some of the structures of both the student and working-class movements suggested alternatives to parliamentarism, extra-parliamentary theory went even further. One of the more interesting exercises was this diagram which originated in Strasburg:[102]

STUDENT CONTESTATION		WORKER CONTESTATION
↓		↓
The putting into question of university structures		The putting into question of industrial structures
	taking the form of	
university occupations		factory occupations
	leading to	
	SOCIAL CONTESTATION	
	↓	
	THE REGIME IN CRISIS	
RECUPERATION OF THE UNIVERSITY by reformist students and professors		RECUPERATION OF THE WORKERS by union bureaucrats
	↓	
	THE DECAY OF THE STUDENT AND WORKER MOVEMENTS	
	The cure:	
	UNIVERSITY AND WORKERS' COUNCILS	
	THE DIRECT EXERCISE OF POWER	

In numerous faculties and institutes, attempts were made to apply the concepts of self-organization, or *autogestion*, and co-determination, or *cogestion*, with varying degrees of success.[103] Again theory could state the desirable goal: "Direct democracy must be present at every level in the functioning of the university. Authority resides in plenary general assemblies. Their right to initiate is enshrined. The system of delegation is only an expedient. Representatives are revocable."[104] Practice would prove less tractable. Yet the concept of *autogestion* was popular, not only in the student movement, but in the ranks of the Confédération française démocratique du travail, France's second-largest trade union federation, and among a good number of technical workers and cadres. It continued to draw support in the post-May period.[105]

[101] *Cahiers de mai*, no 1 (Paris, June 1968). There is a less satisfactory account in Yannick Guin, *La commune de Nantes* (Paris, 1969), chap. 5.

[102] Pierre Feuerstein, *Printemps de révolte a Strasbourg* (Strasburg, 1968), 63–4.

[103] See for example the discussion "Autogestion et la 'Révolution de Mai,'" in *Autogestion* (June 1968), nos 5–6.

[104] [National Charter for French Universities] proposed at Nanterre in June 1968, reprinted in Schnapp and Vidal-Naquet, *Commune étudiante*, 738.

[105] Thus the CFDT, at its 1970 Congress, accepted a report calling for "the democratization of enterprises within a perspective of social transformation and *autogestion*." *Le Monde* (February 5 1970).

Finally, the concept of direct democracy also had applications where national institutions were concerned. "We must decentralize Paris," was one reflection of it.[106] Demands for the autonomy of Britanny, Occitany, and Corsica were another. And at another level, the Situationists could call for "a total decolonization of daily life," for the end to a society based on alienation.[107]

The originality of the May movement and of student extra-parliamentary theory, therefore, lay in its recognition of self-organization and direct democracy as revolutionary principles. "The idea of self-organization, neglected and disdained by the workers and French intelligentsia, reappeared, and with it that old, forgotten idea, 'the factories belong to the workers.' "[108]

V

Whither extra-parliamentary opposition? The student movements of the 1960s have disintegrated, and their enemies of yesterday, liberalism, social democracy, and communism ride high in the saddle. Direct action by students has not been enough to bring the system down, nor have structures of direct democracy broken the stranglehold of bourgeois institutions. On the contrary, there has been much co-option since 1968, much compromise and much retreat.

To be sure, some of the themes which the student movements helped to popularize have come home, but in mutilated form. Universities have been restructured in many western societies; yet they have hardly been democratized from top to bottom, let alone transformed into revolutionary institutions. Anti-imperialism has been toned down to a highly respectable form of bourgeois nationalism in countries like Canada. Participation is a catchword on the lips of men who unleash police forces in the middle of the night, while those who seek revolutionary forms of participation and self-organization are hunted men, as they have always been in bourgeois society.

The history of extra-parliamentarism, however, teaches us that it is a spectre that will not go away. As a theory, admittedly, it suffers from a number of serious weaknesses which I could summarize as follows in reference to student extra-parliamentarism:

1. an exaggerated reliance on spontaneity and on the unmitigated revolutionary consciousness of the masses; this is especially true of the anarchist component of extra-parliamentarism which has rarely been able to face up to the need for disciplined organization.
2. a serious under-estimation of the forces arrayed against it; or to use the phraseology of May 1968, "taking your desires to be reality" always.
3. an absence of precision as to the alternate model it proposes; one knows what one is against more clearly than what one is for.
4. a lack of clarity as to just who might constitute the revolutionary subject, aggravated by the inability of students to forge durable ties with workers and other producers.

[106] *Un Mois de Mai Orageux*, a comment by a student.
[107] See for example the leaflet, "Les étudiants et la révolution," in Schnapp and Vidal-Naquet, *Commune étudiante*, 560–1.
[108] Edgar Morin, "Une révolution sans visage," in E. Morin, C. Lefort, J-M Coudray, *La brèche* (Paris, 1968), 79.

These were some of the reasons student extra-parliamentarism failed to revolutionize western societies.

The other side of the coin must also be stated in reference to the theory generally: (1) extra-parliamentarism is a theory of politics that stresses direct collective action; (2) it represents a revolutionary form of organization, derived from the experience and struggles of the dominated in history, not of those who dominate; (3) it is a critique of the existing, even in socialist societies, hence a call to permanent revolution.

A curious theory, it may be, which savours revolutionary struggle, and might find even the state of direct democracy too routinized for its liking. Yet the utopian quality in extra-parliamentary theory, its Achilles heel where practice is concerned, is at the same time its redeeming feature. For this utopia is not some far-off Platonic ideal reserved for intellectuals or men of power. It is the practical concrete utopia of socialist principles, against which every popular movement can be measured. Unlike liberal, conservative, or social democratic theory, it is not afraid of the role of the masses in history, but is a barometer of their activity. That is why extra-parliamentarism has found its base in both Marxist and anarchist theory.

When mass movements erupt, so too do spontaneity, direct democracy, and militant action. When they decline, the latter decline with them. Extra-parliamentarism is not sufficient to make a revolution, but without extra-parliamentarism there can be no mass movement and no revolutionary subject. "... at moments of great upsurge and the exertion of all human capacities, revolutions are made by the class-consciousness, will, passion, and imagination of tens of millions, spurred on by a most acute struggle of classes."[109]

The concept of extra-parliamentarism, as I have tried to show, is a critique of the class-based, anti-participatory character of bourgeois political institutions. As such, it is an ongoing challenge to a capitalist system which can never satisfy certain basic political needs. At the same time, it represents a challenge to those forces of the left that have seemingly made their peace with capitalism today, social democracy and orthodox communism, and which have often quashed left opposition in their own ranks.

If this is its historical role, extra-parliamentarism is not something which will simply fade away. It will recur, even as examples of direct workers' power have recurred in this century in Russia, in Germany, Italy, France, or more recently Quebec in May 1972. Whether extra-parliamentarism as a revolutionary theory can lead to a permanent transformation in hierarchical and class relations of power and to a working alternative to parliamentarism is another question. Perhaps it is doomed to the labour of Sisyphus. Perhaps its hour is yet to come as part of a socialist revolution in Western societies. *Ich war, ich bin, ich werde sein!*[110]

[109]Lenin, "Left-Wing Communism – An Infantile Disorder," in *Collected Works* (London, 1969), 474–5.

[110]"I was, I am, I shall be!" Rosa Luxemburg, speaking of revolution, in the last essay written before her assassination, "Order Reigns in Berlin," in Rosa Luxemburg, *Politische Schriften*, vol 2, ed. Ossip Flechtheim (Frankfurt, 1966), 209.

Notes de recherche
Research Notes

The 1971 Survey of the Profession

W.H.N. HULL *Brock University*

In the winter of 1970–1, about 1000 questionnaires were sent to members of the Canadian Political Science Association and la Société canadienne de science politique and to known political scientists outside the two associations with a view to procuring information about political scientists and the state of research, publication, and funding in Canada.

The first fruits of the questionnaire appeared in the publication of the CPSA/Société *Directory/Annuaire*. The information obtained on the political scientist was presented as a paper to the CPSA annual meeting in St John's, Newfoundland, in June 1971 and that on research, publication, and funding to the 1972 meeting in Montreal. These papers, in slightly modified form, are published here as documents of record for the information of the profession.

About 64 per cent of those who received the questionnaires returned them. Of that number, about 125 said that they did not consider themselves to be political scientists and 41 returned duplicate forms. As a result, 480 names were included in the *Directory/Annuaire*. For the purposes of analysis, that group was further reduced by excluding from consideration all those not teaching in Canadian universities. Hence, in most of the tables which follow in the "Profile" section, the total number of questionnaires included is 397. According to CPSA records, there were 517 people teaching political science in Canadian universities in 1970. Therefore, from the academic respondents, the response rate was 77 per cent. By province, this percentage breaks down as follows: British Columbia, 71; Alberta, 86; Saskatchewan, 44; Manitoba, 59; Ontario, excluding Toronto, 81; Toronto, 89; Quebec, 72; New Brunswick, 67; Nova Scotia, 70; Prince Edward Island, 67; Newfoundland, 80; total 77.

In the research, publication, and funding section, it should be noted that a total of 319 people answered some, but not necessarily all, parts of questions 18, 19, and 20. Therefore in Tables XXV and XXVIII the figure of 319 has been used as the total figure with a "no response" category included as a balancing figure. In Table XXVI the raw figure of 192 respondents has been used and in Table XXVII the total of 314 appears, that being the number of successful applications submitted by the 192 successful applicants.

A profile of Canadian political scientists

What does the average Canadian political scientist look like? There is a fifty-fifty chance that he (93.2 per cent of us are male, Table III), was born in Canada (Table IV), a somewhat higher chance that he holds Canadian citizenship (62.5 per cent, Table V), and, again, a fifty-fifty chance that he is 35 or under (Table VI), and that he received his secondary education in Canada (Table VII). However, even if he is amongst the 57.2 per cent who received his first degree from a Canadian university (Table VIII), the chances are fairly great that his highest degree is non-Canadian (US, 45.1 per cent; Canadian, 27.4 per cent; British, 17.6 per cent; French, 4.3 per cent; Table IX). Yet again, the chances are just about fifty-fifty that he has received his highest degree within the last five years (Table X), that he is an assistant professor (Table XIII), that he has had five or fewer years of academic experience (Table XIV), and that he has produced at best one publication (Table XV). There is somewhat less than a fifty-fifty chance that he has competence in a language other than his mother tongue (Table XVI), and that two-thirds of the professional associations to which he belongs are Canadian (Table XVII). In terms of academic interest, our model man is most likely to be involved in some aspect of Canadian institutions, processes, and behaviour at the federal level (Tables XVIII and XIX), and is most likely to use libraries, archives, or interview schedules as his main research tools (Table XX).

If what has been outlined above is the profile of our "average" political scientist in Canada, what do his colleagues look like? Our imaginary man will discover that

Canadian Journal of Political Science/Revue canadienne de science politique, VI, no. 1 (March/mars 1973). Printed in Canada/Imprimé au Canada.

9.3 per cent of his colleagues were born in the United Kingdom, .5 per cent in France, 10.8 per cent in other European countries, and 18.4 per cent in the United States (all others, 12.1 per cent, Table IV); that 3.8 per cent of his colleagues retain their British citizenship, .5 per cent their French citizenship, 3 per cent citizenship of other European states, and 18.9 per cent their American citizenship (all others, 8 per cent, Table V). He may wonder at the fact that he has more American colleagues by citizenship than by birth and note the fact that only Americans seem to retain their citizenship whereas others seem more ready to take Canadian citizenship. Of course, in his usual fair-minded and objective way, our imaginary political scientist will note that well over half (58.8 per cent) of those not possessing Canadian citizenship or landed immigrant status have arrived in Canada since 1966 and therefore would not yet be eligible for Canadian citizenship (Table XII).

In terms of their education, our imaginary enquirer might note that 7.3 per cent of his colleagues received their secondary education in the United Kingdom, .8 per cent in France, 6.5 per cent in other European countries, and 21.1 per cent in the United States (all others, 10.4 per cent, Table VII). The corresponding percentages for first and highest degrees are: United Kingdom, 7.3 per cent and 17.6 per cent; France, 1.0 per cent and 4.3 per cent; other European countries, 4.0 per cent and 3.3 per cent; and the United States, 23.9 per cent and 45.1 per cent (Tables VIII and IX).

By this stage of the analysis, our typical political scientist, because he is typical, has begun to tire of statistics; so he eschews further study of his colleagues except for a brief look at their professional interests. While the largest single number shares his interest in Canadian problems (26.8 per cent), he notes that 23.3 per cent favour comparative politics, 10.9 per cent political theory, 9.1 per cent international law and organizations, about 8.5 per cent each public policy and public administration, with political stability and change attracting 6.6 per cent, and methodology of the discipline 5.7 per cent (Table XVIII).

Our imaginary man fortunately remembers the March-Jackson study of 1965–6[1] and makes some revealing comparisons. He notes, for instance, that the number of academic political scientists has increased from 184 to 517 and that, in the process, the number with Canadian secondary education has decreased from 60 per cent to 53.9 per cent. Nevertheless, the number of political scientists in Canadian universities with highest degrees from Canadian universities has increased from 16 per cent to 27.4 per cent at the same time that the number with highest degrees from United States universities has fallen from 51 per cent to 45.1 per cent and from overseas universities from 33 per cent to 27.5 per cent.

On the matter of professional interest, the classifications used in the two studies differ so that complete comparison is not possible. It is possible, however, to observe that the proportion of colleagues expressing an interest in comparative politics has dropped from 36.8 per cent to 23.3 per cent and in international relations from 15.7 per cent to 9.2 per cent, while the numbers interested in political theory have increased from 7.0 per cent to 10.9 per cent, and in public administration from 3.5 per cent to 8.6 per cent.

The art of gazing into the future is indeed difficult and it is impeded by the absence of comparable data collected through time. It is hoped that such data will become available on a regular basis in the near future.

This problem notwithstanding, there are other problems on which the survey has given light and which require some comment. The most fundamental problem is one of definition. What is a political scientist? Those in the *Directory/Annuaire* who identified themselves as political scientists include car salesmen, accounting clerks, and labour research staffs through to PHDs in the discipline. Yet, there seems to be an assumption that only those who teach in a university department can be considered political scientists. Is it not perhaps time to take a look at the profession and to see what constitutes a political scientist and to ask whether or not the Association and la Société might not usefully become professional accrediting bodies?

Another problem raised in the questionnaire is the name of the discipline itself. Obviously, many of our colleagues are upset by the term "political science." Might it not be wise to canvass possible alternative names?

Research, publications, and funding

This section is divided into three broad segments. The first deals with research in progress and significant publications; the second deals with the funding of research in Canada; and the third provides some tentative conclusions.

[1]R.R. March and R.J. Jackson, "Aspects of the State Of Political in Canada," *Midwest Journal of Political Science*, XI, 433–50.

I

Table XXI gives a breakdown by province and by professional interest of the responses to question 16 in which the subject areas of current research projects were sought. Foreign and cross-national studies (25 per cent) and Canadian studies (27.2 per cent) are by far the most popular research subjects. International affairs (11.1 per cent), public policy (10.7 per cent), and political theory (8.5 per cent) follow along in order of popularity. Public administration attracts 6.7 per cent while political stability and change attracts 6 per cent. Methodology (3.8 per cent) and the study of the discipline itself (1 per cent) attract the least amount of attention. The detailed breakdown of the categories of professional interest is given in Appendix I.

A similar set of patterns is reflected in Table XXII where the subject matter of significant research publications is analysed. Subjects dealing with foreign and cross-national topics (28.8 per cent) and Canadian matters (29.6 per cent) again top the lists. International affairs (10.4 per cent), public policy (9 per cent), and political theory (8.1 per cent) continue in their same order of popularity. Public administration shares in publishing popularity with political theory (8.1 per cent) while political stability and change claims only 3.3 per cent of the publications as opposed to 6 per cent of the research projects. This discrepancy may well be explained by the relative newness to the discipline of much of this subject matter and by the inevitable time lag between completion of research projects and publication of the findings. A similarly low rate of publication is evidenced in the areas of methodology (1.3 per cent) and the study of discipline (1.4 per cent).

A breakdown of the countries of publication of the 480 books, monographs, and articles marked as significant is given in Table XXIII. Regrettably a lack of information made it impossible to categorize 26 of the books reported. Table XXIV gives information indicating the journals in which the significant articles have been published.

II

Tables XXV through XXIX show the responses to questions 18, 19, and 20 concerning the attempts to procure research funds, the results, and the reactions thereto.

Table XXV provides a summary of the responses to questions 18*a*, *b*, and *d*, and 19. Two hundred and twenty-six respondents made applications for research funds in the period 1966–70; 122 of these two or more times. Sixteen reported abandoning their projects because of the failure to attract research funds. One hundred and fifty-one indicated they had not. Thirty-six indicated that they had not undertaken projects because they felt that the funds would not be available. Two hundred and thirty-two indicated more optimism.

The projects of those who reported abandoning their work because of unsuccessful grant applications fall into four subject groupings: foreign and cross-national (50 per cent), political stability, instability, and change (18.75 per cent), public policy (12.5 per cent), and Canadian studies (18.75 per cent). The total amount of money involved in these unsuccessful applications was about $67,500, of which $65,000 had been sought from the Canada Council and $2500 from university research sources.

Table XXVI gives the detailed breakdown, by province and by source, of funds requested and granted. Applicants received some 70.3 per cent of funds requested, those applying to the federal government being the most successful (100 per cent of funds requested granted), those applying to non-Canadian sources being the least successful (42.1 per cent of funds requested granted). The Canada Council met 72.4 per cent of requests while universities and private sources showed even greater generosity with 82.2 per cent and 79.7 per cent response rates. Provincial governments provided 45.6 per cent of the funds requested.

On the average, three-quarters of the funds reported came from the Canada Council, but in Alberta, Ontario (excluding Toronto), New Brunswick, and Nova Scotia, the grants received from the Council played a larger than average role. From other federal sources, Quebec was the only province to receive funds above the average whereas universities in British Columbia, Manitoba, Quebec, Nova Scotia, and Newfoundland received above-average support from university research funds. Again, scholars in Quebec were the only ones to receive above-average support from non-university provincial sources, while Ontario (excluding Toronto) and Quebec scholars alone showed above-average performance in gaining research funds from private sources. Non-Canadian funds appeared in above-average amount in Saskatchewan and Toronto.

Table XXVII provides a breakdown of the grants reported in terms of their amount by province. It is noted that about one-third of the grants were for less than $1000, that about two-thirds were for less than $4000, and that of the grants over $10,000 (34 in number) only 4 were made outside Ontario and Quebec. Again, Ontario appears to have attracted relatively more of these large grants than Quebec.

Lack of time from regular teaching duties appears from Table XXVIII to be the largest single detriment to further research in Canada (27.7 per cent) although the three areas dealing with the lack of research funds when lumped together do total 35.9 per cent of the deficiencies listed. (Others include inadequate number of funding agencies, 17.2 per cent; inadequate amount of funds granted, 10 per cent; and inability to obtain financing for more than one year, 8.7 per cent). The lack of adequately-trained research personnel ranks third amongst the deficiencies (18.5 per cent). The lack of research facilities, especially adequate library resources, drew the ire of 9.7 per cent of the respondents.

In Table XXIX an attempt has been made to summarize and to compare on a provincial basis the results of responses to the questions concerning research, publications, and funding. The results may be deceptive but will none the less reinforce existing prejudices and jealousies! Ontario and Quebec appear to be the only provinces to procure research funds in excess of their share of the total number of political scientists – and Ontario seems to be more successful at this than Quebec. In fairness, however, it should be noted that the two provinces together do indicate research in progress (67.2 per cent) and publications (72.3 per cent) both above the provinces' combined share of the estimated professional population (64.4 per cent).

Sixty-one respondents accepted the invitation offered in question 21 to make positive suggestions or complaints about the funding of research in political science. Analysis reveals that some of the complaints are of a general nature and that some, not surprisingly (in light of the large role that it plays in providing funds), are directed against the Canada Council. A compendium of complaints follows. Most were individual comments although a few did receive support from two or three respondents: (1) the absence of an independent funding agency specifically serving the social sciences; (2) the lack of information about existing funding agencies; (3) the tendency of funding agencies to place too much emphasis on the collection of data and not enough on the provision of assistance for analysis and writing; (4) the tendency to discriminate against individual researchers as opposed to the "entrepreneur" who can organize teams and machinery – "the professional applicant"; (5) the tendency to reject topics that are politically sensitive or without sufficient "scientific rigour"; (6) the excessive amount of money spent on voting studies; (7) the heavy teaching load of many academics; (8) the lack of funds for "innovative" research; (9) the fact that American foundations claim to support research in Canada, but do very little.

Those respondents who specifically identified the Canada Council raised the following points:

(1) the Council puts too much emphasis on behaviouralism and systems analysis to the detriment of institutionally-oriented projects; (2) its citizenship requirements are unfair; (3) its application procedures are too cumbersome and slow; (4) it is run by a few snobs about whom the CPSA should do something.

Finally, a complaint against the CPSA: it does too little to help the young researcher find his way through the labyrinth and establish himself.

The following positive suggestions were made, again by individuals or a small number of respondents. It will be noted that some contradict a number of the complaints registered.

1. More funds should be made available for: (*a*) better sabbatical leave support for research and periodic modernizing – including support for families; (*b*) increased exchange fellowship support; (*c*) more group projects and research oriented institutions; (*d*) improved library resources; (*e*) psychological research; (*f*) more in-depth studies of the discipline; (*g*) travel to international conferences; (*h*) regional meetings in Canada; (*i*) secretarial and publication costs; (*j*) software facilities; (*k*) summer stipends; (*l*) PHD students wishing to do field research.[2]
2. Greater efforts should be made to coordinate the research efforts of governments, private enterprise, and universities.
3. Provincial governments should let more contract research. Too much research money is kept "in house."
4. More funds should be made available through universities to reduce the heavy reliance on the Canada Council.
5. As application procedures may not appeal to all, foundations should approach established scholars.
6. Standards should be established so that applicants would compete against them, not against each other.

---

[2]One respondent suggested the following for PHD work: $10,000–$20,000 for each qualified PHD writer, $2,000–$5,000 for each PHD supervisor, 25 per cent off regular teaching duties for each supervisor.

III

Those more experienced in dealing with statistics will undoubtedly be able to draw a wide range of conclusions from the findings presented. Only a few modest comments are attempted now. Before any conclusions are drawn, however, the tentative nature of the findings must be emphasized. An honest effort has been made to reproduce and analyse as accurately as possible the responses to the questionnaire but one must always ask why certain questions were so poorly answered. For purposes of the *Directory/Annuaire*, the response rate from the academic community was about 77 per cent, based on the estimates totaling 517 people shown in Table VI.[3] Perhaps the glamour of being an anonymous statistic in a report on a research funding is less appealing than that of having one's name listed in a professional directory. The response to the research section of the questionnaire was not as great as to the *Directory/Annuaire* section – with the lowest response being from the 175 who took time to indicate whether or not they had abandoned any research projects for lack of funds. Some respondents indicated that they felt that the research section was an undue invasion of their privacy or that the details requested put an excessive demand on their time. Others seemed to consider the questions irrelevant while yet others seemed to tire part way through an admittedly long questionnaire. It was perhaps unwise to combine the *Directory/Annuaire* and research aspect in one survey. Regardless of the reasons for the sometimes low response rate (which even at its lowest was still 34 per cent – high for a mail questionnaire), this limiting factor must be kept in mind in making any statements based on the statistics contained herein.

It is clear that political scientists in Canada owe a debt of gratitude to the Canada Council. Whatever some may consider its shortcomings, it seems obvious that the state of research in the discipline would be immensely different if the Council's funds were not available. This having been said, however, it would seem wise to suggest that alternative sources of funds should be sought so that the dependence of the profession on the Council is not so great. Provincial sources should perhaps be tapped through, for example, an Ontario Social Science Council comparable to the Ontario Arts Council.

Few people seem to have been turned away from research projects because of a lack of research funds. Those reporting their experience seem to have had considerable success in getting funds – although more money could be used. The open question remains as to whether those who failed to fill in the research portion of the questionnaire did so because they did not want to report failure or because they were not research oriented.

From the responses available, it is obvious that many want more funds made available for sabbatical leaves or other means of buying off faculty time for research purposes and for means of retaining recent graduates as trained research assistants. Perhaps the post-doctoral fellowship common to the pure and natural sciences or the internship programme common in the medical sciences could provide useful models. Traditionally, the natural and pure sciences appear to have been in a better position to use for research purposes the talents of the graduate and post-doctoral student than have the social sciences.

It is difficult to draw conclusions about the subject matter of research undertaken by political scientists in Canada or to comment on the form or place of publication. More specific questions about this aspect of research and publication might be asked in future surveys. If comment on the output is difficult, comment on the sources available to produce that output are not. The need to improve Canadian university library resources was widely commented upon.

If the rumblings heard in the Wright Report in Ontario and from other quarters across the land are taken seriously, one cannot help but wonder whether or not we are going to be forced into an agonizing reappraisal of the role of research in our profession. There are certainly voices to be heard which suggest that teaching and the development of teaching skills should be emphasized, that research should be downgraded, and if not downgraded, at least made more project-oriented. One may hope that the excesses of the "publish or perish" tradition have passed, but may we now not be faced with the limitings of research funds to a restricted few in particular areas of interest while the rest of us concentrate on being teachers? What is the role of research in Canadian universities in the seventies? Why do we claim the need for more

[3]It is perhaps worth noting, by way of partial verification of the reliability of the returns, that our respondents show grants totalling $1,184,466 from the Canada Council, about 72 per cent of the grants shown in the Council's reports, 1965–66 to 1969–70, to political scientists in the form of post-doctoral fellowships, leave grants, research grants and Killam Awards ($1,648,000).

money and fewer teaching responsibilities when, for instance, a relatively low percentage of us apply to the Canada Council for the funds already available?

One final comment. This study presents an important challenge to the Canadian Political Science Association and la Société canadienne de science politique. As associations we may not be able to rid the Canada Council of its alleged "snobs," but we can be sure that our own house is in order on a number of difficult issues. Who in the profession is best qualified to conduct research? Should the conduct of research be limited largely to university-oriented people? What of the growing number of political scientists in community colleges and high schools? Is there a way in which the associations might act as a clearing house to assist the young graduate looking for research opportunities, the established researcher looking for qualified assistants, the corporation or governmental department looking for someone to do a job? The time may not be far away when the Martin Arrowsmiths of political science will have to choose between a research-oriented or a teaching-oriented career. What guidance, if any, can his professional associations give him?

Appendix

PROFESSIONAL INTERESTS

00 *Foreign and cross-national political institutions and behaviour*
01 Analysis of particular political systems or sub-systems
02 Decision-making processes
03 Elites and their oppositions
04 Mass participation and communications
05 Parties, mass movements, secondary associations
06 Political development and modernization
07 Politics of planning
08 Values, ideologies, belief systems, political culture
09 Other

10 *International law, organization, and politics*
11 International law
12 International organization and administration
13 International politics
19 Other

20, 30 *Methodology*
21 Computer techniques
22 Content analysis
23 Epistemology and philosophy of science
24 Experimental design
25 Field data collection
26 Measurement and index construction
27 Model building
28 Statistical analysis
31 Survey design and analysis
39 Other

40 *Political stability, instability, and change*
41 Cultural modification and diffusion
42 Personality and motivation
43 Political leadership and recruitment
44 Political socialization
45 Revolution and violence
46 Social and economic stratification
49 Other

50 *Political theory*
51 Empirical theory
52 Formal theory including game theory
53 History of theory
54 Normative theory
59 Other

60 *Public policy: formation and impact*
61 Domestic
62 Foreign
63 Military and national security
69 Other

70 *Public administration*
71 Bureaucracy
72 Comparative administration
73 Organization and management analysis
74 Organization theory and behaviour
75 Personnel administration
76 Planning, programming, budgeting
77 Politics and administration
78 Systems analysis
79 Other

80, 90 *Canadian institutions, processes, and behaviour*
81 Courts and judicial behaviour
82 Elections and electoral behaviour
83 Executives
84 Interest groups
85 Intergovernmental relations
86 Legislatures
87 Political and constitutional history
88 Political parties
91 Public law
92 Public opinion
93 Federal government
94 Provincial government
95 Municipal or regional government
97 Other
99 Political Science

TABLE I

ESTIMATED NUMBER OF POLITICAL SCIENTISTS IN CANADIAN UNIVERSITIES, 1970-71

	BC	Alta	Sask	Man	Ont(ex.T)*	Toronto	Que	NB	NS	PEI	Nfld	Canada	Total
	38	44	18	29	187	72	74	15	27	3	10	—	517

*Excluding Toronto

TABLE II

RESPONDENTS WHO CONSIDERED THEMSELVES POLITICAL SCIENTISTS

	BC	Alta	Sask	Man	Ont(ex.T)	Toronto	Que	NB	NS	PEI	Nfld	Outside Canada	Total
University affiliation													
University	27	38	8	17	151	64	53	10	19	2	8	11	408
Non-University	6	1	1	1	21	20	11	1	2	1	0	7	72
total	33	39	9	18	172	84	64	11	21	3	8	18	480
Sex													
Male	32	34	8	17	163	74	58	11	20	2	7	17	443
Female	1	5	1	1	9	10	6	0	1	1	1	1	37
total	33	39	9	18	172	84	64	11	21	3	8	18	480

TABLE III

POLITICAL SCIENTISTS IN CANADIAN UNIVERSITIES (by sex)

	BC	Alta	Sask	Man	Ont(ex.T)	Toronto	Que	NB	NS	PEI	Nfld	Outside Canada	Total
Male	26	34	7	17	144	57	47	10	19	2	7	—	370
Female	1	4	1	0	7	7	6	0	0	0	1	—	27
total	27	38	8	17	151	64	53	10	19	2	8	—	397

TABLE IV

POLITICAL SCIENTISTS IN CANADIAN UNIVERSITIES (by country of birth)

	BC	Alta	Sask	Man	Ont(ex.T)	Toronto	Que	NB	NS	PEI	Nfld	Total
Canada	12	11	6	8	81	35	32	5	8	1	3	202
United Kingdom	2	1	0	0	17	7	4	1	3	1	1	37
France	0	0	0	0	0	0	2	0	0	0	0	2
other European	3	6	0	0	18	6	8	1	0	0	1	43
United States	8	13	2	6	17	13	3	2	6	0	3	73
Asia	0	6	0	2	9	0	2	0	0	0	0	19
Africa	0	0	0	0	0	0	0	0	1	0	0	1
other	0	0	0	0	3	3	1	0	0	0	0	7
not stated	2	1	0	1	6	0	1	1	1	0	0	13
total	27	38	8	17	151	64	53	10	19	2	8	397

TABLE V

POLITICAL SCIENTISTS IN CANADIAN UNIVERSITIES (by citizenship)

	BC	Alta	Sask	Man	Ont(ex.T)	Toronto	Que	NB	NS	PEI	Nfld	Total
Canadian	14	16	6	8	100	46	38	5	11	1	3	248
landed immigrant	1	4	0	0	9	3	1	0	1	1	1	21
British	2	0	0	0	9	1	1	1	1	0	0	15
French	0	0	0	0	0	0	2	0	0	0	0	2
other European	2	3	0	0	3	1	3	0	0	0	0	12
United States	8	13	2	6	19	11	5	3	4	0	4	75
Asian	0	1	0	2	7	0	1	0	0	0	0	11
African	0	0	0	0	0	0	0	0	1	0	0	1
other	0	0	0	0	0	2	1	0	0	0	0	3
not stated	0	1	0	1	4	0	1	1	1	0	0	9
total	27	38	8	17	151	64	53	10	19	2	8	397

TABLE VI

POLITICAL SCIENTISTS IN CANADIAN UNIVERSITIES (by age)

	BC	Alta	Sask	Man	Ont(ex.T)	Toronto	Que	NB	NS	PEI	Nfld	Total
less than 25	0	0	0	0	2	0	0	0	0	0	0	2
26-30	5	5	1	5	34	12	8	4	8	1	5	88
31-35	10	13	3	4	43	16	16	1	4	0	0	110
36-40	4	9	1	4	20	13	13	2	1	1	2	70
41-45	3	3	1	3	18	4	4	0	0	0	0	36
46-50	1	3	1	0	14	7	5	0	2	0	1	34
51-55	3	2	1	1	5	5	2	1	2	0	0	22
56-60	0	2	0	0	6	3	1	0	1	0	0	13
61-65	0	0	0	0	1	2	1	0	0	0	0	4
over 65	1	1	0	0	5	1	0	1	1	0	0	10
not stated	0	0	0	0	3	1	3	1	0	0	0	8
total	27	38	8	17	151	64	53	10	19	2	8	397

TABLE VII

POLITICAL SCIENTISTS IN CANADIAN UNIVERSITIES (by secondary education)

	BC	Alta	Sask	Man	Ont(ex.T)	Toronto	Que	NB	NS	PEI	Nfld	Total
Canada	12	11	6	8	84	39	34	5	11	1	3	214
United Kingdom	3	1	0	1	14	5	3	0	1	1	0	29
France	0	0	0	0	2	0	1	0	0	0	0	3
other European	2	5	0	0	11	2	4	2	0	0	0	26
United States	10	15	2	6	21	13	4	2	6	0	5	84
Asia	0	3	0	2	9	0	3	0	0	0	0	17
Africa	0	0	0	0	0	1	1	0	1	0	0	3
other	0	0	0	0	2	3	1	0	0	0	0	6
not stated	0	3	0	0	8	1	2	1	0	0	0	15
total	27	38	8	17	151	64	53	10	19	2	8	397

TABLE VIII

POLITICAL SCIENTISTS IN CANADIAN UNIVERSITIES (by first degree)

	BC	Alta	Sask	Man	Ont(ex.T)	Toronto	Que	NB	NS	PEI	Nfld	Total
Canada	11	10	6	9	94	40	36	5	12	1	3	227
United Kingdom	4	1	0	0	14	5	2	1	1	1	0	29
France	0	0	0	0	2	0	2	0	0	0	0	4
other European	0	4	0	0	5	0	6	1	0	0	0	16
United States	11	18	2	6	25	17	4	2	5	0	5	95
Asia	0	5	0	2	9	0	2	0	0	0	0	18
Africa	0	0	0	0	0	1	0	0	1	0	0	2
other	0	0	0	0	2	1	1	0	0	0	0	4
not stated	1	0	0	0	0	0	0	1	0	0	0	2
total	27	38	8	17	151	64	53	10	19	2	8	397

TABLE IX

POLITICAL SCIENTISTS IN CANADIAN UNIVERSITIES (by highest degree)

	BC	Alta	Sask	Man	Ont(ex.T)	Toronto	Que	NB	NS	PEI	Nfld	Total
Canada	2	9	2	7	40	14	18	3	9	2	3	109
United Kingdom	3	2	1	1	41	13	6	1	2	0	0	70
France	0	0	0	0	7	2	7	1	0	0	0	17
other European	0	4	0	1	2	0	5	1	0	0	0	13
United States	22	23	5	8	55	35	16	3	7	0	5	179
Asia	0	0	0	0	2	0	0	0	0	0	0	2
Africa	0	0	0	0	0	0	0	0	1	0	0	1
other	0	0	0	0	1	0	1	0	0	0	0	2
not stated	0	0	0	0	3	0	0	1	0	0	0	4
total	27	38	8	17	151	64	53	10	19	2	8	397

TABLE X

POLITICAL SCIENTISTS IN CANADIAN UNIVERSITIES (by year highest degree obtained)

	BC	Alta	Sask	Man	Ont(ex.T)	Toronto	Que	NB	NS	PEI	Nfld	Total
1967-71	15	17	4	7	69	29	27	5	10	0	7	190
1962-66	5	7	1	3	27	13	7	1	0	0	0	64
1957-61	2	5	2	0	13	3	4	0	0	0	0	29
1952-56	1	2	0	0	10	4	3	0	5	0	0	25
1947-51	1	2	1	1	4	2	2	0	0	0	1	14
before 1947	1	2	0	0	7	6	2	2	0	0	0	20
expected after '71	2	3	0	6	17	4	8	1	4	0	0	45
not stated	0	0	0	0	4	3	0	1	0	2	0	10
total	27	38	8	17	151	64	53	10	19	2	8	397

TABLE XI

POLITICAL SCIENTISTS IN CANADIAN UNIVERSITIES (by province of birth)

	BC	Alta	Sask	Man	Ont(ex.T)	Toronto	Que	NB	NS	PEI	Nfld	Total
BC	3	1	0	1	7	5	0	1	1	0	0	19
Alta	1	3	0	0	4	3	0	0	0	0	0	11
Sask	1	2	1	0	5	4	0	2	0	0	0	15
Man	1	1	1	3	10	2	0	0	0	0	0	18
Ont	4	3	3	3	29	13	5	0	3	1	1	65
Quebec	2	0	0	0	17	3	25	0	1	0	0	48
NB	0	0	0	0	1	1	2	1	0	0	1	6
NS	0	0	1	1	4	0	0	1	3	0	0	10
PEI	0	1	0	0	0	0	0	0	0	0	0	1
Nfld	0	0	0	0	2	0	0	0	0	0	1	3
not stated	0	0	0	0	2	4	0	0	0	0	0	6
total	12	11	6	8	81	35	32	5	8	1	3	202

TABLE XII

POLITICAL SCIENTISTS IN CANADIAN UNIVERSITIES (by year of entry for those not Canadian citizens or holding landed immigrant status)

	BC	Alta	Sask	Man	Ont(ex.T)	Toronto	Que	NB	NS	PEI	Nfld	Total
1966-70	9	12	2	5	35	10	10	1	3	0	3	90
1961-65	1	5	0	1	8	4	3	2	2	0	0	26
1956-60	1	0	0	0	4	0	0	0	0	0	0	5
1951-55	0	0	0	0	6	1	0	0	0	0	0	7
before 1951	0	0	0	0	8	0	0	0	0	0	0	8
not stated	2	1	0	3	8	1	0	1	0	0	1	17
total	13	18	2	9	69	16	13	4	5	0	4	153

TABLE XIII

POLITICAL SCIENTISTS IN CANADIAN UNIVERSITIES (by rank)

	BC	Alta	Sask	Man	Ont(ex.T)	Toronto	Que	NB	NS	PEI	Nfld	Total
prof.	5	8	1	1	39	19	15	1	6	0	1	96
assoc. prof.	6	11	4	4	29	13	14	2	2	0	0	85
asst. prof.	14	17	3	7	61	21	21	6	9	2	6	167
lecturer	2	2	0	5	18	11	3	0	2	0	1	44
not stated	0	0	0	0	4	0	0	1	0	0	0	5
total	27	38	8	17	151	64	53	10	19	2	8	397

TABLE XIV

POLITICAL SCIENTISTS IN CANADIAN UNIVERSITIES (by years of academic experience)

	BC	Alta	Sask	Man	Ont(ex.T)	Toronto	Que	NB	NS	PEI	Nfld	Total
1-5	13	23	2	9	68	32	22	4	12	1	6	192
6-10	7	4	3	7	33	13	17	4	1	1	2	92
11-15	1	2	1	0	19	2	4	0	1	0	0	30
16-20	3	6	0	0	12	4	5	0	3	0	0	33
21-25	1	2	1	1	9	8	2	0	0	0	0	24
over 25	1	1	1	0	6	4	3	1	2	0	0	19
not stated	1	0	0	0	4	1	0	1	0	0	0	7
total	27	38	8	17	151	64	53	10	19	2	8	397

TABLE XV

POLITICAL SCIENTISTS IN CANADIAN UNIVERSITIES (by number of publications)

	BC	Alta	Sask	Man	Ont(ex.T)	Toronto	Que	NB	NS	PEI	Nfld	Total
0	13	13	3	10	45	19	23	4	7	1	3	141
1	1	7	0	1	21	10	4	3	2	0	2	51
2	2	4	2	3	20	6	2	1	4	0	1	45
3	5	3	0	0	7	6	10	1	1	0	0	33
4	5	6	1	2	13	5	3	0	1	0	0	36
5	1	1	1	0	5	3	3	0	1	0	0	15
more than 5	0	4	1	1	40	15	8	1	3	1	2	76
total	27	38	8	17	151	64	53	10	19	2	8	397

TABLE XVI

RESPONDENTS RESIDENT IN CANADA (by competence in languages other than mother tongue)

	BC	Alta	Sask	Man	Ont(ex.T)	Toronto	Que	NB	NS	PEI	Nfld	Total
1 language other than mother tongue	11	10	5	8	66	31	30	4	16	0	4	185
2 languages other than mother tongue	9	11	1	7	22	11	19	2	1	0	2	85
3 languages other than mother tongue	2	4	0	1	19	5	1	0	0	0	0	32
4 languages other than mother tongue	0	2	1	0	5	5	0	0	2	0	0	15
more than 4 languages other than mother tongue	2	2	0	0	6	0	0	1	0	0	0	11
short form*	7	10	2	1	41	25	11	2	2	3	0	104
not stated	2	0	0	1	13	7	3	2	0	0	2	30
total	33	39	9	18	172	84	64	11	21	3	8	462
OOL*	21	26	7	14	108	50	48	6	17	0	3	300

*SF short form—in which only information to be included in *Directory/Annuaire* was provided.
*Competence in other official language

TABLE XVII

RESPONDENTS RESIDENT IN CANADA (by numbers of professional associations to which they belong)

	BC	Alta	Sask	Man	Ont(ex.T)	Toronto	Que	NB	NS	PEI	Nfld	Total
Canadian	44	48	10	29	258	97	119	21	33	SF*	14	673
British	5	4	0	1	17	5	2	0	1	SF	0	35
French	0	0	0	0	3	3	5	2	0	SF	0	13
American	29	22	4	12	89	48	24	4	11	SF	9	252
other	9	11	1	4	41	12	7	0	1	SF	1	87
total	87	85	15	46	408	165	157	27	46	0	24	1060
CPSA	20	26	6	11	107	37	22	6	16	0	6	257
SCSP	0	0	0	0	0	0	5	0	0	0	0	5
both	2	0	0	1	19	5	19	3	0	0	0	49
neither	4	3	1	5	5	17	7	0	3	0	0	47
short form	7	10	2	1	41	25	11	2	2	3	0	104
total	33	39	9	18	172	84	64	11	21	0	8	462

TABLE XVIII

RESPONDENTS TO SURVEY (by professional interest)

	BC	Alta	Sask	Man	Ont(ex.T)	Toronto	Que	NB	NS	PEI	Nfld	Outside Canada	Total
00-09	25	25	3	8	108	49	47	6	14	2	6	16	309
10-19	12	10	5	7	47	11	22	0	3	0	2	2	121
20-39	5	3	0	3	34	8	11	1	4	0	3	3	75
40-49	8	15	3	2	30	15	3	2	3	0	0	6	87
50-59	8	19	5	4	48	26	14	4	7	2	4	4	145
60-69	10	4	1	4	41	29	13	0	8	0	2	1	113
70-79	9	10	1	4	42	15	19	2	6	0	1	6	115
80-97	18	24	9	17	143	60	39	10	18	3	6	9	356
99	0	1	0	0	2	0	2	0	0	1	0	0	6
total	95	111	27	49	495	213	170	25	63	8	24	47	1327

00-09 foreign and cross national political institutions and behaviour
10-19 international law, organization, and politics
20-39 methodology
40-49 political stability, instability, and change
50-59 political theory
60-69 public policy
70-79 public administration
80-97 canadian institutions, processes, and behaviour
99 other

see Appendix for more detailed codes.

TABLE XIX

POLITICAL SCIENTISTS IN CANADIAN UNIVERSITIES

	BC	Alta	Sask	Man	Ont(ex.T)	Toronto	Que	NB	NS	PEI	Nfld	Total
By "system" of professional interest												
authoritarian												
totalitarian	5	3	0	2	14	7	6	1	0	0	0	38
democratic	6	9	3	9	54	18	26	4	3	0	3	135
developing	5	8	1	4	27	11	13	0	4	0	2	75
federal	4	3	3	2	30	10	17	1	1	0	1	72
other	0	1	1	1	4	1	1	0	0	0	0	9
short form	5	10	1	1	34	15	7	2	2	3	0	80
not stated	8	10	2	6	37	12	7	3	10	0	3	98
total	33	44	11	25	200	74	77	11	20	3	9	507
By "level" of professional interest												
international	6	6	2	5	32	6	17	0	5	0	2	81
federal or national	8	16	3	11	63	20	28	4	9	0	2	164
provincial	1	9	2	3	23	8	17	2	3	0	3	71
regional	2	5	0	1	11	5	3	0	0	0	1	28
metro	2	3	0	0	7	2	3	0	0	0	1	18
municipal	2	2	0	0	9	3	3	1	0	0	1	21
other	0	0	0	0	1	1	0	1	0	0	1	4
short form	5	10	1	1	34	15	7	2	2	3	0	80
not stated	8	8	3	5	36	19	5	3	6	0	2	95
total	34	59	11	26	216	79	83	13	25	3	13	562

TABLE XIX (*Continued*)

POLITICAL SCIENTISTS IN CANADIAN UNIVERSITIES

	BC	Alta	Sask	Man	Ont(ex.T)	Toronto	Que	NB	NS	PEI	Nfld	Total
By "area" of professional interest												
N.America	0	2	0	4	5	5	8	1	3	0	0	28
Canada	6	5	4	5	28	5	8	4	5	0	1	71
prov. or reg.	0	0	0	0	3	2	13	0	1	0	2	21
USA	4	0	1	1	12	4	3	0	0	0	0	25
Caribbean	0	0	0	0	0	2	1	0	1	0	0	4
Lat. America	0	1	0	1	4	0	4	0	1	0	1	12
West Europe	2	2	0	1	19	7	7	0	2	0	0	40
Cent. & East Europe	3	3	1	0	9	8	3	1	0	0	0	28
UK	1	0	0	0	0	2	2	1	0	0	0	6
France	0	0	0	0	0	0	3	0	0	0	0	3
Medit'an	0	0	0	0	0	0	2	0	0	0	0	2
Asia	0	1	0	0	2	0	2	0	0	0	0	5
West. Asia	0	0	0	0	2	0	2	0	1	0	0	5
S. Asia	1	1	0	0	3	1	3	0	1	0	0	10
SE Asia	1	2	0	0	5	0	2	0	0	0	0	10
East Asia	2	1	0	1	2	0	2	0	1	0	0	9
China	2	1	0	0	3	1	1	0	1	0	0	9
Australasia	1	0	0	0	0	2	1	0	0	0	0	4
Africa	1	1	0	1	3	6	2	0	1	0	0	15
Sub-S. Africa	1	1	0	0	0	0	1	0	1	0	0	4
third world	1	0	1	1	0	1	3	0	1	0	0	8
west world	0	0	1	0	3	0	1	0	0	0	0	5
Commonw'th	0	0	0	0	2	1	1	0	0	0	0	4
Eng. speak. dom.	0	0	0	0	1	0	1	0	0	0	0	2
all	0	0	0	0	0	0	1	0	0	0	0	1
short form	5	10	1	1	34	15	7	2	2	3	0	80
not stated	6	13	2	4	50	20	13	2	6	0	4	120
total	37	44	11	20	190	82	97	11	28	3	8	531
N=	27	38	8	17	151	64	53	10	19	2	8	397

TABLE XX

POLITICAL SCIENTISTS IN CANADIAN UNIVERSITIES (by main research techniques employed)

	BC	Alta	Sask	Man	Ont(ex.T)	Toronto	Que	NB	NS	PEI	Nfld	Total
mail questionnaire	3	4	3	3	26	5	9	2	2	0	1	58
interview schedule	9	14	6	7	73	23	26	3	5	0	5	171
telephone interviews	0	3	2	1	13	2	7	1	1	0	1	31
part-observ. techniques	9	6	2	2	40	10	17	2	3	0	1	92
libraries or archives	21	23	7	12	94	36	37	7	13	0	8	258
sample survey	4	7	1	2	31	11	8	1	1	0	2	68
punch cards and sorter	6	6	0	2	24	6	7	0	0	0	0	51
computer	8	7	1	1	37	12	12	0	1	0	3	82
mira-code	0	0	0	0	1	0	1	0	0	0	0	2
content analysis	3	3	2	1	31	13	15	1	1	0	1	71
statistics	10	8	2	4	44	11	9	1	2	0	3	94
other	2	2	0	1	14	4	0	0	3	0	0	26
total	75	83	26	36	428	133	148	18	32	SF	25	1004
N=	27	38	8	17	151	64	53	10	19	2	8	397

TABLE XXI

RESEARCH PROJECTS UNDERWAY (by area of professional interest)

	BC	Alta	Sask	Man	Ont(ex.T)	Toronto	Que	NB	NS	PEI	Nfld	Total	Percentage of total
Foreign and cross-national political institutions and behaviour													
01.*	0	1	0	1	17	12	4	1	0	0	1	37	
02.	0	4	0	0	7	2	1	0	1	0	0	15	
03.	1	2	0	0	2	0	0	0	0	0	0	5	
04.	1	0	0	0	3	0	2	0	0	0	0	6	
05.	4	3	0	0	9	4	3	0	0	0	0	23	
06.	4	4	0	0	6	0	1	0	2	0	0	17	
07.	1	0	0	1	3	1	1	0	0	0	0	7	
08.	4	1	0	0	9	5	1	0	0	0	0	20	
09.	0	1	0	0	2	2	3	0	0	0	0	8	
total	15	16	0	2	58	26	16	1	3	0	1	138	25.0
International law, organization, and politics													
11.	0	3	1	0	3	1	0	0	0	0	1	9	
12.	3	0	0	0	4	0	3	0	0	0	0	10	
13.	3	3	0	2	17	1	8	0	1	0	1	36	
19.	0	0	0	0	2	0	3	1	0	0	0	6	
total	6	6	1	2	26	2	14	1	1	0	2	61	11.1
Methodology													
21.	2	0	0	0	0	0	0	0	0	0	0	2	
22.	0	0	0	0	0	0	1	0	0	0	0	1	
23.	0	1	0	1	1	0	1	0	2	0	0	6	
24.	0	0	0	0	0	1	0	0	0	0	0	1	
25.	0	0	1	0	0	0	0	0	0	0	0	1	
26.	0	0	0	0	0	0	0	0	0	0	0	0	
27.	0	0	0	0	2	0	1	0	0	0	0	3	
28.	0	0	0	0	0	0	0	0	0	0	2	2	
31.	0	0	0	1	0	1	0	0	0	0	0	2	
39.	0	0	0	0	2	0	1	0	0	0	0	3	
total	2	1	1	2	5	2	4	0	2	0	2	21	3.8

TABLE XXI (*continued*)

RESEARCH PROJECTS UNDER WAY (by area of professional interest)

	BC	Alta	Sask	Man	Ont(ex.T)	Toronto	Que	NB	NS	PEI	Nfld	Total	Percentage of total
Political stability, instability, and change													
41.	0	0	0	0	1	1	1	0	0	0	0	3	
42.	0	1	0	0	2	0	0	0	0	0	0	3	
43.	2	0	1	0	1	0	0	0	0	0	1	5	
44.	0	0	0	0	3	4	0	0	1	0	0	8	
45.	1	3	0	0	4	0	0	0	2	0	0	10	
46.	0	0	1	0	1	0	0	0	0	0	0	2	
49.	0	0	0	0	1	1	0	0	0	0	0	2	
total	3	4	2	0	13	6	1	0	3	0	1	33	6.0
Political theory													
51.	0	0	0	0	5	1	3	0	0	0	1	10	
52.	1	0	0	0	0	0	2	0	0	0	0	3	
53.	0	2	0	0	5	6	1	1	2	0	0	17	
54.	0	4	1	1	2	4	0	1	1	0	0	14	
59.	0	1	0	0	0	0	1	0	1	0	0	3	
total	1	7	1	1	12	11	7	2	4	0	1	47	8.5
Public policy: formation and impact													
60.	0	1	0	0	0	1	0	0	0	0	0	2	
61.	1	0	1	1	8	4	0	0	1	0	0	16	
62.	2	0	0	3	11	6	3	0	5	0	0	30	
63.	0	0	0	3	3	1	2	0	0	0	0	9	
69.	0	1	0	0	1	0	0	0	0	0	0	2	
total	3	2	1	7	23	12	5	0	6	0	0	59	10.7

TABLE XXI (*continued*)

RESEARCH PROJECTS UNDER WAY (by area of professional interest)

	BC	Alta	Sask	Man	Ont(ex.T)	Toronto	Que	NB	NS	PEI	Nfld	Total	Percentage of total
Public administration													
70.	0	0	0	0	0	0	1	0	0	0	0	1	
71.	0	0	0	0	3	1	0	1	0	0	0	5	
72.	0	0	0	0	1	0	0	0	0	0	0	1	
73.	0	0	0	1	1	0	3	0	0	0	0	5	
74.	1	0	0	0	3	1	0	0	0	0	0	5	
75.	0	0	0	0	1	0	0	0	0	0	0	1	
76.	0	0	0	1	2	0	2	0	0	0	0	5	
77.	0	1	0	0	6	1	2	0	0	0	1	11	
78.	0	0	0	0	0	0	0	0	0	0	0	0	
79.	0	1	0	0	1	0	0	0	1	0	0	3	
total	1	2	0	2	18	3	8	1	1	0	1	37	6.7
Canadian institutions, processes, and behaviour													
80.	0	0	0	0	0	0	2	0	0	0	0	2	
81.	0	0	0	0	2	0	0	0	0	0	1	3	
82.	1	2	0	0	13	2	2	1	0	0	0	21	
83.	0	0	0	0	2	0	0	0	0	0	0	2	
84.	0	0	1	3	2	1	0	0	0	0	1	8	
85.	0	2	0	1	5	0	0	0	1	0	0	9	
86.	0	1	0	2	2	0	1	0	1	0	1	8	
87.	0	0	0	1	4	0	0	0	1	0	0	6	
88.	0	2	1	0	9	1	2	0	0	0	1	16	
91.	1	0	1	0	2	0	0	1	0	0	0	5	
92.	0	0	0	1	5	1	3	0	0	0	0	10	
93.	0	0	0	1	4	0	1	0	0	0	0	6	
94.	4	3	1	0	3	3	8	0	2	0	0	24	
95.	2	3	0	2	7	3	1	1	0	0	0	19	
97.	0	3	1	0	6	0	1	0	0	0	0	11	
total	8	16	5	11	66	11	21	3	5	0	4	150	27.2
99.	0	2	0	2	1	0	0	0	0	0	1	6	
total	39	56	11	29	222	73	76	8	25	0	13	552	1.0
No. reporting	19	26	6	16	118	43	40	6	17	0	8	299	

*See Appendix I.

TABLE XXII

RESEARCH PUBLICATIONS (by area of professional interest)*

	BC	Alta	Sask	Man	Ont(ex.T)	Toronto	Que	NB	NS	PEI	Nfld	Total	Percentage of total
Foreign and cross-national political institutions and behaviour													
01.	4	4	0	3	18	18	5	2	1	0	1	56	
02.	0	2	1	0	4	1	1	0	1	0	0	10	
03.	1	1	0	0	3	1	1	0	0	0	0	7	
04.	0	0	0	0	5	0	0	0	0	0	0	5	
05.	4	2	0	0	5	3	0	0	0	0	0	14	
06.	2	3	0	0	5	3	1	0	1	0	0	15	
07.	1	0	0	0	1	0	2	0	0	0	0	4	
08.	3	0	0	0	6	3	2	0	1	0	0	15	
09.	0	0	0	0	6	4	2	0	0	0	0	12	
total	15	12	1	3	53	33	14	2	4	0	1	138	28.8
International law, organization, and politics													
10.	0	1	0	0	0	0	1	0	0	0	0	2	
11.	1	2	0	0	3	0	0	0	0	0	0	6	
12.	3	1	0	0	7	2	1	0	0	0	1	15	
13.	3	0	0	1	10	3	9	0	0	0	0	26	
19.	0	0	0	0	0	0	0	1	0	0	0	1	
total	7	4	0	1	20	5	11	1	0	0	1	50	10.4
Methodology													
21.	0	0	0	0	0	0	0	0	0	0	0	0	
22.	0	0	0	0	0	0	0	0	0	0	0	0	
23.	0	0	0	0	0	0	0	0	0	0	0	0	
24.	0	0	0	0	0	0	0	0	0	0	0	0	
25.	0	0	0	0	0	0	0	0	0	0	0	0	
26.	0	0	0	0	0	0	0	0	0	0	0	0	
27.	0	0	0	0	0	1	0	0	0	0	0	1	
28.	0	0	0	0	1	0	0	0	0	0	0	1	
31.	0	0	0	1	0	0	0	0	0	0	0	1	
39.	0	0	0	0	2	0	0	0	1	0	0	3	
total	0	0	0	1	3	1	0	0	1	0	0	6	1.3

TABLE XXII *(continued)*

RESEARCH PUBLICATIONS (by area of professional interest)*

	BC	Alta	Sask	Man	Ont(ex.T)	Toronto	Que	NB	NS	PEI	Nfld	Total	Percentage of total
Political stability, instability, and change													
40.	0	0	0	0	0	0	1	0	0	0	0	1	
41.	0	0	0	0	1	0	0	0	0	0	0	1	
42.	0	0	0	0	0	0	0	0	0	0	0	0	
43.	0	1	0	0	0	0	1	0	0	0	2	4	
44.	0	0	0	0	1	1	1	0	0	0	0	3	
45.	1	1	0	0	0	0	0	0	0	0	0	2	
46.	0	0	0	0	1	0	0	0	0	0	0	1	
49.	0	0	0	0	4	0	0	0	0	0	0	4	
total	1	2	0	0	7	1	3	0	0	0	2	16	3.3
Political theory													
50.	0	1	0	0	1	2	0	0	0	0	0	4	
51.	0	0	0	0	2	0	1	0	0	0	0	3	
52.	0	0	0	0	0	0	2	0	0	0	0	2	
53.	0	4	0	0	7	5	0	1	1	0	0	18	
54.	0	3	0	0	4	0	0	1	1	0	1	10	
59.	0	0	0	0	1	0	0	0	0	1	0	2	
total	0	8	0	0	15	7	3	2	2	1	1	39	8.1
Public policy: formation and impact													
60.	0	0	0	0	0	1	0	0	1	0	0	2	
61.	0	0	0	0	5	6	1	0	1	0	1	14	
62.	2	2	0	1	6	5	1	0	2	0	0	19	
63.	0	0	0	0	0	1	3	0	1	0	0	5	
69.	0	0	0	0	2	1	0	0	0	0	0	3	
total	2	2	0	1	13	14	5	0	5	0	1	43	9.0

TABLE XXII (*continued*)

RESEARCH PUBLICATIONS (by area of professional interest)*

	BC	Alta	Sask	Man	Ont(ex.T)	Toronto	Que	NB	NS	PEI	Nfld	Total	Percentage of total
Public administration													
70.	0	0	0	0	2	1	1	0	0	0	0	4	
71.	0	0	0	0	3	4	0	0	0	0	0	7	
72.	0	1	0	0	0	0	0	0	0	0	0	1	
73.	0	0	0	0	0	0	1	0	0	0	0	1	
74.	1	0	0	0	2	0	0	0	0	0	0	3	
75.	0	0	0	0	2	0	0	0	0	0	0	2	
76.	1	0	1	0	0	2	1	0	1	0	0	6	
77.	0	0	1	1	4	3	0	0	0	0	0	9	
78.	0	0	0	0	0	0	1	0	0	0	0	1	
79.	0	1	0	0	0	2	1	0	1	0	0	5	
total	2	2	2	1	13	12	5	0	2	0	0	39	8.1
Canadian institutions, processes, and behaviour													
81.	1	1	0	0	2	1	0	0	0	0	0	5	
82.	1	1	1	0	10	0	2	0	1	0	0	16	
83.	0	0	0	0	4	0	0	0	0	0	0	4	
84.	0	0	0	1	5	2	0	0	0	0	0	8	
85.	0	1	0	0	4	3	0	0	1	0	0	9	
86.	0	0	1	0	3	4	1	0	0	0	0	9	
87.	0	0	0	1	3	1	0	0	0	0	0	5	
88.	0	1	1	0	9	1	3	0	0	0	0	15	
91.	1	2	2	0	1	0	0	0	1	0	0	7	
92.	0	0	0	0	3	0	0	0	0	0	0	3	
93.	0	0	2	0	7	0	3	0	1	0	0	13	
94.	0	4	0	2	8	2	6	0	4	1	1	28	
95.	1	2	0	0	7	4	3	0	0	0	0	17	
97.	0	1	0	0	1	0	1	0	0	0	0	3	
total	4	13	7	4	67	18	19	0	8	1	1	142	29.6
99.	0	1	0	1	4	0	1	0	0	0	0	7	1.4
total	31	44	10	12	195	91	61	5	22	2	7	480	
No. reporting	16	25	5	8	108	51	34	5	12	1	5	270	

*up to two publications selected by each respondent as his most significant.

SUMMARY OF RESPONSES TO QUESTIONS 16 AND 17

Area of professional interest	*Research* (percentage)	*Publications* (percentage)
foreign & cross national	25.0	28.8
international	11.1	10.4
methodology	3.8	1.3
political stability and change	6.0	3.3
political theory	8.5	8.1
public policy	10.7	9.0
public administration	6.7	8.1
canadian	27.2	29.6
political science	1.0	1.4
total	100.0	100.0

TABLE XXIII

COUNTRY OF PUBLICATION OF "SIGNIFICANT" PUBLICATIONS REPORTED

	Books and Monographs		Articles	
Country	Number	Percentage	Number	Percentage
Canada	120	48.4	118	51.0
United States	52	21.0	61	26.2
United Kingdom	30	12.1	30	12.9
France	6	2.4	5	2.2
other	14	5.6	18	7.7
not stated	26	10.5	—	—
total	248	100.0	232	100.0

TABLE XXIV

JOURNALS IN WHICH "SIGNIFICANT" ARTICLES HAVE BEEN PUBLISHED

Canadian	
Canadian Forum	3
Canadian Journal of African Studies	2
Canadian Journal of Economics and Political Science	12
Canadian Journal of Political Science	24
Canadian Public Administration	16
Cahiers de l'Université du Québec (number unspecified)	—
Dalhousie Revue	2
International Journal	5
Journal of Canadian Studies	5
Osgoode Hall Law Journal	2
Pacific Affairs	3
Queen's Quarterly	3
University of Toronto Law Journal	4
University of Toronto Quarterly	3
34 other titles with one article	34
	118
British	
Ethics	5
Journal of Commonwealth Political Studies	3
Parliamentary Affairs	5
World Today	4
13 other titles with one article	13
	30
American	
American Political Science Review	5
Asian Survey	4
Comparative Political Studies	3
International Organization	3
International Studies Quarterly	2
Journal of Politics	3
Middle East Journal	2
Midwest Journal of Political Science	3
Western Political Quarterly	4
32 other titles with one article	32
	61
French	
5 titles with one article	5
Other	
Australia	3
India	3
Italy	2
10 other countries with one article	10
	18

TABLE XXV

RESPONSES TO QUESTIONS 18 AND 19

	18(A) Have you applied to any organization for research funds during the last five years?			18(B) Number of times applications made:					
	Yes	No	No response	One	Two	Three	Four	Five or more	Total
BC	19	3	—	8	3	5	2	1	19
Alta	20	8	—	12	4	1	—	3	20
Sask	4	3	—	1	—	—	2	1	4
Man	12	3	1	8	2	1	1	—	12
Ont(ex.T)	87	22	9	40	18	16	7	6	87
Tor	32	16	—	17	8	3	3	1	32
Que	31	12	4	11	10	7	2	1	31
NB	5	1	2	2	2	—	—	1	5
NS	12	5	—	3	5	1	1	2	12
PEI	short form			short form					
Nfld	4	3	1	2	—	1	1	—	4
total	226	76	17	104	52	35	19	16	226

18(C) Funds requested and granted: See Table XXVI

	18(D) Have you abandoned your research project?			19. In the past five years have you not undertaken a project because you considered funds unlikely to be available?		
	Yes	No	No response	Yes	No	No response
BC	2	10	10	1	17	4
Alta	2	16	10	2	23	3
Sask	—	6	1	—	7	—
Man	—	8	8	4	11	1
Ont(ex.T)	7	55	56	18	80	20
Tor	1	25	22	2	41	5
Que	3	24	20	6	30	11
NB	—	4	4	—	6	2
NS	1	7	9	2	14	1
PEI	short form			short form		
Nfld	—	4	4	1	3	4
total	16	159	144	36	232	51

The responses to questions 18A, B, and D, and 19 total 319 in each case.

TABLE XXVI

RESEARCH FUNDS, REQUESTED AND GRANTED (1966-70)

	British Columbia				Alberta				Saskatchewan			
	Requested	Granted	A	B	Requested	Granted	A	B	Requested	Granted	A	B
Canada Council	56,770	43,351	76.4	65.4	103,483	88,369	85.4	94.6	2,900	2,900	100.0	19.2
federal gov't	2,500	2,500	100.0	3.8	—	—	—	—	—	—	—	—
universities	20,905	20,455	97.8	30.8	5,670	5,090	89.8	5.4	—	—	—	—
prov. gov'ts	—	—	—	—	—	—	—	—	—	—	—	—
private (Can)	—	—	—	—	2,400	—	—	—	—	—	—	—
non-Canadian	—	—	—	—	32,000	—	—	—	12,300	12,200	99.1	80.8
sub-total	80,175	66,306	82.7	100.0	143,553	93,459	65.1	100.0	15,200	15,100	99.3	100.0
pending	—	—			—	8,000			—	—		
grand total	$80,175	$66,306	82.7		$143,553	$101,459	70.6		$15,200	$15,100	99.3	
applicants reporting		14				14				4		
applications reported		35				22				7		
successful applicants		11				12				4		
successful applications		32				17				7		
applications pending		0				1				0		
size of average grant		$2072				$5497				$2157		
estimated no. of academic political scientists		38				44				18		

A—Amount granted as a percentage of amount requested
B—Amount granted by particular institution as a percentage of provincial sub-total

TABLE XXVI (*continued*)

RESEARCH FUNDS, REQUESTED AND GRANTED (1966-70)

	Manitoba				Ontario(ex.T)				Toronto			
	Requested	Granted	A	B	Requested	Granted	A	B	Requested	Granted	A	B
Canada Council	15,261	7,761	50.9	44.3	697,615	492,472	70.5	82.2	362,732	330,970	91.2	74.7
federal gov't	—	—	—	—	25,500	25,500	100.0	4.3	16,700	16,700	100.0	3.8
universities	19,810	9,358	47.3	53.4	33,042	26,402	79.9	4.4	30,125	29,410	97.6	6.6
prov. gov'ts	—	—	—	—	5,000	5,000	100.0	0.8	—	—	—	—
private (Can)	—	—	—	—	22,340	21,845	97.8	3.7	15,100	8,900	58.9	2.0
non-Canadian	4,400	400	9.1	2.3	126,250	27,650	21.9	4.6	59,100	57,100	96.6	12.9
sub-total	39,471	17,519	44.4	100.0	909,747	598,869	65.8	100.0	483,757	443,080	91.5	100.0
pending	—	2,200			—	38,700			—	22,000		
grand total	$39,471	$19,719	50.0		$909,747	$637,569	70.1		$483,757	$465,080	96.1	
applicants reporting		12				70				30		
applications reported		21				145				56		
successful applicants		9				65				29		
successful applications		13				121				52		
applications pending		1				3				2		
size of average grant		$1347				$4949				$8520		
estimated no. of academic political scientists		29				187				72		

TABLE XXVI (*continued*)

RESEARCH FUNDS, REQUESTED AND GRANTED (1966-70)

	Quebec				New Brunswick				Nova Scotia			
	Requested	Granted	A	B	Requested	Granted	A	B	Requested	Granted	A	B
Canada Council	320,079	160,563	50.1	63.6	22,630	19,430	85.9	93.5	47,517	30,650	64.5	82.7
federal gov't	36,375	36,375	100.0	14.4	—	—	—	—	—	—	—	—
universities	33,113	26,563	80.2	10.5	1,450	1,350	93.1	6.5	8,434	5,934	70.4	16.0
prov. gov'ts	40,600	12,100	29.8	4.8	—	—	—	—	—	—	—	—
private (Can)	14,787	14,787	100.0	5.9	—	—	—	—	3,137	500	15.9	1.3
non-Canadian	2,000	2,000	100.0	0.8	—	—	—	—	—	—	—	—
sub-total	446,954	252,388	56.4	100.0	24,080	20,780	86.3	100.0	59,088	37,084	63.8	100.0
pending		131,000*				2,200				5,000		
grand total	$446,954	$383,388	85.8		$24,080	$22,980	95.4		$59,088	$42,084	71.2	
applicants reporting		31				4				10		
applications reported		56				4				22		
successful applicants		28				4				10		
successful applications		44				3				17		
applications pending		4				1				2		
size of average grant		$5736				$6926				$2181		
estimated no. of academic political scientists		74				15				27		

*Canada Council	102,500
Prov. Gov't	28,500
	$131,000

TABLE XXVI (*continued*)

RESEARCH FUNDS, REQUESTED AND GRANTED (1966-70)

	PEI	Newfoundland				Totals			
		Requested	Granted	A	B	Requested	Granted	A	B
Canada Council	all	8,000	8,000	100.0	54.8	1,636,987	1,184,466	72.4	75.9
federal gov't	short	—	—	—	—	81,075	81,075	100.0	5.2
universities	forms	7,100	6,600	93.0	45.2	159,649	131,162	82.2	8.4
prov. gov'ts		—	—	—	—	45,600	17,100	45.6	1.1
private (Can)		—	—	—	—	57,764	46,032	79.7	3.0
non-Canadian		—	—	—	—	236,050	99,350	42.1	6.4
sub-total		15,100	14,600	96.7	100.0	2,217,125	1,559,185	70.3	100.0
pending		—	—			—	209,100		
grand total		$15,100	$14,600	96.7		$2,217,125	$1,768,285	79.6	
applicants reporting			3				192		
applications reported			8				376		
successful applicants			3				175		
successful applications			8				314		
applications pending			0				14		
size of average grant			$1825				$4965		
estimated no. of academic political scientists			10				517		

TABLE XXVII

SUCCESSFUL APPLICATIONS (by size of grant)

	BC	Alta	Sask	Man	Ont(ex.T)	Toronto	Que	NB	NS	PEI	Nfld	Total
1000	12	5	4	7	38	13	9	1	8	—	6	103
1000–1999	8	3	—	1	26	6	5	1	5	—	1	56
2000–2999	4	3	1	4	16	8	5	—	1	—	—	42
3000–3999	2	1	—	1	9	1	3	—	—	—	—	17
4000–4999	1	1	—	—	7	1	5	—	—	—	—	15
5000–7449	3	1	2	—	5	13	7	—	—	—	—	31
7500–9999	2	—	—	—	7	—	3	—	3	—	1	16
10,000–14,999	—	1	—	—	6	4	4	—	—	—	—	15
15,000–24,499	—	1	—	—	5	1	1	1	—	—	—	9
25,000 and over	—	1	—	—	2	5	2	—	—	—	—	10
total	32	17	7	13	121	52	44	3	17	0	8	314

TABLE XXVIII

RESOURCES CLAIMED TO BE LACKING IN CANADA FOR EFFECTIVE RESEARCH

	BC	Alta	Sask	Man	Ont(ex.T)	Toronto	Que	NB	NS	PEI	Nfld	Total	Percentage of total
A	3	12	1	5	24	8	18	1	—	all	—	72	18.5
B	1	6	—	3	12	4	11	—	1	short	—	38	9.7
C	—	1	—	2	6	1	8	—	1	forms	—	19	4.9
D1	6	7	1	4	29	6	11	1	1		1	67	17.2
D2	2	3	1	2	16	7	5	—	2		1	39	10.0
D3	1	3	—	2	16	4	7	—	1		—	34	8.7
E	8	9	4	6	47	7	17	3	5		2	108	27.7
F	—	—	—	1	6	2	2	—	2		—	13	3.3
	21	41	7	25	156	39	79	5	13		4	390	100.0
1	9	19	4	13	74	17	35	4	9		2	186	
2	13	9	3	3	44	31	12	4	8		6	133	
	22	28	7	16	118	48	47	8	17		8	319	

A lack of adequately trained research assistants
B lack of research facilities (space, libraries, etc.)
C lack of funds for research equipment
D lack of funds for specific research projects because of (1) an inadequate number of funding agencies; (2) inadequate funds granted; (3) inability to obtain long-term funds (more than a year)
E lack of time free from regular duties
F other
1 number of persons responding
2 no responses

TABLE XXIX

PERCENTAGE COMPARISONS OF RESEARCH, PUBLICATIONS, AND FUNDS

	BC	Alta	Sask	Man	Ont(ex.T)	Toronto	Que	NB	NS	PEI	Nfld	Total
research in progress	7.1	10.1	2.0	5.3	40.2	13.2	13.8	1.4	4.5	0	2.4	100.0
publications	6.5	9.2	2.1	2.5	40.6	19.0	12.7	1.0	4.6	0.4	1.4	100.0
research funds requested	3.6	6.5	0.7	1.8	41.0	21.8	20.1	1.1	2.7	0	0.7	100.0
research funds granted	4.3	6.0	1.0	1.1	38.4	28.4	16.2	1.3	2.4	0	0.9	100.0
percentage of estimated no. of political scientists	7.4	8.5	3.5	5.6	36.2	13.9	14.3	2.9	5.2	0.6	1.9	100.0
estimated no.	(38)	(44)	(18)	(29)	(72)	(187)	(74)	(15)	(27)	(3)	(10)	(517)

Federal Funds and University Research

BERNARD S. SHEEHAN *University of Calgary*

The federal government withdrew from the field of direct financial support of universities in 1967 under provisions of the new Act.[1] Along with the full responsibility for university finance, the federal government transferred to each province certain tax revenues and a post-secondary education adjustment payment to bring the total financial transfer to at least 50 per cent of the allowable operating cost of post-secondary education. Costs allowable under the Act exclude capital costs, federal grants, student aid, and income for assisted, sponsored, and contract research.[2] The federal councils and agencies continue to be the primary contributors to university research funds. The purpose of this note is to determine the current financial contribution of the government of Canada to university research. Much of the problem is its definition. To establish the framework for this definition, three sets of ideas are explored. These are: direct and indirect costs of university research, university research as an embedded activity, and the problem of relating university activity costs to incomes received from specific sources. These notions lead to formulae which yield divergent alternatives of the federal contribution depending upon the set of assumptions deemed appropriate. Much of the data needed for these calculations were gathered from primary sources and illustrate the application of the formulae for the four-year period 1966–70.

Direct and indirect costs of university research

This section surveys the concepts of direct and indirect costs of university research. There has been considerable discussion and much writing on the subject of how to calculate overhead or indirect costs and on what portion of these costs should be paid by the federal government[3] as a surcharge on monies contributed to assisted and sponsored research funds.[4] Usually items such as salaries, supplies, equipment, and travel are considered direct costs, while costs connected with space, administration, and university services provided to the research project are indirect. Universities which have a fee for use of a computer, for example, are likely to bill a project for computer time and classify the cost as direct, whereas institutions which do not have a fee-for-service system are more likely to lump this cost into overhead. There are no universal rules for determining which costs are direct and which are indirect. The distinction depends on the institution's internal accounting practice.

On the issue of whether the federal government should pay full or partial indirect

---

[1]*Canadian Statutes*, 14, 15, 16 Elizabeth II, Federal-Provincial Fiscal Arangements Act, 1967.

[2]For a full discussion of the Act, see John R. Cameron, *Financial Assistance to Canadian Universities: A Study of Provisions for Financing Higher Education under the Federal-Provincial Fiscal Arrangements Act, 1967* (Halifax: Dalhousie University, 1969). The Act is currently under review and its expiration date of 31 March 1972, has been extended two years. The constitutionality of federal equalization grants has been challenged. See "BC Challenges Ottawa on Equalization Grants," *Toronto Globe and Mail*, (15 February 1972).

[3]Harold Orlans, *Science Policy and the University* (Washington, 1968); *The Effects of Federal Programs on Higher Education* (Washington, 1962); Alice Rivlin, *The Role of the Federal Government in Financing Higher Education* (Washington, 1961).

[4]V.W. Bladen *et al.*, *Financing Higher Education in Canada: Report of a Commission to the Association of Universities and Colleges of Canada* (Toronto, 1965); John B. Macdonald *et al.*, *The Role of the Federal Government in Support of Research in Canadian Universities*, Special Study no 7 prepared for the Science Council of Canada and the Canada Council (Ottawa, 1969).

Canadian Journal of Political Science/Revue canadienne de science politique, VI, no. 1 (March/mars 1973). Printed in Canada/Imprimé au Canada.

costs, there are several points to consider. The federal government could argue that it should not pay indirect costs on the grounds that if universities provide these funds from general revenue, costs would be held to a minimum. Similarly, university researchers may argue that indirect costs should not be paid so that the amount going "directly" into research is maximized. Arguments for federal payment of indirect research costs include the notion that funds received for indirect costs provide the university administration with flexibility. Overhead charges must otherwise be siphoned off general university funds which could be allocated to other activities. Also, it is said that if basic university research expedites important national goals, then it should be fully funded. Further, if one takes the view that post-secondary education must be more equally and explicitly the responsibility of the federal and provincial governments, then current Canadian circumstances favour the federal government's paying full indirect costs to universities rather than 50 per cent of operating expenses through each province. Provincial governments already have such a massive financial control of education that the flexibility given by a return to straightforward federal involvement might be a healthy counterbalance to the possibility of further erosion of institutional autonomy and internal self-determination.

Concerning the problem of institutional distortion caused by external research funds, there are arguments on both sides. If the federal government pays all costs of its sponsored research, the university will not have to draw funds from other activities. Assuming that overhead costs of scientific research are the most expensive, then funds currently used for the overhead of scientific research could be redistributed; this would tend to lessen distortion between disciplines. On the other hand, the traditional checks and balances which allow the university to determine its own internal growth patterns might be weakened if federal agencies pay indirect costs. Since more federal money is available for scientific research than for other activities, science departments can be built up more "cheaply," in terms of university funds, than non-science departments.

Salaries are usually considered direct costs; however, most federal grants do not allow stipends to the principal investigator. The arguments for and against this policy are similar to those advanced with respect to federal payment of indirect costs. Beyond these arguments is the effect external contributions to the salary of the principal investigator could have on academic freedom and on the institution's internal integrity and autonomy. If a federal government agency paid a salary to the grantee, the professor would become dependent on the agency and relatively independent of his institution; and, consequently, the internal organization of the university would be weakened. This view may not be shared by all professors, especially those capable of commanding considerable outside support.

It seems reasonable that when universities and governments come to grapple seriously with the overhead question, the realistic solution will have governments and universities negotiating the extent of government involvement in all associated research costs.[5] The final agreement should depend upon the nature of the project and of the institution. A flat rate would hurt some institutions; and, if it were to be applied to all funding agencies, could lessen the effectiveness of some agencies because they vary considerably in purpose, available funds, and academic interests.

University research: an embedded activity

A prerequisite to calculating the share of university research costs contributed by the federal government is the determination of the total magnitude of these costs. To be costed, university research must be understood in the context of the complex institutions within which it is performed.

People engaged in research in universities also perform many other activities. The following list of activities to which university "researchers" allocate their time illustrates the complicated fabric within which university research is embedded: (1) instruction at many levels - from freshman through advanced graduate studies to guiding the study of post-doctoral fellows, of students of all ages, in skill-type programs, in service courses and specialist courses, in credit and non-credit courses, in the field, in the laboratory, in the classroom, and on

[5]It is argued in the Bonneau-Corry Report that federal granting agencies should make payments to universities designed to cover indirect costs of research they sponsor, including salaries, and that failing a federal-provincial agreement on an alternative figure, it be set at 45 per cent of the amount of each grant, and paid as contributions to the general revenues of the universities. See Louis-Philippe Bonneau and J.A. Corry, *Quest for the Optimum: Research Policy in the Universities of Canada*, Vol. 1, Report of a Commission to Study the Rationalisation of University Research (Ottawa, 1972), 94.

television; (2) supervision of master's and doctoral students; (3) administration of departments, faculties, the university, and committee work; (4) research whether basic, pure, applied, mission-oriented, development, interdisciplinary, alone or with a team, on campus or off campus; reorganizing existing knowledge; self-study; (5) services to the library, data centre, university planning, student counselling, consulting, and other community and professional service. Not all people are engaged in all these activities at the same time. However, the list demonstrates that those who engage in research perform many other professional functions. The extent to which these functions are interrelated and support one another is an important determinant in questions of costing.

The difficulty of determining which activities contribute to what university output is illustrated by the following example. A professor of medicine is assigned in a certain academic year to teach two advanced courses in endocrinology. The courses treat subjects directly related to his sponsored research project. Several students in his classes are writing theses under his supervision and others are medical residents who also confer with him on matters related to their clinical practice. The theses problems are pertinent to the research project, and the students receive a stipend out of the professor's federal research grant. The professor also carries on a limited consulting practice. How does he assign his resources, for the purposes of costing, to research, to public service, and to instruction? What percentage of his time and effort contributes to his research results, and what percentage can be said to be a contribution to the education of his present students, to the delivery of health care, or to development of his courses? In the end, the professor will have to make a professional judgement, and the ultimate cost allocations will depend on that judgement.

Thus, it can be concluded that not only is research a part-time activity for most people in universities, but also functionally, organizationally, and – more importantly – within the mind of the researcher, activities are not easily separable. Nonetheless, this separation is essential to costing and is thus necessary in determining the share any funding agency contributes to research. This does not imply that costing is impossible – only that the nature of universities means that costing is based on judgement, often the subjective judgement of the cost analyst and the individual researcher. In order to evaluate any particular determination of the "federal share," one must be aware of these judgements. It is not within the scope of this paper to discuss university cost studies. However, accurate determination of costs of university research must be based on a careful study of all university costs.[6] The range of confidence within which these costs are determined will depend upon the costing methodology.

There is another notion which complicates research costing, funding patterns, and internal university operations: the feeling that certain professional activities are more acceptable than others. The idea is summed up in the following quote from the Bonneau-Corry Report. "Partly for reasons of finance and prestige (and partly because the achievements of reflective inquiry are harder to assess) most universities have been induced to bias their policies on promotion and salary increases in favour of those members of the teaching staffs whose activities in frontier research win substantial grants from external agencies, and produce published papers in the learned journals. These, it is thought, can be judged objectively while thinking and teaching cannot."[7]

Relating costs of research activities to university income sources

The federal government is the major contributor to universities' assisted- and sponsored-research funds. Table I summarizes by institution grants made during the four-year period 1966–70. Normally, under current fiscal arrangements, the federal government does not contribute directly to other university funds or to general revenue. Thus, it would appear that the following dichotomy exists: federal funds are spent only on research; money received from all other sources supports all university expenditures, including direct and indirect costs of research not covered by revenue from federal sources. Therefore, to calculate the extent of the federal government's support of university research, one need only add up federal contributions to university research trust funds. Unfortunately, the problem is not solved so simply.

Traditionally, universities have guarded the principle that their essential obligations to society are independent of the disposition of their financial patrons. The institutions have tried to create a campus atmosphere of intellectual detachment so that students

---

[6]Alfred D. Cavanaugh, *A Preliminary Evaluation of Cost Studies in Higher Education* (Berkeley, 1969).

[7]Bonneau and Corry, *Quest for the Optimum*, 32.

TABLE I*

FEDERAL GOVERNMENT ALLOCATIONS IN SUPPORT OF RESEARCH AND GRADUATE STUDENTS IN POST SECONDARY EDUCATIONAL INSTITUTIONS: A FOUR-YEAR SUMMARY BY INSTITUTION ($'000)

Institutions	Council totals†				Federal agencies†				Federal totals†			
	1966/67	1967/68	1968/69	1969/70	1966/67	1967/68	1968/69	1969/70	1966/67	1967/68	1968/69	1969/70
Memorial University of Newfoundland	573	671	932	1282	41	108	162	319	614	779	1094	1601
Newfoundland	573	671	932	1282	112	161	226	341	685	832	1158	1623
Prince of Wales	—	17	6	—	—	—	—	—	—	17	6	—
Saint Dunstan's	9	15	—	—	1	11	10	11	10	26	10	11
Prince Edward Island	9	32	42	56	21	35	79	11	30	67	121	67
Acadia University	53	97	157	169	9	77	19	15	62	105	176	184
Dalhousie University	1420	1431	1750	2500	113	145	190	2281	1533	1576	1940	4781
Mount Saint Vincent University	—	3	—	3	—	—	—	—	—	3	—	3
Nova Scotia Agricultural College	—	—	4	—	—	—	42	38	—	—	46	38
Nova Scotia Technical College	197	267	331	345	18	64	—	54	215	331	331	399
St Francis Xavier University	148	177	177	152	39	43	—	4	187	182	177	156
Saint Mary's University	4	39	54	70	—	—	—	13	4	39	54	83
Nova Scotia	1822	2013	2472	3236	512	2032	1292	3843	2334	4045	3764	7079
Université de Moncton	36	82	105	108	6	5	14	5	42	87	119	113
Mount Allison University	95	145	149	118	8	4	6	8	103	149	155	126
University of New Brunswick	611	828	908	1119	1117	206	110	2670	1728	1033	1018	3789
New Brunswick	742	1055	1161	1345	1678	245	475	2683	2420	1300	1636	4028
Bishop's University	47	53	64	57	1	—	—	—	47	53	64	57
Loyola College	32	50	111	113	1	8	9	12	33	58	120	125
McGill University	6395	8655	11484	12090	2239	1006	806	734	8634	9660	12290	12824
Sir George Williams	63	97	272	357	1	8	—	1	64	105	272	358
Collège Militaire Royal	—	—	—	—	194	306	—	223	194	306	—	223
Institut de Microbiologie	9	9	7	—	36	36	—	—	46	44	7	—
Université Laval	2347	3027	4065	4667	231	300	241	237	2578	3327	4306	4904
Université de Montréal	3646	5201	6358	7358	296	450	566	493	3942	5651	6924	7851
Université du Québec	—	—	—	45	434	—	—	—	434	—	—	45
Université de Sherbrooke	293	590	1051	1738	24	36	64	67	317	626	1115	1805
Quebec	12862	17704	23462	26480	4338	3452	5929	3981	17200	21156	29391	30461

TABLE I (*continued*)

FEDERAL GOVERNMENT ALLOCATIONS IN SUPPORT OF RESEARCH AND GRADUATE STUDENTS IN POST SECONDARY EDUCATIONAL INSTITUTIONS: A FOUR-YEAR SUMMARY BY INSTITUTION ($'000)

	Council totals†				Federal agencies†				Federal totals†			
Institutions	1966/67	1967/68	1968/69	1969/70	1966/67	1967/68	1968/69	1969/70	1966/67	1967/68	1968/69	1969/70
Brock University	81	151	203	233	1	3	4	7	82	154	207	240
Carleton University	565	701	1164	1499	90	105	102	137	655	807	1266	1636
University of Guelph	709	933	1587	1797	133	236	336	447	842	1174	1923	2244
Lakehead University	45	99	163	177	3	10	6	16	48	109	169	193
Laurentian University of Sudbury	52	96	144	156	—	—	—	7	52	96	144	163
McMaster University	2813	4246	5023	5210	169	257	215	313	2982	4504	5238	5523
University of Ottawa	1474	1945	2417	2701	135	166	169	199	1609	2110	2586	2900
Queen's University at Kingston	2280	2863	4027	4089	259	291	358	373	2539	3154	4385	4462
Royal Military College of Canada	14	33	10	1	—	—	198	—	14	33	208	1
Saint Paul University	—	—	—	—	7	8	—	—	7	8	—	—
University of Toronto	8056	11102	14695	16058	896	1136	1034	1199	8951	12239	15729	17257
Trent University	105	215	215	237	1	18	20	26	105	232	235	263
University of Waterloo	1445	2210	3294	3888	145	374	321	378	1590	2484	3615	4266
Waterloo Lutheran University	5	2	17	27	—	5	—	13	5	7	17	40
The University of Western Ontario	2311	3336	3930	4003	283	273	413	421	2594	3609	4343	4424
University of Windsor	543	638	780	949	46	87	121	106	589	725	901	1055
York University	382	778	935	1674	37	82	45	80	418	860	980	1754
Ontario	20887	29370	38605	42698	3970	4599	9177	7742	24857	33969	47782	50440
Brandon University	8	16	16	12	1	4	4	4	9	20	20	16
The University of Manitoba	2562	3506	4457	5248	436	1152	756	809	2997	4658	5213	6057
Winnipeg	4	9	19	15	—	1	1	1	4	10	20	16
Manitoba	2574	3537	4492	5275	1278	1157	761	814	3852	4694	5253	6089
U. Saskatchewan (Regina)	—	47	362	447	—	—	—	—	—	47	362	447
U. Saskatchewan (Saskatoon)	2536	3049	3362	3345	435	—	522	1217	2970	3049	3884	4562
Saskatchewan	2536	3096	3724	3793	701	845	522	1217	3237	3941	4246	5010
The University of Alberta	3423	4833	6146	6270	355	667	564	484	3778	5500	6710	6754
The University of Calgary	858	1366	2088	2779	64	156	156	198	923	1522	2244	2977
The University of Lethbridge	3	14	45	97	—	—	3	3	3	14	48	100
Alberta	4284	6221	8288	9155	661	823	961	801	4945	7044	9249	9956
The University of British Columbia	5288	6910	9118	9186	1253	1059	1059	1019	6541	7968	10177	10205
Notre Dame University of Nelson	9	17	19	17	—	—	—	—	9	17	19	17
Selkirk	2	3	6	2	—	—	—	—	2	3	6	2
Simon Fraser University	451	832	1290	1294	34	94	72	90	485	926	1362	1384
University of Victoria	236	400	627	639	90	59	65	79	326	459	692	718
British Columbia	5999	8167	11062	11140	2359	1729	1834	1606	8358	9891	12896	12746
Other	5495	8554	11230	12391	6858	11488	9026	7485	12353	20042	20256	19876
CANADA	57782	80416	105470	116849	22483	26562	30281	30522	80265	106978	135751	147371

*Bernard S. Sheehan, *Federal Government Support of University Research and Graduate Students 1966-1970* ,(Toronto, 1971).
†Direct grants to provinces are added to provincial subtotals.

and professors can provide independent criticism while developing their own creative and other intellectual abilities. Therefore, it is reasonable to speculate that the internal distribution of activities, and thus resources, is influenced by university traditions as well as by external societal pressures such as changing numbers of students and the demand for more research and public service. Thus, while universities accept sums into trust funds and spend these monies according to rules of granting agencies, internal distribution of university activity may not be altered substantially from what it would be if these funds were received into general revenue without strings.

Consider the following conjecture. *Conjecture 1:* if the present level of research activity is appropriate, it is possible that this level is not directly dependent on the *way* the federal contribution is channelled to universities, that is, through assisted- and sponsored-research funds.

Thus, for example, if the federal contribution were made instead to universities' general revenue funds, there might be comparatively little change in the level (or cost) of research activity. Also, it is suggested that there is no simple correlation between the actual cost of research and contributions to assisted- and sponsored-research funds except that income to these funds forms a proportion of total university income from all sources.

To the extent that the conjecture is valid, it follows that the percentage federal share of university research costs is:

$$(1)\quad \frac{\text{direct federal contribution to research funds}}{\text{total university income from all sources}} \times 100$$

For purposes of the above argument, it was assumed that the 50 per cent contribution which the federal government makes to operating costs of post-secondary education is simply a fiscal transfer between governments. If one takes another view – that the 50 per cent of allowable costs of operating post-secondary educational institutions may be thought of as a transfer to institutions since the refund is claimed by the province *after* the money is spent by the university – then formula (1) is altered as follows:

$$(2)\quad \frac{\text{total federal contribution to university operations}}{\text{total university income from all sources}} \times 100$$

An essential point underlying the second conjecture is that activities which under certain circumstances – for example in a research institute or government laboratory – would be classified as research may not be so classified in a university. An activity must be defined in terms of results or consequences of that activity. The problem of costing is to assign to the output or activities the resources required to sustain those activities. In the case of activities with more than one output, costs have to be logically prorated. If this is not done, it would appear that some outputs are produced without cost – like perpetual motion. *Conjecture 2:* total cost of university research must be determined by a careful study of all academic and support program costs in universities. The magnitude of these costs depends on how much all activities contribute to research output as judged by individual researchers and cost analysts.

The validity of the second conjecture suggests that the dollar value of the federal contribution to research is the appropriate formula percentage times the total cost of research activities objectively determined by a program cost study.

Federal government support of university research

To demonstrate the range of different conclusions one can reach on the amount of the federal contribution to university research, two sets of calculations will be performed. The first follows what will be referred to as the "conventional" method and yields results indicating federal government support of university research which are comparable with those reported previously. Details of this method are evident from the calculations.[8] A second set of calculations based on formulae (1) and (2) gives alternative solutions.

CONVENTIONAL SOLUTIONS

Table II gives data required in the calculations. Table III shows the component sources of university funds contributed expressly for research. The figures under "Direct fed-

[8] The conventional method is implicit in Bladen, *Financing Higher Education*; Macdonald, *Role of Government*; Department of the Secretary of State, Education Support Branch, *Federal Expenditures on Research in the Academic Community 1966–67, 1967–68* (Ottawa, 1968); and W.J. Waines, "Federal Support of Universities and Colleges of Canada," Financing Higher Education in Canada Report no 7 (Ottawa, 1970).

TABLE II*

COUNCILS, FEDERAL AGENCIES, AND PROVINCIAL GOVERNMENT SUPPORT OF RESEARCH IN POST-SECONDARY EDUCATIONAL INSTITUTIONS ($'000)

	Canada Council	National Research Council	Medical Research Council	Federal agencies	Federal total	Total provincial
1966-7	2,907	31,125	13,539	20,446	68,017	11,758
1967-8	4,948	41,624	17,544	24,167†	88,283	15,240
1968-9	7,028	52,237	22,325	27,500†	109,090	17,812
1969-70	7,455	58,095	24,923	27,700†	118,173	18,747

*Sheehan, *Government Support*, section 1.2.
†Estimate.

TABLE III

SOURCES OF UNIVERSITY EXPENDITURES EXPRESSLY FOR RESEARCH*

	Direct federal	Universities' general revenue	Other†	Total
1966-7	68	9	29	106
1967-8	88	12	33	133
1968-9	109	16	36	161
1969-70	118	20	38	176

*All dollar amounts given in following tables and calculations are rounded to the nearest million. This is to emphasize that the data are not known with greater precision. For a discussion of difficulties in gathering national information on higher education, see Bernard S. Sheehan, "Proposal for a National Information System for Higher Education," *The Journal of Educational Thought*, vol. 5, no 3 (December 1971), 142-55.

†These amounts are estimates of university income for research (including contract research) from provincial governments, industry, foundations, endowments, and all other sources. The figures for income from provincial governments are given in Table II. Additional income from all other sources for 1966-7 was $16,800,000 and for 1967-8 was $17,600,000, as reported by Statistics Canada. Amounts for the two following years are assumed to be $18,600,000 and $19,600,000.

eral" are the sums of research grants from councils and federal agencies in the appropriate years as shown in Table II. These do not include scholarships or money given in support of training. However, the proportions of research grants used to pay research assistants who are also research trainees (students) are included. This column is the conventional solution assuming that the statutory fiscal transfers are simply transfers between governments. However, if it is assumed that the Act can be interpreted such that federal-provincial fiscal transfers pay the federal share of all costs associated with university research, then a second conventional solution continues with the calculation of indirect and salary expenses related to all research funds regardless of their source. This is the same assumption followed in the development of formula (2). It suggests that under the Act provincial governments serve as the federal government's agent for auditing allowable costs after expenditures and for advancing funds to the institutions against future allowable costs.

The expenditures from universities' general revenue are assumed to average ap-

TABLE IV

FEDERAL SHARE OF INDIRECT SALARY COSTS CHARGEABLE TO UNIVERSITY RESEARCH

	Indirect costs	Salary costs	Percentage federal share	Federal share
1966-7	$36	$ 70	14	$15
1967-8	47	86	50	66
1968-9	56	105	50	80
1969-70	62	114	50	88

TABLE V

ALTERNATIVE CONVENTIONAL SOLUTIONS TO THE PROBLEM OF DETERMINING TOTAL FEDERAL GOVERNMENT SUPPORT OF UNIVERSITY RESEARCH

	Conventional solution (1)	Conventional solution (2)
1966-7	$ 68	$ 83
1967-8	88	154
1968-9	109	189
1969-70	118	206

proximately two per cent of the operating income of those universities which have significant research funds. The operating income of these universities was calculated using Statistics Canada estimates. Although these expenditures are not allowable[9] under the Act, the associated costs are taken as allowable. In summing the appropriate figures in Table III, it is assumed that "contributions" in a given year equal "expenditures" and "costs" in the same year. This is a common assumption made in the universities as well.[10] Following the suggestion made in the Macdonald Report,[11] indirect costs are assumed to be 35 per cent of direct costs. The definition of indirect costs is therefore the same as in that report,[12] and the results of these calculations are shown in Table IV. The method of calculating the figure for "salary costs" seems compatible with the Macdonald Report,[13] where these results were, in turn, based on the cost study of the Association of Universities and Colleges of Canada.[14] The assumption is that the total of indirect costs and salary costs chargeable to research are together equal to the value of the research grant. In order to determine the federal share for 1966–7, the total university income less all research grants was found. Then the percentage of this amount represented by the total federal contribution less research grants was calculated. For the years within the new fiscal arrangement, the normal 50 per cent was assumed.

The necessary calculations of the components of the conventional solutions are now completed. Table V shows conventional solution (1) which is the total federal contribution expressly for research, and conventional solution (2) which includes the federal share of the associated costs of all research expenditures.

[9]"Federal-Provincial Fiscal Arrangements Act, 1967, Post-Secondary Education Adjustment Payment Regulations," PC 1968–615, Schedule B, *The Canada Gazette*, Part II, vol 102, 10 April 1968 (Ottawa, 1968).

[10]Dominion Bureau of Statistics, *Canadian Universities*. Using the Canadian Association of University Business Officers' definition of specific purpose funds, "These funds are recorded as income only to the extent of the funds expended."

[11]Macdonald, *Role of Government.*

[12]*Ibid.*, 150.

[13]*Ibid.*, 142.

[14]Association of Universities and Colleges of Canada, "An Exploratory Cost Analysis of Some Canadian Universities," Report on the Study of Costs of University Programmes in Canada to AUCC, CAUBO, and CAUT (Ottawa, 1970).

TABLE VI

FEDERAL SHARE OF RESEARCH COSTS BASED ON FORMULA (1)

Year	Total cost of research	Percentage federal share	Federal share
1967-8	$266	14.7	$39
1968-9	322	13.8	44
1969-70	352	11.6	41

TABLE VII

FEDERAL SHARE OF RESEARCH COSTS BASED ON FORMULA (2)

Year	Total cost of research	Percentage federal share	Federal share
1966-7	$212	27.9	$ 59
1967-8	266	54.5	150
1968-9	322	54.6	176
1969-70	352	54.0	190

ALTERNATIVE SOLUTIONS

One possible solution is what might be called the minimum, or trivial, solution. It assumes that "research" activities in universities are either instructional activities or else are done only in support of an instructional or other activity. There is no research output; therefore, no costs can be assigned to research; and thus the federal contribution to research is zero. Since this point of view effectively denies research for its own sake as a legitimate university activity, it will not be pursued further here.

Alternative Solution (1). Assuming that the level of research activities is not dependent directly on the sources of university income, federal support during the period 1967–70 is calculated using formula (1). Since no university cost study was performed for the years under review, it is necessary to approximate the total cost of research. For convenience, it is assumed that the sum of funds given expressly for research, the conventional indirect costs and the conventional salary costs chargeable to research is the total cost of research.[15] For the years under the Act, the federal share is shown in Table VI.

Alternative Solution (2). This solution follows the point of view that fiscal transfers under the Act effectively are from the federal government to the institutions. Application of formula (2) is shown in Table VII.

The calculation of the "total federal contribution to university operations" required by formula (2) was performed as follows. For the years under the Act, the total of all direct external research grants was subtracted from the total of university operating income from all sources. Fifty per cent of the remainder was added to the sum of federal grants expressly for research. Thus, this calculation assumes that all universities' operating expenditures, except those out of sponsored- and assisted-research funds, are allowable under the Act. For the year 1966–7, the figure given in Statistics Canada Catalogue 81-212 for the total federal contribution was adjusted to account for differences in the amounts given there for assisted research and the amounts found by an independent study.[16]

COMPARISON OF SOLUTIONS AND CONCLUSIONS

The solutions summarized in Table VIII rest on the following assumptions: the Act transfers funds either to provinces or to institutions; university traditions and internal integrity influence resource utilization even in the face of specific funds donated

[15]This is a critical assumption. The results that follow from it, like the results of the conventional method, are only as good as it is. The assumption may have one further weakness. The problem of costing is to assign to the output of activities resources required to sustain those activities. Thus, if "total cost of research" means total cost of research activities on campus, costs of research outputs will be less than the assumed figure to the extent that "research" activities contribute to other outputs.

[16]Bernard S. Sheehan, *Federal Government Support of University Research and Graduate Students, 1966–1970* (Toronto, 1971).

TABLE VIII

FEDERAL SUPPORT OF UNIVERSITY RESEARCH

	Assuming fiscal transfers considered as:			
	Contributions to university income		Payments to provincial governments	
Year	Conventional solution	Alternative solution	Conventional solution	Alternative solution
1966-7	$ 83	$ 59	—	—
1967-8	154	150	$ 88	$39
1968-9	189	176	109	44
1969-70	206	190	118	41

in specific ways for specific purposes; the actual cost of university research is not known on any campus or on all campuses collectively – therefore rule-of-thumb estimates must be made. These assumptions yield the wide range of answers to the question, "what is the financial contribution of the government of Canada to university research?" given in Table VIII. The divergence suggests that serious consideration of a number of urgent issues must be undertaken.

Since the current Act was extended only to 31 March 1974, it seems the unresolved issues inherent in the assumptions cannot be removed before new arrangements are made or the old extended. The effective federal contribution is in doubt; therefore, the federal role in university research is ambiguous, as is its ability to integrate university research into a national science policy[17] or into any other endeavours toward agreed national goals and objectives. This uncertainty hinders government educational planning and individual (and collective) university academic planning. Further, the wide range of solutions suggests that new proposed funding schemes such as offered in the Wright Report,[18] for example, must be carefully studied. These schemes, on the one hand, may grossly misinterpret the real cost of university research and, on the other hand, may be insensitive to the embedded nature of university research and so cause strains which distort the university internally and, wittingly or unwittingly, hinder it from attaining its agreed legitimate objectives. The fact that these kinds of calculations must be done without knowing the cost of university research says much about the state of institutional research[19] in Canada. Especially during the current period of fiscal constraint for universities, the lack of cost and other management information can lead to disastrous planning decisions at all government and university levels.

Thus, the determination of federal financial support for university research can only be estimated, and even these estimates vary widely depending on which of a number of reasonable assumptions one cares to make. There is a national need to grapple with the academic implications of any proposed new fiscal arrangements. An initial step in this direction would be taken if in future federal-provincial discussions, post-secondary education, including university research, were thought of as more than a vehicle for fiscal transfers.

---

[17]See, for example, the role of the proposed national research academy in *A Science Policy for Canada, Report of the Senate Special Committee on Science Policy*, Vol. 2 (Ottawa, 1972), 467–8.

[18]Commission on Post-Secondary Education in Ontario, *Draft Report* (Toronto, 1972), 46.

[19]Bernard S. Sheehan, "Institutional Research As Adjunct to University Management, *Stoa* II (1972), 37–45.

Social Position and Interest Recognition: The Voter in Broadview, *or* Are Voters Fools?

J. PAUL GRAYSON *University of Western Ontario*

In a brief footnote in *Political Man*, S.M. Lipset argued that political scientists had, in the past, approached the phenomenon of electoral change in terms of its being "a rational reaction to new situations or factors."[1] Sociologists and social psychologists who had channelled their endeavours in this directtion, on the other hand, had, Lipset argued, placed emphasis elsewhere: when it came to explanations of the vote, group pressures and the fulfilment of personal needs were first in their repertoire.

Since Lipset first made this observation, two major developments have occurred in the area of voting research: (1) there has been a trend away from the study of the interpersonal dynamics involved in the voting decision and a corresponding increase in the number of studies focusing on attitudes as the final determinant of the vote, and (2) there has been an increase in the number of studies focusing on long-term electoral trends. The first of these developments is premised on the assumption that, in the United States at least, the voter has a "sense of attachment with one party or the other" although the strength of this attachment may vary greatly from one individual to the next.[2] Moreover, this attachment – or identification – does not necessarily follow racial, sexual, or other potential lines of cleavage: to this extent it is possible to speak of political groupings within American society. The way in which the individual will cast his ballot in any particular election is, in turn, a function of his party identification and the impact of party stances on issues of relevance to him. The second of the developments was based on the belief that studies of the individual voter made possible a transition to analyses of other problems. As a consequence, Campbell argues, in "the last few years a number of attempts have been made to move 'upward' from the study of micro-political units to an understanding of the flow of the total vote, to apply the insights gained from the study of the individual voter to the explanation of the behaviour of the electorate."[3]

Despite these trends, as L. McDonald has recently pointed out, the notion of the "rational voter" which was implicit in Lipset's typification of the political scientist's orientation to the study of voting – and more particularly to the study of voting change – has not passed out of the lexicon of the social scientist.[4] Perhaps the most forthright statement of this posiiton is given by V.O. Key. "The perverse and unorthodox argument of this little book," he writes in his last work, "is that voters are not fools. To be sure, many individual voters act in odd ways indeed; yet in the large the electorate behaves about as rationally and responsibly as we should expect, given the clarity of the alternatives presented to it and the character of the information available to it."[5]

That this formulation is in fact an "updating," based on an appreciation of recent research, of an ideology which centred on "rational man" is not disputable.[6] What does warrant assessment, though, is the extent to which voters make the link between their interests and the party which supports these interests. In Canada, research has shown, for example, that there is a greater tendency for Catholics to vote Liberal than for non-Catholics to vote Liberal. It does not follow, however, that Catholics tend to vote Liberal *because* they perceive the Liberal party as supporting Catholic interests. In other words, as will be demonstrated in the following pages, it cannot be argued that because members of particular social groupings happen to support particular parties that in all cases they do so out of a calculation of their interests and an appreciation that a particular

[1] (Garden City, 1963), 294.

[2] A. Campbell, *The American Voter* (New York, 1960), 121.

[3] "Voters and Elections: Past and Present," in *Political Opinion and Electoral Behaviour*, ed. E.C. Dreyer (Belmont, 1970), 469.

[4] "Attitude Organization and Voting Behaviour in Canada," *The Canadian Review of Sociology and Anthropology*, 8 (1971), 165.

[5] *The Responsible Electorate* (Cambridge, 1966), 7.

[6] L. McDonald, "Attitude Organization," 165.

Canadian Journal of Political Science/Revue canadienne de science politique, VI, no. 1 (March/mars 1973). Printed in Canada/Imprimé au Canada.

party supports these interests. The relevance of these findings will be discussed later.

Method

The data for the study were collected in the spring of 1971 in a random survey of 275 residents of the federal riding of Broadview. This riding, located in downtown Toronto, was, from its formation in 1933 to 1963, a working-class Tory stronghold. First T.L. Church, a former mayor of Toronto, and later George Hees, who gained prominence in the Diefenbaker administrations, were sent to Ottawa by Broadview residents. In 1963 the situation changed and a Liberal, G.D. Hahn, was elected, but his stay in Ottawa was a short one. In 1965 and again in 1968 and 1972, the NDP candidate, John Gilbert, was victorious at the polls.

Between its formation and the present, considerable demographic changes have occurred in Broadview. Although censuses before 1951 do not provide statistics on the basis of tracts which can be matched with constituency boundaries, there is little doubt that prior to 1951 the area was basically a British origin, working-class, and Protestant section of the city. In speaking of Riverdale, one particular part of the constituency, S. Crysdale comments that "Riverdale was settled chiefly by British immigrants and until recent years it has been thought of as comparatively stable."[7] The "British" quality of Broadview is suggested even by 1951 census figures. In that year, 80.4 per cent of area residents claimed British ethnicity. In addition, 54.9 per cent held working-class jobs, and 75.7 per cent were Protestants. By 1961 the effects of post-war immigration were quite apparent in census statistics: now only 61.2 per cent claimed British ethnicity, 59.0 per cent were Protestants, and 59.9 per cent held working-class jobs. A constituency of such heterogeneity facilitates an examination of a number of variables which have consequences for the vote.

In this paper, attention will focus on the "rationality" of the Broadview voter. Using the operational definition that a voter is rational if he: (*a*) has particular objective interests, (*b*) perceives a particular party as supporting these interests, and (*c*) votes for the party perceived as supporting these interests, an attempt will be made to come to terms with V.O. Key's contention that "voters are not fools." Given the definition being used, it matters little whether the voter supports a party because of specific issues supported by the party or because of a general feeling he has that the party will look out for his interests. A working-class voter, for example, may vote NDP because of its position on taxation or because of a general feeling that the party will take care of his interests. In either case, the vote can be considered rational as defined above. The questions used in assessing rationality appear in the appendix.

Before proceeding to analysis, I should mention two limitations of the study. First, the only interests that will be analysed are those resulting from the individual's religion, place of birth, and class. Clearly, the voter may have other interests that he considers more important than these. Given that a number of Canadian studies have shown that these variables have some importance to an understanding of the vote, this limitation does not invalidate the study. The second limitation is that in some tables, because so few people make identifications between their interest positions and political parties, many of the expected cell frequencies are less than 1 and more than 20 per cent of the cells contain numbers less than 5. Consequently, it is inappropriate to use chi-square. In these cases, measures of significance and measures of association will be omitted from analysis although the actual figures in the tables will be analysed, as they are of relevance to the problem under study. Where numbers permit, both chi-square and Cramer's v will be recorded. Because of over-all statistical limitations, however, the research should be regarded as exploratory.

Religion and voting

In a number of Canadian studies, significant relationships have been found between religion and party preference. By and large, the magnitude of the relationship between these variables has far overshadowed the degree of relationship between party preference and any other variable. Over-all, it appears that Roman Catholics tend to support the Liberal party and Anglicans tend to favour the Conservatives.[8] Generalizations about United Church members and Presbyterians, on the other hand, are more difficult to make.[9] In

[7]S. Crysdale, *Occupational and Social Mobility in Riverdale, A Blue Collar Community* (PHD thesis, University of Toronto, 1968), 15.

[8]John Meisel, "Religious Affiliation and Electoral Behaviour," in *Voting in Canada*, ed. J. Courtney (Scarborough, Ont., 1967), 150. Also see G. Anderson, "Voting Behaviour and the Ethnic-Religious Variable: A Study of a Federal Election in Hamilton," *Canadian Journal of Economics and Political Science*, 32 (1966), 34.

[9]W. Gagne and P. Regenstreif, "Some As-

TABLE I

PARTY PREFERENCE BY RELIGION

	Religion		
Party Preference	Protestant (per cent)	Catholic (per cent)	Other (per cent)
Liberal	36.5	57.9	29.0
Conservative	26.9	7.9	32.3
NDP	25.7	17.1	22.6
undecided	10.8	17.1	16.1
total	100	100	100
N=	167	76	31

Chi-square = 20.67; d*f* = 6; *p* less than .05; Cramer's *V* = .19.

addition, in at least two studies it has been found that non-church-goers tend to give their allegiance to the NDP.[10]

In the Broadview study, the relationship between religion and party preference does not differ greatly from that found elsewhere. For purposes of analysis, in this study, distinctions were made between Protestants and Catholics while all other denominations were placed in the "other" category and because of small numbers will not be systematically included in analysis. Assuming that religion is an interest position, the present inquiry will, first of all, proceed on the assumption that it is an independent variable. Should this assumption prove unwarranted, corrections can be made later in the text.

On the basis of electoral research to the present it is evident that only on some occasions do social groupings parallel political groupings. Perhaps in the present study there is some evidence of this parallelism when it comes to religion and voting preference. As can be seen from Table I, while the single greatest percentage of both Protestants and Catholics support the Liberal party, far more Catholics than Protestants give their allegiance to the Liberals. Concomitantly, far greater percentages of Protestants than Catholics give support to the Conservatives and NDP. Differences are particularly noticeable between the percentage support that Protestants and Catholics give to the Conservatives. Interestingly enough, though, of those in the "other" category, the greatest single percentage support the Conservatives. This latter finding is somewhat inconsistent with other research in this area but over-all it is possible to conclude that a disproportionate percentage of Catholics support the Liberals while few Catholics support the Conservatives. Support for this party is found in the ranks of the Protestants and those of "other" denominations.

While there is this association between religion and party preference, in order to determine whether religion is an interest position which is rationally considered by the voter when marking his ballot, it is necessary to ascertain whether or not individuals of respective religions view their favoured party as supporting their particular religious interests. An examination of Tables II and III gives little support to an argument which emphasizes that a rational appreciation by the voter of which parties support particular religious interests necessarily influences his voting decision. While it may have been shown in other studies that Protestants favour the Conservatives and while it was found in this study that more Protestants than Catholics supported the Conservatives, when asked which party supports Protestant interests, Protestants, independent of the party they support, overwhelmingly reply that they do not know (Table II). On the other hand, as can also be seen from Table II, more Conservatives than supporters for other parties view the Conservatives as supporting Protestant interests. Even more interesting are the figures in Table III. Here it appears as though in all party categories, the greatest single percentage of Catholics, independent of the party they support, answer that they do not know which party supports Catholic interests. On the other hand, a greater percentage of Catholics who vote Liberal perceive the Liberal party as supporting Catholic interests (Table III) than do Protestants who vote Conservative (Table II). Equally interesting is that al-

pects of New Democratic Party Urban Support in 1965," *Canadian Journal of Economics and Political Science*, 33 (1967), 530. Also see J. Wilson, "Politics and Social Class in Canada: The Case of Waterloo South," this JOURNAL, I (1968), 296.

[10]J.A. Laponce, *People vs Politics* (Toronto, 1969). Also see Gagne and Regenstreif, "NDP Urban Support," 530.

TABLE II

PROTESTANTS' PERCEPTION OF PARTY SUPPORT

	Party preference			
Party supporting Protestant interests	Liberal (per cent)	Conservative (per cent)	NDP (per cent)	Undecided (per cent)
Liberal	3.3	8.9	4.8	0
Conservative	8.2	24.4	14.3	0
NDP	1.6	0	2.4	0
mixed	13.1	8.9	16.7	27.8
don't know	73.8	57.8	61.9	72.2
total	100	100	100	100
N=	61	45	42	18

TABLE III

CATHOLICS' PERCEPTION OF PARTY SUPPORT

	Party preference			
Party supporting Catholic interests	Liberal (per cent)	Conservative (per cent)	NDP (per cent)	Undecided (per cent)
Liberal	32.6	0	23.1	7.7
Conservative	7.0	0	7.7	0
NDP	0	0	15.4	0
mixed	11.6	16.7	15.4	7.7
don't know	48.8	83.3	38.5	84.6
total	100	100	100	100
N=	43	6	13	13

though it was found in Table I that the NDP received more support from Protestants than from Catholics, of Catholics who do vote NDP, the largest single percentage still view Catholic interests as being supported by the Liberals.

The picture changes slightly if the frequency of church attendance (which can be taken as a rough index of religious commitment) is taken into consideration. That a consideration of this variable is important in explaining the vote has already been demonstrated in at least one Canadian study.[11] In Broadview, even though respondents were willing to state that they were of a particular faith, few regularly attended church services. For this reason, the perspectives of Protestants and Roman Catholics who mentioned that they had at any time in the past month attended church services were compared with the perspectives of Protestants and Roman Catholics in general.

It is evident from the figures in Table IV that little difference exists between the perspectives of Protestant church attenders and Protestants in general (Table II). In both cases, there is virtually no association made between religion and particular political parties. For the Roman Catholics, the picture is different. The figures in Table III demonstrated that, for Roman Catholics in general, the majority who felt that the Liberal party supported Roman Catholic interests were Liberal supporters themselves. The figures in Table V, which refer to Catholics who attend services, demonstrate that, of this group, a large number still see the Liberals as supporting Catholic interests. But more important is the large percentage of Catholic church-goers who perceive the Liberals as supporting Roman Catholic interests yet vote NDP. It is beyond the scope of this study to inquire into the reasons for this relationship, although, as Meisel points out, one aspect of Canadian political folklore stresses that the Liberal party is the "captive of French Canadians and Catholics who are its principal supporters."[12] Perhaps it is in their interactions with other church-goers that, for Catholics, this myth is re-affirmed. Whatever the case, it is still extremely important to realize that for Protestant and Catholic church-goers, as well as for Protestants and Catholics in gen-

[11] G. Anderson, "Voting Behaviour," 33.

[12] John Meisel, *Working Papers on Canadian Politics* (Montreal, 1972), 34.

TABLE IV

PROTESTANT CHURCH ATTENDERS' PERCEPTION OF PARTY SUPPORT

	Party preference			
Party supporting Protestant interests	Liberal (per cent)	Conservative (per cent)	NDP (per cent)	Undecided (per cent)
Liberal	4.1	10.0	5.5	0
Conservative	10.2	20.0	11.1	0
NDP	2.0	0	5.5	0
mixed	14.3	13.3	11.1	23.5
don't know	69.4	56.7	66.6	76.5
total	100	100	100	100
N=	49	30	18	17

TABLE V

CATHOLIC CHURCH ATTENDERS' PERCEPTION OF PARTY SUPPORT

	Party preference			
Party supporting Catholic interests	Liberal (per cent)	Conservative (per cent)	NDP (per cent)	Undecided (per cent)
Liberal	35.3	0	33.3	0
Conservative	3.0	0	0	0
NDP	0	0	11.1	0
mixed	11.7	0	11.1	14.3
don't know	50.0	100.0	44.5	85.7
total	100	100	100	100
N=	34	4	9	7

eral, the number who actually do make a connection between their religion and the fact that a party may support the interests of their religious group, are small. Moreover, the numbers in Tables IV and V are small and should therefore be interpreted with caution.

Over-all, then, what these findings suggest, is that voters, independent of their religion, are usually unaware of or do not necessarily make a connection between religion and political parties. An argument that Catholics vote Liberal or that Protestants vote Conservative *because* they see these parties as supporting their religious interests, is untenable for all but a minority. Voting based on a rational consideration of which party supports the voter's religious interests, it can be inferred from the above, occurs in very few cases.

Birthplace and voting

A number of studies, as well as historical records, have shown that in Canada relationships between ethnic origin and party preference do exist. Often, relationships vary depending upon the region under discussion, yet at least one pattern has been noted more than once: the tendency of those of British ethnicity to cast their ballots for the Conservative party more so than for the Liberal party.[13]

In the present study, while birthplace rather than ethnicity is being considered, it appears that a similar pattern exists. The British-born tend to support the Conservative party (Table VI). Equally noticeable is the fact that a plurality of voters in the "other" category and a plurality of the Canadian-born disproportionately support the Liberals.

In order to determine whether the voter actually makes the connection between his birthplace and his vote, however, further analysis is required. In this, answers as to the individual's perceptions of which party supports immigrant interests will be examined. Should it be found that the British-born and/or the "other-born" perceive the party they vote for as supporting immigrant interests, statements can be made as to the rationality

[13]H.D. Scarrow, "Three Dimensions of a Local Party," in *Papers on the 1962 Election*, ed. J. Meisel (Toronto, 1965), 64. Also see J. Wilson, "Politics," 297.

TABLE VI

PARTY PREFERENCE BY PLACE OF BIRTH

	Place of birth		
Party preference	Britain (per cent)	Other (per cent)	Canada (per cent)
Liberal	21.2	52.0	41.0
Conservative	33.3	6.7	27.1
NDP	30.3	17.3	24.1
undecided	15.2	24.0	7.8
total	100	100	100
N=	33	75	166

Chi-square = 29.30; $df = 6$; p less than .05; Cramer's $V = .23$.

TABLE VII

BRITISH-BORN PERCEPTION OF PARTY SUPPORT*

	Party preference			
Party supporting immigrant interests	Liberal (per cent)	Conservative (per cent)	NDP (per cent)	Undecided (per cent)
NDP	16.7	36.4	40.0	20.0
mixed	50.0	0	20.0	0
don't know	33.3	63.6	40.0	80.0
total	100	100	100	100
N=	6	11	10	5

*Liberals and Conservatives are not listed in the vertical column of this table as they were not mentioned by respondents answering this question.

of their vote. Obviously, the argument being made here is that, objectively, the British-born are immigrants even though they may not define themselves as such. The fact that some of these individuals immigrated as long as 40 years ago may have reduced any feelings they may once have had as "immigrants."

As is evident from Table VII the British-born, whether they are Conservative or not, do not necessarily perceive the Conservatives as supporting immigrant interests; nor, for that matter, do they perceive the Liberals as doing so. When a party is named as supporting immigrant interests, it is usually the NDP. As the number of British-born who make the connection between their birthplace and the position of parties with respect to immigrant interests are few, however, the argument cannot readily be made that the British-born support this or that party because they view them as supporting their interests as immigrants. Again, as was the case when religion was examined, motivation for the British-born to vote for one party or another must be sought elsewhere.

In contrast to the British-born, those of other origins who, as it was shown disproportionately support the Liberals, do make a connection between the Liberals and promotion of immigrant interests. The percentages involved, though, are small (Table VIII).

Over-all, then, while "others" do tend to favour the Liberals, those who vote for other parties tend in approximately equal proportions to see these parties as supporting immigrant interests. Again, it cannot be assumed that, because individuals in a social category tend to vote for a particular party, they necessarily do so because they perceive the party as supporting their interests as, in this case, immigrants. As will be shown, similar statements can be made when class position is analysed.

Class and voting

In a major study, R. Alford has already shown for Canada as a whole that class voting is less evident than in Britain, Australia, and the United States.[14] Furthermore, he found regional, ethnic, and religious con-

[14]R. Alford, *Party and Society* (Chicago, 1963).

TABLE VIII

"OTHER-BORN" PERCEPTION OF PARTY SUPPORT

	Party preference			
Party supporting immigrant interests	Liberal (per cent)	Conservative (per cent)	NDP (per cent)	Undecided (per cent)
Liberal	25.6	0	16.7	16.7
Conservative	5.1	20.0	8.3	0
NDP	5.1	0	25.0	5.6
mixed	38.5	0	8.3	11.1
don't know	25.6	80.0	41.7	66.7
total	100	100	100	100
N=	39	5	12	18

TABLE IX

PARTY PREFERENCE BY OCCUPATION OF HEAD OF HOUSEHOLD

	Occupation		
Party preference	Blue-Collar (per cent)	White-Collar (per cent)	Self-Employed (per cent)
Liberal	48.7	38.1	50.0
Conservative	10.3	27.3	21.4
NDP	28.2	21.0	21.4
undecided	12.8	13.7	7.1
total	100	100	100
N=	78	176	14

Chi-square = 10.36; df = 6; p greater than .05; Cramer's V = .61.

siderations to be more important to an explanation of the vote in Canada than is class. Numerous case studies have confirmed the implication of this statement although in recent years there has been a suggestion that perhaps class plays more of a role, albeit a different one, in electoral behaviour than originally thought. That is, while it has been found that in general the Liberals and Conservatives receive more support from the upper and middle classes than do the NDP,[15] and that religion is a better predictor of party support for Liberals and Conservatives than is class, in at least two studies class has been found to correlate higher with the NDP vote than religion.[16] Knowledge of a person's religion, that is, is helpful in predicting an individual's vote if he is Liberal or Conservative – class is more useful as a predictor if he is NDP.

In the present study, these latter findings are not supported. Judging from the results in Table IX, there is no reason to suspect that class plays a large part in explaining the vote for any party, least of all for the NDP. Religion and birthplace are far more important in explaining the vote than is class.

When analysis is extended to perceptions by the middle class (class being measured by occupation of the head of the household) of which party supports their interests, it is evident that no particular party is perceived by the middle class as supporting their interests (Table X). Hence, for middle-class individuals, regardless of the party they support, no connection is made between class position and the fact that certain parties may support the interests of those in that position. In other words, it cannot be assumed, for the middle-class voter, that he rationally considers his class position before marking his ballot for a particular party.

For working-class individuals the situation is a little different. From Table XI it is obvious that when a party is named as support-

[15]Gagne and Regenstreif, "NDP Urban Support," 537. Also see Pauline Jewett, "Voting in the 1960 Federal Bi-Elections at Peterborough and Niagara Falls: Who Voted New Party and Why?," *Canadian Journal of Economics and Political Science*, 28 (1962), 64.

[16]Wilson, "Politics," 302. Also see, Gagne and Regenstreif, "NDP Urban Support," 536.

TABLE X

WHITE-COLLAR WORKERS' PERCEPTION OF PARTY SUPPORT

	Party preference		
Party supporting white-collar interests	Liberal (per cent)	Conservative (per cent)	NDP (per cent)
Liberal	10.8	8.3	19.4
Conservative	10.8	12.5	2.8
NDP	3.1	4.2	8.3
mixed	26.2	10.4	19.4
don't know	49.2	64.6	50.0
total	100	100	100
N=	65	48	36

TABLE XI

BLUE-COLLAR WORKERS' PERCEPTION OF PARTY SUPPORT*

	Party preference		
Party supporting blue-collar interests	Liberal (per cent)	Conservative (per cent)	NDP (per cent)
Liberal	10.5	12.5	0
NDP	31.6	25.0	63.6
mixed	23.7	25.0	9.1
don't know	34.2	37.5	27.3
total	100	100	100
N=	38	8	22

*Conservatives are not listed in the vertical column of this table as they were not mentioned by respondents answering this question.

ing working-class interests this party tends to be the NDP. This relationship holds independently of the party for which the worker actually votes: Liberal, Conservative, and NDP working-class voters all see the NDP as supporting working-class interests. In toto, 41.2 per cent of all workers perceive the NDP as supporting their interests. But as was indicated in Table IX, only 28.2 per cent of all workers actually vote for the NDP! Of this last percentage, 63.6 per cent of workers voting NDP, or 20.6 per cent of all workers, perceive the NDP as supporting workers' interests. Thus, the relationship for workers between voting NDP and perception that the NDP supports their interests as workers is far higher than any other relationship yet found between interest positions and perception that particular parties support these interest positions, even though the majority of workers do not support the NDP. In other words, while it may not be possible to say that in general a consideration of class position is rationally considered by the voter when casting his ballot, it is fair to say that this consideration is made and then disregarded by a number of workers who vote Liberal and Conservative. In addition, it is possible to argue that the class position of NDP working-class voters *is* rationally considered by them when marking their ballot. Unfortunately, the number of self-employed in the sample was too small to allow similar analysis of this group.

The overall picture

Using the data presented in the tables above, it was possible to construct a rough index of over-all "rationality" for supporters of each of the three parties. This measure was obtained, first of all, by adding the total number of times that supporters for a particular party identified their party as supporting an interest position which they were in. The second step was to then divide this number by the total number of supporters for each party who offered answers as to which party supported this or that interest. For example, Liberals made an identification between their own interest positions and the fact that the Liberal party supported these interests a total of 37 times. In other words, in 37 out of 252 (14.7 per cent) judgements as to which party supported particular interests, Liberals mentioned the Liberal party. This is rather low when compared to figures for the NDP but is higher than the figures for the Conservatives: 18.8 per cent of NDPers and 8.5 per cent of Conservatives named their party as supporting particular interests which they also had. What this means is that while NDPers may make identifications between their interest positions more frequently than do Conservatives or Liberals, it is still only a minority of NDPers who do so.

These findings notwithstanding, it should be kept in mind that measurement here was based on an evaluation of three interest positions – religion, birthplace, and class. It is possible that had other interest positions been considered, the outcomes would have been different. A concentration on these variables is justified, however. In other studies of the voting behaviour of Canadians, great emphasis has been placed on them. The point being made here is that while there may be some association between, for example, being Catholic and voting Liberal, it cannot be assumed that the Catholic voter in Broadview votes as he does because he perceives the Liberals as supporting Catholic interests. More generally, it can be argued that certain social groups in Broadview may tend to cast their ballots for particular parties, but it cannot be concluded from this fact that they perceive the party as supporting group interests.

The implication of these findings is that V.O. Key may be quite correct when he maintains that "voters are not fools." But it is fairly evident from the above analysis that in Broadview voters do not base their decisions to vote for this or that party on a perception that their favoured party supports their religious, birthplace, or class interests. As mentioned previously, it is quite possible that the present study did not include an analysis of the particular "interest" positions which voters might feel that the party they vote for supports. It is equally possible, however, that in trying to explain the vote in Canada, researchers should pay more attention to "group pressures" and irrational factors as outlined by Lipset in the introduction to this article. Unfortunately, studies emphasizing the consequences of group interactions for the vote have not been carried out in Canada. It is high time that they were.

Appendix

The following questions were used in assessing the extent to which individuals were able to make the connection between the interests supported by particular parties and their own religious, ethnic, or class interests.

72 It is generally agreed that people support different parties. The reason for this is that sometimes a certain party may be more concerned with the interests of a particular group of people than are the other parties. Which party would support the interests of the following groups of people? If you feel that more than one of the parties support the interests of any one group please say so. (Repeat question.)
a people who think that unions are a good thing
b people who work in offices or who are not paid by the hour
c people who think that Canada is drifting too far away from England
d people who work in factories, on construction work, and so on.
e immigrants
f the upper class
g people who are self-employed
h Protestants
i people who fear American domination of the economy
j Catholics
k owners of land
l the unemployed
m those who advocate more government control of the economy
n people who oppose communism
o religious people
p home owners
q people who find it hard to get credit when they want to buy things.

6*a* And what is your religion?
10*b* What exactly do you do in your job?
23 Could you tell me what country you were born in please?
66 Which party did you vote for in the last federal election (1968)?

A Shapley Value Analysis of the Proposed Canadian Constitutional Amendment Scheme

D.R. MILLER *University of Florida**

The interactions of a group of non-identical voting units may be studied by applying the concept of the Shapley value from *n*-person co-operative game theory.[1] In this theory one assumes that voting units, or players, may form coalitions of various kinds in order to achieve success in the game, and one may assign a "value" to each such coalition based on what it can accomplish against arbitrary coalitions of the remaining players. The relative value of an individual player is calculated by considering how much he brings to each coalition he might join, that is, by how much the value of that coalition increases because of his membership, and summing this figure over all coalitions of which he could be a part.

The mathematical definition is made by assuming that a coalition S can be assured of obtaining some value from the game, say $v(S)$. The value of player k to this coalition is $v(S)-v(S-k)$, the amount by which its value is changed by his membership. The total value of an individual player is found by multiplying this quantity by the number of ways that such a coalition can form, and summing over all types of coalitions; thus the Shapley value of player k is:

$$(1)\quad \phi(k) = \sum_{\text{all } S} [(n-s)!\,(s-1)!/n!] \times [v(S) - v(S-k)].$$

The Shapley value is by no means the only way to assign a measure of importance to an individual player in an *n*-person game; a number of alternatives, each with its own advantages, exists.[2] The Shapley value, however, has several favourable characteristics. To begin with, it has withstood the scrutiny of game theorists themselves, who still see it as a sound basis for arbitrated settlements and similar problems some 20 years after its formulation.[3] Secondly, it is inherently satisfying mathematically, for the same formula results from a number of quite different lines of reasoning, and can be deduced from a surprisingly simple collection of postulates.[4] Most important for the present discussion, however, is the fact that it is particularly suitable in situations where there is no difficulty in assigning values to the individual coalitions. This means that it is quite useful in voting situations, where the outcome of a particular process can be assumed to have a value of either one or zero for each possible coalition, depending on whether the vote does or does not go the way the players in that coalition wish. The applicability is even more direct when votes can be regarded as essentially isolated events, as they may very well be in a constitutional amendment scheme, as opposed to the situation in governing bodies in which votes are a frequent occurrence and log-rolling must be considered.

It is therefore reasonable to think of applying these concepts to the question of constitutional amendment in Canada, for the scheme proposed in 1971 was characterized by the involvement of a variety of possible coalitions among the provinces. Although a number of features are not allowed for in the calculations to follow (for example, no reference is made to the order in which the voting takes place), it certainly seems worthwhile to examine what sort of measure of voting power is assigned to each province by the Shapley value concept.

Calculations

The assumptions we will make are essentially those of the amendment scheme proposed in 1971. That is, we assume that there are 10 players (the provinces) in the

*Present address: Division of Biological Sciences, National Research Council, Ottawa.

[1]R.D. Luce, and H. Raiffa, *Games and Decisions* (New York, 1957), section 6.8 and chap. 11. For a more recent discussion and an application similar to that presented here, see J.H. Banzhaf III, One Man, 3.312 Votes: A Mathematical Analysis of the Electoral College," *Villanova Law Review*, 13 (1968), 304–12. For a critique see R.J. Sickels, "The Power Index and the Electoral College," *Villanova Law Review*, 14 (1968), 92–6.

[2]G. Owen, *Game Theory* (Philadelphia, 1968), chaps. 8 and 9.

[3]W.F. Lucas, "An Overview of the Mathematical Theory of Games," *Management Science*, 18 (part 2) (1972), 3–19.

[4]Owen, *Game Theory*, 179 ff.

Canadian Journal of Political Science/Revue canadienne de science politique, VI, no. 1 (March/mars 1973). Printed in Canada/Imprimé au Canada.

TABLE I

WINNING COALITIONS (BC = British Columbia; P = prairie province, one of Alberta, Saskatchewan and Manitoba; O = Ontario; Q = Quebec; A = Atlantic province, one of New Brunswick, Nova Scotia, Prince Edward Island, and Newfoundland)

Type	Structure	Members (= s)	No. of ways can be formed
1	BC + 1P + O + Q + 2A	6	18
2	BC + 2P + O + Q + 2A	7	18
3	3P + O + Q + 2A	7	6
4	BC + 1P + O + Q + 3A	7	12
5	BC + 3P + O + Q + 2A	8	6
6	BC + 2P + O + Q + 3A	8	12
7	3P + O + Q + 3A	8	4
8	BC + 1P + O + Q + 4A	8	3
9	BC + 3P + O + Q + 3A	9	4
10	BC + 2P + O + Q + 4A	9	3
11	3P + O + Q + 4A	9	1
12	BC + 3P + O + Q + 4A	10	1
total			88

game. Approval is required of any province that contains (or ever has contained) 25 per cent of the population; at least two of the four Atlantic provinces; and at least two of the western provinces that currently contain (together) 50 per cent of the western population. Currently this means that Quebec and Ontario have vetoes, as have any coalition of three Atlantic provinces, a coalition of British Columbia with any prairie province, and the three prairie provinces taken together.[5]

The value of the game will be one to any winning coalition (any collection of provinces that can get an amendment through) and zero to all others. Thus, to calculate the Shapley value for each province, we consider all the winning coalitions of which it is a member *and* which would not win without its membership, and add these according to equation (1). There are 12 types of winning coalitions, displayed in Table I along with the number of different ways that each can be formed.

When calculating the Shapley value for Quebec or Ontario, each coalition is given the value one, since each becomes a losing coalition without that province's membership. Thus, Quebec is a part of 18 winning six-player coalitions, 36 winning seven-player coalitions, and so forth. The formula (1) becomes:

$$\phi(\text{Quebec}) = 18(5!4!/10!) + 36(6!3!/10!) + 25(7!2!/10!) + 8(8!1!/10!) + 1(9!0!/10!) = 53/168 = .3155.$$

The calculation for Ontario is identical.

For other players the calculation is different since not all the coalitions lose without them and since they are not members of all those listed in Table I. Alberta, for example, is a member of only six of the coalitions of type 1, and cannot count types 2, 5, 6, etc., because with one fewer prairie province these remain winning coalitions. Thus Alberta is critical to six coalitions of type 1, six of type 3, four of type 4, and so forth. We find:

$$\phi(\text{Alberta}) = 6(5!4!/10!) + 10(6!3!/10!) + 7(7!2!/10!) + 3(8!1!/10!) = 1/24 = .0417.$$

Other calculations are carried out in a similar way. The complete results are displayed in Table II.

Results

The critical question one wishes to address in connection with these calculations is that of the "fairness," whatever that means, of the voting scheme. While we are not prepared here to come to grips with this question in detail, it is certainly reasonable to

[5]A veto is also held by the federal government. Here, we consider only the votes of the provinces, justifying the simplification by pointing out that we only want to compare regional voting powers. The inclusion of the federal veto in some sense gives a double voting avenue to some people. The larger problem is certainly of interest, but is considerably more complicated.

TABLE II

SHAPLEY VOTES-PER-PERSON

Province	Shapley Value (per cent)	Population (per cent)	"Shapley votes-per-person"
British Columbia	12.50	9.38	1.334
Alberta	4.17	7.33	0.570
Saskatchewan	4.17	4.79	0.872
Manitoba	4.17	4.82	0.865
4 Western	25.01	26.32	0.952
Ontario	31.55	34.85	0.905
Quebec	31.55	28.94	1.092
New Brunswick	2.98	3.09	0.965
Nova Scotia	2.98	3.79	0.786
Prince Edward Island	2.98	0.54	5.53
Newfoundland	2.98	2.47	1.208
4 Atlantic	11.92	9.89	1.206

Population figures are for the ten-province voting area only.
Source: Canadian Almanac and Directory 1972 (Toronto, 1972).

compare the calculated power distribution with some measure that is traditionally used. The obvious one would seem to be the one person / one vote principle, and Table II also displays the results of dividing the Shapley value, expressed as a percentage, by the percentage population of each region. The result, which we call "Shapley votes-per-person," would be uniformly equal to one if the one person / one vote principle were perfectly applied.

In general, the results are surprisingly close. The lowest figure is for Alberta, with only 0.570 Shapley votes-per-person. However, if we assume that Albertan interests are likely to be close to those of its neighbours, the figure of 0.952 for the western provinces as a unit provides some consolation. One might also calculate that the two-province combination of Alberta and British Columbia has a population of 16.71 per cent and a Shapley value of 16.67 per cent, resulting in 0.997 Shapley votes-per-person. Thus, although Albertans may appear to be under-represented, the larger groups of which they are a part are certainly not.

The figures for Prince Edward Island are more difficult to rationalize. It would certainly seem that the figure of 5.53 Shapley votes-per-person is excessive, but it appears that this is bound to happen under any scheme which gives provinces comparable voting weights. Combining the vote of two provinces for the sake of constitutional amendments might be suggested in order to equalize things somewhat; for example, if Prince Edward Island and Newfoundland were made a single voting unit, the population involved would be close to a third of the total population of the Atlantic provinces, and in one sense the voting power distribution would be improved. However, in any conflict with Newfoundland, Prince Edward Island would be converted to a totally ineffective player, one which cannot change the value of any coalition. There seems to be an argument to the effect that over-representation is preferable to placing any province in this position.

The author has also calculated the distribution of Shapley values for alternative veto rules, such as one that requires three Atlantic provinces (rather than two) to support an amendment. In that case, the Shapley value of each of the Atlantic provinces increases to 7.74 per cent, giving 30.96 per cent of the Shapley voting power to 9.89 per cent of the population. In each other case examined,[6] similar results were found; no distribution of votes produced results which were as closely in line with population figures as the primary scheme discussed here.

[6]The constraints of regional interests were always maintained. That is, requiring that some sub-coalition have a certain number of members in favour was applied only to sub-coalitions consisting of neighbouring provinces. Abandoning this constraint might lead to closer figures, but it is not clear that there would be any politically workable way of putting such a scheme into practice.

The comment that British Columbia might have an "effective veto," as Quebec and Ontario certainly have, merits some discussion.[7] On the one hand this appears not to be the case, since coalitions of types 3, 7, and 11 do not involve British Columbia but are able to pass any amendment. However, the Shapley value for British Columbia is greater than the combined Shapley values for the four Atlantic provinces, and certainly the latter collectively have a well-defined veto. This seeming discrepancy should be regarded as characteristic of the model; there is no well-defined Shapley value which is equivalent to veto power.

To summarize, we may repeat three observations. First, the proposed scheme produces a distribution of voting power which, according to one standard measurement scheme at least, matches the distribution of population surprisingly well. Second, under the one person / one vote concept, the proposed scheme comes as close to equitable power distribution as any politically feasible scheme which does not reduce any province to ineffective status. Finally, the work provides another example of how relatively simple calculations can help to provide quantitative aids to the judgement of such voting arrangements.[8]

[7]*Toronto Globe and Mail* (10 February 1971), 2.

[8]This paper was prepared while the author was attending an institute on deterministic methods in operations research at Cornell University under the sponsorship of the National Science Foundation. I thank Dr William F. Lucas, Director of the Institute, for many helpful suggestions.

Note bibliographique
Review Article

Les études de la Commission royale d'enquête sur le bilinguisme et le biculturalisme

JEAN-CHARLES BONENFANT *Université Laval*

Dans les analyses déjà publiées des « Documents de la Commission royale d'enquête sur le bilinguisme et le biculturalisme », le Document no. 4, *Constitutional Adaptation and Canadian Federalism since 1945*, de Donald C. Smiley avait été laissé de côté. C'est pourquoi j'y reviens avant d'examiner les deux derniers documents offerts au public.

L'évolution constitutionnelle

Pour plusieurs, les difficultés du fédéralisme canadien exigent des solutions constitutionnelles, et même, si la Commission royale d'enquête sur le bilinguisme et le biculturalisme ne s'est guère prononcée elle-même sur le rôle des institutions politiques à l'intérieur de la dualité canadienne, il reste que l'étude du fonctionnement récent du fédéralisme canadien s'imposait ne serait-ce que pour les moments de crise qu'il a parfois provoqués dans les relations entre Québec et Ottawa. On en a confié la tâche à un spécialiste reconnu, Donald V. Smiley, qui a intitulé son travail *Constitutional Adaptation and Canadian Federalism since 1945*[1].

Dans sa préface, datée de juillet 1967, l'auteur a la prudence de rappeler que son étude fut préparée entre l'été de 1964 et le printemps de 1966, c'est-à-dire à une époque où les relations fédérales-provinciales étaient en perpétuelle évolution. Il a cependant pu ajouter une courte annexe permettant de faire le point jusqu'au milieu de 1967.

L'ouvrage est clairement divisé en huit chapitres. Le premier est une sorte d'introduction qui précise que l'objet principal de l'étude est l'activité de l'Etat à l'intérieur des institutions fédératives canadiennes et plus particulièrement les relations entre les deux ordres de gouvernements qui au Canada exerce cette activité. C'est l'occasion de rappeler les grands principes à l'aide de citations de K.C. Wheare et Carl J. Friedrich et de souligner qu'on ne peut dissocier les facteurs sociologiques et politiques du fédéralisme. Certes le fédéralisme canadien a connu des difficultés avant la seconde grande guerre, mais il est naturel de faire naître au lendemain de celle-ci ce qu'on pourrait appeler l'histoire moderne des relations fédérales-provinciales, d'où un chapitre qui rappelle les propositions qui furent formulées au cours de la session de 1944–5 et surtout toute la politique de rétablissement englobée dans une « nouvelle politique nationale ».

L'auteur examine attentivement ce qu'a été le fédéralisme canadien d'après-guerre en soulignant qu'il y a eu, malgré qu'on en ait dit, une atténuation de la domination fédérale. Il traite particulièrement des nouvelles orientations qui se sont manifestées dans le Québec après l'arrivée au pouvoir, en juin 1960, des Libéraux dirigés par M. Jean Lesage. Au chapitre IV, il étudie plus précisément les mécanismes d'ajustement dans la constitution canadienne. Après avoir rappelé rapidement ce qu'était le règlement de base de 1867, les modifications que les amendements et surtout l'interprétation judiciaire y ont apportés, il arrive à notre époque pour étudier ce nouvel instrument d'activité fédérale que constitue le pouvoir de dépenser. Le chapitre traite aussi de la possibilité de la délégation intergouvernementale du pouvoir d'urgence pour conclure que, historiquement, le fédéralisme canadien, vu sous un éclairage légaliste, a joui d'une admirable faculté d'adaptation. Ce chapitre III constitue une excellent synthèse à la fois politique et juridique de la transformation du fédéralisme canadien. Grand spécialiste des subventions conditionnelles, le professeur Smiley ne pouvait manquer d'y consacrer un chapitre ainsi qu'un autre à l'histoire complémentaire de ces subventions, c'est-à-dire la possibilité accordée aux provinces de se retirer des programmes conjoints. Un chapitre porte aussi sur la théorie et la pratique de ce qu'on a appelé le fédéralisme coopératif.

[1]Documents of the Royal Commission on Bilingualism and Biculturalism, 4 (Ottawa, 1970). Ce document n'a pas été traduit en français.

Canadian Journal of Political Science/Revue canadienne de science politique, VI, no. 1 (March/mars 1973). Printed in Canada/Imprimé au Canada.

Dans un chapitre spécial, qui prend parfois figure de conclusion générale, l'auteur évalue ce qu'a été ce fédéralisme coopératif et c'est l'occasion pour lui de traiter du statut particulier du Québec dont on parlait beaucoup au moment où l'étude a été écrite. Il note que dans le système fédératif, tel qu'il a été conçu de 1864 à 1867, aussi bien que dans son évolution postérieure, il n'y avait rien qui prévoyait un statut particulier dans la forme et dans les dimensions qu'ont recherchées au moins deux gouvernements du Québec, celui de M. Lesage et celui de M. Johnson et il doute que, par des accords entre le gouvernement fédéral et le gouvernement du Québec, il puisse être possible d'effectuer des changements constitutionnels suffisants pour que le Québec soit lié avec le reste du Canada par des liens quasi-diplomatiques plutôt que par des liens fédératifs. Les conclusions de l'auteur sont plutôt optimistes et il écrit textuellement (p. 127) : « it seems that Canadian federalism has not yet passed the point of no return ».

L'étude est dense, bien documentée, et on peut regretter qu'elle n'ait pas été traduite en français car elle me semble une des analyses les plus objectives et les plus complètes des problèmes financiers et politiques du fédéralisme au Canada de 1945 à 1967.

La carrière de fonctionnaire

Un des documents les plus importants né de l'enquête sur le bilinguisme et le biculturalisme, tant par son sujet que par son envergure, est certainement celui qui s'intitule *Bureaucratic Careers: Anglophones and Francophones in the Canadian Public Service*[2]. Les auteurs qui l'ont signé sont Christopher Beattie, Jacques Désy, et Stephen Longstaff. Dès les premières lignes, ils expliquent que l'étude de la fonction publique a eu un caractère spécial et, qu'au cours de sa préparation, les experts qui ont travaillé, ont été en perpétuelles relations avec le personnel de la Commission. La plupart des vingt chapitres ont été écrits en anglais mais quelques-uns l'ont été en français. Nous ne pouvons en donner ici qu'une mince image. On y trouve d'abord un arrière-plan historique dans lequel on rappelle que la lutte pour le bilinguisme à Ottawa commença véritablement avec Ernest Lapointe, ministre de la Justice, et représentant du Québec dans le gouvernement que forma, en 1935, M. Mackenzie King. Les chapitres suivants décrivent les mécanismes de la fonction publique et on en arrive aux chapitres de base, c'est-à-dire ceux qui sont consacrés aux éléments humains qui font partie de la vie et du travail des fonctionnaires de carrière. Les éléments étudiés sont nombreux : le lieu de naissance, la langue maternelle, l'appartenance religieuse, l'éducation, l'expérience antérieure, les motifs d'entrée dans la fonction publique, la montée vers les sommets, la satisfaction dans la carrière. On a eu l'heureuse idée de concrétiser, en quelque sorte, l'étude générale par l'étude spéciale, de quatre types de carrières assez variées puisque c'est celle d'officier de finance, celle de recherchiste en agriculture, celle de traducteur, et celle d'examinateur de brevets. L'étude sur la carrière de traducteur, avec un sous-titre, « un certain refuge » qui, déjà est presque un commentaire, a été écrite en français et elle se termine par un délicieux portrait du traducteur dont il convient de citer les quelques lignes (p. 375) : « être insatisfait, cultivé, qui ne peut faire profession de ses connaissances qu'en traduisant; être incompris, dont la susceptibilité doit être ménagée; enfin, être instable, pour qui la fonction publique fédérale représente un havre de paix où il trouve enfin la sécurité professionnelle longtemps recherchée ».

C'est aussi en français qu'ont été écrits un chapitre sur « Les connaissances linguistiques et l'emploi des langues » et un chapitre intitulé « La réaction des francophones aux promesses du bilinguisme et du biculturalisme ». On conclut que la majorité des francophones de l'échelon intermédiaire entretiennent des attitudes optimistes ou mixtes car ils entrevoient des changements réels dans la fonction publique fédérale, mais les auteurs ne craignent pas d'écrire (p. 557) : « le fonctionnairisme fédéral ne pourra pas attirer et retenir dans ses rangs les francophones du pays, en particulier ceux du Québec, différents des autres sur plusieurs points, si de profondes transformations linguistiques et culturelles ne viennent pas modifier le milieu de travail et le milieu de vie du fonctionnarisme outaouais, et si les effets normaux et explicables des rapports majorité-minorité ne sont pas contrés ».

Il est assez difficile de formuler des conclusions générales à la fin d'un document aussi riche et composite. Tout de même, les auteurs ne se sont pas refusés à cette responsabilité et ils ont écrit trois pages réalistes qui se terminent par ces mots (p. 562) : «in few places did we find that the desire for Francophone personnel was complemented by the willingness to provide the intellectual atmosphere and work arrange-

---

[2]Documents of the Royal Commission on Bilingualism and Biculturalism, 11 (Ottawa, 1972).

ments, both formal and informal, that in some way would reflect the language and culture of French Canada. Whether a truly bilingual and bicultural Public Service can be developed is difficult to say, but it is obvious that Canada will not receive the effective administration that it needs until it is ».

La fonction publique québécoise

On est un peu surpris qu'un des documents de la Commission royale d'enquête sur le bilinguisme et le biculturalisme s'intitule *Essais sur la fonction publique québécoise*[3], mais, en le parcourant, on s'aperçoit vite que ce n'est pas un hors-d'œuvre. Le Québec est, en effet, un microcosme dont évidemment la fonction publique n'est pas aussi développée que celle du gouvernement fédéral mais qu'il est quand même intéressant d'étudier sous l'angle de la dualité linguistique. Dans le titre, le mot « Essais » est au pluriel parce qu'en réalité le document rassemble quatre essais qui auraient pu être élaborés et réalisés indépendamment. L'auteur en est Gérard Lapointe qui a bénéficié de l'aide de quelques hauts fonctionnaires provinciaux. Le travail n'était pas facile car non seulement on a peu écrit jusqu'ici sur la fonction publique du Québec, mais, en outre, celle-ci ne s'est guère développée véritablement que depuis un quart de siècle.

Le premier essai porte sur « Les caractéristiques des fonctionnaires provinciaux du Québec », la période étudiée commençant avec le premier rapport annuel de la Commission de la fonction publique du Québec en date du 31 mars 1944 et se terminant avec le rapport de 1965. Pendant cette période, on étudie la répartition des fonctionnaires selon le sexe, l'âge et l'état civil, leurs lieux d'origine, leurs milieux de vie, leurs études, l'évolution de leurs traitements, et leur composition ethno-linguistique. A propos de cette composition, on constate qu'en 1941, on dénombrait proportionnellement plus de fonctionnaires féminins chez les Canadiens anglais que chez les Canadiens français, mais que par ailleurs, en 1961, c'était l'inverse. Signalons qu'on trouve plus de célibataires chez les francophones que chez les anglophones. Le niveau de scolarisation des fonctionnaires ne se différencie pas d'un groupe ethnique à un autre. Enfin, pour la période couverte par l'enquête, c'étaient les fonctionnaires d'origine britannique qui présentaient la plus haute moyenne de traitement.

Le deuxième essai est un exposé sommaire sur la carrière des fonctionnaires provinciaux. Dans l'introduction de cette partie, l'auteur souligne qu'il n'y a pas si longtemps encore on ne parlait guère dans la province de Québec de « faire carrière » dans la fonction publique provinciale et que rares étaient les professionnels ou les techniciens qui envisageaient d'entrer dans cet univers. L'essai décrit ensuite le cadre légal au sein duquel se réalise la carrière du fonctionnaire. Il explique comment du « patronage » d'autrefois on est passé, par l'étape intermédiaire de l'examen individuel, à l'examen groupe. Il analyse les motifs d'entrée dans la fonction publique provinciale à l'aide de réponses à un questionnaire détaillé. On a observé que les jeunes fonctionnaires ont plus souvent que leurs aînés sélectionné le motif « carrière » et qu'un écart important s'est manifesté entre les informateurs des deux sexes, les fonctionnaires masculins étant significativement plus nombreux que leurs collègues féminins à le retenir. La vie de travail des fonctionnaires est aussi étudiée.

Le troisième essai porte sur le bilinguisme et la langue de travail. Après avoir constaté que 93.4 pour cent des informateurs parlent chez eux le français et que, par ailleurs, 30 pour cent des anglophones s'expriment chez eux souvent en français, on constate qu'il y avait alors 44 pour cent de bilingues dans la fonction publique québécoise. L'auteur croit (p. 111) qu'il y a eu chez les informateurs une certaine sur-estimation de leurs capacités. « L'administration québécoise, écrit-il, compte certainement un fort pourcentage de fonctionnaires bilingues, mais les proportions que fournit l'index de bilinguisme doivent être entendues à l'intérieur des limites de confiance pour lesquelles il conviendrait de considérer non pas la marge supérieure des erreurs, mais la marge inférieure à la proportion observée ». Par ailleurs, la connaissance de l'anglais était jugée nécessaire par 37.6 pour cent des fonctionnaires francophones mais 9 francophones sur 10 utilisaient presque toujours le français et 4 anglophones sur 10 l'anglais. Dans leurs communications verbales ou écrites avec des fonctionnaires fédéraux, sur 10 informateurs francophones ou de langue française 6 ou 7 emploient principalement le français, 2 ou 3 le français ou l'anglais et un principalement l'anglais. Les publications et la traduction sont aussi étudiées et l'essai se termine par un certain nombre de conclusions dont il est intéressant de donner l'essentiel : il y a

[3]Documents of the Royal Commission on Bilingualism and Biculturalism, 12 (Ottawa, 1971). Ce document n'a pas été traduit en français.

dans de nombreux secteurs de la fonction publique un unilinguisme français effectif; par ailleurs, presque sans accroc, on observe un bilinguisme de type légaliste; le bilinguisme pratiqué peut aussi parfois être qualifié de courtois; comme on s'est toujours félicité au Québec, du moins officiellement, de respecter les droits des minorités, le bilinguisme des services publics est souvent perçu comme une reconnaissance normale des citoyens de langue anglaise et l'auteur ajoute : « il est cependant regrettable que cette attitude n'inspire pas plus fortement les anglophones des autres provinces vis-à-vis des minorités francophones ». Enfin, l'auteur souligne dans une dernière remarque qu' « un certain bilinguisme s'inspire d'un désir profond d'efficacité ... Si l'on ne peut se faire comprendre qu'en anglais, écrit-il, on utilisera donc cette langue pour ne pas perdre du temps pour arriver à des résultats positifs et pour travailler de façon efficace avec les représentants du gouvernement fédéral ou des organismes anglophones »

Le quatrième essai s'intitule « Profil de l'organisation administrative du Québec ». Après avoir rappelé que « c'est presque devenu un lieu commun de dire que la fonction publique québécoise a évolué selon un rythme accéléré au cours des dernières années », l'auteur étudie la perception de cette évolution par les fonctionnaires. Dans un premier chapitre, il analyse quelques transformations de l'appareil administratif et, dans le second, il traite plus particulièrement des nouveaux spécialistes en fonction de l'évolution de l'administration publique québécoise. Il termine cet essai en posant la question suivante : « Pour un fonctionnaire supérieur au service de l'administration du Québec, existe-t-il des liens entre les transformations intervenues dans la fonction publique provinciale et l'évolution de la société québécoise ? » Les réponses révélatrices peuvent se résumer comme suit : Pour certains, les deux évolutions, tout en ne se confondant pas, s'interpénètrent à un tel point qu'il n'est pas possible d'identifier laquelle est « le moteur de l'autre »; pour d'autres, le gouvernement a réellement assuré le leadership de l'évolution; pour d'autres encore, dans une perspective inverse, l'évolution de l'administration publique n'est qu'un reflet de l'évolution de la société globale et ainsi elle n'a que partiellement concouru au progrès du Québec.

C'était une gageure que de tenter d'écrire ces quatre essais sur la fonction publique du Québec avec aussi peu de matériel, mais l'auteur l'a bien soutenue. Le livre est intéressant; il révèle des constatations intéressantes. Il n'a que le défaut involontaire d'avoir été dépassé rapidement par la précipitation des événements, car déjà la fonction publique québécoise diffère de ce qu'elle était il y a quelques années.

Les associations volontaires

Le treizième et, semble-t-il, le dernier volume des documents a pour titre *Ethnic Relations in Canadian Voluntary Associations*[4]. Il a été préparé par John Meisel et Vincent Lemieux et, malgré son titre anglais, le français et l'anglais y alternent selon les sujets traités. Dès le début, on explique que l'étude des relations ethniques au sein des associations volontaires, ou entre elles, exige un cadre d'analyse qui soit approprié d'une part à l'étude générale de ces associations, et d'autre part, à l'examen de cet aspect particulier de leurs relations internes ou externes. Une typologie des objectifs est tracée et un plan, autant que possible uniforme, est adopté pour chacune des études. Les organismes suivants ont été étudiés : Les Scouts catholiques du Canada et The Boy Scouts of Canada; La Québec Amateur Hockey Association et la Confédération des loisirs du Québec (secteur hockey) et The Canadian Amateur Hockey Association; L'Union générale des étudiants du Québec et The Canadian Union of Students; La Fédération des jeunes chambres du Canada français et The Canada Junior Chamber of Commerce; L'Association des médecins de langue française du Canada et l'Association médicale du Québec et The Canadian Medical Association; The Royal College of Physicians and Surgeons of Canada; La Chambre de commerce de la province de Québec et The Canadian Chamber of Commerce; L'Union des municipalités de la province de Québec et The Canadian Federation of Mayors and Municipalities; Le Conseil canadien de la coopération et The Co-operative Union of Canada; L'Union catholique des cultivateurs et The Canadian Federation of Agriculture.

Un assez long chapitre de conclusions souligne un certain nombre d'observations découlant des enquêtes. En voici quelques-unes qui peuvent être transposées dans d'autres domaines où se pose le problème de la dualité canadienne. Les auteurs remarquent que l'emploi de la langue dans une association n'est pas simplement une question de communcation d'idées. En ef-

[4]Documents of the Royal Commission on Bilingualism and Biculturalism, 13 (Ottawa, 1972).

fet, la langue peut affecter le contenu même de ces idées car on ne peut la séparer de la culture. Une décision prise en anglais et traduite ensuite en français n'est pas toujours tout à fait la même que si elle avait été formulée en français. C'est pourquoi, plusieurs membres francophones des associations volontaires ont exprimé leur mécontentement face aux procédés de prise de décision dans leur organisme. « They felt », précisent les auteurs, (p. 299–300), « that what we might call their cultural tradition was not really able to permeate the substance of the decisions and activities of their associations ».

On note aussi que plusieurs anglophones de bonne volonté ont beaucoup d'admiration et même un peu d'envie pour l'habilité linguistique de leurs collègues francophones, mais on oublie peut-être que s'ils s'expriment avec facilité en anglais ils le feraient sans doute encore mieux en français ou du moins différemment et on continue en formulant l'importante constatation suivante (p. 300–1) : « many Anglophones of goodwill greatly admire and envy the linguistic dexterity of their Francophone colleagues, little realizing that the latter, although they express themselves with ease in English, would nevertheless speak better (and somewhat differently) in French ».

Enfin, soulignons une autre constatation réaliste que les auteurs expriment ainsi (p. 311) : « we have already noted that, if he wishes fully to participate in a pan-Canadian association, the Francophone member must often make the effort of placing himself into an ambience which is linguistically and culturally somewhat alien to him ».

Il semble bien que toutes les études de la Commission royale d'enquête sur le bilinguisme et le biculturalisme qu'on voulait communiquer au public l'aient été. Le bilan en est plutôt positif et, une fois de plus, une Commission d'enquête a enrichi, au Canada, la bibliothèque des sciences de l'homme. La Commission royale d'enquête sur le bilinguisme et le biculturalisme a pu provoquer des polémiques; on a pu l'accuser de n'être pas allée jusqu'au bout de sa tâche, de s'être éloignée avec le temps de l'orientation de ses premiers rapports; on a pu facilement critiquer le coût élevé de l'enquête : il reste qu'avec plus d'ampleur que ne l'avait fait, un quart de siècle auparavant, la Commission royale des relations entre le Dominion et les provinces, elle a mobilisé dans tout les Canada de nombreux universitaires, elle a orienté, jusqu'à un certain point, leurs recherches, et elle a engendré des travaux de valeur inégale mais dont l'ensemble a permis une meilleure prise de conscience de la réalité canadienne et en particulier de la dualité du pays. Pour la première fois peut-être, une foule de problèmes canadiens ont été abordés scientifiquement et sans passion et discrètement des opinions ont été exprimées qui ont pénétré dans les milieux divers. Après avoir rappelé que, « même si les gouvernements n'accordent pas parfois beaucoup d'attention aux recommandations des commissions royales d'enquête, celles-ci exercent une influence réelle dans les milieux universitaires, professionnels et scientifiques », le professeur Khayyam Zev Paltiel, ajoutait : « l'expérience démontre que les opinions qu'une génération n'accepte pas deviennent souvent des « idées reçues » pour les générations suivantes ».[5]

On peut croire qu'il en sera de même des études et des documents aussi bien que des rapports de la Commission royale d'enquête sur le bilinguisme et le biculturalisme et qu'ainsi les idées généreuses qui l'engendrèrent ne sont pas mortes avec la dissolution de l'organisme.

[5] « Les Commissions royales d'enquête » dans *Le Système politique du Canada* sous la direction de Me Louis Sabourin (Ottawa, 1968), 388.

Recensions Reviews

Simeon, *Federal-Provincial Diplomacy* MICHAEL B. STEIN 149
Morin, *Le pouvoir québécois ... en négociation*, et Lalande, *Pourquoi le fédéralisme* JEAN-CHARLES BONENFANT 151
Carter, Canadian Conditional Grants since World War II MARVIN BLAUER 154
Allen, *The Social Passion* WALTER YOUNG 155
Ritchie, *An Institute for Research on Public Policy*, Doern, *Political Policy-Making*, and Rivlin, *New Approaches to Public Decision-Making* PATRICK KYBA 156
Noel, *Politics in Newfoundland* H.B. MAYO 157
Cook, *The Maple Leaf Forever* RICHARD SIMEON 158
Winks, *The Blacks in Canada* EUGENE D. GENOVESE 159
Leiss, *The Domination of Nature* T.J. CARTWRIGHT 160
Binder et al., *Crises and Sequences in Political Development* R.H. JACKSON 161
Gombin, *Les origines du gauchisme* SERGE LATOUCHE 162
Dunn, *Modern Revolutions*, Wilkinson, *Social Movement*, and Rubinoff, ed., *Tradition and Revolution* JOHN ANSON WARNER 164
Miles, *Metropolitan Problems, International Perspectives* RICHARD E. STREN 165
Marx, *L'administration locale en Grande-Bretagne* LOUISE QUESNEL-OUELLET 167
Paulus, *Les milieux dirigeants belges et l'adhésion du Royaume-Uni aux communautés européennes* FERRY DE KERCKHOVE 167
Gunn, *Factions No More* JOHN STEWART 169
Leibniz, *The Political Writings of Leibniz*, Riley, trans. and ed. WILLIAM CHRISTIAN 169

Richard Simeon, **Federal-Provincial Diplomacy: The Making of Recent Policy in Canada.** Toronto: University of Toronto Press, 1972, pp. xvii, 324.

In recent years there has been increasing interest by Canadian political scientists in new approaches to comparative political studies in general and comparative federalism in particular. The earlier emphasis on formal-legal and institutional approaches to Canadian federalism has changed markedly. There are now available a variety of innovative efforts; they define and interpret Canadian federalism in terms of such factors as élite accommodation, the relationship between the political and social structures, the pattern of ethnic-linguistic relationships, patterns of party and group structures, the financial relationships between the federal and provincial party systems, and the pattern of administrative relationships between the two levels of government.

Richard Simeon's stimulating study of federal-provincial patterns of negotiation in the 1960s is a worthy addition to this new genre of federal studies. Simeon imaginatively applies a model of bargaining and decision-making, drawn largely from studies in international politics, to the dominant pattern of federal-provincial governmental relationships in Canada in the 1960s, which he appropriately labels "federal-provincial diplomacy." The major source of his analysis is data gathered from about 120 interviews with participants in three important federal-provincial decision-making events in the last decade: the pension plan negotiations of 1963–4, the financial negotiations of 1966 (determining the tax-sharing and equalization formulas for 1967–72), and the negotiations towards constitutional revision from 1968–71.

Simeon argues cogently that Canadian federalism in the 1960s must be understood as an interaction of variables at three different levels: (1) the social context (including both regional-economic and ethnic differences), (2) the institutional context (including the constitution and formal governmental structures), and (3) interactions between governmental decision-makers. His discussion of the first two levels is drawn principally from the literature on comparative federalism, and shows a keen awareness of the larger context within which federalism operates. He places particular emphasis, however, on the third level, which he describes as "executive federalism," and it is here that his most original contribution is made. He points convincingly to the necessity of bargaining structures between the two levels of government in the absence of alternative outlets in the Canadian federal institutional structure for the regional and ethnic pressures arising from the heterogeneous social environment.

There are two major sections in the book: a historical section and an analytical section. The former is essentially a chronology of events connected with the pension, financial, and constitutional negotiations traced in a concise, informative, and even-handed manner. The dominant role of Quebec in the pension negotiations, and the crisis atmosphere in which the discussions were conducted are well documented. The concessions made to Quebec created a "spillover effect" which helped to produce the more rigidly centralist posture of the federal government in the two subsequent series of negotiations.

In the analytical section which follows, Simeon shows that "executive federalism," which encompasses relations between the federal prime minister and his provincial counterparts, ministers at both levels, and officials at both levels carried out on both a bilateral and a multilateral basis, can be compared to the pattern of bargaining between the representatives of nation-states, particularly in international organizations. One can analyse the patterns of decision-making in terms of: (1) sites and procedures, (2) issues, (3) goals and objectives of actors, (4) political resources, (5) strategies and tactics, (6) outcomes, and (7) consequences. This model enables him to ask many revealing questions about federal-provincial relations and to provide a number of illuminating insights into the negotiating process. For example, he shows that federal-provincial premiers' conferences and continuing committees of officials are far more important in federal-provincial decision-making than are other meetings such as ministers' conferences. And he points out that partisan differences have only a minimal influence in shaping the goals and objectives of actors in the federal-provincial arena.

The most illuminating sections, in my opinion, are the final three chapters dealing with outcomes, consequences, and conclusions. In answer to the frequently asked question as to whether the negotiation process really matters in terms of federal-provincial outcomes, Simeon replies emphatically in the affirmative. He points out that in systems where the central government has exclusive jurisdiction in the policy areas discussed here, or in systems where regional interests express themselves in these matters through federal governmental institutions, the outcomes would tend to be different. The consequences of the federal-provincial negotiation process for the system as a whole are also important. The process tends to limit the role of parliament in a significant area of political decision-making in Canada, to freeze interest groups out of the decision-making process, and to produce constitutional change in the federal-provincial sphere by convention rather than by formal amendment and popular consent. It also has the effect of encouraging incremental rather than fundamental policy change (Simeon might also have mentioned the tendency for the process to reduce the role of parties in policy-making). Finally, although the negotiation process generally has the effect of containing ethnic conflict between French and English Canadians in issues which are susceptible to compromise and trade-offs, it may intensify these conflicts in areas where the value differences between these ethnic groups are fundamental. The failure of the Victoria Conference may be an unhappy foreboding of the weaknesses of the negotiation process in this respect. The results of these outcomes and consequences are an overall pattern of federalism in Canada that is unique and quite distinct from comparable systems in the United States, Australia, or West Germany.

There are a few omissions and weaknesses in Simeon's analysis. In the first place, he might have applied more standardized techniques of analysis to some of the responses of the interviews, particularly where subjective information and attitudinal data are involved. This would have enabled him to assess the relative influence of various factors on the decision-making process. Second, the author should have expanded his discussion of comparative federal systems in order to provide some possible alternative models for federal-provincial decision-making. These might suggest ways of overcoming some of the weaknesses in the existing Canadian system. For example, would a Senate reform involving an increased role for the provinces in the upper chamber comparable to the influence which the Länder governments exercise in the German Bundesrat be desirable or possible for Canada? Third, Simeon appears generally to view federal-provincial relations in Canada as negotiations between 11 more or less co-equal and sovereign authorities representing distinct regional sub-cultures. This has the effect of exaggerating the relative power and cultural autonomy of some provincial governments which are, moreover, not sovereign in a full legal sense.

More important, it places too great importance on the regional variable and too little emphasis on the ethnic-linguistic variable in influencing federal-provincial relationships. It seems to me that the Quebec government has the ultimate trump card in the negotiating process – the credible threat of its secession – and this threat must have acted as a crucial psychological factor in every federal-provincial conference at least since the beginning of the quiet revolution. No federal or provincial government can seriously ignore or underestimate this factor if it values the survival of the federal system itself. Fourth, analogies from international relations bargaining are not always appropriate, since the units in a federal system are not in fact autonomous and share part of the same territory and population; thus the negotiating process is at times a "shadow-boxing" spectacle rather than a genuine bargaining session between co-equals.

In general, however, these minor shortcomings do not mar what is an exhaustively researched, well-organized, clearly written, and illuminating examination of contemporary federal-provincial relations and decision-making in Canada. It is an essential book for students of Canadian federalism to read and makes a major contribution to an understanding of the dynamics of contemporary Canadian politics.

MICHAEL B. STEIN
McGill University

Claude Morin, **Le pouvoir québécois ... en négociation.** Montréal et Québec: Les Editions du Boréal Express, 1972, 212 p.

Gilles Lalande, **Pourquoi le fédéralisme – Contribution d'un Québécois à l'intelligence du fédéralisme canadien.** Montréal : Hurtubise/HMH, Collection Constantes, 1972, 206 p.

Ces deux ouvrages ont paru à quelques jours de distance et, jusqu'à un certain point, ils traitent du même sujet mais de façon bien différente. Le livre de Claude Morin est pragmatique et il est présenté avec une certaine coquetterie; celui de Gilles Lalande est théorique et concis. Je conseillerais volontiers aux lecteurs de commencer par la lecture du premier ouvrage; le second constitue jusqu'à un certain point une réponse.

Claude Morin, a été, de juin 1963 à octobre 1971, sous-ministre des Affaires intergouvernementales du Québec, et, à ce titre, il a été un des principaux conseillers des premiers ministres Jean Lesage, Daniel Johnson, Jean-Jacques Bertrand, et Robert Bourassa. Il a démissionné de son poste en octobre 1971 et il prend bien soin dans son avant-propos de dire qu'il a commencé à écrire son ouvrage après cette démission. La première qualité de cet ouvrage est l'abondance et la précision de l'information. En le lisant, on se rappelle sans cesse que l'auteur était là, qu'il a préparé ou analysé les dossiers dont il parle et que nul, sauf lui, n'aurait peut-être pu écrire un tel livre. Dans son avant-propos, l'auteur explique qu'il n'a pas voulu préparer un ouvrage académique mais qu'il désirait « présenter un livre qui soit moins rebutant ». Il est en effet agréablement présenté avec de nombreuses illustrations et des procédés de mise en page qui attirent l'attention, procédés que pratiquent souvent les Editions du Boréal Express. L'auteur est un excellent vulgarisateur et il n'éprouve aucune difficulté à expliquer clairement, dans un langage quotidien, ce qu'il a dû naguère interpréter aux hommes politiques dont il était le conseiller.

Dès le début, on a l'impression d'une vision manichéenne qu'exprime bien une citation du philosophe tchèque, Karel Kosik, savoir que « la dialectique du maître et de l'esclave s'applique dans le domaine de la politique de telle sorte que le vainqueur contraint le vaincu, non seulement à accepter sa vision du monde, mais aussi à faire siennes les formules par lesquelles il doit accepter sa capitulation ».

L'ouvrage est divisé en dix dossiers, le premier étant consacré au régime de rentes du Québec. On sait que la création par le Québec de son régime de rentes et l'établissement consécutif de la Caisse de dépôt et placement furent regardés comme une grande victoire du Québec à l'intérieur du fédéralisme canadien. L'événement a même inspiré à madame Judy LaMarsh des propos coléreux à l'égard de Claude Morin et du futur ministre Claude Castonguay qui était alors conseiller de M. Jean Lesage. Et pourtant pour M. Morin ce ne fut pas une victoire complète ou du moins il pose la question de savoir « quelle réaction aurait le gouvernement central si le Québec décidait unilatéralement, comme il lui est loisible de le faire, de modifier radicalement son régime de rentes ». « C'est seulement dans un tel cas, ajoute-t-il, qu'on pourrait voir jusqu'à quel point la latitude québécoise est réelle ». Il est intéressant de noter que, depuis que ces lignes ont été écrites, le gouvernement du Québec a effectivement fait adopter le Projet de loi 24 modifiant substantiellement certaines dispositions du régime de rentes du Québec et que malgré quelques protestations du gouvernement fédéral, le projet a été mis en vigueur.

Le deuxième dossier est consacré aux programmes conjoints et plus précisément aux retraits que le Québec a pu pratiquer de ces projets à la suite de l'adoption d'une loi proposée à cet effet par le gouvernement de M. Pearson. Ce fut certainement une concession au Québec mais Claude Morin signale que, malgré ces retraits, l'intervention fédérale demeure considérable. Dans le dossier sur le partage fiscal, l'auteur, après avoir analysé d'une façon particulièrement claire ce problème où habituellement seuls les spécialistes se retrouvent, rappelle que selon une étude qui a été faite par le ministère québécois des Affaires intergouvernementales, « de 1960–1961 à 1967–1968, le Québec n'a pas profité plus des dépenses fédérales faites pour lui qu'il n'a contribué à celles-ci ».

Dans le dossier sur les relations France-Québec, on trouve une bonne synthèse des événements qui dressèrent, l'un contre l'autre, Ottawa et Québec dans des circonstances qui prirent parfois une allure de comédie. Il rappelle qu'en signant des ententes avec la France, le Québec a réalisé un gain, mais il souligne que ce gain n'était pas d'ordre juridique. Le dossier suivant est consacré logiquement aux conférences et organisations internationales, le tout accompagné de l'expression pittoresque « les liaisons dangereuses ». Dans ce domaine, il y eut aussi des événements amusants et le Québec a réalisé certains progrès. « Il serait toutefois erroné de prétendre, précise Claude Morin, que le Québec a, de ce fait, acquis une personnalité internationale, même dans les domaines de sa compétence ». « Disons que, par la force des choses, précise-t-il, il est devenu, parmi les provinces du Canada, le premier conseiller du gouvernement fédéral pour les conférences francophones ».

Dans le dossier sur l'habitation et la rénovation urbaine, l'auteur explique l'entente entre le gouvernement fédéral et celui du Québec relativement à l'administration des sommes versées par Ottawa via la Société centrale d'hypothèques et de logement, la Société d'habitation du Québec prenant l'entière responsabilité de la préparation et de la mise en œuvre des programmes de rénovation et d'habitation. Le dossier est encore ouvert, et, pour Claude Morin, « le problème demeure tout entier ». Dans le dossier 7, il est question de « l'influence du Québec sur les politiques fédérales » et dans le dossier 8, de « la révision constitutionnelle ». C'est dans ce dernier cas une explication intéressante de la faillite de la conférence de Victoria en 1971. Le dossier 9 rappelle ce que sont les mécanismes de relations intergouvernementales et, dans le dernier dossier, l'auteur souligne qu'il y a un certain nombre de questions qui sont en suspens comme les droits miniers sous-marins, la région Ottawa-Hull, l'activité fédérale dans le domaine des Affaires culturelles, les communications, la main-d'œuvre, « et le reste ... » ajoute-t-il. « Le contentieux Québec-Ottawa de 1965, de 1969 ou de 1972 conclut-il est, en substance, toujours le même. Il ne s'amenuise pas, il s'amplifie ».

Au chapitre des conclusions générales, l'auteur répond à la question qu'il avait posée au début de son livre : « Quels gains le Québec a-t-il réalisés depuis 10 ans ? ». Pour lui, la tendance globale révélée par les dossiers étudiés est que, même si on eut l'impression que depuis 1960, le gouvernement du Québec avait réussi à étendre ses compétences, la plupart des gains québécois ont été réalisés non pas dans des domaines jusque là fédéraux, mais dans des secteurs provinciaux qu'avec le temps et avec l'aide de son pouvoir de dépenser Ottawa avait fini par occuper ou qu'il s'apprêtait à contrôler. Reste peut-être comme avantage d'un tel système ce que l'auteur appelle la théorie de l'émulation, savoir que le fédéralisme pousserait grâce à l'action d'Ottawa les gouvernements passifs et traditionalistes à agir. Cette théorie comporte pour lui une certaine dose de vérité mais l'action d'Ottawa aurait agi comme un envahisseur militaire moins équipé forçant « l'attaqué » à faire preuve d'une énergie et d'un esprit d'inventions, l'attaqué étant dans les circonstances l'ensemble des provinces canadiennes. L'ouvrage est complété par une bonne chronologie du Québec 1960–72 préparée sous la direction de l'auteur par Mme Michèle Mongeon-Asselin, assistante de recherche à l'Ecole nationale d'administration publique.

En refermant le livre, on ne peut s'empêcher de constater qu'un des meilleurs témoins des événements de la dernière décennie conclut sans le dire expressément à la faillite du fédéralisme canadien du moins pour autant que le Québec a désiré s'affirmer. Que reste-t-il alors à faire ? M. Morin ne le dit pas dans son livre mais, quelque temps après l'avoir publié, il devenait une des vedettes du parti Québécois qui ne voit comme seule solution que l'indépendance du Québec. Il faut toutefois souligner que, depuis qu'il milite à l'intérieur du parti Québécois, M. Morin s'est montré un des porte-parole les moins radicaux de ce parti. On sent qu'il connaît les dossiers et qu'il sait par conséquent que quelles que soient les solutions, elles ne sont jamais faciles.

Sans le vouloir expressément, l'ouvrage de Gilles Lalande apporte des réponses aux conclusions implicites des dossiers de Claude Morin. Directeur du département de science politique de l'Université de Montréal, Gilles Lalande est l'auteur de plusieurs ouvrages et articles, plus particulièrement dans le domaine des relations internationales. Il croit profondément au fédéralisme, ce qui ne l'a pas empêché de se montrer assez sévère à l'occasion à l'égard de certaines de ses réalisations au Canada. C'est ainsi, qu'il y a quelques années dans un travail extrêmement fouillé, préparé pour la Commission royale d'enquête sur le bilinguisme et le biculturalisme, il avait démontré que le ministère des Affaires extérieurs avait été dominé par une élite de langue anglaise.

Dans son avant-propos, l'auteur écrit que son « petit ouvrage » s'adresse d'abord aux Québécois, « autant, ajoute-t-il, à ceux qui, par ignorance ou par dépit, ont pris l'habitude de dénigrer le fédéralisme qu'à ceux dont l'adhésion naturelle à la formule fédérale de gouvernement cherche des points d'appui qui fassent appel au langage de la raison ». Dans un premier chapitre, il n'a pas de difficulté à montrer que la formule fédérale de gouvernement a connu ces dernières années une grande popularité et beaucoup d'extension. Il dit la variété des régimes fédératifs; il en étudie la nature, les principes opératoires, et les avantages généraux. Cette première partie de l'ouvrage n'est évidemment pas originale; mais elle s'inspire des meilleurs auteurs, elle est à la fois concise et claire et elle fait comprendre qu'on ne peut enfermer le fédéralisme en une formule simple, car c'est un système « ondoyant et divers », comme aurait dit Montaigne. Il peut donc s'adapter à des situations variées, dont celle du Québec.

C'est à « la remise en question du fédéralisme au Québec » qu'est consacrée la seconde partie, et c'est évidemment la plus personnelle et la plus intéressante. D'une façon méthodique, presque sous forme d'un plaidoyer, Gilles Lalande énumère pour y répondre dix assertions courantes au sujet du fédéralisme canadien. Il n'éprouve guère de difficulté à réfuter « une façon de voir qui est largement répandue dans les cercles francophones de l'élite traditionnelle au Québec, savoir que l'AANB est en contradiction avec l'esprit même du fédéralisme » : on oublie trop facilement que le fédéralisme canadien à notre époque ne s'identifie pas avec la lettre de la loi de 1867 mais qu'il a été enrichi par des éléments variés comme les conventions constitutionnelles et l'interprétation judiciaire. D'autres prétendent que l'AANB et par conséquent le régime fédératif canadien sont aujourd'hui dépassés : cela pourrait être vrai si la dynamique politique ne s'était pas chargée de le mettre constamment à jour.

La troisième assertion est intéressante parce que jusqu'à un certain point, elle incarne des griefs des dossiers de Claude Morin : dans le régime fédératif canadien, c'est le pouvoir central qui est le plus fort et par conséquent les provinces, dont le Québec, sont réduites au rang de partenaires mineurs ou inférieurs. A cela, Gilles Lalande répond que le véritable fédéralisme précisément « écarte par définition tout élément de subordination entre échelons de gouvernement » mais il admet que « le gouvernement central ne doit surtout pas se fermer à toute revendication légitime de nouveaux pouvoirs législatifs et administratifs de la part des provinces ». On affirme parfois que le fédéralisme canadien ne repose pas sur le libre choix des parties contractantes et que, par conséquent, il n'assure pas au Québec le droit de décider librement de son avenir politique. Cela n'a guère d'importance car, en fait, « le droit d'un Etat-membre d'une fédération de décider librement de son avenir politique se traduit habituellement par l'exercice de tous les pouvoirs que lui reconnaît l'acte constitutionnel de même que par le recours à la procédure d'amendement ». On répète souvent que dans le système fédératif canadien, le Québec ne peut être que minoritaire : à cela on peut répondre qu'il n'y a pas lieu de prétendre, si on en juge par toute l'expérience acquise, que notre système fédératif subordonne le Québec à Ottawa en le rendant minoritaire. Au point de vue historique, il est facile de prouver qu'est fausse l'assertion souvent répétée que « le fédéralisme est un mode de gouvernement qui a été imposé au Canada français par le conquérant anglais ». On répète aussi que le fédéralisme canadien ne reconnaît pas l'existence de deux nations et nie le droit des Québécois à l'autodétermination. Laissant de côté ce qu'il appelle moqueusement « la féerie sémantique », Gilles Lalande rappelle que « le fédéralisme fait en pratique disparaître toute antinomie fondamentale entre la qualité de citoyens d'un Etat-membre et celle de citoyens de la fédération ». Par ailleurs, si le fédéralisme constitue pour le Québec et plus particulièrement pour les Canadiens français un instrument de colonialisme ou en d'autres termes engendre ce qu'on qualifie « d'insécurité psychologique de la société canadienne française », il ne faudrait pas oublier que celle-ci « tient certes à la condition minoritaire du Canada français en Amérique du Nord, mais plus encore à l'interaction culturelle et aux croisements interculturels qui caractérisent la société moderne ».

Reste la dernière assertion, celle qui a été formulée par la plupart des chefs du parti Québécois, et qu'on retrouve dans l'ouvrage de Claude Morin savoir que « le fédéralisme est source d'inefficacité administrative et de tensions politiques qui sont à la fois stériles, coûteuses et épuisantes ». Cette assertion tient trop compte peut-être de l'histoire même du fédéralisme canadien et, par conséquent, elle ne peut ébranler la confiance au fédéralisme lui-même; elle traduit un goût de la facilité qui ne convient pas au règlement des difficultés politiques et elle oublie les avantages certains de la co-existence de deux échelons de gouvernement. Dans de brèves pages de conclusion, l'auteur répond à la question : pourquoi le fédéralisme : c'est pour lui « la meilleure adéquation possible au réel »; c'est l'avenir et, précise-t-il, « ce n'est pas un état, ni une condition, en tant que tel, c'est un instrument d'avenir et comme tout instrument celui-ci ne peut être valable ou profitable qu'à condition de vouloir et de savoir s'en servir ».

Il est évident que le lecteur qui aura été convaincu, par la lecture du livre de Claude Morin de la faillite du fédéralisme canadien à résoudre le problème des aspirations du Québec contemporain, ne changera pas immédiatement d'idée à la lecture de l'ouvrage de Gilles Lalande. On peut croire, cependant, que s'il est honnête, il admettra que le fédéralisme en lui-même est loin d'avoir vécu, qu'il est une formule féconde et que s'il n'a pas mieux réussi au Canada c'est peut-être parce qu'on l'a mal pratiqué.

Pour paraphraser un mot célèbre de Winston Churchill à propos du parlementarisme, le fédéralisme est peut-être pour les Canadiens et pour les Québécois le pire de tous les régimes, exception faite de tous les autres.

JEAN-CHARLES BONENFANT
Université Laval

George E. Carter, **Canadian Conditional Grants since World War II.** Toronto: Canadian Tax Foundation, 1971, pp. xi, 130.

In the tradition of similar publications issued by the Canadian Tax Foundation in recent years, Professor Carter's little book is very useful for anyone wishing to review the details of this important aspect of the operation of Canadian federalism. In essence, it is a handbook containing a concisely written history (supported by a useful collection of well-presented data) of the major measures and schools of thought that have shaped federal-provincial financial relations since World War II. Despite its origins (PH.D. thesis for Clark University, 1969), it suffers from the lack of a central thesis or argumentative theme. It is almost a totally descriptive work.

The most useful contribution made by Professor Carter is his careful analysis of equalization. He starts with a conventional review of the various forms of unconditional equalization grants that have been used since 1957 and then develops a rather original analysis of the *implicit* equalization that stems from conditional (program) grants. In this analysis, he defines three types of implicit equalization. These are: (*a*) the equalizing effect produced by the fiscal system whenever grants, financed by a progressive tax, are distributed on a flat sum or per capita basis; (*b*) the equalizing effect produced whenever the federal share of a program's cost is inversely related to each province's personal income, as with the use of national average costs in the Canadian hospital insurance and medicare schemes; (*c*) the equalization inherent in the provision, by federal officials, of free access to consultative and advisory services. The author then proceeds to present a simple but useful method of measuring the magnitude of implicit equalization attributable to the existing pattern of Canadian conditional grants. The overall degree of equalization arising from this source (a question of some political import) is shown to be small and basically the result of provincial disparities in per capita contributions to federal funds rather than to any basic equalization factor governing the allocation of conditional grants.

The major shortcomings of this work are almost all in the form of omissions. Although it would be easy to criticize Professor Carter for his refusal to examine any aspect of the subject matter that might possibly be classified as "political" (I was particularly irritated by the author's seemingly unquestioning acceptance of "provincial autonomy" as a bit of mischievous irrationality continually bedeviling the federal structure), I have restricted my criticisms to omissions clearly related to economics.

On page four, Professor Carter acknowledges that: "the failure of national policies in the late 50s to achieve full employment and an acceptable rate of economic growth largely explains provincial assumption of these new activities." Later on he notes, quite properly, that by 1966 the federal authorities were making a basic distinction between "social" grants (such as medicare and social assistance) and "economic" grants (such as ARDA and FRED). This new preoccupation with growth and development would appear to be an area of considerable concern in terms of public finance generally and the economics of federalism in particular. Yet Professor Carter offers no critical analysis of it. Needless to say, his failure to explore this question is rendered more unfortunate by the subsequent institution of DREE grants.

In his chapter on the "opting-out formula," Professor Carter brings up the old question of the minimum fiscal powers necessary if Ottawa is to continue its vital role in countercyclical financing. Again, consideration of the question is advanced no further than the conventional wisdom.

In his conclusions, the author summarizes the factors which led the provincial premiers to challenge the conditional grant system built up after World War II as: "the dramatic rise in provincial-municipal expenditure responsibilities compared to those of the federal government ... a more vigorous provincial leadership supported by a more highly-trained and aggressive public service ... a new self-determination evident in the provincial assumption of an important role in regional economic planning and development ... strong pressure from Quebec for a greatly enlarged provincial autonomy." None of these factors is examined in light of its potential influence in the future. This lack of analysis would, perhaps, be less noticeable if the author had not devoted a good deal of space to such things as a detailed indifference curve analysis on the basic nature of conditional grants (something which could be readily left to an appendix) and a prolonged discussion of the Breton theory of "spillovers" (a highly speculative approach not in keeping with the practical orientation of the rest of the work).

Therefore, in an overall sense, the publication is a concise, well-documented and adequately-presented source book on conditional grants from 1946 to 1970. However, the reader who has a genuine interest in this area will find it difficult to restrict himself to the narrow scope adopted in this and similar works. The need for a comprehensive analysis of federal-provincial finances since World War II covering conditional grants, unconditional grants, tax sharing, expenditure patterns, and access to capital sources remains a very real one.

MARVIN BLAUER
Brock University

Richard Allen, **The Social Passion: Religion and Social Reform in Canada 1914–28.** Toronto: University of Toronto Press, 1971, pp. xxv, 385.

The growth of political radicalism in Canada, in Western Canada especially, cannot be fully explained without reference to the influence of the social gospel, for, as the British Labour party owed more to Methodism than to Marx (as Clement Attlee pointed out), so the varieties of Canadian radical parties – from the Non Partisan League to even the Communist party – owed a good deal to clerics like Salem Bland, J.S. Woodsworth, and A.E. Smith. These men and clergymen like them preached and worked earnestly to bring the Christian doctrine of brotherhood out of the pulpits and into the community. For the most part they came from the Methodist church, although the Baptists and Congregationalists had their social gospelers too.

Starting from the conviction "that Christianity required a passionate commitment to social involvement," the social gospel developed three strains during its hey-day in Canada from 1914 to 1928. As Professor Allen points out, these were the conservative, with its emphasis on "personal-ethical issues"; the radical, which viewed society as organic and emphasized social salvation; and the progressive, which spanned the two extremes. It is the cleric who espoused the radical view that we are most familiar with for these were the men who left, or were forced from their pulpits and lecterns, and who worked for social salvation through politics.

As institutions, the churches flirted with the social gospel. The great Social Service Congress in Ottawa in 1914 seemed to herald a new dawn of church activism and the twenty-four year history of the social gospel is studded with periodic resurgences of official ecclesiastical concern. But the bourgeois backlash of congregation and clerics alike built up, fueled by the spectre of bolshevism and trade unionism, and the church backed away – not ungraciously or unsympathetically – but firmly. In 1920, the position of the Methodist church on the Labour Churches was based more on congregational antipathy and RCMP intelligence reports than it was on biblical injunctions of fellowship and love.

Richard Allen has assembled his facts meticulously and provided in this book not a single study of a single theme, but a series of more or less discrete essays on aspects of the social gospel, dealing less with its impact on society and more with its impact on organized religion and on the Methodist church in particular. The detail is staggering and the documentation impressive. Clearly the author left little out and for students of church history in Canada this is a valuable work.

It is, however, less successful as social history. Indeed the relationship between religion and social reform anticipated by the book's title is never thoroughly canvassed and were it not for a portfolio of photographs of working and living conditions in Canada during this period, it would be difficult to discover just what it was that generated "the social passion." There is, in fact, little of a passionate nature that emerges from this study. This is not, however, a serious flaw; it is clear that the author did not set out to convey a sense of the times; his goal was to examine the events within the churches concerned, centring on the social gospel and the labour churches. This he does with an even and objective hand. He might have been more caustic, the church is such an easy target: the Angolan missions soothed the consciences of the rich, the labour churches did not.

It is perhaps just as well that Professor Allen took this course for he is at his weakest when dealing with matters outside the church. He mistakenly includes Woodsworth and Irvine as part of the Ginger Group and even associates Mackenzie King with the social gospel, suggesting that this played some part in his accession to the Liberal leadership. And while Allen does state that this is a debatable matter, it seems clear that the reader's knowledge of the social gospel in Canada would not suffer if the four pages on King were left out.

Students of this period will not be able to ignore this book and perhaps Professor Allen will one day write a short and pithy history of the social gospel, one that speaks with the passion that motivated men like Bland, Smith, Irvine, and Woodsworth, with the passion that became so distant from the councils of the Methodist church.

WALTER YOUNG
University of British Columbia

Ronald S. Ritchie, **An Institute for Research on Public Policy.** Ottawa: Information Canada, 1971, pp. 95.

G. Bruce Doern, **Political Policy-Making: A Commentary on the Economic Council's Eighth Annual Review and the Ritchie Report.** Montreal: The Private Planning Association of Canada, 1972, pp. 25.

Alice M. Rivlin, **New Approaches to Public Decision-Making.** Ottawa: Information Canada, 1972, pp. 37.

These three volumes have a common purpose – to improve the existing system of public policy formation in Canada. Their major concerns, however, are not the same. The Rivlin study is concerned with *short-term* decision-making; the Ritchie report with *medium-* and *long-term* policy formation; and the Doern article with decision-makers and policy formulators in all situations. Rivlin and Ritchie suggest means by which the quantity and quality of information available to decision-makers can be improved; Doern warns those responsible for public policy formation not to ignore the political nature of their task.

Although the Rivlin study is valuable for its listing of several techniques available to decision-makers to improve their sources of information, the Ritchie report and Professor Doern's commentary must be given more weight in this review for Ritchie proposes the creation of an institution new to the Canadian scene and Doern gives pertinent advice to its future directors. It is difficult to object to Ritchie's recommendation that an institute for research on public policy be established in Canada. The experience of other countries where such institutes already exist has demonstrated their value. Nor can one quarrel with the further recommendations that the Institute provide impartial service and that it be funded in a way that enables it to guarantee its neutrality. One must question, however, the tasks Mr Ritchie sets his institute and the assumptions which underlie its stated objectives. In the first place, despite his contention that "Canadians should plan to choose and chart their future, and not simply be swept into it by forces and contingencies insufficiently foreseen" (p. 42), Ritchie gives no indication of the desired destination of this national "flight plan." He seems to assume either that these national goals are so well known they do not require reiteration or that the comprehensive list of current problems he supplies provides adequate direction. In either case, it must be pointed out that any set of goals must be constantly reviewed and revised, and that to tackle specific problems prior to establishing one's priorities can only lead to confusion, lack of coordination, and the misuse of limited resources. Secondly, one must question the value of a public policy research institute which "is aimed not at making or proposing policies but at adding to the information and the tools of analysis of those who do make them ..." (p. 5). No doubt the additional information and the new techniques will be of great use to decision-makers, but, as Doern rightly points out, it is "an alarmingly simplistic assumption that merely 'adding information' is a function distinct from 'making or proposing policies' " (p. 7). These functions are not separate, and it is difficult to imagine government departments funding research that will contain no policy recommendations. It is even more difficult to imagine the Institute attracting to it mission-oriented people who will not be able to draw the conclusions their research suggests to the attention of those who have the political power to implement them. Lastly, it must be pointed out that the tasks Ritchie sets the Institute will not permit it to evaluate the effects of existing policies. Although the Institute will provide "ingredients for policy appraisal" (p. 42), it is prohibited from applying these criteria to present and future policies for fear that the Institute will be tarred with the brush of partisan politics. For the same reason the Institute will be unable to propose methods of coordinating government policies so that duplication of effort and conflict of objectives are avoided. Undoubtedly, there are potential dangers when an Institute of the type suggested, especially one in a monopoly position, evaluates the policies of governments and recommends specific courses of action. The Economic Council of Canada is living proof of this. However, I submit that there is more to be gained from learning to live with the problem than in so circumscribing the Institute at its inception that it cannot perform what should be its most valuable functions. If governments will agree to regard the Institute's research and recommendations merely as another source of information on which to base their decisions, and if the Institute will remember Professor Doern's caveat that governments have to take into account the political realities of the time when making their decisions, then the difficulties should not be impossible to overcome. Mr Ritchie, in over-rating the Institute's possible political problems underrates its potential contribution to public policy formation in Canada.

In conclusion, the three volumes together pose as many questions as they provide answers. It is indeed unfortunate that none of the authors treats, or, given his publisher's requirements, was able to treat his subject in greater depth. Nevertheless, they do suggest valuable guidelines for future study and debate in the area of public policy formation. The Rivlin study indicates the need for better techniques of decision-making; and the Doern article demonstrates the necessity of further research into the political nature of policy-making. As well, the Ritchie report requires careful examination before its recommendations are implemented.

PATRICK KYBA
University of Guelph

S.J.R. Noel, **Politics in Newfoundland.** Toronto: University of Toronto Press, 1971, pp. x, 328.

In my judgement this is the best of the books that have appeared so far on the politics of the Canadian provinces.

For one thing, it is a literate work, done in a lucid and easy flowing style that few social scientists can command. The author has a "feel" for politics that prevents the history from slipping into mere narrative, and the historical training that prevents the political analysis from degenerating into pseudo-science.

Newfoundland is the poorest of the provinces. There are good reasons for this. The province is isolated, and the climate is harsh ("ten months winter and two months bad weather," as the saying goes). There is very little agricultural land and, except in Labrador, not much mineral wealth or water power. Only the forests and the fisheries form substantial natural resources. The people, almost wholly of English and Irish ancestry, are scattered around the coast line in a thousand "outports."

Meanwhile, the population explosion goes marching on. Newfoundland has the highest birth rate and the lowest death rate (although not the lowest age specific death rate) in Canada. Far more people come onto the labour market each year than can find jobs. The massive unemployment and the high cost of living are rendered tolerable only by the high amount of federal aid, federal social services, and emigration.

Religious cleavages, chiefly Catholic versus Protestant, have divided the people, and the divisions were reflected (and exploited) in politics and in the education system. (The divisions may be dying now, as religious indifference grows.) The class conflict of fishermen and merchant was usually muted, and only occasionally broke into the open. The best instance of this open struggle is seen in the political career of a charismatic demagogue, William Coaker, and of his Fishermen's Protective Union – a tale well told in this book. The Union was undermined by the prosperity of the First World War and was destroyed by the collapse of the market for dried codfish after the war.

Patronage, corruption, even graft, were deeply embedded in political life. So was the reckless "giveaway" of forest resources. The building of the CPR in Canada is not without scandal, but the buccaneering of the Montreal interests who built the Newfoundland railway, and the eagerness of local interests to join the piracy, is almost beyond belief. The only politician who, by contrast, seems to have had less selfish ideas of the public interest is Robert Bond. Noel does full justice to his memory, though Bond's curious withdrawal from public life after 1913 is still something of a mystery.

During the 1920s one government after another went its merry way without regard for the economic facts of life. As Noel puts it, they lived "hopefully on borrowed money." With the great depression Newfoundland's house of cards collapsed after a century or so of independence. In 1934, faced with default on its public debt, the government (perhaps mistakenly) yielded its independence and came under a trusteeship. The former Dominion was then ruled by a commission of six, plus a governor, appointed by the United Kingdom. The light of democracy went out in Newfoundland, as Harold Innis remarked. But there were few to notice and none to mourn. Noel gives an excellent brief analysis of this unique arrangement of commission rule.

In 1949 Newfoundland became a province of Canada. Insofar as this union was brought about by one man, that man was Joseph R. Smallwood. Noel is fair, perhaps even generous to Smallwood. One could easily be more severe on this flamboyant ex-premier: to criticize him for his personality politics, which did so little to prepare the people for self-government; to condemn as grotesque his attempts to make Newfoundland into an industrial province by the reckless disposal of Labrador resources and public money.

There is no doubt that Confederation has integrated Newfoundland into Canada and North America. It is no longer a "traditional" society, with the simple ways of life so beloved by rural romantics. It is more and more a province "like the others." Whether this is a good thing or not, who can say? But if mainlanders, and Newfoundlanders themselves, are seriously interested in the tenth province, this admirable book is required reading.

H.B. Mayo
Carleton University

Ramsay Cook, **The Maple Leaf Forever: Essays on Nationalism and Politics in Canada.** Toronto: The Macmillan Company of Canada, 1971, pp. 253.

This collection of essays, touching on such diverse matters as Pierre Trudeau's political ideas, the options in Canada's continuing debate on the constitution, and the nature of French- and English-Canadian historiography, is knit together by the now-familiar central theme of Ramsay Cook's work: the attack on nationalism in all the forms it has manifested itself in Canada. Nationalism diverts debate from the "real" social and economic issues to sterile abstractions; whatever the protestations of its adherents, it is inherently conservative; it mystifies and perverts the writing of history. Most important, in the Canadian context of geographic diversity and ethnic division, it is necessarily a divisive force since by nature it excludes those who are different and tends to enforce homogeneity. In Canada, moreover, nationalism, French and English, involves competing visions of what the appropriate boundaries and definitions of the nation are.

Within this framework, the essays, most of which have appeared before, range from commentary on current political developments to more substantial reflections on the place of nationalism in Canada. By far the best are those assessing French- and English-Canadian historiography. They are especially lucid guides for the non-historian. Cook suggests that in Quebec especially the historian has always played a major role as the shaper of the national self-image. He traces the preoccupation with *la survivance* from the traditional historians who stressed the need to maintain the values of Catholic, agrarian French-Canada to the post-war generation who stress the need to come to terms with and to embrace secularism, industrialism, and the like. Similarly, despite the wide variety of views, from the continentalism of Underhill to the pessimistic anti-Americanism of Creighton, Cook finds that survival – in the face of British dominance, American influence, or internal dissension, depending on the author – has been the central preoccupation of English-Canadians. The result, he suggests, is a history which usually fails to see the past on its own terms, which has underplayed social and economic history, and over-emphasized constitutional events. Nationalist historians interpret the past in the light of their present goals; history becomes a weapon, an instrument for persuasion. This is effective intellectual history, though occasionally Cook seems to have to squeeze the authors rather hard to force them into the mould. He also begs the question as to whether it is possible *not* to interpret the past in light of preoccupations of the present, and fails to elaborate what issues a "non-nationalist" Canadian historiography would have stressed. Is it "nationalist" indeed to be preoccupied with the conditions of Canada's survival? It would also have been useful to have probed more deeply how influential these historians have been in shaping perceptions of Canada in the wider population.

Cook does go after nationalism with a blunt instrument, lumping together a wide variety of phenomena. The search for national identity of an A.R.M. Lower or Michel Brunet is hardly the nationalism of National Socialism. Nationalism is not clearly defined, and it is not distinguished from other related phenomena such as "national identity," "patriotism," "ethnocentrism" and so on. Is concern about foreign-ownership of Canadian industry merely nationalism and hence reprehensible? When does it cross the line? Cook asserts that nationalism in Canada is always divisive, because it is always exclusive, but gives short shrift to those who have attempted to define a Canadian identity which is inclusive. He asserts that nationalism is always conservative, but, apart from a few offhand swipes, makes no effort to come to terms with the resurgence of what might be called left-wing nationalism which has emerged recently in both French and English Canada. Cook's use of the term is polemical, rather than analytical, and, while suggestive, it is no substitute for more careful assessment of the nature of Canadian identities, or of the role of nationalist ideas in the integration or disintegration of the Canadian communities.

As a commentator on current events, Cook is less effective. Perhaps the most generous comment to make on his extensive, and almost sycophantic, paeans of praise to Prime Minister Trudeau is that they sound very dated. His critiques of alternative futures for English and French Canada – independence, associate states, special status – are thoughtful, but his prescription, essentially the same as Trudeau's, is no more persuasive.

Cook is a perceptive essayist; his style is easy and lucid. His book is pleasant and stimulating reading, even when one disagrees, but except for the analysis of the role of the historian, it does little to advance our understanding of Canadian politics.

RICHARD SIMEON
University of British Columbia

Robin W. Winks, **The Blacks in Canada: A History.** New Haven and London: Yale University Press [Montreal: McGill-Queen's University Press], 1971, pp. xxii, 546.

Although black people have lived in Canada since the seventeenth century they have never formed a statistically significant portion of the population or been at the centre of Canadian political life. Under the circumstances we need not be surprised that the historical and critical literature is so slight. Yet, as Professor Winks had the acuteness to realize, the Canadian black experience deserves full and respectful attention. The swelling interest in what many call the Black Diaspora requires study of the development of black communities in other than the plantation belts of the New World and the great urban centers if only to help control generalizations. Professor Winks, in this useful book, demonstrates, however, that his subject has even greater significance. To his credit he constructs the story of Canada's blacks as worthy of sympathetic attention in its own right, although his own major interest centres on the light it sheds on the social and racial attitudes of Canadians.

Professor Winks tells a disheartening story. Blacks went to Canada in waves. Refugees from the American Revolution, the War of 1812, and the Marroon Wars in Jamaica had no easy time but, for the most part, were accorded a decent reception. Conditions worsened with the influx of escaped slaves from the United States, especially when racist attitudes began to spill over the border. Subsequently, West Indian blacks came as settlers and especially as students. Professor Winks tells this complicated story well and without sentimentality. He matches his forthright criticism of Canadian racism and complacency with tough-minded criticism of the inadequacies of black efforts to build their own communities. In particular, his account of chronic black disunity speaks to American as well as Canadian black history. Among his special achievements is a superb account of the career of Josiah Henson in Canada, which he unravels in a delightful piece of historical detective work.

Admiration for Professor Winks' painstaking and intelligent effort does not, however, imply agreement with his fundamental viewpoint. There is a good deal of ambiguity in his interpretation, which suffers especially from a series of dubious liberal assumptions. In particular, he discusses the problem of integration in Canada with an eye on the situation in the United States – a procedure that weakens his performance, not because comparison need be thought intrinsically misleading, but because he never stops to consider the legitimacy of black-nationalist claims in the United States. Were Professor Winks willing to reflect on the duality of the black experience in the United States as part of the American nation and yet as a nation-within-a-nation, he would have to reconsider his treatment of the black experience in Canada. One of the greatest difficulties faced by Canadian blacks has been their physical, ideological, and historical proximity to the blacks of the United States. But if I am correct in suggesting that black Americans confront an especially painful problem, then the question of "integration" necessarily appears in a unique form. Canadian blacks, on the other hand, clearly have no claims to separate nationality and constitute a racial minority drawn from several separate nationalities and suffering from discrimination and prejudice. The struggle of Canadian blacks for social justice consequently takes on a fundamentally different character from that of American blacks. The development of the Canadian black churches, schools, and press, which Professor Winks discusses with a wholesome combination of sympathy and critical detachment, would look like a different story were it to be re-examined by someone who begins with different ideological assumptions, for it is one thing to try to build separate institutions as part of a developing national personality and quite another to try to do so as part of a minority thrust toward the cultural expression and political defence of a racial minority. Professor Winks' book, however, is meant to open, not close, discussion of these questions. He has written his own book, and written it well.

EUGENE D. GENOVESE
Center for Advanced Study in the Behavioral Sciences, Stanford, California

William Leiss, **The Domination of Nature.** New York: George Brazziler, Inc. [Toronto: Doubleday], 1972, pp. xiii, 242.

This is an unusual book in at least two respects. One is that its author, William Leiss, is currently teaching political science (at the University of Saskatchewan) with a degree in philosophy not political science. The other unusual feature is that the book deals with a subject not normally thought to fall within the boundaries of political science: the natural environment. For both of these reasons *The Domination of Nature* is an interesting and thought-provoking book.

By all accounts, it would seem that man's dominion over nature is being increasingly realized. But it would be a mistake, Leiss contends, to conclude that man is getting any better at it as a result. This is what he calls "the persistent illusion that the undertaking known as 'the mastery of nature' is itself mastered" (p. 23).

There are several reasons for this paradox, but one of the most important is essentially a *political* reason. As man's capacity to bend nature to his needs increases, the range of options among which he may choose also increases. The result, Leiss concludes, is "that the social struggles among men gradually absorb the struggle of men with nature ..." Following Marcuse, Leiss concludes that "the instruments through which men transform the resources of nature into means for the satisfaction of desires are regarded more and more as a crucial object of *political* conflict, both domestically and internationally" (p. 22).

The subject of this book, therefore, is the political content of the idea of the domination of nature by man. Most of the book is what Leiss calls a "fragmental biography" of this idea. He cites its "mythical, religious and philosophical roots"; he deals at length with the views of Francis Bacon; and he provides interesting essays on Max Scheler, Edmund Husserl, and Max Horkheimer.

Finally, in a provocative last chapter, Leiss turns to more contemporary matters and tries to explain the current disillusionment with "conquering nature" – from the Club of Rome and the Stockholm Conference to local citizens' protest movements. Leiss suggests that the disillusionment is due to the failure of our ideology to "transcend the contradictions between positive and negative aspects" of the domination of nature. And, he goes on, "since, in terms of its usual formulation, mastery over nature cannot satisfy the expectations that are associated with it, one day it may fall victim to a counterideology promising a different road to happiness" (pp. 170–2). Leiss is not out to champion a new counter-ideology to replace the old so much as to urge us to take a careful look at both of them and to recognize the inherent weaknesses of each. For it is their "concealed ambiguities" which turn "a once-creative idea into a rhetorical slogan that is repeated endlessly in a mechanical fashion ... [and] the medicine feeds the disease" (p. 178).

In itself, the book is open to a number of criticisms. It is a bit too "fragmental" in nature; the link between its two major parts is not developed as clearly as it might have been, for example, and there are obviously many other philosophers (such as Aristotle, for instance, who is never once mentioned) whose views could have been explored. There is the usual mistake (p. 61) over Bacon's name: it should be Lord Verulam or Viscount St Alban's but not Lord Bacon. And there is somewhat more dogmatism in the book than is reflected in this review (for example, chapter 8, *passim*). But the real significance of the book, it seems to this reviewer, lies in the way in which it extends the traditional conception of politics and political science.

There is much talk these days about "the quality of life" in our cities and indeed on our planet. It is quite clear that, for Leiss, this is the stuff of politics. Politics for him refers in the broadest sense to the way in which men make choices about the quality of their lives. As such, it is a conception of politics worthy of Aristotle. For Aristotle believed (to put it in contemporary phraseology) that the state represents some sort of shared perception as to the meaning of the "quality of life" – no more and no less.

Aristotle, it should be remembered, also claimed that political science was the master science. The fact that it has, in recent times at least, taken a back seat to most of the other social sciences in its approach to virtually everything connected with "the quality of life" – from poverty to the development of natural resources – is simply the result of a less-than-Aristotelian conception of the nature of politics. It is to this book's great credit that it takes politics for all its Aristotelian worth. The result is a stimulating new perspective on a matter of considerable academic as well as public concern. As a final comment, it is interesting to note that the author is a philosophically-oriented political scientist in the vanguard of a movement towards "relevance" in political science.

T.J. CARTWRIGHT
York University

Leonard Binder, James S. Coleman, Joseph LaPalombara, Lucian W. Pye, Sidney Verba, and Myron Weiner, ed., **Crises and Sequences in Political Development.** Princeton: Princeton University Press [Don Mills: Saunders], 1971, pp. xi, 326.

This is the seventh volume in the "Studies in Political Development" series sponsored by the Committee on Comparative Politics of the (US) Social Science Research Council. With individual contributions by most editors of earlier volumes in the series, it probably represents the current state of knowledge about that most complex and elusive subject: political development.

Readers of earlier volumes in the series who might have hoped that this one would provide a more thoroughly integrated and consistent treatment of the subject will be disappointed. While often interesting, informative, and not without helpful insights, the several essays presented here fail in their general aim to provide a straightforward and unambiguous set of concepts and terms for analysing political development. Part of the difficulty doubtless can be attributed to this book's collaborative character and the problem of achieving coordination and control among a group of equally prominent contributors. A more fundamental flaw is the generally vague and imprecise conceptual language which no amount of collaborative co-ordination could have overcome.

The book contains not one but three conceptual frameworks which fit together imperfectly if at all. The basic one is a notion of political development "crises" outlined by Leonard Binder in the introductory chapter and elaborated afterwards in separate chapters dealing with an individual crisis: Identity and Political Culture (Pye), Legitimacy (Pye), Political Participation (Weiner), Penetration (LaPalombara), and Distribution (LaPalombara). These are the key benchmarks of the study. But the book also contains two other conceptual approaches whose relationships with the primary one are never made entirely clear. These are "The Development Syndrome" chapter in which James S. Coleman suggests that political development can be understood as a contrapuntal interaction among the processes of "structural differentiation," the imperative of "equality," and the adaptive "capacity" of a political system. In the final chapter Sidney Verba provides what seems to be yet another conceptual approach which stresses the importance of "sequential models" in the study of political development. While some attempt is made to connect these models – at several places it is suggested that the "crises" are tensions within the "development syndrome" – the exact reason for their inclusion and their functional importance to the book as a whole is never satisfactorily dealt with. Of the three models, this reader found Coleman's notion of a development sydrome involving changes in values, changes in social structure, and changes in the performance of the political system the most convincing and, it should be added, the most consistent with previous theoretical discussions of the subject.

Since the "crises" model dominates the others, it might be worthwhile briefly to consider only a few of the problems attending its use. First, we really never know how to distinguish a crisis from a non-crisis of identity, legitimacy, etc. If the term is meant to imply a critical time of limited duration when a decisive change can or does occur (derived dictionary meaning) then it seems ill-suited to the persistent problems of a major nature that confront developing countries. Second, the several political development crises dealt with – identity, legitimacy, political participation, penetration, and distribution – strongly resist clear definition. This reader was struck by not a few but repeated instances of overlap and ambiguity in the meanings attributed to these terms. Consider the following quotations: "When changes in political participation confront an elite with extreme difficulties – such as those associated with communalism in India or tribalism in Africa – a penetration crisis of unanticipated dimensions and proportions is set in motion" (p. 206), or "The second dimension [of penetration] has to do with the existing or modified ability and predisposition of the objects of policy to receive information regarding policy accurately and to *wish* to conform to such policies voluntarily. Varying degrees of such ability and predisposition are obviously inextricably tied to what we mean by legitimacy" (p. 209); or "... the question of legitimacy is closely linked to all the other crises because the resolution of each does in part contribute to the building of government. The question of identity is one of providing the basic sense of unity for the nation and of, in a sense, filling the physical space with a coherent society, and thus of creating the foundations for supporting the governmental structure which in turn becomes the basic mechanism for converting the consequences of 'participation' into the output of 'distribution' and which expands its own capacity through greater 'penetration' " (p. 137).

What we have in each crisis chapter is a discussion of a particular crisis in relation to all, or most, of the others. The reader is left with the impression that each chapter deals with the same topic (that is, all the crises) though with varying emphases (that is, an individual crisis in relation to all the others). When it is remembered that the first chapter itself deals with all the crises, the result is all too often repetition and overlap. The quite understandable concern of each author to relate 'his' variable to all the others – it is interesting to compare the sub-headings of each chapter – accounts for much of the difficulty, but it also reflects the limited utility of blunt conceptual tools and a language that permits similar phenomena to be denoted by the use of different terms.

As an integrated and consistent whole this volume suffers from these kinds of limitations. However, the individual essays considered alone are frequently lively and helpful, most notably Coleman's and Weiner's. Weiner's contribution is particularly thoughtful on the relationships between political participation and political development. His discussion of ethnic group "incorporation" and "corporate representation" was most suggestive. Still, the overall weakness of the book as a joint conceptual enterprise remains. We still await a precise and straightforward model for studying political system change.

R.H. JACKSON
University of British Columbia

Richard Gombin, **Les origines du gauchisme.** Paris: Editions du Seuil, Collection Politique, 1971, 189 p.

Le livre de Richard Gombin, *Les origines du gauchisme*, est une analyse des sources idéologiques du gauchisme (essai d'explicitation de la « théorie gauchiste », comme dit l'auteur). Cette analyse est faite essentiellement à partir d'une exégèse pertinente de textes et une revue d'auteurs selon la tradition française des études de pensée politique. Ceci résume assez l'intérêt et les limites de cet ouvrage.

En avertissement, l'auteur annonce son projet : expliciter la théorie gauchiste. Dans l'Introduction, la conception du gauchisme qui sera analysée est précisée : « Par gauchisme, écrit Gombin, nous désignerons cette fraction du mouvement révolutionnaire qui offre, ou veut offrir, une alternative radicale au marxisme-léninisme en tant que théorie du mouvement ouvrier et de son évolution » (p. 18). Sont exclus du gauchisme à quelques nuances près les sociaux démocrates et le PSU mais aussi les maoïstes et les trotskystes pour lesquels l'auteur propose le concept d'extrémisme. Les seuls groupuscules qui méritent donc l'étiquette de gauchistes sont pratiquement les situationnistes, certains anarchistes, et certains trotskystes dissidents (le groupe socialisme et barbarie).

L'objet de l'analyse de Gombin va donc être : *l'origine des divers éléments de la doctrine diffusée par ces groupes.* L'ensemble de ces éléments ne constitue pas une unité synthétique mais une mosaïque de thèmes et d'analyses dessinant les contours d'une théorie révolutionnaire possible autre que le marxisme-léninisme. Gombin regroupe toutes les influences autour de quatre thèmes : la critique du régime bureaucratique de l'URSS, la critique philosophique du marxisme orthodoxe, la critique de la vie quotidienne, l'importance des conseils ouvriers.

La critique du régime bureaucratique de l'URSS découle de la critique trotskyste, mais elle fut renouvelée et complétée en France par l'influence de Sartre et des Temps Modernes qui constitue une des sources de cet aspect du gauchisme.

Le révisionnisme philosophique concerne surtout le courant de l'hégéliano-marxisme avec Georg Lukacs et Korsch qui, dès l'entre-deux guerres, ont dénoncé la sclérose du marxisme dans la pratique théorique de la social démocratie mais indirectement dans le léninisme et le stalinisme. La conception du matérialisme dialectique d'Engels appliquée à la nature est pulvérisée; la conception *réaliste* du matérialisme d'Engels et de Lénine est dénoncée tandis que l'accent est mis sur la philosophie de la praxis, l'importance de l'aliénation, et le rôle de la prise de conscience du prolétariat pour la révolution. Ces analyses reprises et diffusées par la revue *Arguments* dans les années 1950 en France constituent le nerf d'une théorie gauchiste.

Le troisième thème, la critique de la vie quotidienne, nous amène à l'aspect le plus original du gauchisme. Heureusement formulée par Henri Lefebvre, diffusée, reprise et repensée par les situationnistes, la dénonciation de l'aliénation du vécu dans la représentation rejoint la tradition des écrivains maudits et les sources originales du dadaïsme et du surréalisme.

Le dernier thème, la théorie du communisme de conseils, nous introduit dans les discussions de secte sur le rôle de l'autogestion et sa conception. Les débats de socialisme et barbarie par delà l'analyse d'Anton Pannekoek renouent avec la tradition anarchiste et le spontanéisme de Rosa Luxembourg.

Dans un dernier chapitre, un peu terne, Richard Gombin tente d'évaluer l'impact du gauchisme sur les événements de mai 1968. De la constatation d'une coïncidence manifeste, d'une interrelation parfois vérifiable, l'auteur se garde de conclure à une causalité et achève son ouvrage en posant la question de savoir si le gauchisme est le chant du cygne du mouvement révolutionnaire ou le point de départ d'une nouvelle forme de contestation.

Il faut reconnaître à Richard Gombin le mérite de s'être attaqué à un problème difficile et de s'en être tiré honorablement pour ce qui est de la présentation des influences idéologiques. Sa définition restrictive du gauchisme est conforme au clivage théorique (et non au clivage politique), elle aboutit à ne donner cette étiquette qu'aux seuls groupes qui *se* reconnaissent comme gauchistes. Les analyses de Korsch, Lukacs, Pannekoek sont, me semble-t-il, correctes. Des filiations moins connues sont mises à jour. On notera l'intéressante critique de la bureaucratie de Rizzi très en avance sur son temps et généralement méconnue, le rapprochement inattendu des thèses trotskystes et de celles de Burnham, la transformation du mouvement Lettriste d'Isidore Isou en Internationale situationniste. L'auteur met en évidence certaines ambiguïtés, divergences ou contradictions de la pensée gauchiste. Le travail est considéré comme moyen de réalisation de l'homme par les fidèles de la tradition marxiste et classé comme la pire des aliénations par les situationnistes. Les paradoxes de l'hypostase du prolétariat sont vus; personne ne peut résoudre ses problèmes à sa place mais il se voit attribuer un rôle messianique par une théorie (celle de Marx). Les difficultés de certains conseillistes, qui préconisent des organisations pour lutter contre les organisations, sont bien soulignées.

Face à ces mérites, il faut signaler quelques oublis qui tiennent peut-être en partie à la problématique de l'auteur. On est étonné de voir que la brochure de Lénine, « Le Gauchisme, la maladie infantile du communisme », et ses analyses sont complètement oubliées ainsi que les révoltes de Kronstadt et la fameuse décision d'interdiction des tendances au sein du parti (votée par Trotsky entre parenthèses). Ceci est d'autant plus étonnant que la définition étroite du gauchisme retenue par l'auteur évoque les liens avec l'opposition de gauche en URSS et que le qualificatif de gauchiste a été donné par les communistes pour stigmatiser leurs adversaires en référence à l'analyse de Lénine. Une influence plus discutable, mais peut-être non négligeable, qui est passée sous silence, est celle qu'Althusser a exercée sur les intellectuels marxistes. Si ses conclusions renforcent le dogmatisme officiel, sa lutte contre l'empirisme a contribué à miner le positivisme du marxisme-léninisme orthodoxe. La place faite au freudo-marxisme, curieusement bâclé dans le dernier chapitre, est sans doute insuffisante. On relèvera (p. 106) une appréciation très discutable sur l'orthodoxie de l'analyse économique de Rosa Luxembourg. En analysant de façon originale l'impérialisme, Rosa Luxembourg s'écartait très fortement de la tradition marxiste et fournissait les bases d'un renouvellement du marxisme qu'on n'a guère pu expliciter jusqu'à maintenant.

Ceci nous amène à une critique beaucoup plus fondamentale de l'ouvrage de Richard Gombinet qui tient à l'étroitesse d'une méthode très conformiste. Cette méthode repose sur un cloisonnement des disciplines et amène à analyser certains aspects d'un phénomène social et à disloquer l'unité de celui-ci.

La façon dont est conçu l'économisme et le rôle de l'économie politique chez Marx en est un symptôme. L'économisme dans le marxisme ne résulte absolument pas du fait que Marx a consacré la plus grande partie de sa vie à écrire le Capital. L'économisme, comme conception du matérialisme historique attribuant un rôle déterminant exclusif et presque mécanique à l'instance économique, n'est pas du tout présent dans le Capital. Il est beaucoup plus manifeste dans l'Idéologie Allemande et chez Engels. Si Marx a fait la critique de l'économie politique, c'est uniquement parce qu'à l'époque du capitalisme qui réifie tous les rapports humains, c'est à travers la critique de cette idéologie-là (et non plus la critique de la religion ou de la philosophie) que l'on pouvait démasquer la réalité du système social. L'excuse de l'auteur est que les gauchistes font souvent la même confusion et échouent en partie de ce fait à analyser la contradiction au sein de la réalité sociale à l'époque de l'impérialisme. Mais l'inconvénient d'étudier les seules origines idéologiques du gauchisme se révèle à l'évidence dans la tentative maladroite d'évaluation de l'influence du gauchisme sur l'événement. La définition étroite du gauchisme éclate alors car il est clair que maoïstes et trotskystes ont eu autant et plus d'impact sur la réalité. Le gauchisme est plus que ce qu'il est ... la conception de l'auteur frise l'idéalisme car on tente d'expliquer la production de la réalité à partir de l'idéologie. On pourrait d'ailleurs prétendre que l'échec des événements provient d'une insuffisance de développement de la théorie.

A n'avoir pas étudié les origines du phénomène gauchiste dans la réalité, ni même analysé le phénomène, ne fût-ce qu'à travers la production idéologique, on est condamné à analyser les différences subtiles d'opinion de plumitifs gauchistes de troisième ordre qui ne représentent rien.

Personnellement, le principal reproche que nous adresserions à l'ouvrage de Richard Gombin c'est que sur le plan de la méthode (ou de son absence de méthode), ce livre sur le gauchisme n'est malheureusement pas un livre gauchiste ... ni même un livre orthodoxe ...

SERGE LATOUCHE
Université de Lille (France) et Ottawa

John Dunn, **Modern Revolutions: An Introduction to the Analysis of a Political Phenomenon.** Cambridge: Cambridge University Press [Toronto: Macmillan], 1972, pp. xiii, 346.

Paul Wilkinson, **Social Movement.** London: Macmillan Press [Toronto: Macmillan], 1971, pp. 176.

Lionel Rubinoff, ed., **Tradition and Revolution: The Frank Gerstein Lectures, 1970.** Toronto: Macmillan of Canada, 1971, pp. 173.

Here, collectively viewed, are three recent volumes on the general subject of social movements and social change. While there is a generic similarity in the subject matter at hand, each book approaches the problem of understanding this phenomenon in a distinctive manner and with highly variable results. It is this reviewer's opinion that John Dunn's excellent treatise stands head-and-shoulders above them all both in terms of a lucid explanation of the material and suitability for classroom use.

While Dunn's book does not provide the reader with an elaborate explanatory theory or ideological assessment of revolutions, it does provide a fine substantive description of those revolutions and movement-regimes which have occurred in Russia, Mexico, China, Yugoslavia, Vietnam, Algeria, Turkey, and Cuba. Dunn obviously has a superb command of knowledge about the data of each of these historic cases and his examination of the implications of each is searching and insightful. The book would be ideal for any classroom where an instructor could augment these informative essays with lectures and discussions oriented more to theories and concepts about revolutions. In a provocative introductory chapter, Dunn notes that "revolution appears as a reasonably frequent type of social change, occurring intermittently throughout history and becoming rather more frequent in recent years" (p. 5). Insofar as this is so, "revolutions must be taken seriously because they represent (or may represent) profoundly important and in some ways distinctively successful attempts to improve the human social condition – at particular times and in particular places" (p. 20). He speculates upon the causes, cycles, and ideologies of revolutionary process in an interesting fashion – even though not everyone will want to agree with everything he says. Overall, an excellent choice for any course dealing with political revolutions or social movements and social change.

Not nearly so much can be said for the volume of Frank Gerstein Lectures (delivered in 1970 at York University in Toronto) edited by Lionel Rubinoff. Unfortunately, this book possesses virtually all the vices and almost none of the virtues found in collections of this sort. It is not as if the cast of speakers is not stellar enough: Ivan Illich, C.S. Holling, George Grant, Robert J. Lifton, Harold Taylor, and Jacob Bronowski would pack any Canadian lecture auditorium with eager listeners. Moreover, the subject of "tradition and change" in matters having to do with the learning and educational process in society is also an important field of concern. The problem lies not in the choice of contributors nor in their subject matter *per se* but in the inadequacy of exposition relating to the ideas mentioned. Too often these occasions serve only as an opportunity for the "greats" to pontificate in very general ways about some very serious and intricate questions which demand (and deserve) careful development and exposition. The lecture format contains certain structural limitations on the rigorous examination of ideas and those limitations are abundantly evident here. If one were interested in the notions of these distinguished contributors, one would do far better to consult their more extensive writings than the bits and pieces to be encountered in these recorded lectures. Furthermore, the book has no index, no bibliography, and no footnotes.

Finally, the effort by British political scientist Paul Wilkinson – appearing in a "Key Concepts in Political Science" series – raises other nagging questions. Wilkinson attempts nothing less than to give the beginning undergraduate reader a critical introduction to the concepts, literature, and theories of social movements. This is a tall order for anyone. Wilkinson complicates his formidable task by trying to suggest that he will do it with due regard for "flexibility," "ideological neutrality," and "cultural interchangeability." He does not succeed in sustaining such an impartial stance. Indeed, his proclivities for controversial typologies like "pluralism and mass society" and "revolutionary and totalitarian movements" suggest a very clear penchant for pluralist and structural functionalist ideological analysis. Insofar as there are very clear biases and prejudices which inform the author's writing throughout, the book has to be read with extraordinary care and precision. In getting so involved, Wilkinson does both too much and too little. For instance, he feels motivated to examine and provide a critique of major theories of social change propounded by such a diverse lot as Rousseau, Marx, Sombart, Tonnies, Heberle, Smelser, Truman, Bentley, Downs, LaPalombara, Finer, Almond and Coleman, Weber, *et. al.* He does this with such a facile glibness that a reader can end up not quite knowing in detail what these men actually had to say, why or if Wilkinson finds them useful, or why he borrows this or that from them. A clear danger here is that a student will emerge from a reading of this book more confused than informed. Because of further problems of a cryptic and less than lucid prose style, I found myself putting this book down with a troubled sense of having taken little from the experience. If a teacher is searching for a good theoretical work on social movements, I would recommend Barrington Moore, Jr.'s brilliant, if flawed, *Social Origins of Dictatorship and Democracy*. Nevertheless, Wilkinson's footnotes, index, and bibliography are quite good.

In sum, the interested teacher is urged to consult John Dunn's book for an unusually useful discussion of revolutions in various nation states during the twentieth century.

JOHN ANSON WARNER
University of Saskatchewan, Regina Campus

Simon R. Miles, ed., **Metropolitan Problems, International Perspectives: A Search for Comprehensive Solutions.** Toronto: Methuen, 1970, pp. xx, 534.

In 1966 the Toronto Bureau of Municipal Research took a step that was to have significant consequences for the comparative study of urban development. Having decided to sponsor a centennial study and training programme on metropolitan problems, the Bureau commissioned eleven background papers on various structural and functional problems. It proceeded to set up "study groups" to discuss the papers as well as matters of purely local interest in 40 metropolitan centres throughout the world. This lengthy volume is the result of a large conference held in August 1967 at York University, at which the authors of the background papers came together with representatives of the study groups in a search for possible solutions. Out of this, INTERMET (International Association for Metropolitan Research and Development) was born in 1968, and has since acted as the co-ordinating secretariat for the study groups and the sponsor of a number of comparative urban research projects. Simon Miles, INTERMET's executive director, has edited the original papers and, in additional chapters and commentaries, has broadened their scope by relating them to the points raised by the conference participants.

The papers are divided into three main sections and a conclusion. The substantive sections consist of a descriptive introductory paper on worldwide demographic, economic, and governmental characteristics of the contemporary metropolis; a section dealing with the major services – transportation, utilities, housing, education, welfare, and public health; and a group of papers focusing on different political/administrative aspects. The fourth, and final section consists of an argument by the editor for comprehensive urban planning and a discussion of the process by which this might be achieved.

The intention of the volume is to present as much factual material as possible on functional and administrative issues, describe and to some extent categorize the range of solutions attempted, and, in the light of this, suggest optimal strategies to policy-makers. At this level the book succeeds very well and the editor is to be congratulated for a clearly-written, informative presentation. Although many of the papers and commentaries are only tenuously related within major sections, the book does gain considerable unity from a number of recurring themes and arguments. The most important theme is the necessity for comprehensive urban planning. "Comprehensive" involves the interrelations among the social, economic, physical, and administrative dimensions of urbanization; the linking of metropolitan planning mechanisms to more local political/administrative groupings on the one hand, and to regional and national planning agencies on the other; and the development of decision-making procedures based on a well-articulated information system. The argument for comprehensive planning joins forces with a second theme: the importance of encouraging local involvement and participation in metropolitan problem-solving. Here we catch a glimpse of the rationale for INTERMET's study groups, made up of leading citizens, experts, and politicians. A final major theme is the concern for devising political/administrative structures (notably a two-tier approach) that would maximize the major goals of metropolitan government – participation, liberty, and the efficient provision of services.

In a book of this size there are inevitably uneven spots. The papers fall roughly into three qualitative groupings: a select few which really sparkle with original analysis (for example the paper by Dupré on intergovernmental relations, and by Gorynski and Rybicki on the "functional metropolis"); a larger number that are competently written and present, in a lively fashion, a good deal of useful information (Sazanami's paper on housing, Bakacs on public health, Rose on welfare services, Smallwood on political systems); and a third group of rather tedious recitations and comparisons of international experience with little or no central argument to guide the reader through a morass of detail (the papers by Hicks and Hanson are the worst offenders here). Without the discipline of specific case studies, the articles all too easily fall back on flaccid truisms ("The development process is complex, and the man-made factors influencing development are diverse. As countries attain new levels of development, much research is needed to improve decision-making and implementation ..." Weissmann, p.433) or oversimplified armchair prescriptions ("If human progress is to [be] achieved ... [economic, social, and environmental] changes must be guided by policies designed to realize society's consensual goals. Such policies have to indicate the desired direction, location, nature and pace of change ... In short, these policies will be expressed as a comprehensive plan." Miles, p.493).

More substantively, the volume suffers from a lack of clear definition of the unit under analysis. Assuming there is something special about the "metropolitan area" – cities having a population of over a million – then why include in the analysis, as the book has done, cities like Belgrade, Ibadan, Hanover, Winnipeg, Edmonton, and Vancouver, all of which had populations well under a million at the time the articles were written? The ostensible reason for this inconsistency is that these cities had been chosen, partly on political grounds, for the Centennial Program, but their inclusion in this book seems to undermine its whole logic. On the other hand, perhaps there is no watertight case to be made for considering all the world's largest cities as a common category. Insofar as the authors try to justify an exclusive focus on the metropolitan area, they almost invariably stress that the problems of the metropolis are the problems of all large, growing cities, only more so. And one author, Hugh Philp, writing on education, cogently questions whether in fact the planning of metropolitan educational systems should have anything to do with the metropolitan unit as such. A more consistent focus on functions and problems in *all* large urban areas would have lent more coherence to this volume than the attempt to base analysis on a purely (and in this case, unevenly applied) statistical definition of the "metropolitan area."

The definitional problem is related to another ambiguity in the presentation of material. Since all metropolitan areas are presumed to present similar, and in principle soluble problems, there is little sensitivity to the very considerable differences between cities in developed and underdeveloped regions of the world. The poverty of the masses, combined with a lack of capital and skills, creates different problems and demands different kinds of solutions. Of course, a rigid application of the developed/underdeveloped distinction can be self-defeating, but many of the solutions suggested in the volume as being universally applicable in principle (such as the encouragement of a wide range of private interest groups, a comprehensive planning process, extensive expressway systems) are for various reasons inappropriate or impractical in most of the world's poorest cities. This bias might have been expected in view of the overwhelming weight of literature and experience in developed areas, though it could have consciously been reduced by some sensitive use of case studies of third world cities.

But to this reviewer, the most serious shortcoming in this book is its failure to come to grips with the first of Lasswell's famous questions, "Who gets what?" With the notable exception of Albert Rose's paper on welfare services, the book is for the most part silent on the very serious problems of slum housing, maldistribution of income, massive unemployment, and racial violence which beset so many of the world's largest cities. The papers offer, by and large, technocratic and administrative solutions to "functional" problems, and as such, ignore both the interests served by existing structures and the political implications of different approaches. If these questions are more difficult to deal with, they are also more important. But while the book stops short of considering possibilities for radical change, it is a valuable addition to the literature on comparative urban development, and deserves careful reading by anyone concerned with urban and regional planning.

RICHARD E. STREN
Ministry of Lands, Housing, and Urban Development, Dar es Salaam

Frédéric Marx, **L'administration locale en Grande-Bretagne.** Paris : Presses Universitaires de France, 1972, 92 p.

Cette récente publication s'insère parfaitement dans la série des Dossiers Thémis dont elle fait partie. Les Dossiers se proposent, en effet, de fournir les données d'un problème plutôt que les conclusions des différents analystes. Dans cette perspective, le petit volume de Frédéric Marx donne les structures administratives actuelles du gouvernement local britannique en insérant, ici et là, quelques commentaires sur ces structures et leur fonctionnement.

Une présentation aussi dégagée des faits est justifiée, puisque les essais critiques sur le sujet sont déjà assez nombreux et que le rapport Redcliffe-Maud serait difficilement remplaçable. En trente-huit pages de textes (les cinquante-quatre autres étant consacrées à la reproduction de documents), l'auteur parvient à résumer les principales coordonnées du problème, soit les structures de l'administration locale et celles du Grand Londres, le fonctionnement par commissions, le contrôle du gouvernement central sur les administrations locales, les finances locales, le contrôle judiciaire, et l'administration locale en Ecosse.

Certains points ont semblé particulièrement intéressants, notamment le développement des institutions locales britanniques par évolution plutôt que par révolution, le problème de la prolifération des commissions et les contraintes imposées par le caractère obligatoire de certaines commissions.

L'originalité du volume tient essentiellement à sa composition, c'est-à-dire à l'addition de documents de base au texte lui-même. Frédéric Marx présente, en effet, quatorze documents qui sont soit des textes législatifs, soit des documents de la jurisprudence locale, soit des extraits d'analyse de la situation actuelle et de propositions de réforme. Ces documents sont un complément indispensable au texte puisqu'ils précisent certains points obscurs et décrivent clairement le processus de sélection du personnel politique.

L'image de l'administration locale en Grande-Bretagne demeure cependant incomplète, par le fait que Frédéric Marx ne traite pas du fonctionnarisme local, ne serait-ce qu'au niveau des structures des services et du personnel de ces services. Un chapitre sur ce sujet aurait permis une meilleure compréhension du mode d'administration.

Signalons aussi une imprécision importante dans la description des bourgs du Grand Londres. L'auteur oublie de mentionner la différence entre les bourgs dits du Londres extérieur et les bourgs dits du Londres intérieur (p 18).

Malgré ces quelques remarques, le volume de Frédéric Marx est une description habile du gouvernement local en Grande-Bretagne. Pour être parfaite, cette image aurait dû être plus complète et, surtout, être accompagnée d'une bibliographie qui aurait permis au lecteur intéressé d'approfondir son étude.

LOUISE QUESNEL-OUELLET
Université Laval

Daniel Paulus, **Les milieux dirigeants belges et l'adhésion du Royaume-Uni aux communautés européennes.** Bruxelles, Editions de l'Institut de Sociologie, Institut d'Etudes européennes, Université Libre de Bruxelles, 1971, 331 pages, bibliographie, annexes.

Ce sont des études comme celle de M. Daniel Paulus qui contribuent à détruire des mythes. Dans cet ouvrage fouillé, on découvre en effet que la vision traditionnelle des élites belges unanimes à réclamer l'admission de la Grande-Bretagne dans le Marché Commun mérite d'être tempérée quelque peu. La simple existence de motivations différentes sous-tendant cette volonté d'accueillir le Royaume-Uni permet déjà de supposer des nuances dans cette unanimité.

On sait que la politique agricole est un des piliers, si mal construit soit-il, de la Communauté et les réactions des milieux agricoles belges sont intéressantes. Sur le principe de l'adhésion britannique, il y a quasi-unanimité; sur les conditions et sur le moment de l'entrée, les divergences abondent. Entre 1961 et 1963, on voudrait voir la Communauté adopter des mesures communes avant de courir le risque « d'entrer dans le Commonwealth » à cause des innombrables concessions accordées à la Grande-Bretagne, En 1966–7, au contraire, on a peur de voir la politique commune remise en question. L'auteur en profite pour dissiper un autre mythe, celui de l'identité entre l'entrée de la Grande-Bretagne à la CEE et l'adhésion de la Grande-Bretagne *plus* le Danemark, la Norvège, et l'Irlande. En effet, ce que les agriculteurs peuvent gagner par l'entrée britannique, ils peuvent le perdre, toutes proportions gardées, par l'entrée du Danemark.

Quant aux syndicats belges, l'espoir de s'associer aux *trade unions* britanniques et de voir la fine fleur de la démocratie, les Scandinaves, renforcer le pouvoir ouvrier en Europe, les poussait à soutenir l'adhésion britannique. Mais M. Paulus montre bien combien les syndicats belges sont conservateurs et raisonnent en termes nationalistes traditionnels (c'est ce qui explique les scissions de plus en plus fréquentes en Belgique entre la base et la direction syndicale). Aussi le souci de préserver les intérêts acquis au sein de la Communauté, même s'ils sont les premiers à juger qu'ils sont insuffisants, ne leur permet d'accorder qu'un soutien passif à la candidature britannique.

La réaction du monde des affaires belge, favorable, témoigne néanmoins du caractère protectionniste de ces milieux et de leurs angoisses devant le changement qu'entraînerait l'entrée de la Grande-Bretagne dans le Marché Commun. Faute d'une véritable politique industrielle, ou plutôt à cause de ses innombrables contradictions (par exemple, le désir d'arriver à créer des industries européennes et celui de mener une vigoureuse politique anti-trust), la CEE encourage indirectement le vieillissement des entreprises à cause des barrières tarifaires dont elle s'entoure. A la crainte de voir la Grande-Bretagne orienter le Marché Commun vers une zone de libre-échange, s'ajoutaient de vives inquiétudes sur la situation économique et monétaire du candidat.

Le monde politique belge, comme nous l'apprend M. Paulus, est d'accord sur le principe de l'adhésion et l'on ne peut s'empêcher de se demander si cet accord de principe résulte d'une véritable foi européenne ou si, au contraire, c'est l'image « d'européaniste » convaincue que projette la Belgique à l'extérieur, qui « oblige » les milieux dirigeants à réciter leur profession de foi.

Pour les Socialistes (PSB), deux aspects méritent d'être soulignés : d'une part, l'influence prépondérante de Paul-Henri Spaak qui élaborait la politique européenne du PSB pratiquement en dehors des structures du parti, ce qui limitait passablement les possibilités d'action du PSB. D'autre part, l'opposition, qui remonte à 1945, des socialistes anglais à l'intégration (en raison des avantages sociaux acquis dans le cadre national, qu'ils ne veulent pas voir s'atténuer dans le cadre supranational) déçoit les socialistes belges. En 1967, M. Spaak avait quitté l'arène politique et le PSB était dans l'opposition; la politique européenne du parti manquait de force. Nonobstant la présence des travaillistes au pouvoir en Grande-Bretagne en 1967, le PSB estimait que, paradoxalement, seul un gouvernement conservateur pouvait mener le Royaume-Uni dans la CEE. Par contre, l'aile flamande du PSB était plus favorable à la Grande-Bretagne et condamnait plus volontiers le général de Gaulle que l'aile wallonne pour qui, en 1967, l'argumentation française paraissait plus pertinente qu'en 1963.

S'il y a fidélité au "Spaakisme" au PSB, au Parti Social Chrétien, l'absence de toute doctrine européenne, alliée à une fédéralisation croissante des ailes flamande et wallonne, va conduire à des différenciations verticales (presse et milieux informés vs gouvernement) et horizontales (flamands et wallons). La plupart des représentants de la presse catholique francophone reprochent au gouvernement son manque de réalisme dans le soutien inconditionnel apporté à l'adhésion britannique. En 1963, au contraire, les milieux, catholiques flamands sont résolument « Spaakistes ». En 1967, le PSC finit par « se trouver » une doctrine pro-britannique pour aussitôt voir la presse francophone affiliée au PSC dénoncer les excès gouvernementaux tandis que l'aile flamande se sent parfois prête à construire l'Europe sans la France. On en vient peu à peu à se demander (1) si la Belgique a eu une politique européenne et (2) si les problèmes extérieurs ont jamais su ébranler le conformisme au jour le jour des partis politiques belges. Nous avons vu que le PSB (en dehors de P.H. Spaak) et le PSC avaient été « passifs ». Or voici que le PLP (Parti de la Liberté et du Progrès) est taxé d'une « passivité » encore plus grande face aux problèmes internationaux. Seul le libre-échangisme propre aux libéraux, allié au conformisme atlantique allait activer le soutien du PLP en faveur de la Grande-Bretagne.

Comme on pouvait s'y attendre, la Volksunie (Parti nationaliste flamand) est anti-française et pro-anglaise, donc favorable à la *politique gouvernementale* même si elle est hostile à la *structure* du gouvernement unitaire. Au contraire, le Front démocratique des Francophones et le Rassemblement Wallon sont des gaullistes « culturels » et des « européens » convaincus par opposition à l'unitarisme.

Grâce à Daniel Paulus, on parvient ainsi à faire un tour complet de l'horizon un peu étriqué de la politique extérieure belge quant à l'admission de la Grande-Bretagne à la CEE. Le problème général est celui de la compatibilité entre le renforcement des institutions et l'élargissement de la communauté. Il demeure qu'après la lecture de cet ouvrage, on se sent désemparé par l'absence de débats véritables dans la plupart des milieux sur la philosophie et les buts de l'intégration. Serait-ce, comme l'écrivait en 1952 Georges Rigassi, qu'encore maintenant « l'idée de l'Union européenne n'est pas rentrée dans la conscience des peuples d'Europe » ou bien cette idée est-elle devenue tellement commune, voire dépréciée, qu'il n'est plus nécessaire de constamment la renouveler, par delà les contingences quotidiennes ?

FERRY DE KERCKHOVE
Université Laval

J.A.W. Gunn, **Factions No More: Attitudes to Party in Government and Opposition in Eighteenth-Century England.** London: Frank Cass, 1972, pp. xii, 275.

The constitution which eventuated from the struggles of the seventeenth century in England was almost, but not quite, unworkable. The duty to govern was still vested in the King; but the House of Commons could deprive the King (and his ministers) of the means with which to govern. The solution was for the King to select as ministers those men who could get business, especially money business, done in the House. But should he select them from one party – unless, of course, all parties were to be suppressed as dangerous to national integrity at home and to national strength abroad? If so, how was an opposed party to be regarded – as traitorous, as merely covetous, or as patriotic, doing its duty in the adversary process? After the electoral reforms of 1832 the complex role of organized parties would be evident, but in the long meantime – from about 1688 until at least 1800 – how parties, especially opposed parties, were to be regarded was a debatable question.

Professor Gunn is out to show that, contrary to conventional wisdom, Edmund Burke was not the first to wrestle earnestly with that question. He is out to show, also, that it must be kept separate from discussions about the merits of mixed governments and of the separation of powers. What he has done is to plunge again and again into the stream – sometimes a trickle, sometimes a torrent – of eighteenth-century polemics to retrieve notable examples of the attitudes prevalent at various periods. Undoubtedly, he makes his case: any student of English politics, or of the British constitution, who ignores this book will do so at peril.

It is possible that a reader may complain that Professor Gunn's introduction is too terse, that the procession of extracts from 74 works has a dazing effect, and that the footnotes are located inconveniently at the end of the book. A reader may wonder if the argument could not have been presented better in a different kind of book, in a kind of political history with the changing views on factions, parties, and opposition as its central theme. If at any point Professor Gunn considered such a possibility, he was wise to reject it. The book he has produced has the merit – which the alternative would have lacked – of making readily available, as the end product of herculean research, the very words of the writers. They come to us with little of the twentieth century interposed. Professor Gunn's rebuttal against the criticism that his introduction is too restrained could be that anybody who wants more can turn to a political history of England. His comment on the complaint that his learned footnotes have been hived at the end could be that in our day publishers defer but little to the wishes of mere writers.

To propose in either Britain or Canada nowadays that government be conducted without parties would be comparable to suggesting that football be played without teams. But how many parties can the playing field of responsible government accommodate? How far ought those in the opposition go in opposing the government's legislative programme when they believe that it is wrong? Are separatist parties, whose declared aim is to end the game, to be regarded as genuine parties? Parties may be factions no more; but not all the basic questions have been answered. As Canadian politicians debate the unanswered questions in the 1970s, the views of their eighteenth-century forbears, as revived by Professor Gunn, may take on a very lively relevance.

JOHN STEWART
St Francis Xavier University

Gottfried Willhelm Leibniz, **The Political Writings of Leibniz**, trans. and ed. Patrick Riley. Cambridge: Cambridge University Press [Toronto: Macmillan of Canada], 1972, pp. viii, 206.

Cambridge University Press advances the claim that the texts in the series in which the book under review appears "are modern, critical editions of major texts in political thought." The editors, however, have chosen to present the works, for the most part, of men such as Wilhelm von Humboldt, Fitzjames Stephen, Kant, and in the present case, Leibniz, whose more serious claims to immortality lie in other fields. Even Leibniz's editor is a trifle apologetic about the quality of the political thought he is presenting. As he says in the Preface (p. vii): "while it is true that no one can pretend that Liebniz' political writings are equal to those of his contemporaries, or even to his own writings on logic, metaphysics and theology, they are at least intriguing and worthy of some attention." And later in the Introduction (p. 22), in a defence of Leibniz, he suggests that "Bertrand Russell ... was not altogether justified in calling Leibniz' social thought a 'mass of inconsistencies' ..."

The problem with this short collection, however, does not lie with the editor and translator. The lengthy introduction, about forty pages long, attempts to put some order and coherence into Leibniz's political and social ideas. Perhaps, though, Riley tries too hard. With a minor political thinker it is more interesting to see his relationship in comparison both to his times and to the great writers who wrote before him and contemporaneously. A collection such as this is useful to the extent that it helps us better to appreciate Hobbes' successes rather than Leibniz's failures: "at the end, Leibniz knew that some of his ideals had become impossible – without, however, being able to give them up" (p. 33).

Besides the introduction, which is well worth reading, there are 154 pages of translations of short works by Leibniz written between 1677 and 1715. The book concludes with a useful critical bibliography and a short, spotty index. Even if this collection were intrinsically interesting, at a published price in this country of $16.50 the sales are more likely to be to librarians than dedicated scholars.

WILLIAM CHRISTIAN
Mount Allison University

NOTICE RE ANNUAL MEETING

On an exceptional basis, the 1973 Annual Meeting of the Canadian Political Science Association will *not* be held in June along with the other Learned Societies. Instead, it will be held at Sir George Williams University in Montreal on 18 and 19 August, the two days preceding the World Congress of the International Political Science Association, which runs 20–25 August. In addition, this year's annual meeting will be sponsored jointly with the Société canadienne de science politique and the program will consist of French, English, and bilingual sessions. It is our current expectation that the usual grant made to us by the Canada Council to support travel to the Learned Societies meetings will be transferred to the August meeting. In addition, we have requested a specific grant this year to help defray some of the extra costs associated with the long stay in Montreal for the World Congress.

These funds are particularly designed to help younger members on the assumption that those presenting, discussing, or chairing papers will be subsidized by their own university. Those requesting CPSA/ACSP grants are urged to obtain finance from their own institutions in order to allow the Travel Fund to be spread widely. Requests, stating the cost of the economy return air fare, the grants you expect to receive from other sources, and the academic rank of the member must reach the Secretary-Treasurer, Professor John Trent, Canadian Political Science Association, c/o University of Ottawa, 30 Stewart Street, Ottawa, Ontario, K1N 6N5, *by May 30th, 1973.* Please enclose a self-addressed, stamped envelope with your request.

AVIS CONCERNANT LA REUNION ANNUELLE

Exceptionnellement cette année la réunion annuelle de l'Association canadienne de science politique ne se déroulera *pas* en juin, comme celle des autres Sociétés Savantes. Elle aura plutôt lieu à l'Université Sir George Williams de Montréal les 18 et 19 août, c'est-à-dire durant les deux jours qui précèdent immédiatement le Congrès mondial de l'association internationale de science politique, qui se tiendra du 20 au 25 août. De plus, la réunion de cette année sera patronée conjointement par la Société canadienne de science politique et le programme comprendra des séances en langue française, en langue anglaise, et des séances bilingues. Nous espérons que la subvention que nous accorde habituellement le Conseil des Arts afin de défrayer le coût des voyages pour permettre aux gens d'assister aux réunions des Sociétés Savantes sera reportée pour notre réunion en août. Nous avons en outre demandé au Conseil une subvention majorée cette année afin de nous aider à rencontrer les coûts plus élevés entrainés par un séjour prolongé à Montréal à l'occasion du Congrès Mondial.

Ces fonds sont d'abord mis à la disposition des membres plus jeunes, attendu que le voyage de ceux qui présentent ou discutent une communication, ou qui y président sera vraisemblablement défrayé par leur propre université. Ceux qui désirent se prévaloir de cette aide devraient tâcher d'obtenir d'abord une subvention de leur employeur, ce qui permettrait à CPSA/ACSP de répartir son assistance plus largement. Les demandes de subvention devraient, après avoir précisé le coût du transport aérien (aller-retour, classe économique) et déclaré les autres sources de financement escomptées, ainsi que le statut académique du demandeur, être envoyées au secrétaire-trésorier, Professeur John Trent, Association canadienne de science politique, Université d'Ottawa, 30 rue Stewart, Ottawa, Ontario, K1N 6N5, *pour le 30 mai 1973*, accompagnées d'une enveloppe aflranchie.

nadian Journal of
olitical science
vue canadienne de
cience politique

MARK SPROULE-JONES and KENNETH D. HART Political Participation

LOUISE QUESNEL-OUELLET Changement dans les structures municipales

K.L. MORRISON The Businessman Voter in Thunder Bay

CONRAD WINN and JOHN MC MENEMY Political Alignment in a Polarized City

BRYAN H. MASSAM Local Government in the Montreal Area, 1911–71

JEAN CRÈTE Analyse stratégique du choix d'un candidat

H.T. WILSON Rationality and Decision in Administrative Science

MORTON SCHOOLMAN Further Reflections on Marcuse and Marx

JEAN PIERRE RICHERT Political Socialization in Quebec

June 1973 juin VI no. 2

Canadian Journal of Political Science / Revue canadienne de science politique

Editorial correspondence in English should be directed to Professor David Hoffman, Division of Social Science, York University, 4700 Keele Street, Downsview 463, Ont. Subscription and business correspondence should be directed to the University of Toronto Press, Periodicals Department, Front Campus, Toronto 181, Ont.

On doit adresser toute communication en français, au sujet de la rédaction, à M. Vincent Lemieux, Département de science politique, Faculté des sciences sociales, Université Laval, Québec 10e, Qué. Les communications à caractère commercial, y compris celles concernant les abonnements, doivent être adressées à : University of Toronto Press, Periodicals Department, Front Campus, Toronto 181, Ont.

The Journal acknowledges with gratitude the generous assistance of the Canada Council. / La Revue tient à remercier le Conseil des Arts du Canada pour la généreuse subvention qu'il a bien voulu lui accorder.

Subscriptions: Membership in either the CPSA/ACSP or the SCSP includes subscription to the journal. Ordinary membership $15. Student membership $5. Joint CPSA and SCSP membership $17. Joint CPSA and Canadian Economics Association (two journals) $26.

Abonnement : la souscription à l'un des organismes ci-dessus (CPSA/ACSP ou SCSP) tient lieu d'abonnement. Montant de la souscription : tous $15, étudiants $5, conjointe aux deux organismes $17, conjointe à l'Association canadienne d'Economique (valant abonnement à *Revue canadienne d'Economique*) $26.

Postage paid in cash at third class rates — Permit no C-71, University of Toronto Press, University of Toronto, Toronto 181, Ont. / Les frais de poste sont payés au comptant selon le tarif de troisième classe — Permis no C-71, University of Toronto Press, Toronto 181, Ont.

Indexed: Index to *Canadian Legal Periodical Literature* / Indexée au *Catalogue des périodiques juridiques canadiens.*

Published by University of Toronto Press / Publiée par University of Toronto Press.

Contents

A Public-Choice Model of Political Participation
MARK SPROULE-JONES and KENNETH D. HART 175

Situations et attitudes face au changement dans les structures municipales
LOUISE QUESNEL-OUELLET 195

The Businessman Voter in Thunder Bay: The Catalyst to the Federal-Provincial Voting Split?
K.L. MORRISON 219

Political Alignment in a Polarized City: Electoral Cleavages in Kitchener, Ontario
CONRAD WINN and JOHN MC MENEMY 230

Forms of Local Government in the Montreal Area, 1911–71: A Discriminant Approach
BRYAN H. MASSAM 243

Analyse stratégique du choix d'un candidat dans une circonscription urbaine
JEAN CRÈTE 254

Rationality and Decision in Administrative Science
H.T. WILSON 271

Further Reflections on Work, Alienation, and Freedom in Marcuse and Marx
MORTON SCHOOLMAN 295

Note

Political Socialization in Quebec: Young People's Attitudes toward Government
JEAN PIERRE RICHERT 303

Recensions / Reviews 314

A Public-Choice Model of Political Participation*

MARK SPROULE-JONES *University of Victoria*
KENNETH D. HART *York University*

The study of political participation is largely guided by sociological and social-psychological perspectives. Citizens are seen to vote, and to press their claims on public officials in other ways, as a result of their resolution of social and group forces and/or inner personality predispositions. The high water mark in this orientation was the 1965 publication of *Political Participation* by Lester W. Milbrath, a volume which was intended "to summarize the state of our knowledge about political participation."[1]

In recent years an economic approach to the study of political participation has gathered pace. This approach takes two forms. In one form, attempts are made to examine the economic rationality (in the sense of consistency) with which voters choose, at election time, on the basis of their own perceptions of the policy stands of the candidates or parties.[2] Party identification, for example, is not conceptualized as a traditional attitude passed down through generations, but instead as a device learned from one's parents that is instrumental for the advance of the voter's own particular set of values.[3] And the supposed lack of knowledge and interest displayed by the voter about electoral issues is seen as partly contingent upon the methodology of electoral behaviour research, which has tended to use closed item questions rather than open ended items designed to tap the issues which each voter (rather than the researcher) decides are salient.[4]

*This is a revised version of a paper entitled "The Political Economy of Political Participation: Model and Analysis," presented at the Public Choice Society, 1972 Annual Meetings, Carnegie-Mellon University, Pittsburgh, 3–6 May 1972. The research in this paper was financed, in part, by a Faculty Research Grant from the Committee on Faculty Research, Leave and Travel of the University of Victoria. We wish to acknowledge the aid and/or helpful comments of a large number of persons, including Donald E. Blake, Garry Curtis, Norman Frolich, Gordon J. Haywood, Donald S. Lutz, Elinor Ostrom, Vincent Ostrom, L.J. Sharpe, and Neil A. Swainson. We regret that not all of the suggestions could be incorporated into our analysis.

1(Chicago, 1965), 4. A comparable effort using 1965 Canadian federal election data is Rick Van Loon, "Political Participation in Canada," this JOURNAL, 3 (1970), 376–99.

2Like so many other areas of electoral behaviour research, these attempts were given a large stimulus by the work of V.O. Key. See his posthumously published, *The Responsible Electorate*, Cambridge, Mass. 1966. See also Michael J. Shapiro, "Rational Political Man: A Synthesis of Economic and Social-Psychological Perspectives," *American Political Science Review*, 63 (1969), 1106–19.

3Arthur S. Goldberg, "Social Determinism and Rationality as Bases of Party Identification," *American Political Science Review*, 63 (1969), 5–25.

4David E. Repass, "Issue Salience and Party Choice," *American Political Science Review*, 65 (1971), 389–400. See also Peter B. Natchez and Irvin C. Bupp, "Candidates, Issues and Votes," *Public Policy*, 1 (1968), 409–37; John C. Pierce, "Party Identification and the Changing Role of Ideology in American Politics," *Midwest Journal of Political Science*, 14 (1970), 25–42; John O. Field and Ronald E. Anderson, "Ideology in the Public's Conceptualization of the 1964 Election," *Public Opinion Quarterly*, 33 (1969), 380–98; Herbert

Canadian Journal of Political Science/Revue canadienne de science politique, VI, no. 2 (June/juin 1973). Printed in Canada/Imprimé au Canada.

The second form that the economic approach to political participation takes is to examine the extent to which various voting rules and electoral arrangements precisely aggregate voter preferences for collective-consumption goods. There has been, of course, a continuous debate among political scientists for over a hundred years as to the value of proportional representation versus other electoral schemes,[5] but the thrust of the economic approach in recent years has been to examine and search for ways around the paradox of voting, first discovered by Borda in the eighteenth century and rediscovered by Kenneth Arrow in 1951.[6] One set of theorists strives to explain why at least some of the ciitzens in a political community accept the imposed choice of others.[7] Robert A. Dahl, for example, hypothesizes that some citizens have to be socialized into such an acceptance on pain of the survival of the "democratic" game itself.[8] Another set of theorists modify one or more of Arrow's conditions for collective choice. Duncan Black, for example, assumes that individual preferences are ordered on an underlying dimension (such as the liberal-conservative dimension of political issues), and shows that, if the preferences of each individual are single peaked or bell shaped on the dimension, then majority rule can produce a non-imposed collective decision.[9] Anthony Downs, as a second example, adds competing political parties to a variety of preference distributions on the dimension of issue space and shows that citizen irrationality can actually be fostered by the parties.[10] Finally, a third set of theorists imply that majority rule and other voting rules are merely alterna-

F. Weisberg and Jerrold G. Rusk, "Dimensions of Candidate Evaluation," *American Political Science Review*, 64 (1970), 1167–85; Symposium, "Issue Voting," *American Political Science Review*, 66 (1972), 415–70.

5For a useful summary of some of the older literature, see Harry Eckstein, "Introduction. The Impact of Electoral Systems on Representative Government," in *Comparative Politics: A Reader*, ed. Harry Eckstein and David E. Apter (New York, 1963), 247–53. For the most complete empirical analysis, see Douglas W. Rae, *The Political Consequences of Electoral Laws* (2nd ed. New Haven, 1971). For the (recently revived) debate in Canada, see Alan C. Cairns, "The Electoral System and the Party System in Canada, 1921–1965," this JOURNAL, 1 (1968), 55–80; J.A.A. Lovink, "On Analysing the Impact of the Electoral System on the Party System in Canada," this JOURNAL, 3 (1970), 497–516; and Cairns, "A Reply to J.A. Lovink, 'On Analysing the Impact of the Electoral System on the Party System in Canada'," this JOURNAL, 3 (1970), 517–21.

6*Social Choices and Individual Values* (New York, 1951).

7Only some of the key features of the voluminous literature spawned by Arrow's work will be noted here. For an old but useful survey of much of the remainder, see William H. Riker, "Voting and the Summation of Preferences," *American Political Science Review*, 55 (1961), 900–11.

8*A Preface to Democratic Theory* (Chicago, 1956).

9*Committees and Elections* (Cambridge, 1958). Black had, in fact, anticipated the Arrow theorem and published his solution prior to 1951. Gordon Tullock, *Toward the Mathematics of Politics* (Ann Arbor, Mich., 1967), chap. 3, showed that Black's solution of single peakedness can be generalized to multiple dimensions.

10*An Economic Theory of Democracy* (New York, 1957). Downs, in fact, modified a solution for ideological differentiation between parties first suggested by Harold Hotelling in 1929 and applied it to the Arrow Problem. [See Harold Hotelling, "Stability in Competition," *Economic Journal*, 39 (1929), 4–57.] Downs was, however, one of the first theorists to suggest that Arrow's theorem could be solved once conditions of perfect certainty were modified. Since the publication of Downs' work, there has been a rapid increase in the literature on multi-dimensional models of spatial competition. Some of the more important works in this literature are reviewed and extended in Otto A. Davis, et al., "An Expository Development of a Mathematical Model of the Electoral Process," *American Political Science Review*, 64 (1970), 426–48.

Un modèle de participation politique dérivé de la théorie des « choix publics »

Les auteurs entendent utiliser l'approche économique pour expliquer la participation politique. Ils conçoivent les diverses activités politiques des citoyens comme étant le reflet collectif, à l'intérieur des multiples encadrements institutionnels, des « ressources », des « coûts » et des « bénéfices », tant « publics » que « privés », des citoyens-consommateurs. Le modèle théorique construit à partir de cette conception est soumis à une vérification empirique à l'aide de données, provenant en partie d'un sondage sur les activités politiques d'un échantillon des habitants de Saanich en Colombie-Britanique. Cette vérification démontre que le modèle permet de prédire une proportion importante de la variance dans les indices de participation des citoyens, et qu'il apporte, de plus, une meilleure contribution à la compréhension de la participation politique qu'un autre modèle de type sociologique présentement en vogue.

Cette étude se veut une tentative de démonstration qu'il est possible et utile pour le chercheur en science politique de se dégager premièrement de l'approche économique des choix publics, qui met surtout l'accent sur la façon dont les mécanismes de votation transforment en choix collectifs les préférences individuelles ayant trait aux biens publics et, deuxièmement, de l'approche socio-psychologique où la participation devient fonction des forces sociales et/ou des prédispositions et personnalités des individus.

tives to the rule of unanimous consent, the rule under which economic (private market) exchange takes place. As a consequence, unanimity should be used as a benchmark (or constitutional rule) for evaluating other (operational) voting rules since it, and it alone, is the rule whereby any voter can ensure that he will not have to accept the imposed choice of others.[11]

This paper also employs an economic perspective on political participation. It, however, differs in a number of respects from current work in the field. First, it includes under the rubric of participation, diverse strategies used by the citizen as a means to reveal preferences for public goods and services. The existing analyses from this economic perspective are inordinately concerned with the voting process, and although some studies have examined other strategies (migration,[12] apathy and alienation,[13] group activity,[14] and protest and revolu-

[11]James M. Buchanan and Gordon Tullock, *The Calculus of Consent* (Ann Arbor, Mich., 1962). Subsequent modifications of the theory in this book will be found in Elinor Ostrom, "Some Postulated Effects of Learning on Constitutional Behavior," *Public Choice*, 5 (1968), 87–104; Herbert J. Keisling, "Potential Costs of Alternative Decision-Making Rules," *Public Choice*, 4 (1968), 49–58; and Mark Sproule-Jones, "Toward a Dynamic Analysis of Collective Action," *Western Political Quarterly* (forthcoming).

[12]Charles M. Tiebout, "A Pure Theory of Local Expenditures," *Journal of Political Economy*, 64 (1956), 416–24; Wallace E. Oates, "The Effects of Property Taxes and Local Public Spending on Property Values: An Empirical Study of Tax Capitalization and the Tiebout Hypothesis," *Journal of Political Economy*, 77 (1969), 957–71; Brian Ellickson, "Jurisdictional Fragmentation and Residential Choice," *American Economic Review*, 61 (1971), 334–39; Albert O. Hirschman, *Exit, Voice and Loyalty* (Cambridge, Mass., 1970); John M. Orbell and Toru Uno, "A Theory of Neighborhood Problem Solving: Political Action vs Residential Mobility," *American Political Science Review*, 66 (1972), 471–89.

[13]Downs, *An Economic Theory*; Gerald Garvey, "The Theory of Party Equilibrium," *American Political Science Review*, 60 (1966), 27–38; Clarence M. Stone, "Local Referendums: An Alternative to the Alienated Voter Model," *Public Opinion Quarterly*, 29 (1965), 213–22.

[14]Mancur Olson, Jr, *The Logic of Collective Action* (Cambridge, Mass., 1965); Richard Wagner, "Pressure Groups and Political Entrepreneurs," *Papers on Non-Market Decision Making*, 1 (1966), 161–70; Albert Breton, "A Theory of the Demand for Public Goods," *Canadian Journal of Economics and Political Science*, 32 (1966), 455–67; Samuel H. Barnes,

tion[15]), they examine them in isolation rather than as part of a mutually interdependent set of ways in which citizen preferences are revealed.[16] It is one of the major assumptions of this paper that a citizen-consumer will use a variety of such strategies depending, among other things, on the strength of his preferences for the public goods and services of the political system. Moreover, it is important to note that an entire electorate can be characterized by scales of participation that reflect their collective preferences for public goods and services. Perhaps it may be through scales of political participation, such as constructed in this paper, that a way may be found to conceptualize and measure the elusive social welfare function of a given community.

Secondly, a theoretical model of political participation is developed, which represents an extension of the logic of voting contained in Downs's "An Economic Theory of Democracy."[17] Downs wrote before the modern theory of collective-consumption goods was largely formalized, and some of the inferences that can be made from this theory about the nature of the benefits and costs of government can usefully extend our understanding of the participation process.

"Party Democracy and the Logic of Collective Action," in *Approaches to the Study of Party Organization*, ed. William J. Crotty (Boston, 1968), 105–38; Ronald Manzer, "Selective Inducements and the Development of Pressure Groups: The Case of Canadian Teachers' Associations," this JOURNAL, 2 (1969), 103–17; Robert H. Salisbury, "An Exchange Theory of Interest Groups," *Midwest Journal of Political Science*, 13 (1969), 1–32; Philip M. Burgess and James A. Robinson, "Alliances and the Theory of Collective Action: A Simulation of Coalition Processes," *Midwest Journal of Political Science*, 13 (1969), 194–218; David L. Shapiro, "Pressure Groups and Public Investment Decisions," *Public Choice*, 10 (1971), 103–8; Stephen Clarkson, "Barriers to Entry of Parties in Toronto's Civic Politics," this JOURNAL, 4 (1971), 206–34; Andrew M. Scott, *Competition in American Politics* (New York, 1970), chaps. 2 and 3.

[15]Thomas Ireland, "The Rationale of Revolt," *Papers on Non-Market Decision Making*, 3 (1967), 49–66; Michael Lipsky, "Protest as a Political Resource," *American Political Science Review*, 62 (1968), 1144–58; Edward Luttwak, *Coup d'Etat: A Practical Handbook* (London, 1968); Albert and Raymond Breton, "An Economic Theory of Social Movements," *American Economic Review*, 59 (1969), 198–205; Anthony Scott, "Investing and Protesting," *Journal of Political Economy*, 77 (1969), 916–20; Michael Lipsky, "Community Organization as a Political Resource," paper delivered at the 69th Annual Meeting of American Political Science Association, Los Angeles, 8–12 Sept., 1970; Michael Parenti, "Power and Pluralism," *Journal of Politics*, 32 (1970), 501–32; Gordon Tullock, "The Paradox of Revolution," *Public Choice*, 11 (1971), 89–99; Charles J. Cicchetti et al., "On the Economics of Mass Demonstrations," *American Economic Review*, 61 (1971), 719–24.

[16]This point has been made in Mark Sproule-Jones, "Strategic Tensions in the Scale of Political Analysis," *British Journal of Political Science*, 2 (1972), 173–91. There are a few exceptions in the literature to this general comment, such as, Robert O. Warren, "Federal-Local Development Planning: Scale Effects in Representation and Policy Making," *Public Administration Review*, 30 (1970), 584–95; Madelyn L. Kafoglis, "Participatory Democracy in the Community Action Program," *Public Choice*, 5 (1968), 73–85, and "Equality of Opportunity in Decision Making: Its Scope in Economic, Social and Political Processes," *American Journal of Economics and Sociology*, 29 (1970), 1–16; Louis F. Weschler and Robert O. Warren, "Consumption Costs and Production Costs in the Provision of Antipoverty Goods," paper delivered at the 69th Annual Meeting of the American Political Science Association, Los Angeles, 8–12 Sept. 1970; Hirschman, *Exit, Voice and Loyalty*; Orbell and Uno, "Neighborhood Problem Solving."

[17]In a theoretical work being pursued concurrently with most of our empirical research, Norman Frolich and his colleagues extended some of Downs' logic to the economic analysis of organized groups made by Mancur Olson. As a result, they derived a theory of political leadership that is based upon concepts that are similar to our own concept of "public benefits" explained below. This theory is now published as *Political Leadership and Collective Goods* (Princeton, 1971).

Thirdly, the economic approach is largely analytical rather than empirical. This study, however, both constructs an economic model of political participation and also tests it empirically, with the use of survey and unobtrusive data. It does not, like the few economic approaches that have looked at the empirical world, rely upon aggregate data with the concommitant problems of valid inference about individuals. The study makes extensive use, for example, of tax data about the individuals in a survey, rather than attempting to break down aggregate tax data collected by government authorities for other purposes.[18] In addition, the study does not, like many political science approaches, concern itself with participation at the nation state level alone. Citizens derive benefits and costs from political agencies at different levels of government, and an attempt is made to incorporate this fact into our analysis.

The paper proceeds as follows. In section I our economic model of political participation is explicated, and a general proposition about the benefits and costs likely to lead to variable rates of participation is derived. In the next section the data and variables used to measure these benefits and costs are discussed at length, while in section III some of the research findings are presented. It will be shown that our model is successful in explaining large proportions in the variations in the scope of participatory activity on the part of the citizens in our sample. It will also be shown, at this time, that our economic model is a better predicator of participation than is the sociological model that appears to dominate the field of political science at the present time.[19] The conclusion will follow in section IV, and some of the implications of our study will be drawn at that time.

I. An economic model of participation

Citizens will participate in politics according to an economic perspective if their expected benefits from so doing will exceed their expected costs. This axiom will hold under all conditions provided citizens possess sufficient resources to expend at least some of them in political activity. A minimal level of education may be conceptualized, for example, as a resource which citizens can use in dealing with public officials, even if this only involves going to the polls to vote for or against political candidates every year or so.[20] In symbolic terms, we may state that:

(1) $P = f(EB, EC, R)$ where P is the degree of political participation,
EB, the expected benefits from participation for an individual citizen,
EC, the expected costs of participation for a citizen,
R, the personal resources of an individual.

[18]Rather peculiarly, the economic studies of referenda voting also have relied on aggregate data. See, for example, James Q. Wilson and Edward C. Banfield, "Public Regardingness as a Value Premise in Voting Behaviour," *American Political Science Review*, 58 (1964), 876–87; William C. Birdsall, "A Study of the Demand for Public Goods," in *Essays in Fiscal Federalism*, ed. Richard C. Musgrave (Brookings, 1965), 235–94; Mark Sproule-Jones and Adrie Van Klaveren, "Local Referenda and Size of Muncipality in British Columbia," *B.C. Studies*, 8 (1970), 47–50.

[19]Norman H. Nie et al., "Social Structure and Political Participation: Developmental Relationships," *American Political Science Review*, 63 (1969), 361–78, 808–32.

[20]See Harold D. Lasswell and Abraham Kaplan, *Power and Society* (New Haven, 1950), 55–

Of course, the expected benefits, expected costs, resources, and degree of political participation will vary from one individual citizen to the next.[21]

What are the types of benefits and costs that are likely to enter any individual citizen's decision to participate in politics? We may postulate two types of benefits and two types of costs: public and private benefits, and public and private costs. Each will be described in turn.

The public benefits from participation for an individual are the changes that he expects in the quantity and quality of public goods and services as a direct result of changes in the rate of his participation. For any individual these benefits are likely to be fairly low in magnitude for the following reason. Public goods are by nature "unpackageable," that is, every citizen can consume the good or service and still leave some available for consumption by other citizens.[22] When certain police services are provided in a community, for example, everyone benefits to some degree from these services, and no one can be excluded from enjoying the benefits. As a consequence, there is little incentive for an individual to participate, other things being equal, since he knows the goods or services will be available anyway. Of course, if participation rates for the entire community were very low, then any citizen might feel he had a "citizen duty" to participate, particularly by voting, in case the democratic process were itself made inoperative. But as a generalization, we may postulate that an individual will only change the scope of his participation (were this change costless), if he felt the change would be decisive in producing favourable adjustments in the service levels of the public goods.[23]

The second type of benefits from participation are private benefits. Besides producing public goods and services, governments also provide a whole range of packageable or private goods to which any individual may lay exclusive claim. One such benefit is the stipend attached to elective or appointive office-holding. Another is the entertainment value of participation in political campaigns. A third might be a business contract with a public agency. Other things being equal, the prospect of private benefits from government will induce, we postulate, participatory activity on the part of the citizen-consumer.

There are also two types of costs associated with participation. First, there are the private costs of time and effort expended in participation. These tend to be extremely high when participation goes beyond the mere voting stage, particularly in terms of marshalling and evaluating information in face-to-face encounters with

62, 67–73, 74–97 for an extensive treatment of the role of resource values in political life. Resources are also treated at length in the writings of R.A. Dahl.

[21]Downs, *An Economic Theory*, and most economists use the term "expected utility" because of this factor.

[22] Public goods differ in the degree to which their benefits are packageable. A sterile debate on the applicability of the logic of public good analysis to goods varying in their degree of packageability immediately followed Samuelson's original explication of the theory in 1954. See Paul A. Samuelson, "The Pure Theory of Public Expenditure," *Review of Economics and Statistics*, 36 (1954), 387–90, "Diagramatic Exposition of a Theory of Public Expenditure," *Review of Economics and Statistics*, 37 (1955), 350–6, and "Aspects of Public Expenditure Theories," *Review of Economics and Statistics*, 40 (1958), 332–8; Julius Margolis, "A Comment on the Pure Theory of Public Expenditure," *Review of Economics and Statistics*, 37 (1955), 347–9; Gerhard Colm, "Comments on Samuelson's Theory of Public Finance," *Review of Economics and Statistics*," 37 (1956), 408–12.

[23]In small groups where the proportion of benefits to costs for any member is likely to be large there will be a greater probability of making decisive contributions by changing the level of one's political activity. See Olson, *Logic of Collective Action*.

public officials.[24] These private opportunity costs fall differentially on the mass of citizenry, and appear, empirically, to reinforce the existing unequal distribution of resources among them. We would anticipate, *ceteris paribus*, that participation will be restrained by such private costs.

The public costs associated with participation rates are the so-called "welfare losses" associated with the provision of public goods and services. When individuals buy private packageable goods, they can vary the level purchased to match their own different preferences. When individuals consume public (unpackageable) goods, they cannot adjust the level consumed to meet their own preferences, since this would lead anyone to understate his preferences in the hope that others would be charged for it and he could consume it for nothing (exclusion being infeasible for public goods). As a consequence, public goods are provided at a particular tax price/unit which may or may not reflect accurately the marginal valuation that an individual may place on this good.[25] The extent to which a tax price/unit does not match any individual citizen's marginal valuation for a public good is termed a "welfare loss," and it is likely that a large number of welfare losses or consumption costs are associated with each public good or service. As a consequence, each individual citizen will bear a net level of consumption costs spread among the various public goods and services provided by the collectivity, and we should expect that changes in the level of these consumption costs will induce changes in the scope of an individual's participatory activity.[26]

We may summarize our discussion of the particular types of benefits and costs associated with participation rates by means of the following equations. We have already stated that:

(1) $P = f(EB, EC, R)$ where P is the degree of participation,
EB, the expected benefits,
EC, the expected costs,
R, the individual resource levels.

Since there are two types of benefits and costs, then:

(2) $P = f(EP_uB, EP_rB, EP_uC, EP_rC, R)$

where EP_uB are the expected public benefits from participation,
EP_rB, the expected private benefits from participation,
EP_uC, the expected public (consumption) costs associated with a level of participation,
EP_rC, the expected private (opportunity) costs of participation.

[24]See, especially, Warren, "Federal-Local Development Planning"; and Weschler and Warren, "Consumption Costs."

[25]For technical proof of these statements, see Gordon Tullock, "Social Cost and Government Action," *American Economic Review*, 59 (1969), 189–97; *Private Wants, Public Means* (New York, 1970), chap. 1; James M. Buchanan, "Notes for an Economic Theory of Socialism," *Public Choice*, 8 (1970), 29–44; Robert L. Bish, *The Public Economy of Metropolitan Areas* (Chicago, 1971), chap. 3.

[26]See Breton, "Demand for Public Goods."

Diagramatically, equation (2) for any individual citizen participating within a given set of system or institutional arrangements, is shown in Figure I. The box indicates the system variables within which an individual citizen operates. The arrows indicate the paths that the various causal factors are hypothesized to take in determining variations in political participation within a political system. The operationalization of these six conceptual sets is the subject of the following section of the paper.

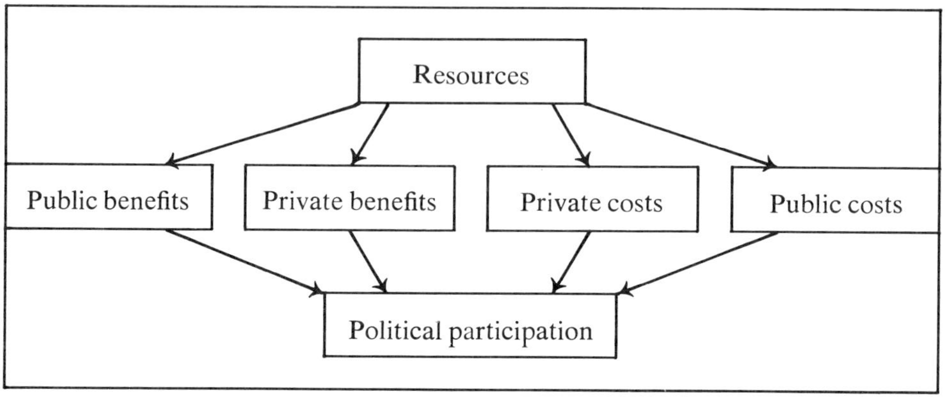

FIGURE I

II. Data sources and variables

The model was examined as follows. Three types of data were gathered for a random sample of 109 individual voters located in the municipality of Saanich, British Columbia. An opinion survey of this sample was conducted in the spring of 1970. Secondly, municipal records on turnout in the 1969 local elections for each individual in our sample were examined in the spring of 1970.[27] Thirdly, each individual was cross checked with the municipal records to discover precisely how much he or she was assessed and levied for 10 different tax items for the years 1964, 1968, 1969, and 1970. This last exercise was completed in the summer of 1971.

The conceptual causal sets represented in Figure I and expressed in equation (2) were measured by the following multiple indicators.[28]

POLITICAL PARTICIPATION

Eight modified versions of the Woodward-Roper scale of political activity were developed for use as indicators of participation.[29] The scale was modified for two reasons. First, in its original form, it did not fit either the Canadian or local political contexts. Secondly, the availability of high quality unobtrusive data afforded an opportunity to replace a respondent's memory of voting with the actual record

[27]As an indicator of reliability, 25.70 per cent of the sample turned out to vote in 1969 compared to 23.27 per cent of the entire Saanich electorate.
[28]See Eugene G. Webb et al., *Unobtrusive Measures* (Chicago, 1966), for a discussion of the value of multiple indicators in social research.
[29]Julian L. Woodward and Elmo Roper, "Political Activity of American Citizens," *American Political Science Review*, 44 (1950), 872–85.

of his voting or non-voting in the civic elections prior to the administration of the survey. Of the eight modified versions of the Woodward-Roper scale, four pertained to participation in general and four to participation in local politics. The four general participation scales used the municipal record of voting and are called general objective participation. Two of the four local scales used the municipal record and two used memory of past voting record; they were labelled respectively, local objective participation and local subjective participation.

Additional modifications to the Woodward-Roper scale must also be noted. First, the local scales used items about memory of past voting record (or the municipal record), contacts with public officials, and financial contributions to political groups. One of the two local objective and one of the two local subjective scales also supplemented those items with an item on the number of memberships in political organizations. The Woodward-Roper scale also used a similar item, but instead of trichotomizing the data, we allowed it to reflect the actual number of memberships reported by the respondent. This modification did not, for the sample at hand, change the variance on four pairs of the eight scales of participation, but we retained all eight as essential concomitants of our theoretical proposition about the multiple strategies of participation. The four general participation scales used (1) the items on the municipal record of votes, contacts with public officials, financial contributions, and in addition, memory of voting at the last federal and provincial elections; (2) all of the four previous items plus the Woodward and Roper item on frequency of discussion of political issues with friends (although modified in the direction of greater variability by making both "occasionally" and "frequently" accepted responses); (3) all of the four items included in the first general participation scale plus the additional item on number of memberships in political organizations, as were used for two of the local participation scales; and (4) all of the five items used in the second general participation scale plus the membership item used in the third general participation scale. All eight scales of participation used in our study were of the additive kind, with the item weighting for each scale taking place only through the varying ranges of the items.

PUBLIC BENEFITS

Three indicators of public benefits were included in the study. First, a political efficacy scale was included, the items of which were designed to tap the decisiveness that each individual thinks his participation might have on the course of governmental activity, rather than to determine a set of attitudes to government in general. Our theory predicted that an individual will change the scope of his participation if he feels that this will be decisive in producing changes in public action. Our items were derived from the political efficacy scale used extensively in the Survey Research Center's election studies.[30] The second indicator was an additive scale tapping consumer satisfaction with the quality of public services in the municipality. It comprised survey items asking the respondent how he felt about Saanich as a community to live in, how well he thought services compared in his area of the municipality to other areas, how he rated the performance of the local government, and how much impact he thought any particular candidate could have if elected to local office. The third indicator was the Survey Research Center's citizen duty

[30]See Angus Campbell et al., *The Voter Decides* (New York, 1954), 187–9.

scale,[31] which was included because a citizen may feel he has a duty to participate in elections regardless of the impact of his participation on the service levels of public goods.

PRIVATE BENEFITS

An additive scale was devised as an indicator of the private benefits that a citizen feels he derives exclusively from the activities of government. This scale was based on two items. The first was a respondent's evaluation of the effect of local governmnt on his *own* day-to-day life. (When the scale as a whole was used in conjunction with the four general participation measures, the item was supplemented with an equivalent question about the effect of the national government.) The second item was an open ended question on the important issues facing the municipality, with three salient issues being the maximum number recorded in the survey. Unfortunately, the sample did not pick up any respondents (apart from one alderman) who derived a direct financial emolument from the government, nor did the survey reveal any additional information that could logically be construed as further indicators of such private benefits.

PUBLIC COSTS

Five scales of the consumption costs associated with government activity were developed for analysis. These were derived from the unobstrusive tax data, specifically land assessments, improvement assessments, school taxes, general taxes, and local improvement taxes, for each individual in our sample for the years 1964, 1968, 1969, 1970. A principal components factor analysis was used to collapse the 20 variables. Scores for all the factors with an eigenvalue greater than one were developed, and the factors most highly correlated with political participation were selected for use. The resultant five scales were all based on either the absolute tax levels in 1968, 1969, and 1970, or on the absolute tax change between 1964 and 1970. In our analysis, we labelled these five scales as Tax Level 1968 Factor 1, Tax Level 1969 Factor 1, Tax Level 1970 Factor 1, Tax Change 1964–1970 Factor 1, and Tax Change 1964–1970 Factor 3.

PRIVATE COSTS

Four indicators of private costs of participation were included. Two pertained to local participation, and two pertained to general participation. The first scale, called local political knowledge, was derived from items asking the respondent to name the mayor and aldermen of the municipality, to name major local government projects, and to name the date of the last local election. The general political knowledge scale supplemented these items with questions designed to elicit knowledge of the national parties and national party leaders.[32] The third and fourth scales were labelled local political attentiveness and general political attentiveness. They both included items on information received from candidates at the last local election, on information about candidates in the last local election that was received from the mass media, on attendance at political meetings in the previous four years,

[31]*Ibid.*, 194–9.

[32]These political knowledge scales were derived and made applicable to the Canadian and local contexts after a review of the scales reported in John P. Robinson et al., *Measures of Political Attitudes* (Ann Arbor, Mich., 1968), chap. 10.

on the regularity with which the respondent receives the local papers, on whether he finds information about Saanich in these papers, and finally on whether he reads the articles on Saanich in the local papers. The general attentiveness scale supplemented all these items with ones about the attention that a respondent reported he paid to political affairs in general.[33] The rationale for including these four particular indicators of private costs was derived from Anthony Downs' *An Economic Theory of Democracy*. We would suggest that persons who rank high on these scales are more likely to bear or have already borne the opportunity costs associated with high rates of participation and, conversely, that persons with low levels of political knowledge and attentiveness are less likely to expend or to have expended the time and effort associated with highly active levels of political participation.[34]

RESOURCES

Besides drawing the sample so that each individual citizen would possess at least one common resource level, that of enfranchisement, to use when operating in the political system, we also included seven indicators of resources. The seven indicators were all personal attributes which an individual citizen could use to increase the net benefits he may derive from a variety of public agencies, as well as indirectly affect the rate of his own political participation (see Figure I). The indicators were, first, socio-economic status, namely the scale derived by Bernard R. Blishen and associates for Canadian occupations,[35] as modified by using decile scores and assigning scores to respondents with missing values by using income and education as predictors. Secondly, an education scale was incorporated, which was simply the last grade of schooling completed by each respondent. Thirdly, a four-point scale of monthly income was included. Also, the age of the respondent, the number of years he was a resident in Saanich, and the number of years he had lived at his present address were included as further indicators of personal resources. And, finally, the number of memberships in local and political organizations were included in a scale labelled organizational involvement, since such memberships may be of considerable value to any citizen when he deals with the personnel and policies of the various levels of government.

All of the 29 variables used in the analysis are described statistically in Table I. It should be noted that two of the variables (D_2 and D_3) are collinear ($R = 0.92$), but they were retained in the analysis because, while theoretically important, they made little change in the predictive efficacy of the model. The nature of the analysis, and the findings themselves, are presented in the next section of the paper.

III. Analysis and findings

The analysis may be divided into two basic stages. First, we examined the predictions between the four causal variable sets (public benefits, private benefits, public

[33]The attentiveness scales were, again, derived and modified from information reported in *ibid.*, 450.
[34]Interestingly, this conclusion is also used in some of the more traditional political sociology analyses of participation. See, for example, the references to "stable communication networks" and the "existence of networks of access to ... political leaders" in Robert R. Alford and Eugene C. Lee, "Voting Turnout in American Cities," *American Political Science Review*, 62 (1968), 806.
[35]"Canadian Society," *Sociological Perspectives* (3rd ed., Toronto, 1968), 748–53.

TABLE I

STATISTICAL DESCRIPTION OF VARIABLES IN THE MODEL

Conceptual set indicators	Designation for other tables	Minimum	Maximum	Range	Mean	Mode	Median	Std. error	Std. deviation	Variance	Kurtosis	Skewness	Valid observations
Resources													
Income	A1	1.00	4.00	3.00	2.610	2.000	2.563	0.093	0.931	0.867	−0.902	0.016	100
Education	A2	2.00	18.00	16.00	11.255	12.00	11.569	0.270	2.781	7.735	0.389	−0.086	106
Socio-Economic Status	A3	0.0	10.0	10.0	5.20	1.00	5.00	0.313	3.130	9.798	−1.462	0.022	100
Age	A4	25.0	75.0	50.0	48.778	46.00	47.167	1.187	12.338	152.232	−0.663	0.179	108
Years in Saanich	A5	0.00	56.00	56.00	12.889	2.000	9.500	1.150	11.955	142.922	1.737	1.396	108
Years in present home	A6	1.00	31.00	30.00	8.128	2.000	5.438	0.668	6.972	48.613	0.336	1.029	109
Organizational involvement	A7	0.0	6.0	6.0	0.713	0.0	0.0	0.109	1.128	1.272	5.277	2.112	106
Public benefits													
Citizen duty	B1	0.00	4.00	4.00	3.294	4.000	3.406	0.080	0.831	0.691	2.538	−1.466	109
Political efficacy	B2	0.0	4.00	4.00	2.780	3.00	2.875	0.099	1.031	1.062	−0.754	−0.417	109
Consumer satisfaction	B3	3.00	7.00	4.00	5.170	5.000	5.176	0.147	1.007	1.014	−0.522	−0.087	47
Private benefits													
Impact of government – local	C1	0.0	5.0	5.0	2.943	3.00	3.014	0.109	1.117	1.247	−0.251	−0.345	105
Impact of government – general	C2	1.0	7.0	6.0	4.647	5.00	4.813	0.127	1.287	1.656	0.023	−0.609	102
Public costs													
Tax level 1968 factor 1	D1	−5.312	17.078	22.390	0.0	−2.693	−0.330	0.334	3.393	11.513	6.798	1.833	103
Tax level 1969 factor 1	D2	−5.088	12.091	17.179	0.0	−2.516	−0.190	0.245	2.519	6.344	3.734	1.097	106
Tax level 1970 factor 1	D3	−4.364	11.779	16.143	0.00	−2.344	−0.400	0.227	2.341	5.479	4.680	1.285	106
Tax change 1964–70 factor 1	D4	−7.248	5.126	12.373	0.00	−0.545	−0.189	0.146	1.381	1.908	10.778	−0.453	90
Tax change 1964–70 factor 3	D5	−7.569	2.848	10.417	0.00	−0.311	−0.101	0.109	1.036	1.073	31.088	−3.743	90
Private costs													
Political knowledge – local	E1	0.0	14.0	14.0	4.426	4.00	4.00	0.260	2.704	7.312	0.867	0.859	108
Political knowledge – general	E2	0.0	20.0	20.0	9.654	10.00	9.632	0.330	3.418	11.681	1.567	−0.187	107
Political attentiveness – local	E3	0.0	7.0	7.0	5.093	5.00	5.203	0.120	1.242	1.543	2.317	−1.058	108
Political attentiveness – general	E4	0.0	9.0	9.0	6.509	7.00	6.656	0.136	1.411	1.991	3.065	−1.072	108
Participation													
General-objective vote	F1	0.0	9.0	9.0	3.314	2.00	3.068	0.181	1.725	2.975	0.427	0.623	91
General-objective vote – modified discussion	F2	0.0	9.0	9.0	3.681	3.00	3.482	0.175	1.666	2.775	1.023	0.659	91
General-objective vote – modified membership	F3	0.0	9.0	9.0	3.314	2.00	3.068	0.181	1.725	2.975	0.427	0.623	91
General-objective vote – modified discussion and membership	F4	0.0	9.0	9.0	3.681	3.00	3.482	0.175	1.666	2.775	1.023	0.659	91
Local objective vote – modified discussion	F5	0.0	5.00	5.00	1.547	1.00	1.333	0.134	1.303	1.697	0.650	0.970	95
Local subjective vote – modified discussion	F6	0.0	5.00	5.00	1.800	1.00	1.586	0.132	1.285	1.651	0.451	0.892	95
Local objective vote – modified discussion and membership	F7	0.0	5.00	5.00	1.547	1.00	1.333	0.134	1.303	1.697	0.650	0.970	95
Local subjective vote – modified discussion and membership	F8	0.0	5.00	5.00	1.800	1.00	1.586	0.132	1.285	1.651	0.451	0.892	95

Note:
In the Tables II–IV, the label "Local" for an independent variable set includes C1, E1, and E3; excludes C2, E2, E4.
In the Tables II–IV, the label "General" for an independent variable set includes C2, E2, and E4; excludes C1, E1, E3.
In the Tables II–IV, the label "Local" applied to the dependent variable refers to the indicators F5, F6, F7, F8.
In the Tables II–IV, the label "General" applied to the dependent variable refers to the indicators F1, F2, F3, F4.

costs, private costs) and the eight dependent variables of political participation. Secondly, we examined the partial correlations between resources and participation, controlling for the four benefit and cost causal sets. We found that this relatively uncomplex causal modelling procedure constituted an adequate method for explaining a large amount of variance in our economic model of political participation. Secondly, we found that the model represents an explanatory improvement, in the sense of "goodness of fit," on the Nie, Powell, and Prewitt "sociological" model.[36]

Table II summarizes the results of the first stage of our analysis. We were able to explain between 48 per cent and 21 per cent of the variance in political participation by our four causal variable sets, depending on the particular scale of participation and depending also on whether the regression analysis was multiple or stepwise in nature. A number of other important points also emerge from Table II.

In the first place, we were able to explain consistently more of the variance in political participation by using the general participation scales as dependent variables than by using the local participation scales. Not only were the R^2s greater for the general participation scales, but also when using stepwise regression, considerably fewer independent variables entered the equations for the local participation models than for the general participation ones. Since the general participation scales merely supplemented the local ones with additional items, this probably indicates that a relatively larger proportion of the variance in the local participation scales is due to uniqueness and unidimensionality.[37]

Secondly, when multiple rather than stepwise regression methods were employed, and consequently all of the independent variables forced into the equations, only 4 of the 16 models (the eight participation scales for two sets of independent variables, those including items pertaining to politics in general and those including items pertaining solely to local politics) gave R^2s significantly different from zero. These 4 can be increased to 8 in number by removing either the tax level measure for 1968 or the tax level measure for 1969. These four additional models yield R^2s of 0.449, 0.449, 0.456, and 0.456, compared to R^2s of 0.468, 0.468, 0.482, and 0.482 for the four complete models. This discussion merely reflects the problems in defining appropriate indicators and refining the existent variables in such a pathbreaking analysis as ours.

Thirdly, it should be noted that four of our pairs of dependent variables (pairs in the sense of being regressed by independent variable sets pertaining solely to local politics and also to politics in general) yield identical R^2s. These four pairs are increased to six pairs when the tax level measures for 1968 or 1969 are omitted from the regression equations, as our previous discussion indicated. This point reflects, again, the fact that our item on memberships in political organizations did not discriminate between solely local ones and organizations operating at the local and other levels of government.

In sum, our first stage of analysis, one of an analysis of variance between our

[36] "Social Structure and Political Participation."

[37] Future research on the models should probably, as a consequence, attempt to tap activity in *solely* community based organizations, activity which may have been obscured in our survey items. Such community oriented organizations appear to be increasing in number, size, and apparent effectiveness in many urban areas of Canada. See, especially, John A. Draper et al., *Citizen Participation: Canada. A Book of Readings* (Toronto, 1971).

TABLE II

ANALYSIS OF VARIANCE FOR 16 MODELS OF PARTICIPATION

Participation (dependent) variable	Independent variable group: local or general	Multiple or stepwise mode of regression	Omitted variables (stepwise mode only)	R^2	Standard error	F	Required F
F1 General	Local	M		0.46750	1.49321	2.15494	2.20 > F > 2.13
		S		0.46750	1.49321	2.15494	2.19
	General	M		0.45878	1.50538	2.08068	2.20 > F > 2.13
		S	D2	0.45564	1.48253	2.34369	2.19
F2 General	Local	M		0.45237	1.46248	2.02760	2.20 > F > 2.13
		S	D1	0.44901	1.44054	2.28175	2.19
	General	M		0.48244	1.42177	2.28800	2.20 > F > 2.13
		S	D1	0.48207	1.39664	2.60618	2.19
F3 General	Local	M		0.46750	1.49321	2.15494	2.20 > F > 2.13
		S		0.46750	1.49321	2.15494	2.20 > F > 2.13
	General	M		0.45878	1.50538	2.08068	2.20 > F > 2.13
		S	D2	0.45564	1.48253	2.34369	2.19
F4 General	Local	M		0.45237	1.46248	2.02760	2.20 > F > 2.13
		S	D1	0.44901	1.44054	2.28175	2.19
	General	M		0.48244	1.42177	2.28800	2.20 > F > 2.13
		S		0.48244	1.42177	2.28800	2.20 > F > 2.13
F5 Local	Local	M		0.33233	1.26287	1.22172	2.20 > F > 2.13
		S	B1,C1,E3,D1,D2,D3,D5	0.24363	1.19781	2.73785	2.69 > F > 2.61
	General	M		0.33519	1.26016	1.23755	2.20 > F > 2.13
		S	E2,E4,B1,D1,D2,D3,D5	0.25196	1.19119	2.86310	2.69 > F > 2.61
F6 Local	Local	M		0.30592	1.26998	1.08185	2.20 > F > 2.13
		S	B1,E1,C1,E3,D1,D2,D3,D5	0.20935	1.19051	3.08916	2.92 > F > 2.84
	General	M		0.33536	1.24275	1.23489	2.20 > F > 2.13
		S	B1,E2,E4,D1,D2,D5	0.27630	1.17300	2.51975	2.53 > F > 2.45
F7 Local	Local	M		0.33233	1.26287	1.22172	2.20 > F > 2.13
		S	B1,C1,E3,D1,D2,D3,D5	0.24363	1.19781	2.73785	2.69 > F > 2.61
	General	M		0.33519	1.26016	1.23755	2.20 > F > 2.13
		S	B1,E2,E4,D1,D2,D3,D5	0.25196	1.19119	2.86310	2.69 > F > 2.61
F8 Local	Local	M		0.30592	1.26998	1.08185	2.20 > F > 2.13
		S	B1,C1,E1,E3,D1,D2,D3,D5	0.20935	1.19051	3.08916	2.92 > F > 2.84
	General	M		0.33536	1.24275	1.23849	2.20 > F > 2.13
		S	B1,E2,E4,D1,D2,D5	0.27630	1.17300	2.51975	2.53 > F > 2.45

Note: See Table I for labels of the variables included in the independent and dependent variable sets.

five causal variable sets of resources, public benefits, private benefits, public costs, and private costs, yielded promising results in terms of explaining the proportion of variance found in our participation scales, especially the general participation scales. For those practitioners of the science of economics who would not interpret an R^2 of 0.482 for our best model as a "promising result," we would remind them that the Nie, Powell, and Prewitt "sociological" model was able to explain only 43 per cent of the total variance in their own best measure of participation.[38] We shall return to this point later.

The second stage in our analysis was to examine the partial correlations between resources and participation, when controlling for our benefit and cost causal variable sets; that is, we applied the methodology of verification developed by Blalock and Simon.[39] In Figure I we expected that resources would be reflected in varying degrees of political participation, but that these resources would operate only indirectly, through the four benefit and cost sets. Table III summarizes our findings.

First, it should be noted that three of our seven resource variables did not correlate, even at the zero order stage, with any of our eight scales of participation. (All correlations were made at a significance level of 0.05.) These resources were age, years in Saanich, and years resident in current home. Apparently, values affecting traditional ways of operating in politics, even at the local level of government, do not exist in our sample.

Thirdly, the two resource variables of income and socio-economic status, which correlated with all eight of our participation measures, plus the education variable, which correlated with the four local participation scales, all disappeared when our posited intervening variables were controlled. This one result appears highly important. In an extensive review of the literature on political participation at all levels of government, we have yet to run across any study that did not postulate, or find empirically, some direct link between class variables and participation.

Finally, the only resource variable that did not disappear when we controlled for the benefits and costs of participation was the organizational involvement scale. It showed a slightly decreased correlational level with the dependent variable in 10 models, and a slightly increased correlation in 6 models. We suspect that this unusual behaviour is a function of data flaws used in the construction of the organizational involvement scale.

Again, the results of our second stage of analysis, that of controlling for the intervening variables of benefits and costs in the expectation that the partial correlations between resources and participation will disappear, have proved highly promising. Our economic model of political participation appears a fruitful line of research.

Our final stage of analysis was to see whether our economic model was more fruitful than the traditional "sociological" models that dominate the political science literature on participation. Our general strategy was to apply a deductive methodology to a series of ad hoc propositions about participation derived from the literature. To be precise, we took the 1969 model of Nie, Powell, and Prewitt,

[38]"Social Structure and Political Participation," 818.
[39]Hubert M. Blalock, Jr, *Causal Inferences in Nonexperimental Research* (Chapel Hill, N.C., 1964).

TABLE III

LINKAGES BETWEEN RESOURCES, BENEFITS AND COSTS, AND PARTICIPATION

		Causal Variable (Control) Set			
		Local		General	
Participation (Dependent) Variable	Resource indicator	Zero-order correlation (R)	Partial correlation (controlled)	Zero-order correlation (R)	Partial correlation (controlled)
F1 General	A1 Income	0.2978	—	0.2978	—
	A2 Education	—	—	—	—
	A3 SES	0.1788	—	0.1788	—
	A4 Age	—	—	—	—
	A5 Years in Saanich	—	—	—	—
	A6 Years in home	—	—	—	—
	A7 Org. involvement	0.5276	0.5367	0.5276	0.5697
F2 General	A1 Income	0.3476	—	0.3476	—
	A2 Education	—	—	—	—
	A3 SES	0.2042	—	0.2978	—
	A4 Age	—	—	—	—
	A5 Years in Saanich	—	—	—	—
	A6 Years in home	—	—	—	—
	A7 Org. involvement	0.5171	0.5045	0.5171	0.5504
F3 General	A1 Income	0.2978	—	0.2978	—
	A2 Education	—	—	—	—
	A3 SES	0.1788	—	0.1788	—
	A4 Age	—	—	—	—
	A5 Years in Saanich	—	—	—	—
	A6 Years in home	—	—	—	—
	A7 Org. involvement	0.5276	0.5367	0.5276	0.5697

TABLE III (*Continued*)

		Causal Variable (Control) Set			
		Local		General	
Participation (dependent) variable	Resource indicator	Zero-order correlation (*R*)	Partial correlation (controlled)	Zero-order correlation (*R*)	Partial correlation (controlled)
F4 General	A1 Income	0.3476	—	0.3476	—
	A2 Education	—	—	—	—
	A3 SES	0.2042	—	0.2042	—
	A4 Age	—	—	—	—
	A5 Years in Saanich	—	—	—	—
	A6 Years in home	—	—	—	—
	A7 Org. involvement	0.5171	0.5045	0.5171	0.5504
F5 Local	A1 Income	0.3546	—	0.3546	—
	A2 Education	0.1790	—	0.1790	—
	A3 SES	0.2059	—	0.2059	—
	A4 Age	—	—	—	—
	A5 Years in Saanich	—	—	—	—
	A6 Years in home	—	—	—	—
	A7 Org. involvement	0.4876	0.4542	0.4876	0.4686
F6 Local	A1 Income	0.3906	—	0.3906	—
	A2 Education	0.1980	—	0.1980	—
	A3 SES	0.1884	—	0.1884	—
	A4 Age	—	—	—	—
	A5 Years in Saanich	—	—	—	—
	A6 Years in home	—	—	—	—
	A7 Org. involvement	0.4203	0.3589	0.4203	0.3812

TABLE III (*Continued*)

Participation (dependent) variable	Resource indicator	Causal Variable (Control) Set: Local — Zero-order correlation (*R*)	Local — Partial correlation (controlled)	General — Zero-order correlation (*R*)	General — Partial correlation (controlled)
F7 Local	A1 Income	0.3546	—	0.3546	—
	A2 Education	0.1790	—	0.1790	—
	A3 SES	0.2059	—	0.2059	—
	A4 Age	—	—	—	—
	A5 Years in Saanich	—	—	—	—
	A6 Years in home	—	—	—	—
	A7 Org. involvement	0.4876	0.4542	0.4876	0.4686
F8 Local	A1 Income	0.3906	—	0.3906	—
	A2 Education	0.1980	—	0.1980	—
	A3 SES	0.1884	—	0.1884	—
	A4 Age	—	—	—	—
	A5 Years in Saanich	—	—	—	—
	A6 Years in home	—	—	—	—
	A7 Org. involvement	0.4203	0.3589	0.4203	0.3812

Note: See Table I for statistical description and labelling of the participation variables.

TABLE IV

ANALYSES OF VARIANCE: SOCIOLOGICAL MODEL AND PARTICIPATION

Participation (dependent) variable	Independent variable set*	R^2	Standard error	F	Required F
F1	General	0.45469	1.38800	4.66702	2.42 > F > 2.34
F1	Local	0.44218	1.40383	4.22769	2.42 > F > 2.34
F2	General	0.44022	1.35820	4.19419	2.42 > F > 2.34
F2	Local	0.40271	1.40297	3.59581	2.42 > F > 2.34
F3	General	0.45469	1.38800	4.44702	2.42 > F > 2.34
F3	Local	0.44218	1.40383	4.22769	2.42 > F > 2.34
F4	General	0.44022	1.35820	4.19419	2.42 > F > 2.34
F4	Local	0.40271	1.40297	3.59581	2.42 > F > 2.34

*The variables were political efficacy, citizen duty, political knowledge, political attentiveness, organizational involvement, and socio-economic status. See Table I for the difference between "general" and "local" modifications of these variables.

and developed this further by applying Blalock's theory construction and theory selection procedures to the model and to the "sociological" propositions about participation compiled by Milbrath.[40] We then derived the "best" model (in the sense of possessing the highest degree of fit to the structural prediction) from all the resultant permutations.[41] We finally took the regression equation of the resultant "best" sociological model and applied it to our own set of general political-participation dependent variables. The independent variables, we derived, were political efficacy, citizen duty, political knowledge, political attentiveness, organizational involvement, and socio-economic status. The results of this exercise are summarized in Table IV. We found that our own economic models consistently explained more of the variance in general political participation than did the sociological model.

In sum, our economic model was capable of predicting a considerable proportion (at the best, almost one-half) of the variance in political participation. As such it appears to possess the capacity to be a superior approach to a sociological one. And, we would add, it appears superior both in terms of fitting the real world (the instrumentalist philosophic position) and in terms of resting, in a deductive sense, on a series of potentially falsifiable premises and assumptions.[42]

IV. Conclusion

The critical problem in both the practical provision of public goods and services, and also in the public choice literature, is to devise a valid and reliable signalling

[40]Hubert M. Blalock, Jr, *Theory Construction*, (New York, 1969); Milbrath, *Political Participation*.

[41]For full details of this procedure, see Kenneth D. Hart, "Social Structure and Political Participation: A Critical Response," Institute for Behavioural Research, York University (forthcoming).

[42]Both views on the appropriate development of a scientific enterprise are set out in Karl R. Popper, "Three Views Concerning Human Knowledge," *Contemporary British Philosophy* (London, 1956), 350–88. We would not, of course, take issue with the statement that higher level generalizations in a deductive theory are inherently more difficult to verify than lower level ones.

mechanism of individual preferences comparable to the way the monetary system operates in the perfectly competitive private marketplace. The most popular candidate to date is a voting mechanism. But votes, as a "political currency," is subject to many flaws. It does not, for example, precisely register the strength of preferences that a citizen-consumer may have over a whole range of public goods and services provided by any one political institution. Such flaws have, at the present time, severely limited the value of political economy in solving some of the policy problems of government.

In this paper, we have used as our "political currency" not votes but political participation in the broad sense. The citizen-consumer has a whole set of interdependent ways in which he reveals his preferences for public goods and services. Besides voting, he may telephone or write to a public official, attend political meetings, join interest groups, contribute money to a political candidate, read about political affairs in the press and discuss these matters with friends and co-workers, or indulge in various other strategies depending on, among other things, the strength of his preferences for different public goods and services. What is equally as important, an entire citizenry can use such a range of strategies, and their collective behaviour can be characterized by interval scales of participation that reflect their collective scale of preferences for the public goods and services. In other words, a scale of political participation may be a superior device both for registering the intensity of individual preferences (if not their direction) and for providing an interpersonal comparison of utilities than the alternatives, such as a voting mechanism, which currently dominate the literature of public choice.

Our paper has been content to show that scales of political participation can be interpreted as the collective reflection of the benefits and costs that individual citizens incur in the provision of public goods and services. Our theoretical model postulated that participation was a function of the public and private benefits, the public and private costs, and the resources of a set of citizen-consumers operating within a given mix of public institutional arrangements. Our empirical modelling showed that such a conception of the political world fitted, with a promising degree of success, the actual participatory behaviour of our sample. It was also shown to be a superior paradigm in terms of predictive efficacy than are the sociological interpretations which, at the present time, dominate the field of political science.

The task of any pathfinding analysis is always beset by unforeseen problems. Our major problem was finding appropriate operationalizations for our theoretical concepts. We resorted to the general strategy of using multiple indicators or proxies of the concepts, and we were aided in this regard by the availability of reliable unobtrusive tax data for each member of our admittedly small sample. But we would hope that future research will be able to refine our variables and develop some more appropriate new ones that can, as a consequence, extend our re-interpretation of a subject lying at the very core of a responsive political system.

Situations et attitudes face au changement dans les structures municipales*

LOUISE QUESNEL-OUELLET *Université Laval*

La région métropolitaine de Québec traverse depuis quelques années une phase de réorganisation municipale dont un point marquant fut sans doute la création de la Communauté urbaine de Québec (CUQ) en 1970[1]. La mise en marche de cet organisme supra-municipal semble avoir favorisé un mouvement vers la fusion et l'annexion des municipalités du territoire, qui sont passées de 27 à 23 en un an et demi. Ce mouvement est venu se juxtaposer au processus de régionalisation qui oblige plusieurs municipalités à s'affirmer et à se renforcer devant leur nouvel adversaire régional.

Cette vague annexionniste, dont la force d'impulsion a comme point d'origine surtout la ville centrale, attire l'attention d'une part par l'impact qu'elle peut avoir sur la région, et d'autre part, par ses implications au niveau de la théorie du gouvernement local. Cet article se limite au second aspect, en se proposant d'insister sur le lien qui unit le citoyen à sa municipalité et à sa région. Le problème fondamental est le suivant : la population des municipalités est-elle favorable à une réforme des structures municipales qui pourrait signifier l'annexion à une ville voisine ou la fusion de plusieurs municipalités pour former une plus grande ville ?

La réponse à cette question pourrait se trouver soit dans les agissements soit dans les attitudes de la population des municipalités. Du côté des agissements, il serait intéressant de voir comment certaines expériences de collaboration volontaire ont été acceptées, et pourquoi certains projets du même genre ont été rejetés. Du côté des attitudes, il serait souhaitable de découvrir la sensibilisation de la population à l'égard des problèmes étudiés et ses préférences. Ces deux optiques sont évidemment complémentaires puisque la première (les agissements) permet en quelque sorte de vérifier si les attitudes sont transposées dans les faits. Il semble cependant que l'étude des attitudes ait avantage à précéder celle des agissements. C'est pourquoi nous avons entrepris l'analyse de ce que pensent les gens de quelques municipalités face à régionalisation et à l'annexion ou la fusion.

De plus, cette approche nous semble pertinente puisque les citoyens ont déjà eu l'occasion de se sensibiliser au sujet, ne serait-ce que par le débit d'information

*Cette étude a été rendue possible grâce à une subvention du Conseil canadien de recherches urbaines et régionales. L'auteur tient à souligner la contribution indispensable de Monsieur Louis-Marie Asselin au titre de conseiller en statistiques, à remercier Monsieur Jacques Léveillée pour ses commentaires fort utiles, et Monsieur Jacques Hamel qui fut assistant de recherche. Merci aussi aux étudiants du département de science politique qui ont fait les entrevues. Une première version de ce texte a été présentée lors des assises annuelles de l'Association canadienne de science politique, à l'Université McGill de Montréal, le 3 juin 1972.

[1]Pour plus de détails concernant le fonctionnement de la CUQ, voir l'article de l'auteur « Régionalisation et conscience politique régionale : la communauté urbaine de Québec », cette REVUE, IV, no 2 (juin 1971), 191–205.

Canadian Journal of Political Science/Revue canadienne de science politique, VI, no. 2 (June/juin 1973). Printed in Canada/Imprimé au Canada.

journalistique et aussi par la création de la Communauté urbaine de Québec qui a permis de discuter d'une restructuration au niveau de la région.

Avant d'aborder l'analyse de ces attitudes, nous présentons une problématique de l'étude du regroupement municipal, en insistant sur les travaux américains qui sont particulièrement féconds quand il s'agit du lien qui unit les citoyens entre eux et à leur région. L'analyse elle-même comprendra trois parties dont la première portera sur les variables primaires, la deuxième sur les attitudes, et la troisième sur les relations entre les variables primaires et les variables d'attitudes.

Problématique du regroupement municipal

Dans la région de Québec, les projets d'annexion et de fusion[2] présentent certaines analogies avec les expériences qui sont analysées par Thomas R. Dye, Brett W. Hawkins, ou Basil G. Zimmer et Amos H. Hawley[3], en ce qu'il s'agit d'une ville centrale autour de laquelle gravitent des municipalités de banlieue dont le degré d'attraction à la ville centrale varie extrêmement. Cependant, la situation québécoise est susceptible d'engendrer des considérations nouvelles du fait que des noyaux sous-régionaux se sont constitués, ou sont en voie de le faire, et que la ville centrale n'est pas la seule à tendre une main annexionniste.

Un autre élément nouveau semble être l'hétérogénéité des villes de banlieue. Contrairement au cas américain où les villes centrales se distinguent de leurs banlieues par un niveau socio-économique plus bas[4], la région de Québec englobe des banlieues dont les niveaux de revenu, d'occupation et de scolarité sont supérieurs dans certains cas, mais aussi, dans d'autres cas, égaux et même parfois inférieurs à ceux de la ville centrale.

De plus, l'hétérogénéité des banlieues tient à l'âge de ces municipalités. Quelques-unes sont, en effet, aussi vieilles que la ville de Québec, alors que d'autres se sont développées très récemment. Aux Etats-Unis, au contraire, le besoin de réorganisation municipale s'est fait sentir à la suite d'une excroissance de la ville centrale, de sorte que, en général, les banlieues sont plus « jeunes » que cette dernière.

Ces quelques considérations indiquent qu'il sera peu pertinent d'utiliser le schème d'analyse le plus fréquent dans les travaux américains, soit le traitement dichotomique des données. En effet, il semble difficile de poser d'un côté les

[2]Par fusion, nous entendons l'union de plusieurs parties pour former une entité municipale nouvelle. L'annexion signifie l'addition à une ville déjà constituée d'un territoire voisin de façon à agrandir cette même ville. Dans le cas de l'annexion, le territoire annexé se fait représenter au sein du conseil municipal de la ville annexante. Dans le cas de la fusion, les conseils municipaux existants sont abolis, et les citoyens de la nouvelle ville élisent des représentants.

[3]Parmi les travaux les plus pertinents sur le sujet, signalons : Thomas R. Dye, qui analyse les annexions dans les villes américaines, entre 1950 et 1960, dans « Urban Political Integration : conditions associated with annexation in American cities », *Politics in the Metropolis*, éd. Thomas R. Dye and Brett W. Hawkins (2nd ed. Columbus, Ohio, 1971), 500–14. Brett W. Hawkins revient sur le cas de Nashville en appuyant sur l'attitude de la population à l'égard de la réorganisation de 1962 dans « Public Opinion and Metropolitan Reorganization in Nashville », *Journal of Politics*, 28 (May 1966), 408–18. Basil G. Zimmer et Amos H. Hawley étudient l'attitude de la population banlieusarde à l'égard d'une annexion éventuelle à la ville centrale dans « Local Government as Viewed by Fringe Residents », *Rural Sociology* (December 1958), 363–70.

[4]Dye, « Urban Political Integration : conditions associated with annexation in American Cities », 507.

Situations and attitudes toward municipal reorganization

This paper focuses upon municipal reorganization as a process involving community values and attitudes. Its main objectives is to test current hypotheses concerning the influence of population characteristics upon attitudes toward local government and annexation, and to compare attitudes toward services and taxes with attitudes toward metropolitan government and annexation. The study actually shows that some of the hypotheses are not confirmed in the Quebec region and that the system of relationships between variables is not the same in every community.

caractéristiques et les tendances de la ville et de l'autre côté celles de l'ensemble des banlieues[5].

L'étude des municipalités de la région de Québec suggère, en effet, que les villes autres que Québec ne sont peut-être pas, au sens strict, les banlieues de la ville centrale. La banlieue se définirait essentiellement par sa relation avec la ville centrale, étant le résultat d'un débordement de la population du centre vers l'extérieur. La banlieue au sens strict est donc plus « jeune » que la ville centrale, et se caractérise par un développement relativement accéléré.

Dans la région de Québec, certaines municipalités sont aussi vieilles que la ville centrale, et ces mêmes municipalités se sont peu développées, du point de vue démographique, depuis quelque cinquante ans[6]. Par conséquent, il semble qu'à priori, il soit impossible de considérer les municipalités de la région de Québec comme un ensemble de banlieues au sens traditionnel. L'étude du changement dans les structures municipales dans ce contexte revêt un intérêt particulier du fait qu'elle jettera de la lumière sur une nouvelle expérience de restructuration. Elle permet également de considérer le problème de l'annexion et de la fusion à l'intérieur d'un territoire qui a déjà subi un certain changement par la création d'un organisme régional (ou supra-municipal).

Malgré leur spécificité propre, les municipalités constituent une entité désignée par le mot région, et à laquelle on applique les concepts de régionalisation et de gouvernement régional. Dès le point de départ, cette expression doit être clarifiée. On assimile parfois la régionalisation à un processus d'intégration, que l'on qualifie ensuite de sociale, d'économique, de politique ou d'administrative. Ceci suggère que la région pourrait être située par rapport à un potentiel ou à l'existence réelle d'une intégration. Un auteur français, Jean-François Besson, apporte quelques précisions, en basant sa théorie de l'intégration sur la théorie des systèmes[7]. Selon cet auteur, l'intégration sera le fait d'un ensemble de parties liées entre elles. Ce lien social et économique, politique et administratif caractérise la région. Le centre nerveux de ce système se situe habituellement dans une ville centrale, qui constitue le cœur de la région.

[5]Comme exemple de cette approche voir : Zimmer et Hawley, « Local Government as Viewed by Fringe Residents ».

[6]L'accroissement en pourcentage de la population de chaque municipalité de 1921 à 1969 est le suivant : Québec, 75.4; Ste-Foy, 3885.1; Giffard, 907.1; Orsainville, 919.8; Beauport, 378.4; Sillery, 725.0; Charlesbourg, 2307.3; Loretteville, 384.1; Vanier, 7207.7. Accroissement moyen (municipalités autres que Québec) 1191.2 pour cent. Sources : Recensement du Canada, Bulletin 1.1 (Bureau fédéral de la statistique, 1961). *Renseignements statistiques, Municipalités du Québec 1969* (Bureau de la statistique du Québec, 1971).

[7]*L'intégration urbaine* (Paris, 1970).

La région implique par conséquent l'existence d'un réseau de communication qui assure le lien entre les parties. Dans le cas québécois, les communications sont rendues difficiles par le partage transversal du territoire par le fleuve St-Laurent. En se basant sur ce qui a été appelé cette « barrière naturelle », les législateurs n'ont pas retenu la rive Sud du fleuve à l'intérieur du territoire de la CUQ. Le mouvement d'annexion respecte ce choix, de sorte que les études actuelles posent comme postulat que la rive Sud est exclue du territoire à annexer à la ville centrale, du moins pour le moment. Il est donc question ici de la région de Québec entendue au sens restreint, englobant les municipalités présentement incluses dans la CUQ.

Cette délimitation de la région revêt un aspect arbitraire évident. Cependant, la recherche d'une définition plus systématique et plus explicite de la région s'est avérée peu fructueuse. On ressent généralement le besoin de préciser un cadre régional, et la question de l'étendue du territoire est reconnue comme primordiale[8], mais les dimensions de la région demeurent encore insaisissables. « If there is such a concept as a natural region, it is a city and its hinterland. As we have seen, however, there may be several hinterlands of different sizes depending upon the number and variety of functions performed by an individual city. Therefore, any delimitation of economic areas will be arbitrary and will not depict a true natural economic region »[9].

Devant les difficultés de trouver une région dont les limites seraient sinon naturelles, du moins relativement évidentes, des efforts ont été faits pour préciser ce que devrait être la région idéale. Une contribution intéressante a été apportée sur ce point par le Ontario Committee on Taxation[10] qui distingue cinq critères à respecter dans la formation d'une région. Le premier de ces critères retient notre attention de façon spéciale : le partage de certaines caractéristiques sociologiques par la population englobée dans la région (caractéristiques économiques, géographiques, historiques).

Ce critère nous semble utile parce qu'il réfère à un ensemble de facteurs dont l'utilisation est fréquente dans l'analyse des attitudes et des comportements politiques, surtout en ce qui concerne les indicateurs socio-économiques. De plus, il permet de rejoindre directement la population qui est touchée par la régionalisation et le processus d'intégration que cela suppose.

Dans cette perspective, Charles R. Adrian constate que:

The metropolitan reform leader, then, has typically spent his years in constructing models which are unconcerned with belief systems other than his own, and he has built into his models assumptions about psychological motivation and rationality that are as unrealistic as were those of John Locke, Jean-Jacques Rousseau, or Adam

---

[8]Dans une discussion du processus de formation de la nouvelle ville de Saint John (NB), Stanley Price mentionne que « in preparing for amalgamation a major decision made by the Conjoint Council was the total size of the enlarged city. The history of annexations and amalgamations in Canadian cities has shown a common mistake of taking over too small an acreage outside the built-up areas ». « Amalgamation of Municipal Governments : Metropolitan Saint John, NB », présenté à la Conference of Provincial Ministers of Municipal Affairs, Fredericton, NB, août 1969, 7–8.

[9]Hugh O. Nourse, *Regional Economics* (Toronto, 1968), 129.

[10]*Report* (Toronto, 1967).

Smith. No wonder that he has so often gone around the day after an election muttering about « selfish narrow minded voters » and self-seeking politicians[11].

Afin d'éviter l'erreur condamnée par l'auteur dans ces lignes, nous croyons essentiel d'aborder le problème du changement dans les structures municipales en empruntant les yeux des gens qui vivent dans les municipalités concernées. Pour comprendre *leur* rationalité, il est important de voir les caractéristiques socio-économiques de ces gens, leur degré d'intérêt au problème traité de même que leur attitude à l'égard des changements envisagés.

Nous espérons ainsi vérifier les deux hypothèses de base de ce travail, à savoir, premièrement, qu'il existe un lien entre les variables socio-économiques (variables de situation) et les variables d'attitude, et que ce lien prend la forme d'un réseau de relations ; deuxièmement, que le réseau de relations n'est pas le même pour toutes les municipalités. Cette seconde hypothèse est basée sur la différence qui existe entre les municipalités, quant à leur population, quant à leur situation par rapport à la ville centrale, par rapport aux noyaux sous-régionaux et par rapport à la CUQ (Tableau IV en annexe).

Méthodologie

L'analyse comprend alors deux types de variables, soit des variables de situation (en l'occurrence le revenu familial annuel, l'occupation et le lieu de travail du chef de famille, et le degré de scolarité du répondant) et des variables d'attitude. Dans l'étude du changement dans les structures municipales, les variables du second type qui semblent pertinentes sont les suivantes : attitude à l'égard des services municipaux, attitude à l'égard du niveau des taxes municipales, attitude à l'égard du changement entraîné dans l'accès des élus au centre de décision, attitude à l'égard des modalités d'annexion et de fusion, et attitude à l'égard de l'organisme régional existant (la Communauté Urbaine de Québec). Enfin l'intérêt des répondants à l'égard des annexions et des fusions nous semble important et il est classé parmi les variables de situation. Cette classification paraît justifiée puisque nous privilégions ici le rôle de variable de situation que peut jouer cet indicateur, tout en reconnaissant qu'il s'agit fondamentalement d'une variable intervenante et non de situation au sens strict.

Nous posons donc une hypothèse de causalité entre les variables, de sorte qu'une variation dans une variable X entraînera une variation dans une autre variable Y qui lui est reliée[12].

L'étude de la relation causale exige alors l'isolation de deux variables, en supposant que l'influence de toutes les autres variables introduites dans le modèle global est considérée comme constante. Cette supposition impose évidemment des limites à la validité de l'analyse, puisque les variables retenues dans le cas présent ne constituent pas une structure simple (variables explicatives naturellement indépendantes entre elles) mais une structure complexe (variables explicatives interdépendantes)[13]. En effet, les variables de situation sont reliées entre elles :

[11] Charles R. Adrian, « Public Attitudes and Metropolitan Decision-Making », *Politics in the Metropolis*, ed. Thomas R. Dye et Brett W. Hawkins, 529.
[12] Vittorio Capecchi, « Causalità e correlazione nella problematica sociologica », *Studi di Sociologia*, II, fasc. 3, 232–3.
[13] Raymond Boudon, *L'analyse mathématique des faits sociaux* (Paris, 1970), 138.

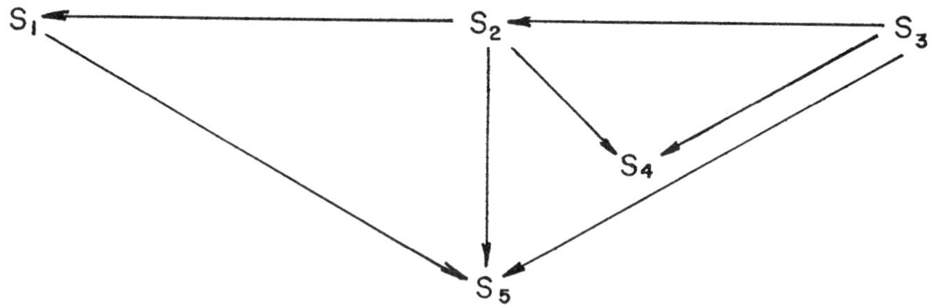

FIGURE 1. Inter-influence des variables de situation.
Légende : S_1 lieu de travail, S_2 occupation, S_3 niveau de scolarité, S_4 revenu familial, S_5 intérêt.

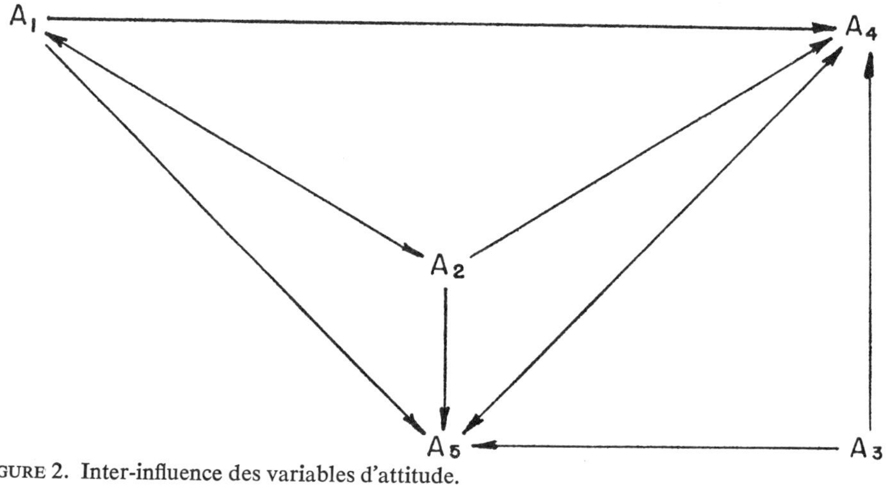

FIGURE 2. Inter-influence des variables d'attitude.
Légende : A_1 attitude à l'égard des services municipaux, A_2 attitude à l'égard du niveau des taxes municipales, A_3 attitude à l'égard de l'accès des élus aux centres de décision, A_4 attitude à l'égard des fusions et des annexions, A_5 attitude à l'égard de la CUQ.

le revenu est fonction de la scolarité, l'occupation est fonction de la scolarité – et les variables d'attitude sont reliées entre elles : l'attitude à l'égard des services municipaux est influencée par l'attitude à l'égard des taxes municipales, l'attitude à l'égard de l'annexion est influencée par l'attitude à l'égard de l'organisme régional – et enfin les variables d'attitudes sont elles-mêmes influencées par les variables de situation.

La structure des relations intervariables est par conséquent très complexe. Nous tenterons d'aborder le problème avec plus de simplicité en distinguant trois types de réseau : d'abord, le réseau des variables de situation (Figure 1), en deuxième lieu, le réseau des variables d'attitude (Figure 2), et en troisième lieu, l'ensemble des réseaux d'influence des variables de situation sur les variables d'attitude. La relation entre les variables prises deux à deux sera analysée à l'aide d'un coefficient de corrélation. Il ne s'agit donc pas d'une analyse de dépendance qui permettrait « de préciser en isolant les effets directs des effets adventices, et de dire que l'effet de X_1 sur X_3 est *n* fois plus important que l'effet de X_2 sur X_3 »[14]. L'analyse qui

[14] *Ibid.*, 105.

suit ne donne pas une image d'ensemble des relations causales, mais elle permet de dire que X_1 paraît avoir une influence sur X_2, et que l'influence de X_3 sur X_2 semble moins forte que celle de X_1 sur X_2. L'intérêt de cette analyse nous semble résider surtout dans la comparaison qu'elle permet entre les municipalités étudiées. Le réseau de relations entre les variables d'attitude varie-t-il d'une municipalité à l'autre ? Le réseau de relations entre les variables de situation et les variables d'attitude change-t-il selon les municipalités ?

Pour tenter de répondre à ces questions, nous utilisons les données qui ont été recueillies par entrevues auprès d'un échantillon de 75 électeurs dans chacune des municipalités de la CUQ comptant au moins 10,000 habitants en 1970. Ces municipalités sont toutes limitrophes à la ville centrale à l'exception de deux municipalités (Figure 3). Les entrevues ont été faites de février à juin 1971, soit de 14 à 17 mois après la création de la CUQ. L'échantillon a été tiré de la liste électorale préparée pour les élections provinciales d'avril 1970. Cette liste comprend tous les citoyens canadiens âgés de 18 ans et plus, résidants dans la municipalité. Deux municipalités disposaient d'une liste électorale municipale récente et nous l'avons utilisée. Au total, 591 entrevues ont été faites, soit 87.5 pour cent de l'échantillon.

Les données sont traitées par municipalité, de façon à déceler les tendances propres à chacune. Les corrélations ont été étudiées à partir du chi-carré, auquel est venu s'ajouter, pour fin de comparaison, le coefficient de Cramer :

$$C = \sqrt{x^2/N \min (R-1)(C-1)}.$$

Plus le coefficient se rapproche de 1, plus la relation qu'il indique est forte. Ce coefficient est intéressant ici puisque, variant toujours entre 0 et 1, il permet de comparer l'intensité de la relation observée. Une référence constante au chi-carré laisse croire que, dans la plupart des cas retenus, un coefficient de Cramer égal ou supérieur à 0.350 correspond à un chi-carré indiquant une probabilité d'erreur $p < 0.01$. Toutefois par mesure de précaution, nous utilisons le coefficient de Cramer comme indicateur d'une intensité relative et non comme reflet exact du degré de signification statistique d'une relation.

I. Les variables de situation

L'analyse a comme point de départ un ensemble de réseaux d'influence qui ont été bâtis soit à partir d'études antérieures sur un sujet semblable, soit de façon intuitive. Ce travail revêt par conséquent un caractère de vérification pour certaines hypothèses, et d'exploration pour certaines relations nouvellement considérées. Par ailleurs, les relations entre les variables de situation ne nous intéressent pas comme telles, puisqu'il ne s'agit pas d'une analyse strictement sociologique. Elles retiennent notre attention, brièvement, parce qu'il a été souligné que les réseaux que nous analysons ont des structures complexes et qu'il importe de voir jusqu'à quel point les variables indépendantes telles l'occupation, le revenu, etc. ... sont elles-même reliées à d'autres variables.

Le Tableau V (annexe) montre en effet que les trois variables identifiant le statut socio-économique des répondants sont rattachées les unes aux autres, dans toutes les municipalités. On note que la scolarité semble toujours avoir plus

TERRITOIRE DE LA
COMMUNAUTÉ URBAINE DE QUÉBEC
Echelle
LAC
SAINT - CHARLES
VAL-
SAINT MICHEL
QUEBEC
LORETTEVILLE
BELAIR
QUEBEC
NOTRE-D
AEROPORT
SAINTE FOY
SAINT - AUGUSTIN
C.N.
C.P.
CAP ROUGE
FLEUVE
ST LAWRENCE RIVER

FIGURE 3.

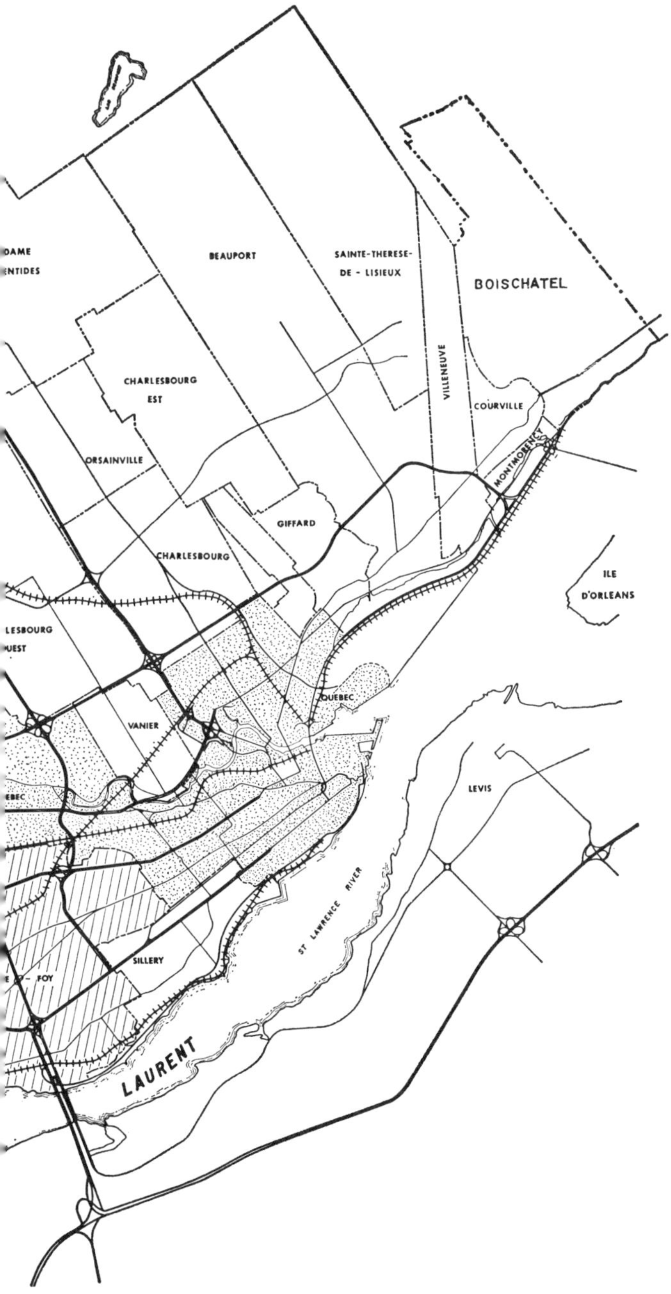
BEAUPORT
SAINTE-THERESE-DE-LISIEUX
BOISCHATEL
VILLENEUVE
COURVILLE
MONTMORENCY
CHARLESBOURG EST
ORSAINVILLE
GIFFARD
CHARLESBOURG
ILE D'ORLEANS
QUEBEC
VANIER
LEVIS
ST LAWRENCE RIVER
SILLERY
LAURENT

d'influence sur l'occupation que sur le revenu. On voit aussi que dans six municipalités sur neuf, les liens de la scolarité avec l'occupation sont plus forts que ceux de l'occupation elle-même avec le revenu. De plus, l'occupation et le lieu de travail sont reliés entre eux de façon assez intense dans toutes les municipalités à l'exception d'une seule.

La cinquième variable de situation, soit l'intérêt à la restructuration municipale, semble relativement indépendante des variables socio-économiques, sauf dans une municipalité. L'influence du lieu de travail se fait rarement sentir sur cet intérêt, de sorte qu'il est possible de conclure qu'il s'agit ici d'une variable autonome, ou du moins qui n'est pas reliée de façon générale aux variables socio-économiques que nous avons retenues.

II. Les variables d'attitude

Plusieurs des hypothèses reliées aux attitudes ont déjà été vérifiées dans des études comparables à celle-ci. En nous basant sur ces travaux, nous analysons les relations qui existent entre les attitudes en les considérant deux à deux. Au besoin, nous tenterons de préciser ces relations, comme c'est le cas pour cette première interrelation entre l'attitude à l'égard des services municipaux et l'attitude à l'égard du niveau des taxes municipales.

SERVICES ET TAXES

Hypothétiquement, ces deux variables devraient être reliées entre elles par une influence réciproque. En effet, la satisfaction à l'égard des services municipaux sera accompagnée d'une satisfaction à l'égard du niveau des taxes, même si celui-ci est relativement élevé. Par contre, une insatisfaction à l'égard du niveau des taxes sera reliée à une insatisfaction à l'égard des services qui sont jugés inadéquats eu égard aux taxes qui sont perçues.

La relation d'interinfluence entre l'attitude à l'égard des services municipaux et l'attitude à l'égard des taxes municipales semble intéressante dans presque toutes les municipalités (sept municipalités sur neuf, Tableau VI, annexe). Les données montrent en effet qu'une attitude prépondérante de satisfaction à l'égard des services est accompagnée d'une attitude de satisfaction à l'égard du niveau des taxes. On note aussi, à la lumière d'une analyse comparative du niveau des taxes dans les municipalités étudiées (Tableau IV, annexe) que la plus grande proportion de gens satisfaits à l'égard des taxes municipales se trouve dans les municipalités où le fardeau fiscal est assez élevé, soit Loretteville et Charlesbourg. Mais on constate que les deux municipalités où le niveau de taxes est le plus bas (Sillery et Vanier) comptent aussi une majorité de répondants qui se disent satisfaits du niveau des taxes.

Par conséquent, il est possible de dire que l'insatisfaction n'augmente pas nécessairement avec le niveau des taxes, mais qu'elle est surtout fonction de l'attitude à l'égard des services municipaux. Il est important de souligner cependant qu'il n'est pas question d'analyser ici la qualité réelle des services municipaux, mais la perception que s'en font les citoyens. Il n'y a pas nécessairement correspondance entre la réalité et cette représentation. Pareille constatation a déjà été faite par Basil G. Zimmer et Amos H. Hawley dans leur analyse de l'attitude des citoyens de banlieue à l'égard des services qui leur sont offerts par leur municipalité. « The judgments in these three instances (police, fire, garbage disposal) are so at odds with any objective comparison which might be made that they suggest a very low level of expectation on the part of the fringe residents »[15].

SERVICES ET REGROUPEMENT

Une seconde hypothèse concerne l'attitude à l'égard des services municipaux et l'attitude à l'égard des annexions et des fusions.

L'attitude à l'égard des services municipaux semble a priori reliée à l'attitude que le citoyen adoptera face à une fusion ou à une annexion de sa municipalité à une autre. En effet, les réformes municipales ont généralement comme objectif de permettre aux citoyens d'une même région de bénéficier de services de qualité égale, ou de meilleurs services que ceux qui leur sont offerts dans les conditions du moment. L'insatisfaction à l'égard des services municipaux sera un indice de l'existence de besoins auxquels la municipalité ne répond pas, et conséquemment d'un certain vide à combler. La population qui n'est pas satisfaite des services qui lui sont offerts aurait tendance à se montrer favorable à l'annexion à une autre municipalité.

Cette hypothèse a été vérifiée par Brett W. Hawkins dans son étude sur la restructuration à Nashville[16]. Elle se vérifie dans la moitié des municipalités étudiées dans la région de Québec. On note ici le cas de Loretteville où les deux variables sont très reliées. Les gens sont très satisfaits à l'égard de leurs services municipaux et ont aussi une attitude peu favorable à l'annexion ou à la fusion. Le Tableau VI (annexe) montre la prépondérance de la relation entre ces deux mêmes variables sur l'ensemble du réseau de relations à Vanier. Chez les répondants de Vanier, les relations entre variables d'attitude semblent faibles, et il devient important dans un tel réseau de souligner l'influence de l'attitude à l'égard des services municipaux sur l'attitude à l'égard des annexions et des fusions, bien que cette relation demeure imprécise.

Si l'attitude à l'égard des services municipaux n'explique pas, dans certaines municipalités, l'attitude à l'égard des annexions et des fusions, est-il possible de déceler une autre relation significative ? La réponse est positive dans le cas de Ste-Foy, mais non dans les trois autres cas (Charlesbourg, Giffard et Orsainville). Dans ces trois dernières municipalités, les variables d'attitude retenues n'expliquent pas l'attitude à l'égard des fusions et des annexions. Deux possibilités s'offrent alors : soit que l'explication de cette attitude se trouvera dans une variable primaire, et nous pourrons le vérifier dans la prochaine partie, soit qu'elle se trouvera dans des variables autres que les dix qui ont été retenues dans cette étude, et dans ce cas, il faudra remettre en question la pertinence des variables retenues.

Il semble par conséquent, qu'il soit impossible de conclure à la vérification de l'hypothèse suivant laquelle l'attitude à l'égard des taxes municipales influencerait de façon significative l'orientation des citoyens d'une municipalité à l'égard

[15] « Local Government as Viewed by Fringe Residents », 365.
[16] « Public Opinion and Metropolitan Reorganization in Nashville », 410.

d'une annexion ou d'une fusion. La relation existe dans certaines municipalités, alors que, dans certaines autres, il semble possible de dire que l'annexion ou la fusion n'est pas envisagée strictement en fonction des répercussions financières.

PARTICIPATION ET GOUVERNEMENT RÉGIONAL

Le changement dans les structures municipales peut être vu d'un œil soucieux de démocratie plutôt que d'économie (entendu dans son sens restreint). En effet, l'un des objectifs du gouvernement local est d'assurer un lien efficace et rapide entre le citoyen et son gouvernement, et même de lui permettre de participer à la solution de certains problèmes particuliers[17]. Il apparaît logique pour les partisans de cet idéal de craindre que l'élargissement des structures municipales n'entraîne une diminution des possibilités de consultation et de participation. Dans cette perspective, l'hypothèse suivante est formulée : l'attitude à l'égard de l'annexion et de la fusion est influencée par les effets anticipés de ces changements sur l'accès aux centres de décision. Ceci revient à dire que les effets de la restructuration ne sont pas vus uniquement en terme de services (rationalité au niveau des extrants) mais aussi en terme de processus décisionnels. Dans la restructuration, le citoyen est peut-être soucieux de la possibilité de faire connaître ses besoins plutôt que de l'amélioration des services. Charles R. Adrian précise cette idée en ces termes : « I think that there is ample, if unsystematic, evidence to show that these (efficiency and economy) are not goals for many citizens, indeed that the citizen is cynical about efficiency if it interests him at all, and that he therefore concentrates on what is, in any case, a higher order of values to him – access to decision-makers, and a sense of having councils and boards that are representative »[18].

L'accès aux centres de décision peut-être le fait des citoyens eux-mêmes ou des représentants qu'ils élisent. Nous faisons donc l'hypothèse que l'attitude à l'égard de la fusion ou de l'annexion sera favorable chez ceux qui voient en ce changement une amélioration de l'accès de leurs élus auprès des centres de décision. Le Tableau VI (annexe) indique que cette hypothèse se vérifie dans le cas de Sillery seulement, et que, dans les autres municipalités de banlieue les citoyens ne semblent pas croire qu'une annexion ou une fusion pourrait faire varier l'accès de leurs élus auprès des centres de décision. Le réseau de relation est très intéressant sur ce point, puisqu'il indique clairement non pas une influence de A_3 sur A_4 mais une influence de A_3 sur A_5.

En effet, les variations attendues dans l'accès des élus aux centres de décision semblent influencer plus intensément l'attitude à l'égard de l'organisme régional. La relation est particulièrement forte à Charlesbourg et à Loretteville où la proportion de ceux qui prévoient un accès moins facile des élus aux centres de décision est plus élevée que dans les autres municipalités. Ces municipalités comptent également une part relativement plus considérable de gens qui sont opposés ou indifférents à l'organisme régional.

[17]Plusieurs auteurs se sont penchés sur cette question, notamment : L.J. Sharpe, « Theories and Values of Local Government », *Political Studies*, XVIII, no 2 (1970), 153–74; G. Langrod, « Local Government and Democracy », *Public Administration*, XXXI (1953), 25–34; H. Whalen, « Democracy and Local Government », *Canadian Public Administration*, III (mars 1960), 1–13.

[18]« Public Attitudes and Metropolitan Decision-Making », 528.

Nous pouvons, par conséquent, conclure de ces données que l'attitude à l'égard de l'organisme régional est reliée à la façon dont les gens évaluent l'influence de la création de cet organisme sur l'accès des élus locaux aux centres de décision.

SERVICES ET GOUVERNEMENT RÉGIONAL

L'attitude à l'égard de l'organisme régional peut par ailleurs être influencée par d'autres variables, notamment l'attitude à l'égard des services municipaux (A_1). La CUQ a, en effet, pris en charge des services dont la responsabilité reposait auparavant entre les mains des municipalités, de sorte que les gens qui étaient satisfaits des services tels qu'offerts par leur municipalité auraient tendance à ne pas se montrer très favorables à l'égard de l'organisme régional.

Selon le Tableau VI (annexe), il existe une relation intéressante entre les variables A_1 et A_5 dans cinq cas sur neuf. Le coefficient n'est pas très fort dans le cas de Giffard, mais nous le retenons puisqu'il est le plus significatif du réseau de relations entre variables d'attitude dans cette municipalité.

L'intensité relative des coefficients permet de noter ici que, sauf dans le cas de Giffard, la relation $\overrightarrow{A_1 A_5}$ est toujours surpassée par une relation plus forte qui est soit $\overrightarrow{A_3 A_5}$, soit $\overrightarrow{A_4 A_5}$. Ce qui revient à dire que l'influence des variations dans l'accès des élus aux centres de décision (A_3) et l'influence de l'attitude à l'égard de l'annexion et de la fusion (A_4) sont plus intenses que l'influence de l'attitude à l'égard des services municipaux (A_1) quand il s'agit d'analyser l'attitude à l'égard de l'organisme régional (A_5). L'attitude à l'égard des services municipaux ne semble pas être le facteur dominant dans l'explication de l'attitude à l'égard du gouvernement régional.

REGROUPEMENT ET GOUVERNEMENT RÉGIONAL

L'annexion et la fusion sont en effet des modalités de restructuration municipale, au même titre que la formation d'un organisme régional[19]. Il semble alors normal qu'il y ait une relation entre l'attitude à l'égard d'une modalité et une autre de ces modalités. A titre d'exemple, on se rappelle l'expérience de Nashville, Tennessee, où le recours de la ville centrale à l'annexion eut pour effet de renverser la majorité qui s'était prononcée, lors d'un premier référendum, contre la création d'un organisme régional[20].

Cette hypothèse se vérifie dans trois municipalités seulement (Sillery, Loretteville et Beauport, Tableau VI, annexe), alors que, dans les autres, l'attitude à l'égard de la CUQ s'explique davantage par l'effet que peut avoir l'organisme régional sur l'accès des élus aux centres de décision.

Le Tableau VI (annexe) montre aussi qu'un système identique de relation semble exister à Sillery, Loretteville et Beauport. La variable A_5 est influencée de façon significative et simultanément par les quatre variables A_1, A_2, A_3 et A_4. L'attitude à l'égard de l'organisme régional fait l'objet de multiples influences dans ces trois municipalités, tandis que les influences sont plus sélectives et moins intenses dans les autres municipalités.

[19]Roscoe Martin précise ces « méthodes d'adaptation locale » dans *Metropolis in Transition* (Washington, DC, 1963).

[20]John C. Bollens et Henry J. Schmandt, *The Metropolis, its People, Politics, and Economic Life* (New York, 1965), 510.

III. Les relations entre variables de situation et attitudes

L'incidence des variables socio-économiques sur les attitudes et les comportements politiques est sans doute l'un des secteurs les plus analysés de la science politique. Cette remarque s'applique aussi au domaine de la politique municipale où plusieurs recherches s'intéressent de façon particulière à l'influence du statut socio-économique[21]. Celui-ci constitue en effet un élément spécificateur de la banlieue par rapport à la ville centrale, et a comme avantage de se présenter sous une forme statistique facilement disponible. Dans cette troisième partie, nous allons faire le lien entre les variables de situation et les variables d'attitude, en voyant successivement la relation entre chaque variable de situation et l'ensemble des attitudes retenues.

REVENU ET ATTITUDES

Le revenu semble avoir exercé une influence pertinente sur l'attitude à l'égard de la restructuration municipale, par exemple dans la région de Cleveland.

> Voters in the wealthier dormitory cities or villages have a record substantially more in favor of metropolitan government than those in the less wealthy communities. Future studies might examine the hypothesis that the more wealthy voters as well perceive the community of interest which exists throughout the metropolis. They understand that the productive unit in which they have a stake is not limited to the municipality in which they have a home. On the other hand, the larger disposable income which they possess may be the most significant factor; they know that if new taxes are needed to improve the government of the entire county they can afford them without personal deprivation. Voters with less disposable income will be most pressed by any new taxes even if their own communities are the ones which would benefit most. This may be the reason they vote against the improved government while their neighbors in the more affluent communities vote for it[22].

Le Tableau VII (annexe) montre que le revenu n'est en aucun cas relié de façon significative à l'attitude à l'égard des fusions et des annexions, ni même à l'attitude à l'égard de l'organisme régional, sauf à Giffard où le coefficient indique une faible relation.

Si le revenu n'influence pas l'orientation à l'égard de la restructuration, des recherches antérieures ont montré qu'il peut avoir une autre conséquence. Edward L. McDill et Jeanne C. Ridley ont en effet constaté que les gens dont le revenu est peu élevé ont plus de difficulté que les autres à se forger une opinion ou à adopter une attitude bien définie sur les questions de restructuration[23]. Cette hypothèse se vérifie dans trois des quatre municipalités dont le revenu est le plus bas (soit Loretteville, Vanier et Beauport). La ville de Québec fait exception, puisque la grande partie des répondants semble s'être fait une opinion sur la

[21]Signalons l'étude de Richard A. Watson et John H. Romani, « Metropolitan Government for Metropolitan Cleveland : an analysis of the voting record », *Midwest Journal of Political Science*, V (nov. 1961), 385.

[22]James A. Norton, « Referenda Voting in a Metropolitan Area », *Western Political Quarterly*, XVI (March 1963), 201. Cette hypothèse est aussi vérifiée dans le cas de Nashville, Tennessee, par David A. Booth, « Metro and the Suburbanite », in *Politics of Metropolitan Areas*, éd. Philip B. Coulter (New York, 1967), 278.

[23]« Status, anomia, political alienation and political participation », *American Journal of Sociology*, LXVIII, no. 2 (Sept. 1962), 207.

restructuration. Cette exception peut s'expliquer parce qu'il s'agit de la ville centrale et elle n'exige pas alors le rejet de l'hypothèse.

OCCUPATION, NIVEAU DE SCOLARITÉ ET ATTITUDES

Selon les données du Tableau VIII (annexe) l'occupation semble plus pertinente que le revenu comme variable explicative dans plusieurs municipalités, surtout en ce qui concerne l'attitude à l'égard de l'organisme régional. Par contre le niveau de scolarité (Tableau IX, annexe) n'est relié de façon significative à aucune variable d'attitude, quelle que soit la municipalité.

LIEU DE TRAVAIL ET ATTITUDES

Parmi les caractéristiques individuelles, nous retenons aussi le lieu de travail. La ville centrale constitue en fait le lieu de travail d'une grande partie de la main-d'œuvre régionale. Ceci nous porte à croire que les gens qui ne travaillent pas dans leur municipalité de résidence mais à la ville centrale ou dans d'autres localités avoisinantes, seraient moins attachés à leur « clocher » et par conséquent plus favorables à une restructuration municipale. Nous faisons donc l'hypothèse que le lieu de travail influence les attitudes à l'égard des annexions et de l'organisme régional.

A ce sujet, Robert C. Wood affirme que les citoyens « mobiles » (ceux qui doivent se rendre dans une autre municipalité tous les jours pour travailler) sont les plus susceptibles de posséder quelques germes de sentiment d'appartenance à une région. « ... the only identifiable metropolitan political community at present is likely to be found, in H.G. Wells' happy phrase, among the de-localized inhabitants, popularly known today as the commuters. These are, perhaps, the only citizens who, through their daily journey to work, are constantly aware of what it means to live in the larger area, who are unfranchised in their places of residence. All other more static notions of community it seems, fragment as rapidly as the present governments themselves »[24].

Selon le Tableau X (annexe) seuls les citoyens de Giffard et de Loretteville sont influencés dans leur attitude à l'égard de l'organisme régional par le fait qu'ils travaillent ou non dans leur municipalité de résidence. Le peu de signification de la variable « lieu de travail » surprend puisqu'elle semblait a priori devoir influencer plusieurs des attitudes étudiées. Selon cette information, la mobilité quotidienne (telle que définie par Robert C. Wood) ne serait pas, de façon générale, une variable pertinente dans l'ensemble des municipalités retenues dans ce travail.

INTÉRÊT ET ATTITUDES

Enfin, les variables dites primaires comprennent également l'intérêt aux problèmes de fusion et d'annexion. Bien que nous n'ayons pas trouvé de développement sur cet aspect dans les travaux consultés, il est possible d'imaginer une relation entre l'intérêt et l'attitude. Il est plus difficile toutefois, de dire dans quel sens se fait sentir l'effet appréhendé. L'intérêt sera-t-il caractéristique de celui qui est favorable ou de celui qui est défavorable au changement dans les structures municipales ?

[24] « Division of Powers in Metropolitan Areas », *Area and Power*, ed. Arthur Maass (Glencoe, Ill., 1959), 67.

TABLEAU I

FRÉQUENCE D'INFLUENCE PERTINENTE (c ⩾ .350) DES VARIABLES DE SITUATION SUR LES ATTITUDES, PAR MUNICIPALITÉ

	Intérêt	Occupation	Revenu	Lieu de travail	Scolarité
Québec	3	0	2	1	0
Sillery	0	5	0	0	0
Ste-Foy	0	3	2	1	0
Charlesbourg	0	1	0	0	0
Giffard	2	1	1	1	0
Loretteville	2	3	2	1	0
Orsainville	0	3	1	1	0
Vanier	0	3	2	0	0
Beauport	1	2	0	0	0
Total	8	21	10	5	0

Les données du Tableau XI (annexe) indiquent que la variable « intérêt aux problèmes de restructuration municipale » est pertinente dans quatre municipalités sur neuf. Deux d'entre ces municipalités sont très intéressées et favorables à l'organisme supra-municipal, tandis que les deux autres sont moins intéressées tout en étant moins favorables. Il semble par conséquent que là où la variable exerce une influence significative, elle soit reliée à une attitude précise, et que, de plus, cette attitude tende à être favorable chez les gens qui se sont dits les plus intéressés.

Conclusion

Dans la première partie de cette analyse, nous avons vu que les variables de situation ont tendance à être reliées entre elles, et ceci dans la plupart des municipalités. La deuxième partie a fait ressortir l'interdépendance des attitudes, et la troisième partie a souligné l'influence de certaines variables de situation sur les attitudes. Est-il possible maintenant de tirer des conclusions concernant les réseaux de relations observées ?

Le tableau de la fréquence de l'influence des variables de situation (Tableau I), quelle que soit l'attitude, montre que l'occupation est nettement la variable dont l'influence se fait le plus souvent sentir avec pertinence.

Le Tableau I fait ressortir une différence entre l'influence des variables de situation à Québec et dans les autres municipalités. L'intérêt et le revenu sont en effet plus influents que l'occupation dans la ville centrale. Mais le Tableau I ne permet pas d'affirmer que les réseaux de relations des banlieues sont identiques. Ceci confirme la variation anticipée dans l'influence des variables socio-économiques sur les attitudes et l'existence d'un modèle propre à chaque municipalité.

Le Tableau II permet de compléter le réseau de chaque municipalité en compilant la fréquence de relations intenses entre les variables d'attitudes. L'importance de l'attitude à l'égard des services municipaux et à l'égard du niveau des taxes municipales est confirmée par ce tableau. En effet, pour ces deux variables, le total des relations réelles intéressantes est plus de la moitié du total des relations théoriques qui avaient été posées à la Figure 2 (16 sur 27 et 15 sur 27).

TABLEAU II

FRÉQUENCE D'INTER-INFLUENCE PERTINENTE ($c \geqslant .350$)
DES ATTITUDES, PAR MUNICIPALITÉ

	Services municipaux	Taxes municipales	Accès des élus	Fusion annexion	CUQ
Québec	2	2	1	—	—
Sillery	3	3	2	1	1
Ste-Foy	1	2	1	0	0
Charlesbourg	1	1	1	0	0
Giffard	1	0	0	0	0
Loretteville	3	3	1	1	1
Orsainville	1	1	1	0	0
Vanier	1	0	1	0	0
Beauport	3	3	1	1	1
Total *f* réelle	16	15	9	3	3
f théorique/municipalité	3	3	2	1	1
Total *f* théorique	27	27	18	9	9

En retenant, en dernière analyse, seulement les liens les plus intenses entre les variables de situation et les attitudes (Figure 4) nous pouvons comparer les réseaux ainsi obtenus d'une municipalité à l'autre.

La Figure 4 montre que les attitudes à l'égard de l'accès aux centres de décision (A_3) et à l'égard de l'organisme régional (A_5) sont soumises à l'influence la plus intense. La variable A_3 est en effet reliée à au moins une variable de situation dans toutes les municipalités. Par contre les attitudes à l'égard du niveau des taxes (A_2) et à l'égard des annexions et des fusions (A_4) sont moins souvent reliées intensément à au moins une variable de situation.

Selon la Figure 4, le réseau théorique de relations entre les attitudes se retrouve tel quel dans une seule municipalité, soit Sillery. Quatre des neuf municipalités ont une structure unique, plus ou moins complexe, soit Québec, Sillery, Loretteville et Beauport. Dans ces cas, les attitudes sont reliées entre elles de façon assez intense, et sont elles-mêmes influencées par des variables indépendantes de situation.

Les cinq autres municipalités se caractérisent par l'existence de deux réseaux plus ou moins complexes, non reliés l'un à l'autre. Les réseaux sont complexes à Ste-Foy, alors que leur structure est relativement simple à Charlesbourg. A Ste-Foy, les services municipaux, les taxes et l'attitude à l'égard de la fusion et de l'annexion forment un réseau intéressant. L'accès des élus aux centres de décision et l'attitude à l'égard de la CUQ forment un second réseau dont l'indépendance à l'égard du premier est aussi intéressante. Le cas de Ste-Foy est unique, puisqu'il ne compte pas de variable isolées, mais deux réseaux indépendants qui intègrent toutes les attitudes retenues.

Les quatre autres cas de double réseau comprennent au moins une variable isolée, qui est l'attitude à l'égard des fusions et des annexions (Charlesbourg, Orsainville et Giffard) et l'attitude à l'égard des taxes municipales (Giffard et Vanier). Non seulement ces variables ne sont pas reliées de façon significative à aucune autre attitude, mais elles ne sont pas influencées par aucune des variables de situation retenues. Nous constatons qu'à Charlesbourg, Giffard et Orsainville

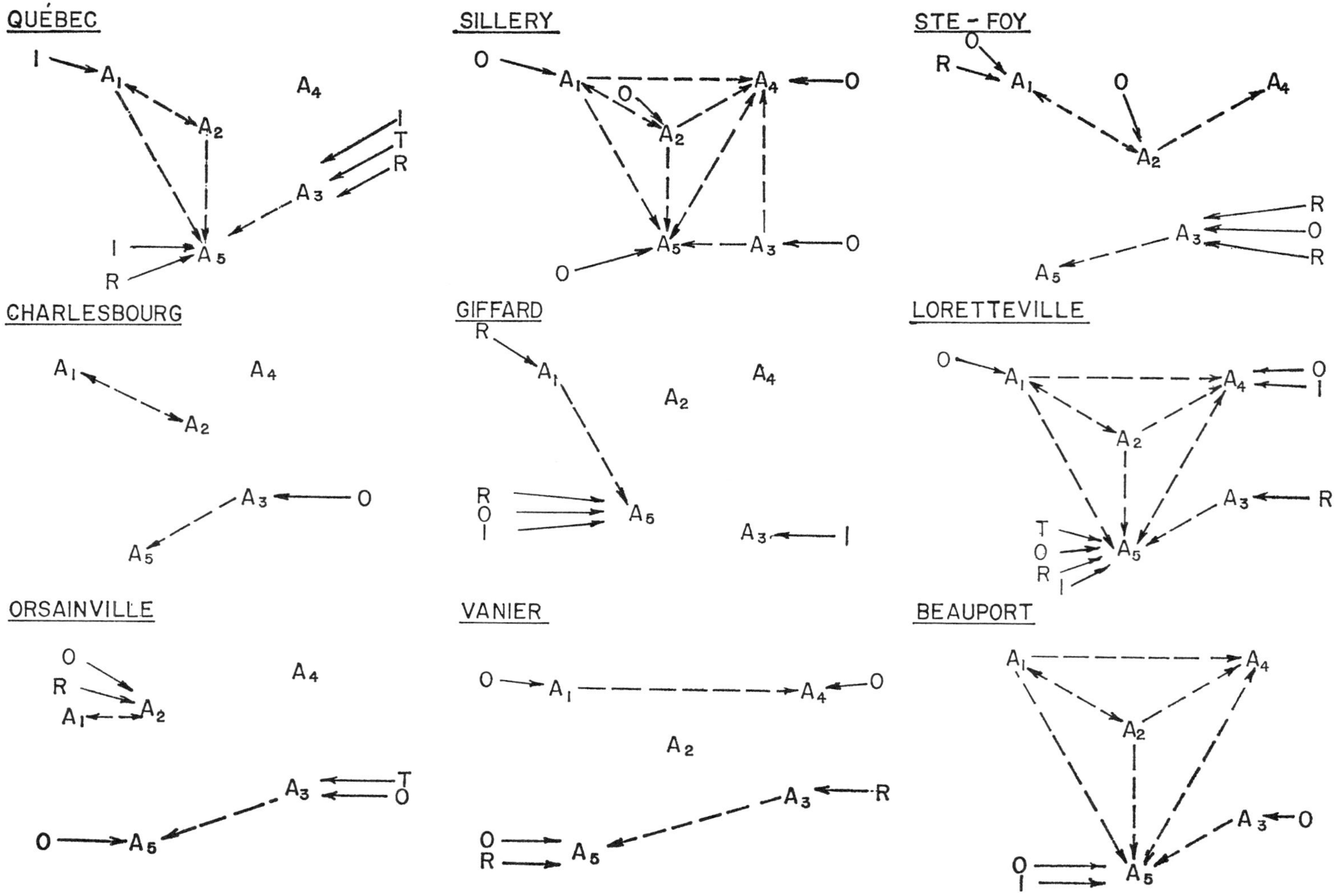

FIGURE 4. Influence des variables de situation et des attitudes, par municipalité.

Légende : la ligne pointillée indique une relation entre deux attitudes; la ligne pleine indique une relation entre une variable de situation et une attitude. *O*, occupation, *T*, lieu de travail, *R*, niveau de revenu, *I*, intérêt, A_1 attitude à l'égard des services municipaux, A_2 attitude à l'égard du niveau des taxes, A_3 attitude à l'égard de l'accès des élus aux

TABLEAU III

FRÉQUENCE DES RELATIONS PERTINENTES (c $\geqslant$ .350) ENTRE LES ATTITUDES

Relations	Fréquence
A_1A_2	7
A_1A_4	4
A_1A_5	5
A_2A_4	4
A_2A_5	4
A_3A_4	1
A_3A_5	8
A_4A_5	3

l'attitude à l'égard des fusions et des annexions (A_4) demeure tout à fait inexpliquée.

Par ailleurs, l'influence des caractéristiques de situation sur les attitudes est vérifiée par la présence dans chaque municipalité de l'une ou l'autre des variables qui sont ordinairement retenues comme indicateurs du niveau socio-économique (occupation, revenu). Il est ainsi possible de vérifier l'existence d'une relation entre le niveau socio-économique de la population et ses attitudes face aux changements dans les structures municipales.

Les variables socio-économiques doivent cependant partager leur influence sur les attitudes avec une autre variable de situation : soit l'intérêt au problème de la restructuration. Mais cette variable n'est pas pertinente dans toutes les municipalités, de sorte que les variables socio-économiques semblent plus importantes.

Du côté de l'inter-influence des attitudes, le Tableau III montre que la relation la plus fréquente est celle qui unit l'attitude à l'égard de l'organisme régional au changement anticipé dans l'accès des élus aux centres de décision ($\overrightarrow{A_3A_5}$).

La relation entre les services municipaux et le niveau des taxes municipales est aussi établie de façon significative dans la plupart des municipalités. Il est par ailleurs étonnant de constater que l'attitude à l'égard des fusions et des annexions et l'attitude à l'égard de l'organisme régional ne sont reliées fortement que dans trois cas sur neuf.

Ces différentes constatations montrent avec évidence que les hypothèses qui ont été formulées concernant la restructuration municipale et les attitudes qu'elle inspire ne sont pas vérifiées dans tous les cas. Parmi les neuf municipalités étudiées, la ville de Sillery respecte le mieux la structure de relations entre attitudes qui fut posée comme point de départ. La population de Charlesbourg manifeste des attitudes dont la structure correspond le moins à celle que nous avons imaginée.

La communauté d'intérêt existe selon des intensités variables d'une municipalité à l'autre. Certaines localités sont opposées au regroupement sous forme de fusion et d'annexion et favorisent plutôt l'organisme régional qui respecte le niveau local. Ces municipalités présentent un ensemble d'attitudes complètement structurées et liées les unes aux autres. Par contre, quelques municipalités ont des opinions plus partagées que les premières, et ces opinions ne sont pas toujours reliées entre elles.

Ces constatations montrent que les hypothèses qui sont couramment formulées concernant le regroupement municipal devront encore être soumises à l'épreuve avant d'être élevées au statut de théories. Cette étude présente tout de même un certain intérêt puisqu'elle permet de confirmer partiellement l'une des hypothèses, à savoir l'existence d'un réseau de relations, et entièrement l'hypothèse concernant l'existence de réseaux propres à chaque municipalité.

Il faut cependant souligner un échec partiel dans quelques municipalités où certaines attitudes demeurent inexpliquées et hors réseau. Ce constat constitue, toutefois, une incitation au prolongement de la recherche et à l'exploration de nouvelles relations, à l'aide de nouvelles variables. La compréhension des attitudes dans certaines municipalités aurait peut-être été plus complète s'il avait été possible de mesurer l'intensité de l'esprit communautaire et la fréquence des communications avec la ville centrale. Ces variables demandent encore à être opérationnalisées et à être traduites en des indicateurs facilement observables avant de pouvoir être intégrées dans une analyse de ce genre.

TABLEAU IV

CARACTERISTIQUES DES MUNICIPALITES

Municipalités	Population 1969	Superficie en acres 1970	Type de gouvernement	Evaluation moyenne maison unifamiliale	Nombre de compagnies	Dette nette/hab.	Dépenses totales/hab.	Nombre d'employés réguliers	Taxes mun., Propriététype**
Québec	166,984	6080	cons.-gér.	$13,000	1938	$311	$198	2069	$285.00
Sillery	15,000	1767	maire-cons.	—	20	224	118	75	$231.00
Ste-Foy	58,700	7360	cons.-gér.*	16,970	—	597	140	347	$318.50
Charlesbourg	30,500	2600	cons.-gér.*	10,000	81	388	82	92	$347.00
Giffard	12,629	1700	cons.-gér.*	14,000	41	297	95	38	$322.50
Loretteville	10,000	1771	maire-cons.	8,500	23	448	122	53	$350.00
Orsainville	10,341	1702	maire-cons.	10,500	45	457	81	38	$374.50
Vanier	9,500	1158	maire-cons.	10,800	49	151	56	41	$267.00
Beauport	15,500	9000	maire-cons.	14,000	55	287	65	—	$272.00

SOURCE: *Renseignements statistiques, Municipalités du Québec, 1969* (Bureau de la statistique du Québec, 1971). Statistiques inédites, ministère des affaires municipales, 1970.

*Note: Ces municipalités sont considérées comme ayant un gouvernement de type conseil-gérant même si celui qui est chargé des fonctions de gérance porte le nom d'administrateur ou de directeur des services.

**Note: Le calcul est basé sur la propriété type définie de la facon suivante : terrain valant $5000, mesurant 100 pieds de front; maison valant $10,000. Le taux de taxation pour l'année 1971 a été fourni par le service d'Informatique de la CUQ. Il s'agit d'une approximation qui ne tient pas compte des taxes d'améliorations locales.

TABLEAU V

INTER-INFLUENCE DES VARIABLES DE SITUATION, PAR MUNICIPALITÉ

	$\overrightarrow{S_1S_5}$	$\overrightarrow{S_2S_1}$	$\overrightarrow{S_2S_4}$	$\overrightarrow{S_2S_5}$	$\overrightarrow{S_3S_2}$	$\overrightarrow{S_3S_4}$	$\overrightarrow{S_3S_5}$
Québec	.379	.438	.476	.314	.485	.347	.276
Sillery	.338	.384	.391	.404	.464	.410	.297
Ste-Foy	.322	.389	.368	.329	.409	.299	.231
Charlesbourg	.295	.380	.387	.286	.414	.295	.214
Giffard	.223	.462	.453	.348	.431	.334	.349
Loretteville	.324	.412	.426	.342	.386	.358	.171
Orsainville	.234	.302	.498	.258	.360	.277	.273
Vanier	.250	.382	.348	.345	.506	.311	.215
Beauport	.351	.391	.357	.298	.372	.258	.246

S_1 lieu de travail; S_2 occupation; S_3 niveau de scolarité; S_4 revenu; S_5 intérêt.

TABLEAU VI

INTER-INFLUENCE DES VARIABLES D'ATTITUDE, PAR MUNICIPALITÉ

	$\overleftrightarrow{A_1A_2}$	$\overrightarrow{A_1A_4}$	$\overrightarrow{A_1A_5}$	$\overrightarrow{A_2A_4}$	$\overrightarrow{A_2A_5}$	$\overrightarrow{A_3A_4}$	$\overrightarrow{A_3A_5}$	$\overrightarrow{A_4A_5}$
Québec	.351	—	.382	—	.362	—	.447	—
Sillery	.596	.442	.458	.429	.422	.431	.365	.502
Ste-Foy	.466	.260	.324	.418	.293	.241	.368	.278
Charlesbourg	.389	.207	.248	.206	.285	.226	.586	.337
Giffard	.212	.214	.350	.219	.163	.295	.312	.326
Loretteville	.532	.640	.492	.500	.431	.315	.483	.553
Orsainville	.397	.311	.236	.251	.296	.257	.368	.227
Vanier	.287	.363	.285	.232	.265	.200	.355	.319
Beauport	.431	.382	.417	.383	.356	.307	.373	.535

A_1 attitude à l'égard des services municipaux; A_2 attitude à l'égard du niveau des taxes municipales; A_3 attitude à l'égard de l'accès des élus aux centres de décision; A_4 attitude à l'égard des fusions et des annexions; A_5 attitude à l'égard de la CUQ.

TABLEAU VII

INFLUENCE DU REVENU SUR LES VARIABLES D'ATTITUDE, PAR MUNICIPALITÉ

	RA_1	RA_2	RA_3	RA_4	RA_5
Québec	.318	.275	.352	—	.303
Sillery	.313	.330	.344	.310	.336
Ste-Foy	.372	.330	.373	.322	.317
Charlesbourg	.226	.316	.268	.323	.317
Giffard	.368	.234	.312	.234	.374
Loretteville	.344	.315	.357	.335	.322
Orsainville	.315	.398	.277	.297	.335
Vanier	.349	.184	.400	.300	.309
Beauport	.255	.280	.237	.285	.348

R revenu; A_1 attitude à l'égard des services municipaux; A_2 attitude à l'égard du niveau des taxes municipales; A_3 attitude à l'égard de l'accès des élus aux centres de décision; A_4 attitude à l'égard des fusions et des annexions; A_5 attitude à l'égard de la CUQ.

TABLEAU VIII

INFLUENCE DE L'OCCUPATION SUR LES VARIABLES D'ATTITUDE, PAR MUNICIPALITÉ

	OA_1	OA_2	OA_3	OA_4	OA_5
Québec	.292	.293	.333	—	.288
Sillery	.379	.399	.357	.383	.385
Ste-Foy	.452	.357	.377	.249	.375
Charlesbourg	.268	.225	.383	.296	.298
Giffard	.250	.291	.299	.298	.405
Loretteville	.394	.326	.318	.388	.399
Orsainville	.321	.417	.429	.303	.367
Vanier	.421	.264	.318	.454	.359
Beauport	.340	.306	.386	.314	.379

O occupation; A_1 attitude à l'égard des services municipaux; A_2 attitude à l'égard du niveau des taxes municipales; A_3 attitude à l'égard de l'accès des élus aux centres de décision; A_4 attitude à l'égard des fusions et des annexions; A_5 attitude à l'égard de la CUQ.

TABLEAU IX

INFLUENCE DU NIVEAU DE SCOLARITÉ SUR LES VARIABLES D'ATTITUDE, PAR MUNICIPALITÉ

	SA_1	SA_2	SA_3	SA_4	SA_5
Québec	.196	.215	.300	—	.263
Sillery	.219	.315	.275	.241	.341
Ste-Foy	.242	.238	.264	.259	.304
Charlesbourg	.141	.220	.231	.234	.242
Giffard	.251	.206	.244	.273	.303
Loretteville	.232	.181	.242	.207	.320
Orsainville	.229	.209	.224	.175	.218
Vanier	.302	.313	.211	.297	.225
Beauport	.213	.206	.324	.231	.219

S niveau de scolarité; A_1 attitude à l'égard des services municipaux; A_2 attitude à l'égard du niveau des taxes municipales; A_3 attitude à l'égard de l'accès des élus aux centres de décision; A_4 attitude à l'égard des fusions et des annexions; A_5 attitude à l'égard de la CUQ.

TABLEAU X

INFLUENCE DU LIEU DE TRAVAIL SUR LES VARIABLES D'ATTITUDE, PAR MUNICIPALITÉ

	TA_1	TA_2	TA_3	TA_4	TA_5
Québec	.299	.250	.414	—	.323
Sillery	.267	.337	.280	.342	.330
Ste-Foy	.285	.307	.358	.319	.277
Charlesbourg	.260	.271	.278	.285	.339
Giffard	.259	.174	.256	.238	.372
Loretteville	.246	.257	.324	.281	.370
Orsainville	.181	.326	.362	.224	.267
Vanier	.339	.268	.260	.289	.276
Beauport	.305	.278	.305	.197	.271

T lieu de travail; A_1 attitude à l'égard des services municipaux; A_2 attitude à l'égard des taxes municipales; A_3 attitude à l'égard de l'accès des élus aux centres de décision; A_4 attitude à l'égard des fusions et des annexions; A_5 attitude à l'égard de la CUQ.

TABLEAU XI

INFLUENCE DE L'INTÉRÊT SUR LES VARIABLES D'ATTITUDE, PAR MUNICIPALITÉ

	IA_1	IA_2	IA_3	IA_4	IA_5
Québec	.393	.266	.371	—	.478
Sillery	.259	.286	.309	.278	.347
Ste-Foy	.239	.248	.243	.332	.335
Charlesbourg	.199	.210	.196	.227	.209
Giffard	.211	.218	.353	.310	.475
Loretteville	.199	.207	.207	.520	.456
Orsainville	.121	.234	.254	.226	.240
Vanier	.164	.233	.292	.216	.328
Beauport	.157	.226	.278	.247	.400

I intérêt; A_1 attitude à l'égard des services municipaux; A_2 attitude à l'égard du niveau des taxes municipales; A_3 attitude à l'égard de l'accès des élus aux centres de décision; A_4 attitude à l'égard des fusions et des annexions; A_5 attitude à l'égard de la CUQ.

The Businessman Voter in Thunder Bay: The Catalyst to the Federal-Provincial Voting Split?

K.L. MORRISON *Lakehead University*

Why do Canadians vote for one party to form the federal government and then so frequently vote for another to form the government in a provincial legislature? While the problem has been ably restated by George Perlin and Patti Peppin, a satisfactory answer still eludes us.[1] One widely regarded explanation, the so-called balance theory, appears to rest on the assumption that Canadian voters in the mass agree, by some mysterious process, to maintain a balance between federal and provincial powers.[2] Since this process is not spelled out, it must be regarded, as it stands, as a mere extension of the market mythology of classical political economy and, as such, of little value. A better explanation needs to be found. One unexplored possibility is that the very nature of the British North America Act creates tensions within the Canadian polity which find their expression in the contradictory voting patterns. Might, for example, the division of powers between the federal and provincial governments create different, and frequently contradictory and antagonistic, blocks of economic power, which would be most active politically either in the federal or the provincial sphere, and which would express their antagonisms by supporting opposing parties at the two levels of government?

The city of Thunder Bay in Ontario seemed to be an ideal place to explore this suggestion. The city's economy is fairly evenly balanced between the federally oriented grain-handling and transportation industries, and the provincially oriented forest and tourist industries. The area has a well-organized business community whose principal agency is the Thunder Bay Chamber of Commerce. The city is relatively isolated, being some 440 miles east and west from the nearest Canadian cities and 200 miles north of Duluth, Minnesota. Opinions expressed would thus tend to be those of the business leaders of the community itself and not mere echoes of some larger community nearby. Finally, and most important, the city (and its original constituent cities, Fort William and Port Arthur, after whom both the federal and provincial riding are named,[3]) has a well-established pattern of voting one way federally, and then with a new party established in power in Ottawa promptly voting for candidates of the opposition parties to sit in Queen's Park (see Table I).

1"Variations in Party Support in Federal and Provincial Elections; Some Hypotheses," this JOURNAL, IV (June 1971). Also, John Wilson and David Hoffman, "The Liberal Party in Contemporary Ontario Politics," this JOURNAL, III (June 1970).
2Perlin and Peppin, "Variations in Party Support," 282.
3The constituency of Thunder Bay, federally and provincially, encompasses, in the main, the provincial District of Thunder Bay and is wholly outside the city by the same name. Both city ridings at one time included parts of the present riding of Thunder Bay. The larger urban populations so effectively dominated these ridings that past variations in riding boundaries can be safely ignored.

Canadian Journal of Political Science/Revue canadienne de science politique, VI, no. 2 (June/juin 1973). Printed in Canada/Imprimé au Canada.

TABLE I

THUNDER BAY VOTING PATTERNS

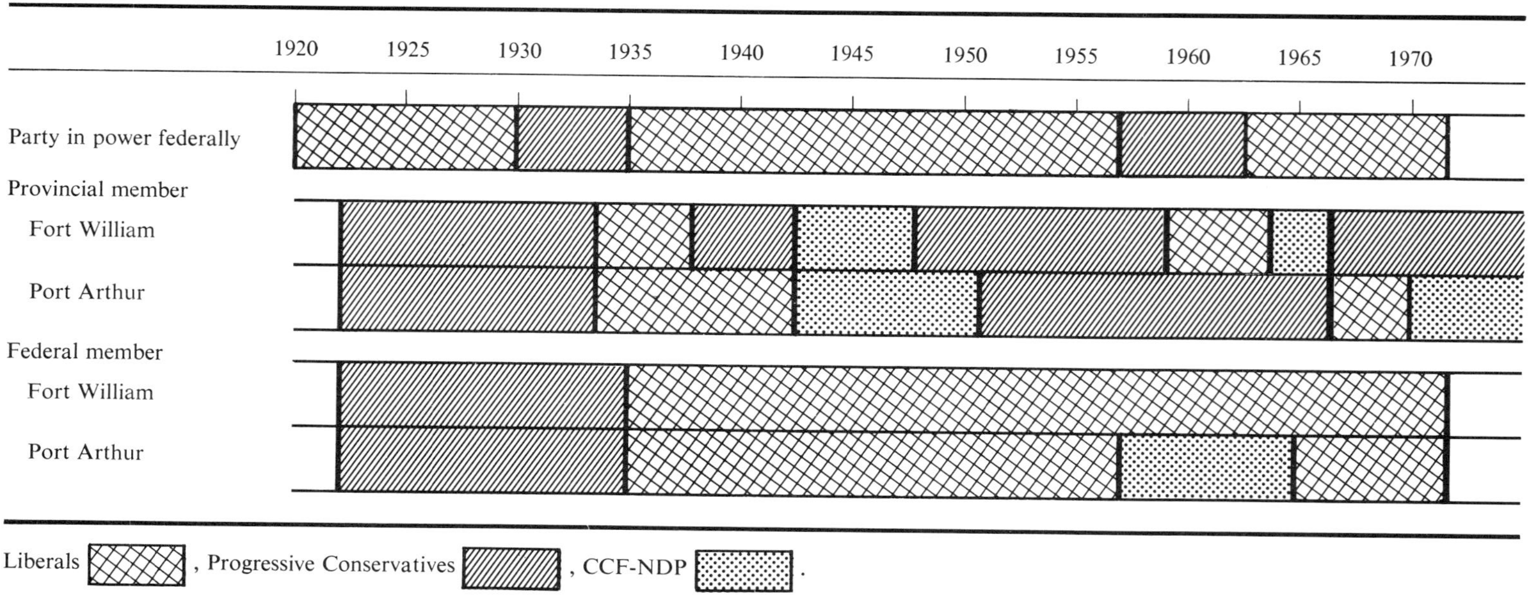

Source: *Canadian Parliamentary Guide 1969*, pp. 294–447.

L'homme d'affaires en tant catalyseur du dédoublement électoral ontarien entre le parti libéral fédéral et le parti conservateur provincial : le cas de Thunder Bay

Cette étude du comportement électoral des hommes d'affaires de Thunder Bay démontre : (1) qu'ils accordent leur appui à l'élite d'un parti sur le plan fédéral et à l'élite d'un autre parti sur le plan provincial; (2) que cet appui prend la forme non seulement de votes et de contributions financières, mais aussi d'une pratique qui consiste à mettre à la disposition du parti favorisé un candidat de choix, en l'occurrence un ancien président de la Chambre de Commerce locale.

L'auteur suggère que ce comportement dédoublé trouve sa source dans la perception différenciée qu'ont les hommes d'affaires des pouvoirs fédéraux et provinciaux, eu égard à leurs implications en ce qui concerne les politiques de taxation et de fiscalité.

The instrument used to test our hypothesis was a questionnaire mailed out to every fourth member on the Thunder Bay Chamber of Commerce and to every fourth lawyer not on this list.[4] Two questions were posed: one sought to uncover the businessman's conception of the importance of federal or provincial government activity to his economic well-being while the other, it was hoped, would uncover discernible federally oriented as against provincially oriented economic groupings. The first was a four-choice question on the importance of federal and provincial government activity to the businessman scaled from "Absolutely vital. They make or break me" to "On the level of the average citizen." It was assumed that if the difference hypothesized existed, it would show up here. No such difference appeared. With few exceptions those who felt that provincial government activities were "very important" or "absolutely vital" felt the same way about the activities of the federal government. Nor is there any evidence that those who put the activities of either level of government in the top two categories felt impelled to extra political exertions as a result. On the contrary, these respondents showed themselves to be slightly more politically quiescent than those for whom government activity was indicated as being less urgent.[5] Thunder Bay businessmen, at least, do not tie their political exertions to their perceived assessment of the importance of government activity to their business or professional life.

A second question that might have produced evidence of a strong federal or provincial orientation was an omnibus one covering the respondent's reasons for voting for the party of his choice in the most recent federal and provincial elections. For the provincial vote, each respondent was given the opportunity to indicate that the party chosen would best defend Ontario interests against federal

[4]Our rationale for adding lawyers was the intimate connection between the legal profession and the business community and the traditional importance of lawyers as leaders in business-supported parties. The leaders of the Progressive Conservative party of Ontario from 1943 to the present, for example, have all been lawyers. In the event, the addition was not significant. Only half-a-dozen names were added to the list and these could not significantly affect the results of the survey based on 211 questionnaires and 83 replies or a 39.3 per cent return. One respondent tore off the sheet which contained the provincial questions and another ignored the federal page. We are thus effectively dealing with 82 returns.

[5]In the provincial sphere, although 45 per cent of respondents reported donating to the party of their choice, only 38 per cent of the most government-affected businessmen did so. Federally, 21 per cent of respondents reported making donations, but only 16 per cent of those most government-affected did so. Distance from the federal election may have dimmed memories somewhat, although, as we shall see, our respondents showed a surprisingly strong memory for past political activity.

encroachment. A strong provincial bias failed to appear. Only 2 respondents out of 82 gave this question first choice, and 10 others mentioned it at varying levels of importance. This reason ranked tenth among the 14 possibilities with a weighted score of 19, and so cannot be considered to be a matter of prime importance for those concerned.[6]

If there was not a strong anti-federal sentiment among respondents, neither was there a strong pro-federal sentiment in so far as this questionnaire was a legitimate device of elicitation. Two questions touched on this matter. The first asked which party could best maintain national unity; and the second which party could best keep the provinces in line. Neither question received a first choice answer, and while 21 respondents indicated with variations in enthusiasm that their party could best maintain national unity, giving this question a score of 34 and a rank of 4, only 9 backed the tougher question that the federal government kept the provinces in line, giving this question a score of 12 and a rank of the same number. Significantly these replies referred to an election in which federal-provincial relations were considered to be an issue of the first rank.[7] One interesting figure in this area is the differing financial support offered provincial Conservatives as against federal Liberals. Twenty-nine businessmen indicated that they had contributed personally to the provincial party's coffers in 1971, while only 11 indicated similar support for the federal Liberals in spite of the fact that businessmen gave both parties almost equal voting support.[8] However, this may merely reflect the businessman's natural affinity to the Progressive Conservative party, which is indicated by the fact that while provincially only 20 per cent of respondents identified with the Liberal party, 63 per cent identified with the Conservatives. Federally, in spite of their propensity to cross party lines and vote Liberal, 35 per cent of respondents identified with the Progressive Conservative party as against 48 per cent who identified themselves with the Liberals.[9] It may also reflect the fact that in the 1971 provincial election the NDP ran energetic campaigns in Thunder Bay which culminated in their taking Port Arthur. In the federal election of 1968, by contrast, the NDP ran a lackluster campaign, with two previously defeated candidates running against popular and well-entrenched sitting members. It was not a circumstance to cause a businessman to give sacrificially.

[6]While respondents were invited to rank their reasons for voting as they did, the methods of responding to this question were so varied as to nullify useful tabulation based directly on respondent ranking. We therefore adopted a scheme of weighting the responses in order to produce a meaningful rank order of importance. First or only choices were given a weight of three; second and third choices, and one of three unranked choices, a weight of two, and all other indications of support a weight of one. On this basis the most popular choice was the local candidate in the 1968 federal election. He received 21 choices of the first category, 15 of the second, and 4 of the third for a score of 97. The most popular provincial choice was the provincial leader with a score of 80.

[7]*Canadian Annual Review for 1968*, ed. John Saywell (Toronto, 1969), 41.

[8]Sixty-one voted Progressive Conservative provincially, 54 Liberal federally; 7 contributed to the provincial Liberals and 4 to the federal PCs; 2 contributed to the NDP in both elections.

[9]Or perhaps this is an indication of the claim that while the Liberals are able to depend upon "funds raised mainly from anonymous (so far as the public is concerned) corporate donors" (George Bain, *Toronto Globe and Mail*, 10 February 1972) the Conservatives depend more on small and medium-sized businessmen.

Thus, while our survey failed to produce the expected information it did provide some interesting evidence that the business community does develop a consensus in the field of political activity and that this consensus is transmitted into support for the chosen candidate of an élite party[10] and is made manifest by the nomination of a Chamber-groomed candidate by that party – a person of substance and a "strong candidate" by reason of his professional or business success, public exposure, network of connections, and financial backing. In short, the perfect "available candidate."

The most striking evidence of this consensus and its political results has already been alluded to. In the federal election of 1968, 30 of the 82 respondents indicated identification with the Progressive Conservatives, including 15 who claimed party membership.[11] But in 1968 only 22 of these Conservative-leaning businessmen trooped to the polls and loyally supported that party. Eight, plus six from the ranks of the uncommitted, voted with the Liberals. The 10 defecting Conservatives included 5 party members, 2 of whom were among the rather select group of 5 who reported influencing a contribution to any party.[12] This tendency was evident in the federal election of 1963 when the Liberals out-polled the Conservatives 34 to 21 and became a stampede in the 1965 election when Robert Andras, the first president of the newly amalgamated Chamber, joined Hubert Badanai, a former president of the Fort William Chamber, on the Liberal ticket. This time the ratio was 52 to 16, and the NDP lost the seat formerly held by Douglas Fisher. With the NDP out of the way, Conservative strength picked up slightly in the election of 1968, but respondents still favoured the Liberals 54 to 22.

In the provincial arena a similar but reversed situation pertains. Here the Progressive Conservatives are the chosen party, and only 16 respondents identified with the Liberals. Of these, 5 voted Conservative, 2 contributed money personally, and 2, including one of the contributors took part in other pro-Conservative election activity.[13] Here again earlier voting trends were confirmed with the Conservatives receiving 61 of the respondents' votes to the Liberals 13, with 6 going to the NDP. Both in 1967 and 1971 voters were offered Chamber past presidents as Progressive Conservative candidates. If Dr Charles Johnston had won Port Arthur, as he came close to doing,[14] all four sitting members would have been past presidents of the Thunder Bay Chamber of Commerce or its predecessors in the pre-amalgamation cities. Since the Second World War, four of the six successful élite party provincial candidates have been past presidents of one of the chambers and the two exceptions are instructive.[15]

[10]Duverger uses the term "cadre" to describe parties which are "groupings of notabilities for the preparation of elections, conducting campaigns and maintaining contact with the candidates." Maurice Duverger, *Political Parties* (London, 1954), 64. Since "cadre" is not in common use in Canada we will use the more popular word "élite" for these parties and "the élite" to describe the "notabilities" who manage such parties.

[11]Forty indicated that they were Liberal-inclined and four NDP; 14 of the Liberals indicated party membership as did 2 for the NDP.

[12]One to the Conservatives, the balance to the Liberals.

[13]Fifty-two identified with the Conservatives, five with the NDP and nine abjured party identification.

[14]Dr Johnston received 10,092 votes; Jim Foulds of the NDP received 11,461.

[15]The exceptions are John Chapple (Liberal), the scion of an important local merchant

This candidate and voting pattern suggests a possible answer to the problem already mentioned concerning the balance theory – its failure to identify the process by which ridings swing from one party in the federal field to another in the provincial and by cumulation swing a province against the federal party in power. Perhaps the businessman is the catalyst of the swing. Our data suggest that he is in a strong position to influence the results in many ridings and we would suggest that he has many and valid reasons for voting provincially against a federal party in power.

To begin with, a businessman is in a position to influence an election by his availability as a candidate, which must say something both about his appreciation of his chances of winning, including his appreciation of the support which may be forthcoming from his fellow businessmen, and also about his concern and commitment to a party and its policies. We have already noted the tendency of Thunder Bay businessmen to vote for a prominent Chamber of Commerce member and this support for the candidate was underlined both in comments on the returns and in private. Conversely, in Thunder Bay the non-chosen élite party finds it difficult to get a prominent businessman to run, certainly not one as prominent as a former Chamber president, and in the last federal and provincial elections the federal Conservatives and the provincial Liberals were reduced to running more or less token candidates who looked as if they came from the traditional NDP stable of preachers and teachers rather than from the traditional élite party stable of lawyers and businessmen.[16]

---

family, and Ron Knight, also Liberal. Chapple was in the line of offices which would have led to a Chamber presidency when he fell out with his colleagues over the proposed amalgamation of the two cities and stepped aside (information supplied by Mr Chapple personally). Knight achieved local fame as the host of an open-line radio talk show. His discernible political convictions would have made him an ideal Social Credit candidate, but as Social Credit has never been able to offer even a token candidate in Thunder Bay he had to look elsewhere. After the élite of the Fort William Liberal Association moved heaven and earth to deny him their nomination (according to a past president of that association) he moved over to Port Arthur and managed to become the choice of the candidate-hungry Port Arthur Liberals. (One of his nominators admitted ruefully to the writer later that neither he nor his wife listened to Knight's radio show and thus did not know what they were getting their party into.) Swept along by adoring housewives for whom his program provided a platform to articulate grievances and frustrations, Knight won the seat for the Liberals. But it was not a Liberal seat for long. He quickly fell out with his party's caucus at Queen's Park and ended up sitting as an independent, or as he preferred to call it as a "free" member. He did not seek re-election. It is significant that both of these "deviants" were Liberals, the unchosen élite party provincially, both lasted only one term, and both were succeeded by CCF/NDP. In both cases it may be noted that the PCs started with candidates who lacked status in the business community. In Fort William in 1963 the candidate was C. Assef, a local billiard hall owner and school trustee who was Lebanese by origin, not a large ethnic group in the Lakehead. In Port Arthur in 1971 the PCs started with Gordon Crompton, owner of a fried chicken concession, but shortly before the election was called switched to Chamber past-president and physician Dr Charles Johnston. The palace revolution involved is known to have created dissatisfaction among rank-and-file PCs and undoubtedly aided the hard-running NDP candidate to slip in.

[16]Three were teachers and one was a mildly maverick dentist, school trustee, and Chamber member. Twenty-five per cent of the city's dentists are Chamber members. Similarly 13 per cent of the doctors and 25 per cent of the lawyers belong. However, many doctors are in clinics and many lawyers in firms both of which by the Chamber constitution only register a limited number of their personnel as members. As a result, these figures do not indicate the full measure of Chamber support from among these professions. In the 1968 federal election, the Ontario candidates of the NDP included 27 school teachers or university instructors, 9 clergymen, 9 businessmen, and 5 lawyers. In the same campaign successful Liberals in

Even when not serving as candidates businessmen are very influential by their activity. With elections becoming increasingly expensive it is obvious that the candidate who has the support of those in the community with access to large sums of money is at a real advantage. We have already noted that many businessmen indicate their political support by financial contributions. But this is not the only, or perhaps even the most significant, aspect to their political commitment. Chamber members take their citizenship responsibilities seriously. Our respondents represented almost 40 per cent of the sample polled. Of the 82, only 2 in the last federal and provincial elections respectively did not vote. When one considers the pressures of business and the normal hazards of illness and disaster, this is a remarkable turnout. Again, 37.8 per cent indicated party membership. It is just possible that our questionnaire was returned by the most politically active and informed among Chamber members and that the other 60 per cent were relatively politically quiescent. Even at that, 125 of the 844 members considered would be party members. If the returns were not biased the number could be as high as 319. Since our best information indicates that even in the height of a hard fought election the membership of all parties in the two city ridings does not exceed six thousand, the potential influence of Chamber members, aside from their influence as prominent citizens and employers, is considerable.

Moreover, their position as employers and civic leaders cannot be overlooked. At the time of writing 9 out of 13 members of the Thunder Bay city council are members of the Chamber of Commerce. Businessmen and their families are traditionally prominent in service clubs, lodges, churches, and other community organizations. Inevitably many people look to them for political guidance or feel impelled to move their way.[17] It is probably safe to assume that counting family, friends, business associates, and employees who can be influenced or pressured the average Chamber member can carry at least 10 people with him when his peers develop a policy, a political 'line," and especially when, by whatever means, the business community decides to throw its weight behind one party and/or one

Ontario numbered in their ranks 26 lawyers and 14 businessmen out of a total of 64, and successful Progressive Conservatives included 3 lawyers and 8 businessmen from 17 winners. Six teachers won for the Liberals and four lost, but the Conservatives appeared to offer teachers and housewives only to lost causes; all of them, six and two respectively, lost. The provincial pattern is much similar with the Conservative winners including 17 lawyers and 32 businessmen. Winning Liberals included 7 lawyers and 9 businessmen out of 21. Both parties elected 3 teachers. Sources: *28th General Election 1968. Report of the Chief Electoral Returning Officer* (Ottawa) and *Canadian Parliamentary Guide.* Not all members list occupations so the Ontario statistics which depend on the *Guide* are incomplete.

[17]When the writer lived in the Ottawa area he was impressed by the number of public servants who felt impelled to vote, federally and provincially, for the party in power lest a hint of deviation threaten their jobs or their promotions. This in spite of the well-established secret ballot and the equally well-established political activity of the wives of some "non-political" civil servants. We feel that it is safe to assume that at least some of the employees of a politically committed employer will feel pressed to go his way. (Some, of course, will deliberately vote against him as has been the tradition in Cardinal, Ontario, where the main employer was a prominent Conservative and the town Liberal.) Similarly, a colleague tells how during the 1930s his father habitually went through his factory on the day before election inquiring after the voting plans of his employees. After the event he carefully checked the poll returns looking for "liars." This was more possible in days gone by and in small open-shop communities than in the unionized urban centres of today, but we suspect this type of political pressure is not entirely absent even now.

candidate.[18] These 10 represent approximately one out of every eight voters in the city. When this fact is combined with the voting dedication of Chamber members, their party activity, and their economic strength, it is hardly surprising that candidates who receive their backing do so well.

Why do businessmen throw their support behind the candidate of one party and then another? One factor is doubtless the desire to be on the winner's side, and a bandwagon effect is created when one élite party or the other is seen to be the probable winner. With contracts, concessions, and a variety of other favours available to the businessman from the party in power, it would be amazing if shrewd calculating concerning probable election results was not a considerable pre-election preoccupation of many businessmen.

A second factor related to the above is the desire to keep the socialists out. Not only are the New Democrats less friendly to business than are the élite parties, but their history of always being to the left of the speaker of the House at Toronto and Ottawa makes them even less desirable as members from a business point of view. Anti-NDP sentiment appeared to be an important factor in the 1971 Ontario provincial election where, as we have noted already, the NDP ran a strong local campaign while a series of election upsets of incumbent governments in other provinces gave some credence to the NDP slogan of "Ontario next." Twenty-eight respondents indicated that anti-socialist sentiment was a factor in their voting, giving this question a score of 49 and a rank of 5. Nine specifically named the New Democrats as the party they were voting against while only one indicated voting against another party, the Progressive Conservatives. Federal voters were not asked a specifically anti-socialist question, but five named the New Democrats as the party they were voting against, as opposed to two anti-Conservative votes, and one anti-Liberal vote.

A final factor affecting businessmen's voting habits can only be speculated upon since the questionnaire was circulated during a period when neither level of government was doing, or failing to do, anything which would particularly aggravate Chamber members.[19] This factor is related to the traditional business belief in free enterprise and in the mystique that state intervention in the world of business is evil or at least unwise. There can be no doubt that governments in the pursuit

[18]

Federal election 1968:	Percentage of popular vote	Percentage of Chamber vote
Liberals	45.4	67.5
NDP	30.7	5.0
PC	23.4	27.5
Other	.5	0
Provincial election 1971:		
Liberals	16.0	16.3
NDP	38.4	7.4
PC	45.6	76.3

The closeness of the Chamber vote to the popular vote for the non-chosen élite party candidates in federal PCs and provincial Liberals is striking. It would seem to indicate that the hard core party faithfuls among Chamber members is very similar to that of the general population, while the less-committed Chamber members swing sharply one way and then the other.

[19]The time was January 1972. Provincially the Progressive Conservatives had just been returned to the great satisfaction of the business community. Federally, the government was taking a number of measures to assure business of its good will. A business delegation was met and was assured that tax reform measures would be modified to meet businesses' most serious objections; Mr Benson was the hero of the hour for his handling of the international monetary crisis as it affected Canada, and federal-provincial relations were quiet. Locally, the

of the most desirable social objectives – a fair distribution of the tax burden, reasonable income minimums, reasonable standards of education and health, an unpolluted environment, and protection of the weak and handicapped – do create problems for business. It is hardly surprising that for many businessmen their dearest wish is that government would leave them alone.

But the businessman would be the first to protest, and loudly, if the government left him alone. He needs the aid and succour of government desperately and continuously – police and tariffs to protect him, subsidies to help him, contracts to sustain him, and regulations to control his labour relations and his market. It is hardly surprising to find that the businessman is very ambivalent in his attitude to government, and especially ambivalent in his attitudes to the federal government. This would seem to be reflected in the answers to our questionnaire where respondents showed much more enthusiasm for the federal party, its leaders and its candidates, than for their provincial counterparts, but much less enthusiasm for claims that the federal party had done a good job while previously in office, was best for business, or related questions (see Tables II and III). In light of the responsibilities and taxing powers of the federal government under the British North America Act this is hardly surprising. The federal government is the big tax collector while, relatively speaking, the provinces are the big spenders.[20] Everybody loves the generous uncle, but few revere the Scrooge who accumulated the family wealth. Again, the types of taxes traditionally collected by the federal government – income and corporation taxes, succession duties, tariffs, and the federal sales tax – are all imposts to which the businessman is peculiarly sensitive, while the direct taxes traditionally levied by the provinces strike at a more oblique angle. Finally, the responsibilities of the federal government for the management of the national economy, including foreign trade, the money supply, interest rates, and the value of the dollar, are all matters of prime importance to business. Few of the areas of provincial responsibility strike the whole business community so directly and so urgently. It can come as no surprise, therefore, that in spite of the presence in the federal cabinet of such luminaries from the world of business as a C.D. Howe, a Wallace McCutcheon, a Robert Winters, or a Mitchell Sharp, it is a rare federal government indeed that is not charged with being insensitive to the needs of business. Provincial governments are less frequently so charged.

If a business community feels that the federal government is insensitive to its needs or is not acting to promote general business interest, what can it do? One answer is to vote in the federal élite opposition party at the next general election. But this has its difficulties. One is that the next federal election may be some time away, and meanwhile, irreparable damage could be done. The other is that opposition parties, once they have taken their place on the speaker's right, have

---

grain boats had been standing off in the harbour like members of a wartime convoy all season signifying an almost-record grain shipping year. Thunder Bay businessmen had little to complain about concerning either level of government.

[20]In 1962 the federal government collected $6.4 billion in taxes while the provinces collected under $3.6 billion. The provinces spent $3.4 billion against the federal government's $6.8 billion. This provincial spending power was assisted by $279 million from the federal government in transfer payments which the federal government probably had the odium of collecting while the provinces received the kudos for spending. Recent fiscal arrangements whereby the provinces are getting increasingly into income and corporation taxing, succession duties, and the like may modify business attitudes toward the two levels of government in time. Source: *1967 Canada Yearbook* (Ottawa).

TABLE II

RANKING OF THE RESPONDENTS' MOST PRESSING REASON FOR VOTING IN THE 1968 FEDERAL ELECTION

Reason	(Scores indicated in brackets)
1 This party offered the best local candidate.	(97)
2 The leader of the party of my choice would make the best Prime Minister of Canada.	(92)
3 I always vote federally for this party.	(48)
4 The party of my choice would best maintain national unity.	(34)
5 The party of my choice would best maintain Canadian independence and integrity.	(33)
6 The party of my choice had done a good job when last in office.	(31)
7 The party of my choice was best to maintain high employment and prosperity.	(26)
8 The party of my choice had the best platform.	(25)
9 The party of my choice was the most reform-minded.	(17)
10 The party of my choice was the best to deal with foreign affairs.	(15)
11 The party of my choice was the best for business.	(15)
12 The party of my choice would keep the provinces in line.	(12)
13 I voted to keep the candidate of — party from winning.	(14)
14 Other.	(6)

notorious habits of acting very much like their predecessors in office. Might it not appear much more useful to elect the federal opposition party to provincial office at the next opportunity, which could come quickly as a result of the more frequent provincial elections? In power in the province such a party is not only more effective than Her Majesty's Loyal Opposition in checking the federal government, but it also has the power and patronage of provincial office at its disposal.

This is at least one logical explanation of the voting tendencies in Thunder Bay mentioned earlier. The community is peculiarly sensitive to the sins of omission and commission, real or imagined, of the federal government, dominated as the city is by two export-oriented industries, grain and pulp and paper. When something goes wrong there will be disenchantment and even backlash against the federal party in power. The temptation to register this disapproval by voting for the opposition party provincially, or at least to support the provincial wing of the federal party in power less enthusiastically, must be very strong. The result will

TABLE III

RANKING OF THE RESPONDENTS' MOST PRESSING REASONS FOR VOTING IN THE 1971 PROVINCIAL ELECTION

Reasons	(Scores indicated in brackets)
1 The leader of the party of my choice would make the best Premier of Ontario.	(80)
2 This party offered the best local candidate.	(76)
3 The party of my choice had done a good job when last in office.	(68)
4 The party of my choice could best act to maintain higher employment and prosperity.	(50)
5 The party of my choice was best able to keep Ontario from becoming more socialist.	(49)
6 The party of my choice is best for business.	(31)
7 The party of my choice had the best platform.	(29)
8 I always vote provincially for this party.	(25)
9 I voted to keep the candidate of — party from winning.	(21)
10 The party of my choice would best defend Ontario's interests against federal encroachment.	(19)
11 The party of my choice could best act to maintain good labour relations in the province.	(13)
12 Other	(10)
13 The party of my choice would help maintain national unity.	(9)
14 The party of my choice was the most reform-minded.	(7)

either be a victory for the provincial wing of the federal opposition party, or a split in the ranks of the élite which will aid an NDP victory. In either case, it will appear as a contradiction to the federal voting pattern.

This then may be the kernel of truth behind the traditional balance theory explanation of the federal-provincial voting split. It is not that the voters in the mass decide that federal power is to be checked by provincial opposition, but that the business communiy for its own good and sufficient reasons tends to opt for this arrangement and to make it possible.

We do not suggest that our case is proven. Much more research in Thunder Bay and elsewhere will need to be done, especially in a period when party support by the business community is more fluid than at present. But we do suggest that Thunder Bay's businessman voter does indicate one reasonable explanation of the phenomenon that is worthy of further study.

Political Alignment in a Polarized City: Electoral Cleavages in Kitchener, Ontario*

CONRAD WINN *Waterloo Lutheran University*
JOHN MCMENEMY *Waterloo Lutheran University*

Urban unrest is an increasingly significant aspect of everyday life and is therefore a developing concern to policy-makers and policy-scientists alike. Historically, Canadian cities have been the site of tense and sometimes violent industrial disputes. They currently experience tamer divisions over issues like urban renewal and the location of obnoxious public and private installations. Kitchener's impassioned conflict over development of its downtown core conforms to the present Canadian pattern. Homeowners' groups, ratepayers' associations, citizens' groups, and individuals at large were mobilized as a direct or indirect result of the central debate. The conflict touched on many contentious issues, ranging from the organization of community power to the neutrality of the press and the propriety of urban renewal.

The redevelopment scheme achieved formal public acceptance at the time of the municipal election of December 1971, when public protagonists were elected or defeated and when the measure was approved by referendum. The use of common polling divisions for the municipal election and the referendum assisted the ecological analysis of the similarity of electoral cleavage on the two ballots. Kitchener's polling structures had been largely the same for the previous provincial election (October 1971) as well as for the preceding municipal elections. This continuity of polling structures facilitated the testing of hypotheses about the historical development of the electoral cleavages and their isomorphism between municipal and provincial levels.

Setting

With a population of 110,000, Kitchener is the business centre for a region of one-quarter million population, southwest of Toronto. Known as part of the Twin Cities area, the city is adjacent to the less populous and more suburban municipality of Waterloo. Together, the two cities form the core of the regional municipality of Waterloo, instituted 1 January 1973. Kitchener's citizens tend to be blue collar in social class, central European in ethnicity, and homeowners rather than tenants. Germans constitute almost one-half of the population while Britons represent one-third.[1] Smaller ethnic population groups include Poles, French-Canadians, Ukrainians, and Dutch. One-third of the population is Roman Catholic while the largest Protestant denomination is Lutheran. Kitchener has a large

*Research was made possible by a grant from Waterloo Lutheran University. Data collection was assisted by Charles Ireland (Waterloo Lutheran). Of the many civic officials who generously agreed to interviews, Aldermen Morley Rosenberg and Robert Wagner deserve our special thanks. Our colleague, Dr John Redekop, took time to critically review an earlier draft.
[1]Census tables, DBS, 1961.

Canadian Journal of Political Science/Revue canadienne de science politique, VI, no. 2 (June/juin 1973). Printed in Canada/Imprimé au Canada.

La stabilité des clivages électoraux à Kitchener, Ontario

L'élection municipale d'octobre 1971, à Kitchener, Ontario, de même que le référendum sur un projet de rénovation urbaine, qui y fut parallèlement tenu, furent l'occasion d'un conflit face auquel peu de citoyens sont restés indifférents.

Les clivages électoraux qui ressortent de ces deux conflits sont analysés quant à leur nature et leurs origines historiques, puis comparés aux clivages qu'avait fait apparaître, chez la même population, l'élection provinciale précédente. Les auteurs appliquent l'analyse factorielle et la corrélation canonique à des données écologiques provenant de trois élections municipales, d'un référendum municipal et d'une élection provinciale.

L'analyse révèle que le conflit au sujet du projet de rénovation n'a pas eu d'influence sur la structure du vote sinon celle d'accentuer l'historique polarisation droite-gauche. La religion, la situation géographique et la personnalisation des campagnes électorales se sont avérées être des facteurs secondaires de partage des voix. Chaque ensemble de facteurs de décomposition de l'électorat accuse un degré acceptable de « manque à expliquer », degré attribuable, selon les auteurs, au caractère non partisan des élections municipales. Enfin, il appert que les clivages au niveau provincial et au niveau municipal semblent substantiellement isomorphiques.

working class and a smaller middle class with the result that average weekly income has been below the urban national average.[2]

The three national parties have strong organizations in the region. The city is represented in the federal and provincial legislatures by Liberals. In the surrounding county, a New Democrat holds the federal seat while a Liberal and a Progressive Conservative hold the two provincial seats.

At the municipal level, Kitchener's administrative organization is best described as a modified council-manager system. Elections are nonpartisan, with independent candidates competing in a single, multimember constituency. At the same time, many political party activists occupy informal roles in the municipal system. Several organizers, policy advisers, and a number of aldermen have been veteran members, executives, and candidates of party associations. Conservative-minded and Liberal-minded aldermen doubt if there exists a systematic pattern of party behaviour at the municipal level. Yet the most active New Democratic-minded alderman believes that a full-fledged party system operates both in Council and during elections.[3]

The market debate

The market debate concerned the massive redevelopment of an area including the city hall, the historic farmers' market,[4] and an adjacent region in the central busi-

[2]The urban national average refers to the mean for a sample of cities selected by the Department of National Revenue in *Taxation Statistics* (Ottawa: Queen's Printer, 1970), Summary Table 1.

[3]Alderman Morley Rosenberg, interview, April 1972. For a study of party alignment in municipal legislative behaviour, see Barry J. Kay, "Voting Patterns in a Non-partisan Legislature: A Study of Toronto City Council," this JOURNAL, IV (June 1971) 224–42.

[4]The farmers' market is associated in the public mind with the old order Mennonite community of Waterloo County. For a popular account of the market prior to the development, see Edna Staebler, "Why gourmets flock to Kitchener's wonderful Mennonite Market," *Maclean's*, 4 September 1965, 15–17, 38–9.

ness district. Existing structures would be replaced by a department store, a parking garage, and a 10-storey office tower. The farmers' market would be accommodated in the parking garage, and the municipal offices in the 10-storey tower. The development plan was first publicly announced in June 1971, after it had been passed secretly by Council. Subsequently, the quasi-judicial Ontario Municipal Board[5] sponsored public hearings on the subject, and then ordered a referendum to be held. The referendum and the municipal election took place simultaneously in December 1971, both experiencing relatively high voter turnout.[6] The provincial election had been held the preceding October at the time of the Ontario Municipal Board's deliberations.

The market debate was heated and acrimonious. On the surface, there existed many points of view (see Table I). The mayor proclaimed the importance of progress; unionists proclaimed the importance of employment; conservationists proclaimed the importance of thrift. Views were expressed in an atmosphere charged with tension and emotion. One especially dramatic element of debate was the implication that financially interested businessmen influenced the project through their control of negotiations and through their control of the mass media.

Canada Trust owned 10 per cent of the developer's parent company. A vice-president and deputy chairman of Canada Trust had been chairman of Kitchener's Urban Renewal Committee, the body largely responsible for the development plan.[7] The same man was also a board member of one of the two broadcasting companies in Kitchener; both companies had participated in a news embargo on the development. At the time of the negotiations, the head of the Urban Renewal Committee as well as the chairman of the city's planning board were executives or directors of Canada Trust. Another director of that firm was the publisher of the *Kitchener-Waterloo Record*. The only daily in the Twin Cities, the *Record* had joined the broadcasting companies in a news embargo on the negotiations.

A report by the Toronto *Globe and Mail* characterized the negotiations as "wheeling and dealing ... in the private offices of the privileged and powerful and behind the closed doors of municipal government."[8] In an issue substantially devoted to politics in Kitchener, the editor of *Maclean's* magazine accused the *Record* and the broadcasting companies of abusing press obligations in a democracy.[9]

The *Record*'s publisher pleaded ignorance of Canada Trust's connections with the developers, attributing the presence of Kitchener notables in the firm to a

[5]The Ontario Municipal Board was created by the provincial government to oversee such municipal matters as debenture issues, zoning, annexation, and amalgamation. Its rulings may be appealed to the courts and the provincial cabinet. See Lionel D. Feldman, "Legislative Control of Municipalities in Ontario," *Canadian Public Administration*, IV (1961) 296–9.

[6]In the referendum, the "yes" proportion was 56.7 per cent, the "no", 43.3 per cent. Slightly more than 40 per cent of eligible voters cast ballots. In 1967 and 1969, 38 per cent and 27 per cent of the electorate voted. The low 1969 turnout is commonly attributed to the absence of a mayoral contest while the high 1967 vote is attributed to a close mayoral race. In 1971, the mayoral contest was noncompetitive, with the incumbent receiving four-fifths of the vote. The high 1971 turnout may therefore be attributed to the market crisis itself.

[7]Hugh Winsor, "A Power Elite Gets its Way in Kitchener," *Globe and Mail*, 7, 8 February, 1972.

[8]For detailed elaboration, see *ibid*.

[9]Peter C. Newman, "The View from Here," *Maclean's*, June, 1972, 3. See also Senator Keith Davey, "How the Media Withheld the Message in Kitchener," *ibid*.

TABLE I

TAXONOMY OF OPINIONS ON THE MARKET PLAN AND TYPICAL ADVOCATES

Catch-word	Opinion	Advocates
Progress	growth and development will ensue	Mayor McLennan; his leading supporters
Jobs	the market development will raise employment in the construction industry	Alderman Mitchell; some union members
Renewal	the city core including city hall and the market building is decrepit, unsafe, and unhealthy	appointed city officials
Low taxes	the enhanced corporate tax base resulting from the development will permit lower personal taxes	sundry
Conservationist	the development is inherently wasteful; structures could be refurbished instead of replaced	individuals associated with Pollution Probe
Traditionalist	beautiful old buildings have intrinsic value	architect of the old city hall; "old-timers"
High taxes	the project will increase the public debt and cause higher taxes	sundry
Classic left	the project is undemocratic, having been designed by an unrepresentative, self-interested business clique	Alderman Rosenberg

formality resulting from an earlier take over of a Waterloo-based trust company.[10] The news embargo was apparently intended to facilitate negotiations and to forestall land speculation. "Premature disclosure would have torpedoed the whole venture," asserted the *Record's* editor. "This ... is a case of putting the community welfare above the news story."[11] "The Record has been a resident of Kitchener for a long time. It has always acted in the city's best interests. It will continue to do so."[12]

Whatever the merits of the debate on the propriety or significance of the Canada Trust connection or of the communications embargo, this debate appears to have overshadowed finer discussions of ecology, tax bases, tax rates, real estate law, and other esoteric matters. Discussions of the origins and nature of the negotiations appeared to polarize the electorate on the market issue. It remains to be seen whether this municipal alignment was of the left-right type, whether it was a new or old alignment, and whether it corresponded to provincial voting. This is the subject of our inquiry.

Hypotheses

The following are the hypotheses to be tested.

Hypothesis 1: the electorate was polarized on a left-right axis related to the market debate. From the earlier review of the issue, the intent of this hypothesis may al-

[10]Winsor, "A Power Elite." [11]*Ibid.*

[12]First you need some muck," editorial, *Kitchener-Waterloo Record*, 9 February, 1972. The editorial was a response to Winsor's articles, particularly his "Viewpoint," (8 February), and to the *Globe and Mail* editorial, "The citizens' right to know," also published 8 February, 1972.

ready be clear. Those voters who identified with established élites and their procedures were pitted against those who questioned the wealth, power, and democratic values of those who made the decision. This is the classic left-right conflict and we expected this cleavage to be the dominant one. An alternate hypothesis might be that there was no single dominant cleavage but many cross-cutting cleavages.

Hypothesis 2: the left-right alignment is historical. The hypothesis assumes that the Kitchener voters have continuous class or left-right identities and, normally, weak opinions on specific issues lacking in clear class significance. They probably had no opinions or perceptions of the market issue until mobilized by the élites or counter-élites to which they held prior allegiance.[13] An alternate hypothesis might be that the market issue engendered strong, independent opinions, creating a new alignment on ecological and/or urban renewal matters.

Hypothesis 3: the market crisis heightened the left-right cleavage. Because of the great emotional turmoil during the market debate, the historic left-right polarization would be accentuated.

Hypothesis 4: the principal auxiliary cleavages are religious, geographic, and personalist. In separate research on the national electoral patterns in the 1960s, one of the authors identified three continuous electoral cleavages in voter perceptions of the federal party system. These cleavages were religious-cultural, geographic, and left-right in nature.[14] In an American overview of divisions at the urban level, James S. Coleman discerned a similar set of cleavages.[15] On the basis of the preceding findings, we expected to uncover in Kitchener auxiliary religious (Roman Catholic-Protestant), geographic, and/or personalistic cleavages.

Hypothesis 5: the total set of cleavages contains a certain level of impurity and redundancy. In their study of middle-size cities in Michigan, Oliver P. Williams and Charles R. Adrian observed that nonpartisan elections reduced class-based consensus about which candidates to support.[16] In partisan elections, candidate cues are provided by parties themselves as well as by major interest groups such as business associations and trade unions. However, in nonpartisan elections, voters – particularly in the working class – are primarily dependent on cues given by neighbourhood acquaintances. This dependence on the neighbourhood for electoral cues would be expected to increase heterogeneity in the perceptions of voters, especially when the electoral unit is a single multimember constituency, the case of Kitchener. As a result, some electoral cleavages might be expected to be redundant or impure. Two or more statistically independent left-right cleavages

[13]For a classic statement on the instability and obscurity of public opinion, see Philip E. Converse, "The Nature of Belief Systems in Mass Publics," in *Ideology and Discontent*, ed. David E. Apter, (New York, 1964).

[14]Winn, "Spatial Models of Party Systems: An Examination of the Canadian Case," doctoral dissertation, University of Pennsylvania, 1972.

[15]*Community Conflict* (Glencoe, Ill., 1957). See also Edward C. Banfield and James Q. Wilson, *City Politics* (Cambridge, Mass., 1967), especially 35–46.

[16]"The Insulation of Local Politics Under the Nonpartisan Ballot," *American Political Science Review*, LIII (Demember 1959), 1052–63.

might be manifested, as might be geographic or personalist divisions with partial left-right content.

Hypothesis 6: the provincial and municipal voting alignments are isomorphic. If the polarization is historical, we would find it expressed consistently at provincial and municipal levels of voting. Otherwise, an alternate hypothesis might be that people distinguish between the two levels of voting, and manifest different alignments. In their American study devoted to this problem, Williams and Adrian uncovered a significant level of isomorphism between municipal and state elections.[17] Despite city manager systems and the noninvolvement of state parties in municipal elections, the authors found that state party alignment anticipated alignment in each of the middle-size cities they studied. Our hypothesis suggests a similar conclusion about Kitchener.

The data

The data consist of the 1967, 1969, and 1971 aldermanic votes, the 1971 referendum ballots, and the 1971 provincial votes in 103 polling units in Kitchener. The majority of the polling units were, in fact, official polls used continuously in all four contests. Some polls were clustered into somewhat larger polling units. Because of the varying sizes of polling units, all votes were transformed to percentages.

Statistical tests

Hypothesis 1: the electorate was polarized on a left-right axis related to the market debate. There are basically three elements to this hypothesis: the presence or absence of polarization, the left-right nature of the principal cleavage, and the association of the market debate. The common factor analysis model provides adequate requirements for testing these three elements.[18] In a factor analytic test, if the principal rotated factor were to account for a substantial amount of variance, if that factor could be interpreted as a left-right cleavage, and if the referendum variable loaded highly on it, then the hypothesis would be validated.

A varimax rotation was performed on the 1971 municipal data set consisting of aldermanic, mayoral, and referendum votes.[19] The first factor is clearly the left-right axis. The highest loadings, all above 0.65, belong to leading conservatives and socialists (see Table II).[20] On one hand, George Mitchell (− 0.81) and Morley Rosenberg (− 0.74) are previous New Democratic party candidates for provincial office, Rosenberg being the leader of the antidevelopment faction as well. On the other hand, Harold Chapman (+ 0.66) and Frank Hoddle (+ 0.85) were leading initiators and proponents of the development. New Democratic Rosenberg has referred to Hoddle as "the house leader of the [de facto] Progres-

[17] *Ibid.*
[18] See R.J. Rummel, *Applied Factor Analysis* (Evanston, Ill., 1970), 104–12 and *passim.*
[19] The association matrix consisted of product moment correlations; the communality estimates were SMC's; and the rotation criterion was eigenvalue one. The actual program was BMDO3M, performed at the computer centre of the University of Waterloo.
[20] See Appendix for a list of aldermen and their party and religious affiliations.

TABLE II

ROTATED FACTORS, 1971 MUNICIPAL VARIABLES

	I	II	III	IV
Left-right factor				
Hoddle	0.85	0.05	0.11	0.09
Chapman	0.66	0.04	−0.01	−0.37
McLennan	0.52	−0.37	0.27	−0.30
Barron	0.52	−0.20	*0.44*	−0.12
"Yes" (Referendum)	0.50	−0.34	0.19	*−0.47*
Rosenberg	−0.74	0.30	−0.19	*0.42*
Mitchell	−0.81	0.33	−0.03	0.07
Religious factor				
Cardillo	0.08	−0.78	0.09	−0.09
Villemaire	0.19	−0.76	−0.07	0.00
Geographical factor				
Honsberger	−0.01	0.18	−0.85	0.23
MacIntosh	0.23	0.39	0.70	0.21
Personalist factor				
Wagner	0.15	−0.02	0.05	−0.92
Percentage total variance	33*	19	16	16
Percentage common variance	39	22	19	19

*Error due to rounding.

sive Conservative municipal government."[21] Alan Barron and Mayor Sidney McLennan are located on the right side of the cleavage, each with loadings of + 0.52. They, too, are supporters of the Progressive Conservative party.[22] Finally, in its "yes" version the referendum variable has a loading of + 0.50.

Two types of aldermen failed to correlate highly with this factor: those lacking in salient party images and Liberals. Edith MacIntosh, a candidate for the Progressive Conservative party in the provincial election in October, has long been a welfare and consumer advocate, roles not often taken by Conservative supporters. Prior to the election, she was not widely known as a Conservative and was frequently entreated by Liberal notables to seek office under their banner.[23] Russell Honsberger, a lumber entrepreneur, old-time socialist politician, and CCF candidate, has apparently mellowed with age, acquiring a reputation among Conservatives and Liberals for his "responsible" views.[24] Dominic Cardillo is the only member of Council whose party affiliation is generally unknown. His basis of support, like that of Mervyn Villemaire (Liberal), is disproportionately religious, while the basis of support for Robert Wagner (Independent Liberal) is singularly personal.[25]

[21]Interview, April 1972.
[22]In 1972 McLennan was an unsuccessful candidate for the federal Progressive Conservative nomination in Kitchener.
[23]An anonymous source in the Kitchener Liberal Association.
[24]See Table II, factor II.
[25]See Table II, factor IV. Alderman Wagner is identified as an *Independent* Liberal because his real partisan affiliation is not widely known and because, by his own admission, his partisanship is not fierce. One fellow alderman is certain that Wagner is a Conservative.

Generally, the hypothesis seems validated. The first factor accounts for a substantial amount of variance, suggesting some degree of polarization. More important, the factor can be interpreted as a left-right cleavage. The loading of the referendum variable on this factor was significant and moderately high, and the factor accounts for almost two-fifths of the common variance. The only important reservation about the full acceptance of the hypothesis might be the fact that the amount of variance explained is not monopolistic.

Hypothesis 2: the left-right alignment is historical: (A) factor comparison. One of the ways of investigating the historical nature of the electoral alignment was to compare varimax rotations for the 1971, 1969, and 1967 data sets (see Tables II, III, and IV). Had the variables been identical for all data sets, then the corresponding factors of each data set could have been compared using a coefficient of similarity. However, electoral defeats changed slightly the universe of aldermen at each election so that the similarity of factors could only be assessed in an informal way.

A glance at the left-right dimensions in the three data sets suggests that they are remarkably alike. Rosenberg and Mitchell, the two leftwing protagonists in 1971, load highly on the left-right factors in 1969 and 1967. Hoddle and Chapman, the aldermen with the highest rightwing loadings in 1971, load moderately or highly on the left-right dimensions of the other data sets.

All the other loadings on the left-right factors can be accounted for as well. Jack Young, who has a moderate, rightwing loading on the 1967 factor, has been a federal Progressive Conservative candidate and member of the Urban Renewal Committee. Robert Wagner, who has moderate-to-strong rightwing loadings in 1967 and 1969, but none in 1971, has always identified himself as part of the Kitchener establishment. In 1971, he continued to hold the same attitudes, but through his aggressive campaign style he apparently projected a forceful individual character.

Syd McLennan, an insurance agent, had a leftwing loading on the 1967 factor,[26] when his mayoral opponent was Harold Chapman, a prosperous businessman with considerably higher social standing in the community. In 1972, McLennan actually sought the federal Progressive Conservative nomination and failed. However, in the 1971 municipal election McLennan was opposed by John Ranisav, a vigorous critic of the market project, who was frequently viewed as a protégé of New Democrat Morley Rosenberg. This fact explains McLennan's rightwing loading on the 1971 left-right factor.

The preceding comments serve to show that each of the first factors of the three factor structures represent left-right cleavages. From the preceding observations, it also seems safe to conclude that the three left-right dimensions share a somewhat common structure. This common structure is historically determined in part. For example, Alderman Mitchell retained a leftwing loading in 1971 although he had become a moderate supporter of the market development. On the other hand, the left-right cleavage accommodates some changes in élite behaviour. Thus, Mayor McLennan was able to move from a leftwing position in

[26]In 1967 McLennan and Chapman were the only candidates for mayor; therefore, their loadings are similar except that the signs are opposite.

TABLE III

ROTATED FACTORS, 1969 MUNICIPAL VARIABLES*

	I	II	III	IV
Left-right factor				
MacIntosh	0.76	−0.23	0.09	0.09
Hoddle	0.57	0.42	0.25	−0.15
Mitchell	−0.74	−0.17	0.32	0.01
Rosenberg	−0.61	*−0.60*	0.13	0.16
Class-associated personalist factor				
Honsberger	−0.04	−0.75	0.32	0.03
Barron	0.01	0.84	0.06	−0.01
Religious factor				
Cardillo	0.14	0.04	−0.83	0.02
Villemaire	−0.18	0.16	−0.66	−0.42
Geographical factor				
Stoner	0.06	0.07	0.21	0.88
Wagner	0.41	0.31	0.19	−0.51
Percentage total variance:	21†	20	15	13
Percentage common variance:	30	29	22	19

*The mayoral variable is excluded since McLennan won by acclamation.
†Error due to rounding.

TABLE IV

ROTATED FACTORS, 1967 MUNICIPAL VARIABLES

	I	II	III	IV
Left-right factor				
Mitchell	−0.83	−0.18	0.06	−0.04
Rosenberg	−0.79	−0.13	−0.36	−0.21
Chapman*	0.50	−0.02	−0.30	0.16
Wagner	0.58	*0.42*	0.08	0.08
Class-associated personalist factor				
Mattson	0.11	−0.94	0.02	−0.31
Young	*0.50*	0.61	0.03	0.01
Hoddle	*0.37*	0.61	0.22	−0.26
MacIntosh	0.24	0.64	0.36	−0.11
Religious factor				
Villemaire	−0.09	−0.05	−0.89	0.08
Honsberger	−0.27	0.32	0.64	0.43
Personalist factor				
Cardillo	0.38	0.00	0.00	0.85
Percentage total variance:	26†	24	16	11
Percentage common variance	33	31	21	15

*Mayoral candidate defeated by McLennan.
†Error due to rounding.

1967 to a rightwing position in 1971 as a result of the change in the structure of mayoral alternatives available to the electorate.

(B) Canonical correlation.[27] The previous section focused on the continuity of the left-right cleavage between elections. The concern of that section was based on the assumption that it is important to study the persistence of individual electoral cleavages over time. It also seems important, however, to examine the continuity of the total set of patterns constituting electoral alignment. In practice, the historical dependence of the 1971 electoral patterns can be assessed by means of canonical correlation, which is a linear measure of consonance between two independent sets of variates.[28] Canonical correlations were therefore computed between the 1971 and 1969, and the 1971 and 1967 data sets.[29] The correlations were, respectively, 0.85 and 0.81, both statistically significant at the 0.01 level. A value of 0.85 means that 72 per cent of the variance of one set of variables is anticipated by the other set.[30]

Hypothesis 3: the market crisis heightened the left-right cleavage. The hypothesis appears validated by the increase in variance accounted for by the left-right factor in 1971 (see Tables II, III, and IV). The common variance explained by that dimension rose from 33 per cent and 30 per cent in 1967 and 1969 to over 39 per cent in 1971. The hypothesis is also supported by the decline of the auxiliary, class-associated, personalist cleavages of 1967 and 1969. Factor II (1967) opposes Joseph Mattson, a nonprogrammatic populist, to three middle or upper status Conservatives (see Table IV). Factor II (1969) opposes Conservative Barron to New Democrats Honsberger and Rosenberg (see Table III).

In 1971, by contrast neither factor II nor factor III can be easily attributed left-right content. Cluster II embodies religious cleavage. Factor III, a geographical factor, appears to arise from different regions of commercial and residential activity for the two aldermen with loadings on the factor.[31] Factor IV has a slight left-right component insofar as the referendum and Rosenberg variables exhibit modest loadings. However, the factor's main character comes from the variable with by far the strongest correlation, popular support for Robert Wagner.

In summary, in 1967 and 1969, factor I represents a classic left-right cleavage and factor II embodies personalist cleavages with possible left-right or class content. In 1971, the classic left-right cleavage increased substantially in strength whereas the category of personalist, class-associated cleavages disappeared altogether, or manifested itself as a weak factor IV, depending on one's interpretation.

[27]The assistance of Jennifer Uttley, Computer Centre, University of Waterloo, and Bill and Janet Ableson, then in the Department of Statistics, University of Waterloo, is gratefully acknowledged.

[28]See William W. Cooley and Paul R. Lohnes, *Multivariate Data Analysis* (Toronto, 1971), chap. 6, and Donald F. Morrison, *Multivariate Statistical Methods* (Toronto, 1967), chap. 6.

[29]The computer program was BMDO6M. See W.J. Dixon, *BMD-Biomedical Computer Programs* (Berkeley and Los Angeles, 1967).

[30]Of course the correlation value is dependent on the particular coefficients associated with each variable in each set. Interested readers may write the authors for a copy of the output.

[31]Honsberger's well-known family lumberyard is in the Northwest, MacIntosh's residence, in the Southeast.

Hypothesis 4: the auxiliary cleavages are religious, geographic, and personalist. Factor II (1971), factor III (1969), and factor III (1967) are all religious cleavages with Catholicism at one pole. Villemaire, who is active in the Knights of Columbus and in charitable associations on the periphery of the Roman Catholic church, loads highly on these dimensions. Cardillo, also a Catholic, exhibits high loadings on this factor in the two more recent data sets. In the 1967 data set, Russell Honsberger, a Protestant, has a high loading opposite to that of Villemaire.

One objection to the preceding religious interpretation is that Joseph Mattson, a Catholic alderman, lacks loadings on the religious factor in 1967. In the first instance, not all aldermen, Protestant or Catholic, need to display loadings on the religious factor. In the second instance, Mattson's low loading may have resulted from his particular personality and lifestyle. Mattson was a criminal lawyer who resigned from the Law Society of Upper Canada. Because he was part of the Catholic community, Catholic voters may have been more aware of and sensitive to unconventional aspects of his career.

Generally, the non-left-right and nonreligious factors appear to combine elements of personalism, geography, and class. Most of these factors can be accounted for informally in terms of the personalities, locations, class identities, and party affiliations of the aldermen. However, the relative importance of the different components is difficult to assess. For example, factor II (1967) may reflect the exceptional popularity of Mattson among sporting groups in some of the lower status regions. However, without survey data it is moot whether the operational components were Mattson's personal charm, athletic interests, class disposition, populism, or electoral organization. The same uncertainty applies to factor IV (1971). Without further information, it would be difficult to weigh accurately the relative import of Robert Wagner's forceful personality, his strong support among service clubs and in the large insurance industry in the city, and his exceptional identification with the market development.

Hypothesis 5: the total set of cleavages contains a certain level of impurity and redundancy. As the preceding paragraphs revealed, each set of factors contained some degree of impurity or redundancy. In general, the non-left-right and nonreligious factors involved some ambiguity of interpretation because they appeared to embody more than one type of social cleavage. Following Williams and Adrian, we have attributed this phenomenon of cleavage impurity to heterogeneity in voter perception resulting from the dependence of municipal electors on neighbourhood acquaintances for electoral cues.[32] However, survey information would be required to evaluate this secondary hypothesis.

Hypothesis 6: the provincial and municipal voting alignments are isomorphic. The hypothesis was evaluated in two ways. In the first place, product-moment correlations were computed between the percentage of votes for each of the three

[32]"The Insulation of Local Politics."

provincial candidates – Breithaupt, MacIntosh, and Mitchell – and each of the successful municipal candidates in 1971.[33] There were no substantial correlations between support for the winning candidate, Breithaupt, and support for any of the municipal officials. However, there were substantial correlations between support for MacIntosh in her two elections, and support for Mitchell in his. The value for MacIntosh was + 0.47, for Mitchell, + 0.44, both statistically significant at the 0.01 level. These correlations cannot be attributed with certainty to isomorphism between provincial and municipal voting since MacIntosh and Mitchell, who experienced correlations, were each municipal and provincial candidates whereas Breithaupt contested only the provincial election. On the other hand, the failure of Breithaupt's provincial vote to correlate with any of the municipal votes could be attributed to the relative absence of Liberal aldermen, to the overwhelming extent of Breithaupt's victory, or to the possibility that Liberal electoral support is uniquely diffuse and mobile.

A canonical correlation was also computed between the 1971 municipal and provincial data sets. The achieved value was 0.84, which suggests that 71 per cent of the variance in one set of variables is anticipated by the other set. Like the preceding findings, this finding implies some degree of isomorphism between the two levels of voting.

Conclusion

Using Kitchener's market crisis as its point of departure, our study investigated the structure of electoral cleavages in that city, their historical development, and their similarity at municipal and provincial levels of voting. For each municipal election, the factor analysis of poll data revealed four cleavages. Two divisions were continuous and important: a left-right cleavage and a religious cleavage. The religious division isolated the Catholic population. The left-right cleavage was associated with and accentuated by the market controversy. It divided Conservatives from New Democrats, and supporters of the development plan from opponents. Not all cleavages delineated by the factor analysis were found to be pure. We attributed the impurity of cleavages in nonpartisan elections to the dependence of voters on neighbourhood acquaintances for electoral cues, and to the resulting heterogeneity of voter perceptions. Finally, the study demonstrated a certain level of similarity between provincial and local patterns of voting.

To the extent that our theoretical objectives coincided with those of Williams and Adrian, our findings were congruous with theirs. Both studies discerned a certain level of isomorphism between the two levels of voting. Both studies found that as local contests became more competitive and issues more salient, the structure of local cleavages became more clearly defined. The congruity between the two studies adds weight to the significance of replication in research; it also suggests the importance of further replication and elaboration in urban electoral investigation. Wherever possible, further research should, however, use survey rather than ecological data. Like many of our predecessors, we found that eco-

[33]The provincial results were Breithaupt, Liberal (42.2 per cent), MacIntosh, Progressive Conservative (29.8 per cent), Mitchell, NDP (27.0 per cent).

logical analysis involved uncertainties and ambiguities of interpretation that are sometimes absent from survey analysis.

Appendix: mayor and aldermen, their party affiliation, religion, role in market debate, 1971

Name	*Party Affiliation*	*Religion*	*Market Plan*
McLennan	Progressive Conservative	Protestant	Actively Pro
Barron	Progressive Conservative	Protestant	Passively Pro
Cardillo	Independent	Roman Catholic	Passively Pro
Chapman	Progressive Conservative	Protestant	Actively Pro
Hoddle	Progressive Conservative	Protestant	Actively Pro
Honsberger	New Democrat	Protestant	Passively Pro
MacIntosh	Progressive Conservative	Protestant	Passively Pro
Mitchell	New Democrat	Protestant	Passively Pro
Rosenberg	New Democrat	Jewish	Actively Anti
Villemaire	Liberal	Roman Catholic	Actively Pro
Wagner	Independent Liberal	Protestant	Actively Pro

Forms of Local Government in the Montreal Area, 1911-71: A Discriminant Approach*

BRYAN H. MASSAM *McGill University*

This essay is a development of an earlier paper by John Mercer[1] in which an evaluation of the relationship between a set of socio-economic variables and the form of local government for approximately 80 municipalities in the Montreal area was undertaken. The author used data for 1961 to test a series of hypotheses developed from the ethos theory of E.C. Banfield and J.Q. Wilson,[2] which states that the form of local government is directly related to the ethos that is valued by a community, and that this ethos is directly related to the socio-economic status (SES) variables that characterize the community. More specifically the higher SES municipalities adopt city-manager government, whereas those with lower status use the traditional mayor-council structure. Further hypotheses after the work of J.H. Kessel[3] and L.F. Schnore and R.R. Alford[4] regarding the size of municipalities were tested. Also, suggested relationships concerning the rate of growth, the percentage of foreign born, and the form of local government after Kessel[5] and E.L. Sherbenou[6] were examined.

The results of the analysis were encouraging though, as Mercer points out, the use of 1961 socio-economic data to describe a municipality in which the decision may have occurred some 40 years earlier can lead to spurious conclusions. In an attempt to add the time-dimension to the problem, the work presented here will examine the relationship between the form of local government and a set of variables that describe the size and the social and economic attributes of each municipality for the following years: 1911, 1921, 1931, 1941, 1951, 1961, 1966, and 1971. At each point in time a set of municipalities will be defined such that the members of the set have the alternative of a manager-style of government open to them. It should be noted that only cities and towns have the option; villages and rural municipalities have therefore been excluded from the analysis.

Further comments on the city-manager plan in the Canadian context are pro-

*This research was funded by a grant from the Social Sciences Division, McGill University and the Canada Council. The author wishes to acknowledge the help of his research assistant, Diana Bouchard, in this study, also the work of Ruth Hood and Max Barlow, graduate students in the Department of Geography.

1"The Structure of Local Government in the Montreal Area," University of Chicago (mimeo, undated).

2*City Politics* (Cambridge, Mass., 1963).

3"Government Structure and Political Environment," *American Political Science Review*, 56 (1962), 615–20.

4"Forms of Government and Socio-economic Characteristics of Suburbs," *Administrative Science Quarterly*, 8 (1963), 1–17.

5"Government Structure."

6"Class, Participation and the Council Manager Plan," *Public Administrative Review*, 21 (1961), 131–5.

Canadian Journal of Political Science/Revue canadienne de science politique, VI, no. 2 (June/juin 1973). Printed in Canada/Imprimé au Canada.

vided by D.A. Young,[7] T.J. Plunkett,[8] and O. Nicholson.[9] The latter deals specifically with the growth of the plan in Quebec, and the author suggests that those communities that have opted for this system are those that have grown rapidly since 1945 and are the homes of executive and professional classes. The latter of these claims will be evaluated in the present study. However, it is within the context of the USA that this manager form of government has been examined most extensively. B.W. Hawkins[10] has drawn attention to the environmental base of urban government forms and has summarized much of the work that was undertaken by political scientists in the 1960s.

A variation on the socio-economic theme, which explains the adoption of the city-manager plan, has been posited by Sherbenou.[11] He suggests that diffusion of the plan among municipalities is characterized by a distance-decay function from the original adopting municipality. This distance-decay relationship can be tested for Montreal by examining the contiguity patterns of municipalities. The municipalities that adopted the plan have been noted and a check has been made to determine whether boundaries were shared with a previously adopting municipality. In the Montreal metropolitan census area, 60 per cent of the adopting muncipalities were contiguous to previously adopting municipalities at the time of adoption. The distance-decay function diffusion hypothesis seems plausible. In this regard as well some note should be made of the fact that Quebec is unique in Canada for having the first municipalities to adopt the city-manager plan, for the number of adopting municipalities (55 of the 84 in Canada in 1970), and for the fact that almost half of these municipalities are towns rather than cities (as is more usual in the other provinces). The amount of clustering is also notable: 26 of the 55 adopting municipalities are in the Montreal metropolitan census area, 6 (of 7 possible ones) are in Saguenay county, and all 3 municipalities in St Maurice county have city managers.[12] While we must allow for the status of Montreal, such a concentration of city managers in a province of lower than average socio-economic status seems also to support the hypothesis that diffusion proceeds by contiguity.[13]

The Montreal study: 1911–71

The major aim of this paper is to present an analysis of variables for the municipalities, for the period 1911–71, in an attempt to search for statistically significant relationships between attributes of each municipality and its form of local government. The years chosen coincide with census years, as census data from Statistics Canada were used in this study.

The specific problem treated here falls within the general class of discrimination-type problems; that is, given a set of attributes for a group of objects and an a priori classification of the objects the problem is to search for the function that

7 "Canadian Local Government Development: Some Aspects of the Commissioner and City Manager Forms of Administration," *Canadian Public Administration*, IX (1966), 55–68.
8 *Urban Canada and its Government* (Toronto, 1969).
9 "The C.M. Plan and How it Grew," *Public Management* (Oct. 1970), 10–11.
10 *Politics and Urban Policies* (New York, 1971).
11 "Class, Participation."
12 *Canadian Almanac*, 1970.
13 As evidenced by per capita income. See P.E. Lloyd and P. Dicken, *Location in Space: A Theoretical Approach to Economic Geography* (London, 1972), 207–9.

Les types de gouvernements locaux dans la région de Montréal

Plusieurs articles portant sur les gouvernements locaux suggèrent que les structures de ces gouvernements reflètent « l'éthos » des municipalités, tel qu'engendré par les caractéristiques socio-économiques de leurs populations. La présente étude tente de vérifier ces énoncées eu égard aux municipalités de la région de Montreal pour les années allant de 1911 à 1971. Certaines données socio-économiques permettent de classifier ces municipalités selon deux types de communautés : celles dont la gouverne repose essentiellement sur une gérance municipale et celles dont ce n'est pas le cas. La méthode de « l'analyse discriminatoire » (discriminant analysis) permet d'établir des distinctions très précises entre les deux types de gouvernements municipaux et une étroite corrélation entre les variables socio-économiques et les formes de gouvernements. Cependant, les équations combinatoires d'attributs socio-économiques varient trop dans le temps pour qu'il soit possible d'établir une équation unique qui puisse servir de modèle général pour toute la période étudiée.

C'est pour la période allant de 1931 à 1961 que les fonctions discriminatoires trouvent leur meilleure application, les données pour 1966 et 1971 ne s'avérant pas significatives. De plus, l'auteur tente, sans grand résultat, d'établir une relation discriminatoire entre, d'une part, des projections, pour 1966, des données socio-économiques de 1961, et d'autre part les types de gouvernements tels qu'ils étaient en 1966.

Enfin, une analyse de la diffusion géographique du type de gouvernement à gérance municipale pour la région métropolitaine de Montréal entre 1911 et 1971 a démontré que 60 pour cent des municipalités qui avaient adopté ce type étaient adjacentes, au moment de l'adoption, à au moins une municipalité qui le pratiquait déjà.

describes the way in which the attributes are combined together to predict the given classification. For the problem tackled in this paper the attributes refer to a set of socio-economic and size variables for each municipality; the objects refer to the municipalities; and the classification system provides two groups. The first group is the set of city-manager municipalities, and the second group is the set of mayor-council municipalities.

Symbolically we can write a linear discriminant function LDF (variables are combined in a linear sequence) as follows: $Y = a_i x_i + a_2 x_2 + ... + a_n x_n$. In this case we have n variables; the weighting of each variable is given by the coefficients a_i to a_n. This LDF is calculated in such a way as to minimize the error of misclassifying municipalities into the two a priori groups. Essentially an attempt is made to look for the discriminatory power of a set of variables that describe the social and economic status of each municipality. By determining LDF's for different time periods, it is hoped that we can reveal the relative importance of attributes over time. This point will be developed towards the end of the paper when a lag effect will be examined. Because of data restrictions, the variables do not coincide with the years of adoption of the manager plan. This is demonstrated in Table I; for example, census data for 1951 are used to choose 9 municipalities from the set of 32. The step-wise method of analysis of W.J. Dixon[14] was used in this paper.[15] More specific references on the use of discriminant analysis are provided by L.J. King.[16]

[14] *Computer Programs Manual* (Los Angeles, 1964).

[15] A similar problem using this method is treated by T.J. Bell, "A Test of the Adoptive Hypothesis of Spatial Economic Pattern Development," *Proceedings* of the Association of American Geographers, 2 (1970), 8–12.

[16] "Discriminant Analysis: A Review of Recent Theoretical Contributions and Applications," *Economic Geography*, 46, no. 2 (1970), 367–78.

TABLE I

ORDER OF ENTRY OF VARIABLES – STEP-WISE DISCRIMINATION

1911		1921		1931	
Basic	Per Capita	Basic	Per Capita	Basic	Per Capita
1 population	1 population	1 TRE	1 liabilities p/c	1 payments	1 British origin
	2 TRE per capita (p/c)	2 Can. born*	2 assets p/c	2 value of new factories*	2 TRE per capita*
		3 liabilities*	3 payments p/c	3 TRE**	3 payments p/c**
		4 assets*	4 Can. born*	4 other origin**	4 assets p/c**
not included		5 total payments**		5 assets**	5 liabilities p/c**
taxable real estate (TRE)				6 population**	6 other origin**
				7 French origin**	7 value of new factories**
		not included	*not included*	8 liabilities**	8 value of new houses**
		population	population	9 British origin**	9 no. of new factories**
			TRE p/c	10 value of new houses**	10 no. of new houses**
				11 no. of new houses**	11 population**
				12 no. of new factories**	
				13 tax rate per $100**	*not included*
					tax rate per $100
					French origin

Significance level of function: * 5 per cent, ** 1 per cent.

TABLE I (*Continued*)

ORDER OF ENTRY OF VARIABLES — STEP-WISE DISCRIMINATION

1941		1951		1961	
Basic	Per Capita	Basic	Per Capita	Basic	Per Capita
1 no. of new factories	1 no. of new factories	1 median rent	1 liabilities p/c	1 income $6000+	1 expenditure p/c
2 French origin	2 French origin	2 tax per $100	2 TRE p/c	2 revenue*	2 TRE p/c
3 population*	3 population*	3 British origin	3 English only*	3 man/prof/tech.*	3 English only
4 value of new houses**	4 value of new houses**	4 males – income $4000+*	4 males – income $1000–**	4 English only**	4 income $6000+**
5 assets**	5 other new construction – number**	5 revenues*	5 nonschool pop.**	5 TRE**	5 French only**
6 value of new factories**	6 value of new factories**	6 occupation males-prof.**	6 occupation – males-labour**	6 expenditure**	6 elem. education**
7 value of other new construction**	7 value of other new construction**	7 liabilities**	7 other origin**	7 univ. education**	7 man/prof/tech.**
8 no. of new houses**	8 British origin**	8 median earnings**	8 British origin**	8 crafts/lab/prac.**	8 univ. education**
9 British origin**	9 other origin**	9 French only**	9 education – 13+years**	9 French only**	9 debt. p/c**
10 other origin**	10 assets p/c**	10 nonschool pop.**	10 assets p/c**	10 Foreign born**	10 crafts/lab/prac.**
11 liabilities**	11 expenditures p/c**	11 occupation – males – labour**	11 median rent**	11 income $3000–**	11 foreign born**
12 other new construction**	12 revenues p/c**	12 education – 13+years**	12 tax per $100**		12 revenue p/c**
13 tax per $100**	13 no. of new houses**		13 occupation – males-prof.**		
	14 liabilities**		14 revenues p/c**		
	15 TRE p/c**		15 expenditures p/c**		
not included	*not included*	*not included*	*not included*	*not included*	*not included*
revenues	tax per $100	population	population	population	population
taxable real estate		English only	French only	elem. education	income $3000–
expenditures		males – income $1000–	Males – income $4000+		
		education 1–4 yrs.	median earnings		
		French origin	1–4 yrs. education		
		other origin	French origin		
		taxable real estate			
		assets			
		expenditures			

Significance level of function: * 5 per cent, ** 1 per cent.

TABLE I (*Continued*)

1966		1967	
Basic	Per Capita	Basic	Per Capita
1 debt	1 TRE p/c	1 tax per $100	1 contrib. & subr.
2 assets	2 revenues p/c	2 contrib. & subr.	2 p.t. revenue
3 revenues	3 debt p/c	3 p.t. revenue	3 population
4 TRE	4 assets p/c	4 population	4 expenditure p/c
5 population	5 expenditures p/c	5 TRE	5 other tax revenue
	6 population	6 expenditures	6 TRE p/c
		7 debt payments	7 revenues p/c
not included			8 debt payments p/c
expenditures			9 tax per $100
		not included	
		revenues	
		other tax revenue	

Significance level of function = * 5 per cent, ** 1 per cent.

The variables that were used to describe the municipalities are shown on Table I, and it will be noted that the same sets were not available for all years. However, in order to allow some comparisons to be made between years, two groups of variables have been used throughout. The first incorporates the ones labelled *basic* on Table I, and includes variables that refer to the socio-economic status and the level of financial prosperity of the municipality. The second group adds fiscal variables that have been standardized to remove the influence of the varying size of the municipalities. This table also shows the order of entry of variables into the discriminant function; those that were not included in the function are also listed. Significant levels are attached to the variables. On Table II the discriminant functions are given for all years except 1911, 1966, and 1971. Data for 1911 did not yield a function because of the small number of city-manager municipalities. With respect to 1966 and 1971, the implication is that the values for the variables at these times are inappropriate to classify municipalities into groups when the grouping process in fact has been going on since 1913, when the first city-manager municipality was created. For each year attempts have been made to derive two functions, the first using the basic data and the second using basic and the standardized per capita financial data. The per capita data for 1921 did not yield a significant function.

In general, the levels of discrimination are high. There are two misclassifications in 1921 and 1951, perfect discrimination in 1931 and 1941, but in 1961 there are six misclassifications. Also, whereas only two variables were needed in the 1921 function, the number increased to six in 1941 and to nine in 1951, though only five were needed using per capita data for this year. Five variables were also needed to produce the functions in 1961. As noted above functions could not be derived for 1966 or 1971. The misclassifications are shown in Table III.

Between 1921 and 1961 there were eleven misclassifications out of a total number of 201. Thus we can conclude that the discriminant functions appear to have captured the major socio-economic and financial variables that correlate with the form of local government. A caveat should be added at this point: we are unable to show cause by the relationships, only that certain types of municipalities, as defined by sets of variables used in this work, allow us to distinguish between types of municipal government. However, when we look more closely at the order of entry on Table I it is difficult to determine consistencies from one time period to another or in the sets of variables that have higher values for city-manager or for mayor-council municipalities. This is complicated because variables used at different times were not precisely the same. Examination of the standard deviations of variables for the mayor-council group reveals that they are generally higher than for the city-manager group. This suggests that the city-manager group is more homogeneous.

We should also draw attention to the fact that the power of this analysis in the early years is limited by the relatively small number in the city-manager group. Also the tests applied so far have not explicitly examined the time-lag factor. From the literature cited earlier, it is suggested that the larger the municipality, the higher the socio-economic status, the faster the rate of growth, and, generally, the more prosperous the municipality, the greater the probability of adoption of the manager plan. However, the order in which all of these events may occur is

TABLE II

DISCRIMINANT FUNCTIONS

1921 *Basic data*

$Y = -0.52782X_1 + 0.00038X_2$

where X_1 = taxable real estate 10^{-4}

X_2 = Canadian born 10^{-4}

Per capita data

function not significant

1931 *Basic data*

$Y = 0.00003X_1 - 0.00002X_2 + 0.01165X_3$

where X_1 = payments 10^{-4}

X_2 = Value of new factories 10^{-4}

X_3 = Taxable real estate 10^{-4}

Per capita data

$Y = 2.05549X_1 + 0.00001X_2 + 0.00027X_3$

where X_1 = British origin 10^{-6}

X_2 = TRE per capita 10^{-6}

X_3 = payments per capita 10^{-6}

1941 *Basic data*

$Y = 0.27009X_1 + 0.06013X_2 + 1.10338X_3 + 0.84967X_4 - 0.00017X_5 - 0.95706X_6$

where X_1 = population 10^{-4}

X_2 = assets 10^{-6}

X_3 = value of new houses 10^{-6}

X_4 = number of new factories

X_5 = value of new factories 10^{-6}

X_6 = French origin

Per capita data

$Y = 0.42786X_1 + 0.87849X_2 + 0.01073X_3 - 0.56285X_4 + 0.00479X_5 - 0.95329X_6$

where X_1 = population 10^{-4}

X_2 = value of new houses 10^{-6}

X_3 = number of new factories

X_4 = value of new factories 10^{-6}

X_5 = other new construction – number

X_6 = French origin 10^{-4}

1951 *Basic data*

$$Y = -0.00680X_1 - 0.00413X_2 - 3.68990X_3 + 1.39523X_4 + 12.85655X_5 + 0.51105X_6 - 0.11105X_7 + 0.03304X_8 - 0.41270X_9$$

where X_1 = French only 10^{-4}

X_2 = median rent

X_3 = males-income over \$4000 10^{-4}

X_4 = median earnings 10^{-4}

X_5 = occupation-males-professional $\times 10^{-4}$

X_6 = British origin 10^{-4}

X_7 = tax (regular + special) per \$100

X_8 = liabilities 10^{-6}

X_9 = revenues 10^{-6}

Per capita data

$Y = -0.01623X_1 - 0.00022X_2 + 2.73523X_3 - 0.00921X_4 + 0.01414X_5 + 0.21378X_6$

where X_1 = English only 10^{-4}

X_2 = median rent

X_3 = occupation-males-professional 10^{-4}

X_4 = taxable real estate per capita 10^{-6}

X_5 = liabilities per capita 10^{-6}

X_6 = revenues per capita 10^{-6}

TABLE II *(Continued)*

1961	*Basic data* $Y = 0.05169X_1 + 0.39424X_2 + 0.52617X_3 - 0.00001X_4 - 0.00021X_5$ where X_1 = official language French only X_2 = income \$6000 + X_3 = occupation-management/professional/technical X_4 = revenue X_5 = expenditure
	Per capita data $Y = -0.03685X_1 + 0.02732X_2 + 0.42221X_3 - 0.00001X_4 + 0.00037X_5$ where X_1 = English only X_2 = French only X_3 = Income \$6000+ X_4 = Taxable estate per capita X_5 = Expenditure per capita

not clear; nor are the differences in time between them clear. In an attempt to examine a specific time-lag element we have used data for 1961 to explain the groupings that existed in 1966. Using these data, it was not possible to derive a significant discriminant function. As there were only two additions to the manager-group between 1966 and 1971, Laval and Dollard des Ormeaux, it was decided not to run the analysis of 1961 data against 1971 groupings. This preliminary test of a time-lag gave disappointing results, and we suggest that change indicators used as variables may produce better results, as they would be more in line with the hypotheses stated above concerning rates of growth.

Experimental removal of the City of Montreal from the 1951 data set noticeably improved results. The city dominates the 32 municipalities included at this time with very large values for the majority of variables. Financial variables per se were of very little importance in discriminating between manager and council municipalities in this analysis; for example, six socio-economic variables gave perfect discrimination. The variables were French-only speakers, males'-income more than \$4000, value of median earnings, 1–4 years education, amount of nonschool education, and numbers in professional occupation group. The discriminant function is shown below. It is significant at the 1 per cent level.

$$Y = -0.79293X_1 + 2.83157X_2 + 0.74495X_3 - 2.73129X_4 + 0.61638X_5 + 1.46387X_6$$

X_1 = French only
X_2 = income \$4000+
X_3 = median earnings
X_4 = 1–4 years education
X_5 = non-school population
X_6 = males – professional occupation

A similar approach was used for the 1961 data set, which had increased by 34 municipalities over the 1951 set. The removal of the City of Montreal allowed a discriminant function to be calculated which, though significant at the 1 per cent level, fails to classify correctly the following municipalities: Montreal West, Roxboro, Cote St Luc, Laval sur le lac, Longueuil, Hampstead, Anjou, and Chateau-

TABLE III

MISCLASSIFICATIONS OF MUNICIPALITIES

			CM	MAYOR
1911	insufficient	data		
1921	basic data	Outremont		x
		Montreal East	x	
	PC data	function not significant		
1931	basic data			
	PC data			
1941	basic data			
	PC data			
1951	basic data	Longueuil		x
		Pointe Claire	x	
	PC data	Longueuil		x
		Pointe Claire	x	
1961	basic data	Hampstead		x
		Anjou		x
		Chateauguay Centre		x
		Montreal West	x	
		Laval Sur le Lac	x	
		Cote St Luc	x	
	PC data	Hampstead		x
		Chateauguay Centre		x
		Longueuil		x
		Cote St Luc	x	
		Montreal West	x	
		Lasalle	x	

guay Centre. This list is very similar to the one provided by the discriminant function that was derived from the complete basic data set, shown on Table III. However, whereas the latter discriminant function incorporated revenue and expenditures, the revised function, which did not use data for the City of Montreal, excluded these variables. The revised function is shown below.

$$Y = +0.04160X_1 + 0.42125X_2 + 0.05555X_3 + 0.39236X_4 - 0.00111X_5$$

X_1 = official language French only
X_2 = income \$6000+
X_3 = university education
X_4 = males – management, professional, technical occupation
X_5 = value taxable real estate.

Conclusions

The primary conclusion is that socio-economic variables can be used with a fairly large degree of success to classify municipalities into city-manager or mayor-council types. The direction of the relationship is harder to distinguish, though in the first period until 1931 the value of taxable real estate appears to have a direct correlation with the city-manager group and in 1931 British origin shows a strong link. However, in this same year the basic data function suggests a negative relationship between the value of new factories and the city-manager plan. The direction of this link appears to remain the same using 1941 data. In the second period, 1941 and 1951, discrimination is of a high order, though almost twice as many variables are needed in each function. In 1941 the size of the municipality as measured by the population appears to be a significant variable, together with general prosperity as measured by assets, value of new houses, and the number of new constructions; all correlate with the city-manager form of local government. By 1951 the ethnic character, which was hardly noticeable in 1941, is beginning to be of some significance. British origin, together with high median earnings, high tax per $100, and large liabilities typify the city-manager municipality. The variables English only (language spoken) and French only show weak links to the mayor-council municipality form. By 1961 the language spoken in a municipality and the income allow fairly good discrimination, revenues and expenditures are of less importance, though they are incorporated into statistically significant discriminant functions. During the last period, that is since 1966, the use of socio-economic or size variables provided little help in explaining the form of local government, and it is in this period that the classification system breaks down. The implication is clear. The forms of local government currently used reflect a melange of factors of varying importance over time. In the early days of the city-manager plan it was the more prosperous municipalities that opted for it, later the larger, faster-growing municipalities. Superimposed upon this sequence is the spatial contiguity notion, that the explanation of the diffusion pattern can be partially explained by a neighbourhood effect, though this introduces the element of autocorrelation into the explanation. Further work could be undertaken to isolate the specific influence of location of a municipality while holding constant its other attributes.

The lagged analysis was disappointing, though intuitively and experientially the author feels that this is an important element in the process. For example, we might pose the question: to what extent is there a relationship between the fact that Pointe Claire appointed a city-manager in 1955 and shortly afterwards there was a rapid growth in industrialization in the area?

In this study no attempt was made to define or evaluate the efficiency of municipal government. Traditionally the view was held that the mayor-council structure lacked the expertise to handle complex organizational and technical problems. However, the validity of this claim should be examined in precise terms now that consulting agencies can be called in on an ad hoc basis to solve local servicing problems. Also the large municipalities are not infrequently served by experienced civil service personnel. Thus we might suggest that it is the intermediate-sized, prosperous municipality that can afford the relative luxury of a fulltime manager.

Finally, though it has been argued that socio-economic and size attributes of a municipality can be used for constructing discriminant functions of municipalities into two groups, we have no real understanding of the decision-making process. We are unable to answer questions about the power of various groups in a community, the influence of the incumbents, and the role of governments outside the locality. The perception of the relative merits of alternate forms of local government also remains untouched. It is in these fields that much remains to be done that will help us to understand thoroughly the reasons for the diffusion of forms of local government over space and time.

Analyse stratégique du choix d'un candidat dans une circonscription urbaine*

JEAN CRÈTE *University of Oxford*

La sélection, par les partis politiques, des candidats à une élection dans une circonscription électorale a attiré bien peu l'attention des politicologues tant au Québec qu'au Canada[1]. Pourtant, dans plusieurs circonscriptions, c'est souvent la seule sélection importante ; l'élection proprement dite n'étant que la ratification du choix fait par le parti[2]. Si les chercheurs se sont peu préoccupés de ce phénomène, c'est peut-être que, comme en Grande-Bretagne et contrairement aux Etats- Unis, on considère que le processus de sélection des candidats par les partis est du domaine privé[3].

Quant à nous, par une étude de cas[4], nous voulons contribuer à l'analyse, encore à venir, de la sélection des représentants de la population. Pour ce faire, nous emprunterons à l'analyse stratégique, elle-même dérivée de la théorie des jeux, quelques concepts. Dans le cadre d'une partie – elle-même extraite d'un Grand Jeu – des agents, dans la poursuite des objectifs d'une organisation, interagissent. Il arrive parfois que les règles du jeu ne prévoient pas exactement les actions qui doivent être posées par les agents. Il y a des zones d'incertitude. Si les agents entrent alors en conflit à propos de l'action à suivre, il y a point clef. Autour d'un point clef s'organise un jeu particulier qui peut mener à plusieurs résultats. Les agents ont des préférences envers ces résultats et ils tentent, grâce à leurs ressources, d'imposer leurs préférences aux autres. Afin de ne rien laisser au hasard, ces agents rationnels établissent des stratégies qui guideront leurs actions.

*Cet article est tiré de ma thèse de maîtrise « Choix d'un candidat dans une circonscription urbaine », Université Laval, 1971. Les données ont été recueillies en collaboration avec Jean Daoust que je remercie. Mes remerciements vont aussi à messieurs M. Gilbert, V. Lemieux, F. Renaud ainsi qu'aux lecteurs de la Revue dont les commentaires furent utiles dans la redaction finale de ce texte.

[1]Pour le Québec, on peut noter l'étude de Brigitte Dodier, Marc Pigeon et François Renaud, « Les conventions dans la région de Québec à l'élection fédérale de 1968 », dans *Recherches Sociographiques*, x, no. 1 (janvier–avril, 1969), 83–93. Pour le Canada, voir H.A. Scarrow, « Three Dimensions of a Local Political Party », *Papers on the 1962 Election*, éd. John Meisel (Toronto, 1965), 53–68 ; et J. M. Beck, « The Nomination of Candidates in Nova Scotia », *Dalhousie Review*, 36, no. 4 (1957), 361–8.

[2]En effet, au Québec, aux élections provinciales de 1956 à 1966, le Parti Libéral a pu compter sur 13 circonscriptions sûres et l'Union Nationale sur 21. Chiffres tirés de Vincent Lemieux, *Quatre élections provinciales au Québec* (Québec, 1969), 201–2. Aux élections fédérales, le Parti Libéral peut compter sur 15 circonscriptions sûres, les Progressistes Conservateurs sur 2, et le Ralliement des Créditistes sur 6 ; voir A. Blais, H. Cantin et J. Crête, « Les élections comme phénomène de décision collective : les élections fédérales de 1957 à 1965 au Québec », cette REVUE III, no. 4, (déc. 1970), 528.

[3]A ce sujet, voir entre autres Leon D. Epstein, *Political Parties in Western Democracies* (New-York, 1967), chap. 8.

[4]Les données que nous utilisons ici ont été recueillies par observation-participante, par des entrevues, et par l'étude des documents publiés par les diverses organisations des candidats en présence.

Canadian Journal of Political Science/Revue canadienne de science politique, VI, no. 2 (June/juin 1973). Printed in Canada/Imprimé au Canada.

Strategic analysis of candidate choice in an urban constituency

Strategic analysis is used in this article to report on a case study of candidate choice in an urban constituency. Several concepts are presented first. During a game, several agents, pursuing the objectives of a partisan organization, interact. It sometimes happens that the rules of the game do not anticipate completely the actions that ought to be advanced by the agents. There exists then a zone of uncertainty. If the agents come into conflict over the action to be taken there is a "crisis point." Around a "crisis point" there occurs a particular play that can lead to several results. The agents have preferences regarding the results and they try, with the help of their resources, to impose their preferences on others. In order to leave nothing to chance, these rational agents establish strategies that guide their actions.

The game described in this article has at stake the choice of a candidate for legislative elections. The agents are activists (or groups of activists) of the partisan constituency association. At the outset of the study there is one aspirant to the candidature; certain activists, for diverse reasons, reject the aspirant as candidate. They form a coalition and present another candidate. The two aspirants and their organizations campaign among members of the association who will decide the choice of candidate. In the course of the campaign several "crisis points" emerge: the two rival organizations oppose each other.

Conclusions were drawn about the utility of case studies when they are made within a certain theoretical framework such as strategic analysis.

Avant de procéder à la description de cette partie, qui a pour enjeu le choix d'un candidat dans une circonscription urbaine, nous définissons plus précisément les quelques concepts empruntés à l'analyse stratégique.

I. Le cadre d'analyse

On dit de la théorie des jeux que c'est une théorie de l'agent social. Elle adopte le point de vue de l'agent plutôt que celui de l'observateur. Cet agent, qu'on qualifie de social, est en interaction avec d'autres agents.

LES OBJECTIFS

Ces agents ou individus sont membres d'une organisation qui poursuit des objectifs. Dans le cas qui nous occupe, ce sont des objectifs propres aux organisations partisanes. Vincent Lemieux[5], à la suite de Frank J. Sorauf[6], les regroupe en trois types : électoraux (acquisition des postes d'autorité par des élections), gouvernementaux (mesures politiques appliquées à l'environnement), organisationnels (maintien et renforcement de l'organisation partisane elle-même). Pour atteindre ces objectifs, parfois conflictuels, ces individus ou ensembles d'individus agissent dans un cadre qui est défini par des règles.

LES RÈGLES DU JEU

Un anthropologue, F.G. Bailey, qualifie ces règles de normatives lorsqu'elles expriment des valeurs socialement acceptées, et de pragmatiques lorsqu'il s'agit des règles du savoir faire ou « comment utiliser habilement ses ressources ».

[5] *L'analyse des organisations partisanes* (Québec, 1969, miméo), 3–4.
[6] *Party Politics in America* (Boston, 1968), 10–11.

Les règles du jeu sont d'abord des règles normatives. Bailey les classe en cinq catégories[7]. On peut résumer chacune comme suit : *Règles de type un* : des règles définissent les enjeux et prévoient « what actions or qualities shall be deemed to have merited the prize » ou, pour employer le vocabulaire de la théorie des jeux, des règles prévoient comment se fera le règlement[8]. *Règles de type deux* : des règles prévoient quels agents peuvent participer au jeu. *Règles de type trois* : d'autres règles prévoient la formation de coalitions. *Règles de type quatre* : des règles définissent les façons de jouer, entre autres ce qui est honnête et ce qui ne l'est pas. Ces règles normatives limitent ainsi le champ des règles pragmatiques. *Règles de type cinq* : des règles prévoient le changement des règles (c'est ce que nous appelons les méta-règles). La « structure » du jeu étant définie par les règles normatives, les règles pragmatiques déterminent la stratégie.

LA STRATÉGIE

Une stratégie, c'est un plan formulé par le joueur avant de jouer, plan qui prévoit les décisions qui devront être prises au cours des différentes étapes que permettent les règles du jeu. C'est l'ambiguïté des règles normatives et/ou le manque d'information qui limitent l'établissement de stratégies efficaces. Bien qu'il ne soit pas faux de parler de stratégie d'un coup, on conçoit plus facilement que cette notion renvoie à une suite d'actions plutôt qu'à une seule.

Au cours d'une partie, ces actions stratégiques se retrouvent lors de jeux particuliers. Un jeu se produit lorsque les règles normatives laissent aux joueurs la liberté de choisir entre plusieurs actions. C'est ce que Michel Crozier nommait la « zone d'incertitude »[9]. Si une action doit être posée pour la poursuite de la partie mais qu'on se trouve en zone d'incertitude, et que les préférences des acteurs envers les résultats possibles de l'interaction ne sont pas similaires, il en résulte un point clef. Jean-Louis Peaucelle définit le point clef : « action ou ensemble d'actions nécessaires aux buts de l'organisation, qui nécessitent l'intervention de membres de l'organisation dans leur zone d'incertitude »[10]. Nous proposons ici de généraliser le concept de point clef de sorte qu'il ne s'applique pas seulement à l'étude de l'organisation, mais aussi à toute autre situation qui intéresse l'analyse stratégique. Le point clef se définit donc par rapport aux règles de type quatre portant sur la façon de jouer et par rapport à celles de type un qui définissent les enjeux.

Bref, lorsque les règles normatives laissent aux joueurs une certaine latitude (donc possibilité de conflit) mais que pour la poursuite de la partie une action doive être posée, il en résulte un point clef. Autour de ce point clef s'organise un jeu. Les joueurs établissent la liste des actions possibles pour chacun et les interactions qui en résultent.

LES PRÉFÉRENCES

Les résultats des ces interactions sont hiérarchisés par l'agent en un ordre de préférences fondé sur une échelle de valeurs. La théorie des jeux ne s'intéresse

[7]*Stratagems and Spoils* (Toronto, 1969), 19–20.
[8]Le mot règlement est pris ici au sens de distribution des dépouilles et non pas au sens de « l'ensemble de règles ».
[9]*Le phénomène bureaucratique* (Paris, 1963), 211–14.
[10]*Essai d'application de la théorie des jeux en tant que moyen d'analyse sociologique* (Paris, 1968, miméo), 4.

pas au système de valeurs ; elle ne cherche pas non plus à montrer comment ces préférences se sont formées mais les considère comme données. Pour les fins de cette étude, il suffira de pouvoir établir pour chaque individu une échelle ordinale de préférences, ce qui suppose qu'une condition spécifique soit respectée : la transitivité.

A partir des échelles individuelles de préférences, on peut construire pour un ensemble déterminé d'individus un ordre collectif des préférences en ne retenant que ce qui est commun à tous les individus. Cependant, il est possible qu'un individu de l'ensemble n'ait pas de préférence envers un résultat donné. G. Th. Guilbaud[11] suggère alors de procéder par classe d'indifférence ce qui, en pratique, revient à ne considérer que les préférences exprimées. Lorsque les ordres de préférences ne coïncident pas, on considérera les individus comme en conflit.

Ce qui précède s'applique en situation d'information complète, c'est-à-dire où chacun des individus connaît tous les résultats possibles de l'interaction, son ordre de préférences envers ces résultats ainsi que l'ordre des préférences des autres individus qui sont de la partie. Lorsque les agents ont établi leurs préférences envers les résultats des interactions possibles, ils « jouent » en essayant d'atteindre le meilleur résultat possible pour eux.

L'AGENT RATIONNEL

L'analyse stratégique postule en effet que l'agent est rationnel. Qu'entend-on précisément par rationalité ? Cela ne semble pas trop clair comme le notent d'ailleurs Luce et Raiffa : « ... it seems to include any assumption one makes about the players maximizing something, and any about complete knowledge on the part of the player in a very complex situation »[12].

Deux éléments se dégagent : la maximisation de quelque chose et l'information. Etant donné que nous allons considérer que le cas observé se déroule en situation d'information parfaite, nous ne discuterons pas ici de cet élément de la rationalité.

L'autre élément réfère quant à lui aux préférences de l'agent. Prenant pour acquis que les agents ont un ordre cohérent de préférences envers les résultats des interactions possibles, on dit qu'ils sont rationnels lorsqu'ils agissent en accord avec ces préférences.

LES RESSOURCES

Pour faire valoir leurs préférences, les individus disposent d'un ensemble de moyens d'action que nous avons appelé ressources. Nous emprunterons aussi au professeur Lemieux une typologie des ressources[13]. Ces ressources peuvent favoriser soit la maîtrise de sa propre action soit le contrôle de l'action de l'autre. Cette maîtrise et ce contrôle peuvent s'exercer au niveau de la pratique ou au niveau de la motivation.

Lorsque nous aurons une ressource de contrôle qui portera sur la motivation de l'autre, on parlera de ressource *symbolique*. La ressource *intellectuelle* sera la ressource de maîtrise qui porte sur sa propre motivation. Elle peut être ou informationnelle ou idéologique. Lorsque les ressources porteront sur la pratique,

[11]*Eléments de la théorie mathématique des jeux* (Paris, 1968), 116.
[12]R. Duncan Luce et Howard Raiffa, *Games and Decisions* (New-York, 1967), 5.
[13]Voir *Une sémiologie politique des organisations* (Québec, 1971, miméo), chap. 2.

elles seront dites *jurales* (ou juridiques), si elles sont de contrôle et *matérielles*, si elles sont de maîtrise.

Ces ressources peuvent se convertir les unes dans les autres soit par transformation chez l'agent lui-même, soit par transaction entre deux agents.

LES INCITATIONS

Lorsqu'un agent A utilise ses ressources pour amener l'agent B à poser une action, on peut dire que l'agent B est incité à agir par l'acquisition (ou la non-perte) de ressources. On s'est le plus souvent borné à étudier les incitations offertes par un seul des agents[14]. Dans ce contexte, étant donné que ce qui motive l'action d'un agent c'est l'acquisition de ressources, on peut utiliser la même typologie pour les motivations que pour les ressources. Nous aurons donc des incitations d'ordre symbolique, intellectuel, jural et matériel.

Cependant, l'expérience quotidienne nous suggère qu'à l'occasion, certaines personnes ne sont pas motivées dans leur action par l'acquisition (ou la non-perte) de ressources qui résulte de l'interaction, mais plutôt par l'interaction elle-même. Ce sont, par exemple, les incitations de « ceux qui font de la politique parce qu'ils aiment cela, par vengeance politique ou parce qu'ils recherchent l'efficacité dans la poursuite des objectifs de l'organisation »[15]. Ces incitations entrent dans une cinquième catégorie, dite politique. Ces incitations politiques de même que les incitations d'ordre symbolique, intellectuel, jural ou matériel peuvent être pour soi ou contre l'autre.

Comme le lecteur s'en sera rendu compte, ce que nous retenons de l'analyse stratégique, ce sont principalement des catégories, des concepts utiles à décrire et à analyser les éléments clefs d'un ensemble de comportements en situation de conflit ou de coopération. Par ailleurs il est certain qu'en employant un modèle ou un cadre de référence nous laissons tomber bien des aspects de la « réalité ». Nous croyons cependant ne pas avoir simplifié abusivement les descriptions, ni trop idéalisé les hypothèses, si bien que leur fonction scientifique demeure discernable.

II. Le contexte

L'ASSOCIATION LOCALE

L'association partisane locale du Parti Québécois compte à ce moment environ 200 membres dont la très forte majorité habite le même quartier ; se sont surtout des fonctionnaires, des universitaires et des étudiants. A la tête de cette association, un conseil est élu par l'assemblée générale des membres ; ce conseil élu nomme les responsables des divers comités permanents ou spéciaux. Durant la période que nous étudions, les membres doivent choisir leur candidat ; ce choix a des aspects idéologiques et organisationnels, et de personnalité.

LE PARTI

L'organisation du Parti Québécois est structurée sur une base d'associations locales relativement indépendantes du niveau national. Il y a cependant un en-

[14]On peut noter le cas de James G. March et Herbert Simon, *Organisations* (New-York, 1958), chap. 4, ainsi que Peter B. Clark et James Q. Wilson, « Incentive Systems : A Theory of Organizations », *Administrative Science Quarterly*, 6, no. 2 (juin 1961), 129–66.

[15]François Renaud, *Sociogramme et incitations à l'intérieur d'une organisation partisane de circonscription* (Université Laval, thèse de maîtrise, 1970), 95.

semble de règles impératives[16] pour assurer le respect de certains principes et l'uniformité de fonctionnement des associations locales. Par exemple, les statuts prévoient qu'il y aura dans chaque circonscription un congrès pour le choix du candidat du parti aux élections législatives. Donc des règles de type un définissent l'enjeu, et des règlements prévoient les modalités du déroulement de ce congrès ; il s'agit ici de règles s'appliquant à la façon de jouer (règle de type quatre).

A cause de l'idéologie, dans ce parti plus encore que dans les partis traditionnels au Québec, l'organisation centrale ne peut contrôler la motivation des membres à la base et imposer le « candidat du parti » à une organisation locale[17]. Dans certains cas cependant elle va laisser paraître ses préférences pour un candidat en lice. L'organisation centrale peut toutefois contrôler la pratique des membres du parti et s'opposer « pour des raisons graves à la présentation de toute candidature au congrès pour le choix d'un candidat du parti »[18]. Il s'agit d'une règle de type deux prévoyant qui peut jouer ou plus exactement qui ne peut jouer.

III. La situation

DUPONT, CANDIDAT

Dès janvier 1969[19], Arthur Dupont informe le conseil de l'association partisane de ladite circonscription de son intention d'être candidat du parti. Le conseil exprime à ce moment son appui à Dupont mais n'engage pas pour autant l'association ; Dupont rend publique sa décision et le congrès, à ses yeux, ne sera qu'une formalité.

Dupont est avocat. Depuis cinq ans il est à l'emploi d'une centrale syndicale qui a son siège social dans la circonscription ; sa famille est avantageusement connue dans la région. Il y a quelques années, à l'Université située dans la région, il avait été président de l'association des étudiants. Dupont a aussi été officier du parti au niveau régional et secrétaire-exécutif d'un parti politique municipal. Déjà différents partis lui avaient demandé de se présenter sous leur étiquette respective. Il avait décliné toutes ces offres. Voilà quelques ressources symboliques qui font de lui, aux yeux du conseil de l'association un candidat valable. Aux yeux de l'organisation centrale, Dupont était d'ailleurs considéré dans la région comme un candidat « vedette ». Les ressources juridiques dont il peut se prévaloir se limitent à son appartenance au parti et à son « membership » dans l'association locale. Du côté des ressources informationnelles, il lui est permis d'assister aux réunions du conseil de l'association, réunions auxquelles il est invité au même titre que les membres du conseil (sans droit de vote cependant). Il compte, au

[16] Il s'agit des statuts du parti adoptés par le congrés national annuel et des règlements adoptés par le conseil national, formé de l'exécutif national et des présidents de chaque association.
[17] Ce que Epstein dit des partis anglais à propos de l'indépendance des « local constituencies » par rapport à l'organisation centrale s'applique en gros à la situation du Parti Québecois, voir Leon D. Epstein, *Political Parties in Western Democracies* (New-York, 1967), 218. Voir aussi Austin Ranney, « Candidate Selection and Party Cohesion in Britain and the United States », dans *Approaches to the Study of Party Organisation*, éd. W.J. Crotty (Boston, 1968), 150.
[18] Extrait des statuts, préambule aux règlements régissant le choix des candidats du Parti Québécois.
[19] Le congrès de mise en nomination a lieu en septembre 1969 en vue de l'élection d'avril 1970 (dont la date n'est pas encore connue).

niveau régional et au niveau central de l'organisation du parti, des amis qui le renseignent. Les resources matérielles jouent un rôle peu important ; toutefois notons qu'il demeure loin en banlieue.

FORMATION D'UNE OPPOSITION

La candidature de Dupont cause le départ de deux membres du conseil de l'association. A cause de son manque de collaboration, Dupont mécontente à peu près tous les militants les plus actifs.

Après plusieurs mois, les membres temporairement éloignés par la présence de Dupont cherchent un nouveau candidat pour le remplacer[20].

Plusieurs raisons motivaient la défection de ces militants. Certains ne voulaient pas Dupont pour des raisons personnelles ou par vengeance politique. On peut dire de ces gens qu'ils étaient mus par des incitations « politiques ». D'autres le refusaient parce qu'il était avocat ou issu d'une famille bourgeoise, ou encore à cause de son style jugé « pompeux » et « prédicateur ». Dans la même ligne de pensée, mais pour des raisons plus positives, d'autres auraient voulu un candidat aux idées plus nouvelles. Ces derniers se préoccupent davantage des idées et du comportement du candidat que de son élection. Ce sont ceux qui sont mus par des incitations idéologiques. Ces incitations leur sont fournies par le parti, via son programme et surtout son approche participationniste.

D'autres désiraient avant tout un candidat déjà connu de la population ou du moins qui pouvait s'appuyer sur un certain prestige (comme Dupont). Si ces gens avaient de telles incitations face aux symboles, c'est qu'ils privilégiaient avant tout les objectifs électoraux de l'organisation partisane de circonscription. Ces militants, au hasard de leurs rencontres, se sont rendus compte qu'ils envisageaient trois solutions possibles : (1) s'opposer à Dupont ; (2) présenter un candidat aussi connu ou prestigieux que Dupont ; (3) présenter un candidat aux idées nouvelles.

Du point de vue de l'observateur, il y a cependant cinq types de candidat possibles. D'abord, il y a Dupont. Puis, en utilisant les deux critères mis de l'avant par les dissidents, soit prestige et idées nouvelles, on peut déduire quatre autres cas.

A	Dupont	
	Prestigieux	*Idées nouvelles*
B	oui	oui
C	oui	non
D	non	oui
E	non	non

Tous ces militants n'avaient pas le même ordre de préférence par rapport à ces solutions. En prenant pour critère leur ordre de préférences, on peut dire qu'ils formaient trois groupes. Le groupe primus comprend ceux qui s'opposaient à Dupont sans se soucier des qualités du candidat de remplacement. Ces gens préféraient indifféremment B, C, D, E à A (B, C, D, E $>$ A). Le groupe secundus ne voulait pas de Dupont mais désirait trouver un candidat aux idées nouvelles pour le remplacer. Les incitations symboliques étaient faibles chez ces gens. Ils ne faisaient

[20] Un second candidat s'était annoncé : Tournesol. Il voulait recueillir le vote des insatisfaits. Ces derniers ne prirent pas sa candidature au sérieux. Etant donné que ce candidat ne joue aucun rôle important, nous allons l'ignorer dans cette étude.

pas de différence entre Dupont et un candidat sans idées nouvelles. Leur ordre de préférence était donc B ou D > A, C ou E. Quant au groupe tertius, beaucoup plus préoccupé par la rentabilité électorale, il préférait d'abord un candidat prestigieux pour remplacer Dupont. Les incitations idéologiques étaient réduites chez ces gens. Il en résultait l'ordre de préférence suivant : B ou C > A > D ou E. On peut trouver l'ordre collectif des préférences en traçant un schéma pour chacun des ordres individuels et en superposant ceux-ci.

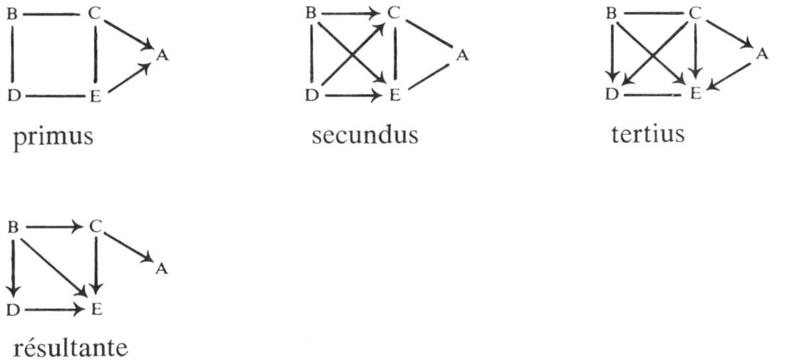

FIGURE 1. L'ordre de préférences des militants insatisfaits envers un type de candidat.

Comme ces trois groupes se rendent compte que leurs préférences ne pourront être atteintes qu'en s'unissant entre eux, ils forment une *coalition*. Selon Jacob Marshak[21], trois conditions définissent la coalition : (1) chaque ordre individuel de préférénce est connu ; (2) un ordre collectif partiel peut résulter de l'ensemble des ordres individuels ; (3) l'optimum de Pareto s'applique. Il y a optimum de Pareto lorsque le résultat pour chacun des participants n'est pas pire dans la coalition que dans l'ordre individuel et que la situation de l'un ne peut être améliorée sans nuire à un autre. C'est la situation devant laquelle se trouvent les groupes primus, secundus et tertius. Si les trois groupes d'insatisfaits forment alors une coalition, tous ne travaillent pas avec la même ardeur. En effet, si on regarde les ordres de préférences de chaque faction, on constate que la possibilité A est plus nettement rejetée par certains que par d'autres. Il ne faut donc pas se surprendre que les gens des factions primus et secundus travaillent avec plus d'entrain.

La première tâche qu'entreprend la coalition[22] c'est de faire circuler la rumeur d'un autre candidat. On profite aussi de l'occasion pour inscrire quelques nouveaux membres dans l'association, avant la date limite, de sorte que la coalition puisse compter sur le plus de votes possibles au congrès de mise en nomination[23]. Cette manœuvre restera fort limitée car un règlement du parti, ou règle normative de type deux, prévoit le gel de la liste des membres trente jours avant la tenue du congrès.

[21]« Towards an economic theory of organization and information », dans *Decision Process*, éd. R.M. Thrall, C.H. Coombs, R.L. Davis (New-York, 1960), 188–9.

[22]Lorsque nous employons l'expression « la coalition » sans autre qualificatif, il faudra entendre le groupe des insatisfaits et leurs nouveaux adhérents, par opposition à la coalition Dupont.

[23]Sur ces trois on quatre nouveaux membres, un votera pour Dupont et un autre ne se présentera pas au congrès.

TABLEAU I

PRÉFÉRENCES DES COALITIONS FACE AUX CANDIDATURES

La coalition	Dupont (a) reste	Dupont (b) se retire
A. se rallie	5 (1)*	
B. trouve un candidat prestigieux	1 (5)	3 (3)
C. trouve un autre candidat	2 (2)	4 (4)

*Le chiffre entre parenthèse indique la préférence de Dupont; l'autre chiffre, celui de la coalition.

IV. La lutte électorale

L'ENJEU

Si la coalition rassemble le maximum de ressources, elle n'a pas encore décidé de les employer. En effet, la lutte se déroule ici à l'intérieur d'une certaine rationalité : tous sont membres d'un même parti politique qui aspire à prendre le pouvoir. La coalition s'oppose à Dupont et voudrait l'humilier, mais pas au point de proposer n'importe qui comme candidat[24]. Depuis que la coalition s'est formée, les militants rebelles se rencontrent plus souvent. La faction qui voulait un candidat aux idées nouvelles s'avère la plus articulée et bientôt elle assimile le groupe primus, c'est-à-dire ceux qui s'opposaient à Dupont mais sans avoir une idée précise du genre de candidat de remplacement. La troisième faction se désagrège peu à peu. Certains membres de cette faction modifient leur ordre de préférences et donnent priorité au critère « idées nouvelles ». Les autres ne quittent cependant pas la coalition car ils espèrent trouver un candidat à la fois prestigieux et aux idées nouvelles. De plus, ils veulent garder le contact avec ces militants pour des activités futures dans une autre partie – les élections. La coalition dispose alors de trois tactiques : (1) elle peut toujours se rallier à Dupont sans lui faire opposition ; (2) elle peut appuyer un candidat prestigieux et aux idées nouvelles ; ou (3) elle peut trouver un candidat aux idées nouvelles qui, bien que non prestigieux, puisse vaincre Dupont au congrès. Pour Dupont, il y a deux tactiques possibles : (1) rester en lice, ou (2) se retirer de la course. Ce que Dupont préférerait par-dessus tout, c'est qu'il y ait unanimité sur sa personne. Contre un candidat quelconque, il estime qu'il pourrait facilement gagner. Cependant, si un candidat prestigieux devait se présenter, il préférerait se retirer pour assurer l'unité de l'association, et surtout il n'aimerait pas être défait par un tel candidat car un échec diminuerait son prestige. Pour sa part, la coalition aimerait bien défaire Dupont, si possible grâce à un candidat prestigieux. Se rallier à Dupont vient nettement au dernier échelon de ses préférences. Si Dupont se retire, la coalition espère que ce soit devant un candidat prestigieux plutôt que devant un candidat quelconque.

On peut résumer les possibilités de règlements, avec l'ordre de préférences de chacun (Tableau I).

[24]Par exemple, il ne vient pas à l'esprit des membres de la coalition d'appuyer le candidat Tournesol, voir note 20.

La coalition, désirant atteindre ses premières préférences (1 et 3 étant supérieurs à 2 et 4) décide de jouer d'abord le candidat prestigieux. On se met donc à la recherche de ce candidat ; nous sommes à un mois du congrès de mise en nomination et il est difficile de trouver un candidat idéal. Il faudrait passer par l'organisation centrale pour obtenir un tel candidat ; or, les membres de la coalition estiment que l'organisation centrale appuie Dupont et qu'elle refuserait de jouer avec la coalition.

LE CHOIX DE L'ADVERSAIRE

Une contrainte importante limitait l'action de la coalition. En effet, quinze jours avant le congrès, la mise en candidature est fermée. Il ne reste que deux semaines à la coalition pour trouver un opposant à Dupont.

Comme la période s'achève et qu'aucune des personnalités approchées n'a encore accepté de se présenter, l'on se demande quel autre candidat, moins prestigieux, mais satisfaisant aux attentes des membres de la coalition, pourrait se présenter. C'est alors qu'on songe sérieusement à Victor Thibault. Certains militants avaient déjà suggéré à Thibault de se porter candidat du parti, mais il avait décliné cette offre.

De fait, Thibault avait été depuis quelque temps le coordonateur de la coalition[25] et de l'opposition à Dupont. Si Thibault n'est pas connu du public, il n'est pas sans ressources.

Thibault est un militant actif depuis la création de l'association. Il est issu du milieu même de l'organisation, ce qui est une ressource symbolique à ne pas dédaigner. Il est sociologue à l'emploi d'une université. En plus de ces ressources symboliques, il est bien informé. Il est au courant de ce qui se passe à toutes les réunions de l'exécutif, soit qu'il y assiste, soit que des informateurs lui fassent des comptes rendus. Il est en contact avec les différents groupes qui se retrouvent dans l'association : l'exécutif, le groupe dit des sociologues, les ex-Rinistes ; il compte aussi parmi ses informateurs des personnes proches de Dupont ; enfin, il faut reconnaître, dans tout bon réseau d'information, le rôle très utile (sinon primordial) que jouent les femmes, confidentes les plus « sûres » des bons militants. Thibault est aussi en bonnes relations avec des individus importants dans l'association. Pour des raisons professionnelles ou personnelles, il est en rapport avec un certain nombre de ces personnes en dehors des activités partisanes.

Il faut noter deux ressources juridiques précises dont jouit Thibault : il est membre en règle de l'association et responsable du comité du programme de l'association. Cette dernière ressource peut facilement se transformer en ressource symbolique (prestige d'être responsable d'un comité) et intellectuelle, plus précisément idéologique. Comme ressource matérielle, il habite la circonscription et son appartement peut servir de lieu de rencontre.

Depuis quelques semaines Thibault songe à se porter candidat : il ne manque aucune activité de l'association. Il sait qu'un candidat, pour être victorieux, doit être plus qu'un nom. Il doit être connu. A l'occasion de l'inauguration d'un nouveau local de l'association, il parcourt des centaines de milles pour venir

[25]Nous employons ici l'expression coordonateur de la coalition, plutôt que « leader de la coalition », parce que Thibault n'est pas l'initiateur de la coalition. Voir William H. Riker, *The Theory of Political Coalitions* (New-Haven, 1965), 107.

TABLEAU II

LES POSSIBILITÉS OFFERTES Á CHAQUE COALITION

La coalition	Dupont (a) reste	Dupont (b) se retire
A. se rallie	x	x
B. présente Thibault	x	x

TABLEAU III

ORDRES DES PRÉFÉRENCES DES DEUX COALITIONS

La coalition	Dupont (a) reste	Dupont (b) se retire
A. se rallie	3 (1)	
B. présente Thibault	1 (2)	2 (3)

participer à cet événement qui rassemble une bonne partie des membres de l'association.

Thibault s'efforce de participer aux mêmes activités du parti que Dupont. Et lorsque Tournesol annonce sa candidature lors d'une conférence de presse, Thibault s'y rend et laisse planer le doute sur la venue d'un troisième candidat.

Aussi, lorsque la coalition cherche un candidat qui peut s'opposer à Dupont, elle choisit un militant très en vue, Thibault. Les délais étant écoulés, et la coalition n'ayant pu jouer la préférence qui venait au premier rang de son ordre, le problème se pose alors tel qu'indiqué au Tableau II.

Quel est l'ordre de préférences de la coalition ? Et celui de Dupont ? La coalition, on s'en souvient, s'est formée contre Dupont au profit d'un candidat éventuel qui aurait davantage d'idées nouvelles. Quant à Dupont, dont nous n'avons pas beaucoup parlé, disons qu'il sous-estime le mouvement que la coalition essaie de provoquer et qu'il considère les insatisfaits comme des marginaux peu dangereux. Les deux ordres de préférences qui en résultent sont ceux du Tableau III.

Face à une telle situation, la stratégie de Dupont se réduit à une seule tactique : rester. Etant donné ses préférences, c'est en jouant la colonne « rester » qu'il s'assure le minimum de perte et possiblement le maximum de gain.

Aussitôt que Thibault est officiellement candidat, Dupont tente alors de contrôler l'action de la coalition. Il téléphone à Thibault et lui demande de se rallier. Si Thibault se rallie, la coalition, faute de ressources pour trouver un autre candidat, n'aurait plus qu'une tactique : se rallier. Dupont exercerait alors sa maîtrise en jouant l'option « rester », et contrôlerait l'adversaire en le contraignant à jouer « se rallier », c'est-à-dire que Dupont aurait du pouvoir.

Thibault cependant refuse de se désister. La coalition garde donc ses deux tactiques comme possibles. Toutefois, à cause de la structure du jeu, elle joue nécessairement la candidature de Thibault. C'est en effet en jouant la rangée inférieure de la matrice qu'elle s'assure le minimax. Dupont reste donc en lice et la coalition présente Thibault.

Une fois ce choix effectué, on ne le dévoile pas immédiatement. En effet, la coalition préfère recruter d'autres membres avant de faire une première démonstration de sa force. Dupont pour sa part n'a pas intérêt à répandre la nouvelle, ce qui ferait davantage connaître Thibault. La coalition, qui devient l'organisation Thibault, essaie d'élargir le cercle de ses sympathisants. On commence par intégrer les amis, puis les militants que l'on connaît le plus. Thibault visite les membres jugés importants dans l'association et qui sont quelque peu réticents à la candidature de Dupont. Peu à peu, le cercle s'étend. Thibault visite les membres de l'association sans faire de distinction[26].

Pour obtenir l'appui des militants, Thibault offre des incitations idéologiques, son programme et ses idées. Les membres ainsi attirés à son organisation lui fournissent des ressources qui lui assurent la maîtrise de sa propre pratique et qui, espère-t-il, pourront ultimement permettre le contrôle de la pratique de son adversaire. On peut même ajouter, à titre d'hypothèse, que dans la mesure où l'incitation idéologique est plus grande que la contribution des membres, ceux-ci sont satisfaits et ne songent pas à quitter l'organisation[27].

L'ASSEMBLÉE DES MEMBRES

Une assemblée générale des membres de l'association est convoquée pour préparer le congrès national du parti. A l'occasion de cette assemblée, les militants pourront se prononcer sur des projets de résolutions à proposer au Congrès national. On élira aussi les délégués de l'association à ce congrès.

La coalition Thibault décide de se préparer en vue de cette assemblée. On veut y démontrer que Thibault est fort et appuyé par les militants et qu'il sera un candidat sérieux à la convention. Pour sa part, Dupont ne prépare rien de spécial.

L'assemblée regroupe de 50 à 60 militants. Pendant la première partie de la réunion, les militants sont appelés à voter des résolutions préparées par les ateliers du comité du programme présidé par Thibault. La seconde partie de la réunion consiste à élire les délégués. La veille, la coalition Thibault a mis au point une tactique. La coalition votera pour une liste préparée à l'avance. Si une tactique similaire n'est pas mise en œuvre par Dupont, Thibault s'assure non seulement le choix des délégués mais aussi l'ordre de leur choix.

En établissant la liste, on s'est demandé si le nom de Dupont devait y apparaître. Dans le camp Thibault on fait le raisonnement suivant : si on place Dupont le premier sur la liste, il sera très fort et la coalition Thibault pourra continuer à cacher son jeu pour ne dévoiler sa force qu'à la toute fin. L'inconvénient de cette tactique – Dupont choisi délégué par une trop grande proportion de militants – est qu'on ne pourra peut-être plus le déloger.

Si, au contraire, Dupont ne se fait pas élire comme délégué au congrès national, il peut fort bien se retirer de la lutte et il n'y aurait alors pas de campagne, de

[26]La coalition Thibault avait plus ou moins systématiquement catalogué les membres de l'association à la manière de Downs, selon le degré d'information et d'intensité des préférences. A Downs, *An Economic Theory of Democracy* (New-York, 1957), chap. 6, spécialement les pages 84 et 85.

[27]Dans la typologie que Riker fait des « side-payments », ce cas-ci référait au type « promises on policy », Riker, *Theory of Political Coalitions*, 111. Les adhérents à la coalition sont payés, ou plus exactement seront payés, si la coalition est victorieuse, par le fait même de la victoire.

mobilisation des militants, de publicité à l'occasion du choix du candidat. Il faut donc que Dupont soit élu délégué, mais avec un nombre de voix inférieur à Thibault. Tout ceci, dans l'éventualité où Dupont veut être délégué au Congrès national. La probabilité qu'il refuse est faible.

Sous forme arborescente, le problème se pose ainsi :

L'intention de Dupont d'être délégué	*Résultats possibles du scrutin*	*Ordre de préférence de la Coalition Thibault*
oui	Dupont plus fort que Thibault	3
	Dupont plus faible que Thibault	1
	Dupont non élu délégué	2
non		

Le soir de l'assemblée, Dupont accepte d'être candidat au poste de délégué. Le résultat du scrutin lui cause toute une surprise : Thibault a réussi à imposer la solution qui venait au premier rang de son ordre de préférences.

A la suite de cette assemblée, Dupont s'inquiète et songe à se retirer ; sa position est beaucoup moins assurée qu'il ne l'avait estimée. Inversement, la coalition Thibault prend confiance et recrute de nouveaux supporteurs, impressionnés par la force de Thibault et la faiblesse de Dupont.

LA CAMPAGNE

De l'assemblée des membres au congrès de mise en nomination, les deux équipes font campagne. Analysons celle-ci sous l'aspect des rapports des organisations avec les membres et avec l'adversaire.

Relations avec les membres

Durant leur campagne, les organisations communiquent avec les membres par correspondance, par téléphone et par contact personnel lors de rencontres avec le candidat ou avec des organisateurs du candidat.

1. La correspondance. Dupont fait parvenir trois lettres aux membres ; Thibault, deux, auxquelles il faut ajouter celle du secrétaire de l'association qui se prévaut de son statut pour « rectifier » certains faits au grand détriment de Dupont.

Le contenu de ces lettres indique quelles ressources chaque candidat a privilégiées. Dupont insiste sur deux thèmes principaux : son travail à l'intérieur du parti et de l'association ; ses activités professionnelles extérieures au parti, c'est-à-dire son engagement syndical. Le premier thème lui est imposé par la campagne elle-même ; les « rumeurs », les « attaques » ... de l'équipe adverse soulignent l'aspect « extérieur » de la candidature de Dupont. Dans son deuxième thème, Dupont recourt à des ressources symboliques externes au parti (les ressources symboliques de Thibault sont internes à l'association), faisant allusion à l'objectif électoral du parti.

Très différents sont les deux arguments principaux développés par Thibault : il s'agit de son « programme » et des appuis dont il bénéficie dans l'association. Par son « programme », c'est aux ressources informationnelles que recourt

Thibault, insistant par là sur les objectifs idéologiques et gouvernementaux du parti. Le deuxième argument important de Thibault consiste à énumérer les noms des membres influents qui l'appuient ; il s'agit d'une symbolisation d'une ressource jurale interne à l'association. Ces ressources symbolisées sont utilisées lors des rencontres avec les membres de l'association pour promouvoir des objectifs organisationnels, à la différence de Dupont, qui, nous l'avons vu, utilisait des ressources symboliques externes à l'association en vue d'objectifs électoraux.

2. *Rencontres.* Les organisateurs de Dupont tiennent quelques réunions de leur candidat avec les membres de l'association pour solliciter des appuis. Thibault pour sa part tente de rencontrer personnellement les militants. Pendant toute la durée de la campagne, les deux organisations multiplient les appels téléphoniques auprès des militants jugés indécis. Pendant la dernière fin de semaine de la campagne, des équipes du groupe Thibault visitent un nombre important de militants.

3. *La presse.* Thibault est le seul à recourir aux média d'information durant la campagne : un communiqué de l'organisation, une conférence de presse du candidat et une entrevue d'un organisateur à un journal. C'est plusieurs mois auparavant que la presse avait fait état de la candidature de Dupont.

Relations avec l'adversaire

Au niveau des rapports entre les deux candidats, Thibault semble avoir joué gagnant plus souvent que son adversaire, en particulier sous trois aspects.

Thibault bénéficie d'un réseau d'information complet sur les déplacements, les manœuvres, et les points de vue de Dupont, ce qui peut lui permettre de prévoir les « coups » et de porter les siens aux moments opportuns. Par exemple, au cours d'une réunion de l'adversaire, Thibault communique avec lui, retient son temps et réplique à ses « coups ».

C'est d'ailleurs le deuxième aspect de ces rapports : Dupont répond aux arguments de Thibault dans une lettre qu'il envoie aux membres, tandis que ce dernier répond directement à Dupont sans mettre tous les membres au courant des arguments adverses[28].

Thibault prend aussi l'initiative de proposer un débat public entre les deux candidats. Il croit en effet qu'il peut plus facilement affronter l'assemblée des membres de l'association que Dupont. Si Dupont accepte, l'affaire est dans le sac ; s'il refuse, il aura l'air de se défiler.

Quant à Dupont, il estime que s'il y avait un débat entre les deux candidats, ou bien la salle serait vide ou bien elle serait remplie de gens des deux organisations rivales. Il espère donc qu'il n'y aura pas de débat, mais surtout, il espère que son adversaire n'en proposera pas. La situation se résume donc au Tableau IV.

Etant donné leur échelle respective de préférences et étant donné qu'aucun d'eux ne contrôle l'autre, on en arrive nécessairement à la situation suivante [2, (2)] : Thibault propose un débat public et Dupont refuse. Thibault peut alors laisser entendre que Dupont craint de rencontrer les membres de l'association.

[28]Les arguments de Thibault portent sur le manque de présence et de travail de Dupont à l'intérieur de l'association (insuffisance de ressources symboliques internes et insuffisance de recrutement) tandis que les arguments de Dupont contre Thibault portent sur l'absence de ressources symboliques externes à l'association (son âge et son inexpérience professionnelle ; son statut de célibataire ; son origine extérieure à la région).

TABLEAU IV

LES PRÉFÉRENCES DES CANDIDATS POUR UN DÉBAT PUBLIC

	Dupont	
Thibault	(a) pour un débat	(b) contre un débat
A. propose un débat	1 (4)	2 (2)
B. ne propose pas de débat	4 (3)	3 (1)

TABLEAU V

PRÉFÉRENCES DES ORGANISATIONS ENVERS LES LISTES DE VOTEURS

	Dupont	
Thibault	(a) liste officielle	(b) ajouter groupe non inscrit
A. liste officielle	2 (3 ou 4)	3 (2)
B. ajouter groupe no inscrit	1 (3 ou 4)	4 (1)

LE CONGRÈS DE MISE EN NOMINATION

Au terme de cette campagne, on procède au congrès de mise en nomination. On peut dégager trois points de cette assemblée ; le droit de vote, le déroulement et l'ambiance, les discours.

Le droit de vote

« Toutes les personnes qui sont membres d'une association du comté, trente jours avant la tenue d'une convention, et qui sont domiciliées dans le comté sont habilitées à voter ». (Règlement régissant le choix des candidats du Parti Québécois.)

Le secrétariat national établit la liste officielle de ceux qui ont droit de vote, mais des personnes convaincues d'être membres en règle (certaines ont leur carte de membre) n'apparaissent pas, pour des raisons impossibles à déterminer, sur la liste officielle du secrétariat national. Si les candidats sont d'accord, ce groupe non inscrit sur la liste officielle aura droit de vote, mais si un seul des candidats s'oppose, seule la liste officielle prévaudra.

Chaque organisation doit donc évaluer son avantage à donner droit de vote au groupe « non inscrit » sur la liste officielle. L'organisation Dupont y est favorable, mais l'organisation Thibault préfère qu'on s'en tienne à la liste officielle. Voici parmi les quatre jeux possibles, les préférences de chaque organisation (Tableau V).

Si Thibault ne connaissait pas déjà le choix de Dupont, son propre choix pourrait être difficile. Il aurait en effet le choix entre une solution prudente (rangeé du haut) et une solution où il peut tout perdre ou tout gagner. Comme il sait que Dupont jouera « non inscrit » il ne peut que jouer « liste officielle ». Comme il n'y a pas accord entre les candidats, c'est la liste officielle qui prévaudra. Thibault qui se disait le candidat de la participation, utilise ici des méthodes (pour éloigner des participants) qu'il aurait en d'autres circonstances dénoncées avec énergie.

L'assemblée

Il ne semble pas, selon les deux organisations, que l'assemblée ait été un élément déterminant dans le résultat. Bien que chaque candidat ait pu être inquiet du déroulement, ce n'est, ni pour l'un, ni pour l'autre, un élément important, prévu et organisé dans la stratégie.

Les membres se prévalant de leur droit de vote sont au nombre de 126, mais plus de 1000 partisans de la région assistent au congrès. Cette ouverture au public profite à Thibault car le Parti Québécois a une audience forte chez les jeunes, les universitaires – auxquels est d'avantage identifiée l'équipe Thibault[29].

Le discours

Les contenus des discours ne varient guère par rapport aux thèmes déjà développés durant la campagne.

A titre d'incitation, Dupont utilise des ressources externes au parti (son engagement syndical ; le fait qu'il est connu du public) qu'il transforme en ressources symboliques; Thibault utilise comme incitations des ressources intellectuelles (son « programme ») et symboliques en s'identifiant au parti, à son objectif réformiste.

Au niveau des objectifs, Dupont insiste sur les objectifs électoraux du parti soulignant sa rentabilité, tandis que Thibault, pour répliquer à cet argument, insiste sur les objectifs organisationnels (par exemple : le travail du candidat est plus important que sa notoriété) et sur les objectifs gouvernementaux du parti.

Les résultats du scrutin

Thibault, 64; Dupont, 58; Tournesol, 4. Thibault obtient de justesse la majorité absolue exigée par les règlements.

Conclusion

Le but de cet article était de rapporter nos observations sur la manière dont un candidat avait été choisi en vue de l'élection québécoise de 1970. Pour ce faire, nous avons utilisé le cadre de l'analyse stratégique.

En cette décade consacrée aux études comparatives et statistiques, il est quelque peu risqué, si on ne veut pas être banni de la profession, de faire une étude de cas. Les études de cas, dit-on, sont presque impossibles à reproduire, ne se prêtent pas facilement à la comparaison, fournissent peu de généralisations et, du point de vue théorique, sont strictement stériles. Nous croyons que l'analyse stratégique, lorsqu'elle peut être utilisée, permet d'éviter, en bonne partie, ces écueils.

Au point de vue théorique, l'analyse stratégique se retrouve dans la filiation immédiate de la théorie des jeux à qui elle emprunte un appareil mathématique. Appareil fort élémentaire, il est vrai, mais qui nous a paru mener à une plus grande précision de l'observation et du traitement des données que le simple énoncé verbal. Cette précision se retrouve principalement lorsqu'on établit l'existence des solutions, dites stratégiques, dans les situations de conflit (ou de coopération) ou lorsqu'on essaie d'expliquer la formation des coalitions.

[29]Un certain nombre de jeunes, d'universitaires, appuient Dupont, et Thibault ne recrute pas ses appuis uniquement dans ces groupes.

L'analyse stratégique, grâce à ses concepts de règles du jeu, de zone d'incertitude, d'objectifs, de ressources, etc., nous permet de décrire systématiquement nos observations, sans pouvoir toutefois les transcrire toutes sous forme algorithmique, tout en demeurant dans la perspective de l'acteur. C'est l'un des avantages de l'analyse stratégique de s'intéresser non seulement au cadre de l'action mais aussi à l'action elle-même et aux relations entre le cadre et le comportement des agents. Bien sûr, ces concepts doivent être plus abstraits que les données brutes elles-mêmes si ces dernières doivent être codifiées de façon à être comparées. Le passage des données empiriques à la catégorisation nous fait perdre certaines informations secondaires, mais malgré son niveau d'abstraction relativement élevé, l'analyse stratégique conserve, de façon générale, une assez forte prise sur la réalité. On peut penser qu'un niveau intermédiaire de concepts, entre la description très factuelle et le niveau le plus abstrait de la théorie, commence à se faire sentir.

Rationality and Decision in Administrative Science

H.T. WILSON *York University*

To a surprising degree, Max Weber has prefigured in his work the contemporary problem of the meaning and significance of rationality for Western society.[1] This does not mean that the contemporary formulation of the problem of human action debates it at its proper boundaries. On the contrary, "administrative science" and organization theory, two terms used to represent a subdiscipline of the social sciences in North America peculiarly concerned with behaviour in organized groups,[2] have largely presumed certain aspects of the problem, with the result that rationality becomes a given within which the issue of decision and decision-making is often debated as if *it* alone were the problem.[3]

Particular imperatives toward generalization, quantification, and theory at any price have eventuated in a full-fledged effort to develop a predictive and interventionist science of administration and organization far beyond the explanatory function of earlier efforts in social inquiry. Devotion to what social scientists conceive of as the scientific paradigm indicates the *possibility* of engineered change and environmental manipulation; elaborate mechanisms and devices which effectively self-confirm in the process of hypothesis-testing a vision of the world of social relationships as ordered, regularized, and stable provide a built-in *valuation* on the basis of "results."[4] Distended from larger philosophical questions, administrative science produces a world of careers for its initiates within an organiza-

[1]*Theory of Social and Economic Organization*, ed. Talcott Parsons (Glencoe, Ill., 1947); *From Max Weber*, ed. Hans Gerth and C. Wright Mills (New York, 1946); *Methodology of the Social Sciences*, ed. Edward Shils and H.A. Finch (Glencoe, Ill., 1949); *Max Weber on Law in Economy and Society*, ed. Max Rheinstein (Cambridge, Mass. 1954); *The Protestant Ethic and the Spirit of Capitalism* (New York, 1958). A useful discussion of Weber oriented to his concept of rationality is Reinhard Bendix, *Max Weber* (Garden City, N.Y. 1962), chap. 12; and Julian Freund, *The Sociology of Max Weber* (New York, 1969).

[2]See Dwight Waldo, "Organization Theory: An Elephantine Problem," *Public Administration Review*, 21, no. 4 (1961), 216–21; "Theory of Organization: Status and Problems," paper presented at the Annual Meeting of the American Political Science Association, New York, 1963; William G. Scott, *Organization Theory* (Homewood, Ill. 1967), especially prologue and chap. 5, 6, and 10; and Alvin Gouldner, "Organizational Analysis," in *Sociology Today*, ed. Robert Merton, Leonard Broom, and Leonard Cottrell (New York, 1959), 400–28. D.S. Pugh, "Modern Organization Theory: A Psychological and Sociological Study," *Psychological Bulletin*, 66, no. 4 (October 1966), 235–51 provides a survey of types of organization theory.

[3]What was presumably a conceptual means to the analysis of larger order questions having to do with human reason becomes self-justifying as a focus for analysis in its own right. This effective delimitation of a field of inquiry carries with it an expansion of the area of the taken for granted, as something to be handled by "philosophers" or "intellectuals" rather than "specialists" and "professionals."

[4]Robert Boguslaw, *The New Utopians* (Englewood Cliffs, N.J. 1965), chap. 2, 3, 4; Alfred McClung Lee, "The Concept of System," *Social Research*, 32 (Autumn 1965), 229–38.

Canadian Journal of Political Science/Revue canadienne de science politique, VI, no. 2 (June/juin 1973). Printed in Canada/Imprimé au Canada.

tional society where the world views that sustain modern technological advance remain unquestioned, except by individuals whose alleged distance from empirical reality makes them unfit critics and analysts.

The academic (sub)division of labour comes to reflect the way the social world really is for many academics; the university is seen as a microcosm of society where efforts at interdisciplinary synthesis are at best ameliorative. The social sciences become knowledge technologies, their methodological and strategic difficulties evidence of "technological lag" in academic organizations.[5] In few areas can the case for such a view be made as strongly as it can be in administrative science and organization theory. The very idea of an administrative science suggests the significance of application, of intervention, of dynamic change and manipulation of the work environment. This view of the relation between knowledge and society is part of an American tradition which has given the United States leadership in most areas of the social sciences.[6]

The purpose here is not to dispute the value of this historic undertaking. Nor is it to argue that the idea of such a social science is worthless. Rather I want to suggest that this view of the relation between society and knowledge about it is symptomatic of a failure to articulate *within the field* certain underlying assumptions about human nature, sociability, and progress which are as important to our understanding of the limits of social intervention as an administrative science is to the success of such efforts.[7]

Rationality, for reasons already alluded to, seems to me to be a good base point for the analysis of the philosophical position of administrative science and organization theory as represented by those individuals particularly interested in decision and decision-making. This focus on decision continues to be significant because here the interface between philosophy and the normative on the one hand and "empirical" science and "the facts" on the other is most severely strained. The work of Herbert Simon and his associates is a case in point.[8]

I want to look at Simon's conception of an administrative science, what he accepts and what he rejects in the tradition as he received and interpreted it. I am concerned particularly with his contribution to the subdiscipline up to the point of his apparent departure from the field after 1960. Next I want to argue for the relevance of a view of social science at once an alternative and a complement to Simon and his critics provided jointly by the phenomenologist Alfred Schutz and the ethnomethodologist Harold Garfinkel.[9] Then I shall endeavour to demonstrate why most if not all criticisms of Simon's position by American social scien-

[5]H.T. Wilson, "Continentalism and Canadian Higher Education," *Canadian Review of American Studies*, 1, no. 2 (Fall 1970), 89–100. Francis Rourke and Glenn Brooks, *The Managerial Revolution in Higher Education* (Baltimore, 1966) give a most thorough survey of automation in *American* universities.

[6]John Madge, *The Origins of Scientific Sociology* (New York, 1962), especially chap. 1, 6, and 14. But see Loren Baritz, *The Servants of Power* (New York, 1964) for a critical analysis of industrial psychology and sociology.

[7]George Grant, "In Defence of North America," "The University Curriculum," and "A Platitude," in Grant, *Technology and Empire* (Toronto, 1968), 15–40, 113–33, 137–43.

[8]Especially Simon's *Administrative Behaviour* 2nd ed. (New York, 1957); Herbert Simon, David Smithburg and Victor Thompson, *Public Administration* (New York, 1950); Simon and March, *Organizations* (New York, 1958); Simon, *Models of Man: Social and Rational* (New York, 1957), especially chaps. 6, 10, 14, and 15.

[9]Alfred Schutz, *The Phenomenology of the Social World* (Evanston, Ill. 1967); Schutz, *Col-*

Rationalité et décision dans la science des administrations

La science des administrations et la théorie des organisations sont deux secteurs des sciences sociales particulièrement affectés par les problèmes inhérents à la conception positiviste de la connaissance de l'univers social. Le statut relatif de la théorie et de la méthode, l'interrelation que l'on présume exister entre les deux, et les postulats selon lesquels on peut « appliquer » la connaissance des phénomènes sociaux en vue d'améliorer la condition humaine, tout cela se présente souvent de façon fort simpliste et quelquefois même dangereuse. A l'aide des arguments avancés par Herbert Simon dans Administrative Behavior *et dans ses ouvrages subséquents, l'auteur veut attirer l'attention sur les plus sérieux écueils que recèle l'approche positiviste dans l'étude des processus administratifs parmi les groupes organisés.*

Le débat sur l'œuvre de Simon, entre 1947 et 1959, a permis de constater que la majorité des critiques, tout en mettant en cause l'accent qu'il plaçait sur des prémisses « décisionnelles » et la dichotomie faits-valeurs qui les soustend, étaient pour l'essentiel d'accord avec Simon quant à la nature de la rationalité humaine, au rôle de l'individu dans un groupe de travail, et à la contribution que l'intellectuel universitaire, par le biais de ses préoccupations cognitives, pouvait apporter à l'amélioration des processus administratifs au nom d'une certaine conception du progrès. Ce n'est qu'à partir du moment où l'on prend conscience que la distinction entre fait et valeur est à la fois une conséquence et une cause de l'établissement et du maintien de la dichotomie entre, d'une part, une soit-disant objectivité sur laquelle l'intellectuel universitaire non engagé aurait une emprise privilégiée et, d'autre part, la subjectivité telle que caractérisée par les valeurs, les préjugés, les préférences et, en général, « l'irrationalité » des participants engagés, que les implications de cette singulière réduction deviennent évidentes.

Une analyse plus phénoménologique de l'organisation du travail amène l'auteur à suggérer, entre autres choses, que les « manquements » à la rationalité tels qu'ils se produisent dans la vie de tous les jours soient considérés non pas comme des déviations par rapport à l'idéal défini dans la tour d'ivoire universitaire, ni comme des facteurs de sabotage de la rationalité optimale, mais bien comme composantes intégrales des données d'une situation bien mieux connue par l'acteur-participant qu'elles ne peuvent l'être par l'analyste extérieur à la situation. En contrepartie de cette conception de l'acteur comme cherchant à satisfaire ses besoins eut égard à sa propre connaissance de l'état d'une situation donnée, on retrouve la préférence des acteurs pour des décisions et actions collectives plutôt qu'individuelles, préférence dont l'auteur souligne, en conclusion, quelques implications.

tists are really family squabbles seen from a perspective outside the structured confines within which the debate took place. Finally, I shall attempt to tie together the analysis and articulate a new paradigm that links the problem of rationality in organization theory to issues traditionally dealt with in political economy and political theory.

I

Simon's initial effort in the first edition of *Administrative Behaviour* was to construct the rudiments of a science of administration predicated on the model of rational man provided by classical economics.[10] Because he equated the discipline of psychology largely with the study of the individual, his focus on the decision and upon decision-making in organized groups tends to favour psychological

lected Papers, Vols. 1–3 (The Hague, 1962); Harold Garfinkel, *Studies in Ethnomethodology* (Englewood Cliffs, N.J. 1967).

[10]See especially the introduction to the second edition, xxiv–xxvii, to be discussed later on.

research and evidence. As a consequence, aspects of the situation or context within which decisions occurred were largely ignored, perhaps, because by scientific canons, structural, that is sociological, findings did not constitute sound evidence.[11] The preoccupation with "hard data," terminological clarification, and an unambiguous technical vocabulary mark Simon's support for the view of science forwarded by logical empiricism. The alleged theoretical objectivity and neutrality of the intellectual making sense of commonsense understanding is also clearly in evidence in Simon's writings. Difficulties and inconsistencies with Simon's commitment to a "science" at once descriptive and explanatory have already been noted in considerable detail by Herbert Storing, whose work needs little elaboration.[12] At the same time, there are several points about Simon's analysis of decision and view of human rationality that have not been adequately touched upon, although Storing comes the closest to explicitly doing so.

Initially forwarding a conception of human rationality based upon the dichotomy between ends and means, Simon reverted quickly to a discussion of rationality in terms of behaviour alternatives where the ends are given rather than problematic for the administrator. It is precisely because the language of means and ends fails to support the *complete* separation of facts and values, "the only valid distinction" according to Simon, that it must be complemented by a behaviour-alternative model of human choice if "inaccurate conclusions" are to be avoided.[13] Every end turns out to be a means to something beyond it, conjuring up an image of an eternal escalator that "ascends and ascends but arrives nowhere."[14] Space and time dimensions suggest further the inadequacy of a conception of human choice that is predicated upon an *isolated* individual attempting to meet the high standards of a normative model of calculated capacity while possessed of the unfortunate baggage of "values" that incessantly sabotage his efforts to gain objectively valid knowledge of the world.[15] Simon recognized this, but did not at first allow it to fundamentally alter his original conception of rationality. Caught between the conflicting conception of man as literally superhuman (for Simon would not admit until 1957 that the "maximizing" model of man was *normative*) and man as a bundle of needs, wants, and desires, the analysis in *Administrative Behaviour* oscillates between a positivistically inspired ideal and a utilitarian reality.[16].

The behaviour-alternative model, when combined with a residual of means-end optimality, is still a maximizing model for Simon however, but one that settles the

[11]See Victor Thompson, *Modern Organization* (New York, 1961), 6–8; Thompson, *Bureaucracy and Innovation* (University, Ala. 1968); Murray Edelman, *The Symbolic Uses of Politics* (Urbana, Ill. 1964), 49–51; and Harold Wilensky, *Organizational Intelligence* (New York, 1967), 75–82 for a critique of "isolated actor" decision-making.

[12]"The Science of Administration: Herbert A. Simon," in *Essays on the Scientific Study of Politics*, ed. Storing (New York, 1962), 63–150. While much of the analysis is sound, Storing tends to place too much emphasis upon the fact-value dichotomy (rationality versus "non-rational preferences") for this writer, a point to be discussed critically further on.

[13]*Administrative Behaviour*, 64–6.

[14]Dwight Waldo, "Replies and Comments," *American Political Science Review*, 46 (June 1952), 503, note 5.

[15]This point is implicit in the alleged "standpointlessness" of logical empiricism to be discussed further on. Simon focuses on values as necessary to explain *departures* "from the norms of rationality." See *Administrative Behaviour*, 149.

[16]See Storing, "Science of Administration," 70.

fundamental policy question of who formulates values by concentrating on the *psychology* of human choice rather than upon the logic. The behaviour alternative model, in short, is an effort to "provide a way of ordering facts that is not dependent on values."[17] Although not yet really committed to the "limits to rationality" approach which would later be so fundamental to his reconstruction of administrative behaviour,[18] Simon side-steps the problem of discretion by arguing that the behaviour alternative model scales down the task of the decision-maker by protecting him against having to deal with values as ends at all. This accords much better with the ostrich-like simplicity that treatment of the problem of administrative discretion was receiving at the time Simon wrote.[19] Indeed, it fits in quite nicely with the robot view of administrative man so central to many political science studies. Relieved of the necessity to concern himself with values, Simon's model liberates administrative man to gather the facts, *given* limits to optimal rationality.[20]

Now the trouble with this concept of rationality is that it *has* to be normative. One can *never* know whether its standards have been realized in any decisional situation. There is no way that anybody could ever be sure they had "really" optimized. The staggering character of the demand is only one aspect of the issue at hand. The *incentive* to optimize, to aim at the ideal of maximal rationality no matter how short of the mark the approximation, makes it easy to understand why Barnard's contribution-satisfaction equilibrium is so central to Simon's analysis.[21] There is, then, no way to determine just how short of the mark one in fact might be, as opposed to the claim that one *is* short of the mark somehow because certain alternative means were not, in retrospect, contemplated or given proper consideration. The ideal as such remains unspecifiable, except in the vague ways that ideals have always been specifiable.

Some idea of the standards that man cannot meet, yet that are not, for Simon, sufficient reason to scale down the maximizing model in his first edition of *Administrative Behaviour*, is evident from the following excerpt. In addition to physical and biological limitations, human rationality is bounded *cognitively*:

> The subject, in order to perform with perfect rationality in this scheme, would have to have a complete description of the consequences following from each alternative strategy and would have to compare these consequences. He would have to know in every single respect how the world would be changed by his behaving one way instead of another, and he would have to follow the consequences of behaviour through *unlimited stretches of time, unlimited reaches of space, and unlimited sets of values.* Under such conditions even an approach to rationality in real behaviour would be inconceivable.[22] (Emphasis mine.)

[17] *Ibid.*, 75.
[18] Preface to the second edition of *Administrative Behaviour* (1957), especially xxii–xxvii.
[19] Both political scientists and administrative law specialists were attempting to deal with "discretion" by administrators as a problem in legislative definition of standards. See Charles Hyneman, *Bureaucracy in a Democracy* (New York, 1950) and the earlier analysis of the problem by Wayne Leys, "Ethics and Administrative Discretion," *Public Administration Review*, 3 (1943), 10–23. Also see H.T. Wilson, "Discretion in the Analysis of Administrative Process," *Osgoode Hall Law Journal*, 10, no. 1 (August 1972) 117–39, for a discussion of the limits of a "discretion" focus in the analysis of administrative behaviour.
[20] *Administrative Behaviour*, 149.
[21] *Administrative Behaviour*, 110–18, inspired largely by Chester Barnard, *The Functions of the Executive* (Cambridge, Mass. 1938), especially chap. 12.
[22] *Administrative Behaviour*, 69.

This would seem to be indicative of the futility of the maximizing model altogether, yet at the very point that this view cries out to be modified or scrapped, Simon decides to stay with it by arguing that human beings in fact delimit their respective spheres of relevance by constructing a "closed system containing only a limited number of variables and a limited range of consequences.[23] Such a working procedure is sometimes discussed by Simon as if it were something that individuals did in full knowledge that they were acting rationally only in this conditional sense. Other times, there seems to be an awareness of the need to define rationality in terms of *intended* action where an individual believes that he is maximizing even though Simon knows that he is not.[24]

Simon then states how fortunate it is that "the consequences of human activities are so strictly segregated; if they were not, the problem of reaching rational decisions would be impossible."[25] This, as Storing notes, is a return to the means-ends schema, albeit within an effort to make it compatible with a conditional conception of rationality in harmony with the behaviour alternative model. Simon's concern for language almost provides him with a way out of the dilemma that results from his effort to reconcile the two schemes: the decision-maker is to maximize *within* this simplified system which puts out of consideration "stretches of time," "reaches of space," and "sets of values" he (or somebody else) does not consider *relevant*. Simon's maximizing model stresses the very sort of complex societal interdependence between means-ends, facts and values, policy and administration which his focus on the isolated individual allegedly closing his own universe of values, variables, and discourse in advance or in process ignores.

At best, one might argue that it is in the situated or contextual aspects of group structure and culture that individuals decide to decide, thereby establishing for that situation the bounds to rationality. And it is precisely the effort to distinguish the significant from the trivial that, particularly during periods of crisis, *demands in the interests of rationality* that certain values and certain realms of fact be excluded from consideration.[26] Sometimes, to be sure, it is a conscious decision to decide that closes further debate and discussion. Often, however, the idea of formal closure turns out to be a view of the process by a non-participant "outside" it, that is, a view from the perspective of the scientific observer who attempts to recast decision-makers in his own image even while he decries their failure to meet his standards.

This is more than simply a problem of scaling down expectations that are really prescriptions, for it indicates an inability to comprehend how decision-making actually occurs. Environmental constraints become "limits" to rationality only

[23] *Ibid.*, 83.

[24] For instance, note Simon's characterization of man contemplating "all the possible patterns of behaviour that an individual might underake" and the way in which his rationality would be defective no matter what his intent. *Administrative Behaviour*, 84.

[25] *Administrative Behaviour*, 185.

[26] Again this may not be a *conscious choice to delimit*, but a necessity. See Harold Wilensky, *Organizational Intelligence*, 77, where March and Simon, *Organizations*, 169, are criticized for their over-reliance upon psychological evidence linking "good" decisions with slowness and deliberateness. Wilensky claims, I think with merit, that such views "tend to overrate the payoff from 'slow deliberation' and underestimate the effect of attributes of structure and culture that transcend individual psychology-hierarchy, specialization, centralization, occupational ideology and other barriers to communication."

for a highly formalized and abstract idealization of reason with little or no empirical anchorage in concrete situations perceived as real by participants in and to them. The situation, constraints and all, is the basic datum in any process of rational decision-making rather than an impediment to it. In order for the formal correctness of an abstract decision procedure to acquire empirical accuracy as it stands, it would have to modify the environment so totally that there would be no environment at all, just an empty universe devoid of chance and possibility. Simon's failure to render empirically meaningful this everyday life process of group and individual decision-making is partly a function of the direction he sees himself heading when he revises his conception of human rationality "down."

This is most clearly evident in his preface to the second edition of *Administrative Behaviour*,[27] where he chides his critics for making too much of his dependence upon the fact-value dichotomy, then goes on to apologize for expecting too much from administrative, as opposed to economic, man. Remember that he is referring to the already-scaled-down "behaviour-alternative" model of human rational possibility, not to the view initially forwarded in means-ends language at the start of the book. Economic man still remained the model of man for Simon in the first edition, however much "closure" was thought to be necessary to decision and action. It is not until 1957, in his preface to the second edition, that we find Simon recasting his theory of administrative rationality, but with an interesting twist: "Administrative theory is peculiarly the theory of intended and bounded rationality – of the behaviour of human beings who *satisfice* because they have not the wits to *maximize*."[28]

This sudden emphasis on intent, we are told, was always implicit in the original essay. Notice, however, that *intendedly* rational action is an example of *bounded* rationality for Simon. Arguing that behavioural scientists have either ascribed to man "a preposterously omniscient rationality" (which clearly includes Simon) or have attempted to "reduce all cognition to affect" in line with psychoanalytic theory (plainly a straw man), Simon sounds ever so briefly like a phenomenologist when he states:

> To anyone who has observed administrative organizations, or has concerned himself with their theory, it seems obvious enough that human behaviour in organizations is, if not wholly rational, at least in good part *intendedly* so. Much behaviour in organizations is, or seems to be, task oriented – and sometimes efficacious [from both the actor's and the observer's perspective] in attaining its goals. Hence if we are to give a psychological explanation of human behaviour in organizations, the psychological theory we employ must be one that has room in it for rational behaviour.[29]

But not "really," that is, "globally" rational behaviour, only a pale and limited variety of it, given the scientific observer's perspective "outside." If economic theory is discovered to demand too much of man the satisficer, psychological theory (but *not* psychoanalysis) is ready to take account of a human rationality which is limited and bounded *because* it is intendedly rather than "objectively" rational.[30] While Simon does concern himself with intent and the definition of the

[27] *Administrative Behaviour*, xxii–xxvii.
[28] *Ibid.*, xxiv. [29] *Ibid.*, xxiii–xxiv.
[30] See notes 84 and 89 for a discussion of "objective" rationality. On the one hand it is defined in comprehensive terms, on the other in terms of the objectives of a given group in the

situation from the standpoint of the actor, this remains second best. The contrast between maximizing and satisficing (satisfy + suffice = good enough) rationalities attests to the fact that even in the later edition, as well as in subsequent works up to 1960, Simon's perspective was still that of the scientific observer, albeit now a disappointed observer to be sure. He remains in the custody of an idealized and prescriptive model of rationality looking down on "administrative man" and occasionally confusing this idealization with social reality. This is evident in the path Simon took in chapters 4 and 5 of *Administrative Behaviour*, which, according to him:

prepares the way for the description of human rationality in organizations by depicting the more global rationality of economic man, and by showing *what conditions would have to be met* for a man to make his choices in the manner assumed by economic theory. Chapter v then undertakes to specify the ways in which actual behaviour *deviates* from the economic model, and the role that the organizational environment plays in such behaviour.[31] (Emphasis mine.)

Simon's compromise between the global rationality of economic theory and the affective reductionism of psychoanalysis does constitute a rapprochement of sorts. He admits that this was only possible because he began to realize after 1947 the need to "construct a model of rational choice that would *incorporate* the actual properties of human beings (!) and at the same time retain some of the *formal clarity* of the economic model" (emphasis mine).[32] That this revised view remains in the grip of the maximizing model of the scientific observer is evident then, in his formulation of the problem of rationality where intendedness is equated with limit and boundary, where the ideal precedes the real in order to highlight "deviations" from it, and where the "actual properties of human beings" come into the theory largely as an afterthought and succeed, or so Simon claims, in "scaling down" what is admittedly a *formal* clarity inhering in the crisp, clear concept of rational man in economic theory.[33]

II

Yet there is a further indication of the problem of the scientific observer with his intellectual construction of social reality. If Simon appears to be arguing that economic theory conceives of human reason in over-simple as well as omniscient terms, this is misleading. Nowhere in the book is his commitment to an objective reality which is complex rather than simple and uncomplicated clearer than in the following statement:

Economic man deals with the "real world" in all its complexity. Administrative man recognizes that the world he perceives is a drastically simplified model of the buzzing, blooming confusion that constitutes the real world. He (administrative man) is content with this gross simplification because he believes that the real world is mostly

organization. See *Administrative Behaviour*, 119 and 62. The latter definition suggests, but does not develop, the possibility that "objective" rationality may mean in the last analysis an intersubjectively shared world view on the matter of both ends and specific means to their attainment.

[31] *Ibid.*, xxiv. [32] *Ibid.*, xxv.

[33] See V. Subramaniam, "Fact and Value in Decision-Making," *Public Administration Review*, 23 (1963), 236.

empty – that most of the facts of the real world have no great relevance to any particular situation he is facing, and that most significant chains of causes and consequences are short and simple. Hence, he is content to leave out of account those aspects of reality – that means most aspects – that are substantially irrelevant at a given time. He makes his choices using a simple picture of the situation that takes into account just a few of the factors that he regards as most relevant and crucial.[34]

Surely this is a confusing construction of the actual situation. Seen from the scientific observer's point of view, it is doubtless true that satisficing means leaving certain "chains of cause and consequence" out of account, but is this done consciously and purposely by organizational actors? What does it mean to argue that an idealized model of man from economic theory "deals with the 'real' world in all its complexity"? Anyone can point out how "complex" the real world is by post hoc reference to factors that might have been considered prior to decision and action. From the standpoint of the scientific observer, whose ideals real people never quite measure up to, it may even make sense to characterize administrative man's view of this "buzzing, blooming confusion" as "a drastically simplified model" of what we must take on faith from Simon constitutes the "real" world. But I would have put most of this the other way around.

Again, Simon has no way of telling us, nor does anyone else, what would constitute an ideally, globally, totally, optimally, maximally rational decision because he could never know for sure whether all "relevant" premises had been included.[35] Secondly, Simon's imputation of conscious simplification of the real world to administrative man won't work. It is *economic models* of globally rational choice that are simplifications, and usually peripherally useful only for the most low level trivial decisions in large organizations. This is supported by recent "advances" in data processing where the program depends upon a view of rationality where the system is unrealistically static and simple.[36] A third point has to do with the subjectivity of Simon and of the scientific observer generally. Here the assumption that the intellectual's construction of social reality is fundamentally and finally more valid than the actor's must again become problematic.

When Simon speaks of limited and bounded rationality he is often (though not always) putting himself into the decisional or action situation with his knowledge of economic theory, then indicating how far short of the ideal his own action *might* fall.[37] The intellectual, however disinterestedly scientific he may be, can no more escape the values that influence his view of reality than can the actor. Actors without such idealized notions of what might be may be intendedly *and maximally* rational from their own standpoint, or alternatively they may not come up to *their own standards*. The difference is that the actor generally has realistic standards, not absurdly idealized ones which effectively blind him to his tasks.[38]

[34]*Administrative Behaviour*, xxv–xxvi. See also Simon, *Models of Man*, 199, where intentionality, equated with interests and values, does not constitute "even approximately optimal" behaviour. See Adolph Lowe, *On Economic Knowledge* (New York, 1965), especially chap. 3, 4, and 6.

[35]As the behaviour-alternative model recognizes.

[36]Boguslaw, *New Utopians*, chap. 2.

[37]*Administrative Behaviour*, xxiii–xxiv, xviii.

[38]Here "realistic" standards would recognize the constraints, when considered as such, as part of the situation to be dealt with, not interfering conditions. To the extent that "cognitive limits" are reformulated in terms of "environmental complexity," some but not all the bias of Simon's discussion of satisficing is sidestepped. See March and Simon, *Organizations*, chap. 6.

The claim that administrative man *rather than economic* man "believes that the real world is mostly empty" indicates further the problem of imputing to organizational actors a conscious effort at delimitation and a commitment to satisficing as a positively chosen method, given "limits" to perfect formal rationality.

There is a third problem in Simon's work that, although it bears upon the confusion of the ideal and the actual in the intellectual's construction of social reality as objectively there and scientifically determinable, deserves to be treated on its own. It is the fact-value dichotomy so central to the logic of Simon's position in all his work, yet dismissed in the revised edition of *Administrative Behaviour* as something which his critics have made too much of.[39] I submit that Simon is correct on this score, but that the reason why he is correct can only be appreciated once the criticisms of his work are seen as "family squabbles" where nobody, with the possible exception of Dwight Waldo, fundamentally challenges Simon's commitment to science and to the role of the intellectual in making sense of everyday life. Yet this is precisely where treatment of the fact-value dichotomy becomes of peripheral significance. Critics got embroiled in its relation to the means-ends language that Simon himself had considered unsatisfactory and had broken with *in the first edition.*[40] Or they involved themselves in the extent to which it was valid to argue that the fact-value dichotomy should be reflected in the distinction between those who administer (appointees, civil servants) and those who make policy (those elected).[41]

What was left out of the consideration, even by such astute critics and commentators as Victor Thompson, Murray Edelman, and Harold Wilensky, was the way in which logical empiricism reduces the distinction between facts and values to the objectively real and to the subjectively and emotively desired. I submit that the reason some of the more serious consequences resulting from adherence to this dichotomy have been so consistently overlooked by Simon's critics (and others) is that most if not all *agree* with it, at least in principle if not in practice.[42] Logical empiricism is the methodological basis for the development of Simon's "science" of administration. He accepts all its basic tenets; indeed he puts it forward in *Administrative Behaviour* (chapter 3) as his alternative to the common sense "proverbs" and principles of administration (chapter 2) which constitute the same kind of barrier to "science" that folk cures and quack remedies allegedly do to the advance of medicine.

This does not mean that Simon is impervious to certain aspects of the difference between the human and the "hard" sciences.[43] It does mean, however, that he is on the whole committed to the view that the study of man can benefit from the terminological, conceptual, and methodological rigour of physics. Without dwell-

[39] *Administrative Behaviour*, xxxiv. [40] *Ibid.*, 62–73.

[41] Dwight Waldo, *The Administrative State* (New York, 1948), especially chap. 6–8; Waldo, "Development of Theory of Democratic Administration," *American Political Science Review*, 46 (1952), 81–103. Notice Simon's statement in the context of his treatise on *public* administration in Simon, Smithburg, and Thompson, *Public Administration*, 58, and Storing's discussion, "Science of Administration," 101–4.

[42] To the extent that categories of analysis "match," the existence of a terminology in common, at least where the fact-value distinction is involved, suggests the outer boundaries of the argument by Simon's "critics." See, for instance, Robert Dahl, "The Science of Public Administration: Some Problems," *Public Administration Review*, 7 (1947), 1–11.

[43] *Administrative Behaviour*, xiv.

ing on the possibility that Simon and the logical empiricists have misconstrued or ignored significant features of scientific inquiry, we can usefully compare Simon's position on basic tenets to that of A.J. Ayer, whose work continues to inspire many philosophers of science, and probably still inspires Simon himself.[44]

Like the logical empiricists, Simon takes as his point of departure the need to analyse and identify modes of oral and written expression in the field being scrutinized. Since Simon is trying to prepare the way for a science where no science has existed before, namely, in a particular area of human social inquiry called administration, he must focus upon some phenomenon or event central to what might be called the administrative process. He finds the key in the analysis of decisions and decision-making, or more properly in the analysis of the *premises* of decision.[45] Simon's commitment to the dichotomy between factual and ethical premises as the twin components in human decision-making is never stronger than in his discussion of whether such a rigid distinction "leaves any room" for human judgment. Like other linguistic analysts, this becomes a peculiar sort of problem for one dedicated to the analysis of the sentences of any endeavour worthy of the name of science.

Arguing like the logical empiricists that one cannot derive ethical propositions from factual ones temporarily compels Simon to conclude that "in a strict sense, the administrator's decisions cannot be evaluated by scientific means."[46] But most so-called ethical propositions "have admixed with them factual elements," which is really to say that the dichotomy does not reflect an actual distinction between types of sentences used by administrators in everyday life. Simon finds "room for human judgment" (!) in the fact that there is rarely if ever time for administrators to maximize by resort to means-end rationality.[47] Thus the behaviour alternative model alluded to before which is the point of departure for Simon's reconstruction of the problem of rationality in administrative decision-making. The further along the mean-end chain one goes, according to Simon, the more residual and secondary become "the facts" and the more primary become the ethical elements.[48] Simon distinguishes the ethical element and judgment as follows:

> In ordinary speech there is often confusion between the element of judgment in decision and the ethical element. This confusion is enhanced by the fact that the further the means-end chain is followed, i.e. the greater the ethical element, the more doubtful are the steps in the chain, and the greater is the element of judgment involved in determining what means will contribute to what ends.[49]

If both types of element (or premise) seem to be on a par in this statement the

[44]See especially *Language, Truth and Logic*, 2nd ed. (New York, 1946). His addendum to the original text, published in 1935, is as theoretically significant from the standpoint of the canons of logical empiricism, as is Simon's preface to the second edition of *Administrative Behaviour*. Also Ayer, "On the Analysis of Moral Judgments," *Horizon*, 20 (1949), 165–81, and *The Revolution in Philosophy* (London, 1956). Simon's reference to Ayer and others in *Administrative Behaviour* is at p. 46.

[45]He puts forward this distinction as a significant one in his preface to the second edition of *Administrative Behaviour*, xii. "It is therefore the *premise* (and a large number of these are combined in every decision) rather than the whole *decision* that serves as the smallest unit of analysis" (emphasis his). This suggests the significance of the fact-value distinction since premises on analysis turn out generally to be either factual or valuational. See p. 46.

[46]*Ibid.*, 47. [47]*Ibid.*, 49–50. [48]*Ibid.*, 50–1. [49]*Ibid.*, 51.

parity is illusory. As a logical positivist, Simon is virtually required to reduce the ethical element to "subjective" judgment where the latter is equated with "values." This is *even more true* for the satisficing view of administrative (as opposed to economic) man advanced in the preface to the second edition of *Administrative Behaviour* than it is for the behaviour-alternative model which seriously compromises means-end rationality in the first. What we are left with is a view of the character of administrative decision-making which makes the commitment to a science of administration meaningless save for the fact that it exists as an observer's ideal on the basis of which actual processes are evaluated. It also casts serious doubt on the view that the *premises* of decision rather than the situated aspects of the process are the proper focus for analysis.[50] Simon's commitment to a normative model of decision, which is allegedly more real because it concerns itself with logical analysis, "hard" data, and the actual complexities of the process, not only manifests serious inconsistencies with respect to the confusion of the ideal and "real," and the artificial separation *in everyday life* of facts and values which are so interwoven in human interaction that even linguistic analysis cannot separate them. It is the tendency to confuse logical truth with empirical evidence that is perhaps the most problematic of all, yet it is one which is endemic to logical empiricism, even in its watered-down form.[51].

According to A.J. Ayer, whom Simon cites authoritatively and with approval in the section on facts and values in decision, the following propositions constitute the central tenets of logical empiricism: (1) all knowledge is empirical and is derived from our experience of sensory reality; (2) the meaning of any empirical (synthetic) proposition is to be discovered in the observations that we would need to make to determine its truth or falsity; (3) the truth of an empirical proposition is never certain, only probable; (4) logical and mathematical (analytical) propositions are tautologous; (5) ethical assertions (metaphysical, theological, normative) are scientifically irrelevant because they are factually meaningless.[52] Propositions (1), (2), and (5) need to be looked at more closely.

In the first place, to say that all knowledge is "empirical" and derived from "our experience of sensory reality" is really to raise the point that human beings derive from their experience in the world a stock of knowledge which is at hand for them in day to day interaction. But this does not mean that there is an objectively real social world which everyone perceives the same way. It serves to raise

[50]See Edward Banfield, "The Decision-Making Schema," and Simon's "The Decision-Making Schema: A Reply," in *Public Administration Review* (autumn 1957), 284, note 5 and (winter 1958), 62. Also, Waldo, "Development" and "Replies and Comments," *American Political Science Review*, 46 (1952), 97 and 494–5, 503.

[51]This extends to the work of Simon and his associates where logically rigorous models are used as a basis for *describing* an organization rather than suggesting a standard to which individuals and groups might address themselves. See *Administrative Behaviour*, xiv (preface to the 1st ed.) where Simon begins by noting that "we do not yet have, in this field, adequate linguistic and conceptual tools for *realistically and significantly describing* even a simple administrative organization – describing it, that is, in a way that will provide the basis for scientific analysis of the effectiveness of its structure and operation. Among the studies of administrative organizations that I have read, few have caught and set down in words *the real flesh and bones of an organization* ..." And further on: "Before we can establish any immutable 'principles' of administration, we must be able to describe, in words, exactly how an administrative organization looks and exactly how it works" (emphasis mine).

[52]For clarification see Luther Binkley, *Contemporary Ethical Theories* (New York, 1961), 59–102 at pp. 64–70.

the problem of intersubjectivity which, while it is the fundamental point of departure for phenomenological social science, is taken to be non-problematic in the positivistic presupposition that there is an objectively real social world which individuals know with varying degrees of truth and falsity.[53]

But social and physical worlds are different precisely because in the former there exists a component of human action which arises out of different and often conflicting constructions of social reality which cannot be treated simply as deviations from the "real" if only because such constructions of social reality are "real" for given individuals and are therefore *the basic datum* of any sociological analysis committed to "scientific" rigour.[54] The dichotomy between facts and values, rigidly adhered to, provides the illusion of scientific verification where the demand that competent observers agree on "truth or falsity" may simply indicate the effect of scientific and intellectual training in developing an intersubjectively shared world where similar or harmonious constructions of social reality are highly likely.[55]

To argue that ethical assertions are scientifically irrelevant because they are nothing more than emotional outbursts or at best statements of preference is to effectively guarantee that the social science which results from adherence to such canons of inquiry will, with the model of the hard sciences well in hand, completely miss the point of social inquiry – to render the common sense world of everyday life meaningful.[56] It is *because* human action is intended and premised on these allegedly irrational preferences and feelings that these aspects must constitute the data for social inquiry, however much they may sabotage logic and "deviate" from normative models which *begin* by presuming an objective reality about which one *ought* to have full information.

III

It is at this point that a reformulation of the problem of rationality in the social world compels a total break with any view which takes as its point of departure the usefulness of the fact-value distinction in any of its various guises. It is precisely because its acceptance is indissolubly linked *not* to the means-ends or administration-policy dichotomies but rather to the object-subject distinction that it must be scrapped as evidence of the limited relevance of the unified science

[53]Here no (or little) distinction is made between the character of knowledge about social and about physical reality from the standpoint of the knowing subject. The social sciences are simply suffering from a methodological (that is, a *technological*) lag which subsequent improvements in technique will permit us to master. See Ernest Nagel, *The Structure of Science* (New York, 1961), especially chap. 1, 2, 6, 13, and 14 for one of the most sophisticated statements of this position.

[54]See especially Alfred Schutz, "Concept and Theory Formation in the Social Sciences," *Journal of Philosophy*, 51 (1954), and Aron Gurvitsch, "The Common Sense World as Social Reality," *Social Research*, 28 (1961), 50–72. Also see Adolph Lowe, *On Economic Knowledge* (New York, 1965), 61–2.

[55]Here the definition of "objective" reality, whether physical or social, takes the form of agreement among colleagues, with the proviso of tentativeness embodied in hypothesis. Interestingly enough, it was logical empiricism which asserted in straightforward *rather than hypothetical* fashion the absolute value of their "standpointless" position beyond values. On schools generally, see Florian Znaniecki, *The Social Role of the Man of Knowledge* (New York, 1940), especially pp. 91–163.

[56]Gurvitsch, "Common Sense World."

model of inquiry for the social sciences. Instead of *beginning* with an intellectual presumption about the existence of a world of objectively knowable facts which is variously responsible for producing human beings whose only barrier to greater knowledge is their "values" and "subjective emotions," we must focus our attention on individuals who act, who construct their social reality, who simultaneously produce a world and endow it with relevances and meanings which are the basis for both their thoughts and their actions.[57] It is because *both* the other's actions and *his knowledge of the world* are problematic that, in Garfinkel's words, the social scientist "cannot avoid *some* working decision about the various phenomena intended by the term 'rationality.' "[58]

The objective here is to provide an alternative view to the positivistic polarization of human action as rational if it conforms to scientific predefinitions and irrational if it does not. Rather than looking down on irrational man from the heights of scientific "objectivity," it is suggested that science as an enterprise depends ultimately upon certain prescientific assumptions which do not simply reduce to "values" but constitute a foundational human basis for reason as it relates both to knowledge and to action. There is, in other words, a more basic kind of rationality which characterizes the common sense world in which we all reside and on which we draw for continued sustenance even in the scientific or theoretical attitude. The Schutz-Garfinkel inventory of the various meanings given to rationality in everyday as well as scientific usage makes this point clear.[59] We shall be particularly concerned with those meanings which appear in the various formulations in Simon's work.

While rationality from the standpoint of the theorizing scientific observer and scholarly analyst is defined to include the compatibility of ends-means relationships with the canons of formal logic, with semantic clarity and terminological precision, and with the information-seeking and cost-calculating model of man in economic theory, common sense usages relevant to the "natural attitude" of everyday life define as rational *any concern or effort whatsoever* to categorize and compare present to past experience, to isolate and review methods or means to a desired end, to analyse and evaluate possible avenues of action and their likely consequences, to rank-order given lines of action and to evolve strategies in advance of anticipated situations, to attempt to schedule or time the release of one's actions by reference to expected events, to attempt to predict outcomes, and to

[57]"Socialization" in this formulation is not referenced ultimately to the system but rather to "significant others," specific individuals in a person's biographical development who influence his view of the world even while they produce their own. Society, in effect, is *both* subjective and objective reality for the actor. See Peter Berger and Thomas Luckmann, *The Social Construction of Reality* (Garden City, N.Y. 1968); Burckart Holzner, *Reality Construction in Society* (Cambridge, Mass. 1968) and Herbert Blumer, *Symbolic Interactionism* (Englewood Cliffs, N.J. 1969), especially chap. 1, "The Methodological Position of Symbolic Interaction."

[58]Harold Garfinkel, "The Rational Properties of Scientific and Commonsense Activities," in Garfinkel, *Studies in Ethnomethodology* (Englewood Cliffs, N.J. 1967), 262–83 at p. 262. Also see Garfinkel, "Studies of the Routine Grounds of Everyday Activities," and "Commonsense Knowledge of Social Structures," in Garfinkel, *Studies in Ethnomethodology*, 35–75, 76–103.

[59]Alfred Schutz, "The Problem of Rationality in the Social World," in Schutz, *Collected Papers*, Volume 2 (The Hague: Martinus Nijoff, 1962), pp. 63–88, and Garfinkel, *The Rational Properties*.

TABLE I

A SUMMARY OF THE PROPOSITIONS RELATING THE RATIONALITIES TO THE CONDITIONS OF THEIR OCCURRENCE*

	For all actions that are governed by the rules of relevance of daily life can the rationalities occur IF			For all actions that are governed by the rules of relevance of scientific theorizing can the rationalities occur IF		
	Considered as an ideal standard of action?	Considered as an operative standard of action?	Considered as a property of actual practice?	Considered as an ideal standard of action?	Considered as an operative standard of action?	Considered as a property of actual practice?
Categorizing and comparing	yes†	yes	yes	yes	yes	yes
Tolerable error	yes	yes	yes	yes	yes	yes
Search for "means"	yes	yes	yes	yes	yes	yes
Analysis of alternatives and consequences	yes	yes	yes	yes	yes	yes
Strategy	yes	yes	yes	yes	yes	yes
Concern for timing	yes	yes	yes	yes	yes	yes
Predictability	yes	yes	yes	yes	yes	yes
Rules of procedure	yes	yes	yes	yes	yes	yes
Choice	yes	yes	yes	yes	yes	yes
Grounds of choice	yes	yes	yes	yes	yes	yes
Compatibility of end-means relationships with formal logic	no	no	no	yes	yes	yes
Semantic clarity and distinctness	no	no	no	yes	yes	yes
Clarity and distinctness "for its own sake"	no	no	no	yes	yes	yes
Compatibility of the definition of a situation with scientific knowledge	no	no	no	yes	yes	yes

*From Harold Garfinkel, *Studies in Ethnomethodology* (Englewood Cliffs N.J. 1967) 271.

†"Yes" is to be read, "Is empirically possible either as a stable property and/or a *sanctionable* ideal." "No" is to be read, "Is empirically possible only as an unstable property and/or an *unsanctionable* ideal." By this is meant that attempts to stabilize the feature or to compel adherence through systematic administration of rewards and punishments, are the operations required to multiply the anomic features of the interaction. What these propositions state for the rationalities when considered singly, they state as well for the set of them taken in any combination.

make choices premised on what would constitute rational grounds for the actor. Notice that rationality in this "natural attitude" is concerned not so much with scientific predefinitions having objective validity in terms of procedural requirements or outcomes (consequences, "success") but rather with intentions, attempts, and efforts where the actor's concern with calculation, anticipation, and prediction is oriented to likelihoods, probabilities, and only occasionally to certainties.[60]

Drawing attention to the difference between the *cognitive* interest of the scientific observer and the *practical* interest of the actor in everyday life, Schutz asks whether we are to classify the latter examples as rational or irrational.[61] The scientist, he argues, is compelled, barring comprehension of the *limiting character* of his interest, to reference such behaviours as at best marginally rational and at worst non-rational or even "irrational." Citing this as indicative of "scientific conceit," Garfinkel suggests that such rigid definitions of rationality be understood as ideal norms of and operative strategies in scholarly and scientific work. Indeed, the concept of rationality may itself be problematic as the basic point of departure for the analysis of human action because such a methodological principle of interpretation presupposes it to be a peculiar and isolated feature of daily life rather than part of a less easily demarcated stream of events which *includes* the intentions and efforts of the actor.[62] Stepping into the scenario with economic theory, psychology, logic, and anything else not comprehensible *to the actor* as an explanation of his action, therefore, is the *scientist's* problem. Schutz formulates it the following way: "Each term used in a scientific system referring to human action must be so constructed that a human act performed within the life world by an individual actor in the way indicated by the typical construction would be reasonable and understandable for the actor himself, as well as for his fellow-man."[63]

This postulate of adequacy constitutes the phenomenological response to and reconstruction of the requirement of procedural verifiability in logical empiricism so central to "progress" in the natural sciences but so incomplete in its usual

[60]See Schutz, "The Problem of Rationality in the Social World," 74–7, and Garfinkel, "The Rational Properties of Scientific and Commonsense Activities," 263–71. Chester Barnard, whom Simon cites with great respect, criticizes scientific predefinitions of rational behaviour on the grounds that they are excessively narrow. See *Functions of the Executive*, appendix, "Mind in Everyday Affairs." For this reason, among others, I would tend to disagree with Sherman Krupp, who places Simon and Barnard together in his analysis of administrative science and organization theory in favour of a view which sees Simon a "rationalist" and Barnard a merger of "rationalist" and "natural systems" approaches as presented by Gouldner, "Organizational Analysis." See Sherman Krupp, *Pattern in Organizational Analysis* (New York, 1961), especially chap. 8.

[61]Schutz, "The Problem of Rationality in the Social World," 74, 69–70. Compare to Simon's dilemma, *Administrative Behaviour*, 76.

[62]Garfinkel, "The Rational Properties of Scientific and Commonsense Activities," 278; Schutz, "The Problem of Rationality in the Social World," 79. Compare Simon's requirements for optimally rational behaviour by the actor in *Administrative Behaviour* (p. 69) with Garfinkel's requirements for the sociological theorist concerned with rational behaviour (p. 270, note 5).

[63]"The Problem of Rationality in the Social World," 85, 19. "What makes it possible for a social science to refer at all to events in the life-world is the fact that the interpretation of any human act by the social scientist might be the same as that by the actor or by his partner." *Ibid.*, 85–6. Notice also Schutz' discussion of the "principle of relevance" and the "postulate of subjective interpretation," also on 85–6.

formulation and transplantation into the social sciences.[64] The idea here is to *discipline* analysis by making all human actions data, without a predefined scheme for classifying them as rational or non-rational given the scientist's characteristic but temporary escape from the common-sense "recipe" knowledge he possesses by virtue of his experience of everyday life. And, let it be noted, this is not a problem which adherence to the phenomenological approach automatically eliminates. On the contrary, the very effort to render the common-sense world meaningful and to guard against scientific and scholarly predefinitions which fail to meet the postulate of adequacy by resort to theoretical constructs indicates the scope of the problem implicit in the attempt to deal with it.[65]

Having contrasted the characteristics of rationality in the natural and theoretical attitudes, let us return again to the question of *directionality* revealed in the process of scientific investigation. Simon, it was noted, tended to first construct a model of a person as a "type" who conforms to idealized standards of rationality, then to compare the "actual" behaviour of individuals against the model.[66] The "discrepancies," though already problematic for Simon in the first edition of *Administrative Behaviour*, become virtually intolerable for him in the preface to the second edition 10 years later. One might argue that, having discovered that administrative man "satisficed," the desire to continue utilization of the maximization model of man thereafter necessitated his virtual abandonment of the field of administrative theory and subsequent move into decision theory and formalism after 1960.[67] It is important to notice that Simon's critics almost to a man do not fundamentally challenge the directionality of this research procedure, with telling consequences for the analysis and assessment of man the satisficer.

In "The Science of Muddling Through"[68] Charles Lindblom describes the way administrators in the public sector *might* go about the task of policy formulation, then compares this to the way they actually do it. He is discussing "good" administrators here, not satisficers who "get by" in Simon's comparison and contrast by doing the minimum necessary for the task without concern for efficiency and effectiveness criteria. Lindblom argues that it is the very complexity of such an enterprise that requires resort to a "branch" rather than a "root" approach. With Simon clearly in mind in his definition of the root approach as "rational-compre-

[64]See Ayer, *Language, Truth and Logic*, 2nd ed. 5–16, where the author modifies his more stringent "principle of verification" (the meaning of a statement lies in the observations necessary to confirm or disconfirm it), which originally required *direct observation*, to require only that the scientist "know what observations *would* decide it for me, *if*, as is theoretically conceivable, I *were once* in a position to make them." See 36–7. Ayer's effort to get around the "scientific conceit" implicit in this requirement, even in its watered down form, has required him to argue that logical positivism never put forward the verification principle as an empirically verifiable proposition but as a *definition*. Ayer, *The Revolution in Philosophy*, 75.
[65]But does not, of course, warrant, or even excuse, failure to deal with these problems on the grounds that it seriously delimits the scope and potential ambit of the social sciences as knowledge technologies concerned with *prediction* and control as well as explanation.
[66]See Garfinkel, "The Rational Properties," 279–80.
[67]Simon, *The New Science of Management Decision* (New York, 1960) indicates his disillusionment with administrative science and organization theory. Much of his subsequent work is summarized in *The Sciences of the Artificial* (Cambridge, Mass. 1968) and by Richard Cyert and James March in *A Behavioural Theory of the Firm* (Englewood Cliffs, N.J. 1964).
[68]*Public Administration Review*, 19 (1959), 79–88. See also David Braybrooke and Charles Lindblom, *A Strategy of Decision* (Glencoe, Ill. 1963).

hensive," Lindblom asserts that what at first glance may seem to constitute *the absence of method* in administrative decision-making is really itself a method or technique after all.[69] The "branch" approach, called the "successive limited comparisons" model, is contrasted with the root approach because *in fact* one cannot separate temporally facts and values and means and ends in ongoing human activity. In addition, the limited (as opposed to the comprehensive) character of administrative pre-decisional analysis replaces much abstract theory with past experience, with the determination and evaluation of policy becoming more a matter of agreement among analysts than a comparison with maximization models. With special reference to *public* adminstration, Lindblom claims that it is as much a question of financial resources as one of cognitive limits, thus *apparently* (but not actually) failing to catch the drift of trends already visible when he wrote toward the use of comprehensive management systems in Western governments.[70]

That Lindblom is trapped in the maximizing model is evident in his insistence upon the fact that administrators do have *a* method, *a one best way* even if it is characterized by "limits" and is not considered worthy of the label "rational" in his analysis. Administrators need not apologize for their approach (as if there were only one), even considering all its "imperfections." While he does attack Simon's (and other's) confusion as to which model really deals with the world in all its complexity, his concentration upon the fact-value, and especially the means-ends dichotomies, is almost a straw man given the fact that even in the first edition, but certainly by the second, Simon had abandoned all efforts to use these two sets interchangeably as a description of the administrative process in favour of the behaviour-alternative model.[71]

The actual still falls short of the ideal, of what might be in the absence of special considerations and features *of the situation* which are as responsible for limiting maximization as is the fact of limited human capacity. Ultimately, of course, cognitive limits and environmental complexity come together in the form of a decision-maker as policy formulator who cannot possibly master all criteria which may possibly (!) be relevant and therefore must act in the knowledge and with the acceptance of these limitations.[72] There is a hint in Lindblom that maximization, *given these limits*, may be *irrational* as well as a recognition of the *decreasing* relevance of the comprehensive approach the further one moves away from the kinds of questions where the presumption of system stability and order can safely be made.

John Pfiffner and Nicolas Nicolaidis come the closest to breaking with the language of rationality and the maximizing model in Simon,[73] but even here the

[69]*Ibid.*, 87–8.
[70]See Symposium, "Governmental Decision-Making," *Public Administration Review*, 24 (1964), 153–65, and Yehezkel Dror, *Public Policy-Making Re-examined* (San Francisco, 1965).
[71]*Administrative Behaviour*, 64–73.
[72]Thus are "cognitive limits to rationality" in March and Simon, *Organizations*, chap. 6, especially 169–71, transformed into attempts to minimize the problem of "uncertainty" given environmental complexity in James Thompson, *Organizations in Action* (New York, 1968) as closed system "administrative science" becomes open system "organization theory." See Waldo, "Organization Theory: An Elephantine Problem."
[73]John Pfiffner, "Administrative Rationality," *Public Administration Review*, 20 (1960), 125–32.

latter's concept of administrative man the satisficer is once again confirmed as it was in Lindblom's study. Pfiffner, summarizing Nicolaidis's "study of 332 actual administrative decisions in the Los Angeles area"[74] claims that administrative rationality differs from "orthodox" concepts because "it does take into account an additional spectrum of facts" relevant to "emotions, politics, power, group dynamics, personality and mental health." The "data of social science," it is argued, "are facts just as much as the carbon content of steel or the dollars and cents in the salary fund." It is because organizations are pluralistic "federations of cooperation" rather than monocratic chains of command that the orthodox formulation of rationality is inapplicable and even irrelevant.

The administrative decision-maker tries to please as many persons as possible, including himself, thus adding a strong political tinge to the decision process. But he also *clothes his decisions with reason.* The politics of the situation requires him to abandon a simple "engineering solution," but he saves face by supporting his decision with reasons which possess face validity. Hence it would be wrong to say that administrative decision-making is either non-rational or irrational. If looked at from one standpoint it is *even more rational* [emphasis mine] than the classical model because it takes into consideration a greater variety of data. It considers psychological and social data which are virtually ignored in the classical model. This being the case, is the politician less rational than the engineer?[75]

The actual decision process in organized groups takes place, according to Pfiffner, along a continuum with classical rationality at one end and intuition and hunch at the other. Proverb selection and "advice" would presumably be somewhere along the continuum and could conceivably be closer to norms of rationality.[76] This is probably the clearest statement within the group of critics about the actual character of decision-making as a *substantially rational* enterprise where multiple criteria of validity obtain, where both information and decision points in the organization are many, and where a commitment to empiricism rather than to formal *logic,* and to experience rather than to abstract theory, makes administrative man far more rational *given the context.*[77]

That he must "clothe his decisions with reason" suggests another dimension of the issue of complexity, yet one not always characterized by such a commitment on the part of the actor to "clothing" as a strategy. Again we may find that we are really speaking from the frame of reference of the scientific observer. Nowhere else does the positive character of administrative activity as situated, political and complex come through as well as it does here. Instead of speaking of cognitive limits, Pfiffner concentrates on both intent and necessity and appears to meet the postulate of adequacy in the process:

The failure of the administrator to gather all available data and to list every possible alternative is not due only to the mechanical limitations of the human mind, as some members of the classical school of rationality have suggested. It is due rather to the fact that the administrator has learned to be selective and to utilize cumulative knowledge just as the scientist has. This, combined with the realization that there may be more than one satisfactory solution, has led to the utilization of common sense short-

[74]*Ibid.*, 125. [75]*Ibid.*, 128.

[76]This differs substantially from Simon's characterization of proverbs as *non-rational* given his scientific-logical perspective on *isolated* rather than situated actors in *Administrative Behaviour*. See especially chap. 2 and this study, notes 11, 26, and 38.

[77]Pfiffner, "Administrative Rationality," 126–30.

TABLE II

RATIONALITY DICHOTOMIES:* WEBER AND HIS SUCCESSORS

	Rationality as Thought	Rationality as Action
Types and polarities	scientific (scholarly) versus common-sense rationality	formal (functional, technological, organizational) versus substantial rationality
Institutional reference point	science as a method; scholarship and intellectual activity	capitalism; bureaucracy; the legal order; the "administrative state"
Problem classification	disenchantment of the world; belief in objective rational order	"rationalization"; organization of action
Problem from actor's standpoint	with reference to his knowledge of "the world"	with reference to his participation in the division of labour
Subsequent intellectual developments and offshoots	phenomenology† (Weber, Husserl, James, Dewey, Schutz); ethnomethodology (Garfinkel); sociology of knowledge (Mannheim, Berger and Luckmann, Holzner)	neo-Marxism; Frankfurt school of Hermeneutic science†† (Horkheimer, Marcuse, Habermas); sociology of knowledge (Mannheim)

*This dichotomy is *implicit* in Weber, who was careful at the level of sociological analysis to define rationality always in terms of *action* (behaviour meaningful to the actor *viz* intended).

†Weber's presuppositions concerning intersubjectivity are the starting point for much of phenomenological sociology.

††The Marcuse-Habermas critique of Weber, and especially the latter, builds more upon *Weber's* implicit dichotomies than on Marx's sub and superstructure distinctions (work, interaction) as alleged.

cuts. The administrative decision-maker is constantly striving to reduce the number of alternates, but by means other than the laborious covering of ground already trodden by others.[78]

IV

We are now ready to bring together the threads of this argument by comparing Simon's formulation of the problem of rationality in terms of decision analysis with the work of Max Weber, who is perhaps the social scientist more concerned than anyone else with rational action and its relation to Western historical development. Weber attempted to avoid the pitfalls inherent in a rigid distinction between thought and action on the grounds that while it might be analytically useful for the scientist it did not conform to the way individual actors went about their business in everyday life.[79] At the same time his twin concerns with sociological methodology and social structure and historical development characteristically compelled him to conceive of rationality from the standpoint of knowledge as distinct from rationality as behaviour meaningful to the actor in given social situations. As a consequence, Weber in fact formulated *two* sets of rationality

[78] *Ibid.*, 130.
[79] *Theory of Social and Economic Organization* (Glencoe, Ill. 1947), 88–98, 104–11.

typologies, one concerned with the actor's knowledge of the world and the other with his participation in the social division of labour.[80] The first is the one we have been dealing with here.

The second has only been alluded to in passing to this point, yet its importance is attested to by the fact that individuals more recently interested in a critical reconstruction of the social sciences from a Marxian perspective have necessarily been compelled to revisit and confront the work of Max Weber, especially as it bears upon technology as an expression of rationality.[81] Herbert Simon has also concerned himself with the relationship between individual rationality and the rationality of the organized group, but has tended to extend the satisficing argument from the actor's knowledge of the world to participation in joint endeavour. Simon sees organizations, that is, organized groups of individuals, as devices for overcoming the cognitive limits to rationality in individual human beings.[82] The very fact that individuals can desire to accomplish given tasks and to achieve given ends yet need the cooperation of others if they are to do so is the basis for group organization and division of labour. The irrelevance of the fact-value dichotomy in the day to day process of administrative decision-making is evident in Simon's attempt to clarify what he means by the use of the term "rational":

> Perhaps the only way to avoid, or clarify, these complexities is to use the term "rational" in conjunction with appropriate adverbs. Then a decision may be called "objectively" rational if *in fact* it is the correct behaviour for maximizing given values in a given situation. It is "subjectively" rational if it maximizes attainment relative to the actual knowledge of the subject. It is "consciously" rational to the degree that the adjustment of means to ends is a conscious process. It is "deliberately" rational to the degree that the adjustment of means to ends has been deliberately brought about (by the individual or by the organization). A decision is "organizationally" rational if it is oriented to the organization's goals; it is "personally" rational if it is oriented to the individual's goals.[83]

What about a conflict between the individual's and the "organization's" construction of the situation? In the first place there is no organization as such. Simon, while no nominalist, does reduce the organization to specific groups of individuals. Secondly, the individual is seen to be either interested in maximizing "personal" goals or acting in a limitedly rational capacity which is bound to be inferior to the capacity of the organized group. Thirdly, however, the idea that there is one technically correct behaviour alternative which constitutes "objective" rationality in a given situation is problematic, especially when that alternative is judged to be the more closely approximated the further one moves away from the individual

[80] *Ibid.* Compare Weber's discussion of the concept of "action" with his distinction between formal and substantive rationality, 184–6, 211–18.

[81] For instance, Herbert Marcuse, *One Dimensional Man* (Boston, 1964); "Industrialization and Capitalism in the Work of Max Weber," in *Negations* (Boston, 1968), 201–26; Jurgen Habermas, "Technology and Science as Ideology," in *Toward a Rational Society: Student Protest, Science and Politics* (Boston, 1970); Karl Loewith, "Max Weber's Interpretation of the Bourgeois-Capitalist World in Terms of the Guiding Principle of 'Rationalization,'" in *Max Weber*, ed. Dennis Wrong (Englewood Cliffs, N.J. 1970), 101–22.

[82] *Administrative Behaviour*, especially chap. 4. It is through *group* action that uncertainty is minimized where total control and predictability remains the scientist's (but not necessarily the politician's or the administrator's) ideal.

[83] *Ibid.*, 76–7.

and the more one widens his constituency of expert calculation and deliberation.[84] The individual's "subjective" rationality is still conceived of in second-best terms; he is a bundle of needs and desires whose values cognitively limit his objective knowledge of the world and render it imperative that he be coordinated into the larger rationality of the group.

> A decision is rational from the standpoint of the individual (subjectively rational) if it is consistent with the values, the alternatives, and the information which he weighed in reaching it. A decision is rational from the standpoint of the group (objectively rational) if it is consistent with the values governing the group, and the information that the group possesses relevant to the decision. *Hence, the organization must be so constructed that a decision which is (subjectively) rational from the standpoint of the deciding individual, will remain rational when reassessed from the standpoint of the group.*[85] (Emphasis mine)

Thus the "basic task of administration" is "to provide each 'operative' employee with an environment of decision of such a kind that behaviour which is rational from the standpoint of this environment is also rational from the standpoint of the group values and the group situation"[86] seen as objectively given.

There is, it would seem, a one best way to design an organization such that harmony will prevail and conflict be virtually structured out. It is probably easier to do this in the name of organizational rationality once the group has become the arbiter of *objective* rationality.[87] The individual's "problem" with respect to knowledge of the world thus shades into his "problem" with respect to participation in the organization. In the first case he is confronted by *scientific* rationality and the intellectual or theoretical attitude which is definitive of a cognitive rather than a practical interest in everyday life events and phenomena. In the second, the actor comes face to face with organized technological rationality where the price he must pay for participation in a division of labour may well be the suspension of his own substantial reason rather than simply the control of his impulses.[88] The idea of a prior rationality, common sense in the first instance, substantial in the

[84]"Organizational" and "objective" rationality virtually become one for Simon to the extent that the "constraints against maximization" become *part of the situation* for him. At this point, objectivity becomes synonymous with the idea that *given groups* in control of the organization intersubjectively share particular orientations to and views of the world. This does not happen very often, however; the technically correct "one best way" is still a *scientific* predefinition of possibility and ideal.

[85]*Administrative Behaviour*, 76–7.

[86]*Ibid.*, 243; see this study, note 84.

[87]This idea of the group, tied as it is to organizational design by a directorate, is quite different from the solidarity emphasis placed by human relations specialists on cooperation in the performance of relatively routine tasks.

[88]There is always a danger that the discussion of the rationalities in the context of an analysis of formal organizations will reduce individual action to non-rational behaviour based on "impulses." Of course, this view is only valid from the perspective of the scientist who supports organizational rationality as the "one best way" and characterizes "deviations" from it as non-rational given the *desire* of given groups to maximize their values. Simon makes his position clear on 75–6 of *Administrative Behaviour* when he excludes intention to be rational *by the individual* from his definition of rationality, then goes on (77, 243) to accept *intentionality* as a basis for defining rationality where it is a *group* which is in question. But even Karl Mannheim, clearly a supporter of the sort of critical analysis in this study, "reduces" common-sense rationality to "control of impulses" in his definition of "self-rationalization." See *Man and Society in An Age of Reconstruction* (London, 1940), 55–6.

second,[89] which is foundational and from which both *scientific* and *organizational* rationality derive their meaning and significance, is totally lacking in Simon's "not good enough" view of the individual whose very cognitive limits become the starting point and justification for rational organization design.

Perhaps the clearest formulation of the built in conflict between substantial and "functional" rationality is to be found in the work of Karl Mannheim, whose concern was to extend Weber's critique of centralized state planning with an eye to attaining a harmony between it and the needs of the individual.[90] Instead of the individual's rationality being "personal," "subjective," and essentially residual in character it becomes primary, with organized action both derivative from and dependent upon it. The problem of rationality with reference to situated human action can be configured quite differently from the standard positivistic formulation once it is realized that the individual brings to the group something more than expert training on the one hand and values, needs, and impulses requiring sublimation or suppression on the other.

> Increasing industrialization, to be sure, implies functional rationality, i.e. the organization of the activity of the members of society with reference to objective ends. It does not to the same extent promote "substantial rationality," i.e. the capacity to act intelligently in a given situation on the basis of one's own insight into the interrelations of events. Whoever predicted that the further industrialization of society would raise the average capacity for independent judgment must have learned his mistake from the events of the past few years. The violent shocks of crises and revolutions have uncovered a tendency which has hitherto been working under the surface, namely the paralyzing effect of functional rationalization on the capacity for individual judgment.[91]

According to Mannheim only those who direct the process of rationalization benefit substantially from increases in functional rationality. Synonyms for functional rationality include formal (Weber), technical or technological, and organizational rationality.[92] Participation in any group endeavour characterized by division of function and the organization of technical sequences and repertoires demands that the individual adjust himself to a rationality of which he is only a part. This becomes critical at certain points of size, complexity, and technical sophistication when the organization of action seems to take on a life of its own.[93] The argument that there exists an always present potential conflict

[89]"A decision is rational from the standpoint of the group (objectively rational) if it is consistent with the values governing the group, and the information that the group possesses relevant to the decision." *Administrative Behaviour*, 243. Compare to: "Then a decision may be called 'objectively' rational if *in fact* [emphasis his] it is the *correct* behaviour for maximizing given values *in a given situation* [emphasis mine]. *Ibid.*, 76.

[90]Mannheim, *Man and Society*, especially 49–75. Compare to Weber, "Theory," 211–18.

[91]Mannheim, *Man and Society*, 58. Compare to Thorstein Veblen, *The Vested Interests and the Common Man* (Boston, 1919), especially chap. 8.

[92]If organization is seen as a device for imposing logic on unorganized externality, then participation in this logic demands that one master given technical repertoires as a precondition to the compensated performance of a stipulated function (or range of functions) in a specific division of labour. Thus this sort of rationality is *formal* or logical, *functional, technological* or technical, and ultimately *organizational.*

[93]See Jacques Ellul, *The Technological Society* (New York, 1964). I have compared and contrasted this critique of technology with the so-called rationalist critique of Weber, Mannheim, Marcuse, and Habermas in "The Sociology of Apocalypse: Jacques Ellul's Reformation of Reformation Thought," *Human Context* (Summer 1973).

between the individual and the social division of labour is not directed to *all* group participation. It is rather directed to the development of complex organizations manned by specialists where dependence upon those who are expert in technical skills, knowledge, and experience renders substantial rationality suspect. Small groups with rudimentary division of labour and relatively simple technologies do not necessarily constitute settings for the confrontation of the individual and the group. Substantial rationality often remains functional for participation in such a division of labour.[94]

Technique is rationality embodied in action against externality. There have always been techniques and rudimentary repertoires of techniques (technologies) based on the organization of persons by abilities and experience. It is the size and scale of organization and organizational dependence upon specialists with technical skills, professional training, and intellectual knowledge that may render common sense rationality so dysfunctional in the work environment that it spills over into other areas of human life where judgment is still necessary.[95] Again it is not that conflict is inevitable, nor does it mean that a pessimistic attitude is warranted. It is rather the assumption of harmony between the individual and the organization where the former must be adjusted (self-rationalization) to the latter that is problematic. Once "the organization" becomes the arbiter of a rationality allegedly possessed of objective validity, the division of labour in a given organized group may well be frozen.[96]

The social sciences, though necessarily a part of the rationalization process they seek to comprehend and render meaningful, must not so completely give themselves up to this process that their practitioners come to conceive of themselves as uncritical specialists in technique whose socialization for careers commits them unequivocally to the values of the social system. In the effort to render social structure and development comprehensible, social scientists must not lose sight of the prescientific and preorganizational character of human action in everyday life. This problem is especially acute in the case of administrative science and organization theory, where positivistic approaches and technological rationality have virtually co-opted the field.

It is the possibility that such knowledge technologies may effectively self-confirm the vision of the ideal held by many of their practitioners that gives this situation added urgency. Simon became disillusioned with administrative science when he discovered the discrepancies between his ideal and the actual process of day-to-day administration. Whether this means that administrative science is obsolete and about to be superseded by the "new science of management decision" is a question whose answer may be of interest to a considerably wider audience than a strictly academic readership.

[94]This not to say that subsets *within* large organizations like those dealt with in the human relations studies can count on such a harmony. Here it would appear that the design imperative which creates subgroups in the organization to meet criteria of technical rationality constitutes a sufficient factoring of organizational goals to be more legitimately perceived as a subset than as a set. Victor Thompson, *Modern Organization*, 15–16.

[95]Mannheim, Man and Society, 58–60.

[96]At this point, a strictly instrumental concept of rationality will be threatened by the rigidity of any system of authority overly dependent on a bureaucratic role hierarchy. See for instance, Victor Thompson, *Modern Organization*, and H.T. Wilson, "The Dismal Science of Organization Reconsidered," *Canadian Public Administration*, 14 (Spring 1971), 82–100.

Further Reflections on Work, Alienation, and Freedom in Marcuse and Marx

MORTON SCHOOLMAN *Brown University*

Recent issues of the *Canadian Journal of Political Science* have contained several articles dealing with a variety of significant topics in the writings of Marcuse and Marx, including excellent discussions on work, freedom, alienation, human emancipation, historical "projects," and technological rationality.[1] Taken together these essays illustrate the controversial nature of these subjects, and, the sound merit of these efforts notwithstanding, I believe the authors would be the first to agree that what has been written is not the final word.

A point of argument is Edward Andrew's contention that Marx "did not believe, as does Marcuse, in the abolition of work, in complete automation."[2] I will try to show that, contrary to this consideration, Marx and Marcuse are in complete agreement regarding the desirability of and the necessity for the abolition of work. This agreement naturally extends to the common underlying assumption pertaining to the domination of nature and the development of a completely automated society. A careful and thorough reading of the *Grundrisse* would easily sustain this interpretation, which is, in fact, so incontestable on the basis of that particular work that further reluctance to accept it is tantamount to intellectual luddism. Over a decade ago Ernest Mandel convincingly argued a similar position while relying heavily on Marx's other middle writings and *Capital*.[3] But the real difficulty presenting the greatest obstacle to reaching an accord among Marx scholars on whether his socialist man becomes increasingly homo ludens or remains continually homo faber is the task of reconciling the *Economic and Philosophic Manuscripts* with the later works. Once again the question of continuity in Marx's work arises, but it results this time from a lack of uniformity in interpretation.

In my opinion, there is also evidence in the *Manuscripts* suggesting that what Marx means by nonalienating human activity is similar to Marcuse's notion of play, but in no respect resembles Andrew's understanding of Marx's notion of work as being "either an activity of freedom or of bondage."[4] Human freedom for Marx is not realized through "radical improvements in the conditions under which men labour,"[5] but requires free activity to be differentiated qualitatively

[1]In addition to the article focused upon here, Edward Andrew, "Work and Freedom in Marcuse and Marx," III (June 1970), 241–56, see also in this JOURNAL, Bentley Le Baron, "Marx on Human Emancipation," IV, (Dec. 1971), 559–70; J.J. Clarke, " 'The End of History': A Re-appraisal of Marx's Views on Alienation and Human Emancipation," IV (Sept. 1971), 367–80; Bernard Solasse, "La démarche critique d'Herbert Marcuse ou un nouveau type de critique sociale," II (Dec. 1969), 448–70; for a critique of Andrew's article, see William Leiss, "Technological Rationality: Notes on 'Work and Freedom in Marcuse and Marx,' " IV (Sept. 1971), 398–400.
[2]"Work and Freedom in Marcuse and Marx," 242.
[3]*Marxist Economic Theory* (New York, 1968), II, 679–86.
[4]Andrew, "Work and Freedom in Marcuse and Marx," 242.
[5]*Ibid.*, 245.

Canadian Journal of Political Science/Revue canadienne de science politique, VI, no. 2 (June/juin 1973). Printed in Canada/Imprimé au Canada.

from work. Using this reassessment of the relationship between work and freedom, I would like to offer a brief suggestion for future reconsideration of Marx's concept of man, which is likely to be more compatible with life in a society freed from work. If we continue to maintain that work for Marx can become an end in itself, then there is indeed "a vacuum in the Marxist utopia. Unless there is no utopia, unless history is never abolished, unless labor continues to be ... some other and truer definition of the essence of man must be found."[6] I am not suggesting a revision of Marx's ideas on work and freedom, but arguing that no new definition of the nature of man is needed beyond Marx.

In his introduction to his edition of *The German Ideology*, C.J. Arthur remarks that although Marx was quite clear in his characterization of alienation and its relation to private property, he failed to provide a clue to its origin.[7] Arthur notes the following passage from the *Manuscripts*: "Just as we have found the concept of private property from the concept of estranged labor by analysis, in the same way every category of political economy can be evolved with the help of these two factors; and we shall find again in each category, e.g. trade, competition, capital, money, only a definite and developed expression of the first formulation."[8]

Arthur erroneously concludes from this statement that as "Marx allows, this kind of analysis still leaves the problem of the roots of estrangement in the process of human development; but unfortunately the manuscript breaks off unfinished before he begins to answer this question." Yet, that Marx believed he had provided sufficient explanation for the genesis of alienation is clearly and explicitly indicated by his statement near the end of "Alienated Labor": "How does it happen, we may ask, that *man alienates his labor*? How is this alienation founded in the nature of human development? We have already done much to solve the problem in so far as we have transformed the question concerning the *origin of private property* into a question about the relation between *alienated labor* and the process of development of mankind. ... This new formulation of the problem *already contains the solution*."[9]

Thus Marx unmistakably confirms that his analysis of alienated labour discloses the sources and the very beginnings of alienation in human development. In addition, the analysis circumscribes the properties of work, illuminates its affinity or lack of affinity for unalienated human expression, and determines the position of labour in his vision of a free society.

Just as private property is derived from alienated labour (actually implied in the concept of alienated labour), so is alienation derived from the labour process; "For labor, *life activity, productive life,* now appear to man only as a means for the satisfaction of a need, the need to maintain physical existence."[10] Hence, alienation originates in the act of sustaining life – which is the origin of labour itself. Compare this point to Marx's statement in *The German Ideology* that "life involves before everything else eating and drinking, a habitation, clothing and many other things. The first historical act is thus the production of the means

[6]Norman O. Brown, *Life Against Death* (Middletown, Conn. 1970), 17.
[7](New York, 1972), 19.
[8]Karl Marx, *Economic and Philosophical Manuscripts of 1844,* (London, 1959), quoted in Arthur, *ibid.*, 19.
[9]Marx, *Early Writings*, 133 (italics added in last line).
[10]*Ibid.*, 127.

Considérations additionnelles sur les concepts de travail, d'aliénation et de liberté chez Marcuse et Marx

Le socialisme tel que décrit par Marx donnerait-il naissance à un « homo ludens » ou à un « homo faber » ? Cette question a fait l'objet d'une vigoureuse controverse entre les critiques de l'œuvre de Marx depuis plus d'une décade, controverse qui portait principalement sur les premières œuvres de Marx dont l'absence de rigueur philosophique pouvait accréditer les interprétations les plus diverses. Une lecture attentive du Grundrisse *de Marx, écrit dont on a peu fait cas jusqu'à tout récemment, permet de résoudre la controverse. Le présent article analyse le concept de travail chez Marx, tel qu'exposé dans le* Grundrisse, *et établit un rapport d'identité entre ce concept et la notion marcusienne de « loisir » (play). Il appert que Marx et Marcuse partagent la même opinion sur la nécessité de l'abolition du travail tel que nous l'avons connu jusqu'à présent, de même que sur les postulats ayant trait à la domination que l'homme est appelé à exercer sur la nature et au développement d'une société complètement automatisée.*

De plus, l'auteur suggère que certains passages des Manuscrits économiques et philosophiques *permettent de croire que ce que Marx entendait par « l'activité humaine non-aliénante » peut également se rapprocher sensiblement de la notion marcusienne de « loisir » (play) mais diffère en tout point de l'entendement que Edward Andrew avait de la notion marxienne de « travail » (work) comme « activité soit de liberté, soit de servitude ». La liberté humaine, selon Marx, n'est pas engendrée par les « améliorations, même radicales, des conditions du travail », mais elle repose plutôt sur la liberté des activités elles-mêmes, liberté qu'il est qualitativement impossible de retrouver dans le « travail ».*

A partir de cette réévaluation des rapports entre le travail et la liberté, l'auteur suggère une reconsidération de notre entendement du concept marxien de l'homme afin de le rendre plus compatible avec une pratique sociale qui serait libérée du travail.

to satisfy these needs, the production of material life itself."[11] The real and primary external attribute of labour is reduced to a definite utility that marks the historical feature of all other types of alienation and forms their bases. Consequently, alienation occurs in any human labour process whereby the products and therefore the activity of labour assume a utilitarian character. Though utilitarian labour constitutes the origin of alienation, it is not easily superseded, for it is obviously recapitulated in every stage of history that requires socially necessary work. Alienation thus continues into communist society, for although "communism is the necesary form and the dynamic principal of the immediate future, [it] is not itself the goal of human development – the form of human society."[12]

Obviously, socio-economic reorganization under communism would have taken strides to eliminate most social and political manifestations of alienation, particularly those caused by the separation of the ownership of the means of production from the working classes; those caused by the existence of private property; and those forms that resulted from the oppressive specialization and regressive egoism of bourgeois capitalism, which robbed man of his political role and subordinated his public existence to private interests. But the genuine preconditions for freedom suppose the realization of an historical project far in advance of a communist system, for "man produces when he is free from physical need and only truly produces in freedom from such need."[13] At the very least, to be "free from physical need," that is, free from the necessity of producing to satisfy such needs,

[11]Ed. R. Pascal (New York, 1967), 16. [12]Marx, *Early Writings*, 167. [13]*Ibid.*, 128.

presumes the partial elimination of scarcity through the domination of nature and an automated economy artificially producing basic human requirements.

We must first conclude from this examination of the *Manuscripts* that the fulfilment of authentically free and unalienated labour requires that the utilitarian character of work be eradicated. But it does not *necessarily* follow for Marx, as it does for Marcuse (and this point is decisive), that automation is the equivalent of the elimination of all work. It is conceivable that labour *might* persist in a society that has succeeded in annulling its utilitarian value through the realization of an advanced historical project. Man, freed from need, might continue to produce the identical objects he produced when there existed a need for them. Objects of human production would no longer possess a use value, in fact, all relative criteria distinguishing the worth of one object over another would disappear. All products would be, regardless of previous standards, human products. The constitution of work would continue essentially unchanged, with the important exception that labour would be stripped of all ulterior and utilitarian purpose, and working conditions would be improved.

Such reasoning bears three principal weaknesses. If labour were perpetuated beyond the utilitarian need for it, labour as life activity, as productive life, would be gratuitous. Secondly, labour must always be studied in relation to man's creative faculties. Utility is a trait Marx ascribed to labour by virtue of the type of basic need it satisfied *and* the creative powers it did not. The abolition of the utilitarian quality of labour would not alter its fundamental relationship to man, that is, it would still not avail man of the opportunity to labour as a means of artistic or creative expression. Finally, the rather paradoxical development of labouring for the sake of labouring, though its utility is precluded by automation, conflicts with Marx's, as well as Marcuse's, belief in a broadly based aptitude for human expression realized in a fully matured communist autarchy. The paradox can be further resolved through the following suggestion for a reassessment of Marx's concept of man.

The expressions that have been used to describe Marx's definition of the essence of man have been extremely vague and abstract, almost entirely void of intelligible empirical content, and have at best been impressionistic. Andrew says, for example, that Marx believed that through work "men objectify their 'subjectivity,' externalize inner needs and talents, actualize their potential, give concrete form to their latent capacities, or realize their human nature. Productive activity is men creating and defining themselves; it is the means whereby men obtain an identity."[14] *Subjectivity, inner needs and talents, potential, latent capacities,* and *human nature,* are cryptic and relative terms that fail to distinguish between alienating or free activity and could be applied to either condition with equal plausibility. I will not go into Eric Fromm's well-known description, but it is similarly obscure to the point of being tautological; for example, he says; "What Marx means by 'species-character' is the essence of man ..."[15] Innumerable examples of cloudy sketches of Marx's notion of human personality could be provided, but it is unnecessary. What I mean to underscore, however, is a lack of certainty about what Marx meant by man's true identity.

[14]Andrew, "Work and Freedom in Marcuse and Marx," 244.
[15]*Marx's Concept of Man* (New York, 1971), 34.

These encumbered descriptions are not initially problematic in the interpretations themselves, for the difficulty is obviously inherent in Marx's patently metaphysical portrayal of human nautre, which often lacks philosophical rigour and clarity. It is conceivable that Marx as dialectician was reluctant to furnish an answer to the question of man's historically matured capabilities. A detailed specification would surely place his concept in danger of obsolescence in the future. For this reason it may be unfair or even presumptuous to consider Marx's vision of a future society. In the same vein, there was certainly a lack of evidence prohibiting Marx, or anyone else for that matter, from developing an accurate and plausible formulation of the nature of man. But, besides the obvious empirical difficulties, certain tendencies did manifest themselves in the early industrial age permitting Marx to generalize in *The German Ideology*, depicting man, for example, as doing "one thing today and another tomorow, to hunt in the morning, fish in the afternoon, rear cattle in the evening, criticize after dinner, without ever becoming a hunter, fisherman, shepherd, or critic." This passage has been construed in many ways, though most commentators agree that Marx is analogically alluding to the profile of human activity under communism.[16] However, if we compare this excerpt from *The German Ideology* with Marx's contemporaneous and trenchant observation in *Capital*, we begin to recapture the complete significance of Marx's ontology. "Modern Industry ... imposes the necessity of recognising ... variation of work, consequently fitness of the labourer for varied work, consequently the greatest possible development of his varied aptitudes ... Modern Industry, indeed, compels society ... to replace the detail worker of today ... by the fully developed individual, fit for a variety of labours, ready to face any change of production, and to whom the different social functions he performs, are but so many modes of giving free scope to his own natural and acquired powers."[17]

Both of these passages should be meaningfully understood symbolically or figuratively rather than literally, as they imply a sort of non-exclusive, non-fixated social activity that suggests a multiplicity of human potentialities bordering on Proteanism. The metaphor, Protean, is in this context a more meaningful expression than "species-being."[18] There is no danger of falsely concretizing Marx's notion of man; its content is merely defined through the negation of the existing division of labour. Man individually performs at will the activities mankind executed as a collectivity.

This metaphorical view of Marx's concept of man contains two concrete aspects. Although this view remains indefinite in so far as explicit categories of human action are not prescribed, in a free society the ranges of human action are determined by the individual's free will, and not by material or other external

[16]See, *ibid.*, 42; Shlomo Avineri, *The Social and Political Thought of Karl Marx* (London, 1968), 231; Adam Schaff, *Marxism and the Human Individual* (New York, 1970), 186, and fn. 7, under "Endnotes," pp. 267–68; Herbert Marcuse, *Reason and Revolution* (Boston, 1968), 278–79.

[17]International Publishers ed. (New York, 1970), I, 487–88.

[18]The term Protean is not being employed as a surrogate for species-being. I have resorted to the use of metaphor to clearly illustrate and to emphasize the autonomous character of human freedom in Marx, as opposed to its social character, which is more properly distinguished by "species-being," "species life," or "species-consciousness." See Bottomore's fn. 2 in his edition of *Early Writings*, 13.

necessities. Necessity serves as the determinant for action as long as utility is the rationale for social organization. The abolition of utilitarian labour ushers in the realm of free choice, which is only qualified by a residual factor – free forms of human expression will not correspond to activity conditioned by physical need. Secondly, the perpetuation of labour in a society that has eliminated its necessity would constitute the perpetuation of alienation. This point is confirmed by Marx when he declares that utilitarian work "is not voluntary but imposed, *forced labor*. It is not the satisfaction of a need, but only a *means* for satisfying other needs. Its alien character is clearly shown by the fact that as soon as there is no physical or other compulsion *it is avoided like the plague*."[19]

Marx demands, in a free society, the complete departure from past manifestations of human powers and demands that nonalienating activity must be qualitatively differentiated from work.

It is quite apparent in *Capital* that Marx is an ardent proponent and zealous advocate of the benefits issuing from automation. He at once recognized the staggering contrast between the "cyclopean" potential of machinery as opposed to the comparatively meager productive output of archaic manufacturing processes. The superiority of machine over man is resolutely affirmed, a superiority engendering the emancipation of the process of production from the "restraints of human strength," from "organic" limitations that "cripple" modern industry.

Marx's exceptionally detailed and exhaustive documentation of the abuse of machinery under capital should not be confused with an indictment of machinery per se. Through a rather elementary dialectical exposition, Marx discloses "the economic paradox, that the most powerful instrument for shortening labour-time, becomes the most unfailing means for placing every moment of the labourer's time and that of his family, at the disposal of the capitalist for the purpose of expanding the value of his capital."[20] Thus when the reader is cautioned and instructed that it is "an undoubted fact that machinery, *as such*, is not responsible for 'setting free' the workman from the means of subsistence,"[21] Marx's argument also implies that machinery, as such, is also not responsible for the workman's enslavement. Marx was sympathetic to and patient with a distressed and apprehensive working class mistakenly directing "their attacks not against the bourgeois conditions of production, but against the instruments of production themselves";[22] striking out blindly and ignorantly by "smashing machinery to pieces, setting factories ablaze," at a modern industrial system that mercilessly displaced their labour with the machine, reduced their earnings below the level of subsistence, and forced them to seek occupations that failed to take advantage of their skills, for he realized that it "took both time and experience before the workpeople learnt to distinguish between machinery and its employment by capital, and to direct their attacks, not against the material instruments of production, but against the mode in which

19 Marx, *Early Writings*, 125 (italics added in the last line).
20 *Capital*, I, 408.
21 *Ibid.*, 441 (italics added). Note, too, in this passage, the deliberate equation between "machinery" (automation), "setting free" the workman, and freedom from providing for a "means of subsistence." In other words, automation under communism or socialism becomes singularly responsible for man's liberation from utilitarian labour.
22 Marx and Engels, *Communist Manifesto*, ed. Samuel Beer (New York, 1955), 18.

they are used."[23] No doubt Marx would be less patient with his modern interpreters who today fail to make this distinction.

In order to realize its end, human labour must then bring about its own negation by transferring its duties and obligations to machinery. Marx saw this transference as an inevitable development in bourgeois economy, and through it a sizable proportion of man's total time is converted into free time. Under ideal conditions all the individual's time would become free time, but until such a completely automated state is achieved, society would economize or distribute time to meet the general material needs and to facilitate the further development of man's higher faculties. In any case, time would be maximized to meet the real needs of the individual.

Marx emphasizes the importance of the relationship between freedom and the social organization of time. In *The German Ideology* he describes history in terms of a series of successive confrontations of each generation of men with a predetermined set of objective material conditions. These objective factors place a limitation upon the orientation of man's intellectual and physical energies, in that they must be brought to bear and concentrated on the provision of the means for material production through the transformation of nature. Man's time must therefore be rationalized to meet the priorities determined in light of external conditions. His maturation is constrained within time and it is not until he is released from the organization of a time continuum shaped by need that he may begin to develop freely. This last supposition is supported in the *Grundrisse*. "If we suppose communal production, the determination of time remains, of course, essential. The less time society requires in order to produce wheat, cattle, etc., the more time it gains for other forms of production, material or intellectual. As with a single individual, the universality of its development, its enjoyment and its activity depends on saving time. In the final analysis, all forms of economics can be reduced to an economics of time."[24]

Automation, using the least time society requires to produce necessities, would ideally allow man to be completely free from the world, from any exogenous considerations in the cultivation of his powers. Without the necessity for response to the outside world, man is transformed into a completely independent and autonomous figure. He is no longer dependent upon nature or upon other men as in the process of production. His will and action have no specific goals or aims, and the ranges of human development would be, in principle, limitless. Protean becomes a symbol for the general manifestation of human powers that have no direction, no purpose other than manifestation itself. Thus man's abilities will be fully exhibited, he "will live in display rather than need";[25] his creative faculties and potentialities will be given, in Marcuse's sense, "free play," they will "be represented and judged *not in terms of [their] usefullness, not according to any purpose [they] may possibly serve ... [but] represented as free from all such relations and properties*."[26] Obviously, progress, real "human" progress, continues beyond the domination of nature.

[23]Marx, *Capital*, I, 429.
[24]Ed. and tr. David McLellan (New York, 1971), 75–6.
[25]Herbert Marcuse, *Eros and Civilization* (New York, 1962), 171.
[26]*Ibid.*, 162 (italics added).

We see that for Marcuse and Marx unconditional development of man's noetic talent is in irreconcilable opposition to work. It is often assumed that because the elimination of labour depends upon the achievement of an automated society, an achievement that is concomitant with a highly centralized control and administration of technology, that the centralization of decision-making might well constitute the further alienation of the means of production from the major segments of society. But, as Marx explained in the *Grundrisse*, automation results in alienation when the disposable time it creates (capital creates "despite itself") is reconverted into surplus labour. Where automation supposes the elimination of all labour, it is proper to conceive of the separation of an automated means of production from the individual to be the same as his separation from work. Since the separation from work establishes the conditions of freedom, the centralized supervision of technology is in harmony with the individual's free will. It does not necessarily follow that in a technocracy the "physical" separation of the individual from the productive process is a violation of his sanction, for this separation is itself sanctioned and ratified by all those concerned with a free and unfettered human state of affairs.

Note

Political Socialization in Quebec: Young People's Attitudes toward Government

JEAN PIERRE RICHERT
Richard Stockton College, New Jersey

Social scientists have for some time been interested in the socialization of young people. An increasing number of studies are available which deal with Western Europe, Japan, South America, and the United States.[1] However, little empirical research has been done on the socialization of Canadian children.[2] The purpose of this paper is to consider the development of English- and French-Canadian children's attitudes toward government in Quebec and to determine, in particular, the impact of their cultural membership on their perception of government.[3] The ultimate goal of this research – though not of this paper – is to investigate empirically the development of national identity in Canada, a concept that has been singled out by several scholars as crucial in political development and nation building.[4]

The data on which this paper is based were gathered during a survey of elementary school children in Quebec, undertaken between October 1970 and March 1971. The major data gathering instrument was a paper and pencil questionnaire which was submitted to 960 pupils, supplemented by essays written by children, and by personal interviews.

I. The sample

The sample is a non-probability quota sample selected in order to facilitate subgroup comparisons. An effort was made to equalize the population's distribution by cultural membership, residence, sex, and socio-economic status.[5]

1See for example "Special Issue on Political Socialization," ed. Jack Dennis and M. Kent Jennings, *Comparative Political Studies*, 3 (1970). The issue includes studies on Japan, Peru, Chile, and Western Europe. See also Fred I. Greenstein and Sidney Tarrow, "Political Orientations of Children: The Use of a Semi-Projective Technique in Three Nations," *Sage Professional Papers in Comparative Politics*, 1 (1970); these writers focus on Great Britain, France, and the United States. The best known American studies are those of Greenstein and Easton and Hess. See Fred I. Greenstein, *Children and Politics* (New Haven, 1965); David Easton and Jack Dennis, *Children in the Political System* (New York, 1969); and Robert Hess and Judith Torney, *The Development of Political Attitudes in Children* (Chicago, 1967).

2On the socialization of young people in Canada see John C. Johnstone, *Young People's Images of Canadian Society* (Ottawa, 1969); and Jon H. Pammett, "The Development of Political Orientations in Canadian School Children," this JOURNAL, 4 (March 1971), 132–41. Johnstone deals with teenagers while Pammett surveyed children enrolled in grades four through eight.

3Culture is a factor that has been relatively ignored by scholars interested in socialization. Thus the study by Pammett on Canadian children does not even raise the issue of the impact of cultural membership. That culture is an intervening variable in the socialization process has been established by such writers as Greenberg, Lyons, and Jahoda. See Edward S. Greenberg, "Children and Politics: A Comparison across Racial Lines," *Widwest Journal of Political Science* (May, 1970), 249–75; Schley R. Lyons, "The Political Socialization of Ghetto Children: Efficacy and Cynicism," *Journal of Politics*, 32 (1970), 288–304; Gustav Jahoda, "The Development of Children's Ideas About Country and Nationality, Part II: National Symbols and Themes," *The British Journal of Educational Psychology*, 33 (1963), 143–53.

4See Gabriel A. Almond and G. Bingham Powell, *Comparative Politics* (Boston, 1966), 52–3; Sidney Verba, "Comparative Political Culture," in *Political Culture and Political Development*, ed. Lucian W. Pye and Sidney Verba (Princeton, 1965), 529–41; Richard A. Dawson and Kenneth Prewitt, *Political Socialization* (Boston, 1969), 34–5.

5I am not claiming that the sample is representative of the entire elementary school population in Quebec.

Canadian Journal of Political Science/Revue canadienne de science politique, VI, no. 2 (June/juin 1973). Printed in Canada/Imprimé au Canada.

TABLE I

DISTRIBUTION BY GEOGRAPHIC AREA AND CULTURAL MEMBERSHIP

	French Canadians		English Canadians	
	Percentage	*N*	Percentage	*N*
Montreal	43.2	248	49.3	190
Sherbrooke	42.0	242	35.1	135
Stanshead	14.8	85	15.6	60
Total	100.0	575	100.0	385

GEOGRAPHIC AREAS

Three regions of Quebec were selected for inclusion in the sample: Greater Montreal, Sherbrooke, and Stanshead. These geographic regions were chosen for two reasons. The first is that they allow for control of the data for urban-rural differences. The second is that all three areas are populated by members of both major language groups and, therefore, have two school systems. Within each geographic area both an English- and a French-Canadian school commission were contacted. A total of nine local commissions were approached. The usual pattern of approach consisted in contacting the director of elementary education in each school system. All school systems contacted included more than one elementary school. As a result, the actual choice of the schools that were to participate in the survey was left to local officials who selected schools on the basis of the socio-economic background of the attending students. In total, 13 schools in 6 school districts participated in the project. Two schools, one English-, one French-Canadian, both in Sherbrooke, were chosen for the pilot work but were excluded from the final analysis. Of the 11 elementary schools that are included in the final sample, 5 are "English-Canadian," and 6 are "French-Canadian." It is, strictly speaking, inaccurate to speak of "English" and "French" schools in Quebec since schools are formally organized along confessional rather than linguistic lines. In reality, Hughes' observation that protestant schools are often called "English" schools remains largely true today.[6]

Cultural membership was assigned on the basis of subjective criteria rather than such objective criteria as the language spoken by children, or the school attended. Both were deemed deficient since many children were bilingual, and since some parents, it appears, send their children to schools of the other cultural group. Consequently, children were asked what they considered themselves to be, either Francophone or Anglophone. Table I shows the distribution of the sample by residence and cultural membership.

SEX, GRADE, AND AGE

The sample was about equally divided according to sex, with about 50 per cent boys and 50 per cent girls in each group. Children were enrolled in grades four, five, six, and seven. The lower limit was dictated by practical reasons since most third graders (who were exposed to only two and half years of formal teaching at the time the questionnaire was submitted) were unable to complete a pilot questionnaire in the available time without considerable help. As a result, it was decided to omit them from the survey since school officials allocated only one class period for the submission of the questionnaire. The upper limit was dictated by the set-up of the elementary school system in Quebec.[7]

Age and grade were highly correlated. The reason for this is that schools are gradually implementing a recommendation of the Parent Commission that children be promoted on the basis of age rather than achievement. Ten out of the 11 schools included in the sample had already implemented this proposal. Consequently nearly all children enrolled in grade four were 8 years old, while those in grades five, six, and

[6]Everett C. Hughes, *French Canada in Transition* (Chicago, 1943), 118.

[7]In the past, elementary education included grades one through seven, and high school began with grade eight. The Parent Commission, which was appointed in order to review the provincial educational system, recommended that the elementary cycle include only grades one through six. Some of the recommendations of the Parent Commission are now being gradually implemented. As a result some elementary schools still include grade seven in the sample because it allows a clearer developmental pattern and because most schools in the sample still included grade seven.

TABLE II

DISTRIBUTION BY CULTURAL MEMBERSHIP AND GRADE

	French Canadians		English Canadians	
Grade	Percentage	*N*	Percentage	*N*
Four	25.3	146	36.1	139
Five	23.0	132	26.0	100
Six	27.5	158	27.8	107
Seven	24.2	139	10.1	39
Total	100.0	575	100.0	385

seven were 9, 10, and 11 years old, respectively. Table II shows the distribution of the population by cultural membership and grade.

SOCIO-ECONOMIC STATUS

Since children's files could not be consulted without parental permission, the father's job, which is taken as the principal indicator of socio-economic status, had to be determined by other means. The primary technique utilized to obtain this information was to ask children to indicate their father's occupation in an open-ended question. This method proved adequate in most cases since over 95 per cent of the children were able to provide a usable answer. For the remaining cases two methods were utilized. First, teachers were asked, and, in the event they were not available or could not provide the answer, individual socio-economic status was assigned on the basis of the status of the school, as rated by school officials. In those cases in which the father was unemployed or deceased, children were asked to indicate his last occupation. When the father did not live at home, the mother's occupation was substituted.

The basis for the classification of children into various socio-economic categories was provided by a six item scale developed by Robert D. Hess and Judith V. Torney.[8] It was decided not to incorporate the scale into the questionnaire because the pilot work indicated that most children were unable to answer the questions without help. Instead, children's answers to the open-ended question asking for their father's occupation were grouped into three categories, based on the Chicago scale, and scored individually. Low socio-economic status was assigned to occupations listed in items two, three, and four (skilled jobs, clerical, low civil service, most teachers, small businessmen, middle range executives); high status was assigned to occupations of type five and six (professionals, owners of large enterprises, etc.). Overall, middle-status children were over-represented in both groups as Table III shows.

II. Attitudes toward government

CHILDREN'S PERCEPTION OF POLITICAL AUTHORITY

Most Canadian children perceived government in terms of authority. Such references to government as "government rules," "it decides," "government tells people what to do" were common. Here is an excerpt from a typical essay: "When someone says government I think of rules. The government tells people what to do. My mother said when they get their pay at work the government takes some money out of their pay. The government also runs the country and has a lot of responsibility." (French Canadian, grade six, boy.)

In addition, political authority was perceived by children largely in personal rather than institutional terms. In other words, Quebecois children, as American children, viewed authority as vested in people rather than in structures or institutions.[9] The following question was asked: "What do you think of when I say government?" Children's answers fell into five categories listed in Table IV. The first category, persons, includes all references to individuals or groups, whether they were specifically identified or not. As a result, it includes, for example, such references as "government is a man," "government is a group of people," or "gov-

[8]The scale is reproduced in their book *The Development of Basic Attitudes and Values Toward Government and Citizenship During the Elementary School Years*, Part I (Chicago, 1965), 32–3.

[9]On American children's attitudes toward political authority see, for example: Greenstein, *Children and Politics*, chap. 3; Easton and Dennis, *Children in the Political System*, chap. 6–14. On the personalization of authority see *ibid.*, 281ff; Hess and Torney, *Basic Attitudes and Values*, 38.

TABLE III

DISTRIBUTION BY CULTURAL MEMBERSHIP AND SOCIO-ECONOMIC STATUS

	French Canadians		English Canadians	
Status	Percentage	*N*	Percentage	*N*
Low	43.0	247	23.4	90
Middle	49.8	286	59.5	229
High	7.2	42	17.1	66
Total	100.0	575	100.0	385

ernment is Trudeau." The second category, institutions, includes parliament, the courts, political parties, and the law. A number of children also referred to what Gabriel A. Almond called the conversion process, that is to say, the process of translation of inputs into outputs.[10] These responses were placed into a third category which includes references to political contestation as well as references that deal with the political process and feedback mechanism. Some specific examples were the following: government "runs things," "it works hard," "politics," government "helps people," it listens to people." The fourth category, norms, includes such references as "freedom," "democracy," "might," and "power." Finally, some children viewed government in terms of symbols such as the flag or the national anthem.

The data presented in Table IV confirm, first of all, that a majority of the children displayed a personal, rather than an institutional, conception of government since all categories other than "persons" were cited by less than 12 per cent of the children of either group. Table IV shows that the major differences between the two groups involved two categories: "persons" and "norms." More French-Canadian children (59.0 per cent) referred to government in terms of persons than did English-Canadian children (51.6 per cent). Anglophone children, however, were more likely to view government in terms of norms (8.9 per cent) than were Francophone children (4.2 per cent). Another minor difference was that more English- than French-Canadian children (3.2 per cent versus 0.7 per cent) referred to political symbols.

The data, when controlled for age, indicated that the pattern of development of the two groups differed. Older English-Canadian children perceived political authority as vested more in political institutions and less in people, while there was little change in the attitudes of French pupils. The difference between the two groups was most significant at grade seven level, at which only 41 per cent of English-Canadian children, as opposed to 57.8 per cent of French-Canadian children, viewed government in terms of people. On the other hand, 23.1 per cent of English-Canadian children saw government in terms of institutions at the same level, while only 10.3 per cent of French-Canadian children did.

The most significant finding that Table IV reveals was that a higher proportion of French-Canadian children than of English-Canadian children viewed government in personal terms, since 59 per cent of Francophone, as opposed to 51.6 per cent of Anglophone, children saw government as a person. The analysis may be carried one step further by distinguishing between those children who viewed political authority as being vested in *one* person and those who thought of it as being vested in a *group* of people. Table V breaks down the answers of those children who displayed a personalized conception of government (first item, Table IV) into two categories; the first includes all responses viewing government as the attribute of one person, for example those children who saw government as "a man." The second category includes all responses referring to government as a *group* of people, for example "government is a group of busy men in Ottawa."

Table V shows that among those children who displayed a personalized conception of authority, a much larger proportion of Francophone children (73.9 per cent) than of Anglophone children (56.0 per cent) thought that political authority was the attribute of one person. Conversely more English-Canadian children (44 per cent) than French-Canadian children (26.1 per cent) saw government in terms of a *group* of people. The data showed, furthermore, that in both

[10]Gabriel A. Almond and G. Bingham Powell, Jr., *Comparative Politics* (Boston, 1966), 11–12.

TABLE IV

CHILDREN'S PERCEPTION OF GOVERNMENT

	French Canadians		English Canadians	
	Percentage	*N*	Percentage	*N*
Persons	59.0	271	51.6	163
Institutions	10.4	48	11.7	37
Processes	5.3	24	5.1	16
Norms	4.2	19	8.9	28
Symbols	.7	3	3.2	10
Other	9.9	45	8.2	26
Unsure	10.5	48	11.3	36
Total	100.0	458	100.0	316

$df = 6$
x^2 29.213$P < .05$

TABLE V

CHILDREN'S PERCEPTION OF THE GOVERNMENT IN TERMS OF INDIVIDUALS OR GROUPS (IN PER CENT)

	French Canadians		English Canadians	
	Percentage	*N*	Percentage	*N*
Individuals	73.9	204	56.0	94
Groups	26.1	72	44.0	74
Total	100.0	276	100.0	168

$df = 1$
X^2 14.46$P < .05$

groups, older children were more likely than younger ones to perceive authority as something that is *shared*, rather than as the attribute of a single person, but the differences between English- and French-Canadian pupils persisted. At grade seven level, for example, 49.8 per cent of Anglophone, as opposed to 37.8 per cent of Francophone, pupils thought that governmental authority was shared by a group of people. This compares with 27.2 per cent of English-Canadian and 17.3 per cent French-Canadian responses at grade four level. An examination of children's perception of the function of government, as well as their evaluation of governmental performance, will shed additional light on their attitudes toward government.

THE FUNCTION OF GOVERNMENT

Easton and Dennis suggest that the development of children's images of political authority affects their perception of the function of government. Children, for example, extend to the government role attributes of the father, particularly his role as provider for the family. Easton and Dennis write that children see "the authorities as possible sources of nurturance resources to which a person can turn in very much the same spirit that a child expects to be able to turn to his parents."[11] According to this view, government becomes a sort of surrogate parent for the child, an institution that helps and protects. As Easton and Hess write, government is perceived by the child as the "family writ large."[12] It stands to reason that the more personalized a conception of government children have, the more they will view government in these terms. This hypothesis may be tested by examining children's attitudes toward the function of government.

Children were asked the following open-ended question: "What does government do?" Their answers were divided into two substantive categories: one that views government as a policy or input agency; and one

[11]Easton and Dennis, *Children in the Political System*, 96.

[12]David Easton and Robert D. Hess, "The Child's Political World," *Midwest Journal of Political Science*, 6 (1962), 242.

TABLE VI

CHILDREN'S EVALUATION OF THE FUNCTION OF GOVERNMENT

	French Canadians		English Canadians	
Government is a	Percentage	N	Percentage	N
Policy agency	41.8	176	49.1	144
Distribution agency	45.1	191	37.9	111
Other	13.1	55	13.0	38
Total	100.0	422	100.0	293

$df = 1$
$X^2 4.03 P < .05$

that perceives government as an output or distribution agency.[13] The first category includes all references to government as a problem solving agency, or as a decision maker, while the second refers to the government as an institution that "helps people," "helps widows and orphans," or "provides jobs," and so on. A third category was used to include those references that could not be meaningfully classified in terms of the previous two categories. Table VI shows that more English-Canadian children (49.1 per cent) than French-Canadian children (41.8 per cent) referred to government as a policy-making agency, and therefore confirms a previous suggestion that they were more likely to view government as a "manager." On the other hand, more Francophone (45.1 per cent) children than Anglophone (37.9 per cent) children referred to government as a distribution agency. While the difference is statistically significant ($x^2 = 4.03$, $p < 0.05$), the percentage difference is not very large.[14] In addition, since the sample is not a probability sample, additional research on this issue is clearly desirable. Nonetheless it is possible to state, albeit in tentative terms, that Anglophone children appeared more input oriented, while Francophone pupils were more output oriented in the sense that the former viewed government as a problem-solver, hence a policy agency, while the latter were more likely to think that the government sends welfare cheques or provides jobs, hence viewed it as a distribution agency. Table VII includes three specific activities of government to which children have referred in the questionnaire. The specific references included in each category vary somewhat in terminology since the question was an open-ended one. Table VII shows that in the cases presented, more English- than French-Canadian children viewed government as a problem-solver, hence a policy, agency, while more Francophone than Anglophone children thought that government sends welfare cheques or provides jobs, hence was a distribution agency.

The data furthermore showed that age tended to reinforce this pattern. Older English-Canadian children referred more often to government as a policy agency than a distribution agency, while there was little change among French-Canadian children. At grade seven level, for example, 61.1 per cent of English-Canadian children viewed government as a policy agency but only 40.6 per cent of French-Canadian children did. On the other hand, 44.3 per cent of French-Canadian children still saw government as a distribution agency at that level, compared to only 33.3 per cent of English-Canadian pupils.

Interview and essay data confirmed the finding that the two groups differed in their evaluation of the function of government. An English-Canadian child's essay illustrates the perception of government as a policy agency: "The government of Canada, they have sessions in Ottawa mostly; they make sure things go right, that industrial processes go on." (Grade six.) This description by a

[13] I am borrowing the term "distribution" from Almond who distinguished four kinds of outputs: regulative, symbolic, extractive, and distributive. The term distribution refers to government as an agency allocating goods, services, and concerned in general with the welfare of citizens. See Almond and Powell, *Comparative Politics*, 27.

[14] Strictly speaking, sampling must be random in order to test meaningfully for statistical significance. However, as Greenstein and Tarrow note, statistical significance tests are also useful in non-random sampling as "rules of thumb, in order to determine which variables are worth discussing." See Fred I. Greenstein and Sidney Tarrow, "The Study of French Political Socialization: Toward the Revocation of Paradox," *World Politics*, 22 (1969), 102ff.

TABLE VII

CHILDREN'S REFERENCES TO THREE SPECIFIC GOVERNMENTAL ACTIVITIES

	French Canadians		English Canadians	
	Percentage	*N*	Percentage	*N*
Government solves problems	1.4	6	8.7	28
Government sends welfare checks	5.6	25	2.3	8
Government provides jobs	9.5	43	5.6	18

$df = 2$
$X^2 30.97 P < .05$

TABLE VIII

DOES GOVERNMENT MAKE MISTAKES?

	French Canadians		English Canadians	
	Percentage	*N*	Percentage	*N*
The government of Canada makes mistakes	88.2	499	93.9	355
The government of Quebec makes mistakes	87.2	495	94.7	357

X^2 not significant

French-Canadian boy manifests a view of government as a distribution agency: "The government fixes the roads for the people who have to travel to work every day. The government makes sure that the highways have been plowed so that the people can get to work. The government gives out old age pensions and welfare to people who need it. It helps people find jobs and other things too." (Grade five.)

THE PERFORMANCE OF GOVERNMENT

Several American scholars report that children frequently see political authority in idealistic terms.[15] The Canadian data showed, on the other hand, that most children sampled did not view political authority in such terms. To begin with, it appeared that the overwhelming majority of children of both groups felt that government makes mistakes, as Table VIII shows. In the second place, there was no indication that any children thought that "government is love," as one American child put it. Greenstein reported that only one or two out of a total sample of 659 children made derogatory comments about government officials.[16] In the Quebec sample ($N = 960$), 71 children made negative remarks which were all spontaneous, since this dimension was not specifically probed. References such as the government "robs us," "it lives in luxury," it "does nothing for the people," it "is lazy," for example, were encountered in the questionnaire responses; a few comments were considerably more derogatory. Interview data and essays the children wrote confirmed the suggestion that children had a non-idealistic conception of government. The following excerpts from essays illustrate this well: "I don't know much about our government, but I know that they make many mistakes, just as we do." (English Canadian, grade seven.) "Our government to me, all they do is rob people and build roads. My father hates the government. If I put down what my father thinks of the government I'd be kicked out of school. Today the taxes are so high you have to be a millionaire to afford a house

[15]See, for example: Greenstein, *Children and Politics*, 31–7; Easton and Dennis, *Children in the Political System*, 287 and 356–58; Hess and Torney, *Basic Attitudes and Values*, 44–5. For a critique of these interpretations see Dean Jaros, Herbert Hirsch, Frederic Fleron, Jr. "The Malevolent Leader: Political Socialization in an American Sub-Culture," *American Political Science Review*, 62 (1968), 564–75.

[16]Greenstein, *Children and Politics.*

and land." (English Canadian, grade five.) This reference to taxes was not an isolated one. It appears that taxes were a major focus of discontent and prompted many critical remarks about the government. Here is another example, this time from a French-Canadian pupil: "Trudeau has the taxes high on everything, so after people pay taxes they don't have much left over." (Grade six.) Overall, 9.5 per cent of French-Canadian children and 5.6 per cent of English-Canadian children in the sample referred to taxes in one way or another.[17]

The differences between the two cultural groups remained when the data were controlled for sex and residence. However, as one might have expected, socio-economic status had some impact on children's perception of the function of government. Within each cultural group, low status children were more likely (45.9 per cent of French Canadians, 41.3 per cent of English Canadians) than high-status children (40.0 per cent of French Canadians, 36.4 per cent of English Canadians) to view government as a distribution agency, that is, a structure that "helps people." Yet even in this case cultural membership had a stronger impact on children's perceptions than socio-economic status, measured in percentage point difference.

III. Political socialization in Quebec

Two major findings were reported in this note. The first is that children in Quebec displayed a non-idealistic conception of government, which contrasts with the findings reported by several studies dealing with the United States. Second, the data showed that Anglophone and Francophone children in Quebec differed in their attitudes toward government. In general, Francophone pupils displayed a more personalized view of government than did Anglophone children, and age appeared to reinforce this pattern. In addition, French-Canadian youngsters were more likely to view government in authoritarian terms, while English-Canadian young people tended to perceive it to be more like a "manager." The two groups differed also in their attitudes toward the function of government: French-Canadian children were more inclined to see government as an output agency, or what was called a distribution agency, while English - Canadian pupils tended to see it as an input, or policy agency.

These findings raise some questions about, first the generalization advanced by some scholars that children view government in idealistic terms and, second, the reasons why English- and French-Canadian children differ in their perceptions of government.

IDEALIZATION OF POLITICAL AUTHORITY: A RE-EXAMINATION

Two explanations accounting for children's idealization of political authority have been advanced.[18] The first is that, in the US, the family acts as a shield which prevents any derogatory or negative information from reaching children. Since the data clearly showed that children were critical of government, one must assume either that the role of the family is different in Canada, or that the family does not act like a protective shield. Since it does not appear that families in the United States and Canada play significantly different roles, one must conclude that the second explanation is plausible. This explanation is reinforced by additional data: for example, the fact that children were aware of the details of such events as the kidnapping of James Cross and the murder of Pierre Laporte carried out by members of the FLQ.[19] Finally, the following quote illustrates perhaps best the idea that the family is not a protective shield; the comment was made by a French-Canadian fifth grader, after criticizing the government: "I don't know much about the government, only what I *hear*" (emphasis added.)

The second hypothesis advanced to explain the idealization of government by children is that children project the qualities of parents, in particular those of the father, onto the occupants of political roles. Since Canadian children did not idealize government, the validity of this explanation would imply that Canadian children do not view their parents as endowed with any ideal qualities. Such an explanation of the idealization of political authority by children does not stand up. It is much more likely that the idealistic view of government that Greenstein and the Chicago group report is due primarily to the fact that much of their data were gathered during the late fifties and early sixties, a period of minimal political contesta tion in the history of the United States, a time during which government may have appeared as "love" to some children. It is unlikely that surveys that would be undertaken today would report such an idealized conception of government.[20]

[17]The question asked was, "What does the government do?"

[18]Jaros, *Malevolent Leader*, 564–65.

[19]See Jean Pierre Richert, "English and French-Canadian Children's Perception of the October Crisis," *Journal of Social Psychology*, 89 (Feb., 1973), 3–13.

[20]Preliminary information derived from a study by the writer presently underway in

PERSONALIZATION OF POLITICAL AUTHORITY

The fact that so many children, especially young children, saw authority in a personalized manner seems to confirm a hypothesis that has been advanced by Harold D. Lasswell.[21] Lasswell conceives of a child's environment in terms of two circles. The primary circle consists of his immediate or family environment. The secondary circle encompasses anything beyond the primary circle, in particular the social system at large. Lasswell argues that children's perception of authority in the secondary circle, that is, social and political authority, is shaped by that of the primary circle. He writes that: "Images of the secondary environment acquire meaning by extension or compensation."[22] In other words, Lasswell says that children perceive political and social authority on the model of family authority. The Chicago Group and Greenstein share this point of view.[23] Greenstein, for example, writes that the president of the United States is perceived unconsciously by children as "the analogue of parents and other immediate environment authorities."[24] As Hess and Torney point out, people, especially the family, are the major intermediaries between the political system and the child.[25] It is through them that children are socialized and become aware of political authority. The following excerpt from an essay written by a fifth grader supports this analysis: "There are many kinds of government, like the local government, the provincial government. The local government is a group of people. In your home your *parents* are the government." (English-Canadian child, emphasis added.) Greenstein adds that authority is primarily perceived in terms of "father figures" and points to several studies of adults who saw the president in such terms.[26] Roberta Sigel has shown that children view the president in terms very similar to those offered by Greenstein and that a majority of them felt that the death of the president has the same effect on them as "the loss of someone close and dear."[27]

The data clearly indicated that political authority was perceived by both groups as a masculine rather than a feminine attribute, since nearly all children gave answers such as government was a "man," and "old gentleman," a group of "men," or something similar. The only exceptions were 1.5 per cent of Francophone and 2.4 per cent of Anglophone children who referred to the Queen of England as the head of the government.[28] The fact that political authority was perceived by children as a masculine attribute is hardly surprising since formal political authority in Canada (as in most Western nations) is in the hands of men. It is indicative, therefore, of a sexist conception of political authority which is viewed, in most Western countries, as "male."

THE IMPACT OF CULTURAL MEMBERSHIP

It may be recalled that French-Canadian children were more likely to see authority in personalized terms and that age did not significantly change this perception. Furthermore, political authority was perceived by members of this group as an attribute that is not shared. These conclusions are based on the findings reported in Tables IV and V which showed that, when asked what government represented for them, Francophone pupils were more likely than Anglophone children to respond that it was a man, or as one child put it, "a man who tells you what to do."[29] The following excerpt from an essay written by a sixth grader is a good illustration of this attitude: "The government is a man who commands all other people. He decides what is good and what is bad." (French Canadian.)

Anglophone children, on the other hand, were more likely to view political authority as being vested in a group of men, and at a later age, in a structure such as parliament or the cabinet. Consequently, this group perceived political authority as something that is *shared*. Here is how one fifth-grade

---

Atlantic County, NJ, designed to measure young people's attitudes toward the police, shows that young people (both black and white) are overly critical of police and other government officials.

[21] *Power and Personality* (New York, 1948), 156ff.

[22] *Ibid.*, 157.

[23] The term Chicago groups refers to Easton and Hess and their associates, many of whom were associated with the University of Chicago in the late fifties and early sixties.

[24] *Children and Politics*, 46.

[25] *Basic Attitudes and Values*, 48.

[26] *Children and Politics*, 47.

[27] *Learning About Politics* (New York, 1970), 188ff.

[28] Previous research suggests that the Queen's role and personality tend to be fused in children's minds, and thus that she is not perceived in sexual terms. See Fred I. Greenstein, "French, British, and American Children's Images of Government and Politics," paper delivered at the meeting of the Northeastern Political Science Association, 13–14 November 1970, Philadelphia, 12.

[29] The question asked was, "What do you think of when I say government?"

English-Canadian pupil described the government: "If the men in the government don't agree on something, they have a meeting and they talk it over." The description of the government by French-Canadian children suggested a perception of government as an omnipotent and arbitrary institution, whereas the statements of English-Canadian children revealed a view of government as an institution which is considerably more flexible since it can encompass both disagreement and consensus.

French-Canadian children frequently referred to the authoritarian features of government. Such references as "he bosses around," "he tells you what to do," "he commands," were common. Overall, 12 per cent of the French-Canadian children referred to government in authoritarian terms while only 5.9 per cent of the English-Canadian children did. The latter viewed government much more often in terms of a manager or problem solver. It is interesting to note that French-Canadian children's perception of political authority closely resembled that of children in France. Greenstein and Tarrow, in a paper dealing with political socialization of children in France, England, and the United States, report that French children perceive political authority in terms of a command.[30] Thus the president of the Republic "commands" everyone, "he orders people around." American children, on the other hand, described the president of the United States as the "chief executive," or as the "leader of the people." This conception of authority is much closer to that displayed by English-Canadian children.

The personalization of children's perception of political authority may be explained by the theory of transference of authority from the family to other structures, a theory that Lasswell and Greenstein have outlined.[31] The greater incidence of such views in the Francophone subsample, and particularly the greater tendency of French-Canadian pupils to view government in authoritarian terms, may be explained by the impact on the socialization process of the political tradition of French Canada which, it has been suggested, is authoritarian.[32] More specifically, it may be argued that children's attitudes toward government in Quebec may be shaped by the differing styles of authority which characterize the English- and French-Canadian cultures.[33]

While it is undeniable that Quebec has undergone considerable political, social, and economic change during the past 50 years, several authors suggest that the pattern of authority in French Canada remains authoritarian, or at least paternalistic.[34] For example, while Dumont and Rocher write that new elites arise, Falardeau and Guindon state that older elites, in particular the clergy, retain positions of leadership.[35] Falardeau notes that, on the one hand, the behaviour of the family reflects a desire for emancipation while, at the same time, the French-Canadian family also manifests a "strict adhesion to the traditional norms."[36] In particular, while the quasi-patriarchal family has all but disappeared in Quebec, the father continues to occupy a position of relative

[30]"Political Orientations of Children: The Use of a Semi-Projective Technique in Three Nations."

[31]Lasswell, *Power and Personality*, 156, 157; Greenstein, *Children and Politics*, 46.

[32]Arthur Maheux, "French-Canadians and Democracy," in *Quebec Today*, ed. Douglas Grant (Toronto, 1960), 341–51.

[33]See the following on the style of authority and its impact on political socialization: Stanley Hoffman, "Heroic Leadership: The Case of Modern France," *Political Leadership in Industrialized Societies*, ed. Lewis Edinger (New York, 1967), 111ff. William R. Schonfeld, *Youth and Authority in France: A Study of Secondary Schools* (Beverley Hills, 1971), 10–12. Harry Eckstein, *A Theory of Stable Democracy*, research monograph 10 (Princeton, 1961).

[34]See, on the general question of authority in French Canada, *Le Pouvoir dans la Société Canadienne-française*, ed. Fernand Dumont and Jean-Paul Montminy (Quebec, 1966). In here, Gerald Fortin, in particular, contrasts two élites in Quebec: the old, which he labels the "technicians" of the preindustrial agrarian society, and the new "technicians" of the postindustrial society. He argues that while the latter are "perhaps less paternalistic than their predecessors they nonetheless see a privileged role for themselves in the new society" based on knowledge and information. Thus the setting changes, and new élites are arising, but the *pattern* of authority does not appear to change since it remains *hierarchical*. See "Transformation des structures du pouvoir," 93ff.

[35]See Fernand Dumont and Guy Rocher, "An Introduction to a Sociology of French-Canada," in Marcel Rioux and Yves Martin, *French-Canadian Society* (Toronto, 1964), 199ff.; Jean C. Falardeau, "The Changing Social Structures of Contemporary French-Canadian Society," in *Essais sur le Québec contemporain*, ed. Jean C. Falardeau (Laval, 1953), 137ff. Hubert Guindon, "The Social Evolution of Quebec Reconsidered," in Rioux and Martin, *French-Canadian Society*, 137–61.

[36]See Falardeau, *Essais*, 116.

preeminence in many Francophone families with respect to decision making.[37] The role of the clergy has also changed, yet the type of change that occurred affects more the setting of the relationship between clerics and population, rather than their authority.[38] In other words, priests still occupy positions of leadership but they do so in new environments: in youth groups or labour movements, for example.[39] Norman Taylor provides a further illustration of the French-Canadian style of authority in the business world.[40] The following statement by a French-Canadian businessman is revealing on this point: "I have a secretary, an assistant general manager, a sales manager, an accountant, a plant superintendent and a plant engineer. I try to leave them with responsibility, but I hate like hell to do it."[41]

The French-Canadian style of authority, then, suggests a pattern in which the decision-making process is *not shared*, but rather is concentrated in the hands of selected individuals interacting with other members of a given social structure in terms of a hierarchy. This model first applies within the family, and is later reinforced in other social situations such as schools, the Church, the work world, and finally carries over into the political sphere by the transference process hypothesized by Lasswell. This pattern would explain why French-Canadian children's perception of government is more likely to be "a man who orders you around" and a provider for personal needs.

Conversely, following Maheux, it may be argued that the Anglophone style of authority is more democratic, in part, because its development was largely unaffected by such authoritative structures as the *ancien régime*, the Catholic Church, and the civil law (strongly influenced by the French *ancien droit*), which had a major impact on the development of French-Canadian society.[42]

[37]See Marcel Rioux, "Kinship Recognition and Urbanization in French-Canada," in Rioux and Martin, *French-Canadian Society*, 372ff.

[38]For a discussion of the traditional role of the *curé* in French Canada see Horace Miner, *St Denis, A French-Canadian Parish* (Chicago, 1939); Everett C. Hughes, *French-Canada in Transition* (Chicago, 1943).

[39]For specific examples see Falardeau, "The Changing Social Structures of Contemporary French-Canadian Society," in Rioux and Martin, *French-Canadian Society*, 106–22; see in addition by the same author "The Role and Importance of the Church in French Canada," 342–57; see also Hubert Guindon, "The Social Evolution of Quebec Reconsidered," 137–61.

[40]Norman W. Taylor, "A Study of French-Canadians as Industrial Entrepreneurs," (PH D Dissertation, Yale University, 1957).

[41]*Ibid.*, 73.

Summary

The data reported in this paper showed that English- and French-Canadian children differed in their perception of government and its function. But the data did not reveal any significant difference in children's evaluation of government. The data generally indicated that while most children perceived government in terms of authority, Francophone pupils displayed a more personalized view of government than Anglophone children and that age reinforced this pattern. In addition, French-Canadian youngsters were more likely to view government in authoritative terms, while English-Canadian young people tended to perceive it more a "manager."

The two groups differed also in their attitudes toward the function of government: French-Canadian children were more inclined to see government as an output agency, or what was called a distribution agency, while English-Canadian pupils tended to see it as an input, or policy agency. Finally, the data showed that there was no significant difference between French- and English-Canadian children's evaluation of the performance of the government: both groups displayed an unidealistic conception of government.

It was argued that children's critical view of government raises some questions about the contention of some writers that children see government idealistically. In addition, it was suggested that the differing styles of authority that characterize the two cultures account for the differing attitudes toward government of children in Quebec.

[42]See the following on the history of codification in Quebec and the impact of French law: J.E.C. Brierley, "Quebec's Civil Law Codification," *McGill Law Journal*, 14, no. 4 (1968), 522–89.

Recensions
Reviews

Tucker, *The Radical Left and American Foreign Policy* BLEMA S. STEINBERG 31
Smiley, *Canada in Question* J.R. MALLORY 31
Desrosiers, *Le personnel politique québécois* RÉJEAN PELLETIER 31
Boily, *Québec 1940–1969. Bibliographie* GILLES CARON 31
Painchaud, *Francophonie, bibliographie 1960–1969* GORDON MACE 31
Khan, MacKown, McNiven, *An Introduction to Political Science* H.G. THORBURN 31
Heeney, *The Things that are Caesar's* KENNETH KERNAGHAN 32
Hodgetts, et al., *The Biography of an Institution* A. PAUL PROSS 32
Swainson, ed., *Oliver Mowat's Ontario* JOHN WILSON 32
Johnson and MacNutt, *Aberhart of Alberta*, and Hooke, *Thirty Plus Five* F.Q. QUO 32
Clarkson, *City Lib* JAMES LIGHTBODY 32
Price, ed., *Regional Government in Ontario* CAROLINE ANDREW 32
Granatstein and Stevens, eds., *Forum* PAUL FOX 32
Canada's 28th Parliament W.F. DAWSON 32
Piotte, *Sur Lénine* ANDRÉ KUZMINSKI 32
Pelczynski, ed., *Hegel's Political Philosophy* FREDERICK M. BARNARD 32
Corry, *The Power of the Law* FREDERICK VAUGHAN 32
Debbasch, *Science administrative* NASIR ISLAM 33
Cotteret et Emeri, *Les systèmes électoraux* FRANÇOIS RENAUD 33
Cotteret et Emeri, *Le budget de l'Etat* RICHARD BERGER 33
Mazrui, *Cultural Engineering and Nation-Building in East Africa* GEOFFREY F. ENGHOLM 33
Wilcox, Rose, and Boyd, eds., *Asia and the International System* SHELDON W. SIMON 33
Smith, *Germany beyond the Wall* KLAUS J. HERRMANN 33
Greenstein and Lerner, eds., *A Source Book for the Study of Personality and Politics* JOHN WOODS 33
Blalock, ed., *Causal Models in the Social Sciences* W.P. IRVINE 33

Robert W. Tucker, **The Radical Left and American Foreign Policy.** (Studies in International Affairs no. 15), Baltimore: The Johns Hopkins Press [Toronto: Copp Clark], 1971, pp. ix, 156.

In a slim volume of 156 pages, Professor Robert Tucker has written a penetrating and cogent critique of the radical left and American foreign policy. Tucker set himself two main tasks: (1) to explore the way in which conventional and radical critiques of American foreign policy differ, and (2) to assess the validity of the radical explanation for that policy.

Conventional critics of American foreign policy (the liberal-realist school) view the American diplomatic record as marked by confusion, uncertainty, and oscillation between isolationism and globalism. They interpret it as having been misguided – compounded of sentimentality and intellectual error (for example, the domino theory), but not as having been malevolent. Its leitmotif was one of "misplaced altruism." The validity of these observations has been sharply challenged by the radical historiographers who see a pattern of clarity and consistency in American foreign policy. America, in their view, has effectively pursued an expansionist policy aimed at stabilizing the world in a pro-American equilibrium. Tucker does not dispute the evidence of a clear and consistent pattern of American expansionism; where he parts company with the radicals is in terms of their explanations for these developments.

In Tucker's opinion, notwithstanding individual differences amongst various writers of the radical left, what is unique to this school of thought is its emphasis upon economic determinism. It insists not only that Americans have defined their security in economic terms, but that American predominance in the world has been sought to preserve and strengthen capitalism at home. The argument is a determinist one because American foreign policy is seen essentially as an inevitable response to the structural needs of American capitalism.

Methodically and painstakingly, Tucker demolishes the economic-determinist arguments of the radical left. In particular, the writings of Harry Magdoff and Gabriel Kolko, with their emphasis on America's need for strategic raw materials as an explanation for its persistent expansionism, are examined and the illogic of their arguments is devastatingly exposed. Moreover, the radicals' refusal to consider other explanatory variables for American foreign policy, such as the structure of the international system, etc., can only lead, in Tucker's view, to a distortion of reality. Professor Tucker does not, however, wholly denigrate the contribution that radical critics have made to our understanding of American foreign policy. "If nothing else, the radical critique has forced us to acknowledge (1) the extent to which an obsessive self-interest has been central in American foreign policy" and (2) the fact that "America has behaved very much as other great nations have behaved."

But if the sources of American foreign policy are not to be found in the forces generated by capitalism, how can American behaviour be explained? In an all-too-brief comment, Tucker suggests that explanations for America's expansionist and counter-revolutionary behaviour "must be sought in the variety of motives that have always led preponderant powers to identify their preponderance with their security and above all, perhaps, in the fear arising simply from the loss of preponderance itself." One could, of course, raise the question, how does this type of explanation differ from traditional explanations of state behaviour offered by the power theorists? But to be fair to Professor Tucker, the main purpose of his study was to explore the validity of the explanations offered by the radical left, not to construct his own set of alternative hypotheses. If Tucker is as good at theory-building as he is at theory-demolition, then we can look forward with anticipation to any future essays dealing with multi-variate analysis of hegemonial behaviour.

BLEMA S. STEINBERG
McGill University

D.V. Smiley, **Canada in Question: Federalism in the Seventies.** Toronto: McGraw-Hill Ryerson, 1972. pp. 190.

Federalism may well be the most difficult form of constitutional government. This is partly because it depends for its strength on a reasoned political nationalism which must coexist with institutionalized cleavages. Partly it is because federalism is a balancing-act in which the weights are perpetually changing. Thus the rather formal structures so lucidly and elegantly set out by Sir Kenneth Wheare give the whole thing a greater air of rationality than it actually has. It is unfair to Wheare to dismiss his analysis as too formal because it must be obvious to anyone who has taken the trouble to read him seriously that he is in fact quite sensible of the role of political forces in his system. Those who, like Riker, see the essence of the matter in a federal bargain the terms of which shift in response to behavioural change do not advance the argument much. Institutional changes, and changes in the role of institutions, are very close to the heart of the matter.

Donald Smiley, who by his careful and perceptive observation of Canadian federalism over the past 20 years has done more than anyone else to make it intelligible, has in this book brought his perceptions to a further, but still evolving, stage of refinement. In the process he has not only drawn his earlier analysis of the key role of executive federalism into perspective, but has succeeded in linking it firmly to the historical roots of our contemporary problems. That there lingers over the whole a distinct air of pessimism, clearly implied in the title, places him firmly in the Canadian intellectual tradition.

Underlying the crisis of Canadian federalism is a weakening of legitimacy as social change undermines old patterns of authority and new economic configurations lead to a questioning of traditional objectives of national policy. Professor Smiley is inclined to think that much of the federal government's apparent objective in the discussions of constitutional revision leading up to the Victoria Conference was misconceived. Since the "older and more collectively oriented purposes of 'Peace, Order, and Good Government'" seem to have been displaced by a greater emphasis on the entrenchment of human rights, a new and heavy weight was to be placed on the constitution itself as a "focus of Canadian political allegiance." The determination to embark on a thorough review of the constitution entailed a serious risk, the costs of which had not been fully calculated. When this approach failed at

Victoria, the existing constitution's legitimacy had been seriously undermined "without replacing it by something allegedly better."

Meanwhile the institutional supports of the system now seem in many cases to undermine rather than to nourish it. Thus he finds nothing in the Canadian system to support Riker's belief that the political parties perform an effective role in adjusting the terms of the federal bargain. The fact of the matter is that the electoral system, in conjunction with the regionalization of the party system, may well be – as Cairns has argued – a source of serious strain on the federal structure. The results of recent elections have suggested that this is the case.

One consequence is that "executive federalism," the continuous process of piecemeal adjustment carried out by intergovernmental negotiation, has had to bear a disproportionate share of the strain. The capacity of these arrangements to respond to regional pressures has at the same time been further limited by the growing "rationality" of federal decision-making under the impact of PPBS.

One would have preferred that Professor Smiley had been willing to develop further his highly suggestive discussion of the need for greater regional decentralization and deliberate representativeness in the federal bureaucracy. While his first discussion of this point, which appeared in the February 1971 issue of *Canadian Public Administration*, was no doubt read by many of the right people, it would have been worthwhile elaborating the argument in greater depth in a book which is destined to be much more widely read.

The analysis in the book bears particularly on the two major problems of the Canadian political environment, regionalism and dual nationalism. The author is both cool and sensible in his discussion of the new dimension that the drastic alterations in the relations of French and English Canada have imposed on the whole nature of Canadian federalism. He is rightly pessimistic about the possibility that the difficulty will disappear if only a sufficiently aggressive bilingual policy can make French Canadians feel at home in English-speaking Canada. If there was a time when this was so, it has passed. This does not of course diminish the importance of the objective, but the problem is much deeper. There are two communities in Canada, and the political system must adjust itself to accommodate them. The problem is – how? He is clear enough about the dangers of commonly discussed solutions, but nobody yet knows the direction in which the answer lies.

Not least of the merits of the book is that it returns to a way of looking at Canadian federalism that has been out of fashion for too long. That way is through what he describes as political economy, which of course takes us back to Harold Innis. It was Innis who pointed out a quarter of a century ago that the strains on the Canadian constitutional system came in large measure from the fact that the economically dominant central Canadian region had succeeded in imposing a political structure and a national policy that corresponded to an economy "built in relation to Great Britain and Europe." Western and northern resource development, and increasing economic integration with the United States, have now put the majority of provincial governments on a collision course with the surviving political framework of the old National Policy. As a consequence, Canadians are now in search not only of an identity, but of a country.

J.R. MALLORY
McGill University

Richard Desrosiers, **Le personnel politique québécois.** Montréal : Editions du Boréal Express, 1972, 143 pp.

Ce volume, paru dans la collection « Etudes d'histoire du Québec », est avant tout un recueil d'articles déjà publiés sur le personnel politique québécois, introduit par un texte de Richard Desrosiers, professeur au département d'histoire de l'Université du Québec à Montréal.

La présentation déborde le cadre de ce seul volume et met en lumière trois grandes approches théoriques qui fondent les études sur le personnel politique : l'une met l'accent sur le comportement individuel de l'homme politique, l'autre sur les classes sociales, et la troisième sur les élites politiques ou les catégories dirigeantes. Cette dernière approche domine l'ensemble du volume puisque les différentes études réunies par l'auteur cherchent avant tout à repérer ceux qui jouent un rôle ou exercent une influence dans la vie politique et à en dégager l'origine sociale et les caractéristiques socio-économiques.

Malheureusement, ces analyses se bornent trop souvent à « décrire » les hommes politiques – essentiellement, députés et ministres – détenteurs du pouvoir politique, sans les rattacher aux autres détenteurs du pouvoir, les élites sociales, religieuses et surtout économiques. Ce qui aurait permis de mettre à nu la « réalité » du pouvoir des hommes politiques québécois.

Certes, Jean-Charles Falardeau ne circonscrit pas le débat aux seuls hommes politiques, mais entend traiter des élites traditionnelles et des élites nouvelles du Québec autant sur le plan économique, culturel et même syndical que sur le seul plan politique. Mais il ne fait qu'effleurer le problème des élites qui sont dominantes, sans être dirigeantes.

Le professeur Bonenfant, pour sa part, s'en tient à l'évolution du statut de l'homme politique canadien-français, en montrant que le député exerce de moins en moins ses fonctions de législateur et d'intermédiaire entre le pouvoir et les électeurs pour exercer plutôt une fonction de contrôle des activités du législateur. Si le député cesse donc d'être un titulaire du pouvoir, c'est pour devenir un instrument de contrôle. Ce qui nous éclaire sur le rôle nouveau joué par les députés, mais non pas sur l'étendue et l'efficacité de ce contrôle dans notre système parlementaire et sur les limites imposées par l'affiliation partisane des députés.

L'analyse de Robert Boily est probablement la plus intéressante du volume puisque l'auteur rattache les hommes politiques du Québec à leur origine sociale, tout en soulignant le décalage entre la faible représentation des classes paysanne et ouvrière et le personnel politique québécois issu du secteur des affaires et des professions libérales. Bien plus, cette étude montre que la classe socialement dominante occupait autrefois le pouvoir politique, alors que les nouveaux dirigeants de l'appareil politique ne sont d'aucune manière « détenteurs d'un pouvoir social ou économique dominant », mais des hommes « qui choisissent comme métier de s'emparer du pouvoir politique et de l'exploiter dans l'intérêt général » qui coïncide d'ailleurs avec l'intérêt du parti et leur intérêt personnel (p. 82). Ce qui amène naturellement le professeur Boily à poser le problème de la réalité du pouvoir des hommes politiques québécois considérés comme une « élite dirigeante » ou comme une « élite simplement dominante ». Sa réponse permet seulement de poser les jalons d'une étude plus vaste qui analyserait les rapports, de dépendance ou non, entre l'élite politique et les élites sociales et économiques, tout en soulignant le caractère international et ethniquement différent du pouvoir économique au Québec, ainsi que les limites sociales, culturelles et constitutionnelles dans lesquelles ont dû évoluer les autorités politiques québécoises.

Le recueil se termine sur une étude de l'évolution de l'élite politique montréalaise, de l'aristocratie à la démocratie, depuis les débuts du pouvoir municipal à Montréal et sur une analyse purement descriptive des cabinets provinciaux où les auteurs tentent de cerner les influences qui président à la formation d'un cabinet et cherchent à montrer comment ce cabinet doit être une synthèse des différentes tendances au sein du parti.

Bien que la plupart de ces textes s'appuient sur la théorie des élites considérées comme catégories dominantes, il ne s'en dégage pas nécessairement une impression d'unité pour l'ensemble du volume. On pourrait croire d'ailleurs que cette impression d'unité peut plus facilement ressortir d'un recueil d'articles déjà publiés que d'une collection de textes originaux ou inédits qui se fondent sur des approches différentes. Dans ce dernier cas, toutefois, l'originalité des textes peut suppléer en grande partie au manque d'unité quasi inévitable dans ce genre d'ouvrage.

En outre, un volume doit avant tout rencontrer le but pour lequel il a été conçu, ce qui ne semble pas le cas ici. La collection « Etudes d'histoire du Québec » veut mettre à la portée de tous des textes parfois difficiles d'accès ou injustement oubliés. Que les textes réunis dans ce volume soient « difficiles d'accès » ou « injustement oubliés », il est permis d'en douter puisqu'ils ont été publiés entre 1965 et 1967 et sont parus dans des revues connues, comme *Recherches sociographiques.* Ce qui d'ailleurs ne minimise en rien l'importance et l'intérêt de chacun de ces articles.

On pourrait souhaiter qu'un prochain volume, portant sur le même sujet, présente vraiment des textes « difficiles d'accès » et « injustement oubliés » ou, bien mieux, qu'il rassemble sous ce thème des textes originaux ou inédits, en dépit de leur caractère parfois disparate.

RÉJEAN PELLETIER
Université d'Ottawa

Robert Boily, **Québec 1940–1969. Bibliographie : Le système politique québécois et son environnement.** Montréal : Presses de l'Université de Montréal, 1971, 208 pp.

Au delà de 2000 entrées individuelles portant sur le système politique québécois, six annexes (éléments bibliographiques, biographies, mémoires, rapports des commissions d'enquête du Québec 1867–1968, rapports des comités d'enquête du Québec 1867–1968, travaux en cours – thèse de maîtrise et de doctorat, thèses de maîtrise et de doctorat terminées en 1968–9), table des matières, index, auteurs et sujets, tel est globalement l'ouvrage du professeur Boily.

Précisons dès le début que cet ouvrage, par le seul fait qu'il existe, représente un apport certain à l'inventaire encore à faire des ressources documentaires en politologie québécoise. Mis à part l'ouvrage de monsieur Philippe Garigue, *Bibliographie du Québec,*

1955–1965, lequel tout en couvrant un champ beaucoup plus vaste, date déjà passablement, il n'existait pas à proprement parler de bibliographie pertinente sur le sujet. Monsieur Boily vient combler ce vide.

Ceci dit, il est certains points que j'aimerais souligner qui, sans vouloir diminuer l'intérêt de l'ouvrage, méritent je crois que l'on s'y attarde. Je glisse rapidement sur le contenu formel du travail comme sur les cas particuliers auxquels on pourrait s'objecter. La bibliographie est un de ces champs où les limites du travail et plus spécifiquement le choix même des titres retenus sont autant d'éléments qui prêtent à trop de subjectivité et d'arbitraire pour qu'on y place le débat ; d'autant plus qu'il serait futile selon moi dans un domaine où si peu a déjà été fait, tant en terme de publications que de repérage, de discuter de l'opportunité ou de la valeur de tel ou tel titre particulier. Je crois qu'à date, sur le sujet en question, tout titre qui existe mérite d'être retenu et ce par le seul fait même qu'il existe.

Là où je m'interroge, c'est sur la qualité des sources documentaires utilisées. Je trouve curieux qu'au strict chapitre des ouvrages documentaires consultés on ait négligé des instruments tel que *Canadiana* et *l'Index Analytique* pour ne nommer que ceux-là. Il aurait existé de nombreux ouvrages indispensables à consulter avant de s'attarder sur *Social Sciences and Humanities Index* que l'on identifie comme l'un des huit principaux index consultés dans l'élaboration de cet ouvrage. (Pour plus d'éléments relatifs aux sources bibliographiques sur le Québec voir : Peter Southam, *Bibliographie des bibliographies sur l'économie, la société et la culture du Québec, 1940–1971*. Québec : Université Laval – Institut supérieur des sciences humaines, 1972, 86 pp.) De fait, la qualité des sources consultés m'apparaît comme la principale faiblesse de cette bibliographie.

La table des matières que l'on retrouve présentée « à la française » à la fin de l'ouvrage, fort complète et très détaillée, m'apparaît comme l'un des points forts de cette bibliographie. Les entrées y sont claires et suffisamment détaillées pour que l'on n'ait pas à effectuer des recoupements excessifs pour retrouver ce que l'on cherche. Le chapitre B traitant des institutions politiques aurait gagné à être un peu plus étoffé. L'administration publique, qui s'y rattache directement, demeure le parent pauvre de cet ouvrage. (Voir : Germain Julien, *Bibliographie : Administration Publique québécoise*. Québec : Ecole Nationale d'Administration Publique, 1971, 196 pp.)

Des différentes annexes que nous propose l'auteur, les plus intéressantes demeurent assurément les deux listes de rapports des commissions d'enquête et de comités d'enquête du Québec de 1867 à 1968. Les annexes D 5 et D 6 portant sur un inventaire des travaux de maîtrise et doctorat sur le Québec en cours et terminées en 1968–9 ont déjà en grande partie perdu de leur exclusivité originale avec la parution en 1971 de *Thèses canadiennes en sciences politiques complétées et en cours de rédaction*, par l'Association canadienne de science politique.

Dans l'ensemble donc, un ouvrage indispensable qui malgré ses faiblesses se devait d'exister et mérite d'être consulté. C'est une première ébauche, un ouvrage de base dans un champ, la bibliographie sur le Québec, où se multiplient depuis quelque temps les ouvrages de valeur avec la parution presque simultanée des travaux de messieurs Boily, Julien, Southam, et enfin Durocher-Linteau (*Histoire du Québec : bibliographie sélective, 1867–1970*) en histoire. L'ouvrage de Robert Boily est de cette classe et à ce titre le bienvenu.

GILLES CARON
Université Laval

Paul Painchaud, **Francophonie. Bibliographie 1960–1969.** Montréal : Presses de l'Université du Québec, 1972, 136 pp.

Dans ce domaine immense que constituent les relations internationales (l'emploi du mot interétatiques nous semblerait plus approprié), la francophonie forme un champ d'intérêt relativement nouveau. De plus, les recherches qui portent sur se sujet ont été jusqu'ici assez fragmentaires. C'est pourquoi il était nécessaire de fournir aux intéressés un instrument permettant une vision d'ensemble sur ce qui a déjà été écrit et pouvant en même temps constituer un guide pour les recherches à venir.

Le but que l'on cherche à atteindre en présentant cette bibliographie est de rendre compte de l'information sur la francophonie que contiennent les principales bibliographies générales employées en sciences humaines. Précisons qu'une attention spéciale a été accordée aux études scientifiques sans qu'un préjudice soit toutefois causé à l'information factuelle. M. Painchaud prévient cependant le lecteur que l'on n'a retenu que peu d'information concernant la vie interne des etats composant la communauté francophone ; il s'agit là d'un choix délibéré puisqu'il a été décidé de placer l'accent surtout sur la francophonie en tant que communauté et sur les relations qu'entretiennent entre eux les divers états francophones. A l'intérieur de ce cadre, une place particulière a été faite aux ouvrages traitant des programmes de coopération ainsi que des rapports entre les états africains et certaines institutions telles que la Communauté économique européenne. Il faut noter enfin que malgré la décision de ne pas retenir d'ouvrages concernant les territoires non souverains, une exception a été faite pour le cas du Québec. Ceci s'explique par ce phénomène particulier d'une collectivité ethnique non souveraine, mais possédant quand même un gouvernement comme instrument principal de défense de ses traits spécifiques.

La bibliographie que nous présente M. Painchaud contient 1602 titres regroupés sous deux thèmes généraux : concept de la francophonie et rapports entre pays francophones. Le premier thème rassemble les ouvrages qui s'intéressent à l'aspect civilisation de la francophonie (langue, culture) et aux organisations internationales issues de ou ayant des rapports avec la communauté francophone. Dans la deuxième partie nous retrouvons des ouvrages qui traitent des différentes relations entre les pays francophones, soient-elles du domaine politique, économique, culturel, ou technique. De plus, il faut retenir que même si les bibliographies générales constituent les principales sources de référence, certaines sources directes ont été incluses afin que cet ouvrage soit le plus complet possible. Enfin, la présentation technique, quant à elle, est faite selon trois sources d'entrée principales : les ouvrages, les revues, et les journaux.

Il est évident que cette bibliographie contient des failles plus ou moins importantes ; d'une part, elle s'adressait au départ à un groupe particulier de lecteurs, de l'autre, elle constituait un des premiers efforts du genre tentés au Québec. C'est ainsi que pour combler ces lacunes, et afin de présenter un recueil de plus en plus complet de la littérature concernant la francophonie, M. Painchaud nous annonce que le Centre Québécois de relations internationales (CQRI) publiera une bibliographie annuelle appelée « Chronique de la francophonie ». Cette publication ne sera pas le seul effort fourni par le CQRI en ce domaine, puisque déjà les structures du Centre contiennent un Bureau d'information sur la francophonie (BIF) et que des recherches sur ce sujet sont actuellement en cours. Au Québec, le CQRI fait œuvre de pionnier dans le domaine des études et de la diffusion de l'information sur la francophonie, et cette bibliographie qu'il nous présente est un jalon indispensable pour faciliter les recherches à venir.

GORDON MACE
Université Laval

R.A. Khan, S.A. MacKown, J.D. McNiven, **An Introduction to Political Science.** Georgetown, Ont.: Irwin-Dorsey Ltd., 1972, pp. xiii, 467.

Instructors in introductory political science courses seeking a textbook that includes the methods and terminology of modern systems analysis have been faced with the dilemma of confining their teaching to Canadian government alone because the materials were available, or else using an introductory text intended for students in the United States or Britain, which lacked Canadian material. Professors Khan, MacKown, and McNiven have sought to supply the missing ingredient that they have long heard their colleagues pray for. They have laboured diligently, presenting some 451 pages of text, supplemented by two indexes. The chapters are followed by supplementary reading lists. The book is encyclopaedic in scope, beginning with two chapters on the discipline, followed by six on the functions of government (socialization, articulation and aggregation of interests, constitutions, rule-making, rule-implementation, rule adjudication). Then follow discussions of political change, authoritarianism, international relations, and four chapters on political ideas: liberalism, conservatism, socialism, and nationalism.

The book is "good in parts." The discussion of roles, structures, and functions (p. 34 et seq.) is clear and concise, and the chapter on political culture, socialization, and public opinion makes excellent use of the Almond and Verba data, supplemented by Johnstone's Canadian material. The treatment of one party systems (p. 92 et seq.) is clear, balanced, and fair.

In general the writing is clear, if uninspired, but the authors tend to squeeze in too much unelaborated factual information. In particular they include too many names of people with so little about each that the treatment at times comes close to name-dropping. Also this pressure to include everything assumes too much knowledge on the part of students (most of whom will, after all, be freshmen, newly arrived from Canadian high schools!). They will find the parade of characters overwhelming, especially when so little is said of each one. And some are pretty remote, for example, Michael Bakunin, Gabriele D'Annunzio, J.B. Duvernay, Eugen Ehrlich, Joseph Gobineau, Johann Herder, E.A. Hoebel, George Lukacs, Joseph de Maistre, Fernand Pelloutier, Karl Wittfogel, etc.

The real problem, however, is the success or failure of the Almond vocabulary and analytical method when applied to teaching introductory courses to students, most of whom have no background in social science. This is a matter of individual judgment, and many political scientists are to be found on either side of the question.

In matters of substance, the students are expected to have some familiarity with Marx (p. 64) if they are to follow the argument, and to be able to profit from a superficial overview of vast areas of political thought and a critique of all important ideologies without significant elaboration. There is not enough explanation to produce comprehension – but too much ground is traversed in space and time. The student is likely to finish like the tourist who "did six countries in five days."

This problem is compounded by overly generalized comment, which is often unclear when precision is required. For example, about the democratic principle: "This assumption underlies the constitutions of most political systems today, though it is honoured more often in the breach than in the practice" (p. 134). Or, "A free man is one who is motivated by his purpose, activated by his rationality, and capacitated by his competence" (p. 136).

One must justify, if one favours it, the addition of the many terms and concepts of politics that are new to the students, the esoteric jargon. In this case I found it greatly added to the prolixity, complexity, and heaviness of the text. The writers are tempted into lengthy expositions of the obvious, using a vocabulary that will burden the students unduly. The justification that it must be learned later if not sooner is not correct – for many the course will be terminal.

In short, to accomplish the task, the text must be of an exceptional quality in both exposition and content. While in many ways and in several parts this book is good, it does not attain, or rather maintain, the required level. Apart from the uneven writing (no doubt in part traceable to the number of authors), there are too many errors, especially in the Canadian material. For example, we are told (p. 116) that "the names of the candidates but not their parties are listed" on the ballot, that "the Governor-General is the representative of the *British* Crown" in Canada, Australia, and New Zealand, and that he *is* head of state (p. 144), and that he "*must approve* bills passed by Parliament before they can become law" (p. 158). The prime minister "is more bound by tradition, law, and convention than other ministers" (p. 161). We are not told how or why. The Canadian Senate "on paper possesses considerable political power, similar to that of the British House of Lords" (p. 173). And "Confederation ... introduced responsible government in British North America" (p. 364); "The *British* ensign was replaced by the maple leaf as the national flag" (p. 366): the terms "English" and "British" are used without discrimination. There are too many small errors in names and usage, for example, R. MacG. Dawson becomes R.W. Dawson, and Laurier comes out "Lourier."

The authors took on a heavy task and have produced a book that provides a modern general introduction to political science. The flaws are remediable so let us look forward to the second edition.

H.G. THORBURN
Queen's University

Arnold Heeney, **The Things that are Caesar's: The Memoirs of a Canadian Public Servant.** Toronto: University of Toronto Press, 1972, pp. xiv, 218.

Historians and political scientists have for too long been deprived of the recollections and insights of senior public servants in Canada. These memoirs of Arnold Heeney, which have been edited by his son Brian, mark a praiseworthy beginning to efforts to remedy this serious gap in the literature on Canadian public affairs.

In the first three chapters, Arnold Heeney recounts with candour and humour his family background, his education, and his work experience before he became principal secretary to Prime Minister Mackenzie King. In the subsequent 11 chapters, he provides a largely chronological account of his remarkable career as a Canadian public servant. Few other public officials in Canada have matched Heeney's extraordinary record of achievement. He served the Canadian government in a variety of high-level positions, including that of Canada's first secretary to the cabinet.

Heeney reveals little of substance about Canada's domestic and external affairs that has not been documented elsewhere. From the perspective of an active participant, however, he does provide important evidence to substantiate assertions made in other writings. Moreover, his fascinating reminiscences about historic events and public personalities, primarily in Canada and the United States, are interspersed with delightful and insightful anecdotes.

Perhaps of greatest contemporary interest are Heeney's observations on Canadian-American relations during his two terms as ambassador to the United States (1953–7) and (1959–62) as well as during his years as co-chairman of the International Joint

Commission (1962–70) and Canadian chairman of the Permanent Joint Board on Defence (1967–70). He became well acquainted with such government leaders as Eisenhower, Dulles, and Nixon as he went about the frequently unenviable task of explaining the Canadian government's position on United States foreign policy.

In the context of current difficulties in Canada's economic negotiations with the United States, it is significant that Heeney concludes that in his "experience of Canadian-American negotiations, which stretches over thirty years, Canadian delegations have, in most cases, been outmanoeuvred by those on the US side of the table" (p. 201). He contends further that it is only in such joint agencies as the IJC and the PJBD "that the inherent inequality in our relations with our giant neighbour is reduced to a minimum" (p. 201).

During his lengthy public service career, Heeney was personally involved in many of the most significant public policy decisions in Canada's history. As secretary to the cabinet from 1940 to 1949, he could aptly be described as Canada's foremost "Man of Secrets" – a term applied to Lord Hankey, Britain's first secretary to the cabinet, by his biographer. Heeney's account of his relations with Canadian politicians (Mackenzie King, St Laurent, Diefenbaker, Pearson) and bureaucrats (Skelton, Clark, Bryce, Ritchie) and of specific periods (the conscription crisis, the public service during the Diefenbaker years) are absorbing and informative. More significantly, Heeney portrays himself as a comfortable inhabitant of the corridors of power and demonstrates the influence he and his administrative colleagues exercised on the content of public policy.

Heeney also made extremely important contributions to the internal management of the Canadian public service, particularly in the sphere of personnel administration. During his brief period as chairman of the Civil Service Commission, from spring 1957 to January 1959, the commission produced the influential *Report on Personnel Administration in the Public Service*. And in 1963, Heeney was appointed chairman of the Preparatory Committee on Collective Bargaining in the Public Service. The *Report* of the committee, submitted in 1965, was the foundation for the unique form of collective bargaining for public servants introduced in 1967.

It is regrettable that certain of the most admirable qualities of the senior bureaucrat – discretion, circumspection, optimism, and generosity – are much less praiseworthy characteristics of an author from whom one is seeking revelations about specific events and personalities. It would be a cause for amazement in academic quarters and concern in official circles, however, if what a retired public servant was inclined to reveal corresponded with what academic scholars wished to learn.

Yet, the concluding chapter, consisting of two and a half pages, is disappointingly brief and superficial. From his enormous wealth of experience close to the core of government, Heeney provides few judgments or prescriptions relating to the nature and direction of Canadian politics and public administration. He could have taught us much more.

On the final page of his book, Heeney expresses the hope that Canadian public servants will acquire "the sense of vocation" to the public service "which is so important to the quality of human achievement" (p. 203). In a modest and self-deprecating fashion and with admirable literary skill, Heeney demonstrates in this book that he possessed the commitment to public service which he wished for others. It is to be hoped that senior public servants who have retired recently or who are about to retire will be inspired to follow Arnold Heeney's example by committing their experiences and insights to paper.

KENNETH KERNAGHAN
Brock University

J.E. Hodgetts, William McCloskey, Reginald Whitaker and V. Seymour Wilson, **The Biography of an Institution: The Civil Service Commission of Canada, 1908–1967.** Montreal: McGill-Queen's University Press, 1972, pp. xi, 532.

This is a courageous and largely successful attempt to meet a long-standing need for a sophisticated analysis of one of the central institutions of the Canadian federal government.

Drawing upon a mass of documentation – by far the major part of it in primary sources – the authors present a fascinating account of the development of the Civil Service Commission from its creation in 1908 to its official demise and reincarnation as the Public Service Commission in 1967. During most of this period the Commission was a central agency in the fullest sense of the word, exercising through its control of the personnel function an extraordinary influence over the evolution of the entire federal public service. It was not, however, always a beneficial influence. Too frequently the Commission's organizational capacity outlasted the need for the services it was intended to provide, a condition that fostered a mechanistic application of the Civil Service Act and a tendency to rigidly defend existing policies and procedures in the face of repeated criticism.

The authors' candid treatment of the resultant paper wars and their occasional more violent eruptions should become a hallmark of studies of Canadian public administration. It is a treatment that adds to a perceptive analysis of the interminable barrages of memoranda, reports, speeches, and letters that characterize policy formation, a human dimension that lightens a formidable study. Throughout the book the authors display a pleasing willingness to dispense with the usual coy reticence of officially sanctioned studies. This approach is particularly effective in their discussion of the Commission's perpetual battles with Treasury Board and its unwilling self-appraisal following the attack of the Glassco royal commission.

At times, though, the vigorous treatment of these events comes close to partisanship. It may well be that Treasury Board "had always looked with considerable favour upon many of the Glassco recommendations since they had the effect of increasing its power at the expense of that of the CSC," (p. 320) but the assertion is not proven and cannot be proven here because the authors have not studied the Treasury Board as they have the CSC. Such displays of bias are minor flaws in a major work. They are engaging rather than disturbing, and if they goad other federal agencies to rebut with their own institutional biographies they are commendable.

It is more difficult to accept the authors' general assessment of the commission's performance during the late 1950s and the early 1960s. Their view is that "the elaboration of the concept of the central staffing agency and its development into specific plans and programs of action, while perhaps long overdue in many respects, essentially stand as a credit to the organization's ability to reassess itself critically and to renew its goals and purposes," (p. 342). Surely an organization possessing the capacity for self-renewal claimed for the commission would have acted upon the advice of men such as J.D. Love and S.H. Mansbridge long before outspoken criticism from elsewhere in the service and the censure of two royal commissions threatened emasculation. In the circumstances the interpretation seems too generous.

Compared with the solid accomplishments of the book, such criticisms are minor. They merely testify to the fact that the biographer of an institution, no less than the biographer of an individual personality, may be unable to resist identifying with his subject. In this instance the distortion is not excessive and to set against it there is a major achievement. For many years the study of Canadian political life has suffered for want of an authoritative account of the development of the country's central administrative machinery. Their terms of reference did not permit Hodgetts, McCloskey, Whitaker, and Wilson to quite fill the gap, but their treatment of one of Ottawa's most influential institutions has made the rest of the task a lot easier. They have contributed immensely to our understanding of Canadian public administration, particularly the development and application of personnel policy, the processes of policy formation, and the relationships between the CSC and the Treasury Board during an important period in Canadian history.

The organization of the book requires comment. It is a hard task to reduce to manageable proportions the long and involved story of a prominent agency. Harder still to indulge in analysis of specific policies and issues without appearing to ramble. The problem is dealt with by devoting the major part of the book to an historical account and the latter and shorter part to an analysis of policies (management development, special problems associated with maintaining the merit principle), and organization (internal administration and commission leadership). Undoubtedly other subjects might have been included – political scientists will regret the failure to follow up the analytical promise of the first chapter – but the topics chosen will probably be considered generally to be most deserving of separate summary and review.

As one of the first two volumes in the Canadian Public Administration Series sponsored by the Institute of Public Administration of Canada under the editorship of J.E. Hodgetts, *The Biography of an Institution* sets a pace in scholarship and institutional cooperation that will be hard for successive volumes to match.

A. PAUL PROSS
Dalhousie University

Donald Swainson, ed., **Oliver Mowat's Ontario.** Toronto: Macmillan of Canada, 1972, pp. 235.

The essays in this collection are largely drawn from a colloquium held at Queen's University in 1970 to mark the 150th anniversary of Sir Oliver Mowat's birth.

They seek to cover a number of different aspects of Ontario history in the later nineteenth century, from treatment of the standard themes of conflict between federal and provincial authorities (both between governments and within the Liberal party) to discussion of several important questions related to the province's social and economic development during a critical period of its growth.

Each essay in its way is extraordinarily well done, and it seems invidious to single out any of them for comment. But surely the most intriguing question for the political scientist interested in the nature of Ontario politics is to find some trace of evidence from the past which brings a light of greater understanding to examination of the modern political system in the province.

In this respect two of the essays in this volume stand out. Professor Armstrong's account of the way in which a set of rules for the conduct of federal-provincial relations established by Sir Oliver Mowat has been handed down almost intact to later Ontario premiers puts flesh on a political tradition that many have regarded as unique to Ontario without really knowing why. Professor Nelles' fascinating study of the attempts of the Ontario government to deal with the problems of resource development at the turn of the century adds to our understanding of this tradition.

Perhaps the most outstanding elements of recent Ontario political history have been the tremendous importance of the office of prime minister – or indeed of any party leader – and the extraordinary political success of governments that have professed what Margaret Evans describes as that "particular blend of conservatism and reform, of caution and advancement" that is the hallmark of Ontario politics. There can hardly be any doubt that this aspect of the Ontario political tradition acquired its significance during Sir Oliver Mowat's premiership, and Professor Armstrong's essay is a delightful illustration of the continuity of that tradition. In his turn Professor Nelles not only describes in detail a particular application of what may be called "the Mowat principles" but puts them in the context of the special circumstances of the development of the Ontario economy.

Other essays in the volume add to this interpretation, particularly Michael Bliss's attempt to find in the Ontario experience an understanding of the problems associated with the development of capitalist economies in general.

It is a rich and varied collection that will add considerably to the growing stock of materials dealing with Ontario politics, and as such makes a valuable contribution to a better understanding of the nature of the Canadian political experience as a whole.

JOHN WILSON
University of Waterloo

L.P.V. Johnson and Ola MacNutt, **Aberhart of Alberta.** Edmonton: Institute of Applied Arts Ltd., 1970, pp. 252.

Alf Hooke, **Thirty Plus Five: I Know, I Was There.** Edmonton: Institute of Applied Arts Ltd., 1971, pp. 265.

Whether the 1971 election upset will prove to be the end of Social Creditism in Alberta remains to be seen. However, to new Albertans – the younger generation and late arrivals – names such as Bible Bill, Major Douglas, and jargon such as "social dividends" and "A + B theorem" sound historical. *Aberhart of Alberta,* written by Dr Johnson, a professor of genetics and a devoted follower of Aberhart, and Mrs MacNutt, a daughter of Aberhart, should be of interest to those who have never known the founder of the Alberta Social Credit movement through their personal life experience. This biographical sketch of Aberhart is more useful to the general public than to political scientists whose interest would be an in-depth analysis of the man's political theory or a detailed account of the Socred movement.

It is Alf Hooke's book which provides many of the hitherto little-known inside stories of the Social Credit government which ruled the province for an uninterrupted 36 years. Though Hooke's book is intended as an autobiography, it turns out to be an exposé of Social Credit administration, particularly that of E.C. Manning. Little wonder the manuscript was turned down by some publishers, as it contains many controversial statements that affect many Alberta politicians who are still living and well today. Hooke, a school teacher at the time, was one of the "one hundred honest men" presented to Aberhart as potential candidates for the Social Credit movement in 1935. Until the 1971 election, in which he did not run, Hooke held a seat in the Alberta Legislative Assembly for 35 years, 30 of which were spent close to the centre of power in various capacities.

Some important conclusions about the Alberta Social Credit can be drawn from the two books reviewed here. First, neither Aberhart nor Manning – for that matter, any politician in the Social Credit movement – is too different from politicians of other persuasions. To capture power, Aberhart did not mind distorting Major Douglas's theory, nor did Manning decline the opportunity to become a board director of banks and corporations – the arch-enemies of Social Crediters – as soon as he retired from provincial politics. In spite of the religious flavor added by Aberhart, Social Credit politics, after all, remained secular.

Secondly, the internal problems of the Social Credit party, like those of other ideological parties, centre around the issue of revisionism. For Alf Hooke and "thousands of others" who "believed [Manning] to be so saintly and so God-guided that anything he did or anything he recommended to be done had to be right" (p. 197), the history of Social Credit government is simply a revolution betrayed. Hooke's indictment, however, is not the first ever brought against the Socred leaders. When Aberhart failed to deliver his Social Credit promises, the backbenchers revolted and the centre of power shifted from the cabinet to the newly-created Social Credit Board of which Hooke was a member (1938–40) and chairman (1940–3).

Thirdly, the generation gap and transition of power seem to be the hardest problems for an ideological party like the Alberta Social Credit to overcome. The 1960s were years in which the Alberta Social Credit attempted, in vain, to adapt itself to a modern environment. When the Socred bid for national power failed, Manning dreamed of using the then-divided Progressive Conservative party as his vehicle to Ottawa. Inside Alberta, Manning's government struggled to create a new image by passing more welfare legislation, allowing more representation from the urban centres and including more young people in the power élite of the Social Credit. Indeed, these were all necessary preparations for Manning to leave the Alberta scene, for, it was hoped, Ottawa. But the call never came from the Progressive Conservatives. The young "brain trust" consisted of some graduate students of political science at the University of Alberta and a few sociologists in Edmonton and Calgary who prescribed the medicine for the party's rejuvenation. Indeed, those young practitioners had neither the confidence of the old-timers in the party nor much credit with the public at large. The leadership passed on to Harry Strom, a compromise candidate between the old and the young.

The conclusions derived from the books reviewed have some serious implications for students of Alberta politics. Will Alberta now move from Macpherson's "quasi-party system" (C.B. Macpherson, *Democracy in Alberta*) into a more conventional party politics? The conclusions presented above seem to suggest that a "quasi-party system" cannot survive the pressure of modern society. But who can say whether the recent victory of the Progressive Conservatives in the province is not merely a substitution of one protest movement for another? The answer remains in the ballot boxes of the near future.

F.Q. Quo
University of Lethbridge

Stephen Clarkson, **City Lib: Parties and Reform.** Toronto: A.M. Hakkert, Ltd., 1972, pp. xi, 227.

This short book is not pretentious in any sense. Basically it is a personal record of Clarkson's 1969 campaign, as a municipal Liberal, for the Toronto mayoralty. As simply such, whatever its other shortcomings, it forms a helpful addition to the burgeoning writing about our urban centres.

Probably the pointed absence of academic sophistication is responsible for the major shortcomings. It is not an insignificant quibble to observe that the book is very wrongly titled for, as a minimum, any liberation "movement" (the municipal Liberal party?) requires a clearly defined oppressor as target. Mayor Dennison is an unlikely candidate for this role: we find substituted a poorly defined conspiracy of shades – ubiquitous developers, realtors, and technocrats – familiar antagonists to readers of other recent writing of this genre. These simple conclusions are not as yet justified by substantive research on the interest aspects of Canadian urban policy-making.

Similarly the matter of the nature of the urban crisis is never directly confronted. It is true that glimpses of the problems in transportation, pollution, and drug abuse appear, as do comments on the fractionalized nature of local authority. But all this is developed outside any over-all appreciation of the inexorable urbanizing pressures of the postwar period upon Canadians and their governments. Without providing clearer reference points against which to measure the total dislocations caused by such rapid population shifts, Clarkson takes too much for granted in advancing the (assumed) altruistic local involvement of party organizations as the sole proper response. A review is not the proper context in which to resolve the apparent contradictions of "ministerial" and "neighbourhood" government, both municipal Liberal planks and assumed by the author to be desirable and compatible.

Professor Clarkson, leaving much unquestioned, treats such fundamental issues underlying his campaign as given, as though by tacit agreement between his audience and himself. It is as if the book were undertaken as a post-mortem for discussion by his Sunday morning candidate caucus.

Apart from his personal notes on organizational problems of finance, campaign coordination, recruitment of personnel, and so forth, Clarkson's discussion of the local electoral system ("The Art of the Impossible") and media relations ("The Mangled Message") are the most commendable aspects of the volume. For a person unfamiliar with either the limitations of the local franchise or the symbiotic association of the press with local governors there is illuminating reading here. His gentle wit and careful organization of material add another plus to the over-all value of the book.

Clarkson is neither Frank Skeffington nor Norman Mailer. The impression left by the book is of a sincere man suddenly overwhelmed by a system whose every act violates his rules of liberal rationality. But, at the same moment, it covers a need in the reporting of Canadian local government and ought to be noted by serious students of these processes.

JAMES LIGHTBODY
University of Alberta

Trevor Price, ed., **Regional Government in Ontario.** Don Mills: Science Research Associates Ltd., 1971, pp. 145.

Regional Government in Ontario comes out of a seminar held at the University of Windsor in 1970 on the question of regional government with particular application to Windsor and Essex County. Upon learning this one is somewhat apprehensive as proceedings of meetings do not always make good books. But in this case the apprehension is unnecessary as the book has both coherence and order; Trevor Price deserves full marks for his editing. With the exception of the piece by the mayor of Detroit, which seems irrelevant to the book, the articles do fit together and do offer an over-all view of the movement towards regional government in Ontario.

The major theme of the book is the importance of regional government for the maintenance of local autonomy: "The regional centre ... would greatly enhance the role and influence of local government" (p. 32), and the more oratorical, "If we fail, I am convinced that local government as a real participant in making community decisions, will wither away to irrelevance within twenty years" (p. 58). What is significant is that this argument has completely replaced the earlier economy argument for regional government. Regional government is no longer being argued as a way to save money but as a way to save independence. The experience so far has at least taught the proponents of regional government not to make their arguments strictly in terms of economy.

The book also brings out some of the specific characteristics of the regional government experience in Ontario. One of these has been the slowness with which regional government has come about; in most of the existing cases a four- to five-year period. This characteristic has if anything increased since the seminar was held, and the 1975 or 1980 date suggested in the book (p. 14) for province-wide coverage now seems completely unrealistic. Another point well-illustrated in the book is that the Ontario government has been willing to be flexible and even innovative in choosing structures for the various regional governments. This can be seen from the differing requirements for direct and indirect election of the regional representatives.

Unfortunately, *Regional Government in Ontario* is not successful in evaluating the regional government experience. In part, but only in part, this is due to the newness of the experience. Little serious work seems to have been done on the evaluation of this experience, a fact reflected in the weakness of the section, "The Operation of Regional Government to Date." But in providing a view of the reasons for, and methods of, regional government in Ontario, the book is both successful and a useful addition to the literature.

CAROLINE ANDREW
University of Ottawa

J.L. Granatstein and Peter Stevens, eds., **Forum: Canadian Life and Letters 1920–70: Selections from the Canadian Forum.** Toronto: University of Toronto Press, 1972, pp. xv, 431.

Since it is virtually impossible to review in 400 words a book of essays spanning a period of 50 years and written by something like 200 contributors (including the reviewer, a fact that raises the delicate issue of conflict of interest), this assessment will settle for a few comments about the role of *The Canadian Forum* in the intellectual life of the country during nearly half of Canada's existence.

The first point to be made is that it is a remarkable fact that *The Forum* (as it usually was called) survived for so long and is still extant. Very few of its peers have withstood that test. The half century of its existence was the age of the collapse of magazines. Yet *The Forum* defied the plague that swept away many of its contemporaries, although most of them were better heeled financially. Its impecuniosity no doubt had much to do with its longevity since the stark truth was that financially speaking there was nothing to sweep away. For years, during the period this writer was associated with the editorial board, *The Forum* teetered on the nether side of bankruptcy most of the time. It tottered on sustained by Kay and Lou Morris's modest book business, the unpaid efforts of the editorial board and the contributors, and occasional benefactions from a number of individuals including such unlikely persons as J.S. McLean, the wealthy meat-packing free enterpriser, whom *The Forum* often attacked and who attached to one of his cheques a note which said, "If your magazine was as good as my sausages, you wouldn't have any financial problems." So much for the laws of economics. Chalk one up for Horowitz's Red Tories.

The second point is that *The Canadian Forum* survived because the editorial staff and the contributors believed in what they were doing. There were periods of passion and moral righteousness in the history of the magazine but by the 1950s when I joined it the emotional gin had run out and we survived like Gunga Din on water, or at least on the pure spring of reason. The effort was not as noble as it sounds since this was before the affluent sixties and there was nowhere to sell our masterpieces.

Third, the last remark is not entirely facetious. *The Canadian Forum* provided an outlet for the expression of opinion and creativity by a host of talented Canadian intellectuals – pundits, poets, essayists, short story writers, and assorted professors – who otherwise would have remained mute because the opportunity to speak publicly was so limited. It was nice to know that *The Forum* was prestigious, but it was even better to know that it was there and would publish one's work.

The Canadian Forum became a national institution that kept the flame of poetry, creative writing, and political and social criticism alive and flickering during the lean and hungry years of our country's adolescence.

PAUL FOX
University of Toronto

Canada's 28th Parliament: A Guide to the Members, their Constituencies and their Government. Toronto: Methuen, 1971, pp. 336.

This is an unusual mishmash of a book. Beginning with three sections on "what Parliament is," "how Parliament works," and "the politics of Parliament," it passes on to full-page descriptions of each member of Parliament and eight appendices listing governors general, prime ministers and speakers, cabinet precedence, departmental functions, parliamentary secretaries, parliamentary committees and their chairmen, senators, and members' party affiliations.

There are some admirable features. It contains maps of the electoral districts. For each member there is information provided on the population of the constituency, the number of registered voters, the actual voters and the winning vote, the two last expressed both in absolute terms and as percentages. On some occasions, but not all, it adds further information on the predominant language of the constituency, ethnic groups, religious affiliations, and dominant industries.

Beyond this it is difficult to praise the compilation. Undoubtedly it suffers (as does the *Parliamentary Guide*) from too great dependence on the members themselves. The long descriptions of the constituencies may have a certain value to some users, but it seems unnecessary for the book to note that Burnaby-Richmond includes the Vancouver Island ferry terminal, that Seymour Mountain is the site of a park with recreational facilities, or that Coast Chilcotin has 200 inches of rain on the coast, less than 10 inches inland, and has mountain peaks up to 13,260 feet. Similarly, it may be wondered what value can be attached, for example, to a brief résumé of the 1968 disputed election in Comox-Alberni, to a statement of local concerns in Elgin ("the pollution of Lake Erie, shore erosion, a water pipeline to serve St Thomas, and education"), or to the fact that Essex has a daily railway freight service to Buffalo.

An attempt has been made to give a history of the political fortunes of the major parties in each riding. The last redistribution makes this largely a futile effort except in the most general terms. Finally, for unexplained reasons, the Senate is restricted to a mere listing in an appendix – no pictures, no biographies, no statement of aims in life or political interests in Parliament, simply political affiliation.

It is difficult to know what this book is intended to do or what market it is aimed at. The publisher notes in his foreword that it was conceived when he was asked to write a sketch on a newly appointed minister's background and constituency. He failed to find the material necessary and this book is his answer. It may indeed be the answer for a hard-pressed newspaperman hurrying to make a deadline. For a political scientist wanting a consistent and useful body of material on Parliament, it is not worth the $12.50 price.

W. F. Dawson
University of Western Ontario

Jean-Marc Piotte, **Sur Lénine.** Montréal : Editions Parti Pris, 1972, 300 pp.

Ce livre participe à plusieurs égards aux deux ouvrages antérieurs de l'auteur. En premier lieu, il s'inscrit dans la suite logique du mouvement de « déstalinisation » qui pour l'auteur s'est manifesté par la publication remarquée d'un Gramsci en 1970. Dans ce sens, il était « normal » que cette démarche soit poursuivie avec un Lénine. En second lieu, sans qu'elle soit clairement explicitée, il puise à la même perspective génétique qui lui a bien réussi dans son premier livre. Elle devrait donner des résultats heureux au niveau de l'analyse de l'ensemble de la pensée de Lénine, si on poursuivait dans le sens que l'auteur indique. Finalement, cet ouvrage n'est pas l'œuvre d'un pur « intellectuel », il a des racines québécoises comme en témoignait son « Québec occupé » (1971) écrit en collaboration. Plus précisément, la sélection des thèmes qui structurent son analyse renvoie à des jugements sur l'éthos de la société québécoise. Ainsi notre degré d'urbanisation l'amène à ne pas traiter d'une façon autonome la question paysanne et à consacrer par ailleurs un chapitre à la question nationale. Cette mise en situation est d'autant plus nécessaire que le débat théorique marxiste a rarement été divorcé d'idéologies politiques explicites ou sous-entendues et du contexte social dans lequel il se produit.

La thèse de l'auteur est que la pensée de Lénine est totalement étrangère au « marxisme-léninisme » tel que fondé exclusivement par Staline sur une interprétation des écrits d'une période qu'il est convenu d'appeler les « Grands classiques » et qui n'est en fait qu'un moment d'une pensée qui a subie des variations importantes en fonction de la conjoncture. C'est donc toute l'œuvre que l'auteur propose d'étudier chronologiquement et non les seuls « Grands classiques » si l'on veut saisir sa pensée politique et faire éclater l'interprétation stalinienne. On voit combien l'approche génétique peut ici rencontrer ses objectifs.

Inscrire un autre ouvrage à une bibliographie déjà imposante consacrée à Lénine constituait en soi tout un défi que l'auteur de Gramsci était peut-être en mesure de relever. Paradoxalement la gageure n'a pas été tenue. Paradoxalement, disons-nous, parce que cela tient en grande partie à la facture du livre que l'auteur ne réussit pas à maintenir dans les limites de sa problématique fondamentale : montrer que la pensée de Lénine est vivante et diffère de la « théorie achevée et complète, valable pour tout pays et dans toute conjoncture » (p. 9). D'autant plus paradoxal que J.-M. Piotte dans l'introduction de son Gramsci, justifiant explicitement la perspective adoptée, élabore à cette occasion des normes qu'il n'a pas suivies dans ce cas-ci. Dans ce sens, comme nous allons le voir, son Lénine se situe en quelque sorte à l'opposé de son Gramsci.

L'ensemble du livre est structuré autour de quatre thèmes qui forment autant de chapitres : la tactique, le parti, l'état et la question nationale. Dans une conclusion générale, il établit très rapidement une comparaison entre l'interprétation stalinienne et la pensée de Lénine telle qu'elle se dégage de l'ouvrage. En somme, il s'agit d'une organisation générale parfaitement conforme aux objectifs de l'ouvrage. La critique a prise au plan de la structuration du traitement de chaque thème. Ceux-ci sont en fait abordés par le biais d'un double régistre que l'auteur a appelé « l'analyse interne de l'œuvre » et « l'analyse externe » (Gramsci, p. 14). Dans le premier cas, il s'agit du matériau fondamental de sa problématique : un ensemble de passages significatifs et de résumés qui collent à la pensée de Lénine et qui sont mis en rapport avec la conjoncture sur laquelle réfléchit Lénine. Cette dialectique pensée-conjoncture donne lieu à un découpage en périodes qui couvrent les fluctuations de sa pensée politique. Cette démonstration est toujours suivie dans chaque chapitre d'une conclusion où il résume ordinairement très schématiquement l'évolution de la pensée. Cependant ces conclusions deviennent en fait une « analyse externe » où intervient la critique à Lénine et la comparaison entre son œuvre et celle d'autres marxistes : Gramsci, Kautsky. On se serait attendu à une conclusion critique en fonction de la « déstalinisation » et cela d'autant plus que l'auteur permet au lecteur d'inventer son propre ordre de lecture.

Comme au niveau du premier registre, l'auteur fait une très large part à la conjoncture concrète dans l'exposition de la pensée de Lénine et que son découpage en périodes donne lieu à une localisation très précise dans le temps, cela lui permet de démontrer la qualité des textes utilisés, à savoir qu'ils constituent des réponses politiques concrètes à des situations concrètes. Ce qui nous apparaît être un apport particulièrement positif à la compréhension de Lénine. Mais comme l'auteur intervient de l'extérieur dans le débat léniniste, cela contribue à masquer justement la pensée spécifique de Lénine et à faire éclater son cadre d'analyse. On passe à un objet second. De sorte qu'on ne sait plus si l'auteur est préoccupé d'exposer la signification interne d'une œuvre ou s'il cherche à contribuer à l'analyse théorique des pratiques politiques. Bref, c'est dans le rapport de l'analyse interne à l'analyse externe que se perd le pari d'un auteur dont on attendait davantage à la suite de sa thèse sur Gramsci. Mais peut-être est-ce justement ce que l'auteur a voulu faire, son livre n'est-il pas intitulé « Sur Lénine » ? Si c'est le cas, cette perspective n'est nullement explicitée.

A cette critique sur la facture du livre, on peut en ajouter une autre qui concerne plus spécifiquement le premier thème abordé : la tactique. Vouloir traiter de ce thème au même niveau que les autres amène un certain flottement dans ce chapitre. Il est peut-être significatif que l'auteur parle de « cinq étapes dans la formulation de la tactique » et non d'une stratégie et de tactiques ou plus simplement de cinq périodes caractérisées par des variations de tactiques en fonction de la conjoncture. Glissement de termes ou intention théorique qui consisterait à situer la place de la tactique dans une structure de concepts, cela n'apparaît pas clairement. Cette ambiguïté se manifeste d'ailleurs dans la conclusion de ce chapitre qui est très sommaire et qui est la seule à ne pas faire l'objet d'une critique externe. C'est aussi le seul thème qui ne soit repris par rapport à la position de Staline. Il y a bien sûr des raisons objectives au difficultés de cette partie de l'ouvrage. « La tactique » ne se situe pas au même niveau que les autres thèmes et la distinction entre le théoricien, le stratège et le tacticien n'est pas facile à établir dans le mesure où théorie et pratique sont liées et dans la mesure où les textes sont aussi des réponses idéologiques. S'il y a un concept de tactique, il devra être construit.

Finalement nonobstant quelques remarques mineures qui ont déjà été traitées lors de la publication de « Gramsci », on peut adresser un dernier reproche à l'auteur, celui de n'avoir pas mieux structuré l'interprétation stalinienne qui ne repose pas uniquement sur les écrits d'une période mais qui se fonde, comme le signale l'auteur, sur des « déformations » de textes antérieurs à la période de la « guerre civile exacerbée ». Cela aurait permis de dégager davantage la spécificité de Lénine au niveau de sa pensée politique.

Voilà un ouvrage dont le matériau de base est excellent et l'exposé interne de l'œuvre bien fait, mais que l'objectif de « déstalinisation » tronque faute d'avoir été mieux défini.

André Kuzminski
Université Laval

Z.A. Pelczynski, ed., **Hegel's Political Philosophy: Problems and Perspectives.** Cambridge: Cambridge University Press [Toronto: Macmillan], 1971, pp. viii, 246.

The editor of this collection is to be congratulated on his success in soliciting essays specially written for the volume by scholars from Britain, France, Germany, Canada, and the United States. Readers will also appreciate his cross references on overlapping or contrasting approaches. "Political philosophy" is conceived in a broad sense; the contributions extend over law (K.-H. Ilting, David Cooper, and Manfred Riedel), history (John Plamenatz and W.H. Walsh), ethics and social theory (Judith N. Shklar, J.-F. Suter, and Eugène Fleischmann), as well as war and the state (D.P. Verene, Z.A. Pelczynski, G. Heiman, and R.N. Berki). Since, however, Hegel's political philosophy forms (at least after 1800) an integral part of a philosophical *system*, any of the areas covered is bound to shed some light on its problems, in so far as philosophical analysis is being applied to them. It is not surprising, therefore, that the essays converge more or less directly on Hegel's principal conceptual categories. Indeed, roughly half the essays focus on the interpretation and analysis of these categories, while the other half probe into their classical, medieval, and modern sources and subsequent influence on later thinkers such as Marx and Stirner. In this connection it may be noted that, while such modern predecessors as Rousseau, Montesquieu, Kant, and Fichte rightly command attention, Herder, whose ideas were seminal in significant areas of Hegel's philosophy (although Hegel, it is true, seldom acknowledged his indebtedness), is mentioned but once throughout the book.

Hegel emerges in these pages as a much more pragmatic thinker than he is commonly held to be. Although his dislike of empiricism is acknowledged, it is also recognized that he preferred empirical thinking to purely formal thinking. Thus the state is to be explained, not by its real or fictitious origin in terms of a solemn agreement or compact, but rather in terms of the process of its actual functioning. It is the degree of its operative actuality that interests Hegel, and he discerns this in light of a state's inherent rationality. This disclosing quality, in turn, is defined by the manner in which laws, mores, traditions, and institutions are consciously, and hence for Hegel, *creatively* experienced as shared forms of life by the members of a polity. The core problem posed, therefore, in the sharing of such a community consciousness or ethos is the interrelationship of the subjective (individual or sectional) realm and the objective (political or universal) realm. Concerning this interrelationship, some contributors stress the significance given to the individual "particularist" realm in Hegel's thought, while others stress the primacy of the political, "universalist" realm. In contrast to these opposed emphases, a third line of approach attaches considerable, if not decisive, importance to the mediating role of social associations. In this view, the attainment of a shared community consciousness is the result of a process of accommodation and bargaining between diverse groups and organizations; and Hegel's dialectic is simply equated with compromise, that is, with a method of negotiated conflict resolution. Judging by this interpretation, Hegel might almost be regarded as a precursor of modern American pluralism with its "group politics" and "civic culture" underpinnings. Perhaps this is a perfectly valid presentation and not merely the reflection of an excessive zeal to prove Hegel's contemporary pertinence. At any rate, emphasis on Hegel's pluralistic tendencies serves as a salutary corrective to the widespread belief that Hegel's monistic tendencies were such as to promote totalitarian ideologies.

No one would deny that Hegel's mode of expression, opaque and tortuous as it frequently is, provides ample scope for diverse and, indeed, conflicting interpretations of a kind just noted. But why question or obscure his intended meaning when this is transparently clear? Hegel emphatically considered participation in sectional "constituencies," such as corporations, to be qualitatively so different from participation in universal constituencies, such as the state, that training in the former could not be readily transferred to the latter. Hence it is one thing to make certain educative claims for participation in subpolitical or nonpolitical groupings, but quite another to imply that what is involved in political participation is merely a matter of replication. Hegel explicitly recognized this crucial difference. He can, therefore, scarcely be credited with presaging contemporary theorists of participation who wish to play down or altogether ignore a distinction on which he so clearly insisted.

Since Hegel did identify the modern state with a highly differentiated social configuration, his notion of a "universal will," or will of the state, raises the problem of what kind of diversity is to be reconciled with what kind of unity. Clearly, "diversity" can refer to structural differences and conflicts of interest that are amenable to compromise, and thus capable of demonstrating the latency of a consensual "will" that might approximate the meaning of Hegel's universal will. But "diversity" can also refer to principles and standards that defy compromise and hence cannot be bridged by negotiation and bargaining, as Marx was the first to point out in his devastating critique of Hegel's political philosophy. Putting it differently, diversity can exist not only *amidst* unity, but also *over* unity, and the latter frequently forms the substance of intense political and ideological confrontation. Conceivably, Hegel's will of the state is consistent with both types of diversity, but to bear this out a convincing case has yet to be made.

Students of social and political philosophy, interested in the continuing debate over Hegel's complex thought, should find this a thought-provoking book.

FREDERICK M. BARNARD
University of Western Ontario

J.A. Corry, **The Power of the Law.** (Massey Lectures), Toronto: CBC, 1971, pp. 63.

This small volume is the printed version of Dr J.A. Corry's CBC Massey Lectures delivered in the fall of 1971. Professor Corry has had a long and distinguished career as a professor of law and political science and as principal of Queen's University. He is known widely throughout Canada and abroad as a scholar of the highest repute. His first book, *Democratic Government and Politics* (1946) was the major textbook in political science for Canadian students for almost two decades. He is the author of a number of books on law and government. This collection of lectures is his latest work and can be said to be a compendium of his thought in so far as it relates to government and the use of law.

The Power of the Law consists of six chapters entitled: "Law as Reason and Custom," "Due Process of Law," "Law as Command," "Obedience and Disobedience," "Civil Rights," and "The Constitution." The underlying concern that permeates these lectures is reflected in the first sentence. Corry writes: "In a revolutionary age, respect for law always declines." Professor Corry is clearly concerned about, even preoccupied with, the modern demands being made on the law in the interest of major social change. In many respects it could be said to be a treatise on "law and order." In the lecture on "obedience and disobedience," Professor

Corry acknowledges that a minimal "disrespect of the law is healthy." But he eschews any efforts to seek major changes in the fundamental democratic creed sustaining the process. There is never the slightest inclination to suggest that the law (including lawyers and the judiciary) can be subverted to narrow partisan ends; never a disposition to concede that revolutionary changes may be justified. All changes must be accomplished "within the rules of the game" (p. 23).

What renders this matter disturbing is the content of the key lecture, "due process of law." This lecture confirms the impression of the earlier lectures which all say something about the means open to dissidents as well as the limits of dissent. Not only are dissidents counselled to seek redress within the rules of the game; they are channelled within the traditional legal procedures, such as the right to counsel, the right to cross-examination and the right to a reasoned judicial judgment (p. 35). This is the rational means of seeking social and political change, says Corry. All other means are irrational. Corry warns of loose-talking revolutionaries who claim that "the evils of our society are so appalling that they must be dealt with in the streets rather than in legislatures, courts and other duly constituted bodies operating under due process of law" (p. 38). He further asserts that "Good causes cannot afford strong-arm methods" (p. 39). The exception appears to be when the constituted authority deems it necessary in the interest of maintaining the present regime to resort to instruments such as the War Measures Act even though this entails the abrogation of the main provisions of due process of law.

In the lecture on civil rights Corry makes it clear that individuals or combinations of individuals may conspire to change the law. But, he hastens to add, "The only limitation – a significant one but not oppressive for most persons – is that they must not organize to pursue directly activities that are forbidden by law" (p. 44). And since Corry does not acknowledge the possibility of a *substantive* due process by which procedural due process can be challenged, even in the courts, he leads squarely to the judicial equivalent of catch 22. Is it any wonder that he supports the application of the War Measures Act?

It is my judgment that this little book could more appropriately be entitled: "The Power of the Law to Maintain the Status Quo." The major deficiency is the persistent indisposition to acknowledge the need for a *substantive* due process at a time when there is a growing dissatisfaction or loss of faith in the democratic process, especially the judicial aspect.

Despite the above reservations, I think these lectures provide a first-rate synopsis of a widely held view of the role of law as an instrument of social control. It should prove to be a valuable little volume if for no other reason than that it provides a concise statement of the predominant view of the community – a statement against which professors of law and political science can react. Would it be too much to expect or hope that the CBC would invite someone to react publicly to these lectures? In all probability it would.

FREDERICK VAUGHAN
University of Guelph

Charles Debbasch, **Science administrative : administration publique.** Paris : Edition Dalloz, 1971, 682 pp.

La rédaction d'un manuel dans un champ d'étude qui souffre d'un grave problème de crise d'identité, n'est pas une vile besogne. Le problème pratique de délimiter les frontières du sujet s'avère énorme. La plupart des classiques contemporains s'en tiennent encore à l'approche du processus administratif, avec certaines modifications pour adapter la théorie de la décision de Simon et/ou aux approches écologiques, behavioristes et de politique publique. L'ouvrage de Debbasch n'est pas une exception à cette règle générale.

Divisé en sept parties, chacune comprenant plusieurs chapitres, le livre offre un énorme étalage de concepts et de données factuelles. La première partie est consacrée à l'information générale. On assiste à la discussion de questions traditionnelles comme science versus art, public versus privé, politique versus administration, sans aucun apport original. L'auteur commence avec une définition de l'administration publique qui semble inspirée de la dichotomie politique-administration. Selon lui, « l'administration publique est l'appareil de gestion des affaires publiques » (p. 1) et « elle constitue l'instrument de réalisation des choix politiques ». Plus loin, il modifie sa position pour affirmer « ... toutes les actions administratives sont la concrétisation des choix politiques effectués par le pouvoir politique ». La « décision administrative » comme telle, n'existe pas. Il établit une relation à sens unique et il ignore totalement l'influence de l'administration publique sur la politique publique.

Les chapitres 3 à 6 offrent une intéressante discussion sous l'aspect de la théorie. Ici, c'est la décision administrative qui est l'unité de l'analyse. Une organisation doit répartir les pouvoirs de décision en se souciant de l'efficacité. La spécialisation et l'unité de commandement sont les deux principaux déterminants de la répartition de ce pouvoir. On peut classifier les décisions administratives selon la position hiérarchique d'où elles proviennent, leur degré de généralisation ou de pouvoirs discrétionnaires de leurs auteurs. La communication s'avère essentielle à la prise de décision mais cette relation n'est pas présentée en détail. On retrouve deux étapes de décision : l'élaboration et l'exécution. La première concerne surtout la collecte de l'information et le développement de l'aspect rationnel. La deuxième constitue le « domaine » véritable de l'administration publique. Mais on cherche en vain des détails sur cette étape. Le chapitre intitulé « exécution de la décision » ne contient qu'un seul paragraphe.

La troisième partie, de loin la plus longue dans l'ouvrage, est consacrée à la description de l'organisation administrative aux niveaux central, régional, et local. Les organismes autonomes et la réforme administrative se voient consacrer chacun un chapitre. Les données présentées concernent principalement l'appareil administratif français. Mais parfois l'auteur présente des données descriptives sur l'URSS, le Royaume-Uni, les Etats-Unis et quelques autres pays. La comparaison reste à un niveau superficiel. L'auteur tente de présenter une image des structures administratives de plusieurs pays au détriment de la profondeur de l'analyse. La quatrième partie, qui traite de l'administration du personnel, est présentée exactement de la même manière.

Les trois dernières parties traitent de problèmes de productivité et d'O et M, de contrôle et de relations entre l'administration et les administrés. La discussion est très étendue au sujet du contrôle politique, juridictionnel, et administratif en France. On retrouve une section sur l'institution de l'Ombudsman dans divers pays d'Europe.

Le livre ne donne pas assez d'importance à la théorie et au comportement administratifs. L'administration financière est un autre secteur qui a été ignoré. Enfin, il n'est fait aucune mention de la nouvelle optique sur l'analyse de la « public policy ». L'approche de l'auteur est fondamentalement descriptive, juridique, et institutionnelle. Parfois, même la description ne se rend pas au-delà d'un niveau très superficiel. On peut difficilement l'utiliser comme manuel de base, sans l'aide de lectures supplémentaires spécialisées.

NASIR ISLAM
Université Laval

Jean-Marie Cotteret et Claude Emeri, **Les systèmes électoraux.** Paris : Presses universitaires de France, 1970, 128 pp.

Depuis que l'élection est devenue la procédure la plus usuelle pour permettre aux gouvernés d'intervenir dans le choix de leurs gouvernants, les systèmes électoraux ont retenu l'attention des politistes, des mathématiciens, des réformateurs, et surtout des hommes politiques. Tout citoyen un peu politisé a son opinion sur le meilleur système électoral. Cependant aucun ouvrage en français ne présentait de façon un peu générale l'ensemble des mécanismes institutionnels permettant aux gouvernés d'exprimer leurs préférences et à ces préférences d'être traduites en postes de commandement. Le petit livre que consacrent Cotteret et Emeri à ces questions veut combler cette lacune, mais il n'y parvient que partiellement.

Dans un premier chapitre, les auteurs brossent à grands traits le tableau de ce qu'ils appellent l'opération électorale. Après avoir décrit succintement l'extension du droit de suffrage en France et en Grande-Bretagne et avoir énuméré les restrictions contemporaines à ce droit, ils passent à une description des différents types de votation. Ils distinguent les élections nationales, les élections locales, et les procédures référendaires. Un des problèmes majeurs des élections nationales dans le cadre des circonscriptions territoriales (et aussi des élections locales, mais les auteurs ne le mentionnent pas) est de déterminer des circonscriptions dont le poids démographique soit identique. Les hommes politiques craignent toujours de modifier les cadres géographiques de la compétition et quand ils s'y aventurent, ils essaient d'en affaiblir au maximum l'impact sur leur carrière politique. La solution idéale, comme le souligne l'ouvrage, consiste à recourir à un organisme extérieur indépendant des législateurs. Par contre Cotteret et Emeri oublient d'insister sur la relation très étroite qui existe entre la carte électorale et le mode de scrutin. Le type de carte qu'on découpera dépend en bonne mesure du mode de scrutin qui sera adopté.

Cette omission est d'autant plus surprenante qu'à partir du deuxième chapitre les modes de scrutin occupent une place prépondérante. Il s'agit d'ailleurs de la meilleure section du livre et de celle qui rendra le plus de services aux étudiants et à tous ceux que la question intéresse. En quelques pages claires et précises les auteurs expliquent le fonctionnement du scrutin majoritaire à un et à deux tours, de la représentation proportionnelle et de ses nombreuses variantes (méthodes du plus fort reste, de la plus forte moyenne, d'Hondt, de Sainte-Lagüe, Hagenbach-

Bischof), et des systèmes mixtes qui tentent de combiner les avantages des deux précédents tout en évitant leurs inconvénients (système des apparentements utilisé en France en 1951 et 1956, système de Hare en usage en Irlande, système japonais, et système de l'Allemagne fédérale).

Les développements sur les modes de scrutin laissent cependant dans l'ombre une variable dont l'importance a été soulignée par les travaux de Douglas W. Rae. Cet auteur montre que plus le nombre de sièges à pourvoir dans une circonscription est élevé, moins l'écart entre le pourcentage des voix et la proportion des sièges obtenus par un parti est prononcé. Après de tels oublis, on est en droit de se demander si les auteurs connaissent les travaux de Rae sur les conséquences politiques des lois électorales.

On découvre la même lacune quand on passe, dans le dernier chapitre, à l'étude des rapports entre les systèmes électoraux et le système politique. Là encore on réduit les systèmes électoraux aux modes de scrutin et on exclut de l'analyse des variables comme le nombre de sièges à pourvoir dans les circonscriptions et la nature du bulletin de vote. L'essentiel du chapitre cherche à mettre en évidence l'impact que peuvent exercer les différents modes de scrutin sur la représentation des partis politiques, leurs structures, et leur nombre. Cette synthèse des idées communément acceptées en science politique nous laisse avec l'impression que, depuis les années 1950, notre connaissance des interactions entre ces deux variables n'a pas progressé de façon significative.

Dans le cours de leur analyse de l'influence du scrutin majoritaire à un tour sur le nombre de partis, Cotteret et Emeri affirment que « si, au Canada, le scrutin à un tour n'empêche pas la présence de quatre partis au plan fédéral, le bipartisme est la règle dans chacune des provinces » (p. 97). Le système partisan de la plupart des provinces est loin de correspondre à cette description. Qu'on se place au niveau du système politique fédéral ou à celui de chaque système provincial, plusieurs provinces, dont les trois plus importantes (Québec, Ontario, Colombie-Britannique), ont succombé à la vague du multipartisme. Seules les provinces maritimes ont su résister aux assauts des tiers-partis et conserver le bipartisme.

L'analyse que développent Cotteret et Emeri tout au long de leur étude révèle les mêmes faiblesses méthodologiques que la plupart des ouvrages consacrés au même sujet. Des propositions d'ordre général ne sont à peu près jamais confrontées avec l'ensemble des données électorales disponibles. Les catégories d'analyse sont souvent définies de façon imprécise, ce qui accentue encore les difficultés de comparaison. Trop souvent on n'a recours qu'à un ou deux exemples pour démontrer une hypothèse et on n'attache pas trop d'importance aux exceptions qui pourraient l'infirmer.

Malgré ces faiblesses méthodologiques, l'ouvrage de Cotteret et Emeri vient combler une lacune. Les étudiants et les professeurs seront heureux de disposer d'une étude en français présentant, de façon claire et accessible à tous, les mécanismes des principaux modes de scrutin en usage dans les démocraties occidentales.

FRANÇOIS RENAUD
Université Laval

Jean-Marie Cotteret et Claude Emeri, **Le budget de l'Etat.** Paris : Presses Universitaires de France, 1972, 128 pp.

Ce livre répond sûrement à un besoin puisque nous n'avions aucune synthèse française sur le processus budgétaire. L'auteur ne s'est pas limité aux aspects les plus populaires, telle la rationalisation des choix budgétaires, mais a abordé les différentes étapes du processus budgétaire (préparation, structure, vote, exécution, et contrôle) en intégrant les considérations théoriques et pratiques. Dès les premières pages, nous bénéficions d'une discussion bien étoffée des évolutions parallèles du budget et de l'Etat, discussion enrichie par des références nombreuses françaises et autres.

A travers des divisions traditionnelles mais normales pour un petit livre de vulgarisation, l'auteur se préoccupe constamment de questions fondamentales : le budget comme instrument de politique économique, le budget et le Plan, etc. Contrairement à tant d'ouvrages récents qui se répètent longuement au sujet de la RCB, l'auteur nous présente une synthèse originale qui réussit à démystifier les nouvelles procédures budgétaires.

Après avoir discuté des problèmes de préparation du budget, l'auteur s'attache à sa physionomie en discutant des différents procédés de classement. Les explications sur le budget des moyens et sur le budget fonctionnel reposent sur des extraits de documents budgétaires des années 1970–1, ce qui facilite la compréhension. Le lecteur sera cependant très déçu de la partie sur le budget des recettes qui est très courte pour ne pas dire inexistante. Cette lacune est d'autant moins acceptable qu'il n'aurait fallu que quelques pages pour satisfaire à un tel ouvrage de synthèse.

La troisième partie du livre porte sur le

vote du budget. Nous y découvrons un auteur très critique : « Le vote du budget est une sorte de spectacle que la classe politique se donne à elle-même, destiné à faire croire – et à croire, pourquoi pas ? – qu'elle est restée maîtresse des destinées de la nation » (p. 51). Nous croyons que de telles affirmations sont trop fréquentes dans la littérature française, les vieux débats sur la montée de la technocratie et le déclin du Parlement ne reposent pas suffisamment sur des études empiriques. Il faudrait un Wildavsky français pour étudier empiriquement les attitudes et comportements des parlementaires. Parler des illusions des parlementaires est vraiment trop facile, il faudrait que de telles affirmations reposent sur des études empiriques.

La discussion des limites qui frappent les parlementaires pour les propositions de dépenses publiques est bien menée et repose sur une vue comparative France – Grande-Bretagne (pp. 56–7). Cette troisième partie se termine par une discussion de quatre principes budgétaires, discussion nuancée par la présentation des pratiques concrètes en vigueur sous la Vième République, pratiques qui viennent souvent réduire à peu de choses les principes officiellement acceptés.

Dans une quatrième partie sur les procédures d'exécution, l'auteur semble rejoindre les idées de la Commission Glassco au Canada et celles des Commissions Plowden (1961) et Fulton (1968) en Grande-Bretagne : « Trop d'autonomie conduit à l'anarchie, trop de centralisation provoque la paralysie. Une des solutions possibles peut passer par une responsabilité totale des exécutants principaux, dégagée de règles strictes, mais soumise à des sanctions rigoureuses » (p. 97).

Enfin dans une dernière partie portant sur le contrôle du budget, l'auteur nous situe bien au centre du dilemne principal d'un processus budgétaire en mutation : « L'organisation administrative, la nomenclature budgétaire et les règlements de comptabilité publique reposent sur une économie de moyens. Les agents d'exécution du budget sont plus soucieux, au regard du contrôle, d'avoir géré sans contrevenir aux textes plutôt que de chercher à atteindre un objectif ou d'accomplir une mission » (p. 108).

RICHARD BERGER
Université Laval

Ali A. Mazrui, **Cultural Engineering and Nation-Building in East Africa.** Evanston, Ill.: Northwestern University Press, 1972, pp. xviii, 301.

Although the phrase nation-building requires no explanation, the notion of social and cultural engineering is not so obvious, particularly to anyone who may have retained memories of Professor Sir Karl Popper's excursions into this area. In Professor Mazrui's argument, cultural engineering emerges from the conceptual framework generated from different aspects of nation-building, but nation-building itself, from another viewpoint is no more than a metaphor that derives from the "simple fact" that independent African nations are newly invented, fragile, and need to be more secure and to become integrated (p. xiii). Moreover, "The strength of metaphor lies in its transphenomenal comparative utility" and "the validation of the concepts of nation-building and cultural engineering" also spring from that same utility. Cultural engineering turns out to be "a special approach to the problems of social engineering" (p. xv) and these problems arise from the impact of cultural factors "on issues of social reform and national development" (ibid). Thus, cultural engineering may involve changing peoples' habits in constructive directions (presumably made clear by the ends the political regime is pursuing) so that institutions may survive, or it may involve "attitudinal" change in the direction of "enlarged empathy."

Professor Mazrui's forte is not the development of social science theory but rather the manner in which he takes up the theories and views expressed by others to illuminate and explain the evolving destinies of African nations. His approach is essentially impressionistic and aesthetic, and he is remarkably fair in his judgments concerning the three main areas in which cultural engineering has a role to play: the printed word, political recruitment, and socio-economic change. It would be a pity if the reader were put off by the introduction to this book, for the main body of it consists of a series of very valuable insights into a whole range of cultural, military, literary, political, and economic problems currently confronting East Africa.

Take for instance the contrasting notions of structural and systemic transformation. In Kenya, there is evidence of a heightened experimentation and innovativeness "which is releasing structural change without the aid of revolutionary planning"; thus a revolution is taking place without revolutionaries at the helm (p. 205). By contrast, in Tanzania systemic change is accompanied by structural innovations such as the *ujamaa* villages. In Uganda, Obote was poised on the edge of a systemic upheaval just before his deposition by General Amin. These ideas are found in a chapter entitled "Political Culture and Concepts of Revolution," which affords a good example of the author's use of many concepts to build up a pointillist impression of revolution and political culture. Mazrui divides revolutions themselves into structural (Meiji Restoration in Japan) and systemic (Russian, Chinese) the latter entailing an overthrow of institutions and a transformation of values. In the East African context, an explanation is required to account for the relative amounts of systemic or structural change displayed by each territory and this Professor Mazrui finds in the intensity of the struggle for independence. The more that was suffered, the less revolutionary and leftist will the government be, and that argument places Nyerere the moderate carrying the torch of socialism in East Africa, while Kenyatta is moving toward a form of African capitalism. Next, an unexpected new theme is introduced: the values and customs of the Kikuyu are described to show how political conservatism rejects excessive rationalism and egalitarianism but encourages economic innovativeness. These ideas are then woven into another line of enquiry. Does being a heartland tribe produce a self-confidence that psychologically promotes economic assertiveness? On the other hand, does a Nilotic propensity to radicalism stem from a feeling of underprivilege in relation to other Bantu tribes? Will there be a clash between political radicals and economic innovators? With history in the making, Professor Mazrui wisely leaves such questions unanswered. This book is the best so far produced by Professor Mazrui and is essential reading for all students of African politics.

GEOFFREY F. ENGHOLM
Lakehead University

Wayne Wilcox, Leo E. Rose, and Gavin Boyd, eds., **Asia and the International System.** Cambridge, Mass.: Winthrop Publishers, 1972, pp. x, 383.

In recent years, North American specialists in international and comparative politics have sought to tie their two subfields together in a synthesis dubbed comparative foreign policy. A salutary effect of the new movement has been to sensitize the country specialist to the impact of the external environment on foreign policy decisions and to force the international relations specialist to concern himself with domestic determinants of international configurations. The volume under review is a capable effort in that direction, whose contributors include Asian experts competent in both domestic and foreign policy. The editors have imposed a loose organizational framework upon the authors, requiring that they deal with salient internal political characteristics, important features of foreign policy decision-making, and those international features deemed most important for each country's future policies in Asia for the 1970s. The book is divided into four sections: one on the major states of Asia; a second on the smaller states; a third on the superpowers, and the final dealing with Asia as a region.

Given the rapidity with which events have altered the features of much of Asian international politics since 1971, the book's substantive discussion holds up remarkably well. The American and Japanese détente with China is presaged as is the growing role of the USSR in Asian affairs through the Bangla Desh War and its aftermath. The discussion of the smaller states of the region is more tentative, however, perhaps because their capacity for independent action is more constrained than that of the major Asian countries and those outside powers involved in the region.

It is impossible to assess adequately all of the contributions in this brief review. Rather, I shall focus on those that seem most important for developing an understanding of Asia as a region. Gavin Boyd's chapter on China, although a competent account of Peking's recent international history, suffers from an inability to explain China's Asian détente policy inaugurated in 1971–2. Similarly, Hans Baerwald's useful discussion of Japan does not explore the implications of Sino-Japanese normalization on Tokyo's military policy or on its relations with Taiwan – both major concerns for Japan's Asian position. Leo Rose provides an insightful analysis of the geopolitics of India's foreign policy. And Wayne Wilcox lucidly explains Pakistan's balance of power foreign policy despite its formal alignment with the West.

Perhaps the best effort at explaining the internal determinants of foreign policy is Franklin Weinstein's assessment of the cyclical tension in Indonesian politics between the solidarity makers (such as Sukarno) and the developers (such as Suharto), which, in turn, correlates with a bellicose versus cooperative international demeanor. Robert Tilman's analysis of Malaysian politics helps to explain Kuala Lumpur's interest in Southeast Asian neutralization and Singapore's more cautious endorsement of the concept.

Wayne Wilcox's discussion of the American role in Asia has some good moments, particularly in explaining President Johnson's calculations and desire to convert the Vietnam conflict into a Korean-type confrontation. However, this reviewer was somewhat nonplussed when Professor Wilcox referred in the staunchest cold warrior fashion to "the Sino-Soviet bloc which had shown in eastern

Europe that it was bent upon world hegemony" (p. 255). One need not be an historical revisionist to balk at the accuracy of that description.

Messrs Thorton, Gelber, and Wriggens together present a provocative series of alternative viewpoints on Asia's future power configurations and particularly on how China, the USSR, and the United States might interact to enhance regional stability, each for its own particular ends.

Finally, if I may be permitted some pedantry, there are some annoying errata: that the *38th* parallel divides North and South Korea (p. 154); that the Ussuri River clash occurred in *1969* (p. 258); and that World War II occurred between 1935 and 1945 (p. 282).

SHELDON W. SIMON
University of Kentucky

Jean Edward Smith, **Germany Beyond the Wall: People, Politics ... and Prosperity.** Boston, Toronto: Little, Brown & Co., 1969, pp. xiv, 338.

Professor Smith has written this book with the kind of professional expertise that is difficult to surpass. He has combined impeccable scholarly research and encyclopaedic scope with the irreplaceable ingredient of living in the German Democratic Republic for an extended period of time. The 11 chapters of this book are filled with perceptions and insights of life in the GDR as it is actually lived, and the author spared himself no effort in providing detailed descriptions and analyses for macropolitical observations. Written five years before the historic recognition of the German Democratic Republic by the Federal Republic of Germany was effected in the GDR's capital city of Berlin, the material has lost none of its political significance. Indeed, the author presciently noted the emerging succession of Erich Honecker when Walter Ulbricht's demise was anything but certain. The full sovereignty of the GDR as a separate and independent state has, of course, since 21 December 1972 been recognized by nearly all of the world's governments, and the GDR awaits its impending admission into the United Nations. The GDR's long march into acceptance by the comity of nations, therefore, has finally been crowned with success even though the German Democratic Republic's existence as a sovereign state dates back to August 1949.

"Impressions of a country that does not exist," the first chapter, summarizes well the absurd status quo ante when the Hallstein Doctrine, a document now thrust into the trash bin of history, insured that diplomatic recognition of the German Democratic Republic by nations other than the Soviet Union would lead to Bonn's severance of relations with those nations. No longer may the German Democratic Republic be referred to with impunity as a so-called state or as the GDR in quotation marks, even though this practice appears to be continued by certain irredentist newspapers in West Germany who persist in playing the role of the ostrich.

The author has punctured a series of mythologies that have largely been accepted as truths even in sophisticated political science circles. "It is tempting to assert that the refugees from the GDR fled for ideological reasons. A more cynical – and doubtless more accurate – answer involves the increased opportunity in the West" (p. 87). Another fiction that the writer exploded pertains to church-state relationships in the GDR. Thus, so far from wanting to annihilate or cripple religion, the GDR government continues to give most generous financial subsidies to the Roman Catholic, Protestant, and Jewish religions; nor did it expropriate the lands of the church (510,000 acres) – they remain under full Church operations. But, regrettably, Smith's account of the Jewish religious community in the GDR lacks substance and is entirely too simplistic in its non-differentiation of Judaism and Zionism.

As he commendably indicated on another level, political parties other than the *Socialist Unity Party* do have important influence on government decision-making, contrary to generally held views of the monolithic Communist state. Thus, parties like the Christian Democrats, Liberal Democrats, National Democrats, and Farmers Union have been effective in promoting certain of their constituents' views and interests, even though this is accomplished by negotiation and persuasion within the Council of State. Thus, the GDR remains the only Communist state that permits deferment of conscientious objectors to military service. Also, against the wishes of leading Communist government officials, the Christian Democratic Union succeeded in retaining the most important Christian holy days as official State days of rest. While sovereign in terms of its status as an independent state, the German Democratic Republic remains nevertheless a "socialist state of German nation" as its 1968 constitution postulated. Professor Smith has done admirably in emphasizing the realities and concomitants of this status. His book represents an invaluable and fluently written contribution to an understanding of GDR existence.

KLAUS J. HERRMANN
Sir George Williams University

Fred I. Greenstein and Michael Lerner, eds., **A Source Book for the Study of Personality and Politics.** Chicago: Markham Publishing, 1971, pp. xvi, 572.

This collection of previously published articles provides a good supplement for teaching purposes to Greenstein's own *Personality and Politics.* This is in part because it complements the latter through sharing its frame of reference, and in part because the editors have succeeded in selecting "contributions that are *basic*, not in the sense of being definitive, but rather in the sense of raising fundamental issues."

The volume's coverage of contemporary materials is quite adequate, although one can question its emphasis on psychoanalytic approaches. A more serious problem is its exclusion of the classics and any materials that are not formally psychological. Surely the striking of a phrase such as "personality and politics" does not signal commencement of concern for the subject matter, yet this book opens with the statement that "Four decades have passed since Harold Lasswell ...". Work in the field is thus deemed to date from the publication of Lasswell's *Psychopathology and Politics.* A line demarcating the field must be drawn somewhere, of course, but it is drawn too narrowly here as elsewhere in the contemporary literature. The student is liable to be left with the impression that nothing of value was done prior to the behavioural revolution or outside of the areas it has affected.

The introduction calls attention to the field's fundamental problem, that of inferring a system's nature from what is known of its parts. Our understanding of aggregation has not moved far beyond the national character approach and any number of fragmentary viewpoints and ideas can be found in the literature today. The editors wisely avoid trying to resolve the situation at a stroke, and rather than putting forward a formal model relating personality to politics they introduce the field much as it stands. In spite of this, however, they achieve an admirable brevity and coherence, quite adequate to the average student's needs.

The book is divided into four sections along common-sense lines, in keeping with the field's lack of conceptual refinement. The first is on theoretical and methodological considerations. The articles selected should together provide an adequate treatment for the well-prepared student although there are pitfalls here, as wherever students must address methodological concerns independently of their application. The student who has not yet gone far enough in his own work to exhaust his *intuitive* methodological capabilities has no basis for appreciating method as a formal concern. If he does not regard method as problematical, its study is an imposition and a bore.

The second section, on personalities of politically significant individuals, seems almost quaint in today's more strictly behavioural context because of its heavily psychoanalytic emphasis. Most of it is devoted to Alexander George's widely circulated critical recapitulation of his work on Woodrow Wilson (the only selection not previously published), and to a selection from, and accolades to, Eric Erickson. There are also pieces by Lane, Janis, and Edwin, of which only Janis's work falls well outside the Freudian stream.

The Freudian emphasis continues in the third section, personality analysis of types of political actors. The authoritarian-personality literature is central to the section and the other psychoanalytically rooted items even include an article by Greenstein on cooperation between psychoanalysts and political scientists. There are also articles by Lasswell and Katz, one by Richard Flacks on the personality characteristics of student radicals, and James D. Barber's very economical model for examining American presidential behaviour. Barber's simplicity provides an attractive, not to mention instructive, counterbalance to the intricate conceptualizations of the psychoanalysts.

The final section returns attention to the fundamental problem of aggregation. A total of nine selections with diverse subject matters and points of view, including those of Inkeles, Parsons, Osgood, and Lasswell, make this section the best balanced, as well as the most methodologically important and the most compelling.

In spite of a certain narrowness, the book is valuable because it makes signal works available under one cover and places them in context without forcing a premature order on them.

JOHN WOODS
University of Calgary

H.M. Blalock Jr., ed., **Causal Models in the Social Sciences.** Chicago: Aldine-Atherton, 1971, pp. xi, 515.

This book is a collection of articles dealing with some of the assumptions required and the issues involved in making inferences about causality from evidence consisting of correlations between data usually gathered at the same point in time. This is not a book for the novice: familiarity with the basic statistics of correlation and regression and with the conceptual issues involved in the notion of causality is assumed. Also, most of the articles are purely formal, though the editor has sought to include at least one concrete application in each section. Those with some background in the field will find the book an invaluable collection of the leading articles from a wide variety of sociological, economic, and biological journals, which our university libraries sometimes tend to scatter all over the campus. In addition to this feature of convenience, there are also eight previously unpublished articles.

Unlike another book in this series, Morrison and Henkel's *The Significance Test Controversy*, this collection is not designed so much to highlight and analyse the controversies in the field but rather seeks to analyse the problems encountered in relaxing the excessively restrictive assumptions of the simplest case. Thus, after presenting two ways of analysing the case of recursive causal models whose variables are measured with a high degree of precision on clearly interval scales, the editor shifts to a series of readings dealing with the estimates of causal arrows in systems characterized by one or more feedback loops. The fourth section examines the problem of making causal inferences in models whose variables may be partly unmeasured and partly measured with considerable inaccuracy. The concluding section deals in part with causal models whose variables are measured on no better than an ordinal scale but also includes a discussion of multicollinearity and of aggregation.

The quality of the material is, in all cases, high and stimulating, but a consequence of the decision to ignore controversy is to make the editor appear either partisan or indecisive. For example, a proposed solution to the problem of ordinal variables is preceded by an article that is critical of the very article reprinted. No editorial guidance is offered as to the grounds of the disagreement or the limits within which each argument might be true. On the differences between path analysis and the Simon-Blalock technique or between path coefficients and path regressions, the editor's comments strike one as unbalanced in each case. Blalock tends to argue, on the first point, that the two techniques are generally equivalent, where it seems that path analysis is both more general and less sensitive to mis-specification. On the second point, Blalock tends to underestimate the value of standardized coefficients particularly where, as in many variables used in political science or sociology, the units of measurement are arbitrary. Apart from these three lapses, however, the editorial comments tend to equal the high quality of the other work represented.

W.P. Irvine
Queen's University

nadian Journal of
olitical science
vue canadienne de
cience politique

J.A.A. LOVINK Is Canadian Politics too Competitive?

DAVID SANKOFF et KOULA MELLOS L'amplification des proportions

GRAHAM WHITE One-Party Dominance and Third Parties

ANDRÉ BLAIS Third Parties in Canadian Provincial Politics

MAURICE PINARD Third Parties in Canada Revisited

RUTH ANN PITTS Parliamentarianism among the French Working Class

BENTLEY LEBARON Three Components of Political Obligation

WILLIAM B. MOUL The Level of Analysis Problem Revisited

FRANK STARK The Prime Minister as Symbol

GEORGE SZABLOWSKI The Prime Minister as Symbol: A Rejoinder

HENRI BRUN Le Labrador à l'heure de la contestation

September 1973 septembre VI no. 3

Canadian Journal of Political Science / Revue canadienne de science politique

Editorial correspondence in English should be directed to Professor David Hoffman, Division of Social Science, York University, 4700 Keele Street, Downsview 463, Ont. Subscription and business correspondence should be directed to the University of Toronto Press, Periodicals Department, Front Campus, Toronto 181, Ont.

On doit adresser toute communication en français, au sujet de la rédaction, à M. Vincent Lemieux, Département de science politique, Faculté des sciences sociales, Université Laval, Québec 10e, Qué. Les communications à caractère commercial, y compris celles concernant les abonnements, doivent être adressées à : University of Toronto Press, Periodicals Department, Front Campus, Toronto 181, Ont.

The Journal acknowledges with gratitude the generous assistance of the Canada Council. / La Revue tient à remercier le Conseil des Arts du Canada pour la généreuse subvention qu'il a bien voulu lui accorder.

Subscriptions: Membership in either the CPSA/ACSP or the SCSP includes subscription to the journal. Ordinary membership $15. Student membership $5. Joint CPSA and SCSP membership $17. Joint CPSA and Canadian Economics Association (two journals) $26.

Abonnement : la souscription à l'un des organismes ci-dessus (CPSA/ACSP ou SCSP) tient lieu d'abonnement. Montant de la souscription : tous $15, étudiants $5, conjointe aux deux organismes $17, conjointe à l'Association canadienne d'Economique (valant abonnement à *Revue canadienne d'Economique*) $26.

Postage paid in cash at third class rates — Permit no C-71, University of Toronto Press, University of Toronto, Toronto 181, Ont. / Les frais de poste sont payés au comptant selon le tarif de troisième classe — Permis no C-71, University of Toronto Press, Toronto 181, Ont.

Indexed: Index to *Canadian Legal Periodical Literature* / Indexée au *Catalogue des périodiques juridiques canadiens.*

Published by University of Toronto Press / Publiée par University of Toronto Press.

Contents

Is Canadian Politics too Competitive?
J.A.A. LOVINK 341

La régionalisation électorale et l'amplification des proportions
DAVID SANKOFF et KOULA MELLOS 380

One-Party Dominance and Third Parties: The Pinard Theory Reconsidered
GRAHAM WHITE 399

Third Parties in Canadian Provincial Politics
ANDRÉ BLAIS 422

Third Parties in Canada Revisited
MAURICE PINARD 439

Parliamentarianism among the French Working Class
RUTH ANN PITTS 461

Three Components of Political Obligation
BENTLEY LEBARON 478

The Level of Analysis Problem Revisited
WILLIAM B. MOUL 494

Notes

The Prime Minister as Symbol: Unifier or Optimizer?
FRANK STARK 514

The Prime Minister As Symbol: A Rejoinder
GEORGE SZABLOWSKI 516

Note bibliographique / Review Article

Le Labrador à l'heure de la contestation
HENRI BRUN 518

Recensions / Reviews 521

Is Canadian Politics too Competitive?*

J.A.A. LOVINK *Queen's University*

For some interesting reason, political science (unlike economics) has until recently invested very little energy in building and testing theories in which competition is a major explicit variable, be it dependent or independent. As a result, we still have no agreement on the most appropriate ways of measuring the various kinds of political competition, little knowledge of the links between levels or intensities of political competition and their socio-economic and political environment, and no hard information about its consequences for political behaviour and decisions. To be sure, we have long had a number of hypotheses seeking to account for political competition (or its absence) expressed in terms of the number and ideological polarization of political parties, or in terms of the distribution of power within organizations, and positing vaguely formulated consequences for the stability, decisiveness, sensitivity, and responsibility of government, or for the way group goals are (re)defined and pursued. Yet none of these propositions, developed by such early greats as Ostrogorski, Michels, and more recently Duverger and Key, has as yet been sufficiently refined to permit a rigorous comparative testing; where such refinement was unnecessary, as in Duverger's ideas about the effect of the electoral system on the number of parties, they have been shown to be wrong.

In the last decade, an increasing effort has been made to fill these gaps in our knowledge. With respect to the one kind of political competition with which we are concerned in this article, the competition for votes between political parties, there is a rapidly growing literature proposing and applying alternative means of measurement, seeking to discover the major determinants of variations in the "closeness" of such competition, and examining the significance of such differences for the kinds of policies that are adopted.

I shall begin with a critical review of this literature (most of which has to do with American politics), in order to provide a comparative perspective for the Canadian data under study. I shall then quickly summarize the Canadian literature on the subject, partly to point up how the data to be presented confirm or deny existing perceptions, and partly as a source of ideas to explain the findings themselves. The sections that follow present a measurement of inter-party competition in Canadian federal elections between 1925 and 1972, explore its rela-

*I am very grateful to William P. Irvine for his very helpful criticisms of an earlier version of this paper, to John Dingwall and André Carrier for their judicious and cheerful assistance as parliamentary interviewers, and to John Dingwall and Christopher Thomson for their competent help in writing many of the computer programs required to process the data. My thanks also go to the Canada Council for financial assistance and to Queen's University for computer services.

Canadian Journal of Political Science/Revue canadienne de science politique, VI, no. 3 (September/septembre 1973). Printed in Canada/Imprimé au Canada.

tionship to the process of urbanization, examine its significance for turnover in the membership of the House of Commons, and investigate its impact on party policy and campaign strategy, as perceived (in this last case) by about one hundred federal politicians.

Existing propositions about the significance of electoral competition

The first item one might reasonably expect to find under this rubric is the proposition that electoral competition – implying *choice* among aspirants to public office – is indispensable to democracy. But the widespread agreement that this proposition would undoubtedly evoke would be purely a function of the ambiguity of the asserted linkage. Under a little probing, the apparent harmony would evaporate like morning mist, revealing gross disagreements about the conditions that such competition must satisfy to produce a truly "democratic" result. Probable points of contention have been identified most clearly in R.A. Dahl's *A Preface to Democratic Theory*, and turn mainly on differential willingness to tolerate deviations from the equality principle and from the requirement that the scheduled alternatives for choice virtually exhaust the range of desired alternatives.

I propose to leave to one side this prickly controversy about the relationship between electoral competition and democracy. More prosaically perhaps, the focus will be restricted to propositions (explicit or implicit) that make some claim about the significance of the *level* of electoral competition, defined in terms of the objective probability that elected officials will be defeated at the next election. Put differently, the question being asked is what consequences have been attached to variation or differences in the objective security of tenure of elected officials, given rough comparability in the democratic quality of the rules of the game under which their tenure is determined.

Undoubtedly, one of the largest claims to be made for the significance of electoral competition (as delimited above) has been that it increases the responsiveness of politicians to the electorate's needs and wishes. A representative affirmation of this belief may be found in the following paragraph.

> Aside from casting extremists out beyond the pale, free elections and a two-party system operate to bring governmental policy roughly in line with intense public preferences over a reasonable span of time ... The "out" party has a built-in incentive to propose policies more popular than [those of] the "in" party in order to assume office. And the "in" party is highly motivated to respond by adopting the policy itself or by proposing others which it believes may be even more popular. *Party competition for votes brings public policy into accord with private preferences.* This calculus of support is far from precise; it is necessarily based more on hunch and guesswork at any point in time than on hard facts.[1]

The theoretical grounds for this proposition are probably stated most explicitly in the influential book by Anthony Downs, *An Economic Theory of Democracy.*

Although it appears to have been widely accepted for many years, this extension to politics of the Manchester liberal faith in the public advantages of rivalry

[1]N.W. Polsby and A.B. Wildavsky, *Presidential Elections*, 2nd ed. (New York, 1968), 280–1, (italics added).

La politique canadienne est-elle trop compétitive?

Bien peu de recherches ont été faites sur la compétition électorale canadienne afin d'en mesurer le niveau, les conséquences et les relations avec d'autres variables. Aux Etats-Unis, malgré l'intérêt récent pour ce genre d'études, il apparaît à l'analyse critique que ces écrits sont empreints de sérieuses faiblesses méthodologiques et n'ont pu accoucher de découvertes concluantes. Dans ces circonstances, l'auteur avoue ne pas vouloir apporter plus qu'une ébauche de réponse à la question générale qu'il se pose sur la compétition électorale au Canada.

En résumé, il a trouvé qu'au Canada (a) la lutte électorale est très compétitive par rapport aux Etats-Unis et à la Grande-Bretagne eu égard au moindre nombre de sièges qui sont « de facto » réservés à un parti donné; (b) que le degré de compétition n'est pas affecté par le facteur régional; (c) que le degré de compétition semble s'être stabilisé depuis cinquante ans; (d) et qu'il n'y a pas de relations entre l'urbanisation et la compétition électorale.

L'auteur a de plus tenté d'évaluer l'impact de la compétition électorale, telle qu'indiquée par la distribution spatiale des sièges réservés (safe) et des sièges non réservés (marginal), sur les programmes des partis et sur leur stratégie électorale. Des interviews recueillis auprès d'une centaine de politiciens fédéraux tendent à démontrer que cet impact est minime.

En conclusion, il est suggéré que la compétition électorale est peut-être trop grande au Canada puisqu'elle a un effet négatif sur les travaux du Parlement dont les effectifs n'ont guère le temps de se familiariser avec ses rouages. L'auteur met en doute l'idée qu'une diminution du degrée de compétition électorale pourrait s'accompagner d'une diminution de la sensibilité politique (responsiveness) des élus.

has never had a firm empirical basis. Apart from its ideological congeniality (at least in a North American setting), a major reason for the widespread academic acceptance of this notion appears to have been V.O. Key's research on Southern politics, which led him to suggest that one-party politics, especially where factions were "loose," gave politicians fewer incentives to appeal to the have-not sectors of society than a competitive two-party system, mostly because it hindered the disadvantaged elements in the population in identifying and penalizing those who had so systematically ignored their needs.[2] Yet (contrary to many interpretations) Key remained far from imagining that close electoral competition offered anything approaching a guarantee of responsiveness to the mass of the electorate. In fact, he seems to have seen party competition (unspecified as to level) as only one of many variables influencing public policy, possibly capable of stimulating a stronger welfare orientation *only in the long run.* In his own words:

Differing patterns of competition, whether they be interparty or intraparty, also have differing consequences for the substance of public policy. The difficulty comes in establishing what those varying consequences are. The expectation from general democratic theory would be that competition between leadership cliques for mass support would tend to result in the adoption of policies for mass benefit. Over the long run such results may accrue, yet the conditions necessary for such results in the short run do not always exist. Imperfections in the flow of information, frailties in political leadership, the unremitting efforts of special interests to protect or advance their causes, the capacity of side issues to divert the electorate, and other factors may affect

[2] *Southern Politics in State and Nation* (New York, 1949), esp. 302–10.

the character and results of competition. Political competition may be a condition precedent to government in the public interest; it does not invariably produce that result.[3]

It is some distance from this cautious assertion to the confident statement of faith by Polsby and Wildavsky quoted earlier.

In the past decade, there has been a spate of studies whose aim has been to find out, through a variety of indices and statistical tests of association, whether the level of electoral competition does indeed vary independently and positively with the relative generosity of social welfare policies.[4] The findings reported in this research, all of which is based on comparisons among American state governments, are sharply at variance. Five of these studies conclude that state differences in the level of electoral competition are so weakly associated with differences in social welfare expenditures, when controlled for state differences in socio-economic development and affluence, that electoral competition must now be discarded as an important explanatory variable for state commitment to social welfare or income redistribution.[5] But three other studies come to contrary conclusions. One finds that the level of the electoral competition has a significant positive relationship to differences among states in expenditures on education and public welfare.[6] Another finds a significant direct association with differences in aid to dependent children and unemployment compensation, but not with differences in old-age assistance and per-pupil education expenditures, a contrast which is explained in terms of the allegedly greater centrality of the former types of expenditure to "the struggle between the haves and have-nots."[7] The third study, in similar fashion, finds electoral competition (coupled with turnout) to be more significantly associated with state differences in education and welfare policy than with differences in highway and natural resource policy, and also accounts for this distinction by suggesting that education and welfare policies are more prone to "array taxpayers and the economic *haves* against recipients of services and the *have-nots*."[8]

[3]*Politics, Parties and Pressure Groups*, 5th ed. (New York, 1964), 298–9.

[4]Some of these studies have also examined the association between the level of electoral competition and other policies, not directly related to the so-called "have–have-not struggle" in society. One, by Fry and Winters (cited in n. 3), uses as its policy variable not the level of social welfare expenditures per recipient but the allocation of the burdens and benefits of state revenue and expenditure policies across income classes, that is, the *redistributive* character of state policies.

[5]R.E. Dawson and J.A. Robinson, "Inter-Party Competition, Economic Variables, and Welfare Policies in the American States," *Journal of Politics*, 25 (1963), 265–89; R.I. Hofferbert, "The Relation between Public Policy and Some Structural and Environmental Variables in the American States," *American Political Science Review*, 60 (1966), 73–82; T.R. Dye, *Politics, Economics and the Public* (Chicago, 1966); R.E. Dawson, "Social Development, Party Competition and Policy," in *The American Party Systems*, ed. W.N. Chambers and W.D. Burnham (Toronto, 1967), 203–37; B.R. Fry and R.F. Winters, "The Politics of Redistribution," *American Political Science Review*, 64 (1970), 508–22.

[6]A.G. Pulsipher and J.L. Weatherby, jr., "Malapportionment, Party Competition, and the Functional Distribution of Governmental Expenditures," *American Political Science Review*, 62 (1968), 1207–19.

[7]C.F. Cnudde and D.J. McCrone, "Party Competition and Welfare Policies in the American States," *ibid.*, 63 (1969), 858–66.

[8]I. Sharkansky and R.I. Hofferbert, "Dimensions of State Politics, Economics, and Public Policy," *ibid.*, 867–79, at 878.

A measure of support for this second set of findings has also been provided by a recent

An elaborate analysis of the relative merits of the studies just reported might show which of these two contradictory assessments of the significance of electoral competition for public policy has the greater validity. However, such an analysis would not only lead us too far afield, but it would also have limited utility given that all of these studies share a major methodological weakness. This deficiency turns upon the validity of the assumption, common to all of this research, that the association between the level of electoral competition and the nature of public policy can be measured satisfactorily by taking a policy reading for all states at one point in time and relating that measure (controlled for differences in socio-economic development and affluence) to an average of one or more indices of electoral competition over the preceding 15, 20 or 30-odd years.[9]

This procedure would have been quite reasonable if the level of electoral competition in most states had been more or less stable in secular terms and if variations about the mean had been fairly small. In that case, the year for which the policy reading is taken would matter little. But this assumption is surely extremely weak, and is moreover logically at odds with the fact that all but one of the writers cited rely on fairly long electoral time series.[10] If, on the other hand, the level of electoral competition varies significantly over time, then it matters greatly *when* the policy measurement is taken. A long-term average of one or more measures of competition might then poorly represent the level of competition actually prevailing at the time the policies in question were adopted, while a policy measurement at some remove from that same date might hide an important lag or inelasticity in the relationship being tested.

This danger can be illustrated by means of the hypothetical example in Figure 1. Here, it is assumed that the policies observed by the researcher at time Z were actually adopted by state A at time Y, by state B at time X and by state C at time W (see Figure 1). Now if it is further assumed that the researcher finds that at time Z state A ranks very high on his index of responsiveness to popular demands, while states B and C rank very low and mid-way respectively, then he will conclude, given that his measure of electoral competition will yield about the same average over the time series V-Z for all three states, that electoral competition is unrelated to political responsiveness. In fact, however, the relationship

study by Prewitt and Eulau. Based on interviews with some 400 city councilmen in the San Francisco Bay area, this research led its authors to conclude that the more seriously councilmen were threatened by electoral defeat the more likely they were to *see* themselves as responding to the wishes of their constituents rather than to their own image of the public interest. K. Prewitt and H. Eulau, "Political Matrix and Political Representation: Prolegomenon to a New Departure from an Old Problem," *ibid.*, 427–41. No data are presented on the fit between the responsiveness of councilmen as seen by themselves and as judged by their constituents. See also K. Prewitt, "Political Ambitions, Volunteerism, and Electoral Accountability," *ibid.*, 64 (1970), 5–17.

9In most of these studies, the measurement of competition is based on one or more *state* offices, an appropriate restriction given that only state policies are being considered. In two cases (Hofferbert, "Public Policy and Structural and Environmental Variables," and Fry and Winters, "Politics of Redistribution"), however, the measure of competition includes the outcomes of elections for U.S. president and senator as two of its three components, thereby casting considerable doubt on the validity of the relationships observed.

10The exception is the study by Sharkansky and Hofferbert, "Dimensions of State Politics," whose index of competition includes several components measured at a single point in time. Some of their other components are measured over time, however, without any explanation of the rationale involved.

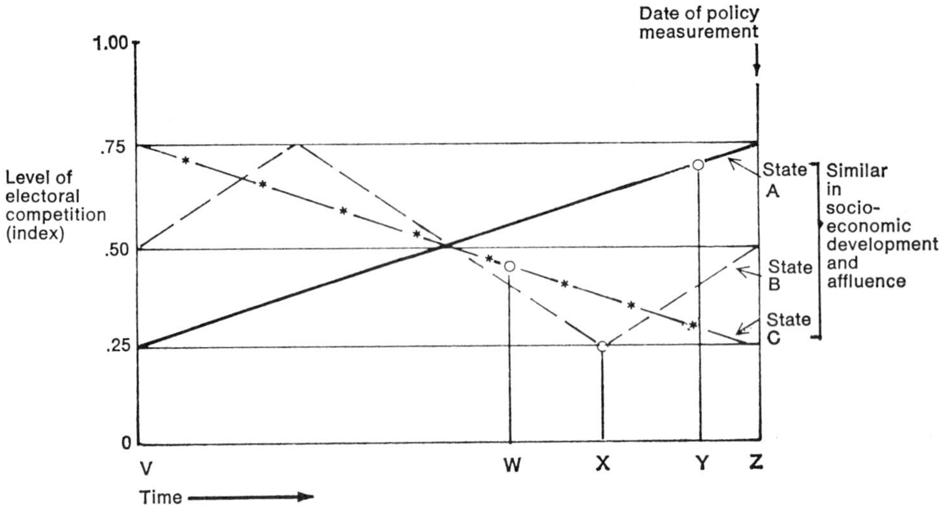

FIGURE 1

would have been much more complex. Thus, State A would have chosen its relatively responsive policies when very highly competitive electorally, state B its relatively unresponsive policies when very uncompetitive electorally, and state C its policies of average responsiveness when about average in electoral competitiveness, thereby yielding a high positive relationship. Yet this association would have been badly marred by the fact that for both states B and C the significant changes in competition between times X-Z and W-Z (respectively) would have been unaccompanied by policy changes in the expected direction. That finding would have necessitated further analysis to determine whether there might not be a consistent lag in what would then appear as the response of policy orientation to changes in the level of electoral competition.

The conclusion is, therefore, that for any state where electoral competition has varied significantly studies of the relationship between this variable and the character of public policy must be longitudinal in nature, exploring the articulation over time between variations in electoral competition and changes in policy orientation. Until some of this research has been done, it seems reasonable to hypothesize: (1) that the two variables (to the extent that they are related at all) will *interact*, increases in competitive pressure tending to stimulate responsiveness to the mass of the electorate, and up-swings in responsiveness tending to diminish competitive pressure; and (2) that the relationship will typically be marked by significant lags.

Closely related to the traditional hypothesis that electoral competition affects public policy is the belief that it also influences the propensity of politicians to innovate. Thus, Theodore Lowi has suggested that innovation, which he defines roughly as "coopting new interests, expressing new ideas, making changes in established commitments or 'definitions of the situation,'" is most likely to occur in an "*alternating* modified one-party system."[11] In the latter situation, he argues,

[11]"Toward Functionalism in Political Science: The Case of Innovation in Party Systems," *American Political Science Review*, 57 (1963), 570–83, at 575.

neither party is likely to make more than marginal changes, for fear that a misreading of the electorate's preferences may deprive it of a victory that already lies too temptingly close at hand. "When party leaders think their party is within a few percentage points of victory, they are likely to see their rational strategy as one of intensification of existing commitments, tightening of ranks, activation of existing followings."[12] By contrast, if one of the two parties is relatively weak (securing around 40 per cent of the vote and 30 per cent of the seats, and likely, on the basis of past performance, to win a majority of the seats only about once in 12 years), then for that party the incentive to innovate is likely to be very high. A good guess may put it in office; a bad one will merely guarantee a defeat that is likely in any event.

Directly contrary to this hypothesis runs an argument recently presented by Joseph Schlesinger. Schlesinger agrees that little innovation can be expected from a two-party system when competition is very close, but posits that in non-competitive situations (and tacitly assuming American political conditions) a rational minority party will not resort to innovation. Schlesinger claims that in such circumstances the appropriate strategy for the minority party is to make itself acceptable to the majority party's identifiers by erasing the differences setting it off from the majority party. The latter, by extension, seeks to prevent such defections by doing the opposite.[13] In this analysis, innovation thus seems a function of factors other than the level of electoral competition.

So far, there appears to have been very little research into the validity of these last two competing hypotheses. An important exception is a study by Jack L. Walker in which this question is one of a variety of fish being fried. In this inquiry, Walker's main tool of analysis is an index of innovation derived for each state of the United States by averaging the time lags between its own adoption of a wide variety of policies and the acceptance of similar-type policies by the first state to do so.[14] For present purposes, it suffices to note that he finds the independent statistical association between these indices and electoral competition to be very weak.[15]

Here again, scepticism is in order. In the first place, Walker's innovation scores are based solely on differences in the speed or timing with which various states ventured into new fields of public policy, to the exclusion of comparisons of the actual innovative content of programs adopted. Secondly, many of the programs included in his innovation index (like the adoption of accountants licensing, advertising [control] commissions, and agricultural experiment stations, to take only the first three in a list of 88 programs) are not ones for which any known hypothesis would suggest a relationship between early adoption and close electoral competition. Without some evidence that the timing and content criteria of innovation would yield roughly the same results, particularly in the case of the more politically salient and redistributive programs on which the level of electoral competition has been thought to have a bearing, it seems premature to

[12] *Ibid.*
[13] *Ambition and Politics* (Chicago, 1966), 121–5.
[14] "The Diffusion of Innovations among the American States," *American Political Science Review*, 63 (1969), 880–99, at 882–3.
[15] *Ibid.*, 885–7.

reject the hypothesis that innovation and competitive pressure are independently and significantly related.[16]

The remaining propositions about the significance of differences in electoral competition may be passed in review more quickly, if only because less effort has thus far been expended in testing them. One of these hypotheses links the level of electoral competition to the rise of new parties, positing that "whenever the opposition party (or the strongest of many opposition parties) fails to retain at least a third of the votes while in opposition, it tends to be replaced [as the main avenue for the expression of protest] by 'third' parties."[17] The idea is that political discontent is likely to be funnelled into the strongest opposition party only if that party is perceived by protest voters as reasonably strong and within striking distance of power. Where this is not so, opposition to the "in" party will tend to express itself through the formation of new third parties or through an upsurge of support for existing third parties.

It is evident that this hypothesis, in treating a low level of competition as a necessary though not sufficient condition[18] for the rise of third parties, presupposes not only that most protest movements will be sufficiently pragmatic to be satisfied with expression through a strong minority party where one is available, but also that the leading minority party will be of the "brokerage" type. It presumes, furthermore, an institutional context in which support for a strong minority party is likely to provide superior access to power than formation of a third party. All of these premises are likely to restrict the theory's validity to a few cases like the Canadian, and even there its fit with history is open to serious question.[19]

Several other hypotheses focus on another facet of the level of electoral competition, the rate of forced turnover in elective office. On one side, there is the large school of thought (carried to practical extremes in the limited terms of office typical of American elected executives) that regards power as corrupting and thus favours the regular displacement of the reputedly powerful. Those sharing this belief also often hold that "significant" political reform almost always requires a wholesale prior change in personnel. In effect, these propositions

[16]In support of this conclusion, doubts may also fairly be expressed about Walker's measures of electoral competition (borrowed from Hofferbert), which rely on gubernatorial elections in one instance, and on a combination of presidential, senatorial, and gubernatorial elections in another. Short of a demonstration that competition for these offices is a good proxy for competition for the state legislature, this does not seem satisfactory.

As far as the coincidence between the content and timing criteria of innovation is concerned, Professor Walker has pointed out in a letter to the writer that secondary sources he has consulted assert that in many cases the content of state programs is very similar (sometimes being based on model bills that are circulated among the states). He is confident, on that basis, that in "the majority of cases" no significant differences exist.

In so far as his list of programs includes many relatively uncontroversial items like accountants licensing, this confidence is probably well founded. It is less plausible, however, with respect to the more politically salient programs like fair housing, resale price maintenance (fair trade laws), and right-to-work legislation, precisely those to which the level of electoral competition has been presumed most significant.

[17]M. Pinard, *The Rise of a Third Party* (Scarborough, Ont., 1971), 37. In the author's own words, one-party dominance is "conducive" to the rise of new parties. *Ibid.*

[18]*Ibid.*, 39.

[19]Kimberly Wakefield, "Measuring One-Party Dominance" (MA thesis, Queen's University, 1972).

may be seen as important amendments to the earlier-mentioned hypothesis that political responsiveness benefits from stiff electoral competition, in that they insist that close competition will have the desired effect only where it in fact produces frequent turnover among political decision-makers, a consequence that may not always arise. Like the principal hypothesis, this amendment still awaits a rigorous comparative testing.

On the other side, reasons may be found for regarding rapid turnover less favourably. Most important of these is the adverse effect that severe insecurity of tenure may have on the quality and socio-economic variety of individuals recruited to political life, on their ability to develop enough political and technical know-how to reduce their dependence on bureaucrats and other established advisers, and on their capacity to pursue their own goals effectively. In this connection, John Porter has argued for a British-style *cursus honorum* in Canada:

> In the process the politician would increasingly become a public figure with a following in the party and in the country, who would articulate for the society particular values and goals. The political leadership role would call for certain skills in persuasion and in the management of party and of Parliament. Like all skills, political ones require training and experience within the political system ...
>
> Without these elements in the political career it is unlikely that the political system becomes sufficiently differentiated to be a system of social power strong enough to make claims on behalf of the total society.[20]

Another common concern about rapid turnover is that it may lead to undue instability and discontinuity of policy. Whether this is so mainly depends, presumably, on whether governments are typically formed by single parties or by party coalitions, on how deeply the parties are disagreed on policy, and on the extent to which policy-makers are bound by objective environmental constraints. Finally, the possibility exists that as turnover approaches its logical extreme (where the "in" party *always* suffers defeat), the response of politicians may not be an ever-growing responsiveness but its opposite, an expanding devotion to self-gratification.[21] But here again, much empirical research remains to be done.

Two reasons remain for treating the level of electoral competition as a significant political datum. One of these is the established, positive association between the level of electoral competition and popular political involvement and voter turnout. These correlates of electoral competition are important not only because of their possible impact on the decisions of politicians (and as such subsumed above), but also in their own right, because of their bearing on the democratic quality of election outcomes. The second reason arises from the linkage between the level of electoral competition and the democratic validity of the process of candidate selection. Wherever electoral competition at the constituency level is close, the democratic salience of party nominating procedures is presumably rela-

[20]John Porter, *The Vertical Mosaic* (Toronto, 1965), 405–6. In accounting for the scarcity of political careerists and what he sees as the consequent lack of autonomy in the Canadian political system, Porter is not satisfied with the uncertainty of a Canadian political career as an adequate answer. He also cites the absence of a financially secure élite willing to make a career of politics, as well as the allegedly bureaucratic outook of many Liberal leaders, beginning with Mackenzie King.

[21]Cf. Downs, *An Economic Theory of Democracy*, chap. 4, esp. 62–3.

tively small. Where competition is very low, however, the democratic case against élite selection and for some sort of primary election is impressive.

To sum up, there is plainly a wide range of more or less untested hypotheses that attribute considerable significance to the level of electoral competition. Sadly, no less than a major, book-length study could adequately examine each of these propositions in the light of the Canadian experience, especially if it were to cover provincial as well as federal politics, as it obviously should do. Within the limited scope of this article, no more can be attempted than to lay part of the groundwork for such studies by measuring the level of electoral competition in federal elections since 1925, and to inquire in a preliminary way into the significance of this factor for the policy decisions of Canadian federal politicians.

Explaining the level of electoral competition

If the level of electoral competition has (or is assumed to have) important political implications, then it becomes interesting to search for conditions with which that level may be systematically related. It comes as no surprise, therefore, that in the past 15 years considerable research has been devoted to this objective.

As is common in the study of parties and elections, the initial impetus for this line of enquiry was given by V.O. Key. In his *American State Politics*, Key suggested that in the American states a high level of electoral competition in national and state politics would be likely to occur only under the following conditions:

> First, within the electorate itself two major groups must exist with each possessed of the capacity to maintain a corps of political leaders. Such groups are, of course, the product of an interaction between the issues of politics and the characteristics of the people. Second, a substantial similarity should prevail between divisions created among the people of a state by the issues of both national and state politics. If the issues of national politics, for example, tend most strongly to unite the people of a state, divisions on questions of state politics may be pushed back into the primaries of the state's major party in national affairs.[22]

Elaborating on this hypothesis, he took care *not* to imply that to meet these conditions would always be sufficient. There is mention, for instance, of the probable significance of state differences in "political histories, traditions, and experiences." But apart from these sources of irregularity, Key clearly believed that a major clue to the level of electoral competition in the states at large would be found to lie in the diversity of their populations. To quote him again:

> In the demographic patterns of the states are to be found the raw materials with which politicians work in the construction of party systems. Conflicts of politics arise between country and city, between farm and factory, between rich and poor, between Protestant and Catholic, between early arrivals and recent immigrants, between descendants of the South and of the North. From such materials party systems are fashioned. The proportions and distribution of all these ingredients of political systems vary from state to state and those variations account in part for the differences in the political organization and practice of states.
>
> As politically significant diversity develops in the proper proportions it tends, outside a few rather peculiar one-party states, to reflect itself in a more evenly matched, more continuous, and often more spirited contest between the major parties.[23]

[22]*American State Politics: An Introduction* (New York, 1956), 229.
[23]*Ibid.*, 228–9.

In support of this view, he noted that the more urban and industrial states were generally more politically competitive, *at the state-wide level*, than the predominantly rural ones. In the former, metropolitan-rural contrasts formed a basis for a political dualism that derived its "vitality from the abiding, though sometimes subtle, differences between the followers of Republicanism and the cohorts of the Democracy."[24]

There is no suggestion, in Key's analysis, that the apparently positive relationship between the process of urbanization and industrialization and electoral competitiveness might be linear. To the contrary, Key explicitly notes that American metropolitan areas varied considerably in electoral competitiveness, some being predominantly Democratic in elections for governor while others divided their votes more evenly.[25] Whether further concentration of population in already heavily urban states would enhance their electoral competitiveness is a question he carefully left moot.

These nuances of Key's position have unfortunately been lost on later tillers of the field who have, to a man, posited a simple positive relationship between the two variables in question. All have gone ahead, without further theoretical investment, to gather relevant data in one form or another, and to subject them to various tests of association, sometimes very crude. The results of this research have been contradictory: some studies report confidently that electoral competition does increase with urbanization and industrialization, others just as firmly state the opposite.[26] Regrettably, none of the writers concluding to the contrary has tried to explain his finding theoretically.

There is neither need nor space to review these studies here.[27] Instead, it seems more fruitful to question the hypothesis itself, to ask why the two variables should be related at all. In approaching this question, it seems simplest first to ask what the most immediate or direct correlates of an increase in electoral competition are likely to be, and then to consider whether these correlates are likely to be affected by urbanization and industrialization.

Logic suggests that the following conditions are necessary (and probably in the long run sufficient) for a rise in the level of electoral competition: (1) a general

[24] *Ibid.*, 240–41. [25] *Ibid.*, 230–42.

[26] Reporting a clearcut relationship between the two variables are: R.T. Golembiewski, "A Taxonomic Approach to State Political Party Strength," *Western Political Quarterly*, 11 (1958), 494–513; H. Eulau, "The Ecological Basis of Party Systems: The Case of Ohio," *Midwest Journal of Political Science*, 1 (1957), 125–35; P. Cutright, "Urbanization and Competitive Party Politics," *Journal of Politics*, 25 (1963), 552–64; Dawson and Robinson, "Inter-party Competition ...," 283–5; A. Ranney, "Parties in State Politics," in *Politics in the American States*, ed. H. Jacob and K. N. Viner (Toronto, 1965), 61–99, at 68–9.

The following arrive at contrary findings: D. Gold and J.R. Schmidhauser, "Urbanization and Party Competition: The Case of Iowa," *Midwest Journal of Political Science*, 4 (1960), 62–75; T.R. Dye, *Politics, Economics and the Public*, 57–8; G.M. Bonjean and R.L. Lineberry, "The Urbanization-Party Competition Hypothesis: A Comparison of All United States Counties," *Journal of Politics*, 32 (1970), 305–21.

For conflicting views on the relationship in Canada, see H.A. Scarrow, "Patterns of Voter Turnout in Canada," *Midwest Journal of Political Science*, 5 (1961), 351–64, at 360; L.R. Grossman, " 'Safe' Seats: The Rural-Urban Pattern in Ontario," *Canadian Journal of Economics and Political Science*, 29 (1963), 367–71; A. Kornberg, "Parliament in Canadian Society," in *Legislatures in Developmental Perspective*, ed. A. Kornberg and L. Musolf (Durham, N.C., 1970), 55–128, at 71.

[27] For a convenient review article, see P. Coulter and G. Gordon, "Urbanization and Party Competition: Critique and Redirection of Theoretical Research," *Western Political Quarterly*, 21 (1968), 274–88.

weakening of party identification among the electorate at large; and/or (2) a partisan realignment and/or spatial redistribution among party identifiers yielding greater equality of support between the parties at the constituency level. The second of these hypothesized correlates seems to need no explanation. The first is derived from the well-known observation that weak identifiers and independents tend to be more open to information and appeals that run counter to their party preference in the preceding election than are strong identifiers, and are thus more likely, for any given information flow, to switch their vote to another party at the next election.[28] A weakening of party loyalties should thus raise the potential for reversing past election results, even if, as is likely, it simultaneously raises the frequency of landslide victories and large legislative majorities.

How far do urbanization and industrialization appear to be associated with either of these preconditions of a more competitive politics? As far as the strength of party loyalty is concerned, no clear-cut relationship appears to exist. Although for a variety of reasons rural and small-town politics is typically dominated by a single party, it appears not to follow that party loyalties in these areas are necessarily any firmer than in the city. To the contrary, the data reported in *The American Voter* suggest that in the United States it is in fact the rural voters (farm and non-farm) who are on the whole somewhat more variable in their party preference (considerably so if one restricts the comparison to rural and urban voters with the same [low] education and income).[29] If anything, urbanization may thus heighten party commitment somewhat, an effect that (*ex hypothesi*) is inimical to increased electoral competition.

It follows from these findings that if urbanization and industrialization are to lead to closer electoral competition, then the linkage between these variables must be through the second hypothesis, that is, via a partisan realignment and/or spatial redistribution of party identifiers. But here again, the grounds for expecting a significant relationship seem weak. This becomes clear when one considers that the impact of urbanization and industrialization on the level of electoral competition will depend on how many and how quickly migrants from country to city and from city to suburb change or weaken their party identification in response to their changed life situation and their parties' (possibly changing) appeals, on how non-migrants respond politically to the changes around them, and on the effects of such shifts in population and (perhaps) party identification on the number of voters identifying strongly, weakly, or not at all with each party *within each electoral division*. It seems dubious that such changes should produce just the right kind of political mix for close electoral competition (or what Key called "politically significant diversity in the proper proportions") more often than by chance.

If this analysis is valid, then the problem of explaining the extent of electoral competition at any given level of politics will vary in complexity depending on the pattern of voter identification with the parties at that level. Where party loyalties are typically strong, such explanations will call for detailed knowledge

[28] Particularly relevant to this point are D.E. Stokes, "Party Loyalty and the Likelihood of Deviating Elections," and P.E. Converse, "Information Flow and the Stability of Partisan Attitudes," in A. Campbell *et al.*, *Elections and the Political Order* (New York, 1966), 125–35 and 136–57 respectively.

[29] A. Campbell *et al.*, *The American Voter* (New York, 1966), chap. 15.

of the number, commitment, and spatial distribution of each party's identifiers, a question to which the degree of urbanization and industrialization probably offers no reliable guide. Where party identification is generally weak, on the other hand, the problem should be simpler: competitive pressure on elected politicians will generally be high.

It stands to reason that such explanations cannot stop at this level. For the next problem is obviously to account for the pattern of party identification itself. At this point, however, practically insuperable problems of causal analysis present themselves. Thus, although it is valuable to know that the strength of party identification (expressed in terms of the consistency with which identifiers support their party electorally) tends to be greater where the parties differ more clearly in ideology and policy,[30] this linkage diminishes in explanatory potential when one recalls that such differences are themselves to varying degrees a function of the number of parties and of the cleavages among the population in question, variables that are loosely related and in turn the products of complex historical circumstances.[31]

It may be concluded from the foregoing discussion that in attempting to explain the level of electoral competition in Canada the accent probably has to be placed directly on the nature of party loyalties among Canadians, not on changes or variations in urbanization and industrialization. It also follows that in the apparent absence of relevant theory the character of party identification in Canada will have to be explained *ad hoc*.

Past research on the level of electoral competition in Canada

To date, very little research on the level of electoral competition in Canada has been published. A good deal of analysis has of course been done by the political parties for their own electoral ends, but for obvious reasons their findings have remained private.[32] As an example of only one of the errors that have arisen from this situation, writers on Canadian politics have typically described the period 1935–57 as one of one-party dominance federally, a label that correctly

[30] A. Campbell and H. Valen, "Party Identification in Norway and the United States," in Campbell *et al.*, *Elections and the Political Order*, 245–68. See also R. Rose and D. Urwin, "Social Cohesion, Political Parties, and Strains in Regimes," in *European Politics: A Reader*, ed. R. Rose and M. Dogan (Toronto, 1971), 217–37, at 228, where the authors present data suggesting that for heterogeneous political parties the vote fluctuates much more than for parties which have a more clearly defined, restricted appeal. It has been noted, on the other hand, that once party identifications are firmly established a diminution in the ideological or political distinctiveness of the existing political parties need not (in fact, does not usually) bring about a decline in the prevalence or intensity of party identification. See, generally, *Political Oppositions in Western Democracies*, ed. R.A. Dahl (New Haven, 1966), and esp. 380–6.

Variations in the pattern of party identification have also been related independently to differences in the politicization process. See P.E. Converse and G. Dupeux, "Politicization of the Electorate in France and the United States," in Campbell *et al.*, *Elections and the Political Order*, 269–91; but cf. D.R. Cameron and L. Summers, "Non-Family Agents of Political Socialization: A Reassessment of Converse and Dupeux," this JOURNAL, 5 (1972), 418–32.

[31] This point is made more fully in Campbell and Valen, "Party Identification in Norway and the US," 265–8.

[32] For a brief discussion of the ways in which the parties have approached this task, see below, pp. 372–3.

TABLE I

MARGINS OF VICTORY IN CANADIAN FEDERAL GENERAL ELECTIONS, 1925–58

	Margin of victory (percentage of vote)					
	0–4.9	5.0–9.9	10.0–14.9	15.0–19.9	20.0–29.9	30.0+
Election	(percentage of seats)					
1925	17.6	17.6	19.6	12.7	13.9	18.8
1926	17.1	19.6	15.1	11.0	15.5	21.6
1930	29.4	20.8	17.1	9.4	11.4	11.5
1935	19.6	19.2	17.1	13.1	13.1	18.0
1940	21.2	19.2	15.9	8.6	16.7	18.4
1945	20.8	24.9	13.5	10.6	18.4	11.5
1949	22.1	16.8	12.6	9.9	18.7	19.9
1953	19.6	16.6	15.1	11.3	15.1	22.3
1957	20.4	17.0	13.6	11.3	21.5	16.3
1958	15.1	16.6	14.0	11.3	14.0	29.1

SOURCE: H.A. Scarrow, *Canada Votes* (New Orleans, 1962).

renders one important aspect of the level of electoral competition in those years while overlooking a score of others.[33]

It is only in the past decade that published data have begun to probe behind the crude totals of votes and seats won. In 1962, Howard Scarrow worked out (for each federal general election from 1921 to 1958) the provincial distribution of margins of victory, and the party and provincial distribution of the most closely contested seats.[34] As measured by the proportion of seats falling into each plurality category, his data suggested that over that period the level of electoral competition had remained remarkably stable (Table I). Some time later, Jorgen Rasmussen compared the outcomes of federal and provincial elections within each province between 1921 and 1964 in terms of (1) the percentage of elections in which the leading party changed, and (2) the percentage of elections in which the dominant party for the whole period won the most votes. By these standards, he found Canadian federal elections to have been considerably more competitive than provincial elections, and more competitive than American presidential elections as well (comparing results on a provincial-state basis).[35]

Since Rasmussen's study no further research on the subject has appeared, although brief mention should be made of an ingenious statistical enquiry by Duff Spafford examining the impact of fluctuations in the number of minor-party candidates on the number of seats won by the two largest parties. Combining all 14 federal general elections from 1921 to 1965, Spafford discovered that this variable has indeed had an important systematic effect, second only to the major parties' share of the vote itself, and that it has touched the two of them *in about the same way*.[36] For present purposes, the latter finding could be of great inter-

[33]Alternative approaches to measuring electoral competition are discussed below, pp. 356–61.
[34]*Canada Votes* (New Orleans, 1962).
[35]"A Research Note on Canadian Party Systems," *Canadian Journal of Economics and Political Science*, 33 (1967), 98–106.
[36]"The Electoral System of Canada," *American Political Science Review*, 64 (1970), 168–76.

est, were it only more clearly interpretable. As it stands, it might mean that the supporters of the two major parties have been about equally ready (or reluctant) to defect when minor party alternatives have presented themselves (an important indicator of the nature of party identification). Or their propensity to defect may in fact have been quite different, in which case the even-handed impact of minor parties could only be explained in terms of the particular spatial distribution of major-party supporters and defectors and of the behaviour and distribution of floating voters. Being unable to resolve this puzzle, we can only note that over time neither major party seems to have lost or gained more in seats than the other as a result of the incursions of minor parties.

What, lastly, does the literature on Canadian politics tell us about the pattern of party identification? One of the earliest empirical studies of this question was done by Peter Regenstreif in 1960. His survey of known supporters of the two largest parties (as identified by the parties themselves) tentatively suggested that nearly half had at some time voted for another federal party, that only about one-quarter were prepared to vote for their party regardless of their assessment of its leader or local candidate, and that almost half saw no policy differences between their own party and the others or thought one of the others "would do more."[37]

Similar results emerged from a national sample survey directed by John Meisel and others in 1965. In that instance, the data showed again that nearly half of the party identifiers interviewed had voted for different federal parties, while only about one-third said that they would vote for the party they identified with even if it favoured a policy they did not like.[38] Although strictly comparable data for other countries do not appear to exist, such indications as there are suggest that the commitment to party implied in these findings is relatively low.[39] According to John Meisel, this fickleness (independence of mind?) of Canadian voters also emerges very strongly from his equally vast 1968 election survey. So much so that he has felt free to state that the concept party identification "may be almost inapplicable in Canada. On the basis of admittedly limited evidence (surveys of only two elections) we have found that party identification seems to be as volatile in Canada as the vote itself."[40] Jane Jenson's analysis suggests

[37]For CCF supporters, comparable proportions for the second and third dimensions were 68 per cent and 4 per cent, respectively. No meaningful comparison is possible for the first dimension, because in many constituencies CCF supporters had no candidate of their own on the ballot. S.P. Regenstreif, "Some Aspects of National Party Support in Canada," *Canadian Journal of Economics and Political Science*, 29 (1963), 59–74. Also, by the same author, *The Diefenbaker Interlude* (Toronto, 1965).

[38]Jane Jenson, "Party Identification in Canada: A Rationally Limited Allegiance," (paper presented at the Annual Meeting of the Canadian Political Science Association, St John's, Nfld., June, 1971), 6–7. See also P.E. Converse, G. Dupeux, and J. Meisel, "Continuities in Popular Political Cultures: French and Anglo-Saxon Contrasts in Canada," (paper prepared for the international conference on comparative electoral behaviour, University of Michigan, 1967), 28–35.

[39]Campbell and Valen, "Party Identification in Norway and the US," 264, whose data indicate that among strong party identifiers in the United States two-thirds have always voted for the same party for President, while among weak identifiers about 45 percent have always done so. For both categories, the comparable Norwegian percentages are higher (Christian party identifiers excepted).

[40]*Working Papers on Canadian Politics* (Montreal, 1972), 67. For further evidence on the weakness of Canadian party identifications, see the growing literature on federal-provincial

that this conclusion may put the matter a little too exuberantly, but even so it is reasonably clear that, compared to Americans, Canadians more frequently switch their vote as well as their party identification.[41]

These findings accord nicely with the inferences drawn by others from some of the apparent peculiarities of Canadian political life. Among these characteristics are the unusual instability in the major parties' share of the national vote, the relative openness of the voters to third-party alternatives, and the widespread belief that few seats are so safe as to be uncapturable with a superior party leader, candidate, and organization.[42] As a rule, all of these phenomena are attributed, at least in the first instance, to the lack of clear-cut policy differences between the major parties.

To sum up, the existing (relatively sparse) literature generally presents Canadian federal politics as very highly competitive, and as marked by relatively weak party loyalties. I see no reason to doubt the truth of this image, but its sketchiness cries out for further work. Thus, there is need for better measurement of electoral competition, for data on possible variations in electoral competition over time, between regions and types of constituency, and among the seats held by different parties, and for a sharper comparative perspective to differentiate the Canadian situation more clearly.

Approaches to measuring electoral competition

Measures of electoral competition exist in bewildering variety. Distribution of the vote by party, distribution of seats by party, percentage of elections won by dominant party, percentage of elections producing a change in winning party, percentage of seats changing party hands at each election; these and a score of other measures have been adopted, singly or in combination, for a single office or for several at once.[43]

Faced with the need to choose among these criteria, one may adopt one of two basic approaches. One is to insist on maximum simplicity, usually because a very high premium is placed on ease of calculation and understandability. The rationale for the extreme emphasis placed on these values is dubious, especially in view of the high costs in plausibility which the resulting unidimensional mea-

---

vote switching, notably John Wilson and David Hoffman, "The Liberal Party in Contemporary Ontario Politics," this JOURNAL, 3 (1970), 177–204; George Perlin and Patti Peppin, "Variations in Party Support in Federal and Provincial Elections," *ibid.*, 4, no. 2 (1971), 280–6. Whether such "ticket-splitting" is more common in Canada than in other federations is a moot point. Scarrow's analysis suggests that the reverse may be true, at least for the United States and Australia, but since his findings are based on changes in winning party (not on the popular vote) their validity remains in doubt. H.A. Scarrow, "Federal-Provincial Voting Patterns in Canada," *Canadian Journal of Economics and Political Science*, 26 (1960), 289–98.

[41]"Party Identification in Canada," 9 and *passim.*

[42]See, for example, H.A. Scarrow, "Distinguishing Between Political Parties – the Case of Canada," *Midwest Journal of Political Science*, 9 (1965), 61–76.

[43]For those interested in examining this literature (most of it bearing on the United States), many of the more important studies are cited in D.G. Pfeiffer, "The Measurement of Inter-Party Competition and Systematic Stability," *American Political Science Review*, 61 (1967), 457–67.

sures typically entail.[44] The other approach is based on the premise that a simple measure that leaves room for reasonable doubt that the resulting classification adequately reflects all relevant aspects of reality is inferior to a more complex one that does not. Thus, any measure relying exclusively on the distribution of the vote by party is unacceptable short of clearcut evidence (probably impossible to produce) that the variability or volatility of the vote is virtually the same in all constituencies and for all parties. Reliance on the proportion of seats won by each party (the traditional measure of party "dominance" in the Canadian literature) is perhaps even worse, since it ignores both vote variability *and* margin of victory, both of which are indispensable (barring evidence to the contrary) to any plausible estimate of the prospects of displacing the party in power at the next election. From the standpoint of this second approach, therefore, the optimum measure of electoral competition is one that best combines economy with plausibility, and thus one that may require adaptation over time as standards of plausibility are altered by new behaviour patterns or research findings.

Before we consider what such a measure might look like, simplicity of exposition would be served by a side-glance at two recent studies of electoral competition in the United States and Britain. Although the measures of competition which they use are not ideal, applying them to federal election results in Canada still throws a valuable comparative light on the Canadian situation.

The first of these two approaches gauges the level of electoral competition according to the proportion of legislative seats consistently captured by the same party over a series of elections. If this measure is applied to the five elections for the US House of Representatives from 1952 to 1960,[45] to the six elections for the British House of Commons from 1950 to 1966,[46] and to the six elections

[44] I am well aware of Pfeiffer's claim that electoral competition can be adequately measured using only the party distribution of the vote. In my view, Pfeiffer fails to provide the systematic empirical evidence that would be required to meet the criticisms of such a simple measure that are advanced in this article. Without such evidence, there is no reason to think that vote pluralities by themselves offer a valid basis of comparison, be it over time, between different offices within the same political system, or between comparable offices in different political systems. (Pfeiffer, "The Measure of Inter-Party Competition and Systemic Stability.")

An important contemporary motivation for simplicity (also advanced by Pfeiffer) is the desire to facilitate statistical manipulation of the results. Thus, Bonjean and Lineberry think that the "most compelling" argument for adopting Pfeiffer's simple measure is "that it meets the requirements of all commonly used parametric tests". Bonjean and Lineberry, "The Urbanization-Party Competition Hypothesis," 309. This consideration loses whatever force it may have when a more complex alternative measure (such as the one proposed in this article) is equally easily manipulatable.

Finally, some reference should be made to the evidence recently provided that a variety of existing measures to compare the competitiveness of the American states all yield roughly similar results. This finding does not mean that a simple measure such as Pfeiffer proposes would necessarily also yield similar results, for the measures compared in the study cited are all relatively complex. It also does not obviate the need for the measure to be developed in this paper, for the measures examined were all tailored to institutional conditions peculiar to the United States. See R.E. Zody and N.R. Luttbeg, "Evaluation of Various Measures of State Party Competition," *Western Political Quarterly*, 21 (1968), 723–4.

[45] C.O. Jones, "Inter-Party Competition for Congressional Seats," *Western Political Quarterly*, 17 (1964), 461–76.

[46] J. Rasmussen, "The Implication of Safe Seats for British Democracy," *ibid.*, 19 (1966),

for the Canadian House of Commons from 1953 to 1965,[47] the following results emerge:

	"No-Change" seats as percentage of total
US House of Representatives	78.2
UK House of Commons	77.0
Canadian House of Commons	23.6

The comparability of these data is slightly weakened by the lower number of elections underlying the US figure (thereby tending to overstate somewhat the relative proportion of "no-change" US seats),[48] but there is no denying the enormous gap between Canada and the other two countries in competitiveness measured in this way.

This datum, important as it is, leaves too much room for skepticism: unless the "no-change" seats in each of the three countries are equally secure against capture, and the "change" seats equally changeable, the apparent differences in competitiveness shown above may plainly over- or understate reality by a significant margin. To avoid such objections, the second approach focuses directly on margins of victory and variability in the party vote.[49] Its rationale, put simply, is that a seat should be considered safe for the party holding it only when the margin of victory in the last election exceeds all but the most extreme recent fluctuations in all of that party's margins of victory in the region in which the seat is located. This approach is operationalized by ranking all regional losses and gains in plurality for each party in recent election pairs, from largest loss to largest gain, dropping off 5 per cent of these changes starting with the largest loss, and declaring "safe" any seat won by the party in question with a plurality greater than the largest loss then remaining in the series. To illustrate, if for the British Labour party in English urban seats the largest previous loss in plurality had amounted to 20 per cent, and to 10 per cent after the most extreme losses had been eliminated, then any English urban seat won by Labour in the most recent election with a plurality of over 10 per cent would be considered "safe."

Applied to the results of the 1964 and 1965 general elections in Britain and Canada, respectively, this method yields the fascinating contrasts shown in Tables II and III. These confirm the sharp differences in electoral competitiveness already suggested by the relative rarity of "no-change" seats in Canada, and add an indication of the radical dissimilarity of the two countries in the variability of party support. Furthermore, Table II reveals some highly suggestive differences in the vote variability of the various parties there represented. In both countries, the parties of the left had stabler voting support than the more ideologically and politically amorphous parties confronting them. At the same time, there were

516–29, at 517–9, updating findings reported in C.O. Jones, "Inter-Party Competition in Britain, 1950–59," *Parliamentary Affairs*, 17 (1963–4), 50–6. In both of these studies, only the 453 seats unaffected by boundary revisions are considered.

[47]In this period there were no federal boundary revisions in Canada, so that all 263 constituencies have been included in the calculation.

[48]For a short explanation of this point, see Jones, "Inter-Party Competition for Congressional Seats," 465, n. 14.

[49]Rasmussen, "The Implication of Safe Seats for British Democracy," 519–29.

TABLE II

FIFTH PERCENTILE FLUCTUATION IN THE MARGIN OF VICTORY, BY PARTY: UNITED KINGDOM (1950–64) AND CANADA (1953–65)*

	United Kingdom				Canada					
Party	English urban	English county	Welsh and Scottish	Total	Maritimes	Quebec	Ontario	Prairies	BC	Total
Liberal	n.a.	n.a.	n.a.	n.a.	−22.9	−46.4	−21.8	−35.2	−16.3	−35.2
Conservative	−13.3	−10.4	−17.4	n.a.	−18.5	−20.0	−36.9	−25.4	−43.2	−34.1
Labour/CCF-NDP	−8.8	−6.3	−7.1	n.a.	n.a.	n.a.	−12.8	−25.7	−12.2	−19.7

*Entries represent the largest loss in percentage margin of victory remaining after five per cent of the recorded changes in margin of victory, ranked from the largest loss to the largest gain, have been set aside, starting from the largest recorded loss.

Sources: British data as reported in Rasmussen, "The Implication of Safe Seats for British Democracy," 524–6. Sources of the Canadian data are reported in Table VI.

TABLE III

"SAFE" SEATS IN THE UNITED KINGDOM, 1964, AND IN CANADA, 1965*

Party	United Kingdom	Canada					
		Total	Maritimes	Quebec	Ontario	Prairies	BC
Liberal	n.a.	23	7	0	14	0	2
Conservative	185	17	2	2	0	13	0
Labour/CCF-NDP	244	14	0	0	4	1	9
Total	429	54	9	2	18	14	11
Percentage of House	69.7	20.4	3.4	0.8	6.8	5.3	4.1

*"Safe" seats are defined as those where the winning party's margin of victory in the 1964 British general election and the 1965 Canadian general election exceeded the regional fifth percentile fluctuation in the margin of victory for the same party in the general elections of 1950–64 inclusive for Great Britain and in the general elections of 1953–65 inclusive for Canada.
Sources: see Table II.

also significant differences in this respect between the British Conservative party and its even more brokerage-oriented counterparts in Canada.

Despite the interesting observations which it permits, this variability-of-support measure has two important drawbacks. The first is that it creates thoroughly implausible classifications where the fifth percentile of fluctuations in the margin of victory yields a figure close to zero, not to say a positive figure. In such cases, the measure would declare even seats won by the most narrow of margins to be "safe." Secondly, the measure assumes that the prospect of changing the electoral result in a given seat can be satisfactorily estimated by observing the volatility record of all seats won by the same party within the same region, a proposition whose validity is likely to vary from party to party, region to region, and country to country, and as a function of the way regions are delimited.

I conclude that there is need for a new measure, one that more plausibly reflects the apparent competitive threat encountered by incumbents, be it over differences of time, place, or office. It seems to me that such a measure should include three dimensions: (1) *the percentage of the vote separating the winner from his nearest rival.* The usual presumption is that as this percentage grows, the objective competitive threat diminishes. But for comparative purposes this rule of thumb is a poor guide; differences in the variability of voting preferences or turnout will cause commensurate inequalities in the competitive threat implicit in any given plurality. Comparability requires, therefore, that the margin of victory be adjusted for differences in (2) *the variability in the winning party's percentage of the vote.* Even then, however, the possibility remains that significant competitive differences may remain because of inequalities in the frequency with which incumbents are defeated. Account must also be taken, therefore, of (3) *the turnover rate*, or the number of changes in the winning party as a percentage of the opportunities for such change.

In operationalizing this composite measure, several difficult decisions must be made. Thus, there are at least two reasonable ways of measuring vote variability, at least three possible ways of adjusting margins of victory for vote variability, and innumerable ways in which the three components could be weighted to reflect the observer's assessment of their relative significance to the level of electoral competition.[50] Potentially, each of these options could be tested for its efficiency in predicting the actual pattern of partisan turnover in a subsequent election, with the choice falling on the most accurate measure. In practice, however, this hit-or-miss approach would be too burdensome as well as unworkable: where constituency boundaries are substantially revised each decennium the number of comparable elections will often be too small. We are forced, therefore, to resort to a prudential selection among these options. This means that *the measure chosen must stand or fall on its plausibility*. It can lay no claim to accuracy.

The measure of electoral competition which I propose to apply to Canadian federal elections since 1925 is constructed as follows: (1) for each seat, for a set of elections falling between two redistribution acts, winning party pluralities are summed; (2) to adjust for differences in vote variability, the vote losses or gains of the party(ies) winning the first election, second election, and so on, are summed (ignoring signs) and subtracted from the sum of their pluralities; (3) the outcome of step (2) is adjusted for the frequency with which the seat changed party hands by multiplying it by a turnover score ranging from 0 to 1, and calculated according to the formula $(1 - C/[N - 1])$, where C stands for the number of changes in winning party and N for the number of elections in the set being examined.

In synoptic form, this "index of safety" may be stated as follows:

$$IS_i = \frac{[(W_{i_1} - L_{i_1}) + (W_{i_2} - L_{i_2}) + \dots (W_{i_n} - L_{i_n})] - [|(S_{i_2} - W_{i_1})| + |(S_{i_3} - W_{i_2})| + \dots |(S_{i_n} - W_{i_{n-1}})|]}{N} \times \left(1 - \frac{C_i}{N - 1}\right)$$

where: IS_i Index of safety for elective office i;
W_{i_n} Winning party's percentage of vote for office i in election n;
L_{i_n} Second-running party's percentage of vote for office i in election n;
S_{i_n} Percentage of vote won for office i in election n by party winning office i in election $n - 1$;
N Total number of elections in the set being examined; and,
C_i Number of times office i changed party hands during the elections included in set N.

The properties of this measure, and the reasons for selecting this particular format, are set out in the appendix to this paper. In my judgment, these characteristics make the index of safety a highly plausible measure of electoral competition. In addition, the index has the advantages of broad applicability (to all offices filled by the single-member district cum plurality vote system of election) and of reasonable statistical simplicity.[51]

[50]For an explanation of these options see the appendix to this paper.
[51]David J. Elkins has recently proposed an approach to measuring electoral competition which would use survey data on each party's share of "standpatters" and "switchers" (in V.O. Key's language) to arrive at the statistical probability that the in-party will be displaced at the next election. "The Measurement of Party Competition in Multi-Party Systems" (unpublished manuscript, Department of Political Science, University of British Columbia, n.d. (1973?)). Although theoretically more satisfying than the present approach, the proposal's dependence on survey data disqualifies it for longitudinal studies reaching into the pre-survey era, and makes it too costly for use at the constituency level.

TABLE IV

INDEX OF SAFETY RELATED TO TURNOVER IN WINNING PARTY: ALL FEDERAL CONSTITUENCIES, 1953–65 (six elections)

Turnover in party winning seat	Index of safety			
	to 4.9	5.0–14.9	15.0+	Total
	(Percentage of column total)			
None	—	23.5	97.1	23.6
Once	17.0	42.6	2.9	26.2
Twice	42.0	29.5	—	30.8
Three times	34.8	4.3	—	16.7
Four times	6.2	—	—	2.7
Five times	—	—	—	—
Total	100.0	100.0	100.0	100.0
No. of Constituencies	112	115	36	263*
Percentage of total	42.6	43.7	13.7	100.0

*Includes two two-member constituencies. These were treated as single-member constituencies by summing the votes won by each party's candidates.

Sources: see Table VI.

Electoral competition in Canada measured by the index of safety

In applying longitudinal measures such as the index of safety, the periodic revision of constituency boundaries presents a familiar problem. In Canada, there have been five redistribution acts in the past five decades, in 1924, 1933, 1947, 1952, and 1966. Constituency-by-constituency comparison of election results in this period is therefore possible only for the following sets of general elections: (1) 1925, 1926, and 1930; (2) 1935, 1940, and 1945; (3) 1953, 1957, 1958, 1962, 1963, and 1965; and (4) 1968 and 1972.

Because of this limitation, the election of 1949 has been ignored altogether. In addition, the third set of elections had to be split into two sets of three to get strict comparability with the first two sets. Only a limited comparison could be made on a six-election basis, with the first set containing only 66 constituencies (out of a total of 241) whose boundaries were left unchanged by the reapportionment act of 1933.

In ordering the findings, all constituencies with an index of safety of less than 5.0 were classed as "marginal" (or most highly competitive), those with an index of from 5.0 to 14.9 as "competitive," and those with an index of 15.0 or more as "safe." This classification worked out well when tested against the relative frequency with which constituencies in the three groups changed party hands during the six general elections from 1953 to 1965. Doing so more than once were 83 per cent of the "marginal" seats, 34 per cent of the "competitive" seats, and none of the "safe" seats (Table IV). Appropriately, 97 per cent of the last group were continuously held by the same party.

A summary of the findings, ordered in this way, is presented in Table V. Two points stand out. One is the confirmation lent by these data to the image of Canadian federal politics as extremely competitive. Never in the past 50-odd years

TABLE V

ELECTORAL COMPETITIVENESS OF FEDERAL CONSTITUENCIES, 1925–65*

	Election set					
	Three elections				Six elections	
Index of safety	1925–6–30	1935–40–45	1953–7–8	1962–3–5	1925–45†	1953–65
	(percentage of total)					
To 4.9 (marginal)	42.3	53.1	42.2	35.4	56.0	42.6
5–14.9 (competitive)	29.0	24.7	35.7	32.3	36.4	43.7
15+ (safe)	28.6	22.2	22.1	32.3	7.6	13.7
Total	99.9	100.0	100.0	100.0	100.0	100.0
Mean Index	11.7	8.7	9.9	11.6	5.9	8.4
N	241††	243‡	263‡	263‡	66	263‡

*The general elections of 1968 and 1972 have been excluded from this analysis because the index requires that the election sets being compared contain the same number of elements.

†Includes only those constituencies whose boundaries were left unchanged by the redistribution Act of 1933.

††Includes four two-member constituencies. Treated as single-member constituencies by summing votes won by each party's candidates.

‡Includes two two-member constituencies. Treated as in note ††.

Sources: see Table VI.

has more than one-third of the House of Commons been made up of "safe" seats. Over the two sets of six elections, the proportion turns out to have been closer to one-tenth. The second point worth noting is the absence of any trend toward increased competition, already foreshadowed more crudely in Table I. If anything, there may have been a slight trend in the opposite direction. Those who are unconvinced of the utility of the index may be brought around by a similar absence of any trend in its component variables (Table VI).

Table VII breaks down this over-all image presented in Table V into its provincial facets. This refinement shows that the lack of trend at the national level does obscure several important tendencies provincially. The most notable of these is the rise in the electoral competitiveness of Quebec. Changes in the opposite direction appear to have occurred in Manitoba and Saskatchewan. On this showing, moreover, the three older Maritime provinces do not deserve their traditional reputation of relative electoral stability. As a group they are no more reliable than any other region, while individually Prince Edward Island and Nova Scotia rank among the most competitive of provinces.

Taken together, these findings offer little support for the hypothesis that urbanization and industrialization create closer political competition.[52] On the surface, the changes in Quebec seem to fit the proposition, but the absence of any national trend toward increased competition is not as predicted. A closer look at this supposed relationship confirms the weakness of the hypothesis in its present primitive form. In Quebec, where competition has increased the most, it is the rural

[52]The proportion of Canada's population classified in census statistics as "urban" has increased from 49.5 per cent in 1921 to 76.1 per cent in 1971. Because of a change in definitions in 1956, these figures slightly overstate the actual rate of urbanization. Canada, Dominion Bureau of Statistics, *1961 Census of Canada*, Bull. 7.1–2, Tables III and IV; Statistics Canada, *1971 Census of Canada*, Bull. 1.1–9.

TABLE VI

KEY COMPONENTS OF ELECTORAL COMPETITION: CANADIAN GENERAL ELECTIONS, 1925–72 (excl. 1949)*

General election	Mean plurality†	Election pair	Mean vote shift††	Seats changing party hands‡
1925	18.2	1925–6	7.3	17.8
1926	20.1	1926–30	8.9	30.7
1930	14.2			
1935	17.7	1935–40	9.7	23.9
1940	18.4	1940–45	11.8	30.0
1945	15.2			
1953	19.8	1953–7	9.7	30.0
1957	18.1	1957–8	10.7	37.6
1958	20.3	1958–62	14.4	38.8
1962	14.2	1962–3	5.0	16.3
1963	16.5	1963–5	5.6	18.3
1965	17.4			
1968	16.8	1968–72	7.8	23.9
1972	18.3			

*For the sake of simplicity, standard deviations have been excluded from the table. Like the mean, this measure reveals no trend.

†Mean vote percentage separating winning candidates and runners-up.

††Change in percentage of vote given to the party winning a given constituency in the first of two successive elections, averaged for all constituencies (ignoring sign).

‡Changes in winning party divided by the opportunities for change (number of seats).

Sources: for the general elections of 1925 to 1958, Scarrow, *Canada Votes*. For the general elections of 1962 to 1968, Canada, *Report of the Chief Electoral Officer*, supplemented for the election of 1962 by the party affiliations of candidates as reported in the *Canadian Parliamentary Guide*. For the general election of 1972, Canada, Twenty-ninth General Election, 1972, *Extracts of Part I and Part IV of the Report of the Chief Electoral Officer* (published in advance of the detailed Report of the General Election held on October 30, 1972 ...), December 1972.

constituencies, not the urban ones, that provide most of the electoral excitement (Table VIII). Although it is true that in the rest of Canada urban constituencies do in fact tend to be more competitive than rural ones, the absence of a systematic relationship between the two variables across the country shows again that other factors have to be taken into the proposition.

A partial explanation of the lack of any well-defined relationship between urbanization and electoral competition has been supplied by the large national election surveys directed by John Meisel in 1965 and 1968. Neither survey revealed any major differences in strength of party identification between voters of urban and rural background and residence, or in the proportions among them (close to 50 per cent in both surveys) who claimed to have voted for more than one federal party in the past.[53]

[53]I am grateful to Professor Meisel for letting me see these results of his work. The findings cited were drawn from cross-tabulating variable 271 ("Where grew up") with variables 183 ("Strength of identification") and 214 ("Party vote consistency-federal") of the 1965 survey (N=2721), and variables 002 ("Community size") and 362 ("During schooling where did you live") with variables 123 ("Degree of strength felt to chosen party") and 174 ("What federal party have you always voted for") of the 1968 survey (N=2767).

TABLE VII

ELECTORAL COMPETITIVENESS OF FEDERAL CONSTITUENCIES: BY PROVINCE, 1925–65

	Sets of three elections				Six elections	Sets of three elections				Six elections
Index of safety	1925–6–30	1935–40–5	1953–7–8	1962–3–5	1953–65	1925–6–30	1935–40–5	1953–7–8	1962–3–5	1953–65
			(Percentage of total)					(Percentage of total)		
Newfoundland						*Prince Edward Island**				
To 4.9			14.3	14.3	28.6	66.7	—	100.0	66.7	66.7
5–14.9			14.3	14.3	—	33.3	100.0	—	33.3	33.3
15.0+			71.4	71.4	71.4	—	—	—	—	—
Total			100.0	100.0	100.0	100.0	100.0	100.0	100.0	100.0
Mean index			30.8	30.4	29.6	5.0	8.5	2.8	3.7	2.3
N	—	—	7	7	7	3	3	3	3	3
New Brunswick						*Quebec*				
To 4.9	30.0	50.0	30.0	10.0	30.0	30.8	29.2	42.7	49.3	53.3
5–14.9	40.0	10.0	60.0	60.0	40.0	24.6	27.7	38.7	18.7	33.4
15.0+	30.0	40.0	10.0	30.0	30.0	44.6	43.1	18.6	32.0	13.3
Total	100.0	100.0	100.0	100.0	100.0	100.0	100.0	100.0	100.0	100.0
Mean index	11.1	14.8	8.4	13.4	9.8	16.5	14.7	9.4	9.9	7.3
N	10	10	10	10	10	65	65	75	75	75
*Nova Scotia**						*Ontario*				
To 4.9	30.8	45.5	90.9	54.5	63.6	42.0	53.7	30.6	35.3	37.7
5–14.9	53.8	18.1	9.1	45.5	36.4	29.6	30.5	35.3	38.8	47.0
15.0+	15.4	36.4	—	—	—	28.4	15.8	34.1	25.9	15.3
Total	100.0	100.0	100.0	100.0	100.0	100.0	100.0	100.0	100.0	100.0
Mean index	7.1	10.2	3.7	4.6	3.3	12.4	7.2	12.2	10.0	8.3
N	13	11	11	11	11	81	82	85	85	85

TABLE VII (*continued*)

Index of safety	Sets of three elections 1925–6–30	1935–40–5	1953–7–8	1962–3–5	Six elections 1953–65	Sets of three elections 1925–6–30	1935–40–5	1953–7–8	1962–3–5	Six elections 1953–65
	(Percentage of total)					(Percentage of total)				
Manitoba						*Saskatchewan*				
To 4.9	76.5	58.8	35.7	21.4	42.9	47.6	76.2	70.6	5.9	11.8
5–14.9	11.8	35.3	50.0	35.7	50.0	47.6	14.3	23.5	23.5	82.3
15.0+	11.8	5.9	21.3	42.9	7.1	4.8	9.5	5.9	70.6	5.9
Total	100.1	100.0	100.0	100.0	100.0	100.0	100.0	100.0	100.0	100.0
Mean Index	3.5	5.0	8.1	13.0	8.3	6.4	4.3	4.5	21.9	11.5
N	17	17	14	14	14	21	21	17	17	17
Alberta						*British Columbia*				
To 4.9	47.1	100.0	42.1	15.8	36.8	57.2	75.0	50.0	40.9	50.0
5–14.9	23.5	—	47.4	47.4	57.9	14.3	12.5	31.8	31.8	40.9
15.0+	29.4	—	10.5	36.8	5.3	28.5	12.5	18.2	27.3	9.1
Total	100.0	100.0	100.0	100.0	100.0	100.0	100.0	100.0	100.0	100.0
Mean index	12.1	0.9	6.9	13.7	8.1	8.4	4.7	8.5	10.7	6.3
N	17	18	19	19	19	14	16	22	22	22

*Two-member constituencies are treated as single-member constituencies by summing the votes won by each party's candidate.
Sources: see Table VI.

TABLE VIII

COMPETITIVENESS OF URBAN AND RURAL CONSTITUENCIES IN CANADA*

Index of safety	Rural	Semi-rural	Semi-urban	Urban	*N*
		(Percentage of column total)			
Canada					
To 4.9	42.7	50.0	48.4	36.3	112
5.0–9.9	20.5	21.0	32.3	32.5	67
10.0–14.9	23.9	7.9	12.9	16.9	48
15.0+	12.8	21.1	6.4	14.3	36
Total	100.0	100.0	100.0	100.0	
N	117	38	31	77	263
Quebec					
To 4.9	83.3	54.5	50.0	21.4	40
5.0–9.9	6.7	27.3	33.3	25.0	14
10.0–14.9	6.7	9.1	17.7	25.0	11
15.0+	3.3	9.1	—	28.6	10
Total	100.0	100.0	100.0	100.0	
N	30	11	6	28	75
Canada without Quebec					
To 4.9	28.7	48.2	48.0	44.9	71
5.0–9.9	25.3	18.5	32.0	36.7	54
10.0–14.9	29.9	7.4	12.0	12.2	37
15.0+	16.1	25.9	18.0	6.1	26
Total	100.0	100.0	100.0	99.9	
N	87	27	25	49	188

*For the rural-urban part of this analysis, constituencies were classified according to the percentage of their population living in cities or towns with a population of 10,000 or over. "Rural," "semi-rural," "semi-urban," and "urban" constituencies are those for which this percentage fell in the ranges of 0–24.9, 25–49.9, 50–74.9, and 75–100 respectively. Source: Canada, Dominion Bureau of Statistics, *1961 Census of Canada*, Bull. 1.1-1. Electoral competitiveness was measured for the set of six general elections, 1953 to 1965. Cf. Table IV.

Given the structure of the index of safety, a relatively low index score is likely to be associated with a relatively high rate of turnover in legislative membership.[54] Table IX bears out this expectation. In most of the election pairs for which turnover could conveniently be measured, turnover was not only high (by British and American standards) but electoral defeat was often its most common cause. Combined, all causes of turnover have ensured that after most elections around two-fifths of the members of the House of Commons have been newcomers. Broken down regionally, turnover has often been even more pervasive: displacement of close to half and more of a region's MPs has not been rare.

The impact which this high rate of turnover has had on the legislative experience of MPs may be gauged from Table X. At the start of 7 of the 14 Parliaments constituted by the elections shown, well over half of the members had been in the

[54]Because turnover is only one of the three components making up the index, and because involuntary retirement through electoral defeat is only one of the causes of turnover, the relationship is obviously neither necessary nor likely to be very close. Moreover, its reverse would probably often fail to hold true: in practice, a high rate of turnover has frequently coincided with relatively *uncompetitive* conditions. T.A. Dye, "State Legislative Politics," in *Politics in the American States*, ed. Herbert Jacob and Kenneth Vines, 151–206, at 170; J. Blondel, *Voters, Parties, and Leaders* (Baltimore, 1963), 153–8. Also Schlesinger, *Ambition and Politics*, 60–3.

TABLE IX

ELECTORAL DEFEAT AS A FACTOR IN TURNOVER IN MEMBERSHIP OF THE HOUSE OF COMMONS: SELECTED YEARS, 1925–72*

	Percentage of members elected in first election of election pair					
Election pair	Defeated	Retired for other reasons	Total turnover	Defeated	Retired for other reasons	Total turnover
		Canada			*Maritimes*	
1925–6	13.5	6.1	19.6	17.2	10.3	27.5
1926–30	22.4	18.4	40.8	10.3	24.1	34.4
1935–40	12.2	27.4	39.6	11.5	46.2	57.7
1940–5	15.5	29.0	44.5	11.5	26.9	38.4
1953–7	24.9	16.2	41.1	45.5	3.0	48.5
1957–8	31.3	9.8	41.1	12.1	9.1	21.2
1958–62	33.2	11.7	44.9	18.2	15.1	33.3
1962–3	13.6	7.2	20.8	12.1	9.1	21.2
1963–5	11.7	12.1	23.8	12.1	9.1	21.2
1968–72	16.7	23.1	39.8	3.1	18.7	21.8
		Quebec			*Ontario*	
1925–6	—	4.6	4.6	19.5	6.1	25.6
1926–30	23.1	24.6	47.7	12.2	19.5	31.7
1935–40	9.2	33.8	43.0	11.0	20.7	31.7
1940–5	7.7	33.8	41.5	15.9	28.0	43.9
1953–7	16.0	18.7	34.7	25.9	22.4	48.3
1957–8	44.0	17.3	61.3	5.9	7.1	13.0
1958–62	48.0	13.3	61.3	34.1	14.1	48.2
1962–3	21.3	6.7	28.0	12.9	7.1	20.0
1963–5	18.7	16.0	34.7	10.6	14.1	24.7
1968–72	6.8	21.6	28.4	21.6	25.0	46.6
		Prairies			*BC*	
1925–6	20.0	5.5	25.5	7.1	7.1	14.2
1926–30	40.0	5.5	45.5	35.7	21.4	57.1
1935–40	17.9	25.0	42.9	12.5	12.5	25.0
1940–5	23.2	25.0	48.2	25.0	31.2	56.2
1953–7	22.0	14.0	36.0	27.3	9.1	36.4
1957–8	62.0	6.0	68.0	45.5	4.5	50.0
1958–62	10.0	6.0	16.0	54.5	4.5	59.0
1962–3	6.0	4.0	10.0	9.1	13.6	22.7
1963–5	8.0	4.0	12.0	—	13.6	13.6
1968–72	23.4	25.5	48.9	34.8	21.7	56.5

*No information is given for the election pairs of 1930–5, 1945–9, 1949–53, and 1965–8 because the data gathered for this study were restricted to election pairs governed by the same redistribution act.

SOURCES: see Table VI.

House for less than four years. A more precise idea of the inexperience of these same 14 Parliaments may be had by looking at their initial *median* years of consecutive prior service: it has often amounted to three years or less.[55]

What significance has the level of competition?

To assess the significance of these findings, we plainly need more knowledge than we now have. As has been noted already,[56] deep obscurity still surrounds the

[55]Cf. David Hoffman and Norman Ward, *Bilingualism and Biculturalism in the Canadian House of Commons* (Ottawa, 1970), 27. By comparison, the average parliamentary experience of British MPs at the start of each Parliament was reported in 1963 to be *eight* years. Blondel, *Voters, Parties, and Leaders*, 155–6.

[56]See above, pp. 342–350.

TABLE X

LEGISLATIVE EXPERIENCE OF CANADIAN MPS, 1925–68

General election	Years of previous consecutive service as MP: 0–3	4–7	8–11	12–15	16+	Total	Median (years)	Mean (years)	Total House membership
	(Percentage of all MPS)								
1925	55.1	24.9	11.8	3.3	4.9	100.0	2	3.6	245
1926	58.0	26.1	10.2	2.4	3.3	100.0	1	3.7	245
1930	40.4	35.9	16.3	4.5	2.9	100.0	5	4.5	245
1935	63.7	11.0	15.1	6.5	3.7	100.0	0	3.8	245
1940	37.6	41.6	9.0	6.5	5.3	100.0	5	5.1	245
1945	43.7	24.1	22.8	3.7	5.7	100.0	5	5.3	245
1953	37.3	25.7	15.9	10.2	10.9	100.0	4	5.9	265
1957	41.1	26.4	12.1	8.7	11.7	100.0	4	5.8	265
1958	70.2	13.6	6.4	5.3	4.5	100.0	1	3.7	265
1962	44.9	34.7	10.2	4.9	5.3	100.0	4	4.3	265
1963	57.0	27.9	7.2	4.1	3.8	100.0	1	4.0	265
1965	65.3	13.6	10.9	6.4	3.8	100.0	3	4.6	265
1968	56.8	26.1	12.9	1.9	2.3	100.0	3	4.1	264
1972	40.1	34.8	15.2	8.0	1.9	100.0	4	4.8	264

Sources: for the general elections of 1925 to 1968, the *Canadian Parliamentary Guide*. For the general election of 1972, see Table VI.

implications of electoral competition for the content and continuity of public policy, for political innovation, for the number of parties, and for the recruitment[57] and autonomy of politicians. Furthermore, we know almost nothing about the significance of rapid turnover for the expertise of MP s, or about the impact of competitive pressure upon their choice of roles. Is it true, as is sometimes suggested, that it takes three or four years on the average before the novice legislator begins to reach his full effectiveness? If so, then in the past about half the House has often been unable to work at potential capacity. Is it true, as it appears to be among American legislators, that politically insecure MPs take a very different approach to public policy than their more secure colleagues, investing relatively little effort in becoming informed on national issues and responding to most problems in parochial rather than national terms?[58] If so, then the present high level of electoral competition may have undercut Parliament's performance as a critic of public policy and administration, and have emphasized its role as a forum for local demands and grievances.

To make at least a little headway in coping with this mass of unknowns, I interviewed a sample of MPs to probe their perceptions of the competitiveness of their own constituency and of Canadian politics generally, and of the bearing which the competitiveness of a constituency or group of constituencies might have on the attention that is paid to its political demands.[59]

[57]It is interesting to note that Canada stands midway between Britain and the United States in the proportion of lawyers in its national legislature. Of Kornberg's sample of the 25th Parliament of Canada, 33 per cent were lawyers, while Ward found exactly the same percentage in 1931. Allan Kornberg, *Canadian Legislative Behavior* (Toronto, 1967), 43; Norman Ward, *The Canadian House of Commons: Representation* (Toronto, 1950), 135. The comparable British and American figures are about 20 and 60 per cent respectively. *The Times House of Commons, 1966* (London, The Times, n.d.), 242; David Butler and Anthony King, *The British General Election of 1966* (London, 1966), 208–9; David Butler and Michael Pinto-Duschinsky, *The British General Election of 1970* (London, 1971), 302; Donald Matthews, *The Social Background of Political Decision-makers* (Garden City, 1954), 30 (US data for 1949–51); Roger H. Davidson, *The Role of the Congressman* (New York, 1969), 37 (based on a sample of 87 Congressmen of the 88th Congress, 1962–4). On the face of it, this finding suggests that the link between the level of electoral competition and the occupational make-up of the legislature is rather weak. It may be, however, that closer inspection of each legislature may nonetheless show a certain association between these two variables.

[58]In the early sixties, Kornberg found constituency competitiveness as perceived by MPs to be totally unrelated to their "legislative goals" and "representational focus," and to be only tenuously related to their "representational style." Substituting constituency competitiveness as measured by Kornberg produced no associations whatever. *Canadian Legislative Behavior*, 92–3, 109, 111. For American data on this point, see Davidson, *Role of the Congressman*, 126–33, and J.C. Wahlke *et al.*, *The Legislative System* (New York, 1962), 291–4.

[59]The report that follows is based on open-ended interviews with 90 MPs (frontbench and backbench), out of a sample of 120, stratified by region and party and chosen at random except for minor modifications to ensure that very small minorities (like Quebec Conservative MPs) would be represented. The regional and party composition of the MPs actually interviewed closely resembled that of the sample (and of the House) as a whole.

Of the 90 MPs interviewed 10 were frontbenchers, of whom 7 were currently in the cabinet while the other 3 were former ministers. To supplement the resulting information on frontbench perceptions and attitudes, interviews were also arranged with 5 other frontbenchers to whom the writer happened to have some access. As a result, 95 MPs were actually interviewed.

All interviews were conducted in June and July, 1969, with the very able assistance of John Dingwall, then a graduate student at Yale University, and of André Carrier, then a graduate student at the University of Ottawa.

The most interesting result of this survey was that the vast majority of MPs seemed to have given previous thought only to the first question, about the competitiveness of their own constituency. The other questions clearly took many by surprise, and accordingly evoked responses that typically seemed rather off the cuff. There was, first of all, little knowledge or agreement about the extent and pattern of electoral competition across the country as a whole. About a third of the MPs interviewed said blithely that in Canada "there is no such thing" as a "safe" seat. Others disagreed, often pointing to various seats in Montreal, the Maritimes, rural Ontario, and elsewhere as examples, but about the total number and regional distribution of such seats most of these MPs had no or only the haziest of notions. By the same token, almost all seemed taken by surprise when asked whether the competitiveness of a constituency had any bearing on its MP's freedom of action in the House or in committee. The more thoughtful responses contradicted one another, some members suggesting that a "member in a very competitive constituency is subject to pressures bordering almost on blackmail" (as one of them put it), while a few others believed that very competitive seats were generally more diverse in social composition and thus more likely to leave their MP freer to do as he thought best. The vast majority of MPs had evidently not considered the question before, and their answers (about equally divided between "I don't know," "it makes no difference," and "safe seats leave you freer") therefore amounted to no more than snap judgments.

Much the same thing may be said about their responses when asked whether they thought their party leader was "more sensitive to the needs and wants of those areas where your party has the greatest chance of gaining and losing seats in the next general election?" What sets these answers apart is their remarkable unanimity. Almost to a man, the MPs who were interviewed denied that any such policy strategy was being followed. More significantly, an overwhelming majority rejected a strategy of that kind as dangerous to national unity, as a betrayal of the party's responsibility to serve the country as a whole, as unfair to the party's most faithful supporters, and as bound in the long run to alienate the electorate. As one MP put it: policies should "be based on need, not electoral advantage," contrary to what he saw as typical of the "old politics." In another's formula, parties should "do what is good for the country, and let the chips fall where they may."

Nine Liberal ministers confirmed that in their view this non-electorally oriented approach was indeed the one generally characteristic of the first Trudeau government. In explanation, several described the alternative as too nationally divisive. Others saw the alternative as too difficult to administer: the variables involved were too numerous and the party too "disorganized and disjointed." It would require "real professionalism" to administer a seat-maximizing policy, far more than the widespread "bungling and amateurism" in the party would permit.

This last interpretation was also advanced, quite independently, by four formerly prominent politicians now outside Parliament. One considered the policies of the Trudeau government as devoid of any rational political calculus, but considered that in that respect it was quite typical of all governments. In his view, it was normal for politicians to "behave capriciously" and to ignore "any decent political arithmetic." Outsiders always made the mistake of attributing politicians with far too much intelligence and "malevolence." The other three respondents saw the phenomenon in less general terms, and more as the product of an unusually large contingent of rank "political amateurs" in the first Trudeau cabinet – people who might be described most simply as less interested in what is wanted or not wanted and more interested in doing what they themselves think is needed.[60]

The general thrust of these interview findings on how electoral competition was actually perceived by members of Parliament seems quite clear. The findings do *not* demonstrate that the level of electoral competition is of no significance for the political responsiveness of governments and opposition parties. It remains to be disproved that a government heavily dependent on marginal seats for its hold on office will not typically be more eager to please than one not so tenuously situated, and that it does not take at least three successive election victories before this superior responsiveness gives way (despite continued heavy dependence on marginal seats) to a delusion of indispensability and the arrogance that goes with it. What does emerge is that among MPs elected in 1968 the electoral margin did not command the forefront of attention, and was generally considered unimportant, unworkable, and illegitimate as a major criterion in allocating political benefits.

If this is so, the reader may remark, then doubts may also be in order about the reported significance of the electoral margin for the conduct of election campaigns. Is it actually true, as many laymen believe, that campaign organizers spend long hours in exhaustive analysis of their party's chances of victory in each constituency, and that the allocation of campaign resources is thereafter closely linked to the resulting priority ratings? Or is the process actually much less rational and the significance of electoral competition correspondingly less?

To answer this last question eight men who had served as national party organizers or campaign directors for the two largest parties were interviewed. These discussions revealed that both parties indeed attempt to rank constituencies in terms of their "winability." Neither party bases this rating solely on a seat's electoral history; each also takes account of the estimated relative appeal of the party's candidate, the condition of the local organization, and of any other relevant information that may be available (for example, data on shifts in the socio-economic make-up of the local population). All respondents also agreed in assigning considerable importance to the quality of the local candidate, potentially enough (especially in rural areas) to shift a constituency one category from the rating it would have received on the basis of all other criteria (for example, from "swing" to "safe," or from "hopeless" to "swing," but not from "hopeless to safe").

The consensus ended, however, when it came to the weight to be attached to past election results. Among the Liberals, the volatility of the Canadian electorate was seen as much less than might have been supposed. They thought that as a rule (rural Quebec being one of the exceptions) a plurality of 10 per cent in the

[60]Cf. James Q. Wilson, *The Amateur Democrat* (Toronto, 1966) for a description and analysis of this orientation to politics in the American context; also John P. Roche and Stephen Sachs, "The Bureaucrat and the Enthusiast," in *Policy-Making in Britain*, ed. Richard Rose (Toronto, 1969), 81–96. Cf. also the late V.O. Key's judgment: "The prediction of public reaction to new courses of action is so primitive an art that thoughtful politicians remark that the only course to follow is to take the action that seems right, on the assumption that it will be defensible at the next election." *Politics, Parties, and Pressure Groups*, 544, n.28.

previous election afforded an MP reasonable security. In their "winability" ratings, the immediate electoral past therefore weighed relatively heavy. The Conservatives took the opposite view. In their opinion, population movements in the four years normally separating general elections were sufficient in Canada that all but the most lopsided past results had to be considered reversible. In devising their campaign strategy, they have therefore tended to downplay election statistics as "only one consideration" among many, preferring to rely more heavily on "intuition" and "educated guesses."

A possible explanation for this intriguing conflict in the way the parties read reality may be drawn from Table XI. Considering all six election pairs together, one might advance as a reasonable hypothesis that the volatility of support for the two major parties is probably about the same: in both cases, nearly 50 per cent of seats lost over this period had previously been won by pluralities of 10 per cent or more. But among the Liberals the memory of such traumatic defeats has had longer to dim. On the short-run record, looking back to 1962, it is easier for Liberals than for Conservatives to persuade themselves that a 10 per cent plurality really offers reasonable security.

The practical importance of these party differences in strategic thought obviously depends in part on the extent to which the subsequent allocation of campaign appeals and resources is actually governed by the conclusions of the analysis. In reality, this linkage was reported to be quite loose in both major parties. Demands for special treatment by leading figures in the party, a desire to gain support in certain sections of the country, to demonstrate "national" status, and to preserve party unity, these and a score of other pressures apparently cause election campaigns to deviate rather widely from the dictates of seat-maximization. The best illustration of this point may be the well-known fact that the Conservative party has long distributed the bulk of its national campaign funds among its provincial branches on a simple per-seat basis. Campaigns, as one party director frankly observed, are "not that scientific."

Conclusion

This paper has had two broad concerns. One of these has been to assess how much we already know about the consequences and correlates of variations in electoral competition, and to judge how satisfactorily such variations in competition have been measured. This concern led to the conclusion that the significance of electoral competition remains substantially unknown, and that there is no reason to expect, much of the existing literature notwithstanding, that urbanization and industrialization typically produce a secular rise in electoral competition. In the upshot, two new hypotheses were suggested. In addition, the first part of the paper produced an approach to measuring electoral competition that seemed more plausible than the approaches used so far.

The paper's second concern was to measure the level of electoral competition in Canadian federal constituencies and to make at least a small start in examining its consequences and correlates. Among other things, it was shown that Canadian politics is indeed extraordinarily competitive (safe seats being far fewer than in

TABLE XI

MARGINS OF VICTORY RELATED TO SEAT LOSSES IN THE NEXT ELECTION: SIX ELECTION PAIRS, 1953–72

Plurality in first election%	Seats changing party hands in second election (percentage of total)							Seats changing party hands in second election (percentage of total)						
	1953–7	1957–8	1958–62	1962–3	1963–5	1968–72	Over-all	1953–7	1957–8	1958–62	1962–3	1963–5	1968–72	Over-all
	All parties							*Liberal party*						
0–9.9	50.6	45.5	43.1	79.1	70.8	65.1	54.8	50.0	45.8	88.9	100.0	86.7	60.8	57.1
10–19.9	31.7	28.3	27.4	16.3	16.8	22.2	25.3	32.9	23.7	11.1	—	—	25.5	24.3
20–29.9	6.3	17.2	14.7	4.6	8.3	11.1	11.5	5.7	17.0	—	—	13.3	11.8	10.5
30+	11.4	9.1	14.7	—	4.2	1.6	8.3	11.4	13.5	—	—	—	2.0	8.1
Total	100.0	100.1	99.9	100.0	100.1	100.0	99.9	100.0	100.0	100.0	100.0	100.0	100.0	100.0
N	79	99	102	43	48	63	434	70	59	9	6	15	51	210
Per cent	30.0	37.6	38.8	16.3	18.3	23.9	27.5	41.1	56.2	18.3	6.1	11.7	32.5	29.7
	Progressive Conservative party							*CCF-NDP*						
0–9.9	100.0	—	39.1	88.5	66.7	85.7	53.6	50.0	58.9	—	100.0	100.0	100.0	65.5
10–19.9	—	—	28.3	11.5	25.0	14.3	23.9	25.0	29.4	100.0	—	—	—	24.1
20–29.9	—	—	16.3	—	8.3	—	11.6	25.0	5.9	—	—	—	—	6.9
30+	—	—	16.3	—	—	—	10.9	—	5.9	—	—	—	—	3.4
Total	100.0	—	100.0	100.0	100.0	100.0	100.0	100.0	100.1	100.0	100.0	100.0	100.0	99.9
N	1	0	92	26	12	7	138	4	17	1	3	1	3	29
Per cent	2.0	—	44.6	22.6	12.8	9.7	21.4	17.4	68.0	12.5	15.8	5.9	13.6	25.4

Source: see Table VI.

Britain and the United States), that there are no major regional differences in electoral competitiveness, that there has been no trend over the past fifty-odd years towards increased electoral competition, and (as hypothesized in the first section of the paper) that urbanization *taken by itself* is totally unrelated to the degree of electoral competition. As far as the significance of these findings is concerned, it follows from the primitive state of our present knowledge in this field that not much of importance can be said with assurance. Almost all of the necessary research remains to be done, exploring the impact of electoral competition on such variables as legislators' recruitment, role perceptions and technical expertise. Only its bearings on party policy-making was here explored in a preliminary way.

This last set of findings needs to be considered a little more deeply. For this purpose, the data may be divided into two categories: (1) those relating to the *level* of electoral competition in Canada – as reflected in the proportion of seats where one or more of the out-parties can be optimistic about displacing the in-party at the next election; and (2) those having to do with the *pattern* of electoral competition – as represented by the regional or subregional distribution of such seats.

With respect to the *pattern* of competition, the survey data suggested that in the twenty-eighth Parliament its significance for party policy was small. In other words, very few MPs saw it as legitimate for parties to tailor their policies to favour those regions, areas, or types of constituency where their potential for seat gains and losses was greatest, and thus to assign second priority to meeting the needs of areas classifiable as electorally safe or hopeless. Consistent with this attitude, frontbenchers and backbenchers of all parties typically showed themselves only vaguely informed about the pattern of competition across the country.

This finding raises a flock of interesting questions for further inquiry. Such research should probably begin by pushing beyond the present analysis to establish how the chances of seat gains and losses have varied across the country *for each party*. Presumably, parties can pursue the seat-maximizing strategy described in the previous paragraph only if significant variance in these prospects of gains and losses actually exists, be it by region, province, or type of constituency. If it turns out (as seems likely for all parties except possibly the Liberals) that this partisan potential for seat gains and losses across the country has typically differed a good deal, then the obvious follow-up step would be to examine party policies themselves, to find out whether their implicit distribution of benefits is in fact unrelated to the party's pattern of competition.[61] Assuming, finally, that this research would corroborate the results of the parliamentary interviews conducted for this study, there would be a new reason to dig much deeper into party policy-making to discover by what other distributive criteria, *if any*, it is consistently informed.

The probability that the results of future research will fit this scenario seems to me quite high, for three reasons. One is that a seat-maximizing strategy would in many cases create intolerable intra-party conflict. It is improbable, after all, that the representatives from a party's most faithful constituencies would for long

[61]For a brief discussion of the problems of measuring and explaining regional favouritism in party policies, see my "On Analysing the Impact of the Electoral System on the Party System in Canada," this JOURNAL, 3 (1970), 497–516, at 499–506.

accept a strategy that would be systematically prejudicial to the interests of their supporters, or that many Canadian party leaders would have the power to oblige them to do so.[62] A second obstacle to such a strategy inheres in the very nature of many contemporary policy problems. These tend increasingly to call for relatively general and wide-ranging solutions (policies that Lowi has called "regulatory" and "redistributive"),[63] which lend themselves less readily than the more *ad hoc* and "distributive" solutions typical of the past to the discriminatory targeting of benefits implied by a seat-maximizing strategy. If so, then the scope for such a strategy should be diminishing with time. A final reason for doubting that the pattern of competition has much bearing on contemporary party policies in Canada is the apparent refusal of Canadian politicians to accept it as a guide even in their campaign appeals. One does not normally see the leader of the Progressive Conservative party systematically ignoring Quebec, or the leader of the New Democratic party concentrating exclusively on Ontario and Western Canada, or the leader of the Ralliement des Créditistes confining his appeals to French Canada. To the contrary, Gordon Churchill's view that the Progressive Conservative party should not "reinforce" past failures by making a major campaign appeal in Quebec[64] appears to stand out as the exception among the electoral strategies chosen by leading Canadian politicians. On these three grounds, and barring a radical deepening of existing political cleavages, I would expect that the pattern of competition has a very limited and declining significance for party policy in Canada.

With respect to the *level* of party competition, little insight into its significance for political responsiveness emerges from the evidence gathered for this article. The remaining discussion will therefore be restricted to a refinement of the hypothesis, proposed on p. 346, that the relationship between these two variables (if any) is likely to be reciprocal and marked by significant time lags.

Plainly, one defect of this earlier statement of the hypothesis is that it does not define the level of competition clearly enough. In referring only to the proportion of seats classifiable as safe, competitive, or marginal, our subsequent discussion left out the important *partisan* dimension of this distribution. For any given breakdown of safe, competitive, and marginal seats, the share of each type of constituency held by each party can obviously differ widely, resulting in radically different competitive conditions. Seen in this light, Canadian politics might have been growing much more (or less) competitive even though the proportion of marginal seats has remained substantially unchanged. Superficial inspection of the election results does not suggest that either of these eventualities has arisen, but none the less the point is worth making.

Questions may also be raised about the notion, implicit in the hypothesis as stated, that the relationship between a party's dependence on marginal seats for its hold on power and its political responsiveness might be linear in nature. For

[62]Such conflict is likely to be avoided only in cases where the distribution of a party's safe and competitive seats closely resembles the distribution of its marginal seats won and lost, when pursuit of a seat-maximizing strategy would not be prejudicial to the interests of the party's less competitive constituencies.
[63]See Theodore Lowi, "American Business, Public Policies, Case Studies and Political Theory," *World Politics*, 16 (1964), 677–715.
[64]See John Meisel, *The Canadian General Election of 1957* (Toronto, 1962), 166–8.

this to be true, it would need to matter greatly to a governing party's sense of security in office whether its caucus of (say) 150 members counted among them 50, 75, or 100 marginal constituencies. This is plainly unlikely, or else one would be required to believe that almost any British government has felt more secure, and has been less politically responsive, than almost any Canadian government. It seems plausible, rather, that the relationships between the proportion of marginal seats in a party's caucus, its sense of political insecurity, and its political responsiveness will prove to be extremely loose, and marked by major lags and sudden shifts. This seems all the more likely when one considers that in shaping the behaviour of an MP the competitiveness of his constituency is undoubtedly only one factor among many.

These two refinements to our hypothesis point to an interesting and unusual conclusion. Assuming that the hypothesis stands up to empirical testing, they suggest that a substantial increase in the number of safe seats in Canada, distributed widely among all parties, would not necessarily reduce the political responsiveness of our governors. In fact, the consequences might be the exact opposite: by reducing the turnover among MPs and raising their average political experience, such a change might do wonders for the effectiveness of Parliament as policy critic and administrative overseer, two functions it now performs least well. It is conceivable, therefore, that the high value traditionally placed on close competition will need revision: here, as elsewhere, one can have too much of a good thing.

Appendix

As was noted above, there are many ways in which the three components of the index of safety could be measured and combined. Some of these options have predictable implications for the plausibility of the measure, others do not. In this appendix, I shall briefly explain my reasons for choosing the present format.

MEASURING VOTE VARIABILITY OR SHIFTS

There appear to be two reasonable ways of doing this calculation. Method 1 (that used in the present index) relies on the vote percentages in two successive elections of the party winning the *first* of those two elections. Method 2 bases itself on the two vote percentages of the party winning the *second* election. Where only two parties exist, these two methods will clearly produce identical results. Where there are more than two parties, the results could potentially be very different, depending on the length of the election series to which the analysis is applied, on the frequency and timing within that series of major electoral realignments, and on the incidence and timing of "flash" third parties. Given that Method 1 tends to be more sensitive to electoral losses than gains, while the opposite is true of Method 2, the pattern of major electoral changes in a short series of elections could cause the two methods to give very different pictures of the variability of the vote. These possibilities are illustrated hypothetically in Table XII.

In reality (actual Canadian federal election results from 1925 to 1965), such large gaps did not materialize very often. The differences in vote variability produced by the two methods actually exceeded five percentage points only 9.5 per cent of the time.

TABLE XII

Election	Party	Vote percentage Seat 1	Seat 2	Seat 3	Seat 4	Seat 5
1	A	*60	*60	*60	*60	40
	B	30	30	30	30	10
	C	10	10	10	10	*50
2	A	20	40	*60	40	*60
	B	*45	10	30	10	30
	C	35	*50	10	*50	10
3	A	40	20	40	*60	*60
	B	10	*45	10	30	30
	C	*50	35	*50	10	10
Sum of shifts:						
Method 1		75	35	20	60	40
Method 2		30	75	40	60	20

TABLE XIII

Seat	Σ Pluralities (1)	Σ Shifts (2)	Method 1 $\left[\frac{(1)-(2)}{N^*}\right]$	Method 2 $\left[\frac{(1)}{N} - \frac{(2)}{N-1}\right]$	Method 3 $\left[\frac{(1)}{(2)}\right]$
1	20	5	5.0	4.2	4.0
2	25	10	5.0	3.3	2.5
3	30	15	5.0	2.5	2.0
4	35	20	5.0	1.7	1.7
5	40	25	5.0	0.8	1.6
6	45	30	5.0	0	1.5
7	50	35	5.0	−0.8	1.4
8	55	40	5.0	−1.7	1.4

*Number of elections in set being examined.

Despite this similarity in the outcomes of the two methods in the Canadian context, a choice between them had to be made. Accordingly, Method 1 was chosen on the rationale that past in-party losses (an indication of potential voter infidelity to incumbents) are likely to be more salient to the current in-party's sense of security than its own gains.

ADJUSTING WINNING PARTY PLURALITIES FOR VOTE VARIABILITY

There appear to be three main ways of performing this operation. These are:

(1) (Σ pluralities − Σ shifts)/number of elections;

(2) (Σ pluralities/number of elections) − (Σ shifts/number of shifts); and,

(3) (Σ pluralities/Σ shifts).

The properties of these three approaches can be observed from the hypothetical examples in Table XIII, which assume a set of three elections and no turnover in winning party. These examples show that the three approaches respond very differently to a parallel expansion of pluralities and shifts. Method 1 records these

TABLE XIV

Election	Party	Vote percentage Seat 1	Seat 2	Seat 3
1	A	*60	*60	*60
	B	40	40	40
2	A	*51	49	49
	B	49	*51	*51
3	A	*60	40	*60
	B	40	*60	40
(*a*) Σ Pluralities		42	42	42
(*b*) Σ Shifts		18	20	22
(*c*) Turnover score		1.0 (no change)	0.5 (one change)	0 (two changes)
Index score $\left[\frac{(a) - (b) \times (c)}{3}\right]$		8.0	3.7	0

situations as representing identical levels of electoral competitiveness. In contrast, both Methods 2 and 3 would depict the same phenomenon as a rapid movement toward increasing competitiveness. Because the latter interpretation appears less plausible than that provided by Method 1, Method 1 was selected.

WEIGHTING OF THE COMPONENT VARIABLES

It may plausibly be argued that the three components included in the index of safety should not be treated as being equally salient to the level of electoral competition. In particular, it may be said that in any measure that purports to compare constituencies in terms of the relative probability of their changing party hands in the next election preponderant attention should be given to the frequency with which they have done so in the past.

The plausibility of this argument is recognized in the index of safety, which does in practice assign a disproportionately heavy weight to the turnover variable. Thus, any seat that has changed party hands at every occasion is assigned an index score of zero (signifying maximum competitiveness) no matter how large its adjusted winning party pluralities may be. And even minor differences in vote variability, provided they bring about one or more changes in winning party, are reflected in major differences in the index of safety. These properties of the measure may be illustrated by the hypothetical examples shown in Table XIV. As with all other aspects of the index, the appropriateness of this particular weighting of the turnover variable is a matter of judgment.

La régionalisation électorale et l'amplification des proportions

DAVID SANKOFF *Université de Montréal*
KOULA MELLOS *Université d'Ottawa*

Le rapport entre la proportion des voix obtenues et la proportion des sièges législatifs remportés est une caractéristique importante de tout système électoral; dans le cas du scrutin uninominal à un tour, ce rapport a été l'objet de plusieurs études. D'une part, ce système, où un seul candidat est élu dans chaque comté selon le principe de la pluralité simple des voix, tend à amplifier une faible majorité populaire, et à la transformer en une majorité législative plus confortable, et ainsi contribue à une certaine stabilité gouvernementale. D'autre part, ce système désavantage sévèrement les partis minoritaires, surtout ceux dont l'appui est dispersé au lieu d'être concentré ou régionalisé; ainsi ce système tend à exacerber les scissions et les mécontentements à l'égard du processus électoral. Ces tendances sont discutées dans le contexte canadien par A.C. Cairns[1].

Considérons un Etat hypothétique à scrutin uninominal à un tour, où il n'y a que deux partis, l'un obtient 60 pour cent des voix populaires, et l'autre 40 pour cent. Imaginons ensuite deux façons extrêmes de répartir ces votes parmi les comtés. Dans le premier cas, chaque comté se conforme au modèle général donnant 60 pour cent des voix au premier parti, et 40 pour cent à l'autre. Alors, le premier parti remporte 100 pour cent des sièges et le deuxième n'a aucun siège. Dans le deuxième cas, le premier parti obtient 100 pour cent des voix dans 60 pour cent des comtés et le second toutes les voix dans le reste. De la deuxième hypothèse résulte une représentation proportionnelle. Suivant ces deux manières de répartir les voix on peut varier les rapports d'appui populaire entre les deux partis : 70–30 pour cent, 80–20 pour cent, etc. Le premier cas est toujours caractérisé par une homogénéité des différents comtés et une majorité très amplifiée. Le deuxième cas extrême est caractérisé par une polarisation qui peut prendre la forme d'une régionalisation des comtés, et par une représentation parfaitement proportionnelle. Les exemples réels de scrutin uninominal à un tour se situent entre ces deux extrêmes tel que l'illustre le graphique 1.

Notre intérêt pour la relation entre l'amplification des majorités et la régionalisation électorale a été stimulé par les récentes discussions publiques sur la réforme électorale au Québec. En 1961, analysant les résultats des élections générales du Québec, P. Cliche[2] a montré la tendance suivante : tandis que le vote populaire pour un parti, disons le Parti libéral, peut osciller au cours des années entre 35 et 70 pour cent, le pourcentage des sièges législatifs remportés par le

[1] « The Electoral System and the Party System in Canada, 1921–1965 », cette REVUE, I (1968), 55–80.

[2] « Les élections provinciales dans le Québec de 1927 à 1956 », *Recherches sociographiques*, II (1961), 343–66.

Canadian Journal of Political Science/Revue canadienne de science politique, VI, no. 3 (September/septembre 1973). Printed in Canada/Imprimé au Canada.

Electoral regionalization and the swing ratio

In single-member constituency, simple plurality electoral systems, the disproportion between the popular vote polled by a party and the number of representatives it elects has stimulated much controversy. We review the mathematical and statistical models of two-party systems of this type which have been proposed by Kendall and Stuart, Theil, Lemieux, March, and the present authors. This leads to a detailed empirical study of series of elections in three systems: the provincial systems of Québec and Ontario, and the Canadian federal system. In verifying a "sliding distribution" model more general than that of Kendall and Stuart, we construct the distribution of constituencies according their level of support for a given party, and hence provide an index of electoral regionalization. Less detailed seat-vote data, for longer series of elections in five systems, provide evidence for the persistence of electoral disproportions and the distinguishability of seat-vote characteristics between different systems. The extreme sensitivity of legislative proportions in Québec to small changes in popular vote proportions is shown to be a consequence not of peculiarities in the electoral map, but of the small standard deviation and large kurtosis (peakedness) of the distribution of constituencies.

parti oscille de façon beaucoup plus forte, soit entre 9 et 94 pour cent. Cliche a utilisé des graphiques semblables à notre graphique 2 pour mettre en relief cette tendance que nous nommerons « l'amplification des proportions ».

Il est évident, d'après le graphique 2, que les résultats de certaines élections sont loin de respecter la représentation proportionnelle. Les partisans du parti désavantagé expriment alors leurs ressentiments contre « l'injustice » du système et exercent une pression pour une réforme électorale. Dans le passé, on se préoccupait des inégalités dans la carte électorale; récemment on s'est rendu compte que l'amplification des majorités est une conséquence plus fondamentale du système électoral. Etant donné la mise en question actuelle de ce système, il nous incombe d'assembler autant d'informations que possible relatives au scrutin uninominal à un tour. Le but de cet article est d'étudier le rapport entre la proportion des sièges et la proportion des voix, d'un point de vue à la fois théorique et pratique en procédant à l'analyse de plusieurs cas-types.

D'abord nous résumerons les théories mathématiques et statistiques développées principalement par Kendall et Stuart, March, Sankoff et Mellos, et Thiel[3], portant sur le scrutin uninominal à un tour. Pour évaluer la relation entre l'amplification des proportions et la régionalisation électorale, nous choisissons un indice pour chacun : le premier est le quotient amplificateur sièges/voix; le second, l'écart-type de la distribution des comtés par rapport à leur appui à un parti donné.

Ensuite nous développerons une méthodologie pour estimer l'espérance du quotient amplificateur à partir des résultats d'une suite d'élections. Nous appliquerons cette méthodologie au cas du Québec, et à autres cas de scrutin uninominal à un tour. Nous étudierons comment l'espérance du quotient amplifica-

[3]M.G. Kendall et A. Stuart, « The Law of the Cubic Proportion in Election Results », *British Journal of Sociology*, I (1950), 183–97; J.G. March, « Party Legislative Representation as a Function of Election Results », *Public Opinion Quarterly*, XXI (1957–8), 521–42; D. Sankoff et K. Mellos, « The Swing Ratio and Game Theory », *American Political Science Review*, LXVI (1972), 551–4; et H. Theil, « The Cube Law Revisited », *Journal of the American Statistical Association*, LXV (1970), 1213–19.

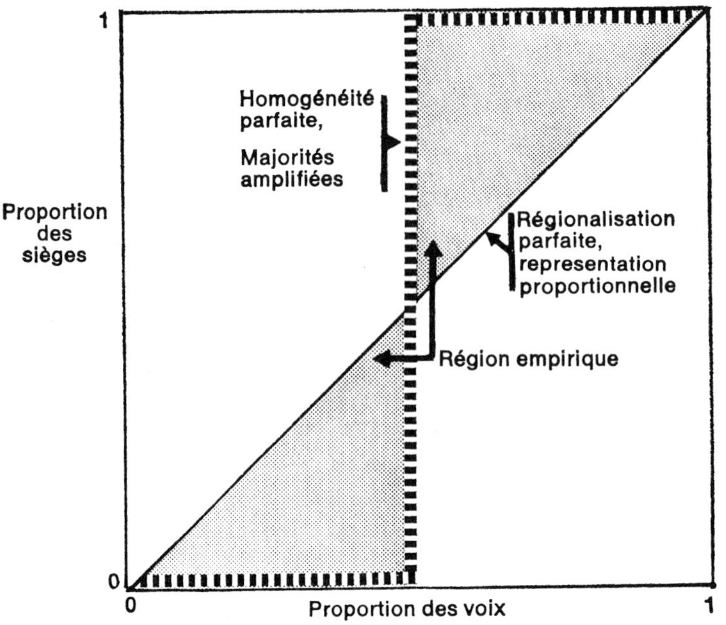

GRAPHIQUE 1. Rapports possibles entre les voix et les sièges. Les bornes représentent les cas extrêmes de régionalisation et d'homogénéité électorale.

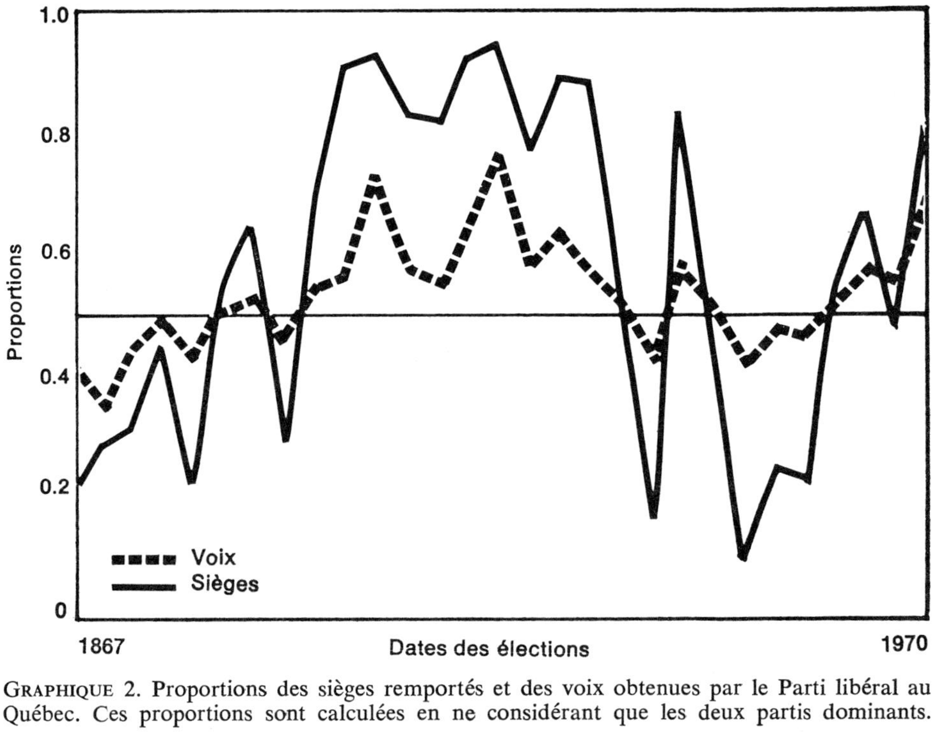

GRAPHIQUE 2. Proportions des sièges remportés et des voix obtenues par le Parti libéral au Québec. Ces proportions sont calculées en ne considérant que les deux partis dominants.

teur reflète l'écart-type de la distribution des comtés, et nous montrerons comment ces statistiques demeurent relativement invariantes d'une élection à l'autre dans un Etat donné.

I. Aspects théoriques

I. LA DISTRIBUTION DES COMTÉS ET LE QUOTIENT AMPLIFICATEUR

Plusieurs chercheurs ont remarqué et étudié l'amplification des proportions dans plusieurs pays du monde où se pratique le scrutin uninominal à un tour. « La loi des cubes » est l'appellation la mieux connue de cet effet. Elle ne décrit cependant adéquatement qu'un cas particulier et c'est pourquoi, pour plus de clarté, nous utiliserons l'appellation plus générale d'« amplification des proportions ». La première étude moderne de ce phénomène a été faite par les statisticiens Kendall et Stuart.[4] Leur travail s'est inspiré d'un article paru dans l'*Economist*,[5] qui a ressucité l'intérêt pour la « loi des cubes » découverte au début du siècle. D'après cette loi appliquée au cas de la Grande-Bretagne à un changement de 1 pour cent dans le pourcentage du vote populaire accordé à un parti donné d'une élection à l'autre, correspond un changement de 3 pour cent dans les sièges législatifs qu'il remporte, ce qui représente un quotient amplificateur de trois. (Quand un accroissement de X pour cent des votes mène à un accroissement de Y pour cent des sièges, on dit que s, le quotient amplificateur sièges/voix, est égal à Y/X.)

Comme nous le montrerons, ce résultat est à peu près constant pour toute une série d'élections en Grande-Bretagne. Kendall et Stuart ont montré que la constance de ce résultat provient du fait que la répartition de la proportion d'appui au parti dans les différents comtés est adéquatement décrite par une distribution normale avec un écart-type toujours assez près de 0.133. L'écart-type reste à peu près constant, même si la moyenne de la distribution, qui est plus ou moins égale à la proportion du vote total obtenu, change.

Le modèle mathématique des systèmes de scrutin uninominal à un tour que nous adoptons ici est basé sur les résultats de Kendall et Stuart. Le modèle s'applique surtout aux systèmes à deux partis, mais il peut également s'appliquer à des systèmes ayant un troisième parti qui soit la plupart du temps beaucoup plus petit que les deux grands partis. Il convient de souligner que cette description est une description idéale, ne tenant pas compte des fluctuations statistiques, parfois très fortes, qui existent dans les systèmes réels.

La pierre de touche du modèle est la distribution des comtés selon leur appui à l'un des deux partis. On postule que cette distribution est normale, c'est-à-dire que la fraction des comtés où le parti reçoit une proportion, disons entre x et $x + 0.01$ des votes, est approximativement

$$\frac{0.01}{\sigma\sqrt{2\pi}} e^{-\frac{1}{2}(x-\mu/\sigma)^2}$$

[4]Kendall et Stuart, « The Law of the Cubic Proportion », et aussi « La loi du cube dans les élections britanniques », *Revue française de science politique*, II (1952), 270–6.
[5]« Electoral Facts », *Economist*, CLVIII (1950), 5–7.

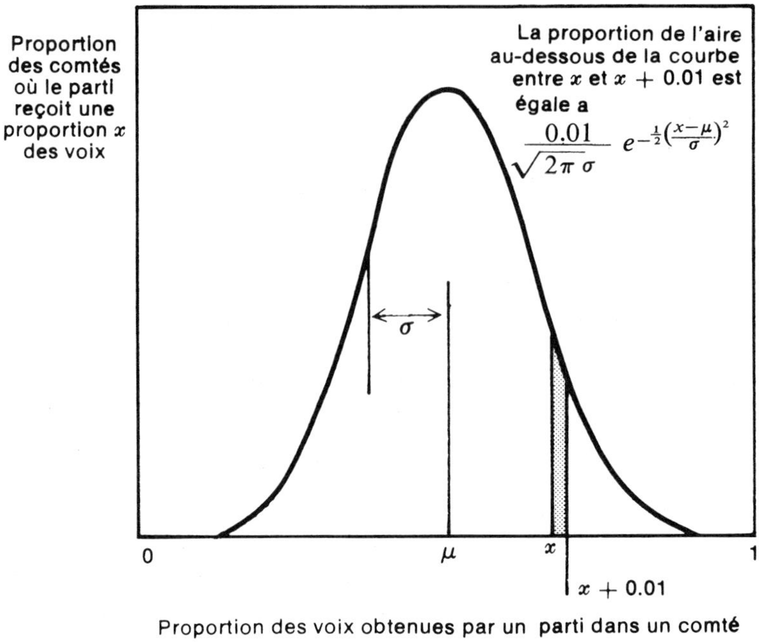

GRAPHIQUE 3. Distribution des comtés selon la proportion des voix accordées à un parti donné.

(où μ représente la proportion du vote populaire total obtenu par le parti, et σ est l'écart-type de la distribution), tel qu'illustré dans le graphique 3.

D'une élection à l'autre, la proportion μ du vote total obtenue par un parti peut changer. Cependant σ ne change pas. Si μ croît, la courbe glisse horizontalement vers la droite; si μ décroît, la courbe glisse vers la gauche. Cet effet est illustré par le graphique 4.

Si μ est trop rapproché de 0.0 ou de 1.0, il devient nécessaire de réajuster le modèle de sorte qu'il n'y ait pas de comtés qui fournissent une proportion de voix à un parti inférieure à 0.0 ou supérieure à 1.0. On peut éviter ces problèmes en utilisant des distributions autres que la distribution normale, telle que la distribution beta, qui peut être fixée à zéro à l'extérieur de l'intervalle 0–1; mais à toutes fins pratiques, on peut ignorer ce problème.

La proportion des sièges obtenus par le parti est, évidemment, égale à l'aire située au-dessous de la courbe de distribution située à droite de 0.5 (50 pour cent), comme l'indique le graphique 5.

Si, par régionalisation électorale, nous entendons le degré général de diversité dans l'appui accordé aux différents partis dans les divers comtés, σ devient une bonne mesure de cette régionalisation. Si la proportion des votes accordé à un parti est à peu près identique dans tous les comtés, la dispersion des comtés, i.e. σ, est faible. D'autre part, quand l'appui à un parti est concentré dans certaines régions, la distribution des comtés est très dispersée et σ est élevé[6].

[6]Que σ soit élevé n'est pas condition suffisante pour l'existence d'une régionalisation. On peut imaginer une situation hypothétique où les comtés qui appuient fortement un parti

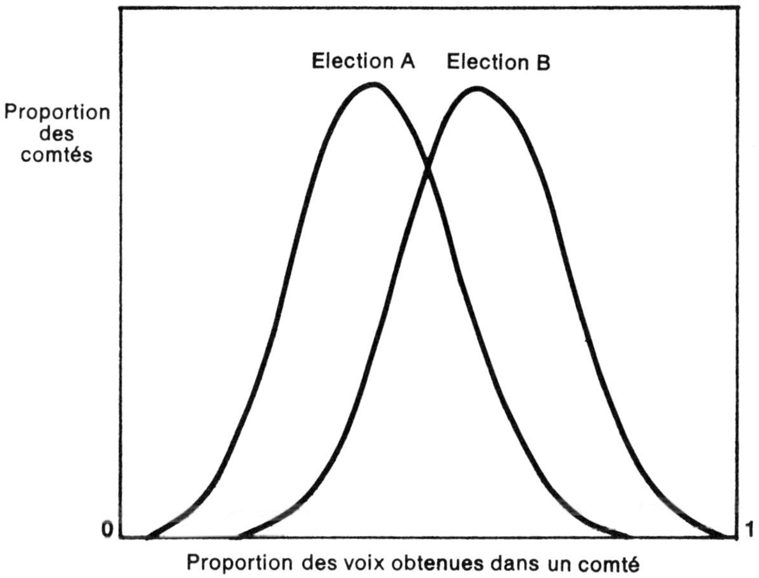

GRAPHIQUE 4. La moyenne de la distribution des comtés change d'une élection à l'autre, mais la dispersion reste constante.

Suivant notre définition du quotient amplificateur, et en supposant que μ_1 et μ_2 sont les proportions des voix, r_1 *et* r_2 les proportions des sièges, obtenues par un parti lors de deux élections successives, nous avons :

$$s = \frac{r_2 - r_1}{\mu_2 - \mu_1}.$$

Nous faisons l'hypothèse que σ est constant pour un Etat donné. Si nous connaissons le vote populaire de deux élections successives (c'est-à-dire μ_1 et μ_2), nous pouvons calculer r_1, r_2 et donc s, au moyen des tableaux de la distribution normale, tel qu'illustré au graphique 5. Un résultat de ce calcul est : lorsque μ_1 et μ_2 sont près de 0.5, s varie très peu. Par exemple, si μ_1 et μ_2 restent de l'ordre de $0.5 \pm \frac{1}{2}\sigma$, s reste entre $3.5/\sigma$ et $4.0/\sigma$. Il s'ensuit que dans la mesure où μ reste près de 0.5, le traitement de s comme étant constant pour un Etat donné serait une bonne approximation, et s apparaîtrait comme une bon indice de l'amplification des proportions, pour les fins comparatives. Pour obtenir la valeur précise de s, nous utilisons la limite de *l'espérance* du quotient amplificateur lorsque μ_1 et μ_2 approchent tous les deux de 0.5. Cette prescription appliquée à une distribution normale nous donne :

$$s = \frac{1}{\sqrt{2\pi}\sigma} \approx \frac{0.40}{\sigma}.$$

---

donné et ceux qui rejettent fortement ce parti sont complètement éparpillés à travers tout le territoire. Néanmoins il est difficile de croire qu'un système politique réel puisse arriver à une telle configuration. En plus, puisqu'une dispersion élevée est une condition nécessaire à la régionalisation, nous sommes justifiés de considerer σ comme indice de régionalisation.

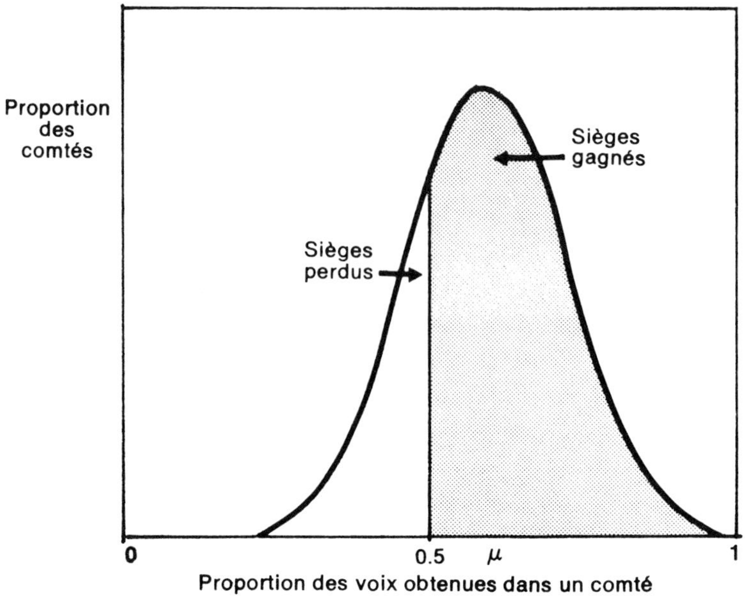

GRAPHIQUE 5. Sièges obtenus en fonction de la distribution des comtés.

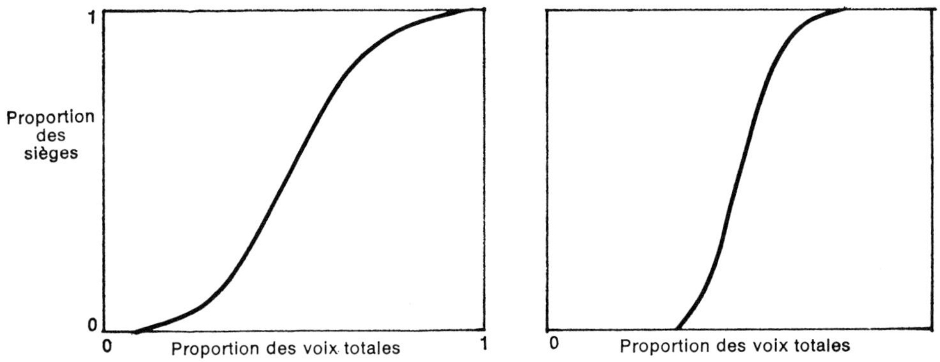

GRAPHIQUE 6. Le rapport entre sièges et voix pour deux systèmes de scrutin uninominal à un tour. A gauche, $\sigma = .167$ et $s = 2.4$. A droite, $\sigma = .083$ et $s = 4.8$.

Une autre façon de voir cette relation est de tracer r (la proportion des sièges gagnés), comme fonction de μ (la proportion du vote populaire obtenu). Cette fonction est, en effet, la fonction cumulative de la distribution normale d'écart-type σ. Pour tracer la courbe de cette fonction, on prend une série de valeurs de μ, et on construit, pour chacune de ces valeurs, une distribution des comtés; ensuite, au moyen du calcul illustré dans le graphique 5, on trouve la valeur de r correspondant à chaque μ. Deux exemples de cette fonction sont présentés dans le graphique 6. La pente, ou dérivée, de la fonction, à μ égale 0.5, n'est autre que s, le quotient amplificateur défini ci-dessus.

Nous avons donc établi un rapport entre la régionalisation électorale et l'amplification des proportions dans notre modèle, à savoir que leurs indices respectifs sont inversement proportionnels. Ainsi Kendall et Stuart ont trouvé qu'en Grande-Bretagne, σ est entre 0.13 et 0.14, tandis que s est près de 3.0.

Rappelons que le modèle que nous avons choisi est une description idéale des systèmes de scrutin uninominal à un tour. En réalité, ces systèmes sont sujets à des fluctuations statistiques très fortes de sorte que, pour une élection particulière, σ et s peuvent dévier considérablement de leurs valeurs idéales. Au moyen de méthodes statistiques précises, et en utilisant les données de plusieurs élections, nous verrons dans la deuxième partie de cet article comment chaque Etat à scrutin uninominal à un tour tend généralement à se comporter comme le modèle idéal, avec ses propres valeurs de σ et s, lesquelles peuvent varier fortement d'un Etat à l'autre.

II. MODÈLES STATISTIQUES

Notre modèle, basé sur la distribution des comtés selon la proportion du vote qu'ils accordent à un parti, n'est pas une explication complète de l'amplification des proportions. Il reste à comprendre comment cette distribution particulière se produit et se maintient, avec un écart-type plus ou moins constant d'une élection à l'autre. J.P. Smith[7] fut le premier à suggérer une explication, à savoir qu'il s'agirait d'une variation d'échantillonnage de l'appui à un parti dans les différents comtés. Si, dans une population, l'appui global est de 55 pour cent à un parti, et que l'on répartit au hasard la population en un nombre de sous-populations (ou comtés), on prévoit que dans certains comtés l'appui sera de moins de 55 pour cent et que dans d'autres il dépassera 55 pour cent. Cependant, Kendall et Stuart ont montré que la variation d'échantillonnage des proportions est presque négligeable dans des comtés qui comptent plusieurs milliers d'électeurs. En plus, ils ont montré que toute explication basée sur la variation statistique nécessite soit des hypothèses spécifiques et quantitatives de corrélations parmi les électeurs, soit des hypothèses également détaillées sur la stratification sociale. En fait, dans ce genre d'analyse, il devient aussi complexe de justifier les hypothèses que d'expliquer la distribution des comtés.

III. MODÈLES ÉQUILIBRÉS

L'amplification des proportions a été également mesurée par Dahl, et par March[8] pour les élections fédérales aux Etats-Unis. Les valeurs trouvées pour le quotient amplificateur varient entre 2.5 et 3.3 en fonction de la chambre législative et en fonction de la méthode de calcul utilisée. March a donné un autre type d'explication à l'amplification des proportions. Afin de simuler une répartition des types de comtés, il a construit un modèle assez complexe où les pressions qui existent à l'intérieur d'un comté sont équilibrées par la formation de coalitions. Comme nous l'avons discuté précédemment, c'est de cette répartition que découle l'amplification des proportions. Son modèle dépend de notions telles que le désespoir des minorités, la confiance des majorités, et les négociations entre les partis.

Plus simplement, nous pouvons attribuer la variation de l'appui à un parti à

[7]Dans les *Minutes of Evidence before the Royal Commission on Systems of Elections* (cmd. 5352), B.P.P. XXVI (1910).
[8]R.A. Dahl, *A Preface to Democratic Theory* (Chicago, 1956), 148, et March, « Party Legislative Representation ».

l'équilibre entre deux forces. D'une part, il y a la diversité régionale et les besoins régionaux qui tendent à concentrer l'appui à un parti en très peu de régions[9]; d'autre part, il y a le désir de remporter la majorité des sièges, désir qui encourage les stratégies du compromis, du « brokerage » et de la formation de coalitions, afin d'élargir les bases d'appui.

C'est la variation dans la pondération relative de ces deux forces selon les régions qui produit la dispersion de la distribution des comtés.

IV. LA THÉORIE DES JEUX

Enfin, il nous reste toujours une question très importante. Pourquoi cette situation équilibrée est-elle toujours caractérisée par des valeurs du quotient amplificateur d'environ 3.0, et de façon plus réaliste entre 2 et 5 ? Pourquoi pas entre 12 et 15, ou entre 0.5 et 1.5 ? Pour répondre à cette question, nous avons développé un modèle simple de théorie des jeux[10]. Nous n'avons fait aucune hypothèse quantitative, afin de ne pas orienter artificiellement le modèle vers un cas particulier. Le modèle est le suivant : il y a n comtés où n peut être égal à 100, 200, etc. Il y a deux partis, munis de ressources R_{I} et R_{II} respectivement. Lors d'une élection, ou bien d'une campagne électorale, chaque parti poursuivant une stratégie secrète distribue comme bon lui semble ses ressources parmi les différents comtés. Dans chaque comté, le parti qui gagne est celui qui y a dépensé le plus de ressources.

Bien entendu, le problème de chaque parti est de trouver une stratégie qui lui permette de remporter le maximum de comtés. Le problème mathématique, pour nous, était de calculer le résultat attendu si les deux partis agissaient rationnellement, c'est-à-dire en employant des stratégies optimales ou presque optimales. Il reste un autre problème, celui de relier le nombre de voix obtenues aux ressources dépensées, dans un comté donné; le modèle le plus simple consiste en une proportionalité simple. Nous avons découvert des stratégies mathématiquement optimales pour ce jeu, dont la propriété principale est que, lorsque les deux partis agissent d'une manière rationnelle, la relation entre voix et sièges est représentée par le graphique 7. Cette relation implique un quotient amplificateur égal à 2.0.

Il est évident que ce jeu est trop simple, car il exclut un certain nombre de facteurs et de complications. Puisque la plupart de ces facteurs sont propres aux différents pays, et varient d'un pays à l'autre, leur effet sur l'amplification des proportions, observée dans une perspective universelle, ne peut être d'une grande importance. D'ailleurs, il est possible d'incorporer dans notre modèle des facteurs importants et universels, tels que la répartition des électeurs non partisans et du noyau des partisans convaincus. L'incorporation de ce type de facteur change la courbe théorique, qui tend à se rapprocher des courbes empiriques; c'est-à-dire que le quotient amplificateur augmente.

Quelles conclusions pouvons-nous tirer de cette approche basée sur la théorie des jeux ? D'abord, il est évident que la disproportion entre les sièges et les votes est générale dans un système de scrutin uninominal à un tour, et qu'elle ne provient pas d'une variation d'échantillonnage parmi les comtés. Malgré la suggestion de

[9]Cairns, « The Electoral System ».
[10]Sankoff et Mellos, « The Swing Ratio ».

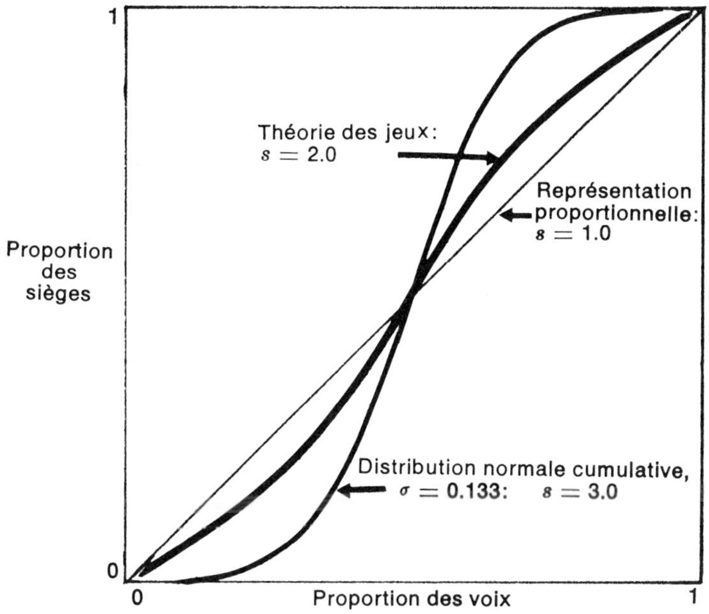

GRAPHIQUE 7. Trois types de courbe sièges-voix.

Cliche[11], la disproportion n'est pas due surtout aux inégalités de la carte électorale[12]. Dans ce type de système électoral, la disproportion est plutôt une conséquence inévitable des problèmes stratégiques rencontrés par les partis au cours de la campagne électorale.

V. RELATIONS AVEC D'AUTRES MODÈLES ÉLECTORAUX

Le modèle basé sur une distribution des comtés dont la forme reste invariante, mais qui peut glisser le long de l'axe horizontal, est lié à plusieurs concepts dans la théorie électorale. Nous nous référons notamment à la « voix normale » de P. Converse[13], au modèle « logit » de Theil[14], et à l'analyse hiérarchique de V. Lemieux[15]. Toutes ces approches attribuent les changements électoraux à de légers ajustements à l'intérieur d'un système stable de répartition des voix, plutôt qu'à des revirements d'appui, d'une élection à l'autre.

La théorie de la voix normale considère que, dans un système à deux partis, les électeurs peuvent être classés sur une échelle comme suit : le noyau convaincu du parti I se situe à un extrême, le noyau du parti II se situe à l'autre, les partisans modérés du parti I, les indépendants, et les partisans modérés du parti II entre les deux extrêmes.

[11]Cliche, « Les Elections Provinciales ».
[12]K. Mellos et D. Sankoff, « Pourquoi les sièges ne sont-ils pas proportionnels aux voix obtenues ? » *Le Devoir* (2 mai 1970).
[13]« The Concept of the Normal Vote », dans *Elections and the Political Order*, éd. A. Campbell, P. Converse, W.E. Miller et D. Stokes (New York, 1966), 9–39.
[14]« The Cube Law Revisited ».
[15]« L'analyse hiérarchique des résultats électoraux », cette REVUE, I (1968), 40–54.

Au moment d'une élection, chaque partisan a une certaine probabilité de voter contre son parti. Cette probabilité est très petite pour les partisans qui se situent dans les deux noyaux, et plus grande pour les modérés. D'une élection à l'autre, tout ce qui change, ce sont les probabilités. Les probabilités des électeurs des deux noyaux changent très peu, et même un petit changement unidirectionnel de la part des modérés suffit pour donner des résultats très différents dans des élections successives.

Cette brève description de la théorie de la voix normale nous montre qu'elle s'accorde très bien avec le modèle d'une distribution des comtés. En effet, suivant le modèle de la voix normale, il nous est possible de prendre comme point de départ une répartition vraisemblable des électeurs de diverses tendances parmi les différents comtés, de calculer la distribution des comtés, et de s'attendre au même type de distribution dans toutes les élections successives. Plus précisement, si le changement du vote populaire d'une élection à l'autre n'est pas trop grand, la forme de la distribution sera relativement invariante, mais la distribution elle-même sera susceptible de se déplacer sur l'axe horizontal. A cette assertion il faut ajouter une qualification mineure, sans importance pour la relation entre s et σ, à savoir que la structure de la voix normale pourrait avoir l'effet de « lier » les extrêmes de la distribution et de permettre seulement au centre de la distribution de bouger. (Pour les raffinements récents de cette théorie, voir l'article de W.L. Miller[16].)

Le modèle « logit » de Theil incorpore l'essence des deux modèles précédents, c'est-à-dire la voix normale et la distribution glissante des comtés. Selon le modèle de Theil, le vote appuyant un parti donné dans un comté i et lors d'une élection t, dépend de deux paramètres α_i et β_t. Le paramètre α_i est spécifique au comté, et il ne varie pas selon l'année t. Il reflète la position du comté dans la distribution des comtés. Le paramètre, β_t, spécifique à chaque élection, est fonction du pourcentage du vote populaire accordé au parti en question lors de cette élection. La proportion du vote en faveur du parti dans le comté i est P_{it} où :

$$\log \frac{P_{it}}{1 - P_{it}} = \alpha_i + \beta_t$$

Selon cette formule, dans les comtés où l'appui au parti est près de zéro ou de 100 pour cent, P_{it} est moins sensible aux variations de β_t que dans le cas des comtés où l'appui est près de 50 pour cent. Le modèle de Theil est conform la théorie de la voix normale en ce qu'il prévoit plus de changements d'affiliation dans les comtés mixtes, et plus d'électeurs fidèles dans les comtés partisans. Il est à noter que la théorie de Theil n'a pas encore subi de vérification empirique.

Les résultats données par ce modèle ne diffèrent de ceux donnés par notre modèle à distribution « glissante » qu'en ce qui concerne les extrêmes de la distribution. L'effet de cette différence sur le quotient amplificateur serait ainsi marginal. La formule proposée par Theil n'est qu'une des nombreuses possibilités qui permettent de tenir compte du vote des noyaux militants et de maintenir les extrêmes de la distribution entre 0 et 1. Par exemple, nous avons exploré la

[16] « Measures of Electoral Change Using Aggregate Data », *Journal of the Royal Statistical Society, Series A*, CXXXV (1972), 122–42.

possibilité d'utiliser une distribution bêta à variance fixe, pour améliorer le modèle basé sur une distribution normale[17].

Une autre recherche qui a produit des résultats s'accordant avec notre théorie et avec celle de Theil est l'étude de Lemieux[18]. La stabilité relative de la forme de la distribution des comtés ne serait guère possible s'il n'existait pas un certain ordre plus ou moins fixe des comtés. Cet ordre serait basé sur le niveau d'appui à un parti donné dans les comtés en question. Le modèle de Theil formalise ces relations au moyen des valeurs fixes des paramètres des comtés, α_i. Pour autant que cette hypothèse soit juste, nous devrions pouvoir produire une échelle Guttman en appliquant la procédure suivante : nous ordonnons les années d'élection d'après le degré de succès global du parti, et nous donnons « 1 » à un comté pour chaque année où il a élu un membre de ce parti; « 0 » autrement. C'est précisément ce que Lemieux a fait, et ses résultats indiquent une échelle ayant un niveau élevé de signification.

II. Aspects empiriques

I. MÉTHODOLOGIE

On ne s'attend pas à ce qu'un système électoral réel suive notre description théorique de façon exacte[19]. Par exemple, dans son étude de l'effet des lois électorales sur le système politique, D.W. Rae[20] a tracé, sur un seul graphique, la relation sièges/voix de 125 élections dans plusieurs pays ayant le scrutin uninominal à un tour. Même si Rae a ajusté une ligne droite à ces données, les points de son graphique sont très éparpillés, et l'on perçoit une tendance vers la forme « S » de notre graphique 6. Par comparaison, les données qui proviennent d'autres modes de scrutin ne montrent pas du tout cette tendance[21], et elles concordent davantage avec un modèle linéaire[22]. Notre tâche ici consiste à examiner la relation sièges/voix dans plusieurs Etats. Le problème méthodologique est de découvrir le système sous-jacent à des données exhibant une grande variabilité statistique.

Dans notre analyse des données, nous aurons à vérifier deux hypothèses. La première hypothèse est que dans chaque système de scrutin uninominal à un tour, on peut découvrir une relation fondamentale sièges/voix, relation qui est caractérisée par un quotient amplificateur donné. La deuxième hypothèse est que cette relation sièges/voix reflète une distribution des comtés qui est caractéristique du système particulier et qui reste relativement invariante (excepté les glissements horizontaux), d'une élection à l'autre.

Pour vérifier la première hypothèse, nous avons recueilli des données provenant de pays ayant le scrutin uninominal à un tour, en mettant l'accent sur ceux qui ont une tradition plus ou moins stable de deux partis. Pour vérifier la

[17]K. Mellos, « The Theoretical Basis of the Cube Law », avec un appendice mathématique par D. Sankoff (ms).
[18]« L'analyse hiérarchique ».
[19]Voir T.H. Qualter, *The Election Process in Canada* (Toronto, 1970), 137.
[20]*The Political Consequences of Electoral Laws* (New Haven, 1967).
[21]*Ibid.*, 90, graphique 5.1.
[22]Selon notre modèle, différents Etats peuvent avoir différentes courbes de forme « S ». La combinaison de ces données sur un seul graphique devrait aussi montrer une forme « S », quoique moins accentuée que sur les graphiques individuels.

deuxième hypothèse nous avons étudié plus en détail les élections récentes aux assemblés législatives du Québec, de l'Ontario et du Canada.

Puisque notre théorie suppose une distribution normale des comtés et donc une distribution normale cumulative pour la courbe sièges/voix, nous avons eu besoin d'une technique pour évaluer les tendances normales cumulatives dans les données sièges/voix. La façon la plus naturelle de procéder est d'employer le papier quadrillé « probit » dont l'axe vertical est gradué de telle sorte qu'une courbe normale cumulative apparaît comme une ligne droite. La pente de cette ligne droite est inversement proportionnelle à l'écart-type de la distribution. Nous portons la proportion des sièges obtenus sur l'axe vertical, et la proportion des voix populaires sur l'axe horizontal[23], pour toute une série d'élections dans un Etat donné. Ensuite nous ajustons une ligne droite aux données, en utilisant la méthode des moindres-carrés. Cette procédure nous permet de voir si les données sont compatibles avec l'hypothèse normale et d'estimer la moyenne et l'écart-type de la distribution. Les résultats de cette analyse sont discutés dans la prochaine section.

Afin d'examiner la distribution des comtés plus en détail, il est nécessaire de considérer non seulement le total des sièges et des voix gagnés, mais également la répartition des voix dans chaque comté. Dans ce cas, le traitement des données devient une tâche considérable, surtout si on considère plus de deux ou trois élections.

Pour cette raison, nous avons concentré notre attention sur les élections du Québec, de l'Ontario et du Canada. Pour chaque élection, les résultats dans chaque comté ont été poinçonnés sur une carte mécanographique individuelle. A partir de cet ensemble de données[24], nous avons calculé la distribution des comtés. Pour vérifier l'hypothèse normale dans ce contexte plus détaillé, nous avons ajusté aux données une distribution normale ayant les mêmes moyenne et écart-type que la distribution empirique. Les résultats de cette partie de l'étude sont discutés dans la section II, partie III.

II. APERÇU MONDIAL DES RELATIONS ENTRE VOIX ET SIÈGES DANS LE SYSTÈME DE SCRUTIN UNINOMINAL À UN TOUR

Bien que le scrutin uninominal à un tour soit un système électoral bien connu et de longue date, il est employé dans peu de pays. Par exemple, c'est le système dominant pour les élections provinciales canadiennes, mais la plupart des provinces emploient (ou ont déjà employé dans le passé), des systèmes considérablement modifiés. Selon H.A. Scarrow[25], parmi les 10 provinces, le Québec et l'Ontario sont les seules qui ont employé exclusivement le scrutin uninominal à un tour dans sa forme pure entre 1920 et 1960. Notre analyse ne portera pas sur les résultats électoraux des autres provinces même si celles-ci utilisaient des systèmes étroitement liés au scrutin uninominal à un tour, la période d'un système stable à deux partis n'étant pas assez longue. Le tableau I présente les

[23]Les proportions sont les proportions des sièges et des voix des totaux des deux grands partis seulement.

[24]La collecte de ces données a été subventionnée par la Faculté des sciences sociales, Université d'Ottawa. Les résultats électoraux sont tirés, pour la plupart, des journaux *Globe and Mail* et *La Presse*.

[25]*Canada Votes, A Handbook of Federal and Provincial Election Data* (New Orleans, 1960).

TABLEAU I

SYSTEMES POLITIQUES ANALYSES

Lieu	Parti I	Parti II	Période de temps	Nombre d'élections
Québec	Libéral	Conservateur/ Union Nationale	1867–1970	29
Canada	Libéral	(Progressistes) Conservateur	1878–1968	25
Grande-Bretagne	Conservative	Labour	1931–70	10
Nouvelle-Zélande	National	Labour	1943–69	10
Etats-Unis	Democratic	Republican	1946–70	13

systèmes politiques et les périodes de temps pour lesquelles suffisamment de données nous étaient disponibles[26].

Le graphique 8 montre les données sur papier probit de la proportion des sièges gagnés par le parti I en fonction de la proportion des voix qu'il a obtenues. Afin de rendre comparables les données se rapportant aux différents cas, les pourcentages de votes obtenus par les partis I et II sont calculés en négligeant les votes accordés à des tiers partis, dont les effets sont différents dans les cinq cas. Ces effets sont discutés plus en détail dans notre conclusion.

Le graphique 8 montre clairement que, malgré le fait que les cinq états ont tous le même type de système, c'est-à-dire le scrutin uninominal à un tour, celui de Québec se distingue nettement par la relation sièges/voix, de quelques autres systèmes, celui utilisé pour élire la chambre basse des Etats-Unis, par exemple. Malgré la grande dispersion statistique sur quelques graphiques, la première hypothèse semble être vérifiée, à savoir que chaque Etat ou pays manifeste sa propre relation sièges/voix. Pour chaque paire de lignes, la méthode des moindres-carrés donne une estimation des pentes qui montre une différence significative ($p < 0.05$), à l'exception des paires Nouvelle-Zélande/Canada et Québec/Grand-Bretagne, où les deux lignes ont des pentes presque identiques; pour la comparaison Québec–Canada, l'oscillation statistique réduit la signification à $p < 0.15$. Néanmoins, dans la plupart des cas, l'oscillation statistique n'est pas assez élevée pour obscurcir des différences entre pays ayant différents quotients amplificateurs.

A quel point les données indiquent-elles une relation normale cumulative entre les sièges et les voix ? Supposons qu'un ensemble de données épouse une courbe normale cumulative comme sur le graphique 6. Lorsque ces données sont exprimées en « probit », elles devraient être linéaires. Une telle linéarité semble être à l'œil nu présente dans tous les cas à l'exception du Québec. D'ail-

[26]Les sources de ces données : le Québec : Cliche, « Les élections provinciales »; Scarrow, *Canada Votes* et *La Presse*; le Canada : J.M. Beck, *Pendulum of Power* (Scarborough, 1968); les Etats-Unis : Department of Commerce, Bureau of the Census, *Statistical Abstracts of the US* (Washington, 1952–71); et Clerk of the House of Representatives, *Statistics of the Congressional Election 1946* (Washington, DC); la Grande-Bretagne : F.W.S. Craig, *British Parliamentary Election Statistics 1918–1970* (Chichester, 1971); la Nouvelle-Zélande : New Zealand Yearbook (Wellington) et *Keesing's Contemporary Archives* (New York). Nous n'incluons pas l'Ontario dans cet aspect de l'étude. La stabilité des proportions des voix libérales et conservatrices pendant les décennies récentes rend impossible une estimation de la relation sièges/voix.

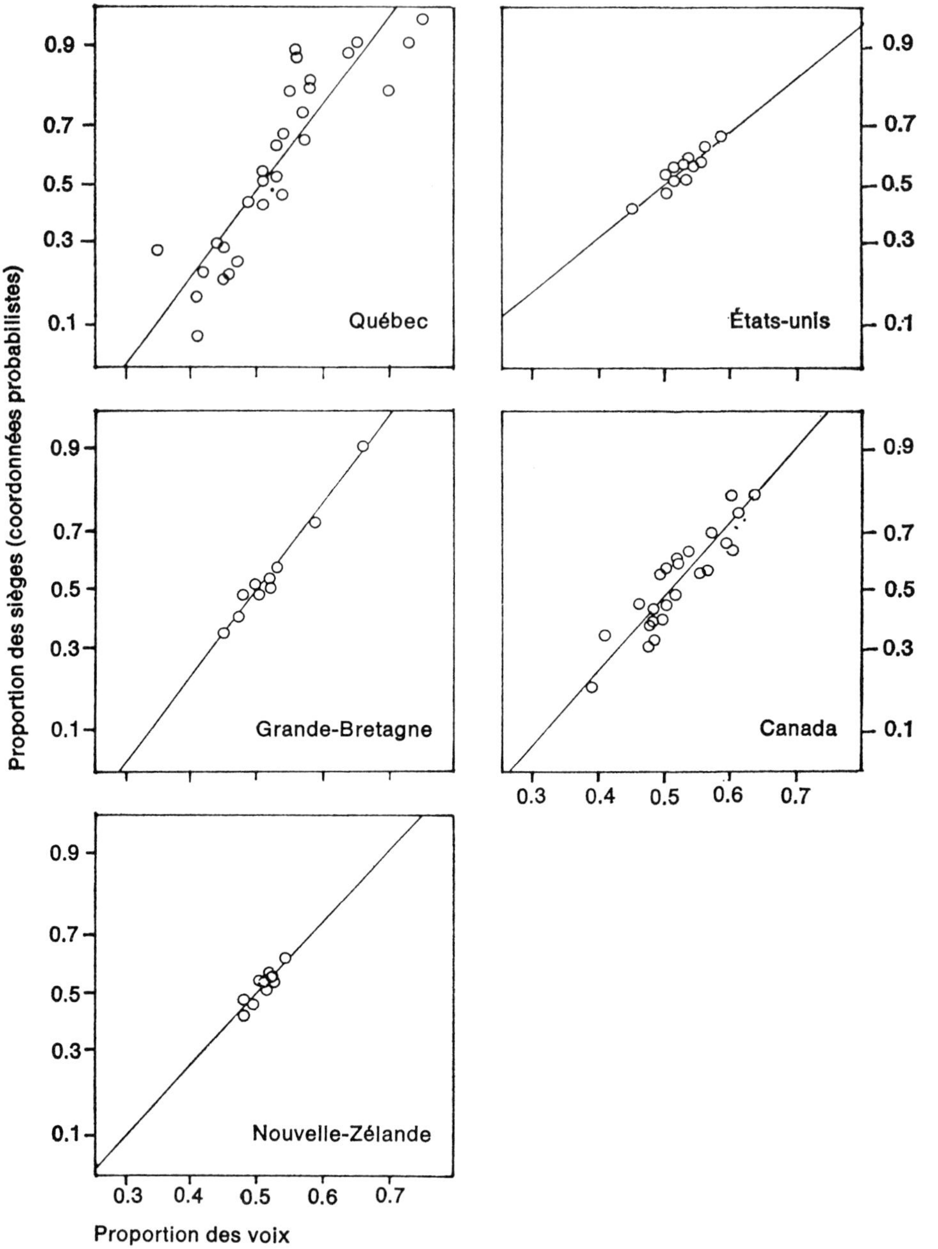

GRAPHIQUE 8. Données sièges-voix dans les systèmes à scrutin uninominal à un tour. Sièges et voix du parti I comme proportions des sommes des sièges et des voix des deux grands partis.

leurs, dans les cas de la Nouvelle-Zélande et des Etats-Unis, l'étendue de la variation sur l'axe horizontale (voix) est trop étroite pour déterminer si la relation linéaire en probit est plus justifiée que d'autres relations; notamment une relation linéaire directe entre voix et sièges. Pour le Canada, l'oscillation statistique est trop grande pour nous permettre d'évaluer l'hypothèse d'une façon non-équivoque. Pourtant, dans ce cas la courbe normale est une approximation plus raisonnable que dans le cas du Québec. En effet, les données du Québec (dans le graphique 8) suggèrent qu'autour de $\mu = 0.5$ la pente est beaucoup plus raide que 3.2, qui est le résultat de l'ajustement par moindres-carrés; cette pente est plutôt 5 ou 6. Cette forte inclinaison pourrait être expliquée par une hypothèse additionnelle, à savoir que la distribution des comtés au Québec est plus pointue que la distribution normale avec le même σ. Nous discuterons davantage de cette distribution dans la section suivante.

III. LA DISTRIBUTION DES COMTÉS AU QUÉBEC, EN ONTARIO ET AU CANADA

Nous avons utilisé deux méthodes pour calculer la distribution des comtés dans plusieurs élections. D'abord, nous avons calculé la distribution des comtés à partir de l'appui accordé au parti I, dans tous les comtés où le parti était en compétition avec au moins un autre parti; nous n'avons donc pas inclu les comtés où le parti en question a gagné par acclamation. La deuxième méthode n'a inclu que les comtés où les partis I et II contestaient l'élection, l'appui au premier parti étant mesuré par sa proportion de la somme des voix des deux partis. Ces deux analyses ont produit des résultats semblables. Nous ne montrons ici que les résultats de la première, qui distinguent de façon plus nette le Québec de l'Ontario.

Le graphique 9 présente les 25 distributions que nous avons calculées, et le Tableau II indique leurs moyennes, écarts-type, et coefficients de dissymétrie et d'aplatissement. Comme nous l'avions prédit dans la section II, partie II, ci-dessus, les estimations de σ pour le Québec sont pour la plupart inférieures à celles du Canada ($p < 0.0001$). Le σ de l'Ontario se trouve entre les deux. D'ailleurs, la tendance du Québec vers une distribution pointue est nettement visible sur le graphique 9, et est confirmé par les valeurs du coefficient d'aplatissement au Tableau II. (L'aplatissement de la courbe normale est 3, et des valeurs plus hautes que 3 indiquent une distribution plus pointue.)

Presque toutes les distributions du Québec sont plus pointues que la courbe normale ayant le même écart-type σ, et les valeurs du coefficient d'aplatissement sont pour la plupart très élevées. Rappellons que cette proprieté a déjà fait l'objet de l'hypothèse additionnelle de la section II, partie II, suggerée par le graphique 8. Les résultats du Tableau II, obtenus par une méthodologie et des données différentes, confirment cette hypothèse. Contrairement à celles du Québec, les distributions du Canada et de l'Ontario concordent avec l'hypothèse de normalité, même si celles de l'Ontario sont plus irrégulières. Cette meilleure concordance est évidente si on se refère aux coefficients de dissymétrie et d'aplatissement des trois systèmes et ceux de la courbe normale. (Pour le cas d'une courbe normale, la dissymetrie = 0 et l'aplatissement = 3.)

Enfin, il nous semble évident d'après le graphique 9 que notre deuxième hypothèse originale se vérifie, c'est-à-dire que la distribution des comtés dans un

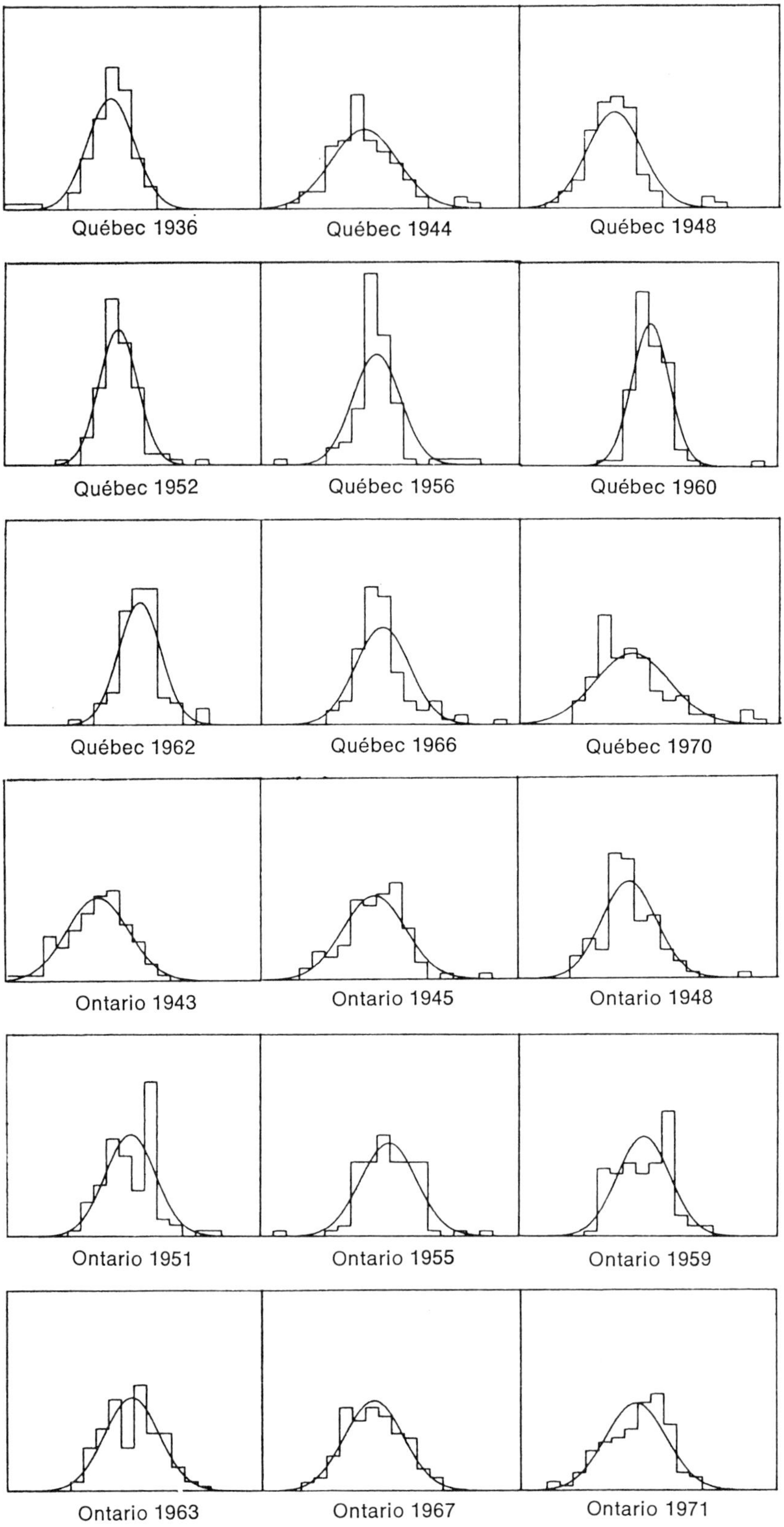
Québec 1936
Québec 1944
Québec 1948
Québec 1952
Québec 1956
Québec 1960
Québec 1962
Québec 1966
Québec 1970
Ontario 1943
Ontario 1945
Ontario 1948
Ontario 1951
Ontario 1955
Ontario 1959
Ontario 1963
Ontario 1967
Ontario 1971

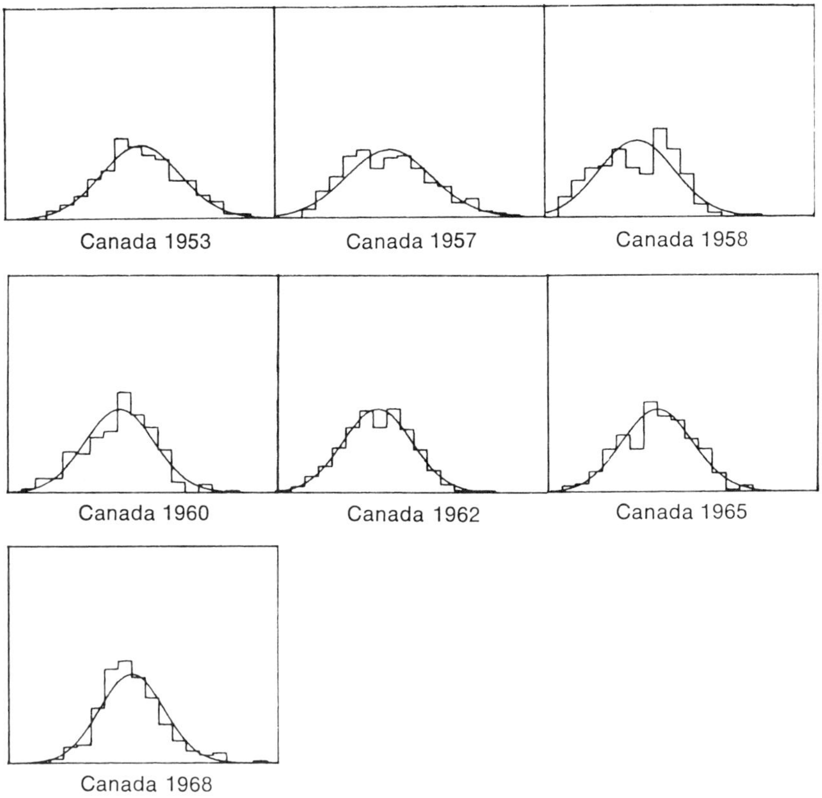

GRAPHIQUE 9. Distribution des comtés selon leur appui au parti I (Québec : Parti libéral; Ontario : Progressive Conservative; Canada : Parti libéral).

TABLEAU II

PROPRIÉTÉS DES DISTRIBUTIONS DES COMTÉS

Lieu	Année	Moyenne	Ecart-type	Dissymétrie	Aplatissement
Québec	1936	0.419	0.092	−1.52	7.10
	1944	0.401	0.129	0.77	4.48
	1948	0.366	0.106	1.08	6.02
	1952	0.449	0.075	0.81	6.07
	1956	0.446	0.092	0.59	8.29
	1960	0.508	0.072	1.71	11.37
	1962	0.530	0.083	0.48	4.81
	1966	0.468	0.105	1.32	5.71
	1970	0.431	0.143	1.15	4.42
Ontario	1943	0.363	0.122	−0.36	2.78
	1945	0.442	0.122	0.17	4.12
	1948	0.429	0.105	0.74	5.17
	1951	0.495	0.100	0.24	3.28
	1955	0.496	0.109	−0.11	5.25
	1959	0.480	0.102	0.03	2.24
	1963	0.492	0.109	0.13	2.37
	1967	0.432	0.113	0.11	2.39
	1971	0.443	0.117	−0.46	2.66
Canada	1953	0.494	0.146	0.18	2.64
	1957	0.419	0.158	0.37	2.56
	1958	0.340	0.140	−0.03	2.25
	1960	0.366	0.128	0.05	2.98
	1962	0.408	0.128	−0.15	3.08
	1965	0.400	0.130	−0.10	2.63
	1968	0.450	0.120	0.61	3.87

système électoral a une forme particulière qui le caractérise, et qui rend compte de la valeur du quotient amplificateur. Cette distribution reste assez invariante, sauf en ce qui concerne le déplacement horizontal.

Conclusion

Dans tout Etat suffisamment grand, il y a une certaine régionalisation géographique et sociale. Par l'entremise du scrutin uninominal à un tour, les aspirations et forces politiques tendent à traduire cette régionalisation sous forme d'une distribution des comtés. Lorsqu'il n'y a que deux grands partis, les divers aspects de cette régionalisation se réduisent à un système uni-dimensionnel. Même s'il y a des changements majeurs dans la structure sociale ou dans l'appui aux différents partis, ils ne seront reflétés que par un glissement de la distribution et non par un changement de sa forme. Cette forme peut se conserver, même après plusieurs redistributions de la carte électorale, des changements de régimes, etc.

L'effet le plus remarquable lié à cette régionalisation électorale est l'amplification des proportions. Une faible majorité des voix populaires devient une majorité écrasante des sièges législatifs. Cet effet, dont l'importance dépend de l'écart-type de la distribution des comtés, et quelquefois de son aplatissement, peut produire un quotient amplificateur de valeur moyenne variant d'un minimum d'environ 2 (la valeur prédite par la théorie des jeux) pour les Etats-Unis, jusqu'à plus de 5 (tel qu'indiqué par les données non-extrêmes pour le Québec sur le graphique 8).

La valeur de 3, donnée par la loi des cubes, se trouve à mi-chemin entre ces deux extrêmes, ainsi que les quotients amplificateurs du Canada, de la Nouvelle-Zélande, et particulièrement de la Grande-Bretagne.

Pour certaines provinces canadiennes telles que l'Ile du Prince-Edouard et la Nouvelle-Ecosse, le quotient amplificateur atteint des valeurs de 10 ou plus. On ne peut conclure dans ces cas si ces valeurs viennent plutôt des modifications du système spécifiques à ces provinces, ou si elles sont dues en fait au scrutin uninominal à un tour. Une autre explication serait que des assemblées législatives ayant un nombre de sièges restreints tendent à réaliser des amplifications plus fortes que celles ayant plus de membres, mais cette hypothèse n'est pas appuyée par les cas étudiés dans le graphique 8.

Une autre question non résolue par cette étude concerne les limites d'applicabilité de notre théorie. Pour les cas de scrutin uninominal à un tour où il y a trois (ou quatre) partis majeurs, les distributions des comtés et l'amplification des proportions sont plus difficiles à étudier[27] et à interpréter. Pour le Québec et l'Ontario l'écart-type est relié à la proportion des voix accordées au troisième parti, même si les données des élections fédérales ne montrent pas cette tendance. La déformation de la distribution des comtés au Québec en 1970 ressemble beaucoup à celle de 1944, année où un troisième parti a attiré un fort appui. Si un système à deux partis était rétabli, il serait intéressant de voir si la distribution des comtés reviendrait à sa forme typique.

[27]T.H. Qualter, « Seats and Votes: an Application of the Cube Law to the Canadian Electoral System », cette REVUE, I (1968), 336–44; D. Spafford, « The Electoral System of Canada », *American Political Science Review*, LXIV (1970), 168–70.

One-Party Dominance and Third Parties: The Pinard Theory Reconsidered

GRAHAM WHITE *McMaster University*

Third parties in this country have long held a special fascination for academics, with the result that over the years a substantial literature has accumulated on them. And while some of these studies have been of very high quality, few have moved beyond description and analysis of one particular party into the realm of general theory regarding third parties. One notable exception is represented by the work of Maurice Pinard, who has endeavoured "to present a general hypothesis concerning the political factors which account for the rise of third parties"[1] at various times and places in Canadian political history. Essentially, Pinard's theory asserts that third parties arise during times of strain, and only in systems which have been structured by periods of one-party dominance.[2]

This article attempts to test both Pinard's structural hypothesis and also a class theory that he suggests, by examining the rise of the following third parties: the United Farmers of Ontario, the United Farmers of Alberta, and the Social Credit party of Alberta.

I. The meaning of one-party dominance

The notion of one-party dominance is crucial to Pinard's theorizing; yet, conceptually and operationally, he deals with it in a rather summary fashion.[3] At the outset of his analysis, Pinard offers as a temporary working definition of one-party dominance in a two-party system ("or a system approaching it") the following: "a situation in which the party in power cannot be seriously challenged by the opposition party; the latter is too weak to replace the former."[4] On the basis of his analyses, he subsequently observes that "a third of the votes seems to be the empirical cutting point below which a situation of one-party dominance is created."[5] In other words, for a condition of one-party dominance, the main opposition party may not attract, on the average, more than 33 per cent of the vote, although Pinard does admit of a "marginal" situation in which an opposition party maintains a greater percentage, but is suddenly weakened.[6]

[1]"One Party Dominance and Third Parties," *Canadian Journal of Economics and Political Science* XXXIII (August, 1967), 356. The theory has been expanded and qualified in chapters 2, 3, and 4 of his *The Rise of a Third Party: A Study in Crisis Politics* (Englewood Cliffs, NJ, 1971).
[2]*Rise of a Third Party,* 23–6.
[3]He also fails to specify what is to be understood by the term "strain," though for present purposes this is a less serious shortcoming.
[4]*Rise of a Third Party,* 22 n.2.
[5]*Ibid.,* 37.
[6]*Ibid.* In all fairness, we must point out that Pinard recognizes that "the proportion of the

Canadian Journal of Political Science/Revue canadienne de science politique, VI, no. 3 (September/septembre 1973). Printed in Canada/Imprimé au Canada.

Such an arbitrary definition would appear unsatisfactory on several grounds. At a minimum, the concept has three important aspects, all of which Pinard implicitly utilizes in his analysis: (1) one-party dominance is an attribute of both the entire political system and its constituent parts – that is, we may speak of one-party dominance in a province or a nation, and also of one-party dominance in a riding or group of ridings within the nation or province; (2) following upon this, one-party dominance in both forms is clearly a *variable* – that is, we may speak of a party in one province as being more dominant than another party in a second province; similarly, ridings within each province may be ordered according to the degree to which they are one-party dominant; (3) finally, and this is the most crucial point (which Pinard indirectly touches upon in his discussion of the differing perceptual horizons of the rural Qubec voter and the Montreal voter[7]), one-party dominance is very much a subjective concept rather than one having any objective definitional standard. Consider what Maurice Duverger has to say in this respect:

> [a dominant party is] first of all a party larger than any other, which heads the list and clearly out-distances its rivals over a certain period of time ... [In a two party system], a party is dominant when it holds the majority over a long period of political development ... every party that is larger than all others over a certain period of time is not necessarily dominant in character: sociological factors are at work as well as the material factor. A party is dominant when it is identified with an epoch; when its doctrines, ideas, methods, its style, so to speak, coincide with those of the epoch ... domination is a question of influence rather than of strength: it is also linked with belief. *A dominant party is that which public opinion believes to be dominant.*[8]

There are at least four considerations which may come into play in an evaluation of the degree to which any given party is perceived as dominant. First, there is the time factor: how long a party has been pre-eminent. It would not seem unreasonable to assume that there is some point after which length of tenure in office ceases to be pertinent – perhaps as little as 10 years, certainly no more than 20 or 25 years.[9] The memory span of most voters being what it is, it is unlikely that there would be, *ceteris paribus*, a significant difference in perceptions of dominance regarding a party which has been pre-eminent for two decades, and one which has been in that happy condition for upwards of half a century. Second, perceived dominance may be affected by the margin of victory of the major party over the minor party (at both the electoral-district level, and in the system considered as a whole). A party that consistently attracts 75 or 80 per cent of the vote should accordingly be perceived as more dominant than a party that is also winning regularly, but by far less substantial margins, perhaps only a few percentage points. On the other hand, it could be argued that in most

---

votes maintained is only an indicator of one-party dominance, though," he adds, "it appears to be a very good one." *Ibid.*, 63, n.2.

[7]*Ibid.*, 28.

[8]*Political Parties: Their Organization and Activity in the Modern State* 3rd. English ed., tr. by Barbara and Robert North (London, 1964), 308. Emphasis added.

[9]"It does not seem possible to specify clearly the length of time one-party dominance must prevail for the system to become conducive to third parties." Pinard, *Rise of a Third Party*, 64, n.5.

Une reconsidération de la théorie de Pinard sur la montée des tiers partis

Afin d'expliquer la croissance des tiers partis au Canada, Maurice Pinard a élaboré une théorie basée sur la notion des « tendances structurales » (structural conduciveness) telle qu'énoncée par Smelser. La théorie soutient que, dans les périodes de tensions sociales, les tiers partis auront tendance à croître dans les systèmes dont la structure est marquée par la prédominance d'un parti. De plus, Pinard suggère qu'une théorie des tiers partis centrée sur les classes sociales pourrait s'avérer plus appropriée dans certaines circonstances. Après avoir examiné la notion de « prédominance » et formulé une version plus explicite de la théorie basée sur les classes sociales, l'auteur applique les deux théories à trois cas bien connus de percée des tiers partis. Il s'avère que, même si on peut déceler des éléments structuraux dans tous les cas, la seconde théorie fournit une meilleure explication que la première dans deux des trois cas, l'inverse étant vrai dans l'autre cas.

cases margin of victory is not salient to the majority of voters, and hence that a third determinant of dominance could be more important: simply how well a party has succeeded in having its candidates elected, regardless of their margin of victory (or defeat) – the operative factor informing popular assessments of party strength is which party a sitting member represents. (In Quebec, to take Pinard's example, between 1917 and 1958, while the Conservative party was able to attract an average of 27.1 per cent of the vote, it was, due to the vagaries of the electoral system, victorious in a meagre 7.8 per cent of the seats.[10]) Inasmuch as the dominant-party candidate's margin of victory and the absence or presence of a dominant-party member sitting for a riding may represent somewhat independent dimensions of one-party dominance, the two variables are employed as separate indicators in the following analyses. Finally, there is a geographical setting to one-party dominance: particular constituencies or regions may, for one reason or another, be more dominated by a party than is the system as a whole. In this respect, it is instructive that Warren Miller has found the degree of one-party dominance at the county level to be meaningful and useful in the analysis of American voting patterns.[11] It remains somewhat unclear, however, in both conceptual and operational terms, what relationship(s) may exist between the perception of region-wide one-party dominance and perceived dominance at the constituency level.[12]

The foregoing comments raise several important conceptual problems with respect to one-party dominance, but provide little by way of definition. This reflects our view that any universal operationalization of the concept must necessarily be artificial and misleading: one-party dominance is in several ways a relativistic concept (since it is dependent on perceptions which may vary widely), and therefore admits of no standard defining formula.

[10]*Ibid.*, 22.
[11]"One-Party Politics and the Voter," *American Political Science Review*, L (September, 1956), 708.
[12]There is a fundamental problem lurking here regarding the proper level at which Pinard's theory should be tested. It will be brought out into the open, though not resolved, in section III.

II. The competing theories: political structure and class conflict

Pinard's theory is built upon Neil J. Smelser's work, which posits *structural conduciveness* as a necessary but not sufficient condition for any episode of collective behaviour.[13] Pinard views Social Credit in Quebec and other Canadian third parties as examples of what Smelser labels "norm-oriented movements" and he posits that their rise is made possible through the structural conduciveness of a party system dominated by one party (and thus characterized by weakness of the other main party).[14] In addition, Pinard contends that third parties will arise only in the presence of serious strain.

The strain, according to the theory, leads to dissatisfaction with the performance of the dominant, governing party. However, voters turning away from the government will tend not to shift their support to the weak opposition party, since it is not perceived as a viable alternative. They will gravitate instead toward a new third party.[15] Discontent will focus around a new third party and not the traditional opposition party since, for tactical and perhaps ideological reasons, potential leaders will not attempt to take over and reconstruct the old opposition party, whose organization and leadership, though moribund, will likely be well entrenched. "Rather than try to subdue and rejuvenate such a machine," Pinard argues, "the new leaders prefer to create an altogether new organization under the charismatic enthusiasm of a popular leader ... from there on, the new party is no longer a weaker party to start with, and its *supporters*, by turning to it, are not choosing an altogether weaker alternative."[16]

Pinard emphasizes that his thesis "does not consider the one-party dominance system – or quasi-party system – as a *concomitant* or *consequent* effect of the rise of political movements, but, on the contrary, as an *antecedent*, necessary condition for the rise of such movements."[17] In other words, the theory contends that third parties cannot arise without one-party dominance. Nonetheless, perhaps the most important and interesting feature of the theory is also its least immediately obvious aspect: the prediction that when a third party does arise, its strength will be *negatively* related (at the electoral-district level) to the previous strength of the opposition rather than of the dominant party.[18]

An approach that interpreted the rise of a third party as essentially a replacement of the opposition party would predict the most pronounced third-party

[13] *Theory of Collective Behavior* (New York, 1963), 15.

[14] Throughout the article, for the sake of simplicity, dominant-party strength will be considered as equivalent to opposition-party weakness; in other words, we will be dealing with two-party systems, though there is no reason why the analysis could not be extended to multi-party systems.

[15] Pinard notes that in some circumstances, such as in Quebec from 1958 to 1962, this may be a two-step process: "after a long period of dominance by a strong party, a dissatisfied electorate turns *in part* to the traditional opposition party. But if this party is *soon* considered to have failed, as the Conservatives were in 1962, then the electorate is not ready to return so rapidly to the dominant party it just repelled; they shift instead to a third party." Pinard, *Rise of a Third Party*, 26. Emphasis in original.

[16] *Ibid.*, 31, emphasis in original.

[17] *Ibid.*, 69, emphasis in original.

[18] The comments in this section are made within the context of elaborating and testing the theory with constituency-level data. See pp. 407–8 below for a discussion of testing it at other levels of analysis.

strength in the areas where the opposition party had formerly received its greatest support. Pinard argues precisely the opposite: that third-party strength will be at a *maximum* in those areas where the opposition had been the *weakest*. The explanation as to why this should be is straightforward: where the opposition party has been weakest there is (and has been) no effective alternative to the government. This may not be of particular significance in normal times, but in periods of strain it leads to an increased likelihood that the discontented will be attracted to a new party, for the traditional opposition party is simply not a realistic alternative. (In this respect, the Pinard thesis may be viewed as a special case of Smelser's assertion that "many norm-oriented movements crystallize when it appears to the discontented that one method of agitation has disappeared or is disappearing."[19]) Where the opposition party does possess a modicum of strength, dissatisfaction with the dominant party will tend to be channelled into the third party to a lesser extent, for the opposition will be seen as an adequate and credible vehicle for rectifying the problems which gave rise to the strain. Clearly, such processes are not uniformly consistent, for even in the opposition party's weakest areas it will still attract some support from those deserting the dominant party. Similarly, the new party will garner some votes in the areas of greatest opposition strength. In over-all terms, however, Pinard predicts a positive relationship between strength of the dominant party and the subsequent strength of the third party.

Pinard develops the theory still further by attempting to account for the factors which originally gave rise to the condition of one-party dominance: "structural cleavages of various sorts or certain types of community structure or widespread and flagrant corruption in very high places – all this possibly reinforced by single-member plurality elections – lead to alienation from one party and to one-party dominance; this, in turn, assuming the presence of strain, becomes a situation conducive to the rise of a third party."[20] We suggest that Pinard is incorrect in equating the origin of one-party dominance with alienation from one major party. It does seem likely that, once established, one-party dominance might be maintained because of structural cleavages or community structure, as Pinard demonstrates.[21] But these factors are not necessary for the *establishment* of one-party dominance. It appears to have been the case, for example, that in Alberta and Saskatchewan, the main factor determining that the Liberals rather than the Conservatives came to enjoy long periods of provincial dominance was the Liberal party's possession of national power at the time of the granting of provincial status in 1905. For this meant that the Liberal party, in addition to dispensing federal patronage, appointed the first lieutenant-governors. Not unexpectedly, they summoned Liberal premiers, who in turn put the provincial patronage to good use. As one authority on the period has written, "what perhaps was the decisive factor in the outcome of the [1905 Alberta] election was the Liberal possession of the machinery of provincial and federal administration."[22] In any event, it is not essential to the theory that it be able to account

[19]Smelser, *Theory of Collective Behavior*, 283.
[20]Pinard, *Rise of a Third Party*, 66.
[21]*Ibid.*, 66–9.
[22]L.G. Thomas, *The Liberal Party in Alberta: A History of Politics in the Province of Alberta, 1905–1921* (Toronto, 1959), 29.

for the origins of one-party dominance, although it would certainly be more impressive if it could do so.

Pinard introduces, in the most fully developed version of his theory, an exception which is of signal importance to this paper.[23] Noting that, on several occasions, the rise of a third party was accompanied by the failure of the strong traditional opposition party to contest a substantial number of seats, he speculates that such cases may not fit the general model. While the opposition party's inability to offer candidates in many ridings is clearly a species of structural conduciveness, it might also, according to Pinard, indicate "the presence of deep-seated unrest in some segments of the population, leading to the abandonment of the old opposition party as a channel for the redress of grievances, and the adoption of a new one."[24] This remark is predicated on his observation that most instances of opposition parties leaving large numbers of seats uncontested in elections marked by the rise of new parties occurred shortly after the First World War, "during a period of intense farmer and labour unrest."[25] Pinard proposes that a "special model," not unlike C.B. Macpherson's, may be required to account for such cases, and states succinctly: "class cleavages lead to the rejection of both old parties and their replacement by a new class party."[26] Beyond this, however, Pinard says nothing about the "special model."[27]

Although the failure of a *strong* opposition party[28] to contest a substantial number of seats prompted the special model, it is apparent that at least some of the supporting cases cited by Pinard[29] were marked by the existence of *weak* opposition parties. By way of illustration, the evidence points unambiguously to the weakness of the Liberal opposition in Ontario before the 1919 rise of the United Farmers of Ontario and also to the enfeebled condition of the opposition Conservative party in Alberta prior to the rise of the UFA.[30]

This being the case, a certain ambiguity develops. In some respects, the differences are more of degree than of kind between a third party that arises as a result both of strain and of an ineffectual opposition (the classic Pinard case) and one whose rise, although predicated on class cleavages, coincides with the traditionally weak opposition party's failure to offer a full slate of candidates.[31] To be sure, the ideal types are readily distinguished and, as will be demonstrated shortly, lead to opposite predictions regarding the direction of the relationship between the strengths of the former dominant party and the new third party. It may be that no middle ground empirically exists between the two cases, but if it does (and the probabilities must lie in this direction), a new synthesis of the structural and class models may be called for.

[23]Pinard, *Rise of a Third Party*, chap. 4, especially p. 65.
[24]*Ibid.*, 65.
[25]*Ibid.*
[26]*Ibid.* See pp. 66–70 for a description of Macpherson's model. See also C.B. Macpherson, *Democracy in Alberta* (Toronto, 1962).
[27]Accordingly, Professor Pinard must be absolved from any responsibility for the extrapolations which will be made about his "special model," which was, in any event, offered in a very tentative fashion.
[28]Pinard, *Rise of a Third Party*, 65.
[29]*Ibid.*, n.10.
[30]See pp. 409–10 and 416 below.
[31]For one thing, and this is an important point in its own right, strain would seem to be present, almost by definition, in the class cleavage model.

Clearly, the problem centres on the confounding effects of class unrest and political action on the one hand and the complete withdrawal of the opposition party on the other. For the most part, the two conditions have occurred together, but it seems unlikely that this must necessarily be the case. This implies that the two are analytically distinct. A crucial question, therefore, involves the effects on a third party – if any – of *the prior strength of an abdicating opposition party.*[32]

If such an opposition had been strong, then structural conduciveness in the form of one-party dominance is no longer at issue. A negative relationship will therefore be expected between former government-party strength and subsequent third-party strength. This negative relationship arises inasmuch as practically all of the former opposition party's supporters may be expected to switch to the new third party,[33] while the proportion of voters deserting the dominant party and coming over to the new party will be essentially a function of class factors and should not vary according to previous levels of party strength. In Pinard's general case, it was the varying proportions of those abandoning the old parties in favour of the third party that led to the positive relationship between dominant-party strength and the success of a rising third party. With the opposition party not fielding candidates, however, there will be no choice to be made by the voter who is discontented with the dominant party.[34] Accordingly, in any given constituency, the support elicited by the new third party should consist of the former opposition's entire electorate, plus a constant (with respect to its level of strength) proportion of the government party's ex-supporters. In short, since by definition one-party dominance will not be a factor, the special class theory predicts, in the case of a formerly strong abdicated opposition, a negative relationship between government-party strength in the previous election and subsequent third-party strength.

Does not an identical conclusion follow if the opposition party has been *weak* prior to its final withdrawal? On this matter, we must answer equivocally. *A priori*, it seems improbable that the previous structuring of the party system (that is, its one-party dominance) would be totally irrelevant to third-party support. And yet it is difficult to say precisely what effects it might have. One structural hypothesis does suggest itself: the greater the strength of the dominant party, the higher the *proportion* of its voters that will defect to the third party.[35] This hypothesis is premised on the belief that the larger, in absolute terms, the dominant party's electorate, the higher will be the percentage of its voters pos-

[32]Although it cannot be considered here, there is a question as to why a strong opposition should be unable or unwilling to contest a substantial number of seats. This would be readily understandable in a previously weak opposition, but it is rather less intelligible in a party that had not been in a weakened condition.

[33]Throughout the paper we make the (admittedly oversimplistic) assumption that voters who harbour ideological disinclinations to support a specific third party – or third parties in general – are not sufficiently numerous to confound the analysis.

[34]The dissatisfied voter of course has the option of abstaining, but abstentions should not, *ceteris paribus*, depend on the strength of any particular party. However, if there is a sufficiently large number of non-voters, it is possible that they will tend to obscure the relationship somewhat.

[35]Pinard's individual-level data indicated that the stronger the dominant Liberal party had been, the higher was the proportion of Liberals who switched to Social Credit (*ibid.*, 30). Since, however, the Conservatives did field a full slate of candidates in the 1962 election, this finding cannot be cited as support for our hypothesis.

sessed of only marginal commitment to it. Such voters would of course be more prone to switch to the new third party. This hypothesis could be tested by correlating, across ridings, the percentage decline in the dominant party's electorate from election A to election B (the third-party election) with its support in election A. The prediction would be that a positive relationship will emerge.[36]

Even if this hypothesis is borne out, however, we will not be able to answer the question posed at the beginning of the previous paragraph with any certainty. For we lack a theoretical basis for predicting the interaction effects of the structural and class variables, though a plausible suggestion might be that they would largely cancel one another out. If this were indeed the case, the over-all relationship between former dominant-party strength and third-party success would be either non-existent or else very weak. If, however, one-party dominance is the more important factor, then a positive relationship should be expected.

To recapitulate briefly, the special theory called for by Pinard to explain the rise of a third party in *purely class* terms predicts, we have argued, a negative relationship between the strength of the former government party and third-party strength. To the extent that the system has previously been characterized by one-party dominance, though, the logic of the structural conduciveness model might still apply, and with it the expectation of a positive relationship. We may thus determine, within broad limits, whether, in the case of the opposition party that contests few seats, a structural or a class model would be more appropriate from the strength and direction of the relationship. A negative association would suggest class as the prime factor, while structural conduciveness (in the form of one-party dominance) would be indicated as more important by a positive relationship.

One of the more evident shortcomings of the discussion thus far is its failure to consider adequately the role of party activists. For Pinard, the activists are at least as important as the voters,[37] although for the most part they are left out in his analysis. They are, it is apparent, the *sine qua non* in the formation of a third party, although once the new party is launched, it is most uncertain how their behaviour will impinge upon the relationships between the parties' electorates.

Party activists are undoubtedly of prime importance in the opposition party's decision whether to run candidates against the new third party. Other than this, however, we would suggest that there is little in the way of generalizations that may be made with any certainty about the effects of party activists. This is not to suggest that they are unimportant – they clearly are not – but that their behaviour is so much less constrained by the structuring of the situation (compared

[36]In this, as in other parts of the paper, we must recognize the dangers involved in making what Converse calls "the assumption of minimal change" – the assumption that the only change is that which is visible as net change in aggregate data. Philip E. Converse, "The Problem of Party Distance in Models of Voting Change," in *The Electoral Process*, ed. M. Kent Jennings and L. Harmon Zeigler (Englewood Cliffs, NJ, 1966), 177. For an insightful discussion of the proportions of voters defecting from parties in more normal times, see David Butler and Donald Stokes, *Political Change in Britain* (New York, 1969), chap. 13.

[37]*Rise of a Third Party*, 31.

with that of the voters) that at present we have no way of incorporating them into either the general or the special theories.

III. The method for evaluating the theories

In order to conduct a complete test of Pinard's theory, we would require comprehensive individual-level data. Ideally, such a data set would contain information on the voters' previous electoral behaviour, on the motivational sources for their behaviour, and above all, on their perceptions of the various parties with respect to their strengths, weaknesses, and political acceptability. The problem is of course that for almost no cases of new third parties is there available any survey data whatsoever, and even where it does exist, unless specifically gathered for the purpose, it would be unlikely to cover more than a few of the key variables. (Even Pinard's own survey data were collected prior to the theory's development.)

If, in the absence of survey data, analysis must proceed at an aggregate level, a fundamental problem, closely related to the "ecological fallacy," arises. "If causal interpretations are attempted on the basis of ecological data," Erik Allardt cautions, "it seems important to use data units which really correspond to areas that people are aware of and with which they identify themselves and others."[38] Now the concept of one-party dominance, as explicated in the first section, is essentially a subjective characteristic of a political system and/or its constituent parts. But the perpetual horizons of voters may vary widely. For some the province represents the salient political unit, while for others the riding or region is more significant. Pinard himself argues that rural voters have much more localized perceptions of party strength than have cosmopolitan urban voters, whose evaluation of party activity and strength tends to be cast in national or provincial terms.[39] This likely represents an accurate appraisal of the perceptual framework for a certain portion of the electorate, but the pattern for the entire population is surely much more complex.

Should the focus of voter perception be mixed (which seems likely) with a resultant variation in the perceived dominance of a party (perhaps more problematical), then the net effect will be a dampening of the relationship between strength of the dominant party and of the third party. The direction of the relationship will remain unchanged, but its strength may be diminished considerably. Unfortunately, the extent to which such conditions are operative may only be determined through survey data, so that for the cases examined in this paper, we can do nothing beyond noting the problem.

Using the province as the unit of analysis, Pinard looked at "all Canadian provincial elections since 1900 in which the party in power was defeated, as well as those elections in which a third party emerged."[40] The results he obtained

[38]"Implications of Within-Nation Variations and Regional Imbalances for Cross-National Research," in *Comparing Nations: The Use of Quantitative Data in Cross-National Research*, ed. Richard L. Merritt and Stein Rokkan (New Haven, Conn., 1966), 340.
[39]*Rise of a Third Party*, 28.
[40]*Ibid.*, 37.

were highly supportive of his hypothesis.[41] He also carried out a detailed constituency-level analysis of the rise of the Social Credit in 1962.[42] And although he was able to demonstrate that the posited associations held at both the riding level and (using survey data) at the individual level, the importance of these findings is somewhat circumscribed in that this case was not a test of the *general* theory. It was, rather, the "two-step" variation of the general theory that was tested.[43] This is perhaps a pointless quibble; nevertheless, it is at least worth mentioning.

By the same token, we must emphasize that, as will be demonstrated shortly, of the three cases considered in the present paper, only one, that of the Social Credit party in 1935, represents a test of Pinard's general theory. The rise of the United Farmers of Alberta was coincident with the total withdrawal of the (weak) Conservative opposition, so that in this instance it is the "special theory" that will be put to the test. The rise of the United Farmers of Ontario in 1919 is something of a hybrid in that its features conform in part to the general model and in part to the special model. For all three, the unit of analysis will necessarily be the constituency. Our findings, then, will by no means constitute a complete evaluation of Pinard's theory, nor of the special-class theory, but should nonetheless provide some indication of their validity.

With respect to the mechanics of testing the hypothesis, there may be serious problems involved in grouping ridings together according to a party's percentage of the vote, and comparing such groupings, as Lemieux and Pinard have done.[44] The cutoff points selected will, of necessity, be arbitrary and largely devoid of theoretical significance, so that results obtained in this way may depend in large measure on the manner in which the ridings have been clustered together. In addition, while in some cases it will be meaningful as an *independent* variable, a party's victory or loss in a constituency, given the distortions inherent in the first-past-the-post electoral system, seems a *dependent* variable of dubious merit. Finally, in those cases in which there are more than two candidates, it may be misleading to use a party's percentage of the vote as a measure of its strength. Since almost by definition, three or more candidates per riding is the norm at the time of the rise of a third party, and at least sporadically prior to this, a different indicator of party strength (*S*-index) was adopted for this paper. This measure is simply the party's plurality in a constituency: the spread in percentage points between it and its nearest rival (if it won the riding) or between it and the winner of the riding (if the party under consideration lost). In all cases the calculation is made in the same manner: for example, the Conservative party's percentage of the vote is always subtracted from the Liberal party's percentage.

[41] *Ibid.* Another study of province-level data, employing more rigorous definitions, examined all elections since the turn of the century and found Pinard's theory to be, on the whole, not supported. See the paper by André Blais, "Third Parties in Canadian Provincial Politics," below.

[42] *Rise of a Third Party*, 23–30.

[43] See n.15 above.

[44] See Vincent Lemieux, "Les dimensions sociologiques du vote créditiste au Québec," *Recherches sociographiques* VI (1965), 185–90; and Maurice Pinard, "La faiblesse des Conservateurs et la montée du Crédit social en 1962," *ibid.*, VII (1966), 360–3. The original operationalization used by Pinard in the Quebec case was rather more ingenious, and apparently more valid (Pinard, *Rise of a Third Party*, 23–5).

Thus, in a riding in which the Liberal candidate obtained 55 per cent of the vote and the Conservative 45 per cent, the index of Liberal strength is +10; in a riding where the figures were reversed, that is, the Liberal candidate obtained 45 per cent and the Conservative 55 per cent, the Liberal *S*-index would be −10; and in a constituency where the results were Liberal 55 per cent, Conservative 30 per cent, Independent 15 per cent, the Liberal *S*-index would be +25. In addition to compensating for the influence of multi-party contests, this index automatically distinguishes, by its sign, between losses and victories, should these be deemed of theoretical importance.[45]

IV. The United Farmers of Alberta

The spectacular rise of the United Farmers of Alberta (UFA) in 1921 has been cited by Pinard as evidence supporting his thesis: "the period prior to 1921 [was] a period of one-party dominance by the Liberals, which permitted the rise of the UFA."[46] On the other hand, according to Pinard, this is one of the cases of class-based political action occurring while the "strong" opposition party effectively left the election uncontested.[47] While the Conservative party maintained more than 33 per cent of the vote during this time, and thus by Pinard's criterion was not weak, he recognizes the weakness which marked the party and its virtually complete withdrawal from the 1921 election in rural areas.[48] Accordingly, this is one of the "special cases" discussed above in which the class theory predicts a negative relationship between Liberal strength in 1917 (the previous election) and that of the UFA four years later. The structural theory would of course predict a positive association.

A review of the secondary literature offered no indication whether the rise of the UFA is better understood in class or in structural terms. That the years from the granting of provincial status to the overwhelming victory of the United Farmers were indeed marked by one-party dominance is suggested by the title of the standard work on the period, L.G. Thomas's *The Liberal Party in Alberta: A History of Politics in the Province of Alberta 1905–1921.* This suggestion receives corroboration in David E. Smith's observation that "*the second major party, the Conservative, never provided a single, viable alternative to the dominant party, the Liberal.*"[49] Continually racked with internal strife and handicapped with uninspired leadership, the Tories were unable to offer an effective challenge to the Liberals, even in the wake of the far-reaching Alberta and Great Waterways Railway scandal of 1910, which should have been enough to

[45]The usefulness and, we would argue, the validity of the *S*-index is suggested in that, while the correlation (Pearsonian *r*) between the index and the actual percentage of vote never fell below +.90, the other correlations were, in every case, higher (and in some cases substantially higher) when they were computed using the *S*-index than they were when the actual percentage was used.

[46]*Rise of a Third Party*, 69.

[47]*Ibid.*, 65, n.10.

[48]*Ibid.*, 42. In only 3 of the 46 constituencies with UFA candidates were there also Conservative candidates.

[49]"A Comparison of Prairie Political Movements in Saskatchewan and Alberta," *Journal of Canadian Studies*, IV (February, 1969), 18. My emphasis.

defeat any government.[50] Both a cause and an effect of this situation was the fact that, in Thomas's words, "between elections, the Conservative organization fell to pieces and had to be improvised anew every four years."[51]

This Liberal pre-eminence notwithstanding, C.B. Macpherson explains the rise of the UFA (and also the later rise of Social Credit) not in structural terms as does Pinard, but ideologically, as a class-based rebellion against both parties. He argues that as a result of Alberta's social homogeneity and its quasi-colonial economy, "the alternate-party system was not indigeneous to Western Canada" for "the political tradition of the Canadian West is a non-partisan tradition."[52] Pinard, citing evidence from Thomas's work, counters that while the élite may have consciously rejected partisanship, it is unlikely that more than a fairly small minority of the mass electorate even entertained, let alone accepted, the non-partisan analysis of politics.[53]

Alberta after the First World War clearly met Pinard's condition of strain. As historian W.L. Morton has remarked, even in the second decade of this century Alberta was still partially a frontier society and, accordingly, "the characteristic frontier malaise of debt, dislocation, and restlessness was active in the province."[54] The provincial government was unable to cope with the instability evident in a socio-economic structure which had been erected "upon confidence in the indefinite continuance of rapid growth."[55] The death blow to the faltering Liberal administration took the form of a recession in 1920, signalled by a sudden drop in agricultural prices.[56]

A final point sheds light on the behaviour of Conservative party activists. This is Thomas's explanation of the fact that only 3 of the 16 Conservative candidates in the 1921 election ran in ridings with UFA candidates: "they [the Conservatives] saw that in the rural areas their whole support, which had always proceeded more from opposition to the government than from true attachment to Conservative principles, had gone over to the UFA."[57]

In the Alberta provincial election of 1921, some 61 candidates were elected from 52 ridings.[58] (In our analyses, the five-member districts of Calgary and Edmonton have been excluded because, as a farmers' movement, the UFA did not run candidates in urban areas. The urban constituencies of Lethbridge and Edson were excluded on similar grounds, while the two-member district of Medicine Hat, in which there was only one United Farmer standard-bearer, was also excluded.) Liberal Premier Stewart was returned unopposed in Sedgewick, and his riding was therefore excluded. The constituency of Claresholm was not considered in the analysis since no candidates from the UFA or from the Liberal

[50]See Thomas, *The Liberal Party in Alberta*, chap. 4.
[51]*Ibid.*, 146.
[52]*Democracy in Alberta: Social Credit and the Party System*, 20.
[53]*Rise of a Third Party*, 70.
[54]*The Progressive Party in Canada* (Toronto, 1950), 37.
[55]Thomas, *The Liberal Party in Alberta*, 154.
[56]*Ibid.*, 189.
[57]*Ibid.*, 203.
[58]Raw electoral data for all Alberta elections were taken from the "Returns of the General Election of the Province of Alberta," various years, kindly supplied by the Clerk of the Alberta Legislative Assembly. Candidates' affiliations for the elections of 1917 and 1921 were taken from Castell Hopkins, *The Canadian Annual Review of Public Affairs 1917* and *1921* (Toronto, 1917 and 1921), 806 (1917) and 854 (1921).

TABLE I

UFA STRENGTH ACCORDING TO PARTY WINNING THE 1913 AND 1917 ELECTIONS (1917 acclamations excluded)

Winner of riding, 1913	Winner of riding, 1917	Mean UFA *S*-index in 1921	*N*
Conservative	Conservative	22.0	5
Liberal	Conservative	29.0	5
Conservative	Liberal	24.0	3
Total for Conservative 'strongholds'		25.1	13
Liberal	Liberal	15.4	22*

*One riding with no UFA candidate in this category (excluded from tabulation).

or Conservative parties ran in 1921. Finally, the mining riding of Rocky Mountain, long a labour stronghold, was excluded on the basis of its social and political deviance from the province's other, rural ridings. Accordingly, 44 ridings remain for analysis.[59]

In most cases, including elsewhere in this paper, acclamations may be considered as indicative of overwhelming strength or weakness on the part of one party or another, and thus theoretically important. The dozen candidates acclaimed in the election of 1917 do not fit the normal pattern, however, inasmuch as they were returned unopposed by virtue of House decree, since they were overseas doing their duty for king and country.[60] For this reason, it is likely not valid to consider ridings with acclamations in 1917 as areas of maximum party strength. Reflecting this, Table I shows, with 1917 acclamations excluded, UFA strength as it relates to the outcome of the two previous elections. The categories of ridings are arrayed in ascending order of Liberal dominance, so that if the class theory holds true, UFA strength should decrease as one moves down the table.

To overcome the problem of small cell sizes, the 13 ridings carried by the Conservatives in either 1917 or 1913 – the Conservative "strongholds" – have also been grouped together. Particularly when these Conservative strongholds are compared with the solid Liberal seats, this table points up the fact that the UFA fared better in formerly Conservative seats than in ridings held by the Liberals. (Even if the strongholds are disaggregated, the results are basically the same.) There is, in other words, a negative relationship between the previous strength of the dominant Liberal party and UFA strength.[61]

59Although there were redistributions in 1913 and 1917, the constituencies under consideration were unaffected.

60At least they were supposed to be overseas – there is some evidence that at least one acclaimed Liberal got no closer to the front than the Saskatchewan border. Thomas, *The Liberal Party in Alberta*, 169.

61It is perhaps significant that the highest mean UFA *S*-index scores were registered in ridings where candidates had been acclaimed in 1917: 31.2 in the five with acclaimed Liberals and 56.0 for the two in which Conservative candidates had been returned unopposed (the remaining acclamations had been in the cities). This suggests that rejection of the old parties may have been most pronounced in areas where the shortcomings of the party system – in the form of highly suspect acclamations – had been most in evidence.

These results are corroborated by the correlations (Pearsonian r) between Liberal strength (S-index) in the two previous elections with UFA strength (S-index) in 1921. Taking first the entire complement of 44 seats, the correlation obtained between 1917 Liberal strength and UFA strength was $-.35$.[62] When the 7 seats in which candidates were granted acclamations in 1917 were excluded, the correlation fell marginally to $-.34$. It will be recalled that the class theory predicted that these correlations would be negative, so that the contention that class factors were indeed primarily important in the rise of the UFA is borne out by the data. Regardless of the manner in which it is analysed, there is a moderate relationship in the direction predicted by our extrapolation of the class theory.

The percentage decline in Liberal vote from 1917 to 1921 correlated with the level of Liberal strength in 1917 at $r = +.49$ ($n = 37$). Accordingly, the hypothesis that the dominant party loses proportionately the largest share of its support in its strongest ridings is also supported. Structural factors would thus not seem to have been completely absent in the rise of the UFA, though judging by the other findings of this section they were not so important as class factors.

V. Alberta Social Credit

The unique phenomenon of Social Credit in Alberta – the only Canadian party with an entire series of books devoted to its study – has been cited by Pinard as providing evidence supportive of his (general) thesis.[63] Social Credit's rise in 1935 is clearly an instance of the theory's general case. Its emergence occurred at the time of severe strain, and in the presence of a weak – even by Pinard's standards – opposition Liberal party, which nonetheless contested every seat in the election.

The literature dealing with Social Credit gives the impression that its rise conforms well with the theory's requirements and predictions. Although the UFA never polled more than 46 per cent of the total vote,[64] it held undisputed sway over the province from its meteoric rise in 1921 to its equally rapid demise 14 years later. Smith cites as an illustration of the impotent, disorganized condition of the opposition the fact that in 1926 the indemnity granted the leader of the

[62]For purposes of computing these correlations, and those presented elsewhere in this paper, a riding in which a party did not run a candidate was assigned an S-index of one less than the party's lowest S-index for any other riding. Similarly, acclamations were scored as one greater than the party's highest index elsewhere. Unless otherwise indicated, though, the correlations reported are those computed excluding acclamations and uncontested ridings. Since we are dealing with the population of ridings (not a sample), significance levels are not appropriate.

[63]*Rise of a Third Party*, 43. The series referred to is the "Social Credit in Alberta: Background and Development" series edited by S.D. Clark. In addition to the volumes by Morton, Macpherson, Thomas, and Irving cited in this paper, the series includes J.R. Mallory, *Social Credit and the Federal Power in Canada* (Toronto, 1954); W.E. Mann, *Sect, Cult and Church in Alberta* (Toronto, 1955); and S.D. Clark, *Movements of Political Protest in Canada 1640–1840* (Toronto, 1959), and others.

[64]Thomas Flanagan, "Ethnic Voting in Alberta Provincial Elections, 1921–1971," *Canadian Ethnic Studies*, III (December, 1971), 150. This figure includes the entire province; if the urban areas, in which the UFA did not offer candidates, were excluded, the UFA vote would be considerably higher. The Flanagan paper, we might point out, provides a useful alternative to the present analysis, the narrow limits of which preclude consideration of a number of important factors, ethnicity being one.

opposition was split three ways.[65] Though he does not mention Pinard's work, Smith concurs with his view of the rise of Social Credit: "the absence of an alternative party in Alberta after 1921 did more to create an environment conducive to accepting Social Credit than any other influence in that society."[66] Prior to the Depression (and to a lesser extent during it) opposition parties in the province were viewed as less than meaningful or indeed, necessary, alternatives to the UFA as a result of the development of a new political norm, rooted in non-partisanship and "delegate democracy."[67] That this was a significant trend in the province may be gauged by the 20 (out of 53) seats left uncontested by the Liberals in the 1930 election, and the 43 ridings with no Conservative candidate in the same year.

As for the presence of strain in Alberta during this period, John Irving's social-psychological study of the Social Credit movement leaves little room for doubt: "as the depression increased in severity, Alberta passed into a phase approaching social disorganization ... thousands of people were socially perplexed, frustrated and angry. They were caught in a steel web from which there seemed no escape. Their social environment, their feeling for the process of life, their hope for the future, all became meaningless."[68]

One further aspect of the Social Credit cataclysm bears mentioning. To a not inconsiderable extent, the well-established political machinery of the UFA was simply usurped by the Social Crediters.[69] On this basis alone, one should expect (as does Pinard's general theory) a positive relationship between Social Credit strength in 1935 and UFA strength in the previous elections.

Seven of the 53 ridings have been excluded from the analysis of the rise of Social Credit.[70] As in the forgoing analysis of the UFA, the Labour outpost of Rocky Mountain, and the urban constituencies of Calgary, Edmonton, Lethbridge, Edson, Medicine Hat, and the new urban riding of Drumheller were not included in the data base. While it is certainly true that the Social Credit was not confined to the rural areas, carrying for example two of Edmonton's six seats and four of a like number in Calgary, we would contend that inasmuch as the dominant party, the UFA, was exclusively a rural phenomenon, the theoretical status of urban constituencies is so unclear that they cannot be meaningfully included in the analysis.

Regardless of the manner of presentation, the data on the rise of the Social Credit are less clear cut than in the case of the UFA, as the following tables illustrate. Table II compares, in terms of the Social Credit party's plurality (*S*-index) in 1935, the effects of Liberal victories in the two previous elections. As the general theory would require, Social Credit fared less well in the ridings where the Liberals, the main opposition, had emerged victorious in 1926 and/or 1930 than in ridings which had been solidly UFA. Moreover, the lowest levels

[65]Smith, "Comparison of Prairie Political Movements," 22.
[66]*Ibid.*, 24.
[67]Macpherson, *Democracy in Alberta*, 142.
[68]*The Social Credit Movement in Alberta* (Toronto, 1959), 336, 4.
[69]*Ibid.*, 341.
[70]The creation of the ridings of Clover Bar and Grande Prairie prior to the 1930 election necessitates that the analysis for the 1926 election be based on only 44 cases. Beyond this, there were no redistributions between 1926 and 1935.

TABLE II

SOCIAL CREDIT STRENGTH ACCORDING TO PARTY WINNING THE 1926 AND 1930 ELECTIONS

Winner of riding, 1926	Winner of riding, 1930	Mean Social Credit *S*-index, 1935	*N*
Liberal	Liberal	15.0	3
UFA	Liberal	30.6	5
Liberal	UFA	29.0	1
Total for Liberal 'strongholds'		25.2	9
UFA	UFA	36.1	37

TABLE III

SOCIAL CREDIT STRENGTH IN 1935 ACCORDING TO LIBERAL STRENGTH IN 1930

Outcome in 1930	Mean Social Credit *S*-index	*N*
Liberal victory	24.7	8
Liberal loss	36.9	20
No Liberal candidate	34.7	18

of Social Credit strength were to be found in the (very few) seats captured by the Liberals in both elections.[71] The table presents UFA strength in ascending order, though the cell sizes are so small that it may only be valid to consider the nine Liberal strongholds together.

The relationship is less clear when the ridings are grouped together as in Table III. The theory predicts a negative relationship between Social Credit plurality in 1935 and Liberal strength in 1930, as indicated by the three categories of ridings. Presented in descending order of Liberal strength, these are: (1) ridings won by the Liberals, (2) ridings contested but lost by the Liberals, (3) ridings uncontested by the Liberals. As may be seen, however, Social Credit was marginally more successful in the ridings in which the Liberals had been at least able to field a candidate in 1930 than they were in those seats uncontested by the Liberals in that election which, it does not seem unwarranted to presume, were areas of more pronounced Liberal weakness. This is not in accordance with the general theory's prediction that greater Liberal weakness in 1930 should be associated with greater Social Credit strength five years later.

Finally, the results of the correlational analysis are interesting, if not always entirely comprehensible. One rather curious result is that while UFA strength in 1926 (*S*-index) correlates moderately well with the Social Credit *S*-index in 1935 ($r = +.37$), and in the general theory's predicted direction, the correlation between 1930 UFA strength and Social Credit plurality is all but non-existent ($r = +.05$), indicating the lack of *any* association between UFA strength and that

[71]The solitary rural constituency which did not drop into the Social Credit maw in 1935, Grouard, was, significantly, the only riding which had remained Liberal throughout the entire period of UFA ascendency. According to Flanagan, Grouard's atypical behaviour was in part attributable to the disproportionately large population of French Canadians in this remote riding. Flanagan, "Ethnic Voting in Alberta," 146–7, 152.

of Social Credit. When the latter correlation is computed only on the basis of the 28 ridings with Liberal candidates in 1930, it rises somewhat, but is still weak: +.18. More solid support for the theory comes from the correlations between pre1935 Liberal strength and Social Credit strength. For all 44 ridings, Liberal strength in 1926 and 1930 correlated with the Social Credit *S*-index at $r = -.38$ and $r = -.32$ respectively. If only the districts that had Liberal candidates in 1930 are considered, the correlations both rise to $-.42$ – all of which are in the direction predicted by the general theory.[72]

The role of structural factors is also pointed up by the very strong relationship between the UFA's vote in 1930 and the percentage decline in its support in 1935 ($r = +.84$; $n = 40$). Again the data support the hypothesis that the dominant party loses proportionately the largest share of its electorate in its (formerly) strongest ridings.

To summarize the analysis of the rise of Social Credit in Alberta, the evidence which has emerged tends to bear out Pinard's theory. Some of the data presented were ambiguous as far as the predictions of his theory were concerned, but on the whole the general, structural, theory was moderately supported.

VI. The United Farmers of Ontario

The unexpected victory of the United Farmers of Ontario (UFO) in the election of 1919 offers another opportunity of testing Pinard's general theory as well as the special class theory. At first blush, the rise of the UFO would seem to be in keeping with Pinard's theory: a period of Conservative dominance resulted in a widespread rejection of the Liberal party as a credible alternative to the government and led, in the presence of serious postwar strain, to the new third party. However, this description omits two salient features of the situation. First, the new third party was stridently class (farmer) in orientation – as was its urban counterpart, the Independent Labor Party.[73] Second, the opposition Liberal party failed to contest some 44 of the 111 seats in the election. Included among these were precisely half (36) of those in which the UFO presented candidates. On this basis, it would appear that the special class cleavage theory might be more germane to the case at hand.

One eminent historian's interpretation of the electoral shifts contributing to the success of the UFO provides unambiguous support for neither Pinard's general, structural theory, nor the special class theory. W.L. Morton writes:

[72]The apparent inconsistency in the correlations between 1935 Social Credit strength and the *S*-indices of the UFA and the Liberal party in the previous election stems from the presence of several Conservative candidates, and also from the different number of constituencies (44 and 28 respectively) on which the correlations were computed.

[73]The relationship between the UFO and the ILP has been stated succinctly: "the two movements had much in common ... [but] disagreed on too many issues to merge. However, they did cooperate in the election campaign." Brian D. Tennyson, "The Ontario General Election of 1919: The Beginnings of Agrarian Revolt," *Journal of Canadian Studies*, IV (February, 1969), 33. The ILP has been excluded from the analysis due to the small number of its candidates in the election (19), and also because it would require, as an urban phenomenon, separate treatment from the exclusively rural UFO, which we do not have the space to present.

the correspondence between the areas of UFO activity and those of the old Grit party was marked. It made evident the basic pattern of the electoral support received by the farmers' candidates. That support was drawn from three sources: the first was discontented rural Liberals disillusioned by the weakness of the provincial Liberals and suspicious of French and clerical influence in the federal party. The second was frustrated rural Conservatives, weary of voting Conservative to no purpose in traditionally Liberal seats. The third was doctrinaire agrarians, who had repudiated the party system and were working for direct representation by farmers of agrarian interests.[74]

Accordingly, the issue of each theory's validity must be resolved empirically.

A prime theoretical concern in the UFO's rise is the status of the Conservative party prior to the 1919 election. It might be objected that it was not a dominant party as Pinard intended the term to mean. Though he observes that the Ontario political scene "was dominated by the Conservatives,"[75] from 1905 to 1919, he does not classify it as being in a condition of one-party dominance inasmuch as the opposition Liberal party averaged more than 33 per cent of the popular vote during this period. Although it is true that the Liberals had held sway in Ontario (provincially) for most of the period from Confederation until 1905, that year marked the beginning of nearly 15 years of unbroken Conservative hegemony during which the Tories carried four successive elections. Though the Liberals averaged only slightly less than 40 per cent of the total vote during these years, this is not a reliable guide to the party's strength in the period leading up to the election. In the later stages of the war, and in the months following it, the Ontario Liberal party was beset by bitter internecine conflict, primarily over the conscription issue and its aftermath of racial division, but also over leadership wrangles and the party's stance on prohibition. Coupled with its recurring inability to terminate the Tory ascendency, this meant that

it was highly questionable whether the Ontario Liberal party was a viable political organization in 1919, so disastrous were its divisions ... perhaps [this] situation was worsened by the fact that the Liberals had spent the past fifteen years in opposition and there appeared no real likelihood of their emerging from the proverbial political wilderness in the near future ... *the Liberals were hopelessly divided and hardly credible as an alternate government.*[76]

Thus if there was not overwhelming Conservative preponderance, there most certainly was abnormal weakness on the part of the sole opposition.

The author of a recent study of the 1919 Conservative debacle agrees that the Liberals were not "a credible alternative to the Hearst Conservatives." However, he also points out that the Tories had serious internal and leadership problems of their own and were accordingly in a markedly weakened condition prior to the election.[77] Nonetheless, our evaluation remains unaltered. For one thing, the extreme debilitation of the Liberal party precluded any effective opposition. Moreover, by the time the Conservative decline had become apparent, the farmers' movement was well under way, so that any lessening in the perception of Conservative dominance would have had a decidedly diminished impact. The

[74]*The Progressive Party in Canada*, 83.
[75]*Rise of a Third Party*, 49.
[76]Tennyson, "The Ontario General Election of 1919," 29–30. Emphasis added.
[77]Peter Oliver, "Sir William Hearst and the Collapse of the Conservative Party," *Canadian Historical Review*, LIII (March, 1972), 34–5.

situation was not unlike that in Alberta in 1935 where the collapse of the UFA was evident to all even before the election.

Concerning the presence of strain, there is widespread agreement that in Ontario (as throughout the nation) severe discontent and social unrest followed in the aftermath of the First World War.[78] One signally important source of farmer agitation was their seeming inability either to stem the tide of rural depopulation or to shake the government from its apparent indifference to the problem which, for both economic and symbolic reasons, was of first-order significance to the farmers. Not only were the cities claiming a relatively larger share of the province's population, but all rural areas, save the newly settled far north, were undergoing absolute population decline and generally had been since the 1880s and 1890s. Rural Ontario's opposition to the federal government's odious conscription policy (in some respects the prime catalyst in the politicization of the UFO[79]) is probably best viewed in the context of the resultant sharp decline in farm manpower.[80]

For this and for other reasons as well, the political outlook throughout much of rural Ontario was distinctly hostile to practically all aspects of the prevailing party system. As one historian has put it, a good many farmers were "caught up in a growing tide of moral indignation, the conviction that the old parties were corrupt and had sold their souls to the protected interests."[81] The period was also marked by continual reference to the scandalous underrepresentation of farmers in both the national and provincial legislatures.[82] In addition, the fear was prevalent that on account of the acceleration in outmigration, the immediate post-war years held the last chance for the farmers to regain something of their political influence.[83] There was, in sum, a pervasive feeling on the farmers' part of inaccessability to governmental decision-making through the traditional channels (that is, the old parties) – a point stressed by Smelser in his discussion of structural conduciveness to norm-oriented movements.[84]

The fact that there were Liberal standard-bearers in some but not all constituencies in 1919 complicates the analysis. If the structural theory is valid, we may expect, for all ridings, a positive relationship between Tory strength prior to 1919 and subsequent UFO success. In those districts contested by the Liberals we have a clear example of Pinard's general case and thus the prediction of a positive association. Where there were no Liberal candidates, the logic of the structural conduciveness interpretation leads to a similar prediction.

If, on the other hand, the special theory is correct, and the underlying political dynamic is one of class, then, as argued in section II, a negative association should emerge in those districts *without* Liberal candidates. Unfortunately, the class theory is indeterminate with respect to the predicted direction of the rela-

[78]Tennyson, "The Ontario General Election of 1919," 27. See also W.R. Young, "Conscription, Rural Depopulation and the Farmers of Ontario, 1917–19," *Canadian Historical Review*, LIII (September, 1972), 290.

[79]R.W. Trowbridge, "War Time Discontent and the Rise of the United Farmers of Ontario 1914–1919," MA thesis, University of Waterloo, 1966.

[80]Young, "Conscription, Rural Depopulation and the Farmers," 318.

[81]Tennyson, "The Ontario General Election of 1919," 29.

[82]*Ibid.*, 27.

[83]Young, "Conscription, Rural Depopulation and the Farmers," 313.

[84]Smelser, *Theory of Collective Behavior*, 282–6.

TABLE IV

UFO STRENGTH ACCORDING TO PARTY WINNING THE ELECTIONS OF 1911 AND 1914

Winner of riding, 1911	Winner of riding, 1914	Ridings with Liberal candidate: Mean UFO *S*-index	Ridings with Liberal candidate: *N**	Ridings with no Liberal candidate: Mean UFO *S*-index	Ridings with no Liberal candidate: *N**
Liberal	Liberal	−7.6	5	24.0	5
Conservative	Liberal	6.0	4	—	0
Total Liberal strongholds		−2.0	10	26.7	6
Liberal	Conservative	12.7	4	25.3	3
Conservative	Conservative	−6.6	22	10.1	23
Total Conservative strongholds		−3.6	26	12.4	30

*The total *N*s for the 1914 strongholds are larger than would be indicated from the 1911–14 breakdown because 1911 data was unavailable for some ridings due to redistribution.

tionship in three-cornered fights. This indeterminacy stems from the fact that it is no longer true that all former opposition supporters have no alternative but to switch to the third party. The option of remaining with the opposition is still available. The implication of this possibility is that the size of the third party's electorate will be a function of *two distinct* proportions: the percentage of the dominant party's supporters deserting in favour of the new party *and* the percentage of the opposition party's voters migrating to the third party. Depending on the magnitudes of these proportions (presumably determined largely by class factors), the *over-all* relationship may be either negative or positive.

The tabulation of UFO strength according to which party won the elections of 1911 and 1914, controlling for the presence or absence of Liberal candidates, is presented in Table IV.[85] If Pinard's general, structural thesis is correct, UFO strength should increase as one progresses down the table, inasmuch as the ridings were arrayed in ascending order of pre1919 Conservative strength. Looking first at those seats in which there were Liberal candidates, it may be seen that this expectation is fulfilled for the first three categories, but that the pattern sharply reverses in the final, most numerous, category. In the latter, the most strongly Tory districts, the UFO was only marginally stronger (or perhaps more accurately, less weak) than it was in the most solid Liberal seats. If the constituencies are dichotomized into Liberal and Conservative strongholds on the

[85]Raw data for Ontario, as well as the exact changes affected by redistributions, are taken from Roderick Lewis, *Centennial Edition of a History of the Electoral Districts, Legislatures and Ministries of the Province of Ontario 1867–1968* (Toronto, 1968). Particularly with respect to candidates' affiliations, this source seems to be more complete than the *Canadian Annual Review* from which Pinard's data were taken; this accounts for the slight discrepancies between our figures and those of Pinard (*Rise of a Third Party*, 49–50). A redistribution was carried out prior to the 1914 election, but in the main it affected only the urban areas. A few ridings have, however, been excluded from some phases of the analysis because their boundaries were substantially revamped at this time. Finally, the 1919 election marked the first full enfranchisement of women. This vast expansion of the electorate was doubtless of major significance, but the problem of dealing with it empirically, as is the case with so many difficulties of aggregate data analysis, can only be recorded, not resolved.

basis of the outcome of the 1914 election alone, a weak negative relationship emerges – directly the opposite of the Pinard theory's prediction.

Turning next to the districts uncontested by the Grits, the existence of a negative relationship between former Conservative strength and UFO strength in 1919 is much clearer – evidence directly supporting the class theory. Table IV also serves to illustrate that the UFO fared considerably better in districts not contested by the Liberals (recall that the *S*-index compensates for the number of candidates). This would seem to indicate that, in the absence of their own party's standard-bearers, most, if not all, Liberal supporters went over to the third party – as was assumed by the class theory.

There were in 1919, 11 rural or semi-rural ridings in which the UFO did not field candidates. Nine of these had been carried by the Conservatives in 1914, and the mean Conservative *S*-index for all 11 in 1914 was 20.2. Areas in which the UFO failed to nominate were, in other words, very strongly Tory. This is, of course, precisely the opposite of the expectation drawn from Pinard's general theory.

Finally, the results of the correlational analysis tend to substantiate the findings already presented. For constituencies with and without Liberal candidates, the relationships between UFO strength in 1919 and that of the Conservative party five years previous were: $r = -.36$ (n=34) and $r = -.40$ (n=33) respectively.

The data, in short, uniformly fail to support the structural theory, and for the most part do support the class theory. As was the case for the two Alberta parties examined earlier, however, there were strong relationships found between level of dominant (Conservative) party strength in 1914 and the percentage decline experienced by the party in 1919: $r = +.67$ (n=34) for ridings with Liberal candidates and $r = +.72$ (n=33) for ridings without Liberal candidates. Structural factors do seem to have played a certain role in the rise of the UFO, but not, it would seem, in the way described by Pinard's general theory.[86]

[86]In an attempt to further illuminate the processes at work in the rise of the UFO, an indicator of social strain was brought into the analysis of the electoral data. The indicator employed was outmigration from rural areas, as a percentage of total population, during the period 1911–21. (Data taken from Young, "Conscription, Rural Depopulation and the Farmers," appendix A; we should like to thank Mr Young for permission to use this data.) Given the importance of rural depopulation as a source of strain (*ibid.*, *passim*, and page 417 above), this would appear a not unreasonable choice.

The migration data, aggregated by county, was matched to the electoral districts as closely as possible, though inclusion of large urban areas in some counties and gross mismatches between some counties and ridings necessitated that the analysis be based on only 50 cases. (In addition, for a considerable number of these rural population movements were not separated out from those affecting incorporated towns and villages; *ibid.*, notes to Appendix A.)

In the 24 ridings with Liberal candidates, results were much as might have been expected. The Conservative *S*-index in 1914 correlated with 1919 UFO strength at $r = -.31$ (the discrepancy between this figure and that in the text, $r = -.36$, is attributable to the different number of cases employed); when the effects of strain (outmigration) were partialled out, r fell to $-.23$, indicating the importance of strain in the causal sequence. Strain correlated with UFO strength at $r = .24$; partialling out previous Conservative strength had virtually no effect ($r = .23$). The simple correlation between Conservative strength in 1914 and outmigration was $-.44$, meaning that the Tories, not unexpectedly, fared worst in areas of heaviest depopulation.

For the 26 ridings not contested by the Liberal party in 1919, the data are frankly in-

Conclusion

Pinard, as it turns out, was correct in his speculation that a class interpretation fits the data on the rise of the two farmers' parties better than does his original structural theory. But, at the same time, structural conduciveness more accurately explains the rise of Alberta Social Credit. These results serve to raise the question of under what circumstances either of the two models is appropriate. Throughout the article we have treated them as virtually polar opposites; in all likelihood this is incorrect. There are quite probably some class factors operating in most instances in which Pinard's structural conduciveness model applies. Similarly, structural processes have been uncovered even in those cases where the class theory offered the better over-all explanation. Indeed, the most consistent finding throughout was the strong positive relationship between former dominant-party strength and its decline in vote at the third-party election, indicating a general tendency for the dominant party to lose proportionately the largest share of its support in its formerly strongest areas.

This, coupled with the positive support found for both the structural and class theories suggests that they are not totally distinct, but may rather be variations on a more widely applicable theory which might account for the development of new (Canadian) political movements in general and third parties in particular. Now, the search for generalizations valid for any time or place carries with it some decidedly suspect methodological assumptions;[87] however, if these are kept in mind, the quest for a more comprehensive theory of third parties in Canada could be expected to produce insights valuable in both theoretical and substantive terms.

One potentially fruitful area for inquiry lies in expanding the notion of structural conduciveness beyond one-party dominance. The ramifications flowing out of the federal arrangement seem especially promising for broadening the concept. Is it not suggestive that in analysing Pinard's original case, Lemieux found Social Credit strength in Quebec to be markedly greater in those ridings which had changed hands either federally *or* provincially between 1956 and 1960?[88] Political developments at one level of government oftentimes are of signal importance to a complete understanding of party dynamics at the other level. Accordingly, any theory of third parties in Canada will have to make provision for the ubiquitous federal-provincial nexus.

---

comprehensible to this writer. The zero-order correlation between 1914 Conservative strength and UFO strength in 1919 was —.43, rising slightly to —.45 when migration was partialled out. Strain correlated with the UFO *S*-index very weakly ($r = .07$), although the partial correlation, controlling for Tory strength in 1914, rose to .23. This unexpected result appears to reflect the influence of the relationship between strain and Tory fortunes in 1914, which was, strange to say, positive ($r = .27$). In other words, in those ridings in which no Liberal candidates were present in 1919, the Conservatives had attracted their greatest 1914 strength in areas *most* affected by outmigration. This finding is puzzling on two counts: (1) why should the relationship be positive? and (2) why should the relationship, *in 1914*, differ according to whether there were or were not Liberal candidates *in 1919*? At the present time, no satisfactory answers – or speculations – can be provided to either of these questions.

[87] T. L. Thorson, *Biopolitics* (Toronto, 1970), chaps. 3–5.

[88] "Les dimensions sociologiques," 187; see also Pinard, *Rise of a Third Party*, 72–8.

Politics is only infrequently given over to submission to simple (if appealing) theoretical explanations. This being the case, we should be neither surprised nor discouraged that Pinard's original theory proved to be of only limited applicability in the analysis of our three third party movements. By the same token, though, it is heartening that all three were fairly well accounted for by the original theory, or by the special class theory sketched out by Pinard. In any event, his efforts, as well as the criticisms and further explorations they have inspired, must be viewed as necessary and important stages in the construction of a theory of Canadian (third) parties.

Third Parties in Canadian Provincial Politics*

ANDRÉ BLAIS *University of Ottawa*

Among the main criticisms addressed to modern social science are that it deals with trivial matters, that it does not study change, and that it is either too abstract or too empirical. Certainly these criticisms do not apply to Maurice Pinard's book *The Rise of a Third Party*. Pinard continuously moves back and forth between his data and his theory, slightly modifying the latter as he goes along. Even on the theoretical side, Pinard moves from middle-range theory to a more abstract level.

The theory is particularly challenging to political scientists. Pinard argues that one-party dominance is a necessary condition of the rise of third parties. It may come as a surprise that a sociologist puts such stress on a "political" variable. This in itself should make the theory attractive to most of us. In chapter 3, which deals with the rise of third parties in Canada, he challenges the usual interpretation of Canadian provincial politics. From the literature,[1] one gets the definite impression that the West and the East have different "political cultures" and that this explains the differences in party politics, third parties being more popular in the West. Pinard rejected this explanation and focused his argument on structural variables. One cannot but welcome such an attempt. Cultural explanations have a conservative overtone, and structural variables cannot be omitted from the study of change.[2]

The hypothesis examined in this article states that one-party dominance is a necessary but not sufficient condition for the rise of third parties. This hypothesis is itself deduced from Smelser's theory, according to which structural conduciveness is one determinant of social movements. Pinard's theory is thus in a way a middle-range theory, but its level of abstraction is still relatively high. Pinard is left with two levels of analysis: a fairly abstract level, where the two basic concepts are one-party dominance and the rise of third parties, and an empirical level. There is a large gap between these two levels, which cannot help but raise serious problems of operationalization. These problems are discussed all too briefly by Pinard. The term "third party" is never precisely defined. The justifi-

*I would first like to thank the students of a graduate seminar at York University for their comments on the first draft of this paper. I would also like to thank Maurice Pinard for the comprehensive list of remarks that he sent me on that draft. Finally I wish to acknowledge the useful discussions I had, at various stages of my inquiry, with Jean Crête, Caroline Andrew, and Carol Charlebois.

1We have in mind several of the books in the University of Toronto Press's Canadian government series and *Canadian Provincial Politics*, ed. Martin Robin (Scarborough, Ont., 1972).

2See Carole Pateman, "Political Culture, Political Structure and Political Change," *British Journal of Political Science* (July 1971), 291–307.

Canadian Journal of Political Science/Revue canadienne de science politique, VI, no. 3 (September/septembre 1973). Printed in Canada/Imprimé au Canada.

Les élections provinciales au Canada et la montée des tiers partis

L'auteur amorce son article par un examen de l'hypothèse de Maurice Pinard selon laquelle la prédominance d'un parti est une condition nécessaire à la montée de tiers partis. Il détecte certaines carences dans la méthodologie de Pinard, en particulier en ce qui a trait à son échantillon d'élections ainsi qu'a sa mesure de la prédominance d'un parti. Il suggère que la prédominance électorale devrait être mesurée à l'aide d'indices multiples.

La théorie pinardienne est vérifiée à l'aide de nouveaux tests dont la plupart en infirment la validité. L'auteur fait cependant observer que l'hypothèse correspond généralement aux connaissances que nous avons du comportement électoral au Canada. Il en conclut qu'une approche plus inductive du problème s'impose.

Une brève analyse historique lui permet de détecter deux phénomènes : le clivage est-ouest et l'existence de nettes tendances historiques. Il lui apparaît que la seule prédominance ne saurait expliquer ces deux phénomènes. Il lui semble donc que la prédominance, bien que pertinente à la croissance des tiers partis, n'est pas un facteur déterminant.

L'auteur tente ensuite d'interpréter la montée des tiers partis dans les provinces canadiennes à l'aide du schéma d'analyse selon la valeur additive (value-added scheme) de Smelser. Il fait valoir que Pinard – de même que toutes les études sur le comportement électoral – n'accorde pas suffisamment d'attention à deux composantes du comportement collectif : la mobilisation et le contrôle social. Il fait donc un bref plaidoyer en faveur d'une réorientation des recherches sur le comportement électoral.

cation for the operationalization of one-party dominance – a most abstract concept – is given in one paragraph. Finally, the choice of the sample is described in one sentence.

We would thus argue that Pinard's hypothesis is most interesting, but that his test is not conclusive.[3] One wonders whether the actual procedure adopted by Pinard is justified within his own theoretical framework. The first part of this article is a close examination of the methodology of chapter 3 in *The Rise of a Third Party*. It questions the validity of some of Pinard's decisions, suggests changes in his indicators and in his sample, and determines how these changes would affect the results. This first part is a look at the theory – and a critique of it – from the inside. The second part of the analysis adopts a different perspective. It discusses the problem at hand – why third parties succeed or fail – in a more general fashion, and in doing so, proposes new ways of testing Pinard's hypothesis.

It could be objected that chapter 3 is not very important in *The Rise of a Third Party*, as it does not deal explicitly with Social Credit. We do not consider the objection to be pertinent. Pinard himself argues in chapter 4 that the main advantage of his theory over that of C.B. Macpherson is that it can account for the rise of third parties everywhere in Canada. Moreover, structural conduciveness is put forward as the first necessary condition and also one of the two crucial determinants of third-party emergence. As we will indicate in the conclusion, if we are to reject the argumentation advanced in chapter 3, an important revision of Pinard's general theory is necessary.

[3]For a similar argument, see W. P. Irvine's review of the book in this JOURNAL, V, no. 2 (June 1972), 313–15.

TABLE I

PREVIOUS STRENGTH OF MAIN OPPOSITION PARTY

Election outcome	A Previously Weak	B Suddenly Weak	C Strong
1. No third party (or third parties less than 10%)	23%	0%	82%
2. Third parties' vote between 10% and 20%	18	10	6
3. Third parties' vote greater than 20%	59	90	12
N (elections)	22	10	33

Gamma: - .70

I. The test of the theory: a re-analysis

Pinard's analysis is based on a whole set of decisions as to the best way to test his theory. In this section each of these decisions is discussed and changes in the procedure are suggested. Particular attention is paid to how each of these changes affects the empirical results.

Central to Pinard's entire analysis is his Table 3.1, reproduced here as Table I, which refers to elections held in Canadian provinces since the beginning of the century. The independent variable is the previous strength of the main opposition party. Category A contains cases in which the opposition party (or the strongest of many opposition parties) failed to retain at least a third of the votes while in opposition; category C contains cases in which the main opposition party succeeded in retaining at least a third of the votes. Category B is discussed below. The measure of the dependent variable, election outcome, is explicit. As can be seen, the relationship between the two variables is very strong (gamma: -.70).[4]

Category B of the independent variable raises some problems. In six of the cases, "the main opposition party though having maintained an average of more than 33 per cent of the votes, had generally been out of power for a long time but above all, found itself suddenly weakened, as indicated by its failure to contest a large proportion of the seats."[5] The point, however, is that this "sudden" weakness may have been caused by the emergence of a third party. If this were so, the assumption of one-way causality, on which the test of the theory is based, would fall apart. Moreover, it seems too easy to decide *a posteriori*, when the data do not fit the theory, that the main opposition party was in fact weak. More basically, it can be argued that cases in which a "fairly strong" opposition party does not contest many seats clearly contradict Pinard's theory. The theory is based on the assumption that voters are fairly passive, that the leaders are determinant in the rise of third parties because they define the situation.[6] The theory deals with élite as well as mass behaviour. It predicts that the leaders of a strong opposition party should not decide not to contest some seats. According

[4]Note in passing that Pinard's hypothesis implies a negative relationship between the previous strength of the main opposition party and the rise of a third party; a negative relationship constitutes a positive test of the hypothesis and vice versa.
[5]Pinard, *Rise of a Third Party*, 38.
[6]*Ibid.*, 31.

TABLE II

PREVIOUS STRENGTH OF MAIN OPPOSITION PARTY*

Election outcome	Weak	Strong
1. No third party (or) third parties' vote less than 10 per cent	67%	78%
2. Third parties' vote between 10 per cent and 20 per cent	0	3
3. Third parties' vote greater than 20 per cent	33	19
N (elections)	9	37

Gamma: – .31

*See the text for an explanation of the variables. We would like to thank Maurice Pinard for having kindly lent us his data on elections held prior to 1930. The other sources were Howard Scarrow, *Canada Votes: A Handbook of Federal and Provincial Election Data*, New Orleans, the Hauser Press, 1962; the *Canadian Annual Review*, the *Canadian Parliamentary Guide* and the *Globe and Mail.*

to the logic of the theory, category B should be collapsed with category C. Pinard concedes that such a point could be argued.[7] The fact is not that it would provide a more stringent test but rather that it is the only legitimate test. When B and C are collapsed, the relationship diminishes, but not by very much (gamma: –.58).

Pinard's analysis of provincial elections is extensive; but at the federal level he considers only a few cases. We prefer to stick to the provincial level. This change, a very minor one, does not weaken the relationship – in fact it strengthens it a little. At the provincial level Pinard considered all elections "since 1900 in which the party in power was defeated, as well as those elections in which a third party emerged."[8] It should first be pointed out that Pinard does not always stick to his own criterion. The New Brunswick election of 1948 is a good example. In that election, the Social Credit party obtained less than 1 per cent of the votes, partly, according to Pinard, because there was a strong two-party system. But this election should not have been included since there was no government turnover. Indeed there are four such cases (Quebec: 1948, New Brunswick: 1948, Prince Edward Island: 1947, and Saskatchewan: 1956) that in my opinion,[9] should not have been included.

Why should not all elections be included? The problem is that one-party dominance is only one of the necessary conditions for the rise of third parties; therefore, one ought to control for these other conditions (such as strain and mobilization). Pinard's reasoning seems to be that when there is no government turnover these conditions are not likely to be met. This is of course a questionable assumption, as we will see at a later stage. If this is the reasoning, though, elections in which a third party emerged should not be included unless the party in power is defeated. If the decision not to include all elections is justified there is no reason why we should include all cases of third party emergence. These last two objections to the sample are minor. Table II in which the "corrections"

[7] *Ibid.*, 39.
[8] *Ibid.*, 37.
[9] These comments are based on the assumption that the emergence of a third party implies that it obtains a fair amount of votes (let us say more than 10 per cent). Otherwise, most of the elections left out by Pinard witnessed the rise of some minor third party.

are made,[10] still shows a fairly strong relationship between the two variables. Note, however, that the strength of the relationship decreases.

In addition, we should critically examine the dependent variable. What Pinard is really concerned with is those circumstances under which people will switch to a third party. His interest is thus in change over time. In fact, his operationalization is biased toward confirming his theory. When the main opposition party is weak there is likely to be another weak third party. This is less likely when there is a strong two-party system. The fact that there is already a third party makes it a little more likely that a third party of some strength will emerge. It therefore makes more sense to look at percentage increases in party votes.[11] When we calculate the results according to the increase in the vote for a third party and not the vote itself again the relationship diminishes only slightly.

But let us come back to the independent variable, one-party dominance. How to measure it? As mentioned before, Pinard looked at the average proportion of votes that the main opposition party obtained while in opposition. In order to assess the validity of this measure we must understand what Pinard really means by one-party dominance. According to him, what characterizes a strong opposition party is that it can be perceived as a viable alternative to the party in power. One-party dominance is the absence of a strong opposition party. From this perspective, the issue pertains to the voters' and activists' perceptions of party strength. Many questions may be raised. First, is party strength perceived in terms of seats or in terms of votes? An argument could easily be made that seats are easier to perceive than votes.[12] But it is more likely that both votes and seats are significant. Pinard notes that using seats instead of votes does not yield good results.[13] He concludes that seats are not as good an indicator of party strength but this inference is not really legitimate. The content validity of an indicator cannot be assessed empirically. The mere fact that Pinard tested his theory using seats indicates that he thought seats could be a valid measure. It seems to us that party dominance is an abstract concept that should be measured through multiple indicators. We should note at this stage that with one of the indicators the theory is not supported.

Another question pertains to the number of previous elections the measurement should include. Pinard chose to include all previous elections since the last government turnover. Again it could be argued that the voters' time perceptions are somewhat restricted and that only the last election is significant. We tested Pinard's theory with this last indicator of party strength and found no relation-

[10]Table II incorporates a few other corrections. For instance, the Saskatchewan election of 1944 is described by Pinard as a case of a third-party emergence (the CCF came to power). In the preceding paragraph however (p. 45) Pinard had stated that in 1934 the CCF became the main opposition party. According to us the CCF was not a third party in 1944. This points out the importance of a precise definition of a third party which Pinard does not provide. We suggest that a third party is a non-traditional party that has not managed to obtain a minimum of 10 per cent of the votes in each of the previous two elections. Table III also includes elections (1970–1) that have occurred since Pinard's study. This adds six cases, three of which support the theory.

[11]Pinard acknowledges this possibility. See *Rise of a Third Party*, 24, n.12.

[12]Alan C. Cairns, "The Electoral System and the Party System in Canada, 1921–1965", this JOURNAL, I (March 1968), 58–80.

[13]*Rise of a Third Party*, 63, n.2.

TABLE III

PREVIOUS STRENGTH OF MAIN OPPOSITION PARTY*

Electoral change	Weak	Strong
1. Third parties did not increase their votes by more than 10 per cent	71%	78%
2. Third parties increased their votes by more than 10 per cent and less than 20 per cent	0	4
3. Third parties increased their votes by more than 20 per cent	28	17
N (elections)	21	23

Gamma: – .21

*A weak opposition party is here defined as one that had not been in power in the previous 15 years. Two elections (New Brunswick, 1908, and Prince Edward Island, 1911) had to be deleted because we did not have the data for elections held before 1900.

ship between the two variables. Another potential indicator of one-party dominance is the number of years a party has been in power; this did yield a mild relationship between our two variables, as can be seen in Table III. Finally, party dominance could also be measured by party distances.[14] This last indicator yielded results which did not support the theory.

We have thus mentioned five measures of the independent variable, all of which make some sense. These five measures are: (1) the average proportion of *votes* the main opposition party obtained while in opposition (Pinard's indicator); (2) the average proportion of *seats* the main opposition party obtained while in opposition; (3) the proportion of votes the main opposition party obtained in *the last election*; (4) the number of years a party has been in power; (5) party distances. For three of these measures, the test proved negative. For two other measures the test was positive, although the relationship was now not as strong (when proper corrections are made) as originally indicated by Pinard.

We have suggested thus far that a more stringent test of Pinard's theory is necesary. This had induced us to suggest some minor changes in the sample and in the dependent variable which barely affect the relationship. In addition, we showed that the last two categories of the independent variable had to be collapsed. Moreover we argued that the independent variable should be measured through multiple indicators. We showed that the theory was supported for only two of the five indicators. Pinard's theory is thus in serious doubt. We will now go a step further and discuss what we think is the major flaw in Pinard's analysis.

For this, we must return to Pinard's sample. We speculated earlier on why he limited himself to elections in which there was a government turnover. We did not question his decision at the time, but we will now. It makes sense to assume

[14]At first sight party distances seem to be the most valid measure of party dominance (see for instance David G. Pfeiffer, "The Measurement of Interparty Competition and Systematic Stability" in *American Political Science Review* (1967), 457–68). We now believe, however, that Pinard is right: strength in previous election(s) is a better indicator (though we have doubts about the exclusion of seats and the number of elections included). The advantage of Pinard's operationalization is that when an opposition party has more than 33 per cent of the votes it is likely not to be too far away from the party in power and to have a strong lead over any third party. Party distances do not include this second element. According to us however Pinard's measure is only a little more valid than party distances.

that the other necessary conditions are likely to be met when the party in power loses ground. But losing ground and losing an election are two different things. How is it possible to argue that there are strains when, in a strong two-party system, a minor change in the distribution of votes leads to a government turnover? Moreover a government party can retain its percentage of votes and still lose the election.

It can be shown that the decision to retain only cases of government turnover is biased toward the verification of the hypothesis. The sample includes elections resulting in "ritual" changes in which there is not much strain and in which the government party, though defeated, remains very popular. These cases are very likely to be cases of a strong two-party system. The point is that for a government turnover to occur in a one-party-dominant system, the minimal switch in the vote distribution is fairly large; the party in power has to lose much ground. This is not necessarily the case in a strong two-party system. This means that in such a sample the other necessary conditions are more likely to be met in a one-party-dominant system (much change must occur for an election in such a system to be considered) than in a competitive two-party system. The observed relationship is at least partly spurious; there are relatively fewer third party emergences in a strong two-party system at least partly because more "ritual" elections are included in which there is not much change in the vote distribution and, presumably, not much strain.

A more appropriate decision would be to consider only elections in which the party in power loses a certain minimum of votes. We tested the theory using two different minima, 5 per cent and 10 per cent. Let us first consider the larger sample based on a 5 per cent minimum. We first retained Pinard's own operationalization, the strength of the main opposition party in previous elections. Table IV shows a positive relationship, contrary to the model's prediction. With other measures of one-party dominance, that is, the strength of the main opposition party in the last election or the number of years the government party had been in power, the hypothesis was still not supported. On the other hand, we did find a negative relationship when relying on the smaller sample (including only elections in which the party in power loses at least 10 per cent of its votes), but only with Pinard's own indicator (gamma: – .33). This, however, was partly a function of the cut-off point. We found that, when the latter was 35 per cent (instead of 33 per cent, as Pinard suggests) the relationship vanished. Altogether we had 16 tests of the theory based on different samples, operationalizations, and cut-off points;[15] only three supported the theory. Of course, it could be argued that the positive tests are in fact the only valid ones. To us this argument is not a cogent one. One-party dominance is a very abstract concept and it is generally acknowledged that, when dealing with an abstract concept, one should rely on the use of multiple indicators[16].

A closer look at the data which are combined in table 4 is illuminating: 16 out of the 20 elections from the Maritime provinces are in line with Pinard's

[15]This leaves out two other measures of one-party dominance – the main opposition party's share of seats in previous elections and party distances – that had already been proved not to support the theory.
[16]See Hubert M. Blalock, *Theory Construction* (Englewood Cliffs, N.J., 1969), 152.

TABLE IV

PREVIOUS STRENGTH OF MAIN OPPOSITION PARTY

Electoral change*	Weak	Strong
1. A traditional party increased its votes by more than 10 per cent	46%	35%
2. A traditional party increased its votes by more than 5 per cent but less than 10 per cent	15	23
3. Third parties increased their votes by more than 5 per cent but less than 10 per cent	0	5
4. Third parties increased their votes by more than 10 per cent	38	38
N	13	40

Gamma: .11

*The 1967 Alberta election had to be excluded because both a traditional and a third party increased their votes.

prediction. Thus it is a fact that in the Maritimes party competition has been intense and third parties have been unsuccessful. Outside these provinces, however, the picture is not at all clear. It is my opinion that Pinard paid too much attention to the Maritime provinces. Of course, third parties have been particularly unsuccessful there. The point is, however, that nothing much has happened anyway. Compare the Maritimes with the Prairies; in the latter, third parties have been successful. But is it not because change is part of the game? Twenty-two of the 51 elections held in the Maritimes can be characterized as status quo ones, in that no party gained or lost more than 5 per cent of its votes. In the Prairies, only 7 out of 50 elections can be characterized in the same way.

The fact is that traditional loyalties are very important in the Maritimes and party identification is very low in the Prairies.[17] As a consequence, there is much more quantitative change in the latter than in the former. Pinard's theory deals with the nature of this change, that is, whether it benefits traditional or third parties. It is concerned with the *direction* of change; but the amount of change itself must also be controlled for. Only three times have third parties increased their votes by more than 10 per cent in the Maritimes. One should keep in mind, however, that very seldom has any party increased its share of the votes by such a margin anyway. Pinard, by looking at instances of government turnover, included many elections in which no meaningful change occurred in the vote distribution. In so doing, he did not control for the amount of change and favoured evidence from one region, the Maritimes, in which his theory seems to work best.

In short, we argue that third parties have been more successful in the West basically because party identification is low and people tend to switch more than

[17]This contrast is well described in Peter Regenstreif, *The Diefenbaker Interlude* (Toronto, 1965), 144. Of course Regenstreif is dealing with federal elections, but as he seems to consider it as an aspect of the Western farmer's personality, his comment should apply to provincial elections as well. The difference also appears very clearly in Martin Robin's *Canadian Provincial Politics*. The articles on Maritimes' politics stress the role of a deep-seated tradition of party identification (cf. for instance J. Murray Beck, "The Party System in Nova Scotia: Tradition and Conservatism"). On the other hand, it is noted that partisan loyalties are relatively weak in British Columbia (cf. Martin Robin, "The Politics of Class Conflict," 40). Likewise, the frequency of federal-provincial vote switching in Alberta and Saskatchewan is underlined. See Robin, *Canadian Provincial Politics*.

they do elsewhere. Given this tendency, support for a third party is more likely. The basic factor, then in our view, is cultural: the higher propensity in the West not to identify oneself to a particular party makes it easier for third parties to be successful. At this point, there is no evidence that one-party dominance plays a major role.

Before going any further, some comment on Pinard's two-step theory is required. The latter was elaborated mainly to account for the rise of the Social Credit in Quebec in the 1962 federal election. His argument is that the Conservatives traditionally had been weak in the province of Quebec. One problem, though, is that these same Conservatives had won 50 out of the 75 Quebec ridings in the preceding election (1958); they could hardly be perceived as a nonviable alternative. This fact forced Pinard to develop a more complex theory that would apply "in some instances": "After a long period of dominance by a strong party, a dissatisfied electorate turns in part to the traditional party. But if this party is soon considered to have failed, as the Conservatives were in 1962, then the electorate is not so ready to turn so rapidly to the dominant party it just repelled; they shift instead to a third party."[18] In fact the argument makes a lot of sense. The same basic process may take different forms. However, the problem is that Pinard looked for the possibility of a more complex process only in those cases where his simpler theory did not work out, only when a third party has arisen without there being one-party dominance. The argument is not dealt with systematically; it is used merely to patch the theory. To test it further we constructed a list of all instances in which an election that allowed a traditional party to increase its share of the votes was followed by an election characterized by the rise of third party. We isolated four such cases (New Brunswick, 1917–20; Quebec, 1939–44; Manitoba, 1915–20; and British Columbia, 1916–20). All four cases are instances of a strong two party system. This refinement of the theory is thus dramatically rejected. One would have to look elsewhere to save the theory.

II. Third parties in Canadian provinces: some further comments

At this stage one might be tempted to bury Pinard's theory. We are reluctant to do so however because the theory does have a common-sense validity. Pinard's argument is that when there is one-party dominance the main opposition party is no longer perceived as a viable alternative and people will switch to a third party. The argument makes a lot of sense in so far as activists and voters are concerned with the short term impact of their behaviour; party activists do not want to waste their efforts, nor voters their votes. What we know about Canadian voting behaviour would also support the "psychological basis" of Pinard's theory. Mildred Schwartz, for instance, noted that many immigrants would not even consider voting NDP for the very simple reason that they knew it would not form the government.[19] Similarly, Michel Chaloult has shown that in Quebec provincial elections, mainly in rural ridings, a weak opposition party is hurt by

[18]*Rise of a Third Party*, 26.
[19]"Political Behaviour and Ethnic Origin" in *Papers on the 1962 Election*, ed. John Meisel (Toronto, 1968), 270.

the fact that many voters will not support it because they are afraid of wasting their votes.[20] Finally some survey data on federal elections could be interpreted as an indirect support for Pinard's theory. For instance it would seem that in 1968 many voters were concerned with electing a majority government.[21] It seems to me that this type of concern is closely related to the concern Pinard attributes to the voter: the latter takes into account the relative strength of different parties as well as the likely short-term impact of his vote.

The literature thus provides us with some empirical evidence that Pinard's attribution of rationality to the voter is at least partly valid. We have referred exclusively to research on voters' perceptions because not much has been done on activists. There is some indication however that they, too, are concerned not to waste their efforts; they are more likely to join parties whose chances of forming a government are good so that "party competition seems to condition the operations of organizations based on social and material incentives."[22] Thus Pinard's hypothesis fits well with what we know of Canadian voters and party activists. This fact, coupled with our conception of theory construction, induces us not to reject the theory, at least not at this stage. Up to now, the approach followed here has been a deductive, rigorous one, the kind of approach advocated by Blalock. One should lay down one's theory as precisely as possible, operationalize one's concepts, and test the theory so as to confirm, falsify, or modify it. This is of course based on the assumption that it is possible to design a neat, clear test of a theory; it is also based on the assumption that there are already too many theories around and that we should try to get rid of as many as possible.[23] But there is also a more inductive way of looking at the testing of theories; according to this view no specific test can ever be definitive and one should rather look for a convergence of results obtained through as many approaches as possible.[24] This is, of course, our own view. Even though our rigorous tests are all negative, other kinds of evidence prevent us from discarding Pinard's theory.

One weakness of our approach so far has been our exclusive reliance on a deductive model. We started with a theory, operationalized our concepts, and tested the relationships between our variables. This is, of course, a legitimate procedure but the danger is to lose touch with reality. This is why we shall now proceed to a brief historical review of Canadian provincial elections. It is our contention that the mere fact of reviewing them makes one more sensitive to potential patterns of explanation. In this regard, we would like to point out one drawback in Pinard's own description of these elections. He proceeds province by province, thus obscuring, it seems, some clear historical patterns.

The first fact to consider is that no significant third party ever arose in Canada before 1919. Then, from 1919 to 1925, third parties became very strong;

[20]"Les études locales et régionales" in *Quatre élections provinciales au Québec*, éd. Vincent Lemieux (Quebec, 1969), 129.
[21]See John Meisel, *Working Papers on Canadian Politics* (Montreal, 1972), 18.
[22]Henry Jacek *et al.* "The Congruence of Federal-Provincial Campaign Activity in Party Organizations: The Influence of Recruitment Patterns in Three Hamilton Ridings" this JOURNAL, V (June 1972), 204.
[23]For an elaboration of this view, see Blalock, *Theory Construction*, esp. pp. 1–9.
[24]This view is put forward by E. Webb *et al.*, *Unobtrusive Measures* (Chicago, 1966).

farmer or labour parties emerged in every province except Quebec and Prince Edward Island. In fact, one may distinguish three groups of provinces in that period. First, the two in which third parties were unsuccessful. Second, Nova Scotia and New Brunswick where third parties obtained about 20 per cent of the votes. Third, all the provinces west of Quebec where, at least in one of the elections held within that period, third parties obtained more than 30 per cent of the votes.

The period 1925–30 marked a return to traditional parties, especially to the Conservatives. The latter gained ground in all provinces where third parties had emerged. Third parties receded everywhere but in the two Western provinces, Manitoba and Alberta, where they had taken power.[25] The East-West division becomes particularly striking in the following period. Only three provinces, Manitoba, Saskatchewan, and British Columbia witnessed the rise of third parties, labour parties, in the early thirties.

The pattern in the late thirties is somewhat less clear. Social Credit appeared on the scene in three Western provinces (British Columbia being the exception); its strength, however, varied considerably from 54.2 per cent in Alberta to 9.3 per cent in Manitoba. On the other hand, l'Action Libérale Nationale got 29 per cent of the votes in Quebec.

In the early forties, the CCF made some headway almost everywhere, Prince Edward Island and Quebec[26] again being the exception. In Nova Scotia and New Brunswick it obtained about 10 per cent of the votes. In Ontario, Manitoba, and Alberta, it jumped to about 30 per cent. In the remaining two provinces, Saskatchewan and British Columbia, the CCF was already the main opposition party. It took power in the former but failed in the latter, forcing, however, a coalition between Conservatives and Liberals. The late forties were a sort of repetition of the late twenties. The third parties which had emerged receded everywhere and were not replaced by new ones.

The emergence of third parties has been particularly rare since the early forties. In the fifties Social Credit made some progress in the three Western provinces where it was not in power, and it even won the election in British Columbia. Since then the only instance of the rise of third parties is the Quebec 1970 election, in which the Parti Québécois obtained 24 per cent of the votes and the Ralliement Créditiste, 11 per cent.

This brief historical review should have provided a very important message: once a third party has arisen in a province, it is likely to meet success in the nearby provinces. At the same time, this trend is modified by an East-West division. What happens in Manitoba does not seem to greatly affect Ontario and vice versa. In the above review, we distinguished nine periods and described a certain pattern for each of these periods in the East and in the West. In the

[25]In Ontario, two third parties, the United Farmers of Ontario and the Independent Labor Party, had formed a coalition government in 1919. In 1923, however, the Conservatives had come back to power. For some background on the matter see David Hoffman, "Intra-Party Democracy: A Case Study," *Canadian Journal of Economics and Political Science*, 1961, 223–36; and Peter Oliver, "W.E. Raney and the Politics of Uplift," *Journal of Canadian Studies* (1971), 3–19.

[26]Another third party, however, the Bloc Populaire, obtained 14.4 per cent of the votes.

West, no province deviates from the over-all (Western) trend more than twice. In the East, only in the early twenties and early forties have third parties emerged in Ontario, New Brunswick, and Nova Scotia. Quebec and Prince Edward Island appear to be different. We will argue that the latter is not; a weak Progressive party appeared in 1923 and a weak CCF in 1943. Quebec on the other hand, appears to be genuinely exceptional. The time periods in which third parties arose do not correspond to any Canadian pattern. The nature of these parties should also be taken into account: they were all related to the nationalist issue. We would contend that third parties in Quebec have a different meaning and should be left out of the present analysis.

In respect to the rise of third parties in Canadian provincial history, two important phenomena must be accounted for. First, why is it that third parties have been more successful in the West than in the East? Secondly, why is it that they emerged in certain historical periods rather than in others? We will argue that even if we look at the problem from this more general perspective, Pinard's theory is not supported. Let us start with the East-West cleavage. Have third parties been more successful in the West because one-party dominance has been more prevalent? There is some indication to that effect. If we look at the 53 cases included in Table IV, for instance, the median previous strength of the main opposition party in the West is 33 per cent compared to 40 per cent in the East. This would give support to Pinard's theory. We will argue, however, that the East-West division should be related to a more striking and basic difference. This difference has already been pointed out in section I. In the Prairies especially, change is part of the milieu; very few elections can be characterized as status quo ones. The main difference between the East and the West lies not so much in the nature of electoral change – whether it is a traditional or a third party that gains votes (though there is some difference between the two regions in that respect) – as in the frequency of change. Our conclusion is thus that the greater popularity of third parties in the West could possibly be related to one-party dominance but that another factor (the volatility of the votes in the West) would appear to be more crucial.

The second question pertains to the existence of distinct historical periods. We examined the relationship between our two variables, using time periods as our units of analysis. We looked at all the elections included in Table IV and analysed the East and the West separately. We found that those periods in which third parties were particularly successful were not more likely to be characterized by one-party dominance. Again, there is hardly any support for Pinard's theory. Looking at groups of elections (instead of single elections as in section I), we developed two more tests of the theory; the relationship between one-party dominance and the East-West cleavage and the relationship between the same independent variable and the existence of historical patterns. One test is mildly positive, the other is clearly negative. At this stage we are inclined to conclude that one-party dominance is not a crucial determinant of the rise of third parties.

The East-West cleavage and the existence of distinct time periods can thus hardly be accounted for by one-party dominance. Still another possibility must be examined. It could be that other factors explain the emergence of a trend in a certain region or at a certain point in time, but that given a trend, a third party will be more successful or less unsuccessful depending on whether there is one-party dominance. The logic of our approach should be clarified. Up to now we have assumed, like Pinard, that outside factors do not disturb the relationship between our two variables. Our historical review indicates that this is not a fair assumption. There are clear regional and historical patterns that are likely to be caused by other factors. These factors should be controlled for. We cannot do this directly, at least not at this stage. By looking at provincial elections period by period, however, we are likely to control for many of these outside factors. We will thus examine whether, *given a trend in a certain region at a certain point in time*, the strength of third parties can be related to one-party dominance. From this perspective, it is not the trend itself that needs to be explained but rather "deviations" from the trend. Within each time period, we will look at "exceptional" provinces (those in which electoral results are significantly different from the other provinces in the same region, the East or the West) and check whether these provinces are also "exceptional" in respect to the independent variable, the state of the party system.

We will not present a complete review of these tests here but rather will limit ourselves to two illustrations. We will examine the Western provinces in the early twenties and thirties. In the first period, third parties of course, were very popular. But Manitoba and Alberta could be defined as exceptional, as the United Farmers took over power in both provinces. If one looks at the average strength of the main opposition party in previous years, the hypothesis is confirmed: the average was 33 per cent in Manitoba, 38.7 per cent in Alberta, 40 per cent in British Columbia, and 44 per cent in Saskatchewan. The results with other indicators of one-party dominance are, however, all negative. We would conclude that there is only mild support for the theory in this first period. In the early thirties, only in Saskatchewan and British Columbia did labour parties gain substantial ground. Whatever the measure here, the predictions of Pinard's theory are completely wrong: Saskatchewan and British Columbia were the two provinces in which party competition was the most intense.

Altogether, we discovered 11 "exceptional" cases. Pinard's prediction was supported four times,[27] three times the results were contrary to the theory's prediction, and four times it was at least partially wrong as the "exceptional" province did not differ from the others in respect to one-party dominance. Therefore this further test leads to the same conclusion: one-party dominance does not seem to be conducive to the rise of third parties.

Finally, a different type of argument must be dealt with. It could be that the theory should be tested not at the provincial level, but rather at the electoral-district level. In fact, in his analysis of the rise of Social Credit in Quebec, Pinard argued that the district level was more relevant for the voters outside Montreal, and the federal level for the Montrealers. When it came to testing his theory throughout Canada, he had to make do with the available data, which were at the provincial level. He noted that "a more detailed analysis of the type carried out for Quebec in 1962 would be most useful, but it is beyond the scope of

[27]This includes two cases that do not support the theory if other indicators of one-party dominance (instead of the average strength of the main opposition party) are used.

this study."[28] It could be argued that the most relevant unit of reference is the riding, that local party strength is what counts, and that therefore the theory should not be tested at the provincial level. Our position is that the unit of reference varies from one individual to another and that the theory should be tested at both levels: the expectation should be a weak relationship at both levels. Our findings at the provincial level are thus, in our mind, sufficient to justify the rejection of the theory, but we would still like to discuss the findings at the constituency level.

It seems that the existing data here do not support the theory either. Pinard did provide some evidence according to which Social Credit fared better in the weakest Conservative districts: the evidence, however, was challenged by Vincent Lemieux who used a different measure of Conservative party strength.[29] We also tested the theory in respect to the Quebec election of 1970. We isolated the 4 ridings outside Montreal in which the Liberals had obtained less than 35 per cent of the votes in 1966; the median support for third parties in 1970 in these ridings was 26.3 per cent ($N = 77$) compared to 28.1 per cent for the other more competitive ridings.[30] There is thus hardly any difference between the two sets of ridings. We would conclude that there is not much to support the theory at the district level.[31]

We started this section by asserting that we should not discard Pinard's theory too rapidly because it has some common-sense validity and because there is some indirect support for it in the literature. This induced us to make a historical review of Canadian provincial politics and to design new tests of the theory. The "explanandum" became the existence of historical and regional patterns as well as deviations from these patterns. These tests also tended to be negative. What should we conclude? We do not think the answer is easy. It is still a question of judgment. The indirect evidence supporting the theory which was reported in the beginning of this section cannot be discarded easily. On the other hand, it is difficult not to be impressed with the negative results of the tests applied. We would argue that one-party dominance is not irrelevant but that at the same time it is not a crucial factor in the emergence of third parties. For practical purposes it could be left out of the analysis. We shall have to look elsewhere to explain the success or failure of third parties in Canadian provincial politics.

[28]Pinard, *Rise of a Third Party*, 37.

[29]"Les dimensions sociologiques du vote créditiste," *Recherches sociographiques* (1965), 181–95.

[30]We left the Montreal ridings out because Pinard has done so himself and we wanted to replicate his method. On the other hand, the median support for third parties in the three weak Liberal ridings (where the Liberals got less than 35 per cent of the votes in 1966) was even lower (26.9 per cent). One should note that the 1970 figures refer to the proportion of registered electors and not of actual voters. The data were taken from Vincent Lemieux, Marcel Gilbert, and André Blais, *Une élection de réalignement* (Montréal, 1970) and *Quatre élections provinciales au Québec*, éd. Vincent Lemieux (Quebec, 1969).

[31]Cf. Graham White, above, pp. 399–421. White calls for a revision instead of a rejection of Pinard's hypothesis. My position is different mainly because I have a different interpretation of Pinard's special model, the "class cleavage" one. I can hardly see how one can talk of a revision when the special model's predictions are exactly the opposite of the general model's. Moreover this new interpretation cannot explain why a strong opposition party does not contest a substantial number of seats (see White, n.32). We would thus conclude that, in so far as Pinard's theory deals with élite behaviour as well as with mass behaviour – which is our interpretation – it is clearly falsified.

Conclusion

Pinard's interpretation of the rise of third parties is based on the role of two independent variables: one-party dominance and strains. The analysis has focused on one-party dominance. It was maintained that Pinard's argument was theoretically attractive but methodologically weak. As we believe that replication studies are much too rare in social science, we come to the conclusion that a reanalysis of Pinard's data was necessary. It was argued that the methodology should be improved and some changes were suggested. Many of these changes did not substantially affect the results: the collapsing of the last two categories of the independent variable and a slight modification in the dependent variable still yielded a moderate measure of association (gamma – .21, see Table III). It was then argued that one-party dominance should be measured through the use of multiple indicators. Five indicators were selected and only with two of them was the theory supported. Even with these two, however, the tests proved to be negative when the appropriate changes were made in the sample of elections. Finally a possible revision of Pinard's theory, the two-step model, was rejected.

In the second section, we looked at the problem from a different perspective. We checked whether Pinard's interpretation could account for the emergence of historical and regional patterns and/or exceptions to these patterns. Again our conclusion was negative. It was finally noted that the theory did not fare better at the constituency level. It seems to us that the only support for Pinard's theory is indirect. Some literature on Canadian voting behaviour clearly suggests that the voter does not want to waste his vote. For this reason we do not claim that Pinard's hypothesis is completely disproved. We suggest however, that its validity is dubious. We would also add that the debate must continue, especially since outside Canada the "wasted vote thesis," which had been thought to have been disproved, has recently been given new support.[32]

Still we are much impressed with the number of negative results of the tests used. Nor have all of them been reported thus far in the article. For instance at a certain stage of our inquiry, we formulated the hypothesis that Pinard's theory could apply better in certain types of settings, that is rural ones. But when we tested this hypothesis we did not find any support for it. Our conclusion is thus that one-party dominance is not a crucial factor in the rise of third parties.

In the introduction, we mentioned two positive aspects of Pinard's theory. The first was the stress on a "political" variable; the second was its structural dimension. The latter was felt to be particularly important, as the literature seemed to be committed to strictly cultural interpretations. Our own analysis may appear to support this latter view against Pinard's. At the end of section I, we argued that the basic difference between the East and the West lay in party identification, a cultural factor. We should add, however, that this cultural difference is related to a structural variable. The Western voter is more volatile because his environment itself is less stable. Short-term change in the economy is much more persuasive in the West. Average annual personal income has tended to change more rapidly and sharply. Between 1927 and 1939, it tended

[32] See Stephen L. Fisher, "The Wasted Vote Thesis," *Comparative Politics* (January 1973), 293–301.

to decline in Canada as a whole; however, only in the three Prairie provinces did it decline by more than 2 per cent. On the other hand, personal income increased substantially from 1939 to 1947; the two provinces where it increased the most were Saskatchewan and Alberta.[33] Likewise, the process of urbanization took place in a much smoother way in the East. Since 1900, only in six instances has a province increased its proportion of people living in urban centres by more than 10 per cent within 10 years: the six instances all occurred in the West.[34] Our own interpretation would point to an integration of both cultural and structural dimensions, putting more emphasis, however (and on this we agree with Pinard), on the latter.

Another advantage of Pinard's theory is its stress on a "political" variable. Does our analysis lead to the conclusion that social and economic variables are the only important determinants of the rise of third parties? I do not believe so; rather we should look for more relevant political variables, and for this, we can go back to Pinard's conceptual framework. In his conclusion, he refers to Smelser's value-added scheme which includes six determinants of collective behaviour: conduciveness, strain, generalized belief, precipitating events, mobilization for action, and social control. Pinard's argument is that the first two, conduciveness and strain, are the crucial ones.[35] Our discussion suggests that only the second is really crucial.

On the other hand it is interesting to note how Smelser himself has re-evaluated his theory. In a recent article, he has said that, were he to revise his theory, he would drop precipitating events and put greater stress on social control.[36] For the problem at hand this has clear implications. If one wants to understand why third parties emerge or fail to emerge, one ought to look very closely at the controls exerted or not exerted by traditional parties. To explain the rise of third parties is essentially to explain the failure of traditional parties to maintain their support. The political variable that is related to this failure is not structural (one-party dominance), but rather symbolic. It is through symbols that traditional parties control the mass of voters.[37] Sometimes these parties use inefficient symbols and lose their control – at least for a while. Our argument is thus that social control should replace structural conduciveness as one of the two crucial determinants of the rise of third parties.

Social control is a most abstract concept. Its meaning in respect to a particular problem needs to be clarified. One dimension that appears to be significant in

[33]See S.E. Chemick, *Interregional Disparities in Income*, staff study, no. 14, Economic Council of Canada, table 1, p. 7. See also chart 9, p. 51, where it can be seen that the growth of real personal income is much less linear in the Prairie provinces.

[34]See Daniel Latouche, "Violence politique et crise dans la société québécoise," *Essays on the Left*, éd. Laurier Lapierre *et al.* (Toronto, 1971), 184, table III. This, at the same time, supports Pinard's theory about the role of strains in the rise of third parties. According to him, what is important is not so much the state of the economy itself as the existence of short-term change, for the worse or even for the better. It is our opinion that Pinard's analysis of economic strains and of the response of the poor is the most convincing part of his theory.

[35]*Rise of a Third Party*, 246.

[36]See "Some Additional Thoughts on Collective Behavior," *Sociological Inquiry* (1972), 97–102.

[37]For an elaboration of this view, see Murray Edelman, *The Symbolic Uses of Politics* (Urbana, Ill., 1967).

respect to elections is leadership and there is some evidence that change in leadership brings about electoral change. The Social Credit's loss in Alberta occurred after Manning's departure and the CCF-NDP went through the same experience in 1964 after Mr Douglas decided to enter the federal scene. On a more general level, it has been observed that, of the nine provincial elections held since 1960 in which a party in power had previously changed its leader, six witnessed a government turnover.[38] It is our contention that we will not be able to explain the successes or failures of third parties until we take into account social control and the symbolic uses of politics. It is towards a deeper understanding of such phenomena that we should now direct our attention.

[38]See Eric Mintz, "An Analysis of Canadian Electoral Outcomes," unpublished paper, York University, March 1972. That changes in the leadership of the opposition party did not yield significant results is also interesting. It supports Smelser's view that social control is more important that mobilization.

Third Parties in Canada Revisited: A Rejoinder and Elaboration of the Theory of One-Party Dominance

MAURICE PINARD *McGill University*

If the importance of one-party dominance as a determinant of the rise of third parties were to be evaluated on the basis of the attention it has already received from political scientists, we would have to conclude that it must not be negligible. Obviously, however, this would not be a proper way of evaluating a theory. Fortunately, its importance rests on other grounds. Apart from my own quantitative *and qualitative* evidence, there is now Graham White's evidence, presented above in his article "One-Party Dominance and Third Parties," which, as will be seen, I read to be in line with my own. And while André Blais, in "Third Parties in Canadian Provincial Politics," above, concludes that he was "impressed with the number of negative results of the tests [he] used" (I am not!), he nevertheless showed an unusual reluctance to discard the theory and finally maintained that "one-party dominance is not irrelevant," though it is "not a crucial factor."[1] We shall see later that his evidence is far from being that negative. Another critic of the test of the theory at the district level maintained, nevertheless, that the theory itself was very sound ("inattaquable") and that its tests at the provincial level were convincing.[2]

This is not to say that the formulation of the theory and the presentation of the evidence in *The Rise of a Third Party* represent a final statement. They do not, as indeed they could never do. In fact, some of the cases of third parties in Canada constituted exceptions to the theory. The results of the 1970 provincial election in Quebec – a major concern in my current research – constituted another important exception.[3] In trying to account for these exceptions. I have come to the conclusion that a more general theory is needed and that the theory of one-party dominance is but a subclass of that theory. Another subclass was already hinted at inappropriately as a "special model" in my book (to account for a particular set of exceptions) and has now properly, I think, been given

[1]See his paper above, pp. 435–6. This conclusion is puzzling to say the least: either the appropriate tests are positive or they are not, and, accordingly, the theory is good or not. One can assess how crucial a factor will be not from some implicit average of the number of negative and positive tests, but from the strength of the relationship observed in valid tests.

[2]Vincent Lemieux, "Les dimensions sociologiques du vote créditiste au Québec," *Recherches sociographiques*, VI (1965), 181–95. For his view about the tests of the theory at the provincial level, see his "Réponse," *Recherches sociographiques*, VII (1966), 363–5.

[3]Despite the presence of a strong two-party system (the Liberals in opposition had previously kept 47 per cent of the votes), two new parties together polled in that election 34 per cent of the votes (the Parti Québécois, 23 per cent, and the Ralliement Créditiste, 11 per cent).

Canadian Journal of Political Science/Revue canadienne de science politique, VI, no. 3 (September/septembre 1973). Printed in Canada/Imprimé au Canada.

more emphasis in White's paper, though I find his formulation of it lacking in many respects. Other subclasses should also be considered.

The offer by the Editors of space to comment on the above papers presents me with an opportunity to elaborate on these views. While so doing, I will present my assessment of both White's and Blais's contributions. I will first deal with theoretical matters, then with methodological matters (problems of operationalizations and of sampling, in particular).

I. The theory

Let me start with an important prefatory note. What shall here be called the theory will refer only to conditions of structural conduciveness. It will be recalled however that conduciveness – or any subclass of conducive conditions – constitutes only one of the necessary conditions for the rise of a political movement. While these other conditions cannot be dealt with here, except indirectly, readers should bear them clearly in mind, even if they are not political factors proper.[4] The fact that the presence of conduciveness is not sufficient to account for the rise of a new movement is a particularly central thesis not to be overlooked. Nevertheless, only types or classes of conducive conditions will be of direct concern here.

ONE-PARTY DOMINANCE

In my previous work, I have identified one-party dominance as one of the crucial conducive conditions for the rise of Social Credit in Quebec as well as for the rise of other third parties in Canada. Since, as will be seen below, I do not accept most of Blais's evidence, I still maintain that this factor is an important one. Let me at this point only try to clarify briefly the theory regarding this factor.

A system of one-party dominance is a party system in which the traditional opposition party (or occasionally, parties) cannot be considered a serious challenger, a viable alternative to the dominant government party. Now while this is an objective structural condition, White is correct in suggesting that in the end it is the people's perception of this condition that counts. I had already suggested that this perception may vary depending on the social location of the observer (for example, urban versus rural).

The crucial question, though – and one which has not been sufficiently dealt with previously – concerns the basis of that perception. We contend that early in an electoral campaign voters tend to develop, in a more or less vague way, their own evaluation of the strength of an opposition party and its chances of defeating the incumbent party. What is crucial in this regard is their more or less immediate environment, particularly in rural areas.[5] The important elements would seem to be the past successes or failures of a party in the voters' own riding, the current vigour of the party, the strength and dynamism of its organization and

[4]The general treatment of these conditions is of course to be found in Neil J. Smelser, *Theory of Collective Behavior*, (New York, 1963). They have been dealt with in the case of Social Credit in the *Rise of a Third Party*, (Englewood Cliffs, 1971), chaps. 6ff.

[5]The same is true of urban areas, except that the boundaries of perception are more distant and less well demarcated.

cadres first in their community and then in their riding, the number of its supporters a voter has encountered in the "polls" he has implicitly carried in his immediate milieux. If the party has met repeatedly with resounding defeats in the past, or if, as a result of internal crises (leadership problems, internal conflict, etc.), the party is suddenly in a state of disarray, if (largely as a consequence of these) its organization is in very poor shape, if its cadres have been destroyed and have to be completely reconstituted, if voters find few of their relatives, friends, or acquaintances, at work, in their neighbourhood, or in other areas of participation ready to support that party, then a collective definition of this party as a hopeless contender is likely to develop, and a situation of one-party dominance prevails.

To the extent that, under strain, the situation leaves no avenue for the political expression of grievances, voters, I have argued, will tend to turn to a third party if one becomes available. Pending this availability, however, the incumbent party may maintain itself in power for long periods. Thus both pronounced stability and sudden shifts to third parties are alternative consequences of one-party dominance.

It should be added that the model is not a deterministic one. Under one-party dominance, there is a strong tendency for a new third party to arise during a period of strain. But there remains some possibility that a weak traditional party could be rejuvenated against all odds to the contrary. In my previous work, I identified five such cases, and since then two other instances have occurred (that is, the return of the weak Conservatives to power in both Alberta and Newfoundland in 1971). I had commented that the appearance of strong leaders at the head of these weak opposition parties might help to account for these deviations.[6]

To this mobilization factor, I would now like to add another condition conducive to such returns: this is *the success of the party of the same political family at the other level of government*, or else *the success of the same party* (at the federal level) *in other regions of the country*. The first of these two possibilities was probably involved in the rejuvenation of the Conservatives in Manitoba in 1958 (after their resurgence at the federal level in that province a few months before under Diefenbaker). The new strength of the Conservatives at the federal level in the Prairies had certainly also something to do with the unexpected (according to the one-party-dominance theory) return of the Conservatives to power in Alberta in 1971. The same may hold about their resurgence in Newfoundland the same year. The second possibility (the success of a federal party in some regions) would account for the strong resurgence of the previously weak federal Conservatives in Quebec, the Prairies, and British Columbia in 1958 after the party's victory in 1957 through successes concentrated mainly in Ontario and the Maritimes.

So far, I have considered one type of deviation from the model (the resurgence of a traditional opposition under one-party dominance) which both Blais and White have neglected. Indeed their attention has been entirely focused on the other type of deviation, the emergence of third parties in presumably strong two-party systems. Assuming for the moment that this is really a deviation

[6]*Rise of a Third Party*, 64, and fn.6.

(rather than a practically unrelated phenomenon, as claimed by Blais), we shall now elaborate on an idea which was only succinctly stated in *The Rise of a Third Party*, the so-called "special model" suggesting that in periods of intense class unrest, a previously strong traditional party could abdicate and be replaced by a third, class party.[7] This is the idea that White has tried to elaborate to account for two of his cases.

A MORE GENERAL THEORY

A one-party-dominance system is only one type of a more general condition of structural conduciveness, that of *the political nonrepresentation of social groups through the party system.* While the presence of a single dominant party leaves all groups opposing it without viable channels of political representation, a strong two-party system (or even a multi-party system, for that matter) could as well be nonrepresentative for groups who feel their central ideology and long-term grievances cannot be accommodated through any of the existing parties. In other words, contrary to pluralist views, existing parties can fail to aggregate certain demands and thus leave constituencies without channels of representation. If their feelings about these demands are strong enough to have become imbedded in a strong ideology or an intense group-consciousness, then such a constituency will believe that none of the existing parties can be counted on. In such situations, what is abandoned in favour of a new party is not a weak traditional opposition party, but all existing parties. Indeed, the latter are not only abandoned, they are positively rejected as unsuitable channels for the expression of a rather precise set of concerns.

In ideal-typical terms, the first situation – one-party dominance – will tend to give rise to what we might call protest movements, while the second situation – the rejection of all existing parties – gives rise to what might be called radical movements.[8] Or if you prefer, in terms of Smelser's typology, these two situations could possibly be distinguished in terms of norm-oriented and value-oriented political movements, respectively. Empirical examples approximating such protest movements would be the Social Credit party, the National Union in Quebec, the Provincial party of the 1920s in British Columbia, the Provincial Rights party of the 1900s in Saskatchewan or the United Newfoundland party of the 1950s. As examples of radical movements, one could mention the following parties during their "real" phase[9]: the Farmers and Labour movements and the Progressives of the 1920s and the CCF/NDP party, or the Bloc Populaire, the RIN and the Parti Québécois in Quebec.

The distinction between these two types of movements rests mainly on the intensity, the scope, the extensity, and the determinant character of ideology in these two types of movements. In general, in what I have called protest movements, the ideology will tend to be less encompassing, to call for less fundamental redefinitions of the social order; it will be less intensely adhered to by its followers and, indeed, it may not be shared at all by many of them. The end

[7] *Ibid.*, 65.
[8] It should be obvious that I am here only concerned with political movements acting through political parties.
[9] On the notions of real and derived phases in collective behaviour, see Smelser, *Theory of Collective Behavior, passim*, esp. 356–8. More will be said about this below.

result is that ideology tends to play a lesser role in mobilizing support, while immediate, as opposed to long-term, grievances play a determining role. A good example of this, and one in which these points have been documented, is the Social Credit party in Quebec in 1962.

The obverse of these points tends to hold during the real phase of radical movements. In particular, long-term grievances against the social order, imbedded in an articulated ideology, are the major determinants.

To be sure, these differences may not be very great at the leadership level, where ideology is generally more intense in any movement, though at times even the leaders of protest movements may not be very ideological. Very often however there will tend to exist large differences between the followers of these two types of movements. Mass recruitment to a protest movement is more likely to be based on generalized beliefs of discontent than on a shared, articulated ideology. Moreover, recruitment is not necessarily limited to a particular social class. Conversely, in a radical movement (as here defined), one is more likely to have been recruited on the basis of an ideology shared by the members of a specific social class or communal group (ethnic group, religious group, etc.). Indeed, quite explicit sentiments of class or communal consciousness are likely to have been developed. Finally, in a protest movement supporters are more likely to be rejecting an old dominant party because of their immediate discontent, while in a radical movement all previously existing parties are rejected because of their presumed unwillingness to incorporate the main tenets of the movement's ideology, whether it be socialism, nationalism, or some other value-oriented belief.

Now, this has to be qualified in two important ways. First, the differences just described are not absolute, but involve questions of degrees. For instance, ideology may play some role for some voters in a protest movement, as for instance in the early phases of recruitment to Social Credit in Quebec in the pre-sixties era. Conversely, many followers of a radical movement may adhere quite confusedly to its ideology.

More importantly, any actual radical movement meeting with some success – and by this, we mean in Canada a third party receiving more than 10 to 15 per cent of the votes – is likely to have entered its "derived" phase and to be in fact a combination of two types of voters: some supporting it because of its goals, the others doing it out of a protest orientation.[10]

The implications of this analysis for the rise of third parties in Canada should be obvious. The first and most important implication is that *strong two-party systems cannot be immune to third parties of the radical type* to the extent that the latter imply the rejection of all other parties. This, I suggest, would account, among other cases, for the flurry of third-party activity in almost all provinces of Canada in the early twenties and during the forties. (In the first case, Farmers and Labour groups were mainly involved, in the latter, the CCF was).

This reformulation of the theory now helps to account for most of the devia-

[10]We do not necessarily mean protest orientations due to one-party dominance, but also protest votes which would normally have been channelled into a traditional opposition, but which, given the dynamism of a new radical movement, now take this route. Of course, if one-party dominance also prevails then the derived phase could be of much greater magnitude.

tions of the second type mentioned above (third parties emerging in strong two-party systems). In particular, this can account for the relative success of the CCF in New Brunswick in 1944 (12 per cent of the votes) and in Nova Scotia in 1945 (14 per cent). It can possibly account *in part* for the success of the CCF in Ontario in 1943 (32 per cent), in British Columbia in 1933 (32 per cent), and in Manitoba in 1969, though in these last cases, one-party dominance could also have been in part involved.[11] Moreover, some of the cases classified as "suddenly weak" opposition parties in Table 3.1 of *The Rise of a Third Party* can also be explained in part in this way, as indeed I suggested at the time and as White is arguing along more or less the same lines above. These cases involved Farmers and Labour groups in Ontario in 1919, in New Brunswick and Nova Scotia in 1920, and in Alberta in 1921. It probably also accounts for part of the support for the Independent movement in Saskatchewan in 1921.[12] In all of these instances, the new movements were of course favoured by the failure of traditional opposition parties to contest a large number of seats, so that to class-conscious votes were added protest votes as well as traditional-opposition votes which had now nowhere else to go. (Note however that according to this interpretation, the failure of the opposition party to contest a certain number of seats would no longer be the cause of the emergence of a strong radical movement[13]; but once the partial or total withdrawal of an opposition party has taken place, it cannot but provide great advantages to a new movement.)

Moreover the new factor being considered now can also account for the very moderate success of the Rassemblement pour l'indépendence nationale (RIN) in the 1966 provincial election in Quebec and for part of the success of the Parti Québécois in the 1970 election (it obtained 23 per cent of the votes). It should be of interest to note that, in this last instance, there are survey data supporting the view that only part of the supporters of the PQ were in agreement with its central goal. For instance, on the eve of the election, only 39 per cent of those who intended to vote PQ were in favour of complete separation, while as many as 50 per cent were opposed. And if 70 per cent of these PQ supporters were in favour of sovereignty-association, no less than a quarter (24 per cent) were against.[14]

Finally, the successes of third parties previously attributed to one-party dominance could no doubt, in some instances, be more fully explained if one were to add to the equation the lack of representation due to ideological reasons presently discussed. This could have been involved, for instance, in Saskatchewan in 1925 (where the Progressives obtained 23 per cent of the votes); in the rise of the CCF in the same province during the thirties and forties; in Manitoba in 1920 and 1922 (Farmers and Labour); and finally in the upsurges of the CCF/NDP in Ontario in 1948 and 1967. It must be stressed however that we are not here

[11]See chap. 3, *Rise of a Third Party.*
[12]See *ibid.* for details.
[13]*Ibid.*, 65.
[14]Based on Peter Regenstreif's poll, reproduced in Vincent Lemieux, Marcel Gilbert, and André Blais, *Une élection de réalignement: l'élection générale du 29 avril 1970 au Québec* (Montréal, 1970), 88. The other data presented there are also relevant, 88ff. See also André Blais, Marcel Gilbert, and Vincent Lemieux, "The Emergence of New Forces in Quebec Electoral Politics," in *Canada: A Sociological Profile*, ed. W.E. Mann (2nd ed. Toronto, 1971), 537–44.

offering an alternative interpretation, but only an additional one, and one-party dominance may well have been the main factor in most of these cases.[15]

Two final comments on these two types of conduciveness. First, writers have often commented on the fact that protest movements seem to be able to grow, as well as to decline or even disappear, much faster than radical movements. In view of the theory here developed, this should not be too surprising. To the extent that under one-party dominance it is not unlikely that many more people will feel unrepresented than when this feeling stems from ideological premises, protest movements should have an advantage, compared to radical movements, in rapidly recruiting a large following. Conversely, to the extent that in a protest movement mobilization tends to rest on immediate grievances rather than a lasting ideology, the decline could be quite swift once the grievances have disappeared. (Other factors, of course, such as coming to power, could work against a fast decline.) A comparison of the fate of the Social Credit and CCF/NDP parties would here be interesting. Consider for instance the rapid rise to power of Social Credit in Alberta and the slower success of the CCF in Saskatchewan, or consider the persistence of a certain minimum of votes for the CCF/NDP both federally and provincially, despite repeated failures, even where there are strong two-party systems (to the extent of course that this party puts up more than a few scattered candidates).

Secondly, I would suggest that a movement having some success despite a strong two-party system would disappear faster than a movement *of the same type* appearing under one-party dominance.[16]

OTHER CONDUCIVE CONDITIONS

The lack of representation either through one-party dominance or through the ideological rejection of traditional parties is probably the most important conducive factor for the rise of third parties. But it is not the only one. There are others, some of which I had discussed previously and some of which are dealt with here for the first time.

First, there is the situation in which, due to a crisis, the traditional opposition party (or all opposition parties) enters into a coalition with the governing party. This of course creates another situation in which large groups opposing the government find themselves without party representation. It should be obvious that given discontent such a situation should be very conducive to new parties. Some of the exceptions which I classified as "suddenly weak" opposition parties before[17] can be explained in this way. In suggesting, as I did then,[18] that these cases could be lumped together with all those of a strong two-party system, I was failing to control for this other type of conduciveness, and so does Blais now in his paper above.

Second, I devoted a whole chapter in *The Rise of a Third Party* to the con-

[15]The new factor may have been more important however for the moderate success of the Bloc Populaire in Quebec in 1944 (14 per cent of the votes).

[16]I should add that the comments made previously regarding the similarities and differences between the "special model" which has been more fully developed here and Macpherson's model still hold; see *Rise of a Third Party*, 69–70, in particular fn.28.

[17]*Ibid.*, 64–5.

[18]*Ibid.*, 39.

ducive impact of political changes at the provincial level in Quebec on the rise of Social Credit at the federal level. White completely overlooked this analysis in his suggestion that in the analysis of third parties, more attention ought to be paid to the impact of changes at one level of government on the party dynamics at the other level.[19] The idea developed in that chapter was that rapid political change partly eroded former partisan attachments and rendered the situation conducive to completely new political identifications.[20]

Third, very closely related to that is the hypothesis that the success of an old or new party at one level of government could be conducive to the success of the same party at the other level. The reason for this is the existence of a strong tendency among many voters to vote a straight ticket from one level to the other. I mentioned above how this could have accounted for the resurgence of a traditional party in Manitoba (1958) and Alberta and Newfoundland (1971). But this type of conduciveness could favour third parties as well. Thus, Social Credit polled 47 per cent of the votes in Alberta in the 1935 federal election, two months after it had been voted into office at the provincial level in that province. The same could be said of the federal Progressive and CCF parties in 1921 and 1935 respectively. Closer to us in time, the success of Social Credit at the federal level in Quebec during the sixties is quite important if one wants to understand the moderate success of the Ralliement Créditiste in the Quebec provincial election of 1970 (11 per cent of the votes), despite the presence of a strong two-party system.[21] Thus what appears as an exception if one-party dominance alone is considered turns out not to be so when this other conducive condition is considered.[22] Note however that while under one-party dominance Social Credit at the federal level rose to 26 per cent of the votes in its first drive (1962) and never since fell below 16 per cent, the Ralliement Créditiste, on the other hand, could not mobilize more than 11 per cent of the voters. A strong two-party system may thus have retarded the growth of the latter party, and that conducive factor may be more important than the one just discussed.

In line with this, an important refinement to the one-party dominance model may now be added: that the existence of *a strong two-party system at both levels of government*, where the two parties are of the same families, seems to create an even stronger barrier against third parties than a strong two-party system at one level only. This former condition appears particularly crucial to explain the relative immunity of the three old provinces of the Maritimes to *any* third party and their complete immunity to *strong* third parties. Conversely, the latter situation is in my view important to understand the particularly fast decline of the

[19]Above, p. 420.

[20]*Rise of a Third Party*, chap. 5. Notice how this hypothesis appears contradictory to the one-party dominance hypothesis (*ibid.*, 73). Indeed the "discovery" of the one-party-dominance model was a serendipitous finding emerging from our work on the former hypothesis.

[21]Similar remarks could probably be made about the Ralliement National (also a Social Credit group) in the 1966 Quebec provincial election (*ibid.*, 53).

[22]There are indications that the federal Social Credit party currently keeps pulling up the provincial wing of the party. Moreover, the 1970 provincial election probably marked, with the decline of the Union Nationale, the opening of an era of one-party dominance, which is likely to favour the Ralliement Créditiste; see Maurice Pinard, "The Ongoing Political Realignments in Quebec" in *Quebec Society and Politics*, ed. Dale C. Thomson (Toronto, 1973), 119–38.

Union Nationale in Quebec and its weakness against the challenge of new parties. Its failure to develop a corresponding strong federal party prevented the development among its supporters of partisan attachments which would have been more enduring because they would have been to the same party at the two levels of government.[23]

Fourth, and again closely related to the above, is the diffusion effect mentioned by Blais in his paper: "once a third party has arisen in a province, it is likely to meet success in the nearby provinces."[24] Blais is right that this should also be considered for its conducive effect.

Fifth, something has to be clarified about what I have called the two-step process of the one-party-dominance thesis, which is criticized by Blais and according to which the rise of a third party in a one-party dominance system is at times preceded by some rejuvenation of the weak opposition party.[25] On the one hand, this is not really a different version of the basic model: what has to be stressed is that the third party, at least in Quebec, arose precisely where the traditionally weak opposition party had remained the weakest – that is, where it did not provide a serious alternative even when at its best. On the other hand, there are indications that the failure of both old parties, in rapid succession, to redress serious grievances can also be conducive to third parties. Again in such a situation feelings that neither old party is an appropriate channel of representation are likely to be strong. This could have been an additional factor leading to third parties in the instances which I have explained by reference to the two-step variation of the model.[26] But this could as well be slightly conducive even in a strong two-party system. Again the rise of the Parti Québécois and the Ralliement Créditiste in Quebec in 1970 in a period of severe strain could be attributed to feelings on the part of many discontented voters that since 1960 both old parties had been tried and found lacking.

Sixth, from a comparative perspective, it would seem that the lack of a system of primary elections, as exists in the USA, is conducive to new parties. When primary elections are part of the electoral process, the potential leaders of a new party might well choose to try to take over an old party, or at least gain a hearing in it, rather than launch a new movement. A primary electoral system makes it also more likely that aggrieved groups will be listened to by some of the contending leaders of the traditional parties. Similarly, a parliamentary system is more conducive to third parties than is a presidential system, to the extent that in the former a third party, by having its support geographically concentrated, may expect to win at least a few seats. In the presidential system, the costs of running

[23]On the other hand, what prevented a serious decline of the Quebec provincial Liberals after the rise of the Union Nationale was the existence of a strong federal Liberal wing.

[24]Above, p. 432.

[25]*Rise of a Third Party*, 26 and chap. 3, *passim*. Blais' criticisms can be found in his paper above, p. 430. (Blais grossly misrepresents my position, as any reader can verify, when he writes that I have recourse to this model "only when a third party arises without there being one-party dominance.")

[26]The other factor would of course have been a previously weak opposition party. The reader should note the similarities between some of the cases classified under the so-called two-step model: a long tenure of office by a strong traditional party followed by one term of office by the weak one, this term of office terminating during a period of strain, and finally the emergence of a third party. See in particular *Rise of a Third Party*, 26, 41, and 48.

a third party candidate are so high that they are likely to appear prohibitive, and without such a candidate, the chances of electing representatives at other levels are much reduced.[27]

As can be seen, one-party dominance is not the only type of conduciveness which renders more likely the emergence of third parties. The emphasis which has been placed on it in my previous work stems from the fact that it constituted both a very strong and a completely unexpected determinant in the rise of Social Credit in 1962 in Quebec and that it appeared important enough to deserve more attention than it had heretofore received in the explanation of the rise of other third parties. It may be that in verifying the impact of this factor in other instances I have neglected other conducive factors which in fact would have accounted for some deviations. Indeed as indicated by the examples provided all along this discussion, my view is that often many of the conducive elements reviewed above act in common. In some cases, it may be that one-party dominance was not one of them (for example, the moderate success of the CCF in the Maritimes), in others it may have acted in combination with other elements (for example, political change in the rise of Social Credit in 1962), while in still others it may have been the crucial one (Social Credit in Alberta in 1935 may fit this category). The fact that one-party dominance may not have had the same impact in all instances does not in any way justify the conclusion that it is not a crucial factor worth considering. Indeed, in those instances where one-party dominance seemed to have had an effect, the latter is so strong that to neglect to consider this factor would seriously jeopardize any serious analysis. This is *at least* what the more refined evidence on Social Credit in Alberta in 1935 (see White's paper above) or in Quebec federal politics in 1962 would seem to indicate. As mentioned before, one-party dominance is likely to produce a pool of unrepresented voters probably larger than any of the other factors here considered, and is therefore likely to exert a greater influence than other conducive factors *when present.* Again, the importance of this factor cannot be assessed from some implicit average of its impact in very diverse situations. Is it not revealing that the major victories of third parties, based on unambiguous pluralities of votes – when not clear majorities – have occurred under conditions of very weak traditional opposition parties, as in Alberta in 1935 or in Saskatchewan in 1944? Conversely, is it not striking that radical movements in strong two-party systems have had only limited success, and that generally this was made possible only by the partial withdrawal of the opposition party?

ALTERNATIVE THEORIES

To conclude this section, I shall ask how this reformulated theory fits with those advanced by White and Blais in their papers above.

It should be clear that between White's class model and the relevant part of our theory there are no major differences. His reformulation of the special model as a class model follows the lines I had previously suggested. But given that a class analysis refers at least in part to strains rather than to conduciveness, that

[27]On this last paragraph, see S.M. Lipset, *The First New Nation* (New York, 1963), 294, 300ff. The plurality-electoral system, on the other hand, is more likely to affect the size of the representation obtained by, and the long-term viability of, a third party than to affect its emergence in terms of popular support.

I have indeed carried out a type of class analysis of Social Credit in Quebec (even if that party was not based on a single class), and finally that a communal (ethnic, etc.) basis as well as a class basis could exist under that model, I think that to call it a class model may be in part misleading and I have preferred to refer to it as a model where conduciveness stems from the nonrepresentation of a specific class or communal group due to ideological stances and long-term discontent toward a social order. (Obviously, short-term grievances could also act as a precipitant in a radical movement.)

Blais on the other hand rejects one-party dominance as of no great significance, though he insists that the hypothesis "is most interesting," that it has "common-sense validity," that it "fits well with what we know of Canadian voters and party activists." As an alternative, he offers first the theory that third parties have been successful in Canada wherever the amount of partisan attachments or party loyalties has been low and vote switching has been high. He suggests that third parties have been less successful in the Maritimes than in the Prairies because in the former elections are much more likely to be status quo ones, with no party gaining or losing more than 5 per cent of the votes. In the West, "change is part of the game," the volatility of the votes is much greater.[28]

The only problem with this theory is that it is not really an alternative theory. There is no doubt that attachments to the old parties must be weak whenever third parties arise. But the real question then becomes: why were these attachments weak in the first place? The answer to this question, I suggest, lies in large part in the set of conducive conditions enumerated above. Thus, wherever one-party dominance prevails, identification to the old parties will tend to be weak: those supporting an unlikely winner will tend to be few in number and weakly attached to it; among those supporting the dominant party, on the other hand, there will be many doing it simply for lack of any other alternative rather than out of any positive identification. This means that there will tend to be many more floating voters than there are in a strong two-party system. Hence a lot of party shifting from election to election is likely to take place[29] and a greater readiness for a new alternative to be witnessed when the other determinants (strain, etc.) are present.

Similarly, many of the other conducive conditions reviewed above could produce a large pool of uncommitted voters, as I have often mentioned above. This is true, for instance, in the case of political change. Indeed the argument developed in this regard – and incidentally supported by data at the individual level[30] – has precisely been that rapid political change tended to erode partisan attachments and thus to create a pool of available recruits for a new party. The

[28]Above, pp. 428–9, 432, 436–7. The hypothesis that limited partisan attachments are related to the rise of "flash" parties has also been suggested in a comparison of France and the United States; see Philip E. Converse and Georges Dupeux, "Politicization of the Electorate in France and the United States," *Public Opinion Quarterly*, 26 (Spring 1962), 1–23. We also found of course that nonpartisans were more likely to have turned to Social Credit in 1962; see *Rise of a Third Party*, 167–9.

[29]This is not contradictory to the statement that one-party dominance is likely to lead to long tenures of office. When a weak opposition party has about 33 per cent of the votes, it is relatively easy to gain (or lose) more than 5 per cent of the votes, but this has little chance of producing a change of government.

[30]I found that stable voters were in general less likely to vote Social Credit than were party changers; see *Rise of a Third Party*, 75–8.

same could be said of the situations in which traditional parties are strong at only one level of government,[31] or in which a third party has appeared at one level, or in which both traditional parties have failed in rapid succession, or finally in which a weak opposition party has been rejuvenated for only a short period. In each of these situations, partisan attachments will tend to be weak and as a consequence third parties will be more likely to arise.

The conclusion to draw from this is clear. Weak party-identifications are simply one of the *intervening* factors between many of the conducive conditions we have reviewed and the rise of third parties.[32] Blais should have paid more attention to the fact that two of his findings are related to one another, that is, that in the Western provinces, the main opposition parties tended to be weaker than in the East *and* that fewer elections in the former than in the latter could be characterized as status quo ones.[33]

In the last three paragraphs of his paper, Blais also touches upon a second alternative theory. Third parties would be the result of the lack of control exerted by traditional parties on their supporters. This in turn would result from their use of inefficient symbols and in particular from changes in leadership. While this is all quite vague, I accept that such factors may affect the fate of a traditional party. But then in a strong two-party system this is likely to affect only one party at a time, to be a temporary situation and to lead some of its supporters to shift to the other traditional party. Exceptionally, it will lead to a more serious decline of a traditional party in favour of third parties, but this will be because many of the elements of conduciveness listed above will also be present. Consider as an example the decline of the Union Nationale and the rise of the PQ and the RC in Quebec in 1970. One will recall that many of the factors listed above appear to be involved in this case. So again we fail to see this as an alternative theory; the real question remains: when will a lack of social control by a traditional party lead voters to the other traditional party or to a third party? To this question Blais offers no answer.

With this we come to the end of our re-examination of the various theories

[31]This point is supported by data of the Social Credit study: there were more party changers between the two old provincial parties in weak federal districts than in strong ones; see the marginal *N*'s in Table 5.3, *Rise of a Third Party*, 77.

[32]I grant however that partisan attachments could also be eroded by severe strains, as for instance greater variations in income and more rapid urbanization (Blais, above pp. 436–7). But these strains cannot be the major source of variations in partisanship. Moreover they should manifest themselves in greater political change, which would then have its own effect (*Rise of a Third Party*, 109–11). Note also that Converse and Dupeux saw the limited party identifications of France as resulting from the lack of family socialization and thus as an intervening factor between the latter and the rise of "flash" parties. In my view, they rejected too easily the idea that it could be linked to a fluid and complex multiparty system, on the basis of a simple comparison with Norway. I would suggest that the lack of political socialization simply hides the transmission from generations to generations of limited identifications, which are themselves related to the party system. At least in Canada, as we have argued, a multiparty system is likely to be a one-party-dominance system producing weak party identifications.

[33]Instead, with a surprising lack of rigour for a strict methodologist, the author simply asserted that while the first difference between West and East "would give support to Pinard's theory," the second difference was a "more striking and basic" one (how was this established?), and he went on to conclude a few paragraphs later that the East-West difference in third-party fortunes could "thus hardly be accounted for by one-party dominance"; Blais, above. p. 433.

which have been presented. I shall now turn to a comparative evaluation of the evidence presented by White, Blais, and myself.

II. The evidence

WHITE'S EXAMINATION OF THREE CASES

As with his theory, I have only minor reservations concerning White's evidence. He chose to examine in detail, at the district level, 3 of the 65 elections I had analysed at the provincial level. The rationale for these choices is not presented. But while in my analysis one of these cases (Alberta, 1935) had been found to support the one-party dominance model, the other two (Alberta, 1921, and Ontario, 1919) were already exceptions in my own test.[34] White's more detailed analysis leads to a conclusion which is exactly the same.[35]

White goes wrong, however, in some secondary aspects concerning the expected relationships between the former strength of the traditional parties and the success of a third party. First, the relationships the model predicted concerned the strength of the former opposition party rather than, as he tends to write, that of the former government party. The reason is of course that what is of importance is the strength of the opposition party, not that of the dominant party (though when there are no other candidates, it does not make any difference). Second, he fails to clearly dissociate the abdication of the old opposition party (its failure to contest all or any number of seats) from his so-called class model. While he recognizes that they are analytically distinct, he fails to fully draw the implications of this.

Obviously, the abdication of a traditional opposition party could result from its weakness, that is, a situation of one-party dominance (for example, the rise of the ALN in Quebec in 1935 against only 33 Conservative candidates for 90 seats approaches that situation), but could also result from the strong challenge of a radical movement – a class movement in White's terms – (as often repeated in the early twenties). Conversely, both the rise of a protest movement under one-party dominance and of a radical movement out of ideological conflict could take place *without* any abdication on the part of the traditionally weak party in the first instance (for example, the rise of Social Credit in Alberta in 1935 against a practically full slate of Liberals – 61 candidates for 63 seats), or on the part of any of the old parties in the second instance (for example, the rise of the Parti Québécois in Quebec in 1970 against a full slate from both old parties).

Therefore these cases have to be differentiated. Considering first the case with no abdication, the theory predicts, in the one-party dominance situation, a *negative* relationship between the former strength of the weak opposition party and the subsequent strength of a third party. This is actually what we found in Quebec in 1962 and what White now finds in Alberta in 1935. On the other hand, in the radical movement situation, again without abdication, there is no

[34] They were classified as cases of "suddenly weak" opposition parties and were among those which then led me to suggest the special model I have now more fully developed.
[35] The basis on which Blais can therefore refer to White's evidence to reject the one-party-dominance hypothesis is still a mystery to me.

reason to expect *any relationship* at all between these two variables, since the rise of a radical movement has nothing to do with the strength of an opposition party.[36] This is what a partial test by Blais for the 1970 Quebec election seems to indicate.[37]

In cases where the opposition party is abdicating, the two models can no longer be differentiated. Whether one-party dominance and/or ideological factors are at work, one should always expect a *positive* relationship between the former strength of the opposition party and the subsequent strength of the new party, to the extent that obviously the latter will draw on a larger pool of voters where the abdicating party was strong than where it was weak. White therefore errs in considering a positive relationship (a negative relationship in his terms, since he uses the former strength of the government rather than that of the opposition party) as being in support of his class model.[38] This is what should be observed, whatever the appropriate model, each time there is abdication, as indeed it is the case in the two instances in which he obtains such a relationship. Notice that in the Ontario situation, where he controls for the absence or presence of Liberal opposition candidates, the positive relationship just predicted is clear under abdication (where one also observes a much greater strength of the UFO), while the relationship is ambiguous (and only slightly negative when the data are dichotomized) under no abdication (see White's Table IV).[39] This is in line with what I have just suggested above. More generally, this means that the one-party dominance hypothesis will not yield itself to easy tests at the district level whenever there are abdications. Therefore, White's conclusion that one-party dominance was not important in Ontario in 1919 and in Alberta in 1921 is unwarranted. It may well be true, given that it was already an exception in my own analysis at the provincial level, but whether it played some role remains an open question.

BLAIS'S RE-EXAMINATION OF THE EVIDENCE

If my disagreements with White are limited, the same cannot be said about Blais. Though the latter touches on a few alternative theories in passing, his major exercise was to offer more "rigorous" tests of the one-party-dominance model. But in his efforts to be rigorous, he has shown a great lack of sensitivity to the complexity of the data. I had always thought that a rigorous methodological effort did not mean the blind application of formal rules; otherwise, a research effort becomes nothing but a random search for the unknown. My feelings are that Blais has become the victim of his own technical acrobatics. In the following pages, I shall comment successively on his operationalizations of the independent variable and of the dependent variable, and on his choice of a sample. Since

[36]Unless of course for some reason the emergence of class or communal sentiments were to be related to the former strength of the old parties.

[37]Blais considers not only the PQ vote but the PQ and RC vote together. But the conducive factors for the latter do not lead one to expect any relationship there either. See Blais, above, pp. 434–5.

[38]Above, pp. 403–6, especially p. 406.

[39]The strong correlation-coefficient nevertheless obtained in this case is subject to suspicion given the non-linear distribution to be observed in Table IV. Moreover, one could expect some diffusion impact of the partial abdication of the Liberals even in districts in which they did not abdicate. Finally, I wonder if urban-rural and ethnic controls would not also be appropriate here.

Blais often changes all three of these elements in any one test of the theory he carries out and since we generally do not have the detailed data on which any one test is based, it will be difficult to pinpoint exactly where he went wrong in any specific test. But enough problems will be mentioned below to raise some very serious doubts about his negative tests.

THE INDEPENDENT VARIABLE

Problems first appear in his multiple operationalizations of the independent variable, one-party dominance. Blais started with the idea that one-party dominance is a very abstract concept, like the concept of anomie, for instance – a highly questionable assumption – and that therefore it should be measured by multiple indicators.[40] I will grant that multiple indicators are better than single ones, whatever the degree of abstraction of the theory, and I did indeed use more than one indicator in testing the theory in Quebec. The real issue however is that not all indicators one can put one's hands on are necessarily equally good measures of the nominal concept. This is particularly crucial if one cannot collect one's own data, but must use existing data. What about Blais's indicators? The least that can be said is that the face validity of some of them is questionable.

Blais has not questioned the validity of the measurements I used; he simply added others. It appears to me that the indicator I used – the average proportion of votes which a party has received while in opposition – is at face value a good measure of the strength of a party, of its possibility of providing a viable alternative. Such a measure is likely to reflect the strength and the dynamism of the party's organization and of its cadres and the frequency with which anyone will meet some of its active and enthusiastic supporters in his daily interactions. If that percentage of votes has been very low, a collective definition of that party as a hopeless contender is likely to have developed. The same of course could be said of the indicator derived from my informant's evaluation of the strength of the Conservatives in Quebec.[41]

But how can one seriously consider the average proportion of seats obtained by an opposition party as an equally good measure of one-party dominance? The distortions introduced by the electoral system are so well known that it barely needs any elaboration. The point is that a party with 40 per cent of the votes could easily be left with as few seats as (or even less than) a party receiving 25 per cent of the votes.[42]

Similarly, using the last election results in terms of votes could have some validity, but if a party had not been weak before, a decrease in votes could simply reflect a temporary setback to be followed by a return to normal strength

[40]On this point, Blais cites Blalock, but he misses Blalock's main point which is that in linking a theory to specific indicators one must develop an auxiliary theory which has its own assumptions, See Hubert M. Blalock, jr, *Theory Construction* (Englewood Cliffs, 1969), 151–4. What I will be arguing below is that while my assumptions appear valid, those of Blais are often very questionable.

[41]*Rise of a Third Party*, 25.

[42]Blais contends I had used seats as a test of the model. This is not correct. I simply started collecting the data on seats as I went along collecting data on votes and kept doing it even after that data soon appeared to have no face validity as a measure of the strength of a party. Again compare what Blais says, above, p. 426, with what I actually wrote where he refers to *Rise of a Third Party*, 63, fn.2.

in the following election. Conversely, a weak party could have exhibited a temporary resurgence in only one election.

A fourth indicator used by Blais is whether the opposition party has not been in power in the previous 15 years. Again while this could measure one-party dominance in some cases, it could fail seriously in others. A strong opposition party as well as a weak one – in terms of our nominal definition – could have faced such a situation. Can you equate the strength of the Quebec provincial Liberals during the 15 years prior to 1960 – during which they maintained an average of 42 per cent of the votes – with that of the Quebec provincial Conservatives during the 15 years prior to 1935 in which they succeeded in maintaining an average of 39 per cent of the votes, but only by failing to contest about one seat in every five in 1923 and 1927? Were the PEI Conservatives a weak opposition party during the 15 years prior to 1959, given that they kept an average of 45 per cent of the votes during that period? Can they be compared to the Alberta Liberals who as the main opposition from 1921 to 1935 could not average more than 28 per cent of the votes?[43]

Finally, Blais used party distances as an indicator. Once more, this could be of some validity if this were to be measured as the average distances over a number of years, but it appears that Blais used only the last election so that my comments of the last paragraph apply here too. At any rate, Blais himself cast some doubts on the validity of that measure.[44]

Some additional comments are in order here. First, if all these indicators are equally valid, why do some yield positive results and others negative results? Does this not indicate that they are not all measuring the same underlying factor or that some do it with many errors? What shall we do with the positive tests, some of which are quite strong? What do they reveal? They must mean something. Can it be shown that they are the ones in which there are measurement errors? I suggest it would be difficult to find indications that opposition parties with an average of less than 33 per cent of the votes – my indicator of one-party dominance – were actually strong parties. Conversely, as some of the examples given above indicate, it would be easy indeed to find indications that parties classified as weak by some of Blais's indicators were actually strong. Second, if these indicators are all measuring the same factor, they should be strongly interrelated and a rigorous testing of the theory would require that this be established. Blais is silent on this point.[45] Third, with a concept as difficult as this one to measure, would it not be appropriate: (a) to use an index made of many specific indicators, both quantitative *and qualitative*[46] – something I have implicitly done in chapter 3, and (b) to have the coding done on the basis of all available infor-

[43]Note incidentally how this last redefinition of one-party dominance drastically alters the distribution of cases as weak or strong opposition parties (in Table II there are 9 weak and 37 strong cases; in Table III, these figures become 21 and 23 respectively). See pp. 425, 427, above.

[44]See above, p. 427, fn.14.

[45]I have on the other hand reported that my two indicators in the tests on Social Credit in Quebec were strongly related to one another; see "La faiblesse des Conservateurs et la montée du Crédit Social en 1962," *Recherches sociographiques*, 7 (Sept.-Déc. 1966), 361.

[46]It should be stressed that in the name of rigour Blais, contrary to White, has systematically disregarded any qualitative evidence of the weakness of opposition parties, such as failures to contest seats, factionalism and splits in a party, severe leadership crises, moribund organizations, etc. I agree with him when he finally writes that his procedure involves "the danger [of losing] touch with reality" (above, p. 431).

mation by outside coders who would be unaware of the hypotheses to be tested and who could be checked for reliability – something neither of us has done. Finally, the most important point is that an examination of the data revealed the existence of a *critical threshold* (the 33 per cent cut-off point) above which the strength of opposition parties does not appear to produce differential effects on third parties. This being the case, it is fundamental that the choice of a cut-off point on the independent variable should not be made blindly to maximize the number of cases in each group. Moreover when using an indicator other than 33 per cent the apparent existence of such a threshold should dictate an examination of the data before arbitrarily deciding on cut-off points.

THE DEPENDENT VARIABLE

Blais defines a third party as "a non-traditional party that has not managed to obtain a minimum of 10 per cent of the votes in each of the previous two elections."[47] I simply fail to understand why a third party which would have obtained more than that in the previous two elections (say, 15 or 25 per cent) would stop being perceived as a new, different alternative to dissatisfied voters. I maintain, as I had implied before, that a third party should be defined as any non-traditional party which has not yet been in power. It thus remains in the eyes of the voters as an untried alternative. Notice that Blais's definition seriously limits the number of emerging third parties to be analysed.

Moreover, in his operational definition, Blais contends that we should consider not the level attained at any one election by a third party, but the increase in support over the last election.[48] Again, I completely disagree. What the theory predicts is the absolute level a third party will attain at any one time, not its increase over the previous election. An illustration should make that clear: in one instance, a third party moves from nothing to 15 per cent of the votes, a gain of 15 per cent; in another instance, a third party moves from 25 to 35 per cent of the votes, a gain of only 10 per cent. Now clearly the theory predicts the second instance as more likely under one-party dominance than the first. Blais's measurement will make the first instance as the one to be explained by one-party dominance. Therefore, contrary to his claim, it is his own operationalization which is biased, not mine. Notice that to explain my "bias" Blais adds: "When the main opposition party is weak there is likely to be another weak third party. This is less likely when there is a strong two-party system. The fact that there is already a third party makes it a little more likely that a third party of some strength will emerge."[49] I simply thought these propositions were empirical outcomes which the theory was precisely designed to predict!

Finally, the reader will note that when Blais moves from Table III to Table IV, in which the difference is supposed to involve a change in the sample, the author also surreptitiously introduces a change in his own operationalization and cut-off points on his dependent variable. I recomputed Table IV, reintroducing in the dependent variable the category in which third parties increased their votes by

[47]Above, p. 426, fn.10.

[48]*Ibid.* Blais writes here (fn.11) that I acknowledged this possibility. This is wrong: in the reference he cites, I was discussing the independent variable, not the dependent one; besides even for that variable I mentioned the serious problems involved.

[49]*Ibid.*

TABLE I

ONE-PARTY DOMINANCE, ELECTORAL CHANGE, AND TYPES OF THIRD PARTIES
(with the party in power having lost at least 5 per cent of the votes)*

	Previous strength of main opposition party	
	Weak	Strong
Electoral change:		
(1) A traditional party increased its votes by more than 10 per cent	46%	35%
(2) A traditional party increased its votes by more than 5 per cent but less than 10 per cent	15	23
(3) Third parties increased their votes by more than 5 per cent but less than 10 per cent	0	8
(4a) Third parties increased their votes by more than 10 per cent but less than 20 per cent	8	13
(4b) Third parties increased their votes by more than 20 per cent	31	23
N (elections)	(13)	(40)
Types of third parties increasing their votes by more than 10 per cent (4a and 4b above):		
(1) Radical movements	40	71
(2) Protest movements	60	29
N (elections)	(5)	(14)

*Recomputed from Table IV in Blais, above. I am grateful to him for having given me the details of the cases included in the fourth row of that table. (While recomputing the data, I noticed an error in one case [Quebec, 1936] that should be classified in the third row of the second column rather than in the fourth row.)

more than 20 per cent. Despite the problems I have raised regarding this new dependent variable (increase in third-party votes rather than absolute level obtained) and despite problems with this sample (to be discussed shortly), I obtained the results of Table I. First the reader should note that the positive gamma Blais obtained in his Table IV does not reveal a greater tendency for third parties to arise in a strong two-party system – there is in fact little difference in this regard – but simply a greater tendency for traditional parties to increase their votes by more than 10 per cent in a one-party dominance system. However this is precisely the kind of prediction you could make about a one-party dominance system: a weak party is more likely to increase its vote by 10 per cent if it was before at, say, 30 per cent of the votes than it can if it was before at, say, 45 per cent. Therefore, Blais is wrong in concluding that his Table IV (as he presented it) is "contrary to the model's prediction."

But there is more to it than that. In reintroducing the original cut-off points on the dependent variable, I now find that the relationship with regard to third party is entirely in line with the model's prediction. On the one hand, third parties are more likely to have gained more than 20 per cent of the votes under one-party dominance as indicated in the last line of the first panel in Table I. In fact, four of the five third parties in the first column of Table I increased their votes by more than 20 per cent, as opposed to only about half under a strong two-party system.[50]

[50]We might add that the strong opposition party column includes the following "strong" parties: Newfoundland, 1959, where the Conservatives were at an average of 33.6 per cent

On the other hand, and most interestingly in view of the revised model presented above, 60 per cent of the movements increasing their votes by more than 10 per cent under one-party dominance were protest movements – and actually all increased their votes by more than 20 per cent – while only 29 per cent were protest movements in a strong two-party system – only half of which increased their votes by more than 20 per cent (see the second panel of Table I). Therefore, as predicted above, when a third party made progress under a strong two-party system, it tended to be a radical party rather than a protest one, and to make limited advances rather than strong ones.

THE SAMPLE OF ELECTIONS

The sample of elections to be used in testing the theory presents some tricky problems.[51] In chapter 3 of the book, I started with the idea of testing which of the traditional opposition party or a third party would be the more likely to replace a government party, and I therefore first chose to examine all elections with a government turnover. I also decided to include elections in which a third party improved its position in order to see whether its success would be greater under one-party dominance than under a strong two-party system.[52]

Now Blais raises the serious objection that even if we take only the elections with a government turnover, the sample is biased toward the verification of the hypothesis. The reason for this is that government turnovers are more likely in a strong two-party system even without severe strain, while the same turnover under one-party dominance would be less frequent, but result from more severe strain. Hence the greater chance of a strong third party in the latter situation.

On this score Blais is right. How serious the bias so introduced would be, however, is unknown. At any rate, in order to correct for this, Blais decided to consider only those elections in which the party in power lost 5 or 10 per cent of the votes, so that these elections could be assumed to have taken place under serious strain. Blais fails to realize, however, that in so doing he himself introduces a bias in the opposite direction: strain, presumably, would have to be more severe to produce the same *loss of votes* in a strong two-party system than in a one-party-dominance system, since in the latter there are fewer partisan attachments. So this is not a good solution.

The only way to avoid these biases seems to be to consider all elections (or a random sample of them). Ideally, of course, one might want to simultaneously control for other types of conduciveness (above all, for types of party) as well as for strain, mobilization, etc., if these were to affect the original relationship. Pending such more elaborate tests, however, it is interesting to observe what an analysis involving all elections yields. Table II presents such a test. It again

---

of the votes; Saskatchewan 1956, where the Liberal opposition was at 33.8 per cent; Quebec, 1935 and Quebec, 1936, where the strength of the Conservatives was around 33 per cent (in this case, see *Rise of a Third Party*, 52). This is therefore a conservative test.

[51] I also considered a few elections at the federal level, but they were not chosen randomly. Blais is therefore right in excluding them from a more rigorous test.

[52] I may not have been very rigorous in the latter case, but on the basis of that statement I fail to see how according to Blais I did "not always stick to [my] own criterion." The examples he gives to make his point all witnessed the appearance or improvement of a third party; above, p. 425.

TABLE II

PREVIOUS STRENGTH OF OPPOSITION PARTY AND ELECTORAL CHANGE, 1900–71*

	Previous strength of opposition party†		
	Very weak††	Weak	Strong
Electoral change‡			
(1) Major gains by opposition party	25%	20%	7%
(2) Minor gains by opposition party	10	14	17
(3) Gains by party in power	15	6	17
(4) Status quo elections	10	31	39
(5) Minor gains by third party	5	7	7
(6) Major gains by third party	35	23	13
N (elections)	(20)	(71)	(71)

*Recomputed from unpublished data analysed by Blais. I am grateful for his permission to use these data.

†Very weak: a group of elections classified by Blais as elections with "one-party dominance with no clear opposition party." In most cases, opposition parties are below 30 per cent of the votes, and the party distances are usually very substantial. Weak: the distance between the party in power and the main opposition party is greater than 10 per cent, but excluding the very weak cases. Strong: the party distance is less than 10 per cent.

††Manitoba, 1941, is excluded because of a wide coalition without any clear opposition party.

‡Electoral change: major gains refer to increases of 10 per cent or more; minor gains refer to increases between 5 to 10 per cent; status quo elections refer to elections in which no party increased its votes by more than 5 per cent. (Whenever two parties increased their votes by more than 5 per cent, only the party that obtained the largest increase was considered in the operationalization.)

confirms the one-party-dominance hypothesis, even though the operationalizations of the two variables are not what one would like them to be for reasons previously discussed. Strong opposition parties tend to lead to status quo elections, while weak ones (and particularly very weak ones) lead to major gains by third parties as well as by opposition parties. This is again entirely in line with the theory and the results of Table I.

BLAIS' OTHER TESTS

In the second part of his paper, Blais re-examines the evidence in a less rigorous fashion, dividing his data by historical periods and/or by geographical areas. Let us briefly consider these tests.

The reader will have noted that Blais considered the lack of a relationship between distinct historical periods (in terms of third-party successes) and one-party dominance as evidence against the theory.[53] This simply cannot be so. Different historical periods can at best be indicators of variations in levels of strains. But it has never been suggested – how could it be? – that one-party dominance could exhibit similar variations across the country according to historical

[53] *Ibid.*, p. 433.

periods. To repeat, one-party dominance is a more or less stable feature of the party structure which, given the appearance of strain, during certain periods, will give rise to third parties.[54]

With regard to the geographical patterns, their explanation by one-party dominance remains one of my major conclusions. Otherwise, I have commented above on Blais' idea that these patterns can better be explained by limited partisanship in the West than by one-party dominance.

Finally, with regard to his joint examination of clusters of elections in a particular region at a particular time, Blais barely presents any evidence. Space limitations prevent me from examining more than one of his tests. It concerns the Western provinces during the late thirties.[55] In this test, Blais examined the differences in the fate of Social Credit in these four provinces: it obtained 54 per cent of the votes in Alberta in 1935; 16 per cent in Saskatchewan in 1938; 9 per cent in Manitoba in 1936; and 1 per cent in BC in 1937. Observing that one-party dominance prevailed in all four cases, he concluded that the differences in Social Credit support could not be accounted for by that factor. The obvious problem here is that Blais disregarded everything else. He reasoned as if everything else was the same and as if only Social Credit appeared on the scene. Obviously, this is false. The party systems of these provinces had evolved in quite different directions. Above all, there were other third parties on the scene. For instance, the CCF, not yet present in Alberta, had 19 per cent of the votes in Saskatchewan, 29 per cent in BC, and 12 per cent in Manitoba. And on the whole the weaker the Social Credit party in a province, the stronger the CCF. The one-party dominance model was never intended to explain *which* third party would emerge. Is it not revealing that the sum of the votes for these two parties was not below 20 per cent? Moreover, Manitoba had a popular government born out of an alliance of the Progressive and Liberal parties, and the Liberals were very strong in Saskatchewan, while in BC, and more so in Alberta, both old parties were very weak. To ignore these basic elementary differences is simply to engage in meaningless verifications. Therefore, I fail again to see how this seriously challenges the theory. I will leave it to the reader to examine more carefully the other tests presented in that section and to evaluate the general conclusion once again that the tests carried on there lead to the view that one-party dominance is not conducive to third parties.[56]

CONCLUSION

For many obvious reasons, I checked but a few of the multitude of tests carried out by Blais. I chose instead to discuss what I consider to be serious problems of face validity for some of his indicators and problems of biases in his samples as well as in his cut-off points. I showed more specifically how he was wrong in

[54]Blais seems to finally recognize that logic in the following paragraphs (p. 434ff.).

[55]The results of that test are not presented in his paper, but he has kindly given me the authorization to refer to them.

[56]His final comments concern his negative evaluation of the tests at the constituency level. I have already argued that White's evidence is in line with what I had previously observed and is now better accounted for by the revised model. As for my own evidence, I do not think that Blais can cite Lemieux's comments on it as rejecting the theory; quite the contrary, as noted above. Finally Blais's evidence about the 1970 Quebec election concerns an exception now accounted for in the revisions presented above.

his assessment of the evidence in many cases and finally presented a table with a complete universe of elections. It is left to the reader to now reach his own conclusion. I for one still have no doubts that the evidence supports the theory.

The most useful part of this exercise however has no doubt been the re-examination of the model and the presentation of a more general theory concerning the conducive conditions for the rise of third parties. For those who think the question is still open, I suggest that in future verifications at the provincial level one should use the complete universe of elections, possibly using an index of one-party dominance rather than single indicators (with the coding done as indicated above and using both quantitative and qualitative data), and devise controls on other types of conduciveness, types of party, strain (by controlling for historical periods, for instance), and mobilization (the number of candidates running for a third party – something we have all neglected so far). More verifications of the theory at the district level should also be most useful, though the abdication of the traditional opposition party, whenever it occurs, raises serious problems, as mentioned before. Together with theoretical clarifications, these verifications should enhance our understanding of the rise of third parties and more generally of the type of party systems we have inherited in Canada.

Parliamentarianism among the French Working Class*

RUTH ANN PITTS *Université de Montréal*

Marx defined classes in terms of the relationship to the means of production. For this reason Marxist sociologists, such as Serge Mallet, have differentiated classes among the working class in general in terms of the technology of the enterprises in which they work.[1] Mallet thus defines the new working class as the class which works in enterprises with continuous-process technology. Like Marx, he sees their position in relationship to the means of production determining their political consciousness. Thus he sees them at the forefront of movements to change systems of authority in the society because they are in the forefront of the new industry and therefore see best the contradiction between the modern means of production and the way production is organized.[2] This paper cannot refute his analysis because the definition of class is different from our own. Rather it presents a parallel empirical analysis based upon the stratification concepts of Weber rather than of Marx. However it is concerned with the same problems as Mallet. In what sense can we talk of a new working class? What are the politics of this class with regard to authority within the firm and within the state? How are these politics different from those of the old working class? Because the questions treated are parallel to those of Mallet, our conclusions are pertinent comments on his conclusions and objectives.

Weber defines class as life chances determined by one's relationship to the market. Although he sees common interests determining similar politics among groups so defined, he does not see their developing a group consciousness. Rather he sees group consciousness developing among status groups. Status is defined as life chances determined by the estimation of the degree to which one's life style conforms to a certain code of honour defined by the most powerful groups in the society.[3] To the extent that people are segregated by life style, they recognize others similarly segregated as similar to them. Thus group consciousness which Marx saw as necessary for a class to fight for itself would in Weber's terms be a function of status groups.

Weber points out that status differences of life style may be differentiated by education.[4] In this article different status groups within the working class (as defined by occupation) are determined by degree of education. Three groups are

*The author wishes to thank the Roper Public Opinion Center for the use of the Institut Française d'Opinion Publique surveys.

[1]Serge Mallet, *La nouvelle classe ouvrière* (Paris, 1969).

[2]*Ibid.*, 42.

[3]Max Weber, "Class, Status and Party," in Hans Gerth and C. Wright Mills, *From Max Weber* (New York, 1958).

[4]*Economy and Society* (New York, 1968), I, 305.

Canadian Journal of Political Science/Revue canadienne de science politique, VI, no. 3 (September/septembre 1973). Printed in Canada/Imprimé au Canada.

differentiated: workers with only a primary education, workers with a secondary education, and workers with a technical education. Their consciousness is assumed to be developed in terms of Weber's analysis – that is, they are conscious of their differences from groups with different amounts of education in terms of the differences in life styles which are associated with different levels of education. Thus the worker with a primary education is alienated from the rest of society because he knows his style of life is deprecated by the rest of the society. As Andre Andrieux and Jean Lignon point out, he sees his primary education as an indelible mark of his condition and as one of the reasons why people look down on him.[5] In these terms the worker with a secondary education may approach to a greater extent the life style of the middle class in so far as he can speak their language. Even though he is a worker, he should feel less the discrimination against the workers' life style because he knows how to differentiate himself from it. As such he should be less alienated from the society. The worker with a technical education should be different from both of these. He has more education than the worker with a primary education and thus should not feel that the discrimination against the workers' style of life on the basis of lack of culture applies to him. On the other hand he is not integrated into the general culture of the middle class as is the worker with a secondary education. Rather he is integrated into the production process. This allows him to feel that he is as capable of directing production as is his boss and thus he feels a sense of discrimination that his education is not as valid for acquiring authority as an advanced secondary education. This is the group we will call the new working class.

The use of the term alienation implies something about the politics of these three groups; however theories defining what to expect with regard to their politics can be derived more systematically from two bodies of data. The first theory which relates specifically to the effects of education on political attitudes may be derived from Gabriel A. Almond and Sidney Verba's *The Civic Culture.* They found a relationship between subjective competence and a belief in the effectiveness of parliamentary democracy. They define subjective competence as the degree to which the person feels that he has influence on the government. However their data show that subjective competence is related to education.[6] This means that the person with a primary education believes less in parliamentary democracy because he feels less that he can influence the government. He is thus alienated from the government because of his feelings that he cannot influence it, and these feelings come from his lack of education.[7]

A close look at the way Almond and Verba measure subjective competence integrates their observations into our theory. They measure subjective competence in terms of whether the person feels he will be treated as well as anyone else by the police and by a government office. Here we come up against discrimination based upon differences in style of life. A person who cannot express himself well in middle-class language will not be treated as well by these agencies as a person who can. An explanation of the politics of different educational

[5] *L'ouvrier d'aujourd'hui* (Paris, 1966), 92.
[6] (Boston, 1965), 168–207.
[7] Samuel Barnes also found that within the Italian Socialist party those persons who had more education were less Marxist and that this could be explained by political efficacy. *Party Democracy: Politics in an Italian Socialist Federation* (New Haven, 1967), 179.

Les attitudes des travailleurs français à l'égard du parlementarisme

L'auteur analyse la conscience politique des travailleurs français en se servant de l'appareil conceptuel de Weber plutôt que de celui de Marx. Selon elle, la nature de la conscience politique des travailleurs dépend de leur mode de vie, lequel est grandement influencé par le niveau de leur éducation. Ainsi, les travailleurs qui possèdent une éducation de niveau secondaire sont plus susceptibles d'appuyer des partis de droite alors que ceux qui n'ont pas dépassé le niveau primaire de même que ceux qui ont acquis une spécialisation technique tendent à appuyer des partis de gauche. De l'intériorisation de la mythologie politique de droite ou de gauche dépend l'attitude des travailleurs à l'égard du système parlementaire. Dans la mesure où la mythologie gaulliste implique une diminution des pouvoirs de l'Assemblée Nationale, les travailleurs possédant une éducation de niveau secondaire sont amenés à perdre confiance dans le parlementarisme. Il appert cependant que pour les travailleurs dont le niveau d'éducation est inférieur ou supérieur au niveau secondaire, ce soit la confiance en eux-mêmes et en leur bonne intégration sociale qui les amène à partager la mythologie de gauche à l'effet que l'individu possède une réelle influence sur le gouvernement grâce au système parlementaire. Ainsi, le travailleur qui n'a pas dépassé le niveau primaire et qui perçoit la société comme nuisible à son mode de vie, perçoit également le gouvernement comme un organisme qui lui est étranger et souhaite que le parlement ne possède de pouvoirs que dans la mesure où le Parti Communiste peut les exercer. Par contre, l'ouvrier spécialisé, conscient du pouvoir qu'il a d'influencer les autorités en vertu de sa position dans le processus de production, donne un plus large appui au système parlementaire. D'où l'auteur conclut que le radicalisme de la nouvelle classe des travailleurs spécialisés détenteurs d'une éducation technique visera à transformer l'exercice du pouvoir plus par l'élection d'un parti socialiste à l'Assemblée Nationale que par des moyens non parlementaires.

groups based upon this data would then be that persons with less education believe less in parliamentary government because they believe less that they can influence government, and this view is based in turn upon their anticipation of discrimination by government officials on the basis of their style of life. On the other hand, people with more education should believe in parliamentary democracy because they believe that they can influence government on the basis of being treated well by government officials.

However the theory needs to be further specified. In assuming that subjective competence in itself brings about a belief in parliamentary democracy, Almond and Verba accept the democratic ideology that a person will accept a régime if he participates in it. It seems clear that even if a person participates in a régime by voting and is well treated by government officials, the actual decisions about the society are made by an élite over whom the individual citizen has little influence. Thus the allegiance to parliamentary government brought about by subjective competence is not based upon the actual experience of influencing government but upon the belief that one can do so. This belief is part of democratic ideology which legitimates parliamentary democracy. It describes parliamentary government as the best form of government because it allows citizens to choose their rulers. People support parliamentary government because they believe this ideology. The function of subjective competence is simply to prevent a person from abandoning this belief because he personally feels unable to influence government.

However a distinction must be made in types of democratic ideology. Historically in France deputies were considered an élite which could best rule in the general interest.[8] The people were conscious that they were an élite and chose them in terms of how well they performed their élite function. This continued to be the ideology of the Independents, the Mouvement Républicain Populaire (MRP), and the Radicals during the Fourth Republic[9] and could be considered a middle-class ethic to the extent that a greater proportion of the middle class than of the working class voted for these parties.[10] Here subjective competence may be seen as allowing a person to feel that the élite does not govern against the general interest. One believed in parliamentary government however because one had accepted the ideologies of these parties which described the deputies as ruling in the general interest.

The parties on the Left have had a different definition of democratic ideology. They define the individual's participation as selecting those who are to represent his specific interests. This definition came from the Left parties' criticism that the deputies of the parties on the Right rule more in the interests of the middle class than of the working class. They, by way of contrast, presented themselves specifically as representing the working class.[11] Presumably the individual participates in terms of his own specific interests and the deputies are legitimate only to the extent that they represent these specific interests. The role of subjective competence – or rather the lack of it – in this Left-voting working-class perception of parliament will be further specified in our second theory.

A second theory of the political behaviour of different educational groups has been elaborated in contrast to that presented above. Elsewhere, I proposed that while groups with only a primary education were alienated largely for the reasons postulated by the above theory, they were brought to loyalty to parliamentary government if they were affiliated with the Communist party.[12] The theory needs to be further elaborated. The worker with a primary education sees the state as alien because he sees that it is controlled by people whose style of life is different and who define his style of life as inferior.[13] It is this perception of the state which is the basis of his feelings of subjective incompetence. The Communist party describes the state as alien in terms of class differences which are

[8]Georges Burdeau, *La Démocratie* (Paris, n.d.), 23–33.

[9]Henry W. Ehrmann, "Direct Democracy in France," *American Political Science Review*, 57(1965), 883–4.

[10]Philip M. Williams, *Crisis and Compromise: Politics in the Fourth Republic* (London, 1964), appendix 7.

[11]Raymond Aron, *The Century of Total War* (Boston, 1955), 242. Aron discusses the logic of the Left's criticism of the idea that the deputies rule in the general interest in terms of Left opposition to democracy. We propose that this is also the logic of the Democratic Left.

[12]"De Gaulle and the Parties," doctoral dissertation, Washington University in St Louis, 1968.

[13]As France has been largely governed by parties of the Centre and Right since the Revolution so that the Communist party and other Left parties feel themselves excluded from the political system, they feel that the state is alien because it is in the hands of their class enemies. We are privileging a lack of subjective competence as the source of a feeling that the state is alien here because it is the basis of a perception that the upper class is alien. Because the worker with a primary education feels that his style of life is looked down upon by the upper class he feels that this class is alien. It is his perception that this alien class which controls government does not grant him the personal recognition which leads to a sense of personal efficacy that leads to his subjective incompetence.

customarily seen as differences in styles of life. Thus the Communist party provides a rationale for the alienation which the worker with a primary education feels. The worker then comes to feel that the Communist party protects him from this alien state. He sees the Communist party protecting his specific interests. Early in the Gaullist régime the Communist party argued that if parliament had more power, the régime would be governed less by monopolists and financiers, presumably because the Communist party would have more power. Thus I submit that the Communist party brought the worker to desire parliamentary government by arguing that he would have more power in a parliamentary régime. Communist workers saw themselves better protected from an alien state in a parliamentary régime. If this is so it means that we should find the alienation of workers with a primary education not leading to rejection of parliamentary government but rather to its espousal among those who are identified with the Communist party. Presumably among workers with more education the influence of the Communist party should not be as decisive because they are brought to believe in parliamentary democracy by integration into middle-class norms.

Neither of these theories deals directly with workers with a technical education. The theory must be further elaborated if they are to be seen as a new working class with a different kind of politics. Weberian analysis precisely allows them to be so seen. Weber discusses status honour in terms of the consolidation of the position of authority of persons who have gained power through charisma.[14] We may therefore assume that the code of status honour may serve as a principle of legitimation – that is, a code defining persons in power as having the right to rule. It is not outside Weber's analysis to assume that the code of status honour of the middle class served to legitimate the authority position of the economic élite largely among those persons who had a secondary education. These individuals recognized the values of middle-class culture as valid and saw the élite's greater prowess in these values as a fair justification of their power. Thus traditionally in France members of the lower class with only a primary education did not recognize the validity of the employers' claim to authority because they did not share the values which legitimated the employers' authority. This authority was experienced as alien precisely because it was not legitimated. Workers with a secondary education, as well as others with a secondary education, recognized this authority as legitimate precisely because they shared the employers' status code.

However workers with a technical education are not integrated into the status code of the employer; hence they are not integrated into the values which have traditionally legitimated the authority structure in France. Thus they do not accept the authority of the employer as does a worker with a secondary education. Rather they are taught to know a great deal about the production process. Mallet describes such workers as feeling that this knowledge gives them the right to a professional qualification, a professional autonomy, and the possibility of promotion.[15] All of this indicates that they assume they have a certain prowess which is more relevant to the production process than is the traditional culture of the middle class and that therefore they have the right to a certain authority. This

[14] *Economy and Society*, vol. 1, 251.
[15] *La nouvelle classe ouvrière*, 17.

makes them a new working class. They have a sense of confidence based upon their knowledge of the production process. They do not recognize the validity of traditional claims to authority.

This line of analysis suggests that the worker with a technical education will contest the traditional authority structure within the firm, but it does not indicate his attitude toward parliamentary democracy. That such a worker will have a different attitude from the other two groups of workers can be derived from the theory we have been elaborating. The worker with a technical education should not accept parliamentary government, as does the worker with a secondary education, simply because he believes in the norms of middle-class culture. However he should not be alienated in the sense that he should appreciate his own value and in the sense that he thinks his style of life is as good as that of the governing élite.

We can also derive from our theory some positive indications of the political attitudes of workers with a technical education. Because they are not integrated into middle-class culture, but rather contest this culture, they should be integrated into the political ideology of the Left rather than that of the Right. This means that they should seek power for parliament not because it allows an élite to rule in the general interest but because it allows parties which represent the working class to have power.[16] However their integration into Left ideology should be different from that of workers with a primary education. We indicated that workers with a primary education do not believe in the parliamentary myth of the Left that the worker has influence through his representatives because they see government as alien as a result of the difference between their style of life and that of the governing élite. They then are brought to support parliament only because they want the Communist party which protects them to have power. However the worker with a technical education is confident in his ability to influence persons in positions of power because of his sense of his own worth. He therefore should continue to believe in the parliamentary myths of the Left that working-class individuals may have influence through parliament.[17] His belief in parliament should depend less upon his desire specifically for the Communist party to have power. Because of his basic belief in parliamentary myths, he should be able to criticize the Communist party when it seeks power outside parliament, even though his belief in parliament comes basically from Left myths.

We have several problems now in turning to the data. First, we need to determine whether differences in education among workers indeed involve different styles of life. More specifically we need to determine whether workers with a secondary education are integrated into the political culture of the Right whereas workers with a primary or technical education are integrated into the political culture of the Left. Second, we need to see whether the hypothesis of Almond and Verba that a belief in parliament is based upon subjective competence is

[16]The degree to which parliament is seen as a democratic institution allowing the citizen some influence on the government by the Left is seen in the fact that the Communist ideologue Pierre le Brun included parliament's discussing the plan in his proposals for democratic planning. *Questions actuelles de syndicalisme* (Paris, 1965).

[17]Mallet feels that the new working class will be radical in its trade-union politics but conservative in its politics with regard to the state. (*La nouvelle classe ouvrière*, 15, 41). We see this "political conservatism" in terms of his parliamentarianism. It flows directly from his radicalism in the firm and is in a sense a militantism in the Gaullist régime.

correct. More specifically we need to know whether those with a secondary or technical education, who should have more subjective competence, believe more frequently in parliament. Third, we need to see whether our distinction between workers with a primary education and workers with a technical education is correct. More specifically does the parliamentarianism of workers with a primary education depend solely upon a desire for the Communist party to have power, whereas that of workers with a technical education depends more broadly in a belief in parliamentary myths of the Left.

Table I begins the analysis. It attempts to show that workers with a secondary education are more likely to be integrated into the political culture of the Right than are either workers with a primary education or those with a technical education. This follows from our proposition that workers with a secondary education are integrated into middle-class culture whereas workers with a primary and technical education are not. A general perusal of the percentages in Table I shows that in all years workers with a secondary education are less likely to vote Communist or Socialist than are workers with a primary or technical education. In 1962 they are more likely to vote for the Centre; in 1965 they are more likely to vote Gaullist; and in 1968 they are more likely to abstain.

The data in Table I may be simplified in order to evaluate them. If we collapse the Communist and Socialist categories into Left and Center and Gaullist into Right we can compare Right-Left tendencies between educational groups by means of statistics appropriate to a 2 $\times$ 2 table. This gives us statistics which indeed indicate that workers with a secondary education are more likely to identify with parties on the Right than are workers with a primary or technical education. Thus in 1962 the relationship between Right voting and secondary education as opposed to primary education is (phi) 0.157 which is significant at the 0.05 level.[18] And in 1968 the relationship between Right voting and secondary as opposed to primary education is (phi) 0.124 which is significant at the 0.10 level. Similarly in 1962 the relationship between Right voting and secondary as opposed to technical education is (phi) 0.195 which is not significant. In 1965 it is 0.185 which is significant at the 0.15 level and in 1968 it is 0.100 which is not significant. Thus we may say in general that workers with a secondary education are more likely to identify with parties on the Right whereas workers with a primary or technical education are more likely to identify with parties on the Left although we may have more confidence that this difference exists between workers with a primary education and workers with a secondary education than between workers with a technical education and workers with a secondary education.

Our second problem is to see whether education alone determines the frequency with which workers with different levels of education support parliament as would be predicted from Almond and Verba's theory of subjective compe-

[18]We use phi because it measures the degree to which all As are Bs and all non-As are non-Bs. This concentration along the diagonal is closest to our concept of causality. The choice of this measure means that our coefficients are smaller than they would be with other measures. It also means that we can only speak of causality as a slightly greater probability that As will be Bs and non-As will be non-Bs. Weber claimed no greater definition for the causality of conscious rationalizations in that he saw other factors as perturbing causes as well. In this sense, our interpretations are ideal types. They represent a logical representation of causal relations in terms of conscious rationalizations which explain the real world only with a low level of probability.

TABLE I

PERCENTAGE OF WORKERS PREFERRING VARIOUS POLITICAL FAMILIES BY EDUCATION

	Primary	Secondary	Technical
		1962	
Communist	27	11	5
Socialist	17	25	41
Centre	20	32	18
Gaullist	20	29	13
None	16	3	23
Total	100	100	100
N	(150)	(35)	(22)
		1965	
Communist	15	7	21
Socialist	13	10	9
Centre	12	15	19
Gaullist	19	32	17
None	41	36	34
Total	100	100	100
N	(265)	(67)	(53)
		1968	
Communist	27	8	19
Socialist	13	17	20
Centre	9	15	15
Gaullist	23	28	27
None	28	32	19
Total	100	100	100
N	(258)	(47)	(90)

Sources
1962: IFOP Survey 4435, 4436, 4437, December 1962. Total *N*: 1512.
Question: Avez-vous voté au premier tour des élections législatives, pour désigner les députés ? Le candidat pour lequel vous avez voté appartenait à laquelle des formations suivantes ?
1965: IFOP 9331, October 1965. Total *N*: 1980.
Question: S'il avait à l'heure actuelle des élections législatives pour choisir des députés, parmi les candidats suivants, quel est celui pour lequel il y aurait les plus grandes chances que vous votiez ?
1968: IFOP Survey D881, November 1968. Total *N*: 1851.
Question: If legislative elections for the choosing of candidates were to be held at the present moment, could you tell me which letter corresponds to the candidate for whom there would be the greatest chance that you would vote?
(In this and subsequent tables the questions are taken from the particular version of the questionnaire provided the author by the Roper Center. The questionnaires were, of course, administered in French.)

tence, or whether this varies not only with education but with integration into the political culture of the Right or the Left as was predicted by our theory. Table II addresses itself to this question. A glance at the percentages shows that only in 1962 do workers with a secondary education desire more power for parliament more frequently than do workers with a primary education in significant proportions, whereas in all three years workers with a technical education desire more power for parliament.

TABLE II

PERCENTAGE BELIEVING PARLIAMENT SHOULD HAVE MORE POWER AMONG WORKERS WITH DIFFERENT LEVELS OF EDUCATION

	Primary	Secondary	Technical
1962	39(150)	53(34)	50(22)
1965	30(265)	23(67)	40(53)
1968	30(258)	39(47)	50(90)

Sources
1962: IFOP Survey 4435, 4436, 4437, December 1962. Total *N*: 1512.
Question: Dans l'avenir, souhaitez-vous que le Parlement (Assemblée Nationale et Sénat) ait un rôle plus ou moins important qu'à l'heure actuelle ?
1965: IFOP Survey 9331, October 1965. Total *N*: 1980.
Question: Dans l'avenir, souhaitez-vous qu'en France le Président de la République ait un rôle plus ou moins important qu'à l'heure actuelle ou qu'il ait un rôle égal ? Et le parlement ?
1968: IFOP Survey D881, November 1968. Total *N*: 1851.
Question: Would you like the President of the Republic in France to have a more important role or a less important role or the same role in the future as he does at the present time? And Parliament?

A statistical analysis confirms this impression. Thus in 1962 the relationship between workers with a secondary education and workers with a primary education desiring more power for parliament is (phi) 0.135 which is significant at the 0.10 level. However in 1965 the relationship is −0.042 which is not significant, and in 1968 it is 0.059 which is not significant. On the other hand the relationship between workers with a technical education and workers with a primary education is 0.087 in 1962 which is not significant, 0.076 in 1965 which is significant at the 0.001 level and 0.186 in 1968 which is significant at the 0.001 level.

These findings support our theory that subjective competence is important only in so far as it supports a belief in myths legitimating parliament and that variations in these myths may also influence whether persons support parliament more than it supports the more direct Almond and Verba interpretation that a belief one can influence government alone influences whether persons support parliament. Thus workers with a primary education and workers with a technical education are integrated into Left political culture. However workers with a technical education believe more frequently in parliament than do workers with a primary education because of their own confidence that they can influence persons in power. On the other hand workers with a secondary education are integrated into the political culture of the Right. Even though they should have more subjective competence than workers with a primary education, according to Almond and Verba's data, their belief in parliament varies. This variation must come with changes in the parliamentary myths of the Right.[19] A change in Right myths may explain the difference between the proportion believing in parliament

[19]Georges Dupeux, "Le comportement des électeurs français de 1958 à 1962," *Revue française de science politique*, 14 (1964), 52–71, for a discussion of party changes in the Gaullist régime.

TABLE III

PERCENTAGE DESIRING MORE POWER FOR PARLIAMENT BY PERCEPTION THAT THE Ve PLAN INFLUENCES ONE'S DAILY LIFE AMONG WORKERS WITH DIFFERENT LEVELS OF EDUCATION

Feel the plan influences one's daily life					
Primary		Secondary		Technical	
Yes	No	Yes	No	Yes	No
32(78)	28(187)	16(25)	33(24)	47(15)	35(37)

Source: IFOP Survey 9331, October 1965. Total N: 1980.
Questions: Dans l'avenir, souhaitez-vous qu'en France le Président de la République ait un rôle plus ou moins important qu'à l'heure actuelle ou qu'il ait un rôle égal ? Et le Parlement ? Le ve Plan fixe les objectifs du développement économique de la France de 1966 à 1970. Vous-même, avez-vous le sentiment que l'élévation de votre niveau de vie est lié à la réalisation des objectifs de ce plan ?

in the 1962 samples and in the other two samples. Particularly in the 1965 sample, where the proportion believing in parliament is lowest, the proportion of workers with a secondary education supporting the Gaullist parties is the largest. The political culture of the Gaullists is different from traditional Right political culture in the attitude toward parliament. Whereas the traditional Right believed that parliament was necessary as an élite which could best rule the country in the general interest, the Gaullists believe that the élite best ruling in the general interest is that associated with the president. Thus although the general differences in life styles between workers with a secondary education and those with a primary education did not change in three years, the difference between the proportion of these workers supporting parliament changed because the political culture of the Right changed as workers with a secondary education moved from the traditional Right parties to the Gaullist parties.

This analysis of the difference between parliamentarianism among workers with a secondary education and other workers is furthered by the data in Table III. There are contrasting ideologies between the Left and the Right with regard to economic planning in France that precisely reflect the differences in their perception of the role of parliament. The technocratic élite which formulates the plan is an élite which makes decisions in the general interest from above. We would therefore expect that persons on the Right should desire that this élite have power. On the other hand the discussion on the Left has been that the workers themselves should have some participation in the elaboration of the plan. One of the ways proposed for them to do this was for the parliament to discuss the plan. Thus, in so far as workers are aware of the effects of the plan, we would expect those integrated into the Left political culture to desire more power for parliament and those integrated into Right political culture to desire less power for parliament. The different effects of awareness of the plan may then explain the reduction in the frequency with which workers with a secondary education believed in parliament by comparison with workers with a primary and technical education.

Table III shows this to be the case. Among those workers who are aware of the plan the belief in parliament is much less frequent among workers with a secondary education than among either workers with a primary education or workers with a technical education. The relationship is (phi) 0.332 between workers with a technical education and workers with a secondary education, which is significant at the 0.10 level and (phi) 0.153 between workers with a primary education and workers with a secondary education, which is significant at the 0.20 level. The differences between workers with different levels of education are not significant when they are not aware of the plan.

Workers with a secondary education are thus willing to give up what influence they might have on government through parliament when they recognize that there is outside of parliament an élite which is improving their level of life. This is in the tradition of Right political culture and more particularly the Gaullist version of it. It indicates that the desire to influence government in itself is easily relinquished when workers believe in Right myths. On the other hand workers with a primary or with a technical education are not willing to give up the influence they have on government in the light of such an élite. This is in the leftist tradition which proposes that such an élite should be controlled by the workers themselves.

To demonstrate the effects of Right and Left myths decisively we should show that regardless of education there is a reduction in belief in parliament among those on the Right and a continued belief in parliament among those on the Left, the difference between educational groups being due to different proportions supporting the respective traditions. Unfortunately we do not have enough cases to do this; thus our interpretation remains tentative. We have presented some evidence that workers with a secondary education are more likely to be integrated into Right political culture whereas workers with a primary and a technical education are more likely to be integrated into Left political culture. We predicted this on the basis of our theory that secondary education gave workers access to middle-class culture whereas this access was blocked to those who did not have a middle-class education. We have seen that this integration into Right political culture then influenced the attitudes that workers with a secondary education had toward parliament even though they may be expected to have more subjective competence than workers with a primary education. This furthers our theory that subjective competence is important only in so far as it leads one to believe in parliamentary myths.

We still need to see whether the difference in subjective competence between workers with a primary education and workers with a technical education influences the way they relate to myths of the Left. We predicted that workers with a primary education would be brought to desire parliamentary government only in so far as this would allow the Communist party to have more power because their lack of subjective competence kept them from believing in parliamentary myths that the worker may have power through parliament. On the other hand we predicted that the worker with a technical education would believe in these myths and thus believe in parliament independently of the chances for power of the Communist party because of his general confidence that he can influence those with power. We therefore need to pursue our analysis of the

TABLE IV

PERCENTAGE BELIEVING PARLIAMENT SHOULD HAVE MORE POWER AMONG PERSONS IDENTIFIED WITH THE COMMUNIST PARTY AS OPPOSED TO THOSE IDENTIFIED WITH OTHER PARTIES BY WORKERS WITH DIFFERENT AMOUNTS OF EDUCATION

	Primary		Secondary		Technical	
	CPF	Other	CPF	Other	CPF	Other
1962	65(40)	28(110)	—(4)	48(30)	—(1)	48(21)
1965	68(34)	25(231)	—(5)	26(62)	64(11)	33(42)
1968	33(69)	30(189)	—(4)	40(43)	65(17)	47(73)

Sources
1962: IFOP Survey 4435, 4436, 4437, December 1962. Total *N*: 1512.
1965: IFOP Survey 9331, October 1965. Total *N*: 1980.
1968: IFOP Survey D881, November 1968. Total *N*: 1851.
Questions: Party: see Table I; parliament; see Table II.

difference between workers with a primary education and workers with a technical education within the leftist tradition.

Table IV begins the analysis of the difference between workers with a primary education and workers with a technical education. It shows the degree to which a belief in parliament was dependent upon identification with the Communist party in the two groups of workers. Presumably the stronger the relationship the greater the dependence upon the Communist party to bring persons to support parliament because there is less influence toward a belief in parliament among persons identified with other parties when the relationship is strong. A glance at the percentages shows that both among workers with a primary education and among workers with a technical education the Communist party generally brings persons to support parliamentary government with noticeable exceptions. However our interest is in the difference in the degree to which workers with a primary education and workers with a technical education depend upon Communist identification for parliamentary support. Here a comparison between the strength of the relationships in the two groups shows that in 1962 and in 1965 workers with a primary education were more dependent upon Communist identification to bring them to support parliament than were workers with a technical education. Thus in 1962 the relationship is (phi) 0.345 among workers with a primary education, which is significant at the 0.001 level, but it is only (phi) 0.218 among workers with a technical education, which is not significant. Similarly in 1965 the relationship is (phi) 0.309 among workers with a primary education, which is significant at the 0.001 level, but it is (phi) 0.213 among workers with a technical education, which is significant only at the 0.25 level.

Thus we may say that identification with the Communist party is an important way in which support for parliament is brought about among both workers with a primary education and workers with a technical education. However we may also observe that it plays a less important role among workers with a technical education than among workers with a primary education because workers with a technical education who do not identify with the Communist party support parliament more frequently. Our argument is that this is because they more than workers with a primary education believe that they can influence persons in posi-

TABLE V

PERCENTAGE OF WORKERS APPROVING OF THE CFDT AND THE PCF DURING THE EVENTS OF MAY BY EDUCATION (of those having an opinion)

	Primary	Secondary	Technical
CFDT	78(109)	64(35)	75(33)
PCF	56(124)	45(53)	36(44)

Source: IFOP Survey D101, June 1968. Total *N*: 1903. Question: For each one of the organizations that I am going to quote to you, can you tell me the opinion you have about the part they played since the beginning of last month of May: very good, rather good, rather bad, very bad?

tions of power so that they believe the parliamentary myth that the individual has influence through parliament.

Can we distinguish between a belief in Left myths which we see as characteristic of the worker with a technical education and the desire for a parliamentary régime only for the Communist party to have more power, which we see as characteristic of workers with a primary education? The data presented in 1968 in Table IV allow us to do so. Thus in 1968 the Communist party no longer brought workers with a primary education to support parliament, whereas it continued to do so among workers with a technical education. The relationship among workers with a primary education is (phi) 0.016, which is not significant, whereas it is (phi) 0.142 among workers with a technical education, which is significant at the 0.30 level. Although the statistical support is thin, we see this difference between the groups as indicating that Communist workers with a technical education continued to believe that parliament was the best means for workers to have power whereas the Communist workers with a primary education saw the chance for the Communist party to seize power outside of parliament and they desired that it do so. Their basic desire was power for the Communist party as protection against the upper classes, whereas the workers with a technical education desired participation in a state which they saw as partly their own.

Table V furthers this analysis. We propose that it may show to what degree the parliamentarianism of the workers with a technical education is independent of direct affiliation with the Communist party to the extent that it shows reactions to the actions of the Communist party during the events of May. At one point in the events of May the Communist party broke with the Mitterand-lead Socialist Federation, which was calling for a more parliamentary régime headed by the democratic Left, and declared that what was needed was a popular socialist régime.[20] Table V indicates that workers with a primary education approved of these actions much more frequently than did workers with a technical education. The relationship is (phi) 0.170, which is significant at the 0.05 level. This means that the worker with a primary education was more likely to desire a direct seizure of worker power even if this meant the domination of the Com-

[20]*Partisans* (May-June 1968), 125.

TABLE VI

PERCENTAGE DESIRING MORE POWER FOR PARLIAMENT BY DESIRE FOR MORE POWER FOR PARTIES WITHIN THE GROUPS OF WORKERS DIFFERENTIATED BY EDUCATION

Parties should have more power					
Primary		Secondary		Technical	
Yes	No	Yes	No	Yes	No
62(55)	22(204)	50(6)	37(41)	67(24)	44(66)

Source: IFOP Survey D881, Nov. 1968. Total N: 1851.
Question: Would you like the President of the Republic in France to have a more important role or a less important role or the same role in the future as he does at the present time? and Parliament and the political parties?

munist party, whereas the workers with a technical education continued to believe that the best way for the workers to have power is through parliament. The belief that the workers could have power outside of legal guarantees surrounding parliament is present among workers with a primary education but not among workers with a technical education. The belief in the need for legal guarantees among technical workers is a belief in parliamentary myths that these actually do allow the workers power.

The data on approval of the Confédération française démocratique du travail (CFDT) is presented to show that the parliamentarianism of the workers with a technical education is not due to a lack of militantism as is the parliamentarianism of workers with a secondary education. The CFDT called for continued strikes in order to institute autogestion in the factories after the Confédération générale du travail (CGT) had made a settlement. Workers with a technical education approved of this call for autogestion as frequently as did workers with a primary education and more frequently than workers with a secondary education.[21] The relationship between workers with a secondary education and workers with a technical education is (phi) 0.175 which is significant only at the 0.25 level. This is the only indication we have that our analysis that workers with a technical education wish to have more power within the firm because they are integrated into the production process is true. We base both their integration into Left political culture and their desire to influence government upon this theory. In the present context it is evident that their desire to have more power may be directed toward a seizure of control within the firm but that they believe that the best way to control government is through parliament.

There is one more indication that workers with a primary education desire parliament to have power primarily so that the Communist party which protects

[21]A Fondation nationale de science politique survey does not find that the technicians (defined in terms of occupation) place a priority on autogestion and on control of the firm by the personnel or the union when expressed in these militantly ideological terms. This is in contradiction to our interpretation of their support for the CFDT. However it finds that when worker control is expressed concretely in terms of influence over the organization of production, organization of work positions, and internal discipline they were the most militant. This is in agreement with our position that they reject authority in the production process because they feel they have a prowess in this domain. Gerard Adam, "Introduction à un débat sur la nouvelle classe ouvrière," *Revue française de science politique*, 22 (1972).

them from an alien state will have power, whereas workers with a technical education desire parliament to have power so that they may influence government. Table VI presents this evidence. It shows the degree to which a desire for more power for parliament depends upon a desire for more power for parties. Again this dependence is seen in the strength of the relationship. The stronger the relationship the more dependent support for parliament is on the desire for parties because persons who do not desire more power for parties are not brought to desire power for parliament by other reasons.

Table VI indicates that both workers with a primary education and workers with a technical education are brought to desire power for parliament because they desire power for parties. However it shows that this relationship is stronger among workers with a primary education than among workers with a technical education. Thus the relationship among workers with a primary education is (phi) 0.348, which is significant at the 0.001 level, whereas the relationship among workers with a technical education is (phi) 0.201, which is significant at the 0.10 level. Workers with a primary education are more dependent upon a desire for parties to have power to support parliament than are technical workers because the latter are brought to support parliament for other reasons. Presumably the primary worker supports parliament only because he desires the Communist party to have power. The worker with a technical education may be brought to support parliament for this reason but he may also be brought to support parliament because he believes that it will allow him to influence government. He does not simply feel that he has to be protected from government.

In summary, the amount of education a worker has had influences his political preferences. The worker with a secondary education is more likely to prefer parties on the Right, whereas workers with a primary or technical education prefer parties on the Left. This indicates that occupation alone does not determine political preference but that the life style within an occupation may influence this. More specifically because the life style of workers with a secondary education is closer to that of the middle class their political preferences tend to be more middle class. The political myths into which the person is integrated by his party preference then assume an independent influence upon his political attitudes. More specifically the attitudes of workers with a secondary education varied with regard to the amount of power parliament should have because the myths associated with parties on the Right changed.

However life style may determine whether the worker has the basic amount of confidence in his own worth and in his own integration into the society to believe even the myth of the Left that parliament allows workers to influence government through their representatives. Thus workers with a primary education who feel generally that their life style is deprecated by the rest of society see the state as alien. They vote Communist to protect them from an alien state and desire parliament to have power only in so far as this will give the Communist party power. When the Communist party has the chance to seize power outside of parliament they will abandon their desire for parliament to have power. Workers with a technical education on the contrary have a confidence that they can influence persons in positions of power because they are confident of their prowess in the production process. Although they also contest authority within the society, their confidence that they are able to influence persons in power keeps them from feeling cynical about myths saying that the individual has influence through parliament. They vote for Left parties as their representatives rather than as their protectors because they do not see the society as alien. Thus their support for parliament is more independent of the desire for the Communist party to have power than is the support for parliament of the worker with a primary education.

By way of conclusion, it is perhaps appropriate to compare our argument and conclusions with those of Mallet. Mallet sees the new working class, defined by the new technology, as desiring to fundamentally modify existing social relations because work is becoming more and more the preparation and organization of production thus giving the worker greater professional autonomy which puts him in contradiction with the established status hierarchy.[22] This argument is different from ours in that it sees the source of radicalism of the new working class in the way their jobs are organized rather than in their education. However we did find that the new working class defined in terms of a technical education is radical to the extent that we found that it supported the CFDT during the events of May. Mallet's analysis and ours of the nature of this radicalism are similar. What a technical education does is to give the new worker a professional autonomy which makes him feel that he is as worthy of authority as his boss. Our analysis explains the mechanisms of the illegitimacy of the boss's authority. Because a technical education does not integrate the new worker into the culture that legitimated the boss's authority but rather gives him another culture more related to the production process he sees this authority as illegitimate.

Mallet sees the radicalism of the new working class leading to "l'autogestion généralisée de la production et de l'économie par ceux qui en portent le poids."[23] In this sense he sees the radicalism of the new working class changing the authority relations in the society as a whole but he does not see the focus for this change in terms of the political system. He proposes that the new working class not be revolutionary in the sense of wanting to seize power. Our analysis may further specify and clarify this theory. We see the new working class attempting to influence authority relations within the economy largely through parliamentary means. Indeed we see their greater parliamentarianism as due to their greater desire to influence the government and to their greater faith that they can do so. We see them believing that they can influence government through parliament because they believe in Left myths. Thus we differ from Mallet in not seeing political consciousness as a direct result of economic relations.[24] This means that

[22] *La nouvelle classe ouvrière*, 41.

[23] *Ibid.*

[24] Raymond Aron also sees the political system as independent from particular socio-economic conditions. "Les sociologues et les institutions représentatives," *Archives européennes de sociologie*, I (1960), 152. He would perhaps agree with us that this is in part due to the fact that political ideologies are articulated by ideologues rather than being spontaneously generated by socio-economic conditions in that he sees the ways of thinking of a society determined by intellectuals and party ideologues whom he defines as part of the governing élites. "Classe sociale, classe politique, classe dirigeante," *Archives européennes de sociologie*, I (1960), 269. The independence of political movements from spontaneously generated consciousness is also commented upon by Touraine, *La conscience ouvrière* (Paris: Editions du seuil, 1966), 345.

they should prefer the new Socialist party which calls for autogestion to be instituted through the control of parliament by the parties on the Left. In this respect it should be interesting to see to what degree the new working class contributed to the growth of Socialist votes in the 1973 election.[25]

[25]A survey conducted by the Fondation nationale des sciences politiques, at the time of the 1969 presidential elections, found that the technicians (defined in terms of occupation) represented a greater proportion of the votes for Michel Rocard, the secretary general of the Parti Socialiste Unifié (PSU) than other workers, although an even larger proportion of them voted for Pompidou. We propose that the vote for the PSU secretary-general represents a militant parliamentarism for control of the economy and of authority within the firm. As a high proportion of Gaullist votes were found because the desire to control the economy is of course conditional upon seeing that the plan does indeed control the economy and upon seeing that the person has influence through electing persons on the Left. Adam, "Introduction à un débat," 515–16.

Three Components of Political Obligation

BENTLEY LEBARON *Brock University*

There are questions that persistently recur both in political philosophy and in political experience. The question whether (or when) to obey or disobey the law in one of these, a question which has diminished neither in relevance nor in urgency since Antigone and Socrates.

Behind our justifications and our condemnations of obedience (or disobedience) we uncover our theories of obligation.[1] Often these theories are held implicitly, unselfconsciously, but it is the task of the political philosopher to make them explicit: in Socrates' terms, to help us "remember" that which we unknowingly know. In order to answer particular questions about political action we need to ask general questions about political assumptions. Why do we take it for granted that we "ought" to obey (or what we "owe" allegiance)? How does the state come to have authority over us; how do we come to be obligated by its edicts? What, precisely, are our obligations as men, and as citizens? Most generally, what is obligation anyhow and whence its "binding force"?

In this paper I want to make explicit a general theory of political obligation that will, I hope, dissolve some confusions and illuminate some controversies found in recent literature on the subject.

I

All obligation is not of a piece – it is no seamless web. Various kinds of obligations come into being in various ways. Perhaps more important, various obligations are backed by various kinds of "authority." Some depend on our active personal commitments; some do not. Some are enshrined in rule books, or codes; some are not and cannot be. Some are *merely* formal (for example, a law of the land that is no longer enforced). Others are almost entirely lacking a formal dimension (for example, the obligation that binds an unusually imaginative conscience to avoid stepping on ants or to pray for their souls as they are crushed). With some obligations, an "objective" instrument is dominant (for

[1]It might be argued that while questions of obedience and disobedience were important as recently as the 1950s and early 1960s, they now have been swallowed up by questions of rebellion, revolution, and political terrorism. I would rather investigate the possibility that by keeping creative disobedience alive we might help to achieve much needed social change without quite so much trauma. But, in any case, *both* disobedience and revolution remind us that problems of obligation lie at the heart of political philosophy, and that our theories of obligation require continual rethinking. See the remarks to this effect by Peter Laslett and W.G. Runciman in the introduction to their *Philosophy, Politics and Society* 2nd series (Oxford, 1967), ix.

Canadian Journal of Political Science/Revue canadienne de science politique, VI, no. 3 (September/septembre 1973). Printed in Canada/Imprimé au Canada.

Trois composantes de l'obligation politique

Cet article a pour but de présenter une théorie générale de l'obligation politique et, ce faisant, de dissiper certaines confusions et d'éclairer certaines controverses engendrées par de récents écrits sur ce sujet.

Toutes les obligations ne sont pas de même nature. C'est pourquoi une théorie générale de l'obligation doit rendre compte des différents types d'obligations selon qu'elles ont des origines différentes et qu'elles s'appuient sur des pouvoirs différents. L'obligation politique se présente comme un amalgame composé d'au moins trois types d'obligation : l'obligation légale, l'obligation morale et « l'engagement interpersonnel » (inter-personal commitment) tel la promesse, le contrat et le consentement. Dans la mesure où il y a souvent conflit entre ces trois types primaires d'obligation, les cas intéressants d'obligation politique sont toujours d'une analyse difficile, dont il n'est pas évident qu'on puisse arriver à les solutionner.

On trouvera dans cet article des précisions sur la nature des trois types primaires d'obligations et de leurs modes potentiels d'interaction.

En conclusion, l'auteur démontre brièvement comment son approche triadique de l'obligation politique peut aider à résoudre certaines questions classiques ayant trait à la désobéissance civile, à la légitimité et à la participation.

example, a written contract). With others, a "subjective" relation is dominant (for example, a tacit understanding).

And of course various obligations may conflict. At any given time it may be impossible to say *simply* that my obligation is to do so and so because I may be obligated to do A and at the same time to refrain from doing A. On different grounds, or by different authorities, I may be obligated both to obey the law and to disobey it. This seems to me a plain fact, and hardly in need of argument, though some authors deny that it is so,[2] and others find it trivial.[3] In my view it is far from trivial because, while we may find it relatively easy to know what our obligations are, it is usually difficult and at the same time very important to decide what to do when these obligations conflict. It is the latter problem that requires continual rethinking if we are to become or remain responsible agents.

I propose to distinguish between three primary varieties of obligation and to show that *political* obligation is an amalgam of all three. The three are legal obligation, moral obligation, and "interpersonal commitment." I do not mean to imply that this categorization is exhaustive, but only that these three components of political obligation seem to me the most significant.

By interpersonal commitment I mean those obligations that arise, directly or indirectly, through our personal behaviour, whether words or actions. Because they depend on what an individual actually does, they might also be termed "per-

[2]Hans Kelsen, *General Theory of Law and State* (New York, 1961), 407ff; see also G.E. Moore, *Ethics* (London, 1966), 65: "It seems evident that one and the same action cannot be both right and wrong." But, for support of my argument see, for example, Thomas Pocklington, "Protest, Resistance, and Political Obligation," this JOURNAL III, no. 1, (March, 1970), 13: "A man contemplating disobedience may have both an obligation to disobey and an obligation to obey." See also Michael Walzer, "The Obligation to Disobey," *Obligations: Essays on Disobedience, War, and Citizenship* (Cambridge, Mass. 1970), 14 and passim.

[3]Thomas McPherson, *Political Obligation* (London, 1967), 72. "Conflict between different *kinds* of obligation is a more theoretically trivial matter than it has been supposed. (It can still be serious practically)."

formatives."[4] The most obvious example of interpersonal commitment is a promise. Now some people have found promises and promising very mysterious and have gone to great lengths to explain why promises ought to be kept – why they obligate us. One of the most common moves is to suggest that there is some kind of moral guarantor ("natural law," for example) that stands behind a promise, giving it binding force.[5] Another is the suggestion that behind any particular promise stands a "general promise" or agreement "not to use certain noises except in a certain way."[6] But this is to invent ghosts and goblins when in fact there are none, for a promise requires nothing "extra" to make it an obligation. It just *is* an obligation. A promise *is* a commitment given by one person to another, which is merely another way of saying that when I promise I obligate myself, or bind myself, to perform a particular action.[7] No moral invocation is required to show that I "ought" to fulfil my promise. The fact that I have promised itself establishes the ought, the binding force of which is a very basic social practice or convention. That is, my commitment (my binding myself or promising) cannot be understood, has no substance, except within the context of this convention, which is almost universally taken for granted.[8] In short, one *cannot* promise without creating an ought or obligation, hence it is *necessarily* (tautologically) true that "one ought to keep one's promises."

Now it may well be that on some occasions, perhaps on most occasions, I *also* have a moral obligation to do that which I have promised. (How I come to have moral obligations will be explored presently.) In such cases the moral obligation may be understood as reinforcing the performative, the interpersonal commitment. But it is equally possible, and often happens in fact, that I have a moral obligation to break a promise. For example, I promised not to disturb your nap, but now I see that your house in on fire; or I promised to help rob the corner grocer, but I have since had a revival of social conscience. In such cases two kinds of obligation conflict in an obvious way. And in many cases it will be entirely obvious which obligation would take precedence, but we should not imagine that because I have a moral obligation to break (or, indeed, to refrain

[4]Pocklington has discussed these obligations of interpersonal commitment (or performatives) under the category of "obligation in the narrow sense." "Protest, Resistance, and Political Obligation," 4 and passim.

[5]John R. Carnes, "Whether there is a Natural Law," *Ethics*, 77, no. 2 (January, 1967), 124. "The law of nature, which enjoins the keeping of promises, guarantees that the social contract is binding." Carnes is here expounding John Locke, but he elsewhere asks us to "take seriously" this Lockean argument (p. 127). See also Kurt Baier, "Moral Obligation," *American Philosophic Quarterly*, 3, no. 3 (July, 1966), 212, 213, 218. Baier holds that the binding force of promises arises from a "blank" moral directive: "keep promises" (p. 213).

[6]H.A. Prichard, "The Obligation to Keep a Promise," *Moral Obligation* (London, 1968). I take it that when Prichard's argument is demystified it will turn out to be much like that of Rawls and Searle, to the effect that promising only makes sense as a social "practice" or "institution." Stated thus, the argument is true and helpful. See John Rawls, "Two Concepts of Rules," and John R. Searle, "How to Derive 'Ought' from 'Is,'" both in *Theories of Ethics*, ed. P. Foote (London, 1967).

[7]"Promising is, by definition, an act of placing oneself under an obligation." Searle, "'Ought' from 'Is,'" 103 and passim; See also Rawls, "Two Concepts," 156: "The promisor is bound because he promised."

[8]Searle, "'Ought' from 'Is'" 113. See also Rawls, "Two Concepts," 153ff; Prichard, "Obligation to keep a Promise," passim; and Hannah Pitkin, "Obligation and Consent-II," *The American Political Science Review*, LX, no. 1 (March, 1966), 45–9.

from making) a particular promise, the promise (once made) is therefore no obligation at all. The promise remains an obligation (however formal), and it remains true that "one ought to keep one's promises," even while we see that in this or that particular case I ought to break my promise. Let me generalize here: no particular obligation is to be taken as a final or absolutely authoritative "ought," but neither is its oughtness rendered simply null and void if perchance it encounters an ought that overrides it.

Besides promising, examples of interpersonal commitment are contracts, agreements,[9] oaths, vows, various kinds of consent[10] and borrowing. Borrowing is not merely *taking*, because in borrowing I commit myself to return the object. That too depends on a social convention, establishing an ought. When I use the term "borrow" I bind myself according to the convention, and without any moralizing I know that I am bound. Thus, to say that I have an obligation to return what I borrow is an exercise in redundancy, for "borrow" *entails* "obligation." No doubt this obligation may fail to move me in some cases, and a more conscientious person than myself may try to goad me into action by making a moral issue of it. "You ought to return what you borrow!" he insists, which merely reminds me of what I have known (necessarily) ever since I learned the meaning of the word borrow. Nevertheless, his moral tone of voice may impart to me an urgency which hitherto I did not feel. Apart from puzzled philosophers, the only other people likely to employ the locution "You ought to return what you borrow" are those in the process of teaching children how the convention of borrowing works. Those of us who have learned to use the convention know perfectly well how it is that borrowing obligates (though it may well be the kind of knowing shown through behaviour rather than through articulation of a concept).[11]

There are forms of interpersonal commitment that are less explicit than promises, contracts, oaths, and borrowing. Suppose I accept the office of secretary. In doing so, I commit myself to carry out certain functions; I bind myself; I impose an obligation on myself. And of course I do not need to make explicit promises to attend meetings, record minutes, circulate them, etc. All of this may be taken for granted, for my acceptance of a social role or office entails an undertaking to fulfil its responsibilities.

Even less explicitly, participation in a common enterprise establishes obligations between the participants, whether they are friends, marriage partners, business partners, or team mates. When you and I undertake a project together (say climbing a mountain) we bind ourselves by actions as well as by words. We make "tacit" commitments. One of us does not simply turn around half way and dis-

[9]See chapter 1 of Joseph Tussman, *Obligation and the Body Politic* (New York, 1960). Tussman rightly and unobtrusively *assumes* that rights and obligations follow as a matter of course from "voluntary agreement."

[10]"To consent precisely is to take on an obligation," McPherson, *Political Obligation*, 25. But in the same passage McPherson argues that, in some contexts, promises and consents fail to obligate (that is, if they are mere "acquiescence," or if they are morally blameworthy). I do not see how he can have it both ways, and the first position seems to me the correct one. See also John Locke, *Two Treatises of Government*, ed. P. Laslett, (New York, 1965), 376. "And Thus every Man, by *consenting* with others to make one Body Politick under one Government, puts himself under an *Obligation* ..." (my italics).

[11]For a brief but useful discussion of knowing shown through behaviour see Michael Oakeshott, "Rationalism in Politics," *Rationalism in Politics and Other Essays* (London, 1962).

appear down the mountain with no word of explanation, leaving the other in wonderment. And no moral argument is required to show why this is so, for obligation commitments are embedded so deeply, so ubiquitously, in our patterns of social intercourse that we make scarcely a move that is not in some way guided by them.[12] This, I take it, is the core of good sense in Locke's discussion of tacit consent. I do not agree with his *particular* argument that travelling the highway is to be construed as consent to abide by the laws of the land, nor with the assumption often made today that voting is a type of participation in the activity of the state that necessarily establishes an obligation to obey the laws of the land, but the *general* point still stands, that consent (promises, contracts, etc.) need not always be explicit and formal. And, for the most part, tacit commitments are no more problematic than are explicit commitments. It is only when obligations begin to *conflict*, either with other obligations, or with strong instincts, desires, needs, or rights, that distinctively *moral* issues arise.

II

Legal obligations, like moral obligations, may overlap with and therefore reinforce the obligations established by performatives. For instance, the law normally adds another dimension – a legal dimension – to the performatives that we call contracts. We agree to certain exchanges of goods or services, and our use of the term "contract" usually implies that we sign formal documents that describe the exchange. We are mutually obligated as soon as we have made our agreement, even without the legal dimension, but when we sign papers the law moves in explicitly, to stand behind our performatives. An obligation that might have remained an issue between private persons becomes the business of the state as well. Conversely, the legal obligation may come first (for example, payment of taxes) and when a citizen makes an overt undertaking to obey, then his performative comes to stand behind it. In either case, two kinds of obligation are at work together. It is equally possible, of course, that our performatives will conflict with, rather than reinforce, legal obligations. Oaths may be to disobey as well as to obey. Promises and agreements within the context of a criminal brotherhood are an obvious case in point, for these commonly clash with *both* legal and moral obligations.[13]

Legal obligations are created and imposed on us by laws that are duly enacted by proper authorities, upheld by the courts, etc.[14] Their "binding force" is quite unlike that of promises and other interpersonal commitments, in that we are obligated externally: that is, without the necessity of any performative on our part. That is to say, even the criminal, the anarchist, and the conscientious disobedient are obligated by the laws of the land, even when they strenuously deny

[12]"Having obligations is inseparable from being a social creature." McPherson, *Political Obligation*, 64. For an extended discussion of the reciprocal connections between "community" and "duty" see Stephen Toulmin, *Reason in Ethics* (Cambridge, 1964), 132ff.

[13]For discussion of other kinds of examples see Pocklington, "Protest, Resistance, and Political Obligation," 12 and 13, and Walzer "Obligation to Disobey," 10ff.

[14]Kelson argues that legal norms must inhere within a system and be backed by sanctions. Hart agrees that laws form a system, but denies that they necessarily have sanctions attached. See Kelson, *General Theory* chapters 1 and 2, and H.L.A. Hart, *The Concept of Law* (Oxford, 1961), chapters 2, 3, 5, and 6.

it. The obligation is *imposed* on them; it does not hang on *their* consent or commitment. One need not have taken an oath of allegiance, for example. As suggested earlier, the citizen *may* reinforce his legal obligations by his own commitments (as when public officials swear certain oaths to uphold and obey), but the point is that he is legally obligated even if he does not do so.

As will become clearer later on, this is no argument that (in the last analysis) a man always ought to fulfil his legal obligations, any more than he always ought to fulfil his promises. Quite the contrary! Yet we need to recognize that these obligations exist; that they have *some* claim on us; that they do not simply fade away in the presence of overriding moral imperatives. The law must be understood as imposing its "ought" claim (however attenuated) even when a conflicting ought wins the day and is given preference.

Now in making the argument that legal obligations are binding even on those who deny and resist them, I am adopting what might be called the "insider's" point of view. By this I simply mean to point to *my acceptance* of legal rules as imposing "oughts," as having binding force. If I did not accept them as valid (if I were a thoroughgoing anarchist) I would be termed an "outsider."[15] To be an insider I do not have to believe that I have an absolute duty to obey all laws on all occasions; I need only be willing to accept the proposition that there is such a thing as political legitimacy, that "the law" (in general) is "valid" and therefore imposes oughts or obligations on those within its jurisdiction.[16] This acceptance of legal institutions may be understood as a mild and passive form of *commitment*, and since the existence of a legal system presupposes such acceptance on a fairly widespread basis, it may be said that legal obligations, like promises etc., hang on commitments. But there are important differences between the active interpersonal commitments (performatives) discussed earlier, and this commitment which may be no more than passive acceptance of the law as in some sense obligatory. For example, earlier we looked at a set of commitments *to other persons*, whereas here we are looking at commitment to criteria that define an institution (a set of rules and procedures). Furthermore, interpersonal commitments are typically commitments to *do* this or that, whereas mere acceptance of the law *as law* is not in itself an undertaking to behave in any particular way – specifically it is not an undertaking to obey.

Another important difference has already been stressed; namely, that the obligations created by interpersonal commitments are obligations that I impose on myself, while legal obligations may be imposed on me quite independent of my

[15]For a related distinction – between "internal" and "external" points of view – see Hart, *Concept of Law*, 55–7, 86–9, 99, and passim. A recent argument from the outsider's point of view is that of R.P. Wolff in "On Violence," *Journal of Philosophy*, LXVI, no. 19 (2 October 1969). Wolff holds that "legitimacy" or legal authority is a "myth" (604, 616); that "there is no such thing as legitimate authority" (608); that "there are no legitimate governments" (609); and the like. It follows that he should view legal rules as merely coercive, and not as imposing obligations or "oughts."

[16]It is possible, of course, that one might be an "insider" with respect to law in the abstract (that is, one is not a thorough-going anarchist), yet an "outsider" with respect to a particular legal system. A revolutionary is often, perhaps typically, in this position during the state of insurgency. It is also possible that an "outsider" be neither an anarchist nor a revolutionary, but simply an external observer, for example, a man from Mars or an academic wearing his "social scientist" hat. This is the outsider with which Hart is primarily concerned in his *Concept of Law*.

will. Let me put this another way. With respect to legal obligations I (the writer) am an insider; I do accept law as a valid ought-creating institution. But outsiders are also obligated by the law, whether they like it or not. (In making this statement I am, as it were, *demonstrating* my insider's stance.) And what does the outsider say? He might well say that there is no legal obligation, that it is all an elaborate and cruel hoax. Since he does not accept law as authoritative, but merely coercive, he recognizes only power relations where others recognize obligations. Now who is right, the insider or the outsider? If you answer "the insider" then you *are* an insider, and vice versa. Kurt Baier finds a "dilemma" here, and demands to know: "Can 'outsiders' have obligations or can they not?"[17] He criticises H.L.A. Hart on this point, finding Hart's account of law "untenable" because it "fails to give a satisfactory answer to the question of whether or not those who look upon the rules from the external point of view have obligations."[18] But this is Baier's dilemma, not Hart's, for it is created by insisting on a definitive either/or where there cannot be one. So far as the insider is concerned the law applies even to those who repudiate it; so far as the outsider is concerned the authority of law means only that "they" (insiders) take it as authoritative. There is no "neutral" resolution to this conflict. No doubt this will be a dilemma for the person who is unable to commit himself to one position or the other, but the fact remains that so long as human beings keep both points of view alive it will be a mistake to demand a uniquely "true" resolution. Hart's analysis reminds us that since both possibilities remain open we must understand obligation from two points of view. And this understanding need not prevent us from choosing.

The binding force of legal obligation does not hang on the commitment of any particular citizen, but it does require the commitment of a considerable number. Were this commitment generally lacking, the legal system would simply break down, as happens occasionally when a polity disintegrates into a condition of warlordism or worse. It is not possible, and in any case there is no need, to say precisely how many must accept a given set of legal institutions in order to give them legitimacy or binding force. Suffice it to say, that there must at least be a body of officials sufficiently committed to the law that they proceed to enforce it, and active resistance on the part of the citizens must be the exception rather than the rule.[19]

At this point it should be clear why consent or contract theories break down, especially those that hold that *all* obligation (or at any rate all political obligation) is to be understood as some kind of consent, contract, or agreement. Locke is the classic example; Joseph Tussman and John Carnes are two contemporary examples.[20] In effect, they attempt to subsume all obligation into the category here discussed as interpersonal commitment, with crucial emphasis on performatives. Their problem is the failure to explain how it can be that we are

[17]"Moral Obligation," 217.
[18]*Ibid.*, 216.
[19]Hart, *Concept of Law*, 111, 113 and passim.
[20]It is instructive to note that both Tussman and Carnes are uneasy about their espousal and revival of contract theory, hence neither ask us to take it quite literally. For Tussman, *Obligation*, 7, it is a "model"; for Carnes, "Natural Law," 125ff. it is a "myth."

all (legally) obligated, even those of us who have not consented or contracted. They fail to explain because: (1) they do not clearly recognize different varieties of obligation; and (2) they do not see the significance of the insider/outsider distinction. Hence they do not see how the commitments of insiders can impose obligations on people who have not so much as accepted the validity of legal institutions, still less undertaken to obey. Putting this another way, contract theories cannot explain how it is that I may be legally obligated to do something that I have never in any way agreed to do. *If* I had agreed, then indeed I would be bound, but if I have not? Tussman is well aware of these difficulties and wrestles with them at length, but his one-dimensional model of obligation simply will not bear all the weight that he wishes to place on it.[21]

For anyone who has taken promising or agreement (that is, a performative) as his obligation paradigm, legal obligation as outlined here may seem curiously bloodless. In comparison with contract theory it is less personal, more formalistic or "legalistic." We have already noted that the binding force of legal obligation sometimes withers almost to the vanishing point, either because the law in question no longer serves a social function and remains only on paper, or because it is iniquitous and fails to command the respect of the citizenry, or because the political system as a whole has become unusually rotten. In such cases it may seem strange to speak of obligation at all, especially when the laws and/or régime are obviously repressive and cruel. Some people, following Aquinas, would rather argue that the law then ceases to obligate, ceases in fact to be law.[22] A related contemporary argument holds that the "binding force" of all obligations, including legal obligations, is and must be moral. "No obligation of any type arises unless a morally binding directive is involved."[23] These arguments seem to me mistaken, for if moral correctness is taken as a fundamental criterion of legal validity (that is, of what the law *is*) then in difficult and controversial cases we will find ourselves simply unable to say for sure what the law is. Further, we will find ourselves in a dilemma as to who might settle the controversy: the civil authorities? religious authorities? each man's conscience? Better that we should maintain a consistent, publicly known criterion of legal validity, and that once having established what the law is we should then proceed to criticize it on moral (or other) grounds.[24]

I contend, with John Austin, that "a law without an obligation is a contradiction in terms,"[25] which means (among other things) that "law," like "promise" and "borrow" is *defined* in terms of ought and obligation (though of course not exclusively in these terms). In other words, so long as law exists at all, it necessarily has some degree of binding force; when it is so bloodless as to impose no ought at all, then it has ceased to be law. But here we should acknowledge again

[21]For an extended critique of Tussman in particular, and consent theories in general, see Hannah Pitkin, "Obligation and Consent" (Parts I and II), *The American Political Science Review* LIX, no. 4 (December, 1965) and LX, no. 1 (March, 1966).
[22]*Treatise on Law* (Chicago), 78. Aquinas, in turn, is leaning on the authority of Augustine.
[23]Baier, "Moral Obligation," 213. Note the parallel to the argument, discussed earlier, that promises and other performatives require a moral building force.
[24]Hart makes essentially the same argument *Concept of Law*, 203–7.
[25]John Austin, *The Province of Jurisprudence Determined* (London, 1965), 185.

that some legal obligations are merely formal,[26] and that others, while not merely formal nevertheless ought to be overridden by moral considerations.[27] Indeed, it is arguable that some laws are of such dubious substance that they might well be overridden by considerations of utility, in extreme cases even by personal preference. (For example, laws intended to regulate the private sexual behaviours of consenting adults might well come under this category.)

There is yet another way to get into a muddle by failing to understand relations between various kinds of obligations. John Carnes raises the question "Why should I obey the law?" and answers simply "because it is the law."[28] However, he finds that somehow puzzling and unsatisfying. The problem is not that this answer is on the wrong track, but that it stops short with purely legal considerations. So far as it goes his answer is correct, if, as I have argued, obligation is built in to the very concept of law (and on this point Carnes agrees). But "because it is the law" seems empty because it does not go on to take account of other kinds of obligation that must be considered together with legal obligation. Carnes eventually makes this point too, though not until he has insisted on creating a separation between political-legal theory, on one hand, and moral theory on the other, and on relegating questions of moral obligation to the latter. My argument is that, to avoid confusion, the various kinds of obligation must be considered together. (Following Plato and Aristotle, I take it for granted that moral and political theory are inseparable.)

III

Moral obligations, like legal obligations, may be imposed on us against our will; they do not depend entirely on our individual consent (or other performative), nor entirely on our personal convictions. However, just as there could be no legal institutions without *someone's* commitment (to those legal institutions), so there could be no moral rules or principles unless someone was committed to them. Someone must accept the proposition that A is good and B is bad, or vice versa, for clearly there would be no moral problem if no one cared one way or the other. This someone (Xavier) we will call the "insider." Xavier is a believer with respect to a particular moral code. And the man who holds to a different code (Yves) we will call the "outsider."[29] Clearly Yves is at the same time an

[26]Everyone has heard of anachronistic laws which are no longer enforced, but are still on the books. For example, see Hart's remark that "Americans are accustomed ... to the inclusion among their statutes of much legal lumber in the form of penal provisions no longer enforced, and I am assured that, in California at least, the provision making a conspiracy to corrupt public morals a crime may safely be regarded as a dead letter." H.L.A. Hart, *Law, Liberty, and Morality* (London, 1963), 7. A few pages later, Hart continues: "the existence of criminal laws which are generally not enforced places formidable discriminatory powers in the hands of the police and prosecuting authorities."

[27]Laws requiring or allowing the persecution of minorities are an obvious example; there are, of course, many others.

[28]"Why Should I Obey the Law?" *Ethics*, 71, no. 1 (October, 1960), 16.

[29]We should note that an outsider with respect to the law may deny the very concept of legal validity (though the revolutionary, for example, denies merely the authority of a particular legal system). The outsider with respect to a moral code, however, typically rejects just that particular code (or rule, or principle), not morality as such. A thoroughgoing denial of the very concepts of moral right and wrong is comparatively rare.

insider with respect to his own code, and Xavier an outsider. The problem is that from Xavier's point of view all men, including Yves, may well be obligated by his (Xavier's) moral code – and, of course, vice versa.

But then is Yves "really" obligated by Xavier's moral code? If you answer definitively yes (or no) then you are an insider (or outsider) with respect to that code.

This account of moral obligation does not commit me (the writer) to an ethic of scepticism, nihilism, or radical subjectivism. The man who insists, and truly believes, that "Pushpin is as good as poetry," or that "It's all a matter of personal opinion, and one man's is as good as another's," has made his commitment to *that* moral stance, and it is at least a lazy, if not a pernicious one. He may not recognize it as a moral stance; he may characterize it as a metaethical insight of surpassing objectivity and realism; but if he believes it strongly enough to live by it (and few, if any, do) then this metaethic is also an ethic, and he is an insider with respect to a rather unfortunate moral code. Unlike him, I am committed to a moral code that makes distinctions between just and unjust, beneficial and harmful, etc., and I am prepared to argue that there are some basic moral imperatives that are universally obligatory, that is, that all men ought to recognize and heed. Like Xavier, I am committed to a particular moral code, and probably there are few mature, self-conscious humans who are not so committed, even if some are committed to codes as stultifying as those which we label "relativist" or "nihilist." If my analysis is correct, moral obligations derive from such commitments, and there is no other possible derivation, though of course our commitments may be more or less successfully concealed (especially from ourselves) behind our beliefs in gods or other mysterious sources. In short, moral obligations, like promises and legal institutions, are human creations.

I hold neither that *my* moral principles are absolute and final – the last word on moral obligation – nor that they are "merely" my opinions, preferences, or "emotions." To the extent that they are thoughtful, rational, humane, and generous, they cease to be merely personal, they become objective interpersonal standards. To the extent that they are directed toward the good of all men and not just my personal good, and to the extent that they actually issue in social benefit, these principles are "moral" in a fundamental sense – this much we can discover embedded in the very concept of morality – and they may be taken as morally obligatory on myself and others. (This remains true even though some men remain outsiders with respect to these principles. The fact that I take note of opposing claims does not commit me to the view that they are morally *valid* claims.) The extent to which any particular principles measure up to the above general criteria must remain a matter of discussion without final settlement, but the fact that there are no final answers in moral matters need not detain us here, nor dismay us, for indeed there are no final answers elsewhere either: not in the scientific enterprise, nor in courts of law, nor even in mystic revelations. It is a mistake to imagine that because we cannot judge the final judgment, therefore we cannot judge at all.

How does the binding force of moral obligation compare with that of the two other varieties of obligation examined earlier? It would seem that moral obligation typically is less institutional than legal obligation, though of course it is possible to institutionalize it: "the church." Part of the problem here is that if fully moral action requires personal commitment, and I believe it does, then just to the extent that it is formalized it ceases to be fully moral.[30] Despite the fact that it *may* be imposed on us against our will (as argued above), moral obligation typically is much closer to the obligations that arise from interpersonal commitments in that the involvement of the individual is more active and direct. Indeed, with respect to moral obligation it is often passionate. Whereas legal obligation is maintained by an elaborate set of institutions – in fact its very essence is institutional – distinctively moral obligation may well be atrophied by institutionalization.

In summary, there are three major sources of obligation: interpersonal commitments, legal rules, and moral rules or principles.

The binding force of interpersonal commitments is precisely my performative, my voluntary undertaking. I *bind* myself by my promise, my consent, my participation, and the like.

The binding force of the law is the authority of the state and its legal institutions, which in turn depends on the (more or less passive) commitment of the populace, or a key segment of the populace. (We might also note that the coercive power of the state serves as another kind of "binding force," but whereas it may encourage obedience, it does nothing toward establishing obligation.)

The binding force of moral rules and principles is the more or less passionate commitment of groups and individuals to those rules and principles. Typically, this commitment is like a promise in that it has something direct and personal in it; but it is like the acceptance of the law in that moral rules, like legal rules, are usually deemed binding not only on ourselves but on others as well. Hence there is a sense in which I may be obligated by the moral commitments of others, though I do not recognize it.

IV

Perhaps the most pressing practical question of political obligation is "When should I disobey?" Call this the *disobedience* question. Behind it stand the more theoretical questions: "Why should I obey?" and "When is a state legitimate?" Call these the *legitimacy* questions.

The disobedience question also leads on (or *may* lead on) to problems of rebellion and revolution, while the legitimacy questions lead on to questions about the kinds of laws that the state may rightly pass, and the kinds of punishment that it may rightly exact.

Finally, there is an important *participation* question: "What are my obligations as a (good) citizen?"

I submit that the forgoing three-dimensional account of obligation can help us answer these questions satisfactorily, and that any discussion of political obligation that neglects one or more of these three components, or that attempts to subsume all obligation under one of them, will prove unsatisfactory.[31]

[30] For development of this argument see Michael Oakeshott, *Religion and the Moral Life* (Cambridge, 1927).

[31] "The truth of the matter is that there is no single simple answer to the question why

Let us take a brief look at some of these questions. First, "When should I disobey?" If obligations were derived exclusively from promises, contracts, or other performatives, the answer would be simple: those who have promised or contracted (etc.) must obey; those who have not are at liberty to disobey. Clearly, as a general theory of obligation this is untenable. Indeed, as we have seen, Tussman admits to considerable uneasiness with this position, though he persists in clinging to it.[32]

If the law were the last word on political obligation, then the answer to "When should I disobey?" would be "Never!"[33] It is this position which legal positivists are sometimes accused of holding,[34] though, as Hart has eloquently shown, it is one which positivists need not hold.[35] I am not sure that any interesting theorists actually hold this position, though admittedly there are passages in the writings of Hans Kelsen and T.W. Weldon that might give the impression that any but legal considerations are irrelevant.[36] However, what is truly frightening is that the behaviours of many military men (and others), in probably all modern wars down to Vietnam, would suggest that thousands hold this position as a matter of *practice*. That is: "when legally constituted authority speaks, my duty, plain and simple, is to obey."[37]

If all obligations were moral obligations, then laws and promises would carry no obligations whatever once it were shown that they were immoral, and one should proceed to disobey them. A difficulty with this position is that all sorts of trivial decisions and essentially noncontroversial matters are made into moral issues, and the moral enterprise is considerably debased.[38] No doubt one *might*, for example, make a moral issue out of laws regulating motor traffic – or an agreement to meet at the corner bar for a drink – but normally these are not taken as moral issues, and they need not be. A more serious difficulty is that if resolution of legal questions is held to depend on resolution of moral questions, then either the judgments of the law courts will cease to be authoritative (if all citizens are deemed to have a share in moral decision-making) *or* our responsibilities for moral judgment (with respect to law) will be shifted onto the law courts entirely and legal judgments *ipso facto* will be taken as morally definitive.

we ought to obey the government," McPherson, *Political Obligation*, 22; see also 52: "If we were to insist on having a general theory of political obligation, it would have to be ... an eclectic one."

[32]I am in agreement with the salvage job performed by Professor Pitkin on Tussman's consent theory (and Locke's), except that the result seems to be not consent theory at all, but a quite different theory. This is almost conceded at the end of the first part of the article, where Professor Pitkin suggests that "in one sense this 'nature of government' theory is thus a *substitute* for the doctrine of consent." ("Obligation and Consent," 999, my italics).

[33]Cases of conflict between two laws, or between two levels of legal jursidiction, might be construed as a partial exception to this.

[34]Claude Ake, "Political Obligation and Political Dissent," this JOURNAL, II, no. 2 (June 1969), 247–8.

[35]See the whole of *The Concept of Law*, but especially chapter 9.

[36]Kelsen, *General Theory*, 406–11 and passim; T.D. Weldon, *The Vocabulary of Politics* (Harmondsworth, Middlesex, 1960), 57 and passim.

[37]For a sobering account of the propensities of ordinary citizens to obey orders unthoughtfully, see Stanley Milgram, "Some Conditions of Obedience and Disobedience to Authority," *Human Relations*, 18, no. 1 (February, 1965).

[38]For further on this see McPherson, *Political Obligation*, 25–6 and 50.

Either legality will become as open ended as morality must be (which seems impossibly chaotic) or morality will become so authority-ridden as to lose its "moral" character (which seems disturbingly possible).

It follows from the above that there is no single or simple answer to the disobedience question. A satisfactory answer to "When should I disobey?" must take account of a complex interweaving of all three kinds of obligation, in which legal considerations will *normally* take precedence (that is, in the ordinary course of events), but in which moral considerations will tend to take precedence in particularly difficult and controversial cases, and in which performatives will tend to play a subsidiary role.[39] Needless to say, the disobedience question cannot be answered in the abstract, without reference to the circumstances of particular cases. Perhaps we should consider a particular situation in order to illustrate the above generalizations. Imagine a case in which relevant circumstances include the following: in a small isolated community a mercy flight is being considered, over dangerous terrain, to take a person who is seriously ill to a place where he may receive appropriate medical attention; the flight would be illegal because the pilot is not sufficiently qualified and/or the plane not sufficiently equipped for this particular season, route, and distance; the pilot has promised the sick person that he will undertake the flight.

My suggestion that performatives will tend to play a subsidiary role is meant as a recognition that in cases such as the above, promises will tend to be less weighty than other factors relevant to the decision. In this case the moral and promissory considerations reinforce each other rather than conflict, so there is no real need to delineate a boundary between them, but even when promises conflict with moral imperatives (for example, the pilot had promised to go to a party that night), I think it safe to assume that moral considerations should normally prevail. (One could, of course, counter by thinking of unusually important promises.)

My suggestion that "legal considerations will *normally* take precedence" is based on the assumption that laws are normally beneficial, or at least are not obviously harmful (that is, there are good reasons for restrictions on certain types of planes, flight paths, etc.). I assume, then, that the pilot would not be justified in breaking these laws in the ordinary course of events (when there is no emergency), and this is the case even though he has never made any special promise to obey the law.

My suggestion that moral considerations will tend to take precedence in particularly difficult and controversial cases could be stated in stronger language: when moral and legal obligations conflict, and when upon careful reflection important moral considerations appear to require illegal action, then one ought to proceed with that illegal action. If the law in question is blatantly repressive (or otherwise clearly at fault) and if the moral need is obvious and pressing, there is no great dilemma. But in the case we are considering, the difficulty arises in that the relevant law is no ass, but rather a pragmatic guide which we overrule at our (and other people's) peril. Hence there may well be a moral argument

[39] I note that while McPherson agrees with me about the complexities of political obligation, he does not agree that moral considerations are to be given any privileged position. See *ibid.* 52–4, but also 74ff.

that *reinforces* the legal obligation, and tells *against* the moral obligation to make the flight. No doubt the pilot is morally obligated to try to save a life and relieve acute distress, but he is also morally obligated to avoid a foolish risk of escalating distress and loss of life. In summary, his decision to fly or not to fly in these circumstances, which I characterize as difficult and controversial, will turn on primarily moral considerations, though laws and performatives are not irrelevant.

When the contemplated illegality also has a political dimension (for example, "civil disobedience"), where public policies, passionate grievances, and the well-being of large elements of the population are involved, cases will be still more difficult and controversial – one could imagine that systematic sorting out of all considerations relevant to a particular act of disobedience might require a book rather than a few paragraphs – and my suggestion is that the more complex and difficult the obligation problem, the safer the generalization that moral considerations ought to take precedence.

When we turn to the legitimacy questions, we find once more that our answers must be three sided. In brief, whenever I have explicitly or tacitly consented to obey that is an obligation and a partial answer to "Why should I obey?" In legal terms, I should obey simply because it is the law, for "law" is an obligation-imposing artifice. In moral terms, I should sometimes (perhaps usually) obey because laws sometimes (perhaps usually) promote general security, welfare, and happiness.

Similarly, there are three interlocking answers to "When is a state legitimate?" Some degree of legitimacy, though certainly not unqualified legitimacy, is conferred by virtue of the consent of (large portions of) the citizenry, however expressed. (It is clear that a government that is simply *imposed* will have a much harder time justifying its claims to legitimacy.) In legal terms, a state is legitimate when it succeeds in getting itself *accepted* as legitimate, first within the state itself, and second within the international community. In moral terms, a state is legitimate to the extent that it secures the welfare of its people and of humanity generally. Those who hold that mankind would be better off without national states must deny that they can be morally legitimate (and such people will probably be interested *only* in the moral dimension of legitimacy). Those who see national states as obviously good and necessary must beware of the opposite tendency to reduce legitimacy to legality.

R.P. Wolff has recently revived the old anarchist contention that legitimacy is a myth, that states and governments are *never* truly legitimate. "I have come to the conclusion that philosophical anarchism is true. That is to say, I believe that there is not, and there could not be, a state that has a right to command and whose subjects have a binding obligation to obey."[40] "Men everywhere and always impute authority to established governments, and they are always wrong to do so."[41] If I follow his argument correctly, Wolff has come to this conclusion by way of a reasoning which takes account only of moral obligation. He argues (correctly) that traditional consent theory breaks down. What I have called legal obligation he discusses under the heading of "*de facto* authority," but this turns

[40] Wolff, "On Violence," 607.
[41] *Ibid.*, 608.

out to be simply another form of power, not genuine authority, and the citizens who are led to accept this authority are (on his showing) misled.[42] This leaves only moral obligation and Wolff, following Kant, argues for an account of moral obligation which would preclude legitimacy of states. "Every man has a fundamental duty to be autonomous, in Kant's sense of the term. Each of us must make himself the author of his actions and take responsibility for them by refusing to act save on the basis of reasons he can see for himself to be good. Autonomy, thus understood, is in direct opposition to obedience, which is submission to the will of another, irrespective of reasons. Following Kant's usage political obedience is heteronomy of the will."[43]

This is not the place to get into the question of whether Kant's moral theory is a satisfactory one though it should be clear that speaking generally it is in accord with what I have said about moral obligation. My basic objection to Wolff's argument is that it subsumes political obligation (and legitimacy) entirely under a moral heading. If we assume that the only real obligation is moral obligation, then we can plausibly refuse to acknowledge the claims of legal obligation as anything but a sophisticated form of coercion. The ordinary citizen, according to Wolff, has been duped into thinking that the law obligates, when in fact it does not. But on this point I would rather rely on the judgment of the citizen than on that of the philosopher. One argument that the citizen might use is the one I have used earlier, that terms such as "law," "authority," and "obligation" are mutually self- and other-defining, such that we cannot grasp the meaning of one without at the same time grasping the others. The concept of law presupposes the concept of obligation. But without relying too heavily on arguments from usage we might recall that a citizen requires conceptual tools that will enable him to distinguish between governments that are worth supporting, and those that are so corrupt or oppressive that they should be overthrown. This kind of distinction becomes difficult, if not impossible, on Wolff's *a priori* argument that *all* governments are illegitimate.

The kinds of considerations relevant to justification of revolutions, punishments, good versus bad laws, etc., should be evident from the above, and I shall not take time here to discuss them separately.

Turning, finally, to the participation question, it should be evident that, as a good citizen, I have three kinds of obligations. I have legal obligations wherever valid laws impinge on my conduct. For example I have an obligation to pay taxes. I have moral obligations that sometimes (perhaps in most cases) reinforce legal obligations, but sometimes cut across legal obligations and demand disobedience. In some instances it may be my moral obligation to refuse to pay taxes, or to campaign against and resist iniquitous laws and policies of the state. I may have obligations deriving from explicit promises (for example, an oath of allegiance) and I may have obligations deriving from my activities as citizen (for example, campaigning for or holding public office).

It is hard for me to see how the act of casting a ballot is to be construed as necessarily giving rise to obligations, unless there has been a commitment to abide by majority decisions. I acknowledge that such a commitment can be taken

[42] *Ibid.*, 604ff.
[43] *Ibid.*, 607.

for granted in some genuinely democratic situations,[44] but even here there may well be overriding considerations.

It is hard for me to believe that the citizen has an obligation to vote, unless he has good reason to believe that his voting is meaningful in terms of genuine alternatives, leading to a better life. There is no relevant legal obligation; there is no relevant interpersonal commitment; and a moral obligation must be demonstrated, not merely taken for granted.

It is hard for me to believe that my obligations to those abstractions called "the state" or "the law" ought to take precedence over my obligations to particular persons, or to the general interests of mankind.[45] I recognize no moral obligation to obey the state come what may; my obedience is conditional on the state's good behaviour; it must deserve my obedience. In fact, it may well be the obligation of the good citizen to call the state to account, to protest, or even to defy its authority in some instances.[46]

At the extreme we may sometimes have an obligation to go beyond protest, pressure, and disobedience, to strive mightily to destroy or transform blatantly repressive political régimes. Obviously we can have no such legal obligation; our political obligations here are almost entirely moral obligations.

I do not believe that there is an obligation upon *every* citizen to be frugal, hard working, a diligent taxpayer, a solid pillar of the community, although remnants of these traditional obligations surely remain. On the other hand, I do believe that we have obligations to "study the issues," to be well informed of public problems, and then to work toward public welfare, whether through public office, through persuasion and pressure, through development of alternative life styles, or in some other fashion. No doubt we have an obligation to preserve the social order, but surely we also have an obligation to transcend it. Following Hannah Arendt, I would argue that we have an obligation to create a "public space" where freedom can dwell.[47] Clearly these obligations are not of the legal variety, nor are they likely to derive, in any significant degree, from promises or agreements. They might be understood as moral obligations that arise out of our commitments to be good citizens, and, in a deeper sense, fully human beings. (I do not imagine that the sketchy criteria for what will count as "good citizens" and "fully human beings" will or ought to stand without controversy. The criteria introduced here would have to be defended and developed.)

Discussions of political obligation in the past have been too easily hung up on questions of consent/agreement, and on questions of legal prescriptions and proscriptions, whereas in fact their moral dimension is at once the most important, the most difficult, and the most interesting. At this level our interests as political philosophers should overlap with our commitment as men and as citizens.

[44]For more on this see McPherson, *Political Obligation*, 21ff, and Pocklington, "Protest, Resistance, and Political Obligation," 8, 15.
[45]"If I had to choose between betraying my country and betraying my friend I hope I should have the guts to betray my country." E.M. Forster, *Two Cheers for Democracy* (London, 1951), 78.
[46]For a provocative discussion of these propositions, see H.D. Thoreau, "On the Duty of Civil Disobedience," *Walden and On the Duty of Civil Disobedience* (New York, 1961).
[47]*The Human Condition* (Garden City, N.Y., 1959); and *On Revolution* (New York, 1965).

The Level of Analysis Problem Revisited*

WILLIAM B. MOUL *University of British Columbia*

The state is the most frequently studied unit or level of analysis in international relations.[1] However, especially in more recent empirical research, aggregations or combinations of this basic unit such as dyads,[2] coalitions,[3] military strategic subsystems,[4] the great power system,[5] the central system, and the total international system[6] have been the focus of attention. As J. David Singer stated in his often cited paper on the level-of-analysis problem: "Whether in the physical or social sciences, the observer may choose to focus upon parts or upon the whole, upon the components or upon the system. He may, for example, choose between the flowers or the garden, the rocks or the quarry, the trees or the forest, the houses or the neighborhood ..."[7] The level-of-analysis problem is concerned with the choice and limitations of particular units of analysis.

*This article is a revision of a paper read at the 1972 annual meeting of the Canadian Political Science Association in Montreal. An earlier version was accepted as part of my comprehensive examination in international relations at the University of British Columbia. A number of people have provided me with critical comments. In particular I would like to thank David J. Elkins, Ole R. Holsti, and Michael D. Wallace of the University of British Columbia.

1Unless specifically noted in the text, "level of analysis" and "unit of analysis" are used interchangeably. This is a common practice in the international-relations literature. Less common and possibly more confusing is treating "system" and "aggregate" as synonyms. While the meaning of system is ambiguous, in the empirical studies examined in this paper the characteristics of the international system are built up by aggregating the characteristics of the components. Calculation of the number of deaths resulting from interstate war in the international system by adding the deaths of the individual states is a simple if not trivial example.

2Richard A. Brody, "Some Systematic Effects of the Spread of Nuclear Weapons Technology: A Study through Simulation of a Multinuclear Future," *Journal of Conflict Resolution*, 7, no. 4 (December 1963), 663–753; Roger W. Cobb and Charles Elder, *International Community: A Regional and Global Study*, (New York, 1971); and R. J. Rummel, "Indicators of Cross-national and International Patterns," *American Political Science Review*, 63, no. 1 (March, 1969), 127–97.

3Raymond Tanter, "International Systems and Foreign Policy Approaches: Implications for Conflict Modelling and Management," University of Michigan, *International Data Archive Research Report*, June 1971.

4Michael Hass, "International Subsystems: Stability and Polarity," *American Political Science Review*, 64, no. 1 (March, 1970), 98–123.

5J. David Singer, Stuart Bremer, and John Stuckey, "Capability Distribution, Uncertainty and Major Power War 1816–1965," *Peace, War and Numbers*, ed. Bruce M. Russett (Beverley Hills, in press).

6J. David Singer and Melvin Small, "Alliance, Aggregation and the Onset of War, 1815–1945," *Quantitative International Politics*, ed. J. David Singer (New York, 1968), 247–86; J. David Singer and Michael D. Wallace, "Intergovernmental Organization and the Preservation of Peace, 1816–1965: Some Bivariate Relationships," *International Organization*, 24, no. 3 (Summer, 1970), 520–47.

7J. David Singer, "The Level of Analysis Problem in International Relations," *The Inter-*

Canadian Journal of Political Science/Revue canadienne de science politique, VI, no. 3 (September/septembre 1973). Printed in Canada/Imprimé au Canada.

Le problème du plan analytique dans l'agrégation spatiale et temporelle en relations internationales

Le problème du plan analytique a trait au choix et aux limites des unités d'analyse. En relations internationales, c'est là un secteur fort confus. L'article bien connu de Singer contient la seule discussion des implications méthodologiques de ce problème. Bien qu'il pose le problème en termes de « composantes » et de « systèmes », Singer le transforme en une comparaison des utilités de deux modèles du comportement de l'Etat. Plutôt que d'éclaircir le problème, cet article a engendré encore plus de confusions et d'erreurs dans les recherches tant théoriques qu'empiriques.

Dans les recherches empiriques, l'erreur la plus fréquente est celle du « sophisme contextuel » (ecological fallacy). Ainsi, Singer et Small, dans leur étude sur les relations entre le phénomène de la formation des alliances et les guerres, au niveau du système international, ont inféré que de telles relations existaient également au niveau des Etats, alors qu'une analyse plus approfondie de leurs données suggère que tel n'est pas le cas.

L'agrégation temporelle relève également du problème du plan analytique. On ne devrait pas s'étonner de rencontrer des cas où la relation entre deux variables longitudinales varie elle-même selon la façon dont sont agrégées les périodes. Même s'il est vrai que le temps constitue une forme très utile de catalogue de l'expérience, le problème de l'agrégation temporelle aurait avantage à être élargi par la considération des périodes diplomatiques, sociales et psychologiques en plus des strictes périodes du calendrier.

Singer has presented the only discussion of the methodological implications of this problem in the international relations literature.[8] While I would agree with him that the neglect of this problem is a "significant variable in the general sluggishness which characterizes the development of theory in the study of relations among nations,"[9] I would also argue that his discussion and its uncritical acceptance have added to rather than reduced the conceptual confusion. I hope to clarify the issue and to touch on some related methodological problems. In particular, I will examine the comparability of cross-sectional and longitudinal analysis and discuss, albeit briefly, temporal aggregation and various types of time – physical, social, and psychological.

The level of analysis problem and ecological fallacy

Essentially, the confusion in Singer's discussion, and in much of the literature, results from equating the "parts-whole," "components-system" problem with the "long standing controversies between social psychology and sociology, personality orientated and culture orientated anthropology or micro- and macro-economics."[10] In the former case, the concern is with different units of analysis and in the latter case, aside from micro- and macroeconomics, the concern is with the types of variables that explain a particular unit's behaviour.

In his paper Singer never does delineate the international system-level or unit of analysis. All the research he describes as employing the system as the unit of

---

national System: Theoretical Essays, ed. Klaus Knorr and Sidney Verba (Princeton, 1961), 77–92.

8 *Ibid.*

9 *Ibid.*, 78.

10 *Ibid.*, 77.

analysis actually employs the state as the unit of analysis. These studies differ from those described in the section of the paper dealing with the nation-state level of analysis only in terms of the relative importance ascribed to "systemic," "external," or "environmental" *influences upon state behaviour*. The level-of-analysis problem has been transformed into a debate over the utilities of various models of state behaviour. For example, while Hans Morgenthau posits a billiard ball model in which the size of the ball and the array of balls on the table are the determining factors, others, such as Richard Snyder, stress the significance of national, internal, or domestic influences.

In assessing the utility of each level of analysis he describes, Singer stresses that "we cannot afford to shift our orientation in the midst of a study."[11] In terms of assessing the relative importance of systemic and domestic variables, however, we must do exactly that. Each model of state behaviour concentrates upon one type of variable ignoring others as non-significant. The models should be treated as hypotheses or theories to be examined. This is primarily an empirical question and one must shift back and forth assessing the contribution of particular types of variables to an explanation of a state's external behaviour. There seem to be no major logical difficulties involved here.[12] With reference to the level of analysis problem *as initially posed*, his stricture against shifting levels is correct. Singer does not heed his own warning, and he also states the contrary. The international system as the unit of analysis, he writes, "should prove to be reasonably satisfactory as a basis for prediction even if such prediction is to extend beyond the characteristic of the system and attempt anticipatory statements regarding the actors themselves."[13]

The "system-component" or level of analysis problem in international relations is a familiar one in the literature of other social sciences, logic, and statistics. It involves what has (unfortunately) become known as the ecological fallacy in sociology, the compositional fallacy in logic, and the aggregation problem in economics. Although there are earlier discussions, W.S. Robinson, in a now classic paper, drew attention to the misuse of aggregate information to study the behaviour of individuals.[14] Can ecological correlations (correlations among groups) be substituted for individual correlations? Can accurate inferences be made from ecological relationships to individual relationships and vice versa? His conclusion was that they cannot.

Robinson demonstrated his point by examining the ecological correlations

[11]*Ibid.*, 84.

[12]James N. Rosenau and Wolfram Hanrieder think that there are logical problems. See Rosenau, "Calculated Control as a Unifying Concept in the Study of International Politics and Foreign Policy," *The Scientific Study of Foreign Policy* (New York, 1971, originally published in 1963); Hanrieder, "Actor Objectives and International Systems," *Journal of Politics*, 27, no. 1 (February 1965), 109–32; "Compatibility and Consensus: A Proposal for the Conceptual Linkage of External and Internal Dimensions of Foreign Policy," *American Political Science Review*, 61, no. 4 (December 1967), 971–83; "International and Comparative Politics: Toward a Synthesis?," *World Politics*, 20, no. 3 (April 1968), 480–93. While Rosenau appears to have changed his earlier position, Hanrieder proposes concepts such as "penetrated system" as "cumulative proposition(s) that cover both analytical environments." See his "Compatibility and Consensus," 981.

[13]"Level of Analysis Problem," 82.

[14]W. S. Robinson, "Ecological Correlations and the Behavior of Individuals," *American Sociological Review*, 15 (1950), 351–7.

(relations among groups of individuals) between race and illiteracy in the United States. Using the nine geographical census divisions as the units of analysis, the correlation coefficient was 0.773. The coefficient computed from individual census data was 0.203. The correlation coefficients for nativity and illiteracy varied from 0.118 (individual) to −0.619 (census division). G. Udny Yule and Maurice G. Kendall, in an earlier discussion of the problem, demonstrated that the way geographical units are modified or aggregated may raise the coefficient from near 0.000 to 0.900. "Our correlations will accordingly measure the relationship between the variates for the specified units chosen for the work. They have no absolute validity independently of those units, but are relative to them. They measure, as it were, not only the variation of the quantities under consideration, but the properties of the unit mesh which we have imposed on the system in order to measure it."[15]

Economists have noted the inaccuracies introduced when estimating micro relationships with aggregate relationships. Inaccuracy of estimation however is not the crux of the level-of-anlaysis problem. The important point is the *logical* error involved in making inferences from relationships dealing with an aggregation of units to relationships dealing with the individual units. While this is designated ecological *fallacy*, the logical error is rarely pointed out and the problem is formulated as one of estimation.

In international relations literature, Nazli Choucri's analysis of the behaviour of nonaligned states toward both East and West provides an illustration.[16] As a group, the three nonaligned states considered, India, Indonesia, and Egypt, exhibited no significant difference in behaviour toward either bloc. Individually however, there were important differences in behavioural orientation. One could not legitimately infer that a relationship at one level of analysis is the same as that at another. The point is not that, in this case, the inference would be empirically inaccurate but that it would be logically incorrect. In non-probabilistic terms, the conclusion may be true but the premises are irrelevant.

A proposition may be confirmed (not rejected) at different levels of analysis. The level of analysis problem does not preclude formulating similar propositions for different units. This is apparently not as obvious as it seems. Hanrieder, noting Singer's discussion, severely criticizes Riggs, Masters, Alger and Russett because they used concepts usually employed in the study of domestic politics to analyse international politics. He writes that "they practically ignore the injunction that concepts from different analytical environments can be used interchangeably only with grave methodological consequences. In that respect (they) are too radical in dismissing voices of caution that point out the dangers of interchanging concepts from one level of analysis with those of another."[17] And he states that "concepts from one level cannot be automatically applied to the other"[18] It is often fruitful to employ the same concepts at different levels of

[15]G. Udny Yule and Maurice G. Kendall, *An Introduction to the Theory of Statistics* (London, 1950), 312.
[16]Nazli Choucri, "The Nonalignment of Afro-Asian States: Policy, Perception and Behavior," this JOURNAL, 11, no. 1 (March, 1969), 1–17.
[17]Hanrieder, "Compatability and Consensus," 977.
[18]Hanrieder, "International and Comparative Politics," 491. He argues that the concepts must meet "the crucial test of isomorphism" (*op. cit.*). One is led to wonder how they

analysis. The level of analysis problem does not provide "an injunction that *concepts* from different analytical environments can be used interchangeably only with grave methodological consequences" (emphasis added). While we are often warned of the dangers of misleading analogies, analogy and metaphor are essential in science. Individual relationships can suggest hypotheses to be examined at an aggregate level. The point is that these require independent confirmation. The relationship in the aggregate need not be the same as that for individuals and may be precisely the opposite.

Michael D. Wallace's recent study of war and status inconsistency can be used to further clarify what is and what is not a level of analysis problem.[19] Research on the social and political behaviour of status-inconsistent individuals suggested a hypothesis about the international behaviour of status-inconsistent states: the greater the status inconsistency, the greater the involvement in interstate war. Because of the identification problem noted by Hubert M. Blalock[20] in analyses of status inconsistency, the hypothesis was tested at the total and central system levels of analysis.[21] Strong positive relationships were found. So far so good. However, these findings do not logically suggest that, in order to reduce war, one should "devise various strategies to reduce the salience of these dimensions of international hierarchy for national policy-makers in favor of matters of domestic concern" (p. 33). This suggestion assumes similar relationships between national status inconsistency and war proneness that have not been demonstrated. The existence of such a relationship at the international system level of analysis does not, *in and of itself*, provide evidence that the relationship exists at the national level.

The hypothesis "the greater the status inconsistency, the greater the war involvement" can be probed at both the national and international level. The concepts are the same at each level and so are their properties such as magnitude of status inconsistency, and frequency, duration, and intensity of war. But in order to measure these properties we necessarily impose a unit mesh upon them. In the case of aggregation we expand the unit mesh and in the case of disaggregation we tighten it. The particular unit mesh restricts our inferences. Individualistic or ecological fallacies are, from this point of view, similar to operationalism in reverse. "By operationalism in reverse is meant endowing the measures with all the meanings associated with the concept."[22]

---

should meet this test if they are not permitted to sit the examination. Ironically, Rosenau ("Calculated Control," 199) confronting the same problem and also noting Singer's discussion states "One reason for the lack of conceptual links is that most students in the international field have not treated their subject as local politics writ large."

19Michael D. Wallace, "Power, Status and International War," *Journal of Peace Research*, 8 (1971), 23–5.

20Hubert M. Blalock, "The Identification Problem and Theory Building: The Case of Status Inconsistency," *American Sociological Review*, 31, no. 1 (February 1966), 375–82.

21If the identification problem is thought of in terms of a possible spurious relationship ("Identification Problem," 27), it need only become a problem if covariation is found at the state level. Moving to the system level to avoid the identification problem may be avoiding a "problem" which is not a problem at all. In other words, analysis at the system level does not permit one to find a zero relationship at the state level. If the state level covariation is not zero, *then* the identification problem has to be confronted.

22Clyde Coombs, "Theory and Methods of Social Measurement," *Research Methods in the Behavioral Sciences*, ed. Leon Festinger and Daniel Katz (New York, 1953), 480.

It follows that analyses of the international system cannot be used to determine the degree to which state behaviour is "environmentally" or "systemically" controlled or the degree to which it results from particular attributes of states. Singer and Small, following the former's reasoning in his level of analysis paper, argue that they can make such inferences. Concluding their analysis of "structural" variables at the "systemic level of analysis" (alliance aggregation) and the onset of interstate war in the system, they advocate similar studies: "unless we understand the environment within which inter-nation conflict occurs, and can ascertain the approximate effect of that environment, there is no meaningful way of establishing the controls which are essential to any inquiry."[23] Analyses of structural effects, or more generally contextual studies of state behaviour, are needed but studies relating attributes of the international system hold little promise in this direction. In terms of the amount of variance "explained," Singer's earlier warning that "one would not add these two kinds of statements (nation level and system level) together" is relevant.[24] You cannot add the percentage of variance of interstate war in the system "explained" by attributes of the system to the percentage of variance of interstate war "explained" by national attributes. You would be adding forests and trees, quarries and rocks or gardens and flowers.

A re-analysis of the Singer and Small alliances and war data

Robinson and Yule and Kendall have demonstrated the possible inaccuracies that can result when inferences are made from aggregate to individual relationships. A re-analysis of the alliances and war data in "National Alliance Commitments and War Involvement, 1815–1945" provides a further example.[25]

In this study, Singer and Small found moderate positive correlations between a state's alliance activities and war involvement for the period 1815 to 1945. Their study was cross-sectional and interpretation of the results is difficult because of the length and variations in the length of the time period. For instance, while England was a member of the international system for the 131 years, Iceland had an extremely brief "life" of 2 years. Duration of membership in the system was itself positively correlated with war involvement. Controlling for duration by dividing the alliance and war values by the number of years in the system reduced the original correlation coefficient considerably.

In interpreting these results, Singer and Small recalled the findings of an earlier study of alliance aggregation and the amount, duration, and intensity of war in the international system. At the system level of analysis the correlations

[23]Singer and Small, "Alliance Aggregation," 286. More recently, Singer, referring to studies at the international system level of analysis, has stated "... until certain of the key ecological variables are identified and their own explanatory power ascertained, we will never know exactly how much control remained in the hands of the decision-makers and how much of the variance is accounted for by their environment." See J. David Singer, "From A Study of War to Peace Research: Some Criteria and Strategies," *Journal of Conflict Resolution*, 14, no. 4 (December 1970), 536.

[24]Singer, "The Level of Analysis Problem," 91.

[25]J. David Singer and Melvin Small, "National Alliance Commitments and War Involvement, 1815–1945," *International Politics and Foreign Policy*, ed. James N. Rosenau (New York, 1969), 513–42.

between alliance aggregation and the onset of war beginning within three years were high, but of opposite sign in the nineteenth and twentieth centuries. In the former century, the relationships were negative; in the latter, they were positive.[26]

They then argue that the "late-comers" (those nations not in the system in 1815 and which entered much later) "would have experienced an alliance and war involvement pattern typical of the *modal* nation during that period." The relationship for the modal nation is, by ecological inference, negative in the nineteenth century and positive in the twentieth. "Therefore, when we introduce hypothetical (i.e., not yet existent) nations into the earlier of our periods, via the involvement-per-year computation, it is statistically inevitable that the correlations will be pushed in the negative direction."[27] Granting for the moment the legitimacy and accuracy of ecological inferences, the argument is puzzling. How can one artificially introduce some nations into one of two time periods when, by definition, there is but one time period? If one could do this, why are the numerous "early-comers" not similarly introduced into the twentieth century cancelling out the effects of the late-comers?

The more reasonable procedure, avoiding an ecological inference, would be to divide the 131 years into two time periods – 1815 to 1899 and 1900 to 1945 – and compute the relevant correlation coefficients. In justifying their procedure, Singer and Small state "what holds for the system must also hold, in general, for the nations since they generate the behaviour from which our systemic properties are inferred."[28] Therefore, we would expect the coefficients to be negative in the nineteenth century and positive in the twentieth century. As can be seen from tables I and II, this is definitely not the case. Controlling for duration of membership, the relationships between war involvement and the various indices of alliance activities are positive in the nineteenth century, not negative. In the period 1900–45 the coefficients are generally smaller and, more importantly, some are negative.[29] The size and sign of the coefficients in tables I and II should illustrate the inaccuracy of inferences from aggregate to individual state relationships. As was noted above, however, the Singer and Small ecological inferences were complicated by the equation of cross-sectional and longitudinal analyses.

In comparing their results for alliance aggregation and the onset of war in the system to a cross-sectional study of states, Singer and Small are equating synchronic and diachronic analyses. How comparable are they? Posing the problem as it is usually done, in terms of appropriateness of inferring change from a static analysis, ignores a basic difference. "If we think of a longitudinal relationship as one holding between two time series, then the unit or units for which the longitudinal relationship is hypothesized cannot be the same as those for which the cross-sectional relationship is established."[30]

[26]Singer and Small, "Alliance Aggregation."
[27]"National Alliance Commitments," 542.
[28]*Ibid.*
[29]The Pearson product-moment correlation coefficients and the Spearman rank-order correlation coefficients are not strictly comparable. In controlling for the effect of duration, I have followed the Singer and Small procedure of dividing the national values on each variable by the number of years a state was in the system. This procedure may not be the most appropriate. See Fernando Cortés and Adam Przeworski, "Per Capita or Sin Capita: A Note of Caution," a paper prepared for the Annual Meeting of the American Political Science Association, 1971.
[30]Otis Dudley Duncan, Ray P. Cuzzort, and Beverley Duncan, *Statistical Geography* (Glen-

TABLE I

CORRELATION COEFFICIENTS (SPEARMAN RANK ORDER) FOR ALLIANCE ACTIVITY AND INTERSTATE WAR, CONTROLLING FOR DURATION IN THE SYSTEM: 54 STATES, 1815–99

	No. of wars	No. of wars with major power	Months in war	Months in war with major power	Battle deaths
Years in alliance	0.376	0.524	0.248	0.453	0.287
Years in alliance with major	0.397	0.619	0.206	0.541	0.278
No. of alliances	0.422	0.554	0.266	0.504	0.330
No. of alliances with major	0.448	0.570	0.283	0.577	0.369
No. of defence alliances	0.361	0.565	0.210	0.486	0.260
No. of neutrality alliances	0.279	0.207	0.193	0.290	0.276
No. of ententes	0.576	0.367	0.497	0.511	0.578
No. of defence alliances with major	0.384	0.585	0.229	0.571	0.306
No. of neutrality alliances with major	0.284	0.206	0.200	0.300	0.283
No. of ententes with major	0.577	0.370	0.494	0.510	0.578

TABLE II

CORRELATION COEFFICIENTS (SPEARMAN RANK ORDER) FOR ALLIANCE ACTIVITY AND INTERSTATE WAR, CONTROLLING FOR DURATION IN THE SYSTEM: 70 STATES, 1900–45

	No. of wars	No. of wars with major power	Months in war	Months in war with major power	Battle deaths
Years in alliance	0.192	0.228	0.099	0.153	0.254
Years in alliance with major	0.194	0.197	0.120	0.135	0.275
No. of alliances	0.008	−0.099	−0.042	−0.136	0.041
No. of alliances with major	0.216	0.302	0.133	0.158	0.302
No. of defence alliances	0.385	0.429	0.272	0.364	0.415
No. of neutrality alliances	0.066	0.079	0.029	0.005	0.010
No. of ententes	−0.104	−0.252	−0.064	−0.212	−0.042
No. of defence alliances with major	0.267	0.343	0.238	0.328	0.385
No. of neutrality alliances with major	0.253	0.274	0.107	0.179	0.236
No. of ententes with major	0.119	0.001	0.163	0.051	0.229

In terms of Figure 1, the common ecological fallacies are reasoning from cell II to cell I and reasoning from cell IV to cell III. Singer and Small however move from cell II to cell III, confounding the ecological fallacy with a cross-sectional–longitudinal fallacy. Therefore the accuracy of the simple ecological fallacy has not been examined. I shall so do below and in doing so be in a position to assess the comparability of longitudinal and cross-sectional analysis.

---

coe, 1961), 166. As Somers, for one, has pointed out, the implicit assumption when interpreting a cross-sectional relationship longitudinally is "developmental equivalence." See Robert Somers, "Applications of an Expanded Survey Research Model to Comparative Institutional Studies," *Comparative Methods in Sociology: Essays on Trends and Applications*, ed. Ivan Vallier (Berkeley, 1971), 383–387 and William B. Moul, "On Getting Nothing For Something: A Note On Causal Models of Political Development," unpublished paper, Department of Political Science, University of British Columbia, May 1973. As it will become obvious below, the relationship between alliance involvement and war is not the same for all states.

Time	Unit of Analysis	
	State	International System or other aggregation of states
Longitudinal	I	II
Cross-sectional	III	IV

FIGURE 1. Classification of types of studies of state and international systems.

It would be interesting to explore the entire data matrix which is composed of the alliances and war data of all states for each year in the period 1815–1945. Many different cross-sections of various lengths and time series for each state, substantively interesting subsystems, and the global system could be analysed. However, this task is beyond current resources and needs. Instead, I have examined the relationships between alliance involvement and the onset of war for four states in the period 1900 to 1945. The four states are Italy, Russia, Turkey and Japan.

If the results of studies from cells I, II, and III are to be compared, a common procedure should be employed. At the system level, Singer and Small tested the hypothesis, "the greater the number of alliance commitments in the system, the more war the system will experience."[31] Their use of the product-moment correlation coefficient in effect tested a much more stringent hypothesis, assessing the linearity of the relationship. The hypothesis implies monotonicity, and order statistics would be more appropriate.[32] In their cross-sectional analysis and in the re-analysis above, the Spearman rank order statistic was used. This statistic is essentially the product-moment statistic computed on ranks. The rank values are treated as interval scales. Also, interpretation of near zero values is difficult, particularly when there are a great number of ties on one variable. This is the case with the present time series. There are few unique values, especially in the war measures. While from a humanitarian point of view considerably fewer wars would be desirable, from the data analysis point of view more variation would be appreciated. The four states to be examined were chosen because they had the greatest number of wars in the twentieth century.

The nature of the data can be seen in the following graphs (Figures 2 to 9). Following Singer and Small, the war scores are for the onset of war during a three-year period. For example, in Figure 2, Russia was not at war in 1911, 1912, or 1913 and entered the First World War in 1914. The number of defence alliances in 1911, however, are to be related to the number of wars begun in 1912, 1913, and 1914. Hence the score of 1 in 1911. Similarly, the number of defence alliances in 1912 is matched with the number of wars begun in 1913, 1914, and 1915. The absolute values of the alliance and war involvement measures have been recoded so that the order is preserved. Russia's battle deaths from wars begun within three years are 0, 45,000, 50,000, 1,700,000, 7,500,000,

[31]Singer and Small, "Alliance Aggregation," 251.

[32]See Robert K. Leik and Walter R. Gove, "The Conception and Measurement of Asymmetric Monotonic Relationships in Sociology," *American Journal of Sociology*, 74, no. 6 (May 1969), 696–709.

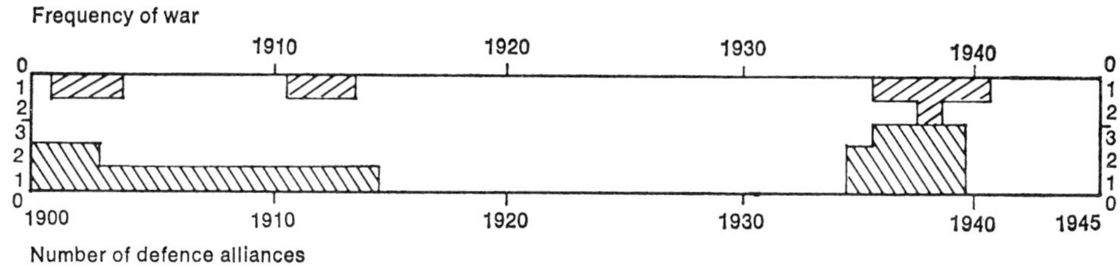

Coefficients:

Gamma	=	0.89
Somers' D	=	0.47
Kendall's tau	=	0.42

FIGURE 2. Russia 1900–1945: relationship between the number of defence alliances and the frequency of war beginning within three years.

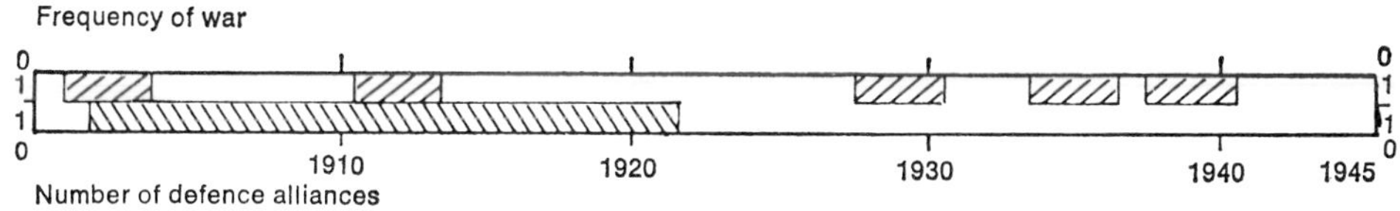

Coefficients:

Gamma	=	−0.30
Somers' D	=	−0.13
Kendall's tau	=	−0.14

FIGURE 3. Japan 1900–1945: relationship between the number of defence alliances and the frequency of war beginning within three years.

and 7,550,000, and they were coded as 0, 1, 2, 3, 4, and 5, respectively. This simplifies graphic presentation and is all that is demanded by the hypotheses. The total graph consists of opposing bar graphs of each variable for the 46 years under consideration. Examination of the graph should reveal the general monotonic association between two variables through time. As one bar graph approaches the mirror image of the other, a stronger positive association is indicated. And as one approaches the complement of the other, a stronger negative association is indicated.[33]

In the case of Russia (Figure 2) the relationship between the number of defence alliances and the frequency of war appears to be positive and strong. Although weaker, the relationship for Italy also appears to be positive. However, in the graphs for Japan (Figure 3) and Turkey (Figure 5), a negative relationship, weaker in the former and stronger in the latter, can be seen. It should be remembered that the number of defence alliances was, in the cross-sectional analysis above, the best predictor of the frequency, magnitude, and intensity of war in the twentieth century. In particular, the correlation coefficient (Spearman rank order) for the number of defence alliances and the number of wars was one of the largest (0.385) of all the coefficients calculated. These four graphs, however, indicate some negative relationships and visual inspection of the other graphs (Figures 6, 7, 8, and 9), using this crude directional test, also suggests

[33]In most cases the number of possible values on one variable is different from that on the other variable in the graph. Therefore, an exact mirror image is not possible.

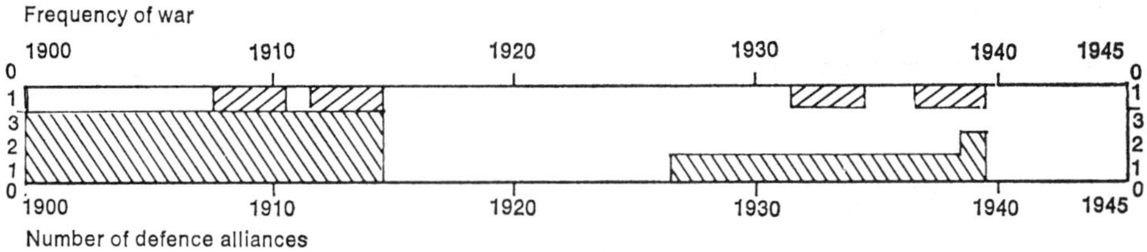

Coefficients:
Gamma = 0.90
Somers' D = 0.47
Kendall's tau = 0.58

FIGURE 4. Italy 1900–1945: relationship between the number of defence alliances and the frequency of war beginning within three years.

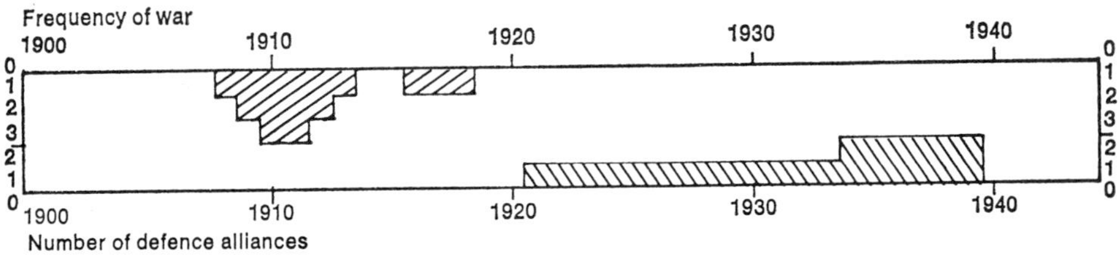

Coefficients:
Gamma = −1.00
Somers' D = −0.29
Kendall's tau = −0.24

FIGURE 5. Turkey 1900–1945: relationship between the number of defence alliances and the frequency of war beginning within three years.

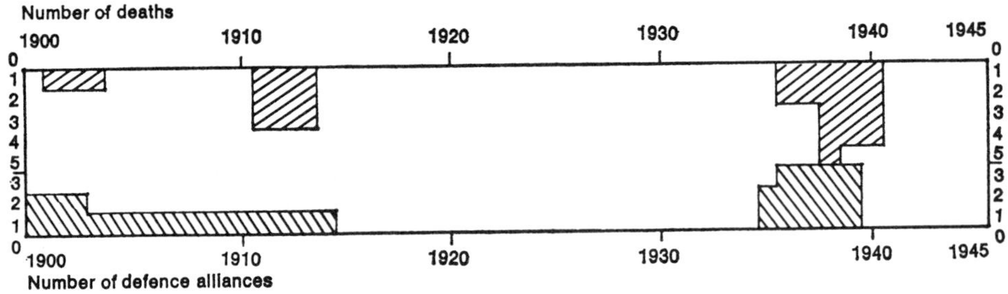

Coefficients:
Gamma = 0.70
Somers' D = 0.32
Kendall's tau = 0.43

FIGURE 6. Russia 1900–1945: relationship between the number of defence alliances and deaths from war beginning within three years.

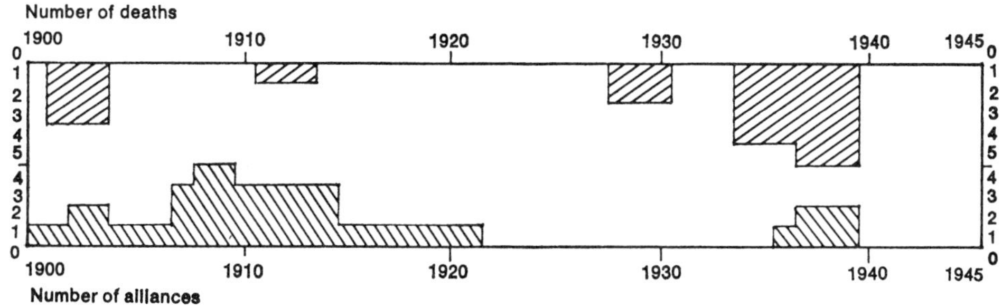

Coefficients:
Gamma = 0.10
Somers' D = 0.06
Kendall's tau = 0.05

FIGURE 7. Japan 1900–1945: relationship between the number of alliances and the deaths from war beginning within three years.

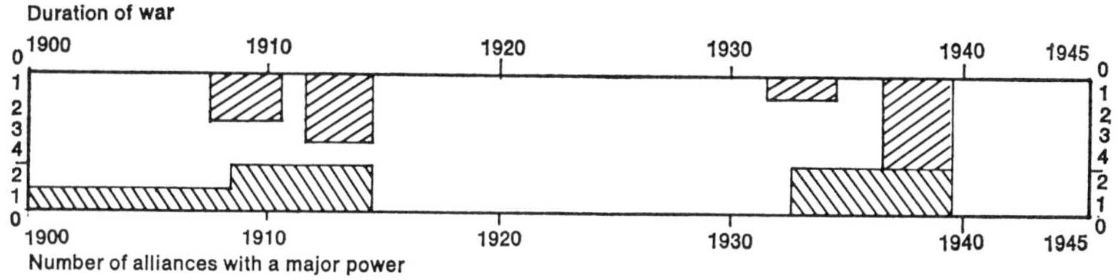

Coefficients:
Gamma = 0.86
Somers' D = 0.48
Kendall's tau = 0.44

FIGURE 8. Italy 1900–1945: relationship between the number of alliances with a major power and the duration of war beginning within three years.

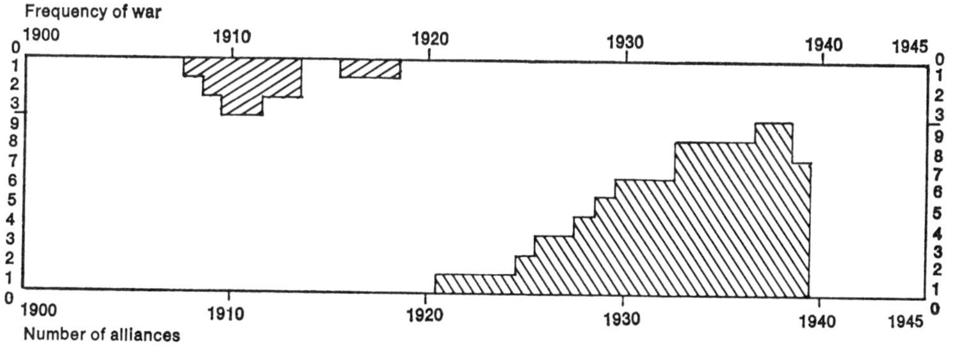

Coefficients:
Gamma = −1.00
Somers' D = −0.26
Kendall's tau = −0.21

FIGURE 9. Turkey 1900–1945: relationship between the number of alliances and the frequency of wars beginning within three years.

that inferences from synchronic to diachronic studies are often inaccurate. The graphs for Turkey (Figures 5 and 9) dramatically illustrate the distortion produced when inferring change from a cross-sectional analysis. Turkey was involved in five wars, all of them before 1920, and had no alliance activity until 1921. This information was lost in analysis of a cross-section 46 years wide. The graphs also illustrate the prior point that inferences from aggregate relationships to individual state relationships are frequently inaccurate.

There are 96 possible relationships between the alliance and war variables for four states. Further visual inspection would be tedious and a summary statistic to describe the degree of association is desirable. Also the directional test is a rather blunt instrument and a statistical measure would permit more precise determination of the degree of cross-national variation in the relationships.

With a limited number of values and consequently a large number of ties in all the variables, computing a measure of association for these time series is equivalent to computing a measure for an ordered contingency table. Kendall's tau, Goodman and Kruskal's gamma and Somers' D are most frequently used in analyses of ordered tables. Each has its advantages and disadvantages and more importantly, while they are related measures of association, each measures a different type of association.

Tau, like the correlation coefficients employed by Singer and Small, is a symmetric measure of mutual association. In the case of no ties and symmetric tables (equal number of possible values for each variable) it has a simple interpretation – the ratio of concordant pairs to total pairs. However, as it was modified to take into account the peculiarities of the present data the simplicity of interpretation was lost.

When there are numerous tied scores gamma is often recommended in place of tau. Gamma discounts ties and is a much more permissive statistic having higher values than tau and reaching its minimum and maximum values more frequently. This can be seen in the tables and is most apparent in the case of Turkey where all the gamma coefficients are −1.000. Gamma is measuring "corner correlation" rather than "diagonal correlation" in this case. Gamma is a measure of one-way association: All A are B, but not all B are A. Given that war is a relatively rare event for a state, the number of alliances may not predict to war while war may predict accurately to alliances. An analogous situation, and common example, exists with rare diseases. Having the disease is probably a good predictor of whether or not the individual was innoculated against it. But because of the rarity of the disease, innoculation may not be a good predictor of the disease. Gamma does not discriminate between these "directions" of prediction and picks the best one-way association. This is not an appealing property when the substantive concern is to predict war from alliances. A measure that distinguishes between independent and dependent variables is necessary.

Somers' D is an assymetric measure of association. That is, the value of this coefficient depends upon which variable is considered to be independent. It is analogous to a regression coefficient rather than to the correlation coefficients used by Singer and Small. Also like regression analysis, it assumes that the independent variable is measured precisely and the error is in the dependent variable.

Therefore, ties on the independent variable – alliances – are penalized and ties on the dependent variable are of no concern. If the number of alliances is considered as a crude measure of the degree of international commitment, this would appear to be appropriate. Although their hypotheses concern the number of alliances, Singer and Small are, in their system level study,[34] measuring the degree of commitment in the system. They use the mean of the number of alliances in year T, T−1, and T−2 as the alliance value for year T.

All three statistics were calculated. Although they are not comparable with each other or with the statistics in the Singer and Small studies, they do indicate the variation in the strength and direction of the monotonic relationships between alliances and war. Large variations in the size of the coefficients and negative values would not augur well for the accuracy of ecological inferences nor for the comparability of longitudinal and cross-sectional analyses. The Somers' D coefficients are reported in full in Table III. They do indicate considerable cross-national variation in the size and sign of the relationships. For example, the coefficients for the number of alliances and the war variables fluctuate between 0.349 and −0.256. Singer and Small on the other hand reported product moment coefficients of approximately 0.500 between the percentage of nations in alliances and the duration of war and the deaths from war in both the central and total systems. In the cross-sectional analysis for 1900 to 1945 presented above, the coefficients (Spearman rank order) hovered around 0.000 – one positive and the other negative. The Somers' D coefficients reported in Table III strengthen the impression derived from visual inspection of the bar graphs. In short, the ecological and longitudinal to cross-sectional inferences made by Singer and Small are inaccurate.

Aggregation problems and the Stanford studies

Ecological fallacies and level of analysis problems are, by no means, limited to the studies by Singer and his associates. The Stanford studies have recently been criticized in this respect by Gordon Hilton.[35] However, much of his criticism is misdirected and indicates a certain misunderstanding of the issues involved. Ole R. Holsti, Robert C. North, and Richard A. Brody correctly state that "each level of aggregation or organization – for example, nation states, populations, or decision-making groups – can be considered potentially useful but for different research tasks."[36] Hilton comments: "The common sense of this approach is compelling, but nevertheless the researcher is failing in his duty if he does not consider and document the possible effects of aggregation. In statistical studies particularly a statement of the statistical effects of aggregation is expected."[37] Dina Zinnes' study of the expression and perception of hostility in the 1914

[34] Singer and Small, "Alliance Aggregation."
[35] Gordon Hilton, "The 1914 Studies – a Re-assessment of the Evidence and Some Further Thoughts," *Peace Research Society (International) Papers*, 13, (1970), 117–41.
[36] Ole R. Holsti, Robert C. North, and Richard A. Brody, "Perception and Action in the 1914 Crisis," *Quantitative International Politics*, ed. J. David Singer (New York, 1968), 126.
[37] "The 1914 Studies," 121. Hilton does have a point with respect to temporal aggregations.

TABLE III

COEFFICIENTS OF ASSOCIATION (SOMERS' D) BETWEEN ALLIANCES AND WARS: RUSSIA, JAPAN, ITALY, AND TURKEY 1900–45

		No. of wars	No. of wars with major	Duration	Duration with major	Deaths from war	Deaths from war with major
No. of alliances	Russia	0.217	0.109	0.204	0.120	0.219	0.120
	Japan	0.089	0.255	0.119	0.278	0.059	0.229
	Italy	0.339	0.191	0.349	0.202	0.327	0.181
	Turkey	−0.256	−0.171	−0.256	−0.171	−0.256	−0.171
No. of alliances with major	Russia	0.224	0.211	0.233	0.199	0.218	0.199
	Japan	0.089	0.255	0.119	0.278	0.059	0.229
	Italy	0.475	0.281	0.483	0.276	0.492	0.285
	Turkey	−0.256	−0.171	−0.256	−0.170	−0.256	−0.171
No. of defence alliances	Russia	0.467	0.323	0.435	0.323	0.454	0.323
	Japan	−0.135	0.096	−0.123	0.108	−0.204	0.061
	Italy	0.297	0.157	0.301	0.145	0.326	0.170
	Turkey	−0.289	−0.193	−0.289	−0.193	−0.289	−0.193
No. of defence alliances with major	Russia	0.463	0.361	0.448	0.350	0.448	0.350
	Japan	−0.135	0.096	−0.123	0.108	−0.204	0.061
	Italy	0.244	0.153	0.250	0.135	0.287	0.171
	Turkey	No defence alliances with major power					

crisis is in contrast praised because it "was the first of all the Stanford studies to consider the problems involved with aggregation."[38]

It is not necessary to consider the effect of aggregation so long as the interest is in the particular aggregates presented, and ecological fallacies are avoided. Holsti, North, and Brody do not make invalid ecological inferences. Zinnes, on the other hand, does. Although her interest was in hostile state behaviour, at one point the perceptions and expressions of hostility for six states were aggregated and displayed in a series of graphs. "It is, of course, possible to question the assumptions inherent in pooling the data over six states. Explicitly, this procedure assumes that the states exhibit similar behavior, or that they would exhibit similar behavior if we could observe them for an unlimited period of time. Whether or not this assumption is valid must depend in part on the results – if we obtain good results, we would consider the assumption warranted, if not, we might wish to revise it."[39] This does not indicate an awareness of the level of analysis problem. To refer to Figure 1 again, throughout the analysis Zinnes moves from cell II to I to III and back again.

Temporal aggregation and types of time

So far, we have only examined the spatial dimensions of the level of analysis or aggregation problem. Although there is little mention of it in the literature, the arguments that have been made also apply to the temporal "unit mesh" we construct. Time is perhaps the ultimate modifiable unit, and how it is modified in analysis affects the results of analysis. We should not be surprised at different relationships between two time series variables if the time slices or aggregations differed.[40]

For example, one would expect the hostile behaviour of Israel toward Egypt to be reciprocated. In statistical terms, a strong positive correlation is to be expected. However, on a daily basis a pattern may be difficult to discern, whereas on a weekly basis of aggregation it may be more visible. Standing back and looking over months or quarters, the pattern would probably be far more striking. In the table below, the correlations between the frequency of violent behaviour of Egypt toward Israel and Israel toward Egypt are displayed. The violent behaviour was dichotomized into "high" and "low" violence and correlation coefficients (Kendall tau) were computed on biweekly, monthly, bimonthly, and quarterly time spans.[41] The patterns in these data, as indicated by the coefficients, do tend to become sharper as the time slice increases.

Some phenomena appear to be patterned over days and some over years, decades, centuries, or millennia. Paul Smoker poses a "time level of analysis problem" which he argues is similar to the "normal" level of analysis problem in international relations. What are, he asks, the interactions between processes that operate at different time scales? "Specifications of these interactions is the time

38*Ibid.*, 138. Dina Zinnes, "The Expression and Perception of Hostility in Prewar Crisis: 1914," *Quantitative International Politics*, ed. J. David Singer (New York, 1968), 138.
39*Ibid.*, 102.
40Yule and Kendall, *An Introduction to the Theory of Statistics.*
41Edward Azar, "Analysis of International Events," *Peace Research Reviews*, IV, no. 1, (November 1970), 90–1, 57–8.

TABLE IV

CORRELATIONS BETWEEN ACTIONS OF ISRAEL AND EGYPT TOWARD EACH OTHER, 1956–7 (Kendall Tau)

	"Low Violence"	"High Violence"
Biweekly	0.446	0.494
Monthly	0.470	0.582
Bimonthly	0.484	0.769
Quarterly	0.982	0.790

Source: calculated from date found in Edward Azar, "Analysis of International Events," *Peace Research Reviews*, IV, no. 1 (November, 1970), 90–1. Definitions of low violence and high violence are on p. 58 of the article.

TABLE V

TEMPORAL AGGREGATIONS IN THE STANDARD STUDIES OF THE 1914 CRISIS

Interval number	Time	Interval width
1	27 June–2 July	6 days
2	3 July–16 July	14 days
3	17 July–20 July	4 days
4	21 July–25 July	5 days
5	26 July	1 day
6	27 July	1 day
7	28 July	1 day
8	29 July	1 day
9	30 July	1 day
10	31 July	1 day
11	1–2 August	2 days
12	3–4 August	2 days

level of analysis problem."[42] This will be discussed further below but it should be noted that it is not the same as the level of analysis problem examined in this paper.

The temporal aggregations in a longitudinal analysis should be uniform. In most of the Stanford studies the data were grouped into twelve intervals as shown in Table V. It is readily apparent that the time slices are not equal. The unit mesh varies from 1 to 14 days. What are the effects of this aggregation procedure? Do the results of the 1914 studies radically depend upon the uneven time intervals?[43] Within the studies there is little discussion of these questions. The justification for the procedure is that "the time periods ... were determined by the amount of the data rather than by the calendar time in order to ensure an adequate number

[42]Paul Smoker, "Anarchism, Peace and Control: Some Ideas for Future Experiment," *Peace Research Reviews*, 4, no. 4 (February 1972), 57. This paper was read to the Faculty Graduate Student Seminar, April 1971.

[43]Ole Holsti's reanalysis of the 1914 data, using daily aggregations, indicates that the results of the Stanford studies do not depend upon the width of the time slices. See Ole R. Holsti, *Crisis, Escalation and War* (Montreal, 1972).

of perceptions for each period."[44] Other methods of grouping the data should be examined.

However, the use of uneven temporal intervals suggests an important question concerning the meaning of "time." As John G. Gunnell, among others, has emphasized, the time is not an entity but "a form of ordering experience." "It is a created order."[45] Granting this, the possibilities of many "times" should be apparent. In the previous discussions we have been dealing with solar time. There are other formal times and also social and psychological times.

We order, or at least we like to think we do, our experience by the movement of a clock. More often than not, we "track time" or order our lives and experiences by events or other experiences.[46] Numerous examples can be found in the ethnographic and sociological literature. For example, the groom at the racetrack measures time "not by the calendar but by the racing season. The past is punctuated by the emergence of a great horse, and the benchmarks of the passing time are referred to as 'the year of Whirlaway, the year of Citation.' and so forth."[47] We have all experienced a dull lecture or seminar and one that "flashed by." The clock time of a dream or hallucination may be relatively brief but the dreamer may encompass "days" of experience. Therefore, the temporal units of clock, social, and psychological time need not coincide. We sometimes speak of "filling time" by doing a number of sometimes trivial things. "Filled time" passes more swiftly than "empty time." The more stimulation or activity, the quicker time passes. (This paper could be evaluated in this way.) In their brief discussion of "diplomatic time," Singer and Small follow the same reason: "there appears to be a marked difference in the amount and rate of diplomatic and military activity between the nineteenth and twentieth centuries, so that while 1899 does not represent an exact chronological midpoint, it is probable that the 85 years prior to 1900 represent an approximate equivalent of the 45 post-century years in term of diplomatic time."[48]

Psychological time may be measured, or fixed, in terms of the amount of activity, stimuli, or information.[49] Perhaps Holsti, North, and Brody have, by reckoning time in terms of documents, unwittingly employed psychological time in international relations. This possibility should be investigated further. The concept of psychological time is intuitively more satisfying for crisis studies employing perceptual data than is solar time.

[44] Ole R. Holsti and Robert C. North, "The History of Human Conflict," *The Nature of Human Conflict*, ed. Elton B. McNeil (Englewood Cliffs, 1965), 161.

[45] John G. Gunnell, *Political Philosophy And Time* (Middletown, Conn., 1968), 17–20.

[46] S. Lyman and M.B. Scott, *A Sociology of the Absurd* (New York, 1971), 189–212.

[47] M. B. Scott, *The Racing Game* (Chicago, 1968), 78. Cited in *ibid.*, 212. For further reading on social time see Pitirim Sorokin and Robert K. Merton, "Social Time: A Methodological and Functional Analysis," *American Journal of Sociology*, 42, no. 5 (March 1937), 615–29; Wilbert E. Moore, *Man, Time and Society* (New York, 1963); Georges Gurvitch, *The Spectrum of Social Time* (Dordrecht, Netherlands, 1964); Georges Gurvitch, "Social Structure and the Multiplicity of Times," *Sociological Theory, Values and Sociocultural Change*, ed. Edward A. Teryakian (New York, 1963), 171–84; and *The Voices of Time*, ed. J. T. Fraser (New York, 1966).

[48] Singer and Small, "Alliance Aggregation," 256. Also see Tanter, "International Systems and Foreign Policy Approaches," 22–4.

[49] Smoker has suggested this measure of psychological time. The literature on time in psychology is immense. See Leonard W. Doob, *Patterning of Time* (New Haven, 1971) for a convenient and extensive bibliography.

Distinguishing between level and unit of analysis

Throughout this paper the terms "level" and "unit" or analysis have been used interchangeably. As noted, this is the conventional usage in the international relations literature. However, given the confusion in this literature, the normal usage does not appear to have permitted, and probably has hindered, conceptual clarity. I will briefly outline another usage which I think would be more fruitful.

The results from the re-analysis of the Singer and Small alliances and war data indicate a considerably more complex situation for states than for the system. After looking at the results, one might be tempted to discontinue further analysis. One might argue that these results for Russia, Japan, Italy, and Turkey illustrate the limited nature of generalizations in international relations. The more reasonable argument develops from asking what it is about these states that accounts for the differences in relationships between alliance activity and war involvement.

> The basic assumption is that the names of nations or of social system in general, are treated as residua of variables that influence the phenomenon being explained but have not yet been considered. Thus such concepts as "culture," "nation," "society," and "political system," are treated as residua of variables, which can be incorporated into a general theory. If the statements reporting particular observations without specifying the spatio-temporal parameters are elliptical, then statements of a historical nature are also elliptical if they do not list the variables that are implicit under the specification of the historical conditions. The often emphasized historical ellipticalness of theoretical statements has its direct counterpart in the theoretical ellipticalness of historical statements.[50]

Do differences in national attributes explain the variations in the effects of alliance involvement on war activity? If so, what are they – geographic area, population size, rate of population increase, resource base, economic development, rate of economic growth, type of government, domestic instability, military capabilities rate of change in military capabilities, etc.? The obvious relational character of alliances should not be forgotten. Or are environmental or contextual factors crucial? What is it about the regional system and/or context in which each state is embedded? To answer this question we "switch levels of analysis." Could it be the distribution of capabilities, the rate of change in capabilities, the number of actors, etc.? The unit of analysis is the state and we are attempting to specify the conditions when alliances will have an effect and the type of effect. The conditions may be found at the state level or system level or combination of both.

What accounts for the difference in the direction of the relationship between alliance aggregation and the onset of war in the nineteenth and twentieth centuries? In this case we cannot "shift up" to a higher level of analysis. There may be an interaction between these variables and longer term social processes. This is an extremely simple example of the time level of analysis problem mentioned earlier.[51]

[50] Adam Przeworski and Henry Teune, *Logic of Comparative Social Inquiry* (New York, 1970), 29.

[51] For a more complex and interesting time level of analysis problem see Paul Smoker and Hugh Miall, "The Arms Race 1952–1958: A Seven Nation Study" paper prepared for Peace Research Conference (Western Division) Vancouver, B.C., February 1972.

Conclusion

Aggregates of states are studied because of an interest in aggregates and this is a legitimate concern of international relations. In voting studies, ecological data were (and still are) used as inexpensive substitutes for individual data which require large expenditures in surveys to obtain, if they are still obtainable. In international relations most of the data are data on states or smaller units. After the initial flurry created by Robinson's paper, methods to assess the accuracy of inferences from aggregates to individuals were proposed.[52] In international relations, because of the readily available state-level data, these methods are irrelevant. We create our aggregates rather than have them ready-made. Although I have examined the accuracy of some ecological inferences, it is for this reason I have stressed the logical problem. Indeed, the relative simplicity of assessing the accuracy of the Singer and Small ecological inferences illustrates the general point.

[52]Otis Dudley Duncan and Beverley Davis, "An Alternative to Ecological Correlations," *American Sociological Review*, 18 (1953), 665–66; Leo A. Goodman, "Some Alternatives to Ecological Correlation," *American Journal of Sociology*, 64 (1959), 610–25; W. Phillips Shively, "Ecological Inference: The Use of Aggregate Data to Study Individuals," *American Political Science Review*, 63, no. 4 (December 1969), 1183–96.

Notes

The Prime Minister as Symbol: Unifier or Optimizer?

FRANK STARK *University of Western Ontario*

One of the most interesting points raised in Thomas A. Hockin's introductory essay to *Apex of Power* was the apparent contradiction he noted between S.J.R. Noel's use of Arend Lijphart's consociational model to describe the "Canadian political network" and the cabinet, and George Szablowski's interpretation of the same political ralationship through the application of F.G. Bailey's models of transactional and bureaucratic leadership. "The traditional transactional interpretation of prime ministerial-cabinet relations emphasizes each Minister's personal (mostly regional) 'representative' role in getting into the Cabinet and explaining his leverage within it ... It may be in keeping with S.J.R. Noel's identification of the necessary attributes of the consociational political network in this volume. Yet George Szablowski in this volume questions whether this transactional dynamic is not threatened in Cabinet by a policy-making system which, with the aid of programme budgeting and clear leadership from the Prime Minister in the Cabinet Committee on Priorities and Planning, emphasizes rationality and the supra-regional functions of policy."[1]

It is a point worth examining in some detail because of the possible usefulness of the consociational model for describing Canadian attempts at unity and the functional difference that centralized planning programs may make to the cabinet system. Both these approaches help to illuminate the work of the cabinet, which needs all the explanatory light we can shed on it. It may not be necessary to put them in opposition to each other.

Professor Noel points out that Lijphart's theory emphasizes that the *élite* links between politicians (rather than *mass* interaction) are a means to bind Canada together. With particular reference to the cabinet, Noel writes, "time after time provincial politicians with no more attachment to the federal system than the mass of their constituents become transformed in Ottawa into Cabinet Ministers intent on making the federal system work." Noel uses the examples of Joseph Howe, the Nova Scotia secessionist who became a cabinet minister at Confederation, and Donald Jamieson of Newfoundland, who underwent the same transformation 82 years later, as "the extreme examples of how the process of elite accommodation in Canada has provided a workable substitute for mass national integration."[2]

The relevant passage in Szablowski's contribution deals specifically with the same subject: "The traditional relationship between the Canadian Prime Minister and his cabinet colleagues has been transactional. It permits the Ministers to retain regional loyalties and to represent regional interests within the cabinet. It does not demand from them a moral commitment to the leader. It leaves them free to bargain and to consolidate their own influence while attending to the business of governing as political heads of their departments. It would appear, however, that this traditional transactional relationship is undergoing a transformation through the means of the cabinet committee system. The Prime Minister divides his leadership role into specialized functions which he then distributes as committee chairmanships to some of his transactional colleagues. For himself he retains the over-all competency ... In this way the transactional ties are modified and new relationships emerge characterized by specialization and inspired by the optimal ethic."[3]

In this passage Szablowski applies directly Bailey's model of the transformation of a transactional model of leadership in which the political "followers" compete for favours from the leader to the bureaucratic model where the specialization of functions binds

---

[1] "The Prime Minister and Political Leadership: An Introduction to Some Restraints and Imperatives", in *Apex of Power*, ed. Thomas A. Hockin (Scarborough, 1971), 13.

[2] "The Prime Minister's Role in a Consociational Democracy," in *ibid.*, 107.

[3] "The Optimal Policy-Making System: Implications for the Canadian Political Process," *ibid.*, 143.

them more closely and effectively by using a normative value as a unifying symbol.

It is precisely on this point of unifying symbols that consociationalism and the bureaucratic model may be put into perspective in the context of the Canadian cabinet. Lijphart, in talking about the necessary willingness of élites to recognize the possibility of fragmentations and jointly seek solutions, is suggesting an élite value system that cuts across subgroup boundaries. This necessitates common symbols of national unity, and discussion, argument, and vigorous interaction about those symbols. It is clear, moreover, that federalism has been the most important of these symbols throughout Canadian history. This importance can be traced over time and the differences in viewpoint about that symbol among cabinet ministers from different regions of the country, east and west, Anglophone and Francophone, are revealing for an understanding of the cognitive basis for federal disputes. However, the general point that federalism does serve as a symbol of national unity or integration is implicit in Noel's concluding paragraph quoted above. The prime minister has himself served as a symbol – a normative one – of national unity and federalism in Canada. Perhaps his success in doing so has been an important aspect of his mass as well as of his élite support, but he does – and here I differ slightly from Szablowski – seek to command allegiance at a moral level on the principle of federalism, or national unity.

For example, Szablowski states that cabinet ministers are not morally committed to the leader. However, cabinet ministers are selected in the name of federalism as representatives of subgroups. They are in my opinion aware of this, and their commitment is both to their leader and to the principle which was the basis of their selection. F. G. Bailey describes moral relationships with a core of supporters as phenomena different from transactional relationships.[4] And so, strictly speaking, it is incorrect to associate Noel's perception of the cabinet's social network with the transactional model.

To both élites and mass, federalism will remain a symbol of national unity as long as the constitution protects provincial rights and national unity remains an issue. In Cameroon, where these rights deteriorated to the point where élites found it more politically profitable to ignore federalism, federalism ceased to be a unifying symbol in élite political culture.[5] But in Canada the problem of unity and federalism as a symbolic solution to that problem – despite the implied centralization of "creative" or "co-operative" federalism – will be with us for a while yet, for there are still political leaders calling out for "real" federalism in the name of unity and with continuing local support.

Therefore, although optimization may be a normative symbol as Szablowski says,[6] it has a rival or a partner in federalism. The cybernetic age may not banish that federal symbol – indeed, advanced communication technology may make the decentralization of government both easier to achieve and more efficient to operate. Sheldon Wolin's statement that "in a post-industrial society the optimal rhetoric replaces the symbols, signs and cults of the past" may itself now be old fashioned. We can hypothesize that men will also be increasingly protective of their cultural identities as they are faced with technology that seems to have a homogenizing effect on culture. Quebec may be an example of this protectiveness: passionately concerned with progress as a goal to eliminate the technological differences between it and the rest of Canada, it is suffering the pangs of the passing of an old life in the search for some kind of new identity. Northern Nigeria underwent a similar experience in the early '60s with important effects for Nigerian unity.[7]

The question of decisional technology is an important one. At the end of his paper Szablowski called for a debate on its effects. But it would not do justice to the explanatory power of the theory of élite accommodation or to federalism as a symbol of national unity to suggest that planning techniques alone will dictate social and political interaction in the cabinet or eliminate the federal symbolic functions of the prime minister's office.

---

[4] *Strategems and Spoils* (New York, 1969), 82–3.

[5] F. Stark, "Federalism as a Symbol of Political Integration in the Elite Political Culture of Cameroon," PH D dissertation, Northwestern University, 1972.

[6] "The Optimal Policy-Making System."

[7] See James O'Connell, "Political Integration, The Nigerian Case," in *African Integration and Disintegration*, ed. D. Hazlewood (London, 1967).

The Prime Minister as Symbol: A Rejoinder

GEORGE J. SZABLOWSKI *York University*

From my perspective, two interesting questions arise from Stark's comment: first, a question concerning the usefulness or explanatory power of Lijphart's élite accommodation theory; and second, a question about the changing nature of *intra*-élite relations (specifically those occurring within the federal cabinet system) as distinct from *inter*-élite relations, primarily at the governmental level in Canada. Bailey's model becomes relevant in the discussion of the second question.

The relevance of a theoretical model hinges on the promise of a discovery that concrete reality may be shown to resemble the "pure" categories and relationships constructed by the analyst. Lijphart felt that for consociational democracy such a promise was limited to the Low Countries, Switzerland, Austria, and Lebanon where " a number of conditions favourable to the establishment and persistence of this type of democracy" exist.[1] Although he was "impressed with an argument that Canada can indeed be considered a consociational system," he admitted that he knew "too little about Canada ... to place it with great confidence in one of the categories of [his] typology."[2]

This of course does not mean that aspects of consociational behaviour cannot be found in other polities. But Lijphart's aim was much broader than that; he sought to correct (in the grand tradition of Comparative Politics) the well-known and much too influential Almondian classification of Western democratic systems dating back to 1956. He attempted also to relate political stability in countries with deeply fragmented political culture and a "low degree of subsystem autonomy" to one overriding variable, namely élite behaviour.

Noel's highly skilful adaptation of the consociational theory to Canada has been widely recognized by Canadian political scientists. It has unquestionably enriched theoretical debate about national unity, stability, and the direction of political change. But, it is time now for a second look at Lijphart's hesitation to consider Canada as a consociational democracy and to question the relevance and the explanatory power of his model.

"Factors conducive to consociational democracy" make up an essential component of Lijphart's theoretical framework. The following questions can be asked about at least four of these important factors. (1) If "external threats" are not perceived uniformly or with largely the same degree of intensity in various regions of the country, how salient is this factor in inducing cooperation among élites? (2) If one subculture within the country is concentrated territorially and its members share distinct socio-political institutions and traditions ultimately expressed in active governmental power, is it possible to speak of "a multiple balance of power among the subcultures"? (3) If the "total load on the decision-making apparatus" of the country is rapidly increasing and governments at all levels tend toward comprehensive policy-making, can the newly emerging institutional forms of conflict resolution be viewed as variants of consociational behaviour? And if not, what are they and how do they fit into the model? (4) If the "perils of political fragmentation" are understood and assessed differently by different regional élites and used by them to force a reallocation of economic and political resources, what precisely is the meaning of the "elite ability to maintain cohesion" and "to transcend cleavages"?

Stark's allusion to "an élite value system that cuts across subgroup boundaries" and to a "vigorous interaction about ... common symbols of national unity" begs for answers to these and similar questions.

In spite of the new institutional and behavioural arrangements at the élite level made within the existing federal framework, the frequency and intensity of conflict in Canada appears to be growing. Clearly, élite behaviour alone cannot account for the rapid political change taking place in an increasingly mobilized society.

F.G. Bailey's theoretical scheme is much less ambitious. Bailey is primarily concerned with *intra*-team (or intra-élite) relationships. He distinguishes not "different phenomena" – as Stark suggests – but different types or categories of such relationships. He readily acknowledges that in a real world (as against a conceptual world) "groups ... are not either

---

[1]"Consociational Democracy", *World Politics*, vol. XXI, January 1969, p. 216.

[2]From private correspondence dated 29 August 1969; see also Arend Lijphart, "Cultural Diversity and Theories of Integration," this JOURNAL, IV (March, 1971), 1–14.

moral or transactional or bureaucratic: leaders may make use of all three principles."[3] The usefulness of Bailey's model, from my point of view, lies in its capacity to depict the impact of technology on political relationships – which become over time institutionalized in an extended bureaucracy. The model is particularly suited to the studies of relatively small political teams, such as the Canadian cabinet. Reliable data about ministerial behaviour are practically unobtainable, but information about structural and procedural modifications in the cabinet system is much more readily available. Bailey's framework permits us to draw from them valuable inferences indicating the direction of change in intra-team relations.[4]

Although the prime minister may be said to "command [from his cabinet colleagues] allegiance at a moral level on the principle of federalism or national unity" – as Stark suggests – this observation must be put in the context of the newly formed pattern of intra-cabinet relationships induced by structural change. In Bailey's terms (which I have adopted), these relationships have become less transactional and more bureaucratic. Nearly all major reforms in the cabinet system brought about in recent years point clearly in that direction. Here are some examples. (1) Functional specialization has been moved upward from budgeting at the level of Treasury Board officials to policy-making at the level of cabinet committees. (2) Cabinet leadership has been divided and made more specialized by the appointment of regular committee chairmen who exercise, within their terms of reference, powers similar to the prime minister. In Britain under Wilson's prime ministership, a minister could "only appeal from the Cabinet committee to Cabinet with the consent of the Chairman of the committee."[5] In Canada, it is not clear whether the formal appeal procedure presupposes adherence to the same practice.[6] (3) The agendas, documents, and procedure at all meetings of cabinet and cabinet committees have been strictly formalized. (4) Additional and more extensive hierarchy has been introduced into the cabinet committee structure. For example, Priorities and Planning is a superior committee in that its membership is restricted; it is chaired by the prime minister; it is designed to deal with issues of higher magnitude (meta-policy questions); its decisions become "guidelines" to be followed by other cabinet committees.[7]

Having recited these innovations, I must issue a warning against too quick and easy assessment of their impact on ministerial behaviour. While they do indicate the direction of change in ministerial relationships, they tell us little about the extent to which these relationships are actually being transformed. Nevertheless, I believe it is appropriate to view the cabinet reforms instituted in Canada as structural and procedural adaptations to technological change. In the future, the cabinet committee system may become an extended bureaucracy – Gordon Robertson already refers to the "blending of the roles" among ministers and officials.

As to the prime minister as symbol, I hope Professor Stark will agree that the prime minister can, and will attempt to, be both a unifier and an optimizer – but with growing difficulty and diminishing effectiveness.

---

[3]*Strategems and Spoils* (Oxford, 1970), 83.

[4]See my "Decisional Technology and Political Process in Canada," forthcoming PH D dissertation, McGill University.

[5]Richard H.S. Crossman, *The Myths of Cabinet Government* (Cambridge, Mass. 1972), 44.

[6]Gordon Robertson, "The Changing Role of the Privy Council Office," *Canadian Public Administration* (Winter, 1971), 491–2.

[7]A.W. Johnson, "The Treasury Board of Canada and the Machinery of Government of the 1970s," this JOURNAL, IV (Sept. 1971), 353.

Note bibliographique
Review Article

Le Labrador à l'heure de la contestation*

HENRI BRUN *Université Laval*

La question du Labrador est une question vieille comme la conquête du Canada par l'Angleterre. Au-delà d'une certaine date, en l'occurence 1825, elle s'est toutefois résumée en la recherche d'une définition précise du Labrador, à l'aide des textes susceptibles d'une interprétation sur ce point. Cette phase, qui a eu ainsi pour objet la délimitation de la frontière Québec-Terreneuve, s'est déroulée surtout en deux temps : 1927 et 1949. En 1927, le Comité judiciaire du Conseil privé a été amené à se prononcer sur la situation de cette ligne frontalière; en 1949, Terreneuve est entrée dans la fédération canadienne en des termes susceptibles, en eux-mêmes, de confirmer le point de vue du Conseil privé. L'étude de la portée de ces textes, de même que d'actes unilatéraux de reconnaissance frontalière dont le Québec aurait pu être l'auteur, constitue l'ouvrage de Luce Patenaude. Etant donné l'enjeu, un territoire immense et riche, cette étude méritait d'être faite, et d'être menée avec minutie, ce qui est le cas.

Bien que le problème étudié comporte des aspects historiques, géographiques et politiques, l'ouvrage demeure essentiellement juridique. L'auteur nous en avertit d'ailleurs. Et il est hors de notre compétence de voir si des aspects extra-juridiques de la question sont susceptibles de porter atteinte au contenu juridique de l'ouvrage.

Dans une première partie de son ouvrage, l'auteur analyse la position juridique du Québec en 1927. Ce travail l'amène logiquement, dans un premier chapître, à s'interroger sur la nature du recours exercé alors auprès du Comité judiciaire du Conseil privé. De cette recherche, l'auteur conclut que le recours de 1927 n'était pas une « reference » au Conseil privé, mais un arbitrage auquel on s'était volontairement soumis.

Pour parvenir à cette conclusion, l'auteur procède à un certain nombre de raisonnements très sérieux, auxquels nous ne sommes pas toujours cependant tout-à-fait prêt à souscrire. Ainsi, il affirme que le Comité judiciaire du Conseil privé refuse, quant il agit à titre de tribunal, que lui soient référées des questions relevant d'autorités autres que les tribunaux. Et il apporte, comme exemple de cette attitude, des cas relatifs, au désaveu des lois provinciales et à la destitution des lieutenants-gouverneurs provinciaux (pp. 44, 45). Sans se justifier, il assimile ensuite tacitement à ces cas les problèmes soulevés par la délimitation des frontières intercoloniales (pp. 46 ss.). Cette extrapolation implicite est d'importance : elle permet à l'auteur de conclure que le Conseil privé n'a pas rendu en 1927 une décision sur « reference », jouissant de toute l'autorité dont est normalement assortie une telle décision (p. 46). Quant à nous, le fondement de ce raisonnement apparaîtrait quelque peu faible, surtout si l'on tient compte de ce que le renvoi au Conseil privé fait expressément état de l'article 4 du Judicial Committee Act de 1933 qui crée la procédure de « reference » au Conseil privé.

A propos d'une question connexe, l'auteur affirme aussi que le Conseil privé exige que le consentent de toutes les parties préside aux demandes d'avis consultatif. Cette affirmation importante n'est toutefois appuyée que sur les dires d'un seul auteur (p. 46). Et pour nous, cette affirmation semble un peu antinomique. Nous ne voyons pas très bien qui sont les parties à une « reference ». Il s'agirait plutôt du fait d'un gouvernement qui a et exerce une faculté que la loi lui a confiée. Or cette affirmation est de taille, car elle autorise également l'auteur à conclure que l'acte posé par le Conseil privé en 1927 n'a pas l'autorité qu'ont habituellement ses décisions (p. 50).

Au début de ce chapître, règne d'ailleurs une certaine confusion au sujet de l'interprétation que veut donner l'auteur de l'article 4 du Judicial Committe Act de 1833 qui institue la procédure de « reference » au Conseil privé. Pour connaître la portée de cet article, il n'y a à peu près rien de mieux que le texte même de l'article. L'au-

---

*Luce Patenaude, Montréal: Les Presses de l'Université de Montréal, 1972, 434 p.

teur le reconnait d'ailleurs (pp. 24, 25). Partant, la « justification » de l'article 4, à laquelle l'auteur se livre à partir de la page 26, ne nous apparaît pas tellement utile ni, à certains égards, pertinente. Il suffit de savoir que le gouvernement britannique avait, en 1927, le pouvoir de référer des questions au véritable tribunal qui était devenu le Comité judiciaire du Conseil privé. L'exécutif n'avait alors plus, en effet, et ceci depuis longtemps déjà, le pouvoir de juger. Cette faculté étant reconnue législativement par le Judicial Committe Act de 1933, elle ne pouvait pas par ailleurs avoir été abolie avant 1931 au Canada. Il n'est donc pas très utile de savoir si ce pouvoir de l'exécutif était de nature ou avait une origine de nature plutôt judiciaire ou plutôt exécutive. Et il est aussi bien difficile d'affirmer que le Judicial Committe Act de 1844 pouvait avoir réduit cette compétence de l'exécutif : il semble que cette dernière loi parlait d'autre chose, en l'occurence l'appel de grâce au Comité judiciaire du Conseil privé. En revanche, la prérogative royale quant aux frontières coloniales, dont l'auteur traite aux pp. 31 ss., n'a rien à voir avec le système des « references » au Comité judiciaire du Conseil privé. Il s'agit là seulement du pouvoir qu'avait le gouvernement britannique de légiférer, à l'époque, relativement à certaines colonies, dans certains cas.

Bref, le caractère convaincant de la démonstration voulant que la décision de 1927 ne soit qu'une sentence arbitrale nous apparaît personnellement un peu douteux. Il nous semble que cette preuve repose sur des bases plutôt précaires et donne lieu à des raisonnements parfois un peu laborieux. Quoi qu'il en soit, cette conclusion amène logiquement l'auteur à consacrer tout un chapître aux conditions de validité du recours considéré comme un arbitrage, c'est-à-dire, essentiellement, aux conditions de validité du compromis d'arbitrage. Et la preuve que cette sentence a été invalidement rendue apparaît beaucoup plus concluante. Toutefois, il nous aurait quand même semblé préférable de retenir aussi l'hypothèse que la démarche de 1927 n'était qu'une simple « reference » au Conseil privé, hypothèse qui n'avait peut-être pas pour effet, elle non plus, de réduire à néant toute possibilité de recours ultérieur de la part du Québec.

La deuxième partie de l'ouvrage de Luce Patenaude est consacrée à l'analyse de la position juridique du Québec en 1971. Cette analyse appelle deux chapîtres essentiels: l'un consacré aux effets juridiques de l'A.A.N.B. de 1949, l'autre aux reconnaissances de la frontière de 1927 dont le Québec aurait pu être l'auteur. Cette partie de l'ouvrage est marquée par de longues digressions qui, souvent, dépassent largement les strictes exigences de la thèse.

Une de ces digressions a pour objet la discussion de l'autorité de l'article 4 du Statut de Westminster de 1931 (pp. 167 ss.). Les exigences de cet article étant respectées par l'A.A.N.B. de 1949, il ne restait, strictement, qu'à interpréter le mot « dominion » dans le cas de la fédération canadienne, afin de savoir si celui-ci vise seulement le fédéral ou encore si, le cas échéant, il vise aussi les membres de la fédération. Bien que non essentiel, ce développement est toutefois fort bien mené. Au point de pouvoir dire que la question s'en trouve définitivement réglée.

Il en est tout-à-fait de même pour le débat sur l'article 7 du Statut de Westminster de 1931 (pp. 171 ss.). Pour que celui-ci paraisse vraiment pertinent, il eut fallu d'abord conclure que l'A.A.N.B. de 1949 portait sur une matière « non rapatriée », spécialement en ce qui a trait à ses dispositions relatives à la frontière du Labrador. Sans quoi il faudrait considérer que c'est l'article 4 du Statut de Westminster qui s'applique à la question, comme semble d'ailleurs l'indiquer le troisième paragraphe du préambule de la loi de 1949. La question est toutefois ici encore traitée d'une façon irréprochable.

Sur cette discussion relative au Statut de Westminster de 1931, il nous apparaît que la distinction entre « matière rapatriée » et « matière non rapatriée » n'est pas assez clairement dégagée. Partant, l'identification de la question de la frontière du Labrador à cet égard se trouve également éludée. A nos yeux, l'importance de cette démarche pourrait être grande. En « matière non rapatriée », les pouvoirs canadiens ne sont que conventionnels. De sorte que devant les tribunaux, une loi britannique visant le Canada ne pourrait pas être attaquée parce que les parlements canadiens n'ont pas été consultés. En « matière rapatriée », la situation est par contre très différente : la participation canadienne est requise par la loi (Statut de Westminster, art. 4). Or comme une loi britannique destinée à s'appliquer au Canada pourrait virtuellement porter sur n'importe quelle matière, la participation canadienne devrait être le fait du ou des parlement(s) compétent(s) en la matière, suivant les dispositions de l'A.A.N.B. de 1867. Sans quoi, le fédéral pourrait toujours envahir les champs de compétence provinciaux par ce biais. Le recours à la procédure de l'article 4 du Statut de Westminster (loi britannique en matière rapatriée) apparaît donc de ce fait largement inutile. A moins, bien sûr, d'y voir le moyen de contourner élégamment les règles fédératives du partage des compétences en cherchant à fondre ou à confondre une question rapatriée avec une question non rapatriée, comme ce pourrait avoir été le cas en 1949. Dégagée plus rigoureusement, la distinction entre « matière rapatriée » et « matière non rapatriée » eut pu peut-être permettre à l'auteur de parvenir à des conclusions moins négatives pour le Québec. Nous sommes parfaitement d'accord avec l'auteur (p. 193) sur le fait que l'A.A.N.B. de 1949 ne viole pas l'A.A.N.B. de 1871. Car il ne s'agit pas alors d'une modification frontalière, mais de la confirmation législative de la décision de 1927. Il resterait cependant à voir si cette confirmation pouvait se faire sans participation législative québécoise en utilisant la procédure de l'article 4 du Statut de Westminster, c'est-à-dire par le biais d'une loi britannique adoptée à la demande et avec le consentement du fédéral seulement.

Finalement, dans un dernier chapître de son ouvrage, l'auteur relate une suite d'actes du gouvernement québécois susceptibles d'avoir un lien quelconque avec la reconnaissance par le Québec de la frontière de 1927. Après quoi, il entreprend de faire ressortir l'autorité respective de ces différents actes. Cette partie de la thèse est typique de l'ensemble de l'ouvrage : l'exposé est global comme il s'agissait d'un ouvrage général, ce qui ne l'empêche pas d'être correct, rigoureux et bien étayé. Les stricts besoins de la thèse sont souvent dépassés. L'autorité des arrêtés en conseil, des ententes intergouvernementales des déclarations ministérielles, des contrats des corporations publiques agents de la couronne, des publications officielles du gouvernement ainsi que des cartes géographiques du gouvernement est étudiée. Sur certains points, on a affaire à la synthèse de notions plus connues; à d'autres moments on profite du résultat de recherches davantage inédites.

Plusieurs passages de l'ouvrage sont ainsi des digressions longues, qui dépassent de beaucoup les exigences de la thèse. Il s'en trouve aussi dans la première partie de l'ouvrage. Par exemple, aux pp. 135 ss., au sujet des rapports juridiques qui existent en droit canadien entre le législatif et l'exécutif. On s'étonne même, dans un ouvrage monographique, de devoir partir de principes aussi généraux et fondamentaux du droit canadien et même de droits étrangers. En l'occurrence, il eut suffii de partir des règles de droit relatives à l' « acte d'état ». De même, aux pp. 145 ss., lorsqu'il est question des moyens de recours contre l'invalidité de la démarche faite en 1927 auprès du Comité judiciaire du Conseil privé. On est alors amené à discuter de sujets aussi éloignés du contexte historique précis de la question soulevée que du système des commissions d'enquête et du rôle de l'ombudsman québécois.

Outre quelques passages particuliers et peu nombreux, toutefois, il faut admettre que ces digressions, étant donné la nature très singulière de la question de droit traitée et les conclusions plutôt négatives auxquelles parvient l'auteur, sont peut-être, paradoxalement, les aspects de l'ouvrage qui contribueront le plus à assurer la pérennité de la valeur de celui-ci. A partir d'un objet très spécifique, Luce Patenaude a greffé une étude remarquable de droit public fondamental, qu'il sera souvent très utile de consulter. Pour décider d'acquérir oui ou non cet ouvrage, il ne faut pas se fier à son seul titre.

Recensions
Reviews

Dion, *Société et politique* DAVID BRAYBROOKE 522
Biot, *Théologie du politique* RAYMOND LEMIEUX 523
Toinet, *Le Congrès des Etats-Unis* EDMOND ORBAN 524
Kwavnick, *Organized Labour and Pressure Politics* FREDERICK C. ENGELMANN 525
Meisel, *Working Papers on Canadian Politics* DAVID EDWARD SMITH 526
Gray, *Canadian Defence Priorities* HARALD VON RIEKHOFF 527
Eayrs, *In Defence of Canada, Vol. III* GEOFFREY PEARSON 528
Burns, *The Struggle for Disarmament* GERRY DIRKS 529
Granatstein and Cuff, eds., *War and Society in North America* and Massey, ed., *The Canadian Military* MARGARET DOXEY 530
Teeple, ed., *Capitalism and the National Question in Canada* THELMA OLIVER 531
Reid, *The Shouting Signpainters*, Jones, *Community in Crisis*, Drache, ed., *Quebec – Only the Beginning*, and Chodos and Auf Der Maur, eds., *Quebec: A Chronicle, 1968–1972* PHILIP RESNICK 532
Borden, *Letters to Limbo* JOHN R. WILLIAMS 533
Westell, *Paradox: Trudeau as Prime Minister* and Trudeau, *Conversation with Canadians* THOMAS A. HOCKIN 535
Touraine, *Le communisme utopique* et *Université et société aux Etats-Unis* DANIEL LA TOUCHE 536
Bourdet, *Figures de Lukacs* ANDRÉ P. DONNEUR 539
Bell, *Resistance and Revolution* WILLIAM LEISS 541
Wood, *Mind and Politics* J. MCCALLA VICKERS 541
Halle, *The Ideological Imagination* BARRY COOPER 542
Meehan, *The Foundations of Political Analysis* M.W. JACKSON 544
Friedrich, *Tradition and Authority*, Partridge, *Consent and Consensus*, and Schapiro, *Totalitarianism* WILLIAM CHRISTIAN 545
Attali, *Analyse économique de la vie politique* et *Les modèles politiques* EDOUARD CLOUTIER 546
Torrelli et Baudouin, *Les droits de l'homme et les libertés publiques par les textes* PANAYOTIS SOLDATOS 547
Brun et Tremblay, *Droit public fondamental* ANDRÉ BERNARD 548
Masclet, *L'Europe politique* MAURICE TORRELLI 550
Hancock and Sjoberg, eds., *Politics in the Post-Welfare State* INGUNN N. MEANS 550
Harris, *Competition and the Corporate Society* ALAN ALEXANDER 551
Richards, *The Backbenchers* ROBERT J. JACKSON 552
Halperin, *The Rise and Decline of Fidel Castro* THOMAS C. BRUNEAU 552
Brecher, *The Foreign Policy System of Israel* TIMOTHY M. SHAW 554
Benjamin, *Les Camerounais occidentaux* LYNN K. MYTELKA 555
Dvorin and Simmons, *From Amoral to Humane Bureaucracy* KENNETH KERNAGHAN 556
Crenson, *The Un-Politics of Air Pollution* T.J. CARTWRIGHT 558
Odegard, *The Politics of Truth* GEORGE J. SZABLOWSKI 559

Léon Dion, **Société et politique – la vie des groupes : Tome 1, Fondements de la société libérale; Tome 2, Dynamique de la société libérale.** Québec : Les Presses de l'Université Laval, 1971, 1972, 444, 616, pp.

"To answer a book effectually," Swift says, in words that apply to reviewing one, "requires more pains and skill, more wit, learning, and judgment than were employ'd in the writing it." Almost all reviews are therefore inadequate; and in some cases, the discrepancy between what can be attempted in the review and what was attempted in the book is so great as to make the review almost inevitably an impertinence. Dion's two volumes represent a truly colossal effort to synthesize the results of the group approach to the study of politics with systems analysis, incorporating – on the way to synthesis – some of the leading ideas of structural-functionalism and a digest both of the literature on participation and of the literature (somewhat less familiar, and not yet so rich) on "consultative politics." In these various connections, Dion draws chiefly on American studies, though he makes substantial use of French sources, too. (By exception) the French sources seem to have taken the initiative in broaching the subject of "consultative politics"; otherwise, it is somewhat disappointing to find that political scientists in France are saying much the same things about much the same topics as are political scientists in the US.

One measure of the size of Dion's effort consists in the range of the literature that he cites. His general bibliographies, which run to 29 pages in the first volume and to 60 in the second, must be the most comprehensive classified bibliographies on the joint anglophone and francophone literature on the topics treated now available anywhere; some of his footnotes constitute bibliographies in themselves, equally valuable in more specialized ways. Another measure of Dion's effort – the one that daunts me most as a reviewer – is the height of his ambition, which amounts to nothing less than providing a comprehensive, theoretical framework for all the chief current concerns of political science as applied (at least as applied from within) to the condition of the liberal democracies. I think that at the height at which Dion chooses to operate, generalities – many of which will seem commonplace, some of them commonplace even to people unfamiliar with the literature, and all of which tend to be unprovocative – inevitably abound. To complain of there being too many generalities is to complain about the rarefied atmosphere, not about the comparative merits of Dion's performance as an astronaut. Furthermore, I am not so much dissatisfied with Dion's attempt to put contemporary empirical theory together as with the character of some parts of that theory itself, especially systems analysis, which is what Dion mainly relies on to create a unifying framework. I am afraid that suspicions engendered in many people besides me come home to roost in a framework like Dion's. There is an uncomfortably wide gap between the mutual relationships plausibly insisted upon as the central topics of systems analysis on the one hand, and interesting particularized hypotheses about the workings of such relationships in actual systems on the other.

Yet the real test of these topics is whether the gap can be filled; and in Dion's case – though with his aim to be general he cannot spare much time to fill the gap – one cannot only hope to supply some suggestions for filling it; his synthesis in at least one crucial connection invites and shapes suggestions that at least foreshadow particularized hypotheses. Dion assigns to interest groups the largest part of the crucial task of mediating between the two great systems that he finds at work in politics – the social system and the political system proper; and he treats interest groups as if they can equally well be assigned to both these systems. They are extensions ("prolongements") of voluntary associations, which are in turn extensions of "real groups" (face-to-face groups; families; multilinked geographical, historical, racial, or religious communities), the roots of the social system. They are also, however, extensions in the other direction, from the political system into the social system. They are often, as Dion points out, fostered, indeed created, by agencies in the political system which has as much need of intermediaries to communicate with the social system as the social system has of intermediaries to communicate with it. Currently, according to Dion, interest groups are doing an adequate job of mediation in neither direction; and their inadequacies are a central feature of the crisis of liberal society, as Dion conceives of the crisis and as his systematic perspective, in assigning interest groups such a central role, inevitably implies.

Even if we put aside the inadequate coverage that active interest groups give to the whole range of "real" groups or to whole men in any group, they fail, Dion argues, to mediate adequately with their own constituents in respect to the interests which the constituents must look to them to articulate. When the groups are the creatures of politicians and bureaucrats they may be mere captive servants of the political system; and one of the dangers of "consultative politics" is that even interest groups which were not originally creatures of the political system may be enticed into captivity. Captivity, however, does not ensure efficiency even in communicating the intentions of agencies in the political system to members of the interest groups. The leadership of the captive groups may know no better than the politicians and bureaucrats themselves what to say to their members, as well as know no better what to say on their members' behalf. On the other hand, freedom of movement in "consultative politics" and in other connections does not imply sensitive attention to the needs and aspirations of members. For reasons now familiar, which Dion recounts in detail from his store of learning, the leadership tends to run away with the policies of interest groups, leaving the members to fall behind and sink into powerless apathy. The most vigorous grass-roots movements are liable sooner or later to be visited by this fate.

These charges are not yet hypotheses, but they are on their way to becoming such. They prompt us to ask, as the next step, how would these inadequacies of mediation and communication manifest themselves in particular instances? We may well wonder how much political sense there is in postulating needs and aspirations which members of interest groups have apart from formulations conferred upon their needs and aspirations by leaders appointed (or self-appointed) to be articulate to just this end. The members of an interest group might be expected to be, at best, like Schattschneider's "the people," a sovereign that "speaks only when it is spoken to," and asked to endorse formulations invented by their leaders. We can surely inquire into the reality of the endorsement by inquiring into among other things the extent to which the members are offered alternative formulations and asked to choose between them. Yet even such choices normally presuppose political initiatives on the part of leaders, who are as much needed to formulate issues as to formulate positions.

Dion inclines to think the chief hope that political parties have of regaining the attention and confidence of voters lies in becoming parties with new skills – parties, functioning as "stratèges-animateurs," which use the mass media and special techniques of participation to create issues and simultaneously engage the voters in effective choices. Evidently interest groups need to remedy their inadequacies in much the same way. But how shall we tell whether, in offering their members issues and choices of position on these issues, and in mobilizing their members behind such positions, the group leaders have done suitable things in the way of "animation," however much excitement and concern has been awakened? Here, I think, we come upon one of the points where systems analysis and Dion's reliance upon it is fully vindicated. Whether the groups have done "suitable things" or not is something that can be discovered only by following the process through full cycles, tracing the effect of the interest groups' representations upon government policy, and then considering the impact of government policy upon the members' satisfactions or dissatisfactions in the daily rounds of the social system. If the members are dissatisfied, and remain dissatisfied through several consecutive cycles, the interest groups are failing in their formulations – possibly failing only to adjust the expectations of their members to realities, but possibly failing much more thoroughly, even though the members themselves have on their own little or no hope of being able to expose the failures by formulating their dissatisfactions in politically more useful ways. What we need at this point are hypotheses searching for ways to express the dissatisfaction as close as possible to exposing what is wrong with the formulations, and hence with the leadership, which the interest groups have been offered; and hypotheses, too, about the fate even of promising formulations on their way through the two systems and back.

I expect there are many connections in which Dion's synthesis invites and shapes suggestions that turn into particularized hypotheses; I have discussed just one connection, which leads out from one of his central themes and happens to interest me especially. I conclude from reflecting upon it that Dion has not only given us an instructive attempt to make comprehensive sense of an immense literature (incidentally making that literature more accessible to more people, especially people in the French-speaking academic world), he has as well succeeded in animating the beginnings of further inquiry.

DAVID BRAYBROOKE
Dalhousie University

François Biot, **Théologie du politique.** Paris : Editions universitaires, 1972, 247 p.

L'intérêt principal d'un tel livre est de représenter une tendance assez nouvelle dans les milieux religieux, surtout ecclésiastiques. Cette tendance traduit, pour parler en termes rapides, d'une part une lecture critique – fort développée depuis le dernier Concile – des rapports traditionnels entre l'Eglise et les Etats ou des articulations habituelles du religieux et du politique; d'autre part elle manifeste une recherche beaucoup plus balbutiante, mais peut être fort significative, d'un langage politique spécifiquement ecclésial. Elle s'inscrit de ce dernier point de vue dans le courant très puissant de renouveau théologique qu'ont lancé les Chenu, Congar, Kung, Rahner, (pour ne mentionner que les mieux connus parmi les catholiques) dont une des principales caractéristiques est de valoriser, pour le bien de la démarche théologique elle-même mais sans chercher à les approprier ni à les réduire, les lectures scientifiques des phénomènes sociaux. Ces lectures sont généralement anthropologiques, sociologiques ou psychologiques. Mais rien n'implique qu'elles ne puissent être aussi politologiques.

La présente théologie du politique reste cependant assez tâtonnante. Elle ne manque pourtant pas de perspective critique. Au contraire la première partie du livre, consacrée à une cueillette de données historiques, est essentiellement un essai de relecture critique de situations assez récentes : les attitudes des catholiques français sous le deuxième Empire, celles des protestants allemands sous le régime national-socialiste, le rôle de l'Eglise dans le Brésil des maréchaux et son statut dans la Pologne et la Hongrie communistes. Cette première partie du livre pose généralement les problèmes de façon très claire, quoique un peu rapide. La volonté de l'auteur n'est pas de faire œuvre historique, mais sans doute politologique. Sa démarche cependant reste historique et on n'y trouve pas de véritables grilles d'analyse qui nous permettent d'accéder à une problématique. L'auteur refuse, de son propre aveu, « une grille de lecture *a priori* », réagissant sans doute alors contre toute lecture « orientée » normativement. Mais cette réaction ralentit énormément la construction d'une grille véritablement politologique. Et faute de cette dernière, on peut se demander ce que représente son effort de « reconnaissance ou de déchiffrage d'une signification, d'une interprétation ou d'une compréhension auxquelles les faits de l'histoire ... peuvent donner lieu », soit son effort théologique lui-même.

Du point de vue politologique, cette première partie du livre est cependant de loin la plus intéressante. Il serait certes important de continuer ces recherches pour cerner les lois de l'articulation du religieux et du politique dans l'histoire, lois qui permettraient alors l'élaboration d'une réflexion critique provenant d'une autre logique, celle d'une « appartenance religieuse ».

La deuxième et la troisième partie du livre s'inscrivent directement dans cette autre logique, relevant les « conceptions politiques de la Bible » d'une part, ce qui nous renvoie à l'observation de d'autres civilisations et « les recherches actuelles pour une théologie du politique ». Ces deux parties ne manquent pas d'intérêt. Au contraire, elles représentent les essais les plus actuels dans le domaine, quand la foi chrétienne trouve une fonction utopique et devient critique nécessaire de toute conjoncture de pouvoir. Nous n'en contestons pas la pertinence et devons plutôt reconnaître leur très grande valeur de stimulation. Leur difficulté réside plutôt dans le lien théorique qui peut les unir à la démarche empirique entreprise initialement. L'interdisciplinarité sous-jacente à la démarche de l'auteur n'est pas poussée à terme : les deux logiques en présence se révèlent de forces inégales.

RAYMOND LEMIEUX
Université Laval

Marie-France Toinet, **Le Congrès des Etats-Unis.** Paris : Presses Universitaires de France, 1972, 230 p.

Une lecture trop rapide de cet ouvrage risque de provoquer des réflexes assez négatifs parmi une infime minorité de lecteurs. Cela pourrait s'exprimer sommairement dans une question de ce genre : « Il y a déjà tant de livres écrits en anglais sur le sujet. Pourquoi ne pas choisir le meilleur et le traduire ? » Ou bien, « ce travail n'apporte rien de bien original pour quiconque suit d'un peu près les écrits américains ».

En fait, pour quelques dizaines de francophones spécialisés dans ce type de problèmes, l'ouvrage en question constituera un apport assez limité.

Par contre, pour la plupart des lecteurs intéressés aux problèmes politiques américains, « Le Congrès des Etats-Unis » représente un excellent outil. D'abord en raison de sa valeur synthétique, ensuite parce que l'approche est suffisamment critique. L'éventail des sources utilisées garantit cette double qualité du travail réalisé. Ainsi, par exemple, la partie consacrée aux commissions sénatoriales fournit une remarquable mise au point. Celle-ci est d'autant plus nécessaire que trop de stéréotypes circulent encore à ce sujet. Les événements récents exigeaient en outre une certaine mise à jour.

Je n'ai relevé qu'une lacune sérieuse. Elle réside dans l'insuffisance des pages analysant les relations du Congrès avec le Président. Il s'agit pourtant de la question la plus fondamentale et la plus critique qui se pose au Congrès actuel. A cette occasion, l'auteur n'a pas suffisamment souligné la faiblesse de la fonction de contrôle du Congrès. L'escalade vietnamienne n'a pas été bien utilisée en tant qu'indice révélateur.

Ceci conduit à des généralités d'une valeur douteuse. Ainsi, parlant de l'invasion du Cambodge (p. 92), M.F. Toinet écrit « Les présidents jusqu'alors avaient eu l'élégance de consulter le Congrès ou ses dirigeants – sinon de demander une autorisation avant de révéler leur décision ».

Une telle affirmation fera bondir la majorité des sénateurs, à commencer par Fullbright l'auteur d'une thèse absolument opposée, reprise dans « The arrogance of Power » (non cité par l'auteur). Les ouvrages les plus récents, publiés aux Etats-Unis accordent une place de plus en plus importante au « War power » du Président et du Congrès. La bibliographie utilisée ici s'avère un peu pauvre. Dans le domaine de la bibliographie, soulignons au passage qu'un ouvrage en français devrait mentionner les rares publications faites dans cette langue, du moins quand elles ont trait à des points de son exposé.

A ce point de vue, les francophones éloignés, ceux de la « périphérie nord-américaine », semblent oubliés. Quand on parle du rôle des lobbyists au Congrès, pourquoi ne pas signaler le livre de L. Dion « Les groupes de pression aux Etats-Unis ». Même remarque à propos de « La télévision américaine » de J. Meynaud.

D'une façon générale, la bibliographie citée à la fin est mal organisée. Elle ne mentionne pas certains ouvrages essentiels. Elle devrait comporter au moins deux pages supplémentaires pour que le lecteur puisse disposer d'un bon instrument de travail en vue d'autres lectures. Ceci dit, l'étude nous semble avoir largement atteint l'objectif assigné à ce type de publication. L'auteur nous paraît même trop modeste dans son introduction.

Quiconque s'engage sérieusement dans un projet de ce genre, se rend parfaitement compte de la somme de recherches et de réflexions qu'elle implique.

Seul un esprit superficiel se permettra de qualifier ce livre d'élémentaire, en utilisant le terme vulgarisation dans le sens un peu péjoratif que l'on peut lui conférer trop rapidement.

EDMOND ORBAN
Université de Montréal

David Kwavnick, **Organized Labour and Pressure Politics: The Canadian Labour Congress, 1956–1968.** Montreal and London: McGill-Queen's University Press, 1972, pp. 287.

"A major factor in the process of group politics," writes Kwavnick in the introduction, "is the pursuit of organizational goals by the participants." They pursue *legitimacy*, "the protection of the status and position of the interest on whose behalf the group's leaders claim to speak"; and *mandate*, "the protection of the position of the group as the recognized spokesman of the interest." The first chapter of his analysis of the activities of the Canadian Labour Congress from 1956 to 1968 is based on these action-oriented concepts. Kwavnick traces the concepts' origins and expounds lucidly how he interprets them. The masterful chapter, which weaves in a minimizing of conflict in group-government relations, and a maximizing of the role of leaders of interest groups, should prove a highly useful addition not only to the literature on Canadian interest groups, but on interest groups in general.

What follows is a painstaking description and analysis of the activities of the CLC as they relate to the two key concepts. Foci of the analysis are the CLC as an organization and its relation to government. Throughout, Kwavnick makes clear that the interest of the leaders takes precedence over the interest of the members, and that the processing of group demands is often subordinated to activities that preserve legitimacy and protect mandate for their own sake. The real struggle of a roof organization like the CLC is with rival labour groups. In an era of welfarism, the government is called upon not so much to keep employers in line, but primarily to make sure that the CLC stays number one in Canadian labour. Policy interests of the CLC tend to be taken care of as long as they follow a welfarist public opinion.

Granting the usefulness of Kwavnick's approach for the analysis of groups, how useful is it for an analysis of the CLC in particular? The main peculiarities of the CLC are its American-based member unions and its attachment to the NDP. The former phenomenon skirts the discussion often; in the discussion of the Banks case, it even occupies the centre. But Kwavnick does not fully discuss the impact of international unions on mandate, and only partially discusses their impact on legitimacy. The second aspect, support of a third party, is only mentioned a couple of times. Kwavnick appears to play down intentionally the role of parties in interest-group life. Considering the actual, though atypical, role of party in CLC activities, such an intentional omission is, in the case of this particular group, the omission of an important part of reality.

These criticisms are tangential. Kwavnick goes about the central part of his task with great competence and clarity. The first chapter remains the pièce de résistance. It deserves to be part of the pattern for future interest-group studies in Canada and elsewhere. Also it strongly merits reprinting in anthologies on interest groups. It should be made accessible to thousands of political scientists who would probably never read a good book on the Canadian Labour Congress.

FREDERICK C. ENGELMANN
University of Alberta

John Meisel, **Working Papers on Canadian Politics**, enlarged edition. Montreal: McGill-Queen's University Press, 1973, pp. xiv, 257.

There are five working papers in this enlarged edition of Professor Meisel's book. In the first edition, published in 1972, there were only four: three based on survey data gathered after the general election of 1968 and one, "'Cancel Out and Pass On': A View of Canada's Options," written "as a quick reaction towards one aspect of Canada's problems – a piece of journalism or pamphleteering more than anything else," which originally appeared in *One Country or Two?*, published in 1971 (p. ix). The fifth, and new, paper, entitled "Howe, Hubris and '72: An Essay on Political Elitism," was writen very shortly after last year's federal election. Its addition to the original volume, which was about to go into a second printing late in 1972, accounts for this enlarged edition.

All of the papers reflect what has come to be expected from Professor Meisel: erudite scholarship and elegant style. In "Howe, Hubris and '72," the author calls style a "weasel" word used "to describe a phenomenon we vaguely understand but find hard to define precisely" (p. 230). Be that as it may, it nevertheless requires style and rigorous precision to translate survey data into the intelligible prose found here. Professor Meisel's expertise in this regard guarantees that with the publication of these working papers, prior to the appearance of the full-fledged study, he will achieve his goal of making as much of the survey data available as quickly as possible. It also assures the realization of another of his purposes: to give students an opportunity to observe "through a paperback peephole ... how one scholar went about ... constructing some political analyses" (p. ix). In fact, this pedagogical intent should provide these papers with a student audience even after the completion of the final work.

Each of the three papers based on survey data breaks some new ground in the study of Canadian politics. The paper on "Some Bases of Party Support in the 1968 Election" goes far beyond simply identifying the personal characteristics of voters, although even at this level some intriguing regional deviations from national patterns of support for the Liberals and Conservatives are notable. Responses to questions about issues and party perceptions and about attitudes linked to political culture also demonstrate striking regional variation in Canada "in many instances, greater than that between the supporters of different parties" (p. 24). These findings suggest once again the pressing need in Canada for a study like Daniel Elazar's on federalism and political sub-cultures in the United States.

Although he deliberately refrains from making theoretical speculations in the working papers, Professor Meisel does break loose long enough to touch on the theme, which he promises will be central to the completed study, of parties in their role as agents helping to convert demands into outputs. The data from 1968 show that a large number of the less privileged in Canada rejected the old parties because of their apparent indifference to the poor and the results of the election in 1972 suggests that an even larger number of the same voters, along with a good many of their more privileged fellow citizens, became disaffected by the arrogance of Liberal policies and spokesmen.

In "Party Images in Canada" Profesor Meisel again looks at voters' perceptions of parties but this time uses the semantic differential approach. Employing 10 pairs of words, which include among others honest-dishonest, good-bad, and competent-incompetent, he establishes the voters' perceptions of the quality, orientation, and performance of existing parties as well as of an Ideal party. Survey data from 1965 permit comparisons over time and reveal startling changes for two of the existing parties when compared to the Ideal: for the Liberals there was a dramatic improvement between 1965 and 1968, for the NDP an equally marked deterioration, but for the Conservatives almost no change. Although it comes as no surprise that over-all the Liberals possess the most favourable image (coming closest to the Ideal and ahead of other parties on most dimensions), it is unexpected that their scores for competence, goodness, and honesty should be relatively low. Why this should be so, Professor Meisel is unable to say but he does suggest that these findings should impel further work into the key mystery of psephology – what makes people vote the way they do?

The paper on "Values, Language and Politics in Canada," which again is based on survey data from 1968, hypothesizes that "social cleavages find expression in differential responses to phenomena" (p. 135). Depending upon the fluency and frequency with which English or French Canadians use the other official language, they will respond with varying intensity to a range of issues from the purely private through the very general to the "ethnically relevant." Professor Meisel rejects as simplistic the old concept of two solitudes because his analysis reveals a variety of contacts which English and French Canadians may experience and in some of which they share a common response.

Concern for relations between Quebec and the rest of Canada occupies Professor Meisel's attention in "Cancel Out and Pass On." Whether or not one agrees with his pessimistic conclusion as to the future, his attempts to specify the divisions of opinion in English Canada as well as to clarify the direction of discontent in Quebec warrant attention. To a resident of the prairies who disagrees with Professor Meisel's opinion, unsubstantiated by any empirical evidence, that this region is populated by pluralists who "normally [see] no great inherent virtue in preserving British patterns in a North American setting," there remains a lingering hope that he is equally mistaken about his final conclusion (p. 199). It is in all probability a false hope.

Although the final paper was occasioned by the results of the 1972 election, its perceptive comments about the Liberal flaw of arrogance originate from Professor Meisel's long observation of Canadian politics. The roots of hubris, it would appear, run deep and in the past have survived the occasional application of humility.

DAVID EDWARD SMITH
University of Saskatchewan, Saskatoon

Colin S. Gray, **Canadian Defence Priorities: A Question of Relevance.** Toronto: Clarke, Irwin, 1972, pp. xv, 293.

It might strain one's patriotic zeal to admit that the two most significant books on Canadian defence policy of the past 15 years have been written by non-Canadians. I am referring to *Canada's Changing Defense Policy* by Jon McLin, an American, and to the work reviewed here. Professor Gray is a young British scholar who has acquired an impressive expertise in the subject of Canadian defence policy. By combining this particular topic with his knowledge of the broader discipline of strategic studies Gray provides us with a most informative and admirably balanced study which avoids the dogmatic defence of the status quo as well as the recent polemic of academic revisionists.

Canadian Defence Priorities concentrates on policy outcomes rather than policy process. It offers a comprehensive discussion of Canada's defence options for the 1970s in conjunction with international strategic conditions and domestic political and economic considerations. The conceptual and organizational focus for this study is derived from the 1971 government *White Paper on Defence.* The author is in over-all agreement with the principal arguments of the *White Paper* and endorses the shift toward domestic considerations in determining Canadian defence priorities. Gray's analysis throughout is firmly rooted in the logic of cost-effectiveness calculations. Past policy choices and current priorities are carefully evaluated in terms of their strategic, economic, and social costs as well as benefits to Canada.

The author recognizes that NORAD has become a symbol of Canadian-American co-operation in the minds of many Americans. Its non-renewal might therefore be viewed as a provocative gesture. To avoid such misinterpretation, the author suggests that Canada renew the arrangements, continue her DEW line warning services, but otherwise show a low profile in NORAD activities and avoid the costly purchase of equipment like AWACS. Gray believes that Canada's continuing membership in NATO and military commitments to the organization provide her with a desirable political foothold in European affairs at a time of anticipated flux in that area. With respect to naval activities, the author suggests that Canada shed her conventional anti-submarine warfare capability and concentrate on developing and installing bottom-based surveillance systems for monitoring sub-surface movements in her coastal waters and arctic channels. According to Gray, no special training or additional equipment is required for international peace-keeping functions beyond what Canada already possesses for other defence activities. The subject of international peace-keeping is accorded no more than peripheral mention, thus reflecting the recent decline of academic and governmental interest in this particular security function.

This book shares the *White Paper*'s essentially benign assessment of the international strategic environment and thus supports the "domestication" of Canadian defence policy. Few would dispute Professor Gray's point that Canada has relied too heavily on foreign sources for its military hardware, as well as the software of strategic thinking, and should engage in more strategic analysis at home. But when he defines Canadian defence priorities almost exclusively with reference to domestic rather than international demands, Professor Gray enters more disputable ground. According to the author, the primary task for Canada's armed forces should be that of domestic peace-keeping during insurrections and civil disturbances. Furthermore, the armed forces should reinforce the efforts of other government departments in protecting and developing arctic resources and in safeguarding the environment. These are honourable tasks, but is it necessary to maintain a military establishment of 80,000 men to perform them and will they be acceptable to the professional interests of the military? I am less inclined to accept this argument, if for no other reason than that one cannot fully "civilianize" the military while making them responsible for planning for externally generated contingencies.

Some unconfirmed skeptics, including this reviewer, will perhaps refuse to accept Gray's thesis that the stationing of military forces in Europe is nothing other than an extraordinarily shrewd finesse whereby the Trudeau government camouflages its preparations for dealing with possible situations of domestic turmoil – even the use of fighter-bombers is included in this scenario – while at the same time earning foreign credit for the appearance of a loyal NATO ally. Governments tend to lack the imagination and sustained rationality to engage in Machiavellian strategies of this kind.

These reservations, however, are minor and they deal more with shadings of emphasis than with substance. Professor Gray has written an impressive book on a complicated subject. In it he has compiled large amounts of technical information while preserving the style of a belletristic essay.

HARALD VON RIEKHOFF
Carleton University

James Eayrs, **In Defence of Canada, Volume III: Peacemaking and Deterrence.** Toronto: University of Toronto Press, 1972, pp. xiv, 448.

The third volume of James Eayrs's study of Canadian defence policy, subtitled *Peacemaking and Deterrence*, deals with postwar-security issues, including the roles and structures of the armed forces, planning for European and world security, continental defence, and the control of atomic energy. A chapter on the Commonwealth, while it contains a fascinating account of Canada's part in finding a solution to the problem of India's remaining in the Commonwealth as a republic, has no apparent structural relationship to the rest of the book. The author explains in his preface that he is reserving for a fourth volume the themes of "North Atlantic ally and global peace-keeper." In view of the references in the preface to the difficulties of gaining access to official files, one may conjecture that the plan of this volume was at least partly determined by the availability of source materials. With the exception of material on the Commonwealth, the files of the Department of Exernal Affairs do not seem to have been consulted beyond 1946 and in regard to atomic energy were apparently not consulted at all. The papers of C.D. Howe, C.J. Mackenzie, and A.G.L. McNaughton fill this gap admirably and of course the King papers provide access not only to policy-making at all levels but to the brooding, enigmatic figure whose personality presides over these pages. One should note also that use of the Claxton papers has added not only an essential dimension to the history of these years but has helped the author to flesh out his portraits of the decision-makers in a superb introductory chapter. Students of Canadian defence policy will be grateful to have made available two key documents on Canada-US postwar defence planning which are printed as appendices.

If unevenness of sources partly explains the rather patchy nature of this study – the United Nations is abandoned in 1945 but the control of atomic energy is pursued into 1950 and the defence of the continent beyond that – one is also left wondering about the focus of the larger enterprise as a cause of distortion. This enterprise is a study of Canadian defence policy in peacetime, and before 1939 it could be treated as virtually synonymous with foreign policy. Both were in short supply, and could in any event be encompassed as pertaining to "security." After the war "security" is of course the dominant concern of Canadian foreign policy but it is a political rather than a military concern. Canada may be under threat but the means of defence exist, if only across the border. What is at stake is Canada's status or role, not the violation of her sovereignty by military means. The expression of this concern takes many forms, of which the most important may have little to do with defence. Thus the analyst of defence policy is bound to be tempted to examine themes which have little or no apparent relevance to the concerns of the Department of National Defence, unless he soldiers on as military historian which no one acquainted with the work of James Eayrs could ever imagine he intended or intends to do. We badly need a good study of Canadian postwar foreign policy. It is too bad that the best one we have is masquerading as a study of Canadian defence policy.

Another aspect of this question of focus is the relationship of the volumes by Eayrs to the series of which they are a part – "studies in the structure of power: decision-making in Canada." Along with the paucity of memoirs by Canadian public men, and perhaps because of it, we have few good studies of decision-making in Canadian government (it is a pity in this regard that the Pearson and Heeney memoirs were unavailable to Eayrs in time). This volume fills a real empirical need because it illuminates the process of decision-making, especially within the Department of External Affairs, by close attention to the *documents du travail.* One is looking over the shoulders of Robertson, Wrong, Pearson, Claxton, *et al.* as they go about the task of making choices between serious alternatives, short-term or tactical as they may be (strategic choices rarely get made in foreign offices). It is regrettable therefore that Eayrs takes little time to reflect on this process and to draw conclusions from it. He approaches the dangerous bridge between "politics" and "science" in his first chapter on the decision-makers themselves but draws back to the safer ground of thumb-nail sketches, well done as they are. The chapters that follow illustrate a remark by an American political scientist, Graham Allison, who has shown no such caution: "we should ask not what goals account for a nation's choice of an action but rather what factors determine an outcome." (*Essence of Decision*, p. 255) It is left to others to speculate what these factors might be.

On the other hand this study is mercifully free of both obscurity and tendentiousness. The author is justly renowned for his clarity of style and asperity of tongue. He lets the actors speak for themselves on the whole although they do not always escape without a flick of editorial chastisement or, on occasion, of applause. The judgments thus pronounced perhaps rest a bit uneasily on the weight of evidence produced to support them but, except for a curious digression apparently intended to portray the young Mackenzie King as a racist, they are circumstantial and not doctrinaire. Nor is there much in these pages to feed the fires of nationalist debate. If Canadian leaders of those days had little hesitation in asserting their suspicion of British attempts to lead or even to advise they had no less compunction in disagreeing with US estimates and assumptions. Their sensitivities were acute and some of the older participants in the international waltz must have wished they could avoid this debutante who refused to go on standing by the wall. James Eayrs is attuned to this ballroom atmosphere. He keeps his eye on all the players from his place in the gallery and he knows that, however familiar the tune, dancing is a matter of mood.

GEOFFREY PEARSON
University of British Columbia

Lt. Gen. E.L.M. Burns, **The Struggle for Disarmament: A Seat at the Table.** Toronto and Vancouver: Clarke Irwin, 1972, pp. 268.

The literature on arms control and disarmament has expanded significantly in recent years, due in part to an increased interest by scholars in peace research, defence policy, and strategic studies. Only a few of the contributors to this literature, however, have brought to the reader the insight and experience acquired in actual arms control negotiations. General E.L.M. Burns, Canada's chief representative to arms-control conferences held under the auspices of the United Nations in the sixties, has set out in this most recent of his books to examine critically the arms limitations proposals put forward by the "super powers." His analysis includes an assessment of the subsequent deliberations of the Ten Nation and Eighteen Nation Disarmament Conferences. Writing with neither unwarranted pessimism nor unbridled optimism, General Burns has presented an exceedingly thorough account of conference proceedings including those debates leading up to the Limited Test Ban and Non-Proliferation agreements of 1963 and 1968 respectively.

The first 6 of the 18 chapters comprising *A Seat at the Table* contain a possibly unnecessarily detailed account of "super power" negotiation tactics and strategic weapons capabilities prior to 1960, the year the Ten Nation Disarmament Conference initially met. At best, these chapters serve the purpose of bringing together a good deal of interesting material for students who are only commencing work in the area of disarmament. The remainder of the book presents an accurate and generally complete examination of arms-control proposals through the use of official document excerpts and numerous welcome excursions into the General's own diary. In addition, the analysis the author brings to the negotiating process, with his assertion of "super power" dominance, provides the student of international relations with empirical data to fit the conceptual frameworks developed by such theorists as Fred C. Iklé and Kenneth Waltz.

Frequently throughout the last two thirds of the book General Burns, in the context of "super power" proposals and conference deliberations, discusses the official Canadian position along with governmental responses to American nudges. The reader should not be surprised to find the General endorsing the traditional or "Pearsonian" approach to Canadian diplomacy based on this state being a mediator or broker between disputants at the conference table. It is while dealing with the Canadian decision to acquire nuclear weapons for defensive purposes that General Burns writes quite candidly about Howard Green, the secretary of state for external affairs during much of the Diefenbaker period, and a fervent supporter of disarmament. In discussing Canada's contribution General Burns also contends that the Canadian decision to adopt nuclear defensive weapons did not injure this country's credibility nor impede the work of the delegation at the arms control conferences.

Despite the over-all strength and value of *A Seat at the Table*, there are some criticisms that might be made. First, while the detailed account or commentary demonstrates fine scholarship by General Burns, the editor's pen should have been in evidence at times when the momentum sagged and the minutia appeared. Second, a more substantive criticism arises from what strikes this reviewer as a disproportionate emphasis upon arms control failures. Specifically, only three chapters directly examine the limited Test Ban and Non-Proliferation agreements while much of the remaining sections of the book expand upon the unacceptable control proposals. Finally, the omission of any significant analysis of the effect the absence of France and the Chinese Peoples Republic had upon arms-control negotiations is unfortunate.

These criticisms are, however, really quite marginal when measured against the worth of this volume. General Burns has written a book which can be warmly welcomed by students and laymen concerned with almost any aspect of the study of international relations.

GERRY DIRKS
Brock University

J.L. Granatstein and R.D. Cuff, eds., **War and Society in North America.** Toronto: Thomas Nelson, 1971, pp. viii, 199.

Hector J. Massey, ed., **The Canadian Military: A Profile.** Toronto: Copp Clark, 1972, pp. vii, 290.

War and Society in North America brings together papers presented at the Canadian Association for American Studies meeting in Montreal in 1970 and the connecting thread is necessarily somewhat thin under a title of such wide scope. Seven of the 12 papers deal with the First World War period, some in relation to United States experience, and others in relation to Canadian. Of the remaining five, one examines Roosevelt's leadership during the Second World War, two concern themselves with literary figures (Hemingway and Mailer) and their attitudes to war and warriors, and two are more up to date, summarizing some thoughts on draft dodgers and investigating aspects of the Canadian response to the Vietnam War. Some of these essays are of particular interest to political scientists. This reviewer found much of interest in Jill Conway's account of the Women's Peace Party and the First World War, with its fascinating allusions to nineteenth century notions of the inherent differences in male and female personalities, which were thought to make women "conservers" and peace lovers.

The lack of – and need for – further studies in the Canadian context is pointed up sharply in several places. For instance, in his essay on Joseph Flavelle, Michael Bliss notes that "generalizations based on a single case are very tentative" (p. 34); it would be valuable to investigate further his hypothesis that Flavelle's "reaction to the war and post-war problems were not untypical of Canadian businessmen." Similarly, in Robert Craig Brown's essay on Borden, it is noted that "the historical record upon which we might base a sound judgment of Borden's leadership" is embarrassingly incomplete. One may hope that some postgraduate work can be directed toward filling these and other gaps.

The second work under review, *The Canadian Military: a Profile*, is a more coherent set of essays related to a central theme. Again, however, the editor points out that it is a beginning – in a field which has been neglected by Canadian scholars. The essays are very short, but well written, and could be of value in classroom work as well as stimulating further interest in the work of the authors and the subjects themselves. One would, for instance, like to see

Richard Preston's essay, "Military Influence on the Development of Canada," expanded so that the twentieth century received much more detailed treatment. Similarly, Denis Stairs' excellent chapter, "The Military as an Instrument of Canadian Foreign Policy," simply whets the appetite for more.

MARGARET DOXEY
Trent University

Gary Teeple, ed., **Capitalism and the National Question in Canada.** Toronto: University of Toronto Press, 1972, pp. xv, 256.

This collection of ten essays is the most important radical Canadian book to be published in many years. All but one of the essays were written especially for this volume by a group, formerly in the University League for Social Reform, who formed SPEC (Studies in the Political Economy of Canada) to "further the radical analysis of Canadian society." This collection is the first result of that effort. It will be especially welcomed by those who have been teaching Canadian politics from a radical perspective without any analytic literature to which students could be referred.

Much of the value of the collection as a whole rests on R.T. Naylor's long essay, "The Rise and Fall of the Third Commercial Empire of the St Lawrence," which describes the nature of capital in relation to the Canadian state. Distinguishing between industrial and commercial capital, Naylor examines Confederation and other questions of Canadian political development convincingly and comprehensively. His interpretation of the economic context of Confederation is an important advance on Creighton and Ryerson, neither of whom provide a satisfactory portrait of the Canadian bourgeoisie during the period 1846–66. Naylor postulates that "Canadian Confederation resulted not from a drive for independence led by a dynamic capitalist class but from the inability of the Canadian bourgeoisie to find a new dependency." In elaborating this view he constructs a treatment of Canadian political economy that should be essential reading for all students of Canadian politics.

An essay by Gary Teeple on land policy, and one on class by Leo Johnson, build on the foundation laid by Naylor. Teeple shows how concentration of land ownership blocked settlement and created a landless class of labourers who were forced either to emigrate to the US or to seek the charity of Canada's towns. A mercantile economy, based on exchange rather than production, was unable to absorb successive waves of immigrants; neither was there much opportunity on the land itself. Teeple integrates what we know about settlement with the basic analysis provided by Naylor, resulting in an impressive new treatment of the subject. Here, and throughout the collection, one is impressed with the tight fit achieved by the authors. The apparent reason for this unity of perspectives is that the group is Marxist; yet, one senses more – perhaps the effects of intensive round-table discussion of the problem posed by the title of the volume. Clearly, the essays were carefully planned to constitute a comprehensive and integrated picture of Canadian political economy.

Leo Johnson's exhortation on class is in the classic tradition of the self-righteous super-left. Readers with delicate stomachs are advised to omit the first four pages of his essay – wherein the sins of liberals, leftists, Marxists, and most of all, Canadian Marxists, are laid bare – and to go straight on to the analysis, which is surprisingly good, and full of new data. Still, the preachy tone may obscure the value of the discussion for many readers.

Three essays treat aspects of labour in politics. Roger Howard and Jack Scott review the interaction among Canadian labour organizations, government, business, and international unions in terms of "ideology" and "class collaboration." Their central argument is that the political culture or "ideology" of Canada's workers must be transformed if any organizational tactic, such as a break from American unions, is to be an effective part of an over-all strategy to transform Canadian society. Unfortunately, the authors neglect to develop a strong strategy for the task of transformation; they resort – predictably – to the weak role of "educators" for a coalition of the powerless. R.B. Morris describes the practical constraints on locals that wish to break away from American unions, including the "reverter clause," the fear of "disunity," loss of bargaining power, and the threat of raiding. The ideological basis of the breakaway movement is also discussed. Charles Lipton argues that genuine solidarity with American workers can only be achieved by Canadians who are *maîtres chez nous*; he also advocates national industrial unions, based on the traditional left-labour values of socialism and populism.

Marcel Rioux's "ethnic class" model of Quebec society is subject to extensive criticism in two essays. Gilles Bourque and Nicole Laurin-Frenette raise the bogey of idealism to exorcise Rioux's thesis, then explore the colonial situation of Quebec in terms of the dialectic it produces between class and nation. Although it is clear that the authors wish to refute Rioux, they achieve an elaboration of his position which strengthens, rather than demolishes. The discussion is hard to follow, probably as a result of bad translation (for example, what is "valorization of national aspects of the social formation," p. 190?). The practical thrust of the discussion is to dismiss the Parti Québécois as a "class project" of the technocratic bourgeoisie who wish to manage state monopolies and seek control of the state to this end. Although this is not new, it is well done and worth reading. Stanley Ryerson's essay is a disappointment. He misjudges the importance of biculturalism, wastes his time throwing tomatoes at other historians, and offers banal conclusions to a mediocre, fragmented treatment of class and nation in Quebec: we are exhorted not to "ignore" such earth-shattering "areas of contestation" as, "the penetration of the crises of class and nation-community by the issues of poisoning of the environment; cultural alienation and educational impasse; the revolt of youth; women's liberation; defence of democratic liberties ..." (p. 226). Is this the table of contents for the June edition of *Chatelaine*?

Three other essays should be mentioned. Agribusiness, corporate farming, and foreign ownership of farmland are the subject of an excellent piece by H.E. Bronson, and Gary Teeple's note on socialism and the CCF/NDP, although marred by a serious misunderstanding of Underhill, is equally good. The brief appendix by Naylor is another *coup*. He asks the question "why Social Credit in Alberta and CCF in Saskatchewan?" and answers it most persuasively in a mere five pages.

This excellent collection will stimulate much discussion and, it is hoped, further work along these lines in years to come.

THELMA OLIVER
Simon Fraser University

Malcolm Reid, **The Shouting Signpainters: A Literary and Political Account of Quebec Revolutionary Nationalism.** Toronto: McClelland and Stewart, 1972, pp. 315.

Richard Jones, **Community in Crisis: French Canadian Nationalism in Perspective.** Toronto: McClelland and Stewart, 1972, pp. xxii, 192.

Daniel Drache, ed., **Quebec – Only the Beginning: The Manifestoes of the Common Front.** Toronto: New Press, 1972, pp. xxviii, 272.

Robert Chodos and Nick Auf Der Maur, eds., **Quebec: A Chronicle, 1968–1972.** Toronto: James Lewis and Samuel, 1972, pp. v, 165.

If there had never been an October Crisis, one can wager there would be a lot less published in English Canada on Quebec. Pierre Vallieres' *White Niggers of America* was published in German translation several years before Toronto publishers noticed its existence. Malcolm Reid's examination of *Parti Pris* lay mouldering in a drawer until Quebec became a hot commodity after October 1970. Richard Jones' account of the roots of French Canadian nationalism, first published in 1966, has now been reissued in the Carleton Library. And the smaller publishing houses have not lagged behind, offering collections, translations, and analyses of Quebec in ever increasing numbers.

This attention paid to Quebec is, of course, long overdue, and is based on a perception of just how basic the national question that divides French from English Canada really is. But French-Canadian nationalism and even separatism are not new, and in their traditional linguistic or cultural guises would not evoke great interest in English Canada. What has suddenly made Quebec politics so explosive is the interplay of nationalism with class consciousness, in particular the consciousness of both French-Canadian middle and working class. It is this interplay, in a context of national-liberation movements and struggles in other corners of the globe, that so clearly sets Quebec off from the provinces of English Canada.

Richard Jones' *Community in Crisis* traces the development of a new middle class in Quebec which "includes the managerial and technocratic bureaucracies of industry and government." It was this new middle class which came to wage battle with Ottawa during the Quiet Revolution and which was the chief beneficiary of the latter's social and economic policies. To be sure, this new middle class had to contend with a more traditional middle class, alarmed at too rapid a rate of change, and with the labouring and farming classes of Quebec for whom, in the words of *Quebec – A Chronicle 1968–1972*, the Quiet Revolution was a failure. At still another level this new middle class was divided in the attitude it should take vis-à-vis Canada, some of its members leaning towards a revamped federalism, others towards outright independence for Quebec.

Jones, writing in 1966, is uncertain what the future of Quebec will hold. "I am no prophet ... I do not know what the final equilibrium between majority and minority will be." The Jones who writes after the October Crisis is a wiser man, "sincerely doubting whether it will ever be possible for English Canada and French Canada to reach some sort of harmonious existence." This is, in fact, the point of departure for Malcolm Reid's *The Shouting Signpainters.*

"I go down from my room in the centre of Montreal and turn east." So Reid begins an account which, in my opinion, is the most perceptive that has been written by an English Canadian on Quebec. What is so striking in Reid's book is the feel he has for the underlying ethnic cleavages in Quebec, which the Montreal poet A. M. Klein once described in a famous line: "The smell of race is in the air." More than that, Reid understands the class cleavages within Quebec society and how Quebec is a hinterland within a larger North American and world capitalist economy. Yet most interesting, indeed the principal merit of the book, is his attempt to analyse Quebec through its language, *joual*, and through its writers, in particular the group that wrote for the magazine *Parti Pris* in the early and middle 1960s.

Parti Pris was a very small magazine, yet just as *Cité Libre* was the vehicle for the development of the liberal ideas of Trudeau, Pelletier and company in the 1950s and early 1960s, so *Parti Pris* was the laboratory of those who were groping towards revolutionary nationalism and Marxism in the early 1960s. As such, it was a *microcosm* of that Quebec left which was to find expression in groupings as diverse as the Union générale des etudiants du Québec (UGEQ), the Movement de libération populaire, and in the early 1970s, the Marxist intellectuals of the Quebec labour movement. Though Reid's book could have done with tighter editing and with some revisions to take account of changes since the middle 1960s, it is a major study of the roots of left nationalism in Quebec.

The collection of articles in *Quebec – A Chronicle 1968–1972* is taken from *The Last Post*, which has been the best English-language journalistic source of information on Quebec in the last few years. The articles, however, are magazine, not book material, and for this reviewer at least, read better between the covers of *The Last Post.*

Finally, *Quebec – Only a Beginning* presents the manifestoes which were widely circulated within the CNTU, the CEQ and the QFL in Quebec in 1971–2. These documents are clear examples of indigenous Quebec Marxist analysis and are evidence of just how quickly Quebec labour became radicalized toward the end of the 1960s. (It is inconceivable that such documents would have been circulated within labour federations in English Canada.) The high points of labour militancy were the *La Presse* strike of 1971 and the general strike in the public service of spring 1972, the latter in particular, evoking the revolutionary syndicalism of earlier European history. Since May 1972, labour unity has been broken, and there may well be a return underway to the business unionism that characterized the Quebec trade-union movements in the early 1960s. Yet the traditions of Quebec labour, especially the CNTU, and the kind of consciousness to which the manifestoes of the common front bear witness, suggest that Quebec labour in the coming years will continue to be more combative and militant than labour elsewhere in North America.

The books under review speak to what, in a sense, has been the perpetual crisis Quebec has been living in since 1960. The question for the future is who is to be the beneficiary of Quebec's national and class awakening of recent years? The left, the centre, or the right? One wing or another of the petite bourgeoisie? The working class? *A suivre.*

PHILIP RESNICK
University of British Columbia

Robert Laird Borden, **Letters to Limbo.** Henry Borden, ed. Toronto: University of Toronto Press, 1971, pp. xii, 310.

Robert Laird Borden: His Memoirs projects the political man while *Letters to Limbo* reveals the whole man. Dictated to his secretary by Sir Robert Borden from 1933 until shortly before his death in 1937, these letters occasionally deal with political issues, such as repudiation by the Ontario government of Quebec power contracts, or discuss political personalities, such as Mitchell Hepburn ("In manners he is a boor, in vindictiveness a savage, and in veracity an Ananias"). However, for the most part they are concerned with reflections on non-political matters of a highly literate, sensitive, and intelligent gentleman.

In these letters are the comments of a perceptive man who had retired from politics, and who, perhaps, if he had been an Englishman instead of a Canadian could have expressed his thoughts in letters to *The Times* or perhaps in the House of Lords where he would no doubt have spent his last years. But being a Canadian, intensely Canadian, he was too conscious of the restraints he had imposed upon his own public utterances to encumber the press with these thoughts; yet he evidently felt the urge of a craftsman in words to express his thoughts and savour them in written form.

His telling comments upon his contemporaries reveal as much about his own standards and perceptiveness as about his subjects. It would be difficult to fault his assessments of R.B. Bennett "as a man of unbalanced and erratic brilliancy; arbitrary ... impulsive" but also a man of "complete devotion to public duty ... resourcefulness and fine courage," or of W.L. Mackenzie King as a man of "less intellectual brilliancy" but "he is more sure-footed than Bennett, a more adroit politician ...." Sir John Ewart, Sir George Foster, Herbert Asquith, David Lloyd George, King George the Fifth are among the prominent figures touched upon sympathetically yet revealingly. He could also be caustic in his remarks upon those who did not measure up to his standards such as a wartime chaplain whom he ticked off as "a self-centered, useless inefficient creature, heedless of his duty and bent solely on gaining higher rank and increased pay."

In a letter to limbo of 22 September 1934, Sir Robert reveals that John Gilman Foster was the close friend of W.L. Mackenzie King who had approached him during the negotiations on the establishment of Union government in 1917, "and assured him that Mr. King was quite prepared to enter Union government. Sir Robert had no doubt that this intimation came directly through Mr. Foster from Mr. King himself." Although both Mackenzie King in the House of Commons and R. MacGregor Dawson in the first volume of *William Lyon Mackenzie King* denied that King ever sought a place in the Union cabinet, there is a persuasive authenticity to Sir Robert's description of the episode.

Throughout the book his philosophic bent for conservatism is quite apparent as in his assertion that he had never been impressed with men's ability to forecast the future, in his recognition that while there are shortcomings and deficiences in the existing social order he preferred "advance by reasonable and gradual methods of the British type ..." or in his quoting of the adage that "Changes are Lightsome, and Fools Like Them." If, as Quintin Hogg has suggested, conservatives do not believe that politics is the most important thing in life, Sir Robert surely qualifies as a conservative, for instead of political affairs he is concerned "with the varying moods of nature, the spring-awakening of Mother Earth, the beauty of the first wildflowers, the lacery of the tree-tops in earliest Spring, the mystery of a cloud-continent as it floats below the morning star and above the dawn."

One hesitates to say that the real Sir Robert Borden has revealed himself in those broader dimensions of his life beyond politics through these Limbo Letters, for undoubtedly politics was a very real part of much of his life, but as Arthur Meighen commented in his introduction to *Robert Laird Borden: His Memoirs*, "though politics was in overwhelming degree his life work ... it was by no means the kind of life he wanted, and certainly not the kind of life he loved." It is this other side of his life, the non-political, which forms the substance of this book illustrating his delight in the world about him. His pleasures in life and awareness of nature manifest themselves in his essay on "Sunsets – in Ottawa and Elsewhere," in his almost compulsive need to describe the beauty of a sunrise, or in the graphic description of the world below during his first plane flight in 1933.

On a par with his love of nature was his appreciation of literature, aided and abetted by a remarkable memory which enabled him to quote at length his favourite poetry from memory. He revealed much about himself in commenting upon an old friend, "That a man of his intellectual force and brilliance should have no interest whatever in the glories of our English literature was inexplicable." Such was not the case with Sir Robert who in his Limbo Letters includes an *olla podrida* of poem titles and quotations for an anthology – all from memory, waxed enthusiastic over the "sheer beauty of thought and expression" of a newly discovered young poet, amazed R.B. Bennett with the diversity and quantity of books he had read, and expressed his pleasure in attending half a dozen plays in New York in April of 1936 and a few months later another dozen in London. Here is the urbane, literate, and witty Sir Robert Borden enjoying the theatre at the age of 82, no doubt with the same cosmopolitan zest he had displayed at his dinner party in the Hotel Majestic in Paris in 1919 when he requested that everyone converse together in French and that no English should be spoken that evening. And then there was the quiet humour of the man who enjoyed the practical joke or who could observe as he set off for a holiday in the midst of the 1935 election campaign that "Perhaps I should regret this absence as an unfortunate deprivation of opportunity for political activities. However, I shall endure it with great equanimity."

It must have been an exhilarating experience for a younger man who was so fortunate as to have known Sir Robert during this period of his life as did his nephew Henry Borden, who edited *Letters to Limbo.* One can issue few caveats on the editing, although on page 234 the editor has repeated a paragraph from one of Sir Robert's letters to John W. Dafoe which had already been quoted on pp. 219–220, but the careful editing confirms that for the editor his task was a "labour of love and token of respect and admiration for a great Canadian" as Henry Borden affirms in the foreword.

JOHN R. WILLIAMS
West Virginia University

Anthony Westell, **Paradox: Trudeau as Prime Minister.** Scarborough: Prentice-Hall, 1972, pp. ix, 262.

Pierre Elliott Trudeau, **Conversation with Canadians.** Toronto: University of Toronto Press, 1972, pp. vi, 214.

Mr. Westell's book, a product hurried to appear before the 1972 federal election, is a change from much journalistic writing on Canadian politics in that it centres as much on the policy issues of the first Trudeau term of office as on the personalities involved. The first two chapters are a lucid narrative of the unfolding of some key issues in federal-provincial relations from 1967 to 1971. Three other chapters, in a somewhat more introductory and abbreviated way, narrate federal government action on other policy problems under the rubrics "the economy," "the just society," and "foreign policy." Two chapters deal with how policy is made. The final chapter is a brief replay of the "FLQ Conspiracy of October 1970."

The author provides more than a review of this term of office, since his narrative is studded with assessments of the Trudeau performance. Most of them are sympathetic. If a theory of political leadership informs these assessments it appears to be the author's sympathy with the pragmatism and unideological approach of Mr Trudeau. Mr Trudeau "counts himself a pragmatist, a man who rows against the current of public opinion to avoid being swept over the falls of extremism. He steers by no compass of ideology ..." Except for a few rare exceptions, neither the views nor the presence of the other federal parties are seen. We are invited to judge the government's performance on the economy against the "troubled times" and "confusion" that preceded it. On the problem of inflation, the author finds the government's record not unsatisfactory given that there was no national "consensus" for wage and price controls. As for unemployment, the Trudeau record is not "out of line with Canadian experience." The federal government's efforts on constitutional reform, social policy, and poverty, if they do not escape criticism, are mostly seen as reflections of the vagaries and tensions of Canadian society at large.

In his discussion of the Trudeau way of making policy, Mr Westell sets out to debunk what he calls, the "myths" about the super-group of advisers, the downgrading of parliament and the arrogant "presidential" style of government. We are reminded of some of the salutary reforms of the House of Commons and of the Liberal caucus. He argues that the newly created cabinet committees and the new centres of influence in the Privy Council Office and the Prime Minitser's Office lead to a system of "checks and balances."

Mr Westell, of course, is not alone among journalists and political scientists in seeming to be temperamentally at odds – as is perhaps Mr Trudeau? – with what the author three times calls the "boring," "guerilla warfare" of Parliament. What distinguishes Mr Westell, however, is the respect, even awe, he reserves for the technical and administrative pragmatists, the mandarins. While we see MPs being "childish," we are shown public servants who "walk briskly," and are "fast-rising young men." Portraits of public servants are flatteringly limned. One is "precise and stylish," another "cool and competent," another is a "soft-talking pipesmoker, a hugely successful lawyer," another "a brilliant lawyer ... who left Harvard when he found it insufficiently challenging."

Conversations with Canadians, a compendium of photographs and of excerpts from Mr Trudeau's speeches is perhaps a good example of what this sort of stylish, cool pragmatism produces as an election booklet. With a few exceptions, the text is wooden, devoid of much metaphor, save those of technological change, dialogue and balance. The photography however provides some nice contrasts to the prose. The visually kinetic prime minister is dressed up as everything from a cool Marlborough man to a hugely successful maritime fisherman.

THOMAS A. HOCKIN
York University

Alain Touraine, **Le communisme utopique; le mouvement de mai 1968.** Paris : Editions du Seuil, 1972, 313 p.

Alain Touraine, **Université et société aux Etats-Unis.** Paris : Editions du Seuil, 1972, 301 p.

Pour comprendre et bénificier de la lecture de ces deux livres, il faut convenir avec l'auteur de l'importance prise dans les sociétés industriellement avancées par les problèmes universitaires, c'est-à-dire « par ceux qui sont liés au rôle de la connaissance dans le fonctionnement de la société, dans sa hiérarchisation, dans son système de pouvoir » (*Université*, p. 186). Il s'agit là pour Touraine d'un axiome fondamental sur lequel malheureusement il ne s'arrête guère. Tout au plus mentionne-t-il qu'en se massifiant, l'université « se lie de plus en plus aux besoins de l'appareil de production et forme .. ceux qui assureront les fonctions d'intégration et de manipulation sans lesquelles le système économique et social ne peut se développer » (*Communisme*, p. 17). Certes l'auteur démontre clairement la dépendance accentuée de l'université, surtout américaine, face aux centres de décision politique et économique mais on aurait souhaité qu'il s'attarde davantage à la relation inverse, c'est-à-dire à cette supposée dépendence des centres de décision envers les universités. En privilégiant l'université comme terrain d'éclosion des conflits sociaux, Touraine n'en arrive-t-il pas à accorder comme il le dit lui-même dans sa postface, « trop d'importance à l'université et aux conduites étudiantes » (*Communisme*, p. 290) ? En 1969–70 donc au plus fort de la contestation étudiante, un bref séjour à l'Université de Chicago m'a laissé l'impression que la classe dirigeante américaine accordait en fait beaucoup moins d'importance aux événements universitaires que les étudiants, administrateurs et professeurs se plaisaient à le croire. Il faut éviter de se leurrer sur l'impact réel de la contestation étudiante sur la conduite de la guerre du Vietnam. Quoi qu'en disent les propagandistes du Pentagone, la guerre n'a pas été perdue à cause de la contestation étudiante mais bien à cause de l'efficacité militaire du FLN et du Nord-Vietnam. De même la révolte étudiante française a certes contribué à immobiliser la France entière pendant cinq semaines mais en fin de compte elle a échoué dans son contre-projet révolutionnaire. Certes, il est toujours possible de transformer cet échec en un succès en se plaçant à un niveau d'analyse plus élevé, mais au niveau très concret et très immédiat de la lutte pour le pouvoir, celui d'ailleurs où se sont placés la majorité des acteurs, il y a eu échec. Echec d'autant plus révélateur des limites d'une contestation universitaire que cette contestation avait effectivement réussi à sortir du cadre étroit de l'université pour opérer une jonction, limitée certes, mais réelle tout de même, avec les revendications ouvrières.

On aurait aussi souhaité que l'auteur use d'un peu moins de globalisme dans sa description de ces sociétés industrielles avancées que sont les Etats-Unis et la France. Alors que l'on est peut-être encore en droit de parler de *la* société et *du* système universitaire français, un tel effort de globalisation est beaucoup plus périlleux dans le cas des Etats-Unis. Certes Touraine ne nie pas l'existence de clivages profonds au sein de la société américaine (noirs-blancs, est-ouest, pauvres-riches, nord-sud, hommes-femmes), mais il perçoit ces clivages comme partie intégrale d'un même système social et non pas comme les fondements de sociétés parallèles à la recherche de leur autonomie propre.

Ces critiques étant faites (puisque tout compte-rendu qui se respecte doit toujours comprendre une ou deux critiques) passons au contenu même de l'analyse de Touraine. Pour Touraine l'université remplit trois fonctions. A un premier niveau l'université contribue une fonction de *production* non seulement en accroissant le bagage scientifique et technologique, mais aussi en définissant les modèles scientifiques et les modèles culturels qui encadrent cette production. A un deuxième niveau, l'université remplit un rôle *d'adaptation* (ou d'intégration) dans la mesure où elle contribue à organiser et à contrôler les changements sociaux qui bouleversent la société. Finalement l'université joue un rôle de *reproduction* (ou de consolidation) dans la mesure où elle réussit à organiser et à interpréter la domination de la classe dirigeante et la dépendance des classes dominées. L'université contribue alors à définir et à maintenir un modèle idéologique qui facilite la reproduction des inégalités en les justifiant.

D'après Touraine, une des originalités majeures de l'université américaine fut de passer successivement d'une fonction d'adaptation à une fonction de reproduction et finalement à une fonction de production. Cette particularité de l'évolution historique des universités américaines explique le caractère particulier, notamment par rapport à la France, des crises qui vont secouter le système universitaire américain à partir de 1964.

Durant la période allant de 1850 à 1890

l'université américaine ne joue qu'un rôle secondaire au niveau de la production car la science et la technologie ne sont pas encore devenues les éléments moteurs du développement économique. Durant ces années l'université n'est liée que de façon intermittente aux classes économiques dirigeantes ou aux centres de décision politique. Mais même si l'université ne joue alors que très partiellement son rôle de reproduction idéologique, elle contribue néanmoins de façon importante à l'adaptation des nouvelles élites à une société nationale en voie de consolidation. Le rôle le plus important des universités et de leurs présidents est d'organiser le changement dans une société qui est à la fois une société de classes et une société ouverte, c'est-à-dire où le modèle culturel sans être complètement autonome n'est pas non plus monopolisé par la classe dirigeante.

Après cette première phase le système universitaire américain a été conduit à se soucier davantage de son fonctionnement interne que de ses relations avec le milieu social. Le thème de la culture générale prend alors le pas sur celui de la consolidation et de l'utilité sociale. Durant cette période l'université joue surtout un rôle de reproduction. Elle cesse d'être marquée par l'activisme de présidents comme Harper à Chicago, Eliot à Harvard ou Butler à Columbia. On n'y retrouve plus un souci de créations institutionnelles comme les Land-Grant Colleges ou d'innovations administratives telles la création des Graduate Schools et de départements. C'est plutôt une période de discussions sur les objectifs de l'éducation (élite ou masse) et d'expansion considérable des effectifs étudiants qui passent de 237,000 en 1900 à 1,494,200 en 1940. L'université ne se préoccupe pas de contribuer à inventer des modèles sociaux et culturels nouveaux comme elle l'a fait à la période précédente. Il s'agit pour elle de justifier et de reproduire l'ordre social qu'elle a elle-même contribué à établir. C'est l'époque de la génération silencieuse où très peu de voix discordantes se font entendre pour dénoncer une société satisfaite d'elle-même et qui en est venue à confondre ordre et progrès.

L'apparition et le développement accéléré de la recherche subventionnée va, à partir de 1940, modifier une fois de plus le rôle de l'université américaine. L'apport massif des fonds de recherches accentue la professionalisation des enseignants qui privilègient maintenant leur rôle de chercheur plutôt que celui d'éducateur. Etant donné le rôle central occupé par la science dans le développement économique et de la puissance politique, l'université se lie de plus en plus étroitement à l'Etat. Son rôle d'éducation et de socialisation diminue en même temps que faiblit sa capacité de décision autonome. Non contente d'adapter ou de reproduire l'ordre social l'université contribue maintenant directement à sa production. Ce rôle de production contribue à accroître l'opulence et l'éfficacité du système universitaire américain (40,000 PHD en 1970). Mais selon Touraine il ne faut pas se laisser aveugler par cette apparente richesse intellectuelle et matérielle. « L'université américaine n'est pas en cela différente des autres. Si elle est mieux organisée, plus riche de moyens et d'institutions, elle est aussi satisfaite de son propre discours et aussi indifférente à un examen sérieux de son rôle social et culturel » (*Université*, p. 178). Aux Etats-Unis comme en France souligne Touraine, l'absence d'une université critique conduit nécessairement à la critique de l'Université.

Touraine distingue dans la contestation étudiante quatre niveaux qui définissent les types de conduite et la nature de ce mouvement social. A un premier niveau il y a la contestation dirigée contre l'université en tant qu'*organisation*. Cette forme de contestation qui se nourrit à partir des problèmes de fonctionnement de l'université (horaires, examens, anomie, discipline) est surtout répandue dans les systèmes universitaires qui s'attachent à reproduire plutôt qu'à produire un ordre social et culturel. Dans les universités où le rôle de production est privilégié, c'est plutôt l'université en tant qu'*institution* qui est remise en question. C'est le système de décision et les règles du jeu universitaire qui sont ici attaquées et non plus seulement leurs aspects extérieurs. A un troisième niveau la contestation dépasse les problèmes organisationnels et institutionnels pour s'attaquer aux problèmes de *pouvoir*, c'est-à-dire à la capacité d'imposer un ordre social et culturel pré-déterminé. La contestation met ici directement en cause les rapports entre l'université et la société et ce au moyen d'une action à la fois défensive et offensive. L'action défensive « est celle qui en appelle à la liberté, à l'expression libre, aux droits de la personnalité contre l'emprise exercée par la machine universitaire placée au service de la techno-bureaucratie » (*Université*, p. 194). L'action offensive par contre vise à renverser le pouvoir de la classe dominante. Cette action offensive se tourne aussi contre le gouvernement universitaire pour faire apparaître clairement la vanité de son discours et sa soumission à la classe dominante. Finalement Touraine distingue aussi un quatrième niveau de contestation plus *culturel* que politique et qui s'adresse aux orientations collectives qui ne peuvent être définies au niveau de la lutte des classes. Se retrouvent ici les thèmes de la qualité de la vie, du respect de l'éco-système du refus de la consommation et de la révolution intérieure.

Le niveau et la forme que prend la contestation universitaire dépendent évidemment du rôle joué par le système universitaire et par le type de société dans lequel l'université est inscrite. C'est ce qui explique les différences importantes entre la contestation de l'université américaine et de l'université française.

En 1964–5 l'université américaine n'est pas en état de crise matérielle ou organisationnelle. Au contraire elle a su, grâce aux millions du gouvernement fédéral et de l'entreprise privée et grâce à d'incessantes initiatives, faire face aux nouveaux problèmes de la société industrielle et de l'éducation de masse. Les présidents des universités jouissent d'une grande capacité de décision tandis que les étudiants et les professeurs ont le sentiment d'appartenir à une institution et à un milieu. Si en 1965, l'université américaine est à son apogée, la société américaine par contre est en état de crise à cause des divisions que suscitent la guerre au Vietnam et les problèmes d'intégration raciale ainsi que l'apparition de la culture pop. D'après Touraine ces trois caractéristiques – richesse de l'université américaine, guerre du Vietnam et culture pop – contribuent à expliquer les trois différences majeures entre la contestation universitaire américaine et sa contrepartie française.

Le fait que les présidents d'université possèdent un haut degré d'autonomie et que les étudiants aient développé un sentiment d'appartenance face à leur institution explique l'importance des problèmes strictement universitaires dans la contestation américaine. Les questions qui touchent à l'organisation et à l'institution ne sont jamais absentes d'une contestation qui se veut aussi une lutte pour le pouvoir et un mouvement culturel. En France par contre la crise organisationnelle aigüe de l'université et le fait que les étudiants n'appartiennent que nominalement à une institution qui est avant tout défini comme une « machine-à-cours » encourage la séparation des problèmes strictement universitaires des problèmes politiques externes. Dans une situation où le système universitaire n'a guère d'autonomie la volonté des étudiants et des enseignants de participer à la gestion de l'institution est immédiatement transformée en confrontation brutale avec le système politique. Aux Etats-Unis les institutions universitaires sont des milieux assez flexibles pour que la contestation puisse s'y développer sans les briser. En France cela s'avéra impossible.

Une deuxième différence entre la contestation universitaire américaine et française réside dans la relation qui s'établit entre la dimension offensive et la dimension défensive de la lutte pour le pouvoir. L'existence d'une crise politique générale dont l'importance dépasse les problèmes internes à l'organisation favorise habituellement un faible degré d'intégration entre l'élite revendicative préoccupée d'action offensive et la masse étudiante ou prolétarienne plus intéressée par une action de type défensif. Ainsi aux Etats-Unis l'état de crise alimenté par les revendications du mouvement noir et par l'opposition à l'aventure vietnamienne tendit à produire un faible degré d'intégration entre d'une part les activités des groupes radicaux en lutte contre le pouvoir politique et son allié universitaire et d'autre part le mouvement de solidarité avec les victimes de ce système, c'est-à-dire les noirs, les jeunes et les étudiants. En France par contre la distance entre les deux faces du mouvement fut plus faible à cause de l'absence de ces grands conflits extérieurs au mouvement étudiant qui en vient à se définir comme un détonnateur de luttes sociales plus générales.

Finalement la rapidité de la pénétration de la culture pop aux Etats-Unis comparée à sa lente pénétration en France explique la séparation qui s'est faite aux Etats-Unis entre l'aspect politique et l'aspect plus culturel de la revendication. L'étudiant français d'après Touraine est beaucoup plus soumis que son confrère américaine à la discipline familiale. Il est plus dépendent culturellement. Il aura donc moins tendance à participer à des mouvements strictement culturels (drogue, musique, communes).

En résumé Touraine suggère que « la crise organisationnelle et la rigidité institutionnelle favorisent la formation d'un mouvement de portée générale, orienté vers l'extérieur, fortement coupé des problèmes universitaires, mouvement où l'idéologie joue un grand rôle, mais qui a peu de chances de pouvoir organiser une action de longue durée dans l'université. Au contraire la situation américaine est telle que le mouvement est fortement lié aux problèmes intérieurs de l'université, mais qu'il éclate lorsqu'il sort de ces limites, éclatement qui renforce (et est renforcé par) l'autonomie de la révolte culturelle » (*Université*, p. 203).

Ce sont là les grands traits de l'analyse de Touraine. Certes il y aurait encore beaucoup à dire sur une analyse que l'on peut sans exagération qualifier de magistrale. Mais par delà la contribution de Touraine à notre compréhension des dynamismes internes de la société post-industrielle, il est un autre aspect qui retient encore plus notre attention soit le témoignage que nous livre Touraine sur sa conception de l'université et du métier de sociologue. Il refuse la dichotomie combien artificielle entre l'activité de recherche et l'action sociale. Il suggère plutôt que « ceux qui ne parlent que de l'essence de l'université et des principes qui fondent l'existence de toute université ne sont pas des réformistes, mais des contre-révolutionnaires. Ceux qui ne veulent voir dans l'université qu'une arme à utiliser pour abattre l'ordre social dominant ne sont pas des révolutionnaires, mais des terroristes » (*Communisme*, p. 272). Si l'université veut continuer à survivre elle doit réussir à intégrer cette double action : critique politique générale et production scientifique. Il s'agit de savoir si l'activité scientifique et pédagogique d'une part et l'activité politique de l'autre réussiront à coexister sans rupture violente et même en interaction constante. Cette nécessaire coexistence définit le rôle du sociologue et de tout chercheur. Son travail consiste par définition « à sortir de la conscience des acteurs et à saisir des rapport sociaux, non des intentions ». A ce titre c'est en « vérifiant des hypothèses qu'il peut être encouragé dans son travail, non pas en étant accepté par les acteurs » (*Communisme*, p. 303). Ce travail de vérification d'hypothèses déplaira nécessairement aux acteurs qu'ils cherchent à maintenir ou à détruire l'ordre établi. La position du chercheur est donc nécessairement inconfortable.

L'œuvre de Touraine est la preuve combien accablante qu'il est possible de faire avancer le combat social tout en faisant œuvre scientifique. Les références, bibliographies, « footnotes » et tout l'appareillage de la démarche scientifique ne sont pas, comme voudraient nous le faire croire plusieurs, les valets de l'ordre établi. Au contraire ...

DANIEL LATOUCHE
Université McGill et
Université du Québec à Montréal

Yvon Bourdet, **Figures de Lukacs.** Paris : Anthropos, 1972, 222 p.

Il convient d'emblée de féliciter Yvon Bourdet d'avoir écrit cet ouvrage. La série d'essais par lesquels il essaie de cerner la pensée et la personnalité de Georges Lukacs témoigne du pluralisme du marxisme. On a trop tendance – et cela me semble particulièrement le cas au Québec où on l'a découvert tardivement – de réduire le marxisme à un certain léninisme. On se prive ainsi des riches recherches d'autres écoles, dont les théoriciens ont eu le malheur d'appartenir à des partis ou à des tendances écrasés par le fascisme ou le stalinisme. On donne ainsi raison à Machiavel, mais certes pas à Marx.

Lukacs est intéressant à divers points de vue. Tout d'abord, son assimilation de la culture marxiste fut précédée d'une éducation universitaire au cours de laquelle il subit l'influence de Dilthey, de Georges Simmel, de Max Weber, de Kierkegaard, de Hegel, de Fichte, de Bergson et de Georges Sorel. Ensuite, son long séjour à Vienne de 1919 à 1930 le mit en contact avec une autre école du marxisme, particulièrement riche en penseurs originaux : l'auxtro-marxisme. Enfin, Lukacs illustre par ses écrits d'après 1929, le triste sort des penseurs communistes aux prises avec Staline : ou ruser comme le fit Lukacs en se soumettant à des autocritiques non sincères et en se réfugiant dans la critique littéraire ou subir le sort des Bela Kun, Boukharine et autres Radek.

En scrutant en quatre essais l'œuvre de Lukacs, Bourdet l'éclaire sous divers angles, ce qui permet d'en restituer la richesse. L'œuvre de Lukacs ne se réduit pas à « Histoire et conscience de classe », même si cet ouvrage est sa contribution la plus importante au marxisme. Lukacs lui-même n'y voyait qu'un jalon dans son cheminement de Hegel à Marx. Son analyse de l'aliénation, par exemple, dans « Histoire et conscience de classe » fut sérieusement corrigée par Lukacs dans des écrits ultérieurs. D'un point de vue hégélien métaphysique, il passa à une analyse marxienne de l'aliénation fondée sur l'exploitation de l'ouvrier dans et par son travail.

Examinons de plus près les quatre essais. Le premier traite du « marxisme du Lukacs » en général. Yvon Bourdet, après avoir décrit le chemin de Lukacs vers Marx, montre la complexité du « marxisme de Lukacs ». Déjà les œuvres publiées présentent des contradictions dues d'une part à l'évolution de Lukacs et d'autre part à ses autocritiques de la période stalienne où se mêlent critiques véritables et critiques non sincères pour sauver sa vie. Mais, en plus il y a les œuvres non publiées, sans compter celles que l'auteur n'a pas pu écrire à cause de la terreur. Il n'est pas ridicule d'évoquer ces écrits cachés ou rentrés, car les interviews données par Lukacs vers la fin de sa vie, dont l'un précisément à Bourdet, ouvrent des aperçus sur ce corpus caché ou tué de l'œuvre de Lukacs. L'orientation générale, sur laquelle il n'a pas varié de 1919 à sa mort, est sa conception du marxisme en tant que méthode. « Le marxisme orthodoxe, écrit-il en 1919 et confirme en 1967, ne signifie donc pas une « foi » en une thèse ou en une autre, ni l'exégèse d'un livre « sacré ». L'orthodoxie en matière de marxisme se réfère bien au contraire et exclusivement *à la « méthode »*. Et il va jusqu'à affirmer dans ce texte que, même si les généralisations ou lois formulées par Marx s'avéraient erronnées par la critique scientifique contemporaine, resterait l'essentiel de l'œuvre de Marx, c'est-à-dire sa méthode. A ce propos, il est assez révélateur que, lorsque Marx nous éclaire sur sa méthode, comme par exemple dans sa préface à la première édition allemande du « Capital » (1867), il la présente comme *la* méthode scientifique, soumettant son œuvre aux mêmes exigences et donc à la même critique que celle du physicien !

Le deuxième essai de Bourdet porte sur le séjour à Vienne de Lukacs et donc de ses rapports avec l'auxtromarxisme. Notons tout d'abord que l'auxtromarxisme ne se réduit pas au néo-kantisme comme l'affirme péremptoirement Althusser (Lire le Capital, Maspero, 1968, p. 92). Lukacs lui-même montre la différence entre le néo-kantisme de Max Adler et l'œuvre d'Otto Bauer. Le long séjour à Vienne de 1919 à 1930, soit entre 35 et 45 ans, est la période la plus productive de la vie de Lukacs. C'est alors, entre autres, que fut publié en 1923 *Histoire et conscience de classe*. Lukacs évolue durant cette période de l'ultra-gauchisme à une position que Bourdet qualifie à juste titre de proche de l'auxtromarxisme. En effet, « De la question de l'organisation des intellectuels » (1920) est spontanéiste et « De la question du parlementarisme » (1920) est qualifié par Lénine, dans une vive critique, de « très gauchiste » puisque Lukacs s'oppose « à la participation au parlement bourgeois. ». Les « Thèses-Blum » (1928) – Blum étant le pseudonyme de Lukacs – sont un projet de programme pour le IIème Congrès du parti communiste hongrois. Contrairement à la tactique stalinienne de l'époque de « classe contre classe », qui considérait les sociaux-démocrates comme les frères-jumeaux des fascistes, Lukacs prétend que toutes les forces de gauche doivent combattre ensemble et que la démocratie bourgeoise, loin d'être un régime équivalent au fascisme est « le meilleur champ de bataille pour le prolétariat ». Bourdet rapproche avec justesse cette position de celle prise par Engels dans la préface des *Luttes de classe en France* et par Otto Bauer lui-même. On peut envisager donc, sinon une influence des auxtromarxistes sur Lukacs, en tout cas une similitude d'analyse des voies et moyens du mouvement ouvrier. Il faut noter que Lukacs, après avoir critiqué les « thèses-Blum » pour éviter l'exclusion, les a réhabilitées en 1956.

Le troisième essai est une étude approfondie du personnage de Naphta dans *La Montagne magique* de Thomas Mann. Même si Lukacs a refusé de se reconnaître dans ce personnage, prototype du stalinien avant la lettre, Bourdet démontre avec brio qu'il n'y a aucun doute possible : Lukacs et Naphta, logés ironiquement chez un tailleur nommé Lukacek, ne font qu'un. Naphta est un jésuite, mais un jésuite qui justifie la dictature du prolétariat. En fait sous le déguisement littéraire du prêtre se cache le militant fanatique ultra-gauchiste qu'était Lukacs à l'époque à laquelle Thomas Mann l'a rencontré à Vienne, soit en 1922. Naphta conçoit la dictature du prolétariat comme violente et sanglante, privatrice de libertés. Tout lui est subordonné. Or, la dictature du prolétariat ne s'incarne pour Lukacs qu'en Russie. Bourdet y voit une justification du stalinisme avant la lettre. D'ailleurs, pour Bourdet il n'y a pas de coupure entre les conceptions léniniste et staliniste car, à partir du moment où la conscience du prolétariat s'incarne dans une avant-garde de révolutionnaires professionnels, ceux-ci se coupent du reste de la société qui est réduite à l'exécution des tâches. Le retour à Lénine, que Lukacs a préconisé dans les dernières années de sa vie, ne mène à rien. En quoi, en effet, Lénine se différencie-t-il de Staline ? Par le fait qu'il est un dirigeant qui reste à l'écoute des masses. Ainsi donc la critique du stalinisme reste au niveau du « testament » de Lénine, qui n'est rien d'autre qu'une critique des personnalités de ces éventuels successeurs. Le bon fonctionnement du régime dépendrait donc des qualités des dirigeants. Il n'a rien de marxien dans tout cela. C'est de plus, d'une pauvreté théorique affligeante ! Bourdet voit, au contraire, dans le stalinisme un substitut à la théorie marxienne après l'échec de la révolution prolétarienne dans les pays industriels, qui a empêche la réalisation d'une société sans classe en Russie.

Le dernier essai est constitué par une interview de Lukacs par Yvon Bourdet, le 16 avril 1971, soit peu de temps avant sa mort. Lukacs y porte un jugement nuancé sur l'auxtromarxisme, louant l'ouverture d'Otto Bauer et l'intelligence et la cohérence de Karl Renner, tout en critiquant son opportunisme ainsi que le kantisme de Max Adler. Dans une critique de la bureaucratie des pays communistes, Lukacs montre le contraste entre les sciences liées aux techniques de guerre qui bénéficient de la liberté scientifique et les sciences humaines où la recherche est limitée aux « intérêts momentanés de la société ». Lukacs prévoit d'autres révoltes ouvrières dans les pays de l'est et ne voit le salut que dans un retour aux soviets de 1917. La critique de la bureaucratie par Trotski n'est la critique que d'un autre bureaucrate pas plus démocrate que Staline. Lukacs reprend également dans cette interview la critique du stalinisme par la personnalité. Enfin, il souligne l'importance de l'éthique dans l'œuvre de Marx et insiste, dans ces dernières paroles que, selon Marx, « la véritable science, au fond, c'est la science de l'histoire ».

L'ouvrage de Bourdet est très riche. A propos de l'œuvre de Lukacs, il discute des questions fondamentales du marxisme. Il invite ainsi à relire dans une autre optique que le léninisme, les classiques du mouvement ouvrier. Il nous rappelle aussi par la plume de Lukacs que, contrairement à nombre de ses prétendus disciples, Marx n'était pas mû par des sentiments (haine du capitalisme) mais faisait confiance à la méthode scientifique.

André P. Donneur
Université du Québec à Montréal

David V.J. Bell, **Resistance and Revolution.** Boston: Houghton Mifflin, 1973, pp. x, 164.

The theory of resistance against established authority, which flourished in the Middle Ages amid the struggle of church and state, has fared none too well since that time. The modern state is Hobbesian to the core: "Right" and "justice" are defined exclusively by secular law, and those who decide to "appeal to Heaven" against it must have something more potent than prayer books in their hands. From the viewpoint of the state, all resistance to authority is by definition a matter of individual or collective psychopathology. Yet the plain facts of contemporary history have compelled governments and social scientists alike to take a serious look at the problems of resistance and rebellion.

David Bell contends that the approaches developed so far have missed the *political* meaning of these events. Unlike social psychology and sociology, political science must take into account the normative dimension – embedded in the tradition of political theory – in which attempts at a rational justification for resistance have been made. The chief value of his book in his insistence that the normative and empirical treatments of this subject must be taken together. Thus to the familiar paraphernalia of the latter – typologies, "systems" interpretations, genera and species, paradigms, and operationalization of categories – he adds a brief historical account of the justifications for resistance.

I think that Bell's approach is both important and correct, but I am not sure that his exposition will please either the political philosophers or those committed to empirical analysis. The former will probably find that he dismisses their essential concerns too quickly, for example in characterizing the question of freedom as speculative and metaphysical. And the latter might well reply that a successful predictive model of the conditions under which revolutions occur would enable them to treat all justifications for resistance *as if* they were epiphenomena.

In the structure of his argument Bell rightly utilizes Barrington Moore's contrast between revolutionary violence and the "normal" everyday violence of established societies. Not so fortunate is his desire to see revolution as an expression of political "instability" or "failure," for the implicit premise – that politics can and should be the realm where social contradictions are reconciled (see Hegel's theory of the state) – is undefended. Likewise his attempt to classify revolution as a form of "internal war" is not argued rigorously (for example, the curt dismissal of Arendt's position): could this classification enable us to distinguish the Chinese revolutionary movement from European fascism?

One omission in the discussion is surprising in view of the author's repeated references to the war in Vietnam – namely the soldier's *obligation* to resist illegal orders that is grounded in the law of war crimes. This is not yet a really effective principle, although many persons may have chosen other forms of resistance (desertion or draft evasion) in awareness of the dilemmas which it poses; in any event it may become a crucial feature of the theory and practice of resistance.

William Leiss
University of Saskatchewan, Regina Campus

Ellen Meiksins Wood, **Mind and Politics: An Approach to the Meaning of Liberal and Socialist Individualism.** Berkeley, Calif.: University of California Press, 1972, pp. 185.

Ellen Meiksins Wood has found still another route through which an attack on the basic theoretical and methodological assumptions of contemporary political science can be made. While it is a somewhat oblique and at times obscure route, the case is well made and presented in a fashion which will be interesting to those who can still remember the ground rules of what Michael Oakeshott has called the philosophic mode.

Basically, the author has taken the problem – so familiar to students of political theory – of the relationships between a theorist's epistemology, his conception of human nature, and his conception of the relationship between the individual and society. At the very root of the argument is the centuries-old problem of whether we are "by nature" social beings or whether it is possible to be human outside of and without society. The author seems to feel that her unique contribution to this discussion is her insistence that we concentrate on the way basic assumptions found in social and political thought about the nature of man and his relationship with society depend on a theorist's epistemology. In fact, she also suggests that a theorist's *choice* of an epistemological position may well *depend* on his views about the nature of the human mind and his wider views about human nature; that is, she states that "theories of mind and cognition are themselves *political* statements."

The particular focus of the approach is the difference so often raised in social science between *action* and *behaviour.* The author attempts to demonstrate that the liberal assumptions that the individual and society are opposed and that the interests and good of the individual are in conflict with the interests and good of society depend ultimately on the empiricist theory of mind and cognition which originates with Locke and in which the mind is seen as a *passive* entity through which natural forces work to produce responses or behaviour. Set in opposition to this is the socialist and "radical" (Rousseauean) liberal conception of the interdependence of individual and society, in which the individual can be neither truly human nor free without society. This alternate conception, the author maintains, depends on an alternate theory of mind and cognition originated by Kant, in which the human mind is seen as an active and creative agent rather than a passive vessel. The author clearly supports this alternative conception of human nature with its implications for social and political thought. She is, therefore, led to argue that the alternative epistemology which supports it is also superior. The basic weakness of the book is revealed at this point. Since the author still seems to view theories of mind and cognition as philosophical problems, she has no real option but to *discuss* the reasonableness of the alternative epistemology originated by Kant. She leaves no doubt in the reader's mind that she considers scientific evidence about human nature and about the nature of mind and cognition to be of limited value – "In the final analysis, ..., we are left with our own perceptions, our own introspection, our own experience of ourselves through which we must interpret our data." In the development of her argument she presents the views of only one psychologist (Piaget) and mentions in passing Noam Chomsky's support for the alternative she prefers.

Certainly in the past theories of mind and cognition were fully within the sphere of philosophy and, one might add, contributed as much to discussions of what human nature *should be like* as they did to discussions of what human nature is like. The author largely ignores the fact that the epistemologies with which she deals contained a strong normative element. She also ignores the fact that knowledge grows by *removing* problems from the philosophical to the scientific disciplines. As a result, the argument is often rather oldfashioned and limited especially in the context of her final question of whether a science of politics should not be concerned with purposeful action (that is, be a moral "science") rather than be a natural science dealing with behaviour. There is little doubt that there is still a role for philosophical discussion concerning what man could be like and what he should be like and that these questions involve both epistemological speculation and elements of a moral science. It is unlikely, however, that a *purely* philosophical approach can contribute a great deal to our knowledge about how man's mind actually operates. Despite these flaws, this book is a useful contribution to the study of political thought and, since the political theories dealt with continue to exist as bases for interpretation and action in the world, it is also useful as part of the on-going process of understanding contemporary political life.

J. McCALLA VICKERS
Carleton University

Louis J. Halle, **The Ideological Imagination.** Chicago: Quadrangle [Toronto: Burns and MacEachern], 1972, pp. xiv, 174.

The intellectual core of Halle's essay is common sense. The ability "to judge of things self-evident," as Thomas Reid (1785) called it, is both a strength and a weakness in the study of political things. The strength of common sense is its ability to inoculate against ideological phantasy; its weakness is that politics is not exhausted by phenomenal externality.

Self-evident appearance is, nevertheless, one of the dimensions of both texts and acts. Marx, Halle argues, eclipsed the evident plurality of men by the abstract notion of a single, huge actor (*Capital* I: 1:4). When the real men who embodied the attributes of the proletariat, namely the European industrial labourers, failed to perform in accord with Marx's recipe, they were displaced by a more recondite term, "the people," on whose behalf revolutionary intellectuals, such as Lenin, presumed to speak. It is refreshing to see an event such as the Russian Revolution called a Bolshevik *coup d'état*: no attempt is made to transfigure phenomena by grinding empirical events through the gears of dialectics. Now, there is nothing necessarily insightful in a refusal to mutilate history, and it is refreshing only because there are so many unskilled intellectual butchers around. In some provinces of the intellect, however, common sense is as tedious as convention and Halle, unable to move beyond either, dutifully announces the commonplace: continental idealism is contrasted with Anglo-Saxon pragmatism and is found wanting; liberals are forever being compared to totalitarians, prudent businessmen to pesky intellectuals. Soon enough we reach the limit to common sense.

Common sense is a limited hermeneutic as well. Rousseau is turned into a romantic totalitarian: his admiration for Lycurgus and Calvin as founders of political regimes is turned into an apologia for Calvin's execution of Michel Servetus much as Machiavelli's discussion of the role of an *ordinatore* has been turned into the perverse principle that the end justifies the means. On the basis of *Die Judenfrage* and a famous misquotation, Marx is suspected of being an anti-Semite with a tragic vision comparable to Aeschylus. We are treated, once more, to the preposterous opinion that Plato may have been a proto-fascist and that Socrates was an agnostic. Other curiosities include the comparison of the Catholic Church to the Masons, the information that Darwin's teaching has made the Genesis myth obsolete and that Halle's knowledge of the universe, that it is 10^{23} kilometres across, has made "what Moses thought" obsolete. More broadly, he says: "Ontological thinking appears not to have caught up with the implications either of evolution or cosmology."

Such a pronouncement is not simply nonsense; it is an expression of faith in the progress of mankind. The "metaphysics" of progress is found in the uncritical opinion that knowledge of the world of phenomena, such as the size of the universe, has an impact on our awareness of our existential participation in being, such as is expressed in the creation story. Amusement at Halle's apparently benign simplicity ends when we read the not-at-all benign conclusions he draws. Because all knowledge is "progressive" no one has a right to claim the truth. Toleration is not a pragmatic compromise but a theoretical principle in the absence of which progress would not be possible. The assumption that sustains the inherently progressive market-place of ideas is that an unseen hand mysteriously sifts correct from stupid opinion. *The* political good, therefore, is the maintenance of what Halle calls "the rules of the game." A *reductio ad Hitlerium* disposes of governmental cheating: it will always be self-evidently anti-liberal. He is coy when it comes to citizen action in the face of less blatant cheating, to say nothing of occasional failures of the unseen hand that result in stupid policy. Halle's example may be illustrative, however. The prudent businessman and the former official in the American Department of State agree that international affairs is a highly complex matter; unlike "the rank and file of intellectuals" who have the regrettable habit of introducing disturbing questions of right and wrong into an otherwise genial and edifying discourse, they know the wisdom of circumstance. "It is significant," Halle says, "that on such issues as arouse public passion, like the American government's decision to intervene in Cambodia in May 1970, free discussion may not be possible on university campuses, where only one position is tolerated, while it continues elsewhere." A common-sense judgment of the Cambodian "intervention" might have been, as Hans Morgenthau suggested recently, to invite Halle to consult a map and observe that the Pacific Ocean stretches between San Francisco and the threat in Hanoi.

What the critical reader can learn from Halle's essay is the following: however indispensable common sense may be for the conduct of politics, in the absence of a genuine, noetic understanding of right and wrong, in the absence of what Kant called the need to think, common sense is indistinguishable from a conventionalist and self-serving justification of existing conditions. The thoughtless discipline of necessity, which surfaces periodically in Halle's essay, suggests that his Hegelian epigraph, which declared his purpose to be both to aid us in understanding what is and to help us ensure it, will do no more than assist his congenial businessmen to endure the sufferings of Cambodians by understanding, like Hegel, the higher imperatives of progress.

BARRY COOPER
York University

Eugene J. Meehan, **The Foundations of Political Analysis: Empirical and Normative.** Georgetown, Ontario: Irwin-Dorsey, 1971, pp. xii, 274.

As Professor Meehan recognizes, "methodological materials have flooded the market in the decade beginning about 1960" (p. 258). Meehan's own contributions to these high waters have not been insubstantial, for this is his fourth methodological book, all from Dorsey.

We are told that this book is aimed at not only political scientists but also social scientists in general (p. 3). Moreover, the methodology which he proposes is not to be limited to the knowing of politics, it is also to be used in the "doing of politics" (p. 4). The basic methodological issue joined by Meehan is one of epistemology, an issue impinging on both knowing and doing.

This epistemology takes as its first tenet the rejection of "the rigid separation of empirical and normative inquiry" because the "focus is on coping with the environment" (p. 1). By "coping" is meant the fulfilment of our utilitarian goals through the use of instruments. Our goals are the normative aspect, our instruments the empirical.

The purpose of inquiry is to enhance human control over the environment (p. 6). Control is enhanced by scientific theories, which Meehan chooses to call explanations (p. 86), and is exercised according to our value judgments. Our values determine what explanations are sought and provide the criteria for the satisfaction of our goals. The resulting explanations in turn stimulate or discourage the pursuit of one item rather than another. Thus, explanations and values are inseparable.

To Meehan's mind explanations and value judgments are not statements about reality, for neither can be directly deduced from or tested against the external world (p. 34). Even the most basic empirical reference is mediated by intellectual concepts before it can be understood and employed. For Meehan these mediating concepts are value judgments (p. 53). Neither explanations nor value judgments are true or false (p. 143). They are alike in being produced by and tested against human purposes and uses (p. 211). This is Meehan's epistemology, instrumentalism.

Where ends are given, Meehan would analyse competing arguments about means. It is undeniably true that normative arguments involve values (the ends) and facts (the means). It is no less true that most political, as opposed to administrative, arguments are about ends, not means. Once ends are stated in any detail this becomes quickly apparent. Certainly Meehan's own basic value of human needs would become more controversial were it formulated in more detail (p. 141). Nor is it always possible for means and ends to be distinguished. For example, which is democracy – an end or a mean? Problems of these sorts are not to be alleviated by the cost-benefit accounting proposed by Meehan (p. 191). Such analysis can only occur after the fundamental questions, such as what constitutes a "need" or an "end," have been settled. However, were these questions answered it would be doubtful that an elaborate method such as Meehan's would be needed any longer.

Although Meehan consciously disavows the mainstream of philosophy of science (p. 1), his epistemology returns to the very headwaters of those currents. His is an attempt to offer a method "in accord with the actual practice of natural science," as Norton Long writes in the foreword (p. vi). Meehan would force all natural science into the Procrustean bed of instrumentalism, which is contrary to much evidence and argument set out in a large body of philosophy, sociology, and psychology of science literature. Meehan's account of the actual practice of science is in some important ways the antiquated "unity of science" doctrine stood on its head. For Meehan all science is unified methodologically in being instrumentalist, as opposed to being unified by a common reality, which was the belief of the doctrine's original advocates.

As the book draws to a close we are told that political science has produced little of use to date because of the purposelessness of its practitioners (p. 244). Without goals success cannot be expected in the instrumentalist activity of inquiry. Eager to rectify the dilemma he perceives, Meehan proposes that the goal of political science should be to change the world (p. 245). This is admirable to be sure, but Meehan would apparently have us change the world even though we are ignorant of it.

This book is indeed unconventional, but not always in the manner intended by the author, for it is also marred by any number of seeming contradictions. For instance, first we read that "there are no formal procedures for ... testing explanations" (p. 64), then that "every explanation must be testable in principle" (p. 70). Then again, Meehan repeatedly calls for reasoned criticism and judgment (p. 1), while dismissing most of philosophy and political science as rot produced by dullards (p. 15).

It is difficult to determine what audience might find a book such as this useful. It would be unsatisfactory as a text because of the nearly complete absence of specific references to other writers and perspectives. The resulting one-dimensional landscape would be misleading to the beginning student. While Meehan feels much embattled, no names of his real or imagined enemies are named nor are their arguments taken up in their original formulations. Such vagueness cannot but impede learning. Mature students could find it a useful reference for some purposes, especially for the instrumentalist position. However, for these purposes the index is not as helpful as might be wished; a problem much compounded by the very personalized vocabulary upon which Meehan insists. Finally, the bibliographic essay with which the book ends is set out without any hint of the criteria by which it was selected. As it stands it presents a confusing array of sources with no visible unification.

M.W. Jackson
University of Alberta

Carl J. Friedrich, **Tradition and Authority.** London: Macmillan [Toronto: Macmillan], 1972, pp. 144.

P. H. Partridge, **Consent and Consensus.** London: Macmillan [Toronto: Macmillan], 1971, pp. 165.

Leonard Schapiro, **Totalitarianism.** London: Macmillan [Toronto: Macmillan], 1972, pp. 144.

The three books under review are contributions to Macmillan's "Key Concepts of Political Science" series, the inspiration of which, according to series editor Leonard Schapiro, is the belief that "all of us who are students of politics ... will be the better for knowing precisely what we mean when we use a common political term." Throughout the series some writers have pursued the goal with signally more success than others. Schapiro also notes that it was "very far from the minds" of those involved in organizing the series to try to impose any pattern on the authors. The diversity of approach displays itself in these books.

Friedrich's *Tradition and Authority* is the least satisfactory. His is the stipulative method. He advances an interesting definition of authority – "What makes a particular course of action authoritative, that is to say, vested with authority, is that convincing reasons may be offered in support of it" – and then proceeds to investigate other writers and schools of thought by the criterion of whether they have used the word in his particular sense. This approach is clearly revealed in his treatment of anarchism when he writes: "it remains to repeat that the anarchist challenge to authority either rested upon a misunderstanding of the true nature of authority, *which the anarchist themselves recognized under another name as based upon reason*, or it became self-defeating" (my italics).

In terms of the aim of the series little is gained by such dogmatism. Friedrich, rather than analysing a concept, is arguing for the adoption of his version of tradition and of authority in both political discourse and political practice. However desirable this might prove to practice, in intellectual history it is bound to have a distorting effect.

There are a number of flaws in the book. Friedrich should have taken more care in the use of some of his terms. For example at one point he argues that "traditionalism" is rightly used as a pejorative term (p. 21), yet at another he lauds Burke as "the great traditionalist" (p. 119). There are a few minor factual errors, but more seriously there is a systematic carelessness of style which often produces needless ambiguity. It is also surprising that Friedrich could have written a book dealing with tradition without once mentioning Michael Oakeshott, the modern writer who has thought most clearly about its value.

P.H. Partridge's *Consent and Consensus* is the more valuable for being less ambitious. Partridge is writing in what might be called the analytical tradition, and his book reveals a great treasure of possible confusion under the apparently simple notion of consent. For example, consent can (1) involve acquiescence under duress, (2) be connected with the manipulation of minds, (3) arise from sheer apathy, indifference, or habit, (4) arise from traditional behaviour, (5) stem from the processes, some of them unconscious, that sociologists call "socialization," (6) follow on the granting of permission, and (7) mean "the kind of situation in which I not only give permission to someone to act in a particular manner but positively will that he should do so." The meaning of the phrase "the consent of the governed," then, is not immediately transparent and Partridge handles well the explication of this difficult concept in democratic theory.

The general thrust of Partridge's argument, however, is to integrate the term consent from political writing with consensus from sociology and show that they are not sharply separable concepts; rather they "refer to attitudes and forms of behaviour that can roughly be arranged along a continuum." Once he has integrated these concepts he can give a satisfying answer to the question: "To what extent is it true to say that consent of the governed is the criterion by which the legitimacy of democratic governments and their policies is to be judged."

Leonard Schapiro's own contribution to the series, *Totalitarianism*, is a masterpiece of clarity and insight. It would be worth studying for its method alone. The pity is that Macmillan did not launch the series with this volume, as it might have provided a model for succeeding writers.

Schapiro's goal is to restrict the use of the term totalitarian to what he calls the three prototype régimes: Hitler's Germany, Mussolini's Italy, and Stalin's Russia. He prefers this approach for two reasons. First, the word itself was not used by Mussolini until 1925 and did not appear in English until 1926; any use of it to régimes before that time is anachronistic. Second, and more important, there were features of those régimes which were genuine novelties in political organization, and the restricted use of "totalitarian" can help elucidate these.

Schapiro analyses the totalitarian régimes with the aid of "five contours from which the map reader in the political wilderness will recognize the 'totalitarian' regime: the Leader; the subjugation of the legal order; control over private morality; continuous mobilization; and legitimacy based on mass support." Schapiro's analysis leads to some startling and penetrating insights. What distinguished these régimes was not that they were glorifications of state power; quite the reverse. "The 'totalitarian' regime is essentially a Leadership regime. Its ideology is in part an instrument to be used in order to overcome the resistance which he would otherwise meet from both state and society." The leader achieves success by using a party which he controls to destroy the normal processes of law and bureaucratic order which we normally identify with a state. The Leader's "apparatus of rule" is quite distinct from the state. "It follows that to speak of 'the totalitarian state' is to use a contradiction in terms ..." and Schapiro prefers "regime" to refer to Hitler's Germany, Mussolini's Italy, and Stalin's Russia.

Equally exciting is Schapiro's analysis of the history and use of the concept. He makes an important distinction between affinity and influence which makes much of the talk about who bears the blame for the rise of Hitler, etc. appear the palpable nonsense it is. Direct affinity exists where there is "a genuine similarity in essential features." In itself this does not prove that an earlier thinker influences a later one. Affinity may arise because of recurrent problems in political thought. "Conversely, where one can show that one man was directly influenced in his outlook by the writings of another, it by no means follows that a case of affinity has been established: the influence is often of a subjective kind in the sense that the man influenced has put his own interpretation of an idea torn out of context, or has consciously or unconsciously perverted the earlier thought." Nietzsche, for example, had an influence on Hitler, in spite of the fact that there was little or no affinity between them. Students of the history of ideas in the future write in peril of their reputations if they overlook Schapiro's distinctions.

WILLIAM CHRISTIAN
Mount Allison University

Jacques Attali, **Analyse économique de la vie politique.** Paris : Presses Universitaires de France, 1972, 219 p.

Jacques Attali, **Les modèles politiques.** Paris : Presses Universitaires de France, 1972, 178 p.

Enfin des livres français sur les modèles mathématiques en science politique ! Au plan de l'enseignement et de la recherche, ils comblent une lacune importante dans la gamme des outils pédagogiques des professeurs et étudiants francophones de la chose politique. Leur principale valeur réside cependant ailleurs : avec le récent volume de Riker et Odershook, *An Introduction To Positive Political Theory*, ils vont constituer la synthèse des applications contemporaines de la mathématique aux phénomènes politiques.

Les deux livres traitent essentiellement des mêmes sujets : la notion de modèle, la relation entre la mesure des attitudes et l'analyse axiomatique des comportements, la formalisation des règles constitutionnelles, des mécanismes d'accession au pouvoir et des stratégies d'exercice du pouvoir par les exécutifs. A celà s'ajoutent, dans le second volume, un chapitre sur les modèles du désarmement international et un autre sur les relations entre modèles et systèmes politiques.

De plus, les deux livres ont été écrits dans une commune optique : celle d'une tentative de synthèse critique.

En ce qui concerne l'aspect synthèse, on retrouve dans l'un ou l'autre les principaux modèles construits depuis la fin des années 50 par les politologues américains (dont le peu connu mais non moins important Kramer). Signalons au passage une nouveauté : l'esquisse, par Attali, d'un modèle de stratégie qui intègre les objectifs tant électoraux qu'idéologiques de l'exécutif. Notons aussi les bons résumés qu'Attali a faits de la théorie des jeux. Il nous semble cependant important de souligner quelques lacunes : les derniers travaux de Sen sur les règles de transformation des préordres individuels en choix collectifs, les recherches pour tenter de déterminer la probabilité de l'avènement du paradoxe de Condorcet, et surtout la pléiade des études théoriques faites par Hinich, Ledyard, Odershook, Riker, Shepsley et d'autres pour développer les modèles spatiaux de compétition électorale dont Downs ne fut que l'initiateur. De même, aurait-il fallu, plus souvent qu'Attali ne le fait, prendre note des applications que les différents modèles ont reçues.

C'est probablement en ce qui concerne l'aspect critique que Attali apporte sa contribution la plus intéressante. Il prend grand soin de bien indiquer la nature normative de la méthode axiomatique en général et le caractère idéologique ainsi que les limites intrinsèques des modèles politiques en particulier. De plus, il suggère les voies nouvelles, tant théoriques que pratiques, qui s'ouvrent aux constructeurs et aux vérificateurs de modèles politiques.

Si la matière exposée et l'optique d'exposition sont en général communes aux deux volumes, il n'en est pas de même quant à leur accessibilité. En effet, le second est d'une facture beaucoup plus abordable que le premier tant par son prix que par sa méthode générale d'exposition. Dans *Les modèles mathématiques*, l'auteur cherche à présenter « en termes littéraires » les axiomatiques plus formellement développés de l'*Analyse économique de la vie politique*. Cette opération – exercice pédagogique toujours périlleux – Attali la réussit avec un bonheur inégal. Cela dépend sûrement du format très limité que l'éditeur impose à la collection dont fait partie le deuxième livre. On sait que l'exposition des axiomatiques est généralement plus longue sous sa forme littéraire que sous sa forme symbolique. En tout état de cause, il aurait été utile que les deux livres comportent un bref lexique explicatif des symboles utilisés, même si, dans l'*Analyse économique*, les démonstrations des théorèmes sont renvoyées en fin de chapitre. Notons aussi que la bibliographie annexée au premier livre est fort incomplète.

Souhaitons que ces deux livres permettent la réintroduction dans la science politique française des problématiques formelles dont les penseurs d'une autre époque s'étaient fort préoccupés. C'est en effet à Condorcet, puis à Borda, que remonte l'étude des axiomes électoraux. Il n'est pas sans enseignement de constater que les aspects formels du libéralisme, que ces auteurs considéraient alors comme des objets valables de recherche fondamentale, soient pendant si longtemps sombrés dans l'oubli, tant en France qu'ailleurs. Mais c'est bien en France cependant où l'on a mis le plus de temps à s'y remettre : peut-être parce que c'est là plus qu'ailleurs que le libéralisme électoral s'est fait décerner par nombre d'analystes un certificat de décès bien prématuré. Il appert toutefois qu'à l'occasion des dernières élections françaises, les esprits même les plus critiques se soient à nouveau éveillés aux propriétés intrinsèques formelles des systèmes électoraux (cf. les analyses du *Nouvel Observateur* et de l'*Humanité-Dimanche*). Il devrait en résulter une compréhension plus approfondie des malfonctionnements de la démocratie électorale.

EDOUARD CLOUTIER
Université du Québec à Montréal

Maurice Torrelli et Renée Baudouin, **Les droits de l'homme et les libertés publiques par les textes.** Montréal : Les Presses de l'Université du Québec, 1972, 387 p.

Les opérations d'identification, de définition et de protection des droits de l'homme sécrètent des problématiques qui demeurent toujours actuelles parce qu'elles sont permanentes. Aussi le recueil de Maurice Torrelli et de Renée Baudoin, consacré à une classification, essentiellement historico-politique, de textes portant sur les droits de l'individu et les libertés publiques, présente-t-il un intérêt permanent pour l'étude des processus systémiques internes et internationaux.

L'importance de la phénoménalité explorée par les deux auteurs pour l'appréciation critique des processus de distribution autoritaire des valeurs systémiques et la richesse de la documentation proposée nous inspirent les quelques réflexions qui suivent et qui répondent à un double objectif : déceler les mérites de la démarche intellectuelle des auteurs, d'une part, relayer vers l'extérieur certains commentaires susceptibles de stimuler la confrontation des idées en cette matière, d'autre part.

Pour ce qui est des mérites de l'étude recensée, nous avons pu retenir l'ampleur de l'effort de recherche accompli ainsi que la pertinence des critères de sélection et de classification des textes recueillis.

Les auteurs ont en effet réussi à exploiter une masse considérable de documents (Constitutions, chartes, déclarations, pétitions, actes constitutionnels, décrets, lois, conventions internationales, etc.) dont ils ont pu ordonner les enseignements d'une manière intelligible, mettant en relief le cadre interne et international des droits de l'homme.

Conscients, par ailleurs, du fait que du choix des données de leur recherche dépendrait le niveau d'approfondissement de leur démarche, ils se sont employés avec persévérance à une entreprise de sélection rationnelle mettant en lumière l'ensemble des réalités idéologiques, juridiques et historiques qui sous-tendent les processus d'établissement et de protection des droits de l'homme.

Quant aux méthodes de classification, un effort de rigueur se manifeste tout au long de l'ouvrage, s'appuyant sur la prise en considération du critère géographique (Europe, Amérique, Afrique et Asie), sans négliger pour autant les dimensions historiques, idéologiques et juridico-institutionnelles des systèmes nationaux (régimes libéraux, régimes dictatoriaux) et internationaux (contrôle politique, contrôle juridictionnel) sélectionnés.

Le travail commenté se veut un recueil de textes et un instrument de recherche plutôt qu'une œuvre de théorisation de la problématique de la reconnaissance et de la protection des droits de l'homme. Aussi cette orientation explicite met-elle les deux auteurs à l'abri de critiques relatives au degré de conceptualisation des vocables « droits » et « libertés » de l'homme.

Cela dit, nous pensons pouvoir indiquer quelques pistes de recherche et de réflexion scientifique, susceptibles, selon nous, d'orienter le lecteur vers l'exploitation théorique du texte de présentation qui introduit le recueil et qui pourrait devenir la partie systématique de l'étude.

Sans vouloir reprendre le débat sur la distinction entre droits et libertés, qui divise les politicologues et les publicistes et que les auteurs n'ont pas manqué d'évoquer, quoique fort brièvement, nous pensons qu'il serait nécessaire de se mettre en état de procéder à une présentation des textes sélectionnés qui distingue, au niveau d'une décomposition analytique des normes, les droits de l'homme des libertés publiques.

Par ailleurs, il ne serait pas sans intérêt d'appliquer la division binaire (reconnaissance et mécanismes de contrôle des droits de l'homme) de la deuxième partie de l'ouvrage (les droits de l'homme sur le plan international) aux textes de sa première partie (les droits de l'homme sur le plan interne), c'est-à-dire d'analyser les droits de l'homme sur le plan interne tant au niveau de leur reconnaissance qu'à celui des mécanismes de protection de leurs titulaires. Car, il y aurait bien lieu de distinguer, même sur le plan interne, les projets juridico-politiques de défense des droits de l'homme des voies de leur actualisation, de comparer la teneur des textes à la réalité de leur mise en œuvre, voire d'opposer les libertés formellement reconnues aux libertés réellement protégées.

Une ébauche d'analyse conceptuelle ayant été à peine amorcée dans le cadre de la note de présentation du recueil, il ne serait pas sans importance de pouvoir préciser les idées quant au contenu exact des termes « droits civils », « droits de l'homme », « droits politiques », « droits individuels », « droits sociaux », « droits juridiques », « droits économiques », « libertés individuelles », « libertés publiques », « libertés fondamentales », et de dégager les cas de tautologie ainsi que les réalités conceptuelles distinctes.

Nous pensons, également, qu'un effort de compréhension et d'analyse approfondie des réalités systémiques des régimes totalitaires du monde occidental et des Etats socialistes nous éviterait le regroupement hétéroclite, dans le cadre de la même rubrique, de systèmes qui, croyons-nous, n'appartiennent pas au même type de régime ni n'obéissent à la même conception de la politique (Espagne, Portugal, URSS, RDA, Pologne, Yougoslavie).

En somme, bien que la démarche de Maurice Torrelli et de Renée Baudouin n'épuise pas sa propre problématique et se prête à un développement analytico-conceptuel, leur ouvrage est certainement appelé à devenir un outil d'investigation scientifique, utilisable par autrui, ce qui ne pourra qu'aiguillonner la réflexion et inciter l'étudiant et le chercheur à l'analyse comparative des actes de reconnaissance et de protection des droits de l'homme et des libertés publiques.

PANAYOTIS SOLDATOS
Université Laurentienne

Henri Brun et Guy Tremblay, **Droit public fondamental.** Québec : Les Presses de l'Université Laval, 1972, xiii, 513 p.

Cet ouvrage, comme l'indiquent les auteurs, a été conçu dans une perspective didactique. Il correspond à l'objet d'un cours de base du programme de licence de droit et il est susceptible d'être utilisé dans le cadre de plusieurs enseignements destinés aux étudiants de diverses sciences sociales dans plusieurs universités. Mais cet ouvrage est davantage un traité qu'un manuel et il peut servir également comme texte de référence, non seulement aux juristes, mais aussi aux cadres de la fonction publique et aux spécialistes de l'analyse politique,

Droit public fondamental a pour objets les concepts fondamentaux du droit public, en général, et les principes premiers du droit public canadien, en particulier. Le droit administratif et les droits municipal et scolaire, bien que recouverts par le concept général de droit public, ne sont pas abordés, car leur spécificité, selon les auteurs, justifie des enseignements et des ouvrages particuliers. Dans les domaincs dont ils traitent, d'ailleurs, les auteurs ne cherchent pas à être exhaustifs : le contenu de leur ouvrage se veut strictement fondamental (p. 7).

Droit public fondamental, en conséquence, est un traité bien différent de l'ouvrage publié en 1965, sous la signature du professeur Louis Baudouin, par l'Institut de droit comparé de l'université de Paris et intitulé *Les aspects généraux du droit public dans la province de Québec*. On se souviendra que, dans cet ouvrage de 432 pages, le professeur Baudouin n'avait consacré qu'une centaine de pages à ce qu'il avait intitulé « le pouvoir législatif » et « théorie générale de la loi » : le reste du texte présentait une étude du pouvoir exécutif, du pouvoir judiciaire, du monde des juristes, du droit administratif et du droit du travail, autant de questions que n'aborde pas *Droit public fondamental*.

Les parties centrales de l'ouvrage de Henri Brun et Guy Tremblay sont précédées de deux sections intitulées respectivement : « Les différents aspects du droit public » (p. 1–7) et « Les sources du droit public canadien » (p. 11–34). Bien qu'il s'agisse là d'une introduction générale, le mot « introduction » n'apparaît nulle part. Ces premières pages n'en comportent pas moins de nombreuses distinctions et définitions qui préparent utilement la lecture des développements subséquents.

La première des parties centrales de l'ouvrage présente les notions de base sur les sujets suivants : la définition socio-politique de l'Etat, la définition juridique de l'Etat, le concept de souveraineté, la propriété publique, le territoire de l'Etat, les conditions d'obtention et de rétention de la citoyenneté, la représentation des citoyens dans les organes étatiques, la classification classique des fonctions étatiques et les principaux types d'organisation de l'Etat qu'elle suppose, et, de façon plus élaborée, le parlementarisme et le fédéralisme. A cela s'ajoute un chapitre sur les moyens dont dispose l'Etat pour protéger son existence et son intégrité territoriale.

La deuxième des parties centrales de l'ouvrage, « la suprématie législative en droit canadien », traite du principe de la légalité et de la *rule of law*, et des limitations que peuvent constituer, dans certaines circonstances, les normes « naturelles », les engagements à l'égard des gouvernements étrangers et les dispositions de l'Acte de l'Amérique du Nord britannique. Cette deuxième partie traite également de l'interprétation judiciaire de la législation et de l'exercice des pouvoirs détenus par les organes exécutifs en vertu de la législation.

La troisième partie de *Droit public fondamental* est intitulée « les organes législatifs canadiens (fédéraux et québécois) ». Après avoir fait état d'une typologie des organes législatifs, les auteurs étudient successivement : le Sénat, la Chambre des Communes et l'Assemblée nationale, le Cabinet fédéral et le Conseil exécutif québécois et, enfin, les rapports entre les organes.

Les diverses sections que les auteurs ont consacrées à l'Etat canadien et aux organes étatiques rappellent parfois les grands développements des traités de droit constitutionnel, qu'ont signé Maurice Duverger ou Marcel Prelot, mais les exemples cités, l'adaptation québécoise et canadienne et, enfin, les rappels de jurisprudence s'inspirent de la littérature juridique canadienne et britannique. L'ensemble est, somme toute, le fruit d'un heureux croisement.

L'ouvrage ne comporte pas de chapitre intitulé « conclusion », pas plus qu'il ne comporte d'introduction proprement dite. Mais il comporte une bibliographie générale, une table des lois citées, une table des arrêts cités, un index analytique, une table générale des matières, et, au tout début, une table des abréviations. Il y a en outre, dispersées çà et là, tout au long des chapitres, 30 bibliographies particulières et 22 sommaires limités. Par contre il n'y a pas de notes infra-paginales. Au total, cet ouvrage compte 330 pages de textes et plus de 160 pages de tables ou de listes diverses.

Certains verront dans tout cela un certain désiquilibre des proportions. Mais, compte tenu des objectifs pédagogiques de l'ouvrage, on ne peut en faire le reproche aux auteurs.

Il convient, somme toute, de saluer la publication de cet ouvrage qui comble largement un besoin qui était devenu de plus en plus évident avec les années.

André Bernard
Université du Québec à Montréal

Jean-Claude Masclet, **L'Europe politique,** dossiers Thémis. Paris : PUF, 1972, 94 p.

Dans ce dossier de la collection Thémis, M. J.C. Masclet réussit en une quarantaine de pages de présentation à donner une idée précise et claire des différentes conceptions et des tentatives qui visent à donner une forme politique unifiée à l'Europe occidentale et plus particulièrement aux Communautés européennes. Un plan chronologique permet d'en suivre les étapes : le premier temps fort : la Communauté politique européenne (1952–4); une occasion manquée, le plan Fouchet (1960–2); les initiatives de la période intermédiaire (1963–9); les premiers efforts de coopération en matière de politique étrangère (1969–72).

Dans une seconde partie, l'auteur a rassemblé 33 documents qui sont des plus utiles car l'on a souvent de la difficulté à les réunir, malgré le recueil de documents de la commission politique du Parlement européen sur ce sujet, qui, publié en 1964, ne comporte évidemment pas certains documents réçents et importants, tel le rapport « Davignon » sur la base duquel a été organisée l'actuelle concertation politique des 9 Etats membres des Communautés européennes.

Ce nouveau dossier, de bonne qualité, est un instrument de travail utile, surtout dans le cadre de cours traitant des questions d'intégration européenne.

MAURICE TORRELLI
Université de Montréal

M. Donald Hancock and Gideon Sjoberg, eds., **Politics in the Post-Welfare State: Responses to the New Individualism.** New York and London: Columbia University Press [Montreal: McGill-Queen's University Press], 1972, pp. xii, 335.

Post-industrial society, that stage in the development of modern society when the industrial system is capable of satisfying all our basic material needs, has attracted increasing attention recently among social scientists. A problem central to the discussion is the role of the individual, as the welfare state, with its automation, affluence, and demands for collective action, reaches maturity. For while the welfare state has enhanced our ability to attain individual fulfilment by increasing the range of our choices, it has also brought into being a bureaucratic machinery which itself often becomes an obstacle to the individual welfare it is charged with protecting. The very size of both public and private bureaucracies, their enormous powers, and their centralized nature, all tend to produce the modern malaise known as alienation. Can we chart a course for the future which provides the individual human being with a meaningful place in society? The present collection of essays probes this question as it presents the reader with varying perspectives on post-industrial politics in the United States, Great Britain, and Sweden, all highly industrialized welfare-state systems. The contributors were asked by the editors to address themselves to several specific questions regarding the "new individualism" and the nineteenth-century variety; whether the present emphasis on the individual will play a part in future ideological struggles in the respective countries; and whether this individualism will contribute to structural changes such as decentralization of government activities.

Since the various authors did not follow the recipe very faithfully, the result is one common to many joint efforts, namely, a certain lack of comparability and coherence in the over-all product. All the writers have, however, dealt with the central issue of the individual's relationship to the group, and the most interesting aspect of the book, from this reader's point of view, is the contrasting picture that emerges, through their presentations, of the post-industrial future in the United States and Europe. Those gazing into the crystal ball for a glimpse of Sweden's and Britain's tomorrow predict relative calm ahead and are confident that the systems possess sufficient adaptive powers to accommodate both individual and group needs. This homogeneity in outlook does not prevail among the observers of American politics, however, on whose part one senses a pervasive pessimism regarding the future. Two of the American contributors, in particular, leave us with little hope for a better tomorrow. Both Christopher Lasch and Dusky Lee Smith see the liberal welfare state as a gargantuan monster pursuing its own peculiar needs and operating according to its own intrinsic laws, not subject to man's rational control. The individual is submerged, incapable of influencing the system.

How, one may ask, is this contrast to be explained? I think that in large measure the explanation may be sought in the different traditions of thought that have marked the two European societies on the one hand, and America on the other. Profound distrust in government and a juxtaposition of the individual and the group are attitudes that have characterized both the right and the left in America's history. In contrast, individualism and collectivism have not traditionally been regarded as contradictory concepts in either Sweden or Great Britain. In both countries, the conservative parties were originally basically collectivist in their orientation, and eventually developed a strong element of social and humanitarian responsibility. The notion that individual self-realization and group needs can be accommodated to each other, and that, indeed, the former is only possible as the latter is achieved, is an old and venerable one in both societies. Because of America's uneasiness about collectivism, even as post-welfare politics is emerging, the controversies over welfare state politics are still continuing. Indeed, as J.M. Cooper, Jr, points out in his essay, the extension of the welfare state in America is now threatened by the convergence of attacks on it from both right and left.

The book, as does any good book, poses more questions than it answers. It is bound to provide stimulus for interesting discussions in any course dealing with the problems of the maturing welfare state in a comparative perspective.

INGUNN N. MEANS
McMaster University

Nigel Harris, **Competition and the Corporate Society: British Conservatives, the State and Industry, 1945–1964.** Agincourt: Methuen Publications, 1972, pp. 384.

The most salient feature of the mythology of Conservatism in Britain is its constant assertion of its continuity – a continuity which finds its most emotive expression in the much used but fundamentally meaningless phrase "the Conservative tradition." As Dr Harris points out, Tories invariably trace the lineage of the "tradition" back to Burke and occasionally to Bolingbroke, with hardly a sideways glance at the problem of reconciling the Burkeian analysis of an agrarian society with the realities of an industrial and technological polity, and their ability to do so derives from a long established pattern of expounding one course of action in theory and doing precisely the reverse in practice.

This study of Conservative attitudes to and actions on the intervention of the state in economic affairs between 1945 and 1964 provides much evidence of the dichotomy between "neo-Liberal" aspirations and "étatiste" or "corporative" achievements. Dr Harris sees the turning point of the post-war period not in the elections of 1950 and 1951 but in the middle of the Labour government's period of office. Until about 1947–8 the neo-Liberals were in the ascendency in the Conservative party and this ascendency found its symbolism in the title of the 1950 election manifesto "Set the People Free." Long before that election, however, there began in the party a retreat from the neo-Liberalism of 1945 and a return to the kind of interventionism which had characterised Conservative policies in the interwar years. It is very significant in this context that of the Labour government's nationalisation measures only those affecting steel and a portion of the road haulage industry were repealed, and that even in the case of steel a large section of the industry remained in public ownership. More important, however, in the context of Dr Harris' argument, is the fact that denationalization (and subsequent renationalization for that matter) made little difference to the economic condition and commercial performance of the steel industry. The conclusion here must be that changing the formal ownership of the industry in 1952 was as much a symbolic act for the Tories as it was 16 years later for the Labour party.

Running through this book is the author's impatience with, and distaste for, what he describes as the sterility of the modern British party system. Dr. Harris is politically on the revolutionary left wing of British politics – a degree of commitment which adds much to the readability of the book without detracting from its academic merit – and his final chapter, which has the same title as the book, is a stimulating critique of a parliamentary system which has made state capitalists out of the Labour party and Social Democrats out of the Conservatives. In the context of the present Conservative government's economic policies, this judgment has its attractions.

Dr Harris' gentle excoriation of the parties is, however, possible only in the context of economic policy, for in the realm of social policy the gap between the parties has, over the last decade at least, steadily increased. There is in this analysis a tendency to generalize a view of the Conservative party (and, by extension, of the Labour party) from the particulars of its economic policies – policies which owed much to the influence of factors extrinsic to the British political system. Despite this, however, Dr Harris has produced a significant and extremely well-researched contribution to the literature of modern British politics. His conclusions about the Conservatives are acceptable, but on the implicit extrapolations about the political and party systems the

Scots verdict of "not proven" is the most appropriate.

ALAN ALEXANDER
University of Reading, England

Peter G. Richards, **The Backbenchers.** London: Faber and Faber, 1972, pp. 248.

The Backbenchers is the most recent and best book by Professor Peter G. Richards on the operations of the British House of Commons. It is somewhat more comprehensive and certainly more subtle than *Honorable Members* (1959). It is more comprehensive in that it deals thoroughly with such new subjects as the impact of the constituencies and the mass media and the various information services for members. It is more subtle because the idea that rewards and punishments are the primary causes of party cohesion has been eliminated and the influence of members on the creation of policy and hence on party cohesion is presented on practically every page of the book.

The Backbenchers is a clear, balanced description of the activities of parliament. It is based on a close reading of Hansard and the British press and a thorough familiarity with the most recent literature on the British parliament. The various institutional arrangements and the steps by which bills and estimates reach fruition are carefully paraded. The newest developments at Westminster and especially the recent reform proposals are both discussed thoroughly. It will be of particular interest to Canadians that Professor Richards has taken to task those scholars who believe in mass participation in the legislative process and has put forward many proposals about how parliamentary machinery could be made to work more effectively. In view of the lack of efficient machinery in the Canadian House a study of the British procedures and organization for parliament would be helpful. Canadian parliamentarians, however, would have to abandon some of their stereotypes of Westminster. These may be found in both the Liberal and Conservative parties and run from Mark MacGuigan's belief that Canada can learn little from the Constitution of the United Kingdom to John Diefenbaker's reverence for a British Parliament which no longer exists.

Unfortunately, perhaps, this is not a book which will be well received by specialists in North America. It lacks even tentative scientific generalizations: there is neither an examination of the concepts employed nor even a primitive research design. One would at least like to know how Professor Richards elected which facts to put in the text and which not to present. For example, the Conservative party "dirts" which he mentions on page 58 were eliminated in 1968–9 shortly after their existence became publicly known. Moreover in the author's attempt to show the role of sanctions in maintaining party cohesion he fails to mention that mildly sanctioned members have usually survived, and even thrived, in British parties. In other words, no relations (statistical or otherwise) are drawn between members' behaviour and party cohesion. And, in those parts of the book which are dominated by such problems, standard common-sense propositions have been accepted even when they contradict each other.

This book should be published in paperback so that students interested in traditional approaches to political science will be well instructed. It is an example of the best form of British descriptive research on a single country and its institutions. As such it shows a mastery of detail which is lacking in most theoretical studies. On the other hand, because *The Backbenchers* lacks comparative generalizations its relevance to theory is missing, and because the author makes no effort to link the legislature to society the reader is deprived of the excitement which comes from broad horizons.

ROBERT J. JACKSON
Carleton University

Maurice Halperin, **The Rise and Decline of Fidel Castro: An Essay in Contemporary History.** Berkeley and Los Angeles: University of California Press, 1972, pp. x, 380.

Revolutions are controversial. Because some classes gain political and economic power to the detriment of others, the obstacles to objectivity are likely to be serious. The chances for objectivity are not increased by the division of the world into two powers, both born of revolutions, holding radically different attitudes toward movements and processes termed revolutionary by either their proponents or opponents. The social scientist who desires to understand revolutions must contend not only with the propaganda produced by these two powers but also with the lack of sophisticated theories in the literature. In fact, the most precise theory is that of Marx which is as much an appeal for revolution as it is a framework for analysis.

The literature on the Cuban Revolution of 1959 is subject to all these impediments to objectivity and tends to be highly polemical. Fortunately, this book by Professor Halperin of the political science department at Simon Fraser is an exception as it offers a realistic interpretation of the revolution. The author spent three years teaching in the Soviet Union and another six (from 1962 to 1968) in Cuba. With such a background one might anticipate either a whitewash of the Cuban and Soviet regimes or one of those furious attacks by erstwhile true believers. The book is neither. We therefore profit from the intimate knowledge of an insider yet one who has retained his objectivity. Professor Halperin has written an excellent book on the development of the Cuban revolution as seen through the person of its initiator and key personality.

In this volume the author is primarily concerned with the period of 1959 to 1964; another volume is now in preparation to cover the period until 1969. Halperin's technique is to discuss the events of the revolution from year to year which at times makes for tedious reading. However, he is not strictly bound by this style and moves back and forth, from the turn of the century until 1971, in order to provide the reader with an integrated analysis of the events and their significance. The chronological approach, moderated by the author's flexibility and deep appreciation of history, has much to recommend it in the analysis of revolution. For one thing we are given insights into the ongoing and eclectic process of the revolution and the personalities that direct it. For another, we can appreciate, in contradiction to those who would propose a single theory to explain revolution, that much of what has happened in Cuba since 1959 is due not to design but rather to accident. The particular timing and configuration of events was crucially important in giving the revolution a direction that could not have been predicted. While generally favourable to Fidel Castro, Halperin does not place him on a pedestal but shows that he is not adverse to making socialist virtue out of accidents and the economic realities of Cuba.

Halperin's understanding of the development of the revolution is stated cogently on page 86: "it was Castro's foreign policy, responding to the impact of the accidents of history on his quixotic temperament and assisted by American diplomacy, which created the conditions leading to the kind of rapid and total restructuring of Cuban society which he himself had not anticipated". There are three main elements which gave the revolution the direction it had assumed by 1964. The first is Castro himself who is the undisputed leader of Cuba. While showing that Castro is an exceptional man in many ways, the author demonstrates clearly that he thought he knew more than he in fact did. With his total control over the direction of the revolution Castro's whims could, and in fact did, have severe implications for economic growth. Castro could always rely on the adulation of the population, despite the errors of his policies, because he is a nationalist leader much in the mould of José Marti and others who have been so important in forming Cuba's revolutionary tradition.

The second element is the United States and it is important in a number of ways. Cuban nationalism since the turn of the century has been anti-American and Castro could easily rest on the support of this nationalism when he had to take what could have been unpopular measures. Halperin indicates that the United States did not fully appreciate the nature of the revolution and by taking measures which did not fit the situation led to its radicalization. It was the tension and even dialectic between the United States and Cuba that gave the revolution its particular direction and very rapid momentum. The author presents convincing evidence that Castro tried several times to signal the American presidents that he was ready to discuss relations between the two countries, and although some progress was made just prior to Kennedy's assassination, little was achieved.

As Castro broke with the Americans he took up with the Soviet Union. The links which were established were by no means predicted by either side but the configuration of events made for the availability of both for the relationship. Many internal changes in Cuba were made in order to attract the Soviets and once they were involved the process of change went all the faster. The break with the United States and subsequent reliance on the Soviet Union is crucial to Halperin's analysis of the dynamic of the revolution. The particular orientation it has taken has been due to the personality of Castro, the behaviour of the United States at specific periods, and shifts in the Sino-Soviet axis. At present the relationship is such that Cuba is becoming increasingly militarized and rigid. A discussion of the Padilla affair suggests that much of the revolution's humanist content has already been surrendered to Marxist orthodoxy.

There is no specific conclusion to this book probably because Professor Halperin intends to provide one in his next volume which will have more distance from the period under study. On the basis of this first volume I look forward with some anticipation to the publication of the next.

THOMAS C. BRUNEAU
McGill University

Michael Brecher, **The Foreign Policy System of Israel: Setting, Images, Process.** Don Mills, Ont.: Oxford University Press, 1972, pp. xxii, 693.

This detailed case study of a new state's foreign policy, the first of a two-volume series (see p. 557), is on the operational and psychological environments of Israel's high-policy élite. It is a notable attempt to integrate the analyses of international systems and foreign policy decision-making. Its analytic framework is the innovative Brecher, Steinberg, and Stein article which provides a suggestive typology of environments, issue areas, and initiative-reactive elements. Its strength is the presentation of exhaustive data on Israel's foreign policy system; its weakness lies in inadequate attention to process. The structures, but not the relationships, of the system are analysed very thoroughly.

The multiplication of jargon has diverted Professor Brecher from the search for causal relationships to over-concentrate on filling conceptual boxes with data. This excessive attention to detail detracts from the book's continuity; it enhances our understanding of the making of foreign policy but it fails to explain Israel's decisions. The focus of research is the "foreign policy decision": "the selection, among perceived alternatives, of one option leading to a course of action in the international system" (pp. 374 and 553). The mode of analysis is verbal rather than quantitative. Many substantive chapters and appendices commence with a brief review of the relevant literature, contributing to the cumulative development of the subdiscipline. The volume is well produced and contains seven appendices, substantial bibliographies, a glossary, and two indexes.

The most valuable theoretical chapters are 1 to 6 and 20. These present the conceptual framework, analyse Israel's dominant bilateral relations within the global system, provide a review of the structure, texture, and power configuration of the penetrated Middle East subordinate system, including a typology of its 20 political cultures, describe the development of Israel's integrated *Tzahal* and those countervailing Israeli assets which invert the "real" balance of power, evaluate the paradoxical economic superiority and vulnerability of Israel and its dependence on external financial aid from western regimes and Diaspora Jewry, interpret the low salience of foreign policy for Israel's coalition politics – the centralized government makes security and foreign policy rather than the *Knesset* or interest groups – and the conclusion reviews the first two decades of Israel's foreign policy. These core chapters might be reissued, along with summaries of chapters 7 through 19, in a more digestable and saleable paperback edition, which would contain the major theoretical products of the research.

The final chapter summarizes the set of independent variables of the preceding 540 pages. It is the most succinct chapter and contains a set of explicit propositions about foreign-policy behaviour based on an informal ranking of variables. Most of the volume is an analysis of the contrasting images of the Israeli "High Policy Elite," the formulation of "High-Policy Decisions," profiles of the Foreign Service and Parallel Technical Elites (FSTE and PTE) and the structure of the foreign ministry. Although this exhaustive treatment is interesting, it is limited in its power to explain, for instance, the pervasive "Ben Gurion complex" and the clustering of generational, educational, and professional cleavages. After this lengthy diversion the following, highly suggestive, hypothesis is welcome: "Israel's images and policy on the core issue of 'the Arabs' since 1948 suggest a general proposition about long-term state behaviour: the Psychological Environment of a decision-making group in foreign policy is in large measure a product or mirror of the Operational Environment" (p. 556). The dominance of its external environment explains Israel's foreign-policy behaviour as indicated by the proportion of external factors in the list of independent variables (p. 555). Therefore, the following observations are interesting but are not theoretically potent: "German and English backgrounds are pre-eminent in the FSTE, while Eastern Europe and Israel are pre-eminent in the PTE. The pre-eminence of Israel is especially striking among 'the Military'" (p. 480); and "Morale within the Foreign Service has been adversely affected by the fundamental gap between the values of a society under siege and the *raison d'être* of diplomacy" (p. 516).

Professor Brecher concludes that the prospects for change in the perceptions underlying Israel's foreign policy are remote due to the "stability of image patterns and minimal circulation in the decision-making élites" (p. 556). Given the dominance of external variables, especially the interrelated threat from the Arab states and the penetrated subordinate system, other approaches might have yielded the same conclusions with greater parsimony. In particular, it is noticeable that this otherwise exhaustive case study of a new state should omit reference to theories of imperialism and structural dependence and to the interdependence of domestic ruling classes and external élites. Israel is clearly an atypical new state. Its origins, population, and ideology are highly distinctive; the intensity of conflict within its subordinate system is unequalled. It abandoned the attempt to be nonaligned in 1950; and the centrality of its transnational ties with World Jewry are unique.

The author acknowledges his "fundamental affinity for Israel and her people" (p. x) and in the uncharacteristic second half of his conclusion is critical of the quest for security through *de facto* alignment with the US. He notes the paucity of Israel's international memberships and advocates diplomatic diversification: "She is, in truth, alone. Thus Israel's policy-makers may be credited with a unique achievement – all the disadvantages of non-alignment and none of the benefits of alignment!" (p. 561). He suggests that relations with the Arabs might begin to improve if the Israeli élite recognized "that Israel's independence is part of a global movement of national liberation in the era of European imperial decline" (p. 561). However, even if such attitudes change, freedom to reinterpret Israeli's genesis is limited as it is "in a condition of near-total dependence on the United States" (p. 565). The foreign-policy approach may be inappropriate if "'*Ein breirah*' (no alternative) is the lynchpin of Israel's political thought and behaviour" (p. 555).

TIMOTHY M. SHAW
Dalhousie University

Jacques Benjamin, **Les Camerounais occidentaux: la minorité dans un Etat bicommunautaire.** Montreal: Les Presses de l'Université de Montréal, 1971, pp. 250.

From the outset we are made aware of Jacques Benjamin's particular identification with his subject matter. "Il est probablement normal," he writes in his introduction, "que ce soit un Québécois qui se penche le premier sur le sort des Camerounais occidentaux ... la minorité dans un Etat bicommunautaire." It is this identification which lends a note of investigative urgency to his study.

In contrast to most students of federalism, the author focuses clearly on this minority and its fate. His is not a global view of the federal system from its centre. Rather his objective is to chart the influence and interaction of institutional factors (nature of the regime, party structure, and form of government) and political culture with a view to determining the extent to which they "favoriser ou décourager la présence de la minorité en tant que force centrifuge" (p. 3). His line of inquiry leads out from a set of provocative questions. How important is the support of a foreign power in assuring the survival of the minority or conversely the domination of the majority? How relevant is the philosophy of federalism held by each community, the type of education of its élites, the presence or absence of common objectives? To what extent is party structure a constraint on the role a minority might play in decision-making at the federal level and even more interestingly at the provincial level?

However suggestive these questions may be, they alone do not constitute the "paradigm" which Benjamin implies they do (pp. 2–4). It is precisely a lack of methodological rigour, moreover, which prevents this study from fulfilling its promise.

Having completed the introduction we are still not at all sure what the author intends his dependent variable to be and how he proposes to measure it. We are aware that the author views federalism as a process but we cannot appreciate the utility he attaches to the notion of a continuum based on Dusan Sidjanski's "degrees of federalism" – a concept which the author fails to develop. Despite their intrinsic interest and the not inconsiderable amount of data contained in the chapters which follow, the reader does not feel a growing sense of "argument being made" or "hypotheses being put to the test." At the end we remain conceptually lost with regard to the way institutional factors and political culture interact to shape the role of the minority in a bicultural state.

In a certain sense the lack of clarity with respect to the core concept of federalism also makes the reader question Benjamin's rejection of a nation-building approach on the grounds that in this approach "le fédéralisme est uniquement retenu comme obstacle à cette construction unitaire" (p. 7). This thorough rejection is curious given that President Ahmadou Ahidjo's own declared interest was, as early as August 1961, in nation-building. "Il ne saurait ... être question de laisser chaque région géographique, chaque groupe ethnique, agir à sa guise," he said, "les deux Etats ... continueront à gérer leurs affaires internes ... dans la mésure où l'exercice de cette prérogative ne risque pas de porter atteinte à l'ensemble de la vie nationale" (p. 10). To Ahidjo's own words can be added the series of actions Benjamin recounts, beginning with the progressive transfer of powers from the federated states to the centre, largely accomplished by 1964, the unification of political parties in 1966, and the replacement of Prime Minister Jua, a partisan of West Cameroonian autonomy, by S.T. Muna, a federationist, in 1968. If as Wheare argues federalism implies two independent governments ruling over the same population then by this definition the Cameroonian system was hardly federal. But this is not Benjamin's definition and given his notion of "degrees of federalism" the author is able to explain away each seeming derogation from classical federalism.

In his first chapter Benjamin sets out to convince us that bicameralism is not essential to Cameroonian federalism and that Cameroon's form of unicameralism can, given its special features, protect the minority. "Avant de crier à l'antifédéralisme, il faut lire l'article 18 de la Constitution," (p. 22) he argues. This article permits the prime minister of a federated state to demand a recall vote during which each state delegation votes as a unit. A simple majority of each delegation is now required. According to this provision it would theoretically be possible for 5 of West Cameroon's 10 deputies to constitute a veto block. Yet in chapter 2, especially on pages 62 and 63 and in footnote 56 on page 171 Benjamin elaborates the weakness of these 10 men from West Cameroon, some of whom hold more pressing ministerial posts in the federal government and many of whom are inexperienced legislators. In his conclusion, moreover, Benjamin emphasizes as the principal weakness of Cameroonian federalism "la relative absence de Camerounais occidentaux dans la prise de décisions à Yaoundé" (p. 148). How federalist, then was the Cameroonian political system during its first decade of independence; which direction was it going in along the "continuum"; and how does this affect the fate of the minority?

One might also add at this point a note on the time span of this study. Although Benjamin frequently refers to "dix ans" as the period of his analysis many of the most important events of 1968–70 are relegated to footnotes. This was the case, for example, in his analysis of West Cameroonian politics to which footnote 50 (p. 170) was appended with the observation that Jua's replacement by Muna in 1968 led to "une situation tout à fait nouvelle." Why was the author reluctant to pursue this analysis in the body of the text? Again in chapter 3 Benjamin leaves us with the impression that an internal frontier continued to exist in Cameroon beyond 1966 and that East Cameroon persisted in receiving higher amounts of per-capita investment at the time of writing despite footnote 13 (p. 176) in which he notes that the 1966–70 Development Plan reverses this situation by allocating more on a per-capita basis to West than to East Cameroon.

While *Les Camerounais occidentaux* has certain methodological flaws, by focussing on the West Cameroonian minority it nevertheless gives an entirely new and welcome perspective on political change in the Cameroon. This focus permits Benjamin, despite the slide toward greater centralization, to get behind these broad evolutionary processes and record the way in which West Cameroonian politics continued to be carried on with relative autonomy within the region during most of the first independent decade.

LYNN K. MYTELKA
Carleton University

Eugene P. Dvorin and Robert H. Simmons, **From Amoral to Humane Bureaucracy.** San Francisco: Canfield Press, 1972, pp. viii, 88.

This brief book is an excellent example of the thought-provoking publications resulting from the revival of interest in normative theory among students of public administration in the United States. The concern of many scholars has shifted from public administration's *crisis of identity* to what the authors of this work describe as the *crisis of imbalance.*

The imbalance exists because the enormous power of bureaucrats is not matched by their devotion to moral principles. Past and contemporary public administration is described as amoral in that its focus has been, and remains, on practice to the detriment of values. The development of moral propositions either by scholars or practitioners has been overwhelmed by the search for improved administrative techniques and processes. Efficiency has been the foremost objective of the study and practice of public administration.

The content of this book has close intellectual bonds with the Minnowbrook papers edited by Frank Marini and published in *Toward A New Public Administration.* The scope of concerns expressed by the authors of the Minnowbrook papers is very broad and it is difficult to discern a concert of opinion on emerging patterns in public administration. However, several of the major emphases of Minnowbrook – relevance, post-positivism (a break with value-free or value-neutral research), and social equity over efficiency – are discussed within a coherent framework in the book under review.

Dvorin and Simmons have written a provocative book in that their premises and hypotheses are a dramatic departure from conventional notions of the appropriate role of practitioners and scholars of public administration.

The central theme of the book is that the prime task of public administration is to develop "an ethical framework based upon fundamental and irreducible values to which the bureaucracy is committed" (p. 34). A theory of public bureaucracy must be founded on an understanding of the public interest which is "indigenous to the bureaucracy." Public servants can and should make as great and as distinctive a contribution to the determination of the public interest as political executives, legislators, and judges. Indeed, moral leadership exercised primarily by political executives is inadequate because they are obliged by electoral circumstances to compromise and to accommodate diverse interests. Career public servants, by way of contrast, are not only more expert and experienced than political executives but are also in more continuous and intimate contact with the citizenry. Moreover, public servants can take a long-run administrative and technical view rather than a short-run political view of public-policy issues.

Dvorin and Simmons believe that a substantive concept of the public interest may evolve in a fashion analogous to the development of common-law concepts, that is, on the basis of decisions made in particular cases over a period of time. To achieve this end, "everyday operational decisions would have to center around the concept of human dignity as the ultimate criterion of the public interest" (p. 55). "Radical humanism" is offered as the frame of reference within which this concept of the public interest may emerge. Radical humanism requires "the ultimate capitulation of operational mechanics and political strategies to a concept of the public interest based on man as *the* most important concern of bureaucratic power" (p. 61).

The authors criticize schools of public administration for their unduly practical orientation and for their over-emphasis on the employment opportunities of their graduates. They regret also that the close structural, theoretical, and psychological links between business and public administration have led to neglect of the uniqueness of "public" as opposed to other forms of administration. Too little research has been done to demonstrate the bonds between political theory and organization theory. To remedy these problems, Dvorin and Simmons contemplate a period of alienation between the theory and practice of public administration. During this period, academic scholars, unhindered by excessive concern for administrative practice and employment opportunities, may develop an ethical framework for administrative decision-making. Once this task has been accomplished, the foundation will have been laid for a "meaningful future rapprochement" (p. 61) between theory and practice.

The primary purpose and the major accomplishment of this book is to focus attention on the significance of values in administrative decision making and on the necessity for bureaucrats to develop a concept of the public interest which provides guidance for their recommendations and decisions. Emphasis is placed on the need for bureaucrats to have an "inner check" or a sense of psychological responsibility in the absence of adequate political and judicial controls over the bureaucracy. However, the theoretical and practical utility of the book depends in very large part on the worth of the criterion set forth to assist bureaucrats to make decisions in the public interest. The criterion which the authors suggest – that of human dignity – is as nebulous and ambiguous as the concept of the public interest itself. Most bureaucrats have at least a rule-of-thumb notion of the public interest which they apply according to the factual and contextual circumstances of the case at hand. Admittedly, it is difficult to formulate specific criteria in terms of which the public interest may be discovered. Nevertheless, exhorting the decision-maker to enhance human dignity provides no more guidance than urging him to pursue the public interest.

The authors are unrealistic in expecting schools of public administration to alter substantially the practical orientation of their programs and courses. Yet they are correct in calling upon teachers to make aspiring public servants conscious of the value conflicts and moral issues involved in administrative decision-making. One of the great benefits of having a variety of institutions engaged in teaching and research in public administration (for example, schools of administration, of public administration, and of public affairs, and departments of political science) is that each institution may bring a different perspective to the study of the field. Political scientists, for example, are comparatively free of pressures toward professionally oriented teaching and research. They have the opportunity therefore to undertake much of the needed research into the value issues of public administration.

Finally, the authors' proposals to resolve the *crisis of imbalance* between administrative power and administrative morality are at odds with the need to reconcile administrative power and political power. Denigration of the elected executive's moral or intellectual capacity to determine the content of the public interest may in many instances be justifiable. Nevertheless, appointed officials have no theoretical or constitutional justification for insisting that their value choices be accepted. In the resolution of value dilemmas, the bureaucrat's recommendation is important – even vital; however, the political executive's decision is overriding – and final. Any other interpretation of relations between bureaucrats and politicians implies a break with traditional democratic theory according to which public-policy decisions are the responsibility of the elected representatives of the people.

KENNETH KERNAGHAN
Brock University

Matthew A. Crenson, **The Un-Politics of Air Pollution: a Study of Non-Decisionmaking in the Cities.** Baltimore and London: The Johns Hopkins Press [Toronto: Copp Clark], 1971, pp. viii, 227.

Since it may well put off a lot of potential readers, the title of this book is most unfortunate. In so far as any meaning at all can be derived from a term like "un-politics," the title does justice to neither the substance nor the subtlety of the author's argument. For what this book deals with is one of the most vital political issues of our time: that is, if some people in a city think that a problem (like, say, dirty air) needs something done about it, what sort of political factors determine whether anything (and if so what) is actually done?

To try to answer this question, Matthew Crenson decided to have a look at the issue of air pollution in American cities. The importance of this choice lies in the fact not that air pollution *is* an issue but rather that air pollution has *not* so far been an issue in most cities. "Though there is a technical capacity to reduce air pollution substantially, a legal ability to take significant action, and considerable financial and technical assistance to support that action, many local governments have remained inactive in the face of a demonstrably serious problem and despite an apparent intensification of public concern about the perils of dirty air" (p. 11).

This focus on a "non-issue" rather than an issue leads Crenson to a sustained critique of the pluralist view of local democracy, as epitomized by Robert Dahl (for example, *Who Governs?*). Crenson quotes (p. 184) Robert Wolff (*The Poverty of Liberalism*) approvingly: "The most significant fact about the distribution of power in America is not who makes such decisions as are made, but rather how many matters of the greatest social importance are not the object of anyone's decision at all." Nor is this (in the case of air pollution, at least) merely a matter of government action lagging behind public opinion, for, as Crenson points out, "the available evidence indicates that, in spite of ... new and expanding sources of pollution, the nation's dirty air is in some ways less serious now than it was twenty, thirty, or forty years ago" (p. 11).

The data on which the study is based come from a National Opinion Research Center survey (the "Permanent Community Sample") of 10 formal leaders in 51 American cities, ranging in population from 50,000 to 750,000. The survey was carried out in late 1966 and early 1967, just before the passage of the US Clean Air Act. Drawing on the results of this survey plus data on the actual level of pollution in each city (three different indices are used to measure suspended particulates, sulphur oxides, and photo-chemical smog), as well as two case studies (in the neighbouring cities of Gary and East Chicago) and a 1963 Department of Health, Education and Welfare study of public attitudes towards dirty air, Crenson arrives at a number of interesting and quite specific conclusions – only two of which will be mentioned here.

First: there *is* a "villain" of the piece (the polluting industries), but its influence is less easy to describe than might be supposed. For one thing, "industrial influence does inhibit the growth of the air pollution issue, but the nature of this inhibiting effect depends on the actual level of pollution" (p. 120). Where pollution is high, industrial influence tends to inhibit the *early* growth of the issue, but where pollution is less severe, industrial influence tends to block the *later* development of the issue (p. 118). For another thing, "industry's perceived influence is not a reflection of its actions. If any aspect of industrial behavior underlies industry's power reputation, it is industrial inaction ..." (p. 123). Paradoxically, too,

Crenson argues, the actual condition of the environment seems to have little effect on this: "when industry speaks up on the matter of dirty air, the growth prospects of the air pollution issue are enhanced ... [but] when industry remains silent ... the life chances of the pollution issue are likely to be diminished" (p. 124).

Secondly: the nature of local politics can affect the salience (or "issueness," as Crenson seems to prefer) of air pollution. Crenson distinguishes between cases where party or machine politics dominate the local scene and those where the bureaucracy is strong and secure. In general, he finds that in conditions of relatively low pollution politics tends to inhibit the growth of the issue, but that in conditions of relatively high pollution, and where industry enjoys a reputation for power, "the life chances of the air pollution issue will be greater in cities where political parties are influential than where they are not" (p. 145). Drawing on the work of Edward Banfield, Mancur Olson and others, Crenson attributes the effect of local politics not so much to the possible existence of "unholy alliances" between politicians and industry but rather to the nature of party politics itself. Clean air is essentially a "collective benefit." As such, the "distribution" of this "good" among the various constituents in a community cannot be controlled by the politician. Unless, therefore, air pollution is a serious issue having almost universal appeal, it is not of much interest or value to the politician. Unlike its benefits, on the other hand, the costs of clean air are usually quite specific in their impact. If, therefore, industry enjoys a reputation for power in a community, the allocation of these costs provides what Crenson calls "entrepreneurial opportunities" for the politician (p. 145). Thus, air pollution is more likely to become a salient issue under such circumstances.

Crenson has run into criticism on two main counts: namely, the adequacy of his data to support the conclusions drawn and his interpretation of the pluralists' position. The first criticism is not really a fair one and it may, in fact, come from not following closely enough the often very clever manipulations Crenson uses to get as much as he can from his data. As to his conclusions, Crenson admits they are "not definitive" (p. 177) even with respect to air pollution – to say nothing of other cases of political neglect or "non-issues" – but he does maintain that his results are "highly probable" explanations of why some cities have ignored their dirty air.

The second criticism is that Crenson does not provide a sufficiently exhaustive treatment of the pluralist approach to community power, and instead relies too much on a single book (Dahl's *Who Governs?*) as his protagonist. This criticism is quite true; the problem is that it misses the main point Crenson is making. This is that "the operation of political power ... is not always revealed in observable political action, nor do community political decisions reveal the full range of local policymaking. One must also consider the non-decisions. To put it simply, there is more to local politics than meets the eye" (p. 178).

It is easy to see how pluralists will be annoyed with Crenson. He talks about the "disturbing paradox" in their studies: "On the one hand, they [pluralists] urge us to attribute no more power to reputed political élites than we can actually see them exercise. On the other, they maintain that the power of non-élites is really much greater than their observable actions would indicate" (p. 182). Moreover, Crenson has some pointed comments to make about the relationship between pluralism and democracy. If (he points out) the existence of democracy depends on there being competition among various leaders or élites (with those leaders or élites varying from issue to issue), then there is no guarantee that democracy will extend to those issues over which leaders or élites choose not to compete – whether this choice be by collusion or mere ignorance. The way a society resolves its problems may be democratic, Crenson is saying, but this by itself cannot ensure that the choice of which problems need resolving will also be democratic. In studying the fate of the dirty-air issue in US cities in the late sixties, Crenson has provided some concrete evidence of how pluralistic communities can be either open or closed with respect to certain kinds of issues. This is an important commentary on contemporary political life.

T. J. Cartwright
York University

Holtan P. Odegard, **The Politics of Truth: Toward Reconstruction in Democracy.** University: The University of Alabama Press, 1971, pp. xi, 439.

Odegard describes himself as "a political scientist by profession and a planner by trade," but in this book he ignores these limitations and chooses to abandon all claims to intellectual modesty. Beginning with "transactionalist" psychology and a theory of perception derived from it ("Knowledge can now be expected to leap eagerly forward in this opening field" p.

53.), he proceeds bravely to an examination of teleological ethics ("Scientific investigation brings a closer understanding of the anatomy and the properties of purpose" p. 73.), then to an inquiry into "moral" science ("Science rises above hierarchy and status; it excludes fame and personal advantage as ultimate aims; it insists upon an equality in the face of experiment" p. 121), only to move on to an analysis of political power ("Power is not simply a relation between men, as Lasswell and Kaplan seem to believe"; rather, it is an "organic bond between Selves, a reciprocal co-relating, a full-dimensioned aspect of transaction" p. 132.). At this point we are still less than half-way through the book and wondering what comes next. Odegard does not disappoint us. Forthcoming topics and issues are organized around key concepts: participation, conservative theory, integration, creative bargaining, scientific mediation. Suddenly we pause before a chapter entitled "Purpose in a Pot," but are reassured by an opening statement that it is "in the nature of an interlude of ventured suggestions" (p. 235) and thus need not be treated with the same degree of seriousness. The four final chapters before "Cloture" focus on the heart of the matter: administrative democracy, responsibility, freedom of speech as fulcrum of control, and control through planning. *The Politics of Truth* and the journey through words have come to an end.

In my view, much of Odegard's theorizing amounts to an exercise in reification. He rejects the distinction between the empirical world and the conceptual world. He orders reality according to his "a priori" definitions of concepts and believes that these abstract distinctions exist as distinctions in concrete action and behaviour. He goes even further. Adopting a simplistically dichotomous approach to ideas, he assigns ethical values to many of his concepts dividing them into moral opposites. For example, "function" is desirable while "structure" is undesirable ("This recognition of the priority of function over structure is basic to progress toward ever more satisfactory human conditions. It goes beyond a mere ranking for precedence" p. 50.). He sets up "control" against "coercion" ("Mistaken 'control' is coercion – trying to attain a set end without knowing how," p. 124; "Control tends to degenerate into coercion in proportion as it is separated from knowing," p. 223; "Control ... cannot be got by coercion," p. 118). Odegard seems to be either unfamiliar or unimpressed with Etzioni's classification of political assets into utilitarian, coercive, and persuasive and also with the possibility of social control through the use of any one or a combination of them. Creative bargaining, according to Odegard, can never result in a compromise because it "does not find a solution to satisfy the old opposing patterns of interest. Rather it finds a new common pattern which is more satisfactory to both parties ... The old is willingly discarded in favour of a more inclusive good" (p. 197). Thus, "creative bargaining is a moral process of inestimable worth. Providing as it does the major viable alternative to compromise, it holds out promise of great achievement in politics" (p. 213). This mode of reasoning substitutes tendentious definition for conceptual analysis and synthesis and contributes little to theory-building.

And this, after all, is Odegard's principal aim: to bridge the gap between politics and administration and offer a unified normative theory to guide a new American administrative democracy. He argues that representative government is a thing of the past; that its institutions – legislatures, political parties, elections – are beyond reform; that nearly all politically significant decisions are taken undemocratically within complex public organizations; and that consequently the thrust of democratization and change must be directed against them. His prescriptions however are as reactionary as they are radical, and are often highly misleading. Perpetual revolution turns out to mean either a "process of moral readjustment" or "a controlled conflict to be organized into administration ... and based in conservative drag" (p. 279); administrative responsibility becomes a "homonomous responsibility ... an acceptance of mature responsibility for the control of human conduct" (p. 304); freedom of speech is not "freedom from" but rather "freedom in the skills of ... self control ... listening ... talking ... objectivizing ... making intentions ... and social purposes" (p. 326); planning is described as an administrative function within which the "dichotomies of politics and execution, policy and performance, value and fact are integrated" (p. 331). The following statement, which concludes this review, can speak for itself: "Social control is built upon human moral knowings. Government that approaches perfection – democracy for our day – as a system of strategic control (not coercion) through the functionalizing of power derives its effectiveness and authority from the organized moral (or should we say political?) knowings of the citizens with whom it deals" (p. 276).

George J. Szablowski
York University

anadian Journal of
olitical science
vue canadienne de
cience politique

MICHAEL B. STEIN Le Crédit social dans la province du Québec

DAVID KWAVNICK Pressure-Group Demands and Organizational Objectives

VIRGINIA MCDONALD Locke the Political Theorist

ROBERT R. GILSDORF Voter Susceptibility to Influence

KRISTIAN S. PALDA Does Advertising Influence Votes?

NORMAN WARD The Representative System and the Calling of Elections

ROBERT VAISON A Note on "Public Policy"

M. JAMES DUNN, RODNEY SCHNECK, and JAN LAWSON
Uni-dimensionality of Political Scales

December 1973 décembre VI no. 4

Canadian Journal of Political Science / Revue canadienne de science politique

Editorial correspondence in English should be directed to Professor David Hoffman, Division of Social Science, York University, 4700 Keele Street, Downsview 463, Ont. Subscription and business correspondence should be directed to the University of Toronto Press, Periodicals Department, Front Campus, Toronto 181, Ont.

On doit adresser toute communication en français, au sujet de la rédaction, à M. Vincent Lemieux, Département de science politique, Faculté des sciences sociales, Université Laval, Québec 10e, Qué. Les communications à caractère commercial, y compris celles concernant les abonnements, doivent être adressées à : University of Toronto Press, Periodicals Department, Front Campus, Toronto 181, Ont.

The Journal acknowledges with gratitude the generous assistance of the Canada Council. / La Revue tient à remercier le Conseil des Arts du Canada pour la généreuse subvention qu'il a bien voulu lui accorder.

Subscriptions: Membership in either the CPSA/ACSP or the SCSP includes subscription to the journal. Ordinary membership $15. Student membership $5. Joint CPSA and SCSP membership $17. Joint CPSA and Canadian Economics Association (two journals) $26.

Abonnement : la souscription à l'un des organismes ci-dessus (CPSA/ACSP ou SCSP) tient lieu d'abonnement. Montant de la souscription : tous $15, étudiants $5, conjointe aux deux organismes $17, conjointe à l'Association canadienne d'Economique (valant abonnement à *Revue canadienne d'Economique*) $26.

Postage paid in cash at third class rates — Permit no C-71, University of Toronto Press, University of Toronto, Toronto 181, Ont. / Les frais de poste sont payés au comptant selon le tarif de troisième classe — Permis no C-71, University of Toronto Press, Toronto 181, Ont.

Indexed: Index to *Canadian Legal Periodical Literature* / Indexée au *Catalogue des périodiques juridiques canadiens.*

Published by University of Toronto Press / Publiée par University of Toronto Press.

Contents

Le Crédit social dans la province du Québec : sommaire et développements
MICHAEL B. STEIN 563

Pressure-Group Demands and Organizational Objectives: The CNTU, the Lapalme Affair, and National Bargaining Units
DAVID KWAVNICK 582

A Guide to the Interpretation of Locke the Political Theorist
VIRGINIA MCDONALD 602

Notes

Cognitive and Motivational Sources of Voter Susceptibility to Influence
ROBERT R. GILSDORF 624

Does Advertising Influence Votes? An Analysis of the 1966 and 1970 Quebec Elections
KRISTIAN S. PALDA 638

The Representative System and the Calling of Elections
NORMAN WARD 655

A Note on "Public Policy"
ROBERT VAISON 661

A Test of the Uni-dimensionality of Various Political Scales through Factor Analysis: A Research Note
M. JAMES DUNN, RODNEY SCHNECK, and JAN LAWSON 664

Recensions / Reviews 670

Le Crédit social dans la province du Québec: sommaire et développements

MICHAEL B. STEIN *Université McGill*

Je présenterai ici un bref sommaire de la thèse principale de mon livre *The Dynamics of Right-Wing Protest: A Political Analysis of Social Credit in Quebec.*[1] De plus, je toucherai à certains développements plus récents dans l'évolution du mouvement (depuis 1970), et à la possibilité d'appliquer mon hypothèse à des phénomènes apparus dans cette province ou dans d'autres sociétés.

L'article sera divisé en quatre parties qui répondent aux questions suivantes : (1) Qu'est le phénomène créditiste ? Est-il un parti ou un mouvement politique ? (2) Quel sorte de mouvement politique est le créditisme ? (3) Comment peut-on expliquer, de ses débuts en 1936 jusqu'à présent, les phases fondamentales du développement de ce phénomène, le mode d'apparition du factionnalisme et des scissions qui se sont produites ? (4) Quelles sont les conséquences de ce phénomène sur la politique au Québec et au Canada, et les applications possibles de cette analyse à d'autres phénomènes, au Québec ou ailleurs ?

I. Le phénomène créditiste : parti ou mouvement politique ?

La plupart des commentateurs voient le phénomène créditiste exclusivement comme un parti politique dont les débuts remonteraient à 1957 avec la fondation du Ralliement des Créditistes sous la direction de Réal Caouette.[2] Mais le phénomène créditiste est un aspect important de la scène politique québécoise depuis la crise des années trente. Et il ne l'est pas comme parti politique mais comme mouvement politique.[3]

La structure originale que s'est donné le Crédit social au Québec a été la Ligue du crédit social, fondée en 1936 par Louis Even, journaliste et traducteur d'une imprimerie à Gardenvale près de Montréal, Armand Turpin, alors directeur de production pour la Compagnie Borden à Hull, et Louis Dugal, jeune avocat montréalais. L'organe principal de propagande de la Ligue était les *Cahiers du Crédit Social*, rédigés par Louis Even. Les *Cahiers* ont paru de façon mensuelle, mais irrégulièrement, pendant trois ans. Le contenu de ce périodique

[1]La référence complète se lit comme suit : *The Dynamics of Right-Wing Protest: A Political Analysis of Social Credit in Quebec* (Toronto, 1973).
[2]Ces remarques sont tirées de ma lecture des revues et des journaux consacrés aux aspects du Crédit social au Québec depuis 1962.
[3]Un parti politique se définit comme toute structure politique dont l'objectif primaire est de prendre le pouvoir politique pour ses membres. Un mouvement politique a des objectifs plus vastes incluant la transformation de la société. Ses moyens d'action sont aussi plus variés. Voir la section II ci-dessous.

Canadian Journal of Political Science/Revue canadienne de science politique, VI, no. 4 (December/décembre 1973). Printed in Canada/Imprimé au Canada.

ressemblait beaucoup aux journaux et périodiques de diverses branches ultérieures du mouvement; c'était un mélange des doctrines de réforme monétaire du Major Douglas d'Angleterre (qui ont été présentées pour la première fois en 1918) et des doctrines sociales de l'Eglise, basées sur les encycliques du pape. Les structures de la Ligue ressemblaient aussi aux structures établies plus tard dans le mouvement : des comités locaux dans les diverses paroisses de la province; un président et un secrétaire, membres des conseils de comté; des districts régionaux composés des membres de ces conseils; et enfin un exécutif provincial formé en partie des présidents nommés dans ces districts et en partie des officiers (président, secrétaire et cinq vice-présidents) élus par les délégués au congrès provincial annuel. Mais la Ligue était principalement un mouvement éducatif, dont le siège était à Montréal, et qui comptait plusieurs milliers de personnes. Il était dirigé et principalement formé par des gens de profession libérale ou commerciale. Ses buts principaux étaient l'éducation et la formation d'une élite d'experts en Crédit social. La Ligue ne réussit jamais à former un mouvement de masse.

C'est avec la fondation de l'Union des électeurs en 1939 que le Crédit social réussit vraiment à s'installer comme mouvement populaire dans la province. Cette branche du mouvement fut créée par Louis Even et par Gilberte Côté, fille d'un famille aisée dont le père était manufacturier de chaussures à Montréal. Elle avait reçu une formation universitaire et elle était de plus très dynamique. Les deux quittèrent la Ligue et lancèrent le journal bimensuel *Vers Demain* en septembre 1939, avec l'intention de faire d'un mouvement réservé à une petite élite un mouvement de masse.

Les créditistes étaient très bien connus au Québec, spécialement dans les villes et villages des régions rurales et semi-urbaines de la province (en dehors de la région métropolitaine de Montréal). Le journal *Vers Demain*, publié bimensuellement à Montréal, était distribué par leurs membres à 60,000 personnes environ au cours des années de leur plus grand succès (c. 1948). Leurs cellules étaient implantées dans les fermes et les usines de plusieurs régions du Québec : l'Abitibi (Rouyn-Noranda), les Cantons de l'Est, la ville de Québec, la Mauricie, et le Saguenay-Lac Saint Jean.

De plus, l'Union des électeurs participa directement à plusieurs élections fédérales et provinciales de 1940 à 1957. Elle ne réussit à gagner qu'un seul siège, celui de Pontiac dans une élection partielle. Réal Caouette en fut le député de 1946 à 1949. Néanmoins, ce mouvement obtint plus de 150,000 votes à son apogée (en 1948), soit presque 10 pour cent du vote québécois.

Mais l'Union des électeurs niait toujours que ses objectifs fussent de gagner le pouvoir, comme les partis politiques conventionnels. Au début, elle avait pour but l'éducation des masses (y compris les classes les plus inférieures et les plus pauvres) à la doctrine du Crédit social. L'objectif du mouvement était de mobiliser un groupe de supporters dans chaque région, de faire pression sur les autorités afin de les persuader d'adopter et implanter la philosophie et la technique économique du Crédit social. A la suite du Major Douglas, l'Union des électeurs rejetait le système des partis, qu'elle considérait comme un jeu de marionnettes manipulé par les grands financiers, les banquiers, etc. Elle hésitait à présenter

Social Credit in the Province of Quebec: Summary and Developments

The article first presents the broad outlines of a recent work of the author. It shows that Social Credit was a movement long before it became a political party, a fact which offers the opportunity to present a brief history of the Social Credit phenomenon in Quebec. This political movement is defined as a protest movement, and its ideology is that of the right in the sense that it makes its appeal particularly to conservatism, with a view to preserving a social and economic order threatened with disappearance. One can distinguish three phases in the evolution of the movement: a mobilization phase, a consolidation phase and a phase of institutionalization. For each of these phases there is a corresponding type of leader. Moreover factionalism acts as the catalyst of change of the movement from one phase to another. The last part of the article presents and discusses the recent developments of Social Credit in Canada and in Quebec. Two different choices appear to be available to the party: to radicalize its appeal as a movement of right-wing protest, or to modernize its ideology in such a way as to become a moderate party of the centre right. Finally the Creditiste phenomenon is examined as a particular species of a broader genus which would include the Parti Québécois as well. One could therefore apply to the latter the same type of analysis that was applied to the Creditiste phenomenon.

des candidats aux élections et elle affirmait publiquement à haute voix qu'ils étaient choisis démocratiquement par une union d'électeurs. Ils n'étaient que des délégués de leur circonscription, sujets à révocation (ce qui était une application de la théorie de la démocratie plébiscitaire).

Même en 1957, quand Réal Caouette et 11 de ses amis quittèrent l'Union des électeurs et fondèrent le Ralliement des Créditistes avec l'intention de participer aux élections et de gagner le pouvoir,[4] les éléments originaux du mouvement dans le phénomène créditiste n'avaient pas disparu. Les structures, le mode de financement, et les moyens de propagande étaient tous basés sur le modèle de l'Union des électeurs. Une grande partie des premiers militants étaient des anciens membres de l'Union des électeurs, qui sont devenus et demeurés les leaders du Ralliement pendant toutes les années soixante. La tension a persisté entre les idées du parti et celles du mouvement pendant ces années. Même le parti provincial, le Ralliement Créditiste du Québec, fondé en 1970, a continué d'être inspiré par certaines idées du mouvement. En février 1973, après un schisme éclatant qui a duré presqu'un an, la plupart des militants se sont tournés vers un « non-créditiste », Yvon Dupuis, pour refaire leur union. A ce moment, les cendres de l'ancien mouvement étaient bien éteintes.

En somme, le phénomène créditiste, au moins durant la période 1936–57, se définit comme un mouvement politique plutôt que comme un parti politique.[5] Les origines du phénomène créditiste en tant que mouvement ont inspiré son processus de développement pendant les 20 premières années de sa vie. Et elles ont continué à déterminer les grandes lignes d'évolution des deux partis politiques créditistes jusqu'à nos jours.

Mais le phénomène créditiste est plus qu'un simple mouvement politique.

[4]La scission complète ne s'est pas produite jusqu'en 1958. Voir la section III ci-dessous.

[5]La définition du concept « mouvement politique » est présentée dans la section II ci-dessous.

C'est un mouvement d'un type spécial, que j'appelle un mouvement de protestation de la droite. D'après moi, ce type de mouvement manifeste des caractéristiques particulières qui déterminent ses modes d'évolution et leurs conséquences pour la société dans laquelle il se trouve.

II. Le type sociologique du créditisme : un mouvement de protestation de droite

Dans la littérature de sociologie politique, un mouvement social est défini comme une forme d'action collective visant à mobiliser des individus pour faire des changements fondamentaux dans l'ordre social.[6] Dans toutes les définitions du concept « mouvement social » les éléments centraux sont les sentiments communs de mécontentement et le désir général de changer la société.

Un « mouvement politique » est un type de mouvement social. Il est dirigé vers un changement de l'ordre politique. Il a un certain nombre de traits en commun avec d'autres structures politiques comme les partis et les groupes de pression, qui sont eux-mêmes en compétition pour exercer de l'influence dans l'arène politique (par exemple, l'organisation des individus autour d'idées et d'intérêts communs qu'ils essayent de promouvoir par des moyens politiques).[7] Mais ce qui est plus important, c'est la façon dont les mouvements politiques se distinguent des autres structures politiques plus conventionnelles.

Premièrement, les mouvements politiques ont des buts plus larges que la plupart des autres structures de compétition politique. Ils visent l'éducation politique, la mobilisation des masses, et d'autres modes d'action dirigés vers un changement général. Deuxièmement, les mouvements politiques sont généralement organisés autour d'une série de croyances ou de buts utopiques concrétisés dans une idéologie politique qui agit comme une force d'unification des membres.[8] Troisièmement, les mouvements politiques manifestent une structuration des rôles politiques et une distribution du pouvoir, de l'influence et de l'autorité parmi ses membres, ce qui les distinguent des autres structures politiques. Les structures d'organisation ont tendance à être plus serrées au niveau du leadership et plus souple au niveau des supporters. Les leaders ont tendance à concentrer le pouvoir et l'autorité entre leurs mains afin de maintenir un contrôle sur les décisions qui définissent la stratégie et les tactiques du mouvement.[9]

Il y a deux types principaux de mouvements politiques, définis par leurs buts : les mouvements de protestation et les mouvements révolutionnaires. Le mouvement révolutionnaire est voué à la destruction du système et à l'obtention du pouvoir afin de transformer complètement l'ordre social. Le mouvement de protestation a des buts plus limités : changer la façon dont les décisions sont prises ou transformer les normes qui délimitent ce processus décisionnel, sans détruire le système lui-même.[10]

Les mouvements de protestation ont comme but de politiser la masse et de

[6]Rudolf Heberle, *Social Movements: An Introduction to Political Sociology* (New York, 1951), 6.
[7]*Ibid.*, 9.
[8]*Ibid.*, 12, 434.
[9]K. Lang and G.E. Lang, *Collective Dynamics* (New York, 1961), 495.
[10]R.J. Jackson and M.B. Stein, *Issues in Comparative Politics: A Text with Readings* (New York and Toronto, 1971), 266.

la gagner à leur idéologie. Par une série d'actions dissidentes contre le régime ou ses autorités ils cherchent à attirer l'attention de la population sur leurs griefs. Leurs objectifs sont, ou de persuader les autorités d'adopter leurs points de vue, ou de les déplacer et de prendre le pouvoir eux-mêmes afin d'appliquer les changements qu'ils désirent. Mais ils n'ont pas pour objectifs de changer fondamentalement les règles du régime ou la base de la société. En ce sens, les mouvements noirs en 1960–5 pour l'obtention des droits civiques, menés par les groupes modérés comme le NAACP et CORE, étaient des mouvements de protestation plutôt que des mouvements révolutionnaires.

Sur le plan idéologique, il y a deux types principaux de mouvements de protestation : les mouvements de droite et les mouvements de gauche. Les mouvements de droite font appel surtout, dans des termes généraux, aux secteurs de la population qui sont à long terme appelés à décliner (par exemple, les paysans dans une époque d'industrialisation et les « cols bleus » dans la société « post-industrielle »). Leurs appels sont caractérisés par un désir de préserver les conditions sociales et économiques actuelles ou de recréer la société du passé. Les mouvements de gauche, par ailleurs, font appel à des secteurs de la population qui augmentent à long terme (par exemple, les « cols bleus » dans la société industrialisée et les « cols blancs » ou les « technocrates » dans la société « post-industrielle »). Ils veulent établir les conditions d'une société future, y compris un revenu minimum garanti, des mesures sévères contre la pollution, des services de santé décentralisés. etc.[11]

Les créditistes peuvent être définis comme un mouvement de *protestation* parce que leur opposition au système financier et politique n'a jamais été révolutionnaire. Ils n'ont jamais voulu plus que changer la méthode de distribution du crédit en pensant que tous les autres changements désirés dans l'ordre économique, social ou politique étaient déterminés par la technique économique. Ils ne veulent pas transformer le régime parlementaire ni le système fédéral canadien. Ils ne veulent pas de grandes transformations dans les méthodes d'organisation des groupes sociaux de la société. Ils ne veulent pas la destruction ni l'abolition du système capitaliste dans l'ordre économique. De plus, à l'exception d'une brève période (de 1944 à 1948) ils n'ont jamais voulu de changements fondamentaux du système démocratique.[12]

De plus, le «créditisme » est un mouvement de protestation *de la droite* parce que son appel est essentiellement conservateur et orienté vers la préservation d'un ordre social et économique qui est en voie de disparaître très rapidement au Québec. Les Créditistes croient que les valeurs traditionnelles comme l'obéissance, le devoir, et la moralité étaient plus répandues dans le système social du passé qu'elles le sont aujourd'hui. Ils croient aussi qu'elles seront rétablies aussi-

[11]Il faut évidemment prendre ceci comme la simple description d'une tendance. En certains cas, des suggestions et des tactiques de gauche peuvent plaire à des gens des secteurs déclinants de la population. De même, des mesures de droite peuvent plaire à des gens d'un segment de la population en pleine croissance. Au reste certaines mesures sont proposées en termes suffisamment vagues et émotifs pour attirer des adhérents de droite comme de gauche.

[12]De 1944 à 1948, les dirigeants créditistes ont demandé la création de corps législatifs parallèles aux parlements fédéral et provincial afin de représenter plus fidèlement les électeurs de chaque circonscription. Cette idée aurait été empruntée à l'expérience russe des soviets et aux essais du gouvernement de Lublin en Pologne. Il y eut une tentative de créer de telles structures (unions d'électeurs), mais ce projet se montra irréalisable et fut abandonné.

tôt que l'influence corrompue du capitalisme monopolistique et les appétits avares des banquiers seront restreints par le système du crédit social. Ils prévoient un nouvel essor de l'agriculteur, du marchand dans les petites villes ainsi que des artisans dès qu'ils auront assez de crédit pour se financer. Ils croient au relèvement de l'église et des institutions religieuses, et demandent la préservation du système d'enseignement confessionnel. Ils dénoncent les ravages de la pornographie et des drogues. Ils veulent que le système des communications dans les petites villes et villages soit protégé des effets trop corrompus des moyens de communication urbains.

III. Evolution du mouvement créditiste : ses trois phases fondamentales et leurs catalyseurs

Les analystes des mouvements sociaux ont rarement essayé de décrire les modes d'évolution de ces mouvements et de mettre en évidence les facteurs responsables de leur transformation. On a généralement observé, cependant, que les mouvements politiques tendent à évoluer en trois phases principales qui peuvent être assimilées à des traits caractéristiques de leurs leaders. On peut, grosso modo, différencier ces phases en (1) mobilisation, (2) consolidation, (3) institutionnalisation. Le processus d'évolution tout entier peut être considéré comme une sécularisation graduelle du mouvement et comme une perte de son élan idéologique, menant à sa transformation éventuelle en une autre forme institutionnelle, ou à sa disparition.

La phase de mobilisation est la période au cours de laquelle les militants du mouvement sont recrutés, la masse de la population est soumise au prosélytisme et à la propagande, les structures de base et les modes d'action sont établis. Le processus-type de cette phase peut être décrit ainsi : un noyau de personnes est attiré par l'idéologie dissidente, pour plusieurs raisons – des griefs d'ordre économique, politique ou social, des besoins et des intérêts personnels ou collectifs, etc.[13] Ces personnes viennent de différentes classes sociales, d'éléments marginaux aussi bien que de groupes intégrés, et même de l'élite. Ils croient fortement aux buts du mouvement et consacrent plus de temps et d'efforts à les définir et à les réaliser que les autres adhérents. Ce groupe soulève et oriente les émotions et les griefs des masses aliénées.[14] Durant cette phase les leaders sont plutôt des « prophètes » ou des « prédicateurs ». Ils doivent leur leadership à leur capacité de concrétiser les principales idées et de convertir à leur cause de nouveaux membres. Leur autorité vient de la supériorité qu'on leur reconnaît dans la formulation ou l'interprétation de la « foi », et dans l'art de la mettre à la portée des masses.[15]

[13] Voir, par exemple, les raisons diverses des adhésions à des mouvements politiques, données par Hadley Cantril, *The Psychology of Social Movements* (New York, 1944), chap. 2, 3; Eric Hoffer, *The True Believer* (New York, 1951), chap. I–III; Heberle, *Social Movements*, chap. 5; et Gabriel Almond, *Appeals of Communism* (Princeton, 1954), chap. IV–XI.
[14] Lang et Lang, *Collective Dynamics*, 495.
[15] Les idées exprimées dans ce passage sont tirées en grande partie de Hoffer, *True Believer*, chap. XV; C.W. King, *Social Movements in the United States* (New York, 1956), 72; Neil Smelser, *The Theory of Collective Behaviour* (New York, 1963), 361, et Lewis N. Killian, « Social Movements », *Handbook of Modern Sociology*, ed. Robert E.L. Faris, (Chicago, 1964), 441–3.

A la phase de consolidation, le mouvement développe ses ressources, augmente le nombre de ses adhérents, affermit ses structures, en précise les rouages et modifie sa stratégie et ses tactiques pour faire face aux situations nouvelles. A cette phase, il est généralement dirigé par des hommes qui ont des talents d'organisateur, d'administrateur ou de propagandiste nécessaires.[16]

A la phase d'institutionnalisation, le mouvement essaie de maintenir et d'augmenter ses appuis par des négociations et des alliances avec d'autres groupes. Sa stratégie et ses tactiques deviennent plus pragmatiques, et moins liées à l'idéologie première et aux buts du mouvement; il accepte des compromis. Il est alors généralement dirigé par des hommes pragmatiques et opportunistes, qui ne sont pas aussi versés dans la doctrine originale que l'étaient les premiers leaders. Ils n'y croient pas autant et sont prêts à sacrifier à des fins immédiates ce qui reste du mouvement original.[17]

Une des caractéristiques dominantes des mouvements sociaux est leur tendance inhérente à favoriser l'apparition de factions. On attribue généralement cette tendance aux conflits inévitables qui s'élèvent entre membres doctrinaires et membres moins doctrinaires quand on essaie de mettre l'idéologie en action. Cette tendance se manifeste particulièrement dans les mouvements politiques. En plus du facteur que nous avons mentionné, il y a à cela plusieurs raisons. Le conflit se développe entre membres dont l'âge et l'expérience politique sont proches, conflit qui se manifeste dans les luttes entre les différents types de leaders et les différents styles de leadership.[18] De plus, de nouvelles bases de pouvoir tendent naturellement à se développer en dehors du groupe des premiers leaders; on peut attribuer cette tendance au fait que l'hétérogénéité s'accroît à mesure que le mouvement évolue.[19] Un autre facteur expliquant l'apparition de factions dans les mouvements politiques est la faiblesse de l'appareil de contrôle, particulièrement dans les mouvements de type non-révolutionnaire ou protestataire. Quant des divergences d'orientation se manifestent, le leadership dominant a peu de récompenses à offrir et peu de sanctions en son pouvoir pour maintenir sa prédominance sur les membres du mouvement.[20]

Quoique ces explications soient valables, elles ne vont pas jusqu'au fond des choses. Et, ce qui est plus important, elles ne font pas vraiment le lien entre le phénomène des factions et la dynamique du changement qui est sous-jacente dans les mouvements politiques. La plupart des analystes ont tendance à considérer les factions comme une cause de faiblesse, comme une force destructrice d'énergie, comme une aberration par rapport à la marche normale des processus d'évolution et de développement de ces mouvements.

[16]Les idées exprimées ici sont tirées en grande partie de Hoffer, *True Believer*, chap. XII, King, Social Movements in the United States, 72–4, Lang et Lang, *Collective Dynamics*, 520; Faris, *Modern Sociology*, 441–2; et Smelser, *Collective Behaviour*, 361.

[17]Les idées exprimées dans ce paragraphe sont tirées en grande partie de Lang et Lang, *Collective Dynamics*, 359, 518–20.

[18]Heberle, *Social Movements*, 118–19.

[19]Lang et Lang, *Collective Dynamics*, 533; Smelser, *Collective Behaviour*, 361; et M. Zald et R. Ash, « Social Movement Organizations : Growth, Decay and Change », *Studies in Social Movements: A Social Psychological Perspective*, ed. Barry McLaughlin (New York, 1969), 478.

[20]Lang et Lang, *Collective Dynamics*, 533, Voir aussi Joseph Nyomarky, *Charisma and Factionalism in the Nazi Party* (Minneapolis, 1961).

Cependant, à mon avis, même si les factions provoquent un conflit interne ou un schisme avoué, elles n'en propulsent pas moins le mouvement vers de nouvelles phases d'évolution, où se produisent le remplacement de ses leaders, la réorientation de sa stratégie et de ses tactiques, et la réorganisation de ses structures. Ces orientations nouvelles peuvent être cruciales et déterminer le succès ou l'échec relatif du mouvement. En d'autres termes, c'est le conflit et non l'accord qui est alors considéré comme la norme des mouvements politiques et l'ingrédient essentiel dans la détermination de leur développement et de leurs effets ultimes sur la société dans laquelle ils opèrent. C'est l'hypothèse que j'ai tenté d'exposer dans mon étude sur le mouvement créditiste au Québec. Il me sera impossible ici de faire une analyse détaillée du phénomène du factionnalisme.[21] Je me contenterai de résumer quelques unes des conclusions de cette étude.

D'abord, puisque le créditisme est le prototype d'une catégorie particulière de mouvement politique, à savoir un mouvement de protestation de droite, on peut s'attendre à ce qu'il présente de nombreuses caractéristiques générales des mouvements politiques. De plus, il se pourrait qu'il présente plusieurs traits particuliers à son espèce. De fait, le Créditisme est déjà passé par deux des trois phases typiques de l'évolution des mouvements politiques, celle de mobilisation et celle de consolidation, et il entre maintenant dans la troisième phase, celle de l'institutionnalisation.

La première phase de développement du mouvement créditiste au Québec, de 1936 à 1957, correspond à peu près au type idéal de la « mobilisation ». C'est durant les trois premières années de la période qui commence avec l'établissement de la Ligue du crédit social et de son journal *Les Cahiers du Crédit Social* que les nombreux militants de la première heure, ceux qui formaient le noyau du leadership de la première génération créditiste, se sont joints au mouvement. Mais le recrutement de militants et d'un segment important de la masse ne se produisit qu'en 1940, avec la création de l'Union des électeurs et de son journal bimensuel *Vers Demain*. De 1939 à 1948 le mouvement créditiste a grandi très rapidement en utilisant une méthode de recrutement très simple mais très efficace : on attribuait à chaque membre un certain quota de recrutement. Les formules d'abonnement se trouvaient dans le journal *Vers Demain*. Quiconque obtenait son quota de 25 membres était automatiquement nommé membre du corps d'élite du mouvement, l'Institut d'action politique, qui à son apogée comprenait 2000 ou 3000 membres environ. Les membres les plus dévoués et les plus efficaces de ce groupe étaient nommés au directorat du mouvement, ayant à sa tête Louis Even et Gilberte Côté-Mercier; ce directorat n'a jamais compté plus de sept membres. Les directeurs, avec l'aide de leurs lieutenants dévoués, prenaient les décisions politiques majeures du mouvement, et maintenaient un contrôle strict sur la troupe. Le nombre des adhérents s'éleva, de 2,000 qu'il était au moment de la fondation de l'Union, à 65,000 (d'après les créditistes eux-mêmes) en 1948.

Louis Even et Gilberte Côté-Mercier étaient les chefs indiscutables du mouvement. Even jouait le rôle de « prophète » et d'idéologue. Il réussit à exprimer

[21]Pour un examen plus détaillé du processus de factionnalisme dans le mouvement créditiste, voir Part III, Introduction, chapitres 6, 7 et Conclusion et Part IV de *The Dynamics of Right-Wing Protest.*

les doctrines abstraites de Major Douglas en termes compréhensibles pour la petite bourgeoisie, les travailleurs et les cultivateurs de Québec. Gilberte Côté-Mercier était l'organisatrice et la propagandiste par excellence : elle prit la majeure partie des décisions de stratégie politique et c'est elle qui choisit la plupart des symboles du mouvement, y compris le béret blanc que les membres portèrent à partir de 1949.

Lors de la première phase les créditistes furent loin d'atteindre leur objectif, qui était d'amener une grande proportion des Québécois à souscrire aux doctrines du crédit social. L'effort le plus intense fut fait aux élections provinciales de 1948, alors que l'Union des électeurs présenta des candidats dans les 92 circonscriptions provinciales du Québec. Mais elle n'obtint que 150,000 votes, sans faire élire un seul candidat. A la suite de cet échec, l'Union s'abstint de toute autre tentative électorale.[22] Pendant quelques années, de 1950 à 1957, les créditistes essayèrent une autre technique d'action politique pour implanter le crédit social : ils firent directement pression sur les politiciens. Quand cette technique échoua également, et que le nombre des membres commença à diminuer, les dirigeants se désintéressèrent des choses temporelles, et l'Union prit un caractère plus religieux.

La seconde phase du mouvement créditiste, celle de consolidation, commença en 1957, avec l'arrivée au leadership de la deuxième génération de créditistes, sous la direction de Réal Caouette. Caoutte s'était joint au mouvement en 1940, et s'était affirmé dès le début comme un propagandiste et un meneur de campagnes électorales de premier ordre.[23] Il se présenta aux élections provinciales de 1944 et aux élections fédérales de 1945 comme candidat de l'Union des électeurs, et se classa en deuxième place dans les deux cas. Mais son appétit électoral fut assouvi pour de bon en 1946, quand il remporta le siège de Pontiac dans une élection partielle. D'autres créditistes de la seconde génération partageaient son point de vue, tels : Laurent Legault, son organisateur dans plusieurs campagnes électorales, Gilles Grégoire, fils de J.E. Grégoire, ancien maire de Québec et leader de l'Union au cours de la plupart des premières campagnes, et François Even, fils de Louis Even. Ces leaders de la deuxième génération étaient convaincus que le meilleur moyen d'établir le crédit social était d'organiser un effort électoral concerté. Ils s'opposaient à l'orientation de plus en plus religieuse du mouvement. C'est pourquoi en septembre 1957, douze personnes, la plupart de la seconde génération créditiste, se réunirent à Montréal pour former le Ralliement des Créditistes.

Les fondateurs du Ralliement n'avaient pas à l'origine l'intention de former une organisation complètement nouvelle. Ils voulaient plutôt créer au sein de l'Union une structure politique parallèle qui rallierait à l'action électorale tous les créditistes de la province, y compris les factions dissidentes.[24] Quand les directeurs de l'Union, Louis Even et Gilbert Côté-Mercier, rejetèrent cette idée,

[22]Les créditistes ont participé, sur une base limitée, aux élections fédérales de 1949, et ils se sont aussi alliés aux Libéraux aux élections provinciales de 1956. Ce furent leurs seuls autres efforts de participation directe aux élections.

[23]Dès 1944, le journal *Vers Demain* décernait à Caouette cette épithète pleine d'admiration : « le tonnerre ».

[24]Les factions dissidentes incluaient la poignée de membres qui restaient de la Ligue et les créditistes expulsés de l'Union par Gilberte Côté-Mercier à cause de leur opposition à sa politique et qui, d'année en année, avaient fini par être assez nombreux.

les leaders de la deuxième génération déclarèrent leur indépendance. A l'origine le Ralliement des Créditistes fut conçu comme parti et comme mouvement à la fois;[25] son objectif principal était d'amener les électeurs à voter pour ses candidats et donc de prendre le pouvoir. Mais il n'abandonna jamais ses objectifs éducatifs.

A ses débuts le Ralliement était surtout composé de membres sécessionnistes de l'Union des électeurs, et, de ce fait, ne se développa que très lentement. Mais en 1960 Caouette et Legault firent alliance avec le Crédit social des provinces de l'Ouest, que Robert Thompson était en train de réorganiser. Caouette fut battu de peu par Thompson au leadership national, et fut nommé député leader du parti national. Fait plus important, dès 1958 le Ralliement établit dans diverses régions du Québec une série de programmes de télévision de 15 minutes qui furent plus tard diffusés sur une échelle plus vaste. Caouette y afficha une personnalité puissante et très populaire. Il gagna au mouvement nombre de nouveaux membres qui n'avaient pas fait partie de l'Union des électeurs. Plusieurs d'entre eux étaient des gens de professions libérales qui donnèrent du prestige au mouvement (par example, Marcoux, Chapdelaine, Côté). Mais les « bérets blancs » demeurèrent l'élément dominant parmi les militants. Sous les conseils de Legault, le « parti-mouvement » se donna les mêmes structures électorales et les mêmes méthodes de financement que celles de l'Union. Il présentait ainsi les deux éléments principaux de la définition du « parti de masse » selon Duverger.[26] Si l'idéologie du Ralliment était essentiellement la même, la stratégie et les tactiques étaient fondamentalement transformées. Les leaders du Ralliement se consacraient maintenant sans équivoque à prendre le pouvoir. Les associations de circonscriptions gardaient leurs cercles d'étude, mais l'organisation des futures élections devenait leur but principal.

Le Ralliement gagna un nombre d'électeurs beaucoup plus élevé que ne l'avait fait son prédecesseur, l'Union des électeurs. L'Union n'avait jamais pu obtenir plus de 10 pour cent du vote populaire, tandis que le Ralliement remporta 26 pour cent des voix au Québec aux premières élections qu'il brigua (1962) et il obtint 29 pour cent des voix aux élections de 1963. Ainsi le Ralliement non seulement consolida la base du mouvement créditiste au Québec, mais il l'élargit également. Mais cette base semble limitée, parfois elle diminue, parfois elle augmente légèrement. Elle atteint rarement plus d'un quart de la population totale du Québec, et elle est limitée aux régions rurales et semi-urbaines. En fait, jusqu'aux élections fédérales de 1972, il semblait que le Ralliement Créditiste était continuellement en déclin.[27]

Il n'est donc pas surprenant de constater que vers 1970, avec le vieillissement

[25]Au cours des interviews faites en 1964, Caouette a indiqué qu'il utilisait les termes « parti » et « mouvement » indifféremment quand il mentionnait le Ralliement. Cependant Legault concevait plutôt le Ralliement comme un mouvement dont l'objectif premier était l'éducation politique et économique d'une élite.

[26]Voir Maurice Duverger, *Les Partis politiques* (Paris, 1964, 5ème éd.), 84–5.

[27]Aux élections fédérales de 1962, le Ralliement reçut 26 pour cent du vote populaire au Québec, obtenant 26 sièges; en 1963 il eut 29 pour cent du vote populaire et 20 sièges; en 1965 il obtint 19 pour cent du vote populaire et 9 sièges. En 1968, il reçut 16 pour cent du vote populaire mais augmenta son nombre de sièges à 14; en 1972 il eut 24 pour cent du vote populaire à Québec et 14 sièges. Aux élections provinciales de 1970, le Ralliement Créditiste du Québec reçut 12 pour cent du vote populaire et 12 sièges.

de la deuxième génération créditiste, une troisième génération, comprenant plusieurs fils des créditistes de la deuxième génération,[28] arriva à maturité et commença à prôner la réorientation des buts du « parti-mouvement ». Pour eux la survivance du créditisme était menacée, et le mouvement ne s'était pas adapté aux nouveaux courants de la population, tel que l'urbanisation, le nationalisme et le désir de modernisation économique et culturelle. Ils conçurent une stratégie destinée à transformer le mouvement de protestation de droite en un parti politique conventionnel, avec une idéologie conservatrice plus pragmatique et une base plus large et plus urbaine. Ils contribuèrent ainsi à amener le mouvement à sa troisième phase, celle d'institutionnalisation.

La troisième phase fut amorcée en mars 1970 par la tenue d'une convention destinée à choisir le leader du parti provincial nouvellement créé. Il est intéressant de noter que ce fut Caouette lui-même qui traça la route de cette nouvelle phase. Il résista à toutes les flatteries et aux efforts les plus intenses pour le désigner comme leader provincial, et il proposa Yvon Dupuis comme son choix personnel au leadership. Mais les militants créditistes présents, pour la plupart membres de la deuxième génération, refusèrent d'accepter un homme qui non seulement n'était pas un créditiste authentique mais qui avait été le pire ennemi du mouvement aux élections fédérales de 1963.[29] Par conséquent, ils ne tinrent pas compte de l'appel de Caouette et votèrent à une majorité écrasante en faveur de Camil Samson, un protégé de Caouette, habitant lui aussi à Rouyn.

Les visées de Dupuis pour le leadership n'étaient cependant pas découragées. Quoique les créditistes provinciaux aient fait bonne figure aux élections de 1970, sous la direction de Camil Samson, les créditistes de la troisième génération n'approuvaient pas le choix de Samson comme leader car selon eux il n'avait ni l'éducation ni la sensibilité nécessaires à l'évolution actuelle de la province, non plus que le raffinement nécessaire pour prendre le pouvoir. C'est pourquoi un groupe de députés provinciaux, menés par le jeune président provincial Phil Cossette, réussit à fomenter un complot pour évincer Samson du leadership provincial. Ils choisirent un vieux créditiste, Armand Bois, comme leader intérimaire, et cherchèrent un candidat plus approprié pour diriger les créditistes de la troisième génération. L'homme auquel ils s'adressèrent finalement, à la fin de 1972, fut Yvon Dupuis. Dupuis a remporté la victoire au deuxième tour de scrutin du congrès créditiste provincial de février 1973.

Dupuis est à bien des égards l'incarnation du leader pragmatique de la phase de l'institutionnalisation. Il projette une image jeune et attrayante, il a de l'expérience politique, du raffinement, et il a prouvé ses dons d'orateur. De plus, il s'est gagné une large clientèle politique dans le ville de Montréal en se servant

[28]Y compris les députés fédéraux, André Fortin, René Matte, Lionel Beaudoin, et les députés provinciaux, Camil Samson, Yvon Brochu, Florian Guay, Antoine Drolet, Ronald Tétrault et Paul-André Latulippe, ces deux derniers étant fils des députés fédéraux.

[29]Dupuis, lorsqu'il était candidat libéral, faisait des imitations de Caouette et se moquait des politiques monétaires des créditistes en utilisant des trucs comme le papier-argent. Il fut récompensé de ses efforts en étant choisi comme ministre sans portefeuille dans le premier cabinet Pearson. Mais il fut destitué peu après, à la suite d'un présumé trafic d'influence dans l'octroi d'un permis de course à St-Jean, Québec. La Cour le disculpa plus tard de cette accusation. En 1970, lorsque Caouette tenta de l'imposer aux créditistes, il se signalait comme animateur d'une ligne ouverte du réseau radiophonique CKVL. Il commença à montrer des attitudes politiques de droite assez semblables à celles des créditistes.

avec succès d'un programme radiophonique et de son journal *Le Défi,* qui publiait des lettres de lecteurs en réponse à ses éditoriaux et à ses commentaires à la radio.

Même s'il partage l'orientation conservatrice des créditistes, Dupuis donne des signes d'un désir de moderniser et de renouveler l'idéologie créditiste pour attirer au parti des éléments nouveaux de la population. Il sera sans doute capable de s'allier à d'autres partis comme l'Union Nationale, pourvu que cette entente se montre avantageuse.[30] Il ne semble pas avoir une grande connaissance ni un grand intérêt pour l'orthodoxie du crédit social, ni pour les traditions passées du mouvement. Ses discours ne s'attardent pas aux questions économiques.[31] Son objectif principal est de conquérir le pouvoir politique, et il semble prêt à prendre tous les moyens nécessaires pour y parvenir. Par exemple, il a déjà commencé à transformer les structures financières du parti, basées sur les souscriptions populaires, en faisant appel ouvertement aux grandes corporations. Il n'y a pas de doute que si éventuellement la responsabilité du leadership repose complètement sur ses épaules et sur celles de la troisième génération, le « créditisme » se transformera d'un mouvement de protestation de droite en un parti politique conventionnel de centre-droite, comme cela existe à l'heure actuelle en Alberta et en Colombie Britannique.

Ainsi le créditisme est passé par les phases typiques des mouvements politiques dans leurs processus d'évolution et d'adaptation aux changements des conditions de la société. Mais nous en savons peu sur le catalyseurs de ces phases. L'expérience créditiste nous suggère un certain nombre d'hypothèses.

Premièrement, chaque nouvelle phase et chaque réorientation du mouvement semblent avoir été causées par une nouvelle génération de leaders, partageant de nouveaux points de vue mais demeurant toujours dans le cadre de la famille créditiste. Ainsi Yvon Dupuis semble être l'instrument de la troisième génération plutôt que son maître. Son succès dépendra de sa capacité d'adaptation aux conditions qui existent à l'intérieur du mouvement. Il y a beaucoup moins de chances qu'il réussisse à changer ces conditions.

Deuxièmement, à chaque phase le changement d'orientation du mouvement a généralement été précédé d'une période de factionnalisme interne qui s'est intensifiée et a provoqué des scissions ouvertes. Ce conflit semble avoir servi de catalyseur premier en créant et en imposant un changement fondamental et une réorientation du mouvement.

Troisièmement, quoique le factionnalisme et les scissions se soient produites pendant toute l'évolution du mouvement, le factionalisme semble avoir atteint son plus haut degré à la phase de consolidation, en dépit du leadership ferme de Réal Caouette. Ceci semble dû à plusieurs facteurs : c'était à ce stage que le

[30]Le leader de l'Union Nationale, Gabriel Loubier, a déjà fait plusieurs déclarations publiques réclamant une alliance des partis d'opposition. Cependant, jusqu'ici, Dupuis a repoussé ces avances, probablement parce que l'opinion publique a tenté de le discréditer juste avant son élection comme leader en disant justement qu'il conduirait les créditistes à ce genre d'alliance. Voir *La Presse*, le 3 février 1973, *Le Devoir*, le 3 février et 23 février 1973, et *The Montreal Star*, le 3 mars 1973.

[31]Ces conclusions sont tirées d'un essai portant sur une analyse du journal *Le Défi* et d'une interview avec Dupuis faite par Mme Vera Murray. Ces travaux ont été faits dans le cadre d'un séminaire de deuxième cycle, conjoint entre l'UQAM et McGill, sur la culture politique au Québec (avril 1973).

conflit entre les adhérents du concept de « mouvement » et ceux de concept de « parti », entre protestataires modérés et protestataires très dissidents[32] (« highly disaffected ») a été le plus intense; les moyens de contrôle interne à la disposition du leadership s'étaient affaiblis lorsque le mouvement avait commencé à se transformer en parti plus conventionnel; les forces externes du milieu québécois – nationalisme, modernisation économique et sociale, conflit économique et linguistique – se sont accrues et ont influencé sérieusement les développements internes du mouvement; le mouvement semblait avoir atteint sa limite extrême d'expansion.

Quatrièmement, même si les causes du factionnalisme à chaque stage sont évidemment complexes, on peut isoler certains sous-groupes de leaders qui peuvent être considérés comme des forces motrices du changement. Lors d'un sondage mené auprès de 69 leaders créditistes en 1967,[33] j'ai pu distinguer deux sous-groupes principaux : les leaders « modérés » et les leaders « très dissidents » (highly disaffected).[34] Ces deux sous-groupes, qui se distinguent non seulement par leurs attitudes politiques mais aussi par leurs origines socio-économiques et leurs modes de participation politique, sont en conflit constant au sujet des objectifs, de la stratégie et des tactiques du mouvement. A la phase de mobilisation, ce conflit est plus facilement contenu puisque le mouvement est en cours d'expansion. Cependant, à la phase de consolidation, il se produit des reculs inévitables, particulièrement dans un mouvement de protestation dont le potentiel électoral est restreint. Les leaders de cette phase, plus politiques que ceux de la première génération et plus modérés aussi, font face à l'opposition des leaders plus dissidents. On peut alors faire l'hypothèse suivante : à ce stage, l'absence de contrôles structurels, sociaux et personnels et l'importance primordiale accordée par les membres aux buts du mouvement laissent libre cours à la tendance naturelle des membres « très dissidents » (highly disaffected) à tourner leur insatisfaction contre le mouvement lui-même et contre les chefs modérés. Il en résulte des conflits insolubles. Quand ces conflits sont renforcés par des différences d'origines et de statut social entre ces deux sous-groupes, le désaccord se produit sur la distribution des statuts et des rôles à l'intérieur du mouvement. Le conflit et les alliances qui en résultent conduisent au schisme.[35]

[32]La définition de ces concepts est donnée à la note 34.

[33]Pour une description de cette enquête, de l'échantillonnage, et du questionnaire, voir les Appendices A et B dans *The Dynamics of Right-Wing Protest*, 240–6.

[34]Les leaders créditistes « très dissidents » ont été définis comme ceux dont les réponses au sondage ont montré une forte désapprobation des systèmes politiques et économiques (c'est-à-dire, que, dans l'échelle de désapprobation, ils arrivaient aux cinquième et sixième rangs). Ils diffèrent aussi des autres créditistes en plusieurs points, tels que leur statut socio-économique, leurs modes de participation aux associations volontaires et au mouvement, leur autoritarisme, leurs tendances à la conspiration, et leur conception de la protestation. Les leaders « modérés » sont les autres créditistes non-inclus dans ce sous-groupe, qui ont répondu d'une façon plus modérée aux questions concernant ces attitudes. Voir les chapitres 5 et 7 dans *The Dynamics of Right-Wing Protest*.

[35]Dans mon livre, je pousse plus loin cette hypothèse basée sur les données de l'enquête, selon laquelle les leaders « très dissidents » peuvent être subdivisés en deux groupes : ceux de statut socio-économique plus élevé, (qui tendent à perdre leur intérêt au mouvement et à diminuer leur participation active dès le début du processus de factionnalisme) et ceux de statut socio-économique plus bas (qui s'allient avec des dissidents plus modérés de bas statut). Ce nouveau sous-groupe, qu'on classifie comme des « dissidents de classe inférieure » conduit le mouvement à un schisme.

Cette hypothèse d'un comportement « schismatique », que nous avons établie d'après les données recueillies au cours de notre sondage, peut être représentée graphiquement comme suit (voir graphique 1).[36]

En utilisant cette hypothèse, on peut expliquer non seulement la scission de 1963, comme j'ai essayé de le faire dans mon livre, mais aussi avec les modifications appropriées, celles de 1966 et 1972.[37]

IV. Conclusions : les conséquences du phénomène sur les politiques québécoise et canadienne et l'application possible de la thèse à d'autres phénomènes

Pour évaluer les conséquences de ce phénomène sur la politique québécoise et canadienne, il est nécessaire de situer le mouvement créditiste dans un contexte socio-économique et politique plus large. Comme nous l'avons indiqué précédemment, il s'agit d'un mouvement idéologiquement de droite, qui représente une réaction conservatrice d'un segment de la population québécoise aux forces inexorables de modernisation qui se manifestent au Québec depuis le début du siècle tout au moins. Les statistiques de l'appui électoral donné aux créditistes, présentées par Vincent Lemieux et Maurice Pinard,[38] montrent que la base électorale du mouvement est restreinte presque exclusivement aux régions rurales et semi-urbaines de Québec, (Abitibi, Cantons de l'Est, sud du Québec, Saguenay-Lac Saint Jean en particulier). C'est essentiellement la même base et le même bastion du mouvement qui existaient au temps de l'Union des électeurs.[39] Aux élections fédérales de 1972, dans la région métropolitaine de Montréal, les créditistes firent une percée pour la première fois, sans toutefois réussir à gagner un seul siège.[40] Quelques indices suggèrent que le choix de Dupuis comme leader provincial a donné un élan aux efforts du parti provincial pour pénétrer les régions fortement urbanisées de Montréal et de Québec, quoique de récents sondages laissent penser que cette expansion n'a qu'une envergure limitée.[41] On peut prédire avec quelque certitude que l'appui électoral au

[36]Ce graphique est une réplique exacte du modèle graphique présenté à la page 182 de *The Dynamics of Right-Wing Protest.* Je suis reconnaissant au Professeur Maurice Pinard de m'avoir aidé à construire ce modèle graphique.

[37]Je ferais l'hypothèse que ces « schismatiques » de 1966, qui ont aidé à former le Ralliement National, étaient en grande partie des leaders « très dissidents » de la seconde génération créditiste. Après le mauvais résultat obtenu aux élections provinciales de 1966, et surtout après la formation du Parti Québécois, en 1968, qui absorba plusieurs créditistes parmi les plus indépendantistes, les « schismatiques » retournèrent au Ralliement Créditiste. De 1968 à 1970 ils furent, avec les créditistes les plus pragmatiques de la troisième génération, les principaux instruments de la formation du parti créditiste provincial. La rupture entre les factions Bois et Samson en 1972 s'est produite essentiellement entre les créditistes très dissidents de la deuxième génération et les créditistes de la troisième génération plus modérés, pragmatiques, et orientés vers la modernisation.

[38]Voir Vincent Lemieux, « Les dimensions sociologiques du vote créditiste au Québec », *Recherches sociographiques*, VI, 2 (1965) 181–95 et Maurice Pinard, *The Rise of a Third Party: A Study in Crisis Politics* (Englewood Cliffs, N.J., 1971).

[39]Voir Lemieux, « Dimensions sociologiques », 182–3.

[40]Les votes créditistes dans la région métropolitaine de Montréal passèrent de 19,188 à 107,172.

[41]Voir le sondage fait par le Centre de Recherche sur l'Opinion Publique (CROP) publié pour la première fois dans *Le Devoir* du 8 juin 1973, et republié dans le même journal après correction d'une erreur de pondération, le 15 juin 1973. Le sondage revisé donne 12.6 pour cent des choix aux créditistes, comparé à 34.7 pour cent aux Libéraux, 17.7 pour cent pour le Parti Québécois, et 3.8 pour cent pour l'Union Nationale. 31.2 pour cent des personnes

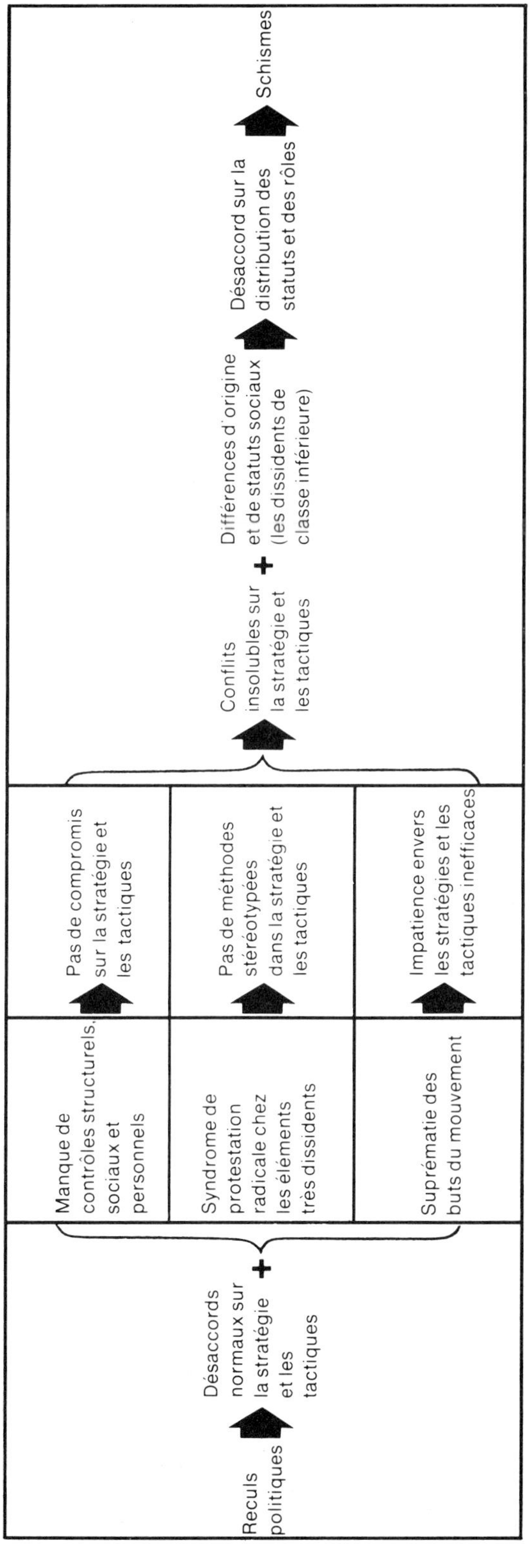

GRAPHIQUE 1. Modèle du comportement schismatique.

créditisme, de même que son leadership, restera dans un avenir proche un phénomène surtout rural et semi-urbain (comme le montrent les résultats de mon propre sondage).[42]

Des tentatives furent faites pour transformer l'idéologie protestataire de droite, qui combinait les doctrines du Major Douglas et les idées sociales catholiques de nature conservatrice, en un conservatisme plus modéré de centre-droite semblable à celui de l'Union Nationale. Par exemple, Caouette prône maintenant un projet de revenu annuel garanti préconisé d'habitude par la gauche (bien que ceci puisse être simplement une adaptation habile de la vieille idée créditiste d'un dividende national). Les appels de Dupuis sont plus négatifs dans leur orientation, quoiqu'ils insistent aussi sur de vagues notions créditistes comme « la personne humaine » et « la démocratie du peuple ». Ses appels s'en prennent surtout aux forces insidieuses du socialisme dans la province, comme les politiques de Claude Castonguay, ministre libéral des affaires sociales, de Jean Cournoyer, ministre actuel du travail, et de Jean-Paul L'Allier, ministre actuel des communications. Il attaque aussi fortement les « communistes », les « felquistes », et les orientations révolutionnaires de leaders syndicaux comme Louis Laberge de la FTQ, Marcel Pépin et Michel Chartrand de la CSN, et Yvon Charbonneau de la CEQ. Il s'attaque aussi aux idées séparatistes et socialistes de René Lévesque, Claude Morin, Jacques Parizeau et d'autres membres du Parti Québécois.[43] Ces appels peuvent aider les créditistes à maintenir leur bastion actuel et leur attirer certains employés non-syndiqués et non-spécialisés des districts ouvriers de Montréal et de Québec, particulièrement ceux qui ont l'esprit de « la classe ouvrière autoritaire » ou au moins sont traditionnels et conservateurs.[44] Cependant, il semble improbable que les créditistes trouvent appui chez les ouvriers de gauche plus organisés et chez les gens plus évolués des professions libérales et de la bureaucratie québécoise de classe moyenne.[45]

Selon moi, tous les mouvements socio-politiques reflètent les forces socio-

---

interrogées refusèrent d'indiquer leurs préférences électorales. En tenant compte du pourcentage habituel d'électeurs qui n'indiquent pas leur choix, ces résultats montrent que depuis les élections de 1970, le RCQ n'enregistre qu'une légère augmentation. Le bastion principal continue à être la région située en dehors des villes de Québec et Montréal. L'appui donné à Dupuis comme leader était un peu inférieur à l'appui donné au parti lui-même.

[42]Pour une description du lieu de résidence des leaders créditistes, voir *The Dynamics of Right-Wing Protest*, 124–5.

[43]Ce sont les impressions personnelles que je retire des discours de Dupuis au congrès de leadership à Québec en février 1973 et des programmes de télévision et radio ultérieurs ainsi que d'articles de journaux tels que *Le Devoir*, du 13 juin 1973. Voir également Vera Murray (voir la note 31).

[44]Le concept de l'autoritarisme de la classe ouvrière est défini par Seymour Lipset, *Political Man* (Garden City, N.Y., 1960) chap. 4. De plus il est possible que les travailleurs récemment arrivés dans les régions urbaines aient gardé leurs attitudes traditionnelles et conservatrices sur bien des questions économiques et politiques, de même que leurs attaches partisanes précédentes. Pour un argument un peu différent sur cette question, voir Maurice Pinard, « Working Class Politics: An Interpretation of the Quebec Case », *Canadian Review of Sociology and Anthropology*, 7 (2), 1970, 87–107 et « The Ongoing Political Realignments in Quebec », *Quebec Society & Politics*, ed. Dale Thompson (Toronto, 1973), 130.

[45]Les récents sondages tendent à confirmer cela. De plus, voir l'enquête faite par Maurice Pinard, « The Ongoing Political Realignments in Quebec », *Quebec Society and Politics*, 119–35. Pinard souligne, cependant, que les appels protestataires des mouvements de droite comme de gauche peuvent être formulés en termes suffisamment vagues pour attirer des électeurs mécontents sans plus. Voir *The Rise of a Third Party*, 95–6.

économiques et politiques plus larges qui sont présentes dans la société ou ils se trouvent. Le mouvement créditiste est un mouvement politique authentiquement québécois qui est apparu dans la province au cours des années de la « crise » et qui répondait aux sentiments d'inquiétude et d'insécurité de certains segments de la population dont la situation économique déclinait. Ils ne pouvaient pas comprendre cela et c'est pourquoi ils craignaient les nouvelles tendances à l'urbanisation, à l'industrialisation, à la bureaucratisation, à la sécularisation et à l'explosion des moyens de communication. Depuis quelque temps au Québec le courant de la modernisation était évident : une société qui, d'après le recensement de 1881, était rurale à 77 pour cent, était devenue, en 1931, urbaine à 56 pour cent.[46] Les premières étapes importantes de l'industrialisation ne commencèrent qu'à la première décade de ce siècle, mais après la première guerre mondiale ils s'intensifièrent de façon remarquable.[47] Ces forces, lentes au début, prirent beaucoup d'expansion après la deuxième guerre mondiale, avec l'encouragement donné par le régime Duplessis aux investissements étrangers. Elles ont contribué à apporter des changements dans les relations entre l'Eglise et l'Etat, dans l'éducation, les communications et l'accroissement de la bureaucratie provinciale, toutes choses généralement associées à la révolution tranquille de 1960.

Le créditisme, avec son idéologie protestataire de droite et sa base rurale et semi-urbaine, est un mouvement qui répond de façon appropriée au segment de la population québécoise qui se sent sérieusement menacé par ces tendances. Ces craintes sont justifiées en ce sens que les traditions rurales et semi-urbaines du Québec sont appelées, à longue échéance, à céder aux forces inexorables de la modernisation. Dans ces régions il y aura une accentuation du déclin économique et de la diminution de la population, ainsi que de la transformation des valeurs adoptées par la jeunesse. Le créditisme lui-même est appelé à décliner en tant que force politique, à moins qu'il ne se transforme en un phénomène fondamentalement différent, soit un parti conservateur modéré qui attirerait des électeurs des secteurs urbains et industriels croissants de la population.

En résumé, le créditisme a actuellement deux choix : radicaliser son appel protestataire de droite en s'éloignant ainsi du Québec d'aujourd'hui; ou moderniser son idéologie, recruter de nouvelles élites urbaines, et se transformer en un parti modéré de centre droite. Le vacuum laissé dans l'éventail politique par l'Union Nationale, un parti modéré de droite, qui semble maintenant en voie de désintégration, a pour effet d'encourager les créditistes provinciaux à faire le deuxième choix.[48] En dépit de leur démagogie et de leur négativisme actuels, il semble évident que les leaders créditistes présents ou futurs trouveront en fin de compte ce choix plus attirant que l'autre.

Cependant, la modernisation elle-même n'a guère de chance d'amener le

[46]Voir Marcel Rioux, « Sur l'évolution des idéologies au Québec », *Revue de l'Institut de Sociologie*, Université Libre de Bruxelles (1968), 108–9.

[47]Voir P. E. Trudeau, *La Grève de l'Amiante*, (Montréal, 1956), Introduction, 3–10.

[48]Le récent sondage de CROP a montré que 3.8 pour cent seulement de la population a l'intention de voter pour l'Union Nationale aux prochaines élections. Voir *Le Devoir* du 15 juin 1973, p. 11. Ceci continue la diminution constante de l'appui donné à l'Union Nationale, indiquée par quatre sondages successifs faits depuis le 18 avril 1970 (*Le Devoir*, le 8 juin 1973, p. 1).

Ralliement Créditiste à son but ultime qui est de prendre le pouvoir au provincial ou au fédéral. Aussi longtemps que trois partis seulement se partageront l'électorat de la province, il faudra plus qu'un tiers de la population pour amener un parti au pouvoir. Dans le contexte québécois d'aujourd'hui le Ralliement Créditiste du Québec, avec son leadership actuel, semble peu susceptible d'enlever suffisamment de votes urbains au Parti Libéral ou au Parti Québécois pour atteindre ses objectifs. Seule une crise économique et politique entraînant un déséquilibre extrême pour le Québec pourrait changer cette conjoncture.

Quant aux créditistes fédéraux, qui constituent le noyau du parti réunifié qui a été rebaptisé « Crédit social du Canada », leur avenir, à long terme, semble encore plus sombre. Quoique le parti ait fait meilleure figure au Québec et dans les autres provinces, aux élections fédérales de 1972,[49] il n'a jamais récupéré les pertes subies dans les provinces de l'Ouest, ce qui était un de ses objectifs majeurs lors de la réunification. Le parti du Crédit social du Canada semble voué à demeurer un parti fédéral à base régionale, dont les bastions seront limités surtout aux régions rurales et semi-urbaines du Québec. Caouette – leader et pilier du parti – a eu récemment des problèmes de santé dus au diabète, et il est possible qu'il s'apprête à se retirer. Par l'appui non équivoque qu'il a donné à Dupuis, dont l'âge et les orientations pragmatiques appartiennent tout à fait à la troisième génération créditiste, Caouette a peut-être indiqué son intention de laisser le fardeau du leadership à des hommes plus jeunes. Il est intéressant de noter qu'àu début de 1973 il a désigné son fiils Gilles, élu pour la première fois au parlement fédéral en 1972, comme porte-parole officiel du parti en son absence.

Etant donné ces perspectives futures plutôt sombres pour le mouvement, on peut s'attendre à ce que les processus de factionnalisme et de schisme se répètent à la troisième phase d'institutionnalisation. Ces conflits internes produiront sans doute de nouveaux leaders qui auront des orientations différentes et pourront peut-être amener une amélioration temporaire dans le parti. Le processus de factionnalisme devrait finalement diminuer lorsque la tension entre l'aspect « mouvement » et l'aspect « parti » ainsi qu'entre les leaders « très dissidents » et « modérés » se résoudra en faveur de ces derniers. Si cela se produit, la survie à long terme du Crédit social, en tant que parti distinct au niveau fédéral comme au niveau provincial sera en danger.[50]

Le mouvement créditiste n'est en aucune façon un phénomène unique au Québec et au Canada. Ainsi que j'ai tenté de le prouver, c'est un prototype d'une forme politique plus générale qui se manifeste dans bien des sociétés en voie de transformation. Ceci est vrai non seulement des mouvements protestataires de droite qui ont surtout la faveur de la petite bourgeoisie, des ouvriers non-organisés et des cultivateurs des régions rurales et semi-urbaines à la périphérie de la société moderne, urbaine et industrialisée. C'est vrai également des mouvements protestataires et révolutionnaires de gauche qui se mani-

[49]Au Québec le Parti est passé de 16 pour cent des votants en 1968 à 24 pour cent en 1972. Dans tout le Canada il a doublé son soutien électoral par rapport à 1968, et obtenu 708,000 votes (*Regards*, vol. 12, nos. 9–10–11, 1972).

[50]Une crise économique ou politique soudaine pourrait aider à améliorer son avenir, à court terme tout au moins.

festent en diverses sociétés chez les ouvriers organisés, les professionnels, les bureaucrates de la classe moyenne et les étudiants. Ces mouvements sont susceptibles de montrer bien des caractéristiques communes avec leur contre-partie de droite, quoique leur mode d'évolution et la dynamique de leurs conflits et de leurs transformations soient susceptibles d'être différents. Par exemple, le Parti Québécois peut être considéré comme un mouvement social-démocrate et nationaliste modéré de gauche, dont le leadership se recrute surtout parmi les étudiants de CEGEP et des universités, les professeurs et autres professionnels. Mais il a une forte base électorale dans les milieux ouvriers de Montréal. On y observe sans aucun doute la même tendance à la formation de sous-groupes à l'intérieur du leadership, ainsi que l'a montré la division entre les « électoralistes » et les «participationnistes » à un récent congrès du Parti Québécois.[51] Si le parti connaît un recul aux prochaines élections provinciales, il pourrait se produire un processus similaire de factionnalisme, de conflit interne et de schisme, qui pourrait avoir pour effet de changer le leadership actuel et de réorienter l'idéologie du mouvement. Son avenir paraît brillant s'il continue sa course actuelle en exposant des idées sociales et économiques nouvelles et modérées et en proposant une politique qui séduit les secteurs en croissance de le société québécoise contemporaine – c'est-à-dire les professionnels, les bureaucrates, les ouvriers organisés et les jeunes.[52] Le modèle exposé ici (distinction de phases fondamentales et de leurs catalyseurs) peut aussi s'appliquer à ce « parti-mouvement », mais je laisserai à d'autres le soin de conclure s'il s'applique ou non, et comment.

[51]Voir *Le Devoir*, le 26 février 1973, 6.

[52]Comme l'a suggéré son manifeste *Quand nous serons vraiment chez nous* et le programme social-démocrate modéré adopté à son congrès de février, 1973. Il y a des conflits entre les objectifs politiques d'indépendance et les objectifs socio-économiques caractéristiques d'une démocratie sociale modérée qui attirent différents segments de la population québécoise. Voir Daniel Latouche, « The Independence Option: Ideological and Empirical Elements ». dans Dale C. Thomson, *Quebec Society and Politics*, 179–94. Ce domaine sera peut être le point le plus vulnérable pour le parti. Les prochaines élections provinciales, qui auront lieu en octobre 1973, devraient montrer clairement si ce conflit peut être résolu facilement ou non.

Pressure-Group Demands and Organizational Objectives: The CNTU, the Lapalme Affair, and National Bargaining Units

DAVID KWAVNICK *Carleton University*

It was pointed out in an earlier paper[1] that students of interest groups have traditionally concerned themselves with the process by which demands are brought to the attention of the political decision-makers, the manner in which the demands are articulated, and the extent to which government activity is influenced by the demands. Consequently, it was noted, students of interest group activity had developed a form of "tunnel vision"; that is, their determination of which demands ought to be studied was made on the implicit assumption that the most important demands, and hence the ones most deserving of their attention, were those which reflected the objectively important needs, or the strongly felt aspirations, of the groups' membership.

That paper went on to suggest, however, that interest group leaders in their relations with government might seek objectives other than the advancement of the interests of their groups' membership: specifically, that objectives related to organizational maintenance and enhancement might be among the more important objectives sought by interest group leaders.

In another work[2] a theoretical framework for the study of the pursuit of organizational maintenance and enhancement was set out at some length. It was stated, in essence, that the organizational objectives of interest group leaders were advanced through the pursuit of legitimacy and mandate. Legitimacy, in this context, refers to the position of the interest as a respectable and accepted part of the political and social system. Mandate, in this context, refers to the position of a particular spokesman group as the recognized and accredited representative of the interest on behalf of which its leaders claim to speak.

One means of strengthening the mandate of a group, it was pointed out, is through expansion of its membership. In the case of labour organizations one of the more convenient means of expanding the membership is by raiding another labour organization.

The works cited above did not go beyond suggesting that interest group leaders pursued objectives related to organizational maintenance and enhancement *concurrently with* or *in lieu of* objectives related to the satisfaction of the needs of the membership. It was not suggested that interest group leaders might pursue organizational objectives *at the expense of* the vital interests of their

[1]"Pressure Group Demands and the Struggle for Organizational Status: The Case of Organized Labour in Canada," this JOURNAL (1970), 56–72.
[2]Kwavnick, *Organized Labour and Pressure Politics: The Canadian Labour Congress 1956–1968* (Montreal and London, 1972) especially chap. 5.

Canadian Journal of Political Science/Revue canadienne de science politique, VI, no. 4 (December/décembre 1973). Printed in Canada/Imprimé au Canada.

La poursuite de fins organisationnelles par un groupe de pression : la CSN et les unités nationales de négociation dans l'Affaire Lapalme

Une article précédemment paru dans cette Revue *(III, 1970, pp. 56–72) avait établi qu'il arrivait que les dirigeants de groupes de pression poursuivaient, dans leurs relations avec les gouvernements, des buts autres que la promotion des intérêts de leurs membres. Ainsi, il apparaissait que le maintien et la croissance des structures organisationnelles pouvaient devenir des objectifs prioritaires pour les dirigeants.*

Le présent article étudie le rôle de la Confédération des Syndicats Nationaux dans l'Affaire Lapalme à la lumière de ses tentatives antécédentes pour faire amender certaines dispositions de la Loi sur les Relations de Travail et les Conflits Industriels. L'auteur y défend la thèse selon laquelle les leaders de la CSN *ont utilisé le conflit opposant les chauffeurs de la Compagnie Lapalme et le gouvernement fédéral pour alimenter leurs propres différends avec le gouvernement fédéral et le Congrès du Travail du Canada en tentant de jeter le discrédit sur le principe des unités nationales de négociations, principe dont l'application contrevenait aux efforts de la* CSN *pour recruter des membres québécois au sein des syndicats affiliés au* CTC *dans des entreprises relevant de la juridiction du gouvernement fédéral.*

groups' membership or that they might sacrifice those vital interests in attempting to secure organizational advantages or in realizing their organizational ambitions. The present paper argues precisely that point.

It is the thesis of this paper that the leadership of the Confederation of National Trade Unions (CNTU)[3] used the Lapalme drivers and their dispute with the government of Canada to pursue their own dispute with the government and with the Canadian Labour Congress (CLC) in the matter of national bargaining units. It is here contended that the CNTU leadership risked, and ultimately sacrificed, the most vital interests of the Lapalme drivers in a dispute which ultimately concerned only those leaders' ambitions for organizational aggrandizement.

Briefly stated, the argument is that the CNTU leadership refused to accept any settlement of the Lapalme drivers' dispute unless that settlement included recognition of a CNTU local as bargaining agent for the drivers. In order to reach a settlement on those terms it would have been necessary for the government of Canada (i) to circumvent the objections of the Public Service Staff Relations Board and the postal unions, (ii) to over-ride the Public Service Staff Relations Act, and (iii) to abandon the principle of national bargaining units. The first two steps could not have been taken without the introduction of special legislation which would have had the effect of realizing the third step. The realization of this third step, the abandonment of the principle of national bargaining units, has been the objective of a long and hard-fought campaign by the CNTU leadership.

The present paper should not be understood to say that interest group leaders continuously and habitually sacrifice the vital interests of their members in order to further their organizational ambitions. It does, however, demonstrate that, given sufficient opportunity and motivation, this can happen.

[3]This organization is known in French as the Confédération des syndicats nationaux (CSN).

I. The CNTU and national bargaining units

The dispute between the CNTU and the CLC over national bargaining units has been described in detail elsewhere.[4] In brief, the CNTU leadership wishes to expand the size of their organization and one way to expand the membership of a union is by raiding another union.[5] During the 1960s, various affiliates of the CLC and the CNTU were almost constantly raiding each other.[6]

The CNTU ran into insurmountable difficulties, however, when it attempted to raid CLC unions in the broadcasting and railway industries. A successful raid requires that the raiding union be certified by a labour relations board as the exclusive bargaining agent on behalf of the newly acquired members. In the case of the broadcasting and railway industries the certifying authority is the Canada Labour Relations Board.

Labour relations boards were originally established to do away with the bitter, and often violent, confrontations between labour and management on the question of union recognition. Certification of a union by a labour relations board places an employer under a legal obligation to recognize that union as the exclusive bargaining agent for the employees for whom it was certified and to bargain with that union in good faith.

Labour relations boards decide a number of questions, but only two are pertinent to this discussion. First, the boards decide whether or not a majority of the workers in a given bargaining unit do in fact wish to be represented by the union seeking certification. This question is normally settled by means of a representation vote. Second, the boards decide whether or not the newly organized workers constitute an appropriate bargaining unit, for example, should a union be certified to represent the employees performing a particular type of work or must the union also organize other workers in the same premises

[4]Kwavnick, *Organized Labour and Pressure Politics*, 123–33.

[5]Union A is said to be "raiding" Union B when Union A's organizers attempt to convince workers already organized and represented by Union B to switch their allegiance to Union A.

[6]For example, the following taken from the *Report of the Executive Council to the Sixth Constitutional Convention of the Canadian Labour Congress* (Ottawa, 1966), 17:

> "During the year 1964 the Confederation of National Trade Unions launched a major general program of raiding against Canadian Labour Congress affiliates ...
>
> Officers of the Congress and the Quebec Federation of Labour decided to establish a jointly-controlled team of organizers directed by a Co-ordinator, which would be mobile enough to serve as a defensive force wherever raids occurred ...
>
> During the early stages of the opposition's raiding activity substantial inroads were made on the membership of Congress affiliates. More than 10,000 members were lost during this period. By the end of 1964 the counter measures taken by the Congress and the Quebec Federation of Labour had begun to take effect. In spite of continued vigorous activity on the part of the CNTU, the unions under attack, with the assistance of the flying squads of organizers from the special team, were able to bring the string of successful raids to a halt ...
>
> The activity of the special team was not confined to defensive activity. In several cases raids against the CNTU were undertaken, which, although not always successful, indicated very clearly that the CNTU is far from invulnerable ...
>
> At the end of the year there were signs of an increase in the tempo of raiding activity by the CNTU and it has become necessary to set up defence programs on behalf of members of affiliate unions in very strategically important bargaining units, such as the Canadian Broadcasting Corporation and the railways."

performing related tasks or, in the case of an employer who has several premises, is it sufficient that the union has organized the workers at one of the premises or is the "appropriate bargaining unit" all of that employer's premises.

The composition of labour relations boards is balanced between labour and management with a neutral chairman appointed by government. The labour and management representatives are appointed upon the nomination of organizations representative of labour and management respectively. In the case of the labour members on the Canada Labour Relations Board, one is appointed upon the nomination of the CNTU, one upon the nomination of the Railway Brotherhoods, which are affiliates of the CLC, and two are appointed upon the nomination of the CLC itself.

In early 1966, a CNTU affiliate succeeded in organizing a group of CBC employees in Quebec who were at that time represented by a CLC affiliate. The Canada Labour Relations Board, however, refused certification to the CNTU union on the grounds that the appropriate bargaining unit in this case was Canada-wide. But the CNTU has virtually no base outside the province of Quebec and so the organizational ambitions of its leaders were stalled, at least temporarily, by the principle of the national bargaining unit and the application of that principle by the Canada Labour Relations Board.

The problem, as it appeared to the CNTU leadership, was to get the Canada Labour Relations Board to alter its view of what constitutes an appropriate bargaining unit in Canada-wide industries. This, in turn, would require that the composition of the labour representation on the Board be altered to do away with the greater representation enjoyed by the CLC, on the not unjustified assumption that the CLC nominees would always act to protect their own organization.

On 4 December 1967, following a vigorous and intensive lobbying campaign by the CNTU, the government introduced Bill C-186. The purpose of the bill was to amend the Industrial Relations and Disputes Investigation Act in such a way as to give the CNTU the substance of what it demanded – the neutralization of the CLC's majority on the labour side of the Board. The CLC responded by launching "a national campaign of unprecedented intensity."[7] The bill was never passed; it died on the order paper when Parliament was dissolved for the general election of 1968. The CNTU leadership was left champing at the bit awaiting, with growing impatience, the bill's reintroduction.

Another factor in the dispute was the unionization of the federal public service. The Public Service Staff Relations Act of 1966 provided collective bargaining rights for federal public servants and established the Public Service Staff Relations Board to perform for the public service the same functions that the Canada Labour Relations Board performs for industries under federal jurisdiction.

The CNTU attempted to organize some of the federal public servants in Quebec and, in particular, some of the many thousands of French-Canadian public servants in the Ottawa-Hull area. However, they were not able to make

[7]Canadian Labour Congress, *Report of the Executive Council to the Seventh Constitutional Convention of the Canadian Labour Congress* (Ottawa, 1968), 3–4.

much headway against the Public Service Alliance (PSA)[8] which already had the allegiance of most federal public servants and which was therefore able to claim certification.

It would have availed the CNTU little even if it had been able to organize the public servants in various work units in Quebec or in the Ottawa-Hull area. It would then have had to seek certification by the Public Service Staff Relations Board whose labour members are nominated by organizations which have as much of a vested interest in preserving national bargaining units as has the Canadian Labour Congress.[9] Thus, again, the organizational ambitions of the CNTU leadership came up against the principle of the national bargaining unit. The organizations whose membership the CNTU coveted, and wished to raid, controlled the mechanisms which would have to legitimize their raids, and the principle of the national bargaining unit provided those organizations with a convenient peg upon which to hang an argument in defence of their own organizational self-interest.

By 1970, four years had passed since the CNTU had begun its assault upon the principle of the national bargaining unit. In December 1967, it had seemed that the victory was won. But their efforts had all come to naught and they were growing impatient with a government which, while remaining committed to the reintroduction of Bill C-186, appeared to be most reluctant to act.

II. The Lapalme affair

THE FIRST PHASE

Since at least 1913, postal trucking services in Montreal had been provided by private entrepreneurs operating under contract to the Post Office Department. Over the years the contract had been awarded to a number of different contractors. However, each new contractor had traditionally taken into his employ the drivers employed by the previous contractor. As a result, some drivers had built up impressive records of seniority. By early 1970, 117 of the 457 drivers had more than 10 years' seniority and one driver reportedly had 43 years of seniority.[10]

In 1954 the mail delivery contract had been awarded to Rod Service Ltd. The drivers were not then represented by a union and this situation continued until October 1965, at which time a local union affiliated with the CNTU was certified by the Canada Labour Relations Board. Disagreements between the union and Rod Service Ltd. led to four annual strikes between 1966 and 1969. Only the first strike was a legal one.

By 1969, the contractor decided that the contract was not worth the labour relations problems involved in carrying it out. On 22 January 1969, Rod Service Ltd. informed the Post Office Department that it had no interest in continuing the contract beyond its expiration date of 31 March, 1969. Afer futile nego-

[8]The Public Service Alliance was formed in 1966, following the introduction of collective bargaining in the public service, by the merger of previously existing organizations. These organizations (the Civil Service Association of Canada and the Civil Service Federation of Canada) had been in existence for many years.

[9]In fact, the Public Service Alliance is an affiliate of the Canadian Labour Congress.

[10]*Le Devoir*, 4 February, 1970, p. 3.

tiations with the contractor, the postmaster-general announced that the Post Office would itself provide mail trucking services in Montreal. This alternative was rejected by the union on the grounds that it would have meant the integration of their members into the public service and the consequent dismantling of the local bargaining unit.

The matter remained unresolved and the drivers remained uncertain about their future employment. The result was a series of strikes and slowdowns during February and March 1969 which ended only when the Post Office revoked the Rod Service Ltd. contract and entered into a temporary one-year agreement with G. Lapalme Inc., a subsidiary of H. Lapalme Transport. The contract between the Post Office and Lapalme required of the new contractor that he hire the former Rod Service drivers and assume the obligations undertaken by Rod Service Ltd. in its contract with the union.

Later that year the Post Office policy on trucking services changed. Until that time trucking contracts had been given out without benefit of public tenders and for short terms, usually only one year at a time. The new policy called for public tenders and five-year contracts. In addition, the Montreal trucking operation was to be divided into five parts with separate tenders being called for each part. The Post Office Department claimed that the division of the service into five parts enabled many small contractors to enter bids. The union later claimed that the sole purpose of the manoeuvre had been to break the union.[11]

In September 1969, G. Lapalme Inc. was informed of the new policy and was asked to inform its employees. Tenders were called in December 1969. However, the documents setting out the conditions of the tenders specified an hourly wage of not less than $2.82, the minimum rate set by the parity committee.[12] Since this was less than the drivers were receiving under the terms of their contract the union refused to co-operate with the employer in the preparation of tenders. As a result, G. Lapalme Inc. did not enter a bid for any of the five contracts.

The new contracts were awarded on 16 January 1970, and signed shortly thereafter. Thus, by the end of January the Lapalme drivers were faced with the fact that their contract with Lapalme and Lapalme's contract with the Post Office would expire simultaneously on 31 March and the new contractors were under no obligation to employ them or to recognize their union. The result was uncertainty and desperation among the drivers who faced unemployment in a city which already had a very high unemployment rate.

On 4 February the drivers acted, disrupting mail services by means of slowdowns and "study sessions." The Postmaster General attempted to circumvent the strikers by contracting for outside help. The drivers responded with sabotage and violence. On 17 February, the CNTU and the Quebec Federation of Labour, the provincial arm of the CLC, announced the formation of a common front to pursue the struggle on behalf of the Lapalme drivers. The disruption of mail services continued through two fruitless meetings between the CNTU leadership

[11]*Le Devoir*, 7 February, 1970, p. 1.
[12]Parity committees in Quebec are empowered to establish minimum wage rates for various trades in different parts of the province. Their rationale lies in the traditional Roman Catholic social philosophy of Quebec and their original purpose was to ensure the payment of a "just wage" in accordance with the various papal encyclicals on the subject.

and the postmaster-general and an abortive mediation attempt by the minister of labour.

On 18 March, in the face of continued disruption and mounting public pressure, the government appointed H. Carl Goldenberg as a commissioner under Part I of the Inquiries Act: "to inquire into the contracts that have been entered into for the vehicular delivery of mail in Montreal ... and the status and rights of all employees presently involved in vehicular mail deliveries, including their collective rights ... and to recommend such measures in that regard as he considers equitable and desirable for the restoration of normal and effective service in Montreal."[13]

THE GOLDENBERG REPORT

The appointment of a commissioner did not bring an end to the disruption of mail services or cause an ebbing of violence. On 26 March, in the midst of a still deteriorating mail delivery situation, Mr Goldenberg submitted his report. Responsibility for the dispute was laid entirely upon the government: "the invitation to tender made no reference to the hiring of present personnel. In my opinion this was a serious omission. Although the Post Office was not their direct employer, its change of policy would directly affect the livelihood of the Lapalme employees. The Post Office was therefore under a moral obligation to seek to protect their employment as far as possible."

The report recommended the cancellation of the five contracts awarded by tender and further:

> that the Post Office should assume operation of the postal transport service throughout the City of Montreal and that the Lapalme employees should be integrated in the Public Service of Canada in the order of their acquired seniority having regard to adjustments in requirements, the necessity of which is admitted.
>
> The recommended integration should be effected jointly by the Post Office Department and the Public Service Commission with due regard to justice and the special requirements of the case. If this is done, the employees concerned will have achieved security of employment and will enjoy the other benefits and working conditions of Public Service employees. Their collective rights should be assured in the normal way by the Public Service Staff Relations Act.

Two days later, the government announced its acceptance of the recommendations. In addition, the press release announcing the government's acceptance virtually assured positions in the Public Service to all the Lapalme drivers: "Because of the high rate of turn-over and an increasing workload in the Post Office, those engaged under these arrangements can be assured of security of employment. Those not engaged will be placed on a waiting list in the Post Office and accorded preference for employment as mail service couriers."

The problem, however, was far from being resolved. Even as the government was announcing its acceptance of the Goldenberg recommendations, Raymond Parent, secretary-general of the CNTU, was outlining the three questions that still remained unanswered. The first concerned wage rates. The union contract with Lapalme had established an hourly wage of $3.25. The contract between the Post Office and the Canadian Union of Postal Workers (CUPW), then being renegotiated, had established a top rate of $3.00 per hour.

[13]Order-in-Council P.C. 1970–492 dated 17 March, 1970.

Second, there was the question of seniority and the related problem of the probationary period for employees entering the Public Service. The Goldenberg Report had made no specific recommendations on these matters although it had contained a general statement about "due regard to justice and the special requirements of the case." The government's offer had mentioned seniority only as the factor which would govern the order in which the drivers would be offered positions in the Public Service; it had made no mention of the probationary period. Meanwhile, the presidents of the CUPW and the Letter Carriers' Union were reported to have taken the position that the Lapalme drivers would have to enter the Public Service as new employees.[14]

The third question dealt with union security. The Goldenberg Report had recommended that the collective rights of the Lapalme drivers "should be assured in the normal way by the Public Service Staff Relations Act." This would normally have meant that the drivers, upon joining the Public Service, would become members of the CUPW, the union which had been certified as the exclusive bargaining agent by the Public Service Staff Relations Board and which had a contract with government. For the drivers to be represented by a union other than the CUPW would require either another certification under section 26 of the Public Service Staff Relations Act or agreement by the CUPW to waive the rights it had acquired by virtue of its certification and under its existing contract with the government. The possibility that either of these alternatives would come to pass was negligible, and the CNTU leadership understood this. Therefore, rather than face the Public Service Staff Relations Board, the CNTU demanded that its representation rights be assured by the government. The leadership of the CUPW, on the other hand, was reported to be adamant in claiming its rights as the exclusive bargaining agent on behalf of all postal drivers employed by the Post Office.[15]

The government gave the Lapalme drivers until 31 March to accept its offer based on the Goldenberg Report. The government's spokesman, Treasury Board President C.M. Drury, announced that if the drivers turned down the government's latest offer other drivers would be engaged to move the mails.

On 30 March, Vincent Prince of *Le Devoir*, in a lead editorial entitled « Le conflit des postes : la CSN se montre trop intransigeante sur certains points »[16] analysed the latest government offer and the position of the CNTU. On the subject of job security and the probationary period he said:

Le gouvernement a aussi accepté de respecter les droits d'ancienneté des employés de Lapalme. La priorité dans le réembauchage sera donnée à ceux qui ont le plus d'années de service.

Tous, évidemment, ne pourront être repris. Mais cela est fort compréhensible. G. Lapalme Inc. avait augmenté ses effectifs de quelque 110 employés environ en ces derniers mois. Il l'avait fait apparemment surtout sous la pression du syndicat et parce qu'il ne lui en coûtait pas plus cher, son contrat étant, en quelque sorte, du type « cost plus ». C'était une situation à corriger.

[14] *Le Devoir*, 28 March, 1970, p. 2.
[15] *Ibid.*
[16] *Le Devoir*, 30 March, 1970, p. 4. This editorial is cited in detail because it appears that the government's offer of 6 April was made with one eye on its recommendations. The probable reasons which prompted the government to make this offer are discussed later.

and made the following recommendations:

> Même si nous reconnaissons qu'il a pris une bonne décision en acceptant de respecter l'ancienneté, il pourrait, disons, convenir de reprendre ceux qui ont au moins deux ans de service.
>
> Ottawa pourrait aussi pousser cette reconnaissance de l'ancienneté un peu plus loin. Dans son offre, l'ancienneté ne s'applique qu'à l'embauchage. Il devrait au moins prévoir que ces employés de Lapalme, une fois passés à la fonction publique, seront considérés dès le départ comme permanents. En d'autres termes, il devrait les exempter de l'année de probation.

With respect to the union demand that the government undertake to provide the various benefits set out in its contract with Rod Service Ltd. and Lapalme, in particular, the demand that the drivers be paid the hourly rate of $3.25, the editorial said:

> Là, nous prétendons que le syndicat se montre trop exigeant. La fonction publique ne peut être tenue de respecter une convention qu'elle n'a pas elle-même signée. Elle créerait, en ce faisant, un précédent dangereux. Il faudrait, au moins, si elle acceptait de payer ces nouveaux camionneurs plus cher que ceux qu'elle emploie déjà ellemême, qu'elle puisse leur refuser certains avantages qu'elle consent aux membres de la fonction publique en contre-partie de salaires moins elévés.

The least justifiable demand, however, according to M. Prince, was that which dealt with union recognition:

> Mais, là où les exigences de la CSN nous paraissent vraiment excessives, c'est quand elle demande au gouvernement de reconnaitre provisoirement son unité de négociation en attendant une décision de la Commission des relations de travail. Le gouvernement qui agit ici comme employeur n'a pas a préférer un syndicat à un autre.
>
> La CSN devrait accepter le transfert de ses syndiqués à la fonction publique sans poser de telles conditions. Ce n'est qu'une fois ce transfert effectué qu'elle devrait s'empresser de présenter une requête à la Commission des relations du travail pour faire reconnaître son syndicat comme agent négociateur à la place de l'union des postiers.

As the deadline approached, the CNTU and the government held a series of eleventh-hour meetings, but without result. On 1 April, the drivers lost their jobs and dug in for a long fight.

THE SECOND PHASE

The withdrawal of the Lapalme drivers and the recruitment of replacements did not end the dispute. The drivers continued to meet daily in an arena in the east end of Montreal. *Le Devoir* ran an editorial on 3 April urging the government to be less rigid and the cabinet met on the same day to consider the possibility of a further offer to the drivers. On 6 April the drivers began what was to become a familiar tactic – picketing the parliament buildings in Ottawa. While the drivers were marching on Parliament Hill, their leaders were meeting with Treasury Board President C.M. Drury who presented them with a revised government offer. The new offer was to be held open until 15 April.

Under the terms of the new offer, the Lapalme drivers employed by the Post Office would be paid at the hourly rate of $3.25, rather than at the lower rate provided in the contract between the Post Office and the CUPW. The fact that the drivers would also receive the full range of public service fringe benefits made this offer more generous than that suggested by the *Le Devoir* editorial of 31 March.

The editorial had also suggested that the standard six-month probationary period be waived; the new government offer reduced it to one day.

In the matter of retention of seniority the government faced a more difficult problem. However, under a special arrangement with the Council of Postal Unions (made up of the CUPW and the Letter Carriers' Union) the drivers would be permitted to retain their relative seniority for a period of three months. The government was unable to go any further in this regard because seniority normally gives a worker rights not only vis-à-vis his employer but also vis-à-vis his fellow workers in such matters as choice of vacation times, choice of shift, etc. Understandably, the Council of Postal Unions was unwilling to agree to the permanent deterioration of the relative position of those workers who were already members of its affiliated unions. The government was unable to act unilaterally because the provisions regarding seniority were incorporated into the contracts which it had previously negotiated with the postal unions.

However, with respect to the major consideration where the recognition of seniority did not prejudice the relative position of other workers – seniority pay scales – the government agreed that "previous service with Lapalme Inc. and Rod Services Ltd. would be recognized in determining their rates of pay in the future."[17]

To the drivers who could not be engaged immediately by the Post Office, the government offered severance pay of up to 28 weeks' salary. Inasmuch as the drivers had never been government employees, the government's offer of severance pay is probably unique in the annals of labour relations. Moreover, the drivers were not entitled to severance pay from their former employer: the contract between the CNTU and Lapalme had made no provision whatever for severance pay.

The drivers hired by the Post Office were to receive the full range of Public Service fringe benefits. The differences in the fringe benefits provided under the CNTU contract with Lapalme and those provided in the Public Service were substantial. The Lapalme contract had made no provision for a pension plan; the Public Service pension plan, financed by equal contributions by employer and employees, provided for pensions of up to 70 per cent of average earnings during the six years of highest earnings. The Lapalme contract had made no provision for severance pay; the Public Service provided severance pay of up to 28 weeks salary. The Lapalme contract had provided for up to two weeks at full salary in the event of industrial accident; the Public Service provided full salary during the entire period of incapacity. The most important fringe benefit, however, derived from the fact that the Public Service offered the drivers a degree of job security that they could never have enjoyed under the contracting-out system.

The only question that remained outstanding related to the retention of representation rights by the CNTU. On this matter Mr Drury said "that the position of the government with regard to the status of the CNTU as the bargaining agent for the drivers was unchanged. He said the government can take no other position than that the law must be observed."[18]

[17]Treasury Board press release, 7 April, 1970 (mimeo).
[18]*Ibid.*

The offer was rejected the next day by the union. At a stormy meeting in Montreal the drivers, harangued by the CNTU leadership and led on by the leaders of other CNTU affiliated unions who promised money, support, and even mentioned the possibility of sympathy strikes, remained united behind the CNTU leadership. Given the urgings of their leaders, it is not difficult to understand the decision of the drivers. Prior to unionization they had worked under appalling conditions and were truly exploited by the mail delivery contractors. In the four years following certification of their union they had gone out on strike four times. Although three of those strikes had been illegal, their leaders had always been able to bring them through the strikes victoriously. Even in the dispute then underway, the drivers had only to compare the position in which they had found themselves in January, when the five new contracts had been awarded, with the government's latest offer to see the extent to which their leaders had forced the government to retreat. Thus, when their leaders told them to reject the government's offer and promised them total victory, they fell into line and followed.

The CNTU leadership had rejected the government's offer "en alléguant qu'elle ne tenait pas compte de trois principes primordiaux : maintien de l'unité de négotiation, droits acquis et sécurité d'emploi."[19]

Of the three reasons cited, only the first, maintenance of the bargaining unit, can have been meant seriously.[20] In the matter of *droits acquis* (seniority and acquired rights) the government had gone as far as it could possibly go without actually violating its contract with the postal unions. The question of job security had initially caused some anxiety, particularly in view of the provision for a one-day probationary period. The more suspicious drivers wondered whether they would be taken into the public service only to be released after their first day on the job. Mr Drury quickly put an end to that speculation when he wrote to CNTU President Marcel Pepin to assure him that "le gouvernement n'embauchera pas les nouveaux employés pour les mettre à pied le lendemain."[21]

With the rejection of the ofer of 6 April, it was evident that no amount of concessions by the government would be acceptable to the CNTU unless those concessions included complete capitulation on the issue of union representation.

The government offer of 6 April, even more generous than the Goldenberg recommendations, presented the CNTU leadership with a problem which had been implicit in their strategy from the moment that the government announced its acceptance of those recommendations. Only if public opinion was convinced of the justice of their cause could the CNTU leadership hope to force the government to retreat still further. However, convincing public opinion was dependent upon demonstrating that the various government offers would still leave the drivers suffering under an injustice. Prior to the appointment of the Goldenberg Commission this had been an easy task. However, it became more difficult after

[19]*Le Devoir*, 8 April, 1970, p. 1.
[20]This view was shared by others, see *Le Devoir*, 13 April, 1970, p. 4, and 8 June, 1970, p. 2. In April 1971, the CNTU published a small book on the affair by a member of its Secrétariat d'action politique, Pierre Vadeboncoeur, entitled *366 Jours et tant qu'il en faudra.* The book dwells exclusively on the issue of preserving the bargaining unit as the stumbling block to an agreement with the government.
[21]*Le Devoir*, 13 April, 1970, p. 3.

the government had appointed one of the most respected labour mediators in the country to investigate the problems and recommend an equitable solution, and almost impossible after the government had accepted his recommendations without reservation even though those recommendations ran counter to its previously stated policy.

The offer of 6 April was so generous that rejection of it threatened to undermine public confidence in the credibility of the CNTU leadership. The strength of the government's position lay in the fact that it had accepted the Goldenberg recommendations without reservation and had even gone beyond them. It was thus evident to the CNTU leadership that an attack upon the government's position would have to be begun by discrediting Mr Goldenberg.

Accordingly, on 9 April the CNTU leadership accused Mr Goldenberg of having prepared his report in accordance with secret instructions from the government: "M. Pépin a accusé M. Goldenberg d'avoir sacrifié son devoir aux intérêts de M. Kierans et d'avoir préparé son rapport avec l'avis de certains ministres."[22] The only evidence offered by the CNTU was the text of what purported to be a leaked cabinet document, prepared before the appointment of the Goldenberg Commission, setting out the rationale behind the government's refusal to accede to the CNTU demand for maintenance of the bargaining unit. It was alleged that a copy of this document had been submitted to the commissioner.

The effect of this accusation was to undermine still further the credibility of the CNTU leadership. An editorial in *Le Devoir* shortly after the accusation was made spoke of "la sortie disgracieuse d'un Marcel Pépin contre le Commissaire – enquêter Carl Goldenberg."[23]

The 15 April deadline passed and the Post Office began hiring new drivers. The Lapalme drivers, with ample encouragement from their leaders, held fast to their demand for complete capitulation by the government. While the Post Office recruited new drivers the Lapalme drivers occupied themselves by committing various acts of vandalism against postal trucks and holding a demonstration on Parliament Hill in Ottawa where Marcel Pépin gave them another pep talk and promised the full support of the CNTU.

On 21 April, the CLC formally withdrew from the common front which its Quebec branch had earlier entered into with the CNTU. It appeared to the CLC leadership that their counterparts in the CNTU had ulterior motives in pursuing the dispute. The release read, in part:

> The situation prevailing among postal truck drivers in Montreal must not be allowed to undermine the collective bargaining process prevailing in the federal public service, nor destroy established national bargaining units.
>
> We have the utmost sympathy for the Montreal workers in their efforts to maintain job security and obtain decent wages and working conditions. It should, however, be recognized that they can obtain full protection of these and other rights through the unions which are now established in the postal service.
>
> We are determined that the interests of the recognized unions now in the service shall not be jeopardized because this particular group has been misled. It may not be unreasonable to assume that efforts to win special recognition for this unit, outside the established unions, is simply a means of attempting to gain inroads in the whole process of national collective bargaining.

[22] *Le Devoir*, 10 April, 1970, p. 3.

[23] *Le Devoir*, 13 April, 1970, p. 4.

Were this back-door approach to succeed, it would have repercussions far beyond the present Montreal situation and would threaten the entire structure of national collective bargaining in transportation, communication and other vital areas.[24]

THE FINAL PHASE

The recruitment of new drivers altered the circumstances of the dispute in a fundamental manner. Before 15 April, while the government's offer remained open, the Post Office had relied upon rented trucks to move the mails. The new drivers recruited by the Post Office after 15 April would, in accordance with the existing contract, become members of the CUPW. This union would then be bound to protect their job security in any settlement between the Post Office and the Lapalme drivers.

The drivers spent the next few months picketing on Parliament Hill in Ottawa and receiving periodic pep talks from the CNTU leadership while they attempted to keep up public interest in their case. They received some encouragement with the appointment, on 24 September, of a new postmaster-general to replace Mr Kierans. The successor, Jean-Pierre Coté, agreed to re-open negotiations. Talks were delayed by the kidnap crisis of October 1970 and it was not until 17 December that the government announced a new offer. The main points of the offer, outlined in a Post Office Department press release, were:

1. The positions currently available in the Post Office Department in the Montreal area, as well as those positions which will become vacant in the next year, for which the former Lapalme employees can qualify, are offered to them on a priority basis as outlined in Paragraph 8.
   At the moment, 109 positions are available, or will be in very short order. In the next year it is estimated that a little over a hundred other positions will be made available.
2. Through the services of the federal Manpower Department, all positions currently available, as well as those positions which will become vacant in the next year, in the Public Service in the Montreal area, for which the former Lapalme employees can qualify, are offered to them on a priority basis as outlined in Paragraph 8.
   A list of available positions will be drawn up by the Manpower and Immigration Department as soon as the ability, the competence and the potential of each former Lapalme employee is evaluated by Departmental advisors.
3. The federal Department of Manpower and Immigration offers to all former Lapalme employees, who do not receive job offers according to paragraphs 1 and 2, training programs to enable them to qualify for positions in the Public Service which will become available in the next year. Those persons taking this training will receive the customary allocations ...

5. The years of service of the former Lapalme employees will be taken into account when the available positions are allocated.

8. The former Lapalme employees will be considered on the same basis as those people on the Public Service layoff list.[25]

This offer, quickly rejected by the union, marked the beginning of a new phase in the affair. To the CNTU leadership it was now clear that the battle was lost, that they would not be permitted to use the Lapalme drivers as a means of attacking the principle of national bargaining units. To the drivers the offer

[24]CLC news release, 21 April, 1970 (mimeo).
[25]Post Office Department news release, 17 December, 1970 (mimeo).

brought a rude awakening. Up to this point, each new government offer had represented an improvement over the previous offer. Moreover, the drivers appear to have believed that, come what may, the government could never go back on an offer once announced, that they would always be able to retreat to the previous government offer. The offer of 17 December demonstrated that their position had deteriorated drastically since the previous April.

The state of affairs as revealed by the offer of 17 December had the effect of dividing the CNTU leadership and the drivers. Once defeat was recognized, the strategy of the CNTU leadership changed, their objective became to disembarrass themselves of the Lapalme drivers as quickly as possible. First, because anything which brought the affair to mind was the remembrance of a grave defeat and as such was an unwelcome embarrassment. A more practical reason was the financial problem. It had been one thing to provide strike pay and expense money to several hundred drivers while it appeared that their long marches on Parliament Hill might yet result in the breakdown of the principle of national bargaining units. It was another matter to bear those heavy expenses in the knowledge that the struggle was hopeless and gave every appearance of being interminable.[26] The drivers, on the other hand, now had very little to lose and they sought a great intensification of the struggle with nothing less than total victory as the acceptable goal, it now being evident that anything less than total victory would leave them very badly off indeed. In accordance with their revised strategy the CNTU leadership attempted to convince the drivers to accept something less than total victory, something which lay within the realm of possibility. The drivers, in turn and in accordance with their own strategy, became increasingly adamant in their refusal to compromise. With each side pushing its own strategy the inevitable result was to embitter the drivers against the CNTU until, by the end of December 1970, it could be said that "les gars de Lapalme s'estiment trahis."[27]

After a month of infighting within the CNTU the drivers acted. On 9 February 1971, they occupied the Montreal headquarters of the CNTU "pour forcer la centrale à faire son ouvrage."[28] The drivers were of the opinion that the CNTU leadership was not exerting itself on their behalf with sufficient vigour. Frank Diterlizzi, president of the Lapalme local, said in an interview:

> On voudrait que ceux qui vivent de l'oxygène du syndicalisme fassent du syndicalisme. Ca fait dix mois qu'on fait des suiveux. La comédie est finie: on se rend à la réalité.
>
> On veut que Trudeau et la CSN mettent fin aux conflits de personnalités entre eux, avec nous pris entre les deux. On ne sera pas les moutons, les victimes du système établi. Ils ont fini tous les deux de jouer avec nous.[29]

It was also reported of Mr Diterlizzi that "(il) estime que la CSN les a délaissés, qu'elle les considère comme un boulet aux pieds, qu'à l'insu des travailleurs elle 'marchand' avec le gouvernement pour trouver une façon élégante de s'en débarrasser." The CNTU, according to its strategy, was attempting to find some

[26]Strike pay alone was costing the CNTU over $12,000 per week.
[27]*Le Devoir*, 30 December, 1970, p. 4. Also *La Presse*, 29 December, 1970.
[28]*Le Devoir*, 10 February, 1971, p. 1.
[29]*Ibid.*, pp. 1 and 2.

way of relieving itself of the Lapalme affair and to this end was negotiating with the government in an attempt to get what it considered a reasonable offer, that is, an offer along the lines of the one rejected in April 1970. The drivers, following their own strategy, were determined not to let the CNTU off the hook.

Negotiations were undertaken between the CNTU and the Lapalme drivers in an effort to end the occupation which the CNTU leadership found particularly embarrassing. The drivers presented three conditions:

1. Que M. Gérard Picard, ancien président de la CSN se joigne aux trois négociateurs désignés par la centrale, MM. Raymond Parent, Pierre Vadeboncoeur, et Maurice Sauvé;
2. Que cette équipe reçoive "carte blanche" et négocie sans pression indue de l'"establishment syndical";
3. Que la CSN verse aux grévistes de Lapalme leurs chèques d'allocation jusqu'à la "victoire totale".[30]

On 16 February, one week after the occupation began, the CNTU and the drivers reached an agreement. Although the terms of the agreement were not made public it appeared that the drivers had been victorious on points 1 and 3. CNTU President Marcel Pépin thereupon sought a meeting with the prime minister and, seeking a scapegoat, stated that the entire affair "repose sur ce qui semble être une politique systématique d'obstruction contre la CSN au niveau du haut-fonctionnarisme fédéral."[31]

There is no need to examine in detail the events of the next 18 months; they constituted a single, simple scenario repeated over and over again. The CNTU had done too good a job of arousing public sympathy for the Lapalme drivers. Despite their resolve on more than one occasion, public sympathy prevented the CNTU leadership from washing their hands of the entire affair. After each such attempt the CNTU leadership found itself forced back into the struggle more firmly committed than ever to finding a solution acceptable to the drivers.

The drivers, though no longer adamant in demanding total victory, remained adamant in rejecting any proposal which did not include immediate mass reinstatement in their jobs. The government, on the other hand, announced its willingness to consider any proposal from the CNTU but was equally adamant in insisting that it would not accept any solution which involved working an injustice upon the drivers then employed by the Post Office. The government had no real choice in the matter, the new drivers were members of the CUPW and their union could be expected to act to protect their job security.

The CNTU leadership was thus caught between the drivers and the government, both remaining adamant in insisting upon mutually incompatible conditions for the settlement of the dispute. The CNTU leadership could not fix the blame for the impasse upon the drivers who, after all, had only acted on the advice of the CNTU leadership and accepted at face value its promises of support and eventual victory. Moreover, blaming the drivers implied the logical step of withdrawing the CNTU's support from them and the CNTU leadership had found, on more than one occasion, that it could not carry out its threats to do so.

The result was that each new confrontation between the CNTU and the drivers

[30] *Le Devoir*, 16 February, 1971, p. 6.
[31] *Le Devoir*, 17 February 1971, p. 10.

ended with the CNTU leadership going back to the government with another proposal which invariably foundered on the government's insistence that the acquired rights of the new drivers be respected. With each failure, relations between the drivers and the CNTU leadership deteriorated further and the latter, in their frustration, became more embittered toward the government. Finally, in February 1972, the CNTU refused to present its customary annual brief to the government.[32]

At the CNTU convention of June 1972, the leadership attempted once again to disembarrass itself of the Lapalme drivers. A report presented to the convention by the leadership stated that the battle was lost and that the entire affair now consisted of the CNTU contributing weekly strike pay in the amount of $12,000, while the drivers, from time to time, picketed the parliament buildings. The report recommended that the affair be declared closed. The drivers were able to prevent acceptance of the report by the convention. Instead, the convention voted to establish a *comité de reclassement* to place the drivers in new jobs and to continue their strike pay until they were so placed.

IV. The CNTU and the Lapalme affair

It is the thesis of this paper that the leadership of the CNTU attempted to use the Lapalme drivers and their grievance against the Post Office as a battering ram with which to break down the principle of national bargaining units, the objective of the exercise being to open up the federal public service and federal crown corporation employees in Quebec, as well as the Quebec employees of other national enterprises, to CNTU raids.

When the Lapalme affair began there were a number of questions outstanding between the drivers and the Post Office, the most important being the right of the drivers to keep their jobs and to enjoy the benefits provided under their union contract. Maintenance of their union was important because it was only by preserving the union that they could assure themselves of continued enjoyment of the benefits which it provided. So long as the Post Office continued to use the contracting-out system, preservation of their union was the only means open to the drivers to maintain decent wage rates and working conditions. Saving the union was thus a means to an end and, with good reason, it became the focal point of the drivers' struggle. The objective of saving the union took on added significance when the CNTU leadership claimed, with at least the appearance of justification, that the division of the Montreal postal delivery region into five separate contracts was nothing more than an attempt to break the union.

The government's acceptance of the Goldenberg recommendations altered the situation radically, especially with the improved offer of 6 April, 1970. The drivers received assurances on the major points under dispute – job security, working conditions and wage rates. Moreover, they were not to be left exposed

[32]It was also during this period (January 1971 to June 1972) that the position of the CNTU leadership changed from one of staunch opposition to separatism [see Richard Jones, *Community in Crisis: French-Canadian Nationalism in Perspective* (Toronto, 1972), chap. III] to one favouring separatism. In September 1972, the CNTU refused to issue a policy statement on the forthcoming federal general election on the grounds that federal elections are "irrelevant" to Quebec.

and unprotected in future. Upon joining the Public Service they were to become members of the CUPW, one of the most militant unions in the entire public service. Union preservation thus ceased to be a necessary part of the drivers' demands, other means were available to protect their interests.

It was soon after the submission of the Goldenberg Report that the CNTU leadership must have perceived the opportunity which the dispute offered to them. They therefore continued to encourage the drivers to hold out for the whole original package including preservation of their union. Union preservation ceased to be a means to an end and became, in so far as the drivers were concerned, an end in itself; an end, moreover, which was not necessary to protect their interests.

The full import of the course adopted by the CNTU leadership is staggering in its implications. They demanded nothing less than that an employer (in this case the Post Office) ignore the decision of a labour relations board as well as the contract with the union certified by that board, and, instead, recognize another union as the representative of some part of its employees. The last union leader in Canada known to have made such a demand was Hal Banks, and the reign of terror which he instituted in attempting to secure compliance led directly to his downfall.[33]

It is possible, indeed probable, that the drivers themselves did not appreciate the fine points of labour relations theory which were being attacked in their name. It is certain, however, that the CNTU leadership did understand what they were doing. It is certain, as well, that they understood fully two further points. First, that the postal unions would never willingly agree to the recognition of a CNTU affiliate, or of any other outside organization, as the bargaining agent for a class of workers over whom they claimed jurisdiction and in respect of whom they had a contract with the Post Office. Second, that in the face of opposition by the postal unions and the virtual certainty that the Public Service Staff Relations Board would refuse to certify the Lapalme local, the government could not possibly grant what the CNTU demanded unless the governing legislation was amended.

The strategy of the CNTU, therefore, appears to have been to force the government to accept a settlement which would require it to introduce legislation to amend the Public Service Staff Relations Act. In effect, it sought to force the government to introduce a public service equivalent of Bill C-186, with one essential difference – that this time the government would be inextricably committed to seeing the bill through the legislative process. The way would thus be open for the CNTU to start raiding the many thousands of federal government employees in Quebec and in the Ottawa-Hull area. Furthermore, once the principle of the national bargaining unit had been done away with in the public service, it would no longer be possible to argue for its retention in other nationwide industries on the grounds of practical necessity. The way would thus be open to secure an amendment to the Industrial Relations and Disputes Investigation Act.

To this end the CNTU leadership risked, and ultimately lost, the jobs of over three hundred workers.

[33]*Organized Labour and Pressure Politics*, 145–66.

Before accepting the conclusions drawn from the Lapalme affair by this paper, it is necessary to ask whether there is any additional evidence to support those conclusions, evidence less circumstantial than that so far presented. Such evidence does exist, from within the CNTU itself.

Following the Quebec public service strike of May 1972, several leading executives broke with that organization and established a rival trade union centre. Amid the charges and mutual recriminations which followed, some dirty CNTU linen was laundered in public. According to Jacques Dion, treasurer of the CNTU for 13 years prior to May 1972, "that business of the Lapalme guys cost us [that is, the CNTU] $2 million."[34] The purpose of the entire affair, according to Mr Dion, was "to embarrass the Trudeau government."[35] If MM. Pépin and Parent spent $2 million of union funds and jeopardized the jobs of several hundred workers in order to embarrass the government, it must be assumed that they had some ulterior motive in doing so, that they were seeking some objective which transcended the immediate problems of the Lapalme drivers. The only other explanation, that MM. Pépin and Parent acted out of malice, spite, or mischief, in addition to raising questions about their sanity, is simply too grotesque to be credible. What then were their ulterior motives, what other objective were they seeking?

The only explanation which provides a credible answer to these questions is that the CNTU leadership was using the Lapalme affair to break the principle of the national bargaining unit; that the CNTU leadership had subordinated the needs and interests of the drivers to the pursuit of objectives which had no relevance to the needs of those drivers and which related only to the organizational maintenance and enhancement ambitions of the CNTU leadership.

A further question imposes itself at this point. Could the CNTU leadership have had any realistic expectation of success? The answer to this question must be in the affirmative. For reasons which go beyond the scope of this paper, the traditions of Quebec society and the Quebec labour movement are such that an industrial dispute can easily escalate and become a full-blown *cause célèbre* with unknown social and political consequences. Thus, the major industrial disputes in Quebec have had a far greater significance for the social development of that province than similar events would have had in other parts of the country. The asbestos strike of 1949, for example, is acknowledged to have been a great watershed in the social development of Quebec – and few people understood the significance of that dispute as well as the present prime minister himself. Similarly, the French language CBC producers' strike of 1959 had politicized, and in some cases radicalized, an entire generation of young French Canadians in the broadcasting industry and beyond, including René Lévesque.[36]

Given the conditions in Quebec in the spring of 1970, the most important of which will be examined below, there was a distinct possibility that the government would give into the demands of the CNTU rather than take the risk that the affair might indeed become a *cause célèbre* with uncertain consequences.

[34] *Globe and Mail*, 10 June, 1972, p. 12.
[35] *Ibid.*
[36] Similarly, the public service strike of May 1972 has been another milestone in the social development of Quebec although the direction in which it will lead is thus far uncertain.

The most important single consideration in Quebec in the early months of 1970, as the Lapalme affair was reaching its crisis, was the fact that René Lévesque was leading a separatist party in the Quebec provincial election set for 29 April. While only Lévesque's most enthusiastic supporters could have thought that his Parti Québécois might win the election, those who opposed separatism were very concerned, almost panic-stricken, at the prospect that the separatists might show considerable strength at the polls.

The Quebec Liberal party, the only credible opposition to the Parti Québécois, based its appeal on a hard-headed calculation of the advantages of federalism, in particular the economic advantages. Under these circumstances the Lapalme affair could not help but be an embarrassment. While the Quebec Liberals expatiated upon the economic advantages of federalism the CNTU was depicting the federal Liberals as a heartless crew depriving several hundred Quebec workers of their jobs over what, to the man in the street, must have seemed an obscure legal quibble. In short, the Lapalme affair was not a good advertisement for the economic advantages of federalism and it appeared, no doubt, that the federalist cause would be helped by a settlement that was both quick and advantageous to the drivers. The drivers themselves spared no effort to keep the affair in the public eye.

Despite earlier statements to the effect that they would not go beyond the Goldenberg recommendations, the government felt constrained, after 31 March, to make still another offer to the drivers. As newspaper reports and pre-election polls showed unexpected and growing support for the Parti Québécois, the CNTU leadership appears to have believed that the federal government would come under increasing and irresistible pressure to settle the affair before election day. The CNTU leadership appears to have believed that time, at least until 29 April, was on their side and that all that was required of them was that they sit tight and wait for the government to come to them.

These then were the circumstances under which the CNTU leadership risked the jobs of over three hundred workers in a desperate attempt to break the principle of the national bargaining unit.

V. Conclusions

The major conclusion to emerge from this examination of the Lapalme affair is that the pursuit of organizational objectives may, in the opinion of interest group leaders, weigh far more heavily vis-à-vis the needs of the membership than was heretofore believed. The Lapalme affair was undoubtedly an extreme case; however, even as such it is useful. The extent to which organizational objectives may plausibly be credited with motivating the behaviour of interest group leaders is now considerably greater than was previously the case.

This paper and the previous studies that called attention to the importance placed upon organizational objectives by interest group leaders examined the activities of organizations representative of organized labour. It is possible to argue that the structure of the labour movement makes it particularly vulnerable to abuses of trust on the part of the leadership, indeed, it may be said that certain aspects of labour organization virtually invite abuse,[37] and that therefore the findings of these studies are of only limited applicability. These points, even if valid, would not detract from the value of the studies. First, if organized labour is indeed particularly vulnerable to abuses of trust by the leadership then it is an excellent subject for the study of that phenomenon. Second, the fact that leaders of groups other than organized labour may not have the same opportunities available to them says nothing about their motivations and may mean only that they must pursue their organizational objectives in a more discreet or more subtle manner. Finally, even if the findings of these studies have no applicability beyond organized labour, it is nevertheless a fact that organized labour is an interest of sufficient importance in Canada and elsewhere that studies which help to explain the actions of its leaders are of value for that reason alone.

[37]The particular vulnerability of the union member to abuses of trust on the part of union leaders has been generally recognized, inside the labour movement as well as outside it. At its 1970 convention, the Canadian Labour Congress established a review board to deal with complaints of individual union members against their leaders. The board was established in spite of the opposition of the CLC leadership which was able, nevertheless, to emasculate it by gaining acceptance of an amendment which stipulated that all members of the board would be chosen from within the CLC itself. The establishment of review boards to protect the union member from his leaders has also been recommended in Ontario by the late Mr Justice I.C. Rand, *Royal Commission Inquiry into Labour Disputes* (Toronto, 1968), 57, 92–4; and at the federal level by H.D. Woods, *Canadian Industrial Relations: The Report of the Task Force on Labour Relations* (Ottawa, 1969), 101–5 and 149–52.

A Guide to the Interpretation of Locke the Political Theorist

VIRGINIA McDONALD *Atkinson College, York University*

Sheldon Wolin has offered the fruitful suggestion that political theories be regarded as paradigms, in the Kuhnian sense, ways of looking at the political world that help us to understand and grasp what we are about in a political context. They offer guidelines for determining what is significant and relevant for our appreciation of that world. There are both normal and extraordinary paradigms, the normal serving as explanations and justifications of the established mode of life, the extraordinary as critiques of such modes of life. The great political theorists were rarely engaged in outlining and justifying normal paradigms. Their work was for the most part stimulated by crises in their political worlds. Their "theories were offered as symbolic representations of what society would be like if it could be reordered."[1]

The Wolin thesis provides, I believe, a key to an understanding of Locke the political theorist. Locke offers, Wolin contends, an extraordinary liberal egalitarian paradigm, natural rights. Its basic concepts, equality and freedom, operate "like that of such abstract concepts as mechanism or atomism in scientific explanation. To say that the world is a machine, or is composed of irreducible particles ... is ... to be committed to a general programme of research, to an ideal of what would constitute a satisfactory explanation ... Such schemes of scientific thought ... are landmarks which give us our bearing as we advance from one particular assertion to another."[2] To see in the utterance "all men are equal" a trivial tautology or a patent falsehood is to do violence to the spirit behind it. Only when, through an act of creative imagination, we view it as the basic concept in a new way of looking at men in social and political relationships, can we grasp the total complex of values, interests, and claims that lie behind it. "To believe in equality is to believe, roughly, that people ought to be treated alike, especially by the state, in certain respects in which they are, or tend to be, treated differently."[3] Equality, seen as a revolutionary liberal paradigm, focusing on the value of human personality, provided a landmark giving men their bearings in moving from one practical assertion to another.

Locke was trying to offer an extraordinary political paradigm in oppostion to the normal paradigm of his time, place and socio-economic milieu. There is an

[1]"Paradigms and Political Theories," P. King and B.C. Parekh, eds., *Politics and Experience: Essays Presented to Professor Michael Oakeshott on the Occasion of His Retirement*, ed. P. King and B.C. Parekh (Cambridge, Eng., 1968), 148.
[2]P. Corbett, *Ideologies* (London, 1965), 184.
[3]*Ibid.*, 180.

Canadian Journal of Political Science/Revue canadienne de science politique, vi, no. 4 (December/décembre 1973). Printed in Canada/Imprimé au Canada.

Guide pour l'interprétation des écrits de Locke en théorie politique

Le paradigme égalitaire et libéral proposé par Locke s'oppose à celui non égalitaire soutenu par les auteurs qui lui sont contemporains. Cette opposition se retrouve non seulement entre ces deux paradigmes mais aussi chez Locke lui-même qui tente de concilier les exigences morales et intellectuelles de son nouveau paradigme avec celles, économiques, sociales et culturelles, du paradigme en vogue à son époque. La pensée théorique de Locke en matière politique doit être interprétée à la lumière de cette double confrontation.

Il existe une polarisation parmi les interprètes contemporains de Locke entre les tenants du constitutionalisme libéral et ceux du marxisme, les premiers mettant surtout l'accent sur ses écrits égalitaires et libéraux et les seconds sur les passages qui reflètent les préoccupations sociales contemporaines à Locke. L'auteur croit qu'il vaut mieux reconnaître et expliquer les contradictions inhérentes à l'œuvre de Locke que de tenter de les résoudre en faveur de l'un ou l'autre pôle. Selon lui, Locke, tout en faisant intellectuellement et moralement siennes la plupart des idées égalitaires, conservait néanmoins une certaine sympathie pour le courant normatif de son époque. Il fut ainsi amené à céder devant les exigences pratiques du paradigme contemporain toutes les fois qu'elles entraient en contradiction avec ses convictions égalitaires. En l'absence d'une telle contradiction cependant, Locke approfondit les implications égalitaires du paradigme libéral.

inherent tension both between the extraordinary and normal paradigms, and within Locke himself, between the moral/intellectual demands of his new normative paradigm and the economic, social, and cultural demands of the normal paradigm of his time and place. In this tension between the paradigms and in Locke himself, in his commitment in part to both, lies, I believe, a clue to the understanding of Locke the political theorist. My position may seem a rather trite one: Locke was not consistent, he was not willing to live with some of the social and political consequences that could plausibly be derived from the assumptions of his new way of looking at the political world. My position is, I believe, rescued from triteness for two reasons.

First, contemporary interpretations of Locke do not attempt to live with his inconsistencies, but are polarised into two extreme interpretations, the liberal-constitutionalist and the Marxian, depending on whether one attempts to carry through consistently the significant and relevant facts of the liberal equality paradigm or of the normal paradigm of Locke's own age and socio-economic milieu. Rather than attempting to smooth out Locke's inconsistencies and fit his political theory into a pattern consistent with either paradigm, I suggest we begin and end with these inconsistencies.

Second, I attempt to show at what stages and why, in the development of his extraordinary paradigm, Locke wavers in commitment to its universalist liberal, egalitarian assumptions. Locke's extraordinary equality paradigm, grounded in a theological metaphysical foundation of the spiritual equality of all men, confronted the normal non-egalitarian paradigm of his own society and his own socio-economic milieu. Locke, while drawn intellectually and morally to much in the egalitarian perspective, could not draw himself away from the normative demands made by his own socio-economic milieu. Where Locke's equality paradigm directly challenged the established paradigm it had to give way to the practical assertions of the settled way of life. Thus we find Locke specifically limiting the election of representatives to men of property. On the other hand, the practical assertions of the equality paradigm regarding the establishment of civil society and opposition to established government never confronted Locke with the inherent contradictions between those assertions and the social and political implications of his day. Locke assumed that the English people could be united in opposition to arbitrary, absolute government.[4] But he was never forced to question or determine who the "people" were. No Putney Debates, no direct confrontation with the rank and file of militia or people, faced Locke with the need to make his egalitarian assertions square with the facts of the norms of his age and milieu. At the various stages of the state of nature and of the establishment of civil society there is thus for him no direct confrontation between his ideal paradigm and the normal paradigm of his day. Even at the stage of revolution there is no bitter confrontation, for the Whig Revolution was a bloodless revolution. Thus at these stages Locke could allow free play to his creative imagination to unwind the implications of his ideal paradigm. I suggest that Locke's egalitarian insights, gained from his theological presuppositions, where undisturbed by direct confrontation with the socio-economic assumptions of his time and place could develop further egalitarian implications allowing for a growing awareness of the potential rationality of the "meaner" sort. This unravelling was made possible simply because no direct challenge from the "meaner" sort forced him to make good those insights in practical social, political, and economic assertions.

In this paper I shall attempt to show the extent of Locke's commitment to his egalitarian paradigm and the extent of his commitment to the presuppositions of the normal paradigm of his time and place. Emphasis upon Locke's theological assumptions is, I believe, of paramount importance to an understanding of the extent of his commitment to his extraordinary paradigm. In reading Dunn, Abrams, and others among recent contributors to Lockean research, I have been particularly struck by the close correlation they found between Locke's religious and political thought and the parallel development from an authoritarian to a libertarian approach in both. I consequently was drawn to a detailed study of Locke's original works on theology and politics. In my assessment of Locke I have sought to reconcile the positions of Dunn, Abrams, and others with that of Macpherson in an effort to transcend the sterile debate which now seems to dominate discussions of Locke.

Five stages occur in Locke's reconstruction of political society from the examination of man in his "Original," that is, in the state of nature: (1) natural equality and natural equal jurisdiction, the state of nature; (2) entering into compact for establishment of civil society; (3) joining an already established

[4]As Laslett has pointed out, Locke's *Two Treatises* was prompted in the first instance by opposition to the Tory monarchical position which was firmly entrenched in 1679 and philosophically defended by reference to Filmer's *Patriarcha*. In the second instance it served as justification of a revolution (1688) against a similar appeal to the rule of despotic will against the rule of law. In the first instance, Locke and Shaftesbury's efforts to make the egalitarian paradigm prevail failed, leading to Shaftesbury's imprisonment and Locke's exile. By 1688 the normal authoritarian paradigm gave way to a growing opposition which found in Locke's *Two Treatises* the justification for their "Glorious Revolution."

civil society as an adult; (4) electing a government; (5) opposing or revolting against an established political system. At which of these stages does egalitarian man give way to inegalitarian man and why?

At each of these stages, except stage 4, Locke speaks of every man, all men. His propositions are throughout universal. All men are naturally equal, all men have a right to execute the law of nature, all men join together to form the civil society, the political community, all men agree to have the majority speak for them all, all men at the age of adulthood are free to express their allegiance or emigrate, all men, acting on majority decision, participate in the decision as to the type of régime or government to be established, all men through their majority have a right to revolt in the face of arbitrary and "rebellious" rule. At stage 4 specific qualifications to such universal language stand out boldly and unmistakably. Only those with property are to elect representatives and only in proportion to the extent of that property (II, s. 158).[5]

The crucial cleavage between a liberal-constitutionalist and Marxian interpretation of Locke, the contemporary extremes of interpretation of Locke the political theorist, centres on the question of whether in fact we can read back into stages 1, 2, 3, and 5 the same limitation of rights and authority to men of property. C.B. Macpherson's interpretation is compelling, with its reading into the Lockean text of the social implications of his time and place and his own socio-economic milieu, as seen in Locke's attitude to the poor, both unemployed and labourers, and in his society's attitude to labourers as not entitled to political rights, as in fact subhuman or "beasts." If we add to these social implications Locke's political limitations of the equality principle, his rare examples of explicit consent as concentrated on such issues as consent to taxation (II, s. 138), and his specific spelling out of correct electoral reform as consisting of people only having "a right to be distinctively represented ... in proportion to the assistance, which [they] afford to the publick" (II, s. 158), which reflect the social implications of his age, the Macpherson thesis is further reinforced and allows for a convincing rendering of Locke as working with those same assumptions at the establishment of political society through compact, at the coming of age of adults in the political society, and at the time suitable for an "appeal to heaven." We could then start from the obvious certainty of Locke's favourable attitude to property qualifications for voters together with the social implications of Locke and his age and move back from this position to make his whole thesis consistent with this certainty.

It is generally agreed that Locke's initial postulates of man include equality of reason in the sense of the rational faculty by which, together with sense, man gains, through the light of nature, access to the law of nature, the rules of right reason whereby man is meant by God to conduct his life. It is also generally agreed that this rationality in both senses, as the discursive faculty and as "right reason," is mere potentiality until by "study," "industry," and application, the faculty of reason is developed and with it the capacity to gain knowledge of rationality as right reason. It is further generally acknowledged that for Locke the

[5]All references to Locke's *Two Treatises* are from *John Locke: Two Treatises of Government: a Critical Edition with an Introduction and Apparatus Criticus*, ed. P. Laslett, (Toronto, 1965).

"greatest part" of mankind are not "studiers" of the law of nature either through indolence or lack of opportunity or both. Where disagreement develops in interpretation is over the crucial question whether knowledge of natural law sufficient to live by, to conduct oneself in a morally responsible way, is accessible to and generally gained by most people or whether such knowledge requires "full" rationality, that is, a thorough grasp of the intricacies of the demonstrative science of morals, the intuitive propositions and deductive inferences Locke argues make up a full understanding of the law of nature as a natural as opposed to a divine law.

For Macpherson Locke believes rationality necessary for understanding the law of nature was at first available to all. But Locke, in "Of Property," comes to confine such rationality to those few "rational and industrious" men to whom God has given the use of the earth and who have made profitable use of it with the introduction of money and a commercial economy. They, by their labour, are entitled to claim that part of the earth they have cultivated and enriched. It was they who, with the introduction of money, and the intelligent use of this for furthering trade, enlarging and increasing the yield of the earth, brought more satisfying subsistence to even the day-labourer than to a king in the wilderness of America.

In time Locke lost his assurance of the possibility or even necessity of full rationality understood as a demonstrative science of morals:

> "Human reason unassisted," Locke argues, "failed men in its great and proper business of morality. It never from unquestionable principles, by clear deductions, made out an entire body of the 'law of nature.' And he that shall collect all the moral rules of the philosophers, and compare them with those contained in the New Testament, will find them to come short of the morality delivered by our Saviour ..." To the repeated insistence of his friend, William Molyneux, that he should write a treatise proving the demonstrability of ethics ... Locke replies: "The Gospel contains so perfect a body of ethics, that reason may be excused from that inquiry, since she may find man's duty clearer and easier in revelation than in herself ... Those things that every man ought sincerely to inquire into himself, and by meditation, study, search, and his own endeavours, attain the knowledge of, cannot be looked upon as the peculiar profession of any one sort of man ... However ignorant he may be of philosophy, or of sophisticated demonstrations of God's existence, simple belief in divine revelation is all that God requires of him."[6]

One can, I believe, detect in the temporal development of Locke's work a moral and spiritual development as well, a more humane, tentative, humble awareness of all men's fallibility, of all men's weakness of will in seeking truth and living by it, together with an awareness of a potentiality in all men for rationality, for moral, rational choice. The recent work of Abrams and Dunn shows the close parallel between Locke's evolution from an authoritarian to a libertarian perspective in religion and politics as revealed in a textual comparison of his early works – *Tracts on Government* (1660), *Essays on the Laws of Nature* (1662–4), and his later religious and political works – his writings on toleration, beginning in 1667, through the *Reasonableness of Christianity* (1695),

[6]R. Ashcraft, "Faith and Knowledge in Locke's Philosophy," *John Locke: Problems and Perspectives: a Collection of New Essays*, ed. J.W. Yolton (Cambridge, Eng., 1969), 219–21.

Of the Conduct of the Understanding (1706), and his *Two Treatises on Government* (1690)[7].

There is a recognition in the *Reasonableness of Christianity* that if men of the meanest sort need commands from God through Christ for guidance in moral conduct, so do the wisest, that the "demonstrative ethics" of Christian revelation was vouchsafed first not to the wisest, the richest, the most powerful, but to the meanest and lowest. If the latter could not be expected to understand the superfine distinctions of the schools, they could "feel" and be moved by and recognize the moral validity of the universal rules of God and Nature as exemplified in the conduct of a Jesus. Note, for example, his recognition in *Of the Conduct of the Understanding* that "the industrious and rational were to be found among Calvinist peasants in France before the Revocation of the Edict of Nantes": "more might be brought to be rational creatures and Christians ... if due care were taken of them. For, if I mistake not, the peasantry lately in France (a rank of people under a much heavier pressure of want and poverty than the day-labourers in England) of the reformed religion, understood it much better, and could say more for it, than those of a higher condition among us."[8] Such knowledge Locke seems to end by acknowledging is sufficient, is all men need for the guidance of their personal and public lives, including their assessment of the general trend and design of their rulers.

Such rendering of Locke brings him closer to the Levellers' ultimate ground of moral and political thought, the priesthood of all believers. Just as Lilburne moved through an intellectual and moral development, from passive obedience to the state, from the arrogance of divine election to become a fiery defender of the rights of man against arbitrary authority and a believer in religious toleration for all, under the moderating and humane influence of Walwyn; so too, I believe, we can see in Locke a similar development, through the moderating influence of a Shaftesbury. Locke moved from an authoritarian elitist interpretation of authority and the masses, through a gradual realization of that new world view of "individuality" that demands from all that they "shift for themselves" not only in assenting to truth, consenting to government on the basis of good reasons achieved through grappling with their own minds and their own souls, but as well, in labouring with their own hands to render a parcel of the earth theirs by title of such exercise. And all this, as with Lilburne, for the glory of God.

Thus, instead of starting my analysis of Locke from his seventeenth-century social assumptions and his voter qualifications, and reading back into the state of nature the implications of those assumptions, I start with Locke's state of nature with its initial postulates of equality, freedom, rationality. With the crucial question of voter qualification for the choice of representatives I find Locke confronted with the uncomfortable demands of his own social and political existence and unprepared to sustain the logic of his universal premises in the face of

[7]For an elaboration of this point see in particular my observations in this paper in the sections "Transition from Tracts to Treatises" and "Stage 5: The Right to Revolt."

[8]Locke, quoted in J. Dunn, *The Political Thought of John Locke: an Historical Account of the Argument of the 'Two Treatises of Government'* (Cambridge, Eng., 1969), 253–4.

those demands. Dunn finds a similar reluctance: "... the most Utopian of the pieces [on "Labour"] suggests a complete social equality of opportunity for cognitive effort (six hours a day for all), before shifting away in alarm at the egalitarian *social* implications of the proposal and substituting a distribution which preserved the opportunities of the poor, while reflecting the existing status differences."[9] Locke grew aware that all men to whom the Christian message had been made available could, through revelation and sincere searching for that essential spiritual and moral relationship with God, be equipped with all the knowledge of the moral law sufficient to guide their private lives and to judge of and share in the creation of polity. But he was unwilling to see his argument through to its logical outcome, a democratic suffrage. His friend Tyrrell, however, recognized the implications of Locke's political theory: "It was Tyrrell, not Locke, who ... admitted there was really no stopping place between the ground he and Locke occupied and logical individualism, final democracy, the sharing of political power with women, children and servants."[10] Others would draw out these implications in defence of practical demands for electoral reform. Such is evident in the speech of Thomas Erskine in defence of Thomas Hardy, leader of the first British working-class political organisation: "[Locke] ... considered universal representation to be such an inherent part of the constitution as that the King himself might grant it by his prerogative even without the Lords and Commons ... The maxim that the King might grant universal representation as a right before inherent in the whole people to be represented stands upon the authority of Mr. Locke."[11] As C.B. Macpherson observes: "His [Locke's] work invites this treatment, for it seems to have almost everything that could be desired by the modern liberal democrat. Government by consent, majority rule, minority rights, moral supremacy of the individual, sanctity of individual property – all are there, and all are fetched from a first principle of individual natural rights and rationality, a principle both utiliarian and Christian."[12] But they are all there only if the God's eye view is also there. Only there could be found such egalitarian sentiments in an age of such gross actual inequality. Locke saw in men what God saw, their equal worth, their equal capacity to know Him and His law. Discount as rationalization or veneer the theological trappings and the theory can well be seen as solely a defence and justification of the new bourgeois values of unlimited accumulation.

As with the interpretation of "differential rationality," so with "property," the rendering we give reflects our belief in Locke's commitment to his theological presuppositions. Man as master of himself, proprietor of his life, liberty, and estate, divorced from the ultimate proprietorship over him of his creator, takes on and will historically acquire the characteristics of the atomic, self-made, individual beholden neither to society nor to any other being or institution, guaranteeing his self-reliance through his capacity for unlimited accumulation. So conceived we *should* start with the explicit restrictive rendering of property

[9] *Ibid.*, 231.
[10] J. Locke, *Two Treatises of Government*, ed. P. Laslett (Toronto, 1965), Introduction, 82–3.
[11] Quoted in Dunn, *Political Thought of John Locke*, 7.
[12] *The Political Theory of Possessive Individualism: Hobbes to Locke* (3rd ed.; Oxford, 1965), 194.

in sections 138 and 158 of the *Second Treatise*. When the chips are down what really matters is property as estate. And how vital the control of political power by those with such assets in the light of the seething resentment of those who with covetousness and quarrelsomeness, refuse to accede to the new rules of the game! Bring back the theological underpinnings, the validity and effectiveness of the moral law and its law-giver, and property as estate recedes in importance before the demands of that law-giver to preserve oneself and one's liberty to allow for the means of realizing a subjective knowledge of God and performing the injunctions which He issues.

What prompted the *Two Treatises*? On the face of it, Sir Robert Filmer's defence of patriarchalism, of the divine right of kings, of absolute, arbitrary power, and, according to Laslett's researches, the efforts of Shaftesbury and the Whigs to persuade Charles II to accept the Exclusion Bill, an effort prompted by a concern for property not as estate but as religious liberty. There were other complaints against Charles's behaviour, against his refusal to call frequent and regular parliaments, his threat to their property as their purse. The *Treatises* seem at best only secondarily a harangue against the quarrelsomeness and contentiousness of those resentful of unlimited appropriators. It reverberates with moral indignation against arbitrary despotic rule of will against the divine command to live by law. It resounds with its revolutionary justification of the people's right to appeal to heaven against any such "wild beast or noxious brute" who would seek to establish and justify an absolute monarchy which "is indeed *inconsistent with Civil Society* and so can be no Form of Civil Government at all." (II, s. 90)

Whatever interpretation of Locke's moral and political theory we advance, we face incoherencies and inconsistencies. If we start, as I do, from the universal initial premises, we inevitably face their incompatibility with his acceptance of the patent social and political inequalities of his own age. If we start with those social and political inequalities and trace them back to his initial postulates we face the same contradictions and inconsistencies, of reconciling these particular recommendations with his overall universal propositions. Rather than trying to smooth out the logically and morally jagged edges of the outline by reading back into Locke's initial postulates a mere gloss to hide those actual inequalities, a more sympathetic rendering is one which Macpherson himself offers: "Locke could not have been conscious that the individuality he championed was at the same time a denial of individuality. Such consciousness was not to be found in men who were just beginning to grasp the great possibilities of individual freedom that lay in the advancement of capitalist society."[13]

The law of nature

No analysis of equality from the state of nature to the right of revolution can proceed without understanding the law of nature. For that law, the declaration of God's will, permeates and regulates every relationship of man to man, in face-to-face relationships, in group relations, within the political community. It is the moral framework within which the human drama is played.

[13]*Ibid.*, 261–2.

The law of nature and its law-giver, God, are known to man through his natural faculties of reason, the discursive faculty, and sense, and the knowledge so gained is as certain and indubitable as that supposedly established by innate knowledge. It is so guaranteed because our Creator, manifesting the attributes of perfect wisdom, beneficence, omnipotence, would not provide us with the human faculties of reason and sense to deceive us, but rather to provide us with the necessary avenues to knowledge of His will, and the declaration of that will, the law of nature, which clearly enjoins us to glorify God, to preserve ourselves, and to love our neighbour.

To say that "man is rational" is, for Locke, to say: man has a rational faculty. He is expected to use it and to use it in accordance with certain standards, before he either "assents" to the truth of a proposition or "consents" to a rule of human behaviour. His whole moral/political/epistemological theory is normative; that is, this is what man can do, is expected to do, at times does not and yet ought to do. It is also normative in Locke's more extended sense. It is commanded by God, the supreme law-giver, Creator and Sustainer of our being and our happiness. J.W. Yolton has summed up concisely Locke's understanding of natural law: "the laws of nature specify the conditions for humanity. To violate these laws is tantamount to renouncing one's humanity ... The laws of nature express the will of God and indicate the normative foundation for all subsequent forms of society ... Society may express these laws well or poorly; it cannot violate them and remain a moral community."[14]

Transition from tracts to treatises

One cannot examine Locke's mature political work, *The Two Treatises*, with its emphasis on natural equality without an understanding of his perspective on natural law or without attempting to resolve the glaring contradictions between his earlier political works, *Two Tracts on Government*, and the *Treatises*. There is a marked contrast between Locke's earlier and later views of the "people." Turning to the *Tracts* and the *Essays on the Law of Nature* we are presented with the image of the seething "multitude," prey to every passing whim of greed, passion, and depravity, an image of a "tempestuous sea" ready to break through the flood gates of political and social morality and law at the slightest encouragement of unscrupulous and designing leaders. There is a blistering denunciation of the opinion that the voice of the people is the voice of God. How to reconcile these sentiments with those of the *Treatises* characterized by natural political virtue which "We all possess ... both because we are disposed favourably towards each other in our very make-up, our nature, and because, when we co-operate, when we discuss things together, the tendency of what we do and what we say will inevitably be towards the politically efficacious, that which will look out for all of us."[15]

Locke begins from a position that a few men have full insight into the law of nature. These few can transcend considerations of self-interest and see what is for the public good in accordance with that law and act on that insight. It is

[14]"Locke on the Law of Nature," *Philosophy*, LXVII (October 1958), 495, 498.
[15]Laslett's Introduction to *Two Treatises of Government*, 123.

the breakdown of his assurance of this knowledge and of the moral uprightness of the few that destroys the ground of his authoritarianism. That authoritarianism was a reaction to the "indecent" disorder caused by ordinary men in their endless disputes over indifferent things and their consequent tendency to disrupt the fabric of society and government. Locke, prompted by fear of insecurity and a return to the revolutionary religious unrest of his childhood, responds as a Hobbist. Anything for decency and order. And the new Monarch, Charles II, our great Restorer, has the public-mindedness and knowledge requisite for this commission.

But as Locke matured, under the influence of Shaftesbury, in the atmosphere of British politics, he became aware that kings and magistrates can err, that ignorance, depravity, interest, partiality or party, are ubiquitous. No man, no class escapes them. If the contrast persists between human rational beings and brutes or wild beasts, the latter can no longer be confined to the multitude. For, as Laslett points out, Locke came to believe that "*Leviathan*, like the royal patriarch, did subordinate all human wills to one will, it made law and government a matter of will, therefore it did treat men as beasts and anyone pretending to its rights and powers could be treated as a beast ... Charles and James Stuart fit easily enough into the role ..."[16] Add to this Locke's increasing recognition that philosophers, even he himself, had not provided and seemed unable to provide a demonstrative ethics comparable to mathematics, through reason alone. If men are to find such a demonstrative ethics, the natural light of reason cannot, unassisted, provide it. Only revelation, faith, the Gospel can do so.

Thus are the gates open for the intrusion of new insights. Men of the highest wisdom assent to the truths of Christianity made known to them by Christ's apostles, the illiterate ones, the meanest sort. It was they who first grasped the truth of the message and gave it to the wise to which their reason assented. If the whole tenor of the *Reasonableness of Christianity* stresses the limited capacity of humble, mean men, it equally attests to their ability to grasp the most essential truth, the law of God, the Gospel, the basic rules of natural law, and that more surely and more unquestioningly than the fully rational few. Abrams argues that as a result of these insights Locke ended by building his "philosophy on two cardinal propositions: the immediate fact of partiality and the ultimate fact of an accessible, rational, God-given order. The actual equality of men in ignorance and self-love had to be complemented by a potential rationality and a potentially accessible rational order ... If men are by nature partial they are also by nature potentially rational."[17] With Locke's growing belief in the need to supplement and confirm reason by faith and revelation, together with a recognition that it was to the "ignorant and lowly" that Christ's message was first delivered and accepted, Locke's attitude to the multitude softened. Turning to *Of the Conduct of the Understanding*, we learn that "We are all short-sighted," that "the use and benefit of this touchstone, which is natural reason, is spoiled and lost only by assumed prejudices, overweening presumption, and narrowing our minds." The "narrow bonds" of perspective is the condition not only of the "day labourer in

[16] *Ibid.*, 109.
[17] J. Locke, *Two Tracts on Government*, ed. P. Abrams (Cambridge, Eng., 1967) Introduction, 96–7.

a country-village," of "porters and cobblers of great cities," but equally and less justifiably of a "country gentleman who, leaving Latin and learning in the university, removes thence to his mansion-house, and associates with neighbours of the same strain, who relish nothing but hunting and a bottle"[18]

My interpretation can be challenged. Locke's *Reasonableness of Christianity* like so many of his other works is open to considerable variation of interpretation. Thus Macpherson has quoted the following observation by Locke as confirmation of Locke's marked distinction between the greatest part who must be commanded and the few who can know: "the day-labourers and tradesmen, the spinsters and dairy-maids, ... hearing plain commands, is the sure and only course to bring them to obedience and practice. The greatest part cannot know, and therefore they must believe."[19] Yet the whole tenor of the *Reasonableness* seems to me to impress upon *all* men, the highest and the lowest, that reason unassisted by revelation, reason unassisted by hope of the rewards of a life hereafter and of the existence of a supreme law-giver, has been and in the nature of the case is unable to offer a plain and intelligible and demonstrative ethic. For Locke continually reiterates that knowledge of and obligation to natural law depend upon belief in and commitment to the existence of a divine legislator. Thus all must be commanded. All must obey. He observes that: "It is not every writer of morality ... that can thereby be erected into a lawgiver to mankind ... He, that anyone will pretend to set up in this kind, and have his rules pass for authentic directions, must show, that either he builds his doctrine upon principles of reason, self-evident in themselves, and that he deduces all the parts of it from thence, by clear and evident demonstration: or must show his commission from heaven, that he comes with authority from God to deliver his will and *commands* to the world"[20] (my italics). Locke had argued earlier that "human reason unassisted failed men in its great and proper business of morality. It never from unquestionable principles, by clear deductions, made out an entire body of the 'law of nature.'"[21] His conclusion is that reason unassisted never will be able to do so. Plain and intelligible morality is available to *all* men only through revelation and faith in a divine lawgiver even though once the commands of such a legislator are made known to them the wisest and most rational will come to acknowledge their reasonableness. I believe the following passage reinforces this interpretation of Locke's position that the only effective accessibility of the reasonableness of Christianity to all men, the low and the high, is through belief and faith and submission to divine *commands.*

To one who is once persuaded that Jesus Christ was sent by God to be a King, and a Saviour of those who do believe in him; all his commands become principles; there needs no other proof for the truth of what he says, but that he said it. And then there needs no more, but to read the inspired books, to be instructed: all the duties of morality lie there clear and plain, and easy to be understood. And here I appeal, whether this be not the surest, the safest, and most effectual way of teaching: especially if we add this farther consideration, that as it suits the lowest capacities of reasonable creatures, so it reaches and satisfies, *nay, enlightens the highest* [my

[18]J. Locke, *Of the Conduct of the Understanding, Works* (Aalen, Ger., 1963), III, 208, 211.
[19]Locke, quoted in *Political Theory of Possessive Individualism*, 225.
[20]*The Reasonableness of Christianity, As Delivered in the Scriptures, Works* VII, 142.
[21]*Ibid.*, 140.

italics]. The most elevated understandings cannot but submit to the authority of this doctrine as divine; which coming from the mouths of a company of illiterate men, hath not only the attestation of miracles, but reason to confirm it: since they delivered no precepts but such, as though reason of itself had not already made out, yet it could not but assent to, when thus discovered, and think itself indebted for the discovery. The credit and authority our Saviour and his apostles had over the minds of men, by the miracles they did, tempted them not to mix ... any conceits, any wrong rules, anything tending to their own by-interest, or that of a party, in their morality ... It is all pure, all sincere; nothing too much, nothing wanting, but such a complete rule of life, as the wisest men must acknowledge tends to the good of mankind, and that all would be happy, if all would practise it.[22]

All men come then to knowledge of a demonstrative, that is, a plain and intelligible ethic, not through reason, which has failed even the fully rational few, but through faith and revelation, Christ's Gospel. But acceptance of the Gospel must come to man not ready-made by authority, custom, tradition, hearsay, but through seeking. It must be an acceptance which is subjective, made through one's own efforts and must be so gained to be considered a truly religious and moral insight. For Dunn, it is Locke's awareness of this need for personal search and assent in religion that sets the stage in the *Essay on Toleration* "for a more subversive politics. The necessary autonomy of individual religious judgement had been proclaimed to the world of politics. The transposition of this theme from theology and epistemology to sociology and politics made each individual man the final judge of how far the society in which he lived had succeeded in avoiding force, the 'way of beasts,' the avoidance of which was its sole end."[23] And again: "because the autonomous emotional commitment was a prerequisite for cognitive competence in the most essential elements of the law of reason, no weight of conceptual complexity or sophistication in any other human being could be any sort of surrogate for it. There could be no normative expertise in religious knowledge because the incidence of faith was determined by the grace of God and the individual's experience of faith was a necessary and a sufficient condition for a grasp of religious duty adequate to secure his salvation."[24]

The stages of political development

STAGE 1: THE STATE OF NATURE

We are now in a position to examine the reconstruction of political society from a consideration of man in his "Original," natural state. In his initial postulates of man in the state of nature, Locke presents a picture of equal, rational beings, equipped with the same faculties and free to lead their lives and preserve their liberties and possessions, within the bounds of the law of nature, without interference from any man. The theological backdrop renders man's equality and freedom of moral significance. The natural descriptive account of man's faculties supplies the important link between "ought" and "can." These faculties are the means God has provided to enable men to fulfil their moral and jural relationship to Him and His declared will, the law of nature.

[22] *Ibid.*, 146–7.
[23] Dunn, *Political Thought of John Locke*, 39.
[24] *Ibid.*, 249.

Textually, the only explicit limitation on the equality of natural political virtue and hence of equal political rights is provided in stage 4, the election of representatives of the government. Macpherson reads similar implications of inequality back into the other stages of the political condition. So interpreted, Locke becomes the apologist of the propertied, even of a new bourgeois morality. I have seen Locke's theological framework as, for him, of vital importance to morality and hence to political life, and have found that this theological framework in his maturer years rendered his attitude to the meaner sort more egalitarian. Taken from this perspective, the relevance and sincerity of his theological framework, he becomes a forerunner of liberal constitutionalism and of the egalitarian assumptions of a future democratic society.

For Locke the state of nature is a description both of a theological normative order and of man's sociological and psychological condition, from both of which arise government and the necessary ingredients for the mix of legitimate political organization. The theological framework is not reducible to a set of propositions about this actual condition of man. The latter merely provides the materials for the possible partial operation of the rules of that normative order in human relationships and even offers a slim possibility of an actualization of lives lived fully in accordance with these rules. This cannot be achieved by men isolated and apart, but it may be feasible within legitimate political society, for there men in forming a political community create a new moral dimension for themselves. Their perspective shifts in a Rousseauist fashion, from a concern for *self*-preservation to the preservation of mankind (see II, s. 6, and s. 134 and s. 212).

The state of nature is a jural relationship between man and God's law. It describes a legal-moral order in which all men naturally stand and determines the rules and standards by which men ought to regulate their relationships with each other. It enjoins that men live together in peace, good will, mutual assistance, recognizing their equal status as the property of the Omnipotent Proprietor, free to conduct their lives, pursue their actions and protect their possessions without the right of any other to interfere with them so long as they act freely, not licentiously, regulating their conduct within the limits prescribed by the law of nature. To act thus is to act humanly. The rule of reason is the rule of man.

The state of war, on the contrary, is a complete repudiation in deed and thought of this normative order and that very repudiation strips man of his humanity. His design to live by force, not law or right, reduces him to the status of inferior creatures, wild beasts that may be enslaved and used as any other lower creatures.

The state of nature as a state of peace and good will describes a jural order, how men ought to and are expected to conduct themselves. And like any other jural order, it is a state in which some men in hasty and ill-considered passion periodically violate the law of nature. Hence the need for some body or bodies to punish such infractions. While historical examples are unnecessary to and logically independent of the validity of the state of nature as a normative order, instances of the historical operation of this condition can in fact be cited: states in their relationships with each other, two men in their relationships with each other on a desert island. While "at best an Argument from what has been, to what should of right be, has no great force" (II, s. 103), Locke uses history "to confirm plain reason":[25] "what ought to be done will appear the more plausible if it can be shown to have been once done or to be otherwise compatible with factual evidence. On these lines Locke combined his reliance on reason and history."[26] In both historical instances deviation from the pattern can be noted. Some states occasionally violate the rules of natural law, as do the two men on the island. Sometimes, their adherence to that normative order breaks down altogether. Force prevails and brings with it the state of war.

If God's jural order is to be a guide for man in his social relations it must be possible for man to aspire and even at times to conform to that order. Otherwise God's order like any legal order loses its point. How men behave is not a criterion of how they ought to behave but it is an index to what they can be expected to live up to, given their actual natural propensities and faculties. And they are all, for Locke in his mature works, a mix of ignorance, party and partiality, but also of potential reason. On occasion, the latter aspect may predominate to the point where co-operation is so natural that civil society is even unnecessary. At other times their self-interest and corruption seem so great that civil society seems impossible.

Locke's rendering of the state of nature, of civil or political society, of society and of government, is extremely difficult to grasp. The state of nature, legally defined, is a condition in which there is "[no] common establish'd Law and Judicature to appeal to, with Authority to decide Controversies between them, and punish offenders" (II, s. 87). Civil society or political society – terms he uses interchangeably – is legally and morally defined as the opposite of this condition: "Whosoever therefore out of a state of Nature unite into a *Community*, must be understood to give up all the power, necessary to the ends for which they unite into Society, to the *majority* of the Community ... And thus that, which begins and actually *constitutes any Political Society*, is nothing but the consent of any number of Freemen capable of a majority to unite and incorporate into such a Society. And this is that, and that only, which did, or could give *beginning* to any *lawful Government* in the World" (II, s. 99).

There are forms of society into which men may enter other than civil or political society – the relation of man and wife, of parent and children, of master and servant, but "each of these, or all together came short of *Political Society*" (II, s. 77). Each of these could prevail even though men were not in civil society, that is, were in fact in the state of nature. Forms of rule, of government, might be established over them but could not be judged legitimate, lawful governments unless "one devests himself of his Natural Liberty, and *puts on the bonds of Civil Society* ... by agreeing with other Men to joyn and unite into a Community ... When any number of Men have so *consented to make one Community* or Government, they are thereby presently incorporated, and made *one Body Politick*, wherein the *Majority* have a Right to act and conclude the rest" (II, s. 95).

Absolute Monarchy by definition is "*inconsistent with Civil Society.*" "Every *Absolute Prince* in respect of those ... under his *Dominion*" is still in the state

[25]M. Seliger, *The Liberal Politics of John Locke* (London, 1968), 231.
[26]*Ibid.*, 231.

of nature (II, s. 90). "For he being suppos'd to have all, both Legislative and Executive Power in himself alone, there is no Judge to be found ... from whose decision relief and redress may be expected of any Injury or Inconveniency, that may be suffered from the Prince ... So that such a Man, however intitled, Czar or Grand Signior ... is as much *in the state of Nature*, with all under his Dominion, as he is with the rest of Mankind" (II, s. 91).

Locke offers us this scenario: Men pass through two stages of the state of nature in the process of establishing a fully developed civil society. Men in a state of nature begin their social relations in a patriarchal milieu. Their condition is one of harmony and peace. They gradually evolve a primitive but legitimate form of civil society in consenting to make their Father-figure the authority over them. This condition deteriorates as commerce and trade and more complicated interhuman relations develop. The Patriarch grows greedy, he expands his prerogative, he denies a common law binding him as well as his people, he enters once again into a state of nature with his people but this time into a state of war against them. This forces his people to reexamine the grounds of legitimate government and to establish a fully developed civil society. They come to see they "could never be safe nor at rest, *nor think themselves in Civil Society*, till the Legislature was placed in Collective Bodies of Men, call them Senate, Parliament or what you please" (II, s. 94).

What is paramount to Locke in his distinction between the two stages of the state of nature is the fact that the early stage of man's development under benevolent patriarchal rule gives way to the stage of irresponsible, arbitrary rule of a despot – to the state of nature as a state of war between the ruler and his people. Here too the difference between his early writings and the *Two Treatises* is marked – his initial deference to Charles II the Great Restorer gives way to a bitter, disillusioned denunciation of that same monarch.

To develop more fully the Lockean scenario:

At the extreme pole of the state of nature defined as peace, good will and co-operation, we find the beginnings of the first form of civil society, that golden age when men's desires were limited by their basic need for survival. That age was one of patriarchalism in which all the members of the group consented to have one man, the father, execute for them all the law of nature (II, s. 106–7).

But in time this idyllic state declined and men tended to move closer to the extreme pole of the state of war (II, s. 94). All men then equally consented to the transformation of their form of government into a collective body of men, in opposition to an arbitrary and absolute monarch, for they now came to see that absolute power, with unlimited prerogative, in the hands of an irresponsible and arbitrary ruler, was worse even than the state of nature men were naturally in. And no men could be judged foolish enough to consent to the establishment of a form of government in which they supposedly "agreed that all of them but one, should be under the restraint of Laws, but that he should still retain all the Liberty of the State of Nature, increased with Power, and made licentious by Impunity. This is to think that Men are so foolish that they take care to avoid what Mischiefs may be done them by *Pole-Cats*, or *Foxes*, but are content, nay think it Safety, to be devoured by Lions" (II, s. 93).

The dividing line for Locke between the first type of political society and the second, the establishment of civil society and its replacement by a more legitimate society, in which political power is vested in a collective body of men, appears to coincide with the change from a society in which possessions were few to a society in which "Government has no other end but the preservation of Property" (II, s. 94). New sociological and psychological factors have intruded. Money has been introduced by tacit consent, men have settled in cities, and trade has flourished. Men have become corrupted by ambition and luxury: "complicated economic transactions gave rise to disputes and controversies among men. Now laws were needed to 'settle the properties of those of the same society.' 'In all collections of men,' Locke observes, a 'variety of opinions and contrariety of interests' emerge. The need for some 'common superior' to act as 'judge' in deciding these 'controversies' obviously grew in proportion to the frequency with which men interacted with each other within the same city and between cities ... With the accrual of material wealth, the Lockean state emerges, with its division of political power, its impartial judges, and a multiplicity of laws."[27] It did so specifically in response to the exorbitancies and abuses of the power granted the monarch. It was the monarch's concupiscence and that of those around him that forced men "to examine more carefully *the Original* and Rights of *Government*" (II, s. 111) and to devise the only legitimate political society, that in which the legislature was placed in collective bodies of men whose laws became the public or community laws to which all, including the legislators themselves, were subject.

In this second phase of the state of nature,[28] with its introduction of money, trade and corruption, which brought with it the first actual form of *legitimate* political organization, new interpretations of the law of nature aroused dissent, misunderstanding, quarrelsomeness not just between the ruler and the ruled but among the people themselves. Yet the introduction of legitimate, or non-arbitrary, civil society did not arise directly from a state of war among the people. There were the few, the wealthy industrious and rational, who understood (and profited from) the new bourgeois interpretation of natural law. They were called upon to "show the way of reason to the rest and thus supply the remedy for the presence of 'the corruption and vitiousness of degenerate Men.'"[29] Their task would not be an easy one. The "persuasion" would border on the coercive. Rousseau paints a picture of how such persuasion could be effected:

the rich man ... conceived at length the profoundest plan that ever entered the mind of man ... "Let us join," said he, "to guard the weak from oppression, to restrain the ambitious, and secure to every man the possession of what belongs to him: let us institute rules of justice and peace, to which all without exception may be obliged to conform; rules that may in some measure make amends for the caprices of fortune, by subjecting equally the powerful and weak to the observance of reciprocal obliga-

[27] R. Ashcraft, "Locke's State of Nature: Historical Fact or Moral Fiction?," *American Political Science Review*, LXII, no. 3 (September 1968), 911.

[28] As Ashcraft notes: "It may be objected that what we have labelled the 'second phase' of the state of nature is not that 'natural condition' of man, but the 'early stages' of civil society. But Locke is quite explicit regarding the conditions under which *political* society comes into being" *Ibid.*, 912. For an illuminating discussion of Locke's shift from historical description to moral prescription in his analysis both of the state of nature and of political society, *see* the above article, 898–915.

[29] H. Aarsleff, "The State of Nature and the Nature of Man," in Yolton, *John Locke*, 102.

tions. Let us, in a word, instead of turning our forces against ourselves, collect them in a supreme power which may govern us by wise laws, protect and defend all the members of the association, repulse their common enemies, and maintain eternal harmony among us" ...

Such was ... the origin of society and law, which bound new fetters on the poor, and gave new powers to the rich; which irretrievably destroyed natural liberty, eternally fixed the law of property and inequality, converted clever usurpation into unalterable right, and, for the advantage of a few ambitious individuals, subjected all mankind to perpetual labour, slavery and wretchedness.[30]

What for Rousseau was the paradigm of an illegitimate civil society was for Locke a paradigm of legitimacy. But Locke did not linger over the social implications of his model of a legitimate society. Such implications were not to be allowed to blur the point at issue. The point to be emphasized was the state of war not of the multitude against the "industrious and rational" few, the unlimited appropriators, but of an arbitrary ruler against his people. Locke was blind to forms of arbitrary, tyrannical sway of the will of man over man other than that of the arbitrary rule of an absolute monarch. Locke's incredible rendering of the wage relationship of compact between the rich and the starving beggar (I, s. 43), bears witness to this insensitivity. And yet on the issue of the unbridled rule of a royal despot Locke was confident that all men, at least all Englishmen, could be persuaded to join in the appeal to heaven against this beast who lived by no law, who degraded all men "from the common state of Rational Creatures" (II, s. 91). On this issue all men were able to see the violation of the law of nature for it was as plain in this case if not plainer than any rule of positive law.

Here Locke's universal statements may be read as written. All men could be convinced of the violation for all men knew that "he who attempts to get another Man into his Absolute Power, does thereby *put himself into a State of War* with him; It being to be understood as a Declaration of a Design upon his Life. For I have reason to conclude, that he who would get me into his Power without my consent, would use me as he pleased, when he had got me there, and destroy me too when he had a fancy to it" (II, s. 17).

Seliger sums up well the function of the state of nature in Locke's political theory: "his theory of the state of nature fulfils quite adequately the purpose of showing that men are as capable of political organization as they stand in dire need of it ... Its specific purpose is to prove that men need, and are capable of providing, not only a remedy for the inconveniences of a state of nature, but a remedy as well for the inconveniences of government. The theory of the state of nature supplies the basis for resistance to arbitrary rule."[31]

STAGE 2: ESTABLISHMENT OF CIVIL SOCIETY

2a: Consent and civil society. There is an inherent ambiguity in Locke's analysis of consent. If we take consent in his stronger sense, as free, deliberate, personal choice, democracy alone seems legitimate. If we take it in its weaker sense, any government would appear to be legitimate so long as no one rebels. Yet consent and mere counting of heads are not equivalent. Neither mere expression of will

[30]*A Discourse on the Origin of Inequality* (London and New York, 1955), 204–5.
[31]*Liberal Politics of John Locke*, 100.

nor submission constitutes consent. A key to Locke's understanding of consent can be found in Rousseau's distinction between the will of all and the general will in the sense that the one is a mere registering of desire, inclination, self-interest, and the other is a normative concept, a will directed to and guided by certain standards and rules. Those standards and rules for Locke are found in the law of nature, God's declared will. This will is the supreme Legislative of the universe. We are entrusted with the execution of that will so long as we fulfil the ends which the supreme Legislative has posited. Those ends for us are the fulfilment of certain duties, to glorify God, to preserve ourselves, and to love our neighbour. It is in relation to His legal and moral order that our status as equal and free rational beings is to be understood. So long as we act and live by that order we are rational beings, members "of the same species and rank promiscuously born to all the same advantages of Nature, and the use of the same faculties, [and] should also be equal one amongst another without Subordination or Subjection" (II, s. 4).

God grants to all men of such equal status "the *Execution* of the Law of Nature ... whereby every one has a right to punish the transgressors ... For in that *State of perfect Equality*, where naturally there is no superiority of jurisdiction of one, over another, what any man may do in Prosecution of that Law, every one must needs have a Right to do" (II, s. 7). But "God having made Man such a Creature, that, in his own Judgment, it was not good for him to be alone, put him under strong Obligations of Necessity, Convenience, and Inclination to drive him into *Society*, as well as fitted him with Understanding and Language to continue and enjoy it" (II, s. 77). Thus political obligation is ultimately grounded not on consent but on God's will. Consent is limited by man's natural rights as deducible from the law of nature, in particular the right to live. Arbitrary absolute power is incompatible with such rights for "no body can desire *to have me in his Absolute Power*, unless it be to compel me by force to that, which is against the Right of my Freedom, i.e. make me a Slave" (II, s. 17). To be reduced to such a condition is to be deprived of that freedom necessary for fulfilment of his religious and moral duties, a virtual destruction of his humanity, of the work of his Creator.

2b: The civil compact. "Political power ... will not be special in the sense that it is different from the power all men continue to exercise in preserving the law of nature ... It will be special only in the sense that it is collective."[32] Laslett sees the incorporation of political society as the active participation of all those given by God the execution of the law of nature, and that means all men. The theological normative legal-moral order against which this executive power of all men must be seen means "that it must be possible to construe the legitimacy of any set of social arrangements in terms of the will of all adult participants in it, each individual counting for one."[33] Yet "This does not indicate that Locke felt any profound yearning to institute mass democracy ... to 'poll the whole nation.'"[34] The political community may decide to entrust the execution of its

[32]Introduction, *Two Treatises of Government*, 121.
[33]Dunn, *Political Thought of John Locke*, 121.
[34]*Ibid.*, 121–2.

affairs to one, to a few or to many, depending on the virtue, goodness, and wisdom of the men available. The government's task was to be a limited one, a fiduciary one, which meant that irresponsible behaviour on their part deprived them of office.

The crucial focus of the political society is, for Locke, the community, the original compact. This remains intact with the dissolution of government. If trust is the operative term between political community and government it is even more relevant within the community itself. As Laslett points out, trust is a corollary of natural political virtue: "'Some Trust one in another,' is an assumption of all who join to make up society."[35]

Yet the whole theological moral-jural order as expressed in the state of nature is conveniently removed from the world of actuality when the rule of reason comes in direct conflict with current history. As Dunn points out, in answer to the query, why did Locke not provide adequate machinery for expressions of consent: "The *Two Treatises of Government* was written not as a set of instructions in how to institute legitimate political societies *ab initio*, but as an abridgement of [British] constitutionalist thought." Dunn quotes Locke's letter of February 1689 regarding the meetings of the Convention Parliament: "the settlement of the nation upon the sure grounds of peace and security is put into their hands, which can no way so well be done as by restoring our ancient government; the best possible that ever was, if taken and put together all of a piece in its original constitution."[36] As reason comes uncomfortably into closer confrontation with history, history, actuality, prevails. It is at this very point that Macpherson's thesis gathers increasing strength. On the suffrage issue Locke is explicit, because it counts. On the right to revolution he can, for Seliger, return to his universal assertions for as Seliger somewhat cynically observes:

> In every context in which he refers to the consent of all members and to the will of the majority, their ascertainability turns out to rest on no other than presumptive evidence. It will not do to attribute this to muddled thinking. Only because he would not admit any other evidence did he deem it expedient, and, above all, safe, to invoke the will of the majority at all. This is what underlies his acceptance of the majority's revolutionary umpirage and his rejection of equal suffrage and removes any contradiction between the two. The umpirage is accepted because it is impossible to ascertain with any accuracy the will of the majority in revolution. Suffrage is limited because through it the will of the majority can be accurately ascertained, at least as regards some issues, including the confirmation of a revolutionary change. Locke's intention to legitimize the management of political society by reference to the will of the majority, his mistrust of the majority's judgement, and his realistic appraisal of its power, are part of a consistent line of thought.[37]

Yet Locke's unwillingness to make history conform to the rule of reason will not deter others. His very universal language, his emphatic declaration that history and precedent are not guides to what ought to be, his insistence that no man is born a natural subject but all are born normatively free, equal, rational beings, obliged to judge the society they live in by the standards of the law of nature and if found wanting, to emigrate or in the last resort to "appeal to

[35]Introduction, *Two Treatises of Government*, 126.
[36]J. Dunn, "Consent in the Political Theory of John Locke", *The Historical Journal*, x, no. 2 (1967), 161.
[37]Seliger, *Liberal Politics of John Locke*, 308–9.

heaven"; all this denies precedent's right to block change and development. And as G.J. Schochet observes: "A further escape from genetic reasoning was provided for Locke by his belief that government power – despite its patriarchal origins – exists only for the benefit of the governed. Political authority could therefore be regarded as part of an on-going process; it is held as a sacred trust for the 'publick Good and Safety.'"[38]

This leads to the next stage in the development of the political process, the coming of age, to the question: "what behavioural criteria must be satisfied for a man to be held a member of a previously existing legitimate community ...?"[39]

STAGE 3: COMING OF AGE OR REAFFIRMATION OF MEMBERSHIP IN POLITICAL SOCIETY

Locke's examples of tacit consent which he cites in II, s. 122, would reduce affirmation of membership to the mere status of resident alien. Yet he insists that full members must give express declarations of allegiance but only one instance is cited and that, the case of heirs of landed proprietors, seems hardly exhaustive of such express promises and engagements. We are left to fall back upon negative evidence. Those who come of age do not emigrate or do not renounce their inheritance. Yet, in being left in this unsatisfactory condition, we are left where, Seliger argues, modern liberal democratic theory still leaves us: "[such affirmation of membership] can be presumed to be implicit in certain actions and abstentions from others. We do, like Locke, infer an affirmative attitude towards a free society from the fulfilment of civic duties and the exercise of civic rights, although none of such acts, including voting, is directly performed to answer the question whether people agree to belong to their political society or accept its regime."[40]

STAGE 4: ELECTING THE GOVERNMENT

It is here that, textually, Macpherson's thesis finds its strongest support and my tentative thesis of a theologically inspired, developing egalitarian, Locke wavers. II, s. 158 could not be more explicit. A "fair and *equal Representative*" according to true reason would include "the *number of Members*, in all places ... in proportion to the assistance, which it [the people] affords to the publick." Macpherson reinforces the fact of the disfranchisement of the poor: "When he addressed himself to questions of economic policy, as in the *Considerations*, he ... assumed as self-evident ... that the wage-labourer has no other property than his labour ... he says taxes cannot fall on 'the poor labourer or handicrafts man.'"[41] In other words, labourers are excluded from voting because they have no assistance to make to the public. Seliger reinforces Macpherson's point that "the *Treatises* had no need to dwell on details where the principles defended were in line with prevailing practices ... For the public that he addressed and the cause which he served, universal manhood suffrage was anything but a pressing issue."[42]

[38]"The Family and Origins of the State," in Yolton, *John Locke*, 95.
[39]Dunn, *Political Thought of John Locke*, 130.
[40]*Liberal Politics of John Locke*, 282.
[41]*Political Theory of Possessive Individualism*, 216–7.
[42]*Liberal Politics of John Locke*, 288.

STAGE 5: THE RIGHT OF REVOLT

It is in his development of his theory of revolution that Locke stands out in greatest contrast to his earlier conservative authoritarianism as revealed in the *Tracts*. Here if anywhere can be found the materials upon which to build a liberal-constitutionalist image. And this is in fact, as Macpherson points out, also the "only effective test of citizenship, as he made no provision for any other method of exercising the right to turn out an unwanted government."[43] It is here that I feel once more on firmer ground in my position that there are in Locke important egalitarian strands which link his theological framework with the world of reality. The whole tenor of his argument is that it is the people, the "multitude" of the *Tracts*, in whose hands lies the ultimate right of appeal to heaven. For to the arguments which he himself had advanced in the earlier work, that such a policy is tantamount to anarchy, inasmuch as "the People being ignorant, and always discontented, to lay the Foundation of Government in the unsteady Opinion, and uncertain Humour of the People, is to expose it to certain ruine" (II, s. 223), Locke in his maturer work, born of his growing awareness of the potential rationality of all men as well as the ubiquity of partiality and ignorance, responds: "such *Revolutions happen* not upon every little mismanagement in publick affairs. *Great mistakes* in the ruling part, many wrong and inconvenient Laws, and all the *slips* of human frailty will be *born by the People*, without mutiny or murmur. But if a long train of Abuses, Prevarications, and Artifices, all tending the same way, make the design visible to the People, and they cannot but feel, what they lie under, and see, whither they are going; 'tis not to be wonder'd, that they should then rouze themselves" (II, s. 225). For this "settled design" against their persons, liberties and possessions is a clear sign of the state of war and a state of war worse than that of "the state of Nature, or pure Anarchy." The greatest evil for Locke lies not in the machinations, passions and criminality potential in his fellow-men. The greatest evil is the same tendencies in government, armed as it is not only with the authority of the political community, but with the force of that community, its wealth, its people united together behind what they had intended to be a responsible and law-abiding regime.

And so Locke advanced to his really "strange doctrine," that "true" rebellion is not the action of the people against arbitrary and illegitimate exercise of authority. Rather it is the latter who are "truly and properly *Rebels*. For when Men by entering into Society and Civil Government, have excluded force, and introduced Laws for the preservation of Property, Peace, and Unity amongst themselves; those who set up force again in opposition to the Laws, do *Rebellare*, that is, bring back again the state of War, and are properly Rebels: Which they who are in Power (by the pretence they have to Authority, the temptation of force they have in their hands, and the Flattery of those about them) being likeliest to do" (II, s. 226). Again: "when either the Legislative is changed, or the Legislators act contrary to the end for which they were constituted; those who are guilty are *guilty* of *Rebellion*" (II, s. 227). To those who say that the People are not justified in taking action against such "authority," Locke retorts: "They may as well say upon the same ground, that honest Men may not oppose Rob-

[43]Political Theory of Possessive Individualism, 224.

bers or Pirates, because this may occasion disorder or bloodshed" (II, s. 228).

In such circumstances no "superfine distinctions" of the schools are necessary to determine a violation of the law of nature. Here the signs are so plain, so visible, no man can ignore them for he can understand them and be moved by them through that very mechanism that moves men to action, the feeling of unease, pain, suffering. When all men's faculties and parts are so affected, can any man be blind to what is afoot?

It is here I believe that Locke's thesis rings sincerely, fervently; and it does so because it is an issue that he believes strikes personally at himself and all Englishmen, in the face of the Filmerian thesis in vindication of absolute and arbitrary authority as alone legitimate.

Locke's commitment to an egalitarian paradigm

Macpherson has rightly observed that for an autonomous ethic to prevail it must find some equality among men more important than their differences which will enable them to live together in a moral and humane way. With Locke the only evidence for such equality was man's relationship to God. Given that metaphysical framework men were equal, free, rational. They were stamped with a worth that transcended the gross, but for Him, irrelevant inequalities of mundane existence.

Locke's moral and theological framework portrays a humane and aspiring humanity, a world of equal, free, rational men. Yet we may ask, why fulfil this vision in the hereafter? If men can be counted upon as sufficiently aware of and obedient to natural law within the state of nature, in the founding of legitimate political communities, and in rebelling against irresponsible mishandling of such communities, why deny them similar responsibility within the political community, in choosing their representatives, in standing as representatives? Is it the demands of his socio-economic milieu that hold him back or is it moral timidity and insensitivity or something of both? We are unsure. Yet this equivocation need not prevent us from admiring the magnificent and morally compelling denunciation of a Locke roused by the prospects and implications of arbitrary, absolute, irresponsible government. On that note he does take with him and can expect to take with him any reasonable human being. Against this call to revolution which men have remembered and looked up to we may excuse his petty social distinctions, his loss of moral nerve in his analysis of the wage relationship. This call to revolution was a practical assertion guided by his egalitarian paradigm. It aroused men to a recognition of the "beastly" and irrational behaviour of irresponsible and arbitrary government. That contribution was prompted by the demands of seventeenth-century England but it is a contribution with a universal appeal and a universal relevance.

Notes

Cognitive and Motivational Sources of Voter Susceptibility to Influence*

ROBERT R. GILSDORF *University of Alberta*

To many political scientists the stuff of the discipline is supposed to be the delineation and comparison of power and influence relationships. Yet I doubt that we have really progressed very far in our empirical analysis of such phenomena; and indeed empirical studies, especially those conducted in the field, or in the "real" world, which have actually demonstrated influence relationships or tested formulations, seem to have lagged far behind the conceptual part of the enterprise. As one leading formulation puts it, one actor has influence over another actor in so far as he can change his behaviour (opinions, etc.) or get him to do something he would not otherwise do.[1] Even to demonstrate that in any given setting certain actors have more influence and others less, let alone to explain the finding convincingly or to attempt comparisons with other settings, requires careful measurement of the motives, skills, and resources of both influencers and influencees. The requirements are very demanding, of course, and it is no wonder that empirical research has not been able to portray and explain the full reciprocal nature of influence relationships. The concession made to the conceptual and empirical difficulties of the problem seems to have been to examine only one of the actors, or half of the relationship; and in practice this seems to have worked out to be a concentration more on the influential than on the influenced. At times it seems that we have been enthralled simply by the thought of having discovered the influence-wielder, and that we have forgotten that there must also be others who are influence-recipients. As a hopeful correction to this one-sided treatment of influence relationships, and also simply to present some evidence on a topic that needs more documentation, my intention in this paper is to examine those influenced in local politics.

In 1968, shortly after the conclusion of the municipal elections in Edmonton, I carried out a survey of electoral and other forms of participation in the local political system. In the analysis of the findings, some rather striking differences in the susceptibility of voters to information, communicated in part by the mass media, emerged. It is this topic that forms the major portion of the paper. Before turning to a conceptual and methodological discussion and then to the findings themselves, I shall present a brief review of Edmonton's recent experience with elections, and the 1968 election in particular.

The 1968 civic election in Edmonton

Along with those of most other Canadian cities, elections in Edmonton are carried out according to the so-called reform rules of nonpartisanship, and until 1971 all of its 12 aldermen were elected at large. Most recent elections have been characterized by ad-hoc groups sponsoring slates of candidates for the council, and in addition to these there has been the usual clustering of community notables around mayoralty and city council candidates. With the major exception of routine labour endorsement of several candidates for the council, overt interest-group activity in election campaigns seems to have been minimal. The presence of slating groups – and there is some evidence that they have been of some effect in past elec-

*I am indebted to the University of Alberta for faculty research grants which made it possible to conduct the survey on which this paper is based. For their comments on earlier drafts, I wish to express my thanks to Jack K. Masson, Fred I. Greenstein, Mildred A. Schwartz, and Steven Brown and the other members of a colloquium of graduate students who carried out a stimulating critique of a previous draft of the paper.

[1]Robert A. Dahl, *Modern Political Analysis*, 2nd ed. (Englewood Cliffs, 1970), chap. 3. See also John C. Harsanyi, "Measurement of Social Power, Opportunity Costs, and the Theory of Two-Person Bargaining Games," *Behavioral Science*, 7 (January 1962), 67–80.

Canadian Journal of Political Science/Revue canadienne de science politique, VI, no. 4 (December/décembre 1973). Printed in Canada/Imprimé au Canada.

tions – means that Edmonton cannot be classified as a pure case of a "nonpartisan" system.[2] But these groups have generally been quite ephemeral, and they have seldom maintained themselves for more than a single campaign. Except for the group that dominated the 1968 campaign, the United Civic Action Party (UCAP), none has attempted to run both a mayoralty candidate and a slate of aldermanic candidates; and the UCAP is the only one that started off with any intention to operate as a "party" after the election. As I shall explain below, even the UCAP backed away from this latter intention; and after the election it faded away just as all of its predecessors did. Pure nonpartisanship may not exist in Edmonton, but it certainly cannot be claimed that it has a party system that is stable over time.

No doubt for most of the reasons usually cited for the indifference of the citizenry to local politics, Edmontonians typically have been quite lackadaisical about their elections.[3] In the survey itself, only about a third of the respondents claimed to be more than moderately interested in local political matters; to this we can compare the one-half of the sample who declared such an interest in national and provincial politics. The difference is quite apparent in the relative turnout figures in the city for civic as compared to national and provincial elections. Of the 20 civic elections held between 1948 and 1971, in only 2 has turnout exceeded a majority of eligible voters; and even if we restrict the examination to the 10 elections involving a mayoralty contest, in only 4 of these has it exceeded 40 per cent. (In the only two cases in which turnout exceeded 50 per cent, what probably sparked participation more than anything else is the fact that each election involved a close mayoralty race with one of the candidates being the colourful and highly controversial William Hawrelak.) Without getting into a detailed comparison of relative turnout figures between civic and federal and provincial elections in the city, I might merely note that turnout in Edmonton for the 1965 and 1968 federal elections was over 70 per cent, and in the 1967 provincial election about 60 per cent.[4]

Even when they do participate in elections it is doubtful that the voters are either very clear in their own minds about the choices they are making or especially concerned over the past and future course of the government of the city. Whether befuddlement or indifference is the key factor accounting for it, one thing is clear: incumbent aldermen are repeatedly endorsed by their re-election to office. With as many as 40 candidates competing for the 12 positions on the city council, incumbency as such has usually given some candidates a clear edge over the others. In the 20-odd years spanning the 1948 and 1971 elections, in which there were 80 individual cases of incumbent aldermen seeking re-election, only 4 of them were defeated. Furthermore, incumbents usually predominate in great majority among the top vote-getters in each election.[5]

Ultimately the 1968 election deviated

[2]As a limiting case, "pure" nonpartisanship would mean the absence not only of parties which contest either provincial or national elections but also of all slate-group activity. Unpublished findings on the vote-clustering of candidates in previous elections, in studies carried out by James G. Allen, indicate that voters must have perceived a common association among candidates sponsored by the same group.

[3]The reasons usually cited for this indifference are the absence of compelling issues and sharp controversy; the attitude of "this is administration not politics"; the scarcity of adequate information defining the issues and linking them with candidates; and the institutions, particularly at-large elections of council members and the absence of competing parties. For amplification, see Edward C. Banfield and James Q. Wilson, *City Politics* (New York, 1968), chaps. 2 and 16, and Willis D. Hawley, "The Partisan Bias of Nonpartisanship," PHD thesis, University of California at Berkeley, 1970.

[4]Studies pointing to the difference between municipal and higher-level voting turnout and analysing municipal voting rates are Robert R. Alford and Eugene C. Lee, "Voting Turnout in American Cities," *American Political Science Review*, 62 (September 1968), 796–813; and M. J. Goldsmith, "Political Structure and Voter Turnout in Local Elections in Ontario," unpublished paper presented to the Annual Meeting of the Canadian Political Science Association, Montreal, June 1972.

[5]For studies noting this tendency, often ascribed to the impact of nonpartisanship itself, see Charles R. Adrian, "Some General Characteristics of Nonpartisan Elections," *American Political Science Review*, 46 (1952), 766–76; and the evidence in Charles E. Gilbert and Christopher Clague, "Electoral Competition and Electoral Systems in Large Cities," *Journal of Politics*, 24 (1962), 323–49, which suggests that at-large electoral systems may be more fundamental to this pattern than nonpartisanship itself. Contrary evidence is provided by Eugene C. Lee, *The Politics of Nonpartisanship* (Berkeley and Los Angeles, 1960), 66.

very little from the norms of low turnout and the return to office of all incumbents. (Thirty-nine per cent of those eligible voted in the election, and all seven incumbent aldermen running again were re-elected.) What looked to be at first a signal departure from the standard form of nonpartisanship, however, was the establishment of the UCAP, which fielded a slate of eight aldermanic candidates and a mayoralty candidate, former alderman Les Bodie, who led the ticket.[6] Moreover, instead of restricting its role to that of electoral alliance, the UCAP made public its aims to continue working after the election as a party. In the end the UCAP functioned as no more than an electoral coalition or pressure group – or perhaps it qualifies as a "quasi-party" – with a strictly limited span of existence, solely that particular campaign. While, as I shall point out below, the UCAP's over-all effectiveness in the campaign was limited, it did succeed in influencing a portion of the electorate; and, for good or ill, it did provide the focal point of the campaign. Several descriptive comments are therefore in order.

Perhaps the most controversial feature of the UCAP was its avowed intention to maintain itself as a coalition during the forthcoming term of office. According to its banner carrier, Bodie, the UCAP would function to "make candidates accountable to the taxpayers in a sense of giving a clear choice of policies upon which results can be measured by all citizens. And it will give council a greater ability to set priorities for all projects and expenditures."[7] Somewhat later one of the UCAP aldermanic candidates explained it more concisely, though hardly in a way to persuade many voters, when he told an election gathering that the group was formed because "we decided we need a concentration of power to make things happen," and that meant "power to move the city when we wanted it moved."[8]

Through a combination of circumstances, the UCAP's attempt to style itself as a political party backfired, and in the end the net effect of doing so was probably negative. In spite of the dire pronouncements of many political scientists on the baneful effects of not having parties, Edmontonians – who are not alone on this – are opposed to anything that smacks of "party politics" at the municipal level.[9] Then to add to this is the fact that no other group actively entered the fray in 1968, which allowed the other contenders for office to court votes by denouncing the "power grab" of the UCAP. As the campaign drew to a close, two things seemed to happen. First, the question of the UCAP as a "party" became the focal issue of the campaign, drowning out substantive concerns. Second, the UCAP itself seemed to be trying to skirt the issue and turn the debate to other matters. In this it does not seem to have succeeded. Despite the very sophisticated and massive advertising campaign mounted by the UCAP and the decidedly favourable press coverage and eventual endorsement given to UCAP candidates by the local paper, the *Edmonton Journal*,[10] the group scored only a partial victory in the election.

In a close three-way race for the mayor's office, the UCAP candidate, Bodie, who obtained 30.3 per cent of the vote, was outpaced by both of his opponents, Reg Easton (30.7 per cent) and the winner, Ivor Dent (39 per cent). UCAP candidates for the council came out with higher-than-average total votes, and five of the eight were elected; however, part of this apparent success in the aldermanic race must be discounted and attributed as much to the mere fact of the incumbency of its leading candidates as to the efforts or appeal of the UCAP as such. For four of its winning candidates were incumbents, and the other had held office only two years before; and whereas the UCAP failed to elect any of its three non-

[6]When Bodie first announced the slate, in early September 1968, there were only seven aldermen on the ticket. Later they gained another one, bringing their complement to eight.

[7]*Edmonton Journal*, 6 September 1968, 3.

[8]*Ibid.*, 10 October 1968, 5.

[9]When asked whether they favoured or opposed having political parties in local elections in Edmonton, only 13 per cent of the respondents in my sample endorsed the idea, while 59 per cent opposed it, and another 29 per cent had no opinion. A post-election survey of the 1971 Alberta provincial election, directed by Professor Richard E. Baird, found that only 25 per cent of the province-wide sample favoured "having political party type organizations run candidates in municipal elections." For a spirited argument in favour of partisan politics in Canadian cities, see James Lightbody, "The Rise of Party Politics in Canadian Local Elections," *Journal of Canadian Studies*, 6 (February 1971), 39–44; and for the United States, see Hawley, "The Partisan Bias."

[10]Though its endorsement both of Bodie and the entire slate of UCAP candidates for city council was pretty lukewarm, the paper did recommend them (and no other candidates) to the voters the day before the election. See the editorial of 15 October 1968.

incumbent candidates, two independent newcomers managed to win seats in their first try for the office.[11]

Cognitive and motivational differences in voter susceptibility to influence

CONCEPTUAL ISSUES

In one way or another, many writers have commented on the fate of the uninformed or uninterested voter, casting doubts on the consistency and stability of his opinions and behaviour, speculating on the extent to which he is dependent upon externally proffered information and advice, and concluding that his voting choices are seldom autonomously made. For Herbert McClosky "awareness" is a crucial factor in "both the amount and the quality of participation"[12]; while for Bernard Berelson the "less informed people are on an issue, the more susceptible they are to opinion conversion through the influence of the communication media."[13] Philip Converse has examined the problem from several angles, all of which converge on the central question of the role played by cognitive factors (for example, level of information, extent of knowledge, etc.) and to a lesser extent motivational ones (such as motivational centrality), in the maintenance of consistency and stability in an individual's attitudes and voting behaviour.[14] Remarking on the dilemma of the voter in local elections, often faced with having to choose out of a long list of candidates about whom he knows very little, Ithiel de Sola Pool captures the essence of the problem investigated in this paper. "He has neither time nor energy to inform himself on all of them. So how he votes on these minor offices is apt to be affected by any information that comes his way about the candidates for them. It is in this situation of low intensity of attention and interest that the endorsement of a candidate by a newspaper is capable of influencing a number of voters."[15]

Certainly there is a consensus among investigators in the United States about the effects of cognitive and motivational factors in mediating the individual's reception of and action on information and cues originating from the mass media and other agencies.[16] That is to say, interest and involvement in politics go together with greater knowledgeability; these factors are mutually reinforcing and make for the greater awareness that enables the voter to ward off messages to which he is exposed. But it is surprising to find so little systematic evidence that could confirm or disconfirm these assumptions, plausible as they are. Donald R. Matthews and James W. Prothro present

[11]Average votes received by aldermanic candidates were as follows: 1 / all incumbents ($N = 7$), 42,527; 2 / UCAP incumbents and former office-holders ($N = 5$), 41,866; 3 / all incumbents and former officeholders ($N = 10$), 40,381; 4 / all UCAP candidates ($N = 8$), 36,546; 5 / UCAP newcomers ($N = 3$), 27,679; 6 / all candidates ($N = 32$), 25,695; 7 / other candidates not included in 1–5 ($N = 19$), 17,695. As we can see, incumbency as such was a major ingredient in vote-getting; but while incumbency was a key factor in the relative success of UCAP candidates, sponsorship by the group also contributed something, as comparisons between 5 and 7, and 2 and 3 show.

[12]"Political Participation," *International Encyclopedia of the Social Sciences*, ed. David L. Sills (New York, 1968), vol. 12, 261.

[13]"Communications and Public Opinion," *Communications in Modern Society*, ed. Wilbur Schramm (Urbana, 1948), 178.

[14]Angus Campbell et al., *Elections and the Political Order* (New York, 1966), "Information Flow and the Stability of Partisan Attitudes," 136–57; "Attitudes and Non-Attitudes: Continuation of a Dialogue," *The Quantitative Analysis of Social Problems*, ed. Edward R. Tufte (Reading, 1970), 168–89; and "The Nature of Belief Systems in Mass Publics," *Ideology and Discontent*, ed. David E. Apter (New York, 1964), 206–61.

[15]"The Effect of Communication on Voting Behavior," *The Science of Human Communication: New Directions and New Findings in Communication Research*, ed. Wilbur Schramm (New York, 1963), 136.

[16]Many other factors besides these bear on this, of course. For a general statement on mediating conditions, see Joseph T. Klapper, "Mass Communication, Attitude Stability, and Change," *Attitude, Ego-Involvement, and Change*, ed. Carolyn W. Sherif and Muzafer Sherif (New York, 1967), 297–310, which summarizes much of Klapper's larger work, *The Effects of Mass Communication* (Glencoe, 1960). Personality factors affecting "persuasibility" or susceptibility to influence are discussed and some pertinent findings presented in Harriet Linton and Elaine Graham, "Personality Correlates of Persuasibility," *Personality and Persuasibility*, eds. Carl I. Hovland and Irving L. Janis (New Haven, 1959); and William J. McGuire, "Personality and Susceptibility to Social Influence," *Handbook of Personality Theory and Research*, ed. Edgar F. Borgatta and William W. Lambert (Chicago, 1968).

some striking findings showing that the lower the level of political information of southern blacks in the United States, the higher the (positive) association between exposure to mass media and rate of political participation.[17] William A. Glaser finds that reminders to vote, regardless of mass medium, have their greatest effect on the voting turnout of the less informed and less well-educated segments of the electorate.[18] But beyond these few fragments, there does not seem to be much evidence one way or the other. In spite of the provocativeness of his conceptual discussion, Converse does not submit his formulation to an adequate empirical test.[19] Nor, surprisingly enough in a study of community power, does Dahl attempt any searching analysis of varying voter susceptibility to influence through the local press.[20]

Perhaps the results of any such testing are assumed to be so obvious that political scientists addicted to survey analysis have not bothered to look for them. This could be an answer, but I am also inclined to suspect that one reason we have not found more evidence of the influence of the mass media is that we have been prone to use inappropriate models and methodologies. Variables such as degree of interest in politics are often conceived of solely as direct or independent variables accounting for extent of exposure to the mass media, level of information, and the like; and amount of information or knowledge is often conceived of solely as a dependent variable in relation to extent of interest or involvement in politics, exposure to the media, and so forth. Even if either cognitive or motivational variables are conceptualized as intervening ones for certain purposes, it is seldom that they are introduced into the analysis to specify mediating conditions in relation to exposure to communications media – or, for that matter, other possible sources of influence. No one really disputes the relationship between, say, interest in politics and following accounts of it in the mass media. But the point is that there are many people who are exposed to political news who are neither particularly interested in politics nor all that well informed. Converse states it well when he says: "It is likely that the individual who is well-informed about an object of controversy can screen out channels of potential incoming information more effectively from 'afar' than the more poorly-informed bystander. The well-informed person *knows* which newspapers columnists are so wrong they are not worth reading; the poorly-informed person, while less likely to read any columnists, perhaps, will be unable to exercise such knowledgeable selection on the occasions when he does."[21] It is this type of formulation of the problem that ought to be tested more often.

METHODOLOGICAL CONSIDERATIONS

The basic design of the analysis is as follows.[22] Exposure to communications media

[17] *Negroes and the New Southern Politics* (New York, 1966), 258.

[18] "Television and Voting Turnout," *Public Opinion Quarterly*, 29 (Spring 1965), 77.

[19] See especially "Information Flow and the Stability of Partisan Attitudes," in which he merely relates stability of voting according to party identification and media usage. Edward C. Dreyer, "Media Usage and Electoral Choices: Some Political Consequences of Information Exposure," *Public Opinion Quarterly*, 35 (Winter 1971–2), 544–53, refutes some of Converse's findings, but, like Converse, he does not attempt to use a more appropriate design for testing the original formulation.

[20] *Who Governs?* (New Haven, 1961). In a survey of voting in an election on a new city charter, he and his associates found that "among those ... who knew of the Register's opposition, twice as many voted against the charter as among those who did not know how the paper stood" (pp. 266–7). He does speculate about the effects of issue salience and the anchoring of voting preferences "in well-established attitudes" (p. 266), as well as that of the ambivalent position of the Democratic party. But none of these assumptions are tested, and he does not attempt to assess the differential impact of the paper on voters of varying orientations to politics.

[21] "Attitudes and Non-Attitudes," 184 (emphasis in original).

[22] The survey was carried out shortly after the 16 October 1968 municipal election. Interviewing, carried out by trained interviewers provided by Verne Hardman and Associates, started about two weeks after the election and was completed about three weeks later. The sample was drawn in the following manner. First, the 276 polls of the city were stratified according to socio-economic and ethnic characteristics of the census tract in which they fell, and then from each stratum a random sample of polls was chosen. Then from each of these polls a random sample of voters was drawn from the enumeration list. If originally designated respondents refused to be interviewed or could not be reached after several call-backs, substitutes chosen randomly from

(which for reasons stated below will be restricted largely to frequency of reading of editorials on local issues) will be related (1) to an information index based on the recognition of candidates of the UCAP and the perception of slating-group activities in recent civic elections, and (2) to voting for aldermanic candidates of the UCAP. The informational variable is conceived of as playing an intervening role, while the latter is the dependent behavioural variable. Next the intervening variable will be related to voting for UCAP candidates. Since the purpose of the analysis is to test the effects of (1) exposure to the media and (2) the possession of relevant information on persons of varying susceptibility to influence, the respondents will be classified according to their motivational and cognitive orientations to local politics, and the relationships within each of the resulting subgroups will be compared.

The voting variable is the percentage of his aldermanic votes (maximum number of 12) the voter cast for candidates of the UCAP. Respondents who reported that they had voted in the election were shown a card listing the aldermanic candidates in the same order as they had appeared on the ballot, and they were asked to indicate which ones they had voted for: 126 respondents did, and the percentage of votes each voter cast for UCAP candidates was calculated. The choice of any particular set of cutting points to group the percentages would inevitably have been an arbitrary decision, so the variable was dichotomized at the median to produce equal-sized groups.[23]

As will be recalled, five of the UCAP candidates were incumbent aldermen or had held the position in the recent past, and incumbency has been shown to be a major factor in re-election. It is virtually impossible to isolate "pure" UCAP-voting from the contaminating effects of incumbency as such, so, given the essential inextricability of UCAP sponsorship and incumbency, some doubts might be raised about what it is we are measuring with the voting variable. But the fact that the presence of incumbents on its ticket may have facilitated the UCAP's campaign – and all of its winners were such types – does not necessarily detract from the findings reported below. UCAP sponsorship seems to have contributed extra support even if the candidate happened to be an incumbent or public figure (former office-holder).[24] Furthermore, when the percentage of votes cast for incumbents and public figures is used as the dependent variable in parallel analyses (data not reported here), the pattern varies from that found when the UCAP variable is used.

There were 32 aldermanic candidates in the election, from which the voter had to make a selection of no more than 12. Anything approaching precise information about the stands of the candidates on the issues – assuming there were any that were particularly salient to the voter and he had some conception about what the city ought to do on any given matter – must have been at a premium.[25] By virtue of having been an alderman or other public personage, or through personal acquaintanceship, some candidates were more visible than others. But as far as informational inputs into the campaign are concerned, the most salient ones appear to have been the continual bombardment of the public with candidate advertising and the endorsement given to the UCAP slate by the *Edmonton Journal*. Of the candidate advertising, that of the UCAP (which used the *Journal* quite heavily) was by far the most intensive and sophisticated.

The primary independent variable in the study therefore is extent of exposure to the local paper, specifically the frequency of reading of editorials on local issues. Since the *Edmonton Journal* did explicitly lend its editorial support to the UCAP ticket, the

the enumeration list of the poll were provided. The eventual sample totaled 255.

[23]In earlier versions of the paper, this variable was trichotomized. While dichotomization has its obvious disadvantage, it has the advantage of facilitating discussion and presentation of findings in terms of percentages, and it affects the findings below only slightly.

[24]For example, the average number of votes won by such candidates on the UCAP ticket ($N = 5$) was 41,866, compared to 38,896 for similar types not sponsored by the group ($N = 5$).

[25]There were several matters on which plebiscites were being held: whether the city should be divided into wards (but with no specific plan being presented); whether city council should regulate store hours; and whether a cost study should be made of a convention and sports centre. Except for the regulation of store hours, none of the plebiscite issues was particularly controversial at that time; and the store hours issue does not seem to have been a divisive one among the candidates. The *Edmonton Journal* favoured doing away with the regulation of store hours and the "omniplex" study and opposed the institution of a ward system. The voters endorsed the position that store hours should not be regulated, that the cost study should be undertaken, and that a ward system should be instituted.

TABLE I

THE EFFECTS OF FREQUENCY OF EXPOSURE TO THE MASS MEDIA (GAMMA)[a]

Frequency of exposure to	Information Level[b]	Percent UCAP Votes[c]
Local newspaper	.487**	.201
Editorials in local paper	.361***	.051
TV news	.049	−.004
Radio news	.277**	.330
$N=$	(254–5)	(126)

[a]Statistical significance of relationships (X^2, using one-tailed test) will be reported in this and the following tables according to the following convention: ***, $p < .01$; **, $p < .05$; *, $p < .10$.

[b]Based on correct identification of at least one UCAP aldermanic candidate and perception that slate groups have been active in recent civic elections in Edmonton.

[c]Dichotomized at median.

choice of editorial-reading as the key independent variable is an appropriate one. But there is also a practical reason for doing so: the fact that general reading of the paper is sharply skewed toward daily usage, and this is also the case for the other media (radio, TV). For example, 83 per cent of the respondents reported that they read the *Journal* every day (the highest frequency category provided for), while only 27 per cent read locally oriented editorials that often. The use of control variables for the main portion of the analysis so badly depletes the number of cases of those less frequently exposed to the paper in general and to the other media, whereas this is not the case with editorial-reading, that any attempt to pursue the effects of these other media had to be abandoned. However, as a gauge of the impact of editorials in comparison to the other media, I present some aggregate findings for the gamut of communications media tapped in the survey (see Table I).

No data were obtained on alternate sources of information specifically related to the campaign, and nothing can be said about the voter's perception of the *Edmonton Journal*'s stand in the election or the receipt or evaluation of information specifically on, or put out by, the UCAP. Consequently most phases of the processing of information by voters must remain unexplored here. Unfortunately there were no information items from which to construct an index of information level that could be credibly conceptualized as antecedent to the campaign. Thus there is no way to test propositions such as Converse's, which postulate lower susceptibility to media influence on the part of the already well-informed voter. But there are two information or cognition items that can be used as the basis for a variable measuring the respondent's level of information or awareness of the campaign. The items consist of the number of UCAP-sponsored aldermanic candidates correctly linked up with the group's mayoralty candidate and the perception that there have been groups sponsoring candidates in recent elections. It is assumed that the respondent derived such cognitions and perceptions from his following of the campaign, which is to say that they are campaign-relevant and can only be conceptualized as subsequent to any exposure to the media.

For the candidate-information item, the respondents were shown the card listing the aldermanic candidates and asked if any of them "were supporting particular candidates for mayor." Probes were used to ask specifically about candidates supporting each of the three mayoralty candidates, but for this item only the number of UCAP candidates correctly identified as supporting Bodie was used. In all, 20 per cent of the respondents were able to recall the name of one or more UCAP candidates as "Bodie supporters," and since only about half of these mentioned more than one name it was decided to consider a respondent informed if he made at least one correct identification.

Perception of group activities in backing candidates was measured by asking the respondents: "What about those local groups that support candidates in civic elections ... do you recall having read or heard something about any of them in recent elections here in Edmonton?" If the answer was affirmative, the respondent was asked to specify the groups and particularly if he knew of any that had supported candidates in the 1968 election. About a third (35 per cent) of the respondents replied in the affirmative to the general question, but only 16 per cent were able to furnish details in response to the follow-up questions (and only 12 per cent mentioned the UCAP by itself or along with other groups). Analysis showed that it made little difference whether the respondent was able to be specific in his answer, so the variable was dichotomized between those who perceived group activities (with or without specific details) and those who did not. This item must of course be interpreted in the broader sense of perception or awareness of group activities in general rather than as an index of cognition of the UCAP as such.

Earlier analyses showed that candidate information and perception of group activities were quite similarly related to media exposure, on the one hand, and voting behaviour on the other; and since it is not my intention to try to draw distinctions between types of information, I have combined the two items into a composite index of information or awareness. Respondents who recalled both facets (14 per cent) were classified as more informed; those who recalled only one (27 per cent) as less informed; and those who could recall neither (58 per cent) as not informed at all.

As measures of the cognitive and motivational dimensions of the voter's orientation to local politics, hypothesized as demarcating those more susceptible from those less susceptible to communications influence, the following variables are used. The motivational aspect is measured by the extent of interest the respondent claimed he had in the 1968 civic election. Those declaring they were extremely or quite interested in the election were classified as being more highly motivated to follow or get involved in local politics (and particularly that election); those who were only moderately or not at all interested in the election were classified as less motivated. The cognitive variable is based on the respondent's agreement or disagreement (combining the "strong" agreement or disagreement responses with the respective weaker response categories) with the statement, "Sometimes local affairs here seem so complicated that a person like me can't really understand what's going on." This is, of course, more a measure of an individual's subjective competence in comprehending the local political scene than one of his knowledge, so it is appropriately labeled as degree of cognitive competence or comprehension.

The use made here of the interest and cognitive competence variables – as mediating variables, or what would be called in the language of survey research control variables – might differ from their more typical employment in other studies, but both variables ought to be sufficiently familiar to most readers that a detailed discussion of their validity can be avoided. As one might expect, persons who were more interested in the election and felt they understood local politics were more likely to follow politics in the media more faithfully, more likely to participate both in politics and in voluntary associations, more likely to be interested more generally in local politics and in national and provincial politics as well, and less likely to be alienated from, or feel powerless toward, local political authorities.[26] If in other studies the comprehension variable has frequently been used in conjunction with other variables as part of a political efficacy or alienation scale, there is no reason why it cannot be used as an indicator of the more strictly cognitive aspects of subjective competence.

The analytical framework thus is basically quite simple. The major independent

[26]Some of the correlates (gamma) of level of interest and cognitive competence (using the full range of values for these variables) with indicators of media exposure, broader political interest, and other attitudes are:

	Interest in election	Cognitive Competence
Frequency of exposure to:		
Local paper	.526	.401
Local editorials	.448	.188
TV news	.204	.049
Radio news	.239	.272
Extent of interest in:		
Local politics generally	.712	.286
National/provincial politics	.608	.475
Frequency of voting in local elections	.449	.238
"People like me don't have any say about what the city government does" (agree)	—.331	—.473
"I don't think public officials here care much about what people like me think" (agree)	—.325	—.611
N =	(254–5)	(251–2)

TABLE II

HYPOTHESIZED COMMUNICATIONS EFFECTS ACCORDING TO INTEREST AND COGNITIVE COMPETENCE

Level of cognitive competence	Level of interest	
	High	Low
High	weakest	intermediate
Low	intermediate	strongest

variable is frequency of editorial-reading on local issues, and its effects will be assessed by observing its correlation, firstly, with the intervening informational variable and, secondly and perhaps most importantly, with voting for UCAP aldermanic candidates. We can then examine the impact on voting of the informational variable itself, even though we do not have complete data as to how the voter came into possession of the information. The assumption throughout is that voters who are less interested and feel themselves less able to comprehend local politics will be most heavily hit not only by their reading of editorials in the local paper but also by having received bits of relevant information. Compared to their more interested and better-comprehending counterparts, they are less attentive to local politics and less informed; but they are exposed to, and pick up cues from, the local paper and other sources, perhaps unknowingly, and these cues ought to make more difference in their behaviour than in that of the others. By dichotomizing both of the mediating variables and employing them simultaneously, we have a four-fold breakdown of the sample in varying combinations of high and low interest and cognitive competence. Satisfactory confirmation of the hypothesis requires that the correlations be strongest in the low-low quadrant of the sample, as shown in Table II.

Findings

To the extent that these data capture some of the more salient effects of the UCAP's campaign through the communications media, it seems that the group did not make a particularly impressive dent in the public consciousness. As we have already seen, only about 4 out of 10 respondents had any awareness of two features that could hardly be ignored by a voter with even minimal discernment – the perception of slating-group activities and the identification of UCAP candidates – and only 14 per cent could be considered at all cognizant of both facets. Among the 126 respondents who indicated which aldermanic candidates they had voted for, the median number of votes cast was about 8. The median proportion of their votes that went to the UCAP was about one-third, and only about one-sixth of the respondents reported having cast more than half of their votes for the group.

Still, if the UCAP's campaign – insofar as it is adequately reflected in the survey – was not an unblemished success, neither was it a complete failure. It may not have reached a majority of the electorate – or if it did any conscious awareness soon lapsed – but those it did reach do seem to have been influenced to vote for its candidates. The more aware a person was of group and candidate aspects, the more likely he was to vote in the election: 97 per cent of those who were aware of both aspects voted, compared to 64 per cent of those who were cognizant of only one aspect and 53 per cent of those who could not recall either of them.[27] Among voters, the possession of UCAP-relevant information is clearly associated with voting in higher proportions for its candidates, although the extent of information possessed does not seem to have made much difference. For voters who could not recall either facet of the campaign, only 31 per cent cast high (above-median) proportions of their votes for the UCAP; whereas 57 and 59 per cent, respectively, of those who recalled one or both facets voted in high proportions for the group.[28] As we

[27]Only about 39 per cent of eligible voters actually voted in the 1968 election, but 62 per cent of the respondents reported having voted. The sample is therefore unrepresentative in this sense, or respondents were giving socially acceptable responses to questions about voting participation. Whether this biases the results here is a moot question, but I do not think it does.

[28]Other factors were associated with voting in the election and for UCAP candidates. Respondents who said they knew candidates personally were more likely to have voted

shall see below, a voter's orientation to local politics played an important mediating role in this process; and in the final analysis there is a certain residual influence on the least-aware segment of the electorate that can be attributed to the direct influence of the press.

Before turning to the more detailed analysis of the effects of editorial-reading and awareness in conjunction with the interest-comprehension dimensions of voter orientations, let us first compare the aggregate effects of the several communications media. As Table I shows, newspaper reading, in both of its aspects, and radio-listening are mildly to moderately associated with awareness and voting for the UCAP, but while none of these relationships could be considered especially strong, they indicate that these media are a good deal more potent sources of information and possible cues influencing voting than television-viewing.[29] The prominent role of the local paper is to be expected, and no doubt also the negligible impact of television, but radio, though it does not match the press as a source of information, seems to be a more effective source of influence over voting. Yet, while both the press and radio seem to play a perceptible role in influencing voters, it must be said that their role in conveying information is generally greater than that of directly persuading voters. In this regard it is particularly instructive to note that general exposure to the local press, and thus to UCAP propaganda, has a heavier impact on voters than the reading of editorials. It appears from this difference that the *Edmonton Journal*'s editorial endorsement of the UCAP had virtually no effect at all in the way its readers voted in the election.[30]

Many factors affect how well or poorly informed a person is about the institutions, processes, and actors in his political systems, but I shall not attempt to catalogue them here. It suffices to point out that the subjective factors of interest and cognitive competence, media exposure, and awareness are all interrelated, but that ultimately the impact of the media is expected to be greatest among those low in interest and competence. Respondents who were more interested in the election were more likely to be aware of groups and/or candidates (gamma $= .41$, $p < .001$), and similarly in regard to their sense of comprehension (gamma $=$ $.36$, $p < .05$). Orientation to local politics is, of course, related to the frequency of following politics in the media, and the latter, as we have just seen, is associated with greater awareness (gamma $= .36$ for editorial-reading). Table III shows the effects of editorial-reading on awareness according to the intersection of the motivational and cognitive dimensions of the voter's orientation. Table IIIa presents the correlations based on somewhat more refined scales (three levels) for the variables, while Table IIIb presents a simplified percentage breakdown of the results, using dichotomies.

Table IIIa shows that awareness and frequency of exposure to editorials are most closely associated among persons who combine a higher degree of interest in the election with a low sense of competence in understanding local politics. At the other extreme, the persons who are both interested and judge themselves able to comprehend the system are the ones least likely to be dependent upon the press for their information. The remaining two cells exhibit relationships intermediate between these two extremes. The percentages in Table IIIb show this quite well too, and they also allow us to assess the contribution of differences in orientation. Just as we saw in Table IIIa, daily, as opposed to less frequent, reading of editorials brings no increment of awareness to the cognitively more competent and more interested citizen; while for the interested

in the election, and also to have cast higher proportions of their votes for UCAP candidates. UCAP-voting was higher among voters who approved of slate groups as compared to those who did not. And, needless to add, there is a definite correlation between voting for Bodie for mayor and UCAP-voting. But, though all of these additional factors were associated with voting preferences, none of them seems to invalidate or override the findings reported below.

[29]Media effects on information level of voters parallel those reported for all respondents in Table I, though the correlations tend to be somewhat lower in strength. The weaker correlations are the result of having eliminated many of the less attentive and cognitively less competent respondents from the analysis; these respondents are, of course, the ones assumed to be most subject to influence from the media. But including data on voters only does not add much to the table, so, in the interest of economy, these correlations have been left out.

[30]Nor did attitudes toward the introduction of a ward system in Edmonton, opposed by the *Journal*, seem to be related to the frequency of reading of editorials. Respondents were also asked whether they generally agreed or disagreed with the position of the paper in its local editorials, but the impact of editorial-reading was no greater among those who agreed with them than among those who disagreed with them.

TABLE III

INFORMATION LEVEL AND FREQUENCY OF EDITORIAL-READING

Table IIIa: Gamma[a]

Level of cognitive competence	Level of interest: High	Low	All
High	−.056	.238	.177
N=	(59)	(47)	(106)
Low	.548***	.349	.444***
N=	(49)	(97)	(146)
All	.253*	.324	.361***
N=	(108)	(147)	(255)

Table IIIb: Percentage informed[b]

Level of cognitive competence	High interest ed. reading: Daily	Less	Low interest ed. reading: Daily	Less
High	66.7	68.6	60.0	32.4
N=	(24)	(35)	(10)	(37)
Low	68.4	26.7	37.5	25.9
N=	(19)	(30)	(16)	(81)

[a]The relationship is between frequency of editorial-reading and level of information, with three values for each variable. N's in the marginals include some cases which could not be classified according to cognitive competence.

[b]Percentage correctly identifying one or more UCAP candidate or perceiving slate groups in recent elections.

but less competent segment it produces the largest increment of all (41.7 per cent). Following editorials more closely brings some improvement in the awareness of the other voters, but the percentage differentials, as with the correlation coefficients, are of intermediate size. We can also see that greater cognitive competence makes no difference at all to the more interested person who follows local editorials more faithfully, whereas it does for other subgroups. Greater interest leads to somewhat greater awareness in all cases, but level of interest is of little importance to the better-comprehending person who reads the editorials every day; and similarly at the other extreme to the less-comprehending person who follows them sporadically or not at all, but who remains quite uninformed irrespective of level of interest.

Let us now consider the relative effects of media exposure and level of information on the voting of persons in the four orientation subgroups. Tables IVa and IVb display the findings regarding the impact of frequency of editorial-reading, and Tables Va and Vb present those for level of information on the UCAP campaign. As with the preceding table, each of the sets of tables presents both the correlation coefficients and a simplified array of percentages. The minor discrepancies in each of the table sets, between some of the correlations and the corresponding percentages, are the result of the dichotomization of the independent variables (for computing the correlation coefficients three levels were used). But these discrepancies do not detract from the basic patterns in the tables.

As is evident from Table IVa, frequency of reading editorials on local issues does not have much of a direct impact on voting behaviour, regardless of the state of the voter's cognitive-motivational orientation to local politics. The pattern does support the hypothesis, however. Furthermore, if the voter is both interested and subjectively competent on the cognitive plane, the "impact," if that is what it could be called, is negative to an equivalent degree. Taken in isolation from each other, both dimensions of the voter's orientation would seem to play comparable roles in determining his susceptibility to media influence (see marginals of

TABLE IV

UCAP-VOTING AND FREQUENCY OF EDITORIAL-READING

Table IVa: Gamma[a]

Level of cognitive competence	Level of interest: High	Low	All
High	−.357	.000	−.266
N=	(43)	(15)	(58)
Low	.209	.328	.306
N=	(29)	(39)	(68)
All	−.134	.249	.051
N=	(72)	(54)	(126)

Table IVb: Percentage high UCAP votes[b]

Level of cognitive competence	High interest ed. reading		Low interest ed. reading	
	Daily	Less	Daily	Less
High	35.3	53.8	40.0	50.0
N=	(17)	(26)	(5)	(10)
Low	54.5	50.0	50.0	37.9
N=	(11)	(18)	(10)	(29)

[a]The relationship is between frequency of editorial-reading and percentage votes for UCAP candidates, with three values for the former and two for the latter. None of the relationships is significant at $p < .10$.

[b]Percentage casting above-median proportions of their votes for UCAP aldermanic candidates.

Table IVa); but when they are introduced together we can see that the cognitive factor is the more important one.

Whatever direct influence the press might have on voting is far overshadowed by that which occurs merely as a result of the uninterested and less-comprehending voters having been reached with appropriate information (Table va). Whether more precisely through frequent exposure to the editorial columns of the paper or simply because they picked up the "right" information, these voters, undoubtedly more passive actors in community politics, reveal themselves to be more dependent on outside agencies; one might venture the guess that they are more manipulable too.[31]

But there are some differences that need to be pointed out. In spite of the weaker (and statistically non-significant) association between voting and editorial-reading for the subgroup expected to be most susceptible to influence, the over-all findings for the impact of editorial-reading on voting are more symmetrical than those for information. In the case of the latter, the subgroup that one might expect to be least strongly affected by possession of information exhibits a relationship as strong as that for editorial-reading. While this relationship is not statistically significant, it does suggest that some voters did make relatively informed and autonomous decisions. In addition, it must be remembered that the information variable measures only the com-

[31]While not necessarily to be taken as proof of their having been manipulated, there is a suggestion that these voters could not discern and follow up their interests or else that they held attitudes that were not at all consistent with the pattern of their voting. Except for the most undiscerning voter, it would have been hard to avoid perceiving the basic business orientation of the UCAP. Yet, while for all other subgroups voting for UCAP candidates was inversely correlated with the belief that business had too much influence in politics in Edmonton, for the less interested and cognitively less competent voters there was actually a slight positive association between the two (gamma = .22, NS).

TABLE V

UCAP-VOTING AND LEVEL OF INFORMATION

Table va: Gamma[a]

Level of cognitive competence	Level of interest: High	Low	All
High	.309	.000	.222
$N=$	(43)	(15)	(58)
Low	.053	.851***	.576**
$N=$	(29)	(39)	(68)
All	.195	.637***	.400**
$N=$	(72)	(54)	(126)

Table vb: Percentage high UCAP votes[b]

Level of cognitive competence	High interest		Low interest	
	Informed[c]	Not informed	Informed	Not informed
High	53.1	27.3	50.0	40.0
$N=$	(32)	(11)	(10)	(5)
Low	50.0	53.3	80.0	16.7
$N=$	(14)	(15)	(15)	(24)

[a]The relationship is between level of information on candidates and groups, using three values, and percent votes for UCAP candidates (dichotomized).
[b]Percentage casting above-median proportions of their votes for UCAP aldermanic candidates.
[c]Informed in the sense of being able to identify at least one UCAP candidate or having perceived group activity in recent elections

bined effect of a number of relationships in which the voter engages and sources of information to which he is exposed. If the voter on the fringes of the system is being manipulated more than others who are more fully integrated, from these data we are not in a position to say much about the actors or agencies that are doing the manipulating. If the data could be broken down according to source of information, we might find that no single source has an influence exceeding that of the local press.

If we look more closely at the effects of editorial-reading and level of information on voting, as they occur in relation to each other, we find that each of the factors operates effectively only in the absence of the other (Table VI). Among those who are informed about the campaign – to what extent they are informed makes no particular difference – if following editorials regularly had any effect at all, it drove them away from the UCAP. The only voters that one might say were influenced by their steady attention to the editorials were those who must not have been at all aware of the UCAP's campaign (gamma = .338, NS). On the other hand, the extent to which the voter was aware of the campaign made virtually no difference at all (gamma = .092, NS) for the steady readers of editorials; but for those who did not do so, the effect was of some consequence (gamma = .591, $p < .01$).

Summary and Conclusions

Despite a substantial body of analytical literature dealing with processes of influence, there have been surprisingly few attempts to test our assumptions in empirical field studies or through secondary analysis of survey data. Most noticeably lacking is any sustained interest in the recipients of influence attempts, and particularly in regard to the factors that affect their susceptibility to influence. In this paper I have marshalled some findings from a survey of the 1968 civic election in Edmonton in an attempt to demonstrate that voters are more susceptible to or dependent on information or cues originating from other agencies if they are lacking in the motivation to follow or become involved in politics and if they feel they cannot cope with the cognitive complexities of the local system. In a four-fold breakdown of the sample, respondents were classified according to their interest in the election (high vs. low) and their subjective

TABLE VI

UCAP-VOTING, INFORMATION, AND EDITORAL-READING
(Percentage High UCAP Votes)[a]

	Frequency of editorial-reading		
Information level[b]	Daily	Less often	All
High	46.7	71.4	58.6
N=	(15)	(14)	(29)
Low	46.2	62.1	57.1
N=	(13)	(29)	(42)
Not informed	40.0	27.5	30.9
N=	(15)	(40)	(55)

[a]Percentage casting above-median proportions of their votes for UCAP aldermanic candidates

[b]"High," correctly identified one or more UCAP candidates and perceived group activities; "low," either of above; "not informed," neither of above.

competence in understanding local politics (high vs. low). To test the assumption that the group of respondents low on both variables would be most susceptible to communications influence, the extent of campaign-relevant information and voting for aldermanic candidates of a slate group, the United Civic Party (UCAP), were related to frequency of reading of newspaper editorials on local issues. Since the group had advertised heavily in the paper and had been endorsed by it editorially just prior to the election, editorial-reading can be plausibly assumed to be a source of influence. In addition, voting for UCAP candidates was related to extent of campaign-relevant information, with the assumption that possession of pertinent information, though not necessarily deriving from the local press or other mass media, would have its most potent effect on the voting of the less interested and cognitively less competent segment of the electorate.

The findings clearly bear out the hypothesis in regard to the greater susceptibility to influence of the cognitively less competent. Those who rated low on this measure showed the closest relationship between the extent of their information and voting behaviour and their reading of editorials; and the extent to which they voted for UCAP candidates was very closely related to the extent of campaign-relevant information they possessed. Conversely, those high in cognitive competence were least influenced. But the mediating role played by level of interest was not as consistent. When the dependent variable was voting, the hypothesis was confirmed, in that it was the subgroup low on both interest and cognitive competence that showed the closest association between voting and both editorial-reading and information. But this pattern did not extend to the impact of editorial-reading on level of information. While no attempt was made to hypothesize about the other subgroups – that is, those high on both variables or high on one and low on another – it was found that individuals who were high on both dimensions were least likely to be influenced by their exposure to editorials. However, this did not occur when voting was related to information.

Editorial-reading led voters to become more informed about the election, and in this case to be informed about group activity such as that of the UCAP and its candidates, and being informed in this sense led voters to cast higher proportions of their votes for the candidates of the UCAP. But the sequence, from exposure to editorials to ultimately voting for the UCAP, was by no means as straightforward as this might suggest. More assiduous reading of editorials did bring about greater awareness, especially in the case of the cognitively less competent yet more interested person, but any influence the paper had on voting through its editorials – virtually none in the aggregate – was on the least-informed voters. One wonders whether these uninformed voters were simply responding to a cue, without any intervening cognitive impact that could later be recalled. On the other hand, the voters among whom information had its greatest impact were at best only occasional readers of the editorial columns of the local paper. Several possible interpretations of this finding come to mind, among them the possibility that their occasional reading sufficed to expose them to relevant cues of which they had some recollection. But it is also possible that they derived their information from sources other than the local press – or at least the editorial side of it – a possibility that raises some tantalizing questions for further research on communications influence.

Does Advertising Influence Votes? An Analysis of the 1966 and 1970 Quebec Elections*

KRISTIAN S. PALDA *School of Business, Queen's University*

I. Introduction

The intensive use of paid time and space in mass media by political parties and candidates during electoral campaigns in Western democracies has given rise to the widespread opinion that advertising expenditures can and do influence the outcome of the voting process. If this were indeed so it could be argued that parties and candidates with rich coffers might, at least in some measure, buy their way into seats of power by lavish outlay on advertising. The continuous debate in Canada and other democratic countries on the desirability of limiting campaign funds attests to the importance of this issue.[1]

It is undoubtedly a problem more central to the democratic process than the analogous issue of consumer sovereignty and sellers' advertising. The influence of mass media commercial messages on buyer behaviour has, however, been repeatedly investigated and assessed while, to my knowledge, the impact of political advertising expenditure on *voting* patterns has not.[2] For this there appears to be a sound enough reason: reliable data on party and particularly candidates' advertising expenses has not been available in any electoral entity.[3]

There is, nevertheless, an exception to this scarcity of data. For reasons to be explained further on, an electoral law requiring a full disclosure of party and candidate advertising as well as other electoral expenditures was put on the statute books of the province of Quebec in 1963. Two provincial elections, in 1966 and 1970, were held under these disclosure rules and published statistics about them provide the raw material upon which this study is based.[4]

The central purpose of this paper is to discover whether advertising expenditures had a measurable and significant impact on the outcome of these two elections. A subsidiary goal of the investigation is to demonstrate the applicability of economic-demand analysis – and more particularly of its econometric version used in the assessment of the net impact of advertising on purchases – to the analysis of an electoral process. (Some readers may conclude that the tests on regression coefficients for the significance of the advertising impact are less interest-

*I benefited from suggestions by William P. Irvine and a referee. J.J. Lambin and his Louvain-Mons marketing econometric workshop provided, as always, a critical sounding board.

[1]Upon being victorious in the October 1972 elections in British Columbia, the New Democratic party announced that its first bill to be submitted to the legislature will severely restrict political advertising outlays.

[2]This phrasing is carefully chosen not to include a vast amount of research done on the influence of mass media on *intentions* to vote.

[3]A recent brief article calculated Spearman rank correlation coefficients between total campaign expenditures and votes cast in the 1970 British elections. It is not clear whether a distinction can be made in Britain between advertising and other electoral expenses and if the major part of such expenses is captured by the reporting requirements. See A.H. Taylor, "The Effect of Party Organization: Correlation between Campaign Expenditure and Voting in the 1970 Election," *Political Studies* (September 1972), 329–31.

[4]I would like to thank Professor Paltiel of Carleton University for drawing my attention to this fact.

Canadian Journal of Political Science/Revue canadienne de science politique, VI, no. 4 (December/décembre 1973). Printed in Canada/Imprimé au Canada.

ing than the potential *predictive* power of the voting demand regressions)

Accordingly the plan of this paper takes the following form. In Part II, I speculate on the specification of the ideal "demand" model to explain the outcome of a democratic election. In Part III, I discuss the variables and data that are available with regard to the two Quebec elections and I revise downward the scope of the ideal demand model. I then outline the models actually fitted to the data. In Part IV, I present results of the estimation and analyse them. Part V carries my concluding remarks.

Lest the reader lose track of the central emphasis of the paper I repeat that my primary purpose is the assessment of the impact of *advertising expenditures* on the *number of votes* obtained by candidates rather than on the full explanation of the electoral outcome.

II. Voting-demand models

Any investigator with experience in measuring the effects of promotional expenditure on consumer-buying patterns knows that the advertising-sales relationship is exceedingly difficult to unearth and that if success is to crown such an enterprise it must be undertaken in the framework of a multivariate analysis. Frequently, however, even a sophisticated approach does not uncover the existence of a measurable relationship between advertising and sales.

A healthy scepticism about the presence of a measurable impact of paid political messages carried by mass media is doubly justified. First, political issues may be more closely linked with an individual's value system than are his buying problems.[5] Thus a *change* in his outward expression of political convictions – in his vote – caused by no matter what stimulus, may require a greater effort on his part than does a change in his buying pattern. That this change may represent a considerable cost to the voter is shown by well-documented evidence on selective exposure to and perception of political messages. Second, most of commercial advertising is concentrated in the area of frequently purchased, low-cost consumer products. A wrong buying decision under the influence of advertising is thus easily corrected on the next round of purchases; a repeat "purchase" to correct is usually offered a voter only once in about every four years.

Thus in order to detect the influence, if any, of paid political advertising on voting, one should be prepared to resort to the use of the best developed tools in the social sciences that are available. In my opinion one such tool is the demand model evolved by economists, adapted to the requirements of the electoral process.

The version of the economic-demand model which approaches most closely the political campaign situation is perhaps that dealing with the oligopolistic firm selling a differentiated product, also called a brand.[6] That demand model attempts to explain and predict the purchases of the average firm's brand. Buying is frequently referred to as "voting with your dollar," but the analogy has its limits in that each voter is endowed with an equal amount of "purchasing power" and has only an infrequent opportunity to "buy." It is nevertheless intriguing to consider a vote for a group of candidates or for a party in the same light as the sale of a unit of a firm's brand in an oligopolistic market.

The variables which determine the sales of a typical brand are usually taken to be its price, quality, and promotional expenditure, the prices, qualities, and promotional expenditures of rival brands, the "non-controllable" tastes of buyers, and, for the market as a whole irrespective of brands, the income of the buyers and prices of substitute commodities.

Assuming, for the purposes of this study, that there are no "substitutes" for the political parties or candidates except for the act of *not* voting (I am not much concerned

[5]For different views see Lester Milbrath, *Political Participation* (Chicago, 1965), chap. 4.

[6]I refer here to the Dorfman-Steiner model and its later market-share versions, particularly that of Lambin. See Robert Dorfman and Peter O. Steiner, "Optimal Advertising and Optimal Quality," *American Economic Review* (December 1954), 826–36; Jean-Jacques Lambin, "Optimal Allocation of Competitive Marketing Efforts," *Journal of Business* (October 1970), 468–84. Economists working in political theory envisage the electoral process in terms of *spatial* competition rather than as set forth above. See Otto Davis, Melvin J. Hinich, and Peter C. Ordeshook, "An Expository Development of A Mathematical Model of the Electoral Process," *American Political Science Review* (June 1970), 426–48. I have been unable to find anything corresponding to my approach in the latest survey of economic analysis applied to political phenomena, Jacques Attali's *Analyse économique de la vie politique* (Paris, 1972).

here with voter turnouts[7]), and since all voters have the same "income" or voting power (one man, one vote), the last two variables can be dropped from the analysis, at least for the moment. A preliminary version of the voting-demand model is:

(1) votes cast for candidate i in district j, $v_{i,j} = f$ (price$_i$, quality$_i$, promotional expenditure$_i$, non-controllable tastes of voters$_j$)

$i = 1,2, \ldots, n$ $\quad n =$ number of candidates standing in the election

$j = 1,2, \ldots, m$ $\quad m =$ number of electoral districts.

The "price and quality" of the candidate (and of his party, as well as of his rivals) can perhaps best be translated into electoral terms as the issues on which he takes a recognizable stand and, if he is an incumbent, as his and his party's past performance. Campaign issues could, conceivably, be separated into those that will have a measurable economic impact – giving rise to a positive or a negative benefit (price) to the voter, and those that will not. Non-economic campaign issues and, if applicable, past performance could be put under the heading of candidate quality.

The awkward expression "non-controllable tastes of voters" can now be explained and dropped. By tastes I mean – and in this I follow standard economic terminology[8] – those characteristics of voters which predispose them to vote for one party (or candidate) or another. Operationally such characteristics can be defined in terms of demographic attributes, such as mother tongue, religion, urban-rural, educational level, and occupation. Two possibly important variables under this heading are unemployment and income levels. The latter thus re-emerges again, but not as a source of purchasing power as in economic analysis, but rather as a "taste-determinant." Finally, the previous or historical voting pattern of the electors can also usefully be included in the category of these determinants. It is, however, already partly captured by the candidates' and parties' past performance. There remains a word of explanation about the adjective "non-controllable." These predispositions are clearly *not* controllable from the point of view of the candidate or his party by any of their *current* activities.

However, it can be hypothesized – and this is the main thrust of my investigation – that some tastes, predispositions or attitudes of voters are amenable to the influence of political manipulation as expressed in monetary terms by the variable "promotional expenditures," which thus becomes an operational proxy variable for "controllable tastes." By promotional expenditures I understand both outlays on paid commercial messages in mass media (advertising) and expenses connected with travel, the renting of meeting halls and campaign offices, office supplies and campaign buttons, and services of campaign assistants which will be called "other expenditures."

A second, more refined, demand model then emerges:

(2) $v_{i,j} = f$[economic issues espoused by candidate i;
non-economic issues espoused by candidate i, electoral
history of candidate i and his party in riding j;
advertising expenditure by candidate i and his party, other expenditures by candidate i and his party, unpaid volunteer effort on behalf of candidate i;
demographic characteristics of riding j]

The four sets of variables correspond to those in (1), but are closer to the estimation needs of electoral evaluation. They will be discussed further in Part III.

So far I have suggested the shape of a voting-demand model for the typical or average candidate. If envisaged in a regression context, the model requires that all variables connected with individual candidates (such as their promotional expenditures) be carried into the estimation procedure. The profile of the typical or average candidate may not, however, be the most enlightening aspect of the electoral process, just as the profile of an imaginary, typical brand may not be of primary interest to the firm selling a specific one. We might therefore wish to construct a voting-demand model for the candidates of one party only, or for candidates possessing a particular identifiable characteristic. I propose to look first at the situation in which the dependent variable is the votes obtained by winning candidates. In constructing a model for this purpose the attributes and efforts of the losing candidates can be fused into indices expressing opposition or rival strength. Foremost among these indices are the promotional

[7]Voter turnout as related to campaign intensity is the subject of a study I am now undertaking.

[8]The economist designates as "tastes" all demand – influencing variables *except* those that can be expressed in monetary terms: prices, income, and, conceivably, product quality.

outlays of the losing rivals. This suggests a competitive voting demand model of the form:

(3) $v_{w,j}$ = *f*[economic issues$_w$, economic issues$_r$;
non-economic issues$_w$, electoral history$_w$,
non-economic issues$_r$, electoral history$_r$;
ad expenditure$_w$, other expenditure$_w$, volunteer effort$_w$,
ad expenditure$_r$, other expenditure$_r$, volunteer effort$_r$;
demographics of riding$_j$]

where the subscripts *w* and *r* designate, respectively, winner and rivals.

An analysis of the voting process for the candidates of *one* political party – whether winners or not – can be carried out in a similar manner.

A further refinement of (3) follows naturally. Until now I ignored deliberately the effect of "getting the vote out." One might speculate that in some electoral districts the victory or defeat of certain candidates hinges on the degree of voter participation. While this effect can be incorporated into the voting demand model, it can be safely ignored if the dependent variable, and some of the determining variables, are converted into a 'market share" index. Thus,

(4) $ms_{w,j}$ = *f*[economic issues$_w$ / economic issues$_r$; non-economic issues$_w$ / non-economic issues$_r$, electoral history$_w$ / electoral history$_r$; ad expenditure$_w$ / ad expenditure$_r$, other expenditure$_w$ / other expenditure$_r$, volunteer effort$_w$ / volunteer effort$_r$; demographics of riding$_j$].

where ms_w, the market share of the winner, is the number of votes obtained by the winner, divided by all votes cast in district.[9]

Finally, one may argue that in a majority-voting system the variable that is of crucial concern to candidates and parties is neither the number of votes, nor market shares, but the size of the plurality received by the winner in a riding. From a strict *short-term* optimization point of view all plurality votes in excess of one are redundant and, what is more, have been obtained at non-negligible cost.

To see to what extent voting plurality is sensitive to electoral expenditure and other factors the following model appears appropriate:

[9]The meaning of the ratios is left deliberately vague; it will be sharpened further on.

(5) plurality$_{w,j}$ = *f*[same variables as in (3)].

III. Data and models for Quebec elections

A description is given here for the background of the two Quebec elections necessary to understand the nature of the available data, of the construction of the variables, and of the revision of the models discussed above in the light of the obtainable information.[10]

In 1960 the Parti Libéral du Québec swept into power, after a quarter-century of uninterrupted rule by the Union Nationale party, on a plank of general reform. Crucial to the survival of the new regime was a thorough electoral reform which, apart from a redrawing of electoral boundaries at the expense of the heavily favoured rural districts entailed three elements of immediate interest here: limitation of campaign funds, their partial reimbursement from the public purse, and full disclosure of the parties' and candidates' electoral expenses. While the individual provisions of the electoral law[11] are quite complex, their rough summary is given in Table I.

The reported electoral expenses which must be thoroughly documented by *vouchers* fall into the following categories:

1 *Personal expenses of candidate.* These expenses are all expenses *paid by the candidate himself*, up to a limit of $2000, and excluding "publicity" expenses. Expenses incurred by the candidate for food and lodging, if they are not reimbursed to him (presumably, but at a guess only, by his party), are not considered election expenses.

2. *Travelling expenses and hire of vehicles.* These exclude the candidate's travel costs. Examples are travel expenses of persons other than the candidate, hire of bus, helicopter, plane, etc.

3. *Hire of premises.* This excludes the renting of a meeting hall for the purpose of selecting a candidate.

4. *Services.* Examples of service expenses are the hiring of temporary office staff, the renting of furniture and office equipment, etc.

[10]For scholarly analyses of the 1966 and 1970 elections see *Quatre élections provinciales au Québec*, ed. Vincent Lemieux (Quebec, 1969); V. Lemieux, M. Gilbert, A. Blais, *Une élection de réalignement* (Montreal, 1970).

[11]Loi électorale du Québec, 11–12 Elizabeth II, 1963, ch. 13 and subsequent amendments (ch. 12 *Statuts du Québec*, 1965 and ch. 5 *Statuts*, 1966).

TABLE I

SUMMARY OF THE QUEBEC LAW ON ELECTION EXPENSES

	Candidate	Party
Expense limitation	60¢ per eligible voter in electoral district up to 10,000 electors, 50¢ per elector up to 20,000 electors, 40¢ per elector in excess of 20,000	25¢ per eligible voter in electoral districts where party has official candidate
Reimbursement	15¢ per elector if candidate: (*a*) has obtained 20 percent or more of valid votes (*b*) has been elected (*c*) whose party placed first or second in preceding election	none
Penalties for non-disclosure of expenses	does not get reimbursed; cannot sit in legislature until disclosure; may be fined and imprisoned	party leader cannot sit in legislature until disclosure; may be fined and imprisoned

5 *Goods supplied.* These might include office supplies and direct mail to electors in the form of circulars (but not any material prepared by an advertising agency), campaign buttons, etc.[12]
6. *Advertising expenses.* While advertising expenses are not directly defined, there is strong evidence that they are indeed expenditures incurred on paid messages by candidates and parties carried by mass media. One source of this evidence is the elimination process carried on under expense headings 1 to 5 (with the minor exception of circulars sent by direct mail). The other source of evidence is the provision that every advertisement appearing in a printed or broadcast media must identify the sponsor; there are further frequent references in the electoral act to the employment of advertising agencies and their obligation to itemize expenses (incurred on behalf of candidate and party) to their official electoral agents. It is interesting to note that expenditures incurred *before* an election is called on materials of an advertising nature are deemed to fall under the heading of electoral expense.

There is, nevertheless, a category of campaign expense which is not, *ex post*, open to quantification. This is the provision of free services by individuals who furnish their own time (not at employers' cost) and use of vehicles. While there are strong provisions against corrupt practices, it is also undoubtedly true that some material inducements to electors are handed out and these, perforce, must be ignored.

For the purpose at hand I have constructed two variables out of the election expenses which were previously designated as "promotional expenses": candidate's advertising outlays and "all other expenses." The candidate's advertising expenditure is used in two versions. The first is merely the candidate's reported advertising expense. The second is the advertising expense incurred by the candidate in his district *plus* apportioned advertising expenditure incurred by party headquarters on a province-wide level.

The party headquarters' advertising expenditure is typically devoted to publicizing the party's stand on important general campaign issues and to the promotion of the party leader. In the 1966 election 80 per cent of the total party headquarters' electoral expense of $1,310,000 went to advertising, while in 1970 the percentage was 71 out of a total sum of $1,964,000.[13] The apportionment was undertaken according to the following formula, deemed the most neutral in the absence of any specific knowledge regarding headquarters operations:

[12]Except for category 1 and 6, the expenses are only identified by title. The examples are taken from a term paper prepared for Vincent Lemieux at Laval University in December, 1971. The student group who authored the paper obtained these examples from the chief returning officer of the province.

[13]Unless otherwise stated all data were taken from the 1966 and 1970 *Rapports du président général des élections* (Québec, no dates).

Party headquarters' advertising expenditure apportioned to party candidate in electorale district j =

$$\frac{\text{Total H.Q. party ad expenditure}}{\text{No. of eligible voters in all districts in which party stood}} \times \left(\begin{array}{l}\text{No. of eligible}\\ \text{voters in district } j\end{array}\right).$$

This is a straightforward per capita allocation and may be reasonably realistic, since substantial sums are spent on "province-wide" diffusion of standardized messages.

"All other expense" is the sum of the candidates' (but *not* the parties') personal expenses, travelling expenses and hire of vehicles, hire of premises, services, and goods supplied in each riding.

Referring back to models (2), (3), and (4) we must now see what data are available with regard to the desired variables. As already mentioned, there is no information available on the volunteer efforts backing each candidate.

Similarly, it is a hopeless task to attempt to construct *ex post* indices of the economic and non-economic campaign issues espoused by the individual candidates. It is, however, by no means impossible to do so if the campaign were followed as it unfolds on the district and province-wide level. Indeed, an index approaching the requirements of our models – albeit on an overall party level – has been compiled for the 1966 election.[14]

The electoral histories of the candidate and party in a given riding are easily obtainable.[15] I have elected to use five measures: party or candidate is incumbent or not in a riding (zero-one variable); the number of previous wins by candidate; the number of previous wins by party (these variables go from zero up to six); candidate was a minister or not in outgoing government (again, a zero-one variable). I have not attempted to find out whether a candidate, when he was not an incumbent, ran but was not victorious in elections preceding that of 1966, for such information is available only from newspaper reports.

I have also not been able to obtain satisfactory data on the demographic characteristics of electoral districts. The fundamental obstacle is the lack of overlap of census and other government statistics with provincial electoral boundaries, particularly severe with regard to metropolitan Montreal (about 25 ridings). The one unequivocal demographic statistic is the urban-rural designation of voting polls stated in the election reports. It is employed in subsequent estimation in the following form:

urban-rural variable for electoral district j, UR_j

$$= \frac{\text{number of urban polling stations in electoral district } j}{\text{total number of polling stations in electoral district } j}.$$

Somewhat less confidence is to be placed in the construction of the next demographic variable, called French-English. Eight electoral districts in which substantial non–French-Canadian minorities or small majorities were identified, were designated as "not French." (This was done by using obsolete 1961 census data and observing the non-French names of candidates in such districts.)[16] The resulting zero-one (1 being employed for French) dummy variable (called F_j) has good discriminating power, for non–French-Canadian groups tended to side solidly with the Liberal party which identified itself with the preservation of the Canadian federal system.

A variable called average per-elector-income was calculated for all electoral districts *except* metropolitan Montreal and Quebec, that is, for 69 out of 108 districts.[17] Official taxation statistics unfortunately report only aggregate figures for metropolitan Montreal and Quebec city districts. Clearly, the influence of income on voting outcome could be tested only in $N = 69$ samples.

Of all the other variables pertaining to demographic characteristics the one that I regret most not having is the electoral district's rate of unemployment, as this is

[14]See Koula Mellos, "Quantitative Comparison of Party Ideology," this JOURNAL, (December 1970), 540–58. An economist would probably choose to tackle the problem of quantifying campaign issues with the help of an analytical scheme that goes under the name of hedonic price index. For its most powerful use to date see Keith Cowling and John Cubbin, "Price, Quality, and Advertising Competition," *Economica*, (November 1970), 378–84.

[15]*Annuaires du Québec*, 1966, 1970, ("Gouvernement et administration").

[16]Brome, D'Arcy McGee, Jacques Cartier, Marguerite Bourgeoys, Notre-Dame-de-Grâce, Ste-Anne, Robert Baldwin, Westmount.

[17]Department of National Revenue, *Taxation Statistics* for 1966 and 1970. Total reported income was divided by the number of the district's electors.

deemed in Quebec a politically sensitive determinant.[18]

Let us, however, keep things in perspective by repeating that we are interested foremost in the effect, if any, of advertising. To possible reproaches that the estimated models may have been misspecified because important variables were omitted – resulting estimates thus becoming biased – there will be, as usual, only one convincing reply: the evidence emerging from the fitted regressions and the residuals they generate.

To summarize, the following actual models have been fitted with data:

(2a) $V_{i,j} = f(PARTINC_i \text{ or } CANINC_i, MIN_i; ADC_i, OTHEXP_i; F_j, UR_j);$

(2a′) $V_{i,j} = f(PARTINC_i \text{ or } CANINC_i, MIN_i; ADCP_i, OTHEXP_i; F_j, UR_j).$

For 69, rather than the total 108 districts, the variable YEL was also employed. The variables are defined as follows (for ease of reference see the compact definitions in Table A in the appendix:

$V_{i,j}$ = number of valid votes received by candidate i in district j.

In 1966 some candidates recorded electoral expenses, but did not list advertising expenses. In such cases candidates were kept in the sample. Those who did not list any electoral expense in 1966 or in 1970 (in the later election whenever a candidate did list electoral expenses he also listed advertising outlays) were not included in the sample. The number of candidates deleted from the sample was 33 in 1966 and 53 in 1970. None of them received more than a handful of votes.

$PARTINC_i$ = candidate i's party was incumbent or not (1 or 0);

$CANINC_i$ = candidate i himself was incumbent or not (1 or 0);

MIN_i = candidate i was minister in outgoing government (1 if yes, 0 if not);

ADC_i = candidate i's advertising outlay. Those 1966 candidates retained in sample who reported electoral expenses but no advertising expense were "provided with" an advertising expense generated as follows:

ADC_k = generated ad expense of candidate k (none of whom were elected)

$$= (S_1 + S_2)/2$$

$$S_1 = \frac{\Sigma ADC_i}{n}, \; k \neq i$$

$$S_2 = \frac{\Sigma ADC_j}{m}, \; k \neq j$$

where ADC_i = ad expense by candidate i of same party;

n = no. of candidates of same party in sample;

ADC_j = ad expense by candidates in same riding j;

m = no. of candidates in riding j (excl. k);

$ADCP_i$ = candidate i's advertising outlay plus apportioned part of his party headquarters' advertising outlay;

$OTHEXP_i$ = candidate i's other expense;

F_j = electoral district j had a predominantly French-Canadian character or not (1 or 0);

UR_j = electoral district j's rural-urban character in percentage;

YEL_j = average income per elector in district j.

(3a) $W_{i,j} = f(WINWIN_i, PARWIN_i, MIN_i; WAD_i, WOTHEXP_i, RIVAD_j, RIVOTHEXP_j; F_j, UR_j)$

(3a′) $W_{i,j} = f(\dots \dots WADP_i, \dots, RIVADP_j, \dots, \dots)$

(Relation 3a′, analogously to 2a′, is different only in having augmented the two advertising variables by the apportioned party headquarters advertising expense.)

New variables are defined as follows:

$W_{i,j}$ = number of valid votes received by winning candidate i in district j;

[18]Stigler, in a recent paper, did not, however, detect any relationship between unemployment levels and outcomes of US congressional elections. See George J. Stigler, "General Economic Conditions and National Elections," *American Economic Review*, (May 1973), 160–7. The fragmentary evidence I have seen points equally to *no* relationship between party electoral performance in a district and that district's unemployment rate.

[19]The definition of this variable suffers somewhat from the fact that new ridings were created. In the 1944, 1948, 1952, and 1956 elections there were 94 ridings; in 1960 and 1962 there were 96 ridings.

$WINWIN_i$[19] = number of previous wins (up to 6) by winning candidate;[19]
$PARWIN_i$[19] = number of previous wins by winner's party in district j (up to 6);[19]
WAD_i = winner's advertising expenditure;
$WADP_i$ = winner's advertising expenditure augmented by apportioned party headquarters' advertising expenditure;
$WOTHEXP_i$ = winner's other expense;
$RIVAD_j$ = sum of advertising expenditures of winner's rivals in district j;
$RIVADP_j$ = sum of rivals' advertising expenditures in district j augmented by apportioned party H.Q. advertising expenditure;
$RIVOTHEXP_j$ = sum of other expenses of rivals in district j.

(4*a*) $MSW_{i,j} = f(WINWIN_i, PARWIN_i, MIN_i; WADSH_i, WOTHEXPSH_i; F_j, UR_j)$

(4*a*′) differs only by having $WADPSH_i$ instead of $WADSH_i$

New variables are:

$MSW_{i,j}$ = market share of valid votes cast in district j obtained by winner i, that is, number of votes cast for winner divided by total number of valid votes cast in district j;
$WADSH_i$ = share of advertising expenditures of winner; that is, dollars spent on advertising by winner divided by total advertising expenditure in district j;
$WADPSH_i$ = same as $WADSH_i$ except that advertising expenditures are augmented by apportioned amount of party headquarters' ad expense;
$WOTHEXPSH_i$ = winner's share of total other expenses incurred in district j.

(5*a*) $PLU_{i,j} = f(WINWIN_i, PARWIN_i; WAD_i, WOTHEXP_i, RIVAD_j, RIVOTHEXP_j; F_j, UR_j)$

(5*a*′) differs from (5*a*) by having $WADP_i$ instead of WAD_i, and $RIVADP_j$ instead of $RIVADC_j$

The only new variable is the dependent one, $PLU_{i,j}$, which is the plurality of valid votes obtained by the winner, or the excess of votes of the winning candidate over his runner-up in the riding.

Finally, appendix Table B presents some important information, such as summary statistics, on the 1966 and 1970 samples and the variables employed.

To complete the above information it should be said that in the 1966 election the pattern of Quebec politics was still in its traditional mould in which power shifted between the Liberal and Union Nationale party. In 1966 the Union Nationale party gained 56 seats, the Liberal party 50, and independents two seats in the provincial legislature. In 1970 the two-party structure cracked under the simultaneous onslaught of the populist Ralliement Créditiste (Social Credit) and the separatist Parti Québécois who gained, respectively, 12 and 7 seats, with the Liberals (72 seats) forming the government and the UN party retaining but 17 seats. The 1970 election has been called an election of realignment, signifying an important structural shift. No doubt further consideration of this interpretation will follow from the results of the most recent Quebec election held in October 1973.

IV. Results and analysis

The functional form of all the models, with the exception of the market-share versions, has been assumed to be linear or linear in logs.[20] For example,

$$(2a) \quad V_{ij} = a + b_1\, PARTINC_i + b_2\, MIN_i + b_3\, ADC_i + b_4\, OTHEXP_i + b_5\, F_j + b_6\, UR_j + u_i$$

where u_i is a random term.

All the models have been estimated by ordinary least squares regression. The sample observations have been arrayed in order of candidate's advertising expenditure, from smallest to largest in order to check on possible heteroskedasticity in the residuals $\hat{u}_i$.

Regression estimation consisted of two steps.[21] In the first, stepwise regression ordered all of a model's variables in decreasing order of statistical significance. In the second step, only those variables were fitted with sample data which showed up as significant at the 5 per cent level in the stepwise regression. It is the results of the second step which are presented here. This procedure tends to preserve the efficiency of estimates which might have been affected by collinearity among variables; it is also

[20] Dummy variables, however, and the urban-rural variable have *not* been used in log form.

[21] I am grateful to Paul H.S. Lau for the excellent computing assistance he has furnished me.

conservative in our context since it does not force the campaign expenditure variables in.

1. VOTING-DEMAND MODELS (2a) AND (2a′)

In these voting-demand models, it will be recalled, the dependent variable is the number of votes cast for an individual candidate i. The prime on ($2a'$) signifies that the advertising expense of the candidate was augmented by the apportioned amount of party headquarters expenditure.

In linear form the regression results for the 1966 and 1970 elections are:

$$(2a)\quad 1966\quad V_{i,j} = \underset{}{-40} + \underset{(24.3)}{.7047\, OTHEXP_i} + \underset{(6.8)}{.3373\, ADC_i} + \underset{(4.8)}{1661\, PARTINC_i} + \underset{(4.4)}{2796\, MIN_i} + \underset{(2.9)}{1179\, UR_j}$$

$$R^2 = .734 \quad DW = 1.80 \quad N = 385$$

$$(2a)\quad 1970\quad V_{i,j} = -521 + \underset{(8.8)}{.4484\, OTHEXP_i} + \underset{(7.2)}{4287\, PARTINC_i} + \underset{(5.6)}{.3729\, ADC_i} + \underset{(4.2)}{3004\, UR_j} - \underset{(3.3)}{3669\, MIN_i}$$

$$R^2 = .478 \quad DW = 1.87 \quad N = 418$$

(Numbers in parentheses are t-statistics; DW is the Durbin-Watson statistic; N is the sample size.)

For the reader not familiar with the dummy variable technique the 1966 results are verbally interpreted first. A candidate whose party was incumbent in the electoral district and who was a minister in the outgoing government picked up, on the average, 1661(1) + 2796(1) − 40 (intercept value) = 4417 votes, without taking into account the urban-rural character of his riding and his electoral expenditures. An additional dollar spent on $OTHEXP_i$ would bring him, on average, 7/10 of a vote; a dollar on advertising expenditure 1/3 of a vote; if his district is of a 50:50 urban-rural character, he would pick up (1179) (0.5) additional votes.

As has been stated, only estimates containing coefficients of variables significant at about the 95 per cent level are being shown.[22] Thus in 1966 and 1970 F_j (French-Canadian majority riding) is not included; the picture changes slightly when variables are presented in logarithmic form, as will be seen later.

R^2, the coefficient of multiple determination, is very high – at 0.734 – in 1966, considering the huge size of the sample and the standard deviation of V_i (=5,360), almost as large as the mean of V_i (=6,008).

The critical value of the Durbin-Watson statistic, *above* which the null hypothesis of no heteroskedasticity need not be rejected, is about 1.7 for a sample of 400 and a regression with 5 conditioning variables at the 1 per cent level of significance. Most of the D-W statistics here comfortably exceed that level and provide evidence that the variance of V_i does not increase with higher levels of advertising expense, ADC_i or $ADCP_i$.[23]

At this point a possible source of specification bias must be considered. It is obvious that the larger the size of the electoral district in terms of registered voters, the higher will be the parties' campaign outlays, if only because permitted expenses are a function of the number of eligible voters. In larger districts candidates will also tend to get a higher vote count. Is it therefore not possible that my models, in which variables are *not* deflated by the district's eligible voters, "blame" advertising and other expenditures for differences in votes which would be better explained simply by district sizes?

To test the effect of the "omitted" variable, district size, the ($2a$) regressions were re-run with V_i, ADC_i and $OTHEXP_i$ deflated by the number of registered voters in the district. (These variables have been

[22] An F=2 value "to remove" was used in the stepwise regression. Its precise equivalent in terms of a t-statistic for regression coefficients changes with sample size and number of conditioning variables. Suffice it to say that here F=2 is the equivalent of $1.5 < t < 1.6$.

[23] Durbin-Watson tables do not list values for samples larger than 100 observations. The D-W test is most commonly employed to find evidence of autocorrelation. For references on cross-sectional employment see Carl F. Christ, *Econometric Models and Methods* (New York, 1966), 527. Obviously, we are testing for homoskedasticity against the advertising variable only. An excellent summary of recent literature on this problem is Dennis J. Aigner, *Basic Econometrics* (Englewood Cliffs, N.J., 1971), 124–31.

given asterisks.) The results are shown below.

(2*a*) 1966 *DEFL*

$$V_i{}^*{}_j = .025 + .641\ OTHEXP_i{}^* \underset{(25.3)}{} + .416\ ADC_i{}^* \underset{(8.9)}{} + .073\ PARTINC_i \underset{(7.3)}{} + .058\ MIN_i \underset{(3.3)}{}$$

$$R^2 = .820 \quad N = 385$$

(2*a*) 1970 *DEFL*

$$V_i{}^*{}_j = .066 + .372\ OTHEXP_i{}^* \underset{(9.5)}{} + .127\ PARTINC_i \underset{(9.4)}{} + .272\ ADC_i{}^* \underset{(5.0)}{} - .063\ MIN_i \underset{(2.5)}{}$$

$$R^2 = .482 \quad N = 418$$

The striking result here is that the UR_j variable does not enter the regression results "significantly," while all conditioning variables retain their hierarchical importance. On reflection, this is what we should expect, as "urbanity" is strongly correlated with district size (the correlation between them being 0.73 in both election years): populous districts are urban districts. (District size varied in 1966 from 6597 to 69,301 registered voters and in 1970 from 7096 to 79,792 such voters.) Similar results were obtained with the "primed" (2*a*′) regressions, in which augmented advertising expense was used.

The question then arose of whether to normalize by district size all regressions except (4*a*), or whether not to normalize and retain the urban-rural variable instead. I chose the latter course, because UR_j fulfils the role of a dual variable. It stands for district size *and* for a cluster of demographic attributes. That it does indeed act in the second role can be seen in its appearance in the market share regressions (4*a*), which by their nature have been purged of the size effect. It will be more opportune to consider a source of possible simultaneous equation bias (do votes influence advertising expenditure?) at a later stage.

Returning now to the interpretation of the results of (2*a*), the coefficient of the urban-rural variable tells us, in this model, that candidates in urban ridings pick up more votes than candidates in the less-populated rural districts. It is interesting to note that being an outgoing minister in 1966 brought the candidate additional votes, but lost him votes in 1970. On both occasions the governments were *not* re-elected.

The most powerful conditioning variable, statistically speaking, appears to be the candidate's other electoral expenditure, $OTHEXP_i$. Note, nevertheless, that while on the average a dollar's increase over the mean sample value in other electoral expense in 1970 "buys" 0.448 votes, a dollar's increase in advertising expenditure from the mean ad outlay of the candidates buys almost 0.38 votes.

When cast in logarithmic form the estimates appear as follows:

(2*a*) 1966

$$\log V_{i,j} = 1.2356 + .2895 \log OTHEXP_i \underset{(11.7)}{} + .3545 \log ADC_i \underset{(10.9)}{} + .1633\ PARTINC_i \underset{(3.9)}{} + .1638\ UR_j \underset{(3.4)}{} + .0861\ F_j \underset{(2.3)}{} + .1110\ MIN_i \underset{(1.5)}{}$$

$$R^2 = .775, \ DW = 1.75$$

(2*a*) 1970

$$\log V_{i,j} = 1.2858 + .3962 \log OTHEXP_i \underset{(14.4)}{} + .1665 \log ADC_i \underset{(6.8)}{} + .2868\ UR_j \underset{(6.2)}{} + .1869\ PARTINC_i \underset{(5.1)}{} + .1550\ F_j \underset{(2.8)}{}$$

$$R^2 = .650, \ DW = 1.89$$

The log transformation leaves the least-squares fit of the data almost unchanged in the 1966 results and improves it extraordinarily in the 1970 results.[24] (In what follows only the "best" –as judged by the evidence of R^2 and DW statistics – regression results will be shown, in the sense that either the linear or the log-log form only will be presented.) In 1970 *MIN* is now replaced by *F*. In this model *F* merely tends to increase the number of votes, for the non–French-Canadian districts are, on the average, less populous than the French-Canadian ones.

The double-log form rests on the multiplicative functional form. Can a multiplicative relationship be theoretically justified? Note that only the expenditure variables are used in log transformation on the right

[24]This statement must be interpreted with a grain of salt. Budgetary reasons prevented me from making an unexceptional comparison between linear and logarithmic R^2's, which requires that the residuals of the log regressions be first converted to anti-logs before calculating a comparable R^2 statistic.

hand side of the equation – suggesting, rather realistically, that a candidate can scarcely hope to gather votes with expenditures confined to one of the two categories only.

The most important result, thus far, is the sturdy performance of the unadjusted-advertising expense variable which invariably shows up as being highly significant in influencing the number of votes cast for a candidate. When headquarters advertising is apportioned to the candidates, advertising becomes even more influential in its effect on voting:

(2a′) 1966

$$\log V_{i,j} = .9477 + \underset{(15.1)}{.5165} \log ADCP_i + \underset{(7.5)}{.1867} \log OTHEXP_i + \underset{(3.5)}{.1218}\, PARTINC_i + \underset{(3.1)}{.1355}\, UR_j + \underset{(1.8)}{.0950}\, F_j$$

$$R^2 = .814,\ DW = 1.93$$

(2a′) 1970

$$\log V_{i,j} = 1.0140 + \underset{(12.5)}{.3538} \log OTHEXP_i + \underset{(9.8)}{.2685} \log ADCP_i + \underset{(5.7)}{.2609}\, UR_j + \underset{(4.4)}{.1568}\, PARTINC_i + \underset{(3.3)}{.1820}\, F_j$$

$$R^2 = .668,\ DW = 1.94$$

We may note here, in addition, that the logarithmic versions tend to perform better than linear ones and strengthen our confidence in the results. For a double-log relationship between votes cast and advertising (and other expenses) implies decreasing returns to promotional outlays – a phenomenon amply documented in marketing research (where, naturally, sales revenue rather than number of votes is the dependent variable). It is rather interesting to observe that the decreasing returns mechanism operates here despite the fact that advertising expenditures cannot be pushed very far on account of the electoral expense limitation.

2. VOTING-DEMAND MODELS (3a) AND (3a′)

With the dependent variable being the number of votes obtained by the winning candidate, W_i, attention now shifts to the competitive aspect.[25] The winner's promotional efforts are assessed in comparison to all his rivals' campaign expenditures. The best (3a) estimates are set out below:

(3a) 1966

$$\log W_{i,j} = 1.3318 + \underset{(11.4)}{.7227} \log WOTHEXP_i + \underset{(7.2)}{.2530} \log WAD_i - \underset{(5.4)}{.2755} \log RIVOTHEXP_j + \underset{(2.6)}{.0727}\, MIN_i + \underset{(1.9)}{.0679}\, UR_j$$

$$R^2 = .767,\ DW = 1.94$$

(3a) 1970

$$W_{i,j} = 7680 + \underset{(8.6)}{1.1027}\, WAD_i + \underset{(8.1)}{.8448}\, WOTHEXP_i - \underset{(6.3)}{9837}\, F_j + \underset{(2.7)}{3894}\, UR_j - \underset{(1.8)}{.1014}\, RIVOTHEXP_j$$

$$R^2 = .797,\ DW = 1.64$$

The R^2's continue highly satisfactory. The 1970 *D-W* statistic dips into the inconclusive region between 1.44 and 1.65 and visual inspection does show some widening of the variance of the residuals at low and at high values of WAD_i.

In the (3), (4), and (5) 1970 models the F_j variable, when it does come in – as in (3a, 1970) – has now the meaning ascribed to it: it has invariably a *negative* coefficient indicating that the number of votes obtained by winners tended to be less in French-Canadian districts, because non–French-Canadian districts gave larger majorities to their Liberal representatives.

We note the negative coefficient of the variable $RIVOTHEXP_j$, other-than-advertising expenses by the rivals of the winner in the riding. While it would seem natural to expect that the more intensive the campaign effort of the winners' rivals, the lower his majority, this expectation is not confirmed in the adjusted (3a′) models. There, the variable representing rivals' combined advertising expense, $RIVAD_j$, comes in but with a positive coefficient. Thus one might *speculate* that the higher the combined expenditure on advertising by rivals, the more are electors stirred to cast votes *and* they cast them in favour of the winner. It is therefore possible that the effect of intensive advertising on the part of all candidates is successful in "bringing the vote out" and this benefits the winner. The same effect is found in all subsequent results whenever $RIVAD_j$ is admitted into the regression; however – and this is an important distinc-

[25]From here on the sample sizes are $N = 108$, corresponding to the number of electoral districts.

tion – coefficients of $RIVOTHEXP_j$ continue to be negative.

Many economists (and, I suspect, political scientists as well) are opposed to advertising on the assumption that individual firms' (and candidates') mass media messages tend to cancel each other out and resources are thus wasted. Yet the phenomenon that emerges here has been not infrequently found in market investigations of product brands: advertising within the industry, internecine though it may appear, stimulates total demand and enlarges the pie from which shares are to be cut. It may well be that advertising in a political campaign stimulates voter interest in general and enhances participation in voting, something perhaps not undesirable.[26] The adjusted models yield the following results:

(3*a*′) 1966

$$\log W_{i,j} = .8212 + .4846 \log WOTHEXP_i + .4043 \log WADP_i - .1697 \log RIVOTHEXP_j + .0495\, MIN_i - .0627\, F_j + .0071\, PARWIN_i\ .1059 \log RIVADP_j$$
$$\qquad (8.2) \quad (6.1) \quad (3.8) \quad (1.9) \quad (1.7) \quad (1.6) \quad (1.6)$$
$$R^2 = .820,\ DW = 1.96$$

(3*a*′) 1970

$$\log W_{i,j} = .5470 + .2344 \log WADP_i + .3527 \log RIVADP_j + .3100 \log WOTHEXP_i - .2224\, F_j + .1198\, UR_j$$
$$\qquad (6.1) \quad (5.9) \quad (5.8) \quad (3.7) \quad (2.1)$$
$$R^2 = .830,\ DW = 1.60$$

It remains to note here that $PARWIN_i$, the number of times the candidate's party was elected previously in the district, shows up as affecting the outcomes in the 1966 elections. (As stated previously, models 3–5 employ both *PARWIN* and *WINWIN*. The twain never turn up together, but neither seems to have inherent superiority.)

3. VOTING-DEMAND MODELS (4a) AND (4a′) In these models the dependent variable is the market share of votes going to the winner, MSW_i. The concept of market share of votes and promotional shares ($WADSH_i$, $WOTHEXPSH_i$) effectively neutralizes the "getting out the vote" influence and is thus worth an effort at estimation. It also dispenses with the need of taking into account the district size. The regression results with advertising unadjusted for headquarters expenditures are:

(4*a*) 1966

$$MSW_{i,j} = .4435 - .2361\, F_j + .3364\, WOTHEXPSH_i + .0209\, WINWIN_i + .1903\, WADSH_i + .0400\, UR_j - .0473\, MIN_i$$
$$\qquad (7.7) \quad (5.5) \quad (3.3) \quad (3.2) \quad (1.7) \quad (1.6)$$
$$R^2 = .627,\ DW = 1.71$$

(4*a*) 1970

$$MSW_{i,j} = 0.4430 - .2389\, F_j + .3854\, WOTHEXPSH_i + .0179\, WINWIN_i + .1587\, WADSH_i + .0458\, UR_j$$
$$\qquad (7.8) \quad (5.8) \quad (3.0) \quad (2.7) \quad (1.9)$$
$$R^2 = .617,\ DW = 1.3.$$

Because of the limited range of the share values no log transformation was undertaken on the (4) models. Note that since the market share was calculated for only one "brand" of candidates, winners, no problems of so-called logical consistency (market shares must add up to one) arise here.[27]

No important change appears when the advertising share augmented by headquarters' expenditures is substituted into the regressions:

(4*a*′) 1966

$$MSW_{i,j} = .2721 + .4226\, WOTHEXPS_i - .1183\, F_j$$
$$\qquad (7.9) \quad (5.1)$$

[26]At this stage it must be acknowledged, however, that these remarks are speculative. Note that in 1966 *RIVADP* is significant at the 5 per cent level only if we postulate *a priori* that its sign is negative. If no assumption is made about its sign, the critical *t*-value for the 5 per cent level rises to 1.96. Ongoing research devoted to the exploration of impact of campaign expenditures on abstentionism does, however, show in preliminary results that campaign intensity influences positively voter participation.

[27]Richard Schmalensee, *The Economics of Advertising* (Amsterdam, 1972), 104–12.

$$+ .2732\ WADPSH_i$$
$$(3.6)$$
$$+ .0099\ PARWIN_i$$
$$(3.5)$$
$$R^2 = .564,\ DW = 1.95$$

(4a′) 1970

$$MSW_{i,j} = .4662 - .2429\ F_j$$
$$(7.8)$$
$$.3450\ WOTHEXPSH_i$$
$$(5.1)$$
$$+ .0165\ WINWIN_i$$
$$(2.6)$$
$$+ .1370\ WADPSH_i$$
$$(2.1)$$
$$+ .0456\ UR_j$$
$$(1.9)$$
$$R^2 = .606,\ DW = 1.61$$

At this point it might be useful to see how the market-share model forecasts. On 4 December, 1968 a byelection was held in the riding of Notre-Dame-de-Grâce. The Liberal candidate won over the only opposing candidate, a UN adherent. The appropriate regression is (4*a*) 1966, since party headquarters did not participate.

Tetley, the Liberal, spent $4667 on advertising and $17,913 on other electoral expenses. Staunton spent $20,574 on advertising and $7,284 on other expenses. The riding is English (F=0), urban (UR=1), neither of the candidates won before ($WINWIN$=0) or was minister (MIN=0). Thus,

$$MSW_{i,j} = 0.4435 + (0.3664)(0.7109) + (0.1903)(0.1848) + 0.0400 = 0.7792 \text{ forecast.}$$

Tetley's actual share was 0.7928.

4. VOTING-DEMAND MODELS (5a) AND (5a′)

Just as the firm is not interested in the largest possible market share or sales revenue obtainable, but in maximum profit so, from a narrow optimization viewpoint the candidate and his party do not seek the largest possible vote. Rather, the candidate wants to be elected and for this a majority of one is sufficient. In a majority representation system, such as everywhere in North America, the party's interest in this matter is identical with its candidate's. It is, therefore, useful to examine how the winners' plurality (excess of his votes over that of his runner-up) is conditioned by the electoral variables on which data are available.

It should be pointed out, nevertheless, that the narrow optimization point of view is adequate only in a static framework. A large plurality may be desirable on dynamic grounds. For instance, a winner who piles up a large majority may discourage, on the next round, highly qualified potential rivals to present themselves in his "safe" riding. He may also have a stronger claim to a cabinet portfolio. The incoming government may wish to gerrymander ridings in which large majorities were realized to weaken opposition in one instance and to offer potential victory to its candidates in ridings adjacent to those in which it gained "unnecessarily" large majorities.

It is appropriate to mention in this connection a phenomenon which is not investigated in this study. One might speculate that campaigning has long-term, lagged effects. Thus a candidate may present himself (and spend funds) several times before he is elected. It would be bold to assert that it was only the last, successful campaign which was responsible for his election. His previous exposure to voters is obviously worth something.[28] We get an indirect echo of this here, since many regressions admit *PARTINC*, *WINWIN*, and *PARWIN* as significant conditioning variables, though of course it seems reasonable to believe that the most important ingredient of these variables is the electorate's experience with the candidate's performance in Parliament.

And now for the results which are, for 1966, surprising to say the least:

(5a) 1966

$$PLU_{i,j} = 4{,}630 - 5{,}648\ F_j$$
$$(5.0)$$
$$- .2385\ RIVOTHEXP_j$$
$$(3.7)$$
$$+ .2656\ RIVADC_j$$
$$(3.20)$$
$$+ 3{,}097\ UR_j$$
$$(3.17)$$
$$+ 2{,}413\ MIN_i$$
$$(3.0)$$
$$+ .1763\ WOTHEXP_i$$
$$(2.0)$$
$$+ 279\ PARWIN_i$$
$$(1.9)$$
$$R^2 = .572,\ DW = 2.06$$

(5a′) 1966

$$PLU_{i,j} = 4{,}250 - 4{,}903\ F_j$$
$$(4.2)$$
$$- .2356\ RIVOTHEXP_j$$
$$(4.1)$$
$$+ .2696\ RIVADP_j$$
$$(4.0)$$
$$+ 2{,}469\ MIN_i$$
$$(3.0)$$
$$+ 2{,}869\ UR_j$$
$$(2.8)$$
$$+ 271\ PARWIN_i$$
$$(1.9)$$
$$R^2 = .568,\ DW = 2.14$$

---

[28]I have examined this phenomenon in a commercial context in *The Measurement of Cumulative Advertising Effects* (Englewood Cliffs, N.J., 1964).

TABLE II

COEFFICIENTS OF VARIATION ($\hat{\sigma}/\bar{X}$) OF WAD AND WADP

	1966	1970
Winner's advertising expenditure (WAD)	0.63	0.70
Winner's adjusted advertising expenditure (WADP)	0.48	0.69

Neither the non-adjusted (5*a*) nor the adjusted (5*a*′) form show the winner's advertising outlay to be a significant conditioning variable. They do show, however, rivals' advertising expense to be influential. Are we then to assume that the winner's plurality was unaffected by his advertising outlay in the 1966 election?

Before we offer a tentative answer we should ask whether the correlation between the winner's advertising outlay and that of his rivals was possibly so high that $RIVADC_j$ (or $RIVADP_j$) pushed out "freakishly" WAD_i (or $WADP_i$). We know that the two sets of variables were employed in (3*a*) and (3*a*′), albeit in logarithmic form. But in both 1966 (3*a*) and 1966 (3*a*′) log WAD_i (or log $WADP_i$) did come into the regression although the simple *correlation* coefficients between them were *higher* (0.597 and 0.811 respectively) than the correlation coefficients between these variables in (5*a*) and (5*a*′) which are, respectively, 0.349 and 0.619. Collinearity is therefore hardly responsible for the poor performance of the winner's advertising in the 1966 (5*a*) and (5*a*′) models.

We are then thrown back to the somewhat unsatisfactory tentative explanation that *WAD* or *WADP* did not vary sufficiently across the cross-sections in 1966 to emerge as significant conditioning variables; whereas, as will be seen, in 1970 they did. Some slight evidence of this are the coefficients of variation in the two elections. (See Table II). Only the 1970 results with adjusted winner's advertising expenditures need detain our attention:

$$
\begin{aligned}
(5a')\ 1970\quad PLU_{i,j} = {} & 11{,}071 - \underset{(7.3)}{13{,}220}\, F_j \\
& + \underset{(4.4)}{.3766}\, WADP_i \\
& + \underset{(2.8)}{.1860}\, RIVADP_j \\
& + \underset{(2.6)}{650}\, PARWIN \\
& - \underset{(2.1)}{.1395}\, RIVOTHEXP_j \\
& - \underset{(2.0)}{3{,}196}\, MIN_i \\
R^2 = {} & .675,\ DW = 1.56
\end{aligned}
$$

Here everything falls again into the accustomed pattern except for the absence of the UR_j variable. If we were to ask the question here (admittedly formulated from the *static* optimization viewpoint) as to how much a typical winner should spend on advertising – taking due account of party headquarters outlays – if he were to desire but a one-vote plurality, we would get a surprising answer: *nothing*.

The typical winner, a mere statistical construct, is endowed with the following "characteristics":

F_j = .9259, $WADP_i$ = \$9969, $RIVADP_j$ = \$19,080, $PARWIN$ = 2.333, $RIVOTHEXP_j$ = \$15,609, MIN = .1019.

When these values, which are obviously the means of the 1970 (5*a*′) variables, are substituted into the regression equation, the value of PLU_i = 5146 votes, again the sample mean as can be verified in the appendix table. By using a value of zero for *WADP*, the forecast plurality reduces to 1392 votes, still a substantial majority.[29]

We come then to the opinion that the typical winner (and his party) *overadvertised* – from the strictly short-term viewpoint. (Since the winner's other expenditure did not come into the regression, we have no means of judging him on $WOTHEXP_i$; note also that rivals' advertising, $RIVADP_j$, increased his vote.)

Supporting evidence for this comes in the 1966 and contradictory evidence in the 1970 elections from a series of regressions, not shown here, in which the market shares of Liberal and of UN candidates were regressed against the usual set of variables, but where instead of advertising and other expenditure shares the *ratio* of each candidate's advertising to his other expenditure was employed as a conditioning variable. The UN regressions for both years showed a significantly *negative* coefficient of this *AD/OTHEXP* ratio, the Liberal regression for 1966 yielded a non-significant coefficient of this ratio and the 1970 regression a significant positive coefficient. With a properly

[29]The average plurality with non-augmented advertising, WAD_i, is 1095 votes.

balanced communications mix we would not expect the coefficient of the ratio to be statistically significant; a significantly negative coefficient implies that too much of the campaign budget is spent on advertising. In 1966 the UN won, in 1970 the Liberals won.

Evidence that firms frequently *over-advertise* is beginning to emerge from econometric literature.[30] However, such evidence must be weighed very carefully, especially if the investigator believes in the informed rationality of economic man. Why should a candidate (or his party) overspend substantially on promotion? He is either acting irrationally, or, more likely, making his decisions in the face of great uncertainty or, even more likely, optimizing over the long run horizon – an aspect we mentioned remains unexplored here.[31]

Before the various findings are placed in perspective in the concluding section, one last issue must be discussed. Known as the problem of identification in econometrics, it arises in our context as the following question: do candidates more likely to win expend larger sums on advertising than those less likely to win? That is, can we be sure that in our equations advertising influences votes rather than *vice versa*?

The matter is difficult to resolve on *a priori* grounds. It could be argued that an incumbent is more likely to invest in what is a safe seat. It could be equally well argued that an unsafe seat or simply a dubious riding would be more likely held or conquered by a higher advertising expenditure. Or, from a party's point of view, it may make sense to urge candidates in marginal ridings to spend more on advertising than to so urge candidates in districts which are either a safe or a poor bet.

Let us see what we can make of the evidence. If, for instance, winners did *not* spend on the average more on advertising than runners-up, there is little reason to suspect causality to flow in reverse direction from votes to advertising. In 1966 winners spent of their own funds an average of $4140 on advertising, but runners-up spent $4352 on average. (When *adjusted* advertising figures are used – less relevant to the issue under consideration – the figures still have the same ranking: winners spent $8801, runners-up $8967). However, the 1970 figures are not as reassuring. In those elections the average advertising expenditure of the winner was $5105 and that of the runner-up $4389. (Corresponding adjusted ad expenditures are $9969 and $7571.)

Since advertising was not the only campaign expense incurred, the question as to what rationale lay behind candidates' outlays was looked at in a regression using 1970 data for all candidates ($N = 418$). The dependent variable was defined as a candidate's total campaign expense divided by the total legal limit on his expenses. The conditioning variable of interest, labelled "marginality," was in the case of a winner his plurality divided by eligible electors, and in the case of a loser the number of votes he fell short of the winner's votes, also divided by the district's eligible voters. The variables which came in determined the following regression form:

Candidate *i*'s total campaign expenditure as percentage of his legal limit
$= f(\text{Marginality}_i, PARWIN_i, F_j)$

Marginality was the most statistically significant variable and had a negative coefficient. It thus appears that the most money was being invested in doubtful electoral districts, just as an economist would prescribe. In this sense, then, the sheer number of expected votes had no positive causal influence on campaign expenditure.

An objection might be raised that actual votes are an unsuitable proxy for expected votes. We can turn to further evidence, this time with the help of the candidates' – or rather their parties' – electoral history. *PARWIN*, the number of times a party won a particular seat in preceding elections, has shown up to be in many cases a variable which is influential in increasing the chance of a candidate's success. Thus a candidate whose party was more often victorious in a given riding had a better chance to win. Should we therefore find that the correlation between *PARWIN* and winners' advertising outlays is significant, there would be reason to suspect that candidates more likely to win do indeed spend more money on advertising and that causality may not have flown in the direction we assumed throughout. Fortunately, the data do not bear this out, as can be seen in Table III. Only the correlation coefficient between *PARWIN* and log *WADP* in 1970 is statistically significant at the 5 per cent level

[30] Jean-Jacques Lambin, "Is Gasoline Advertising Justified?," *Journal of Business* (October 1972), 585–619; Lester G. Telser, "Advertising and Cigarettes," *Journal of Political Economy* (October 1962), 471–99.

[31] As was mentioned, a variable called *YEL*, income per elector, was available in 69 of the 108 ridings. When employed in the stepwise (2*a*) regressions, its coefficient had no statistical significance whatever. The tentative conclusion is therefore that this "taste" characteristic did not affect the outcome of the Quebec elections.

TABLE III

SIMPLE CORRELATION COEFFICIENTS BETWEEN 1966 AND 1970

1966		1970	
PARWIN and *WAD*	−.030	*PARWIN* and *WAD*	.086
PARWIN and log *WAD*	−.002	*PARWIN* and log *WAD*	.105
PARWIN and *WADP*	−.132	*PARWIN* and *WADP*	.161
PARWIN and log *WADP*	−.119	*PARWIN* and log *WADP*	.251

(but not at the 1 per cent level) and *WADP* is adjusted expense, not fully relevant here. Some of the correlation coefficients even have negative signs.

A last remark addressed to non-Canadian readers may be in order. Candidates of the two *major* parties in Quebec traditionally did not have to face what might be called the McGovern problem of *raising* electoral funds. Local support was sufficient to finance their personal campaign while most of their parties' headquarter expenditures were spent on the provincial level. Some candidates spent up to their legal limit and most of them were reimbursed from the public purse according to the provisions of the electoral law. While discussion centred on the willingness of candidates to spend, their *ability* to spend does not seem to interfere with the postulated direction of causality either.

The reasonable conclusion can therefore be reached that causality in our regressions flows in the specified manner from expenditures to votes.

V. Conclusion

For some time now I have been extremely sceptical of the accepted opinion that advertising outlays have a material effect on the outcome of democratic elections. My scepticism was based on two reasons: the findings of mass communication research about resistance to change of deep-seated attitudes and the great empirical difficulty of documenting the influence of advertising on sales.

The discovery of possibly the only satisfactory data available anywhere – the expenditure records of parties and candidates in the 1966 and 1970 Quebec elections – made it possible to test my null hypothesis of no advertising effects.

The test was in the form of ordinary least squares estimates of voting-demand models inspired by econometric market research practice. Guarding against simultaneous equation and specification bias and checking for heteroskedasticity and collinearity, the estimates showed advertising expenditures in various forms (as well as other campaign expenditures) to be a powerful conditioning variable. The null hypothesis thus stands defeated.

This is a finding of some importance for political analysts and party managers, albeit strictly applicable only to one geographic area. One might speculate, for instance, that paid mass media political messages exert but little influence where the candidates and their platforms are well known through news and broadcast reporting, such as in US presidential elections.

Several other interesting issues have been raised but require further study which is now being carried on. Among them are the findings that rival candidates' advertising expenditure increases the number of votes for the winner; that most candidates appear to over-advertise; and that advertising outlay increases in proportion to the narrowness of the winning margin. Three directions for further research are indicated. One is of interest to political scientists, raising questions such as whether abstentions are affected by campaign expenditure intensity and whether rural areas are affected differently from urban areas by mass communication effort. The second may concern party managers, dealing with problems of optimal size of campaign budget and optimal communications mix (between advertising and personal communication). The third direction for further research is of general interest: the possibility of forecasting electoral outcomes with econometric models – a method fully distinct from the short-term forecasts based on opinion sampling.

Appendix

TABLE A

LIST OF VARIABLES (subscripts i designate candidate or his party, j the electoral district)

Dependent variables	Conditioning variables	
V_{ij} = valid votes for i in j W_{ij} = valid votes for winner MSW_{ij} = market share of valid votes of winner PLU_{ij} = plurality of valid votes of winner	(*a*) *Advertising* ADC_i = advertising expenditure of i $ADCP_i$ = augmented ad expenditure WAD_i = winner's ad expenditure $WADP_i$ = winner's augmented ad expenditure $WADSH_i$ = winner's share of ad expenditure in j $WADPSH_i$ = winner's augmented share of ad expenditure $RIVAD_j$ = sum of rivals' ad expenditure in j $RIVADP_j$ = sum of rivals' augmented ad expenditure	(*c*) *Historical variables* $PARTINC_i$ = i's party incumbent $WINWIN_i$ = number of previous wins by winner $PARWIN_i$ = number of previous wins by winner's party in j MIN_i = i was minister in outgoing government
	(*b*) *Other expense* $OTHEXP_i$ = other expense of i $WOTHEXP_i$ = winner's other expense $WOTHEXPSH_i$ = winner's share of other expense in j $RIVOTHEXP_j$ = sum of rivals' other expense in j	(*d*) *District characteristics* UR_j = j's urban-rural character in percentage F_j = French or English YEL_j = average income of elector in j

TABLE B

SUMMARY STATISTICS ON 1966 AND 1970 ELECTIONS

		Σ	$\bar{X}$	s.d.	max.	min.
V_i	1966	2,313,246	6008	5360	24,840	82
	1970	2,832,371	6739	6319	46,169	53
W_i	1966	1,207,515	11,181	4859	24,840	3294
	1970	1,368,667	12,673	8154	46,169	3560
MSW_i	1966		52.0%	8.5%	90.6%	34.7%
	1970		46.3%	12.5%	90.4%	28.6%
PLU_i	1966		3191	4161	23,161	5
	1970		5146	7345	41,316	41
ADC_i	1966	$1,064,482	2765	3026	18,706	3
	1970	1,745,368	4175	3744	21,254	1
$ADCP_i$	1966	$2,114,708	5492	5430	25,784	8
	1970	3,137,252	7505	6341	32,374	1
WAD_i	1966	$ 447,108	4140	2579	11,697	134
	1970	551,340	5105	3507	21,254	333
$WADP_i$	1966	$ 950,555	8801	4196	19,477	1256
	1970	1,076,681	9969	6200	32,374	895
$WADSH_i$	1966		43.5%	14.9%	88.5%	6.8%
	1970		31.6%	13.3%	63.1%	6.5%

TABLE B – *continued*

$WADPSH_i$	1966		45.8%	8.2%	65.3%	11.8%
	1970		34.5%	12.3%	54.0%	4.0%
$RIVADC_j$	1966	$ 616,054	5704	4024	18,706	89
	1970	1,194,028	11,056	5845	25,045	794
$RIVADP_j$	1966	$1,164,185	10,779	5749	27,856	1284
	1970	2,060,618	19,080	9205	44,260	2018
$OTHEXP_i$	1966	$2,072,328	5382	5192	25,129	1
	1970	2,656,639	6335	5021	26,412	1
$WOTHEXP_i$	1966	$ 963,375	8920	4081	25,129	2848
	1970	970,831	8989	4580	26,412	1797
$WOTHEXPS_i$	1966		47.3%	11.3%	86.0%	27.0%
	1970		37.9%	12.1%	83.0%	8.0%
$RIVOTHEXP_j$	1966	$1,110,272	10,280	5342	30,891	1606
	1970	1,685,808	15,609	8444	45,637	1584
UR_j	1966		.6257	.3431	1	0
	1970		.6322	.3343	1	0

	1966	1970
Electoral districts	108	108
Candidates in sample	385	418

The Representative System and the Calling of Elections

NORMAN WARD *University of Saskatchewan*

Sometime between 30 October 1972 and the spring of 1973, the government led by the Rt. Hon. Pierre Trudeau, with fewer than half the members of the House of Commons belonging to the Liberal party, discovered that, unless it was prepared to use maps based on the 1961 census, one of the courses not immediately available to it was the dissolution of Parliament and the calling of another general election. The handicap (and it must also have particularly affected the strategy of the New Democratic party), was not for any constitutional reason; nor was it based on the possibility that the governor general might refuse the prime minister a dissolution. That possibility existed, although no one in the cabinet or Commons appears to have recognized it. Eugene Forsey concluded years ago, after his exhaustive study of the prerogatives governing dissolution: "Even where a great new issue of public policy has arisen, the Crown would be justified in refusing dissolution if Supply had not been voted, or a redistribution or franchise Act had not yet had time to come into operation, provided an alternative Government could be found, or provided the issue was not one which brooked no delay, e.g. a mandate for the despatch of troops overseas."[1] Two of the conditions noted by Dr Forsey three decades ago existed in 1972–3: a redistribution act had not yet had time to come into operation, and an alternative government could be found.

The reason for the government's inability to call an election was simply that, as the law stood, the electoral machinery if based on 1971 maps could not be ready until well on in 1974; technically, Mr Trudeau could have asked for and received a dissolution, and then had to date an election months later, which could have brought him into conflict with the sections of the British North America Act which require Parlia-

[1] *The Royal Power of Dissolution of Parliament in the British Commonwealth* (Toronto, 1968), 262.

Canadian Journal of Political Science/Revue canadienne de science politique, VI, no. 4 (December/décembre 1973). Printed in Canada/Imprimé au Canada.

ment to meet at least once a year. His problem arose from section 23 of the Electoral Boundaries Readjustment Act: "Within five days after the receipt by the Secretary of State of the draft representation order, the Governor in Council shall by proclamation declare the draft representation order to be in force, effective upon the dissolution of the then existing Parliament or effective upon the dissolution of the next following Parliament if upon the issue of the proclamation Parliament is then dissolved, and upon the issue of the proclamation the order has the force of law accordingly."[2] The "draft representation order" – an instrument prepared by the representation commissioner after the various electoral-boundaries commissions have drawn the federal constituencies in each province, reconsidered them after the required public hearings and examinations by members of Parliament, and made their final decisions – had begun its course in the summer of 1972, before the general election of that year had been called. The boundaries commissions have by law one year in which to send their maps to the Speaker of the House, and by July 1973 the maps were in the House of Commons being objected to by members, and the draft representation order, according to its statutory schedule, was certain to reach the secretary of state by November or December 1973. Thereafter, according to the representation commissioner and the chief electoral officer, both experienced administrators of elections, a full year would be needed to organize the new constituencies, to instruct the new returning officers (most returning officers are displaced by a redistribution, many because they no longer reside in the constituency they previously directed), and, on the purely political side, to allow the party organizations to become familiar with the new constituency boundaries and polling divisions.[3]

At the best of times, with the electoral machinery fully manned, instructed, and ready to be used, a Canadian general election takes at least two months, and a prime minister of Canada is never able, as is his British counterpart, to have an election in a scant three weeks. The chief factor in this is the Canadian process for the enumeration of voters, which is done on an *ad hoc* basis for every election and begins on the forty-ninth day before polling day.[4] On top of that, the chief electoral officer needs extra time for last-minute emergencies. That officer, Jean-Marc Hamel, testified in 1970 of the election of 1968: "I believe there were 14 returning officers who resigned or for some reason or other had to be replaced in the week prior to and the week after the issue of the writ ... That is the reason we insist on at least 9 to 10 days between the issue of the writ and the beginning of the enumeration. We absolutely need this period for these particular cases."[5] The chief electoral officer's use of "we insist" is revealing: no prime minister, however large his majority, can have an election if the machinery is not ready, and if (as has happened) an emissary from the chief executive office waits upon the electoral office to sound out the possibilities of an early election he may well be told, "We could have one in two months – provided, of course, you hold it in only 230 constituencies. We're short a few returning officers."

The machinery in 1973, if the new maps were proceeded with, would have been short nearly all its returning officers; the exact number is not known because the redistribution was not completed. The redistribution of 1966 required the re-appointment or replacement of 258 of 264 of them, and "it was done quite expeditiously, but still it took over a year to get the whole group of them appointed."[6] The law, at the urging of the chief electoral officer and a recommendation from the Committee on Privileges and Elections, now requires the Governor-General-in-Council to appoint a returning officer "within sixty days from the date on which the Chief Electoral Officer has been informed of the vacancy,"[7] so that portion of the machinery has been quickened, although there is considerable doubt whether the new provision applies to a redistribution when vacancies *en masse* occur. The machinery as a whole remains geared, in effect, to "majority government," and to elections every four or five years, with ample time between convulsions for the printing and distribution of several tons of supplies, the selection and instruction of personnel, and even the sober consideration

[2] *R.S. Can.*, 1970, c. E-2, s. 23.

[3] Canada, *House of Commons Debates*, 19 July 1973, especially p. 5797. Mr Allen MacEachen, president of the Privy Council, was here speaking on the report stage of the bill to suspend the new redistribution, and gave an excellent summary of the situation.

[4] *R. S. Can.*, 1970, 1st Supp., c. 14, ss. 18(1).

[5] Canada, House of Commons, Standing Committee on Privileges and Elections, *Minutes of Proceedings and Evidence*, 1970, pp. 8:27–8.

[6] *Ibid.*, p. 8:25.

[7] *R. S. Can.*, 1970, 1st Supp., c. 14, ss 7(5).

by prime ministers of the fact that a so-called snap election still requires two months.

With the increasing incidence of "minority government" (surely one of the strangest misnomers one could apply to a cabinet system) increasing pressure has been put on the machinery in a variety of ways. The elections of 1958 and 1963, following so closely on those of 1957 and 1962, put almost inhuman burdens on the administration. Members of Parliament and ministers, though warned of the cost and cumbersome nature of permanent voters' lists (against which the Committee on Privileges and Elections reported in 1970 with unmistakable clarity,[8]) are beginning to look longingly at any system that might eliminate from the Canada Elections Act all assertions like: "The returning officer shall, commencing on Monday, the forty-ninth day before polling day ..." When one adds a redistribution scheme which, twice in its two applications, has complicated the manoeuvrings of consecutive governments drawn from the same political party, dissatisfaction with the whole apparatus is not difficult to understand. The dissatisfaction, expressed rather mildly in 1965–6 but in explicit terms in 1973, now concerns fundamental aspects of the Canadian representative system, on parts of which members of Parliament are almost unanimous, while on others they are profoundly divided.

In 1965–6, when the government of the Rt. Hon. L.B. Pearson, without a majority formed exclusively of Liberals, had been in office only two years and had itself taken the initiative in transferring the redistribution of constituency boundaries from parliamentary committees to independent commissions, the chief problem that arose concerned the timing of the next general election. During 1965 the 10 boundaries commissions were at work, and the government had to consider whether to hold another election on the old constituencies created in 1952 (which rural-urban shifts in population had marvellously skewed[9]), or to await the commissions' maps, and if so for how long. (The commissions, it may be noted, were not anxious to hold public hearings on proposed electoral boundaries during an election campaign.) The chief electoral officer at the time was coincidentally the representation commissioner (Nelson Castonguay) who formally advised the secretary of state on 5 July 1965 that an election on the new maps *could* be held by November (later revised to late October) 1966 provided that all 264 returning officers were available within 30 days of the maps becoming law; a qualification generally forgotten by observers at the time.[10] The government decided not to wait, incurring the displeasure of numerous citizens who were not all non-Liberals, and held its election in 1965. Since the new redistribution system was at work for the first time, and had not yet produced its final maps, criticism of it as such was minimal.

By the 1970s, however, a second set of maps drawn by independent commissions was in the House, and the overwhelming majority of the members had no first-hand experiences of redistribution by any other method; of those who did, only Stanley Knowles (Winnipeg North Centre) strongly defended the new system. Many more-junior members, happily free of encounters with gerrymanders, frequently confused the independent commissions with the constitutional and statutory rules within which they had to draw boundaries and offered some remarkable fresh glosses on the law and interpretations of what the commissions had done. Thus two members of the Committee on Privileges and Elections asked the chief electoral officer in 1971 and 1973, in effect, how he appointed returning officers, and both received the same answer: "I discover the name after he has been appointed."[11] Another asserted roundly in the House, "The act states that because there is a greater concentration of voters in a metropolitan riding a tolerance of 25 per cent above [the] quota is allowed. Rural ridings are allowed a tolerance of minus 25 per cent below the 82,000 quota because of the large land area covered by most of them"; the act draws no such distinction between rural and urban seats.[12]

---

[8]"It is not feasible to introduce a system of Continuous Electoral Rolls in Canada at this time." Canada, House of Commons, Standing Committee on Privileges and Elections, *Fourth Report to the House*, 19 March 1970. See also *Report of the Representation Commissioner on Methods of Registration of Electors and Absentee Voting* (Ottawa, 1968).

[9]See Norman Ward, "A Century of Constituencies," *Canadian Public Administration*, 10(1), 1967, pp. 105–22.

[10]The relevant correspondence is reproduced in Peter C. Newman, *The Distemper of Our Times* (Toronto, 1968), pp. 498–502.

[11]Canada, House of Commons, Standing Committee on Privileges and Elections, *Minutes of Proceedings and Evidence*, 1971, p. 1:22; *ibid.*, 1973, p. 3:21.

[12]Canada, *House of Commons Debates*, 18 July 1973, p. 5770; *R. S. Can.*, 1970, c. E-2, s. 13.

Another member, professing to find a similarity in the 10 commission reports and noting that the representation commissioner was a member of all 10 commissions, saw his fell hand on all 10 maps; Mr Castonguay had already cheerfully scouted his influence (later pointing out that only once in two redistributions had a commission accepted a proposal from him) and recommended the abolition of his office, its routine work to be done by a secretariat attached to the chief electoral officer.[13] Most surprisingly of all, the veteran member for Prince Albert, the Rt. Hon. John Diefenbaker (whose constituents had offered no briefs to the Saskatchewan commission, which had to cancel a scheduled public hearing in the riding) not only described the Saskatchewan map as a gerrymander with "certain of the boundaries [drafted] under Mr. Justice Brownridge [with] political considerations in mind," but accused Judge Brownridge, one of his own appointees to the Bench, of possibly having "some ambition for a higher judicial appointment."[14]

Apart from this kind of aberration, the parliamentary debates on the postponement of the 1972–3 redistribution were a remarkably revealing record of members' problems with representation, and their attitudes toward them. The government, had it wished solely to postpone the redistribution, could have done so with a relatively short amendment to section 23 of the Electoral Boundaries Readjustment Act, quoted above. Instead, under pressure from urban members wanting more urban seats, from rural members who were discontented because in some provinces they were getting them, from westerners losing representation and who thought the guarantees of seats to the Maritime provinces were excessive, and from Newfoundlanders who found the Maritime guarantees discriminatory, the several House leaders reached an all-party agreement which not merely suspended the 1972–3 redistribution until 1 January 1975, but also assumed that before that date a whole new system of rules and devices will have been created; otherwise, the maps already drawn will return from limbo and continue their stately progression toward the statute books. The government, to minimize the chances of that happening, committed itself in July of 1973 to "a formal statement [on] a possible package for redistribution" in the fall.[15]

Allan MacEachen, presenting the bill on behalf of the government, offered no other reasons for the suspension of redistribution than the general desire to keep 1974 free for a possible election and the dissatisfaction expressed by some members with the proposed redistribution. Given the long birth-pangs of the redistribution system theoretically in force in 1973, and the depth of the disagreement shown by members in discussing its suspension, it is not easy to envisage what kind of all-party agreement (which is tacitly taken for granted on all sides) may emerge, or what it may do to the Canadian representative system when it does, whether one considers the commissions themselves, the rules they must follow, or both. Certainly little of the debate offered much hope that any new machinery would simplify the prime minister's task of advising dissolution and timing an election on an up-to-date set of constituencies.

Mr Knowles, as noted, praised the commissions as did several others; Walter Dinsdale, a fellow Manitoban sitting for Brandon-Souris, averred "that there is something fundamentally wrong with our method of electoral boundaries adjustment."[16] John Lundrigan (Gander-Twillingate) asserted that, "anybody who suggests that representation in the Canadian House of Commons should be based totally, primarily and solely on population really does not deserve to enjoy the benefits of a federal system and be part of Canada," and Mr Diefenbaker later added, "representation by population cannot be preserved within this country if confederation is to be maintained."[17] Urban members felt differently, and Ron Atkey (St Paul's) spoke for most of them when he said: "What I am concerned about is the people living in cities generally, about urban politics, and the fact that if we were to derogate from the principle of representation by population, the political process here in Ottawa would become increasingly irrelevant to those people in the cities. I think that is unhealthy. I think that this House is becoming more and more irrelevant to the real power processes in the cities."[18]

---

[13]Canada, *House of Commons Debates*, 10 July 1973, p. 5465; Standing Committee on Privileges and Elections, *Minutes of Proceedings and Evidence*, 1970, p. 20:16; *ibid.*, 1973, p. 4:44.

[14]Canada, *House of Commons Debates*, 10 July 1973, p. 5473. Having twice sat with Mr Justice Brownridge on the Saskatchewan Electoral Boundaries Commission, I should like the record to show that he is one of the fairest and most conscientious chairmen I have ever worked with, and that Mr Diefenbaker's references to both the map and Judge Brownridge were without foundation.

[15]*Ibid.*, 18 July 1973, p. 5770.

[16]*Ibid.*, 5 July 1973, p. 5336.

[17]*Ibid.*, 9 July 1973, p. 5434; July 10, 1973, p. 5473.

[18]*Ibid.*, 18 July 1973, p. 5772.

The rural-urban division in the House, with the population as a whole becoming increasingly urbanized and rural seats inevitably becoming larger and more unmanageable, cut across party lines, as did the attitudes of the members as provincial and regional spokesmen. Quebec members favoured postponement because it would save their province 2 more seats for perhaps at least one more election; British Columbians generally opposed it because the same redistribution allotted 3 more seats to them. Newfoundlanders looked askance at the rules which guaranteed them only 6 seats to Prince Edward Island's 4, or 6 to New Brunswick's 10. Prairie members recalled the days when their region, while growing rapidly in population, had been deprived of seats because the redistribution based on the census of 1911 did not take effect until 1917, and that on the census of 1921 not until 1925; they wanted something done to save prairie seats in the 1970s. Hardly anybody, indeed, appeared satisfied with the representative system and even Mr Knowles, one of the few who always differentiated carefully between the independent commissions and the rules for the distribution of seats among the provinces, pointed out that the rules worked unfairly among their chief beneficiaries, the Maritimes.[19] In his province, incidentally, the commission had so drawn the boundaries that 9 of the province's proposed 12 seats included part of the metropolitan area of Winnipeg.

That map, with its nine counterparts, may yet become law if the Electoral Boundaries Readjustment Suspension Act[20] fails of its purpose. The act does not merely suspend the redistribution of 1972–3; it also abolishes the 10 commissions which drew the maps, and while their re-establishment is also provided for, the president of the Privy Council made clear that any re-established commissions would not necessarily include the same personnel: the reconstituted commissions would pick up where their predecessors left off and be expected to hold new public hearings on the maps in the light of parliamentary objections to them.[21] But it was plain from the 1973 debates that a significant number on both sides of the House wanted more far-reaching changes than that. Randolph Harding (Kootenay West) was one of several MPs critical of the increasing size of rural ridings, many of them rich in resources, and he urged "some type of formula to include consideration of communications, acreage, people, the economy of the area, resource development, etc.;"[22] urban members kept reiterating that acres did not vote, people did. Some members proposed bringing the Senate more closely into a formula which would compensate the less-populous provinces with extra senators rather than extra MPs; but Mr Knowles suggested the abolition of both the senatorial floor and the Senate: "We could develop a system in which we provide for each province a certain number of members, two, three, or four, just because they are provinces. On top of that we could give each province a number of members in proportion to their population. Alternatively, we could decide on quotients that vary. The first 500,000 or one million could represent so many members and after that it would take more population to get additional seats."[23]

Lorne Nystrom (Yorkton-Melville) also proposed a sliding scale for awarding seats to provinces,[24] while Marcel Lambert (Edmonton West), a former Speaker, suggested that at the very least the commissions ought to give reasons for the boundaries they draw. (Since the only possible reasons an honest commission could give are already outlined in the Electoral Boundaries Readjustment Act, that proposal would in effect require each commission to justify obeying the law. The Alberta map in 1973, for example, reversed the traditional trend and made rural seats, on the average, more populous than urban; but the act permits commissions to consider "relative rate of growth of population of various regions of the province," so that the commission could have easily explained its boundaries by pointing to urban rates of growth and citing that phrase.[25]) Still other members wanted to look again at such specifics as permanent voters' lists, enlarging the size of the Commons, and drawing distinctions between urban and rural seats; or, at the other end of the spectrum (and in the light of the bill concerning election expenses introduced in the same session), "a wide ranging bill covering every aspect of the electoral reform."[26] Hardly anybody, incidentally, so much as hinted at the possibilities of using electronic aids for any part of the electoral process.

Whatever the final outcome, the next Canadian general election appears almost

---

[19] *Ibid.*, 5 July 1973, p. 5346.
[20] *Statutes of Canada*, 1973, c. 23.
[21] Canada, *House of Commons Debates*, 5 July 1973, p. 5343.
[22] *Ibid.*, p. 5351.
[23] *Ibid.*, p. 5346.
[24] *Ibid.*, 9 July 1973, p. 5413.
[25] See *ibid.*, 12 July 1973, p. 5558–9; *R. S. Can.*, 1970, c. E-2, s. 13.
[26] Canada, *House of Commons Debates*, 5 July 1973, p. 5352. Incidentally, to save Saskatchewan its current 13 seats instead

certain to be held on constituencies which, despite the massive population shifts of the current era, will be based on the census of 1961; and the immediate cause of this is that the whole machinery, including redistribution, has in fact become so involved that it cannot always be ready for closely spaced elections. In many ways it has always been, though reliable, a strikingly casual apparatus. Down to and including 1973 the structure was so little viewed as an integral whole that while the expenses of the representation commissioner are paid out of the Consolidated Revenue fund, those of the chief electoral officer include estimates which must pass a parliamentary committee. Again, the chief electoral officer told the Committee on Privileges and Elections in 1970 that he was required to publish a list of those key officials, the returning officers, in the *Canada Gazette* each January: "So, every fall around November I circulate my returning officers to find out whether they are still alive or still interested and still consider themselves in the job, and so on. This is the only contact I have with most of them every year." In 1971 the same officer drew the committee's attention to the fact that he had no budget for an election at any time, but had to go to the Treasury Board for funds when one was called; the situation, he testified, was "not exactly unhealthy ... but one which I do not think is normal."[27] The returning officers, as noted above, are appointed by the Governor-General-in-Council without reference to the chief electoral office; yet they are the individuals who actually conduct the 264 separate contests which make up the vast administrative achievement called a general election.

The days when the electoral machinery can be taken for granted appear to have passed, and the parliamentary session of 1973 offered no convincing evidence that any growing consciousness of the machinery will necessarily be for the sole benefit of the electorate. Under the best possible timetable, the Representation Commission and the chief electoral officer agreed in July 1973, the failure of Parliament to take any further action on the suspension of redistribution will mean that the maps drawn by reconstituted commissions could not be ready before December 1975, with another year required for the appointment and training of returning officers, the drafting of polling divisions, and the necessary political reorganization at the local level;[28] if Parliament does act, an election as late as 1975 or 1976 may still have to be based on an old redistribution. The all-party agreement which led to the suspension of redistribution in 1973 was at least partly to suit the convenience of elected members, and more than one pointed out that the political decisions involved in boundary drawing required more "political input"; one went so far as to compare professional politicians with professional doctors making medical decisions. A House of Commons practically full of members with no recollections of the helter-skelter "political inputs" in the redistributions of 1946 and 1952 – and apparently without knowledge of the well-documented cases of 1882, 1891, or 1934 – can too easily forget that parliamentary constituencies belong to electors, not members.

To that suspicion one can add a few more. If Parliament takes the representation commissioner's advice and abolishes his office, attaching its duties to a secretariat under the chief electoral officer; and if Parliament passes Bill C-203 of 1973, which also makes the chief electoral officer the administrator responsible for the new legislation concerning the control of and accounting for election expenses,[29] Canada may soon have a newly centralized electoral system which will have many admirable attributes. The mere fact of its centralization, however, will undoubtedly encourage consideration of electronic aids for the drawing of boundaries (which would be a relatively simple matter if populations alone were involved), the registration of voters, and the counting of their votes, all for cogent reasons connected with efficiency and accuracy. Canada may have before it, therefore, the interesting prospect of an electoral system which may fall short of a desired flexibility whatever the wishes of the prime minister, or of a majority in the House of Commons, or the state of preparations in the chief electoral office, because of an accidental – or contrived – power failure. Anyone who thinks that is a fanciful suggestion would do well to read the debates and committee proceedings on representation during the past decade.

---

of permitting it to drop to 12 would require the total membership of the House to rise from 264 to 296.

[27]Canada, House of Commons, Standing Committee on Privileges and Elections, *Minutes of Proceedings and Evidence*, 1970, p. 8:19; 1971, p. 1:16.

[28]*Ibid.*, 1973, pp. 4:40ff.

[29]Canada, House of Commons, First Session, Twenty-ninth Parliament, 1973, *Bill C-203*, An Act to amend the Canada Elections Act, the Broadcasting Act and the Income Tax Act in respect of election expenses. The bill received second reading on 12 July and was referred to the Standing Committee on Privileges and Elections.

A Note on "Public Policy"*

ROBERT VAISON *Mount Saint Vincent University*

Normally in political studies the term public policy is construed to encompass the societally binding directives issued by a society's legitimate government. We usually consider government, and only government, as being able to "authoritatively allocate values." This common conception pervades the literature on government policy-making, so much so that it is hardly questioned by students and practitioners of political science. As this note attempts to demonstrate, some re-thinking seems to be in order. For purposes of analysis in the social sciences, this conceptualization of public policy tends to obscure important realities of modern corporate society and to restrict unnecessarily the study of policy-making. Public policy is held to be public simply and solely because it originates from a duly legitimated government, which in turn is held to have the authority (within specified limits) of formulating and implementing such policy. Public policy is public then, our usual thinking goes, because it is made by a body defined somewhat arbitrarily as "public": a government or some branch of government. All other policy-making is seen as private; it is not public (and hence to lie essentially beyond the scope of the disciplines of poliitcal science and public administration) because it is duly arrived at by non-governmental bodies. Thus policy analysts lead us to believe that public policy is made only when a government body acts to consider some subject of concern, and that other organizations are not relevant to the study of public policy.[1]

A bit of reflection reveals that public policy is not "public" solely because it is originated by the legislature or another branch of government. It is public precisely because it affects the public, or those citizens who are directly concerned with the particular focus of that policy. It is public because it affects, involuntarily, members of society who had no immediate and direct acquiescence in its formulation. The essence of a policy's "public-ness" is its ability to bind (obviously within certain limits) citizens who have an interest in the area the policy covers.

Consider the contemporary question of abortion. The policy of a national government, as formally and legitimately enacted, may be to prohibit abortions under all circumstances. In fact, though, a number of that nation's hospitals may actually perform abortions under circumstances decided upon by the officials of those hospitals. Abortions thus may be performed for the public, notwithstanding the policy of the government to the contrary; indeed this has long been the *de facto* situation in some nations. The appropriateness of a broadened concept of public policy becomes clearer if the opposite situation is considered. A government may establish a policy allowing abortion under several circumstances, but major hospitals may decide not to perform abortions under any circumstances, or to perform them under different circumstances. Thus the effective public policy may in fact be that abortions are not available to some of the women of that society who, if government policy was the total public, would be eligible. Dictates of the Roman Catholic Church may override government intention in parochial hospitals. What we have is a policy mix in our pluralist society and students of public policy cannot adequately cope here simply by conceding the existence of numerous, relatively autonomous inputs to the political system, or by occasionally mentioning spill-over effects. There are many "black boxes" and sources of policy output.

The value of this suggested reconceptualizing of public policy becomes more apparent when we shift the discussion to the economic sector. Governments often have no specific policy regarding numerous consumer and industrial matters, but a dominant corporation (or an oligopoly of corporations) often has. A particular Canadian television network may for its own reasons decide not to carry some sporting event to the chagrin of numerous sports fans. This decision is clearly public in its effect whether it is made by the Canadian Broadcasting

*I wish to thank several political scientists at Dalhousie for their comments on an earlier draft.

[1]In their recent and seemingly wide-ranging book on public policy-making, Doern and Aucoin, surprisingly at this late date, omit any reference to the dominating influence of multinational corporations in Canadian political economy – surely a key touchstone in areas of public policy ranging from energy to defence, from regional disparity to foreign policy. I refer to *The Structures of Policy-Making in Canada* (1971).

Corporation or by the private network.[2] It is in fact a public policy. So are many decisions taken affecting other goods and services. Making dial telephones available in all areas of the country or limiting them to larger centres directly affects citizens residing in remote or sparsely settled locales, whether the policy is made by a limited liability company, a crown corporation or a government regulatory agency. To call the former case a private decision and the latter two public ones only tells us something about the present legal status of the body making the decisions; it tends to obscure the underlying uniformity of the policy's influence and repercussions. Many decisions made by public servants have limited public effect. Some have only intra-governmental implications. The same limited nature of course holds for actions by private employees. What is important for the social scientist is that some decisions (including, of course, decisions to retain the status quo) of both government and privately-owned organizations have importance and implication extending considerably beyond the boundaries of the organization making the decision. To these only should be reserved the name public policies.

A policy is public, then, not because of the legal status of the particular organization (or individual) formulating it but rather because of the nature and effect of the policy itself. It is public if it directly or indirectly affects members of the society outside the organization initiating the policy. Naturally, it is only of this genre if the affected individuals cannot immediately (in the normal run of things) avoid being so affected. For instance, one may not want to abide by the rules of a stamp club. Obviously one does not have to: one can resign from the club, start one's own, or be a lone philatelist. The policy of the club is not what we have called public policy; one can easily evade it. But the young girl (to return to the example above) with an unwanted pregnancy is not in the same position if either the government or geographically convenient hospitals choose not to make available the sought-after abortion. True, she could leave the country in search of more liberal governments or hospitals. But short of this rather drastic and perhaps quite costly action on her part, she is bound by the public policy in her present location pertaining to abortion – whether that policy was formulated by the legislature, a department of health, a particular hospital, or a medical association.

At some point our analysis runs into the question of whether public policy is still public policy if it can be relatively easily circumvented. Clearly, the delineations put on the qualifying phrase "relatively easy" are germane and in need of continuing re-examination as political economic forces shift. Prohibition in the United States was public policy, formally honoured by government, corporations, churches, and other societal groupings. Yet the ready availability of liquor throughout much of that policy's life is common knowledge. A similar situation exists today regarding the non-medical use of drugs. As another example: most laundry soaps on the market today are sources of obnoxious pollution because it is the public policy of the government not to prohibit or control them and it is the public policy of the corporations involved to produce them. Once again we are faced with a curious situation: non-pollutant or low-pollutant laundry detergents are being produced. If the public opts to purchase these products rather than the more objectionable detergents, what exactly constitutes public policy? Was it the decision of certain firms to produce pollution-reducing detergents? Was it the decision of consumers to buy the product? Was it the government's decision to publicize the obnoxious level of pollution in the old detergents (without actually prohibiting them)? Was it the stand taken by consumer associations or anti-pollution groups? All public policies can be characterized by their purview, their effect, and their ease of circumvention. Some public policies – and some laws – seem made to be broken, or at least are often broken. All policies are upon examination a mix, a concoction in which formal governmental action may be a relatively minor ingredient.

Following this line of thought, a broadened conceptualization of public policy seems needed – one that is more in accord with the political and socio-economic realities that face a social scientist attempting to understand and explain contemporary society. Definition is not an easy task in the realm of social science, but it is one that

[2] Or whether it is made by an American network. This raises the ticklish issue of extraterritoriality which pervades, in various guises, policies enacted by American government bodies as well as private corporations. For the purposes of this brief essay, this question will be ignored. But its relevance for comprehending a wide spectrum of operative public policy is I think self-evident, and a factor that cannot be shielded by reference to "latent elements" or "unusual circumstances" or "extra-systemic forces."

must be faced continually. To this end we might conceive of public policy as any socially authoritative decision or directive that binds or strongly influences those in society outside the boundaries of the particular organization making the policy. Thus public policy would include: (1) statutes enacted by a legislature; (2) decisions handed down by the courts, as finally appealed; (3) rules, regulations, and directives issued by cabinet, or by a government department or agency, acting within its legal capacity; (4) decisions made by a corporation, or cartel of corporations, which are unopposed by any of (1) to (3) above, that affect goods, services, job opportunities, and such available to the public; (5) decisions made by other private organizations (such as professional associations) which similarly affect citizens beyond the organization's membership. The term "socially authoritative" seems broad enough to encompass the contemporary status of governments, large corporations, and respected private groups such as professional associations. To the average citizen all three classes of organizations have an authoritative aura.

As with traditional conceptions of public policy, the inclusion of a host of actions within this proposed classification is moot. Clearly some decisions would not be included, such as that of the voluntary stamp club noted above or rulings made by public officials or private executives which have only intra-organizational effect. This reconceptualization can lead to more comprehensive analysis of the various decisions that together make up a society's mix of public policy. A good part of this work has been done respecting government policy-making, but very little hard examination of public policies made by those organs in the last two categories has been carried out.[3]

Why this call for a broader conceptualization of our notion of public policy? For a number of interrelated reasons. By and large North American social science (especially its recent mainstreams) has seen itself balkanized into narrow disciplinary boxes. Economics, political science, sociology, and other areas of study have largely been content to concern themselves with a conveniently carved-out niche, often oblivious to developments in neighbouring towers. Some efforts have been undertaken to break down and integrate accumulated knowledge into a more meaningful whole; studies of decision making and policy formulation fall into this category. A wider and more realistic (and salient?) comprehension of what public policy actually encompasses in our highly integrated and interdependent society would bolster such efforts, and would give impetus to a return to the political economy tradition, a tradition honourably etched in Canadian scholarly heritage by the work of Innis and others.

But the balkanization of social science (and the retention of a narrow and unrealistic interpretation of which policies and decisions are really public), coupled with their liberal-pluralist bias, has an underlying danger – or advantage, depending upon one's vantage point. It tends to obscure the overriding socio-political reality of modern welfare-capitalism: the dominating presence – both nationally and internationally – of the new imperialists, the huge conglomerate corporations.[4] The current concern of social scientists over formal government decisions (as constituting the only real public-policy decisions) only serves to emaciate these disciplines. Indeed one might argue that government today really operates only in those areas of socio-economic concern in which (*a*) corporate interests are not involved, for reasons of their own, or (*b*) corporate interests allow government to function within unwritten yet very real limits. The evolving continental energy policy – drafted by government officials and corporate interests – illustrates this particularly well. In a nutshell Canada may be able to regulate at an acceptable level of oil pollution in the Arctic, but she will not be able to bar American oil companies from the area. One suspects this latter "public policy" is firmly established, no matter what Ottawa says. This may indeed not be so. But accurate and competent assessment of validity will not come from political scientists operating within an input-output analysis of "black boxes" located within the "political subsystem."

To draw out of the preceding: what seems needed is more than elimination of a euphemistic terminological distinction. An exclu-

[3]For instance, a corporation's policy-making process would appear to have an array of input sources: dominant shareholders, an executive management group, perhaps some governmental agencies, representatives of other corporations in the same field, employee associations, and bodies such as consumers' associations.

[4]Some invaluable reading here: P. Baran, *The Political Economy of Growth* (New York, 1957), Paul Baran and Paul Sweezy, *Monopoly Capital* (New York, 1966); David Horowitz, ed., *Corporations and the Cold War* (New York, 1969). Indispensable for the student of Canada is K. Levitt, *Silent Surrender* (Toronto, 1970).

sive focus upon government policies removes from our purview many of the really crucial public decisions continually being made – or not being made. In the broadened and more realistic conceptualization of public policy being advocated here, a considerable number of the vital public decisions are in fact government non-decisions – and involve a conscious absence of action on the part of government in the face of corporate action. An understanding of contemporary society and its patterns of behaviour requires more than study of how governments, or churches, or unions, or corporations act, and to what ends. It necessitates a comprehensive, meaningful overview of how they interact: how actions of one influences those of another, and the political-economic assumptions of each. To this end, a more pertinent conceptualization of public policy is in order. Such reformulation should open up fruitful avenues for exploration, for instance the interrelation of political and corporate (and other) interests in the formation of public policies over energy transfers and export. Clearly, the respecification of public policy called for here is not a panacea. Indeed it is more akin the opposite: it will only serve to open up troublesome issues that social scientists heretofore have been loathe to touch. Such an event might even convince disciplinary doubters that analysis of public policy is relevant on their own terms. If we are to avoid "apolitical politics," as mainstream political science has been dubbed by some of its critics, we must penetrate beyond the unrealistic segmentation in which subsystem thinking traps us. Hardheaded examination of policy and value-setting decisions offers one opportunity.

A Test of the Uni-dimensionality of Various Political Scales through Factor Analysis: A Research Note

M. JAMES DUNN *University of Alberta*
RODNEY SCHNECK *University of Alberta*
JAN LAWSON *University of Alberta*

Contemporary political science is increasingly interested in the problem of empirical measurement and at various times researchers need scales to measure political attitudes and behaviour. In this process the Canadian political scientist is faced with two alternatives: (1) he can develop new scales, or (2) he can use existing measures from the literature which in most cases mean using scales empirically developed and used in the United States.

The focus of this research, through factor analytic techniques, is to test in a Canadian setting the uni-dimensionality of various political scales developed and used in American social science.[1] An anti-French scale developed by the authors was also used. The results may be useful to political scientists doing survey research in Canada.

The determination of uni-dimensionality is a crucial step in scale construction and can be defined as the degree to which separate scale items can be said to measure a single underlying dimension.[2] Low uni-dimensionality of scale items decreases the researcher's ability to discriminate among responses on a single dimension. Conversely, high uni-dimensionality means items on a scale are grouped along a single dimension or all items measure the intended attribute or have a common component. A uni-dimensional scale more readily permits researchers to rank individuals along a continuum or dimension according to their responses to the scale items.

[1]In this study, uni-dimensionality is equated with homogeneity.

[2]See Harry S. Upshaw, "Attitude Measurement," in Hubert M. Blalock and Ann B. Blalock, *Methodology in Social Research* (Toronto, 1968), 60–108; John P. Robinson, Jerrold G. Rush, and Kendra B. Head, *Measures of Political Attitudes* (Ann Arbor, 1968), 16–18; William A. Scott, "Attitude Measurement," *The Handbook of Social Psychology*, 2nd ed. ed. Gardner Lindzey and Elliot Aronson (London, 1968), 254–6.

Canadian Journal of Political Science/Revue canadienne de science politique, VI, no. 4 (December/décembre 1973). Printed in Canada/Imprimé au Canada.

Political scales

The following political scales were used in this study.[3]

SCALE I – LIBERAL/CONSERVATIVE[4]

1 The way they are run now, labor unions do this country more harm than good.
2 The government should leave things like electric power and housing for private businessmen to handle.
3 We need more government controls over business practices and profits.
4 Canada would be better off without any labor unions at all.
5 Big companies control too much of Canadian business.
6 The government ought to help people get doctors and hospital care at low cost.
7 The government in Ottawa ought to see to it that everybody who wants to work can find a job.
8 The government ought to have special programs so that children from poor families receive help to get as much education as possible.
9 The government ought to see that the poor get good housing at low cost.

SCALE II – POLITICAL INTOLERANCE[5]

10 If a person wanted to make a speech in your community against churches and religion, should he be allowed to speak?
11 Should such a person be allowed to teach in a Canadian university?
12 If a person wanted to make a speech in your community favouring government ownership of all the railroads and big industries, should he be allowed to speak?
13 Should such a person be allowed to teach in a Canadian university?
14 If a Communist wanted to make a speech in your community, should he be allowed to speak?
15 Should such a person be allowed to teach in a Canadian university?

SCALE III – ANTI-FRENCH-CANADIAN[6]

16 Do you feel that the federal government is doing too much for Quebec in relation to other provinces?
17 Do you think French Canadians are making unreasonable demands?
18 Do you agree with the policy of the federal government to make both French and English the official languages of Canada?

SCALE IV – POLITICAL ALIENATION[7]

19 It doesn't matter which party wins the elections, the interests of the little man don't count.
20 Elected officials become tools of special interests, no matter what.
21 Local officials lose touch with the people who elected them.
22 If people knew what was really going on in high places, it would blow the lid off things.
23 People who go into public office are usually out for all they can get.

SCALE V – POLITICAL PARTICIPATION[8]

24 How frequently do you vote in local municipal elections?
25 How frequently do you vote in federal elections?
26 When you get together with your friends would you say that you discuss public issues like government regulation of business, labour unions, taxes, and farm programs?
27 Have you ever written, phoned, or talked to your member on city council, in the provincial legislature, or the House of Commons, or any other public official about some issue or problem?
28 Have you ever gone to any political

---

[3]The scales were "Canadianized" by the authors. For example, Washington was replaced by Ottawa or American was replaced by Canadian.

[4]Variables 1, 2, 6, and 7 are from a questionnaire called "Political Attitudes Study," from the Survey Research Center, University of Michigan. Variables 4 and 5 are from Martin Trow, "Small Businessmen, Political Tolerance, and Support for McCarthy," *American Journal of Sociology*, 64 (1958), 270–81. Variables 3, 8, and 9 have been adapted from Robinson, Rusk, and Head, *Measures of Political Attitudes*, 70–202.

[5]The items in this scale are from a questionnaire called "Political Attitude Study," from the Survey Research Center, University of Michigan. Also see Samuel A. Stouffer, *Communism, Conformity, and Civil Liberties* (Garden City, New York, 1955).

[6]This scale was developed by the authors.

[7]Variables 19, 20, 21, 22, and 23 are from John E. Horton and Wayne E. Thompson, "Powerlessness and Political Negativism: A Study of Defeated Local Referendum," *The American Journal of Sociology*, 67 (1962), 489.

[8]Variables 24 and 25 were developed by the authors, variables 26, 27, and 28 were modifications from Julian L. Woodward and Elmo Roper, "Political Activity of American Citizens," *American Political Science Review*, 44 (1950), 872–85. Variable 29 is from Horton and Thompson, "Powerlessness and Political Negativism," 489.

meetings, speeches, rallies, dinners, or things like that in connection with an election?

29 Would you say that you are:
a person who contributes to community decisions?
a person who is active, but not one of the decision-makers?
just an ordinary person in the community?
not really a part of the community at all?

Factor analysis

William A. Scott has stated that, "To the extent that a test is homogeneous, three basic conditions should obtain:
1. The average intercorrelation among all pairs should be positive.
2. Each item should correlate positively with the total score on the remaining items.
3. The total test variance should exceed the sum of item variances."[9]
From his analysis Scott concluded that these three statements are equivalent.

Normally intercorrelation analysis would be used. However, as the number of attributes measured and the number of observations becomes large, factor analysis or cluster analysis becomes increasingly useful.[10] Therefore, factor analysis was selected as the method for testing the uni-dimensionality of the various political scales.[11]

Oblique and varimax orthogonal axis rotation procedures were used. In oblique rotation (used in determining simple structure solution) the axes are themselves correlated as the angle the axes intersect at is different from 90°. The objective of the oblique rotation is to select axes that pass directly through groups of factor loadings. The varimax rotation holds the intersection of the axes at 90° (orthogonal) thus the axes pass through or close to groups of factor loadings. The objective of varimax rotation is uncorrelated axes. Thus, if one scale clusters around one axis and a second scale clusters around the other axis, it can be inferred that the scales are uncorrelated.

Factor analysis of the items of the scales in this study fulfilled two functions: (1) It took the observations of each item and linked them together into distinct patterns of occurrence. This functions to determine the uni-dimension of the scale. (2) It summarized a large number of items in terms of a smaller set of linear combinations that preserved most of the data in the original set and allowed for easier handling of the data. Once the scale is uni-dimensional one score can summarize all aspects of the attitude measured.

Sample and questionnaire

The survey was not random but a restricted sample of 621 individuals who were taking the Management Development Program offered by the Department of Extension at the University of Alberta. The middle-class nature of the sample is indicated by their education and income levels; 88 per cent had completed high school, 49 per cent had some post-secondary training, and 44 per cent had incomes over $10,000.

The items in the questionnaire were concerned with measuring three types of variables: political, socio-demographic, and organizational (29 items measured political variables, 14 items measured socio-demographic variables, and 40 items measured organizational variables). All items measuring political and organizational variables were stated in terms of a Likert-type scale. Only those items related to political variables were used in this paper.

Results

ANALYSIS OF UNI-DIMENSIONALITY

The results of the oblique and varimax rotation procedures are summarized in Table I. Only factors with eigenvalues greater than 1.0 were reproduced.

When comparing the results of the oblique and varimax rotations, the only shift in the factor patterns was the order of the factors in terms of their relative significance.

---

[9]"Measures of Test Homogeneity," *Educational Psychological Measurement*, 20 (1960), 751.

[10]Robinson, Rusk, and Head, *Measures of Political Attitudes*, 16–18.

[11]Once the sample had been determined and the questionnaires administered the data were subjected to a coding procedure. This was completed and the coded data were introduced into an SPSS computer program for factor analysis. The specific factor analysis program utilized was PA 2 which is principal factoring with iteration. Program PA 2 automatically replaces the main diagonal elements of the correlation matrix with communality estimates. Initial estimates of the communalities are given by the squared multiple correlation between a given variable and the rest of the variables in the matrix. PA 2 then employs an iteration procedure which continues until the difference between two successive communality estimates is negligible. See Norman H. Nie, Dale H. Bent, and C. Hadlai Hull, *Statistical Package for the Social Sciences* (New York, 1970), 208–44.

TABLE I

SUMMARY OF FACTOR ANALYSIS WITH OBLIQUE AND VARIMAX ROTATIONS

	Oblique					Varimax				
Factor	Factor name	Item number	Original scale	Factor loading	Highest factor loading of items not included	Factor name	Item number	Original scale	Factor loading	Highest factor loading of items not included
1	Political intolerance	10	2	0.652	0.120	Political Intolerance	10	2	0.724	0.169
		11	2	0.814			11	2	0.829	
		12	2	0.714			12	2	0.767	
		13	2	0.785			13	2	0.814	
		14	2	0.701			14	2	0.763	
		15	2	0.712			15	2	0.755	
2	Political alienation	19	4	0.439	0.225	Political alienation	19	4	0.558	0.283
		20	4	0.690			20	4	0.752	
		21	4	0.606			21	4	0.697	
		22	4	0.626			22	4	0.712	
		23	4	0.608			23	4	0.697	
3	Anti–French-Canadian	16	3	0.764	0.268	Government welfare	6	1	0.540	0.186
		17	3	0.701			7	1	0.678	
		18	3	0.483			8	1	0.729	
							9	1	0.704	
4	Government welfare	6	1	0.458	0.176	Anti–French-Canadian	16	3	0.799	0.160
		7	1	0.528			17	3	0.778	
		8	1	0.622			18	3	0.661	
		9	1	0.579						
5	Active participation	26	5	0.469	0.126	Active participation	26	5	0.634	0.177
		27	5	0.713			27	5	0.773	
		28	5	0.578			28	5	0.703	
		29	5	0.449			29	5	0.607	
6	Passive participation	24	5	0.903	0.109	Passive participation	24	5	0.897	0.160
		25	5	0.793			25	5	0.885	
7	Government intervention and labour power	1	1	0.397	0.274	Government intervention and labour power	1	1	0.553	0.354
		2	1	0.513			2	1	0.686	
		3	1	0.443			3	1	0.590	
	4 and 5 deleted					4 and 5 deleted				

TABLE II

FACTOR CORRELATIONS AFTER OBLIQUE ROTATION WITH KAISER NORMALIZATION

	Factor 1	Factor 2	Factor 3	Factor 4	Factor 5	Factor 6	Factor 7
Factor 1	1.00000	0.10713	0.09873	0.10016	—0.09676	0.02212	—0.09795
Factor 2		1.00000	0.34164	—0.16134	—0.10155	—0.13617	0.04304
Factor 3			1.00000	—0.04540	—0.04579	0.01351	—0.13453
Factor 4				1.00000	—0.01333	0.10535	—0.24442
Factor 5					1.00000	0.26433	—0.04059
Factor 6						1.00000	—0.15139
Factor 7							1.00000

Factor 1–political intolerance
Factor 2–political alienation
Factor 3–anti–French-Canadian
Factor 4–government welfare
Factor 5–active participation
Factor 6–passive participation
Factor 7–government intervention and labour power

In the oblique rotation the French-Canadian issue was factor three. It became factor four in the varimax rotation. Similarly, factor four (government welfare) in the oblique rotation became factor three in the varimax rotation. All other factors remained in the same pattern and in the same order.

Since the analysis resulted in seven significant factors, some of the original five scales had subdivided. Scales number two (political intolerance), number three (anti–French-Canadian), and number four (political alienation) all held together in their original form. Scale number one (Liberal–Conservative) split into a subscale on social welfare (factor four in oblique solution, factor three in varimax solution) and a subscale on government intervention and labour power (factor seven in both oblique and varimax solutions). Scale number five (political participation) split into two subscales, one indicating active political participation (factor five in both oblique and varimax solutions) and the other indicating passive political participation (factor six in both oblique and varimax solutions).

The splitting of the political participation and Liberal/Conservative scales into two subscales is logical and indicates the sensitivity of these scales to differentiate political attributes. In the political participation scale variables 24 and 25 deal only with the frequency of voting while the other four items (variables 26, 27, 28, and 29) deal with more complex forms of political participation. In the Liberal-Conservative scales four items (variables 6, 7, 8, and 9) all deal with welfare and government spending and three items (variables 1, 2, and 3) deal with government and labour power in the economy.[12]

INTER-SCALE CORRELATION

Once it had been found that the scales were basically uni-dimensional it became necessary to analyse the inter-scale correlation. This was done to determine whether more than one scale was measuring the same attribute.

The first step was to examine the factor correlations determined through the oblique solution. Using a cut-off of ±0.20 as an indication of low correlation, only 3 out of a possible 21 correlations exceeded this level. A positive correlation of 0.34164 was found between factor two (political alienation) and factor three (anti–French-Canadian). It would seem that a condition of negativism or cynicism is common in both scales. A positive correlation of 0.26433 was found between factors five (active participation) and factor six (passive participation). Both factors are measuring an attribute of participation. A negative correlation of —0.24442 was found between factor four (government welfare) and factor seven (government intervention and labour power). This is largely due to the factor loading of variable 6 which loads strongly on factor four and to some degree on factor seven. This is understandable as variable 6 deals with government intervention to provide medical care.

The varimax solution also indicated low inter-scale correlation. The orthogonal axes

[12]Since items 4 and 5 do not load significantly on any factor they were deleted.

rotation indicated the scales were grouped close to an axis and when the scales were compared two at a time, one scale grouped close to the vertical axis and the other scale grouped close to the horizontal axis.

Summary and conclusion

Through factor analysis, using both oblique and varimax factor rotations, this research tested the uni-dimensionality of various political scales. Three scales (political intolerance, anti-French-Canadian, and political alienation) all held together in their original form and two scales (Liberal-Conservative and political participation) each split into two subscales which in turn held together. The splitting of the Liberal-Conservative and political participation scales into two subscales was logical and explainable. This is an indication that the scales were differentiating important attributes. Inter-scale correlation was determined through examination of the factor correlation matrix and through orthogonal axis rotation. These techniques showed the scales are largely uncorrelated and therefore each scale is measuring a different political attribute.

In conclusion, this paper presents some data showing the uni-dimensionality of various political scales. Therefore, Canadian political scientists, who want to use the scales analysed in this research, have some empirical evidence showing their adaptability to the political culture of Canadians.

Reviews
Recensions

Modelski, *Principles of World Politics* CAROL A.L. PRAGER 67
Ehrlich, *Le pouvoir et les groupes de pression, étude de la structure politique du capitalisme* GUY LORD 67
Destler, *Presidents, Bureaucrats and Foreign Policy*, Hilsman, *The Politics of Policy Making in Defense and Foreign Affairs*, and Mennis, *American Foreign Policy Officials* GILBERT R. WINHAM 67
Vincent, *Factor Analysis in International Relations* JAN JØRGENSEN 67
Ørvik *et al.*, *Departmental Decision-Making* HOWARD H. LENTNER 67
Chodorow, *Christian Political Theory and Church Politics in the Mid-Twelfth Century* E. BURKE INLOW 67
Cranston, *The Mask of Politics* WILLIAM CHRISTIAN 67
Prévost, *La crise du fédéralisme canadien* ANDRÉ BERNARD 67
Abella, *Nationalism, Communism, and Canadian Labour* TERENCE MORLEY 67
Mallory, *The Structure of Canadian Government* JOHN STEWART 68
Hodgetts, *The Canadian Public Service* NEIL A. SWAINSON 68
Coombes, *State Enterprise*, and Foster, *Politics, Finance and the Role of Economics* W.H.N. HULL 68
Budge *et al.*, *Political Stratification and Democracy* RICK BUTLER 68
Bouthillier et Meynaud, *Le choc des langues au Québec* ANDRÉ P. DONNEUR 68
Ionescu, *Comparative Communist Politics* STANISLAV KIRSCHBAUM 68
Nayar, *The Modernization Imperative and Indian Planning* JOHN R. WOOD 68
Lee and Larson, eds., *Population and Law*, Commission on Population Growth and the American Future, *Population and the American Future*, and Meadows *et al.*, *The Limits to Growth* PETER SMITH 6

George Modelski, **Principles of World Politics.** New York: Free Press [Don Mills: Collier-Macmillan], 1972, pp. x, 370.

Contemporary scholars of international politics have tended to analyse the phenomena of their field piecemeal. In its place there may be no substitute for this approach. Yet while discrete problems under examination become magnified, other important ones, including some of the most characteristic ones, recede out of focus. In this erudite and original book, George Modelski attempts to redress the balance by directing attention to the whole of what Modelski terms the political constitution of world society. Modelski divides his book into three parts, "The Evolution of World Politics," "The Nation-State System," and "The Principles of World Politics" – that is, roughly, world politics past, present, and future. A useful Introduction tracing the recent professionalization of the discipline of world politics is also included. Drawing upon a broad spectrum of social science, especially sociology, economics, and organizational theory, Modelski sets out to "describe, explain, and appraise" (p. 10) "in the spirit of the social sciences" (p. 21) the world politics that have been and could be.

A central contention of the book is that the ethnocentric perspective of the nation-state is troublesome not only politically but also analytically. In conceding the conceptual supremacy of the nation-state, the analyst loses sight of other factors that condition and set outer limits on alternative forms of political life. The substitution of a "geocentric" view enables one to account for world-scale organizations and networks including global corporations, world revolutionary movements, the international community of diplomats, scientists, and other global élites, and world-wide forces representing ecological interests, among others. If it requires demonstration, Modelski, uncovering new data, shows that these phenomena already have palpable empirical significance and also that their vigor must be a major concern of any emerging study of the politics of world society. This is the case if for no other reason (and there are others, of course) than that increasing competition for scarce resources compels a global perspective. In this absorbing part of the book Modelski ranges freely but discriminatingly over the phenomena that contribute structure and richness to world society isolating new problems and treating perennial ones in new ways.

Making optimum use of deductive and intuitive forms of analysis, *The Principles of World Politics* is ripe with insights and suggestive propositions for further investigation. For example, Modelski questions the notion that world politics are "primitive" because they are non-centralized. To the contrary, he argues, there is good reason to suspect that non-centralized politics presuppose more intricate structures than enforced hierarchical organizational ones. Taking a sweeping view of what he calls "earth politics" Modelski suggests that the quantity and quality of political life at the local, national, and global levels should be viewed together in order to understand the real character of each. Modelski also has interesting observations to make about diplomacy. He considers that the institution has grown beyond workable proportions and in the process has also outlived its usefulness, counterproductively and expensively keeping political interaction to a minimum. "The medium (of diplomacy)," concludes Modelski, "has now become the entire message" (p 186).

Thought-provoking, but requiring more argument, are some of Modelski's economic analogies. Take, for example, the proposition that empires, being the political counterpart of monopolies, must produce less of the good of order and justice more expensively than more competitive systems containing a number of autonomous units (p. 35). It is not immediately apparent why a parallel to the dynamics of the economic situation is to be expected in the political case, although the idea is worth exploring. Also the precise nature of the necessary causal link between war and the nation-state system that Modelski identifies seems to require more explication, especially in the light of modern conditions (p. 253ff.).

An important strength of the book is a judicious blending of history and social science analysis. Methodologically pragmatic, Modelski believes that the history of world politics is largely a human artefact and that deterministic interpretations have limited utility. He also perceives that social science analysis can not do justice to the significance for social science of concrete historical political systems.

It is impossible in a brief review to more than scratch the surface of this intricately conceived and organized book. In addressing himself to the whole of the politics of world society with remarkable stamina and a disciplined imagination Modelski has provided one coherent rationale for the discipline as well as an agenda for its future development.

CAROL A. L. PRAGER
University of Calgary

Stanislaw Ehrlich, **Le pouvoir et les groupes de pression, étude de la structure politique du capitalisme.** Paris : Mouton, 1971, 283 p.

Voici la traduction française revue et augmentée du livre que le professeur Stanislaw Ehrlich de l'Université de Varsovie a consacré aux groupes de pression dans les états capitalistes. Ce livre prolonge les réflexions que l'auteur nous avait livrées sur les rapports entre la structure politique du capitalisme et les groupes de pression dans un article de la *Revue française de science politique*. Il s'agit donc d'une œuvre que nous attendions et qui vient s'ajouter à une littérature de langue française de plus en plus importante dans le domaine de l'étude des groupes de pression.

Ce livre présente un double intérêt. D'abord, il situe l'étude des groupes de pression dans le cadre des recherches marxistes, et à ce titre il inclut d'intéressants développements sur les rapports entre la lutte des classes et l'action des groupes de pression dans le processus politique. La démarche de l'auteur insiste sur le conditionnement de classe des groupes d'intérêt organisés tout en affirmant la nécessité de connaître les oppositions entre les divers intérêts afin de mieux comprendre le sens des conflits de classes fondamentaux. Cette analyse n'amène pas l'auteur à souscrire aux conclusions des tenants de la « group theory » ou du pluralisme. Au contraire, il rejète les tendances « qui tentent de tirer parti des études consacrées aux groupes d'intérêt pour contester la division en classes ou dissimuler les antagonistes sociaux fondamentaux que sont les antagonistes de classes » (p. 4). Le premier chapitre développe cette analyse avec rigueur et constitue, avec l'essai de synthèse de la fin, l'apport le plus significatif de ce livre.

Le deuxième aspect intéressant réside dans l'ampleur du sujet traité. En effet, l'auteur ne confine pas son étude à la seule présentation de considérations théoriques ou méthodologiques et à leur vérification dans le cadre de quelques études de cas mais il se fixe comme objectif l'étude des rapports entre groupes de pression organisés et les structures politiques des principaux états capitalistes du monde occidental : les États-Unis, la France, la Grande-Bretagne et l'Allemagne de l'Ouest. Cette approche comparée lui permet de tirer un certain nombre de conclusions générales sur le comportement et le rôle des groupes d'intérêt dans des sociétés de ce type et à constater leur importance dans le fonctionnement et le maintien des régimes capitalistes. Pour Ehrlich, les groupes d'intérêt constituent une deuxième structure de représentation et forment le complément indispensable de la structure politique. Les divers éléments de la structure des intérêts essaient de s'assurer une influence durable et ininterrompue sur la structure politique dans le but d'atténuer l'aliénation de l'appareil d'état bourgeois.

Le plan du livre découle logiquement de cette approche. La majeure partie de l'œuvre est consacrée à l'étude des rapports entre les groupes de pression et les principaux échelons de la structure politique : les partis politiques, les élections, le parlement, l'éxécutif et le pouvoir judiciaire. Quelques chapitres, toutefois, traitent de problèmes particuliers sans que leur inclusion dans le livre soient clairement justifiée (par exemple, le chapitre IV : « Quelques traits spécifiques du système de parti américain », ou encore, le chapitre XI qui porte sur les groupes de pression internationaux). A la décharge de l'auteur il faut tout de suite préciser que certains de ces chapitres comportent un vif intérêt, entre autres, celui consacré aux intérêts régionaux (chapitre V).

La contribution d'Ehrlich à l'étude des groupes de pression est de premier ordre. Elle propose aux chercheurs et aux étudiants une base de réflexion et des voies de recherche nouvelles en intégrant à l'approche marxiste les aspects les plus révélateurs des études occidentales sur les groupes de pression. Malgré certaine faiblesses inévitables dans ce genre de livre (l'analyse ne s'appuie que sur des sources secondaires et utilise peu les publications des 10 dernières années sur les groupes de pression) il faut souhaiter au livre d'Ehrlich la plus large diffusion possible.

GUY LORD
Université du Québec à Montréal

I. M. Destler, **Presidents, Bureaucrats and Foreign Policy: The Politics of Organizational Reform.** Princeton: Princeton University Press, 1972, pp. xii, 329.

Roger Hilsman, **The Politics of Policy Making in Defense and Foreign Affairs.** New York: Harper and Row, 1971, pp. ix, 198.

Bernard Mennis, **American Foreign Policy Officials: Who They Are and What They Believe Regarding International Politics.** Columbus: Ohio State University Press, 1971, pp. xi, 210.

A reading of the three titles above is convincing evidence that the bureaucratic politics model of policy-making is alive and well among the scholars who study Washington. Ever since Graham Allison drew the distinction between the rational and the bureaucratic politics models, explanations of policy-making in foreign affairs have increasingly been couched in terms of the "tug and pull of politics." Hilsman's little book is an outright description of this process and its institutions, with special emphasis on the Kennedy and Johnson years. Destler's book accepts the bureaucratic politics model explicitly, while offering a polite polemic on how the process can be improved. Mennis's book is concerned with the sort of stuff that makes the bureaucratic politics model possible, namely, the differing values and beliefs among foreign-policy officials.

"Policy making is politics," declares Roger Hilsman, in a ringing challenge to the academics of an earlier era who cringed from words like "politics" and "power." Policy-makers disagree on basic values, we are told, and policy is made through institutions that have their own axes to grind. "As Americans," Hilsman states, "we would like to think not only that policy making is a conscious and deliberate act ... but also that the alternative chosen is aimed at achieving over-arching ends that serve a high moral purpose." But such is not the case in the real world of policy making, and so Hilsman details the events that actually occur.

One cannot disagree with Hilsman's interpretation or argument because he is right. What one can wonder is why so much emphasis is given to an interpretation that is by now neither particularly novel nor controversial. Academic audiences are well used to the bureaucratic politics model of policy-making, and it is dubious whether policy-makers ever were impressed with the argument. To turn the tables for a moment, it would hardly surprise any knowledgeable professor to be told that university policy was a result of the tug and pull of different forces within the institution. It is hard to believe that policy-makers are any less perceptive.

However right he may be, Hilsman's emphasis on the political aspects of policy-making may work a disservice if it blinds us to alternative analyses, or if it becomes an expression of how policy ought to be conducted. As for the first, Hilsman's analysis is inadequate for explaining broad shifts in foreign-policy concerns, or in comparing American foreign policies with the foreign policies of other countries. Not every nation, for example, has experienced the increasing militarization that has characterized postwar American policy. One suspects, as with Huntington, that this is not a result of successful politicking by the military, but rather is caused by an increased willingness throughout the whole foreign-policy establishment to resort to military solutions. Thus policy is based not only on bureaucratic infighting but also on the shared values of the policy élites. Hilsman himself reflects one of these shared values when he laments: "So long as the world is governed not by a single sovereignty but individual nation states ... nations will have not only armies but intelligence organizations as well ... (a)nd these organizations will continue to have power in the making of national policy." Hilsman's statement refers to the CIA, and it better explains why the CIA is employed in American foreign policy than does anything in the bureaucratic politics model.

The question of whether Hilsman's analysis is a description of policy-making or a guide for conducting policy can be fairly raised from his concluding chapters. This is an important distinction. However flawed the rational model is as a description of policy-making, it is valuable as a normative model because it calls upon policy-makers to choose defensible goals, to consider alternatives, and to seek solutions to the vexing problems of co-ordination and control. Kissinger has recognized this concern when he spoke of theme and constancy of purpose in foreign policy, and when he described the problems of the modern state as getting coherence and design in an overwhelming bureaucracy. By comparison, the bureaucratic politics model has little to offer about how policy-making should proceed. Because Hilsman never distinguishes how policy is made from how policy makers should act, his chapters on improving the policy process amount to little more than an exhortation to conduct policy "with an eye to the realities of the political process by which it is made." This is sensible, but obvious. The odd thing is that Hilsman, who draws most of his observations from the Kennedy years, seems to have missed the element of purpose and design in Kennedy's foreign policy, and he has overplayed how far the Kennedy men were realistic about conducting that policy.

Destler avoids Hilsman's tendency to make the bureaucratic politics model into a Good Thing. His proposal to structure foreign policy around a rejuvenated state department accepts bureaucratic politics but seeks to make it responsive to the president, in order to achieve coherence and depth in foreign policy. His proposal is timely, as evidenced by Kissinger's appointment as secretary of state. This move will undoubtedly bring the president's office closer to the foreign-policy bureaucracy, and will meet one of Destler's most effective criticisms of past policy-making.

There is a sense however in which Kissinger's appointment is unrelated to Destler's argument, and here the author may have missed the boat entirely. In press briefings Kissinger described the emphasis of the first term as conducting relations with adversaries, for which a personalized and clandestine structure was appropriate. The emphasis in the second term however was to be on the more regularized problems of international relations, which are complex in nature and require a bureaucratic approach. This argument suggests that choice of organization follows choice of problem, and it is quite out of step with Destler's once-and-for-all approach to structuring the bureaucracy. One feels uneasily that Destler has made a clearer separation between procedure and content in policy-making than exists in reality. He would have benefited from Hilsman's observation that "some organizational arrangements facilitate certain kinds of policy and other organizational arrangements facilitate other kinds of policy."

A similar criticism can be levelled at Destler's analysis of relations between presidents and the state department. State is an organization with its own values, and its usefulness to the presidency has partly depended on the policies pursued by the incumbent. State was too traditional for Kennedy in dealing with developing areas, and was too dovish for Johnson and Nixon on Vietnam. Given this, Destler's suggestion of placing more of the president's men in the state department may simply move a potential split between the president and the state department further down the ladder at state. Far from rejuvenating the state department, such an event might hasten its eclipse.

The value and political beliefs that underlie the state department, as well as the foreign-policy arm of the defense department, have been probed in Mennis's research. Many of the findings are not unexpected, such as the Northeastern and ivy-league background of state department officials, or the fact that defence personnel take harder lines in foreign policy than do their counterparts at state. The most useful contribution is Mennis's conclusion that the attitudinal differences between these two organizations are a function of self-selection of personnel, and not a result of post-recruitment socialization. However Mennis has not probed this issue very far. Organizational socialization is a complex issue which requires a more elaborate research design than the author's survey data provide.

These three books on American foreign policy-making are very different. Destler's is the best of the lot. It will likely be a noble failure, but well worth the effort for its interesting detail and its astute observations on the difficulties of organizing the government. Hilsman's effort is uneven, and he mixes insightful commentary about the policy-making process with very elementary material indeed. Mennis's book spent more time with methodology than substance, and most unfortunately never discussed the implications of what were essentially descriptive findings. It is incidentally at this point – examining the implications of differing values among foreign-policy élites – that further work on the bureaucratic politics model should be directed.

GILBERT R. WINHAM
McMaster University

Jack E. Vincent, **Factor Analysis in International Relations: Interpretation, Problem Areas, and an Application.** Gainesville: University of Florida Press, 1971, pp. 141.

Operationalization of concepts is one of the more persistent stumbling blocks in the behaviouralist quest for empirically grounded theories of politics. Ultimately there is no link between a concept as an analytic unit within a logically coherent theory and the outer world of physical reality other than social conventions of natural language. The problem of operationalization generally arises as a search for quantifiable empirical measures or indices of a given pre-existing concept.

Conversely, factor analysis yields nameless indices of variation in pre-existing data. The operationalization problem is to assign each index or factor a label. In most studies, including *Factor Analysis in International Relations*, the labels assigned to the indices or factors are identical to theoretical concepts such as "underdevelopment" or "democracy." Unfortunately such labeling creates an illusion of precision, or what Rommel has termed the "fallacy of misplaced concreteness." The problem of operationalization arises because there is no link between the labels arbitrarily assigned to factors and the identical theoretical concepts other than "face validity," which is a euphemism for common sense aided by historical and descriptive knowledge.

Vincent attempts to sidestep the issue of operationalization by warning that "any naming of these sets of scores, then, is simply a device to simplify presentation." Nevertheless, the names selected by the author have connotations as concepts in international relations theory. Inevitably he slips into the habit of referring to the labels of factors as if they were accurate measures of the concepts themselves. Furthermore, he invites other researchers to use the factor score results of his study as indices in future studies. As indices of what? Arbitrary labels? No, Vincent would allow other researchers to use the factor scores merely as indices of variation among 129 nations on the 91 original variables in his study. But from a theoretical perspective, this restriction is a nonsensical retreat into data analysis for the sake of data analysis, with no prospect of ever emerging into the world of theory. If factor analysis is to be used as an instrument of index construction, then the problem of operationalization must be faced squarely rather than sidestepped in the manner advocated by the author.

The book illustrates much of what is wrong with the use, or rather abuse, of factor analysis in international relations today. The main abuse is that of substituting analysis of computer techniques for analysis of international relations. In 59 pages of text and almost 70 pages of tables, the author makes a few contributions to the former topic (notably in choice of matrix algorithm for factor scores) and none to the latter.

Supplemented at length by factor analysis of two different sets of data, the text is essentially divided into three parts: an exposition of techniques and technical problems of factor analysis, a rather pedantic critique of 28 previously published factor analysis studies in international relations, and finally an "application" of factor analysis which consists of reducing a mishmash of 91 original variables to 19 orthogonal (linearly unrelated) factors, computation of factor scores for 129 nations and an extremely meagre discussion of the results.

Vincent fails to explain what theoretical, or even empirical, purpose is served by generating 19 *unrelated* indices of variation in a set of data. Such an exercise is equivalent to positing that there exist 19 meaningful absolutely unrelated sources of variation in national attributes – a dubious assumption. Beyond the first factor, "underdevelopment," the results rapidly lose any semblance of face validity. The United Kingdom is ranked lower on "democracy" than Malagasy Republic and Japan. Iceland and Switzerland are ranked lower on "internal peace" than Venezuela and South Africa. The usual problem of interpretation of results has been compounded by Vincent's indiscriminate choice of original variables from scattered sources and time points. These include not only the highly unreliable and ethnocentric Banks and Textor data but also orthogonal factor scores from others' studies. In factor analysis, "you are what you eat." The type of factors which emerge is completely dependent on the original choice of variables and nations. No amount of improvement in computational skills can transform input garbage into a theoretically interesting repast of results.

JAN JØRGENSEN
Dalhousie University
Prio, Oslo

Nils Ørvik and associates: Odd Bruaas, Abraham Hallenstvedt, Jan Jølle, Anders Sjaastad, **Departmental Decision-Making: A Research Report**. Oslo-Bergen-Tromsö: Universitetsforlaget, 1972, pp. 162.

This book is a report of research conducted by the director of the Research Group for International Relations at the University of Oslo and four graduate students. The decision-making process in four departments in three ministries involved in making Norwegian foreign policy was studied. The authors were guided in their research by the approaches and generalizations of theoretical work on decision-making, particularly that of Richard C. Snyder and his associates, Joseph Frankel, Herbert Simon, and James G. March.

The research team focused on three clusters of variables to explain decision-making within the departments: (1) organizational characteristics, (2) personnel characteristics, and (3) communication/information. They analysed documentary materials and conducted interviews. They studied process, rather than cases.

The authors have been painstaking, sometimes to the point of tedium, in explaining their approach, methods, variables, data, findings, and the limitations of each. Although the study does not offer the extensive evidence necessary to verify hypotheses from the literature of organizational behaviour, it does describe the way in which these departments perform in terms of such hypotheses. The book also makes a number of interesting observations both about the way Norwegian foreign policy is formulated and how the bureaucracy relates to its environment and about the comparative study of decision-making.

It seems apparent from this study that the theoretical literature on foreign-policy decision-making can usefully be applied to small countries as well as to large ones. This book will be of most interest to those concerned with public administration and the process of decision-making in foreign policy. It does not deal with any of the issues of Norwegian foreign policy. One particularly good discussion is the explanation of how the time problem affects decision-making at different levels of the hierarchy.

The authors have treated diplomatic missions abroad as part of the international environment. Because these missions are part of the Norwegian government, I think it is a conceptual error to treat them so. Although their location is outside Norwegian territory, they remain domestic institutions. With regard to a minor point, there is a number of errors in names and titles in the bibliography.

The main finding of the book is that people at the lower and middle levels of the ministries are the most influential in decision-making. This conclusion coincides with other independent studies of decision-making in other countries, the United States and Japan being two examples. In particular, under the impetus of Allison's seminal work on the Cuban missile crisis, it is becoming fashionable to look for explanations of foreign-policy decision-making in the bureaucracy. On the other hand, Thordarson's fine study of the foreign policy review in the Trudeau ministry concluded that it was the prime minister who was most influential. From the point of view of democratic accountability and coherent, centralized control of foreign policy, Thordarson is more reassuring. Ørvik's and others' findings are disturbing.

This poses some questions for further scholarship. Are Canada and Norway – so similar in governmental forms – really so different in the locus of control over foreign policy? Are the methods responsible for the different findings: Ørvik and his associates studied process while Thordarson studied a case? Should a distinction be drawn between basic or fundamental decisions and sequential or routine ones (Ørvik holds that even the most important decisions are most heavily influenced at the lower levels of the bureaucracy)? If Ørvik's findings are correct, will this bring about an institutional crisis when a major foreign-policy decision is made by low-level persons who cannot be held accountable? Is there a complex process yet to be explained which will reconcile the divergent findings? Or are these contradictions simply a manifestation of the common problem that scholars tend to identify with those whom they study?

This book obviously stimulates questions as well as answers them. That perhaps is as good a criterion as any for judging that the book makes a significant contribution to the literature.

HOWARD H. LENTNER
Baruch College,
City University of New York

Stanley Chodorow, **Christian Political Theory and Church Politics in the Mid-Twelfth Century: The Ecclesiology of Gratian's Decretum.** Berkeley, Los Angeles, London: University of California Press, 1972, pp. xi, 300.

Twenty years ago in North America, canon law was looked upon as the esoteric concern of Roman Catholics and Anglican chancellors. Outside of the seminaries, little was known of the discipline and such relevant publication as occasionally appeared was confined to religious journals. In 1952–3 the University of California made a valiant attempt to secularize the study of canon law by simultaneously announcing the acquisition of the Robbins collection (Mr Robbins was a well-known Episcopal layman whose hobby was canon law); the visit (a joint invitation with the Episcopal Bishop of California) of the Bishop of Exeter, the leading canonist of the Church of England whose book *Western Canon Law* was soon to be published by the university press; and the endowment by Mr Robbins of a chair of canon law at the university (whatever happened to that one?).

For a brief moment, canon law enjoyed once more the resplendent dignity it had from the twelfth to the fifteenth century when the papacy was the big prize of the "mitred lawyers" – as Maitland once described them. This reviewer, who was present during this period from 1952 to 1953 in the Bay region, can well recall the lionizing of the distinguished bishop from England, the public display of the canon law collection in the university library, the many parties where the clergy and laity mixed freely to talk of canon law's hoary past and uncertain future. It was truly a time to remember.

Under these circumstances, it is only fitting that the University of California Press should announce some 20 years later the publication of Stanley Chodorow's *Christian Political Theory and Church Politics in the Mid-Twelfth Century*. Mr Chodorow, a young historian teaching at the University of California at San Diego would, of course, not have been present in those early days. It does seem less than diplomatic, however, for him not even to mention the Robbins Collection in his 25-page bibliography. But, of course, Mr Chodorow had – by the time the book was complete – fallen into the hands of the Germans. He spent 14 months at the University of Tübingen, that delightful academic resort on the edge of the Black Forest, and his book reflects the best and the worst of German academic tradition. It is ponderous, slow, and solid. It is sufficiently heavy going to recall upon completion of the reading the well-known waggish observation of an Englishman that if the Germans were given their choice of Heaven or lectures about Heaven, they would all flock to the latter.

Mr Chodorow's thesis is that Gratian not only founded the science of canon law – which is hardly in dispute – but that he presented in the *Decretum* the most extensive exposition of Christian political theory in the mid-twelfth century. In advancing this thesis, the author clearly challenges traditional political theory that Gratian was no theorist at all. In very few books in the field is he mentioned. Great names like Dunning, McIlwain, and even Gierke on the continent do not so much as list Gratian's name in their great histories of political theory. The Carlyles do, but only as a canonist. Perhaps these scholars were overlooking a good thing. But this reviewer tends to share their view. The problem is that Mr Chodorow mistakes ecclesiology for political theory. Whatever his training in theology may be, it is not sufficient to carry the burden of what is no doubt his real competence in the field of history. At times his book reads like a catechism. Some statements that appear to the author to have great import are in fact quite commonplace concepts. For example, he states that St Bernard "had much to say about the nature of the Church ... in particular, he calls it the Bride of Christ." Again, "there is no doubt that Gratian saw Christ as the founder of the Church on earth." Or again, "It can be seen that the Eucharist was a focal point for community self-consciousness and cohesion in the Church." Once more, "the Church didn't originate in a kind of social contract; Christ founded the Church." In the vernacular of the day, "what else is new?"

The book consists of 10 chapters. In the opinion of this reviewer chapters IV, V, and VI, dealing with the legal aspects of Gratian's *Decretum*, are the best of the 10 because here at least the subject matter moves to the heart of Gratian's own work and ceases to be peripheral. But even here it would have been helpful if the author had given more consideration to Gratian's methodology, which in its own way was as innovative as that of Aristotle. After the loose compilations of Anselm, Ivo, Burchard, and others, Gratian's systematic development of his *Decretum* was a thing of beauty. Mr Chodorow does not make it come clear. Actually, the *Decretum* consists of two things. On the one hand it consists of a collection far surpassing in completeness and logic all previous canonical collections – the *Hibernensis*, the *Hispana*, even the spurious *Pseudo-Isidorian Decretals*, etc. This, after all, is the meaning of the term *Decretum* (or *Decreta* as the term is used earlier) – the decrees of the Church. The second part of Gratian's work was his own commentary – a didactic textbook which took the controversial texts (*Discordantium canonum concordia*) and gave them a reasoned unity. The manner in which Gratian did this was as follows: He opens with an authoritative proposition. If it is generally accepted throughout the Church, he regards it as valid and it stands. If, however, he finds opinion divided, he takes the opposing statements and tries to reconcile them by determining which is the more recent statement (he considers the law of the Church to be progressive) or which is the more authoritative, or which is the universal rule, or which is the general rule. Logically, he then proceeds with subdivisions and distinctions. The whole matter is quite precise and carefully devised.

One final thing. Gratian was an apologist. This must be understood and it is not clear that the author does. It goes without saying that Gratian's efforts immediately broadened the sphere of ecclesiastical jurisdiction as it applied to the papacy. Indeed, of the entire *Corpus Juris Canonici*, the *Decretum* of Gratian composes a full half. But this is not the canon law of the whole Church (the *Decretum* has not even been translated into English). Its very lack of universality, therefore, places the *Decretum* of Gratian in much narrower perspective than is the normal requirement of good political theory. The author himself finally comes to this conclusion on the last page when he admits the *Decretum* is "a failure from the standpoint of the political theorist." Nevertheless, it was a good walk through the Black Forest.

E. BURKE INLOW
University of Calgary

Maurice Cranston, **The Mask of Politics.** London: Allen Lane [Don Mills: Longman], 1973, pp. 193.

At present there is no one writing in English about politics who does so with the grace and elegance of Maurice Cranston. His aim is to restore to political philosophy "that dreaded clarity" of which he speaks in the essay that gives its title to this volume.

The value he attaches to discussing politics in the language of common speech makes an important philosophical point. In this regard Cranston shows himself a worthy successor to Michael Oakeshott. It is part of Oakeshott's argument that to discuss politics in "value free" terms coined to replace common words is to miss the extent to which politics involves little else than the use of ordinary words. As Cranston puts it: "in talking politics we cannot avoid making value judgements. They are part of the very words in use. Besides, the most serious form of political speech is an argument, and an argument entails an appeal to norms of more than one kind."

Cranston's substantive, as distinct from his methodological, concern, is with liberty. His first book, *Freedom*, was a long essay in the explication and clarification of this concept; and this concern runs through his later published works. It was significant that he chose as the subject of his second book the biography of John Locke, whose conception of liberty he finds both wholesome and appealing.

It is with thinkers whom he finds promoting dangerous theories of liberty that he is preoccupied in these papers which he has brought together and republished. The second essay is concerned to explicate the different meanings of "freedom" in Western thought, a task dictated by two problems. First, the word "freedom" is incompletely descriptive. When a man says he is free, one needs to enquire further, free from what constraint or burden? Second, the word "freedom" "implies liking, approval, some form of favourable attitude toward the situation mentioned." It is the latter aspect that leads the word "freedom" to be much bandied about and much abused as a consequence.

He first turns his attention to Rousseau and identifies the major weakness of his treatment of freedom in the notion that it involves "not being subject to any other *man.*" As a consequence Rousseau ignores the threat that institutions pose. "Is this a philosopher's concept of freedom? Perhaps; but is it not also like that of a footman? The dream of liberty in the servants' hall is the dream of the elimination of the master; translated into political terms, this becomes the republican fantasy that freedom lies in the elimination of the king."

Sartre also comes in for damning scrutiny in an essay which draws on Cranston's longer *Jean-Paul Sartre*, and the danger of a Sartre beguiled with violence is brought out all the more clearly in comparison with the moderation of Albert Camus, the subject of the succeeding essay. He rounds out the internal trilogy of modern French writers with an insightful analysis of Michel Foucault.

However, he ends the collection with his most vigorous assault on the ideologist of intolerance, Herbert Marcuse. Cranston finds the drift of Marcuse's political theory from 1935 to the present wholly disagreeable. He uses his formidable powers of analysis to set out clearly Marcuse's views, and confesses near the end of his essay that he had done so because "one has only to set forth clearly the main lines of his thinking to reveal it as being at once nugatory and dangerous." His criticism of Marcuse is twofold. First, "the analytic devices he introduces are worthless." Second, Cranston is revolted by what he takes to be the attitude underlying Marcuse's call for suppression and a reign of terror: "the idea of mankind appeals to him; real men – most of them – sicken him ... Ideologists, like soldiers, march on their stomachs; and Marcuse has the stomach of a very high-class aesthete, queasy, fastidious, and misanthropic."

In short this is a collection of deeply thought and brilliantly written essays. If more writers on politics, including contributors to this *Journal*, followed Cranston's lead, there would be no need of his fear and warning that we might sometime face the day when politicians are no longer conscious of the norms that govern their activity and when "the triumph of information over knowledge will be complete."

WILLIAM CHRISTIAN
Mount Allison University

Jean-Pierre Prévost, **La crise du fédéralisme canadien**. Paris : Presses universitaires de France, 1972, 96 p.

Comme le dit le feuillet publicitaire, les « Dossiers Thémis », dans lesquels est paru *La crise du fédéralisme canadien*, rassemblent, sous une forme commode, des faits, des textes, des chiffres, des références, des documents relatifs à un problème, le tout accompagné d'un commentaire qui sert de fil conducteur. Une sélection sévère, comme le dit encore le feuillet publicitaire, est nécessaire. Mais une telle sélection est dangereuse : elle peut fausser entièrement les perspectives si elle n'est pas rigoureusement objective.

Présenter un dossier sur « la crise du fédéralisme canadien » était une véritable gageure pour celui qui entend rester fidèle à l'esprit d'objectivité et de rigueur scientifique qui guide la collection des « Dossiers Thémis ». Jean-Pierre Prévost, directeur du service Information de la Chambre de Commerce Internationale, a relevé le pari avec succès. Son recueil présente un ensemble relativement équilibré et le choix des pièces saura donner au lecteur pressé (l'ouvrage a moins de cent pages) une perception assez juste des aspects juridiques et politiques de la crise du fédéralisme canadien.

L'introduction signée par l'auteur est remarquable. Elle situe avec concision et clarté l'ensemble du problème et offre un aperçu prudent sur les perspectives, telles qu'elles pouvaient apparaître au cours de l'année 1971–2. Il s'agit d'un des bons textes qu'il est donné de consulter à titre d'introduction à l'étude du fédéralisme canadien.

Le choix des documents comporte un extrait de l'Acte de 1867, quelques paragraphes sur les mécanismes de coopération intergouvernementale, des textes sur le partage fiscal, quelques mots sur les partis politiques (plus ou moins pertinents d'ailleurs), les points de vue de M. Trudeau, de M. Johnson et de M. Lévesque, et, enfin, quelques pièces relatives aux propositions d'amendement constitutionnel dont on faisait grand cas à l'époque de la conférence de Victoria en juin 1971. L'importance accordée aux propositions de revision constitutionnelle (25 pages, soit près du tiers de la partie « documents ») vient sans doute de l'intérêt que présentaient ces questions au moment où l'ouvrage a été bâti.

Si le tiers de l'ouvrage est consacré à la constitution et aux propositions d'amendement constitutionnel des gouvernements, il n'y a, par contre, pratiquement rien sur les facteurs culturels et sociaux que plusieurs analystes associent volontiers à la crise du fédéralisme canadien. On ne trouve, sur ce sujet, que quelques passages très courts dans l'introduction. Si on considère finalement l'importance accordée aux documents exprimant les points de vue et les préoccupations des gouvernements, on peut conclure que l'auteur a privilégié, dans sa sélection des pièces, les dimensions juridiques du problème.

Il s'agit là, d'un certain point de vue, d'une faiblesse que n'excusent pas entièrement les dimensions réduites de l'ouvrage. La constitution fédérale du Canada a plus de cent ans et le conflit gouvernemental fédéral-provincial existe depuis 1867. Pourtant la crise du fédéralisme canadien n'est réelle que depuis les attentats des années récentes et la fondation de partis politique souverainistes ou, si l'on préfère, séparatistes. Pourquoi la crise se produit-elle aujourd'hui ? Pourquoi n'y a-t-il pas eu d'attentats indépendantistes avant 1963, ni de parti sécessionniste avant 1966 ? La réponse à ces questions ne se trouve pas dans les documents présentés par M. Prévost. Ces questions seront sûrement présentes à l'esprit de ses lecteurs. *La crise du fédéralisme canadien* aurait pu comporter quelques pages sur les hypothèses que formulent certains politologues et sociologues québécois en réponse à ces questions.

La dimension sociologique aurait ajouté à la valeur de ce petit recueil fort bien réussi par ailleurs.

André Bernard
Université du Québec à Montréal

Irving Martin Abella, **Nationalism, Communism, and Canadian Labour: The CIO, the Communist Party, and the Canadian Congress of Labour 1935–1956.** Toronto: University of Toronto Press, 1973, pp. vii, 256.

The book jacket proclaims that this is "not simply an historical survey" of industrial unionism in Canada. In a way that is unfortunate since Professor Abella is revealed by this book as a highly competent exponent of historical fact, but at the same time as a rather confused analyst of his factual data. It is almost as though we have two books here – the one a punctilious recitation of the organizational and structural difficulties encountered by the industrial unions in Canada from 1935 to 1956, the other a Waffle-inspired tract predictably denouncing the betrayal of the Canadian proletariat by international unionists and moderate social democrats from the CCF.

Professor Abella sets out to demolish what he considers to be the three central myths of Canadian labour history. The first is the view that the CIO presence in Canada in the late 1930s and early 1940s was essential to the growth of industrial unionism in this country. Abella, in opposition to this view, contends that during this period of rapid union organizational growth "the personnel, the treasury and the experience were not provided by Americans; they were largely Canadian. All the CIO provided was its name." He concludes from this that the CIO was not needed by Canadian workers, and, if anything, "it can be argued that the CIO connection was as harmful as it was helpful." This is because Canadian industrialists and their political allies like Ontario Premier Mitchell Hepburn were particularly opposed to "CIO" unionism. Professor Abella seems to forget, however, considerable evidence which indicates that Hepburn and his cronies were basically opposed to "powerful" unionism, no matter what the acronym. They opposed the CIO because they saw it as a potentially powerful organization which would likely tame the then unlimited powers of industrial management. To admit, as does Professor Abella, that Canadian workers "thought the CIO was necessary" and then to assert, nonetheless, that the CIO was not necessary because CIO accomplishments in Canada were primarily (though not entirely, it should be noted) the work of Canadians, is to ignore completely the centrality of belief systems to consequent action. If Canadian workers who wished industrial unionization believed that the CIO was necessary to achieve that unionization, then surely, outside of a world of pure imagination, the presence in Canada of the CIO was indeed necessary. To argue otherwise is to put an absurd construction on the meaning of "necessary."

The second myth ripe for Abella's demolition is the view that the Communist party exercised a negative and disruptive influence on the development of industrial unionism in Canada. On the contrary, asserts Professor Abella, "the contribution of the Communists to the CIO in Canada was invaluable." Moreover, he insists that: "in the immediate post-war period these men [that is, the Communists] – and their unions – who had done much to build and strengthen the industrial union movement in Canada were ruthlessly ejected. Caught up in the anti-Communist hysteria which hallmarked the late 1940s and early 1950s ... the Congress [CCL] patriotically decided to rid itself of its left-wing membership." Yet the careful scholarship which characterizes Professor Abella's exhaustive description of the struggles between the Communists and their opponents in the Steelworkers Organizing Committee, in the Mine, Mill, and Smelter Workers union, in the Woodworkers of British Columbia, in the United Electrical Workers, and in the United Auto Workers leads, at least this reviewer, to an entirely opposite conclusion. The myth is not demolished, it becomes reality. The Communists were, according to Professor Abella's own evidence, clearly disruptive; they used every tactic imaginable to win control of industrial unionism in Canada (they failed, as we know), and they opposed as bitterly as it is possible the attempts by democratic socialists to bring the unions into the CCF camp. As Gad Horowitz has already informed us, they even went to the lengths of forming alliances with the Liberals in order to promote the defeat of CCF candidates, both for legislatures and for union office. Much of Abella's account corresponds almost exactly with that of Horowitz and others, and yet after detailing the painful twists and turns of the party line during the 1940s he then produces this amazing and eccentric conclusion that the Communists were expelled from the CCL for "patriotic" reasons. The Communists were expelled because they refused to accept any decisions of the majority (quite rightly by their own lights), and because the enmity between social democrats and Communists inevitably leads to the expulsion of one group by the other from the political life of workers' organizations. In Eastern Europe, of course, it was usually the social democrats who suffered this fate during the same period of history.

Finally, Professor Abella attempts to show that, despite earlier academic views to the contrary, the Canadian Congress of Labour (CCL) was basically in vassalage to CIO chieftains. In contradistinction to his other theories, there is evidence presented that would tend to confirm this view. However, all the evidence is not in, and the evidence that is marshalled by Professor Abella is simplistically analysed. For example, the resignation of Pat Conroy as the CCL's chief executive officer after he lost a series of battles with Charlie Millard, then the National Director of the Steelworkers, is treated by Abella as evidence of international union domination. Conroy, who for years cut a figure as the romantic exile (he recently finished a 20-year stint as Labour Attaché at the Canadian Embassy in Washington) is seen as the noble defender of national unionism whose removal from the scene is indicative of international union control of the CCL. In fact, although the quarrel between Conroy and Millard had some nationalistic overtones, it was primarily one of appropriate trade union structure. Conroy, and his successors in the Canadian Labour Congress, favoured a strong central labour body which would enrol not only affiliated unions but also workers who belonged to directly chartered unions. Millard and the internationals favoured a relatively weak central labour body with few directly chartered local unions. There are, certainly, nationalist implications to be derived from these views on labour structure. However, since most national unions in the CCL, and now in the successor organization the Canadian Labour Congress (CLC), are also opposed to the aggrandizement of Congress power through the formation of directly chartered unions it would seem that this is not an issue that can simply be cast in a black-and-white, nationalist-hero, continentalist-villain mould. Yet Professor Abella does not reveal the organizational implications of the Conroy resignation issue, and by this omission he inadequately treats the very complicated question of CCL autonomy and power.

Much of the material in Professor Abella's book is of value, his style is lively, his descriptions often vivid and, for the most part, accurate. There are a few annoying errors of the sort that Senator Forsey would forgive but not forget – on page 24 Graham Spry is incorrectly identified as Ontario leader of the CCF, and on page 31 Ted Jolliffe is also identified with that office in 1938 while at that time he was only chairman of the party's electoral committee (later, in 1942 Jolliffe would become Ontario CCF leader) – but basically the sequence of events is set down as it happened. (One wonders if historians lie awake at night worrying about these tiny errors of fact?)

Unhappily, Professor Abella's conclusions seem to proceed, not from his painstakingly gathered data, but rather from the currently fashionable academic nationalism which finds beauty and truth only in ultra-leftist movements lately self-stamped with a made-in-Canada label.

TERENCE MORLEY
Queen's University

J.R. Mallory, **The Structure of Canadian Government.** Toronto: Macmillan of Canada, 1971, pp. xii, 418.

This book emphasizes constitutional fundamentals. Professor J.R. Mallory takes us, as did Sir William Anson in the case of the United Kingdom, to the frame and foundations of Canada's national government. For the most part the book is about the formal institutions of constitutional monarchy at Ottawa. Not since W.P.M. Kennedy's study *The Constitution of Canada* have we had a major book with so strong a public-law approach. Kennedy, however, took the easy route; he organized his work historically, thus exonerating himself from having to describe contemporary institutions. Professor Mallory begins with a strong historical introduction, but thereafter turns to the more difficult task of giving a balanced and accurate account of each of our major institutions, providing at once the relevant historical background and an analysis of each institution's current status and operation.

The structure of the book is revealing. The three chapters immediately after the introduction deal with the formal executive, the political executive, and the administrative machine. The next three are on the electorate, the Senate, and the House of Commons. The chapters on the formal executive, the political executive, the electorate, and the House of Commons are all about equal in length, about 40 pages. The chapter on the administrative machine is the longest, covering 70 pages, and the one on the Senate is the shortest, requiring only 25 pages. Then there is a chapter on the courts, in 44 pages. Finally, there are two chapters on Canadian federalism, the first (45 pages) on the federal distribution of power, and the second (35 pages) on stability and change in the federal balance.

The chapters that draw extensively on Professor Mallory's own research set a very high standard; this is notably true of those on the formal executive, the administrative machine, and the courts. The same is true of the chapter on the political executive, within the limits taken by the author. Better informed, more lucid expositions will be hard to find. The "federal distribution of power" is discussed with clarity and authority. The author's erudition may have made him somewhat laconic, at least for the general reader, on the interpretation of the British North America Act before 1949, but he makes amends with his section on the recent work in this field by the Supreme Court. The section on the distribution of financial resources seems short.

Two great elements are held together by the principles of responsible government. The House of Commons is the waist of the hour-glass. Above, there is the Queen, together with those who hold offices under the Crown. Below, we find the people and their representatives. When the structure is viewed exclusively from either the top or the bottom, the other element suffers. Professor Mallory introduces us to the constitution by his historical chapter; there we are given a brief side-view. Then he takes us up to the top, and, starting with the Queen, he works down. This approach is highly successful while we are on the executive and the administration. But thereafter, as the legal component becomes less important, the approach is somewhat unsatisfactory. The relationship between the electorate and the House of Commons, and then between the House and the cabinet eludes us. The author relies on his introduction and on common knowledge to provide the linkages. His chapter on the electorate is followed by the one on the Senate, and when we come to the one on the House, we find that it deals with the speaker, the privileges of members, the legislative process, etc. Perhaps he is right; yet one is confident that he has something important to say about how responsible government operates today.

The only disappointing chapter is the one on the House of Commons. It is important to know how far a governor-general may go in declining to heed the advice of a prime minister, but it is important also to know a good deal about the House as the immediate base of a prime minister's power. The other defects are venial. Too much is attempted in too little space – 38 pages – with the result that the chapter seems hurried. Moreover, at the very time when Professor Mallory was taking its picture, the House was re-ordering itself, so that on some points his account already is outdated. Most notably, if the new role of the standing committees, for better or worse, is to be revealed, the work assigned to them in 1968 must be examined more fully. Appropriately, he devotes a fair amount of space to closure and time allocation; but he understates the problem. "A government," he writes (p. 265), "forced to use it [closure under s.o. 33] is admitting its inability to carry the House by reasoned argument." But political confrontations take place below the level of reasoned argument; witness the instances when closure has been used. Undoubtedly, the British approach to simple closure is far better than ours, but the key difference is not that the speaker at Westminster may refuse to accept a closure motion when he feels that it is premature, but that at Westminster there is a general presupposition that a debate is to end at the sitting at which it began, so that closure there normally relates to the hour, not the sitting, at which the vote is to be taken.

Professor Mallory will not corrupt the young with jargon: he has something to say; he knows what it is; and he says it, often with persuasive grace. His publishers, too, took their obligations seriously. Some dates, all in the 1960s, were put down wrong, but they are obvious.

Inevitably the book will be considered for use as the backbone of courses in Canadian government. Its substance and clarity recommend it. Its brevity would permit the assignment of three or four specialized works as additional reading. However, the most powerful argument in its favour is that this is no mere textbook; rather, it is a work of mature and thoughtful scholarship.

JOHN STEWART
St Francis Xavier University

J.E. Hodgetts, **The Canadian Public Service: A Physiology of Government, 1867–1970.** Toronto: University of Toronto Press, 1973, pp. xiii, 363.

No one is more aware than Professor Hodgetts that books on institutional structure are rather out of style these days, but this, quite unabashedly, and quite justifiably in view of the state of our art, is what he has presented. His focus is on structure, the framework of the Canadian public service, its evolution over the past century, and nothing more. He does not attempt to probe the behavioural roles of most Canadian public servants, the scenarios with which they attack policy-forming and organizational problems, or, at any length, the manner in which these public servants serve as organizational sensors for government. What he does attempt is a definitive institutional study designed to serve as a launching ramp for later work of this sort.

This is not a text in the classic sense, although it will be used as such especially with advanced classes and with public servants themselves. On the other hand it is not simply administrative history, but rather a collection of slightly more than a dozen well-integrated essays, almost all of which contain some of the wry asides and mature reflection for which their author is justly renowned. The first four of these essays, comprising part one of the book, place the Canadian public service in its setting. Here it is related to its physical, economic, technological, and cultural background, to Canadian federalism and political tradition, and to those important legal foundations which the author has often alluded to before, and which are so frequently overlooked by North American, although not by European, scholarship.

The reader not enamoured of organizational anatomy and physiology may well find the six chapters of part two rather taxing, for here, much of the time, the author cuts and recuts his way through the same tissue – this is no corpse. But those who stick with him will be well rewarded. This reviewer cannot recall having read anywhere a more acute interpretation of a century of organizational change, or a saner commentary on the organizational principles, dysfunctional consequences and all, associated with it. Those, particularly, who teach or who are responsible for organizational construction should dig into these chapters on the departmental and non-departmental rubrics, on auxiliary and staff functions, on the internal division of work, and on its geographical dispersion. Some excellent organizational charts add to the merit of this section.

Those seeking insight into the massive organizational changes put in process in the public service in 1966, into the managerial changes launched in 1967, or into the major reassessments of the service conducted from a managerial perspective over the last century, may well want to start reading with the last section of the book, part three. Here four incisive, tightly written essays deal in turn, with the Treasury Board, the Public Service Commission, departmental management, and the employee – "the neglected managerial link."

Professor Hodgetts has kept a tight rein on himself. Even when reflecting on the inception of collective bargaining, for instance, he has not allowed himself (to the reviewer's regret) to wander from his structural perspective. It is only in a short concluding chapter that he indulges in some provocative prescription. He doubts if we have any new structural forms to exploit and is sensitive to the claims advanced recently to the effect that we may have come close to a tolerance level in the public service with our spate of change in the 'sixties, and certainly may have impaired, in the process, some capacity to achieve basic objectives.

Still, he is very concerned about the challenge facing government today to come up with more sophisticated policy responses to ever more demanding and changing communities. He does not pursue at all here (as he does so justifiably elsewhere) the extent to which parties and legislatures in Canada have failed to meet these challenges, and he is not lugubrious in the manner of Norman MacLeod (see *The Economist*, 23 April 1973). He does speculate, nevertheless, that we may need to take the advice of a 1919 Senate committee and create a few small high-status ministries, charged with policy generation, refinement, and coordination, but not direct operating responsibilities. Under these ministries he can see real merit not only in a "loosening up of hierarchy," especially at the operational level, but also in a new look at "contracting out" to other levels of government.

He speculates also about the curious fact that it has been the public service, of all the sectors of government, which has been most adaptive to and perhaps most innovative in building new links with its external environment. Whatever the explanation for this, he suggests that the public service has probably carried too much of the burden of adjustment. Thus he ends on a sombre note, wondering about the continued responsibility of an adaptive public service when the other sectors of government show such limited inclination to change.

Reflections of this sort, and his running commentary on the problems of structural change, provide a research design for a host of studies to be pursued by others. Professor Hodgetts has come up with a first class book, which no serious student of the governing process in Canada will want to miss.

NEIL A. SWAINSON
University of Victoria

David Coombes, **State Enterprise: Business or Politics?** London: George Allen and Unwin [Agincourt: Methuen], 1971, pp. 244.

C.D. Foster, **Politics, Finance and the Role of Economics: An Essay on the Control of Public Enterprise.** London: George Allen and Unwin [Agincourt: Methuen], 1971, pp. 232.

In reviewing these two books on essentially the same topic published by the same publisher in the same year, one is reminded of that vintage year, 1933, when professors Robinson and Chamberlin within months of each other produced monumental works on the theory of imperfect and monopolistic competition. One commences to read the books with anticipation!

From somewhat different perspectives, both authors – Coombes, the political scientist and Foster, the economist – provide a great deal of information on, and insights into, the operation of the nationalized industries in the United Kingdom. Ironically, the economist is primarily concerned with the relationship described as "triangular" (p. 11) between Parliament, ministers, and boards, while the political scientist is concerned about the criteria by which the performances of the public corporations are judged, "the main obstacles to treating state enterprises as businesses," and the means "of setting up nationalized industries on a less politically exposed and more efficient basis" (p. 18). Both cover many of the same topics – the social vs. economic obligations of the nationalized industries, the means of enforcing their public accountability, the role played by Parliament, the minister, competition, and the market place in the lives of the industries. Each praises in some respects, criticizes in others, the work of the Select Committee on Nationalized Industries.

In addition, however, each covers some subjects not treated by the other. Coombes writes at greater length about consultation with workers and the public as a means of control, about alternatives to nationalization as a means of conducting state enterprise, and about examples of such enterprises in Sweden and Italy (Foster looks more to the possibly less suitable American experience when he looks abroad for comparisons). Foster on the other hand, dwells at greater length on such matters as the exercise of the minister's financial powers, the subtle powers of persuasion open to him, the limitations of the present public control of nationalized industries, and the need to expose the many myths that currently surround them. Mr Foster, of course, writes with the advantage not only of an academic perspective, but also that of one who has served in senior advisory capacities of the defunct Department of Economic Affairs and in the Ministry of Transport in the Wilson government.

In their analyses, both authors agree on a number of points. Parliament and the public understand little of the real role and operating conditions of the nationalized industries. Ministers have had far less control over the industries than was expected by public or Parliament, although ministerial influence has grown in recent years. Since 1945, if not earlier, there has been unending confusion between the commercial and social roles of the industries. They have been run on an *ad hoc* basis, reeling from crisis to crisis as short-run expediency has demanded. Neither government nor the industries have been able to do the sector planning which nationalization itself was intended to facilitate. What little planning has been done has been of a largely tactical or short-run nature, not of the desired strategic or long-run variety. Given all these ills, both authors also agree that there is little to be gained from mere tampering with the existing statutory relationships between ministers and boards. Each seeks something more fundamental.

Yet, ironically, the authors seem to argue against each other's major recommendations. Foster argues, amongst other things, for the strengthening of the financial and economic side of the civil service so that members would be better able to advise their ministers and to apply strategic financial control to the boards of the nationalized industries. Coombes suggests the vesting of the nationalized industries in a number of holding companies which "would control the state's interest in the undertakings now vested in the nationalized boards while the undertakings themselves would be constituted as ordinary joint-stock companies" (p. 238). These holding companies would be in a better position to co-ordinate the activities of their particular sector (fuel, transport, etc.) while, at the same time, the individual corporations would be more exposed to the competitive pressures of a private industry. Presumably with no prior knowledge of Foster's specific recommendations, Coombes argues that solutions of the sort Foster suggests are deficient in several respects. Where do the experts come from? Is not narrow professional "tunnel vision" likely to be enhanced? Do the proposals really improve democratic control of the industries? Were not the corporations themselves set up to be the specialists in their particular fields? Foster finds the Coombes-like solution equally unappealing – lacking in *real politic*. He suggests that such a solution, while not necessarily guaranteeing greater efficiency within the industries would certainly weaken the public control of them. A decision as to which view is correct, if either, will depend upon the criteria used for judgment. Coombes is obviously more concerned to remove the industries further from political pressures, to make them more businesslike. Foster is more concerned with the overall public control of them. The disagreement of two such well-informed observers merely highlights the complexities created by state enterprise.

One brief review cannot encompass all the thought or arguments contained in two works of this sort. Nor can it comment upon all of the inevitable shortcomings. Briefly, one can only regret the little quantitative evidence produced to support many of the judgments made – for instance, in connection with the discussion of the use of question time in the Coombes' book – or the minor use of the tools of economic analysis in Foster's essay, an essay which has something of the ring of a memoir rather than a cogent academic study. One feels somewhat uncomfortable that there may be too many generalizations about the *genre* "public enterprise" drawn from the experience of only one.

Regardless, one does gain the feeling that mutual benefit might be derived from some cross-national study. One cannot help but wonder, for instance, if those who advocate the nationalization of the Bell Telephone Company of Canada would be as happy to see it come about after reading Professor Coombes' analysis of the confusion of business and politics in British public enterprise. Conversely, Professor Coombes might benefit from an examination of the rail, airline, or broadcasting industries in Canada and of the regulatory agencies which control them before refining further his concept of the holding corporation. Similarly, Mr Foster might reflect upon the role of the experts in the Prime Minister's Office and upon the experience with PPBS in the Canadian rather than the American context.

It is too early to tell whether these two books will make the impact on academic theory and public policy that the Robinson and Chamberlin books did in the 1930s. One can hazard the guess that they will not, while at the same time suggest that, as competent and informative works on a contemporary subject of vital concern, both books deserve serious examination by policy-makers and students of public enterprise.

W.H.N. HULL
Brock University

Ian Budge, J.H. Brand, Michael Margolis, A.L.M. Smith, **Political Stratification and Democracy**. Toronto: University of Toronto Press, 1972, pp. vii, 322.

The behavioural approach to the study of politics is of course American in origin and has been accepted much less readily in Britain than in Canada. This study of Glasgow local politics is therefore of particular interest, since it represents an exceptionally ambitious and rigorous attempt to apply behavioural methods to the study of local government in Britain. The study was initiated through the University of Strathclyde in Glasgow, which in the past several years has established itself as one of the leading centres of behavioural research in Britain.

The empirical content of the study is based upon questionnaire and interview data drawn from a sample of Glasgow electors, ward chairmen, party members, city councillors, and newspaper correspondents. Though based upon local data the study is broader in scope, being concerned with questions of the bases of political participation and stability. While political stability has frequently been approached at the level of the individual voter, as in much of the political socialization research, the authors of the present study develop the concept of *political stratification* as the primary explanatory variable. "Political stratification is a shorthand item for the differentiation of large democratic populations by their varying levels of political activity and involvement." Three strata of participation are defined: councillors, party workers, and electors. Reducing the model to its essential outlines, members of each stratum will have more in common with each other politically than with members of other strata, including those of the same party. Horizontal ties of common interest and involvement within individual strata will override the traditional cleavages of party, religion, or class. The argument is developed that this cohesion will be especially true of activists who will be in close contact with each other, who have a vested interest in preserving the institutional arrangements that directly benefit them, and who can be shown to value a conciliatory atmosphere in which to function. Intra-stratum cohesion, particularly at the highest level, is seen as exercising a moderating influence on traditional cleavages and is thus a primary contributor to system stability. It is important to note, however, that the concept of political stratification is advanced as the strongest among several influences on political behaviour and stability: "What really emerges is a distinction between stratification as the strongest direct predictor of attitudes unaffected by party competition, and class and religion as the strongest direct predictors of attitudes affected by party competitors."

The effect of political stratification on representation, political communication, and inter-strata agreement on five local issues is examined in what soon becomes excessive detail. The reader is obliged to soldier on through extremely detailed methodological explanations replete with the requisite jargon before arriving at the substance of the findings. While the study must be commended for its rigour, it suffers from an unnecessary lack of clarity and incisiveness. The reformulated model of intra-strata cohesion and party competition (pp. 264–5), for example, is so detailed as to be virtually unintelligible. Two substantive points relative to the findings of the study should also be given consideration. The data is severely bounded by both time and place, being restricted to a single city at one point in time. In addition, there were no particularly contentious issues in Glasgow politics at the time of the study. It is reasonable to expect that socially divisive issues such as a restructuring of the educational system or an adjustment in the relationship between residential and commercial tax rates would intensify party divisions at the expense of activism.

A point unrelated to the study itself but relevant to its publishers should also be made. The book, at $17.50, is overpriced. While not presuming to comprehend the subtleties of present-day publishing and marketing, I think it is clear that this book will be financially beyond the reach of most students. Of course library copies will be available but it seems unnecessary and unfair to deprive many interested students of the opportunity of buying the book.

Overall, the major deficiencies remain those associated with style and presentation and are thus remediable. Since this volume is part of a larger study it is hoped that future findings will be presented in a more lucid manner.

RICK BUTLER
Memorial University

Guy Bouthillier et Jean Meynaud, **Le choc des langues au Québec, 1760–1970.** Montréal : Les Presses de l'Université du Québec, 1972, xiv, 768 p.

Choisir les textes significatifs du débat linguistique qui agite le Canada depuis deux siècles n'était pas une gageure facile à tenir. Guy Bouthillier et le regretté Jean Meynaud l'ont réussi pourtant, en surmontant une difficulté supplémentaire : celle de recentrer le débat sur le Québec, alors que les préoccupations des défenseurs de la langue française s'étendaient jusque vers 1960, au Canada français tout entier, voire même aussi aux Franco-Américains.

La lecture des 119 documents choisis, de la pétition des notables canadiens au roi d'Angleterre (1763) au Mémoire de l'Hydro-Québec, à la Commission Gendron (1970) est fascinante. Ces textes, précédés de notices qui les situent dans le contexte de leur époque et donnent une biographie succinte de leurs auteurs, constituent un point de départ quasiment indispensable d'une étude systématique et scientifique du problème linguistique au Québec, tâche qui, comme l'indiquent Bouthillier et Meynaud, reste à accomplir. Tracer la genèse d'un problème n'est pas un luxe, même si trop souvent en science humaine on tend à négliger à tort le génétique pour se concentrer exclusivement sur le synchronique. Une analyse poussée de ses textes – par la technique de l'analyse du contenu – permettrait sans aucun doute de distinguer avec précision les éléments de permanence, d'évolution et de rupture dans le combat pour la défense de la langue française.

Nos auteurs, sans faire une analyse aussi poussée de la question, discernent dans leur introduction (p. 1–87), « les traits caractéristiques de la bataille linguistique » et « les aspects actuels du combat ». Nous avons déjà noté le « caractère essentiellement défensif » de cette lutte, que ce soit pour conserver le droit au français dans les institutions officielles ou para-officielles – aussi régulièrement remis en cause qu'il est garanti – pour maintenir l'intégrité linguistique contre les anglicismes, pour repousser « les appréciations péjoratives de la qualité du français parlé au Canada » et pour obtenir des services commerciaux en français. Le style de cette lutte est marqué par la prudence et la modération : jusqu'en 1960, la revendication linguistique est très généralement maintenue dans le cadre politique existant; on accepte la dualité linguistique au Québec même si certaines autres provinces n'ont pas hésité à pratiquer « un unilinguisme agressif »; enfin, les Canadiens français utilisent faiblement « l'appareil gouvernemental pour la solution des problèmes et des conflits linguistiques ». Avant 1960, une seule loi : la loi Lavergne (1910) – imposant le français dans les services publics – fut promulguée par le Québec.

Depuis 1960, Guy Bouthillier et Jean Meynaud discernent, à côté du maintien de certains traits caractéristiques de la lutte, des changements importants et aussi l'apparition de nouvelles revendications. Sur le plan des changements, on assiste chez les combattants de la langue au rejet de la dualité linguistique au Québec auquel se substitue la prépondérance du français, voire l'unilinguisme; le cadre politique existant est remis en cause, tandis qu'on renonce également à la défense de la francophonie nord-américaine tout entière pour se concentrer sur le Québec; les gouvernements fédéral et québécois interviennent et légifèrent de plus en plus dans le domaine linguistique. Le style d'action prudent cède le pas à des manifestations, même violentes (contre le bill 63, pour l'école unilingue française à Saint-Léonard).

Une nouvelle revendication, laissée curieusement sous le boisseau jusqu'en 1960, apparaît : le français langue de travail. Il est assez extraordinaire qu'aucun texte d'avant 1960 – Meynaud et Bouthillier n'en ont trouvé vraiment aucun – ne se préoccupe de l'anglicisation des travailleurs par leur travail. Ce silence s'explique par l'étroitesse de vue d'une élite coupée des masses populaires. Jean-Marc Léger avait d'ailleurs déploré dans un article de *L'Action nationale* (sept.-oct. 1952), l'absence de « la classe ouvrière et du travail organisé » au troisième congrès de la langue française tenu à Québec en juin 1952. Or, celle-ci est désormais active dans les luttes de la fin des années soixante et le français, langue de travail, est devenu un objectif, même pour le gouvernement québécois. Facteur nouveau dans la lutte linguistique : les « sentiments de frustration et d'inquiétude chez les anglophones » du Québec qui redoute de voir « limiter les privilèges écrasants » dont dispose la langue anglaise à Montréal.

Ces changements semblent donc traduire une accentuation de la lutte pour le français que révèlerait l'inquiétude des anglophones. En fait, nos auteurs sans contester ces changements, constatent « la persistance d'attitudes profondes » qu'on peut retracer sans peine dans les deux siècles passés. La législation reste timide et n'ose s'attaquer ni au secteur crucial de la langue de travail, ni à l'intégration des immigrants à la majorité linguistique. Les arguments employés pour promouvoir la langue française sont largement à la remorque des sempiternelles objections des anglophones : le français (hier patois, aujourd'hui inapte à suivre le développement technologique) est une langue d'une petite minorité (hier dans l'Empire britannique, aujourd'hui dans le contexte nord-américain). A quoi on répond : nous parlons la langue de x millions d'hommes, comme si une collectivité, « hors de toute autre considération », n'avait pas le droit de parler sa langue et le devoir de la protéger : voir Norvège, Suède, Finlande ... Bouthillier et Meynaud s'inquiètent d'autant plus de la persistance de cette attitude défensive qu'apparaissent des facteurs d'affaiblissement, comme le rejet du « bon parler » français, symbolisé par l'engouement pour le joual que nos auteurs, reprenant le diagnostique de l'ethnolinguiste Gilles Lefebvre, n'hésitent pas à qualifier de « stade avancé d'anglicisation linguistique et culturelle » (p. 80).

Comme nous le disions plus haut, il est évident qu'une analyse systématique des textes reste à faire, mais Guy Bouthillier et Jean Meynaud nous ont fourni les matériaux et tracé la voie. Ils le font également pour l'étude générale du facteur linguistique. Ils dénombrent, en effet, au début de leur introduction, une dizaine de « pistes d'investigation » qui constituent un véritable programme de recherches. Chacun de ses thèmes à lui seul présente déjà une tâche considérable. Pour s'en tenir à l'une de ces pistes, sur laquelle nous nous sommes aventurés, l'étude des « modalités et résultats des politiques (policies) tendant à influer sur les comportements linguistiques » (p. 7), reste à faire au Québec. Mais ce n'est qu'au prix de recherches sérieuses que l'on parviendra à détruire les mythes. Par exemple, les recherches faites dans d'autres pays ont démontré que c'est un mythe de croire à l'inefficacité des lois et règlements pour promouvoir le français comme langue de travail.

André P. Donneur
Université du Québec à Montréal

Ghita Ionescu, **Comparative Communist Politics.** London: Macmillan [Toronto: Macmillan], 1972, pp. 64.

This is a useful little booklet for both students and faculty. The author divides his work into two sections: a recapitulation of the prevalent approaches to the study of communist politics and the framework needed for the study of comparative communist politics. Set within the more general debate on comparative politics, Ionescu shows how the subgroup of communist studies can add to the debate as well as the inherent problems of communist studies in comparison with other subgroups in political science.

In recapitulating the approaches to communist politics Ionescu shows how Western scholars have moved from the totalitarian definition given by Friedrich and Brzezinski to comparative studies of communist politics, using tools often more applicable to other subgroups, with the inevitable consequence of incomplete or counterproductive results. Ionescu's examination of M.C. Lodge's *Soviet Elite Attitudes since Stalin* well illustrates the point. However, the author might have given other examples. Ionescu then goes on to show how others have moved in other directions with Almond's "political capabilities" framework, the modernization framework, or the latest approach, that of the study of groups. From all this the author concludes: "on the positive side, these studies have finally succeeded in extricating the study of communist politics from the limits of sovietology and linking it honourably and profitably with the main orientations and trends of social science in general." But he warns at the same time: "the difficulties of research in communist studies are such that to experiment with only one approach, or to link everything to one approach, would be counter-productive."

After such a *tour d'horizon* of the field, one should not find it surprising to see the author argue that "the state is still useful for comparative political studies." One might think that political science has come full circle; if so, one must add it has also reached a higher level. The point that the author is making is that in order to understand communist politics one should study it from that one vantage-point that also makes comparison with other political systems possible. But more important is the fact that it is around the state that communist politics revolves, ideology notwithstanding. In fact the denial *in principle* of the permanent existence of the state in socialist ideology is the third reason the author gives for his approach, for it allows a possibility of examining the relationship between theory and practice. Thus by using the vantage point of the state, Ionescu shows how cross-area and intra-area studies are possible. In the first case, three features are available: sovereignty, representative government, and parties. In the latter case, the communist states have five characteristics in common which they alone share: war-origins, abolition of private property and ownership, apparats, teleological vocations, and the absence of legitimate opposition.

The author's recommendations open many possibilities, including analysis at various levels of conceptualization. Despite the many difficulties this entails, it offers at least the opportunity of one common approach but also a more varied view of communist politics.

STANISLAV KIRSCHBAUM
Glendon College, York University

Baldev Raj Nayar, **The Modernization Imperative and Indian Planning.** Delhi: Vikas Publications, 1972, pp. ix, 246.

Professor Nayar has taught political science at McGill University since 1964, specializing in comparative politics and South Asian government. His contributions to Indian political research have included studies of state politics, language policy, voting behaviour, religious movements, and business interest groups. The present volume on the politics of Indian economic planning further demonstrates his analytic versatility.

The study examines the aims, motivations, and consequences of Indian planning during the heyday of governmental intervention in the economy from the mid-1950s to the mid-1960s. The central thesis is that planning in India was meant not only to serve welfare ends, but also, and more importantly, the goals of political sovereignty, military security, and economic independence. The latter three elements constitute national power, the pursuit of which is, for Professor Nayar, the modernization imperative heeded by all governments hoping to survive in the international political system. "Modernize or be subjugated" is the predicament for India, as for all underdeveloped states: "there is no other alternative, there is no other choice."

Applying the modernization model of David Apter, the author depicts India's central developmental dilemma as one of trying to implement a mobilizational economic strategy in a reconciliatory political system. Nehru and his chief economic adviser P.C. Mahalanobis sought to propel India forward *via* heavy industrialization. Their limited success was not a fault of the policy but a result of the fact that the policy "was not executed to the point of completion." What success was achieved can be attributed to external assistance, consumer sacrifices, and a polity whose main features were a national hero, a dominant party, and a low level of social mobilization. What undermined the policy, according to Professor Nayar, were the constraints posed by federalism and democracy: the voters wanted *ghee*, not guns.

Professor Nayar's *realpolitik* perspective provides a needed corrective for those who have seen only social justice in the ambitions of Indian planners. Some may find it surprising, however, to read that the concern of Indian planners and politicians for national power in terms of military self-sufficiency dates from the early 1950s, since published defence expenditures remained low and relatively static up to 1962 and the border conflict with China. To others, discussion of India's quest for economic independence must seem ironic in the light of the increasing reliance on foreign aid in the same period. Although Professor Nayar does find some supportive evidence for his national power thesis in Five Year Plan drafts and working papers, he appears occasionally to read post-1962 intentions into the 1950s rhetoric. What is extraordinary is how aptly predictive his analysis is for the early 1970s. But again, how is it that India can progress toward military self-sufficiency and even nuclear capability – as she seems to be doing now – when social mobilization is more advanced and domestic distributive demands are stronger than ever?

Students of international relations will be pleased by Professor Nayar's emphasis on the influence of foreign-policy goals in domestic policy. Those who study domestic political inputs in planning and resource allocation will find his intentional underemphasis of party, interest group, bureaucratic, or leadership politics somewhat puzzling. To fully understand the parameters surrounding decision-making in Indian economic planning one needs to know as much about power realities in subnational as in international politics; the "ruler's imperative" (*pace* Wriggins) affecting élites at lower levels of India's pyramidal polity must be squared with the modernization imperative. Nehru's "grand design" may have been sullied by factional or patronage politics, but frequently the latter have provided opportunities for new developmental initiatives. In any case, they cannot be ignored (nor their study reproached), for whatever their role in the politics of planning, their role in the politics of implementation is crucial.

In the end, Professor Nayar's prescriptions for India are clear: more mobilizational planning, more heavy industry, less foreign aid, more military and economic self-sufficiency. In the wake of the 1971 war with Pakistan they seem prophetic. Doubts raised at Stockholm in June 1972, however, added to India's continuing agricultural and population crises, have left some observers wondering whether modernization for India, by whatever strategy, is not a cruel chimera. To ask for an ecological perspective on India's developmental needs, however, is to ask Professor Nayar for another of his stimulating books.

JOHN R. WOOD
University of British Columbia

Luke T. Lee and Arthur Larson, eds., **Population and Law**. Durham: Rule of Law Press, 1971, pp. xi, 452.

The Commission on Population Growth and the American Future, **Population and the American Future.** New York: New American Library, 1972, pp. 362.

Donella H. Meadows *et al.*, **The Limits to Growth.** New York: Universe Books [Don Mills: Burns and MacEachern], 1972, pp. 205.

Taken together, these three constitute a primer for anyone interested in population and related policies. For the social scientist the least satisfactory is probably the Lee-Larson edition, the first in a series on law and population. This is a book for the practitioner, the legal scholar, and the drafter of legislation. The concluding prescriptive sections should be of particular interest to the drafters of cabinet memoranda. There are 14 case studies of individual nations from Asia, East and West Europe, and the Mid-East. North and South America are not provided for – suggesting the comparatively recent emergence of population questions as an area of public policy there. A further section on the United Nations, which departs from the case-study format, is useful in terms of describing multi-national birth control efforts, but its necessity in a work of this kind is not demonstrated. Better to have expanded the comparative base to North and South America.

The case studies make interesting reading in that they reveal tension within each nation's social legislation. This is caused by the presence of what the authors see as both pro- and anti-natalist elements. As a result, their job of measuring the "impact of laws" becomes difficult. The question of whether an explicitly pro-natalist law leads to an increase in births is never answered. Rather, the editors and contributors assume this, as they do its opposite. Further, they make the assumption that the arrival of the welfare state in developing countries has negated official attempts to limit births – an untested, and probably untestable, assumption. It would seem to be more reasonable to assume that operative law in a sensitive area like birth control follows rather than promotes attitudinal and behavioural change. In any event the job of gauging the law's impact is clearly not as simple as these legal scholars would have us believe, and their treatment of the cultural origins of population policies is simplistic and weak.

For future publications in this series the editors might find it useful to do two further things. First, they should spell out more clearly which variables of population policy they are treating. This work uses "population policy" when only one policy variable, fertility or birth control, is being examined. Secondly, they could revise their organization plan for case studies to make their categories more functional and thus more useful to both the student and the practitioner. Using "suspected pro-natalist" and "suspected anti-natalist" as two main categories could begin this redefinition process.

With the report of the Rockefeller Commission, Americans have now done what the British and the Japanese did in 1949 – they have given legitimacy to public examination of natural population growth. The report has made birth control an appropriate area for public policy debate in the USA, a status the issue lacked before. Whatever the success of the recommendations (and President Nixon has not been amused) it is clear the Commission's minimum goal, "to make population, and all that it means, explicit on the national agenda" (p. 8), has already been achieved.

The report is introduced with a three-part perspective, from which it is claimed the recommendations follow consistently. First, controlling the number of children is a critical component of societal self-steering. Second, unrestrained population growth, particularly among minorities, is a major factor in the persistence of conflict between the stated goals of the American Dream and the reality of life for some Americans. And third, births constitute the basic unit of analysis to which the ecological problem can be reduced. There is a major element missing from this perspective: the American population in world terms. The report later makes token reference in this direction, but they get it backwards: "world population growth is going to make these problems worse before they get better. The United States needs to undertake much greater efforts to understand these problems and develop international policies to deal with them" (p. 56). And later: "we are concerned with population trends only as they impede or enhance the realization of those values and goals cherished in, by and for, American society" (p. 118). Surely the rationale for population stabilization in an overdeveloped nation must make a place for that nation's population and its consumption in relation to the population and consumption of underdeveloped nations. From this perspective the United States and Canada today contribute more to the global population "problem" than do India or Bangladesh. Possibly the Commission omitted this element from their perspective for the pragmatic reason that they had to sell their proposals to American politicians.

Are the recommendations consistent with the stated perspective? Occasionally they pursue a "what's good for General Motors and thus the U.S.A. is fewer births" tangent, attempting to persuade the reader that stability in their capitalist society, with its increasingly capital-intensive economy, means fewer people to be unemployed. However, the major orientation lies in the predictable proposals on child care, education, equal status for women and illegal immigration, and less predictable ones on birth control for minors and abortion on demand. The most knotty proposal, one would think, is a call for national population distribution guidelines. The most meaty one for academics is the massive research envisaged, which would keep a new research cartel busy for at least the next 10 years. In terms of political saleability, most proposals have a good ring to them, but one wonders about the additional clout greater emphasis on the concept of the unwanted child would have brought.

Unlike the narrow scope of these two works, *The Limits to Growth* takes on the world, and the world a century hence at that. This effort of the Club of Rome has already received some of the attention it deserves, most of it from irate economists and mathematicians. With enemies like these there must be something useful here. What the Meadows group offers is "the most useful model now available for dealing with problems far out on the timespace graph," the problems being accelerating industrialization, rapid population growth, widespread malnutrition, depletion of non-renewable resources, and deteriorating environment, all appearing from "the five major sectors of the population-capital system." For them, the application of the model, with the many imperfections it possesses, allows examination of the interrelationships of food, population, capital, nonrenewable resources and pollution sectors in the world scheme of things to come. Their major *argument* – they are not dealing in hard predictions or conclusions – is, given present trends, it will all end with *both* a bang and a whimper, their "overshoot and collapse mode."

There is little in this work which could be lifted and slapped down in a public policy in spite of the claim that, "we feel that the model described here is already sufficiently developed to be of some use to decision-makers" (p. 22). One imagines the undersecretary of state for External Affairs leaning back in his chair and asking himself how many people can be provided for on this earth, at what level of wealth, and for how long. But most of the matters touched on have been known and written about for some time. What these people have done is bring some of it together and give it the ring of computer science, thus reducing the impact of critics flailing away at just another doomsday book. In a sense, this scientific ring aids their goal of public visibility for the limits to growth concept, a goal similar to that of the Rockefeller Commission in population matters.

The core of the study appears in the last three chapters, where they manipulate the five "quantities or levels" of their model with equally depressing effects, and where they call into question the technology-will-save-us school. The latter they do with some cogency, citing among other things the green revolution and its unanticipated social costs. They conclude with a powerful chapter, "The State of Global Equilibrium," which explores packages of policies to deliberately limit growth, and the nature of the society such policies might produce. With births set equal to deaths, capital investment equal to depreciation, increased emphasis on food and services, and with the introduction of certain technology in pollution abatement and land restoration, their model behaves beautifully, envisaging "an equilibrium state sustainable far into the future." Good news at last. Their stable-state notion centres on the resources redistribution which can come only if we stop relying on what growth promises but never seems to deliver. The authors plead for intensive further study of their global equilibrium concept. They, and the concept, deserve that study.

PETER SMITH
St Francis Xavier University

Canadian Journal of Political Science

Revue canadienne de science politique

Volume / Tome VI, 1973

Index

Articles

BLAIS, ANDRÉ. Third Parties in Canadian Provincial Politics 422

CRÊTE, JEAN. Analyse stratégique du choix d'un candidat dans une circonscription urbaine 254

ESBEREY, J.E. Personality and Politics: A New Look at the King-Byng Dispute 37

FAUCHER, ALBERT. La révolution tranquillisante 3

HART, KENNETH D. *See* SPROULE-JONES, MARK

KNIGHT, JONATHAN. Risks of War and Deterrence Logic 22

KWAVNICK, DAVID. Pressure-Group Demands and Organizational Objectives: The CNTU, the Lapalme Affair, and National Bargaining Units 582

LE BARON, BENTLEY. Three Components of Political Obligation 478

LOVINK, J.A.A. Is Canadian Politics too Competitive? 341

MC DONALD, VIRGINIA. A Guide to the Interpretation of Locke the Political Theorist 602

MC MENEMY, JOHN. *See* WINN, CONRAD

MASSAM, BRYAN H. Forms of Local Government in the Montreal Area, 1911–71: A Discriminant Approach 243

MELLOS, KOULA. *See* SANKOFF, DAVID

MORRISON, K.L. The Businessman Voter in Thunder Bay: The Catalyst to the Federal-Provincial Voting Split? 219

MOUL, WILLIAM B. The Level of Analysis Problem Revisited 494

PINARD, MAURICE. Third Parties in Canada Revisited: A Rejoinder and Elaboration of the Theory of One-Party Dominance 439

PITTS, RUTH ANN. Parliamentarianism among the French Working Class 451

QUESNEL-OUELLET, LOUISE. Situations et attitudes face au changement dans les structures municipales 195

RESNICK, PHILIP. The Political Theory of Extra-Parliamentarism 65

SANCTON, ANDREW. The Application of the "Senatorial Floor" Rules to the Latest Redistribution of the House of Commons: The Peculiar Case of Nova Scotia 56

SANKOFF, DAVID, and KOULA MELLOS. La régionalisation électorale et l'amplification des proportions 380

SCHOOLMAN, MORTON. Further Reflections on Work, Alienation, and Freedom in Marcuse and Marx 295

SPROULE-JONES, MARK, and KENNETH D. HART. A Public-Choice Model of Political Participation 175

STEIN, MICHAEL B. Le Crédit social dans la province du Québec : sommaire et développements 563
WHITE, GRAHAM. One-Party Dominance and Third Parties: The Pinard Theory Reconsidered 399
WILSON, H.T. Rationality and Decision in Administrative Science 271
WINN, CONRAD, and JOHN MCMENEMY. Political Alignment in a Polarized City: Electoral Cleavages in Kitchener, Ontario 230

Notes

DUNN, M. JAMES, RODNEY SCHNECK, and JAN LAWSON. A Test of the Uni-dimensionality of Various Political Scales through Factor Analysis: A Research Note 664
GILSDORF, ROBERT R. Cognitive and Motivational Sources of Voter Susceptibility to Influence 624
GRAYSON, J. PAUL. Social Position and Interest Recognition: The Voter in Broadview, *or* Are Voters Fools? 131
HULL, W.H.N. The 1971 Survey of the Profession 89
LAWSON, JAN. *See* DUNN, M. JAMES
MILLER, D.R. A Shapley Value Analysis of the Proposed Canadian Constitutional Amendment Scheme 140
PALDA, KRISTIAN S. Does Advertising Influence Votes? An Analysis of the 1966 and 1970 Quebec Elections 638
RICHERT, JEAN PIERRE. Political Socialization in Quebec: Young People's Attitudes toward Government 303
SCHNECK, RODNEY. *See* DUNN, M. JAMES
SHEEHAN, BERNARD S. Federal Funds and University Research 121
STARK, FRANK. The Prime Minister as Symbol: Unifier or Optimizer? 514
SZABLOWSKI, GEORGE. The Prime Minister as Symbol: A Rejoinder 516
VAISON, ROBERT. A Note on "Public Policy" 661
WARD, NORMAN. The Representative System and the Calling of Elections 655

Notes bibliographiques / Review Articles

BONENFANT, JEAN-CHARLES. Les études de la Commission royale d'enquête sur le bilinguisme et le biculturalisme 144
BRUN, HENRI. Le Labrador à l'heure de la contestation 518

Recensions / Reviews

ABELLA, IRVING MARTIN. *Nationalism, Communism, and Canadian Labour: The CIO, the Communist Party, and the Canadian Congress of Labour 1935–56*. By Terence Morley 679
ALLEN, RICHARD. *The Social Passion: Religion and Social Reform in Canada 1914–28*. By Walter Young 155
ATTALI, JACQUES. *Analyse économique de la vie politique*. Par Edouard Cloutier 546
ATTALI, JACQUES. *Les modèles politiques*. Par Edouard Cloutier 546
BELL, DAVID V.J. *Resistance and Revolution*. By William Leiss 541
BENJAMIN, JACQUES. *Les Camerounais occidentaux : la minorité dans un Etat bicommunautaire*. By Lynn K. Mytelka 555
BINDER, LEONARD, *et al.* (eds.). *Crises and Sequences in Political Development*. By R.H. Jackson 161
BIOT, FRANCOIS. *Théologie du politique*. Par Raymond Lemieux 523
BLALOCK, H.M., JR. (ed.). *Causal Models in the Social Sciences*. By W.P. Irvine 336
BOILY, ROBERT. *Québec 1940–1969. Bibliographie : Le système politique québécois et son environnement*. Par Gilles Caron 317
BORDEN, ROBERT LAIRD. *Letters to Limbo* (ed. by Henry Borden). By John R. Williams 533
BOURDET, YVON. *Figures de Lukacs*. Par André P. Donneur 539
BOUTHILLIER, GUY, et JEAN MEYNAUD. *Le choc des langues au Québec, 1760–1970*. Par André P. Donneur 685
BOYD, GAVIN. *See* WILCOX, WAYNE
BRECHER, MICHAEL. *The Foreign Policy System of Israel: Setting, Images, Process*. By Timothy M. Shaw 554

BRUN, HENRI, et GUY TREMBLAY. *Droit public fondamental.* Par André Bernard 548
BUDGE, IAN, *et al. Political Stratification and Democracy.* By Rick Butler 684
BURNS, LT. GEN. E.L.M. *The Struggle for Disarmament: A Seat at the Table.* By Gerry Dirks 529
Canada's 28 Parliament: A Guide to the Members, their Constituencies, and their Government. By W.F. Dawson 326
CARTER, GEORGE E. *Canadian Conditional Grants since World War II.* By Marvin Blauer 154
CHODOROW, STANLEY. *Christian Political Theory and Church Politics in the Mid-Twelfth Century: The Ecclesiology of Gratian's Decretum.* By E. Burke Inlow 676
CHODOS, ROBERT, and NICK AUF DER MAUR (eds.). *Quebec: A Chronicle, 1968–1972.* By Philip Resnick 532
CLARKSON, STEPHEN. *City Lib: Parties and Reform.* By James Lightbody 324
COMMISSION ON POPULATION GROWTH AND THE AMERICAN FUTURE. *Population and the American Future.* By Peter Smith 688
COOK, RAMSAY. *The Maple Leaf Forever: Essays on Nationalism and Politics in Canada.* By Richard Simeon 158
COOMBES, DAVID. *State Enterprise: Business or Politics?* By W.H.N. Hull 683
CORRY, J.A. *The Power of the Law.* By Frederick Vaughan 329
COTTERET, JEAN-MARIE, et CLAUDE EMERI. Le budget de l'Etat. Par Richard Berger 332
COTTERET, JEAN-MARIE, et CLAUDE EMERI. *Les systèmes électoraux.* Par François Renaud 331
CRANSTON, MAURICE. *The Mask of Politics.* By William Christian 677
CRENSON, MATTHEW A. *The Un-Politics of Air Pollution: A Study of Non-Decisionmaking in the Cities.* By T.J. Cartwright 558
CUFF, R.D. *See* J.L. GRANATSTEIN
DEBBASCH, CHARLES. *Science administrative : administration publique.* Par Nasir Islam 330
DESROSIERS, RICHARD. *Le personnel politique québécois.* Par Réjean Pelletier 316
DESTLER, I.M. *Presidents, Bureaucrats and Foreign Policy: The Politics of Organizational Reform.* By Gilbert R. Winham 672
DION, LÉON. *Société et politique – la vie des groupes : Tome 1, Fondements de la société libérale; Tome 2, Dynamique de la société libérale.* By David Braybrooke 522
DOERN, G. BRUCE. *Political Policy-Making: A Commentary on the Economic Council's Eighth Annual Review and the Ritchie Report.* By Patrick Kyba 156
DRACHE, DANIEL (ed.). *Quebec – Only the Beginning : The Manifestoes of the Common Front.* By Philip Resnick 532
DUNN, JOHN. *Modern Revolutions: An Introduction to the Analysis of a Political Phenomenon.* By John Anson Warner 164
DVORIN, EUGENE P., and ROBERT H. SIMMONS. *From Amoral to Humane Bureaucracy.* By Kenneth Kernaghan 556
EAYRS, JAMES. *In Defence of Canada, Volume III: Peacemaking and Deterrence.* By Geoffrey Pearson 528
EHRLICH, STANISLAW. *Le pouvoir et les groupes de pression, étude de la structure politique du capitalisme.* Par Guy Lord 671
EMERI, CLAUDE. *See* COTTERET, JEAN-MARIE
FOSTER, C.D. *Politics, Finance and the Role of Economics: An Essay on the Control of Public Enterprise.* By W.H.N. Hull 683
FRIEDRICH, CARL J. *Tradition and Authority.* By William Christian 545
GOMBIN, RICHARD. *Les origines du gauchisme.* Par Serge Latouche 162
GRANATSTEIN, J.L., and PETER STEVENS (eds.). *Forum: Canadian Life and Letters 1920–70: Selections from the Canadian Forum.* By Paul Fox 325
GRANATSTEIN, J.L., and R.D. CUFF (eds.). *War and Society in North America.* By Margaret Doxey 530
GRAY, COLIN S. *Canadian Defence Priorities: A Question of Relevance.* By Harald von Riekhoff 527
GREENSTEIN, FRED I., and MICHAEL LERNER (eds.). *A Source Book for the Study of Personality and Politics.* By John Woods 336
GUNN, J.A.W. *Factions No More: Attitudes to Party in Government and Opposition in Eighteenth-Century England.* By John Stewart 169
HALLE, LOUIS J. *The Ideological Imagination.* By Barry Cooper 542
HALPERIN, MAURICE. *The Rise and Decline of Fidel Castro: An Essay in Contemporary History.* By Thomas C. Bruneau 552
HANCOCK, M. DONALD, and GIDEON SJOBERG (eds.). *Politics in the Post-Welfare State: Responses to the New Individualism.* By Ingunn N. Means 550

HARRIS, NIGEL. *Competition and the Corporate Society: British Conservatives, the State and Industry, 1945–1964.* By Alan Alexander 551
HEENEY, ARNOLD. *The Things that are Caesar's: The Memoirs of a Canadian Public Servant.* By Kenneth Kernaghan 320
HILSMAN, ROGER. *The Politics of Policy Making in Defense and Foreign Affairs.* By Gilbert R. Winham 672
HODGETTS, J.E. *The Canadian Public Service: A Physiology of Government, 1867–1970.* By Neil A. Swainson 682
HODGETTS, J.E., WILLIAM MCCLOSKEY, REGINALD WHITAKER, and V. SEYMOUR WILSON. *The Biography of an Institution: The Civil Service Commission of Canada, 1908–1967.* By A. Paul Pross 321
HOOKE, ALF. *Thirty Plus Five: I Know, I Was There.* By F.Q. Quo 323
IONESCU, GHITA. *Comparative Communist Politics.* By Stanislav Kirschbaum 687
JOHNSON, L.P.V., and OLA MACNUTT. *Aberhart of Alberta.* By F.Q. Quo 323
JONES, RICHARD. *Community in Crisis: French Canadian Nationalism in Perspective.* By Philip Resnick 532
KHAN, R.A., S.A. MACKOWN, J.D. MCNIVEN. *An Introduction to Political Science.* By H.G. Thorburn 319
KWAVNICK, DAVID. *Organized Labour and Pressure Politics: The Canadian Labour Congress 1956–1968.* By Frederick C. Engelmann 525
LALANDE, GILLES. *Pourquoi le fédéralisme – Contribution d'un Québécois à l'intelligence du fédéralisme canadien.* Par Jean-Charles Bonenfant 151
LARSON, ARTHUR. *See* LEE, LUKE T.
LEE, LUKE T., and ARTHUR LARSON (eds.). *Population and Law.* By Peter Smith 688
LEIBNIZ, GOTTFRIED WILLHELM. The Political Writings of Leibniz. By William Christian 169
LEISS, WILLIAM. *The Domination of Nature.* By T.J. Cartwright 160
MCCLOSKEY, WILLIAM. *See* HODGETTS, J.E.
MACKOWN, S.A. *See* KHAN, R.A.
MCNIVEN, J.D. *See* KHAN, R.A.
MACNUTT, OLA. *See* JOHNSON, L.P.V.
MALLORY, J.R. *The Structure of Canadian Government.* By John Stewart 680
MARX, FRÉDÉRIC. *L'administration locale en Grande-Bretagne.* Par Louise Quesnel-Ouellet 167
MASCLET, JEAN-CLAUDE. *L'Europe politique.* Par Maurice Torrelli 550
MASSEY, HECTOR J. *The Canadian Military: A Profile.* By Margaret Doxey 530
MAZURI, ALI A. *Cultural Engineering and Nation-Building in East Africa.* By Geoffrey F. Engholm 333
MEADOWS, DONELLA H. *et al. The Limits to Growth.* By Peter Smith 688
MEEHAN, EUGENE J. *The Foundations of Political Analysis: Empirical and Normative.* By M.W. Jackson 544
MEISEL, JOHN. *Working Papers on Canadian Politics.* By David Edward Smith 526
MENNIS, BERNARD. *American Foreign Policy Officials: Who They Are and What They Believe Regarding International Politics.* By Gilbert R. Winham 672
MEYNAUD, JEAN. *See* BOUTHILLIER, GUY
MILES, SIMON (ed.). *Metropolitan Problems, International Perspectives: A Search for Comprehensive Solutions.* By Richard E. Stren 165
MODELSKI, GEORGE. *Principles of World Politics.* By Carol A.L. Prager 670
MORIN, CLAUDE. *Le pouvoir québécois ... en négociation.* Par Jean-Charles Bonenfant 151
NAYAR, BALDEV RAJ. *The Modernization Imperative and Indian Planning.* By John R. Wood 687
NOEL, S.J.R. *Politics in Newfoundland.* By H.B. Mayo 157
ODEGARD, HOLTAN P. *The Politics of Truth: Toward Reconstruction in Democracy.* By George J. Szablowski 559
ØRVIK, NILS *et al. Departmental Decision-Making: A Research Report.* By Howard H. Lentner 675
PAINCHAUD, PAUL. *Francophonie. Bibliographie 1960–1969.* Par Gordon Mace 318
PARTRIDGE, P.H. *Consent and Consensus.* By William Christian 545
PAULUS, DANIEL. *Les milieux dirigeants belges et l'adhésion du Royaume-Uni aux communautés européennes.* Par Ferry de Kerckhove 167
PELCZYNSKI, Z.A. (ed.). *Hegel's Political Philosophy: Problems and Perspectives.* By Frederick M. Barnard 328
PIOTTE, JEAN-MARC. *Sur Lénine.* Par André Kuzminski 327

PRÉVOST, JEAN-PIERRE. *La crise du fédéralisme canadien.* Par André Bernard 678
PRICE, TREVOR (ed.). *Regional Government in Ontario.* By Caroline Andrew 325
REID, MALCOLM. *The Shouting Signpainters: A Literary and Political Account of Quebec Revolutionary Nationalism.* By Philip Resnick 532
RICHARDS, PETER G. *The Backbenchers.* By Robert J. Jackson 552
RITCHIE, RONALD S. *An Institute for Research on Public Policy.* By Patrick Kyba 156
RIVLIN, ALICE M. *New Approaches to Public Decision-Making.* By Patrick Kyba 156
ROSE, LEO E. *See* WILCOX, WAYNE
RUBINOFF, LIONEL (ed.). *Tradition and Revolution: The Frank Gerstein Lectures, 1970.* By John Anson Warner 164
SCHAPIRO, LEONARD. *Totalitarianism.* By William Christian 545
SIMEON, RICHARD. *Federal-Provincial Diplomacy: The Making of Recent Policy in Canada.* By Michael B. Stein 149
SJOBERG, GIDEON. *See* HANCOCK, M. DONALD
SMILEY, D.V. *Canada in Question: Federalism in the Seventies.* By J.R. Mallory 315
SMITH, JEAN EDWARD. *Germany beyond the Wall: People, Politics ... and Prosperity.* By Klaus J. Herrmann 335
STEVENS, PETER. *See* GRANATSTEIN, J.L.
SWAINSON, DONALD (ed.). *Oliver Mowat's Ontario.* By John Wilson 322
TEEPLE, GARY (ed.). *Capitalism and the National Question in Canada.* By Thelma Oliver 531
TOINET, MARIE-FRANCE. *Le Congrès des Etats-Unis.* Par Edmond Orban 524
TORRELLI, MAURICE, et RENÉE BAUDOUIN. *Les droits de l'homme et les libertés publiques par les textes.* Par Panayotis Soldatos 547
TOURAINE, ALAIN. *Le communisme utopique : le mouvement de mai 1968.* Par Daniel Latouche 536
TOURAINE, ALAIN. *Université et société aux Etats-Unis.* Par Daniel Latouche 536
TREMBLAY, GUY. *See* BRUN, HENRI
TRUDEAU, PIERRE ELLIOTT. *Conversation with Canadians.* By Thomas A. Hockin 535
TUCKER, ROBERT W. The Radical Left and American Foreign Policy. By Blema S. Steinberg 314
VINCENT, JACK E. *Factor Analysis in International Relations: Interpretation, Problem Areas, and an Application.* By Jan Jørgensen 674
WESTELL, ANTHONY. *Paradox: Trudeau as Prime Minister.* By Thomas A. Hockin 535
WHITAKER, REGINALD. *See* HODGETTS, J.E.
WILCOX, WAYNE, LEO E. ROSE, and GAVIN BOYD (eds.). *Asia and the International System.* By Sheldon W. Simon 334
WILKINSON, PAUL. *Social Movement.* By John Anson Warner 164
WILSON, V. SEYMOUR. *See* HODGETTS, J.E.
WINKS, ROBIN W. *The Blacks in Canada: A History.* By Eugene D. Genovese 159
WOOD, ELLEN MEIKSINS. *Mind and Politics: An Approach to the Meaning of Liberal and Socialist Individualism.* By J. McCalla Vickers 541

Critiques / Reviewers

Alexander, Alex 551
Andrew, Caroline 325
Barnard, Frederick M. 328
Berger, Richard 332
Bernard, André 548, 678
Blauer, Marvin 154
Bonenfant, Jean-Charles 151
Braybrooke, David 522
Bruneau, Thomas C. 552
Butler, Rick 684
Caron, Gilles 317
Cartwright, T.J. 160, 558
Christian, William 169, 545, 677
Cloutier, Edouard 546
Cooper, Barry 542
Dawson, W.F. 326
Dirks, Gerry 529
Donneur, André P. 539, 685
Doxey, Margaret 530
Engelmann, Frederick C. 525
Engholm, Geoffrey F. 333
Fox, Paul 325
Genovese, Eugene D. 159
Herrmann, Klaus J. 335
Hockin, Thomas A. 535
Hull, W.H.N. 683
Inlow, E. Burke 676
Irvine, W.P. 336
Islam, Nasir 330
Jackson, M.W. 544
Jackson, R.H. 161
Jackson, Robert J. 552

Jørgensen, Jan 674
Kerckhove, Ferry de 167
Kernaghan, Kenneth 320, 556
Kirschbaum, Stanislav 687
Kuzminski, André 327
Kyba, Patrick 156
Latouche, Daniel 536
Latouche, Serge 162
Leiss, William 541
Lemieux, Raymond 523
Lentner, Howard H. 675
Lightbody, James 324
Lord, Guy 671
Mace, Gordon 318
Mallory, J.R. 315
Mayo, H.B. 157
Means, Ingunn N. 550
Morley, Terence 679
Mytelka, Lynn K. 555
Oliver, Thelma 531
Orban, Edmond 524
Pearson, Geoffrey 528
Pelletier, Réjean 316
Prager, Carol A.L. 670
Pross, A. Paul 321
Quesnel-Ouellet, Louise 167
Quo, F.Q. 323
Renaud, François 331
Resnick, Philip 532
Shaw, Timothy M. 554
Simeon, Richard 158
Simon, Sheldon W. 334
Smith, David Edward 526
Smith, Peter 688
Soldatos, Panayotis 547
Stein, Michael B. 149
Steinberg, Blema S. 314
Stewart, John 169, 680
Stren, Richard E. 165
Swainson, Neil A. 682
Szablowski, George J. 559
Thorburn, H.G. 319
Torrelli, Maurice 550
Vaughan, Frederick 329
Vickers, J. McCalla 541
von Riekhoff, Harald 527
Warner, John Anson 164
Williams, John R. 533
Wilson, John 322
Winham, Gilbert R. 672
Wood, John R. 687
Woods, John 336
Young, Walter 155

CANADIAN JOURNAL OF POLITICAL SCIENCE
REVUE CANADIENNE DE SCIENCE POLITIQUE

PREPARED BY ROMAN MARCH MCMASTER UNIVERSITY

THE INDEX HAS BEEN PREPARED IN TWO WAYS. FIRST EACH AUTHOR IS LISTED BY SIRNAME AND THE FULL TITLE OF HIS ARTICLE. THIS IS FOLLOWED BY A GROUP OF THREE NUMBERS. THE FIRST NUMBER IS THE NUMERICAL EQUIVALENT OF THE MONTH IN WHICH THE ARTICLE WAS PUBLISHED. THE SECOND NUMBER IS A TWO DIGIT GROUPING STATING THE YEAR THE ARTICLE WAS PUBLISHED. THE THIRD SET OF NUMBERS IS THE PAGE REFERENCE OF THE ARTICLE.

FOLLOWING THE AUTHOR LISTING IS A KEYWORD LISTING OF ALL RELEVANT WORDS WHICH HAVE APPEARED IN THE TITLE OF THE ARTICLE. THE SEQUENCE OF NUMBERS IS THE SAME AS THE SEQUENCE USED IN THE AUTHOR LIST.

AUTHOR LIST

ADAM, HERIBERT, THE SOUTH AFRICAN POWER-ELITE. A SURVEY OF IDEOLOGICAL COMMITMENT 3/71/76
AKE, CLAUDE, POLITICAL OBLIGATION AND POLITICAL DISSENT 6/69/245
ANDREW, EDWARD, A REPLY TO WILLIAM LEISS, ≠≠TECHNOLOGICAL RATIONALITY. NOTES ON
ANDREW, EDWARD, WORK AND FREEDOM IN MARCUSE AND MARX 6/70/241
BACCIGALUPO, ALAIN, LA PARTICIPATION DES FORCES DEMOCRATIQUES A L≠EXPERIENCE FRANCAISE DE PLANIFICATION REGIONALE 3/72/1
BAIRD, RICHARD, LASKIN, RICHARD, FACTORS IN VOTER TURNOUT AND PARTY PREFERENCE IN A SASKATCHEWAN TOWN (RESEARCH NOTES) 9/70/450
BARNARD, FREDERICK M., BETWEEN OPPOSITION AND POLITICAL OPPOSITION, THE SEARCH FOR COMPETITIVE POLITICS IN CZECHOSLOVAKIA 12/72/533
BAY, CHRISTIAN, NEEDS, WANTS, AND POLITICAL LEGITIMACY 9/68/241
BEEHLER, RODGER, THE WOLFF AT THE DOOR (NOTES) 12/72/553
BENJAMIN, JAQUES, LA MINORITE EN ETAT BICOMMUNAUTAIRE. QUATRE ETUDES DE CAS
BENJAMIN, JACQUES, LA RATIONALISATION DES CHOIX BUDGETAIRES, LES CAS QUEBECOIS ET CANADIEN 9/72/348
BERGERON, GERARD, COMMENTAIRE DE LA COMMUNICATION DU PROFESSEUR AREN LIJPHART 3/71/18
BERGERON, GERARD, STRUCTURE DES ≠FONCTIONNALISMES≠ EN SCIENCE POLITIQUE 6/70/205
BERNARD, STEPHANE, LES FACTEURS DE LA DECISION POLITIQUE EN REGIME DEMOCRATIQUE, 6/68/147
BIXLEY, BRIAN, DEMOCRATIC THEORY AND PUBLIC POLICY 9/70/415
BLACK, ERROLL, ONE TOO MANY REPORTS ON POVERTY IN CANADA ((RA) 9/72/439
BLAIS, ANDRE, THIRD PARTIES IN CANADIAN PROVINCIAL POLITICS 9/73/422
BLAIS, A., CANTIN H., CRETE, J., LES ELECTIONS COMME PHENOMENE DE DECISION COLLECTIVE, LES ELECTIONS FEDERALES DE 1957 A 1965 AU QUEBEC 12/70/522
BLAKE, DONALD E., THE MEASUREMENT OF REGIONALISM IN CANADIAN VOTING PATTERNS 3/72/55
BLONDEL, J., PARTY SYSTEMS AND PATTERNS OF GOVERNMENT IN WESTERN DEMOCRACIES 6/68/180
BONENFANT, JEAN-CHARLES, LES ETUDES DE LA COMMISSION ROYAL D≠ENQUETE SUR LE BILINGUISME ET LE BICULTURALISME (RA) 9/71/406
BONENFANT, JEAN-CHARLES, LES ETUDES DE LA COMMISSION ROYALE D≠ENQUETE SUR LE BILINGUISME ET LE BICULTURALISME (RA) 9/72/444
BROADBENT, J. E., THE IMPORTANCE OF CLASS IN THE POLITICAL THEORY OF JOHN STUART MILL, 9/68/270
BROMLEY, DAVID, KORNBERG, ALLAN, SMITH, JOEL, SOME DIFFERENCES IN THE POLITICAL SOCIALIZATION PATTERNS OF CANADIAN AND AMERICAN PARTY OFFICIALS- A PRELIMINARY REPORT 3/69/64
BRUN, HENRI, LE LABRADOR A L≠HEURE DE LA CONTESTATION (RA) 9/73/518
BRYNE, DOROTHY, SOME ATTENDANCE PATTERNS EXHIBITED BY MEMBERS OF PARLIAMENT DURING THE 28TH PARLIAMENT (NOTES) 3/72/135
BYERS, R. B., PERCEPTIONS OF PARLIAMENTARY SURVEILLANCE OF THE EXECUTIVE, THE CASE OF CANADIAN DEFENCE POLICY 6/72/234
CAIRNS, ALAN C., THE ELECTORAL SYSTEM AND THE PARTY SYSTEM IN CANADA , 1921-1965, 3/68/55
CAIRNS, ALAN C., THE JUDICIAL COMMITTEE AND ITS CRITICS 9/71/301
CAIRNS, ALAN C., A REPLY TO J. A. A. LOVINK, ≠≠ON ANALYSING THE IMPACT OF THE ELECTORAL SYSTEM ON THE PARTY SYSTEM IN CANADA≠≠ 12/70/517
CAMERON, DAVID M., REGIONAL INTEGRATION IN THE MARITIME PROVINCES 3/71/24
CAMERON, DAVID R., SUMMERS, LAURA, NON-FAMILY AGENTS OF POLITICAL SOCIALIZATION. A REASSESSMENT OF CONVERSE AND DUPEUX 9/72/418
CANTIN, H., BLAIS, A., CRETE, J., LES ELECTIONS COMME PHENOMENE DE DECISION COLLECTIVE, LES ELECTIONS FEDERALES DE 1957 A 1965 AU QUEBEC 12/70/522
CAPLAN, NEIL, SOME FACTORS AFFECTING THE RESOLUTION OF A FEDERAL-PROVINCIAL CONFLICT 6/69/173
CARRIER, ANDRE, L≠IDEOLOGIE POLITIQUE DE LA REVUE CITE LIBRE 12/68/414
CASSTEVENS, THOMS W., MORRIS, WILLIAM D., THE CUBE LAW AND THE DECOMPOSED SYSTEM 12/72/521
CASSTEVENS, THOMAS W., DENHAM, WILLIAM A., 111, TURNOVER AND TENURE IN THE CANADIAN HOUSE OF COMMONS, 1867-1968 (RESEARCH NOTES) 12/70/655
CHEVRETTE, FRANCOIS, A LA RECHERCHE DE L≠ESSENCE DU PHENOMENE POLITIQUE 6/69/262
CHEVRETTE, FRANCOIS, REFLEXIONS SUR UNE COSMOGONIE POLITIQUE 9/69/359
CHI, H. H., THE REGRESSION MODEL OF REGIONALISM. A CRITIQUE (NOTES) 6/72/291
CHOUCRI, NAZLI, THE NONALIGNMENT OF AFRO-ASIAN STATES - POLICY, PERCEPTION, AND BEHAVIOUR, 3/69/1
CLARKE, HAROLD, KORNBERG, ALLAN, SMITH, JOEL, ATTRIBUTES OF ASCRIBED INFLUENCE IN LOCAL PARTY ORGANIZATIONS IN CANADA AND THE UNITED STATES 6/72/206
CLARKE, J. J., ≠≠THE END OF HISTORY≠≠. A REAPPRAISAL OF MARX≠S VIEWS ON ALIENATION AND HUMAN EMANCIPATION 9/71/367
CLARKSON, STEPHEN, BARRIER TO ENTRY OF PARTIES INTO TORONTO≠S CIVIC POLITICS. TOWARDS A THEORY OF PARTY PENETRATION 6/71/206
CLARKSON, STEPHEN, SIMULATION IN TEACHING COMPARATIVE POLITICS, PLAYING FRENCH GAMES (RESEARCH NOTES) 9/70/462
COLTON, TIMOTHY, THE ≠≠NEW BIOLOGY≠≠ AND THE CAUSES OF WAR, 12/69/434

COMEAU, PAUL-ANDRE, ACCULTURATION OU ASSIMILATION - TECHNIQUE D≠ANALYSE ET TENTATIVE DE MESURE CHEZ LES FRANCO-ONTARIENS, 6/69/158
COMEAU, PAUL-ANDRE, ANALYSE COMPARATIVE ET INFORMATIQUE, 3/68/81
COOPER, BARRY, VALUES AND THE METHODOLOGY OF POLITICAL SCIENCE.A COMMENT 3/71/119
COPES, PARZIVAL, THE FISHERMEN≠S VOTE IN NEWFOUNDLAND 12/70/579
CRETE, JEAN, ANALYSE STRATEGIQUE DU CHOIX D≠UN CANDIDAT DANS UNE CIRCONSCRIPTION URBAINE 6/73/254
CRETE, J., BLAIS, A., CANTIN, H., LES ELECTIONS COMME PHENOMENE DE DECISION COLLECTIVE, LES ELECTIONS FEDERALES DE 1957 A 1965 AU QUEBEC 12/70/522
CROWLEY, RONALD W., A COMMENT ON PROFESSOR MACPHERSON≠S INTERPRETATION OF FRIEDMAN≠S CAPITALISM AND FREEDOM, 6/69/256
CUNNINGHAM, ROBERT, THE IMPACT OF THE LOCAL CANDIDATE IN CANADIAN FEDERAL ELECTIONS 6/71/287
CUNNINGHAM, ROBERT C., WINHAM, GILBERT R., PARTY LEADER IMAGES IN THE 1968 FEDERAL ELECTION 3/70/37
DENHAM, WILLIAM A., III, CASSTEVENS, M A., III, TURNOVER AND TENURE IN THE CANADIAN HOUSE OF COMMONS, 1867-1968 (RESEARCH NOTES) 12/70/655
DEVALL, W. B., SUPPORT FOR CIVIL LIBERTIES AMONG ENGLISH-SPEAKING CANADIAN UNIVERSITY STUDENTS 9/70/433
DION,LEON, THE CONCEPT OF POLITICAL LEADERSHIP 3/68/2
DION, LEON, POLITIQUE CONSULTATIVE ET SYSTEME POLITIQUE 6/69/226
DION, LEON, A LA RECHERCHE D≠UNE METHODE D≠ANALYSE DES PARTIS ET DES GROUPES D≠INTERET, 3/69/45
DOERN, G. BRUCE, RECENT CHANGES IN THE PHILOSOPHY OF POLICY-MAKING IN CANADA 6/71/243
DUNN, M JAMES, SCHNECK, RODNEY, LAWSON, JAN, A TEST OF THE UNI-DIMENSIONALITY OF VARIOUS POLITICAL SCALES THROUGH FACTOR ANALYSIS, RESEARCH NOTE 12/73/664
EASTON, DAVID, THE THEORETICAL RELEVANCE OF POLITICAL SOCIALIZATION 6/68/125
ENGELMANN, FREDERICK C., PERCEPTIONS OF THE GREAT COALITION IN WEST GERMANY 1966-1969 3/72/28
ELKINS, DAVID J., REGIONAL CONTEXTS OF POLITICAL PARTICIPATION. SOME ILLUSTRATIONS FROM SOUTH INDIA 6/72/167
ESBEREY, J. E., PERSONALITY AND POLITICS, A NEW LOOK AT THE KING-BYNG DISPUTE 3/73/37
FAUCHER, ALBERT, LA REVOLUTION TRANQUILLISANTE 3/73/3
FEAVER, GEORGE, CONTEMPORARY POLITICAL THOUGHT AND THE AMERICAN SCIENCE OF POLITICS, 9/68/357
FRANKS, C. E. S., THE DILEMMA OF THE STANDING COMMITTEES OF THE CANADIAN HOUSE OF COMMONS 12/71/461
GELINAS, ANDRE, LES PARLIAMENTAIRES ET L≠ADMINISTRATION PUBLIQUE AU QUEBEC 6/68/164
GILBERT, MARCEL, L≠INFORMATION GOUVERNEMENTALE ET LES COURRIERISTES PARLIEMENTAIRES AU QUEBEC 3/71/26
GILSDORF, ROBERT R, COGNITIVE AND MOTIVATIONAL SOURCES OF VOTER SUSCEPTIBILITY TO INFLUENCE (NOTES) 12/73/624
GOW, J. I., HISTOIRE ADMINISTRATIVE DU QUEBEC ET THEORIE ADMINISTRATIVE 3/71/141
GOW, J. I., LES QUEBECOIS, LA GUERRE ET LA PAIX, 1945-60 3/70/88
GRAYSON, J. PAUL, SOCIAL POSITION AND INTEREST RECOGNITION, THE VOTER IN BROADVIEW, OR ARE VOTERS FOOLS (NOTES) 3/73/131
GREENBERG, EDWARD S., CHILDREN AND THE POLITICAL COMMUNITY* A COMPARISON ACROSS RACIAL LINES, 12/69/471
GREENE, THOMAS H., VALUES AND THE METHODOLOGY OF POLITICAL SCIENCE 6/70/275
GUNN,J.A.W.,JEREMY BENTHAM AND THE PUBLIC INTEREST 12/68/398
HAHN, HARLAN, VOTING IN CANADIAN COMMUNITIES/ A TAXONOMY OF REFERENDUM ISSUES, 12/68/462
HARASYMIW, BOHDAN, NOMENKLATURA* THE SOVIET COMMUNIST PARTY≠S LEADERSHIP RECRUITMENT SYSTEM, 12/69/493
HART, KENNETH D., SPROULE-JONES, MARK, A PUBLIC CHOICE MODEL OF POLITICAL PARTICIPATION 6/73/175
HAVEL, J. E., GRANDS VILLES, NATIONS ET EMPIRES. UNE CARTE POLITIQUE DE LA NOUVELLE SOCIETE INDUSTRIELLE AVANCEE 3/72/120
HOFFMAN, DAVID, AND SCHINDELER, FRED, THEOLOGICAL AND POLITICAL CONSERVATISM, 12/68/429
HOFFMAN, DAVID, WILSON JOHN, THE LIBERAL PARTY IN CONTEMPORARY ONTARIO POLITICS 6/70/177
HOLSTI, K. J., RETREAT FROM UTOPIA. INTERNATIONAL RELATIONS THEORY, 1945-70 6/71/165
HULL, W. H. N., THE 1971 SURVEY OF THE PROFESSION (NOTES) 3/73/89
IRVINE, WILLIAM P., ASSESSING REGIONAL EFFECTS IN DATA ANALYSIS 3/71/21
IRVINE, WILLIAM P., A REPLY TO PROFESSOR CHI≠S CRITIQUE (NOTES) 6/72/297
IRVINE, WILLIAM P., RECRUITMENT TO NATIONSLISM, NEW POLITICS OR NORMAL POLITICS 12/72/503
JACEK, HENRY, MCDONOUGH, JOHN, SHIMIZU, RONALD, SMITH, PATRICK, THE CONGRUENCE OF FEDERAL-PROVINCIAL CAMPAIGN ACTIVITY IN PARTY ORGANIZATIONS. THE INFLUENCE OF RECRUITMENT PATTERNS IN THREE HAMILTON RIDINGS 6/72/190
JACKSON, M. W., THE APPLICATION OF METHOD IN THE CONSTRUCTION OF POLITICAL SCIENCE THEORY 9/72/402
JENSON, JANE, REGENSTRIEF, PETER, SOME DIMENSIONS OF PARTISAN CHOICE IN QUEBEC, 1969 (RESEARCH NOTES) 6/70/308
JOHNSON, A.W., THE DYNAMICS OF FEDERALISM IN CANADA 3/68/18
JOHNSON, A. W., THE TREASURY BOARD OF CANADA AND THE MACHINERY OF GOVERNMENT OF CANADA 6/71/243
KAY, BARRY J., VOTING PATTERNS IN A NON-PARTISAN LEGISLATURE. A STUDY OF TORONTO CITY COUNCIL 6/71/224
KNIGHT, JONATHAN, RISKS OF WAR AND DETERRENCE LOGIC 3/73/22
KORNBERG, ALLAN, SMITH, JOEL, BROMLEY, DAVID, SOME DIFFERENCES IN THE POLITICAL SOCIALIZATION PATTERNS OF CANADIAN AND AMERICAN PARTY OFFICIALS* A PRELIMINARY REPORT, 3/69/64
KORNBERG, ALLAN, SMITH, JOEL, CLARKE, HAROLD, ATTRIBUTES OF ASCRIBED INFLUENCE IN LOCAL PARTY ORGANIZATIONS IN CANADA AND THE UNITED STATES 6/72/206
KWAVNICK, DAVID, PRESSURE GROUP DEMANDS AND THE STRUGGLE FOR ORGANIZATIONAL STATUS, THE CASE OF ORGANIZED LABOUR IN CANADA 3/70/56
KWAVNICK, DAVID, PRESSURE-GROUP DEMANDS AND ORGANIZATIONAL OBJECTIVES, THE CNTU THE LAPALME AFFAIR, AND NATIONAL BARGAINING UNITS 12/73/582
LAPONCE, J. A., CANADIAN PARTY LABELS - AN ESSAY IN SEMANTICS AND ANTHROPOLOGY 6/69/141

LAPONCE, J. A., DIE-- A DROITE OU A GAUCHE 6/70/257
LAPONCE, J. A., POST-DICTING ELECTORAL CLEAVAGES IN CANADIAN FEDERAL ELECTIONS, 1949-68. MATERIAL FOR A FOOTNOTE (NOTES) 6/72/270
LASKIN,RICHARD, BAIRD, RICHARD, FACTORS IN VOTER TURNOUT AND PARTY PREFERENCE IN A SASKATCHEWAN TOWN (RESEARCH NOTES) 9/70/450
LATOUCHE, DANIEL, ANTI-SEPARATISME ET MESSIANISME AU QUEBEC DEPUIS 1960 12/70/559
LAUNDY, PHILIP, COMMENT ON PROFESSOR C. E. S. FRANKS≠ ≠≠ THE DILEMMA OF THE STANDING COMMITTEES OF THE CANADIAN HOUSE OF COMMONS≠≠ (NOTES) 9/72/437
LAVAU, GEORGE, PARTIS ET SYSTEMES POLITIQUES - INTERACTIONS ET FONCTIONS 3/69/18
LAWSON, JAN, DUNN, JAMES, SCHNECK, RODNEY, A TEST OF THE UNI-DIMENSIONALITY OF POLITICAL SCALES THROUGH FACTOR ANALYSIS, A RESEARCH NOTE 12/73/664
LEBARON, BENTLEY, MARX ON HUMAN EMANCIPATION 12/71/559
LEBARON, BENTLEY, THREE COMPONENTS OF POLITICAL OBLIGATION 9/73/478
LEDUC, JR., LAWRENCE, PARTY DECISION-MAKING. SOME EMPIRICAL OBSERVATIONS ON THE LEADERSHIP SELECTION PROCESS 3/71/97
LEISS, WILLIAM, TECHNOLOGICAL RATIONALITY. NOTES ON ≠≠WORK AND FREEDOM IN MARCUSE AND MARX≠≠ 9/71/398
LEMIEUX, VINCENT, LES ELECTIONS FEDERALES DE 1957 A 1965 AU QUEBEC. UNE REINTERPRETATION 9/71/395
LEMIEUX, VINCENT, L≠ANALYSE HIERARCHIQUE DES RESULTATS ELECTORAUX 3/68/40
LEMIEUX, VINCENT, LE JEU DE LA COMMUNICATION POLITIQUE 9/70/359
LEMIEUX, VINCENT LA COMPOSITION DES PREFERENCES PARTISANES, 12/69/397
LEMIEUX, VINCENT, POUR UNE SCIENCE POLITIQUE DES PARTIS 12/72/485
LESLIE, PETER M., THE ROLE OF POLITICAL PARTIES IN PROMOTING THE INTERESTS OF ETHNIC MINORITIES, 12/69/419
LIJPHART, AREND, CULTURAL DIVERSITY AND THEORIES OF POLITICAL INTEGRATION 3/71/01
LIGHTBODY, JAMES, A NOTE ON THE THEORY OF NATIONALISM AS A FUNCTION OF ETHNIC DEMANDS 9/69/327
LIGHTBODY, JAMES, SWORDS AND PLOUGHSHARES. THE ELECTION PEROGATIVE IN CANADA (NOTES) 6/72/287
LONG, JOHN ANTHONY, MALDISTRIBUTION IN WESTERN PROVINCIAL LEGISLATURES* THE CASE OF ALBERTA, 9/69/345
LOON, RICK VAN, POLITICAL PARTICIPATION IN CANADA, THE 1965 ELECTION 9/70/376
LOVINK, J. A. A., IS CANADIAN POLITICS TOO COMPETITIVE 9/73/341
LOVINK, J. A. A., ON ANALYSING THE IMPACT OF THE ELECTORAL SYSTEM ON THE PARTY SYSTEM IN CANADA 12/70/497
MACPHERSON, C. B., THE CRITICISM OF CONCEPTS AND THE CONCEPT OF CRITICISM, (NOTES) 3/72/141
MACPHERSON, C.B., ELEGANT TOMBSTONES* A NOTE ON FRIEDMAN≠S FREEDOM 3/68/95
MACPHERSON, C. B., INTERPRETATION VS. CRITICISM - A REJOINDER TO PROFESSOR CROWLEY, 9/69/356
MANZER, RONALD, SELECTIVE INDUCEMENTS AND THE DEVELOPMENT OF PRESSURE GROUPS - THE CASE OF CANADIAN TEACHERS≠ ASSOCIATIONS, 3/69/103
MARZARI, FRANK, THE PROSPECTS FOR STRATEGIC STABILITY IN THE 1970≠S 12/71/541
MASSAM, BRYAN H., FORMS OF LOCAL GOVERNMENT IN THE MONTREAL AREA, 1911-71, A DISCRIMINANT APPROACH 6/73/243
MAY, RONALD J., DECISION MAKING AND STABILITY IN FEDERAL SYSTEMS 3/70/73
MCDONALD, VIRGINIA, A GUIDE TO THE INTERPRETATION OF LOCKE THE POLITICAL THEORIST 12/73/602
MCDONOUGH, JOHN, JACEK, HENRY, SHIMIZU, RONALD, SMITH, PATRICK, THE CONGRUENCE OF FEDERAL-PROVINCIAL CAMPAIGN ACTIVITY IN PARTY ORGANIZATIONS. THE INFLUENCE OF RECRUITMENT PATTERNS IN THREE HAMILTON RIDINGS 6/72/190
MCHALE, VINCENT E., RELIGION AND ELECTORAL POLITICS IN FRANCE - SOME RECENT OBSERVATIONS, 9/69/292
MCLELLAN, DAVID S., THE ≠≠OPERATIONAL CODE≠≠ APPROACH TO THE STUDY OF POLITICAL LEADERS. DEAN ACHESON≠S PHILOSOPHICAL AND INSTRUMENTAL BELIEFS 3/71/52
MCMENEMY, JOHN, WINN, CONRAD, POLITICAL ALIGNMENT IN A POLARIZED CITY, ELECTORAL CHANGE IN KITCHNER, ONTARIO 6/73/230
MEANS, GORDON, MICROFILMING TECHNIQUES FOR DATA GATHERING AND FIELD RESEARCH (TECHNICAL RESEARCH NOTE) 9/70/475
MEANS, INGUNN NORDERVAL, WOMEN IN LOCAL POLITICS. THE NORWEGIAN EXPERIENCE 9/72/365
MELLOS, KOULA, SANKOFF, DAVID, LA REGIONALISATION ELECTORALE ET L≠AMPLIFICATION DES PROPORTIONS 9/73/380
MELLOS, KOULA, QUANTITATIVE COMPARISON OF PARTY IDEOLOGY 12/70/540
MILLER, A. J., CONSENSUS AND CONFLICT IN FUNCTIONALISM. IMPLICATIONS FOR THE STUDY OF INTERNATIONAL INTEGRATION 6/71/178
MILLER, D. R., A SHAPLEY VALUE ANALYSIS OF THE PROPOSED CANADIAN CONSTITUTIONAL AMENDMENT SCHEME (NOTES) 3/73/140
MILNE R. S., THE OVERDEVELOPED STUDY OF POLITICAL DEVELOPMENT (RA) 12/72/560
MONGAR, THOMAS M., PERSONALITY AND DECISION-MAKING - JOHN F. KENNEDY IN FOUR CRISIS DECISIONS, 6/69/200
MORRIS, WILLIAM D., CASSTEVENS, THOMAS W., THE CUBE LAW AND THE DECOMPOSED SYSTEM 12/72/521
MORRISON, D. G., STEVENSON, H. M., CULTURAL PLURALISM, MODERNIZATION, AND CONFLICT. AN EMPIRICAL ANALYSIS OF SOURCES OF POLITICAL INSTABILITY IN AFRICAN NATIONS 3/72/82
MORRISON, K. L., THE BUSINESSMAN VOTER IN THUNDER BAY, THE CATALYST TO THE FEDERAL-PROVINCIAL VOTING SPLIT 6/73/219
MOUL, WILLIAM B., THE LEVEL OF ANALYSIS PROBLEM REVISITED 9/73/494
NICHOLLS, DAVID, POLITICS AND RELIGION IN HAITI 9/70/400
NOEL, S. J. R., CONSOCIATIONAL DEMOCRACY AND CANADIAN FEDERALISM 3/71/15
NOLAN, RICHARD L., SCHNECK, RODNEY E., SMALL BUSINESSMEN, BRANCH MANAGERS, AND THEIR RELATIVE SUSCEPTIBILITY TO RIGHT-WING EXTREMISM- AN EMPIRICAL TEST, 3/69/89
ORBAN, EDMOND, LA FIN DU BICAMERALISME AU QUEBEC 9/69/312
OUELLET, LIONEL, CONCEPTS ET TECHNIQUES D≠ANALYSES DES PHENOMENES ADMINISTRATIFS 9/68/310
PALDA, KRISTIAN S, DOES ADVERTISING INFLUENCE VOTES, AN ANALYSIS OF THE 1966 AND 1970 QUEBEC ELECTIONS (NOTES) 12/73/638
PAMMETT, JOHN H., THE DEVELOPMENT OF POLITICAL ORIENTATIONS IN CANADIAN SCHOOL CHILDREN 3/71/132
PAREL, ANTHONY, SYMBOLISM IN GANDHIAN POLITICS, 12/69/513

PASIS, HARVEY, THE INEQUALITY OF DISTRIBUTION IN THE CANADIAN PROVINCIAL ASSEMBLIES (NOTES) 9/72/433
PERLIN, GEORGE, PEPPIN, PATTI, VARIATIONS IN PARTY SUPPORT IN FEDERAL AND PROVINCIAL ELECTIONS. SOME HYPOTHESES 6/71/280
PINARD, MAURICE, THIRD PARTIES IN CANADA REVISITED 9/73/439
PITTS, RUTH ANN, PARLIAMENTARIANISM AMONG THE FRENCH WORKING CLASS 9/73/461
POCKLINGTON, THOMAS, PROTEST, RESISTANCE, AND POLITICAL OBLIGATION 3/70/1
PRESTUS, ROBERT, INTEREST GROUPS AND THE CANADIAN PARLIAMENT. ACTIVITIES, INTERACTION, LEGITIMACY, AND INFLUENCE 12/71/444
QUALTER, TERENCE H., SEATS AND VOTES - AN APPLICATION OF THE CUBE LAW TO THE CANADIAN ELECTORAL SYSTEM, 9/68/336
QUESNEL-OUELLET, LOUISE, REGIONALISATION ET CONSCIENCE POLITIQUE REGIONALE. LA COMMUNAUTE DE QUEBEC 6/71/191
QUESNEL-OUELLET, LOUISE, SITUATIONS ET ATTITUDES FACE AU CHANGEMENT DANS LES STRUCTURES MUNICIPALES 6/73/195
REGENSTREIF, PETER, NOTE ON THE ≠ ALTERNATION ≠ OF FRENCH AND ENGLISH LEADERS IN THE LIBERAL PARTY OF CANADA, 3/69/118
REGENSTRIEF, PETER, JENSON, JANE, SOME DIMENSIONS OF PARTISAN CHOICE IN QUEBEC, 1969 (RESEARCH NOTES) 6/70/308
REILLY, WAYNE G., POLITICAL ATTITUDES AMONG LAW STUDENTS IN QUEBEC 3/71/122
RESNICK, PHILIP, THE POLITICAL THEORY OF EXTRA-PARLIAMENTARISM 3/73/65
RICHERT, JEAN PIERRE, POLITICAL SOCIALIZATION IN QUEBEC, YOUNG PEOPLE≠S ATTITUDES TOWARD GOVERNMENT (NOTE) 6/73/303
ROSENBAUM, NAOMI, SUCCESS IN FOREIGN POLICY, THE BRITISH IN CYPRUS, 1878-1960 12/70/605
ROWAT, DONALD C., THE PROBLEMS OF GOVERNING FEDERAL CAPITALS 9/68/345
SANKOFF, DAVID, MELLOS KOULA, LA REGIONALISATION ELECTORALE ET L≠AMPLIFICATION DES PROPORTIONS 9/73/380
SANTOS, C. R., SOME COLLECTIVE CHARACTERISTICS OF THE DELEGATES TO THE 1968 LIBERAL PARTY LEADERSHIP CONVENTION (RESEARCH NOTES) 6/70/299
SANCTON, ANDREW, THE APPLICATION OF THE ≠≠SENATORIAL FLOOR≠≠ RULES TO THE LATEST REDISTRIBUTION OF THE HOUSE OF COMMONS, THE PECULIAR CASE OF NOVA SCOTIA 3/73/56
SANDBROOK, RICHARD, PATRONS, CLIENTS, AND FACTIONS. NEW DIMENSIONS OF CONFLICT ANALYSIS IN AFRICA 3/72/104
SCHINDELER, FRED,AND HOFFMAN ,DAVID, THEOLOGICAL AND POLITICAL CONSERVATISM, 12/68/429
SCHOOLMAN, MORTON, FURTHER REFLECTIONS ON WORK, ALIENATION, AND FREEDOM IN MARCUSE AND MARX 6/73/295
SCHNECK, DUNN, JAMES, LAWSON ,JAN, A TEST OF THE UNI-DIMENSIONALITY OF VARIOUS POLITICAL SCALES THROUGH FACTOR ANALYSIS, A RESEARCH NOTE 12/73/664
SCHNECK, RODNEY E., NOLAN, RICHARD L., SMALL BUSINESSMEN, BRANCH MANAGERS, AND THEIR RELATIVE SUSCEPTIBILITY TO RIGHT-WING EXTREMISM- AN EMPIRICAL TEST, 3/69/89
SEGAL, DAVID R., STATUS INCONSISTENCY AND PARTY CHOICE IN CANADA, AN ATTEMPT TO REPLICATE (RESEARCH NOTES) 9/70/471
SHEEHAN, BERNARD S., FEDERAL FUNDS AND UNIVERSITY RESEARCH (NOTES) 3/73/121
SHIMIZU, RONALD, JACEK, HENRY, MCDONOUGH, JOHN, SMITH, PATRICK, THE CONGRUENCE OF FEDERAL-PROVINCIAL CAMPAIGN ACTIVITY IN PARTY ORGANIZATIONS. THE INFLUENCE OF RECRUITMENT PATTERNS IN THREE HAMILTON RIDINGS 6/72/190
SIMMONS, HARVEY G., THE PLANNER≠S DILEMMA. REGIONAL REFORM IN FRANCE 9/71/381
SLOANE, JOHN H., POLITICAL INTEGRATION IN THE EUROPEAN COMMUNITY 12/68/442
SMILEY, DONALD V., THE CASE AGAINST THE CANADIAN CHARTER OF HUMAN RIGHTS 9/69/277
SMILEY,D.V., THE NATIONAL PARTY LEADERSHIP CONVENTION IN CANADA 12/68/379
SMITH, JOEL, KORNBERG, ALLAN, CLARKE, HAROLD, ATTRIBUTES OF ASCRIBED INFLUENCE IN LOCAL PARTY ORGANIZATIONS IN CANADA AND THE UNITED STATES 6/72/206
SMITH, JOEL, BROMLEY, DAVID, KORNBERG, ALLAN, SOME DIFFERENCES IN THE POLITICAL SOCIALIZATION PATTERNS OF CANADIAN AND AMERICAN PARTY OFFICIALS A PRELIMINARY REPORT 3/69/64
SMITH, PATRICK, JACEK, HENRY, MCDONOUGH, JOHN, SHIMIZU, RONALD, THE CONGRUENCE OF FEDERAL-PROVINCIAL CAMPAIGN ACTIVITY IN PARTY ORGANIZATIONS. THE INFLUENCE OF RECRUITMENT PATTERNS IN THREE HAMILTON RIDINGS 6/72/190
SOLASSE, BERNARD, LA DEMARCHE CRITIQUE D≠HERBERT MARCUSE OU UN NOUVEAU TYPE DE CRITIQUE SOCIALE, 12/69/448
SOLDATOS, P., LA PROBLEMATIQUE DE L≠INCOMPATABILITE DES FONCTIONS MINISTERIELLES ET DU MANDAT DE DEPUTE EN SYSTEME POLITIQUE DE TYPE PARLEMENTAIRE 6/72/251
SPROULE-JONES, MARK, HART, KENNETH D., A PUBLIC CHOICE MODEL OF POLITICAL PARTICIPATION 6/73/175
STARK FRANK, THE PRIME MINISTER AS SYMBOL, UNIFIER OR OPTIMIZER (NOTES) 9/73/514
STEIN, MICHAEL , LE CREDIT SOCIAL DANS LA PROVINCE DU QUEBEC, SOMMAIRE ET DEVELOPPEMENTS 12/73/563
STEVENSON, H. M., MORRISON, D. G., CULTURAL PLURALISM , MODERNIZATION, AND CONFLICT. AN EMPIRICAL ANALYSIS OF SOURCES OF POLITICAL INSTABILITY IN AFRICA NATIONS 3/72/82
STRICKLAND, D. A.,ON AMBIGUITY IN POLITICAL RHETORIC - DEFEAT OF THE RAT CONTROL BILL IN THE HOUSE OF REPRESENTATIVES, JULY 1967, 9/69/388
SZABLOWSKI, GEORGE, THE PRIME MINISTER AS SYMBOL, A REJOINDER (NOTES) 9/73/516
THORBURN, H. G., TOWARDS A MORE SIMPLIFIED PARTY SYSTEM IN FRANCE 6/68/204
TOURNON, JEAN, LE PLURALISME. UNE MISE A MORT RATEE 6/71/265
TRUMAN, TOM, A CRITIQUE OF SEYMOUR M. LIPSET≠S ARTICLE, ≠≠VALUE DIFFERENCES, ABSOLUTE OR RELATIVE. THE ENGLISH-SPEAKING DEMOCRACIES≠≠ 12/71/497
VACHET, ANDRE, DIVISION DE POUVOIR ET INTEGRATION SOCIAL- DE MONTESQUIEU A LA CRISE ACTUEL DU PARLEMENTARISME, 9/68/261
VACHET, ANDRE, LE PROBLEM DE LA NATION DANS LE MARXISME FRANCAIS 3/70/18
VAISON, ROBERT, A NOTE ON ≠≠PUBLIC POLICY≠≠ (NOTES) 12/73/661
VERNEY, DOUGLAS V., THE EDUCATION OF A POLITICAL SCIENTIST 9/70/345
WAND, BERNARD, C. B. MACPHERSON≠S CONCEPTUAL APPARATUS 12/71/526
WAND, BERNARD, THE CRITICISM OF CONCEPTS AND THE CONCEPT OF CRITICISM. A REJOINDER (NOTES) 6/72/301
WARD, NORMAN, MONEY AND POLITICS. THE COSTS OF DEMOCRACY IN CANADA 9/72/335
WEARING, JOSEPH, THE TRUDEAU PHENOMENON 9/69/369
WHITE, GRAHAM, ONE-PARTY DOMINANCE AND THIRD PARTIES, THE PINARD THEORY RECONSIDERED 9/73/399
WILSON, H. T., RATIONALITY AND DECISION IN ADMINISTRATIVE SCIENCE 6/73/271

WILSON, JOHN, POLITICS AND SOCIAL CLASS IN CANADA - THE CASE OF WATERLOO SOUTH 9/68/288
WILSON, JOHN, TOWARDS A SOCIETY OF FRIENDS, SOME REFLECTIONS ON THE MEANING OF DEMOCRATIC SOCIALISM 12/70/628
WILSON, JOHN, HOFFMAN, DAVID, THE LIBERAL PARTY IN CONTEMPORARY ONTARIO POLITICS 6/70/177
WINHAM, GILBERT, ATTITUDES ON POLLUTION AND GROWTH IN HAMILTON, OR ≠≠THERE≠S AN AWFUL LOT OF TALK THESE DAYS ABOUT ECOLOGY≠≠ 9/72/389
WINHAM, GILBERT R., CUNNINGHAM, ROBERT B., PARTY LEADER IMAGES IN THE 1968 FEDERAL ELECTION 3/70/37
WINHAM, GILBERT R., QUANTITATIVE METHODS IN FOREIGN POLICY ANALYSIS 6/69/187
WINN, CONRAD, MCMENEMY, JOHN, POLITICAL ALIGNMENT IN A POLARIZED CITY, ELECTORAL CLEAVAGES IN KITCHENER, ONTARIO 6/73/230
XYDIS, STEPHEN G., A NOTE ON NAOMI ROSENBAUM≠S ≠≠SUCCESS IN FOREIGN POLICY, THE BRITISH IN CYPRUS, 1878-1960≠≠ 9/71/404

KEYWORD LISTING

ACCULTURATION OU ASSIMILATION* TECHNIQUE D≠ANALYSE ET TENTATIVE DE MESURE CHEZ LES FRANCO-ONTARIENS 6/69/158
ACHESON≠S, DEAN, THE ≠≠OPERATIONAL CODE≠≠ APPROACH TO THE STUDY OF POLITICAL LEADERS, ACHESON≠S PHILOSOPHICAL AND INSTRUMENTAL BELIEFS 3/71/52
ADMINISTRATION PUBLIQUE AU QUEBEC, LES PARLEMENTAIRES ET, 6/68/164
ADMINISTRATIVE (HISTOIRE) DU QUEBEC ET THEORIE ADMINISTRATIVE 3/71/141
ADMINISTRATIVE SCIENCE, RATIONALITY AND DECISION IN 6/73/271
ADMINISTRATIVE (THEORIE), HISTOIRE ADMINISTRATIVE DU QUEBEC ET 3/71/141
ADVERTISING, DOES IT INFLUENCE VOTES, AN ANALYSIS OF THE 1966 AND 1970 QUEBEC ELECTIONS 12/73/638
AGENTS (NON-FAMILY) OF POLITICAL SOCIALIZATION, A REASSESSMENT OF CONVERSE AND DUPEUX 9/72/418
AFRICA, PATRONS, CLIENTS, AND FACTIONS, NEW DIMENSIONS OF CONFLICT ANALYSIS IN 3/72/104
AFRICAN NATIONS, AN EKPIRICAL ANALYSIS OF SOURCES OF POLITICAL INSTABILITY IN CULTURAL PLURALISM, MODERNIZATION, AND CONFLICT, 3/72/82
AFRICAN(SOUTH) POWER-ELITE. A SURVEY OF IDEOLOGICAL COMMITMENT 3/71/76
AFRO-ASIAN STATES, NONALIGNMENT OF* POLICY, PERCEPTION AND BEHAVIOUR, 3/69/1
ALBERTA (CASE OF)*MALDISTRIBUTION IN WESTERN PROVINCIAL LEGISLATURES, 9/69/345
ALIENATION AND HUMAN EMANCIPATION, ≠≠THE END OF HISTORY≠≠, A REAPPRAISAL OF MARX≠S VIEWS ON 9/71/367
ALIENATION, WORK, AND FREEDOM IN MARCUSE AND MARX, FURTHER REFLECTIONS 6/73/295
ALIGNMENT (POLITICAL) IN A POLARIZED CITY, ELECTORAL CLEAVAGES IN KITCHNER, ONTARIO 6/73/230
≠≠ALTERNATION≠≠ OF FRENCH AND ENGLISH LEADERS IN THE LIBERAL PARTY OF CANADA, NOTE ON, 3/69/118
AMBIGUITY IN POLITICAL RHETORIC* DEFEAT OF THE RAT CONTROL BILL IN THE HOUSE OF REPRESENTATIVES, JULY 1967, 9/69/338
AMENDMENT, OF THE PROPOSEWD CANADIAN CONSTITUTIONAL AMENDMENT, A SHAPLEY VALUE ANALYSIS OF 3/73/140
AMERICAN AND CANADIAN PARTY OFFICIALS* SOME DIFFERENCES IN THE POLITICAL SOCIALIZATION PATTERNS OF 3/69/64
ANALYSE COMPARATIVE ET INFORMATIQUE, 3/68/81
ANALYSE HIERARCHIQUE DES RESULTATS ELECTORAUX 3/68/40
ANALYSE STRATEGIQUE DU CHOIX D≠UN CANDIDAT DANS UNE CIRCONSCRIPTION URBAINE 6/73/254
ANALYSIS (CONFLICT), NEW DIMENSIONS OF IN AFRICA, PATRONS, CLIENTS, FACTIONS 3/72/104
ANALYSIS (DATA), ASSESSING REGIONAL EFFECTS IN 3/71/21
ANALYSIS (EMPIRICAL), OF SOURCES OF POLITICAL INSTABILITY IN AFRICAN NATIONS CULTURAL PLURALISM, MODERNIZATION, AND CONFLICT, 3/72/82
ANALYSIS (FOREIGN POLICY), QUANTITATIVE METHODS IN 6/69/178
ANALYSIS (THE LEVEL OF) PROBLEM REVISITED 12/73/494
ANALYSIS (SHAPLEY VALUE) OF THE PROPOSED CANADIAN CONSTITUTIONAL AMENDMENT SCHEME 3/73/140
ANTHROPOLOGY AND SEMANTICS (AN ESSAY IN), CANADIAN PARTY LABELS 6/69/141
ANTI-SEPARATISME ET MESSIANISME AU QUEBEC DEPUIS 1960 12/70/559
ASSEMBLIES, CANADIAN PROVINCIAL, INEQUALITY OF DISTRIBUTION IN 9/72/433
ASSIMILATION OU ACCULTURATION* TECHNIQUE D≠ANALYSE ET TENTATIVE DE MESURE CHEZ LES FRANCO-ONTARIENS 6/69/158
ASSOCIATIONS, THE CASE OF CANADIAN TEACHERS≠* SELECTIVE INDUCEMENTS AND THE DEVELOPMENT OF PRESSURE GROUPS, 3/69/103
ATTENDANCE PATTERNS EXHIBITED BY MEMBERS OF PARLIAMENT DURING THE 28TH PARLIAMENT (NOTES) 3/72/135
ATTITUDES (POLITICAL) AMONG LAW STUDENTS IN QUEBEC 3/71/122
ATTITUDES ON POLLUTION AND GROWTH IN HAMILTON, OR ≠≠THERE≠S AN AWFUL LOT OF TALK THESE DAYS ABOUT ECOLOGY 9/72/389
ATTITUDES ET SITUATIONS FACE AU CHANGEMENT DANS LES STRUCTURES MUNICIPALES 6/73/195
ATTITUDES, YOUNG PEOPLE≠S TOWARD GOVERNMENT, POLITICAL SOCIALIZATION IN QUEBEC 6/73/303
BARGAINING UNITS (NATIONAL), THE CNTU, THE LAPALME AFFAIR AND PRESSURE-GROUP DEMANDS AND ORGANIZATIONAL OBJECTIVES 12/73/582
BELIEFS (PHILOSOPHICAL AND INSTRUMENTAL) DEAN ACHESON≠S, THE ≠≠OPERATIONAL CODE≠ APPROACH TO THE STUDY OF POLITICAL LEADERS 3/71/52
BENTHAM,J., BENTHAM AND THE PUBLIC INTEREST 12/68/398
BICAMERALISME AU QUEBEC, LA FIN DU, 9/69/312
BIBLIOGRAPHIQUES (ELEMENTS)* LE QUEBEC CONTEMPORAIN, 3/68/107
BICOMMUNAUTAIRE (LA MINORITE EN ETAT), QUATRE ETUDES DE CAS 12/71/477
BILINGUISME ET LE BICULRALISME, LES ETUDES DE LA COMMISSION ROYALE D≠ENQUETE SUR 9/72/444
BICULTURALISME ET LE BILINGUISME, LES ETUDES DE LA COMMISSION ROYAL D≠ENQUETE SUR LE 6/72/304

BILINGUISME ET LE BICULTURALISME, LES ETUDES DE LA COMMISSION ROYALE D≠ENQUETE SUR LE 6/72/304
BILINGUISME ET LE BECULTURALISME, NOTE BIBLIOGRAPHIQUE 9/71/406
BIOLOGY (THE NEW), AND THE CAUSES OF WAR, 12/69/434
BOARD (TREASURY) OF CANADA AND THE MACHINERY OF GOVERNMENT OF THE 1970≠S 9/71/346
BRITISH IN CYPRUS, 1878-1960, SUCCESS IN FOREIGN POLICY 12/70/605
BROADVIEW (THE VOTER IN), SOCIAL POSITION AND INTEREST RECOGNITION, OR ARE VOTERS FOOLS 3/73/131
BUDGETAIRES, LA RATIONALISATION DES CHOIX, LES CAS QUEBECOIS ET CANADIEN 9/72/348
BUSINESSMAN VOTER IN THUNDER BAY, THE CATALYST TO THE FEDERAL-PROVINCIAL VOTING SPLIT 6/73/219
BUSINESSMEN (SMALL), BRANCH MANAGERS, AND THEIR RELATIVE SUSCEPTIBILITY TO RIGHT-WING EXTREMISM* AN EMPIRICAL TEST 3/69/89
BYNG-KING DISPUTE (ANEW LOOK AT), PERSONALITY AND POLITICS 3/73/37
CAMPAIGN ACTIVITY IN PARTY ORGANIZATIONS,(THE CONGRUENCE OF FEDERAL-PROVOVINCIAL THE INFLUENCE OF RECRUITMENT PATTERNS IN THREE HAMILTON RIDINGS 6/72/190
CANADA, ATTRIBUTES OF ASCRIBED INFLUENCE IN LOCAL PARTY ORGANIZATIONS, THE UNITED STATES 6/72/206
CANADA, THE COSTS OF DEMOCRACY IN, MONEY AND POLITICS 9/72/335
CANADA, NOTE ON THE ≠≠ALTERNATION≠≠ OF FRENCH AND ENGLISH LEADERS IN THE LIBERAL PARTY 3/69/118
CANADA, ON ANALYSING THE IMPACT OF THE ELECTORAL SYSTEM ON THE PARTY SYSTEM IN 12/70/497
CANADA, ON ANALYSING THE IMPACT OF THE ELECTORAL SYSTEM ON THE PARTY SYSTEM IN A REPLY TO J. A. A. LOVINK 12/70/517
CANADA (POLITICAL PARTICIPATION IN), THE 1965 ELECTION 9/70/376
CANADA, ONE TOO MANY REPORTS ON POVERTY IN CANADA 9/72/439
CANADA, THE DYNAMICS OF FEDERALISM IN CANADA 3/68/18
CANADA, THE ELECTORAL SYSTEM AND THE PARTY SYSTEM, 1921-1965, 3/68/55
CANADA NATIONAL PARTY LEADERSHIP CONVENTION 12/68/379
CANADA (IN), POLITICS AND SOCIAL CLASS* THE CASE OF WATERLOO SOUTH 9/68/288
CANADA, RECENT CHANGES IN THE PHILOSOPHY OF POLICY-MAKING IN 6/71/243
CANADA, STATUS INCONSISTENCY AND PARTY CHOICE IN, AN ATTEMPT TO REPLICATE 9/70/471
CANADA, SWORDS AND PLOUGHSHARES, THE ELECTION PREROGATIVE IN 6/72/287
CANADA, THIRD PARTIES IN CANADA REVISITED 12/73/439
CANADA (TREASURY BOARD) AND THE MACHINERY OF GOVERNMENT OF THE 1970≠S 9/71/346
CANADIAN AND AMERICAN PARTY OFFICIALS* SOME DIFFERENCES IN THE POLITICAL SOCIALIZATION PATTERNS OF, 3/69/64
CANADIAN CHARTER OF HUMAN RIGHTS, THE CASE AGAINST, 9/69/277
CANADIAN COMMUNITIES (VOTING IN)/ A TAXONOMY OF REFERENDUM ISSUES 12/68/462
CANADIAN CONSTITUTIONAL AMENDMENT SCHEME, A SHAPLEY VALUE ANALYSIS OF 3/73/140
CANADIAN DEFENCE POLICY, THE CASE OF , PERCEPTIONS OF PARLIAMENTARY SURVEILLANCE THE EXECUTIVE 6/72/234
CANADIAN FEDERAL ELECTIONS, 1949-68, POST-DICTING ELECTORAL CLEAVAGES IN 6/72/270
CANADIAN FEDERAL ELECTIONS, THE IMPACT OF THE LOCAL CANDIDATE 6/71/287
CANADIAN FEDERALISM AND CONSOCIATIONAL DEMOCRACY 3/71/15
CANADIAN HOUSE OF COMMONS, THE DILEMMA OF THE STANDING COMMITTEES 12/71/461
CANADIAN HOUSE OF COMMONS, THE DILEMMA OF THE STANDING COMMITTEES, COMMENT ON CES. FRANKS 9/72/437
CANADIAN HOUSE OF COMMONS, 1867-1968, TURNOVER AND TENURE IN 12/70/655
CANADIAN PARLIAMENT, INTEREST GROUPS AND. ACTIVITIES, INTERACTION, LEGITIMACY AND INFLUENCE 12/71/444
CANADIAN PARTY LABELS* AN ESSAY IN SEMANTICS AND ANTHROPOLOGY 6/69/141
CANADIAN POLITICS, IS IT TOO COMPETITIVE 12/73/341
CANADIAN PROVINCIAL ASSEMBLIES, THE INEQUALITY OF DISTRIBUTION IN 9/72/433
CANADIAN PROVINCIAL POLITICS, THIRD PARTIES IN 12/73/422
CANADIAN SCHOOL CHILDREN, THE DEVELOPMENT OF POLITICAL IRIENTATIONS IN 3/71/132
CANADIAN TEACHERS≠ ASSOCIATIONS* SELECTIVE INDUCEMENTS AND THE DEVELOPMENT OF PRESSURE GROUPS, 3/69/103
CANADIAN UNIVERSITY STUDENTS (ENGLISH-SPEAKING), SUPPORT FOR CIVIL LIBERTIES AMONG 9/70/433
CANADIAN VOTING PATTERNS, THE MEASUREMENT OF REGIONALISM IN 3/72/55
CANADIEN ET QUEBECOIS (LES CAS) LA RATIONALISATION DES CHOIX BUDGETAIRES 9/72/348
CANDIDATE (THE INPACT OF THE LOCAL) IN CANADIAN FEDERAL ELECTIONS 6/71/287
CAPITALISM AND FREEDOM (FRIEDMAN≠S) A COMMENT ON PROFESSOR MACPHERSON≠S INTERPRETATION OF 6/69/256
CAPITALS (FEDERAL), THE PROBLEMS OF GOVERNING 9/68/345
CASE OF CANADIAN DEFENCE POLICY, PERCEPTIONS OF PARLIAMENTARY SURVEILLANCE OF
CATALYST TO THE FEDERAL-PROVINCIAL VOTING SPLIT, THE BUSINESSMAN VOTER IN THUNDER BAY 6/73/219
CAUSES OF WAR, THE ≠≠NEW BIOLOGY≠≠ AND, 12/69/434
CHANGEMENT DANS LES STRUCTURES MUNICIPALES, SITUATIONS ET ATTITUDES FACE AU 6/73/195
CHARACTERISTICS (COLLECTIVE) OF THE DELEGATES TO THE 1968 LIBERAL PARTY LEADERSHIP CONVENTION 6/70/299
CHI≠S CRITIQUE, A REPLY TO 6/72/297
CHILDREN (CANADIAN SCHOOL), THE DEVELOPMENT OF POLITICAL ORIENTATIONS IN 3/71/132
CHILDREN AND THE POLITICAL COMMUNITY* A COMPARISON ACROSS RACIAL LINES, 12/69/471
CHOICE (PARTY) IN CANADA, STATUS INCONSISTENCY AND, AN ATTEMPT TO REPLICATE 9/70/471
CHOICE (PUBLIC) A PUBLIC-CHOICE MODEL OF POLITICAL PARTICIPATION 6/73/175
CHOIX D≠UN CANDIDAT DANS UNE CIRCONSCRIPTION URBAINE, ANALYSE STRATEGIQUE DU 6/73/254
CIRCONSCRIPTION URBAINE, ANALYSE STRATEGIQUE DU CHOIX D≠UN CANDIDAT DANS 6/73/254
CITE LIBRE, L≠IDEOLOGIE POLITIQUE DE LA REVUE CITE LIBRE 12/68/414
CITY COUNCIL (TORONTO). VOTING PATTERNS IN A NON-PARTISAN LEGISLATURE 6/71/224
CITY (POLITICAL ALIGNMENT IN), ELECTORAL CLEAVAGES IN KITCHNER, ONTARIO 6/73/230
CIVIC POLITICS (BARRIERS TO ENTRY OF PARTIES INTO TORONTO≠S). TOWARDS A THEORY OF PARTY PENETRATION 6/71/206
CIVIL LIBERTIES, SUPPORT FOR AMONG ENGLISH-SPEAKING CANADIAN UNIVERSITY STUDENTS AMONG 9/70/433
CLASS (FRENCH WORKING), PARLIAMENTARIANISM AMONG 12/73/461
CLASS (THE IMPORTANCE OF), IN THE POLITICAL THEORY OF JOHN STUART MILL 9/68/270
CLASS (SOCIAL) POLITICS AND, IN CANADA* THE CASE OF WATERLOO SOUTH 9/68/288

CLEAVAGES (ELECTORAL) IN KITCHNER, ONTARIO, POLITICAL ALIGNMENT IN A POLARIZED CITY 6/73/230
CLEAVAGES (POST-DICTING ELECTORAL), IN CANADIAN FEDERAL ELECTIONS, 1949-68, MATERIALS FOR A FOOTNOTE 6/72/270
CLIENTS, PATRONS, AND FACTIONS, NEW DIMENSIONS OF CONFLICT ANALYSIS IN AFRICA 3/72/104
CNTU, THE LAPALME AFFAIR, AND NATIONAL BARGAINING UNITS, PRESSURE-GROUP DEMANDS AND ORGANIZATIONAL OBJECTIVES 12/73/582
COALITION (GREAT), PERCEPTIONS OF IN WEST GERMANY, 1966-1969 3/72/28
COGNITIVE AND MOTIVATIONAL SOURCES OF VOTER SUSCEPTIBILITY TO INFLUENCE 12/73/624
COLLECTIVE (DECISION), LES ELECTIONS COMME PHENOMENE DE, LES ELECTIONS FEDERALES 1957 A 1965 AU QUEBEC 12/70/522
COMMISSION ROYALE D≠ENQUETE SUR LE BILINGUISME ET LE BICULTURALISME, LES ETUDES DE LA 6/72/304
COMMISSION ROYALE D≠ENQUETE SUR LE BILINGUISME ET LE BICULTURALISME, LES ETUDES DE LA 9/72/444
COMMITTEES(STANDING) OF THE CANADIAN HOUSE OF COMMONS, THE DILEMMA OF, COMMENT ON CES. FRANKS 9/72/437
COMMITTEES (STANDING) (THE DILEMMA OF) OF THE CANADIAN HOUSE OF COMMONS 12/71/461
COMMITMENT (IDEOLOGICAL), A SURVEY OF. THE SOUTH AFRICAN POWER-ELITE 3/71/76
COMMITTEE (JUDICIAL) AND ITS CRITICS 9/71/301
COMMONS (HOUSE OF) THE APPLICATION OF THE ≠≠SENATORIAL FLOOR≠≠ RULES TO THE LATEST REDISTRIBUTION OF THE HOUSE, THE PECULIAR CASE OF NOVA SCOTIA 3/73/56
COMMONS (CANADIAN HOUSE OF), THE DILEMMA OF THE STANDING COMMITTEES 12/71/461
COMMUNAUTE URBAINE DE QUEBEC. REGIONALISATION ET CONSCIENCE POLITIQUE REGIONALE QUEBEC 6/71/191
COMMUNICATION POLITIQUE, LE JEU DE LA 9/70/359
COMMUNIST PARTY≠S (SOVIET) LEADERSHIP RECRUITMENT SYSTEM* NOMENKLATURA, 12/69/493
COMMUNITIES (CANADIAN) VOTING IN CAN. COM./ A TAXONOMY OF REFERENDUM ISSUES, 12/68/462
COMMUNITY (EUROPEAN) POLITICAL INTEGRATION IN, 12/68/442
COMMUNITY (POLITICAL), CHILDREN AND* A COMPARISON ACROSS RACIAL LINES, 12/69/471
COMPARATIVE (ANALYSE) ET INFORMATIQUE 3/68/81
COMPARATIVE POLITICS (SIMULATION IN TEACHING), PLAYING FRENCH GAMES 9/70/462
COMPARISON (QUANTITATIVE) OF PARTY IDEOLOGY 12/70/540
COMPETITIVE, IS CANADIAN POLITICS TOO COMPETITIVE 12/73/341
COMPONENTS (THREE) OF POLITICAL OBLIGATION 12/73/478
CONCEPTS (CRITICISM OF) AND THE CONCEPT OF CRITICISM 3/72/141
CONCEPTS, THE CRITICISM OF AND THE CONCEPT OF CRITICISM 6/72/301
CONCEPT OF POLITICAL LEADERSHIP 3/68/2
CONCEPTS ET TECHNIQUES D≠ANALYSES DES PHENOMENES ADMINISTRATIFS 9/68/310
CONFLICT ANALYSIS (NEW DIMENSIONS OF IN AFRICA), PATRONS, CLIENTS, FACTIONS 3/72/104
CONFLICT (AND CONSENSUS) IN FUNCTIONALISM. IMPLICATIONS FOR THE STUDY OF INTERNATIONAL INTEGRATION 6/71/178
CONFLICT, CULTURAL PLURALISM, AND MODERNIZATION, AN EMPIRICAL ANALYSIS OF SOURCES OF POLITICAL INSTABILITY IN AFRICAN NATIONS 3/72/82
CONFLICT (FEDERAL-PROVINCIAL), SOME FACTORS AFFECTING THE RESOLUTION OF A 6/69/173
CONSCIENCE POLITIQUE REGIONALE (REGIONALISATION ET). LA COMMUNAUTE URBAINE DE QUEBEC 6/71/191
CONSENSUS AND CONFLICT IN FUNCTIONALISM. IMPLICATIONS FOR THE STUDY OF INTERNATIONAL INTEGRATION 6/71/178
CONSERVATISM, THEOLOGICAL AND POLITICAL, 12/68/429
CONSOCIATIONAL DEMOCRACY AND CANADIAN FEDERALISM 3/71/15
CONSTITUTIONAL AMENDMENT SCHEME (CANADIAN), A SHAPLEY VALUE ANALYSIS OF 3/73/140
CONTESTATION, LE LABRADOR A L≠HEURE DE LA CONTESTATION 12/73/518
CONVENTION (THE 1968 LIBERAL PARTY LEADERSHIP), SOME COLLECTIVE CHARACTERISTICS OF THE DELEGATES TO (RESEARCH NOTES) 6/70/299
CONVENTION NATIONAL PARTY LEADERSHIP CONVENTION CANADA 12/68/379
CONVERSE AND DUPEUX, A REASSESSMENT OF, NON-FAMILY AGENTS OF POLITICAL DUPEUX 9/72/418
COSTS OF DEMOCRACY IN CANADA, MONEY AND POLITICS 9/72/335
COUNCIL (TORONTO CITY), VOTING PATTERNS IN A NON-PARTISAN LEGISLATURE 6/71/224
COURRIERISTES PARLEMENTAIRES AU QUEBEC, ET L≠INFORMATION GOUVERNEMENTALE 3/71/26
CREDIT SOCIAL DANS LA PROVINCE DU QUEBEC, SOMMAIRE ET DEVELOPPMENTS 12/73/563
CRISE (A LA), ACTUEL DU PARLEMENTARISME, DIVISION DE POUVOIR ET INTEGRATION SOCIAL* DE MONTESQUIEU 9/68/261
CRISIS DECISIONS (FOUR), PERSONALITY AND DECISION-MAKING* JOHN F. KENNEDY IN 6/69/200
CRITICISM OF CONCEPTS AND THE CONCEPT OF CRITICISM 3/72/141
CRITICS, THE JUDICIAL COMMITTEE AND ITS 9/71/301
CRITIQUE (LA DEMARCHE) D≠HERBERT MARCUSE OU UN NOUVEAU TYPE DE CRITIQUE SOCIALE, 12/69/448
CRITIQUE, A REPLY TO PROFESSOR CHI≠S CRITIQUE 6/72/297
CRITIQUE SOCIALE, LA DEMARCHE D≠HERBERT MARCUSE OU UN NOUVEAU TYPE DE, 12/69/448
CUBE LAW (AN APPLICATION OF THE), TO THE CANADIAN ELECTORAL SYSTEM, SEATS AND VOTES 9/68/336
CULTURAL DIVERSITY AND THEORIES OF POLITICAL INTEGRATION 3/71/01
CULTURAL PLURALISM, MODERNIZATION, AND CONFLICT, AN EMPIRICAL ANALYSIS OF SOURCES OF POLITICAL INSTABILITY IN AFRICAN NATIONS 3/72/82
CYPRUS (THE BRITISH IN), 1878-1960, SUCCESS IN FOREIGN POLICY 12/70/605
DATA ANALYSIS, ASSESSING REGIONAL EFFECTS IN 3/71/21
DATA GATHERING AND FIELD RESEARCH, MICROFILMING TECHNIQUES FOR 9/70/475
DECISION COLLECTIVE, LES ELECTIONS COMMME PHENOMENE DE, LES ELECTIONS FEDERALES 1957 A 1965 AU QUEBEC 12/70/522
DECISION-MAKING (PARTY). SOME EMPIRICAL OBSERVATIONS ON THE LEADERSHIP SELECTION PROCESS 3/71/97
DECISION-MAKING AND STABILITY IN FEDERAL SYSTEMS 3/70/73
DECISION-MAKING (PERSONALITY AND)* JOHN F. KENNEDY IN FOUR CRISIS DECISIONS 6/69/200
DECISION POLITIQUE EN REGIME DEMOCRATIQUE, LES FACTEURS DE LA, 6/68/147
DECISIONS (FOUR CRISIS), PERSONALITY AND DECISION-MAKING* JOHN F. KENNEDY IN 6/69/200
DECISION AND RATIONALITY IN ADMINISTRATIVE SCIENCE 6/73/271
DEFENCE POLICY (CASE OF CANADIAN), PERCEPTIONS OF PARLIAMENTARY SURVEILLANCE OF THE EXECUTIVE 6/72/234

DELEGATES TO THE 1968 LIBEERAL PARTY LEADERSHIP CONVENTION, SOME COLLECTIVE CHARACTERISTICS OF (RESEARCH NOTES) 6/70/299
DEMANDS (ETHNIC), A NOTE ON THE THEORY OF NATIONALISM AS A FUNCTION ,9/69/327
FEMANDS (PRESSURE-GROUP) AND ORGANIZATIONAL OBJECTIVES, THE CNTU, THE LAPALME AFFAIR, AND NATIONAL BARGAINING UNITS 12/73/582
DEMANDS (PRESSURE GROUP), AND THE STRUGGLE FOR ORGANIZATIONAL STATUS, THE CASE OF ORGANIZED LABOUR IN CANADA 3/70/56
DEMARCHE CRITIQUE D≠HERBERT MARCUSE OU UN NOUVEAU TYPE DE CRITIQUE SOCIALE 12/69/448
DEMOCRACIES (ENGLISH-SPEAKING)≠≠, CRITIQUE OF SEYMOUR LIPSET≠S ARTICLE, ≠≠VALUE DIFFERENCES, ABSOLUTE OR RELATIVE. THE...≠≠ 12/71/497
DEMOCRACIES (WESTERN), PARTY SYSTEMS AND PATTERNS OF GOVERNMENT IN, 6/68/180
DEMOCRACY IN CANADA, THE COSTS OF MONEY AND POLITICS 9/72/335
DEMOCRACY (CONSOCIATIONAL) AND CANADIAN FEDERALISM 3/71/15
DEMOCRATIC SOCIALISM (SOME REFLECTIONS ON THE MEANING OF), TOWARDS A SOCIETY OF FRIENDS 12/70/628
DEMOCRATIC THEORY AND PUBLIC POLICY 9/70/415
DEMOCRATIQUE (REGIME), LES FACTEURS DE LA DECISION POLITIQUE EN, 6/68/147
DEMOCRATIQUES (LA PARTICIPATION DES FORCES) A L≠EXPERIENCE FRANCAISE DE PLANIFICATION REGIONALE 3/72/1
DEPUTE, LA PROBLEMATIQUE DE L≠INCOMPATABILITE DES FONCTIONS MINISTERIELLES ET DU MANDAT DE, EN SYSTEME POLITIQUE ETATIQUE DE TYPE PARLEMENTAIRE 6/72/251
DETERRENCE LOGIC, AND RISKS OF WAR 3/73/22
DIEU-- A DROITE OU A GAUCHE 6/70/257
DILEMMA OF THE STANDING COMMITTEES OF THE CANADIAN HOUSE OF COMMONS 12/71/461
DIMENSIONS (SOME) OF PARTISAN CHOICE IN QUEBEC, 1969 (RESEARCH NOTES) 6/70/308
DISPUTE (A NEW LOOK AT THE KING-BYNG DISPUTE PERSONALITY AND POLITICS 3/73/37
DISSENT (POLITICAL) AND POLITICAL OBLIGATION 6/69/245
DISTRIBUTION, THE INEQUALITY OF, IN THE CANADIAN PROVINCIAL ASSEMBLIES 9/72/433
DIVERSITY (CULTURAL) AND THEORIES OF POLITICAL INTEGRATION 3/71/01
DIVISION DE POUVOIR ET INTEGRATION SOCIAL*DE MONTESQUIEU A LA CRISE ACTUEL DU PARLEMENTARISME 9/68/261
DOMINANCE (ONE-PARTY) AND THIRD PARTIES, THE PINARD THEORY RECONSIDERED12/73/399
DROITE (A) OU A GAUCHE--DIEU 6/70/257
DUPEUX AND CONVERSE, A REASSESSMENT OF, NON-FAMILY AGENTS OF POLITICAL SOCIALIZATION 9/72/418
DYNAMICS OF FEDERALISM IN CANADA 3/68/18
ECOLOGY, LOT OF TALK ABOUT, ATTITUDES ON POLLUTION AND GROWTH IN HAMILTON 9/72/389
EDUCATION OF A POLITICAL SCIENTIST 9/70/345
ELECTION (1965), POLITICAL PARTICIPATION IN CANADA 9/70/376
ELECTION PREROGATIVE IN CANADA, SWORDS AND PLOUGHSHARES 6/72/287
ELECTIONS COMME PHENOMENE DE DECISION COLLECTIVE, LES ELECTIONS FEDERALES DE 1957 A 1965 AU QUEBEC 12/70/522
ELECTION (1968 FEDERAL), PARTY LEADER IMAGES IN 3/70/37
ELECTIONS (CANADIAN FEDERAL), THE IMPACT OF THE LOCAL CANDIDATE IN 6/71/287
ELECTIONS FEDERALES DE 1957 A 1965 AU QUEBEC, UNE REINTERPRETATION 9/71/395
ELECTIONS FEDERALES DE 1957 A 1965 AU QUEBEC, LES ELECTIONS COMME PHENOMENE DE DECISION COLLECTIVE 12/70/522
ELECTIONS (QUEBEC) 1966 AND 1970, DOES ADVERTISING INFLUENCE VOTES 12/73/638
ELECTIONS, VARIATIONS IN PARTY SUPPORT IN FEDERAL AND PROVINCIAL, SOME HYPOTHESES 6/71/280
ELECTORAL CLEAVAGES IN KITCHNER, ONTARIO, POLITICAL ALIGNMENT IN A POLARIZED CITY 6/73/230
ELECTORAL CLEAVAGES (POST-DICTING) IN CANADIAN FEDERAL ELECTIONS, 1949-68, MATERIAL FOR A FOOTNOTE 6/72/270
ELECTORAL POLITICS IN FRANCE, AND RELIGION* SOME RECENT OBSERVATIONS,9/69/292
ELECTORAL SYSTEM AND THE PARTY SYSTEM IN CANADA, 1921-1965 3/68/55
ELECTORAL SYSTEM (ON ANALYSING THE IMPACT OF) ON THE PARTY SYSTEM IN CANADA 12/70/497
ELECTORAL SYSTEM (ON ANALYSING THE IMPACT OF) ON THE PARTY SYSTEM IN CANADA A REPLY TO J. A. A. LOVINK 12/70/517
ELECTORALE (LA REGIONALISATION) ET L≠AMPLIFICATION DES PROPORTIONS 12/73/380
ELECTORAUX(DES RESULTATS),L≠ANALYSE HIERARCHIQUE DES 3/68/40
EMANCIPATION (HUMAN) AND ALIENATION, ≠≠THE END OF HISTORY≠≠. A REAPPRAISAL OF MARX≠S VIEWS ON 9/71/367
EMANCIPATION (HUMAN), MARX ON 12/71/559
EMPIRICAL ANALYSIS OF SOURCES OF POLITICAL INSTABILITY IN AFRICAN NATIONS, CULTURAL PLURALISM, MODERNIZATION, AND CONFLICT, 3/72/82
EMPIRICAL OBSERVATIONS ON THE LEADERSHIP SELECTION PROCESS. PARTY DECISION-MAKING 3/71/97
EMPIRES, GRANDS VILLES , ET NATIONS, UNE CARTE POLITIQUE DE LA NOUVELLE SOCIETE INDUSTRIELLE AVANCEE 3/72/120
ENGLISH AND FRENCH LEADERS IN THE LIBERAL PARTY OF CANADA, NOTE ON THE ≠≠ALTERNATION≠≠ OF, 3/69/118
ENGLISH-SPEAKING CANADIAN UNIVERSITY STUDENTS, SUPPORT FOR CIVIL LIBERTIES AMONG 9/70/433
ETHNIC DEMANDS, A NOTE ON THE THEORY OF NATIONALISM AS A FUNCTION OF9/69/327
ETHNIC MINORITIES, THE ROLE OF POLITICAL PARTIES IN PROMOTING THE INTERESTS OF, 12/69/419
EXTREMISM (RIGHT-WING)* SMALL BUSINESSMEN, BRANCH MANAGERS, AND THEIR RELATIVE SUSCEPTIBILITY TO, 3/69/89
EUROPEAN COMMUNITY, POLITICAL INTEGRATION IN, 12/68/442
ENGLISH-SPEAKING DEMOCRACIES, CRITIQUE OF SEYMOUR LIPSET≠S ARTICLE, ≠≠VALUE DIFFERENCES, ABSOLUTE OR RELATIVE....≠≠ 12/71/497
ETAT BICOMMUNAUTAIRE (LA MINORITE EN), QUATRE ETUDES DE CAS 12/71/477
EXECUTIVE, PERCEPTIONS OF PARLIAMENTARY SURVEILLANCE OF, THE CASE OF CANADIAN DEFENCE POLICY 6/72/206
EXTRA-PARLIAMENTARISM, THE POLITICAL THEORY OF 3/73/65
FACTEURS DE LA DECISION POLITIQUE EN REGIME DEMOCRATIQUE, 6/68/147
FACTIONS, PATRONS, AND CLIENTS, NEW DIMENSIONS OF CONFLICT ANALYSIS IN AFRICA 3/72/104
FACTOR ANALYSIS, A TEST OF THE UNI-DIMENSIONALITY OF VARIOUS POLITICAL SCALES 12/73/664
FACTORS (SOME), AFFECTING THE RESOLUTION OF A FEDERAL-PROVINCIAL CONFLICT 6/69/173

FEDERAL ELECTION (1968), PARTY LEADER IMAGES IN 3/70/37
FEDERAL FUNDS AND UNIVERSITY RESEARCH 3/73/121
FEDERAL-PROVINCIAL VOTING SPLIT (CATALYST TO), THE BUSINESSMAN VOTER IN THUNDER
BAY 6/73/219
FEDERAL SYSTEMS, DECISION MAKING AND STABILITY IN 3/70/73
FEDERALES (ELECTIONS) DE 1957 A 1965 AU QUEBEC, LES ELECTIONS COMME PHENOMENE
DE DECISION COLLECTIVE 12/70/522
FEDERAL AND PROVINCIAL ELECTIONS (VARIATIONS IN PARTY SUPPORT), SOME HYPOTHESES
6/71/280
FEDERAL ELECTIONS (CANADA), POST-DICTING ELECTORAL CLEAV AGES IN,1949-686/72/270
FEDERAL ELECTIONS (CANADIAN), THE IMPACT OF THE LOCAL CANDIDATE IN 6/71/287
FEDERAL-PROVINCIAL CAMPAIGN ACTVITY IN PARTY ORGANIZATIONS (THE CONGRUENCE OF)
THE INFLUENCE OF RECRUITMENT PATTERNS IN THREE HAMILTON RIDINGS 6/72/190
FEDERALES (LES ELECTIONS) DE 1957 A 1965 AU QUEBEC. UNE REINTERPRETATION9/71/395
FEDERALISM (CANADIAN) AND CONSOCIATIONAL DEMOCRACY 3/71/15
FEDERALISM IN CANADA, THE DYNAMICS OF 3/68/18
FIELD RESEARCH AND DATA GATHERING, MICROFILMING TECHNIQUES FOR 9/70/475
FISHERMEN≠S VOTE IN NEWFOUNDLAND 12/70/579
FOOLS, SOCIAL POSITION AND INTEREST RECOGNITION, THE VOTER IN BROADVIEW OR ARE
VOTERS FOOLS 3/73/131
≠FONCTIONNALISMES≠ (STRUCTURE DES) EN SCIENCE POLITIQUE 6/70/205
FOREIGN POLICY ANALYSIS, QUANTITATIVE METHODS IN 6/69/178
FOREIGN POLICY (SUCCESS IN), THE BRITISH IN CYPRUS, 1878-1960 12/70/605
FRANCAISE (MARXISME), (LE PROBLEM DE LA NATION DANS LE) 3/70/18
FRANCAISE LA PARTICIPATION DES FORCES DEMOCRATIQUES A L≠EXPERIENCE)
DE PLANIFICATION REGIONALE 3/72/1
FRANCE, TOWARDS A MORE SIMPLIFIED PARTY SYSTEM IN, 6/68/204
FRANCE (REGIONAL REFORM IN), THE PLANNER≠S DILEMMA 9/71/381
FRANCE, RELIGION AND ELECTORAL POLITICS IN*SOME RECENT OBSERVATIONS, 9/69/292
FRANCO-ONTARIENS (CHEZ LES), ACCULTURATION OU ASSIMILATION* TECHNIQUE D≠ANALYSE
ET TENTATIVE DE MESURE 6/69/158
FRANKS,CES., COMMENT ON≠≠THE DILEMMA OF THE STANDIDNG COMMITTEES OF THE
CANADIAN HOUSE OF COMMONS≠≠ 9/72/437
FREEDOM AND WORK IN MARCUSE AND MARX 6/70/241
FREEDOM (FRIEDMAN≠S), A NOTE ON, (ELEGANT TOMBSTONES), 3/68/95
FREEDOM (FRIEDMAN≠S CAPITALISM AND), A COMMENT ON PROFESSOR MACPHERSON≠S
INTERPRETATION OF 6/69/256
FREEDOM , WORK, AND ALIENATION IN MARCUSE AND MARX, FURTHER REFLECTIONS 6/73/295
FREEDOM (WORK AND) IN MARCUSE AND MARX≠≠ (NOTES ON), TECHNOLOGICAL RATIONALITY
9/71/398
FRENCH AND ENGLISH LEADERS IN THE LIBERAL PARTY OF CANADA, NOTE ON THE
≠≠ALTERNATION≠≠ OF, 3/69/118
FRENCH GAMES, SIMULATION IN TEACHING COMPARATIVE POLITICS 9/70/462
FRENCH WORKING CLASS, PARLIAMENTARIANISM AMONG 12/73/461
FRIEDMAN≠S CAPITALISM AND FREEDOM, A COMMENT ON PROFESSOR MACPHERSON≠S
INTERPRETATION OF 6/69/256
FRIEDMAN≠S FREEDOM, A NOTE ON* (ELEGANT TOMBSTONES), 3/68/95
FRIENDS (TOWARDS A SOCIETY OF), SOME REFLECTIONS ON THE MEANING OF DEMOCRATIC
SOCIALISM 12/70/628
FUNCTIONALISM (CONSENSUS AND CONFLICT IN). IMPLICATIONS FOR THE STUDY OF
INTERNATIONAL INTEGRATION 6/71/178
FUNDS (FEDERAL) AND UNIVERSITY RESEARCH 3/73/121
GAMES (FRENCH), SIMULATION IN TEACHING COMPARATIVE POLITICS 9/70/462
GANDHIAN POLITICS, SYMBOLISM IN, 12/69/513
GAUCHE (A), DIEU--A DOITE OU 6/70/257
GERMANY (WEST), PERCEPTIONS OF THE GREAT COALITION IN , 1966-1969 3/72/28
GOVERNING (THE PROBLEMS OF), FEDERAL CAPITALS 9/68/345
GOVERNMENT OF THE 1970≠S (MACHINERY OF), THE TREASURY BOARD OF CANADA 9/71/346
GOVERNMENT (FORMS OF LOCAL) IN THE MONTREAL AREA, 1911-71, A DISCRIMINANT
APPROACH 6/73/243
GOVERNMENT (PATTERNS OF), IN WESTERN DEMOCRACIES, PARTY SYSTEMS AND, 6/68/180
GOVERNMENT, YOUNG PEOPLE≠S ATTITUDES TOWARD, POLITICAL SOCIALIZATION IN
QUEBEC 6/73/303
GOUVERNEMENTALE (L≠INFORMATION) ET LES COURRIERISTES PARLEMENTAIRES AU
QUEBEC 3/71/26
GROUPES D≠INTERET, A LA RECHERCHE D≠UNE METHODE D(ANALYSE DES PARTIS,3/69/45
GROUPS (INTEREST) AND THE CANADIAN PARLIAMENT, ACTIVITES, INTERACTION,
LEGITIMACY, AND INFLUENCE 12/71/444
GROUP (PRESSURE) DEMANDS AND THE STRUGGLE FOR ORGANIZATIONAL STATUS, THE CASE OF
ORGANIZED LABOUR IN CANADA 3/70/56
GROUPES D≠INTERET, A LA RECHERCHE D≠UNE METHODE D(ANALYSE DES PARTIS,3/69/45
GROUPS (PRESSURE), SELECTIVE INDUCEMENTS AND THE DEVELOPMENT OF* THE CASE OF
CANADIAN TEACHERS≠ ASSOCIATIONS, 3/69/103
GROWTH, ATTITUDES ON POLLUTION AND, IN HAMILTON, LOT OF TALK ABOUT ECOLOGY
9/72/389
GUERRE (LES QUEBECOIS), ET LA PAIX, 1945-60 3/70/88
HAITI, RELIGION AND POLITICS IN 9/70/400
HAMILTON (ATTITUDES ON POLLUTION AND GROWTH IN), LOT OF TALK ABOUT ECOLOGY
9/72/389
HAMILTON (THREE RIDINGS), INFLUENCE OF RECRUITMENT PATTERNS IN
THE CONGRUENCE OF FEDERAL-PROVINCIAL CAMPAIGN ACTIVITY IN PARTY 6/72/190
HIERARCHIQUE(L≠ANALYSE) DES RESULTATS ELECTORAUX 3/68/40
HISTOIRE ADMINISTRATIVE DU QUEBEC ET THEORIE ADMINISTRATIVE 3/71/141
HISTORY (THE END OF) . A REAPPRAISAL OF MARX≠S VIEWS ON ALIENATION AND HUMAN
EMANCIPATION 9/71/367
HOUSE OF COMMONS (CANADIAN), THE DILEMMA OF THE STANDING COMMITTEES OF, COMMENT
ON CES. FRANKS
HOUSE OF COMMONS, CANADIAN, 1867-1968, TUROVER AND TENURE IN 12/70/655
HUMAN EMANCIPATION AND ALIENATION, ≠≠THE END OF HISTORY≠≠. A REAPPRAISAL OF
MARX≠S VIEWS ON 9/71/367
HUMAN EMANCIPATION, MARX ON 12/71/559
HYPOTHESES (SOME), VARIATIONS IN PARTY SUPPORT IN FEDERAL AND PROVINCIAL
ELECTIONS 6/71/280
IDEOLOGIE POLITIQUE, DE LA REVUE CITE LIBRE, 12/68/414
IDEOLOGY (PARTY), QUANTITATIVE COMPARISON OF 12/70/540
IDEOLOGICAL COMMITMENT (A SURVEY OF). THE SOUTH AFRICAN POWER-ELITE 3/71/76

INCONSISTENCY (STATUS) AND PARTY CHOICE IN CANADA, AN ATTEMPT TO REPLICATE 9/70/471
INDIA (SOUTH), REGIONAL CONTEXTS OF POLITICAL PARTICIPATION, SOME ILLUSTRATIONS FROM 6/72/167
INDUSTRIELLE AVANCEE (SOCIETE), UNE CARTE POLITIQUE DE LA NOUVELLE GRANDS VILLES, NATIONS ET EMPIRES, 3/72/120
INEQUALITY OF DISTRIBUTION IN THE CANADIAN PROVINCIAL ASSEMBLIES 9/72/433
SOCIALIZATION 9/72/418
INFLUENCE, ACTIVITES, INTERACTION AND LEGITIMACY, INTEREST GROUPS AND THE CANADIAN PARLIAMENT 12/71/444
INFLUENCE (ATTRIBUTES OF ASCRIBED) IN LOCAL PARTY ORGANIZATION IN CANADA AND THE UNITED STATES 6/72/206
INFLUENCE OF RECRUITMENT PATTERNS IN THREE HAMILTON RIDINGS, THE CONGRUENCE OF FEDERAL-PROVINCIAL CAMPAIGN ACTIVITY IN PARTY 6/72/190
INFLUENCE, COGNITIVE AND MOTIVATIONAL SOURCES OF VOTER SUSCEPTIBILITY 12/73/624
INFLUENCE, DOES ADVERTISING INFLUENCE VOTES, AN ANALYSIS OF THE 1966 AND 1970 QUEBEC ELECTIONS 12/73/638
INFORMATION GOUVERNEMENTALE ET LES COURRIERISTES PARLEMENTAIRES AU QUEBEC 3/71/26
INSTABILITY (POLITICAL) IN AFRICAN NATIONS, AN EMPIRICAL ANALYSIS OF SOURCES OF CULTURAL PLURALISM, MODERNIZATION, AND CONFLICT, 3/72/82
INSTRUMENTAL BELIEFS, THE ≠≠OPERATIONAL CODE≠≠ APPROACH TO THE STUDY OF POLITICAL LEADERS, DEAN ACHESON≠S 3/71/52
INTEGRATION (INTERNATIONAL), CONSENSUS AND CONFLICT IN FUNCTIONALISM, IMPLICATIONS FOR THE STUDY OF 6/71/178
INTEGRATION (POLITICAL) , CULTURAL DIVERSITY AND THEORIES OF 3/71/01
INTEGRATION(POLITICAL) IN THE EUROPEAN COMMUNITY 12/68/442
INTEGRATION (REGIONAL) IN THE MARITIME PROVINCES 3/71/24
INTEGRATION (SOCIAL), DIVISION DE POUVOIR ET* DE MONTESQUIEU A LA CRISE ACTUEL DU PARLEMENTARISME 9/68/261
INTERACTION, LEGITIMACY AND INFLUENCE, INTEREST GROUPS AND THE CANADIAN PARLIAMENT 12/71/444
INTEREST GROUPS AND THE CANADIAN PARLIAMENT. ACTIVITIES, INTERACTION, LEGITIMACY AND INFLUENCE 12/71/444
INTEREST RECOGNITION AND SOCIAL POSITION, THE VOTER IN BROADVIEW OR ARE VOTERS FOOLS 3/73/131
INTERESTS, OF ETHNIC MINORITIES, THE ROLE OF POLITICAL PARTIES IN PROMOTING, 12/69/419
INTERNATIONAL INTEGRATION. CONSENSUS AND CONFLICT IN. IMPLICATIONS FOR THE STUDY OF 6/71/178
INTERNATIONAL RELATIONS THEORY, 1945-70, RETREAT FROM UTOPIA 6/71/165
INTERPRETATION OF LOCKE THE POLITICAL THEORIST, A GUIDE TO THE 12/73/602
INTERPRETATION (PROFESSOR MACPHERSON≠S), OF FRIEDMAN≠S CAPITALISM AND FREEDOM, A COMMENT ON 6/69/256
ISSUES (REFERENDUM) VOTING IN CANADIAN COMMUNITIES / A TAXONOMY OF REF. ISS., 12/68/462
JEU DE LA COMMUNICATION POLITIQUE 9/70/359
JUDICIAL COMMITTEE AND ITS CRITICS 9/71/301
KENNEDY (JOHN F.) IN FOUR CRISIS DECISIONS, PERSONALITY AND DECISION-MAKING* 6/69/200
KING-BYNG DISPUTE (A NEW LOOK AT), PERSONALITY AND POLITICS 3/73/37
KITCHENER, ONTARIO, ELECTORAL CLEAVAGES IN, POLITICAL ALIGNMENT IN A POLARIZED CITY 6/73/230
LABELS (CANADIAN PARTY)* AN ESSAY IN SEMANTICS AND ANTHROPOLOGY 6/69/141
LABRADOR A L≠HEURE DE LA CONTESTATION 12/73/518
LAPALME AFFAIR, THE CNTU, AND NATIONAL BARGAINING UNITS, PRESSURE-GROUP DEMANDS AND ORGANIZATIONAL OBJECTIVES 12/73/582
LAW STUDENTS IN QUEBEC, POLITICAL ATTITUDES AMONG 3/71/122
LEADER IMAGES (PARTY), IN THE 1968 FEDERAL ELECTION 3/70/37
LEADERS (FRENCH AND ENGLISH) IN THE LIBERAL PARTY OF CANADA, NOTE ON THE ≠≠ALTERNATION≠≠ OF, 3/69/118
LEADERSHIP CONVENTION (RESEARCH NOTES) 6/70/299
LEADERSHIP CONVENTION (LIBERAL PARTY), SOME COLLECTIVE CHARACTERISTICS OF THE DELEGATES TO THE 1968 (RESEARCH NOTES) 6/70/299
LEADERSHIP NATIONAL PARTY LEADERSHIP CONVENTION CANADA 12/68/379
LEADERSHIP(POLITICAL), THE CONCEPT OF 3/68/2
LEADERSHIP RECRUITMENT SYSTEM, THE SOVIET COMMUNIST PARTY≠S, (NOMENKLATURA), 12/69/493
LEADERSHIP SELECTION PROCESS (SOME EMPIRICAL OBSERVATIONS ON). PARTY DECISION-MAKING 3/71/97
LEGISLATURE (VOTING PATTERNS IN A NON-PARTISAN). A STUDY OF TORONTO CITY COUNCIL 6/71/224
LEGISLATURES (WESTERN PROVINCIAL), MALDISTRIBUTION IN* ALBERTA CASE, 9/69/345
LEGITIMACY, ACTIVITES, INTERACTION, AND INFLUENCE, INTEREST GROUPS AND THE CANADIAN PARLIAMENT 12/71/444
LEGITIMACY (POLITICAL), NEEDS AND WANTS 9/68/241
LIBERAL PARTY OF CANADA, NOTE ON THE ≠≠ALTERNATION≠≠ OF FRENCH AND ENGLISH LEADERS IN 3/69/118
LIBERAL PARTY IN CONTEMPORARY ONTARIO POLITICS 6/70/177
LIBERAL PARTY LEADERSHIP CONVENTION, SOME COLLECTIVE CHARACTERISTICS OF THE DELEGATES TO 6/70/299
LIBERTIES (CIVIL), SUPPORT FOR AMONG ENGLISH-SPEAKING CANADIAN UNIVERSITY STUDEN 9/70/433
LIJPHART, AREND, COMMENTAIRE DE LA COMMUNICATION DU 3/71/18
LIPSET, SEYMOUR, A CRITIQUE OF HIS ARTICLE, ≠≠VALUE DIFFERENCES, ABSOLUTE OR RELATIVE. THE ENGLISH-SPEAKING DEMOCRACIES≠≠ 12/71/497
LOCAL GOVERNMENT (FORMS OF) IN THE MONTREAL AREA, 1911-71, A DISCRIMINANT APPROACH 6/73/243
LOCAL PARTY ORGANIZATION IN CANADA (ATTRIBUTES OF ASCRIBED INFLUENCE IN) AND THE UNITED STATES 6/72/206
LOCAL POLITICS, WOMEN IN, THE NORWEGIAN EXPERIENCE 9/72/365
LOCKE THE POLITICAL THEORIST, A GUIDE TO THE INTERPRETATION OF 12/73/602
LOGIC (DETERRENCE) AND RISKS OF WAR 3/73/22
MACPHERSON, C. B.≠S CONCEPTUAL APPARATUS 12/71/526
MALDISTRIBUTION IN WESTERN PROVINCIAL LEGISLATURES* CASE OF ALBERTA, 9/69/345
MANAGERS (BRANCH), SMALL BUSINESSMEN AND THEIR RELATIVE SUSCEPTIBILITY TO RIGHT -WING EXTREMISM* AN EMPIRICAL TEST, 3/69/89

MANDAT DE DEPUTE EN SYSTEME POLITIQUE ETATIQUE DE TYPE PARLEMENTAIRE, LA PROBLEMATIQUE DE L≠INCOMPATABILITE DES FONCTIONS MINISTERIELLES 6/72/251
MARCUSE, HERBERT, LA DEMARCHE CRITIQUE OU UN NOUVEAU TYPE DE CRITIQUE SOCIALE, 12/69/448
MARCUSE AND MARX (NOTES ON ≠≠WORK AND FREEDOM IN), TECHNOLOGICAL RATIONALITY 9/71/398
MARCUSE AND MARX, WORK AND FREEDOM IN 6/70/241
MARCUSE AND MARX, WORK, ALIENATION AND FREEDOM, FURTHER REFLECTIONS ON 6/73/295
MARX AND MARCUSE, FURTHER REFLECTIONS ON WORK, ALIENATION, AND FREEDOM 6/73/295
MARX AND MARCUSE, WORK AND FREEDOM IN 6/70/241
MARITIME PROVINCES, REGIONAL INTEGRATION IN 3/71/24
MARX AND MARCUSE, NOTES ON ≠≠WORK AND FREEDOM IN≠≠, TECHNOLOGICAL RATIONALITY 9/71/398
MARX ON HUMAN EMANCIPATION 12/71/559
MARXISME FRANCAIS (LE PROBLEM DE LA NATIO DANS LE) 3/70/18
MEASUREMENT OF REGIONALISM IN CANADIAN VOTING PATTERNS 3/72/55
MEMBERS OF PARLIAMENT DURING THE 28TH PARLIAMENT, ATTENDANCE PATTERNS 3/72/135
MESSIANISME ET ANTI-SEPARATISME AU QUEBEC DEPUIS 1960 12/70/559
MARX≠S VIEWS ON ALIENATION AND HUMAN EMANCIPATION (A REAPPRAISAL OF), THE END OF HISTORY 9/71/367
MESURE, TECHNIQUE D≠ANALYSE ET TENTATIVE DE, CHEZ LES FRANCO-ONTARIENS, ACCULTURATION OU ASSIMILATION 6/69/158
METHOD (THE APPLICATION OF) IN THE CONSTRUCTION OF POLITICAL SCIENCE THEORY 9/72/402
METHODOLOGY OF POLITICAL SCIENCE (VALUES AND) 3/71/119
METHODOLOGY AND THE VALUES OF POLITICAL SCIENCE 6/70/275
METHODS (QUANTITATIVE) IN FOREIGN POLICY ANALYSIS 6/69/187
MICROFILMING TECHNIQUES FOR DATA GATHERING AND FIELD RESEARCH 9/70/475
MILL (JOHN STUART), THE IMPORTANCE OF CLASS IN THE POLITICAL THEORY OF 9/68/270
MINISTER (PRIME) AS SYMBOL, UNIFIER OR OPTIMIZER 12/73/514
MINISTER (PRIME) AS SYMBOL, A REJOINDER 12/73/516
MINISTERIELLES (LA PROBLEMATIQUE DE L≠INCOMPATABILITE DES FONCTIONS), ET DU MANDAT DE DEPUTE EN SYSTEME POLITIQUE ETATIQUE DE TYPE PARLEMENTAIRE 6/72/251
MINORITE EN ETAT BICOMMUNAUTAIRE. QUATRE ETUDES DE CAS 12/71/477
MINORITIES (ETHNIC), THE ROLE OF POLITICAL PARTIES IN PROMOTING THE INTERESTS OF 12/69/419
MODEL, THE REGRESSION MODEL OF REGIONALISM, A CRITIQUE 6/72/291
MODEL, A PUBLIC CHOICE MODEL OF POLITICAL PARTICIPATION 6/73/175
MODERNIZATION, CULTURAL PLURALISM, AND CONFLICT, AN EMPIRICAL ANALYSIS OF SOURCES OF POLITICAL INSTABILITY IN AFRICAN NATIONS 3/72/82
MONEY AND POLITICS, THE COSTS OF DEMOCRACY IN CANADA 9/72/335
MONTESQUIEU (DE) A LA CRISE ACTUEL DU PARLEMENTARISME, DIVISION DE POUVOIR ET INTEGRATION SOCIAL 9/68/261
MONTREAL AREA, 1911-71, FORMS OF LOCAL GOVERNMENT IN, A DISCRIMINANT APPROACH 6/73/243
MOTIVATIONAL SOURCES OF VOTER SUSCEPTIBILITY TO INFLUENCE, COGNITIVE 12/73/624
MUNICIPALES (LES STRUCTURES), SITUATION ET ATTITUDES FACE AU CHANGEMENT DANS 6/73/195
NATION DANS LE MARXISME FRANCAISE (LE PROBLEM DE LA) 3/70/18
NATIONAL BARGAINING UNITS, THE CNTU, THE LAPALME AFFAIR AND, PRESSURE-GROUP DEMANDS AND ORGANIZATIONAL OBJECTIVES 12/73/582
NATIONAL PARTY LEADERSHIP CONVENTION CANADA 12/68/379
NATIONALISM AS A FUNCTION OF ETHNIC DEMANDS, A NOTE ON THE THEORY OF, 9/69/327
NATIONS (AFRICAN), AN EMPIRICAL ANALYSIS OF SOURCES OF POLITICAL INSTABILITY IN, CULTURAL PLURALISM, MODERNIZATION, AND CONFLICT, 3/72/82
NATIONS, GRANDS VILLES, ET EMPIRES, UNE CARTE POLITIQUE DE LA NOUVELLE SOCIETE INDUSTRIELLE AVANCEE 3/72/120
NEEDS, WANTS, AND POLITICAL LEGITIMACY 9/68/241
NEWFOUNDLAND, THE FISHERMEN≠S VOTE IN 12/70/579
NOMENKLATURA* THE SOVIET COMMUNIST PARTY≠S LEADERSHIP RECRUITMENT SYSTEM, 12/69/493
NONALIGNMENT OF AFRO-ASIAN STATES*POLICY, PERCEPTION, AND BEHAVIOUR, 3/69/1
NON-FAMILY AGENTS OF POLITICAL SOCIALIZATION, A REASSESSMENT OF CONVERSE AND DUPEUX 9/72/418
NON-PARTISAN LEGISLATURE (VOTING PATTERNS IN). A STUDY OF TORONTO CITY COUNCIL 6/71/224
NORWEGIAN EXPERIENCE, WOMEN IN LOCAL POLITICS 9/72/365
NOVA SCOTIA (THE PECULIAR CASE OF), THE APPLICATION OF THE ≠≠SENATORIAL FLOOR≠≠ RULE TO THE LATEST REDISTRIBUTION OF THE HOUSE OF COMMONS 3/73/56
OBLIGATION (POLITICAL) AND POLITICAL DISSENT 6/69/245
OBLIGATION (POLITICAL), THREE COMPONENTS OF 12/73/478
OBLIGATION (PROTEST, RESISTANCE, AND) 3/70/1
ONE-PARTY DOMINANCE AND THIRD PARTIES, THE PINARD THEORY RECONSIDERED 12/73/399
ONTARIO (KITCHNER), ELECTORAL CLEAVAGES IN, POLITICAL ALIGNMENT IN A POLARIZED CITY 6/73/230
ONTARIO POLITICS, THE LIBERAL PARTY IN CONTEMPORARY 6/70/177
OPTIMIZER OR UNIFIER, THE PRIME MINISTER AS SYMBOL 12/73/514
ORGANIZATIONAL OBJECTIVES, PRESSURE-GROUP DEMANDS AND, THE CNTU, THE LAPALME AFFAIR, AND NATIONAL BARGAINING UNITS 12/73/582
ORGANIZATIONAL STATUS,(PRESSURE GROUP DEMANDS AND THE STRUGGLE FOR, THE CASE OF ORGANIZED LABOUR IN CANADA 3/70/56
ORGANIZATIONS (LOCAL PARTY), ATTRIBUTES OF ASCRIBED INFLUENCE IN , IN CANADA THE UNITED STATES 6/72/206
ORGANIZATIONS (PARTY), CONGRUENCE OF FEDERAL-PROVINCIAL CAMPAIGN ACTIVITY IN THE INFLUENCE OF RECRUITMENT PATTERNS IN THREE HAMILTON RIDINGS 6/72/190
ORGANIZED LABOUR IN CANADA, PRESSURE GROUP DEMANDS AND THE STRUGGLE FOR ORGANIZATIONAL STATUS 3/70/56
≠≠OPERATIONAL CODE≠≠ APPROACH TO THE STUDY OF POLITICAL LEADERS. DEAN ACHESON≠S
PAIX (LES QUEBECOIS, LA GUERREET LA), 1945-60 3/70/88
PARLIAMENT (CANADIAN), INTEREST GROUPS AND, ACTIVITIES, INTERACTION, LEGITIMACY AND INFLUENCE 12/71/444
PARLIAMENT (MEMBERS OF). ATTENDANCE PATTERNS DURING THE 28TH PARL., 3/72/135
PARLEMENTAIRES ET L≠ADMINISTRATION PUBLIQUE AU QUEBEC, 6/68/164
PARLEMENTAIRE (DE TYPE), LA PROBLEMATIQUE DE L≠INCOMPATABILITE DES FONCTIONS MINISTERIELLES ET DE MANDAT DE DEPUTE 6/72/251

PARLEMENTAIRES (COURRIERISTES) AU QUEBEC, ET L≠INFORMATION GOUVERNEMENTALE 3/71/26
PARLIAMENTARISM (EXTRA-), THE POLITICAL THEORY OF 3/73/65
PARLIAMENTARIANISM AMONG THE FRENCH WORKING CLASS 12/73/461
PARLEMENTARISME (DU), DIVISION DE POUVOIR ET INTEGRATION SOCIAL* DE MONTESQUIEU A LA CRISE ACTUEL 9/68/261
PARLIAMENTARY SURVEILLANCE OF THE EXECUTIVE (PERCEPTIONS OF), THE CASE OF CANADIAN DEFENCE POLICY 6/72/206
PARTICIPATION, POLITICAL, A PUBLIC-CHOICE MODEL OF 6/73/175
PARTICIPATION (REGIONAL CONTESTS OF, SOME ILLUSTRATIONS FROM SOUTH INDIA 6/72/167
PARTICIPATION DES FORCES DEMOCRATIQUES A L≠EXPERIENCE FRANCAISE DE PLANIFICATION REGIONALE 3/72/1
PARTICIPATION (POLITICAL) IN CANADA, THE 1965 ELECTION 9/70/376
PARTIES, POLITICAL, THE ROLE OF, IN PROMOTING THE INTERESTS OF ETHNIC MINORITIES 12/69/419
PARTIES (BARRIER TO ENTRY OF) INTO TORONTO≠S CIVIC POLITICS. TOWARDS A THEORY OF PARTY PENETRATION 6/71/206
PARTIES (THIRD) IN CANADA, REVISITED 12/73/439
PARTIES (THIRD) IN CANADIAN PROVINCIAL POLITICS 12/73/422
PARTIES (THIRD) AND ONE-PARTY DOMINANCE, THE PINARD THEORY RECONSIDERED 12/73/399
PARTIS ET DES GROUPES D≠INTERET, A LA RECHERCHE D≠UNE METHODE D≠ANALYSE, 3/69/45
PARTIS ET SYSTEMES POLITIQUES*INTERACTIONS ET FONCTIONS, 3/69/18
PARTISANES (PREFERENCES), LA COMPOSITION DES 12/69/397
PARTY CHOICE IN CANADA AND STATUS INCONSISTENCY, AN ATTEMPT TO REPLICATE 9/70/471
PARTY DECISION-MAKING. SOME EMPIRICAL OBSERVATIONS ON THE LEADERSHIP SELECTION PROCESS 3/71/97
PARTY IDEOLOGY, QUANTITATIVE COMPARISON OF 12/70/540
PARTY LABELS (CANADIAN)* AN ESSAY IN SEMANTICS AND ANTHROPOLOGY 6/69/141
PARTY LEADER IMAGES IN THE 1968 FEDERAL ELECTION, 3/70/37
PARTY (LIBERAL) OF CANADA, NOTE ON THE ≠≠ALTERNATION≠≠ OF FRENCH AND ENGLISH LEADERS IN, 3/69/118
PARTY (LIBERAL) LEADERSHIP CONVENTION, SOME COLLECTIVE CHARACTERISTICS OF THE DELEGATES TO 6/70/299
PARTY (LIBERAL) IN CONTEMPORARY ONTARIO POLITICS 6/70/177
PARTY (LOCAL), ATTRIBUTES OF ASCRIBED INFLUENCE IN IN CANADA THE UNITED STATES 6/72/206
PARTY NATIONAL PARTY LEADERSHIP CONVENTION CANADA 12/68/379
PARTY OFFICIALS* SOME DIFFERENCES IN THE POLITICAL SOCIALIZATION PATTERNS OF CANADIAN AND AMERICAN, 3/69/64
PARTY ORGANIZATIONS, CONGRUENCE OF FEDERAL-PROVINCIAL CAMPIGN ACTIVITY IN, THE INFLUENCE OF RECRUITMENT PATTERNS IN THREE HAMILTON RIDINGS 6/72/190
PARTY PREFERENCE IN A SASKATCHEWAN TOWN, FACTORS IN VOTER TURNOUT 9/70/450
PARTY SUPPORT IN FEDERAL AND PROVINCIAL ELECTIONS, SOME HYPOTHESES, 6/71/280
PARTY SYSTEM IN CANADA, (AND) THE ELECTORAL SYSTEM, 1921-1965, 3/68/55
PARTY SYSTEM IN CANADA, ON ANALYSING THE IMPACT OF THE ELECTORAL SYSTEM ON 12/70/497
PARTY SYSTEM IN CANADA, ON ANALYSING THE IMPACT OF THE ELECTORAL SYSTEM ON A REPLY TO J. A. A. LOVINK 12/70/517
PARTY SYSTEMS AND PATTERNS OF GOVERNMENT IN WESTERN DEMOCRACIES, 6/68/180
PARTY SYSTEM IN FRANCE, TOWARDS A MORE SIMPLIFIED, 6/68/204
PARTY≠S (THE SOVIET COMMUNIST) LEADERSHIP RECRUITMENT SYSTEM* NOMENKLATURA, 12/69/493
PATRONS, CLIENTS, AND FACTIONS, NEW DIMENSIONS OF CONFLICT ANALYSIS IN AFRICA 3/72/104
PATTERNS OF GOVERNMENT IN WESTERN DEMOCRACIES, PARTY SYSTEMS AND, 6/68/180
PERCEPTIONS OF THE GREAT COALITION IN WEST GERMANY, 1966-1969 3/72/28
PERCEPATIONS OF PARLIAMENTARY SURVEILLANCE OF THE EXECUTIVE, THE CASE OF CANADIAN DEFENCE POLICY 6/72/206
PERSONALITY AND DECISION-MAKING* JOHN F. KENNEDY IN FOUR CRISIS DECISIONS 6/69/200
PERSONALITY AND POLITICS, A NEW LOOK AT THE KING-BYNG DISPUTE 3/73/37
PHENOMENE DE DECISION COLLECTIVE 12/70/522
PHENOMENE POLITIQUE, A LA RECHERCHE DE L≠ESSENCE DU 6/69/262
PHENOMENES ADMINISTRATIFS (DES), CONCEPTS ET TECHNIQUES 9/68/310
PHILOSOPHICAL AND INSTRUMENTAL BELIEFS OF DEAN ACHESON. THE ≠≠OPERATIONAL CODE≠≠ APPROACH TO THE STUDY OF POLITICAL LEADERS 3/71/52
PHILOSOPHY OF POLICY-MAKING (RECENT CHANGES IN) IN CANADA 6/71/243
PINARD THEORY RECONSIDERED, ONE-PARTY DOMINANCE AND THIRD PARTIES 12/73/399
PLANIFICATION REGIONALE, LA PARTICIPATION DES FORCES DEMOCRATIQUES A L≠EXPERIENCE FRANCAISE DE 3/72/1
PLANNER≠S DILEMMA. REGIONAL REFORM IN FRANCE 9/71/381
PLURALISM (CULTURAL), MODERNIZATION , AND CONFLICT, AN EMPIRICAL ANALYSIS OF SOURCES OF POLITICAL INSTABILITY IN AFRICAN NATIONS 3/72/82
PLURALISME. UNE MISE A MORT RATEE 6/71/265
POLARIZED CITY, POLITICAL ALIGNMENT IN, ELECTORAL CLEAVAGES IN KITCHNER, ONTARIO 6/73/230
POLICY, CASE OF CANADIAN DEFENCE, PERCEPTIONS OF PARLIAMENATARY SURVEILLANCE OF THE EXECUTIVE 6/72/234
POLICY, PERCEPTION AND BEHAVIOUR* THE NONALIGNMENT OF AFRO-ASIAN STATES, 3/69/1
POLICY-MAKING IN CANADA, RECENT CHANGES IN THE PHILOSOPHY OF 6/71/243
POLICY (PUBLIC), A NOTE ON 12/73/661
POLICY (SUCCESS IN FOREIGN), THE BRITISH IN CYPRUS, 1878-1960 12/70/605
POLITICAL ALIGNMENT IN A POLARIZED CITY, ELECTORAL CLEAVAGES IN KITCHNER, ONTARIO 6/73/230
POLITICAL ATTITUDES AMONG LAW STUDENTS IN QUEBEC 3/71/122
POLITICAL COMMUNITY (CHILDREN AND), A COMPARISON ACROSS RACIAL LINES, 12/69/471
POLITICAL INTEGRATION IN THE EUROPEAN COMMUNITY 12/68/442
POLITICAL LEADERSHIP, THE CONCEPT OF 3/68/2
POLITICAL LEGITIMACY, NEEDS AND WANTS 9/68/241
POLITICAL OBLIGATION AND POLITICAL DISSENT 6/69/245
POLITICAL OBLIGATION (PROTEST, RESISTANCE, AND) 3/70/1
POLITICAL PARTICIPATION, A PUBLIC-CHOICE MODEL OF 6/73/175

POLITICAL PARTIES, THE ROLE OF, IN PROMOTING THE INTERESTS OF ETHNIC MINORITIES, 12/69/419
POLITICAL SCIENCE, VALUES AND THE METHODOLOGY OF 6/70/275
POLITICAL SOCIALIZATION, THE THEORETICAL RELEVANCE OF, 6/68/125
POLITICAL SOCIALIZATION IN QUEBEC, YOUNG PEOOPLE≠S ATTITUDES TOWARD GOVERNMENT 6/73/303
POLITICAL INTEGRATION (THEORIES OF) AND CULTURAL DIVERSITY 3/71/01
POLITICAL INSTABILITY IN AFRICAN NATIONS (AN EMPIRICAL ANALYSIS OF SOURCES OF) CULTURAL PLURALISM, MODERNIZATION, AND CONFLICT, 3/72/82
POLITICAL LEADERS (THE ≠≠OPERATIONAL CODE≠≠ APPROACH TO THE STUDY OF). DEAN ACHESON≠S PHILOSOPHICAL AND INSTRUMENTAL BELIEFS 3/71/52
POLITICAL OBLIGATION, THREE COMPONENTS OF 12/73/478
POLITICAL ORIENTATIONS (THE DEVELOPMENT OF) IN CANADIAN SCHOOL CHILDREN 3/71/132
POLITICAL SCIENCE THEORY, THE APPLICATION OF METHOD IN THE CONSTRUCTION OF 9/72/402
POLITICAL SCIENCE (VALUES AND THE METHODOLOGY OF). A COMMENT 3/71/119
POLITICAL SOCIALIZATION, NON-FAMILY AGENTS OF, A REASSESSMENT OF CONVERSE AND DUPEUX 9/72/418
POLITICAL THEORY OF EXTRA-PARLIAMENTARISM 3/73/65
POLITICS, CANADIAN, IS IT TOO COMPETITIVE 12/73/341
POLITICS, CANADIAN PROVINCIAL, THIRD PARTIES IN 12/73/422
POLITICS (BARRIER TO ENTRY OF PARTIES INTO TORONTO≠S CIVIC POLITICS). TOWARDS A THEORY OF PARTY PENETRATION 6/71/206
POLITICS (COMPARATIVE), SIMULATION IN TEACHING, PLAYING FRENCH GAMES 9/70/462
POLITICS (ELECTORAL) AND RELIGION IN FRANCE*SOME RECENT OBSERVATIONS, 9/69/292
POLITICS (GANDHIAN), SYMBOLISM IN, 12/69/513
POLITICS AND MONEY, THE COSTS OF DEMOCRACY IN CANADA 9/72/335
POLITICS (ONTARIO), THE LIBERAL PARTY IN CONTEMPORARY 6/70/177
POLITICS AND PERSONALITY, A NEW LOOK AT THE KING-BYNG DISPUTE 3/73/37
POLITICS AND RELIGION IN HAITI 9/70/400
POLITICS, WOMEN IN LOCAL POLITICS, THE NORWEGIAN EXPERIENCE 9/72/365
POLICY (PUBLIC) AND DEMOCRATIC THEORY 9/70/415
POLITICS AND SOCIAL CLASS IN CANADA* THE CASE OF WATERLOO SOUTH 9/68/288
POLITICAL PARTICIPATION IN CANADA, THE 1965 ELECTION 9/70/376
POLITICAL SCALES,A TEST OF THE UNI-DIMENSIONALITY OF, THROUGH FACTOR ANALYSIS 12/73/664
POLITICAL SCIENTIST, THE EDUCATION OF 9/70/345
POLITICAL THEORIST (LOCKE), A GUIDE TO THE INTERPRETATION OF 12/73/602
POLITIQUE (COMMUNICATION), LE JEU DE LA 9/70/359
POLITIQUE CONSULTATIVE ET SYSTEME POLITIQUE 6/69/226
POLITIQUE (LES FACTEURS DE LA DECISION), EN REGIME DEMOCRATIQUE, 6/68/147
POLITIQUE REGIONALE REGIONALISATION ET CONSCIENCE). LA COMMUNAUTE URBAINE DE QUEBEC 6/71/191
POLITIQUE (SCIENCE), STRUCTURE DES ≠FONCTIONNALISMES≠ EN 6/70/205
POLITIQUES (PARTIS ET SYSTEMES)* INTERACTIONS ET FONCTIONS, 3/69/18
POLLUTION (ATTITUDES ON), AND GROWTH IN HAMILTON, LOT OF TALK ABOUT ECOLOGY 9/72/389
POSITION (SOCIAL) AND INTEREST RECOGNITION, THE VOTER IN BROADVIEW OR ARE VOTERS FOOLS 3/73/131
POUVOIR (DIVISION DE), ET INTEGRATION SOCIAL* DE MONTESQUIEU A LA CRISE ACTUEL DU PARLEMENTARISME 9/68/261
POVERTY IN CANADA, ONE TOO MANY REPORTS ON 9/72/439
POWER-ELITE (SOUTH AFRICAN). A SURVEY OF IDEOLOGICAL COMMITMENT 3/71/76
PREFERENCES PARTISANES, LA COMPOSITION DES, 12/69/397
PRESSURE GROUP DEMANDS AND THE STRUGGLE FOR ORGANIZATIONAL STATUS, THE CASE OF ORGANIZED LABOUR IN CANADA 3/70/56
PRESSURE-GROUP DEMANDS AND ORGANIZATIONAL OBJECTIVES, THE CNTU, THE LAPALME AFFAIR, AND NATIONAL BARGAINING UNITS 12/73/582
PRESSURE GROUPS, SELECTIVE INDUCEMENTS AND THE DEVELOPMENT OF* THE CASE OF CANADIAN TEACHERS≠ ASSOCIATIONS, 3/69/103
PRIME MINISTER AS SYMBOL, UNIFIER OR OPTIMIZER 12/73/514
PRIME MINISTER AS SYMBOL, A REJOINDER 12/73/516
PROFESSION, 1971 SURVEY OF 3/73/89
PROTEST, RESISTANCE, AND POLITICAL OBLIGATION 3/70/1
PROVINCE DU QUEBEC,LE CREDIT SOCIAL DANS LA,SOMMAIRE ET DEVELOPPEMENTS 12/73/563
PROVINCES (MARITIME), REGIONAL INTEGRATION IN 3/71/24
PROVINCIAL ASSEMBLIES, CANADIAN, INEQUALITY OF DISTRIBUTION IN 9/72/433
PROVINCIAL AND FEDERAL ELECTIONS, VARIATIONS IN PARTY SUPPORT, SOME HYPOTHESES
PROVINCIAL-FEDERAL VOTING SPLIT (CATALYST TO) THE BUSINESSMAN VOTER IN THUNDER BAY 6/73/219
PROVINCIAL LEGISLATURES (WESTERN)*MALDISTRIBUTION IN, ALBERTA CASE, 9/69/345
PROVINCIAL POLITICS (CANADIAN), THIRD PARTIES IN 12/73/422
PUBLIC-CHOICE MODEL OF POLITICAL PARTICIPATION 6/73/175
PUBLIC INTEREST, JEREMY BENTHAM AND THE PUBLIC INTEREST 12/68/398
PUBLIC POLICY, A NOTE ON 12/73/661
PUBLIC POLICY AND DEMOCRATIC THEORY 9/70/415
PUBLIQUE (ADMINISTRATION), AU QUEBEC, LES PARLEMENTAIRES ET, 6/68/164
QUANTITATIVE COMPARISON OF PARTY IDEOLOGY 12/70/540
QUANTITATIVE METHODS IN FOREIGN POLICY ANALYSIS 6/69/187
QUEBEC (LA COMMUNAUTE URBAINE DE). REGIONALISATION ET CONSCIENCE POLITIQUE REGIONALE 6/71/191
QUEBEC CONTEMPORAIN* ELEMENTS BIBLIOGRAPHIQUES, 3/68/107
QUEBEC, LE CREDIT SOCIALS DANS LA PROVINCE DU 12/73/563
QUEBEC DEPUIS 1960, ANTI-SEPARATISME ET MESSIANISME AU 12/70/559
QUEBEC ELECTIONS OF 1966 AND 1970, DOES ADVERTISING INFLUENCE VOTES 12/73/638
QUEBEC (LES ELECTIONS FEDERALES DE 1957 A 1965) . UNE REINTERPRETATION 9/71/395
QUEBEC, LA FIN DU BICAMERALISME AU, 9/69/312
QUEBEC (LES COURRIERISTES PARLEMENTAIRES AU), ET L≠INFORMATION GOUVERNEMENTALE 3/71/26
QUEBEC (LES ELECTIONS FEDERALES DE 1957 A 1965 AU), LES ELECTIONS COMME
QUEBEC (HISTOIRE ADMINISTRATIVE DU) ET THEORIE ADMINISTRATIVE 3/71/141
QUEBEC, LES PARLEMENTAIRES ET L≠ADMINISTRATION PUBLIQUE AU, 6/68/164
QUEBEC, POLITICAL ATTITUDES AMONG LAW STUDENTS IN 3/71/122
QUEBEC, POLITICAL SOCIALIZATION IN, YOUNG PEOPLE≠S ATTITUDES TOWARD GOVERNMENT 6/73/303
QUEBECOIS ET CANADIEN, LES CAS, LA RATIONALISATION DES CHOIX BUDGETAIRES 9/72/348

QUEBECOIS, LA GUERRE ET LA PAIX, 1945-60 3/70/88
RATIONALISATION DES CHOIX BUDGETAIRES, LES CAS QUEBECOIS ET CANADIEN 9/72/348
RECRUITMENT PATTERNS (INFLUENCE OF) IN THREE HAMILTON RIDINGS)
THE CONGRUENCE OF FEDERAL-PROVINCIAL CAMPAIGN ACTIVITY IN PARTY 6/72/190
REGIONAL CONTESTS OF POLITICAL PARTICIPATION, SOME ILLUSTRATIONS FROM SOUTH
INDIA 6/72/167
REGIONALE (PLANIFICATION), LA PARTICIPATION DES FORCES DEMOCRATIQUES A
L≠EXPERIENCE FRANCAISE DE 3/72/1
REGIONALISATION ELECTORALE ET L≠AMPLIFICATION DES PROPORTIONS 12/73/380
REGIONALISM (THE MEASUREMENT OF) IN CANADIAN VOTING PATTERNS 3/72/55
REGIONALISM, THE REGRESSION MODEL OF, A CRITIQUE 6/72/291
REGRESSION MODEL OF REGIONALISM, A CRITIQUE 6/72/291
REPORTS ON POVERTY IN CANADA, ONE TOO MANY 9/72/439
RACIAL LINES, A COMPARISON ACROSS* CHILDREN AND THE POLITICAL COMMUNITY,
12/69/471
RAT CONTROL BILL, DEFEAT OF, HOUSE OF REPRESENTATIVES, JULY 1967 9/69/338
RATIONALITY AND DECISION IN ADMINISTRATIVE SCIENCE 6/73/271
RATIONALITY (TECHNOLOGICAL). NOTES ON ≠≠WORK AND FREEDOM IN MARCUSE AND MARX≠≠
9/71/398
RECENT CHANGES IN THE PHILOSOPHY OF POLICY-MAKING IN CANADA 6/71/243
RECHERCHE (A LA), DE L≠ESSENCE DU PHENOMENE POLITIQUE 6/69/262
RECOGNITION (INTEREST) AND SOCIAL POSITION, THE VOTER IN BROADVIEW OR ARE
VOTERS FOOLS 3/73/131
RECRUITMENT (LEADERSHIP) SYSTEM, NOMENKLATURA* THE SOVIET COMMUNIST PARTY≠S,
12/69/493
REDISTRIBUTION (LATEST) OF THE HOUSE OF COMMONS, THE APPLICATION OF THE
≠≠SENATORIAL FLOOR≠≠ RULES, THE PECULIAR CASE OF NOVA SCOTIA 3/73/56
REFERENDUM ISSUES (A TAXONOMY OF) VOTING IN CANADIAN COMMUNITIES 12/68/462
REFORM (REGIONAL) IN FRANCE, THE PLANNER≠S DILEMMA 9/71/381
REGIONAL EFFECTS IN DATA ANALYSIS (ASSESSING OF) 3/71/21
REGIONAL INTEGRATION IN THE MARITIME PROVINCES 3/71/24
REGIONAL REFORM IN FRANCE, THE PLANNER≠S DILEMMA 9/71/381
REGIONALE (REGIONALISATION ET CONSCIENCE POLITIQUE). LA COMMUNAUTE URBAINE DE
QUEBEC 6/71/191
REGIONALISATION ET CONSCIENCE POLITIQUE REGIONALE. LA COMMUNAUTE URBAINE DE
QUEBEC 6/71/191
REGIME DEMOCRATIQUE, LES FACTEURS DE LA DECISION POLITIQUE EN, 6/68/147
RELIGION AND ELECTORAL POLITICS IN FRANCE* SOME RECENT OBSERVATIONS, 9/69/292
RELIGION AND POLITICS IN HAITI 9/70/400
REPLICATE (AN ATTEMPT TO), STATUS INCONSISTENCY AND PARTY CHOICE IN CANADA
9/70/471
REPRESENTATIVES (HOUSE OF), DEFEAT OF RAT CONTROL BILL IN, JULY, 19679/69/338
RESEARCH (FIELD), MICROFILMING TECHNIQUES FOR DATA GATHERING AND 9/70/475
RESEARCH (UNIVERSITY) AND FEDERAL FUNDS 3/73/121
RESISTANCE (PROTEST), AND POLITICAL OBLIGATION 3/70/1
RESOLUTION (THE), OF A FEDERAL-PROVINCIAL CONFLICT, SOME FACTORS AFFECTING
6/69/173
RESULTATS ELECTORAUX, L≠ANALYSE HIERARCHIQUE DES, 3/68/40
REVOLUTION TRANQUILLISANTE 3/73/3
RHETORIC (POLITICAL)* DEFEAT OF THE RAT CONTROL BILL IN THE HOUSE OF
REPRESENTATIVES, JULY 1967 9/69/338
RIDINGS (THREE HAMILTON), INFLUENCE OF RECRUITMENT PATTERNS IN
THE CONGRUENCE OF FEDERAL-PROVINCIAL CAMPAIGN ACTIVITY IN PARTY 6/72/190
RIGHT-WING EXTREMISM* SMALL BUSINESSMEN, BRANCH MANAGERS, AND THEIR RELATIVE
SUSCEPTIBILITY TO 3/69/89
RIGHTS (HUMAN), THE CASE AGAINST THE CANADIAN CHARTER OF, 9/69/277
RISKS OF WAR AND DETERRENCE LOGIC 3/73/22
ROLE OF POLITICAL PARTIES IN PROMOTING THE INTERESTS OF ETHNIC MINORITIES,
12/69/419
RULES (APPLICATION OF THE ≠≠SENATORIAL FLOOR≠≠ RULES TO THE LATEST
REDISTRIBUTION OF THE HOUSE OF COMMONS, THE PECULIAR CASE OF NOVA SCOTIA
3/73/56
SASKATCHEWAN TOWN, FACTORS IN VOTER TURNOUT AND PARTY PREFERENCE IN 9/70/450
SCALES (POLITICAL), A TEST OF THE UNI-DIMENSIONALITY OF THROUGH FACTOR ANALYSIS
12/73/664
SCHOOL CHILDREN (CANADIAN) THE DEVELOPMENT OF POLITICAL ORIENTATIONS IN 3/71/132
SCIENCE (ADMINISTRATIVE), RATIONALITY AND DECISION IN 6/73/271
SCIENCE POLITICAL, THE APPLICATION OF METHOD IN THE CONSTRUCTION OF
9/72/402
SCIENCE (POLITICAL).. VALUES AND THE METHODOLOGY OF.. A COMMENT 3/71/119
SCIENCE (POLITICAL), VALUES AND THE METHODOLOGY OF 6/70/275
SCIENCE POLITIQUE, STRUCTURE DES ≠FONCTIONNALISMES≠ EN 6/70/205
SCIENTIST (POLITICAL), THE EDUCATION OF 9/70/345
SEATS AND VOTES* AN APPLICATION OF THE CUBE LAW TO THE CANADIAN ELECTORAL
SYSTEM 9/68/336
SEMANTICS AND ANTHROPOLOGY (AN ESSAY IN), CANADIAN PARTY LABELS 6/69/141
≠≠SENATORIAL FLOOR≠≠RULES (APPLICATION OF), TO THE LATEST REDISTRIBUTION OF
THE HOUSE OF COMMONS, THE PECULIAR CASE OF NOVA SCOTIA 3/73/56
SEPARATISME (ANTI-) ET MESSIANISME AU QUEBEC DEPUIS 1960 12/70/559
SHAPLEY VALUE ANALYSIS OF THE PROPOSED CANADIAN CONSTITUTIONAL AMENDMENT
SCHEME 3/73/140
SIMULATION IN TEACHING COMPARATIVE POLITICS, PLAYING FRENCH GAMES 9/70/462
SITUATIONS ET ATTITUDES FACE AU CHANGEMENT DANS LES STRUCTURES MUNICIPALES
6/73/195
SOCIAL POSITION AND INTEREST RECOGNITION, THE VOTER IN BROADVIEW, OR ARE
VOTERS FOOLS 3/73/131
SOCIALE (CRITIQUE), LA DEMARCHE D≠HERBERT MARCUSE OU UN NOUVEAU TYPE ,12/69/448
SOCIALISM (DEMOCRATIC), ON THE MEANING OF, TOWARDS A SOCIETY OF FRIENDS
SOCIALIZATION, POLITICAL, NON-FAMILY AGENTS OF, A REASSESSMENT OF CONVERSE AND
DUPEUX 9/72/418
SOCIALIZATION (POLITICAL), SOME DIFFERENCES IN PATTERNS OF CANADIAN AND
AMERICAN PARTY OFFICIALS* A PRELIMINARY REPORT, 3/69/64
SOCIALIZATION (POLITICAL) IN QUEBEC, YOUNG PEOPLE≠S ATTITUDES TOWARD
GOVERNMENT 6/73/303
SOCIALIZATION (POLITICAL), THE THEORETICAL RELEVANCE OF, 6/68/125
SOCIETE INDUSTRIELLE AVANCEE (UN CARTE POLITIQUE DE LA NOUVELLE)
GRANDS VILLES, NATIONS ET EMPIRES, 3/72/120

SOCIETY OF FRIENDS (TOWARDS), SOME REFLECTIONS ON THE MEANING OF DEMOCRATIC SOCIALISM 12/70/628
SOUTH AFRICAN POWER-ELITE. A SURVEY OF IDEOLOGICAL COMMITMENT 3/71/76
SOVIET COMMUNIST PARTY≠S LEADERSHIP RECRUITMENT SYSTEM* NOMENKLATURA, 12/69/493
STABILITY (STRATEGIC, THE PROSPECTS FOR IN THE 1970≠S 12/71/541
STATUS INCONSISTENCY AND PARTY CHOICE IN CANADA, AN ATTEMPT TO REPLICATE 9/70/471
STATUS, (ORGANIZATIONAL), PRESSURE GROUP DEMANDS AND THE STRUGGLE FOR, THE CASE OF ORGANIZED LABOUR IN CANADA 3/70/56
STABILITY IN FEDERAL SYSTEMS, DECISION-MAKING AND 3/70/73
STRATEGIC STABILITY IN THE 1970≠S, THE PROSPECTS FOR 12/71/541
STRATEGIQUE (ANALYSE) DU CHOIX D≠UN CANDIDAT DANS UNE CIRCONSCRIPTION URBAINE 6/73/254
STRUCTURE DES ≠FONCTIONNALISMES≠ EN SCIENCE POLITIQUE 6/70/205
STRUCTURES MUNICIPALES, SITUATIONS ET ATTITUDES FACE AU CHANGEMENT DANS LES 6/73/195
STRUGGLE FOR(PRESSURE GROUP DEMANDS AND THE) ORGANIZATIONAL STATUS, THE CASE OF ORGANIZED LABOUR IN CANADA 3/70/56
STUDENTS (ENGLISH-SPEAKING CANADIAN UNIVERSITY STUDENTS) SUPPORT FOR CIVIL LIBERTIES AMONG 9/70/433
STUDENTS (LAW) IN QUEBEC, POLITICAL ATTITUDES AMONG 3/71/122
SUPPORT FOR CIVIL LIBERTIES AMONG ENGLISH-SPEAKING CANADIAN UNIVERSITY STUDENTS 9/70/433
SURVEILLANCE (PARLIAMENTARY) OF THE EXECUTIVE, PERCEPTIONS OF , THE CASE OF CANADIAN DEFENCE POLICY 6/72/206
SURVEY (1971) OF THE PROFESSION 3/73/89
SWORDS AND PLOUGHSHARES, THE ELECTION PREROGATIVE IN CANADA 6/72/287
SYMBOL, THE PRIME MINISTER AS, UNIFIER OR OPTIMIZER 12/73/514
SYMBOL, THE PRIME MINISTER AS, A REJOINDER 12/73/516
SYMBOLISM IN GANDHIAN POLITICS, 12/69/513
SYSTEM (CANADIAN ELECTORAL), SEATS AND VOTES * AN APPLICATION OF THE CUBE LAW TO THE 9/68/336
SYSTEM(ELECTORAL) AND THE PARTY SYSTEM IN CANADA,1921-1965, 3/68/55
SYSTEM (ELECTORAL), ON ANALYSING THE IMPACT OF ON THE PARTY SYSTEM IN CANADA 12/70/497
SYSTEM (ELECTORAL), ON ANALYSING THE IMPACT OF ON THE PARTY SYSTEM IN CANADA A REPLY TO J. A. A. LOVINK 12/70/517
SYSTEM (OF LEADERSHIP RECRUITMENT), NOMENKLATURA* THE SOVIET COMMUNIST PARTY≠S 12/69/493
SYSTEM(PARTY) IN CANADA,(AND) THE ELECTORAL SYSTEM, 1921-1965, 3/68/55
SYSTEM (PARTY) IN CANADA, ON ANALYSING THE IMPACT OF THE ELECTORAL SYSTEM ON 12/70/497
SYSTEM (PARTY) IN CANADA, ON ANALYSING THE IMPACT OF THE ELECTORAL SYSTEM ON A REPLY TO J. A. A. LOVINK 12/70/517
SYSTEM (PARTY) IN FRANCE, TOWARDS A MORE SIMPLIFIED, 6/68/204
SYSTEME POLITIQUE, POLITIQUE CONSULTATIVE ET 6/69/226
SYSTEMES POLITIQUES, PARTIS ET* INTERACTIONS ET FONCTIONS, 3/69/18
SYSTEMS (FEDERAL), DECISION-MAKING AND STABILITY IN 3/70/73
SYSTEMS (PARTY) AND PATTERNS OF GOVERNMENT IN WESTERN DEMOCRACIES, 6/68/180
TAXONOMY OF REFERENDUM ISSUES/ VOTING IN CANADIAN COMMUNITIES 12/68/462
TEACHERS≠ ASSOCIATIONS (CANADIAN)* SELECTIVE INDUCEMENTS AND THE DEVELOPMENT OF PRESSURE GROUPS, 3/69/103
TEACHING (SIMULATION IN) COMPARATIVE POLITICS, PLAUING FRENCH GAMES 9/70/462
TECHNIQUE D≠ANALYSE ET TENTATIVE DE MESURE CHEZ LES FRANCO ONTARIENS, ACCULTURATION OU ASSIMILATION 6/69/158
TECHNIQUES ET CONCEPTS , D≠ANALYSES DES PHENOMENES ADMINISTRATIFS 9/68/310
TECHNIQUES (MICROFILMING) FOR DATA GATHERING AND FIELD RESEARCH 9/70/475
TECHNOLOGICAL RATIONALITY. NOTES ON ≠≠WORK AND FREEDOM IN MARCUSE AND MARX≠≠ 9/71/398
TENURE AND TURNOVER IN THE CANADIAN HOUSE OF COMMONS, 1867-1968 12/70/655
THEOLOGICAL ,AND POLITICAL CONSERVATISM, 12/68/429
THEORETICAL RELEVANCE OF POLITICAL SOCIALIZATION, 6/68/125
THEORIE ADMINISTRATIVE, HISTOIRE ADMINISTRATIVE DU QUEBEC ET 3/71/141
THEORIES OF POLITICAL INTEGRATION, AND CULTURAL DIVERSITY 3/71/01
THEORIST (POLITICAL), A GUIDE TO THE INTERPRETATION OF LOCKE 12/73/602
THEORY (DEMOCRATIC) AND PUBLIC POLICY 9/70/415
THEORY (INTERNATIONAL RELATIONS) 1945-70, RETREAT FROM UTOPIA 6/71/165
THEORY (PINARD≠S) RECONSIDERED, ONE-PARTY DOMINACE AND THIRD PARTIES 12/73/399
THEORY (POLITICAL) OF EXTRA-PARLIAMENTARISM 3/73/65
THEORY (POLITICAL) OF JOHN STUART MILL, THE IMPORTANCE OF CLASS 9/68/270
THEORY (POLITICAL SCIENCE), THE APPLICATION OF METHOD IN THE CONSTRUCTION OF 9/72/402
THEORY OF NATIONALISM AS A FUNCTION OF ETHNIC DEMANDS, A NOTE ON, 9/69/327
THIRD PARTIES IN CANADA REVISITED 12/73/439
THIRD PARTIES IN CANADIAN PROVINCIAL POLITICS 12/73/439
THIRD PARTIES AND ONE-PARTY DOMINANCE, THE PINARD THEORY RECONSIDERED 12/73/399
THUNDER BAY, THE BUSINESSMAN VOTER IN, THE CATALYST TO THE FEDERAL-PROVINCIAL VOTING SPLIT 6/73/219
TOMBSTONES (ELEGANT)* A NOTE ON FRIEDMAN≠S FREEDOM, 3/68/95
TORONTO CITY COUNCIL. VOTING PATTERNS IN A NON-PARTISAN LEGISLATURE 6/71/224
TORONTO≠S CIVIC POLITICS (BARRIER TO ENTRY OF PARTIES). TOWARDS A THEORY OF PARTY PENETRATION 6/71/206
TREASURY BOARD OF CANADA AND THE MACHINERY OF GOVERNMENT OF THE 1970≠S 9/71/346
TRUDEAU PHENOMENON 9/69/369
TOWN (SASKATCHEWAN), FACTORS IN VOTER TURNOUT AND PARTY PREFERENCE IN 9/70/450
TURNOUT (VOTER) AND PARTY PREFERENCE IN A SASKATCHEWAN TOWN, FACTORS IN9/70/450
TURNOVER AND TENURE IN THE CANADIAN HOUSE OF COMMONS, 1867-1968 12/70/655
UNIFIER OR OPTIMIZER, THE PRIME MINISTER AS SYMBOL 12/73/514
UNITED STATES AND CANADA, ATTRIBUTES OF ASCRIBED INFLUENCE IN LOCAL PARTY ORGANIZATIONS 6/72/206
UNIVERSITY RESEARCH AND FEDERAL FUNDS 3/73/121
UNIVERSITY STUDENTS (CANADIAN ENGLISH-SPEAKING), SUPPORT FOR CIVIL LIBERTIES 9/70/433
URBAINE (CIRCONSCRIPTION), ANALYSE STRATEGIQUE DU CHOIX D≠UN CANDIDAT DANS 6/73/254

URBAINE (COMMUNAUTE DE QUEBEC). REGIONALISATION ET CONSCIENCE POLITIQUE REGIONALE 6/71/191
UTOPIA (RETREAT FROM). INTERNATIONAL RELATIONS THEORY, 1945-70 6/71/165
≠≠VALUE DIFFERENCES, ABSOLUTE OR RELATIVE. THE ENGLISH-SPEAKING DEMOCRACIES≠≠, A CRITIQUE OF SEYMOUR LIPSET≠S ARTICLE 12/71/497
VALUE (SHAPLEY) ANALYSIS OF THE PROPOSED CANADIAN CONSTITUTIONAL AMENDMENT SCHEME 3/73/140
VALUES AND THE METHODOLOGY OF POLITICAL SCIENCE 6/70/275
VALUES AND THE METHODOLOGY OF POLITICAL SCIENCE. A COMMENT 3/71/119
VILLES (GRANDS), NATIONS ET EMPIRES, UNE CARTE POLITIQUES DE LA NOUVELLE SOCIETE INDUSTRIELLE AVANCEE 3/72/120
VOTE (THE FISHERMEN≠S) IN NEWFOUNDLAND 12/70/579
VOTER (BUSINESSMAN) IN THUNDER BAY, THE CATALYST TO THE FEDERAL-PROVINCIAL VOTING SPLIT 6/73/219
VOTER IN BROADVIEW, SOCIAL POSITION AND INTEREST RECOGNITION, OR ARE VOTERS FOOLS 3/73/131
VOTER SUSCEPTIBILITY TO INFLUENCE, COGNITIVE AND MOTIVATIONAL SOURCES 12/73/624
VOTER TURNOUT AND PARTY PREFERENCE IN A SASKATCHEWAN TOWN, FACTORS IN 9/70/450
VOTES, DOES ADVERTISING INFLUENCE IT, AN ANALYSIS OF THE 1966 AND 1970 QUEBEC ELECTIONS 12/73/638
VOTES (SEATS AND)* AN APPLICATION OF THE CUBE LAW TO THE CANADIAN ELECTORAL SYSTEM 9/68/336
VOTING IN CANADIAN COMMUNITIES/ A TAXONOMY OF REFERENDUM ISSUES 12/68/462
VOTING PATTERNS (CANADIAN), THE MEASUREMENT OF REGIONALISM IN 3/72/55
VOTING PATTERNS IN A NON-PARTISAN LEGISLATURE. A STUDY OF TORONTO CITY
VOTING SPLIT, THE CATALYST TO THE FEDERAL-PROVINCIAL VOTING SPLIT, THE BUSINESSMAN VOTER IN THUNDER BAY 6/73/219
WANTS, NEEDS, AND POLITICAL LEGITIMACY 9/68/241
WAR (THE CAUSES OF), AND THE ≠≠NEW BIOLOGY≠≠, 12/69/434
WAR (RISK OF) AND DETERRENCE LOGIC 3/73/22
WATERLOO SOUTH (THE CASE OF), POLITICS AND SOCAIL CLASS IN CANADA* 9/68/288
WESTERN DEMOCRACIES, PARTY SYSTEMS AND PATTERNS OF GOVERNMENT IN, 6/68/180
WESTERN PROVINCIAL LEGISLATURES* MALDISTRIBUTION IN,ALBERTA CASE, 9/69/345
WOMEN IN LOCAL POLITICS, THE NORWEGIAN EXPERIENCE 9/72/365
WORK , ALIENATION, AND FREEDOM IN MARCUSE AND MARX, FURTHER REFLECTIONS 6/73/295
WORK AND FREEDOM IN MARCUSE AND MARX 6/70/241
≠≠WORK AND FREEDOM IN MARCUSE AND MARX≠≠ (NOTES ON). TECHNOLOGICAL RATIONALITY 9/71/398
≠WORK AND FREEDOM IN MARCUSE AND MARX≠ ≠≠ 9/71/400
WORKING CLASS (FRENCH), PARLIAMENTARIANISM AMONG 12/73/461
YOUNG PEOPLE≠S ATTITUDES TOWARD GOVERNMENT, POLITICAL SOCIALIZATION IN QUEBEC 6/73/303
28TH PARLIAMENT, ATTENDANCE PATTERNS OF MEMBERS OF PARLIAMENT 3/72/135
1867-1968, TURNOVER AND TENURE IN THE CANADIAN HOUSE OF COMMONS 12/70/655
1878-1960, THE BRITISH IN CYPRUS, SUCCESS IN FOREIGN POLICY 12/70/605
1911-71, FORMS OF LOCAL GOVERNMENT IN THE MONTREAL AREA, A DISCRIMINANT APPROACH 6/73/243
1949-68, POST DICTING ELECTORAL CLEAVAGES IN CANADIAN FEDERAL ELECTIONS 6/72/270
1957 A 1965 AU QUEBEC (LES ELECTIONS FEDERALES DE), LES ELECTIONS COMME PHENOMENE DE DECISION COLLECTIVE 12/70/522
1957 A 1965 (LES ELECTIONS FEDERALES AU QUEBEC. UNE REINTERPRETATION 9/71/395
1960, ANTI-SEPARATISME ET MESSIANISME AU QUEBEC DEPUIS 1960 12/70/559
1965 ELECTION, POLITICAL PARTICIPATION IN CANADA 9/70/376
1965 (LES ELECTIONS FEDERALES DE 1957 A 1965 AU QUEBEC), LES ELECTIONS COMME PHENOMENE DE DECISION COLLECTIVE 12/70/522
1966 AND 1970 QUEBEC ELECTIONS, DOES ADVERTISING INFLUENCE VOTES 12/73/638
1966-1969, PERCEPATIONS OF THE GREAT COALITION IN WEST GERMANY 3/72/28
1968 FEDERAL ELECTION, PARTY LEADER IMAGES IN 3/70/37
1968 LIBERAL PARTY LEADERSHIP CONVENTION, SOME COLLECTIVE CHARACTERISTICS OF THE DELEGATES TO (RESEARCH NOTES) 6/70/299
1970 AND 1966 QUEBEC ELECTIONS, DOES ADVERTISING INFLUENCE VOTES 12/73/638
1970≠S, THE PROSPECTS FOR STRATEGIC STABILITY IN 12/71/541
1970≠S, THE TREASURY BOARD OF CANADA AND THE MACHINERY OF GOVERNMENT 9/71/346
1971 SURVEY OF THE PROFESSION 3/73/89

Canadian Collection of Reprints in political science
Collection canadienne de réimpressions en science politique

NOW AVAILABLE AT REASONABLE PRICES – An important aid for teaching courses in political science

EN VENTE À DES PRIX RAISONNABLES – Des textes supplémentaires pour les cours en Science politique

JACQUES BENJAMIN La minorité et Etat bicommunautaire : quatre études de cas (IV, 4) 50¢

ALAN C. CAIRNS The Electoral System and the Party System in Canada, 1921–1965 (I, 1); J.A.A. LOVINK On Analysing the Impact of the Electoral System on the Party System in Canada (III, 4); ALAN C. CAIRNS A Reply to J.A.A. Lovink (III, 4) 75¢

ALAN C. CAIRNS The Judicial Committee and Its Critics (IV, 3) 75¢

PAUL-ANDRÉ COMEAU Acculturation ou assimilation : technique d'analyse et tentative de mesure chez les Franco-ontariens (II, 2) 50¢

C.E.S. FRANKS The Dilemma of the Standing Committees of the Canadian House of Commons (IV, 4) 50¢

K.J. HOLSTI Retreat from Utopia: International Relations Theory, 1945–70 (IV, 2) 50¢

GAD HOROWITZ Conservatism, Liberalism and Socialism in Canada (*Canadian Journal of Economics and Political Science* XXXII, 2) 50¢

A.W. JOHNSON The Treasury Board of Canada and the Machinery of Government in the 1970s (IV, 3) 50¢

GEORGES LAVAU Partis et systèmes politiques : interaction et fonctions (II, 1) 50¢

AREND LIJPHART Cultural Diversity and heories of Political Integration; S.J.R. NOEL Consociational Democracy and Canadian Federalism; GÉRARD BERGERON Commentaire de la communication du professeur Arend Lijphart (IV, 1) 50¢

TOM TRUMAN A Critique of Seymour M. Lipset's Article, "Value Differences, Absolute or Relative: The English-Speaking Democracies" (IV, 4) 50¢

JOHN WILSON AND DAVID HOFFMAN The Liberal Party in Contemporary Ontario Politics (III, 2) 50¢

Copies of these publications may be ordered from the Canadian Political Science Association, University of Ottawa, Ottawa, Ontario, K1N 6N5. Cheques must be enclosed with individual orders.

If there is sufficient interest, other titles taken either from the *Journal* or other Canadian sources, may be added to this series. Send suggestions to the Association.

On peut commander ces articles de l'Association canadienne de Science politique, Université d'Ottawa, Ottawa, Ontario, K1N 6N5. Un chèque doit accompagner les commandes individuelles.

Si une demande suffisante se manifeste, d'autres titres tirés de la *Revue* ou d'autres sources canadiennes peuvent s'ajouter à cette collection. Adressez toute proposition à l'Association canadienne de Science politique.